MOON HANDBOOKS

ARGENTINA

WAYNE BERNHARDSON

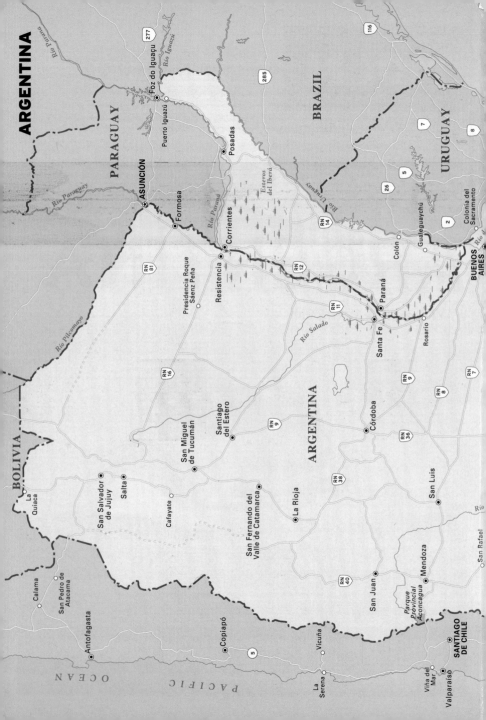

Contents

Discover **Argentina**

Argentina is a land of superlatives and extremes. A geographical jewel that owes its name — from the Latin root for silver — to Spanish settlers' misguided quest for precious metals, it's the world's eighth-largest country, slightly smaller than India.

Argentina's diversity satisfies almost any interest. Famous for the tango, the capital, Buenos Aires, has a European cultural heritage, but even though it is often called the "Paris of the South," it more closely resembles New York in its New World vigor.

Emptying into the South Atlantic, the Río de la Plata is longer than the Mississippi; the gaucho homeland of the flat green pampas stretches west toward the Andes, where the summit of Cerro Aconcagua is "The Roof of the Americas." In the shadow of Aconcagua, the Cuyo region is wine country, where hundreds of bodegas make fine wines for the domestic and international markets, and Mendoza is one of South America's most livable cities.

Among its staggering landscapes, Argentina has Iguazú, higher than Niagara and nearly four times wider, and the ruins-rich polychrome canyon of the Quebrada de Humahuaca, linked to the Andean highlands. The northwestern province of Salta provides a smaller but

intriguing area of high-altitude vineyards, and its namesake capital is home to colonial architectural monuments.

Northernmost Patagonia's forested lakes district reminds visitors of the Alps; in southern Patagonia, hikers can stroll among elephant seals and penguins on wildlife-packed Península Valdés, marvel at the Cueva de las Manos, where pre-Columbian painters created the continent's oldest aboriginal rock art, and behold the Glaciar Moreno, a grinding river of ice that inspires the eyes *and* the ears. Finally, witness Tierra del Fuego's subantarctic fjord lands, which Argentina shares with Chile.

Over the last half of the 20th century, Argentina suffered a long decline, with occasional growth spurts interrupted by economic and political disasters, including a brutal military dictatorship. In the decades since the return to constitutional government, though, it has become an ideal place to travel. Most important, like the melancholy music and dance of the tango, it has retained its identity and mystique.

Planning Your Trip

▶ WHERE TO GO

Physiographically, culturally, and economically, Argentina divides into several different regions, roughly contiguous with political boundaries.

Buenos Aires and Vicinity

Though it's no longer a bargain destination, South America's highest-profile capital is reason enough to visit the country—many visitors spend weeks or even months enjoying its first-rate accommodations, innovative cuisine, cultural resources, all-night entertainment, and nonstop shopping. Despite its international sophistication, it's also a city of neighborhoods where no one is truly anonymous. Nearby suburbs offer rewarding excursions, especially the channels of the Paraná Delta.

The Pampas

Beneath seemingly endless horizons, the grassy pampas were the original gaucho country, now home to sprawling ranches that often open their gates to paying guests. In the south, low mountain ranges give way to an Atlantic coastline where Argentines themselves prefer to holiday.

Argentina's most densely populated region, the pampas are also the most productive economically. Over a third of the

country's population lives in Gran Buenos Aires (Greater Buenos Aires, including the federal capital); nearly half of them live in the capital and Buenos Aires Province.

Geographically, the pampas divide into the humid pampas (most of Buenos Aires Province, plus parts of Santa Fe and Córdoba) and the arid pampas (westerly Buenos Aires Province

Independence hero Manuel Belgrano rests outside Monserrat's Iglesia Santo Domingo.

IF YOU HAVE . . .

- **ONE WEEK:** Visit Buenos Aires, Iguazú, and El Calafate's Glaciar Moreno.
- **THREE WEEKS:** Add Iberá, Mendoza's wineries, and Bariloche's lakes before continuing to El Calafate and El Chaltén.
- **SIX WEEKS:** Add a road trip along Patagonia's RN 40.

and all of La Pampa Province). Coverage here includes Buenos Aires and La Pampa only.

Mesopotamia and the Paraná

One of the world's great river systems supports two spectacular attractions: the world-famous Iguazú Falls and the underrated wetlands of Esteros del Iberá. The region also boasts colonial Jesuit missions extending into Brazil and Paraguay.

North of Buenos Aires, between the Río Paraná and the Río Uruguay, Entre Ríos, Corrientes, and Misiones Provinces consist of rolling lowlands, marshes, and rounded mountains. On the Paraná's right bank, Santa Fe Province prospers from fertile alluvial soils, abundant rainfall, and the industrial port of Rosario—also one of the country's cultural centers.

North of Santa Fe, Chaco and Formosa Provinces belong to the Gran Chaco, a hot lowland that becomes drier as it extends west.

Cuyo and Córdoba

If the pampas are Argentina's breadbasket, the Cuyo provinces of Mendoza, San Juan, and La Rioja are its wine cask—about three-quarters of the country's wine comes from irrigated vineyards on the eastern Andean slope, and exports are increasing. Visitors can spend days or even weeks winery-hopping or fossil-hunting in desert parks.

Colonial Cuyo fell under Chilean administration, but the snows that then blocked winter communications over the Andes—helping forge a distinct regional identity—now welcome skiers. The snow never vanishes from 6,959-meter Cerro Aconcagua, the "Roof of the Americas," which draws climbers and hikers from around the globe. Much of the country's petroleum and natural gas also originates here.

The provincial capital of Córdoba is a center of learning that traces its legacy back to the Jesuits, but it's also an industrial powerhouse. Its rolling backcountry, shared with neighboring San Luis, is one of Argentines' favorite year-round playgrounds, also offering Parque Nacional Quebrada del Condoritos, the Andean condor's easternmost habitat.

The Andean Northwest

In colonial times, the densely populated northwest was the link to the Viceroyalty of Perú

Vines of Mendoza is a great place to introduce yourself to the best wines from Mendoza.

and to Spain, and its indigenous and colonial landmarks—set among incomparable mountain and desert scenery—are the region's strongest assets. Cities like Salta, San Salvador de Jujuy, Catamarca, and Santiago del Estero were thriving when Buenos Aires was a hardship post; only after independence did they reverse their orientation toward the Atlantic.

In addition to its historic and scenic appeal, the Northwest is an underappreciated wine region. The areas around Cafayate can boast distinctive high-altitude wines, including Argentina's top Torrontés.

Northern Patagonia

South of the Río Colorado, northern Argentine Patagonia consists of Neuquén and Río Negro Provinces, plus northwesterly parts of Chubut that correspond to the Andean "lakes district."

Most of the region is arid steppe, but the densely forested sector near the Chilean border boasts numerous national parks. Centered around San Carlos de Bariloche, this is a conventional holiday destination, but activities-oriented travel, including hiking, climbing, rafting and kayaking, and

fly-fishing, has grown rapidly over the past decade. Ski resorts take advantage of a heavy winter snowpack.

For more than three centuries, northern Patagonia was a conflict zone where Araucanian (Mapuche) Indians kept both Spanish and Argentine forces and settlers off guard, until the late 19th century.

Southern Patagonia

For purposes of this book, southern Patagonia comprises the arid Chubut coast and steppe along with all of Santa Cruz Province. South to the Chilean border, the Atlantic coastline is a scenic cornucopia of whales, seals, penguins, and other wildlife, but there are also notable historical sites such as the lower Chubut valley's Welsh colonies.

Santa Cruz is famous for the dramatic Glaciar Moreno, a crackling outlier of the southern Patagonian ice sheet, and some of the continent's most exhilarating hiking near El Chaltén. It also has one of the continent's largest penguin colonies at Cabo Vírgenes and intriguing historical ports in Puerto Deseado and Puerto San Julián.

Most of the population is urban, but the

the Llao Llao peninsula, with Lago Nahuel Huapi and the Chilean border in the background

rural economy supports everything from subsistence plots to extensive grazing of cattle and sheep.

Tierra del Fuego and Chilean Patagonia

Across the Strait of Magellan from the continent, Chile and Argentina share the scenic grandeur of the subantarctic Isla Grande de Tierra del Fuego, where Ushuaia is the world's southernmost city. The biggest draw, though, is the igneous spires of Chile's Parque Nacional Torres del Paine.

Most of Chilean Patagonia in this book consists of jagged snow-covered mountains and islands set among inland seas that bear the brunt of Pacific storms that feed the glaciers of the southern continental ice field, which extends into Argentina's Santa Cruz Province. The only significant city is the regional capital of Punta Arenas, though the town of Puerto Natales is a gateway to Torres del Paine.

▶ WHEN TO GO

Argentina is a year-round destination, but try to avoid Buenos Aires's sticky summer. The spring (September–November) and fall (March–May) may be best, but even winter can see warm, brilliant weather.

Steamy subtropical Iguazú can also get crowded during winter holidays (late July–early August). In the northwestern highlands, winter's warm, dry days are ideal for backcountry travel, despite chilly nights. Cuyo's March wine harvest festival draws throngs to Mendoza and vicinity. Summer is best for mountaineering on Aconcagua, but fossil fanatics should avoid the dangerously hot desert parks.

Besides traditional tourists, Patagonia's lakes district draws hikers, fly-fishing enthusiasts, and skiers (June–August). El Calafate was once a summer destination, but the Moreno Glacier gateway now stays open October–April, and even for July holidays. Península Valdés depends on wildlife—July's right whales bring the first tourists, who keep coming, along with elephant seals, orcas, and penguins, until late March.

right whale in Puerto Pirámides, Patagonia

On Tierra del Fuego, still mainly a summer destination, Ushuaia is the gateway to Antarctica after spring's pack ice breakup.

Before You Go

When planning a trip to Argentina, remember that distances are great and logistics can be complicated. Unless your trip is an open-ended overland excursion, this means choosing among numerous options as to destinations and means of transport. Leaving Buenos Aires to visiting other high-profile destinations like Iguazú and El Calafate can require 2–3-hour flights or 24-hour bus trips. Driving is an option, but for most visitors this will mean a rental car from a provincial airport or city.

Passports and Visas

U.S. and Canadian citizens traveling to Argentina and Chile (whose southernmost sector gets coverage in this book) need passports but not advance visas. Passports are also necessary for checking into hotels, cashing travelers checks, or even credit card transactions. Both countries routinely grant foreign visitors 90-day entry permits in the form of a tourist card. Both Argentina and Chile now collect a variable "reciprocity fee" from

U.S., Canadian, Australian, and Mexican citizens at their main international airport.

Vaccinations and Health Insurance

Theoretically, Argentina and Chile demand no proof of vaccination, but if you are coming from a tropical country where yellow fever is endemic, authorities could ask for a vaccination certificate. Traveling to Argentina or Chile without adequate medical insurance is risky. Before leaving home, purchase a policy that includes evacuation in case of serious emergency.

Transportation

GETTING THERE

Most long-distance visitors arrive by air at Aeropuerto Ministro Pistarini (EZE), better known as Ezeiza. Some will arrive overland and others by ship.

Overland travel from the north can be challenging, but once you reach Argentina or Chile, it's easy enough. There are many crossings from Brazil and Uruguay, fewer from Bolivia and Paraguay. Argentina and Chile share numerous border crossings; in both countries' Andean Lakes Districts, trans-Andean bus service is fairly common, but many southerly crossings lack public transportation. For those choosing an aquatic route, the main option is the cruise between Punta Arenas and Ushuaia.

GETTING AROUND

Argentina has several domestic airports, but traveling between them often requires backtracking to the Buenos Aires hub of Aeroparque Jorge Newbery.

Buses along the principal highways are frequent, spacious, and comfortable—sometimes even luxurious. Rail service is limited and slow. If you're visiting for several months, renting or buying a vehicle is worth consideration.

Explore Argentina

► THE BEST OF ARGENTINA

For first-timers, the big sights are Buenos Aires, Iguazú Falls, and Patagonia's Moreno Glacier. Since most will arrive in Buenos Aires, this simplifies logistics, but great distances mean that flying to Iguazú and Patagonia is unavoidable.

If you have just seven nights, figure at least two in Buenos Aires (at the beginning and end), two in Iguazú, and three at El Calafate, gateway to the glacier. With two or three extra days, you could spend more time in the capital, take an excursion to the Fitz Roy sector of Parque Nacional Los Glaciares, or perhaps overnight at an *estancia* near Buenos Aires or El Calafate.

Day 1

Arrive at Aeropuerto Internacional Ministro Pistarini (Ezeiza) and transfer to a Buenos Aires hotel, with the afternoon free for sightseeing.

Iguazú waterfalls in Misiones Province

Day 2

Catch an early-morning flight to Puerto Iguazú, with the afternoon at the falls; if the timing's right, take the full-moon tour.

Day 3

Take an excursion to the Brazilian side of the falls or, alternatively, hike the rain forest on the Argentine side. Or, visit the historic Jesuit mission of San Ignacio Miní.

Day 4

A morning flight back to Buenos Aires and on to El Calafate eats up most of the day. Take an evening excursion to a nearby *estancia* for an *asado*.

Day 5

Plan for a full-day excursion to the Moreno Glacier in Parque Nacional Los Glaciares.

Day 6

Travel overland by bus or rental car to the Fitz Roy sector of Parque Nacional Los Glaciares, with accommodations at the hamlet of El Chaltén. With an early arrival time and good weather, there's time for a swift hike to view the glaciated needle of Cerro Torre.

Day 7

Stupendous views of Cerro Fitz Roy make strenuous full-day hike to Laguna de los Tres worth it. In the evening, return to El Calafate.

Day 8

Spend a relaxing day at an *estancia* like the rustic Estancia Nibepo Aike or the more luxurious Eolo Lodge on Estancia Alice.

Day 9

After the return flight to Buenos Aires, you'll have the afternoon and evening free for sightseeing and perhaps a tango floor show.

Day 10

Explore Buenos Aires during the day before your evening flight home.

Glaciar Moreno

▶ THE ARGENTINE EPIC

Buenos Aires is the starting point—and flashpoint—of Argentine history. Time has transformed, if not erased, the colonial quarters of Monserrat and San Telmo, but it's the epic of independence, the era of immigration and excess, the populism of the Peróns, and the ruthless 1976–1983 dictatorship that helped create contemporary Argentina.

What is now northwestern Argentina was only an outlier of the fabled Inka empire, but there are plenty of pre-Inka archaeological sites in Jujuy's Quebrada de Humahuaca, the Salta highlands and other Andean provinces, and Córdoba and its Sierras. History plays second fiddle to nature in Mesopotamia, at least at Iguazú, but Jesuit mission ruins tell an epic story in their own right.

Day 1

Arrive at Aeropuerto Internacional Ministro Pistarini (Ezeiza) and transfer to a Buenos Aires hotel. The afternoon is for visiting historic sites like the Plaza de Mayo, the Casa Rosada presidential palace, and the Congreso Nacional.

San Ignacio Miní is the best-preserved of Argentina's Jesuit missions.

Day 2

Take a full-day city tour, including the colonial neighborhood of San Telmo, the colorful immigrant barrio of La Boca, and upscale Retiro.

Day 3

An early-morning flight to Puerto Iguazú allows the afternoon at the falls; if the timing's right, take the full-moon tour.

Day 4

Travel overland to the landmark Jesuit mission at San Ignacio and smaller ruined missions en route, with an overnight at the city of Posadas. From Posadas, time permitting, take an excursion across the Paraguayan border to the well-preserved missions of Trinidad and Jesús.

Day 5

Fly to Buenos Aires and backtrack to the colonial city of Salta, with the afternoon free to visit the city's colonial churches, monuments, and museums.

the valley of the Río Iruya, south of its namesake village

Day 6

Take in a full-day tour of the altiplano high steppe; in the winter dry season, ride the Train to the Clouds.

Day 7

After an excursion to the archaeological sites and colonial monuments of the Quebrada de Humahuaca, a World Heritage Site in Jujuy Province, overnight in scenic Purmamarca or Tilcara.

Day 8

Enjoy a morning tour to the remote and stunningly scenic Andean village of Iruya, returning to Salta in the afternoon.

Recoleta Cemetery is filled with the souls of Argentina's history.

Day 9

Head out by rental car for the town of Cafayate via the colorful desert canyon of the Quebrada de Cafayate, with a side trip to the pre-Columbian ruins of Quilmes. Sample Cafayate's unique white wine, torrontés, at any of several local bodegas.

Day 10

On the return loop to Salta, stop at the scenic Andean village of Cachi and Parque Nacional Los Cardones.

Day 11

A morning flight to Buenos Aires leaves the afternoon for visits to the historical cemeteries at Recoleta and Chacarita. In the evening, take in a tango floor show.

Day 12

Travel overland to the pilgrimage center of Luján, Argentina's single most important religious site, and the gaucho capital of San Antonio de Areco.

Day 13

Ferry across the River Plate to the World Heritage Site of Colonia, Uruguay.

Day 14

Take the morning and afternoon for exploring Buenos Aires, including Palermo's Museo de Motivos Argentinos José Hernández (gaucho museum) and Museo Eva Perón before an evening departure.

▶ ART AND ARCHITECTURE

Early Argentine art is derivative, but today's Buenos Aires is the heart of a vigorous contemporary painting, sculpture, and multimedia scene. The city has only a handful of late colonial constructions around the Plaza de Mayo, as it really came into its own around the turn of the 20th century, when Francophile architects erected mansard-crested *palacetes* for oligarchic families, and proceeds from the pampas funded grandiose public buildings like the Congreso Nacional.

Argentina's finest colonial art and architecture survives in the northwest, on an axis that runs south from Jujuy and Salta through Tucumán and Córdoba. Contrasting with Mesopotamia's verdant subtropical vegetation, bright red sandstone blocks distinguish Mesopotamia's colonial Jesuit missions; Guaraní artisans crafted the elaborate adornments.

Day 1

Arrive at Aeropuerto Internacional Ministro Pistarini (Ezeiza) and transfer to a Buenos Aires hotel. Visit main historic sites like the Plaza de Mayo, the Casa Rosada presidential palace, and the Congreso Nacional.

Day 2

A full day's sightseeing includes colonial San Telmo (home to Buenos Aires's finest *filete* and the Museo de Arte Moderno) and the vernacular architecture of La Boca, a barrio that's also home to the Museo Quinquela Martín and the Fundación Proa.

Days 3-4

Visit the Francophile mansions of Retiro, Recoleta, and Palermo, and any of the key art museums such as the Museo Nacional de Bellas Artes, Museo de Arte Decorativo, and especially the Museo de Arte Latino-americano Buenos Aires–MALBA, and private galleries in Retiro and Recoleta.

Day 5

A morning flight to Puerto Iguazú leaves the afternoon for a visit to the falls. If the timing's right, return for the evening full-moon tour.

Day 6

Travel overland to the historic Jesuit mission at San Ignacio and other ruined missions en route, with an overnight at the city of Posadas. From Posadas, time permitting, take an excursion across the Paraguayan border to the well-preserved missions of Trinidad and Jesús.

Day 7

Fly to Buenos Aires, then on to the colonial city of Salta. Visit the city's key colonial churches, monuments, and museums.

Salta Cathedral was built in 1858.

Day 8

Take an excursion to the archaeological sites and colonial monuments of the Quebrada de Humahuaca, a World Heritage Site in nearby Jujuy Province. Overnight in Purmamarca or in Tilcara, site of several notable provincial art museums.

Day 9

Return to Salta, continuing to Cafayate, the pre-Columbian ruins of Quilmes, and the museums at Santa María. Overnight in Cafayate.

Day 10

Travel overland to Cachi, visiting several colonial churches and Cachi's archaeological museum, returning to Salta via Parque Nacional Los Cardones and the scenic Quebrada de Escoipe. Return flight to Buenos Aires or, if the timing's right, direct to Córdoba.

Day 11

From Buenos Aires take a morning flight to Córdoba, with an afternoon visit to Jesuit constructions at Manzana de las Luces, part of a UNESCO World Heritage Site, and the Jesuit ruins and museum at Alta Gracia.

Day 12

Return to Buenos Aires. Spend the afternoon visiting Belgrano art museums, including Museo Yrurtia, Museo Larreta, and Museo Badii.

Day 13

Full-day excursion to the gaucho capital of San Antonio de Areco, home to many artists and artisans. Alternatively, a ferry across the River Plate to the World Heritage Site of Colonia, Uruguay, a walled city that's one of the Southern Cone's best-preserved colonial sites.

Day 14

Day-trip to La Plata, the Buenos Aires provincial capital created as a planned city in the late 19th century.

Day 15

Spend your last day exploring Buenos Aires before an evening departure.

▶ TRAIPSING THE ARGENTINE VINEYARDS

Visitors who can't make it out of Buenos Aires will find wine bars where they can sample the country's best, and restaurants around the country carry a broad selection.

But true aficionados should spend at least a week in and around Mendoza—not nearly enough time to visit all the 100-plus wineries around the provincial capital.

Day 1
Arrive at Aeropuerto Internacional Ministro Pistarini (Ezeiza) and transfer to a Buenos Aires hotel. In the afternoon, visit central historic sites like the Plaza de Mayo, the Casa Rosada presidential palace, and the Congreso Nacional.

Day 2
A full-day city tour will include the colonial neighborhood of San Telmo, the colorful immigrant barrio of La Boca, and the northern barrio of Retiro. Enjoy a predinner visit to a lively wine bar.

Day 3
Take a morning flight to the provincial capital of Mendoza, center of Argentina's largest wine-producing region. In the afternoon, visit wineries of Maipú, in the city's eastern suburbs.

Casa Rosada – the President's Palace

Day 4
Tour the wineries of nearby Luján de Cuyo, with lunch at Ruca Malén or another winery. Have dinner in the fashionable Chacras de Coria neighborhood before returning to Mendoza.

Day 5
Take a breather from the wineries, with a tour or rental car excursion up the Río Mendoza valley for views of Cerro Aconcagua (the Western Hemisphere's highest summit). Or, check out the view from the statue of Cristo Redentor, a peace monument on the Chilean border near Las Cuevas. Have dinner at 1884, adjacent to Mendoza's Escorihuela winery.

Day 6
An excursion to the provincial capital of San

Juan, home to several lesser-known wineries, allows a side trip to the offbeat Difunta Correa shrine.

Day 7

Travel to high-altitude wineries of the Uco Valley, southwest of Mendoza, with special attention to Bodega O. Fournier or the state-of-the art Bodegas Salentein. Overnight at Salentein or San Rafael.

Day 8

Take a full-day tour of San Rafael wineries, returning to Mendoza in the afternoon.

Day 9

Hop a morning flight to Buenos Aires and on to the city of Salta, with an afternoon city tour.

Day 10

By bus or rental car via the scenic desert canyon of the Quebrada de Cafayate, make your way to the town of Cafayate, home to the finest vintages of the white varietal torrontés. Visit wineries and take a side trip to pre-Columbian ruins at Quilmes in nearby Tucumán Province.

Day 11

Visit additional wineries near Cafayate and travel overland to the picturesque desert

HOTELS ON THE GRAPEVINE

Taking advantage of the wine boom, many Argentine bodegas now boast their own hotels, where wine aficionados can spend an entire vacation sipping the malbec with gourmet food at lunch and dinner.

HOTEL COLOMÉ

In one of world's highest, most isolated vineyards, Swiss winemaker Donald Hess has built an elegant, unpretentious hotel that has put the Salta Province backwater of **Molinos** on the map.

POSADA SALENTEIN

In the **Uco Valley,** about 100 kilometers south of Mendoza, Salentein enjoys an idyllic tranquility and it offers accommodations among its merlot and pinot noir vines.

LA POSADA

On the grounds of Carlos Pulenta's Bodega Vistalba, in **Luján de Cuyo** just south of Mendoza, La Posada could hardly be more exclusive – there are just two sprawling suites. Celebrity chef Jean-Paul Bondoux's La Bourgogne restaurant serves lunch here.

CLUB TAPIZ

On the Maipú wine district's western edge, just across the highway from **Luján de Cuyo,** Tapiz's vineyards surround a 19th-century Renaissance residence transformed into a stylish seven-room guesthouse with subterranean tasting room.

vineyard in Uco Valley, Mendoza, in front of the Andes Mountains

Bodega O. Fournier is one of the Uco Valley's high-altitude wineries.

village of Cachi for an overnight. If possible, detour to Bodega Colomé near Molinos or, alternatively, spend the night at its hotel.

Day 12

Return to Salta via Parque Nacional Los Cardones and the precipitously scenic Quebrada de Escoipe.

Day 13

A morning flight to Buenos Aires leaves the afternoon and evening free for sightseeing and perhaps a tango floor show.

Day 14

Enjoy a full day of sightseeing in Buenos Aires before an evening departure.

► THE BIODIVERSITY EXPEDITION

In its nearly 3 million square kilometers, Argentina offers an astonishing diversity of natural environments. The real can't-miss is the Esteros del Iberá marshes, in Corrientes Province, where the colorful subtropical birds, reptiles, and mammals are reason enough to visit Argentina for a week or more.

Day 1

Arrive at Aeropuerto Internacional Ministro Pistarini (Ezeiza) and transfer to a Buenos Aires hotel. Visit main historic sites.

Day 2

Take a tour to the riverside suburb of Tigre

and the Río Paraná Delta, including the island of Martín García near the Uruguayan border.

Day 3

An early-morning flight to Puerto Iguazú allows the afternoon at the falls; if the timing's right, take the full-moon tour.

Day 4

Travel overland and spend the night at Yacutinga Lodge, with distinctive accommodations on a private nature reserve east of Puerto Iguazú. Alternatively, consider a night at Posada Puerto Bemberg, only half an hour south of Iguazú.

Day 5

Return to Puerto Iguazú and, time permitting, visit the Brazilian side of the falls (visa necessary).

Day 6

Travel overland to the city of Posadas, with a stop at the landmark Jesuit mission at San Ignacio. Continue to Colonia Carlos Pellegrini, in the Esteros del Iberá wetlands, by 4WD vehicle with driver.

Day 7

Enjoy a full-day wildlife-viewing excursion among the floating islands of the Esteros del Iberá.

Day 8

Head to the provincial capital of Corrientes for a flight back to Buenos Aires and on to the colonial city of Salta. Alternatively, spend

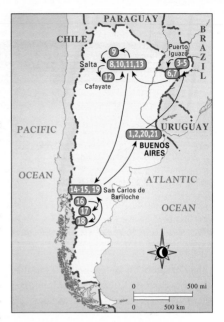

HIKES IN THE ANDES

Stretching for thousands of kilometers from the Bolivian border to Tierra del Fuego, where they disappear beneath the sea, the Argentine Andes offer an infinity of options for hikers.

CERRO ACONCAGUA

South America's most famous summit, the "Roof of the Americas" attracts climbers from around the world with hikes ranging from a quick walk to an overlook to multiday treks.

CERRO LÓPEZ

Parque Nacional Nahuel Huapi has many hikes, but the trailhead for this one near **Colonia Suiza** lies right on the Circuito Chico bus route from Bariloche. It's a stiff climb, and the forested trail is unclear in a couple of spots, but the reward is a breather at Refugio López (1,620 meters), which stocks cold drinks and food.

CERRO PILTRIQUITRÓN

Only a short hop east of **El Bolsón,** the summit of this Andean outlier reaches 2,284 meters above sea level. The reward is a relief-map view of the entire Puelo valley and the string of summits along the Chilean border and beyond.

LOMA DEL PLIEGUE TUMBADO

It's not the highest-profile trail in Santa Cruz's **Parque Nacional Los Glaciares,** but the day hike to the shoulder of this 1,550-meter peak offers some of the finest perspectives on Cerro Torre, Fitz Roy, and the Southern Patagonian Ice Fields.

GLACIAR MARTIAL

On **Tierra del Fuego,** only half an hour outside Ushuaia, it's possible to take a chairlift halfway to the Martial glacier; at that point, a sometimes slippery footpath continues to the glacier's lip, and when the clouds clear there are panoramic views across the legendary Beagle Channel to Chile's Isla Navarino.

view of Lago Verde, Parque Nacional Los Alerces

more time at Iberá and take an overnight sleeper bus to Salta.

Day 9

Travel an overland loop, by rental car, from Salta up the Quebrada del Toro to the altiplano at San Antonio de los Cobres, stopping at enormous salt flats, and then descending to Purmamarca or Tilcara for the night. (In the dry winter, itineraries are easy to stick to, but the wet summer can disrupt overland transportation.)

Day 10

Visit the archaeological sites and colonial monuments of the Quebrada de Humahuaca, a World Heritage Site in Jujuy Province. Return to Salta.

Day 11

Take a full-day excursion to the *yungas* cloud forests of Parque Nacional Calilegua.

Day 12

Depart by rental car for Cafayate via the colorful desert canyon of the Quebrada de Cafayate, with a side trip to the pre-Columbian ruins of Quilmes. Sample Cafayate's unique white wine, torrontés, at any of several local bodegas.

Day 13

On the return loop to Salta, take in the scenic village of Cachi, Parque Nacional Los Cardones, and the precipitous canyon known as the Quebrada de Escoipe.

Day 14

Hop a morning flight to Buenos Aires, continuing to San Carlos de Bariloche, with time for a late-afternoon excursion to Circuito Chico, in Parque Nacional Nahuel Huapi.

Day 15

Day-trip by bus or rental car to Villa la

Angostura; then take the boat to Parque Nacional Los Arrayanes, returning by footpath to Villa la Angostura. If it's a long summer day, consider a side trip to Parque Nacional Lanín and its araucaria forests.

Day 16

Travel by bus or rental car to El Bolsón, with a visit to its Feria Artesanal for organic beer and grazing at various food stands. Take an afternoon excursion to nearby Parque Nacional Lago Puelo or, with an early start, hike to the summit of Cerro Piltriquitrón for spectacular panoramas of the Andes along the Chilean border.

Day 17

Bus or drive to the city of Esquel, gateway to Parque Nacional Los Alerces and its millennial *alerce* forests. Spend the afternoon at the La Hoya ski area, where the chairlift carries hikers to the trailheads in summer.

Day 18

Enjoy a boat excursion (Circuito Lacustre) at Parque Nacional Los Alerces, with an overnight at the park's landmark Hotel Futalaufquen or in more modest accommodations, including camping.

Day 19

Return to San Carlos de Bariloche, stopping at Butch Cassidy's former cabin, with a detour to Parque Nacional Nahuel Huapi's Ventisquero Negro (Black Glacier).

Day 20

A morning flight to Buenos Aires leaves the afternoon and evening free for sightseeing and perhaps a tango floor show.

Day 21

Take a full day for exploring Buenos Aires before heading to the airport for an evening departure.

WILDLIFE ENCOUNTERS

capybara in the wild Esteros del Iberá

Argentina abounds in wildlife that, for most visitors, will be utterly novel.

ESTEROS DEL IBERÁ

In the vast sodden center of **Corrientes Province,** the Iberá marshes are the Everglades of Argentina, with a cornucopia of birds plus caimans, capybaras, marsh deer, the elusive maned wolf, and even the recently reintroduced giant anteater.

THE ALTIPLANO AND THE *YUNGAS*

In the thin air of **northwestern Argentina,** guanacos and vicuñas gallop across the steppe while Andean condors circle above them. Wetlands such as **Laguna Pozuelos** are home to thousands of breeding flamingos; at lower elevations, the *yungas* cloud forests of **Parque Nacional Calilegua** and **Parque Nacional El Rey** support the occasional jaguar and many colorful subtropical birds.

PENÍNSULA VALDÉS

Linked to the mainland by a narrow isthmus, the seas and shores of Chubut's **Reserva Provincial Península Valdés** boast an array of marine mammals – elephant seals, orcas, sea lions, and whales – and an abundance of Magellanic penguins and other shorebirds.

PARQUE NACIONAL LOS GLACIARES

It's most famous for the **Moreno Glacier,** but the lands of Los Glaciares are blessed with abundant wildlife, including the sprinting *ñandú* or rhea, stealthy foxes, galloping guanacos, and even the occasional puma.

BUENOS AIRES AND VICINITY

Cosmopolitan Buenos Aires, South America's highest-profile capital, has changed remarkably since its shaky start as a Spanish imperial backwater. Massive postindependence immigration turned a once cozy "Gran Aldea" (Great Village) into the first Latin American city with a million inhabitants; prosperity made it a "Paris of the South" with broad avenues, colossal monuments, and mansard-capped mansions.

Foreigners often conflate Buenos Aires with Argentina—even as provincial Argentines vociferously protest, "Buenos Aires is *not* Argentina." Like New Yorkers, brash *porteños* (residents of the port) have a characteristic accent that sets them apart from the provinces. Many still identify strongly with their own Gran Aldea barrios. In fact, residents of the city's 47 barrios might even protest that their own neighborhoods are too closely identified with the national capital.

That's because each "Baires" neighborhood has a distinctive personality. The compact, densely built "Microcentro" boasts the capital's major shopping and theater districts, as well as its Wall Street in "La City." Immediately south, in Monserrat, the Avenida de Mayo is the city's civic axis, the site of spectacle and debacle in Argentina's tumultuous 20th-century politics. Monserrat gives way to the cobbled colonial streets of San Telmo, with its tango bars and Plaza Dorrego flea market. Farther south, La Boca is a working-class outpost and a colorful artists' colony known for the Caminito, its curving pedestrian mall.

Northern neighborhoods like Retiro and

© HELGE HØIFØDT

HIGHLIGHTS

Ⓒ Plaza de Mayo: Buenos Aires's historic center is ground zero for Argentine public life (page 34).

Ⓒ Café Tortoni: For nearly a century and a half, the Avenida de Mayo's traditional gathering place has been an island of stability in an ocean of political, social, and economic upheaval (page 39).

Ⓒ Galerías Pacífico: Even nonshoppers will appreciate the vision with which 1990s developers adapted this historic Microcentro building to contemporary commerce while preserving its stunning murals (page 42).

Ⓒ Teatro Colón: Renovated for the bicentennial, the continent's most important performing arts venue retains its style and dignity (page 42).

Ⓒ Plaza Dorrego: Antiques vendors and spirited performers clog San Telmo's principal plaza and surrounding streets every Sunday (page 45).

Ⓒ Cementerio de la Recoleta: For both the living and the dead, the barrio of Recoleta is the capital's prestige address (page 58).

Ⓒ MALBA: For decades, even during dictatorships, Argentina has had a thriving modern art scene, but Palermo's striking Museo de Arte Latinoamericano de Buenos Aires has given it a new focal point (page 62).

Ⓒ Museo Eva Perón: Promoted by Evita's partisans, Argentina's first museum dedicated to a woman is as notable for what it omits as for what it includes (page 63).

Ⓒ Museo Argentino de Ciencias Naturales: In the untouristed barrio of Caballito, this improving museum sheds light on Argentina's dinosaur discoveries of recent decades (page 65).

Ⓒ Isla Martín García: Just off the Uruguayan coast, its bedrock rising out of the River Plate's muddy waters, the historic island of Martín García has been a colonial fortress and even a political prison, but today it's an absorbing getaway from the Buenos Aires bustle. It is reached from the suburb of Tigre, only 45 minutes by train from the capital (page 95).

LOOK FOR Ⓒ TO FIND RECOMMENDED SIGHTS, ACTIVITIES, DINING, AND LODGING.

Recoleta are more elegant and even opulent—the most affluent Argentines elect to spend eternity at the Cementerio de la Recoleta, one of the world's most exclusive graveyards. Beyond Recoleta, Palermo's parks were the property of 19th-century despot Juan Manuel de Rosas, but much of the barrio has become a middle- to upper-middle-class area with some of the city's finest dining and wildest nightlife. North of Palermo, woodsy Belgrano is a mostly residential area that sometimes fancies itself not just a suburb or separate city but a republic in its own right—and it was briefly Argentina's capital.

When *porteños* tire of the city, there are plenty of nearby escapes. The closest are the intricate channels of the Paraná Delta, easily reached from the northern suburb of Tigre, itself a short train ride from the city. One highlight is the island of Martín García, a colonial fortress and onetime prison camp with historic architecture and nature trails.

Even in times of crisis, the River Plate's megalopolis still has much to offer the urban explorer in a city that, as the cliché about New York says, never sleeps. Even during 2002's political and economic meltdown, *Travel + Leisure* named it Latin America's top tourist city. Still, it remains one of the most underrated destinations on an underrated continent.

PLANNING YOUR TIME

Buenos Aires deserves all the time you can give it. Those planning an extended stay, say two weeks or more, should acquire *Moon Buenos Aires,* which has exhaustive coverage of the capital and more detail on excursions in Buenos Aires Province and neighboring Uruguay.

At a minimum, though, figure three days for highlights like the Plaza de Mayo, adjacent sights like the presidential palace and cathedral, and the Avenida de Mayo and Café Tortoni; the southern barrios of San Telmo (preferably on a Sunday) and La Boca; and the Teatro Colón, Recoleta and its famous cemetery, and Palermo (including the MALBA art museum).

But that's pressing it, and at least a week would be desirable for seeing those sights

thoroughly, at a more leisurely pace, and taking in the Puerto Madero waterfront, Palermo's parks and fine arts museums, Chacarita cemetery, and the Paraná Delta. Even that would permit only limited partaking of the rapidly evolving restaurant scene in Palermo Soho, Palermo Hollywood, and Las Cañitas; the vibrant cultural life (including art galleries and theater); the hyperactive nightlife; and even compulsive shopping at Galerías Pacífico and other recycled landmarks.

No matter how much time you spend here, there's always more to see and do.

ORIENTATION

Gran Buenos Aires (Greater Buenos Aires) is a sprawling metropolitan area that takes in large parts of surrounding Buenos Aires Province. The Ciudad Autónoma de Buenos Aires (Autonomous City of Buenos Aires, also known as the Capital Federal) lies within the boundaries formed by the Río de la Plata, its Riachuelo tributary, and the Avenida General Paz and Avenida 27 de Febrero ring roads.

Buenos Aires's barrios give the megalopolis its neighborhood ambience. Its historic center is **Monserrat** (also known as Catedral al Sur, "South of the Cathedral"), whose Plaza de Mayo is ground zero in Argentine public life. Immediately north, part of the barrio of San Nicolás, the **Microcentro** (also known as Catedral al Norte, "North of the Cathedral") is the commercial and financial hub. To the east, stretching north–south along the river, redeveloped **Puerto Madero** is the newest barrio.

South of Monserrat, tourist-friendly **San Telmo** is a Bohemian blend of the colonial barrio, peopled with artists and musicians plus a scattering of old-money families and even more *conventillos* (tenements) abandoned by old money. To the southeast, **La Boca** has never been prosperous, but it has a colorful working-class history, a palpable sense of community, and extravagant vernacular architecture.

West of Monserrat and San Nicolás, **Balvanera** subdivides into several smaller neighborhoods, including Congreso (home to the national legislature), Once (the Jewish

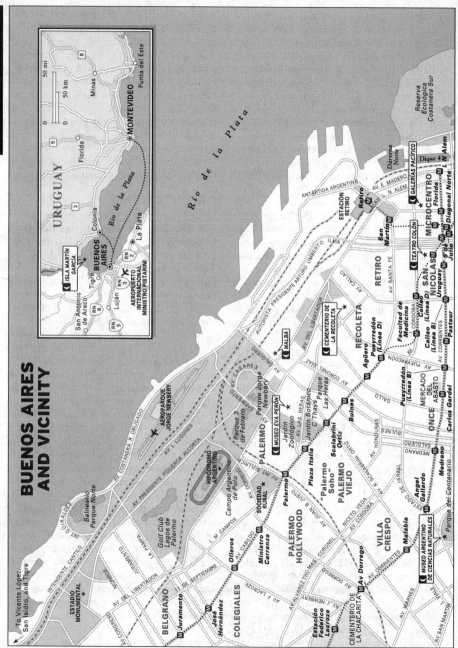

BUENOS AIRES AND VICINITY

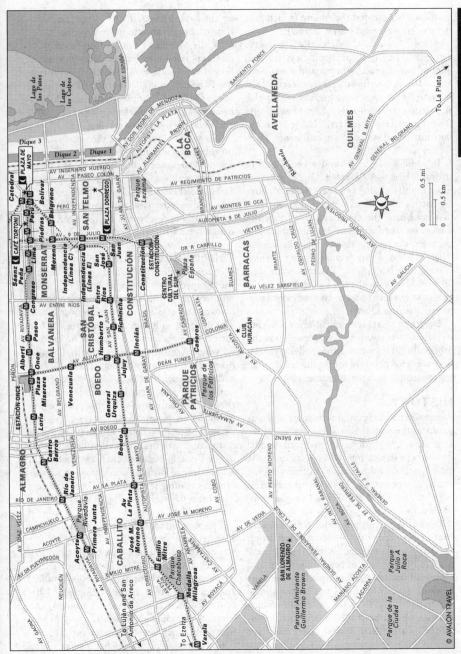

© AVALON TRAVEL

garment district), and the Abasto (which gave the city tango legend Carlos Gardel).

Across Avenida Córdoba, **Retiro** marks a transition to the upper-middle-class residential barrios to the north and northwest. Immediately northwest, elegant **Recoleta** is famous for its even more elegant necropolis, the Cementerio de la Recoleta. Overlapping Retiro and Recoleta, Barrio Norte is an opportunistic real estate fiction rather than a barrio per se.

Beyond Recoleta, several avenues lead to the open spaces of **Palermo.** One of the city's most rapidly changing areas, the city's largest barrio subdivides into several smaller but distinct units: the embassy row of Palermo Chico, between Avenida del Libertador and the river; the residential and nightlife zone of Palermo Viejo, across Avenida Santa Fe, which further subdivides into "Palermo Soho" and "Palermo Hollywood"; and Las Cañitas, on the Belgrano border. There is even a newly designated "Palermo Queens."

Belgrano prizes its residential identity, but its leafy streets also have several museums and other cultural resources. More outlying barrios have scattered points of tourist interest, including museums, parks, and ferias.

HISTORY

Buenos Aires's origins are, in some ways, as murky as the muddy Río de la Plata. Everyone agrees that Querandí hunter-gatherers roamed its southern banks, but their encampments of *toldos* (tents of animal skins) shifted with the availability of game, fish, and other resources. No Querandí site could be called a city, a town, or even a village.

Buenos Aires proper dates from January 1536, when Pedro de Mendoza's expedition landed on its shores, but his short-lived colony withered in the face of supply shortages and Querandí resistance. Traditionally, Argentine histories place Mendoza's settlement on the *barrancas* (natural levees) of present-day Parque Lezama, but author Federico Kirbus has concluded that the first Buenos Aires may have been closer to the provincial town of Escobar,

up the Paraná Delta. The evidence is circumstantial, but it's an intriguing hypothesis.

While Mendoza's initial effort failed, Juan de Garay refounded Buenos Aires on a southbound expedition from Asunción, in present-day Paraguay, in 1580. Garay died at the hands of the Querandí, but his settlement—peopled by *mancebos de la tierra* (offspring of Spaniards and Guaraní Indians)—survived.

The muddy riverbank location made a poor port, but this was almost irrelevant—the new Buenos Aires was subordinate to Asunción, which was subordinate to the Viceroyalty of Lima and the Spanish capital of Madrid via a long, indirect overland and maritime route. It took nearly two centuries for Buenos Aires to match Lima's viceregal status.

Colonial Buenos Aires

Mendoza's expedition had one lasting legacy: the escaped herds of horses and cattle that, proliferating on the pampas, transformed the backcountry into a fenceless feral-cattle ranch. The presence of horses and cattle, nearly free for the taking, spawned the gaucho culture for which Argentina became famous. Durable hides were the primary product; perishable beef had little value.

Buenos Aires lacked accessible markets, though, because low-value hides were too bulky for shipment to Spain via Lima and Panama. But they could support a vigorous contraband with British and Portuguese vessels in the Paraná's secluded channels, and Spain acknowledged Buenos Aires's growing significance by making it capital, in 1776, of the new Virreinato del Río de la Plata (Viceroyalty of the River Plate).

The population, only about 500 in the early 17th century, grew slowly at first. By 1655 it was barely 4,000, and it took nearly a century to reach 10,000, in 1744. By the time of the new viceroyalty, though, it exceeded 24,000, and nearly doubled again by the early 19th century. As Madrid loosened control, the livestock economy opened to European commerce and expanded with new *saladeros* (meat-salting plants). The growing population, which

THE *PORTEÑO* PSYCHE

When Berkeley grad student Mariano Ben Plotkin arrived in Buenos Aires on vacation, his aunt questioned him about California's cost of living, which she found astonishingly cheap. On hearing his item-by-item accounting, the *porteña* psychoanalyst commented, "Oh, now I understand – there you don't need to budget for psychoanalysis."

New Yorkers may chatter about their therapists, but *porteños* can match or surpass them – here, psychoanalysis and other therapies are not for the upper and upper-middle classes alone. During registration at the Universidad de Buenos Aires medical school, a flurry of flyers offers psychoanalysis and psychotherapy with UBA professionals – the first session free – for individuals, couples, and groups. Subte handouts declare that "Asking for help is the start of solving the problem" and tempt commuters with "unlimited sessions."

In recent years the therapy obsession may have been a function of economic crisis, and even the former *corralito* banking restrictions have been interpreted in this context. In an early 2002 interview with National Public Radio's Martin Kaste, a Freudian psychiatrist argued that "Money has a certain symbolic equivalence to the penis. People put their money in the bank, but at the moment they want to withdraw it they lose their money, so this produces a castration anxiety."

Another claimed that "sexual desire has also been caught in the *corralito* – men worry about lack of desire and premature ejaculation, and women are unable to have orgasms." The 2002 Festival de Tango even included a session on Tango de Autoayuda (Self-Help Tango).

Meanwhile, angry real-estate brokers picketed the residence of caretaker President Eduardo Duhalde, himself a former real-estate agent, but not necessarily in hope of any relief for a frozen real-estate market. Rather, proclaimed one protestor, "This turned into our therapy, a place to set our anguish free."

Therapy, though, is not just a function of the times; it began with the 1930s arrival of Jewish refugees from Europe. Ben Plotkin himself has chronicled this tale in *Freud on the Pampas:* *the Emergence and Development of a Psychoanalytic Culture in Argentina* (Palo Alto, CA: Stanford University Press, 2001).

Many of Buenos Aires's thousands of shrinks practice in Palermo's so-called Villa Freud, an area bounded by Avenida Santa Fe, Avenida Las Heras, Avenida Scalabrini Ortiz, and Avenida Coronel Díaz. Patients can top off their meds at the Farmacia Villa Freud (Medrano 1773, tel. 011/4825-2612). One online magazine specializes in listings for professional office rentals, and even acting classes are often exercises in therapy.

Institutions add to the therapeutic ambience. The Asociación Psicoanalítica Argentina (Rodríguez Peña 1674, tel. 011/4812-3518, www.apa.org.ar) once organized a month-long exhibition on "Psychoanalysis, Culture, and Crisis" at the Centro Cultural Borges. The **Museo de Psicología Horacio Piñeiro** (Avenida Independencia 3065, 3rd floor, tel. 011/4931-5434, 9 A.M.–6 P.M. Mon. and Fri.) recounts the experimental efforts of an early-20th-century pioneer.

Villa Freud's locus, though, is **Librería Paidós** (Avenida Las Heras 3741, tel. 011/4801-2860, www.libreriapaidos.com.ar), an inconspicuous bookstore in the Galería Las Heras.

In Argentine cinema, therapy is as common as in Woody Allen films – in Rodolfo Durán's 2007 comedy *Terapias Alternativas* (Alternative Therapies), an apathetic loner psychoanalyst winds up unexpectedly caring for his own son by a brief relationship and simultaneously sharing accommodations with a suicidal patient. Allen himself is a great favorite, and for that matter, he once suggested he might film in Buenos Aires.

More recently, a hit play on Avenida Corrientes went by the title *Therapy: If Only Freud Could See This*, but such matters are not always humorous. In the summer of 2010, after junior lightweight boxer Rodrigo "The Hyena" Barrios killed a pregnant woman in a Mar del Plata hit-and-run, he took several hours to surrender to police, apparently to avoid alcohol and drug tests. In the ensuing days, he managed to remain free on bail as he underwent "psychological testing."

previously consisted of peninsular Spaniards, criollos (creoles, or American-born Spaniards), small numbers of *indígenas* (Indians), and mestizos (the offspring of Spaniards and *indígenas*), soon included African slaves.

Republican Argentina and Buenos Aires

While *porteños* resisted the British invasions of 1806 and 1807, those invasions undercut Spain's authority and helped end Spanish rule in the Revolution of May 1810. The movement reached its climax in 1816, when delegates of the Provincias Unidas del Río de la Plata (United Provinces of the River Plate) formally declared independence, but the loose confederation only papered over differences between provincial "Federalist" caudillos and the cosmopolitan "Unitarists" of Buenos Aires.

In Buenos Aires, the largest province, Federalist Juan Manuel de Rosas ruled from 1829 until his overthrow in 1852. Ironically enough, the ruthless and opportunistic Rosas did more than anyone else to ensure the city's primacy, though it did not become the country's capital until 1880.

By the time Rosas took power, the population was nearly 60,000; in 1855, shortly after he left, it reached 99,000. In 1833 Charles Darwin was impressed with the city's size and orderliness:

> Every street is at right angles to the one it crosses, and the parallel ones being equidistant, the houses are collected into solid squares of equal dimensions, which are called quadras. On the other hand the houses themselves are hollow squares; all the rooms opening into a neat little courtyard. They are generally only one story high, with flat roofs, which are fitted with seats, and are much frequented by the inhabitants in summer. In the centre of the town is the Plaza, where the public offices, fortress, cathedral, &c., stand. Here also, the old viceroys, before the revolution had their palaces. The general assemblage of buildings possesses considerable architectural beauty, although none individually can boast of any.

Rosas's dictatorial rule, obstinate isolationism, and military adventures discouraged immigration, but his defeat at the battle of Caseros (1853) opened the country to immigration and economic diversification. For the city, still a provincial capital, this meant explosive growth—its population more than doubled, to 230,000, by 1875. In 1880, when the other provinces forced Buenos Aires's federalization, irate provincial authorities shifted their own capital to the new city of La Plata, but the newly designated federal capital continued to grow. By the early 20th century, it became the first Latin American city with more than a million inhabitants.

The *Porteños* Get a Port

Buenos Aires was a poor natural port. Its muddy river banks and shallow waters made loading and unloading slow, laborious, expensive, and even hazardous, as freighters had to anchor in deep water and transfer cargo to barges. Before becoming a great commercial port, it had to speed up a process that took months for the average steamship.

Engineer Luis Huergo offered the simplest and most economical solution: to provide better access to existing port facilities in the southern barrios of La Boca and Barracas. Political influence trumped his practical expertise, as congress approved downtown businessman Eduardo Madero's vague plan to transform the mudflats into a series of deep water *diques* (basins) immediately east of the central Plaza de Mayo.

Approved in 1882, Puerto Madero took 16 years to complete, came in over budget, suffered scandalous land dealings, and, finally, even proved inadequate for the growing traffic. Only improvements at La Boca and the 1926 opening of Retiro's Puerto Nuevo finally resolved the problem, but port costs remained high.

From Gran Aldea to Cosmopolitan Capital

Federalization brought a new mayor—Torcuato de Alvear, appointed by President Julio

Argentino Roca—and Alvear immediately imposed his vision on the capital. Instead of the intimate Gran Aldea, Buenos Aires would become a city of monuments, a cosmopolitan showpiece for Argentina's integration with the wider world. Where single-story houses once lined narrow colonial streets, boulevards like Avenida de Mayo soon linked majestic public buildings like the Casa Rosada presidential palace and the Congreso Nacional, the federal legislature.

Newly landscaped spaces like the Plaza de Mayo, Plaza del Congreso, and Plaza San Martín, not to mention the conversion of Rosas's Palermo estate into parklands, reflected the aspirations—or pretensions—of an ambitious country. Some, though, castigated Alvear for favoring upper-crust barrios such as Recoleta, Palermo, and Belgrano over struggling immigrant neighborhoods like San Telmo and La Boca.

As immigrants streamed in from Spain, Italy, Britain, Russia, and other European countries, such differential treatment worsened social tensions. In 1913, Buenos Aires became the first South American city to open a subway system, but in poorer neighborhoods large families squeezed into *conventillos* (tenements) and struggled on subsistence wages. The gap between rich and poor exploded into open conflict—in 1909, following police repression of a May Day demonstration, anarchist immigrant Simón Radowitzky killed police chief Ramón Falcón with a bomb, and in 1919, President Hipólito Yrigoyen ordered the army to crush a metalworkers' strike during the so-called Semana Trágica (The Tragic Week).

Yrigoyen, ironically enough, pardoned Radowitzky a decade later, and his was the first administration to suffer one of the repeated military coups that plagued the country in the 20th century. The dictatorship that followed him continued to obliterate narrow colonial streets in favor of wide thoroughfares like Corrientes, Córdoba, and Santa Fe, and the crosstown boulevard Avenida 9 de Julio. Despite public deference to working-class interests, the populist Perón regimes of the 1940s and 1950s splurged on pharaonic works projects, heavy and heavily subsidized industry, and unsustainable social spending that squandered post–World War II surpluses.

The Dirty War and Its Aftermath

As Gran Buenos Aires grew and sprawled, encompassing ever more distant suburbs, the capital and its vicinity housed more than a third of all Argentines; by 1970 it had over 8 million inhabitants. Continued political instability, though, became almost open warfare until 1976, when the military ousted the inept President Isabel Perón (Juan Perón's widow) in a bloodless coup that became Argentina's bloodiest reign of terror ever.

One rationale for taking power was corruption, but the military and their own civilian collaborators were just as adept in diverting international loans to demolish vibrant neighborhoods and create colossal public works like freeways that went nowhere. Much of the money found its way into offshore bank accounts.

Following the 1983 return to constitutional government, Argentina underwent several years of hyperinflation under President Raúl Alfonsín's Radical government. President Carlos Menem's succeeding Peronist government brought a decade of economic stability with strong foreign investment, and Buenos Aires was one of the main beneficiaries. The financial and service sectors flourished, and ambitious urban renewal projects like Puerto Madero's conversion into a fashionable riverfront of lofts and restaurants brought a sense of optimism through the 1990s. The boom had its dark side, though, in "crony capitalism," through which the president's associates enriched themselves through favorable privatizations.

Even before late 2001's partial debt default, the economy contracted and *porteños* began to suffer. After Menem's hapless successor Fernando de la Rúa resigned in December, the country had a series of caretaker presidents until Néstor Kirchner's election in May 2003. As the economy stagnated and unemployment rose, homelessness also rose and scavengers became a common sight even in prosperous Palermo and Belgrano. Strikes, strident pickets blocking bridges and highways, and frustration with politicians and institutions like the International Monetary Fund (IMF) contributed to the feeling of *bronca* (aggravation).

In the ensuing years, the devalued peso brought a tourist boom and once again encouraged investment in hotels and other real estate, though the benefits were uneven and unemployment remained historically high. The global economic downturn of late 2008 has reversed some of those gains, but the city has not suffered so badly as the provinces and some other countries.

Sights

MONSERRAT-CATEDRAL AL SUR AND VICINITY

In 1580, Juan de Garay reestablished Pedro de Mendoza's failed settlement on what is now the **Plaza de Mayo,** surrounded by most major national institutions. The barrio's axis is **Avenida de Mayo,** linking the **Casa Rosada** presidential palace (1873–1898) with the **Congreso Nacional** (National Congress, 1906); the broad perpendicular Avenida 9 de Julio splits Monserrat in half.

At the northeast corner, renowned architect Alejandro Bustillo designed the **Banco de la Nación** (1939). Immediately south of the Casa Rosada, the marble facade of the **Ministerio de Economía** (Economy Ministry) still bears pockmarks from strafing naval planes during 1955's Revolución Libertadora that sent Juan Domingo Perón into exile.

One of Avenida de Mayo's literal landmarks is Mario Palanti's **Palacio Barolo** (1923), an office building topped by a rotating semaphore visible from Montevideo's Palacio Salvo (the work of the same architect). In 1923, when Argentine heavyweight Luis Angel Firpo fought Jack Dempsey in New York, the Barolo erroneously announced Firpo's victory with a green light from the tower.

South of the Plaza de Mayo, most landmarks are modified colonial buildings. From the roof of the **Casa de la Defensa,** *porteños* poured boiling oil on British invaders in 1806–1807. The building now houses Télam, the official government press agency.

Monserrat's Palacio Barolo is one of the city's most emblematic buildings.

© BEATRICE MURCH

◖ Plaza de Mayo

Colloquially known as the "Plaza de Protestas," the Plaza de Mayo has often played center stage in Argentine history. The Peróns, in particular, used it for spectacle, convoking hundreds of thousands of *descamisados* (shirtless ones), their fervent underclass disciples.

Internationally, the plaza gained fame for some of its smallest gatherings ever. From the late 1970s, the Madres de la Plaza de Mayo marched silently around the **Pirámide de**

Mayo, its small central obelisk, every Thursday afternoon to demand the return of their adult children kidnapped by the military and paramilitary gangs. Most of the disappeared died at their captors' hands, but the mothers brought Argentina's shame to world attention.

Ironically, throngs cheered the dictatorship here when it occupied the British-ruled Falkland Islands in 1982. As the war went badly, though, crowds turned on the de facto regime, whose collapse brought a return to constitutional government.

Following the December 2001 economic meltdown, the Plaza de Mayo witnessed major protests and a police riot that killed several demonstrators and forced President Fernando de la Rúa's resignation. Other demonstrators included leftist groups who deplored the "model" ostensibly imposed by international lending agencies, and bank depositors outraged at banking restrictions that effectively confiscated their savings.

Catedral Metropolitana

On the site of the original colonial church designated by Juan de Garay in 1580, the cathedral opened in 1836; Joseph Dubourdieu's 1862 pediment bas-reliefs compare the biblical reconciliation of Joseph and his brothers with the battle of Pavón, where Bartolomé Mitre's Buenos Aires forces defeated caudillo Justo José Urquiza.

Within the cathedral, a lateral chapel holds the **Mausoleo del General José de San Martín,** the independence hero's tomb. Disillusioned with postindependence turmoil, San Martín lived in exile in France until his death in 1850; his remains were returned to Argentina in 1880, after President Nicolás Avellaneda ordered construction of this elaborate crypt, marked by an eternal flame.

The Catedral Metropolitana (Avenida Rivadavia and San Martín, tel. 011/4331-2845) is open 8 A.M.–7 P.M. weekdays, 9 A.M.–7:30 P.M. weekends.

Museo del Cabildo

The Plaza's only remaining colonial structure, the Cabildo was a combination town council and prison, and the site where criollo patriots deposed Spanish viceroy Baltasar Hidalgo de Cisneros in 1810. The present structure preserves part of the *recova* (arcade) that once ran the plaza's width.

The museum is thin on content—a few maps, paintings, and photographs of the plaza and its surroundings as well as a portrait gallery from the British invasions (1806–1807) and the Revolution of May 1810. Only part of the building survived 19th-century mayor Torcuato de Alvear's wrecking ball (which made the Avenida de Mayo possible).

The Museo del Cabildo (Bolívar 65, tel. 011/4343-4387, US$0.30) is open 10:30 A.M.–5 P.M. Wednesday–Friday, 11:30–6 P.M. weekends. Guided tours (US$0.80) take place at 3 P.M. Friday and Sunday; a free tour takes place at 2 P.M. Sunday.

Casa Rosada
(Casa de Gobierno Nacional)

For better or worse, the presidential palace has been the site of contentious spectacle, the place where Perón and Evita summoned the cheering masses who later jeered the ruthless dictatorship after the 1982 Falklands War. In late 2001 it witnessed the shooting of demonstrators by federal police under the inept De la Rúa administration. The building owes its pinkish hue to President Domingo F. Sarmiento, who proposed blending Federalist red and Unitarist white to symbolize reconciliation between the two violently opposed factions of 19th-century politics.

The Casa Rosada was not originally a single building; in 1884 Italian architect Francesco Tamburini merged the original government house with the former post office to create the present asymmetrical structure. On the east side, facing Parque Colón, pedestrians can view the excavated ruins of the colonial **Fuerte Viejo** (fortress) and early customs headquarters (buried beneath landfill in the 1890s).

Entered from the south side, the basement's **Museo de la Casa de Gobierno** contains memorabilia from Argentine presidents, but unfortunately its charter prohibits material

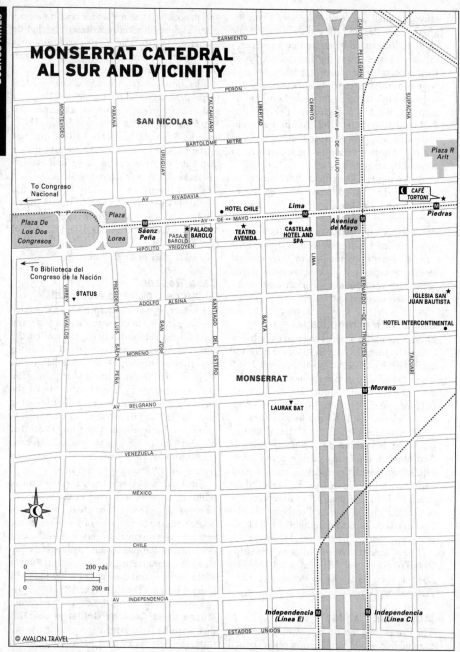

MONSERRAT CATEDRAL AL SUR AND VICINITY

SARMIENTO

PERÓN

LIBERTAD

CERRITO

CARLOS PELLEGRINI

SUIPACHA

SAN NICOLAS

MONTEVIDEO

PARANÁ

TALCAHUANO

AV — 9 — DE — JULIO

BARTOLOME MITRE

URUGUAY

Plaza R Arlt

To Congreso Nacional

AV RIVADAVIA

HOTEL CHILE

Lima

CAFÉ TORTONI

Plaza De Los Dos Congresos

Plaza

AV - DE - MAYO

Avenida de Mayo

Piedras

Lorea

Sáenz Peña

PASAJE BAROLO

★PALACIO BAROLO

TEATRO AVENIDA

CASTELAR HOTEL AND SPA

HIPÓLITO YRIGOYEN

To Biblioteca del Congreso de la Nación

VIRREY

STATUS

PRESIDENTE

ADOLFO ALSINA

SANTIAGO DEL ESTERO

LIMA

SALTA

BERNARDO - DE - IRIGOYEN

IGLESIA SAN JUAN BAUTISTA

CAVALLOS

LUIS SÁENZ PEÑA

SAN JOSE

HOTEL INTERCONTINENTAL

MORENO

TACUARI

MONSERRAT

AV BELGRANO

Moreno

LAURAK BAT

VENEZUELA

MÉXICO

CHILE

| 0 | 200 yds |
| 0 | 200 m |

AV INDEPENDENCIA

Independencia (Línea E)

Independencia (Línea C)

ESTADOS UNIDOS

© AVALON TRAVEL

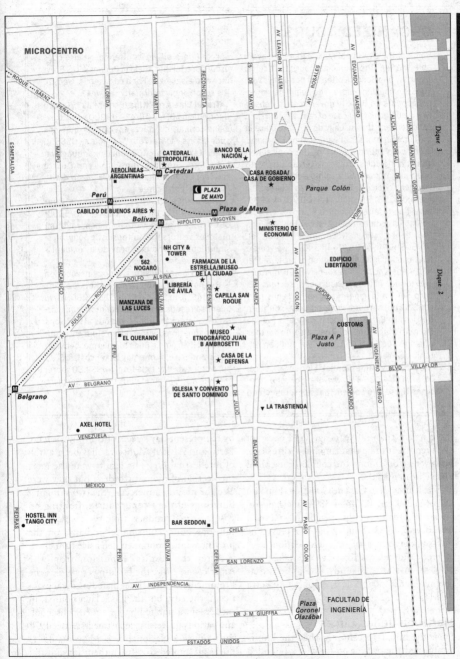

ORGANIZED TOURS

Some of the city's best guided tours are available through the municipal tourist office on Saturday and Sunday, often but not always with English-speaking guides. The complete schedule appears on the city government's website (www.bue.gov.ar). In case of rain, the tours are canceled, and they usually do not take place in the summer months of January and February.

For conventional tours of the capital and vicinity, including the Microcentro, Recoleta and Palermo, and San Telmo and La Boca, a frequent choice is **Buenos Aires Visión** (Esmeralda 356, 8th floor, tel. 011/4394-2986, www.buenosaires-vision.com.ar).

Highly recommended **Eternautas** (Avenida Presidente Julio A. Roca 584, 7th floor, tel. 011/5031-9916 or 011/15-4173-1078, www.eternautas.com) is an organization of professional historians who offer inexpensive walking tours and longer half-day excursions, such as "El Otro Sur," a fascinating three-hour bus tour (US$30 pp) through working-class southern barrios like Barracas, Nueva Pompeya, Parque Patricios, and Boedo. They also go farther afield to such places as La Plata and San Antonio de Areco.

By its very name, **Tangol** (Florida 971, Local 31, tel. 011/4312-7276, www.tangol.com) combines those two *porteño* passions, tango and soccer (*igo-o-ol!*), in its offerings. It also does excursions farther afield in Buenos Aires Province and elsewhere. For a commercial website it's surprisingly informative as well.

Travel Line Argentina (Esmeralda 770, 10th floor, Oficina B, tel. 011/4393-9000, www.travelline.com.ar) conducts specialty excursions such as its "Evita Tour" (4 hours, US$55), which takes in the CGT labor headquarters, Luna Park Stadium, the Perón and Duarte residences, and other locales associated with Evita's meteoric career.

One unique option is **Cicerones de Buenos Aires** (J. J. Biedma 883, tel. 011/5258-0909, www.cicerones.org.ar), a nonprofit that matches visitors with enthusiastic nonprofessional guides who can provide a resident's perspective on the city.

For self-guided visitors, a good new option is **Buenos Aires Bus** (Avenida Roque Sáenz Peña 846, 10th floor, tel. 011/5239-5160, www.buenosairesbus.com), an on-and-off transportation system that links various attractions and destinations, with a dozen stops throughout the city from La Boca to Palermo, between 9 A.M. and 8 P.M. A one-day ticket costs US$13 pp, but a two-day ticket only US$2.50 more; there is also a nightlife bus through Recoleta and Palermo.

more recent than 30 years ago (and does not even require it to be that timely). Visitors can, however, stroll among the colonial catacombs visible from outside.

The Museo de la Casa de Gobierno (Hipólito Yrigoyen 219, tel. 011/4344-3804, www.museo.gov.ar, free) is normally open 10 A.M.–6 P.M. weekdays, 2–6 P.M. Sunday, but as of press time it was undergoing a major reorganization.

Free guided Casa Rosada tours take place 10 A.M.–6 P.M. weekends and holidays, at the main entrance (Balcarce 50) facing Plaza de Mayo.

Manzana de las Luces

Since the mid-17th century, when the Jesuits established themselves on the block bounded by the present-day streets of Bolívar, Moreno, Perú, and Alsina, Monserrat has been a hub of intellectual life. The Jesuits were the most intellectual of monastic orders, but they were also the most commercial—the two surviving buildings of the **Procuraduría,** fronting on Alsina, stored products from their widespread missions, housed missionized Indians from the provinces, and contained defensive tunnels.

After the Jesuits' expulsion from the Americas in 1767, the buildings served as the Protomedicato, which regulated medical practice in the city; but the block later housed, in succession, a public library, a medical school, and various university departments. After 1974 the Comisión Nacional de la Manzana de las Luces attempted to salvage them for cultural purposes, opening the tunnels to the public and restoring part of the "Universidad" lettering along the Perú facade.

The **Iglesia San Ignacio** (1722) replaced an earlier structure of the same name. In 1836 the Jesuits returned, at Rosas's invitation; in 1955, at Juan Perón's instigation, mobs trashed the building, but it has since been restored.

The church shares a wall with the **Colegio Nacional de Buenos Aires** (1908), the country's most prestigious and competitive secondary school, taught by top university faculty. The re-created **Sala de Representantes** housed the province's first legislature.

The **Instituto de Investigaciones Históricas de la Manzana de las Luces Doctor Jorge E. Garrido** (Perú 272, tel. 011/4342-3964, www.manzanadelasluces. gov.ar) conducts a series of guided tours (1 and 3 P.M. Mon.; 3 P.M. Tues.–Fri.; 3, 4:30, and 6 P.M. Sat.–Sun.) for US$1.50 pp. English-language tours (US$3 pp) require 15 days' notice and a minimum of 20 people.

Museo Etnográfico Juan B. Ambrosetti

Affiliated with the Universidad de Buenos Aires, the Ambrosetti museum has first-rate archaeological, ethnographic, and ethnohistorical material on the Andean Northwest (bordering the great civilizations of highland Perú), the northern Patagonian Mapuche, and the Tierra del Fuego archipelago. Well organized with good narration in Spanish only, it does a lot with what it has—and what it has is pretty good.

The Museo Etnográfico (Moreno 350, tel. 011/4345-8196, www.museoetnografico.filo.uba.ar, US$0.30, free for retirees) is open 1–7 P.M. Tuesday–Friday and 3–7 P.M. weekends, except in January, when it's closed. There are guided tours at 4 P.M. Saturday and Sunday.

Museo de la Ciudad

Above the remarkable Farmacia La Estrella, the city museum specializes in elements of everyday urban life, including architecture, floor

Independence hero Manuel Belgrano rests outside Monserrat's Iglesia Santo Domingo.

© WAYNE BERNHARDSON

tiles, furniture, and postcards; the pharmacy's exterior windows have been turned into display cases.

Except in February, when it's closed, the Museo de la Ciudad (Defensa 219, tel. 011/4343-2123 or 011/4331-9855, US$0.80, free Wed.) is open 11 A.M.–7 P.M. daily.

⟨ Café Tortoni

One of BA's most quietly traditional places, Café Tortoni (Avenida de Mayo 825, tel. 011/4342-4328, www.cafetortoni.com.ar) has made no concessions to the 21st century and only a few to the 20th: Upholstered chairs and marble tables stand among sturdy columns beneath a ceiling punctuated by stained-glass *vitraux,* the wallpaper looks original between the stained wooden trim, and walls are decorated with pictures, portraits, and *filete,* the traditional *porteño* sign-painter's calligraphy.

Acknowledged on the walls, past patrons include singer Carlos Gardel, La Boca painter Benito Quinquela Martín, dramatists Luigi

Pirandello and Federico García Lorca, and pianist Arthur Rubinstein; more recently, it has hosted Spain's King Juan Carlos I and Hillary Rodham Clinton. The original entrance faced Rivadavia, on the north side, but Torcuato de Alvear's creation of Avenida de Mayo forced it to reorient itself.

Iglesia y Convento de Santo Domingo

Since late colonial times, the mid-18th-century Dominican church (also known as Iglesia de Nuestra Señora del Rosario) at Avenida Belgrano and Defensa has witnessed some of Argentine history's most dramatic events. It still displays banners captured by Viceroy Santiago Liniers from the Highlanders Regiment No. 71 during the 1806 British invasion, and the exterior shows combat damage from the British occupation of 1807. Near the church entrance, an eternal flame burns near sculptor Héctor Ximenes's **Mausoleo de Belgrano** (1903), the crypt of Argentina's second-greatest hero; Belgrano was an indifferent soldier, but he did design the Argentine flag.

Following independence, President

Bernardino Rivadavia secularized the church, making it a natural history museum and turning one of its towers into an astronomical observatory. In 1955, during the coup against Juan Perón, anticlerical Peronists set it afire.

MICROCENTRO AND VICINITY

Formally known as San Nicolás, the area bounded by Retiro on the north, Puerto Madero on the east, Monserrat on the south, and Balvanera to the west encompasses much of the traditional financial, commercial, and entertainment centers. The area between

Avenida 9 de Julio and the riverfront, immediately north of the Plaza de Mayo, is commonly called the Microcentro and, on occasion, Catedral al Norte.

Named for Argentina's independence day, **Avenida 9 de Julio** literally separates the Microcentro from the rest of the barrio—only a world-class sprinter could cross all 16 lanes of seemingly suicidal drivers fudging the green light. At the corner of Corrientes, the 67.5-meter **Obelisco** (Obelisk, 1936) is a city symbol erected for the 400th anniversary of Pedro de Mendoza's initial encampment.

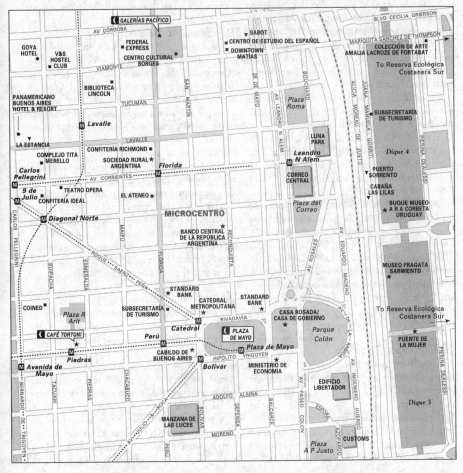

One of the Microcentro's foci is the pedestrian **Calle Florida,** once the city's major shopping street. Originally a private residence dating from 1910, the **Sociedad Rural Argentina** (Florida 460) houses an organization that has voiced the interests of large landowners—some would say "the oligarchy"—since 1866. The traditional axis of *porteño* nightlife, **Avenida Corrientes** has taken a backseat to trendier areas, but the recent widening of sidewalks has encouraged pedestrians to return.

Calle San Martín, with its banks and exchange houses, is the axis of **La City,** the financial district that's home to the Italianate **Banco Central de la República Argentina** and its **Museo Numismático Dr. José E. Uriburu** (Reconquista 266, tel. 011/4393-0021, 10 A.M.–3 P.M. weekdays, free), which helps explain the country's volatile economic history. After the events of late 2001 and early 2002, angry protestors expressed their *bronca* by defacing even the elegant Spanish Renaissance **Standard Bank** (1924).

Across Avenida 9 de Julio, on Plaza Lavalle, the **Palacio de Justicia** (Tribunales or Law Courts, 1904) has lent its colloquial name to the neighborhood. North of the landmark **Teatro Colón** (1908), protected by bulky concrete planters, the **Templo de la Congregación Israelita** (1932) is the city's largest synagogue and home to the small but impressive **Museo Judío Dr. Salvador Kibrick** (Libertad 769, tel. 011/4132-0102, ext. 105, museojudio@judaica.org.ar); from 3 to 5:30 P.M. Tuesday and Thursday it offers guided tours (US$8 pp) in Spanish, English, and Hebrew. Having ID is obligatory; do not photograph this or any other Jewish community site without explicit permission.

◖ Galerías Pacífico

As Calle Florida became an elegant shopping district in the late 19th century, Francisco Seeber and Emilio Bunge were the main shareholders in the proposed Bon Marché Argentino, inspired by Milan's Galleria Vittorio Emmanuelle II. Unfortunately, their French investors backed out, but Seeber resurrected the project by 1894 as the Galería Florida.

One of the era's biggest buildings, with a double basement and four upper stories, it covered an entire city block bounded by Florida, Avenida Córdoba, San Martín, and Viamonte. In 1908, though, the British-run Ferrocarril de Buenos Aires al Pacífico acquired the Córdoba side for business offices; within two years it controlled the rest of the building. It later passed to Ferrocarriles Argentinos, the state railroad enterprise created by Juan Perón in 1948.

Meanwhile, in 1945, Argentine artists gave the cupola its most dramatic feature: 450 square meters of murals, including Lino Spilimbergo's *El Dominio de las Fuerzas Naturales* (the Dominion of Natural Forces), Demetrio Urruchúa's *La Fraternidad* (Brotherhood), Juan Carlos Castagnino's *La Vida Doméstica* (Domestic Life), Manuel Colmeiro's *La Pareja Humana* (The Human Couple), and Antonio Berni's *El Amor* (Love). Linked to Mexican muralist Davíd Alfaro Siqueiros, all belonged to the socially conscious Nuevo Realismo (New Realism) movement.

For most of the 1980s the Galerías languished until, in 1992, the murals became a highlight of a newly fashionable shopping center—appropriately enough, its original purpose. Well worth a visit even for anticonsumers, the Galerías (www.galeriaspacifico.com.ar) offers free guided tours at 11:30 A.M. and 4:30 P.M. on weekdays from the street-level information desk. On the basement level, it has a fine food court and the city's best public toilets.

◖ Teatro Colón

Possibly the continent's most important performing arts venue, the ornate Colón (1908) reopened in 2010—though it is not yet ready for opera. Even as work proceeded, it managed to offer top-tier international opera, ballet, and symphonic performers, as well as first-rate local talent in opera, ballet, and symphony in alternative venues.

Argentine lyric theater dates from the early 19th century, with the first European artists arriving in the 1820s. The original Colón, on the Plaza de Mayo, seated 2,500 people and opened with Verdi's *La Traviata* in 1857. As the earlier theater became the Banco de la Nación, authorities chose the site of the country's first-ever railway station for Francesco Tamburini's Italian Renaissance design.

Occupying a lot of more than 8,000 square meters, with floor space of nearly 38,000 square meters on seven levels, the Colón opened with a performance of Verdi's *Aída*. Seating 2,478 patrons, with standing room for another 700, it's one of the country's most ornate buildings, its **Gran Hall** outfitted with Verona and Carrara marble, its **Salón de los Bustos** studded with busts of famous figures from European classical music, and its **Salón Dorado** (Golden Salon) modeled on palaces like Paris's Versailles and Vienna's Schönbrunn.

The main theater itself follows lines of French and Italian classics, with world-class acoustics; a rotating disc aids rapid scene changes. The orchestra accommodates up to 120 musicians. Seating ranges from comfortably upholstered rows to luxury boxes, including a presidential box with its own phone line to the Casa Rosada and a separate exit. Presidential command performances take place on the winter patriotic holidays of May 25 and July 9.

Since its opening, the who's who of performers has included Igor Stravinsky, María Callas, Mikhail Baryshnikov, George Balanchine, and Yo-Yo Ma, not to mention world-renowned orchestras and dance companies. At times, though, the administration has let its hair down to accommodate performers like folk-singer Mercedes Sosa, the *porteño* rhythm-and-blues unit Memphis La Blusera, and rock guitarist-songwriter Luis Alberto Spinetta.

The Teatro Colón (box office at Libertad 621, tel. 011/4378-7344, www.teatrocolon.org.ar) presents some 200 events per annum between May and November. Both events and guided tours were suspended until the theater reopened, but for the latest information contact the Teatro Colón (Viamonte 1168, tel. 011/4378-7132, visitas@teatrocolon.org.ar, US$3 nonresident adults, US$1.50 Argentine residents, US$0.75 children up to age 10); tours last 50 minutes and go behind the scenes as well.

PUERTO MADERO

Born amidst 19th-century corruption, modern Puerto Madero is an attempt to reclaim the riverfront, which languished off-limits during the military dictatorship of 1976–1983. Comparable in some ways to Baltimore's Inner Harbor and London's Docklands, it has recycled the handsome brick *depósitos* (warehouses) around its four large *diques* (basins) into stylish lofts, offices, restaurants, bars, and cinemas. The late director Fabián Bielinsky used its promenade for an entertaining chase scene in his con-man film *Nine Queens*.

Built on landfill east of the river's *barrancas*, what is now Puerto Madero expanded during the dictatorship as the military dumped debris from its massive public works projects east and southeast of the *diques*. Ironically enough, as native plants and animals colonized the rubble and rubbish, it became the **Reserva Ecológica Costanera Sur** (Avenida Tristán Achával Rodríguez 1550, tel. 011/4893-1597), now a popular destination for Sunday outings, cyclists, and joggers—not to mention a cruising area for the capital's gays. Hours are 8 A.M.–7 P.M. Tuesday–Sunday, when reservations can be made by phone; there are guided tours weekends and holidays at 10:30 A.M. and 3:30 P.M., and moonlight tours at 8:30 P.M. on given Fridays—by previous Monday's reservation only.

Sequentially numbered from south to north, the four rectangular basins include a 450-berth yacht harbor at Dique No. 3; docked here, the **Museo Fragata *Sarmiento*** (tel. 011/4334-9386, 10 A.M.–7 P.M. daily, US$0.60, children under 5 free), an early-20th-century naval training vessel, is a national historical monument.

Spanish architect Santiago Calatrava's **Puente de la Mujer** is a modernistic pedestrian suspension bridge whose rotating center section allows vessels to pass between Dique No. 3 and Dique No. 2. At the northernmost Dique No. 4, the **Buque Museo A.R.A. *Corbeta Uruguay*** (tel. 011/4314-1090, 10 A.M.–7 P.M. daily, US$0.60) rescued Norwegian explorers

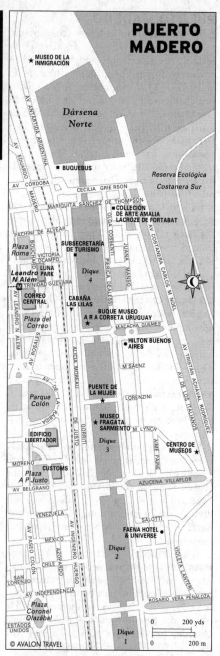

PUERTO MADERO

Carl Skottsberg and Otto Nordenskjöld from Antarctica in 1903. Dating from 1874, it's the oldest Argentine vessel still afloat.

Several original cranes remain in place along the west side of the basins, where British engineers designed the redbrick warehouses. Work on the east-side buildings was slower to progress during the economic crisis, but the riverfront is finally making a contribution to Buenos Aires's livability.

Colección de Arte Amalia Lacroze de Fortabat

On the east side of Dique No. 4, aging cement heiress Amalia Lacroze de Fortabat (widely considered Argentina's wealthiest woman) has erected a modern four-story display space for her personal art collection. Despite a reputation for cultural conservatism—she once indignantly retracted a fiction prize because she considered the novel her independent judges chose to be pornographic—the collections include some of Argentina's most cutting-edge modern artists, including Antonio Berni, Jorge de la Vega, and Xul Solar, as well as European masters and contemporaries. Even a Warhol portrait of Fortabat herself is on display.

New in late 2008, the Colección de Arte Amalia Lacroze de Fortabat (Olga Cossettini 141, tel. 011/4310-6600, www.coleccionfortabat.org.ar) is open noon–9 P.M. Tuesday–Friday, and 10 A.M.–9 P.M. weekends. Admission costs US$4, with US$1 discounts for children under age 12, students, educators, and retired people. Guided tours (in Spanish) take place at 3 and 5 P.M. on open days; English-language tours require advance reservations.

Museo Nacional de la Inmigración

Toward the barrio's north end, the **Hotel de Inmigrantes** was Argentina's Ellis Island for European immigrants. From 1911 until 1953, Old World arrivals could spend five nights here before heading into the Argentine unknown.

Building on lessons from earlier mistakes, this reception facility for immigrants was an exemplary institution when it opened. While still a work in progress, the current museum details sample family histories and panels on immigration procedures and the treatment of new arrivals.

At present, the only areas open to the public are the reception area, the dining room, and a small part of the upstairs dormitories. Part of the dining room provides access to a computerized archive on 3.7 million immigrants from 60 countries who arrived by boat after 1882.

The Museo Nacional de la Inmigración (Avenida Antártida Argentina 1355, tel. 011/4317-0285, museodelainmigracion@migraciones.gov.ar, free) is open 10 A.M.–5 P.M. weekdays, 11 A.M.–6 P.M. weekends.

SAN TELMO AND VICINITY

After yellow fever drove elite families to northern barrios like Palermo and Belgrano in the 1870s, San Telmo's narrow colonial streets became an area where impoverished immigrants could find a foothold in *conventillos*, abandoned mansions where large families filled small spaces—often a single room. Today, it's a mixed neighborhood where *conventillos* still exist but young professionals have also recycled crumbling apartment buildings and even industrial sites into stylish lofts. Famous for its Sunday street fair, a favorite among Argentines and foreigners alike, it's one of the city's best walking neighborhoods.

While colonial Spanish law dictated a city plan with uniform rectangular blocks, in practice things were not quite so regular. North-south **Calle Balcarce,** for instance, doglegs between Chile and Estados Unidos, crossing the cobblestone alleyways of **Pasaje San Lorenzo** and **Pasaje Giuffra.** The **Casa Mínima** (Pasaje San Lorenzo 380) takes the *casa chorizo* (sausage house) style to an extreme: Now open to the public as part of tours of the nearby **El Zanjón de Granados** (Defensa 755, tel. 011/4361-3002, www.elzanjon.com.ar), the width of this two-story colonial house is barely greater than the an average adult male's arm-spread.

To the east, on Paseo Colón's **Plaza Coronel Olazábal,** sculptor Rogelio Yrurtia's *Canto al Trabajo* (Ode to Labor), is a tribute to hardworking pioneers, is a welcome antidote to pompous equestrian statues elsewhere. Across the avenue, the neoclassical **Facultad de Ingeniería** (Engineering School) originally housed the Fundación Eva Perón, established by Evita to aid the poor—and her own political ambitions. Three blocks south, beneath the freeway, the so-called **Club Atlético** was a clandestine torture center during the Proceso dictatorship; it is now a memorial park.

San Telmo's heart, though, is **Plaza Dorrego** (Defensa and Humberto Primo), site of the colorfully hectic weekend flea market. A few blocks south, in a cavernous recycled warehouse, the **Museo de Arte Moderno** (Avenida San Juan 350, tel. 011/4361-1121) was closed for remodeling but was to reopen in late 2010.

◀ Plaza Dorrego

Six days a week, Plaza Dorrego is a quiet shady square where *porteños* sip *cortados* and nibble lunches from nearby cafés. On weekends, though, it swarms with Argentine and foreign visitors who stroll among dozens of antiques stalls at the **Feria de San Pedro Telmo,** the most famous and colorful of the capital's numerous street fairs. Items range from antique soda siphons to brightly painted *filete* plaques with *piropos* (aphorisms), oversized antique radios, and many other items.

The plaza and surrounding side streets also fill with street performers like the ponytailed Pedro Benavente ("El Indio"), a smooth *tanguero* (dancer) who, with various female partners, entrances locals and tourists alike—even though his music comes from a boom box. Up and down Defensa, which is closed to cars on Sunday, there are also live tango musicians and other dancers, not to mention puppet theaters, hurdy-gurdy men with parrots, and a glut of *estatuas vivas* (costumed mimes, some original and others trite).

The Feria de San Pedro Telmo takes place every Sunday, starting around 9–10 A.M. and continuing into late afternoon. Even with all the antiques and crafts stands, there's room to

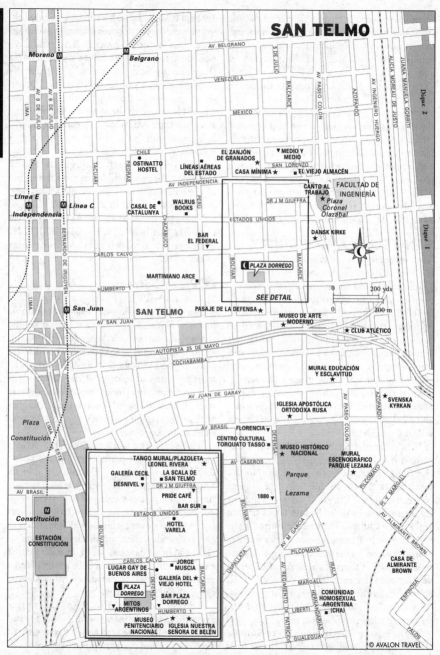

SAN TELMO

© AVALON TRAVEL

enjoy lunch and the show from the sidewalk cafés and balconies overlooking the plaza.

Parque Lezama

The presumptive but unlikely site of Pedro de Mendoza's founding of the city, famed landscape architect Carlos Thays's Parque Lezama is an irregular quadrilateral above the old river course (now covered by landfill). Shaded by mature palms and other exotic trees and studded with monuments, it's the place where aging *porteños* play chess, working-class families enjoy weekend picnics, and a Sunday crafts fair stretches along Defensa to Avenida San Juan.

On the capital's southern edge in colonial times, the property came into the hands of Carlos Ridgley Horne and then Gregorio Lezama, whose widow sold it to the city in 1884. Horne built the Italianate mansion (1846) that is now the national history museum; at the northwest entrance, Juan Carlos Oliva Navarro finished the **Monumento a Don Pedro Mendoza** (1937) a year too late to mark the 400th anniversary of Buenos Aires's original founding.

Opposite the park's north side, architect Alejandro Christopherson designed the turquoise-colored onion domes and stained-glass windows of the **Iglesia Apostólica Ortodoxa Rusa** (Russian Orthodox Church, 1904, Avenida Brasil 315), built with materials imported from St. Petersburg.

Museo Histórico Nacional

Like many Argentine museums, Parque Lezama's Museo Histórico has undergone an overhaul for Argentina's 2010 bicentennial, with new and surprisingly evenhanded material on Peronism (note Juan Perón's Grundig tape recorder, which he used to communicate to his faithful), the state terror of the Dirty War, and the 1980s democratic restoration.

There are also thematic exhibits, such as early daguerreotypes of famous but also anonymous figures from early-19th-century Argentina, that border on a social history that's often overlooked in museums of this sort. More conventionally, there's a re-creation of liberator José de San Martín's French bedroom-in-exile, portrait galleries of figures such as San Martín and independence intellectual Mariano Moreno, and massive oils that romanticize the brutal Patagonian campaigns of General Julio Argentino Roca.

The building itself is a well-kept landmark whose subterranean gallery hosts special exhibits and occasional concerts. The Museo Histórico (Defensa 1600, tel. 011/4307-1182, informes@mhn.gov.ar, free) is open 11 A.M.–6 P.M. Wednesday–Sunday.

LA BOCA

On the west bank of the twisting Riachuelo, the working-class barrio of La Boca owes its origins to mid-19th-century French Basque and Genovese immigrants who worked in packing plants and warehouses during the export-beef boom. Perhaps more than any other city neighborhood, it remains a community, symbolized by fervent—or rather, fanatical—identification with the Boca Juniors soccer team.

Socially and politically, La Boca has a reputation for disorder and anarchy, but it's also an artists' colony, a legacy of the late Benito Quinquela Martín, whose oils sympathetically portrayed its hardworking inhabitants. It is literally BA's most colorful neighborhood, thanks to brightly painted houses with corrugated zinc siding that line the pedestrian **Caminito** and other streets. Initially at least, these bright colors came from marine paints salvaged from ships in the harbor.

The starting point for most visits remains the cobbled, curving Caminito, once the terminus of a rail line, where artists display watercolors on weekends and sometimes on weekdays. On either side of the Caminito, along Avenida Pedro de Mendoza, several landmarks lend character to the neighborhood. Immediately east, for instance, high-relief sculptures stand out above the display window of the ship chandler **A. R. Constantino.** Farther on, the former restaurant **La Barca** retains a batch of Vicente Walter's well-preserved bas-reliefs on nautical themes.

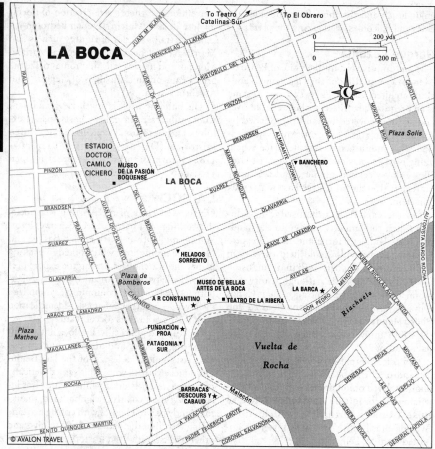

La Boca's gateway, though, is Avenida Almirante Brown, at Parque Lezama's southeast corner, where the Catalinas del Sur theater group has erected the **Mural Escenográfico Parque Lezama,** a three-dimensional mural depicting community life through colorful caricatures. Some consider the barrio dangerous and recommend guided tours, but anyone with basic street smarts should be able to visit without incident, at least in daytime.

Museo de Bellas Artes de la Boca

Boca's artist-in-residence, Benito Quinquela Martín (1890–1977), was an orphan who

became a son of his barrio, living and painting in the building that's now an homage to his life and work promoting the community. His well-lighted studio displays his oils of working-class life (Quinquela himself labored as a stevedore before devoting himself to painting). There is also a collection of brightly painted bowsprits reflecting the barrio's maritime orientation, and a selection of works by notable Argentine painters, including Antonio Berni, Raquel Forner, Eduardo Sívori, and Lino Spilimbergo.

The Museo de Bellas Artes de la Boca Benito Quinquela Martín (Pedro de Mendoza 1835, tel. 011/4301-1080, US$0.80) is open 11 A.M.–5:30 P.M. Tuesday–Sunday.

Museo de la Pasión Boquense

For residents, the barrio's key landmark is the home of the Boca Juniors, **Estadio Doctor Camilo Cichero,** better known by its nickname **La Bombonera** (Brandsen and Del Valle Iberlucea); murals of barrio life cover the walls along the Brandsen side of the stadium. In La Bombonera's catacombs, its museum is a thunderous homage to the passion for soccer and its role in the community.

Professionally organized, its 1,800 square meters include photographs of almost every player who ever took the pitch; it also includes roster cards, trophies, and even a photograph of Eva Perón in a blue-and-gold Boca jersey. Boca's ultimate icon and idol, though, remains retired striker Diego Maradona, who, despite drug problems and other erratic behavior, evokes a near-messianic loyalty. He now coaches the national team.

Interactive video timelines integrate local, national, and international events—even the Dirty War that the military dictatorship waged as Argentina hosted the 1978 World Cup—with those in the sporting world. Except for its depiction of the barrio, though, it tests the patience of non–soccer fans.

The Museo de la Pasión Boquense (Brandsen 805, tel. 011/4362-1100, www.museoboquense. com, 10 A.M.–6 P.M. daily) charges US$5 pp, or US$8 pp with a guided stadium tour.

Fundación Proa

Immediately south of the Caminito, the cavernous Fundación Proa (Avenida Pedro de Mendoza 1929, tel. 011/4104-1000, www.proa. org, 11 A.M.–7 P.M. Tues.–Sun.) is a literally state-of-the-art display space that showcases abstract and figurative works by Argentine and international painters and sculptors. In addition, it includes an auditorium that hosts a regular schedule of lectures, live music and dance, film, and other cultural events.

Admission costs US$2.50 for adults, US$0.80 for children and seniors, but children under age 12 accompanied by an adult do not pay; free guided tours take place Tuesday–Friday at 3 and 5 P.M., with an additional noon tour on weekends. English-language tours cost US$8 extra pp, for up to ten people.

BALVANERA (ONCE AND THE ABASTO)

Rarely mentioned by its official name, Balvanera subsumes several smaller neighborhoods with scattered sights: The bustling area commonly known as Congreso overlaps Monserrat and San Nicolás, while the Once and Abasto neighborhoods have their own distinctive identities.

Once, the garment district, is also the capital's most conspicuously Jewish enclave, where men and boys in yarmulkes, Orthodox Jews with their suits and beards, and even Hassidic Jews with their side curls are common sights. There are several Jewish schools, noteworthy for the heavy concrete security posts outside them—Once suffered the unsolved terrorist bombing of the **Asociación Mutualista Israelita Argentina (AMIA)** (Pasteur 633), which killed 87 people in 1994.

West of Once, Abasto was the home of tango legend Carlos Gardel, whose restored residence is now the **Museo Casa Carlos Gardel** (Jean Jaurés 735, tel. 011/4964-2071, www.museocasacarlosgardel.buenosaires. gov.ar, 11 A.M.–6 P.M. Mon. and Wed.–Fri., 10 A.M.–7 P.M. weekends and holidays, US$1, free Wed.), a tango museum dedicated to the barrio's favorite son.

In Gardel's time the magnificent **Mercado del Abasto** (1893), bounded by Avenida Corrientes, Anchorena, Agüero, and Lavalle, was a wholesale produce market that fell into disrepair before its rescue as a modern shopping center by international financier George Soros in the late 1990s. Its food court features a kosher McDonalds.

Palacio del Congreso Nacional

Balvanera's largest landmark, the neoclassical Congreso Nacional, was one of the last major public works projects undertaken before

Palacio del Congreso Nacional

© EDUARDO RIVERO/123RF.COM

Francophile architecture became the norm. The Italianate building faces the Plaza de los dos Congresos and, in the distance, the Casa Rosada.

Argentines view their legislators with skeptical and even cynical eyes, and the Congreso has always given them reason. Progressive mayor Torcuato de Alvear chose the site in 1888; the Italian Vittorio Meano won a controversial design competition, but he overshot the budget and, following a congressional inquiry, died mysteriously by a gunshot from his maid in 1904.

Functional by 1906, the building didn't receive its final touches until 1946. Its 80-meter bronze cupola still bears marks from the 1930 military coup against Hipólito Yrigoyen. Presidents who have died in office, such as Perón, have lain in state here (so did Evita, in 1952).

Phone at least an hour ahead for free guided tours of the upper-house Senado (Hipólito Yrigoyen 1849, tel. 011/4010-3000, ext. 3855, www.senado.gov.ar), which take place weekdays at 11 A.M. in Spanish, English, and French; for English speakers, there is another tour at 4 P.M., and for Spanish speakers, additional tours at 5 and 6 P.M.

In Spanish only, free guided tours of the lower-house Cámara de Diputados (Avenida Rivadavia 1864, tel. 011/4370-7532, www.diputados.gov.ar) take place weekdays except Wednesday at 10 A.M., noon, and 4 and 6 P.M.

Palacio de las Aguas Corrientes

Perhaps the capital's most photogenic building, the former waterworks (1894) glistens with 170,000 rust-colored tiles and 130,000 enameled bricks imported from Britain, crowned by a Parisian mansard. Filling an entire city block, the extravagant exterior masks a utilitarian interior of 12 metallic tanks that held more than 60 million liters of potable water.

Swedish architect Karl Nystromer conceived the building, popularly known as Obras Sanitarias, whose tanks became superfluous as engineers developed subterranean tunnels for moving water through the city. At present, the building houses offices and the small but interesting **Museo del Patrimonio Aguas Argentinas** (tel. 011/6319-1104), a museum open 9 A.M.–1 P.M. weekdays only, with free guided tours at 11 A.M. Monday, Wednesday, and Friday. The tanks now hold archives of city maps and plans that were created in conjunction with the waterworks.

The official street address is Riobamba 750, but the museum entrance is on the Rivadavia side; follow the arrows to the elevator, which takes you to the 1st floor.

RETIRO

Commonly describing the area surrounding **Plaza San Martín** but taking in everything north of Avenida Córdoba and parts of Barrio Norte, Retiro was home to an isolated 17th-century monastery and then a slave market, bullring, and cavalry barracks. After independence, it became a zone of *quintas* (country houses); by 1862, General San Martín's equestrian statue marked its definitive urbanization, and on the centenary of his birth in 1878, mayor Torcuato de Alvear turned the plaza into a public park.

From the late 19th century, the surrounding streets became the city's elite residential area.

The most extravagant residence, dating from 1909, was the **Palacio Paz** (Avenida Santa Fe 750, tel. 011/4311-1071, ext. 147, www.palaciopaz.com.ar), a 12,000-square-meter Francophile mansion built for *La Prensa* newspaper founder José C. Paz. It now houses the **Círculo Militar** (www.circulomilitar.org) and is open for guided tours (US$5 pp) in Spanish at 11 A.M. and 3 P.M. Tuesday–Friday and 11 A.M. Saturday; English-speaking tours (US$9 pp) take place at 3:30 P.M. Wednesday–Thursday. Another part of the building serves as the army's **Museo de Armas** (Weapons Museum, Avenida Santa Fe 702, tel. 011/4311-1071, ext. 179, 3–7 P.M. weekdays only, US$0.80).

On the plaza's north side, dating from 1905, the art nouveau **Palacio San Martín** (Arenales 761, tel. 011/4819-8092, free) was originally a three-house complex built for the Anchorena family. When not needed for protocol and ceremonial purposes, it's open for guided tours at 2:30 P.M. Tuesday–Wednesday.

© WAYNE BERNHARDSON

Retiro's Palacio Paz was the largest private residence ever built in Argentina.

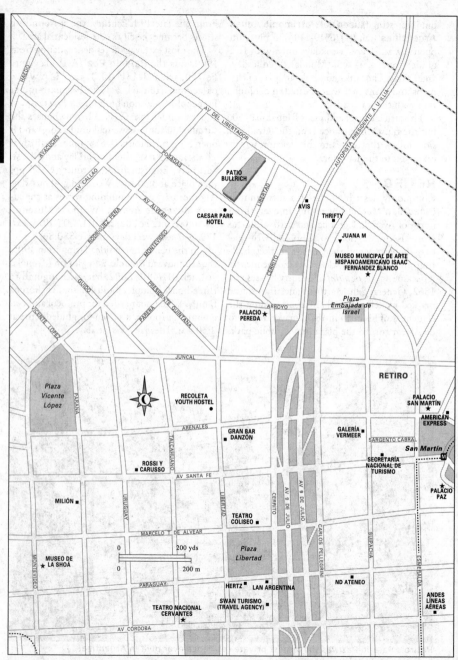

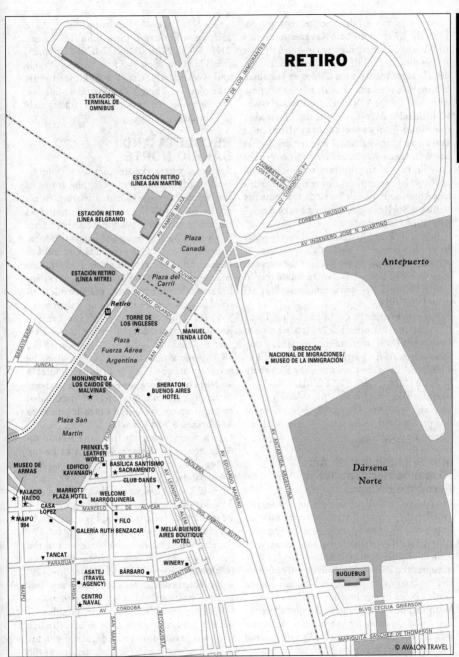

RETIRO

ESTACIÓN TERMINAL DE OMNIBUS

AV DE LOS INMIGRANTES

AV COMODORO PY

COMBATE DE COSTA BRAVA

CORBETA URUGUAY

AV INGENIERO JOSÉ N. QUARTINO

Antepuerto

ESTACIÓN RETIRO (LÍNEA SAN MARTÍN)

AV RAMOS MEJÍA

ESTACIÓN RETIRO (LÍNEA BELGRANO)

Plaza Canadá

DR G M ZUVIRÍA

ESTACIÓN RETIRO (LÍNEA MITRE)

Plaza del Carril

GILARDO GILARDI

Retiro M

★ TORRE DE LOS INGLESES

■ MANUEL TIENDA LEÓN

Plaza Fuerza Aérea Argentina

SAN MARTÍN

DIRECCIÓN NACIONAL DE MIGRACIONES/ ■ MUSEO DE LA INMIGRACIÓN

BASAVILBASO

JUNCAL

★ MONUMENTO A LOS CAÍDOS DE MALVINAS

■ SHERATON BUENOS AIRES HOTEL

Plaza San Martín

FLORIDA

AV ANTÁRTIDA ARGENTINA

Dársena Norte

FRENKEL'S LEATHER WORLD

DR R ROJAS

MUSEO DE ARMAS ★

■ EDIFICIO KAVANAGH ★

■ BASÍLICA SANTÍSIMO SACRAMENTO

AV LEANDRO

PAOLERA

AV EDUARDO MADERO

CLUB DANÉS ▾

PALACIO ★ HAEDO ★

■ MARRIOTT PLAZA HOTEL ●

WELCOME ■ MARROQUINERÍA

N ALEM

ING ENRIQUE BUTTY

★ CASA LÓPEZ ■

MARCELO DE ALVEAR

★ MAIPÚ 994 ■

▾ FILO

■ GALERÍA RUTH BENZACAR

● MELIÁ BUENOS AIRES BOUTIQUE HOTEL

▾ TANCAT

PARAGUAY

WINERY ■

MAIPÚ

■ ASATEJ (TRAVEL AGENCY)

▾ BÁRBARO

FLORIDA

TRES SARGENTOS

BUQUEBUS

★ CENTRO NAVAL

AV CÓRDOBA

SAN MARTÍN

RECONQUISTA

BLVD CECILIA GRIERSON

MARIQUITA SÁNCHEZ DE THOMPSON

© AVALON TRAVEL

At the plaza's southeast edge, dating from 1935, the 33-story **Edificio Kavanagh** (Florida 1035) was BA's first skyscraper—and its first air-conditioned building. At the northeast corner, the **Monumento a los Caídos de Malvinas** is a marble monument with names of those who died in the 1982 Falkland Islands War with Britain. Across Avenida del Libertador, the **Plaza Fuerza Aérea Argentina,** once known as Plaza Britania, was renamed after the war, when Argentina's air force was the only branch of the military that performed credibly; its centerpiece, though, is still architect Ambrose Poynter's **Torre de los Ingleses** (1916), a Big Ben clone donated by the Anglo-Argentine community.

South of Plaza San Martín, literary great Jorge Luis Borges resided in an apartment at **Maipú 994,** immediately south of the weapons museum. The beaux arts **Centro Naval** (Naval Center, Florida 801, www.centronaval.org.ar) dates from 1914.

Across Avenida 9 de Julio, facing Plaza Lavalle, the Plateresque **Teatro Nacional Cervantes** (1921) is one of the capital's key theater venues. At the barrio's southwestern edge, a block north of the Cervantes, the **Museo de la Shoá** (Montevideo 919, tel. 011/4811-3537, www.fmh.org.ar, 11 A.M.–7 P.M. Mon.–Thurs., 11 A.M.–4:30 P.M. Fri., US$1.30) is a small but professional Holocaust museum with an Argentine focus.

Museo Municipal de Arte Hispanoamericano Isaac Fernández Blanco

Housing the collections of its namesake founder, the municipal art museum contains an impressive array of Spanish- and Portuguese-American religious painting and statuary, as well as exquisite silverwork and furniture. It occupies the Palacio Noel, an equally impressive neocolonial residence built for city mayor Carlos Noel by his brother Martín in 1921. With its nods to Andalucía, Arequipa (Perú), and especially Lima for its balconies, the house was an antidote to the period's fashionable Francophile architecture.

The Museo Municipal de Arte Hispanoamericano (Suipacha 1422, tel. 011/4327-0272 or 011/4327-0228, US$0.25, free Thurs.) is open 2–7 P.M. Tuesday–Friday and weekends 11 A.M.–7 P.M. Guided tours take place at 3 and 5 P.M. Saturday–Sunday, but the museum may be closed in January and/or February.

RECOLETA AND BARRIO NORTE

Recoleta, where the line between vigorous excess and opulent eternity is thin, is one of Buenos Aires's most touristed barrios. In everyday usage, it's the area in and around its namesake cemetery, but the sprawling barrio is bounded by Montevideo, Avenida Córdoba, Avenida Coronel Díaz, Avenida General Las Heras, and the Belgrano railway. Recoleta also encompasses much of Barrio Norte, a residential area of vague boundaries that extends westward from Retiro and north into Palermo.

Once a bucolic outlier of the capital, Recoleta urbanized rapidly when upper-class *porteños* fled low-lying San Telmo after the 1870s yellow fever outbreaks. Flanking the cemetery are the Jesuit-built baroque **Iglesia de Nuestra Señora de Pilar** (1732) and one of the city's top cultural centers, all surrounded by green spaces, including **Plaza Intendente Alvear** and **Plaza Francia.**

In a former skating rink, the **Palais de Glais** houses the **Palacio Nacionales de las Artes** (Posadas 1725, tel. 011/4804-1163, www.palaisdeglace.org, noon–8 P.M. weekdays, 10 A.M.–8 P.M. weekends, admission cost depends on the program), a museum with a steady calendar of artistic and historical exhibits, plus cultural and commercial events.

Four blocks north and a block west of the cemetery, architect Clorindo Testa's **Biblioteca Nacional** (Agüero 2502, tel. 011/4806-4729, www.bibnal.edu.ar, 9 A.M.–9 P.M. weekdays, noon–7 P.M. weekends) is a concrete monolith on the grounds of the former presidential palace; the last head of state to actually live there was Juan Domingo Perón, along with his wife Evita (whose ghost, legend says, roams the

EVITA ON TOUR

Eva Perón became famous for her visit to Europe in 1947 when, as representative of an Argentina that emerged from World War II as an economic powerhouse, she helped legitimize a shaky Franco regime in Spain and, despite missteps, impressed other war-ravaged European countries with Argentina's potential. But even her death five years later did not stop her from touring.

Millions of Argentines said adios to Evita in a cortege that took hours to travel up Avenida de Mayo from the Casa Rosada to the Congreso Nacional, where her corpse lay in state. She then found a temporary resting place at the Confederación General del Trabajo (CGT, the Peronist trade union), where the shadowy Spanish physician Pedro Ara gave the body a mummification treatment worthy of Lenin in preparation for a monument to honor her legacy.

Evita remained at the CGT until 1955, when anti-Peronist General Pedro Aramburu took power and ordered her removal. Eventually, after a series of whistle-stops that included the office of an officer who apparently became infatuated with the mummy, Aramburu shipped her to an anonymous grave near Milan, Italy – even as a cadaver, Evita was a symbolic reminder of Peronism's durability.

Despite banning the party, Aramburu had reason to worry. For many years Argentines dared not even speak Perón's name while the former strongman lived in luxury near Madrid. In 1970, though, as Argentine politics came undone in an era of revolutionary ferment, left-wing Montoneros guerrillas kidnapped Aramburu and demanded to know Evita's whereabouts.

When Aramburu refused to answer, they executed him and issued a statement that they would hold the body hostage until Evita was returned to "the people." A common slogan of the time was *"Si Evita viviera, sería Montonera"* (If Evita were alive, she would be a Montonera); Perón, however, detested the leftists even as he cynically encouraged them to assist his return to power.

The police found Aramburu's body before any postmortem prisoner swap could take place, but a notary in whom Aramburu had confided came forward with information as to Evita's whereabouts. In September 1971, Perón was stunned when a truck bearing Evita's casket and corpse arrived at his Madrid residence; remarried to dancer María Estela (Isabelita) Martínez, he neither expected nor wanted any such thing. With the mummy in the attic, meanwhile, Perón's bizarre spiritualist adviser José López Rega used the opportunity to try to transfer Evita's essence into Isabelita's body.

In 1973, Perón finally returned – leaving Evita in Madrid – and was soon elected president with Isabelita as his vice president. Meanwhile, the Montoneros once again kidnapped Aramburu – from his Recoleta crypt – until Evita's return.

Angry but ill and senile, Perón died the next year, and succeeding president Isabelita flew Evita's corpse on a charter from Madrid to the presidential residence at Olivos, just north of the capital. It stayed there until March 1976, when General Jorge Rafael Videla's junta overthrew Perón's living legacy.

At Recoleta, Evita finally achieved the respectability that she envied and resented during her rise to power. Though she was an illegitimate child who went by her mother's surname, Ibarguren, she landed in the family crypt of her father, Juan Duarte, a provincial landowner – only a short walk from Aramburu's tomb.

Even that may not end Evita's wanderings. In mid-2002 there were rumors of yet another move – to San Telmo's Franciscan convent at Defensa and Alsina (ironically enough, it was set on fire by Peronist mobs in 1955, but it's also the burial place of her confessor Pedro Errecart). Another possibility is the new mausoleum at Juan Perón's *quinta* (country house) in the southern suburb of San Vicente, which holds his remains after a chaotic move from Chacarita in late 2006 (when a brawl between rival unions erupted into gunfire).

Isabelita, for her part, was even willing to see Evita lie alongside her late husband. The main objection, it seems, is that Isabelita, former caretaker president Eduardo Duhalde, and other Peronist politicians like the idea better than the Duarte heirs do.

hallways). The website has a regularly updated events calendar.

Writer Ricardo Rojas (1882–1957), who showed greater respect for South America's indigenous civilizations than any other Argentine literary figure, lived at the **Casa Museo Ricardo Rojas** (Charcas 2837, tel. 011/4824-4039, 10 A.M.–6 P.M. weekdays), and his house's architecture communicates that respect. Admission includes guided tours conducted by motivated, congenial personnel.

Centro Cultural Ciudad de Buenos Aires

In the 1980s, architects Clorindo Testa, Jacques Bedel, and Luis Benedit turned the 18th-century Franciscan convent alongside the Iglesia Nuestra Señora del Pilar into a cultural center with multiple exhibition halls and an auditorium that's one of the most important sites for late summer's Festival Buenos Aires Tango. They added the **Plaza del Pilar,** a stylish arcade housing the upscale Buenos Aires Design shopping mall and a gaggle of sidewalk restaurants and cafés.

Interestingly enough, immediately after independence, General Manuel Belgrano established an art school on the site. Thereafter, though, it served as a beggars prison until Torcuato de Alvear cleaned it up in the 1880s; Italian architect Juan Buschiazzo turned the chapel into an auditorium and transformed adjacent walls and terraces into an Italianate style. Until its 1980s remodel, it served as a retirement home.

The Centro Cultural Ciudad de Buenos Aires (Junín 1930, tel. 011/4803-1040, www.centroculturalrecoleta.org) is open 2–9 P.M. weekdays and 10 A.M.–9 P.M. weekends and holidays. Admission is free except for the Museo Participativo and for some film programs.

Museo Xul Solar

Despite his blindness, Jorge Luis Borges left vivid descriptions of paintings by Alejandro Schulz Solari, better known as Xul Solar. Obsessed with architecture and the occult, Xul Solar (1897–1963) produced vivid abstract

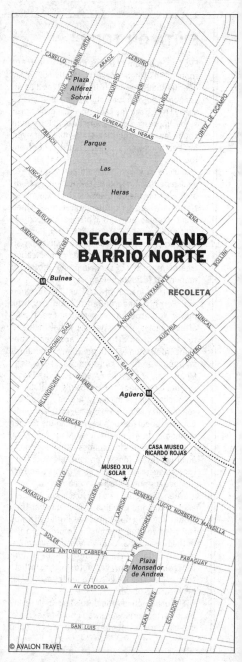

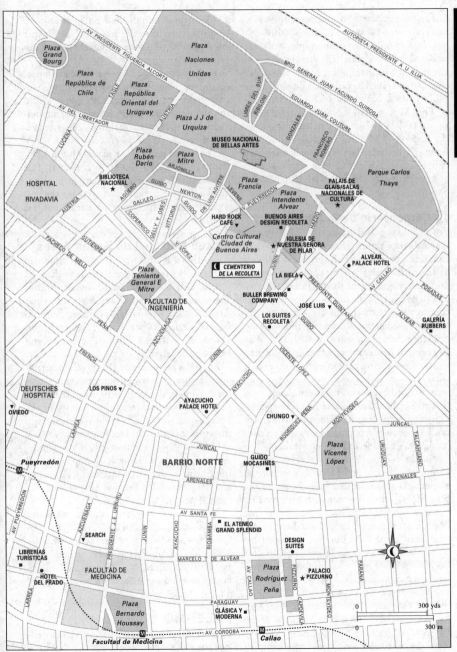

AUTOPISTA PRESIDENTE A U ILLIA

Plaza Grand Bourg

Plaza República de Chile

Plaza República Oriental del Uruguay

AV PRESIDENTE FIGUEROA ALCORTA

TAGLE

AUSTRIA

AV DEL LIBERTADOR

LUCENA

Plaza Naciones Unidas

Plaza J J de Urquiza

Plaza Rubén Darío

Plaza Mitre

ARJONILLA

BRIG GENERAL JUAN FACUNDO QUIROGA

LIBRES DEL SUR

BILLONI

GONZALES

EDUARDO JUAN COUTURE

FRANCISCO ROMERO

MUSEO NACIONAL DE BELLAS ARTES

Parque Carlos Thays

BIBLIOTECA NACIONAL ★

HOSPITAL RIVADAVIA

AUSTRIA

GUTIERREZ

AGUERO

GUIDO

GALILEO

COPERNICO

GELLY Y OBES

NEWTON

VITTORIA

GUIDO

DR LUIS AGOTTE

LEVENE

AV PUEYRREDÓN

Plaza Francia

Plaza Intendente Alvear

PALAIS DE GLAIS/SALAS NACIONALES DE CULTURA ★

HARD ROCK CAFÉ ▼

BUENOS AIRES DESIGN RECOLETA

ALVEAR PALACE HOTEL ●

PACHECO DE MELO

V LÓPEZ

Centro Cultural Ciudad de Buenos Aires

IGLESIA DE NUESTRA SEÑORA DE PILAR ★

AV CALLAO

POSADAS

Plaza Teniente General E Mitre

☾ CEMENTERIO DE LA RECOLETA

LA BIELA ▼

PRESIDENTE QUINTANA

ALVEAR

GALERÍA RUBBERS ■

FACULTAD DE INGENIERÍA

BULLER BREWING COMPANY ■

JOSÉ LUIS ■

JUNIN

GUIDO

PEÑA

LOI SUITES RECOLETA

FRENCH

AZCUENAGA

VICENTE LÓPEZ

DEUTSCHES HOSPITAL

▼ OVIEDO

LOS PINOS ▼

JUNIN

AYACUCHO

AYACUCHO PALACE HOTEL ●

CHUNGO ▼

RODRÍGUEZ PEÑA

MONTEVIDEO

JUNCAL

TALCAHUANO

URUGUAY

Plaza Vicente López

ARENALES

LARREA

JUNCAL

GUIDO MOCASINES ■

BARRIO NORTE

ARENALES

Pueyrredón Ⓜ

AV PUEYRREDON

AZCUENAGA

PRESIDENTE J E URBURU

JUNIN

AYACUCHO

RIOBAMBA

AV SANTA FE

EL ATENEO GRAND SPLENDID ■

MARCELO T DE ALVEAR

DESIGN SUITES ●

PARANA

▼ SEARCH

LIBRERÍAS TURÍSTICAS ■

HOTEL DEL PRADO ●

FACULTAD DE MEDICINA

LARREA

AV CALLAO

Plaza Rodríguez Peña

PIZZURNO

PALACIO PIZZURNO ★

MONTEVIDEO

CAPDEVILA

Plaza Bernardo Houssay

PARAGUAY

CLÁSICA Y MODERNA ■

AV CORDOBA

Facultad de Medicina Ⓜ

Callao Ⓜ

| 0 | 300 yds |
| 0 | 300 m |

oils and watercolors. This museum displays an assortment of his work, mostly smallish watercolors, in utilitarian surroundings with plasterboard walls and dim light that contrast with the painter's intense colors. It also shows personal effects, such as postcards directed to famous writers such as Friedrich Nietzsche.

The Museo Xul Solar (Laprida 1212, tel. 011/4821-5378, www.xulsolar.org.ar) is open noon–7:30 P.M. Tuesday–Friday and noon–7 P.M. Saturday; it's closed in January. Admission is US$2.50. Guided tours take place at 4 P.M. Tuesday and Thursday, and 3:30 P.M. Saturday.

◖ Cementerio de la Recoleta

For the living and dead alike, Recoleta is Buenos Aires's prestige address. Its roster of cadavers represents wealth and power as surely as the residents of its Francophile mansions and luxury apartment towers hoard their assets in overseas bank accounts. Arguably, the cemetery is even more exclusive than the neighborhood—enough cash can buy an impressive residence, but not a surname such as Alvear, Anchorena, Mitre, Pueyrredón, or Sarmiento.

Seen from the air, the cemetery seems exactly what it is—an orderly necropolis of narrow alleyways lined by ornate mausoleums and crypts that mimic the architecture of BA's belle epoque. Crisscrossed by diagonals but with little greenery, it's a densely *de*populated area that receives hordes of Argentine and foreign tourists.

Nearly everyone visits the crypt of Eva Perón, who overcame her humble origins with a relentless ambition that brought her to the pinnacle of political power with her husband, General and President Juan Perón, before her death from cancer in 1952. Even Juan Perón, who lived until 1974 but spent most of his post-Evita years in exile, failed to qualify for Recoleta; he now reposes at his former country house at San Vicente.

There were other ways into Recoleta, though. One improbable resident is boxer Luis Angel Firpo (1894–1960), the "wild bull of the Pampas," who nearly defeated Jack Dempsey for the world heavyweight championship in 1923. Firpo, though, had pull—thanks to sponsor Félix Bunge, a powerful landowner whose family owns some of the cemetery's most ornate constructions.

Endless economic crises have had an impact on one of the world's grandest graveyards, as once-moneyed families can no longer afford the maintenance of their mausoleums, but municipal authorities are making a concerted effort to restore them.

The Cementerio de la Recoleta (Junín 1790, tel. 011/4803-1594, 7 A.M.–6 P.M. daily, free admission) is the site for many guided on-demand tours through travel agencies; the municipal tourist office sponsors occasional free weekend tours.

Museo Nacional de Bellas Artes

Argentina's traditional fine arts museum mixes works by European artists such as El Greco, Goya, Klee, Picasso, Renoir, Rodin, Toulouse-Lautrec, and Van Gogh with their Argentine counterparts, including Antonio Berni, Cándido López, Raquel Forner, Benito Quinquela Martín, Prilidiano Pueyrredón, and Lino Spilimbergo.

In total it houses about 11,000 oils, watercolors, sketches, engravings, tapestries, and sculptures. Among the most intriguing are López's detailed oils, which relate the history of the Paraguayan war (1864–1870)—even though the artist lost his right arm to a grenade.

Oddly enough, architect Julio Dormald designed the 1870s building as a pump house and filter plant for the city waterworks; renowned architect Alejandro Bustillo adapted it to its current purpose in the early 1930s.

The Museo Nacional de Bellas Artes (Avenida del Libertador 1473, tel. 011/4803-0802, www.mnba.org.ar, free) is open 12:30–8:30 P.M. Tuesday–Friday; weekend hours start at 9:30 A.M. Guided tours take place Tuesday–Friday at 4 and 6 P.M., and weekends at 5 and 6 P.M.

PALERMO

Buenos Aires's largest barrio, Palermo enjoys the city's widest open spaces—thanks to

© WAYNE BERNHARDSON

a corner fruit market in Palermo

19th-century dictator Juan Manuel de Rosas, whose private estate stretched from Recoleta to Belgrano, between present-day Avenida del Libertador and the Río de la Plata. After his defeat at the battle of Caseros in 1852, Rosas went into exile in Great Britain, and his properties became **Parque Tres de Febrero.**

Once part of the capital's unsavory *arrabales* (margins), its street corners populated by stylish but capricious *malevos* (bullies) immortalized in Borges's short stories, Palermo hasn't entirely superseded that reputation—some poorly lighted streets still make visitors uneasy. Yet it also has exclusive neighborhoods such as **Barrio Parque,** the embassy row also known as **Palermo Chico,** immediately north of Recoleta.

Across Avenida del Libertador, the **Botánico** is an upper-middle-class neighborhood that takes its name from the **Jardín Botánico Carlos Thays** (Avenida Santa Fe 3951, tel. 011/4831-4527, 8 A.M.–6 P.M. daily, free), an otherwise appealing botanical garden infested with feral cats. Opposite nearby Plaza Italia, the **Jardín Zoológico** (Avenida Las Heras s/n, tel. 011/4806-7412, www.zoobuenosaires.com.ar, 10 A.M.–6 P.M. Tues.–Sun.) is an ideal outing for visitors with children (free up to age 12). General admission costs US$3 per adult.

The real center of action, though, is across Avenida Santa Fe at **Palermo Viejo,** where **Plaza Serrano** (also known as **Plaza Cortázar**) is a major locus of local nightlife. Palermo Viejo subdivides into **Palermo Soho,** a trendy term to describe the area south of Avenida Juan B. Justo, and the more northerly **Palermo Hollywood,** where many television and radio producers have located their facilities. Shaded by sycamores, many Palermo Viejo streets still contain *casas chorizo* (sausage houses) on deep, narrow lots. One of the most interesting private residences is the **Casa Jorge García** (Gorriti 5142), whose garage facade features Martiniano Arce's *filete* caricatures of the García family.

Palermo's most conspicuous new landmark is the controversial **Centro Cultural Islámico Rey Fahd** (Avenida Bullrich 55, tel. 011/4899-1144, www.ccislamicoreyfahd.org.ar), built with Saudi money on land acquired from the Menem administration. It's open for guided tours only Tuesday and Thursday noon–1 P.M. To the north, overlapping Belgrano, **Las Cañitas** is a gastronomic and nightlife zone challenging Palermo Viejo among *porteño* partygoers.

Parque Tres de Febrero

Argentine elites got their revenge on dictator José Manuel de Rosas with Parque Tres de Febrero. Not only does the equestrian **Monumento a Urquiza** (Avenida Sarmiento and Avenida Figueroa Alcorta) commemorate Rosas's military nemesis, but President Domingo F. Sarmiento's name graces one of the main avenues. Sarmiento, Rosas's implacable foe, oversaw the transformation during his presidency (1868–1874); a Rodin statue of Sarmiento now stands at the site of the dictator's bedroom (the Roman-style villa was dynamited).

In the early 20th century, noting Sunday's spectacle of horse-drawn carriages and motorcars, British diplomat James Bryce remarked that "Nowhere in the world does one get a stronger impression of exuberant wealth and extravagance." Today, though, it's a more democratic destination, where the automobiles move slowly and picnickers, walkers, joggers, in-line skaters, and cyclists can enjoy its verdant serenity.

The park's sights include the **Jardín Japonés** (Japanese Gardens); the **Rosedal** (Rose Garden, Avenida Iraola and Avenida Presidente Pedro Montt); the **Museo de Artes Plásticas Eduardo Sívori** (Avenida Infanta Isabel 555, tel. 011/4772-5628, www. museosivori.org.ar, noon–8 P.M. Tues.–Fri., 10 A.M.–8 P.M. weekends, US$0.30), a fine painting and sculpture museum; the **Hipódromo Argentino** (racetrack, Avenida del Libertador and Avenida Dorrego); and the **Campo Argentino de Polo** (polo grounds), directly across Avenida del Libertador.

Jardín Japonés

An oasis of calm in the city's rush, Buenos Aires's Japanese garden opened in 1967, when Crown Prince Akihito and Princess Michiko

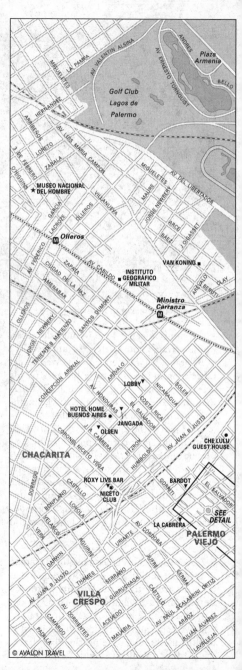

© AVALON TRAVEL

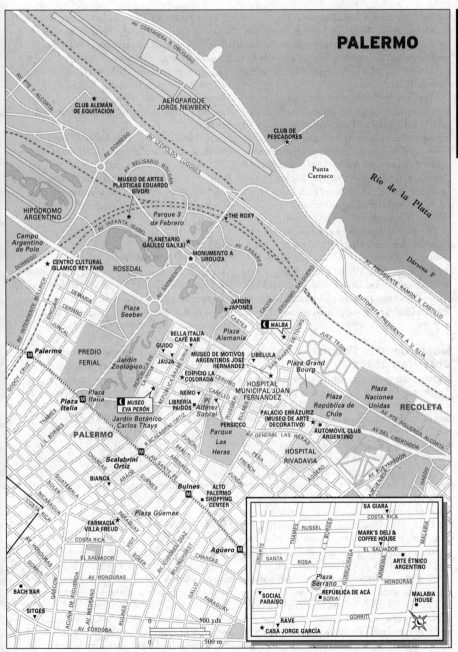

PALERMO

AV COSTANERA R OBLIGADO

AEROPARQUE JORGE NEWBERY

CLUB ALEMÁN DE EQUITACIÓN ★

AV PTE F ALCORTA

AV DORREGO

AV LEOPOLDO LUGONES

CLUB DE PESCADORES ★

Punta Carrasco

Río de la Plata

AV BELISARIO ROLDÁN

MUSEO DE ARTES PLÁSTICAS EDUARDO SÍVORI ★

Parque 3 de Febrero

THE ROXY ★

HIPÓDROMO ARGENTINO

AV INFANTA ISABEL

PLANETARIO GALILEO GALILEI ★

Dársena F

Campo Argentino de Polo

AV CASARES

MONUMENTO A URQUIZA ★

AV PRESIDENTE RAMON S CASTILLO

DORREGO

CENTRO CULTURAL ISLÁMICO REY FAHD ★

ROSEDAL

AV SARMIENTO

CALVIA

JERONIMO SAGUERO

AUTOPISTA PRESIDENTE A U ILLIA

AV INTENDENTE BULLRICH

DEMARIA

CERVIÑO

SINCLAIR

JUNCAL

Plaza Seeber

JARDÍN JAPONÉS ★

CASTEX

Plaza Alemania

MALBA

JUEZ TEDIN

GODOY CRUZ

Palermo M

PREDIO FERIAL

Jardín Zoológico

BELLA ITALIA CAFÉ BAR ▼

GUIDO

JAUJA

REPÚBLICA DE LA INDIA

MUSEO DE MOTIVOS ARGENTINOS JOSÉ HERNÁNDEZ ★

SAN MARTIN DE TOURS

LIBÉLULA ▼

Plaza Grand Bourg

SALGUERO

Plaza Naciones Unidas

RECOLETA

EDIFICIO LA COLORADA

CERVIÑO

HOSPITAL MUNICIPAL JUAN FERNÁNDEZ

Plaza Italia M

Plaza Italia

MUSEO EVA PERÓN

NEMO ▼

LIBRERÍA PAIDÓS

CABELLO

RUGGIERI

BULNES

PI ▼

Alférez Sobral

Plaza República de Chile

THAMES

J L BORGES

Jardín Botánico Carlos Thays

PALERMO

R SCALABRINI ORTIZ

PALACIO ERRÁZURIZ (MUSEO DE ARTE DECORATIVO) ■

AUTOMÓVIL CLUB ARGENTINO ■

AV DEL LIBERTADOR

AV PTE FIGUEROA ALCORTA

PERSICCO ▼

CHARCAS

Scalabrini Ortiz M

AV SANTE FE

ARENALES

JUNCAL

BERUTI

PEÑA

Parque Las Heras

AV GENERAL LAS HERAS

FRENCH

HOSPITAL RIVADAVIA

AV PUEYRREDÓN

AZCUENAGA

HAEDO

BIANCA ▼

ARAOZ

GÜEMES

Bulnes M

JUNCAL

GUATEMALA

SOLER

NICARAGUA

COSTA RICA

AV HONDURAS

GORRITI

ALTO PALERMO SHOPPING CENTER M

Plaza Güemes

PARAGUAY

VIDT

CORONEL DÍAZ

SOLER

AV CORDOBA

FARMACIA VILLA FREUD ▼

COSTA RICA

EL SALVADOR

BILLINGHURST

Agüero M

CHARCAS

BACH BAR ■

GASCON

ACUÑA DE FIGUEROA

AV MEDRANO

BULNES

GALLO

PARAGUAY

SITGES ▼

AV CORDOBA

0   500 yds

0   500 m

URIARTE

THAMES

RUSSEL

J L BORGES

GURRUCHAGA

SA GIARA ■

COSTA RICA

MALABIA

MARK'S DELI & COFFEE HOUSE ▼

EL SALVADOR

ARTE ÉTNICO ARGENTINO ■

SANTA

ROSA

ARMENIA

HONDURAS

Plaza Serrano

REPÚBLICA DE ACÁ ■

SORIA

MALABIA HOUSE ●

SOCIAL PARAÍSO ▼

GORRITI

RAVE ▼

CASA JORGE GARCÍA ★

visited Argentina. Administratively part of the Jardín Botánico, the Jardín Japonés enjoys better maintenance, and because there's chicken wire between the exterior hedges and the interior fence, it's full of chirping birds rather than feral cats.

Like Japanese gardens elsewhere, it mimics nature in its large koi pond, waterfall, and "isle of the gods," and also Japanese culture in features like its pier, lighthouse, and "bridge of fortune." In addition, the garden contains a **Monumento al Sudor del Inmigrante Japonés** (Monument to the Effort of the Japanese Immigrant). Argentina has a small but well-established Japanese community in the capital and the suburb of Escobar.

The Jardín Japonés (Avenida Casares and Avenida Adolfo Berro, tel. 011/4801-4922, www.jardinjapones.com.ar, 10 A.M.–6 P.M. daily) charges US$1.50 for adults, US$0.25 for children (above age six) on weekdays; weekend and holiday rates are US$2 for adults, US$0.75 for children. There are guided weekend tours at 3 P.M.

Museo de Arte Popular José Hernández

It's tempting to call this the "museum of irony": Argentina's most self-consciously gaucho-oriented institution sits in one of the country's most urbane and affluent neighborhoods, also home to many foreign embassies. Named for the author of the *gauchesco* epic poem *Martín Fierro,* it specializes in rural Argentiniana.

Even more ironically, land-owning oligarch Félix Bunge built the derivative French-Italianate residence with marble staircases and other extravagant features. Originally named for the Carlos Daws family, who donated its contents, it became the Museo de Motivos Populares Argentinos (Museum of Argentine Popular Motifs) José Hernández until the 1976–1983 dictatorship deleted the potentially inflammatory *populares* (which in context means "people's") from the official name. Thus, perhaps, it could depict gentry like the Martínez de Hoz family as part of a bucolic open-range lifestyle.

That said, the museum has many worthwhile items, ranging from magnificent silverwork and vicuña textiles created by contemporary Argentine artisans to pre-Columbian pottery, indigenous crafts, and even a typical *pulpería* (rural store). Translations of Hernández's famous poem, some in Asian and Eastern European languages, occupy a prominent site.

The Museo de Arte Popular José Hernández (Avenida del Libertador 2373, tel. 011/4803-2384, www.museohernandez.org.ar, 1–7 P.M. Wed.–Fri., 10 A.M.–8 P.M. weekends and holidays) charges US$0.30 admission except Sunday, when it's free. It's normally closed in February.

Museo Nacional de Arte Decorativo

Matías Errázuriz Ortúzar and his widow Josefina de Alvear de Errázuriz lived less than 20 years in the ornate beaux arts building (1918) that now houses the national decorative art museum. Its inventory consists of 4,000 items from the family's own collections, ranging from Roman sculptures to contemporary silverwork, but mostly Asian and European pieces from the 17th to 19th centuries. Many items are anonymous; the best-known are by Europeans like Manet and Rodin.

The Museo Nacional de Arte Decorativo (Avenida del Libertador 1902, tel. 011/4802-6606, www.mnad.org.ar, 2–7 P.M. Tues.–Sun., US$1.25, free Tues.) offers guided English-language tours Tuesday–Saturday at 2:30 P.M. The museum is closed the last week of December and first week of January.

◖ MALBA

Buenos Aires's most deluxe museum, the Museo de Arte Latinoamericano de Buenos Aires is a striking steel-and-glass structure dedicated to Latin American art rather than the Eurocentric contents of many—if not most—Argentine collections. Designed by Córdoba architects Gastón Atelman, Martín Fourcade, and Alfredo Tapia, it devotes one entire floor to the private collection of Argentine businessman

Eduardo F. Constantini, the motivating force behind the museum's creation; the 2nd floor offers special exhibitions.

The most prominent artists on display are the Mexicans Frida Kahlo and Diego Rivera, but there are also works by Antonio Berni, the Chilean Robert Matta, the Uruguayan Pedro Figari, and others. It also has a cinema and hosts other cultural events.

The Museo de Arte Latinoamericano de Buenos Aires (Avenida Figueroa Alcorta 3415, tel. 011/4808-6500, www.malba.org. ar, US$4, US$1.25 Wed.) is open noon–9 P.M. Wednesday, noon–8 P.M. Thursday–Monday and holidays.

Museo Eva Perón

At her most combative, to the shock and disgust of neighbors, Eva Perón chose the affluent Botánico for the **Hogar de Tránsito No. 2,** a shelter for single mothers from the provinces. Even more galling, her Fundación de Ayuda Social María Eva Duarte de Perón took over an imposing three-story mansion to house the transients.

Since Evita's 1952 death, middle-class apartment blocks have mostly replaced the elegant single-family houses and distinctive apartment buildings that then housed the *porteño* elite (many of them moved to northern suburbs). Half a century later, on the July 26th anniversary of her death—supporting Tomás Eloy Martínez's observation that Argentines are "cadaver cultists"—her great-niece María Carolina Rodríguez officially opened this professionally organized museum to "spread the life, work, and ideology of María Eva Duarte de Perón."

What it lacks is a critical perspective to help, again in Rodríguez's words, "understand who this woman was in the 1940s and 1950s, who made such a difference in the lives of Argentines"—a goal possibly inconsistent with her other stated aims. Rather than a balanced assessment, this is a chronological homage that sidesteps the issue of personality cults of both Evita and her charismatic husband.

The Museo Eva Perón (Lafinur 2988,

tel. 011/4807-9433, www.museoevita.org, 11 A.M.–7 P.M. Tues.–Sun., US$3) has a museum store with a selection of Evita souvenirs and a fine café-restaurant as well. Guided English-language tours, bookable in advance, cost US$5.

BELGRANO

North of Palermo, linked to central Buenos Aires by Subte, bus, and train, Belgrano remains a barrio apart. In fact, it was once a separate city and then, briefly in the 1880s, the country's capital; both the executive and legislative branches met at what is now the **Museo Histórico Sarmiento** (Cuba 2079, tel. 011/4781-2989, www.museosarmiento.gov. ar, 1–5:30 P.M. Sun.–Fri.), honoring President Domingo F. Sarmiento. Sarmiento never lived here, but the exhibits contain many personal possessions and a model of his provincial San Juan birthplace; it also chronicles the near–civil war of the 1880s that resulted in Buenos Aires's federalization. Admission costs US$0.60 but is free Thursdays. Guided tours take place Sunday at 4 P.M.

Immediately west, **Plaza General Manuel Belgrano** hosts a fine crafts market open on weekends and holidays; nearby, the landmark **Iglesia de la Inmaculada Concepción** (1865), colloquially known as **La Redonda** for its circular floor plan, figures prominently in Ernesto Sábato's psychological novel *On Heroes and Tombs.*

North of the plaza, set among impressive Andalusian gardens, the **Museo de Arte Español Enrique Larreta** (Juramento 2291, tel. 011/4783-2640, www.museolarreta.bue-nosaires.gov.ar, 2–8 P.M. weekdays, 2–10 P.M. weekends, US$0.30, free Thurs.) reflects the Hispanophile novelist who built it. Like many other museums, it closes in January.

A few blocks northwest, the **Museo Casa de Yrrutia** (O'Higgins 2390, tel. 011/4781-0385, www.casadeyrurtia.gov.ar, US$0.30) was the residence of sculptor Rogelio Yrurtia (1879–1950), creator of San Telmo's *Canto al Trabajo* and other works that challenged the traditional pomposity of Argentine public

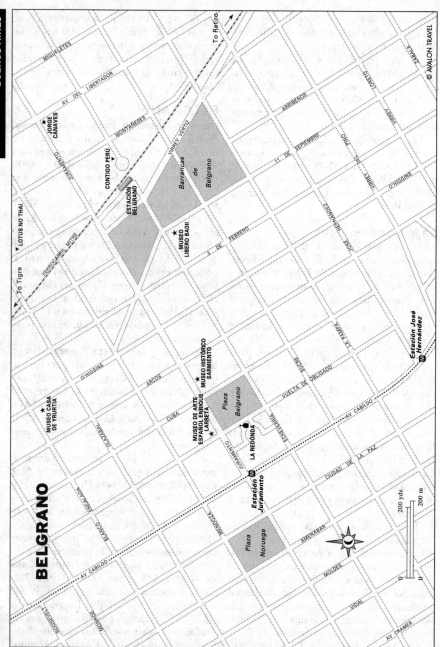

BELGRANO

© AVALON TRAVEL

To Retiro

To Tigre

FERROCARRIL MITRE

LOTUS NO THAI

JORGE CANAVES

CONTIGO PERÚ

ESTACIÓN BELGRANO

Barrancas de Belgrano

MUSEO LIBERO BADII

MUSEO CASA DE YRURTIA

MUSEO DE ARTE ESPAÑOL ENRIQUE LARRETA

MUSEO HISTÓRICO SARMIENTO

LA REDONDA

Plaza Belgrano

Estación Juramento

Plaza Noruega

Estación José Hernández

MIGUELETES

AV. DEL LIBERTADOR

MONTAÑESES

VIRREY VÉRTIZ

3 DE FEBRERO

ARRIBEÑOS

11 DE SEPTIEMBRE

VIRREY DEL PINO

O'HIGGINS

JOSÉ HERNÁNDEZ

LA PAMPA

SUCRE

VUELTA DE OBLIGADO

AV. CABILDO

CIUDAD DE LA PAZ

ECHEVERRÍA

JURAMENTO

CUBA

ARCOS

O'HIGGINS

OLAZÁBAL

ESCALADA

BLANCO

MENDOZA

AV. CABILDO

ROOSEVELT

MONROE

AMENÁBAR

MOLDES

VIDAL

AV. CRAMER

ZABALA

LORETO

TURREY

YURBE

DEL PINO

0   200 yds

0   200 m

art. Hours are 3–7 P.M. Tuesday–Friday and Sunday. Guided tours, at no additional expense, take place Tuesday–Friday at 3 P.M. and Sunday at 4 P.M.

The famous landscape architect Charles Thays turned **Barrancas de Belgrano,** three blocks east of Plaza Belgrano, into a shady public park. Just across from the park, the **Museo Líbero Badii** (11 de Septiembre 1990, tel. 011/4783-3819, 10 A.M.–4 P.M. weekdays, closed in Jan., free) exhibits the work of one of the country's most innovative sculptors (ring the bell for entry). Across the tracks from the Barrancas, along Arribeños north of Juramento, Belgrano's **Barrio Chino** (Chinatown) has grown rapidly since the 1990s, with an impressive new gate donated by the Chinese embassy. Belgrano residents who need feng shui consultants can find them here.

OUTER BARRIOS

Beyond its most touristed barrios, Buenos Aires has a variety of sights that range from the relatively mundane to the morbid. Some are less easily accessible by Subte but have regular *colectivo* (city bus) service.

◖ Museo Argentino de Ciencias Naturales

Once on the city's outskirts, the barrio of Caballito gets few tourists, but its largest open space, heavily used **Parque Centenario,** is a good area for visitors to see an unadorned but improving neighborhood that's popular with urban homesteaders. The park's natural history museum, housing one of the country's largest and best-maintained collections of its type, veers between the traditional stuff-in-glass-cases approach and more sophisticated exhibits that provide ecological, historical, and cultural context. Dating from 1937, its quarters are only a third the size of the original grandiose project but include decorative details such as bas-relief spiderwebs around the main entrance and sculpted owls flanking the upper windows.

The main floor contains geological and paleontological exhibits, including a reconstruction of the massive Patagonian specimens *Giganotosaurus carolini* (the world's largest carnivorous dinosaur) and the herbivore *Argentinosaurus huinculensis* (whose neck alone measures about 12 meters). The 2nd floor stresses mostly South American mammals (including marine mammals), comparative anatomy, amphibians and reptiles, birds, arthropods, and botany.

The Museo Argentino de Ciencias Naturales Bernardino Rivadavia (Angel Gallardo 490, tel./fax 011/4982-0306, www.macn.secyt.gov.ar, 2–7 P.M. daily, US$0.80 for visitors age 7 and older) is about equidistant from the Malabia and Angel Gallardo stations on Subte Línea B.

Cementerio de la Chacarita and Vicinity

Buenos Aires's second cemetery may be more affordable than Recoleta, but eternity at the Cementerio de la Chacarita can still mean notoriety. Its residents include high-profile Argentines in fields ranging from entertainment to religion and politics—and the lines between these categories are not always obvious.

The most beloved is tango singer Carlos Gardel, who died in a plane crash in Colombia in 1935. Hundreds of admirers from around the globe have left plaques on the tomb, many thanking him for miracles, and every June 26 they jam the cemetery's city-like streets to pay homage. As often as not, the right hand of his bronze statue holds a lighted cigarette, and a red carnation adorns his lapel.

In terms of devotion, only Spanish-born faith-healer-to-the-aristocracy Madre María Salomé comes close to Gardel; on the 2nd of most months—she died October 2, 1928— white carnations cover her tomb. Other famous figures include aviator Jorge Newbery, for whom the city airport is named, killed in a plane crash in 1914; tango musicians Aníbal "Pichuco" Troilo and Osvaldo Pugliese; poet Alfonsina Storni; La Boca painter Benito Quinquela Martín; and theater and film comedian Luis Sandrini.

Certainly the most famous, though, was Juan Domingo Perón, who was recently moved to a new mausoleum at his San Vicente country house. In June 1987, stealthy vandals entered the family's Chacarita crypt, amputating and stealing the caudillo's hands in a crime since linked to Italian financier Lucio Gelli. Anti-Peronists speculated, despite lack of evidence, that the thieves sought Perón's fingerprints for access to supposed Swiss bank accounts.

Only a short walk from the Subte Línea B's Estación Federico Lacroze, the Cementerio de la Chacarita (Guzmán 680, tel. 011/4553-9338, www.cementeriochacarita.com.ar, 7 A.M.–6 P.M. daily) covers 95 blocks with a total of 12,000 burial vaults, 100,000 gravesites, and 350,000 niches. The website is unofficial but useful.

In addition to Chacarita, there are two contiguous but formally separate cemeteries: the **Cementerio Alemán** (German Cemetery, Avenida Elcano 4530, www.cementerioaleman.org.ar, tel. 011/4553-3206) and the **Cementerio Británico** (British Cemetery, Avenida Elcano 4568, tel. 011/4554-0092, www.cementeriobritanico.org.ar). Both are open 7 A.M.–6 P.M. daily.

The Británico is more diverse, with tombs showing Armenian, Greek, Irish, Jewish, and many other immigrant nationalities. The Anglo-Argentine Lucas Bridges, son of Anglican missionaries in Tierra del Fuego and author of the memoir *The Uttermost Part of the Earth,* was buried here after dying at sea en route from Ushuaia to Buenos Aires. The Alemán features a large but politically neutral monument to Germany's World War II dead—no German or German-Argentine wants to be publicly associated with the Third Reich.

Entertainment

Buenos Aires is a 24-hour city with as much to offer as New York or London. Argentines in general and *porteños* in particular are night people—discos and dance clubs, for instance, may not even *open* until 1 A.M. or so, and they stay open until dawn. Not everything takes place at those hours, though, and since a deadly fire in late 2004 there are more municipal restrictions on live music venues and hours.

Every Buenos Aires daily has thorough event listings, especially in end-of-the-week supplements. For tickets to events at many major venues, contact **Ticketek** (tel. 011/5237-7200, www.ticketek.com.ar). The company adds a US$1 service charge to most tickets. It has outlets in the Microcentro (Viamonte 560, Locales 6 and 8), in Barrio Norte at Lee-Chi (Rodríguez Peña 1034), in San Telmo at La Trastienda (Balcarce 460), and in Recoleta at the Centro Cultural Recoleta (Junín 1930).

For discount tickets to tango shows, cinemas, and live theater, try *carteleras* such as **Cartelera Espectáculos** (Lavalle 742, Local 2, tel. 011/4322-1559); **Cartelera Baires** (Avenida Corrientes 1382, Local 24, tel. 011/4372-5058, www.cartelerabaires.com); and **Cartelera Vea Más** (Avenida Corrientes 1660, Local 2, tel. 011/6320-5319).

CAFÉS
No single place embodies tradition better than Monserrat's historic **Café Tortoni** (Avenida de Mayo 825, tel. 011/4342-4328, www.cafetortoni.com.ar). Most tourists come for coffee and croissants, but there's live tango and the bar serves good, reasonably priced mixed drinks accompanied by a sizable *tabla* of sliced salami and longaniza, pâté, Vienna sausages, cheese, and olives that easily feeds two people.

Though it has undergone a partial rehab, the worn-about-the-edges **Confitería Ideal** (Suipacha 384, tel. 011/5265-8069, www.confiteriaideal.com) remains one of the most traditional settings for coffee and croissants. Despite worn upholstery and cracked floors, the Ideal served as a set for Madonna's *Evita* debacle, and it hosts downstairs tango shows (for spectators) and upstairs *milongas* (for aspiring dancers) Wednesday and Thursday around 3 P.M. By contrast, the elegant **Confitería Richmond** (Florida 468, tel. 011/4322-1341), one of Borges's favorites, looks nearly as good as the day it opened.

Recoleta's **La Biela** (Avenida Quintana 596/600, tel. 011/4804-0449, www.labiela. com) is a classic breakfast spot, but it remains a pricey place to eat. In good weather try the patio, beneath the palm and *palo borracho* trees, and the giant *gomero* or *ombú,* which needs wooden beams to prop up its sprawling branches. It's slightly more expensive to eat outside, where the service can be inconsistent.

BARS AND CLUBS

The distinction between cafés and bars is more a continuum than a dichotomy. Some of the more stylish (or pretentious) bars call themselves pubs, pronounced as in English, though many call themselves Irish.

Relocated to Monserrat after the demolition of its classic Microcentro locale, **Bar Seddon** (Defensa 695, tel. 011/4342-3700) has made a successful transition to the capital's oldest neighborhood. Behind its street-side restaurant, **La Trastienda** (Balcarce 460, tel. 011/4342-7650, www.latrastienda.com) has recycled a Monserrat warehouse into an attractive theater that hosts both live music and drama.

Downtown Matías (Reconquista 701, tel. 011/4311-0327, www.matiaspub.com.ar) is the Microcentro branch of BA's oldest Irish-style pub; there's live music in various styles, including Celtic, and a 7–11 P.M. happy hour.

San Telmo's **Mitos Argentinos** (Humberto Primo 489, tel. 011/4362-7810, www.mitosargentinos.com.ar) has retooled as a *rock nacional* pub that hosts live music Friday and Saturday nights. **Bar Plaza Dorrego** (Defensa 1098, tel. 011/4361-0141) makes an ideal break from Sunday flea-marketeering or for a beer on its namesake plaza any other day.

In new quarters, the artsy **Foro Gandhi** (Avenida Corrientes 1743, tel. 011/4374-7501, www.casonadelarte.com.ar) is a hybrid bookstore-coffeehouse–cultural center whose offerings include films, poetry readings, tango shows, and theater.

BA's ultimate sports bar is the Abasto's **Café Bar Banderín** (Guardia Vieja 3601, tel. 011/4862-7757, www.elbanderin.com.ar). Decorated with soccer pennants dating decades back, it recalls the era when *porteños* argued about rather than gawked at *fútbol.* There's TV now, but the mid-1950s setting survives.

Retiro's **Bárbaro** (Tres Sargentos 415, tel. 011/4311-6856, www.barbarobar.com.ar) takes its punning name from a *lunfardo* (street slang) term roughly translatable as "cool." And it is, but unpretentiously so.

Bordering Barrio Norte, **Milión** (Paraná 1048, tel. 011/4815-9925, www.milion.com.ar) is a tapas bar occupying three stories of a magnificent 1913 mansion; minimally altered for its current use, it offers garden, patio, and interior seating. There's a 6–9 P.M. happy hour, for beer only, on weekdays; it keeps late hours Monday–Saturday, but closes at 1 A.M. Sunday.

The nearby **Gran Bar Danzón** (Libertad 1161, tel. 011/4811-1108, www.granbardanzon.com.ar) is a sophisticated wine bar that doubles as a restaurant, with a sushi special at happy hour (7–9 P.M.), though the sushi chef takes Mondays off. Drinkers can lounge on the comfy chairs and sofas or at the long bar; the dining area is separate. The music could be better and the volume lower, but the staff is cordial and the wine selection impressive.

Recoleta's **Buller Brewing Company** (Presidente Ramón Ortiz 1827, tel. 011/4808-9061) is a brewpub that produces seven different types of beer served with tapas, seafood, and pizza. The nearby **Hard Rock Café** (Avenida Pueyrredón 2501, 011/4807-7625, noon–3 A.M. daily) is the barrio branch of the worldwide hamburger and rock-and-roll memorabilia chain.

Palermo Hollywood's cavernous **Niceto Club** (Niceto Vega 5510, tel. 011/4779-6396, www.nicetoclub.com) has become one of the area's top live music venues over the last several years; it's open Thursday, Friday, and

Saturday nights. The musical offerings cover many styles, including electronica.

In Las Cañitas, **Van Koning** (Báez 325, tel. 011/4772-9909) is an Amsterdam-style pub that capitalizes on the Argentine fixation with all things Dutch since the country acquired its own royalty with the marriage of Máxima Zorreguieta to Crown Prince William in 2002. Dutch expats gather here the first Wednesday of every month.

Restored to its old Palermo location, beneath the railroad tracks in Parque Tres de Febrero, **The Roxy** (Avenida Casares and Avenida Sarmiento, www.theroxybsas.com. ar) traditionally draws performers of the stature of Charly García. It also operates Palermo Hollywood's **Roxy Live Bar** (Niceto Vega 5542), down the block from Niceto Club.

JAZZ

Clásica y Moderna (Avenida Callao 892, tel. 011/4812-8707) is a hybrid bookstore-café–live jazz venue that has occupied the same Barrio Norte location since 1938. Performers here have included Susana Rinaldi, Mercedes Sosa, and Liza Minnelli. Regulars get better service than strangers; it's open 8 A.M.–2 A.M. Sunday–Thursday, 8 A.M.–4 A.M. Friday–Saturday.

TANGO AND *MILONGA*

Many but not all tango venues are in the southerly barrios of Monserrat and San Telmo. Professional shows range from straightforward, low-priced programs to extravagant productions at high (often excessive) cost. *Milongas* are participatory bargains for those who want to learn.

One of the best values is Monserrat's legendary **Café Tortoni** (Avenida de Mayo 825, tel. 011/4342-4328, www.cafetortoni.com.ar) Live song-and-dance shows at its Sala Alfonsina Storni, separated from the main part of the café, cost around US$10–18 pp plus drinks and food.

Dating from 1920, the elegant **El Querandí** (Perú 302, tel. 011/5199-1770, www.querandi. com.ar) is another classic; for US$80 pp, the nightly dinner (starting at 8:30 P.M.) and show (starting at 10:30 P.M.) occupies the upper end of the scale.

San Telmo's **Bar Sur** (Estados Unidos 299, tel. 011/4362-6086, www.bar-sur.com.ar) is a relatively spontaneous and informal venue open late Monday–Saturday nights. The show costs US$48, the dinner another US$19 pp, including unlimited pizza, with drinks extra.

One of San Telmo's classic venues, occupying a late-18th-century building, **El Viejo Almacén** (Balcarce and Avenida Independencia, tel. 011/4307-6689, www.viejo-almacen.com.ar) charges US$78 pp including dinner at its restaurant, directly across the street.

Literally in the shadow of the Mercado del Abasto, part of a project to sustain the legacy of the "Morocho del Abasto" in his old neighborhood, the **Esquina Carlos Gardel** (Carlos Gardel 3200, tel./fax 011/4867-6363, www.esquinacarlosgardel.com.ar) has nightly shows from US$65 (show only) to US$92 pp (with dinner); there are also more expensive VIP seats.

In the southern barrio of Nueva Pompeya, **El Chino** (Beazley 3566, tel. 011/4911-0215) has become a tourist hangout for its rugged authenticity. Inexpensive shows (around US$8) with live music start around 11 P.M. Friday and Saturday nights, with an à la carte dinner an hour earlier. The food is working-class Argentine.

For those who want to learn instead of watch, the best options are neighborhood *milongas*. Organized events charge US$2–3 with a live orchestra, less with recorded music. For classes, a good clearinghouse is Monserrat's **Academia Nacional del Tango** (Avenida de Mayo 833, tel. 011/4345-6968, www.anacdel-tango.org.ar). For the truly committed, it even offers a three-year tango degree.

San Telmo's **Centro Cultural Torquato Tasso** (Defensa 1575, tel. 011/4307-6506, www.torquatotasso.com.ar) offers outstanding live tango music (but no dancing) Friday- and Saturday-night shows at 11 P.M. several nights every week, a free Sunday-night milonga at 10 P.M., and tango lessons every day.

Balvanera's **Italia Unita** (Perón 2535, tel. 011/4953-8700, www.saboratango.com.ar) hosts tango floor shows, but after 10:30 P.M. Saturday night it hosts a *milonga* that often features live music. Constitución's **Niño Bien** (Humberto Primo 1462, tel. 015/4147-8687) has an elegant Thursday-night *milonga* from 10:30 P.M. that gets crowded early, as it has one of the city's best dance floors.

Palermo's **Salón Canning** (Scalabrini Ortiz 1331, tel. 011/4832-6753) hosts the **Parakultural** (www.parakultural.com.ar), a more avant-garde *milonga* that incorporates electronica, on Monday, Tuesday, and Thursday from 11 P.M. On Wednesday and Friday from 8 P.M., Villa Nearby Crespo's **Tangocool** (Avenida Córdoba 5064, tel. 011/4383-7469, www.tangocool.com) offers lessons and a *práctica* (apprenticeship) that becomes a quasi-*milonga*.

CLASSICAL MUSIC AND OPERA

The classical music and opera season lasts March–November but peaks in winter, June–August. For nearly a century the premier venue has been the **Teatro Colón** (Libertad 621, tel./fax 011/4378-7344, www.teatrocolon.org.ar).

Other options include the Microcentro's **Teatro Opera** (Avenida Corrientes 860, tel. 011/4326-1335), which seats 2,500 spectators; Monserrat's **Teatro Avenida** (Avenida de Mayo 1212, tel. 011/4381-0662, www.balirica.org.ar), which has handled the opera during the Colón's closure; and Retiro's **Teatro Coliseo** (Marcelo T. de Alvear 1125, tel. 011/4816-5943).

La Scala de San Telmo (Pasaje Giuffra 371, tel. 011/4362-1187, www.lascala.com.ar) is an intimate high-culture performing arts venue focused on theater and classical music plus occasional folkloric indulgences.

CINEMA

Buenos Aires's traditional commercial cinema district is in the Microcentro along the Lavalle pedestrian mall west of Florida and along Avenida Corrientes and Avenida Santa Fe. In addition, there are multiplexes in the shopping malls of Puerto Madero, Retiro, and Palermo, and in barrios such as Belgrano.

Imported films generally appear in the original language with Spanish subtitles, except for animated and children's movies, which are dubbed into Spanish. Spanish-language translations of titles are often misleading, but the *Buenos Aires Herald* prints the original English title and translations of other foreign-language titles.

In the Microcentro, the Instituto Nacional de Cine y Artes Visuales (www.incaa.org.ar) operates two central cinemas mostly promoting Argentine films: the four-screen **Complejo Tita Merello** (Suipacha 442, tel. 011/4322-1195) and the three-screen **Cine Gaumont** (Rivadavia 1635, tel. 011/4371-3050). At the Teatro San Martín's **Sala Leopoldo Lugones** (Avenida Corrientes 1530, 10th floor, tel. 011/4371-0111, www.teatrosanmartin.org.ar), Werner Herzog is as mainstream as it gets.

The two-screen **Complejo Cine Lorca** (Avenida Corrientes 1428, tel. 011/4371-5017) shows mostly European films and the occasional off-center Hollywood flick (in the *Bad Santa* vein).

In Palermo, within a much larger art facility, the screening room at the **Museo de Arte Latinomamericano de Buenos Aires** (MALBA, Avenida Figueroa Alcorta 3415, tel. 011/4808-6500, www.malba.org.ar/web/cine.php) shows up to half a dozen classics, documentaries, and obscurities daily.

THEATER

Despite Argentina's countless economic crises, Buenos Aires remains the continent's theater capital. The district's traditional heart is Avenida Corrientes, between Avenida 9 de Julio and Avenida Callao, but many venues are showing the effects of economic hardship. Avenida de Mayo and many Microcentro side streets are also home to important theaters, many of them historic.

Winter is the main season, but events can take place at any time of year. For discount tickets, check *carteleras* or online ticket-purchasing

© WAYNE BERNHARDSON

Teatro Avenida

services. All major *porteño* newspapers provide extensive listings and schedules.

The single most notable facility is the **Teatro General San Martín** (Avenida Corrientes 1530, tel. 011/4371-0111, www.teatrosanmartin.com.ar), a multipurpose complex that lacks architectural merit but compensates with its diverse offerings.

Other notable theater institutions include the **Sala Pablo Neruda** (Avenida Corrientes 1660, tel. 011/4370-5388); **Teatro Avenida** (Avenida de Mayo 1212, Monserrat, tel. 011/4381-3193); and the **Teatro Nacional Cervantes** (Libertad 815, tel. 011/4815-8883, www.teatrocervantes.gov.ar).

There are several smaller and less conventional "off-Corrientes" venues, some of which might be called microtheaters—**Teatro El Vitral** (Rodríguez Peña 344, tel. 011/4371-0948, www.teatroelvitral.com.ar) seats only about 40 people in front of each of its three small stages. Part of a politically and socially conscious bookstore, **LiberArte** (Avenida Corrientes 1555, tel. 011/4375-2341, www.

liberarteteatro.com.ar) offers weekend theater programs.

Before his death in 1977, La Boca artist and promoter Benito Quinquela Martín donated the building that serves as headquarters for La Boca's **Teatro de la Ribera** (Pedro de Mendoza 1821, tel. 011/4302-9042, www.teatrosanmartin.com.ar). Their barrio compatriots **Teatro Catalinas Sur** (Benito Pérez Galdós 93, tel. 011/4300-5707, www.catalinasur.com.ar) form one of the capital's most entertaining and creative companies, worth seeing for those who don't know a word of Spanish.

CULTURAL CENTERS

Adjacent to the Galerías Pacífico, the **Centro Cultural Borges** (Viamonte and San Martín, tel. 011/5555-5359, www.ccborges.org.ar, US$2.50 pp) features permanent exhibits on Argentina's most famous literary figure as well as rotating fine arts programs and performing arts events. Hours are 10 A.M.–9 P.M. Monday–Saturday, noon–9 P.M. Sunday.

Recoleta's **Centro Cultural Ciudad de Buenos Aires** (Junín 1930, tel. 011/4803-1040, www.centroculturalrecoleta.org) is one of the city's outstanding cultural venues, with many free or inexpensive events. It's open 2–9 P.M. Tuesday–Friday, 10 A.M.–9 P.M. weekends and holidays; there are guided visits (tel. 011/4803-4057) Wednesday at 6 P.M. and Saturday at 3 and 5 P.M.

In recent years the **ND Ateneo** (Paraguay 918, tel. 011/4328-2888, www.ndateneo.com.ar) has set the standard for seeing top-quality musicians in an intimate theater setting. Styles include jazz, rock, folklore, and others.

GAY VENUES

Buenos Aires has a vigorous gay scene, centered mostly around Recoleta, Barrio Norte, and Palermo Viejo, with a handful of venues elsewhere. Lots of gay men hang out on Avenida Santa Fe between Callao and Pueyrredón, a good area to meet people and learn the latest. The monthly publication *La Otra Guía* lists gay-oriented and gay-friendly businesses.

The capital's gay venues are mostly tolerant

FERIAS OF BUENOS AIRES

For sightseers and spontaneous shoppers alike, Buenos Aires's diverse ferias (street fairs) are one of the city's greatest pleasures. The most prominent is Sunday's **Feria de San Pedro Telmo**, which fills Plaza Dorrego and surrounding streets – authorities close Calle Defensa to vehicle traffic – with booths full of antiques, *filete* paintings, and other crafts. There are professional tango musicians and dancers, and dozens of other street performers range from embarrassingly mundane to truly innovative. Running roughly 10 A.M.-5 P.M., it also involves sidewalk cafés and nearby upscale antiques shops.

So successful is the Feria de San Pedro Telmo that it has aided the now-thriving **Feria Parque Lezama**, a Sunday crafts fair that has gradually spread north from its namesake park up Defensa and under the freeway; only the broad Avenida San Juan has managed to stop it. Parque Lezama also gets Sunday street performers, though not as many as in Plaza Dorrego.

In La Boca, the **Feria Artesanal Plazoleta Vuelta de Rocha** (Avenida Pedro de Mendoza and Puerto de Palos) takes place weekends and holidays 10 A.M.-6 P.M.; along the length of the nearby Caminito, painters, illustrators, and sculptors sell their works in the **Feria del Caminito**, open 10 A.M.-6 P.M. daily.

After San Telmo, the most frequented feria is Recoleta's crafts-oriented **Feria Plaza Intendente Alvear**. Immediately northeast of the Centro Cultural Recoleta, also strong on street performers, it has begun to stretch south along Junín; hours are 9 A.M.-7 P.M. weekends and holidays.

On weekends and holidays, crafts stalls cover most of Belgrano's main square at the easygoing **Feria Artesanal Plaza General Manuel Belgrano** (Juramento and Cuba). Hours are 9 A.M.-7 P.M. or even later, when it gets better.

Gauchesco traditions thrive in the weekend **Feria de Mataderos,** where city-bound *paisanos* (countrymen) and would-be *paisanos* immerse themselves in the nostalgia of the *campo* (countryside). In addition to a diverse crafts selection, this spirited street fair features open-air *parrilladas* (mixed grills) and regional delicacies like tamales along with live music and dancing in rural styles such as *chamamé*, horseback races, and even – during Carnaval – a neighborhood *murga* (troupe) to kick off the season in the style of northwestern Jujuy Province. In the southwesterly barrio of Mataderos, in the streets surrounding the arcades of the former Mercado de Hacienda (Lisandro de la Torre and Avenida de los Corrales), the feria (www. feriademataderos.com.ar) is about an hour from the Microcentro by *colectivo* No. 180 and *ramal* (branch) 155 from Tucumán, Talcahuano, or Lavalle. In summer it takes place 6 P.M.-midnight Saturday; the rest of the year, it starts at 11 A.M. Sunday.

and even inclusive of nongays. When non-Argentine heterosexual women tire of Argentine machismo, they sometimes even prefer gay bars for dancing, but *porteño machistas* are catching on to this.

San Telmo's **Pride Café** (Balcarce 869, tel. 011/4300-6435) is a corner café and meeting place that draws plenty of straight folks for sandwiches, sweets, specialty drinks, and the 7–9 P.M. happy hours.

Barrio Norte's **Search** (Azcuénaga 1007, tel. 011/4824-0932) is a well-established gay bar open nightly with live entertainment.

In Balvanera/Once, the durable **Angel's** (Viamonte 2168, www.discoangels.com.ar) is a gay male bar and dance club that's open Thursday–Saturday after midnight to the beat of electronica.

On the edge of Palermo, one of BA's most popular gay bars, **Sitges** (Avenida Córdoba 4119, tel. 011/4861-3763, www.sitgesonline. com.ar), packs them into three large but distinct spaces almost until daybreak. Known for drag shows, it offers some mainstream entertainment and gets celebrity clientele.

Palermo Soho's **Bach Bar** (Cabrera 4390) is

a predominantly lesbian locale that doesn't advertise the fact—there's no sign outside—but there's usually a crowd. It's open from about 11 P.M. Tuesday–Sunday.

Also in Palermo Soho, **Bulnes Class**

(Bulnes 1250, tel. 011/4861-7492, www.bulnesclass.com.ar) is a comfortable, spacious locale with contemporary style and drag shows in the Liza Minnelli mold that also draw women and mixed crowds.

Events

Buenos Aires observes all the usual holidays and many special events on top of that. The summer months of January and February, when most *porteños* leave on vacation, are generally quiet; things pick up after school starts in early March.

Dates for the pre-Lenten **Carnaval** (Carnival), in February or March, vary from year to year; unlike Brazil's massive festivities, Carnaval here means neighborhood *murgas* (street musicians and dancers), and celebrations take place on weekends rather than during the entire week.

Since 1998, when it began on Gardel's December 11 birthday, the **Festival Buenos**

Aires Tango (www.festivaldetango.gov.ar) has moved twice before appearing to settle around mid-August, immediately before the Mundial de Tango (World Tango Championships), which run to the end of the month. Despite its recent beginnings, the tango festival has already become one of the city's signature events, spanning two weekends and including music, song, and dance that ranges from traditional and conservative to imaginative and even daring. Unlike the mass spectacle of Carnaval, it's a decentralized series of performances at smaller, often intimate venues around the capital. As such, it offers opportunities to see and hear

© WAYNE BERNHARDSON

Murga dancers and drummers parade down Avenida Corrientes at Carnaval.

not just established artists but also developing performers. Most funds for the city-sponsored festival go to pay the artists, and admission is either free or inexpensive; tickets are usually available on a first-come, first-served basis on the day of the performance.

Mid-April's three-week book fair, the **Feria del Libro** (www.el-libro.com.ar), is Latin America's largest and has been a fixture on the literary scene for nearly three decades. Most exhibitors at Palermo's Predio Ferial (entrances at Cerviño 4474 and Avenida Sarmiento 2704, tel. 011/4777-5500, US$1) are from the region, but authors of international stature, including the English-speaking world, make notable appearances.

Late April's **Festival Internacional de Cine Independiente** (International Independent Film Festival, www.bafici.gov.ar) has become a fixture over the past decade. Featuring independent films from every continent, it takes place at various cinemas but mostly at the Mercado del Abasto.

For nearly two decades, now at Palermo's Predio Ferial, mid-May's **Feria de Galerías Arte BA** (www.arteba.com) has shown work from dozens of Buenos Aires art galleries.

Not an official holiday, June 24 commemorates the **Día de la Muerte de Carlos Gardel**, the anniversary of the singer's death in an aviation accident in Medellín, Colombia. Pilgrims crowd Chacarita cemetery to pay tribute, and there are also tango events.

For more than a century, late July's **Exposición Internacional de Ganadería, Agricultura y Industria Internacional** (www.ruralarg.org.ar), the Sociedad Rural's annual agricultural exhibition at the Predio Ferial, has been one of the capital's biggest events.

Though the tango festival has moved to late February and early March, the city still closes the street near the Central Cultural San Martín on Gardel's December 11 birthday for the **Milonga de Calle Corrientes,** dancing to live and recorded music.

Shopping

The main shopping areas are the Microcentro, along the Florida pedestrian mall toward Retiro; Retiro, around Plaza San Martín and along Avenida Santa Fe; Recoleta, near the cemetery; and the tree-lined streets of Palermo Viejo, where stylish shops sit among the newest restaurants and bars. Street markets take place in San Telmo, Recoleta, and Belgrano.

SHOPPING CENTERS

Over the past decade-plus, many older buildings have been recycled into upmarket malls for one-stop shopping. The most notable is the Microcentro's magnificent **Galerías Pacífico** (Florida and Córdoba, tel. 011/5555-5100, www.galeriaspacifico.com.ar).

Once a livestock auction house, Retiro's **Patio Bullrich** (Avenida del Libertador 750, tel. 011/4814-7400, www.shoppingbullrich.

com.ar) has become a palatial 24,000-square-meter commercial space with nearly 70 shops, plus restaurants and cinemas, on four levels.

Buenos Aires Design Recoleta (Avenida Pueyrredón 2501, tel. 011/5777-6000, www.designrecoleta.com.ar) is a 3,000-square-meter complex of shops and restaurants on two levels alongside the cultural center and cemetery. As its name suggests, it focuses on design and interior decoration.

ANTIQUES

Sunday's **Feria de San Pedro Telmo,** one of the city's biggest tourist attractions, fills Plaza Dorrego with antiques and bric-a-brac. There are also many dealers in galleries with small street-side frontage, including **Galería Cecil** (Defensa 845, tel. 011/4307-0259) and **Galería de la Defensa** (Defensa 1179).

ART GALLERIES

Buenos Aires has a thriving modern-art scene, with the most innovative galleries in Retiro and Recoleta. Retiro's **Galería Ruth Benzacar** (underground at Florida 1000, tel. 011/4313-8480, www.ruthbenzacar.com) showcases some of the capital's and the country's most avant-garde artists.

Galería Rubbers (Avenida Alvear 1595, Recoleta, tel. 011/4816-1864, www.rubbers.com.ar) is an excellent contemporary gallery. **Galería Vermeer** (Suipacha 1168, Retiro, tel./fax 011/4393-5102, www.galeriavermeer.com.ar) is less up-to-date but still a good one.

BOOKS AND MUSIC

Bookstores are where Buenos Aires shopping really shines; they are as much—or more—cultural as commercial institutions, and they take that role seriously.

Buenos Aires's signature bookstore is the Microcentro branch of **El Ateneo** (Florida 340, tel. 011/4325-6801, www.tematika.com.ar), which has a huge selection of Argentine history, literature, and coffee-table souvenir books, plus domestic travel titles (it is also a publishing house).

The most elegant, though, is the affiliated **El Ateneo Grand Splendid** (Avenida Santa Fe 1880, Barrio Norte, tel. 011/4813-6052), which made *The Guardian's* list of the world's ten best bookstores. Opened in December 2000, it occupies a recycled cinema that deserves a visit simply to see its seamless transformation—the stage is a café, readers can relax in the opera-style boxes, and floor-to-ceiling bookshelves line the curving walls of the upper levels.

In a notable art deco building, Monserrat's **Librería de Ávila** (Adolfo Alsina 500, tel. 011/4311-8989, www.libreriadeavila.servisur.com) is a classic book dealer specializing in history, ethnology, travel literature, tango, folklore, and the like; it also hosts book presentations and even musical events, and it has a café.

San Telmo's **Walrus Books** (Estados Unidos 617, tel. 011/4300-7135, www.walrus-books.

boots for sale in Palermo

© WAYNE BERNHARDSON

com.ar) carries an ample selection of English-language books well beyond the usual Stephen King potboilers. Hours are 10 A.M.–8 P.M. Tuesday–Sunday.

Librería Platero (Talcahuano 485, Tribunales, tel. 011/4382-2215, www.libreriaplatero.com.ar) may be BA's best specialist shop, with an enormous stock of new and out-of-print books (the latter in the basement stacks). It does good trade with overseas academics and libraries.

Librerías Turísticas (Paraguay 2457, tel. 011/4963-2866 or 011/4962-5547) has an outstanding choice of Argentine maps and guidebooks, including its own guides to neighborhood cafés.

In addition to books, **El Ateneo** and **El Ateneo Grand Splendid** carry quality CDs. **Zivals** (Avenida Callao 395, tel. 011/5128-7500, www.zivals.com) has a large and varied bargain bin in addition to its regular stock. For alternative music, try **Disquería Oid Mortales** (Avenida Corrientes 1145, Local 17, tel. 011/4382-8839, www.oidmortalesdiscos.com.ar) or **Free Blues** (Rodríguez Peña 438, tel. 011/4373-2999), which deals in used CDs, cassettes, and even vinyl.

CRAFTS

In the Galerías Pacífico, **El Boyero** (Florida 760, tel. 011/5555-5307, www.elboyero.com) sells items ranging from leather bags, boots, and belts to gaucho and Mapuche silverwork and *mate* gourds, but also ceramics.

Monserrat's **Arte Indígena y Criollo** (Balcarce 234, tel. 011/4343-1455, www.arteyesperanza.com.ar) stocks a representative sample of indigenous crafts from around the country. Palermo's **Arte Étnico Argentino** (El Salvador 4656, tel. 011/4832-0516, www.arteetnicoargentino.com) specializes in

textiles, specifically clothing from the Andean Northwest and woolen rugs from the Mapuche of Patagonia, along with rustically styled furniture.

LEATHER GOODS AND FOOTWEAR

Retiro has several leather specialists, starting with **Frenkel's Leather World** (Florida 1055, tel. 011/4311-2300, www.frenkelsleather.com.ar), which sells crafts as well. Try **Casa López** (Marcelo T. de Alvear 640/658, tel. 011/4311-3044, www.casalopez.com.ar) for women's handbags and accessories in particular.

Welcome Marroquinería (Marcelo T. de Alvear 500, tel. 011/4313-7847, www.welcome-leather.com.ar) and **Rossi y Carusso** (Avenida Santa Fe 1377, Barrio Norte, tel. 011/4811-1965, www.rossicaruso.com) are among the best-established leather-goods sellers.

Italian immigrant Luciano Bagnasco created one of the capital's most enduring shoemakers in **Guido Mocasines** (Rodríguez Peña 1290, Barrio Norte, tel. 011/4813-4095, www.guidomocasines.com.ar).

WINE

Retiro's **Winery** (Avenida Leandro N. Alem 880, tel. 011/4311-6607, www.winery.com.ar) sells Argentine wines by the glass and also carries a stock of imported wines. It has several other branches around town.

Palermo Soho's **Lo de Joaquín Alberdi** (Borges 1772, tel. 011/4832-5329, www.lodejoaquinalberdi.com.ar) is the retail outlet of the Cabernet restaurant across the street. Near the U.S. Embassy, **Terroir** (Buschiazzo 3040, tel. 011/4778-3408, www.terroir.com.ar) is the city's elite wine shop, with access to limited vintages in addition to the usual fine wines, but it's not utterly unaffordable.

Sports and Recreation

Not just a city for sightseeing, Buenos Aires also offers activities ranging from the calm of a chess match to language study to the energy of a soccer game.

RUNNING

Many *porteños* have taken up running, but the largest open spaces suitable for it are in the northern suburbs of Palermo and Belgrano. The major exception is the Reserva Ecológica Costanera Sur, the former rubbish tip near Puerto Madero.

CYCLING AND MOUNTAIN BIKING

Buenos Aires's densely built city center, ferocious traffic, and monotonous terrain limit recreational cycling, but a surprising number of *porteños*—even some police officers—get around on bicycles. There is a growing network of paved bicycle trails, and Palermo's parks and the roads of suburban Buenos Aires Province encourage some riders.

San Telmo's **La Bicicleta Naranja** (Pasaje Giuffra 308, tel. 011/4362-1104, www.labicicletanaranja.com.ar) offers bicycle rentals and tours of the city; it has an additional Palermo branch (Nicaragua 4825).

Rental bikes are also available along Avenida de Infanta Isabel in Palermo's Parque Tres de Febrero (on both sides of the Museo de Artes Plásticas Eduardo Sívori), and at the Reserva Ecológica Costanera Sur.

HORSEBACK RIDING

In addition to tourist-oriented *estancias,* the city itself offers several riding options: try the **Club Hípico Mediterráneo** (Avenida Figueroa Alcorta 4800, Palermo, tel. 011/4772-3828), or the **Club Alemán de Equitación** (Avenida Dorrego 4045, Palermo, tel. 011/4778-7060).

GOLF

The 18-hole **Golf Club Lagos de Palermo** (Avenida Tornquist 1426, tel. 011/4772-7261) is open 7 A.M.–5 P.M. Tuesday–Sunday. Greens fees are low, but reservations are almost essential.

SOCCER

Soccer-mad Buenos Aires has six first-division teams, and it seems there's a match every night. For participants, there are pickup games in Palermo's parks and elsewhere.

For spectators, *entradas populares* (standing-room tickets) are cheapest, but *plateas* (fixed seats) have better security. The most popular clubs are **Boca Juniors** (Brandsen 805, La Boca, tel. 011/4309-4700, www.bocajuniors.com.ar); **River Plate** (Avenida Presidente Figueroa Alcorta 7597, Núñez, tel. 011/4789-1200, www.cariverplate.com.ar); and **San Lorenzo de Almagro** (Avenida Perito Moreno and Varela, tel. 011/4381-8095, www.sanlorenzo.com.ar).

HORSE RACING

The country's major track is the **Hipódromo Argentino** (Avenida del Libertador 4101, Palermo, tel. 011/4788-2800, www.palermo.com.ar). Races take place any day of the week, but mostly Friday–Monday. General admission costs US$1, with minimum bets about the same.

Accommodations

Buenos Aires has abundant accommodations in all categories. Since 2002's economic implosion, some opportunistic hoteliers have established higher rates for foreigners; if they insist on this, there's little you can do except go elsewhere or, if your language skills are good enough, try to argue the point. Advertised rates at top-end hotels often exclude the 21 percent IVA, but prices listed here do include taxes.

UNDER US$25

Over the past several years, youth hostels have sprung up like tango halls in Gardel's time, and most of them are good to excellent at modest prices. Some but not all are Hostelling International affiliates.

It actually lies within Retiro, but HI affiliate **Recoleta Youth Hostel** (Libertad 1216, tel. 011/4812-4419, www.trhostel.com.ar, US$10–12 pp dorm, US$39–50 d with private bath) still boasts an excellent location—arguably the most prestigious address of any hostel in the city. Rates are higher on weekends.

Congreso's **St. Nicholas Youth Hostel** (Bartolomé Mitre 1691, tel. 011/4373-5920, www.snhostel.com, US$10 pp dorm, US$41–46 s or d in private rooms) is another rehab with ample common spaces; those common spaces, though, are so close to the dorms that it can be hard to get to sleep at an early hour.

Near the Facultad de Medicina, **Hotel del Prado** (Paraguay 2385, tel. 011/4961-1192, www.hoteldelprado-ba.com.ar, US$25 s or d) is a plain but tastefully remodeled older building with a quiet interior, good beds, and friendly owner-operators. Rooms have private bath, cable TV, telephone, and ceiling fans but no air-conditioning; there are discounts for extended stays.

US$25-50

In the Microcentro, the independently operated **V&S Hostel Club** (Viamonte 887, tel./fax 011/4322-0994 or 011/4327-5131,

---

THERE'S NO PLACE LIKE HOME

Rather than renting a hotel room, visitors spending at least a week in Buenos Aires should consider renting an apartment and living in a neighborhood. Shopping in the same place every day, buying a newspaper from the corner kiosk, learning the bus lines and Subte system, and establishing a rapport with the *portero* (doorman) give a traveler the chance to be part of local society. It's especially good if you wish to stay in a neighborhood like Palermo or Belgrano, which have relatively few accommodations.

Daily newspapers like *Clarín*, *La Nación*, and the *Buenos Aires Herald* all have rental listings. For short-term rentals, though, the best option is an agency, such as **B y T Argentina Travel & Housing** (tel. 011/4821-6057, www.bytargentina. com); its online inventory of apartments and other housing is a good way to familiarize yourself with the options. Other possibilities include **BA House** (tel. 011/4851-0798, www.bahouse.com.ar), with a smaller selection of housing in a more geographically restricted area, and **Alojargentina** (tel. 011/5219-0606, www. alojargentina.com.ar).

---

www.hostelclub.com, US$11–19 pp dorm, US$65 s or d) has both dorms and rooms with private baths. The century-old structure has central heating, air-conditioning, and large, attractive common areas that include a kitchen, a dining room, and a *parrilla* for barbecues.

It's not quite the design hostel it aspires to be, but San Telmo's **(Ostinatto Hostel** (Chile 680, tel. 011/4362-9639, www.ostinatto.com. ar, US$10 pp dorm, US$47–49 d with private bath) has done some daring innovations while keeping prices modest, even low, in an ideal location. It features a bar-restaurant, a rooftop terrace that hosts barbecues, and even a mini-cinema, and offers at least one free-of-charge activity per day.

Rates at Monserrat's **Hostel Inn Tango City** (Piedras 680, tel. 011/4300-5776, www.hostel-inn.com, US$11 pp dorm, US$42 d), an HI affiliate, includes breakfast, kitchen facilities, free Internet, and even dinner Monday–Thursday. It's even dog-friendly, but owners must take responsibility for their canine companions.

Congreso's **(Hotel Chile** (Avenida de Mayo 1297, tel./fax 011/4383-7877, www.hotelchile.com.ar, US$37 s, US$45 d) is an art nouveau monument offering modernized rooms with private baths, cable TV, and telephones. Corner balcony rooms on the upper floors enjoy panoramic views of the Congreso and, by craning your neck eastward, the Plaza de Mayo and Casa Rosada; the decibel level rises from the street, though.

US$50-100

The **(Goya Hotel** (Suipacha 748, tel./fax 011/4322-9311, www.goyahotel.com.ar, US$40–60 s, US$55–75 d) is one of the Microcentro's best small hotels. Rates include private bath, cable TV, and air-conditioning; some slightly dearer rooms have whirlpool tubs. It may be advantageous to pay pesos in cash, as their exchange rate is unfavorable.

The **Ayacucho Palace Hotel** (Ayacucho 1408, tel./fax 011/4806-1815, www.ayacucho-hotel.com.ar, US$60 s, US$70 d) offers some of the exterior style of more elegant *porteño* hotels without extravagant prices. Its 70 rooms are plainly but comfortably furnished.

On a block-long street, Palermo Soho's **(Che Lulu Guest House** (Emilio Zolá 5185, tel. 011/4772-0289, www.luluguest-house.com, US$20 pp–US$70 d) is an artist-inspired B&B where eight small but colorful rooms go for bargain prices. The spacious common areas, well isolated from the bedrooms in this three-story house, make staying here a sociable experience.

Only half a block off Plaza Dorrego,

catering exclusively to gay men, San Telmo's **Lugar Gay de Buenos Aires** (Defensa 1120, tel. 011/4300-4747, www.lugargay.com.ar, US$40–60 s, US$50–80 d) is nicely recycled eight-room B&B with secluded rooftop terraces. Payment is by cash only.

At **(Hotel Dos Congresos** (Rivadavia 1777, tel. 011/4372-0466, www.hoteldoscongresos.com, US$79 s, $US84 d), the stately exterior is a misleading approach to a refurbished interior, where spacious and comfortable rooms with cable TV, air-conditioning, telephones, and other standard amenities come with a buffet breakfast. Reservations are advisable for the loft rooms, which have spiral staircases and whirlpool tubs.

US$100-150

Monserrat's "hetero-friendly" **Axel Hotel** (Venezuela 647, tel. 011/4136-9400, www.axelhotels.com, from US$110 s or d) is the city's first full-service hotel built and run with the gay community in mind. Architecturally, the creative use of transparent glass in common areas suggests its guests have nothing to hide, but the 48 midsize rooms evince a discreet boutiquey sensibility. Its staff are expert in local nightlife, and it has both indoor and outdoor pools.

Devaluation briefly made Monserrat's four-star **(562 Nogaró** (Diagonal Presidente Julio A. Roca 562, tel. 011/4331-0091, www.562nogarohotel.com, US$121 s or d) a bargain, but prices have returned to international levels. Dating from 1930 but renovated a few years ago, this French-style 150-room hotel offers all contemporary amenities, including Wi-Fi, air-conditioning, and in-room safes.

Just south of Plaza de Mayo, the **NH City & Tower** (Bolívar 160, tel. 011/4121-6464, www.nh-hoteles.com, US$130–146 s or d) is a spectacularly modernized 300-room building dating from 1931 that had the misfortune to reopen at the nadir of Argentina's 2001–2002 meltdown. That bad timing meant good rates for beautifully appointed rooms with all modern conveniences, plus luxuries like a rooftop pool, gym, and sauna, but it's making up for the business it lost then. It also has an exceptional Spanish restaurant.

One of the capital's most historic lodgings, dating from 1929, Monserrat's four-star **Castelar Hotel & Spa** (Avenida de Mayo 1152, tel. 011/4383-5000, www.castelarhotel.com.ar, US$131 s or d) has hosted the likes of Spanish dramatist Federico García Lorca (who lived in room 704 for six months), Chilean Nobel Prize–winning poet Pablo Neruda, Nobel Prize scientist Linus Pauling, and many Argentine politicians. Embellished with Carrara marble, it offers comfortable, well-equipped rooms with breakfast and access to its own spa. There are entire nonsmoking floors.

In a painstakingly remodeled *casa chorizo,* ◖ **Malabia House** (Malabia 1555, tel./fax 011/4832-3345, www.malabiahouse.com.ar, US$140–188 s or d) is a stylish bed-and-breakfast with magnificent natural light, glistening wood floors, handsome furnishings, and small but attractive patio gardens. Standard ground-floor rooms have external private baths; the slightly more expensive upstairs rooms have air-conditioning and interior baths.

Near the Obelisco, the **Panamericano Buenos Aires Hotel & Resort** (Carlos Pellegrini 525, tel. 011/4348-5000, www.crowneplaza.com.ar, US$144–277 s or d) consists of an older south tower and a newer north tower. Both are comfortable, but the north-tower rooms are no longer technologically superior to the others.

US$150-200

Ever since the Bush twins partied in Palermo while their father's Republican party took a thumpin' in the 2006 U.S. midterm elections, every taxi driver in town knows where to find **Hotel Home Buenos Aires** (Honduras 5860, tel. 011/4779-1008, www.homebuenosaires.com, US$150–210 s or d). Even U2 stayed here (and welcomed other guests to their party) when they played Buenos Aires, but you needn't be a big name to enjoy its imaginative design, spacious rooms and suites, and ample common spaces, including a large garden with

pool that's uncommon in this part of town. With neighboring properties it forms a mini-greenbelt that's remarkably quiet for such a lively neighborhood. A secluded garden apartment goes for US$460.

Retiro's **Meliá Buenos Aires Hotel** (Reconquista 945, tel. 011/4891-3800, www.solmelia.com, US$152 s or d) has 209 rooms, including 18 suites, in a modernistic hotel with luminous rooms, a gym and business center, and entire nonsmoking floors. Rates include a sumptuous buffet breakfast; there are discounts from mid-December through February.

OVER US$200

Barrio Norte's bright boutique-style **Design Suites** (Marcelo T. de Alvear 1683, tel./fax 011/4814-8700, www.designsuites.com, US$218–254 s or d) has a heated pool, gym, restaurant room service, and daily newspaper delivery (of the guest's choice). Each of its 40 suites has cable TV, a telephone, Internet and fax connections, a kitchenette, a minibar, air-conditioning, a strongbox, and a hot tub.

Near Puerto Madero, across from the Plaza Fuerza Aérea Argentina, the mammoth 742-room high-rise **Sheraton Buenos Aires Hotel** (San Martín 1225, tel. 011/4318-9000, www.starwoodhotels.com, US$240–301 s or d) gets the international business trade but also many tourists. It offers a large fitness center and swimming pools as well as two restaurants.

Now under international-chain control, Retiro's landmark (dating from 1909) ◖ **Marriott Plaza Hotel** (Florida 1005, tel. 011/4318-3000, www.marriott.com, US$224–345 s or d) has undergone modernization without losing its German baroque charm and elegance.

Monserrat's **Hotel Intercontinental** (Moreno 809, tel. 011/4340-7100, www.buenos-aires.intercontinental.com, US$215–350 s or d) consistently makes best-hotels lists in magazines like *Travel + Leisure.* Affordable for what it offers, two-thirds of its 315 rooms are nonsmoking.

The **Loi Suites Recoleta** (Vicente López 1955, tel. 011/5777-8950, www.loisuites.com.

ar, US$303–520 s or d) is the toniest link of a stylish four-hotel chain. With some of BA's most innovative design, it makes magnificent use of natural light.

Favored by business travelers and international entertainment figures, Retiro's highly regarded **Caesar Park Hotel** (Posadas 1232, tel. 011/4819-1100, www.caesar-park. com, US$339–526 s or d) now belongs to a Mexican luxury hotel chain. Rates include an extravagant breakfast buffet, but it can't match the established historical elegance of competitors like the Four Seasons and Alvear Palace.

Since 1928 the ❰ **Alvear Palace Hotel** (Avenida Alvear 1891, tel. 011/4805-2100, www.alvearpalace.com, from US$393 s or d) has symbolized elegance and luxury—not to mention wealth and privilege. This is one place that, despite devaluation, maintains both its standards and its prices—ranging upwards of US$5,000 for the royal suite—for accommodations with Egyptian-cotton sheets and Hermès toiletries. Francophobes may find the ancien régime decor cloying, but it consistently ranks among the world's best hotels in *Travel + Leisure* and *Condé Nast Traveler.*

Rivaling the Alvear Palace, but with French architect Philippe Starck's own distinct style, Puerto Madero's **Faena Hotel & Universe** (Marta Salotti 445, tel. 011/4010-9000, from US$425 s or d) has recycled a historical granary into a cutting-edge hotel and "experience" whose interior is a hybrid of Parisian classicism and avant-garde sensibility.

Food

Almost everything remains affordable at present, at quality ranging from good to world-class, but some places are more affordable than others. The listings below are arranged geographically.

MONSERRAT/CATEDRAL AL SUR AND VICINITY

Peruvian food is becoming more common in the capital, and plain-Jane **Status** (Virrey Cevallos 178, tel. 011/4382-8531) is one of the best budget options, with home-style central Andean dishes such as *ají de gallina* (chicken in a walnut sauce over rice, with potatoes) in the US$5 range. Spicy items and garnishes, such as *papa a la huancaína,* are also available.

According to *Buenos Aires Herald* restaurant critic Dereck Foster, BA's best Spanish food comes from the restaurant at the **NH City Hotel** (Bolívar 160, tel. 011/4121-6464). Other Spanish/Basque seafood options include the classic (and author favorite) ❰ **Laurak Bat** (Avenida Belgrano 1144, tel. 011/4381-0682, www.laurakbat.com.ar, US$10–20).

Near Monserrat's western border, San Cristóbal's **Miramar** (Avenida San Juan 1999, tel. 011/4304-4261) is a reliable *rotisería* (deli) that's also a decidedly unfashionable *bodegón* restaurant that's ideal for unpretentious lunches or dinners with poised service. Prices are moderate, even low, for items such as *gambas al ajillo* (garlic prawns) and *lechón* (roast pork).

MICROCENTRO AND VICINITY

❰ **Pizzería Guerrín** (Avenida Corrientes 1372, tel. 011/4371-8141) is a one-of-a-kind that sells by the slice at the stand-up counter—the *fugazza* (and *fugazzetta*) are exquisitely simple and simply exquisite. **La Continental** (Callao 361, tel. 011/4374-1444, www.lacontinental.com), which has more than a dozen branches around town, is a good backup.

Several tourist-oriented *parrillas* make a fetish of staking their steaks over hot coals in circular barbecue pits, tended by bogus gauchos in full regalia, behind picture windows. While they play for the cliché and serve too many

COOLING DOWN WITH *HELADOS*

Buenos Aires has two kinds of *heladerías* (ice creameries). The first are chains producing large industrial batches; some of these are good, some are awful, and most fall in between. The other is the neighborhood ice creamery that creates *helados artesanales* in smaller quantities.

Gradually overshadowing the fading Freddo, **Chungo** (tel. 0800/888-24-8646, www.chungo. com.ar) is probably the best industrial-quality ice cream; the most convenient branches are in Recoleta (Avenida Las Heras and Rodríguez Peña) and Palermo (Olleros 1660). **Bianca** (Avenida Scalabrini Ortiz 2295, tel. 011/4832-3357) is the Palermo locale of a midsized chain with a wide selection of flavors. Founded by Freddo's former owners, the always-crowded **Persicco** (Salguero 2591, Palermo, tel. 011/4801-5549) is challenging the other chains.

Over the past couple of decades, **Cadore** (Avenida Corrientes 1695, Congreso) has consistently been one of the best (don't miss the dark chocolate and lemon mousse), but even its renovated storefront hasn't remedied its low profile. Across from Parque Lezama, **Florencia** (Brasil and Defensa, tel. 011/4307-6407) is San Telmo's best (and one of the cheapest). In Belgrano, try the hole-in-the-wall **Gruta** (Sucre 2356, tel. 011/4784-8417).

New in late 2009, Palermo's **Jauja** (Cerviño 3901, tel. 011/4801-8126, www.heladosjauja. com) is the BA branch of El Bolsón's landmark ice creamery, with wildly imaginative flavors such as *calafate* (Magellan barberry) with sheep's milk and *mate cocido* – not to mention *cerveza* (beer) and *crema de maní* (peanut). It trucks its product in from its northern Patagonian home – more than 1,700 kilometers and 20-some hours south.

people for individual attention, the quality is good and prices are reasonable at **La Estancia** (Lavalle 941, tel. 011/4326-0330, www.asador-laestancia.com.ar).

Possibly downtown's best restaurant, the banker's favorite **◖ Sabot** (25 de Mayo 756, tel. 011/4313-6587) serves Italo-Argentine dishes of the highest quality in a very masculine environment—women are few but not unwelcome—with good-humored professional service. Moderately expensive by current standards, most entrées, like *matambre de cerdo* and *chivito,* plus some fish dishes, cost in the US$10–15 range. A pleasant surprise is the *mate de coca* from fresh coca leaves (for digestive purposes only). It's open for weekday lunches only.

PUERTO MADERO

Over the past few years, redeveloped Puerto Madero has had an impact on the restaurant scene, but more because of its overall tourist appeal than its quality—with a couple of exceptions, the food is unimpressive. Most restaurants, though, have outdoor seating along the yacht harbor, and when the weather's fine it's ideal for people-watching. Because the area draws foreigners from nearby luxury hotels, restaurants here are accustomed to dealing with dinnertimes as early as 7 P.M.

Opposite Dique No. 4, the best *parrilla* is **◖ Cabaña Las Lilas** (Alicia Moreau de Justo 516, tel. 011/4313-1336, www.laslilas. com). Often packed for lunch despite soaring prices, it offers complimentary champagne and snacks while you wait; its *bife de chorizo* (which has skyrocketed to US$30) may be the finest in town.

Puerto Sorrento (Alicia Moreau de Justo 410, tel. 011/4319-8731, www.sorrentorestaurant.com.ar) is the best seafood choice, and at midday it has an excellent three-course *almuerzo ejecutivo* (US$18 including soft drink, beer, or wine). The service is exemplary.

SAN TELMO AND VICINITY

Despite the barrio's tourist allure, San Telmo's gastronomy lags behind that of other barrios. Most restaurants here are better lunchtime bargains than dinnertime indulgences.

Medio y Medio (Chile 316, tel. 011/4300-1396) bursts with lunchgoers seeking the Uruguayan caloric overload *chivito*, a steak sandwich piled high with lettuce, cheese, tomato, and bacon; a fried egg crowns the *chivito al plato*, which includes a slab of beef plus potato salad, green salad, and fries.

Dating from 1864, **(C) Bar El Federal** (Carlos Calvo 399, tel. 011/4300-4313) looks its age—in a positive way, with its worn tiled floors and intricate carved wooden bar. The menu is large, but the house specialty is turkey ravioli (US$5), with a choice of sauces; there's refreshingly cold hard cider on tap.

Despite the capacity of the multiple dining rooms at **DesNivel** (Defensa 855, tel. 011/4300-9081), Sunday visitors to the Plaza Dorrego market form long queues outside for *parrillada* and pasta at bargain prices; it's open for lunch Tuesday–Sunday and dinner daily. Opposite Parque Lezama, **1880** (Defensa 1665, tel. 011/4307-2746) is a traditional *parrilla* with plenty of barrio atmosphere, including *filete* ornaments by Martiniano Arce. Most

entrées fall in the US$6–10 range, including pasta dishes like *ñoquis* (gnocchi).

Recently reopened in its classic dining room—dark mahogany woodwork and Spanish tiles—the **Casal de Catalunya** (Chacabuco 863, tel. 011/4361-0191, cuinacatalana@fibertel.com.ar) specializes in Catalonian seafood, other Spanish dishes, and the occasional standard Argentine item. Many dishes are made with garlic, about which Argentines are unenthusiastic.

LA BOCA

La Boca is not an enclave of haute cuisine, but there's good enough food for lunch—most people visit the barrio during the daytime—and even an occasional dinnertime foray.

Banchero (Suárez 396, tel. 011/4301-1406) is the original locale of the pizzeria that claims to have invented the onion-and-mozzarella *fugazzetta*. Whether or not that's true, theirs is one of the best.

In an area where taxis are obligatory at night and maybe advisable even in the

a midday tapas bar at a San Telmo restaurant

daytime (though some cabbies have trouble finding it), **☾ El Obrero** (Agustín Cafferena 64, tel. 011/4362-9912) is where celebrities go slumming for steaks. Its walls plastered with images of soccer icon Diego Maradona and little else, it draws an international clientele on the order of Bono and Robert Duvall, and they haven't even removed the photo of disgraced ex-president Fernando de la Rúa. There's no printed menu—check the chalkboards, where most items run around US$5–6.

At the other end of the spectrum, celebrity chef Francis Mallman has placed **Patagonia Sur** (Rocha 801, tel. 011/4303-5917, www.restaurantepatagoniasur.com), one of his several gourmet restaurants in Argentina and Uruguay, in the barrio. It might seem out of place here, and it's expensive (around US$80 pp for a three-course dinner without wine), but Mallman's blend of Argentine beef, seafood, and other regional dishes are always worth consideration.

RETIRO

For most Buenos Aires visitors, Danish *smørrebrød* might seem an improbable alternative, but the **Club Danés** (Avenida Leandro N. Alem 1074, 12th floor, tel. 011/4312-5442) is both cheap and appetizing, with lunch specials in the US$8 range and exceptional views of Puerto Madero. The city's hippest and most adventurous pizzeria is garishly decorated **Filo** (San Martín 975, tel. 011/4311-0312, www.filo-ristorante.com).

Inconspicuous **Juana M** (Carlos Pellegrini 1535, tel. 011/4326-0462) is a cavernous basement restaurant that serves beef and pasta dishes, with unlimited access to a diverse salad bar. While prices are rising, it's still worth consideration, with a quick kitchen and friendly service.

☾ Tancat (Paraguay 645, tel. 011/4312-5442) is a first-rate and wildly popular *tasca*, an informal Spanish bar (usually with hams hanging on strings from the ceiling and bottles of wine lined up along the walls). It offers good-natured service and lunches around

US$8–15 pp; don't miss the *jamón serrano* (cured ham) appetizer. Reservations are almost essential for the few tables, but lunchgoers can jam into the long wooden bar, backed by shelves of wine covered with business cards, posters, and photos. It's open noon–12:30 A.M. Monday–Saturday.

RECOLETA AND BARRIO NORTE

José Luis (Avenida Quintana 456, tel. 011/4807-0606) is an Asturian seafood restaurant that stresses fresher and lighter dishes than most of its counterparts. Entrées are mostly in the US$10 range and up; it's open Monday–Saturday for lunch and dinner.

The Barrio Norte favorite **Los Pinos** (Azcuénaga 1500, tel. 011/4822-8704) occupies an old-fashioned apothecary, its wooden cases still stocked with antique bottles and rising nearly to the ceiling. Fixed lunch and dinner specials, with substantial choice, fall into the US$6–10 range; the à la carte menu of beef, seafood, and pasta is not much more expensive, as the comparably priced entrées include a side order. Service is well-intentioned but inconsistent.

Internationally recognized **Oviedo** (Beruti 2602, tel. 011/4822-5415, www.oviedoresto.com.ar) is a formal restaurant that specializes in seafood such as a shrimp risotto (US$17) but also serves Patagonian lamb and standards like beef, with most entrées in the US$15–25 range.

PALERMO

Palermo is, without question, the center of innovation in Argentine dining, mostly in Palermo Soho but also in Palermo Hollywood, the Botánico, and Las Cañitas.

Among the Botánico's best, **☾ Bella Italia Café Bar** (Repúblic Arabe Siria 3330, tel. 011/4807-5120, www.bellaitalia-gourmet.com.ar) is the moderately priced (but cash-only) café version of the eponymous nearby restaurant. For around US$7 it has outstanding squash gnocchi with a subtle cream sauce, along with fine cannelloni and salads.

Having recently changed hands, but remaining in the same family, **Guido** (Bulevar Cerviño 3943, tel. 011/4802-1262, www.guidorestaurant.com.ar) is a trattoria that has expanded an already outstanding menu notable for a nightly risotto (US$10) and a separate three-course dinner (also US$10), as well as inexpensive pizzas. The decor is cinematic, the service is attentive, and there's an extensive list of wines by the glass.

Mark's Deli & Coffee House (El Salvador 4701, tel. 011/4832-6244) is a U.S.-style deli, bright and cheerful with indoor and patio seating and outstanding sandwiches (about US$5); there's a small selection of wines by the glass and large and tasty glasses of lemonade. It closes early, around 9:30 P.M. Monday–Saturday and at 7 P.M. Sunday.

For quality-to-price ratio, the hands-down best choice for empanadas and regional dishes is **La Cupertina** (Cabrera 5296, tel. 011/4777-3711). The service may be inconsistent, but the chicken empanadas and *humitas en chala* (similar to tamales, wrapped in corn stalks) are exquisite and so cheap that price is no object, even with wine; there are also individually sized pizzas. Don't miss the desserts, especially the Spanish custard *natillas* and *arroz con leche*. It keeps limited hours: 11:30 A.M.–3:30 P.M. Tuesday–Sunday and 7:30–11 P.M. Tuesday–Saturday; it's also small, seating only about 20 diners in simple but attractive surroundings.

In the Botánico, cozy **Nemo** (Cabello 3672, tel. 011/4802-5308, danieljosecid@hotmail.com) serves light entrées, including seafood-based pastas (around US$8–12) and a diverse fish menu (US$10–15) that includes at least one freshwater catch. It has limited sidewalk seating. *Buenos Aires Herald* food writer Dereck Foster calls it the capital's "consistently best seafood restaurant."

In spacious new—but slightly less intimate—quarters across Avenida Libertador, **Libélula** (Salguero 2983, tel. 011/4802-7220, www.libelularestaurant.com.ar) is a Japanese-Peruvian restaurant serving seviche, spicy (on request) sushi, and traditional dishes such as

ají de gallina (chicken breast with creamy walnut sauce).

Just when it seems that Peruvian food here can't get any better, along comes **Bardot** (Honduras 5237, tel. 011/4831-1112, www.restobardot.com.ar, daily for lunch and dinner), with dishes such as *mero a lo macho* (grouper with a shrimp sauce, US$13), BA's best pisco sours (two-for-one on Wed.), and near flawless service. For those who want to sample Peru's gastronomic diversity, there's a Sunday buffet (1–4 P.M., US$18) that includes a bit of everything, including the pisco sour.

Unique in the city, Palermo Hollywood's **Jangada** (Bonpland 1670, tel. 011/4777-4193, www.restaurantejangada.com) specializes in two-person platters (US$20–25) of Paraná river fish such as *boga, pacú,* and *surubí.* Reservations are advisable.

The *parrilla* of the moment is **La Cabrera** (Cabrera 5099, tel. 011/4831-7002, www.parrillalacabrera.com.ar), where the *bife de chorizo* (US$10) is big enough for two hungry diners and comes with a sampler of side dishes including pureed potatoes, pumpkin and applesauce, and several salads. Reservations are advisable at dinnertime, when it has a more formal branch a few doors north, across Thames.

Nearby **Rave** (Gorriti 5092, tel. 011/4833-7832, www.restaurantrave.com.ar) opens at 8:30 P.M. nightly, but it's not unusual to find its split levels packed with 2 A.M. diners. Good choices include *mollejitas* (sweetbreads) and chicken or mushroom risotto. It can get loud, but not deafening.

Sa Giara (Gurruchaga 1806, tel. 011/4832-5062, www.sagiara.com.ar) brings something new to Italo-Argentine cuisine with Sardinian *curligionis,* which resemble Chinese or Japanese pot stickers but stuffed with sweet potato (US$11) or three meats (beef, lamb, pork, US$13), or other items. The villa-style venue also offers inexpensive sandwiches of prosciutto, artisanal cheeses, and the like.

At the casual **Social Paraíso** (Honduras 5182, tel. 011/4831-4556, www.socialparaiso.com.ar), the US$7 lunch specials feature items like *bondiola* (pork loin) with a tabbouleh salad;

entrées such as stuffed chicken breast with mozzarella and bacon, or Patagonian lamb with grilled vegetables, fall into the US$8–11 range. It also has innovative desserts and a respectable selection of wines by the glass.

One of BA's most creative restaurants, Palermo Hollywood's **Olsen** (Gorriti 5870, tel. 011/4776-7677, olsen@fibertel.com.ar) serves what might be called Scandinavian criollo cuisine, with dishes like ravioli with goat cheese and pork roast with raspberry sauce, for upwards of US$10. The bar serves the standard aperitifs but also a literally dizzying variety of vodka-based cocktails. Notable for its ambience as well as its food, Olsen has devoted part of its deep lot to a sculpture garden that replicates a Scandinavian boreal forest of birches, cypresses, and pines. It's open for lunch and dinner Tuesday–Sunday, and at 10 A.M. Sunday for brunch.

It's not the fashionable scene that Olsen is, but Hollywood's **Lobby** (Nicaragua 5944, tel. 011/4770-9335) is a hybrid restaurant, wine bar, and wine retailer with inexpensive but outstanding breakfast and lunch menus, including sandwiches, vegetarian dishes, and seafood salads. The by-the-glass wine options are excellent, but they also sell bottles off the wall for a token corkage fee, and there is sidewalk seating.

BELGRANO

Belgrano has many decent restaurants—the city's Chinatown is here, and Chinese is the default option. Still, choices such as **Contigo Perú** (Echeverría 1627, tel. 011/4780-3960), in a cul-de-sac near the railroad tracks, are worth considering. Having grown from humble origins to become a neighborhood success and now something of a design restaurant, its prices have risen, though, and it has lost much of its former authenticity.

Recently relocated to Chinatown, (**Lotus Neo Thai** (Arribeños 2265, tel. 011/4783-7993) is Argentina's Thai pioneer and one of few places in the country where it's possible to taste truly spicy dishes. Still with soothing music and lotus-themed decor, it's now open for lunch as well as dinner; though it's smaller than its former Las Cañitas location, the rooftop terrace provides extra space in fine weather. Lunches are a bargain at around US$10.

One of the city's elite restaurants, the stylish (**Pura Tierra** (3 de Febrero 1167, tel. 011/4899-2007, www.puratierra.com.ar) is expensive but worth the splurge for creative dishes prepared with the freshest local ingredients, such as *bondiola* (pork loin with fruit garnishes), and remarkable service (including one of the city's most knowledgeable and communicative sommeliers).

Information and Services

TOURIST INFORMATION CENTERS

The **Secretaría Nacional de Turismo** (Avenida Santa Fe 883, Retiro, tel. 011/4312-2232 or 0800/555-0016, www.turismo.gov.ar) is open 9 A.M.–5 P.M. weekdays; there's a branch at Aeropuerto Internacional Ezeiza (tel. 011/4480-0292) and another at Aeroparque Jorge Newbery (tel. 011/4771-0104). Both airport branches are open 8 A.M.–8 P.M. daily.

The municipal **Subsecretaría de Turismo** (www.bue.gov.ar) maintains several information kiosks: in the Microcentro (Florida 100, 8:30 A.M.–6:30 P.M. daily); in Retiro (Florida and Marcelo T. de Alvear, 9 A.M.–5 P.M. Mon.–Sat.); in Recoleta (Quintana 596, 10 A.M.–5 P.M. daily); at Puerto Madero's Dique 4 (Avenida Alicia Moreau de Justo 200, tel. 011/4315-4265, 9:30 A.M.–7:30 P.M. daily); and at the Retiro bus terminal (tel. 011/4313-0187, daily 7:30 A.M.–1 P.M. weekdays only). All distribute maps and brochures, and they usually have English-speaking staff.

LIBRARIES

The **Biblioteca Nacional** (National Library, Agüero 2502, Recoleta, tel. 011/4808-6000, www.bn.gov.ar) is open 9 A.M.–9 P.M.

weekdays, noon–7 P.M. weekends. It holds frequent special exhibitions, lectures and literary events, and free concerts.

At the Microcentro's Instituto Cultural Argentino-Norteamericano (Maipú 672, tel. 011/5382-1500, www.icana.org.ar), the **Biblioteca Centro Lincoln** (tel. 011/5382-1536, www.bcl.edu.ar) has English-language books, magazines, and newspapers.

BANKING

Most visitors find the ubiquitous ATMs most convenient for changing money. In the La City financial district, numerous *casas de cambio* along San Martín between Corrientes and the Plaza de Mayo usually offer the best exchange rates for U.S. cash, euros, and travelers checks. For travelers checks, they normally charge a commission or pay a lower rate than for cash, but **American Express** (Arenales 707, Retiro, tel. 011/4310-3000) cashes its own checks for no commission.

POSTAL SERVICES

The **Correo Central** (Sarmiento 151, 8 A.M.–8 P.M. weekdays, 10 A.M.–1 P.M. Sat.) is a landmark building worth a visit in its own right; there are many other branch offices. International parcels exceeding 1 kilogram must go from the **Correo Internacional** (Antártida Argentina near the Retiro train station, tel. 011/4316-7777, 11 A.M.–5 P.M. weekdays).

Federal Express (Maipú 753, tel. 011/4393-6054) offers private courier service.

COMMUNICATIONS

Locutorios for faxes and long-distance calls are so plentiful that it's hardly worthwhile to mention any in particular. Many have Internet connections, but there are also countless locales devoted exclusively to Internet service, and Wi-Fi is almost ubiquitous.

TRAVEL AGENCIES

North of Plaza San Martín, Retiro's **American Express** (Arenales 707, tel. 011/4310-3000, www.americanexpress.com.ar) offers the usual services of a travel agency.

Swan Turismo (Cerrito 822, 9th floor, Retiro, tel. 011/4129-7926, www.swanturismo.com.ar) is a full-service agency that's earned a reputation for navigating some of the Argentine travel system's eccentricities.

In the Galería Buenos Aires, affiliated with STA Travel, the nonprofit **Asatej** (Florida 835, 3rd floor, Retiro, tel. 011/4311-6953, fax 011/4311-6840, www.asatej.com) is good at searching out the best airfares for anyone, not just students; it is also an affiliate of Hostelling International. Another good choice is **Say Hueque** (Viamonte 749, 6th floor, tel. 011/5199-2517, www.sayhueque.com), which is particularly good with independent travelers.

LANGUAGE STUDY

Buenos Aires has a growing number of language schools at competitive prices, starting with the Universidad de Buenos Aires's **Centro Universitario de Idiomas** (Junín 222, Balvanera, tel. 011/4823-6818, www.cui.edu.ar). Others include the **Centro de Estudio del Español** (Reconquista 715, 11th floor, tel./fax 011/4315-1156, www.cedic.com.ar); **Coined** (Suipacha 90, 2nd floor, tel. 011/4331-2418, www.coined.com.ar); the **Instituto de Lengua Española para Extranjeros** (ILEE, Avenida Callao 339, 3rd floor, tel./fax 011/4782-7173, www.argentinailee.com); and the **International Bureau of Language** (Florida 165, tel. 011/4331-4250, www.ibl.com.ar).

For individual tutoring, contact English-speaking **Dori Lieberman** (tel./fax 011/4361-4843, dori@sinectis.com.ar).

IMMIGRATION

For visa extensions, the **Dirección Nacional de Migraciones** (Avenida Antártida Argentina 1355, tel. 011/4317-0237) is open 8 A.M.–1 P.M. weekdays.

MEDICAL

Public hospitals include Recoleta's **Hospital Rivadavia** (Avenida Las Heras 2670, tel. 011/4809-2000) and Palermo's **Hospital Municipal Juan Fernández** (Cerviño 3356, tel. 011/4808-2600).

The **Hospital Británico** (Perdriel 74, Barracas, tel. 011/4304-1082, www.hospitalbritanico.org.ar) is a highly regarded private hospital. Argentine presidents have had arthroscopies and soccer star Diego Maradona did detox at Belgrano's **Clínica Fleni** (Montañeses 2325, tel. 011/5777-3200, www.fleni.org.ar), but it does not serve every specialty.

Getting There

Buenos Aires is the main port of entry for overseas visitors and the hub for domestic travel within the country.

BY AIR

Most international flights arrive and depart from the suburban airport at Ezeiza, though a handful from neighboring countries use close-in Aeroparque.

Aerolíneas Argentinas (Perú 2, Monserrat, tel. 011/4320-2000) flies to destinations ranging from Puerto Iguazú on the Brazilian border to Ushuaia in Tierra del Fuego.

LAN Argentina (Cerrito 866, tel. 0810/999-9526) is the local affiliate of Chile's successful and reliable international airline. It serves a growing number of domestic destinations.

Aeroparque-based **Andes Líneas Aéreas** (Avenida Córdoba 775, tel. 0810/7772-6337, www.andesonline.com) is a new private airline flying to Córdoba, Puerto Iguazú, Salta, Jujuy, and Puerto Madryn.

Also Aeroparque-based, **Sol Líneas Aéreas** (tel. 011/5031-4211, www.sol.com.ar) is a budget carrier serving Rosario, Santa Fe, Córdoba, and Mendoza.

Líneas Aéreas del Estado (LADE, Perú 714, San Telmo, tel. 011/4361-7071, www.lade.com.ar) is the Argentine air force's commercial aviation branch. Miraculously surviving budget crises and privatizations, it flies to southern Buenos Aires Province and Patagonia on a wing and a subsidy.

BY BUS

Buenos Aires's main bus station is Retiro's **Estación Terminal de Ómnibus** (Avenida Ramos Mejía 1860, tel. 011/4310-0700, www.tebasa.com.ar). The sprawling three-story building hosts nearly 140 separate bus companies that cover the entire country and international destinations as well. It's walking distance from the northern terminus of Subte Línea C, at the Retiro train station.

The ground floor is primarily for freight; passengers leave from the 1st-floor *andénes* (platforms). Companies operate out of more than 200 *ventanillas* (ticket windows) on the 2nd floor, roughly arranged according to geographical regions: Zona Sur (South, windows 1–21, 23, 25, 27–30, 32–34, 101); Cuyo (windows 31, 33, 35–43, 45, 47), Zona Noroeste (Northwest, 44, 46–59, 148); Centro (Center, 59–94, 103, 105); Zona Noreste (Northeast, 95–101, 105, 107, 109, 111, 113–153); Costa Atlántica (Atlantic Coast, 152, 154–178); Internacional (International, 179–206).

On the departure level, the Centro de Informes y Reclamos (tel. 011/4310-0700) provides general information and also oversees taxis; direct any complaint about drivers to them. There is a separate tourist office, open 7:30 A.M.–1 P.M. only.

For long-distance and international buses, reservations are a good idea, especially during the summer (Jan.–Feb.) and winter (late July) holiday periods, but also on long weekends like Semana Santa.

When pickets aren't blocking the bridges, several carriers take the roundabout overland route to Montevideo, Uruguay, via the Colón-Paysandú border crossing, which takes longer (ten hours) than the ferry but costs less (US$40): **Bus de la Carrera** (four nightly, tel. 011/4313-1700); **Cauvi** (once nightly, tel. 011/4314-6999); and **General Belgrano** (once nightly, tel. 011/4312-4933). All leave between 9:30 and 11:30 P.M.

To the Paraguayan capital of Asunción (18 hours, US$50–69), the main carriers are **Nuestra Señora de la Asunción** (tel. 011/4311-7666) and **Chevallier Paraguaya** (also tel. 011/4311-7666). For Brazilian destinations such as São Paulo (40 hours, US$125), and Rio de Janeiro (48 hours, US$167), try **Pluma** (tel. 011/4313-3880) or **Crucero del Norte** (tel. 011/4315-1652).

For the trans-Andean crossing to Santiago, Chile (19 hours, US$68), carriers include **Fénix Pullman Norte** (tel. 011/4313-0134), **Buses Ahumada** (tel. 011/4313-0134), and **Pullman del Sur** (tel. 011/4315-0010). For the Peruvian capital of Lima (via Chile, a 72-hour marathon, US$190), the choices are **El Rápido Internacional** (tel. 011/4311-3757) and **Ormeño Internacional** (tel. 011/4313-2259).

BY TRAIN

Railroads were once the pride of the transportation system, but most Argentines now get around by bus. There are still long-distance trains to the southern beach resorts in and around Mar del Plata, northwest to the cities of Rosario, Córdoba, and Tucumán, and to the Mesopotamian city of Posadas.

From Constitución, **Ferrobaires** (tel. 011/4304-0028, www.ferrobaires.gba.gov.ar) goes to Mar del Plata and, in summer, to Pinamar. One-way fares range from US$14 (in stiff-backed *clase única*) to US$19 (reclining Pullman seats). The less frequent Expreso del Atlántico (US$23) and El Marplatense (US$25) are more comfortable.

From Retiro, **Trenes de Buenos Aires** (TBA, tel. 011/4317-4400 or 0800/333-3822, www.tbanet.com.ar) goes to Rosario Norte (5.5 hours, US$10) and points along the way weekdays only at 6:43 P.M.

Also from Retiro, **Ferrocentral** (tel. 011/4312-2989, www.ferrocentralsa.com.ar) goes to Rosario Norte (6 hours, US$6–15) and Córdoba (14.5 hours) at 8:50 A.M. Monday, Wednesday, Friday, and Sunday. Rates to Córdoba are US$6 *turista,* US$8 *primera,* and US$25 Pullman. Ferrocentral also goes to Rosario and Tucumán (25 hours) Monday and Friday at 10:40 A.M. Rates to Tucumán are US$13 *turista,* US$18 *primera,* US$34 Pullman, and US$78 d with breakfast in *camarote* sleepers. Tickets go fast because it's cheap; the office is open 10 A.M.–6 P.M. weekdays and 9 A.M.–1 P.M. Saturday.

BY BOAT

At Puerto Madero's Dársena Norte, **Buquebús** (Avenida Antártida Argentina 821, tel. 011/4316-6405, www.buquebus.com) sails to Colonia and Montevideo; it also has a ticket office at Avenida Córdoba 789, Retiro. Services and fares vary, depending on the vessel—the *Eladia Isabel,* for instance, has the cheapest but slowest crossing to Colonia (3 hours, US$25–45 pp), while the high-speed ferries *Juan Patricio* and *Patricia Oliva II* cover the longer distance to Montevideo (2.5 hours, US$67–111) in roughly the same time. Fares and frequencies vary according to the season.

Buquebús now has competition from Colonia Express (Avenida Córdoba 753, tel. 011/4317-4100, www.coloniaexpress.com), which leaves from its own Terminal Fluvial Colonia Express (Dársena Sur, Avenida Pedro de Mendoza 330, La Boca). Fares to Colonia range US$27–34, to Montevideo US$35–54, but there are occasional Web specials as low as US$5 to Colonia and US$10 to Montevideo.

Getting Around

AIRPORTS

Buenos Aires has two airports, both operated by the private concessionaire **Aeropuertos Argentinos 2000** (tel. 011/5480-6111, www.aa2000.com.ar). The main international facility is **Aeropuerto Internacional Ministro Pistarini**, 35 kilometers southwest of downtown, popularly called Ezeiza after its namesake suburb. The other is Palermo's **Aeroparque Jorge Newbery** (Avenida Costanera Rafael Obligado s/n), which is primarily domestic but handles a few international flights from neighboring countries.

International passengers leaving from Ezeiza pay a US$30.50 departure tax, payable in local currency or U.S. dollars; US$18 of this is normally collected on departure. On flights shorter than 300 kilometers to neighboring countries, such as Uruguay, the tax is only US$6; on domestic flights from Aeroparque, it's about US$3. These latter fees are normally included in the ticket price.

There is a variety of options for getting to and from the airports, ranging from *colectivos* (city buses) to shuttles, metered taxis, and *remises* (meterless taxis).

Colectivos are the cheapest option, but they are more practical for close-in Aeroparque than distant Ezeiza, as they take circuitous routes on surface streets. To Aeroparque (about US$0.30), the options are No. 33 from Plaza de Mayo, the Microcentro, and Retiro; No. 37-C ("Ciudad Universitaria") from Plaza del Congreso, Avenida Callao, Avenida Las Heras, and Plaza Italia; No. 45 northbound from Plaza Constitución, Plaza San Martín, or Retiro; and No. 160-C or 160-D from Avenida Las Heras or Plaza Italia. Return buses leave from the Avenida Costanera Rafael Obligado, a short walk outside the terminal.

To Ezeiza (about US$0.75), the backpackers' pick is the No. 86-A ("Aeropuerto"), from La Boca to Plaza de Mayo, Plaza del Congreso, and onward, but the roundabout route takes up to two hours. *Servicio Diferencial* buses cost more (US$2.60) but have comfortable reclining seats. At Ezeiza, both leave from just outside the Aerolíneas Argentinas terminal, a short distance from the main international terminal.

Manuel Tienda León (Avenida Madero and San Martín, Retiro, tel. 011/4315-5115 or 0810/888-5366, www.tiendaleon.com.ar) runs frequent buses to and from Ezeiza (US$12) and to Aeroparque (US$4); buses from Ezeiza make connections to Aeroparque for domestic flights, and also include door-to-door taxi service from Tienda León's Retiro terminal.

Taxis and *remises* offer door-to-door service and are no more expensive than shuttles for three or more people. Manuel Tienda León and many other companies, such as **Transfer Express** (tel. 0800/444-4872) and **Naon Remises** (tel. 011/4545-6500), have *remises* to Aeroparque (US$6) and Ezeiza (US$25–35). Both *remises* and taxis usually tack on tolls to Ezeiza (about US$1).

COLECTIVOS (BUSES)

More than 200 separate bus routes serve the Capital Federal and Gran Buenos Aires, but most visitors and even residents need to know fairly few of them. It's helpful, though, to have one of the annually updated city atlases, such as the *Guía Lumi* or *Guía T,* with detailed itineraries; abbreviated pocket versions are also available. Newsstand kiosks and bookstores normally sell these.

Route signs, at fixed stops, do not always indicate the bus's itinerary. In the absence of a written guide, ask someone—*porteños* often know the system by heart and are generous with information. Fares depend on distance traveled, but most are US$0.35 or less; on telling the driver your destination, he will enter the fare in the automatic ticket machine, which takes only coins but does give small change. Rechargeable electronic tickets are in the works.

RIDING THE SUBTE

Operated by the private concessionaire Metrovías, the state-owned Subterráneos de Buenos Aires comprises five alphabetically designated lines (*líneas*), four of which (A, B, D, and E) begin in Monserrat or the Microcentro and serve outlying northern and western barrios with numerous stations in between. Línea C is a north-south connector line between major railway stations at Retiro and Constitución.

An additional north-south connector line, Línea H, now links Once and outlying southern barrios, beneath Avenida Pueyrredón and Avenida Jujuy, to Avenida Caseros. Línea E is undergoing a 2.1-kilometer extension from Bolívar station (Plaza de Mayo) to Retiro, due to be completed in 2012.

Subte hours are 5 A.M. to about 11 P.M. Monday-Saturday, but the system opens later (around 8 A.M.) and closes earlier (about 10:30 P.M.) Sundays and holidays, when services are less frequent. Fares are US$0.30; to save time, purchase magnetic tickets in quantities of 2, 5, 10, or 30 rides, or a rechargeable Monedero ticket. Two or more people may legally use the same ticket by passing it back and forth across the turnstile; you do not need a ticket to exit the system.

Before going through the turnstiles, be sure of which direction you're headed; at some stations, trains in both directions use the same platform, but at others the platforms are on opposite sides. Some stations have one-way traffic only; in those cases, the next station down the line usually serves one-way traffic in the other direction.

For complaints or problems, contact Metrovías's Centro de Atención al Pasajero (tel. 0800/555-1616 toll-free).

SUBTE ROUTES

Línea A begins at Plaza de Mayo in Monserrat and runs beneath Avenida Rivadavia to Primera Junta, in the barrio of Chacarita.

Línea B begins at Avenida Leandro Alem in the Microcentro and runs beneath Avenida Corrientes to Federico Lacroze in the barrio of Chacarita, where it connects with the suburban Ferrocarril Urquiza. A recent northwesterly extension continues to Tronador and Avenida los Incas and is due to reach Villa Urquiza.

Línea C connects Retiro (which has northern suburban commuter surface rail lines) with Constitución, the transfer point for southern suburban commuter surface lines; Línea C also has transfer stations for all other Subte lines.

Línea D begins at Catedral on Plaza de Mayo and runs beneath Avenida Santa Fe and Avenida Cabildo through Palermo and Belgrano to Congreso de Tucumán in the barrio of Núñez.

Línea E begins at Bolívar on the Avenida de Mayo (though a northern extension to Retiro is under construction) and goes to Plaza de los Virreyes in the barrio of Flores. At Plaza de los Virreyes, there's a light-rail extension known as the Premetro.

TRAINS

Buenos Aires has two rail systems: the subway that serves the Capital Federal, and a series of surface commuter trains, connecting downtown with more distant suburbs.

Privatized in 1994 and popularly known as the Subte, the Buenos Aires **subway** opened in 1913 and is still the fastest way to get around town. South America's first underground railway, the 13th in the world, has modernized and expanded in recent years, but some antique cars, with their varnished but worn woodwork, and stations with elaborately tiled but chipped murals recall early-20th-century Argentina's prosperity and optimism.

The private concessionaire **Metrovías** (www.metrovias.com.ar) operates the six existing underground lines, including the new (but incomplete) transverse Línea H. At present there are 76 stations for 44.1 kilometers of track; the system carries about 262 million passengers per year.

Since taking over the system, Metrovías has also improved the rolling stock, extended existing lines, modernized many stations, and built new ones. Electronic tickets have replaced the traditional Subte *fichas* (tokens), but while this may be more efficient than in the past, it also means lots of litter; rechargeable electronic cards may change this. Ventilation remains poor in many stations, though some newer cars are air-conditioned.

The most useful and best **suburban rail line** is the Ferrocarril Mitre, operated by **Trenes de Buenos Aires** (TBA, tel. 011/4317-4400 or 0800/333-3822, www.tbanet.com.ar), which connects the classic Estación Retiro (Avenida Ramos Mejía 1302) with Belgrano and Zona Norte suburbs including Vicente López, Olivos, Martínez, San Isidro, and Tigre.

TBA also operates the Ferrocarril Sarmiento from Estación Once (Avenida Pueyrredón y Bartolomé Mitre; Subte: Plaza Miserere), which goes to western destinations like Moreno, with connections to Luján. Unlike the immaculate Mitre, this is a run-down line.

In mid-2007 the Kirchner government re-nationalized the Ferrocarril Roca, then run by **Transportes Metropolitano** (tel. 0800/362-7622, www.ugofe.com.ar), which operates from Estación Constitución (Avenida Brasil and Lima) to the Buenos Aires provincial capital of La Plata and intermediates. The government has spoken of creating a new state rail system with private partners.

CAR RENTAL

For reasons of safety (ferocious traffic) and practicality (no parking and cheap taxis), driving in Buenos Aires makes no sense, but a car can be useful for excursions. Rental agencies include **Avis** (Cerrito 1527, Retiro, tel. 011/4326-5542); **Dollar** (San Martín 945, Retiro, tel. 011/4315-8800); **Hertz** (Paraguay 1138, Retiro, tel. 011/4815-6789); **Localiza** (Lima 969, Constitución, tel. 011/4382-9267); and **Thrifty** (Carlos Pellegrini 1576, Local 24, Retiro, tel. 011/4326-0418).

Vicinity of Buenos Aires

When the pressures of city living grow great, *porteños* escape to the suburbs and countryside of Buenos Aires Province and across the river to Uruguay. When the capital swelters in summer heat, the Paraná's maze of forested channels is just close enough for an afternoon off, but there's plenty to do for a day trip, a weekend, or even longer. Fewer than 4,000 people, many of whom traditionally bring their produce to Tigre's Mercado de Frutos, live in the 950 square kilometers of "the islands."

TIGRE

After decades of decay, the flood-prone riverside city of Tigre itself seems to be experiencing a renaissance. The train stations are renovated, the streets clean, the houses brightly painted and many restored, and it remains the point of departure for delta retreats and historic Isla Martín García. In a decade, the population

zoomed from a little more than 250,000 to some 300,000.

From its beginnings as a humble colonial port for Buenos Aires–destined charcoal from the delta, Tigre languished until the railroad linked it to the capital in 1865. From the late 19th century, it became a summer sanctuary for the *porteño* elite, who built imposing mansions, and prestigious rowing clubs ran regattas on the river. After the 1920s, though, it settled into a subtropical torpor until its recent revival.

Tigre is 27 kilometers north of Buenos Aires at the confluence of the north-flowing Río Tigre and the Río Luján, which drains southeast into the Río de la Plata. The delta's main channel, parallel to the Río Luján, is the Río Paraná de las Palmas.

East of the Río Tigre, the town is primarily commercial. West of the river, it's largely residential.

© DAVID WILBANKS/FLICKR.COM

Buenos Aires Rowing Club in Tigre

Sights

On the Río Tigre's right bank, along Avenida General Mitre, two classic rowing clubs are symbols of bygone elegance: dating from 1873, the Anglophile **Buenos Aires Rowing Club** (Mitre 226), and its 1910 Italian counterpart the **Club Canottierri Italiani** (Mitre 74). Both still function, but they're not the exclusive institutions they once were.

Unfortunately, Tigre's revival has also brought fast-food franchises and the dreadful **Parque de la Costa** (Pereyra s/n, tel. 011/4002-6000, www.parquedelacosta.com. ar, 11 A.M.–midnight, Wed.–Sun.), a cheesy theme park. Open admission, valid for all rides and games, costs US$10–17, but is free for children under three.

East of Parque de la Costa is the **Puerto de Frutos** (Sarmiento 160, tel. 011/4512-4493, www.puertodefrutos-arg.com.ar); though its docks no longer buzz with produce transported by launches from the deepest delta, it is home to a revitalized crafts fair that's open 11 A.M.–7 P.M. daily but is most active on weekends. Handcrafted wicker furniture and basketry, as well as flower arrangements, are unique to the area.

In the residential zone across the river, the **Museo de la Reconquista** (Liniers 818, tel. 011/4512-4496, 10 A.M.–6 P.M. Wed.–Sun., free) was the Spanish Viceroy's command post while the British occupied Buenos Aires in 1806 and 1807. More than just a military memorial, it chronicles the delta, ecclesiastical history, and Tigre's golden age from the 1880s to the 1920s.

Several blocks north, fronting on the Río Luján, the **Museo Naval de la Nación** (Paseo Victorica 602, tel. 011/4749-0608, US$0.80) occupies the former **Talleres Nacionales de Marina** (1879), a cavernous naval repair station that closed as military vessels got too large for its facilities; it now chronicles Argentine naval history from its beginnings under Irishman Guillermo Brown to the present. Despite occasional jingoism, it houses a remarkable collection of model ships, along with maps and colonial portraits (including Spanish scientist Juan de Ulloa). An open-air

TRAVEL IN URUGUAY

The picturesque Uruguayan town of Colonia del Sacramento is an easy day trip or overnight excursion from Buenos Aires. The capital city of Montevideo and the resorts of Carmelo and Punta del Este require a little more investment in time and money. For details, see *Moon Buenos Aires*, which covers most of the Uruguayan coastline.

VISAS AND OFFICIALDOM

Very few nationalities need advance visas for Uruguay, but requirements can change – if in doubt, check with the consulate in Buenos Aires. Ordinarily, border officials give foreign tourists an automatic 90-day entry permit.

HEALTH

Uruguay requires no vaccinations for visitors entering from any country, and public health standards are among the continent's highest. Tap water is safe to drink, but short-term visitors who may have sensitive stomachs should be cautious.

MONEY AND PRICES

When Argentina sneezes, Uruguay catches cold, and the Argentine political and economic meltdown of 2001-2002 had severe repercussions on the economy. As both economies have recovered, Argentines have returned, but not in the numbers seen prior to the collapse. Uruguayan prices are somewhat higher than in Argentina.

The U.S. dollar operates as a parallel currency in Uruguay, at least in the tourist sector, where hotel and restaurant prices are often quoted in both currencies. Away from the heavily touristed coast, this is less common.

Traditionally, Uruguay has the continent's most liberal banking laws; exchange houses are numerous, and bureaucracy is minimal for U.S. cash and travelers checks. Banks, though, keep limited hours – approximately 1-5 P.M. weekdays only. ATMs are common in Montevideo, Colonia, and Punta del Este, but in smaller towns they may not work with foreign plastic.

COMMUNICATIONS

Uruguayan communications remain under the state monopoly Antel, despite privatization pressures, and long-distance phone and Internet offices are fewer than in Argentina. The country code is 598; each city or town has a separate area code, ranging from one to four digits.

GETTING AROUND

Distances in Uruguay are short, and the roads are good. Rental cars are readily available, but the cost of gasoline is high, about US$1.50 per liter. Diesel is slightly cheaper.

Uruguayan buses resemble those in Argentina – modern, spacious, and fast – and service is frequent on most routes. Most, though not all, towns have a main bus terminal, usually on the outskirts; some bus lines have separate ticket offices in conveniently central locations.

---

sector includes naval aircraft and the bridge of a ship destroyed during the 1982 Falklands war. Hours are 8:30 A.M.–5:30 P.M. weekdays, 10:30 A.M.–6:30 P.M. weekends.

The city's newest landmark is the **Museo de Arte Tigre** (Paseo Victorica 972, tel. 011/4512-4528, www.mat.gov.ar, US$1.25), which houses figurative works by Argentine artists from the late 19th to the 20th century. Showcasing artists such as Benito Quinquela Martín and Juan Carlos Castagnino, it occupies the spectacularly restored Tigre Club

(1913), a belle époque edifice that once housed a hotel-casino. Hours are 9 A.M.–7 P.M. Wednesday–Friday, with guided tours at 11 A.M. and 4 P.M., and noon–7 P.M. weekends and holidays, when guided tours take place at 1, 3, and 5 P.M.

Practicalities

In a recycled mansion on the west side of the Río Tigre, the family-run **Casona la Ruchi** (Lavalle 557, tel. 011/4749-2499, www.casonalaruchi.com.ar, US$55 d with shared bath)

has five spacious rooms, attractive gardens, and a pool.

Standard Argentine eateries are a dime a dozen at locales like the **Mercado de Frutos.** For a more sophisticated menu on a shady riverside terrace with good service, try **María Luján** (Paseo Victorica 611, tel. 011/4731-9613, www.ilnovomariadellujan.com). Homemade pastas cost around US$7–10, more elaborate dishes around US$9–12.

In the Nueva Estación Fluvial, the **Ente Municipal de Turismo** (Mitre 305, tel. 011/4512-4497 or 0800/888-8447, www.tigre. gov.ar) is open 9 A.M.–5 P.M. daily. The private website **Tigre Tiene Todo** (www.tigretienetodo.com.ar) is also useful for services.

Getting There and Around

Tigre is well connected to Buenos Aires by bus and train, but heavy traffic on the Panamericana Norte makes the bus slow. Through the delta, there are numerous local launches and even international service to the Uruguayan ports of Carmelo and Nueva Palmira.

The No. 60 *colectivo* from downtown Buenos Aires runs 24 hours a day, but when traffic's heavy it takes two hours to reach Tigre.

Tigre has two train stations. From Retiro, Trenes de Buenos Aires (TBA) operates frequent commuter trains (US$0.40) on the Ferrocarril Mitre from the capital to **Estación Tigre**; it's also possible to board these trains in Belgrano or suburban stations.

Also from Retiro, a separate branch of the Mitre line runs to Estación Bartolomé Mitre, where passengers transfer at Estación Maipú to the Tren de la Costa (www.trendelacosta.com. ar), a tourist train that runs through several riverside communities and shopping centers to its terminus at **Estación Delta,** at the entrance to the Parque de la Costa. This costs about US$3, including intermediate stops.

From Tigre's Nueva Estación Fluvial (Mitre 319), several companies offer *lanchas colectivas,* river-bound buses that drop off and pick up passengers at docks throughout the delta. Among them are **Interisleña** (tel. 011/4749-

0900), **Líneas Delta Argentino** (tel. 011/4749-0537, www.lineasdelta.com.ar), and **Jilguero** (tel. 011/4749-0987). **Marsili** (tel. 011/15-4413-4123) and **Giacomotti** (tel. 011/4749-1896) use smaller *lanchas taxi.*

Cacciola (Lavalle 520, tel./fax 011/4749-0329, www.cacciolaviajes.com) has daily launches to Carmelo, Uruguay, at 8:30 A.M. and 4:30 P.M. (2.5 hours, US$16), with bus connections to Montevideo (US$8.50 more). Fast, new catamarans make the trip quicker and more comfortable than it once was, but it also means they use broader, less scenic channels to get there.

Líneas Delta Argentino also operates launches to the Uruguayan town of Colonia (3.5 hours, US$20) daily at 7:30 A.M.; it also goes to Nueva Palmira, Uruguay (3 hours, US$15), west of Carmelo, at 7:30 A.M. daily, with an additional Friday sailing at 5 P.M. While launches leave from Cacciola's international terminal, sales take place at Delta Argentino's, across the river.

THE DELTA

Tigre itself may have been revitalized, but many rusting hulks still line the Paraná's inner channels. Farther from Tigre, where colonial smugglers often hid from Spanish officials, summer houses stand on *palafitos* (pilings) to prevent—not always successfully—their being flooded.

Many operators at Tigre's Nueva Estación Fluvial and the Puerto de Frutos offer 40- to 90-minute excursions that are, metaphorically speaking, enough to get your feet wet in the delta. It's also possible to use the *lanchas colectivas* to get where you want to go, including hotels and restaurants. A word of warning: powerboaters, especially on "personal watercraft," can be as reckless as motorists—don't jump in the water without looking around first.

A favorite excursion is the **Museo Histórico Sarmiento** (Río Sarmiento and Arroyo Los Reyes, tel. 011/4728-0570). Dating from 1855, built from fruit boxes and now encased by glass, President Domingo F. Sarmiento's onetime summer residence preserves some of his personal effects. Open 10 A.M.–6 P.M. Wednesday–Sunday, it charges no admission; a one-kilometer footpath leads through a typical gallery forest.

Accommodations and Food

Both accommodations and dining options are increasing in the delta. The following is just a sample of what is now available.

On the Río San Antonio, about 50 minutes from Tigre by Interisleña, rates at **Hotel l'Marangatú** (tel. 011/4749-6765, www.i-marangatu.com.ar, US$50–65 s, US$66–79 d) include breakfast and dinner.

About 80 minutes from Tigre by Delta Argentino launch, the **Marco Polo Inn Náutico** (Paraná de las Palmas and Cruz Colorada, tel. 011/4728-0395, www.marcopoloinnnautico.com, US$63–73 s or d) is a Hostelling International affiliate with its own sandy beach, a separate pool, a restaurant, and a spa in the works. The accommodations are simple and relatively small, but bright and cheerful; the higher-priced rooms have air-conditioning.

On Canal Honda off the Paraná de las Palmas, about 90 minutes from Tigre by Delta Argentino, **Río Laura Hotel & Resort** (tel. 011/4728-1019, www.riohotellaura.com.ar, US$100–167 s or d) has ample standard rooms and a handful of larger suites with whirlpool tubs. Its restaurant offers river fish such as *surubí*.

On Río Tres Bocas, about 25 minutes from Tigre by Interisleña, **La Riviera** (Río Sarmiento 356, tel. 011/4728-0177) offers outdoor dining in good weather, with a wide selection of beef, fish, and pasta dishes.

◖ Isla Martín García

Almost within swimming distance of Carmelo (Uruguay), the Precambrian bedrock island of Martín García boasts a fascinating history, lush woodlands, and an almost unmatchable tranquility as a retreat from the frenzy of the federal capital and even provincial suburbs.

Only 3.5 kilometers off the Uruguayan coast but 33.5 kilometers from Tigre, 168-hectare Martín García rises 27 meters above sea level. Its native vegetation is dense gallery forest; part of it is a *zona intangible* provincial forest reserve.

HISTORY

Spanish navigator Juan Díaz de Solís was the first European to see the island, naming it for one of his crewmen who died there in 1516. In colonial times it often changed hands before coming under firm Spanish control in 1777; in 1814 Guillermo Brown, the Argentine navy's Irish founder, captured it for the United Provinces of the River Plate. For a time, mainlanders quarried its granite bedrock for building materials.

For a century (1870–1970) the navy controlled the island, and it served as a political prison and a regular penal colony; it was also a quarantine base for European immigrants. While serving as Colombia's consul in Buenos Aires, Nicaraguan poet Rubén Darío (1867–1916) lived here briefly.

Political detainees have included presidents Marcelo T. de Alvear (in 1932, after his presidency), Hipólito Yrigoyen (twice in the 1930s), Juan Domingo Perón (1945, before his election), and Arturo Frondizi (1962–1963). In World War II's early months, Argentina briefly incarcerated German crewmen from the battleship *Graf Spee,* scuttled off Montevideo in December 1939.

While the island passed to the United Provinces at independence, it was not explicitly Argentine until a 1973 agreement with Uruguay (one of the United Provinces). After the navy departed, the Buenos Aires provincial Servicio Penitenciario used it as a halfway house for ordinary convicts, but it was also a detention and torture site during the 1976–1983 dictatorship.

SIGHTS

Uphill from the *muelle pasajero* (passenger pier), opposite the meticulously landscaped **Plaza Guillermo Brown,** the island's **Oficina de Informes** was, until recently, the Servicio Penitenciario's headquarters. It now houses provincial park rangers. Several antique *baterías* (gun emplacements) line the south shore.

At the plaza's upper end stand ruins of the onetime **Cuartel** (military barracks), which later became jail cells. Clustered together nearby are the **Cine-Teatro,** the former theater, with its gold-tinted rococo details; the **Museo de la Isla** (Island Museum); and the former **Casa Médicos de Lazareto,** the quarantine center that is now the **Centro de Interpretación Ecológica** (Environmental Interpretation Center).

Opposite the Cuartel, the **Panadería Rocío** (1913) is a bakery that makes celebrated fruitcakes; farther inland, the now-unused *faro* (lighthouse, 1881) rises above the trees. To the north, the graves of conscripts who died in an early-20th-century epidemic dot the isolated *cementerio* (cemetery).

At the island's northwest end, trees and vines grow among the crumbling structures of the so-called **Barrio Chino** (Chinatown), marking the **Puerto Viejo,** the sediment-clogged former port. Across the island, beyond the airstrip, similar vegetation grows in the **Zona Intangible,** which is closed to the public.

RECREATION

Though the island offers outstanding walking and bird-watching, the river is not suitable for swimming. The restaurant Comedor El Solís, though, has a swimming pool open to the public.

ACCOMMODATIONS AND FOOD

Crowded in summer and on weekends, **Camping Martín García** (tel. 011/4728-1808) charges US$3 pp for tent campers, with discounts for two or more nights; reservations are advisable for hostel bunks with shared bath (US$5 pp) or with private bath (US$7 pp). Cacciola's **Hostería Martín García** charges US$85 pp for full-board packages that include transportation from Tigre. Each additional night costs US$44 pp.

Cacciola's restaurant **Fragata Hércules** is decent enough, but **Comedor El Solís** is at least as good and a bit cheaper; in winter, however, the Solís may be closed. **Panadería Rocío** is known for its fruitcakes.

GETTING THERE AND AROUND

On the Río Tigre's west bank, **Cacciola** (Lavalle 520, tel. 011/4749-0329, www.cacciolaviajes.com) offers day trips Tuesday, Thursday, Saturday, and Sunday at 9 A.M., but passengers should get there half an hour earlier. Arriving around noon, the tour includes an aperitif on arrival, a guided visit, and lunch at Cacciola's *Fragata Hércules.* It returns to Tigre around 5 P.M., but again, get to the dock early. There is ample time for just roaming around.

Cacciola also has a Microcentro office (Florida 520, 1st floor, Oficina 113, tel. 011/4393-6100). Fares for a full-day excursion are US$37 for adults, US$28 for children ages 3–9, including port charges. Transportation alone costs US$20 per adult, US$19 per child.

THE PAMPAS

West of the Capital Federal, Buenos Aires Province is gaucho country, transformed by the herds of cattle that proliferated on the pampas after the Spanish invasion and by the horsemen who subsisted off those herds. Eventually and ironically, those free-spirited gauchos became peons on the sprawling *estancias* (cattle ranches) that occupied almost every square inch of prime agricultural land.

La Plata, a planned city created when Buenos Aires became a separate federal district, is the provincial capital and a worthwhile excursion from BA. San Antonio de Areco is Argentina's unofficial gaucho capital, and the *estancias* (guest ranches) that surround it are some of the country's most historic. Between Buenos Aires and San Antonio, the equally historic city of Luján has outstanding architecture and museums, and it is also a major devotional center.

To the south, the coastal city of Mar del Plata and a string of nearby beach resorts comprise Argentina's—or rather Buenos Aires's—traditional summer vacation destination. This area, though, also boasts the humid pampas' greatest scenic diversity, thanks to the rolling ranges of Tandilia and the steeper Ventania, north of Bahía Blanca. Scattered around the area are several other *estancias* open to the paying public.

Thinly populated La Pampa Province boasts the off-the-beaten-track attraction of Parque Nacional Lihué Calel. Some of the strongest resistance to Argentina's 19th-century incursions into Mapuche territory took place here.

© KEVIN DYER/ISTOCKPHOTO.COM

HIGHLIGHTS

◖ **Museo de La Plata:** In Buenos Aires Province's capital city of La Plata, Argentina's premier natural history museum makes a great day trip from Buenos Aires (page 104).

◖ **Complejo Museográfico Enrique Udaondo:** This complex of historical museums in the pilgrimage city of Luján is among the country's best (page 109).

◖ **San Antonio de Areco:** In the placid pampas west of Luján, Argentina's "gaucho capital" celebrates its heritage during November's Fiesta de la Tradición, but it's a great excursion in any season (page 110).

◖ **Tandil:** The most attractive city in southern Buenos Aires Province's interior is located at a granite mountain range that's ideal for mountain biking, rock climbing, and other activities (page 118).

◖ **Parque Provincial Ernesto Tornquist:** Near the sleepy town of Sierra de la Ventana, Buenos Aires Province's most mountainous terrain offers its best hiking. There are also outstanding *estancias*, such as Cerro de la Cruz (page 126).

◖ **Mar del Plata:** Argentina's traditional beach resort has become one of its biggest tourist traps, but it still shows its elegance and sophistication in its historical neighborhoods and cultural offerings – especially outside the touristy summer months of January and February (page 126).

◖ **Museo del Automovilismo Juan Manuel Fangio:** More than just a tribute to the legendary Formula One champion, this automotive museum near Mar del Plata takes an expansive view of transportation technology (page 137).

◖ **Museo del Puerto:** On Bahía Blanca's outskirts, this whimsical self-styled "community museum" in Puerto Ingeniero White does a lot with a little to illuminate the immigrant experience (page 142).

◖ **Parque Nacional Lihué Calel:** Surrounded by the arid pampas that become Patagonian desert toward the southwest, Lihué Calel's resistant granite summits and canyons are an archipelago of biodiversity (page 147).

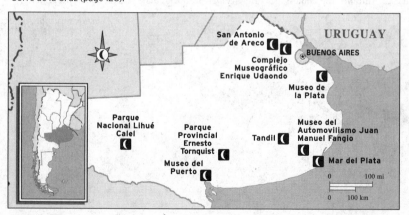

LOOK FOR ◖ TO FIND RECOMMENDED SIGHTS, ACTIVITIES, DINING, AND LODGING.

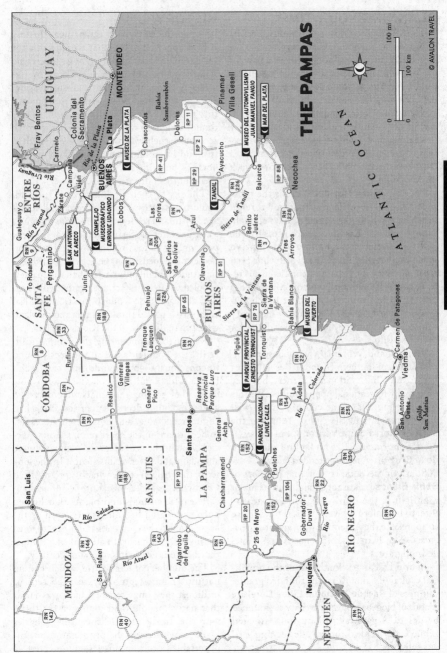

THE PAMPAS

URUGUAY

MONTEVIDEO

Fray Bentos
Carmelo
Colonia del Sacramento
Gualeguaychú
ENTRE RÍOS
Gualeguay

Fray Bentos

Río Uruguay

Río Paraná

Zárate
Campana
Luján
BUENOS AIRES
La Plata

Río de la Plata

MUSEO DE LA PLATA

Chascomús
Dolores
RP 11
Bahía Samborombón

Pinamar
Villa Gesell

MUSEO DEL AUTOMOVILISMO JUAN MANUEL FANGIO

MAR DEL PLATA

Ayacucho
RP 2
RP 41
RP 29
Balcarce
RP 88

Necochea

TANDIL
RN 226
Azul
Sierra de Tandil
RN 228

Las Flores
RN 3

SANTA FE

Pergamino
SAN ANTONIO DE ARECO
RN 9
COMPLEJO MUSEOGRÁFICO ENRIQUE UDAONDO
Lobos
RN 205

To Rosario

CÓRDOBA
RN 8
RN 7
Rufino
Junín
RN 188
Pehuajó
RN 226
RP 65
Trenque Lauquen
RN 33
RN 5
San Carlos de Bolívar
Olavarría
RP 51
BUENOS AIRES
Sierra de la Ventana
Sierra de la Ventana
RP 76
Benito Juárez
RN 3
Tres Arroyos
Bahía Blanca
MUSEO DEL PUERTO

Pigüé
PARQUE PROVINCIAL ERNESTO TORNQUIST
Tornquist
RN 22

General Villegas
General Pico
Realicó
RN 35
Reserva Provincial Parque Luro
La Adela
RP 154
Río Colorado
Carmen de Patagones
Viedma

SAN LUIS
San Luis
RN 188
RP 10
LA PAMPA
Santa Rosa
General Acha
RN 152
PARQUE NACIONAL LIHUÉ CALEL
Puelches
RP 106
Gobernador Duval
Río Negro
San Antonio Oeste
Golfo San Matías
RN 251
RN 250
RN 23

Chacharramendi
RP 20
25 de Mayo
RN 152
RP 151
Algarrobo del Aguila
RN 143
Río Atuel
Río Salado
MENDOZA
San Rafael
RN 146
RN 143
RN 40

RÍO NEGRO

Neuquén
RN 22
NEUQUÉN
RN 231

ATLANTIC OCEAN

THE PAMPAS

100 mi
100 km
0

© AVALON TRAVEL

PLANNING YOUR TIME

Buenos Aires Province is enormous, and La Pampa is large enough that travel in the region can be time-consuming without a base for exploration. Some destinations, like **La Plata, Luján,** and **San Antonio de Areco,** make ideal day trips from Buenos Aires, but San Antonio's ambience and accommodations, and the *estancias* in the vicinity, make it an ideal getaway (it's calmer and quieter midweek). Some overseas visitors make properties like **Estancia El Ombú** destinations in themselves for a week or even more.

For Argentines, **Mar del Plata** is the province's highest-profile destination; foreign beachgoers will find a couple of days enough, though the city has an active cultural scene and a day trip to the **Fangio Automotive Museum** in nearby Balcarce is worthwhile even for nondrivers. The chain of cookie-cutter resorts northeast and southwest of "Mardel" has pockets of peacefulness for quiet beach getaways, at least outside the January–February summer peak, but they're not major draws for overseas visitors.

Tandilia and Ventania, the modest mountain ranges of southern Buenos Aires, fall short of the Andes in elevation and scenery, but they offer many recreational opportunities. Visitors spending months in the country might well enjoy some days in the city of **Tandil** or the town of **Sierra de la Ventana,** but guests at prestigious *estancias* like **La Isolina** and **Cerro de la Cruz** often relish extended stays.

South of Sierra de la Ventana, the port of **Bahía Blanca** is pleasant enough, but its major highlight is the quirky museum at nearby **Puerto Ingeniero White.** This is the best place to appreciate the Argentine immigrant experience—even better than Buenos Aires's Hotel de Inmigrantes.

In arid La Pampa, southwest of the provincial capital of Santa Rosa, the rounded granite summits of **Parque Nacional Lihué Calel** are islands of biogeographical diversity surrounded by desert. A gateway to Patagonia, isolated Lihué Calel is ideal for anyone seeking serious solitude.

HISTORY

It's tempting to say that the pampas' history is beef and wheat, but that would omit the Querandí, the aboriginal hunter-gatherers who stalked guanaco, rhea, and other game over its grassy horizons before the Spanish invasion. Though they used bows, arrows, and spears, they primarily hunted with *boleadoras,* sinewy thongs weighted with stones. When thrown accurately, such *bolas* were effective enough to trip and immobilize an animal as large as a horse or bull; in fact, the gauchos later used them for this purpose.

Thanks to their mobility, the Querandí could harass early Buenos Aires and discourage any inland settlements for more than half a century after the Spaniards arrived. Imperial policy played a role in this slow development, as the crown focused on the densely settled central Andean highlands rather than the sparsely peopled pampas. In fact, for nearly two centuries, all legal trade—not to mention political authority—passed through Lima and overland rather than directly to the Río de la Plata.

Rather than conquering the pampas militarily, the Spaniards did so indirectly—and unconsciously—by abandoning cattle and horses, which multiplied on grasslands whose only other grazing mammals were deer and guanaco. Unlike deer and guanaco, cattle had commercial value, and horses were necessary to herd them; in the short term, the new species brought the peoples of the pampas a more abundant and diverse subsistence. In the long term, they helped create what historian Alfred Crosby has called a "neo-Europe" of ecologically exotic animals and plants that helped open the region to immigrants, even as the horse enabled the Querandí and others to resist the invaders militarily. In areas like La Pampa, they held out nearly into the 20th century.

The numbers of feral cattle, which had no natural enemies, probably reached tens of millions; they impoverished lush grasslands that native peoples had managed skillfully with fire. In the early 19th century, Charles Darwin, witnessing the proliferation of impenetrable European thistles, commented, "I doubt whether any case is on record of an invasion on so grand a scale of one plant over the aborigines."

As cattle overwhelmed wild game, the hunter became a mounted herdsman, but this was a gradual process—the rangy cattle were wild enough in the beginning that hunting was hazardous, and gauchos (as the riders became known) were often gored. Living off the herds, the free-roaming gaucho became a symbol of *argentinidad* (Argentine identity) even as his role diminished with political and economic change.

In the early independence years gauchos could kill cattle for food as long as they left the hides, which had some economic value, to the landholder. As Argentina became integrated with the global economy, though, more-intensive land-use practices like sheep- and wheat-farming meant the fencing of the pampas and the end of the autonomous gaucho, who became a dependent laborer on the *estancias.*

By the late 19th century, sharecroppers and permanent settlers had further displaced the gaucho, Argentina was becoming Europe's granary, and the British-built railroads had fanned out from Buenos Aires to transport beef, maize, and wheat to the port. Tensions between the capital and its hinterland nearly led to civil war in the 1880s, when provincial authorities moved the seat of government to the new, planned city of La Plata.

Through much of the 20th century, the richest *estancias* retained a stranglehold on rural social and economic life; their lavish *cascos* (mansions) embodied the pretensions of an aspiring aristocracy. Successive crises in the last 30-plus years, though, have weakened their grip, and many traditional landholders have had to open their portals to tourists (often, though not always, the most affluent tourists).

Argentina remains a major beef and grain producer, but as in Australia and North America, its mechanized agriculture relies on fossil-fuel fertilizers and pesticides. Renewed antagonism between the farming sector and the federal government over export taxes for soy and beef has characterized the past few years. Smaller farms near Buenos Aires and other cities have benefited from access to urban markets for their fruits, vegetables, and dairy products, but the contemporary gaucho is more symbol than substance.

La Plata and Vicinity

In 1882, after barely avoiding civil war following the federalization of the city of Buenos Aires, indignant provincial authorities expropriated six square leagues in the Municipio de la Ensenada to create the new capital of La Plata. Provincial Governor Dardo Rocha commissioned Pedro Benoit's orderly grid, superimposed with diagonals like those of Washington, D.C., for the city plan. Embellished with pretentious neoclassical and Francophile buildings, it has somehow achieved a remarkable harmony over time.

While government is its reason for existence, La Plata has become one of the country's major cultural centers, with first-rate universities, theaters, concert halls, libraries, and museums. In January and February, though, when politicians go on vacation and university students return home, the cultural calendar thins out.

ORIENTATION

La Plata (pop. about 667,000) is 56 kilometers southeast of Buenos Aires via freeway, the Autopista Buenos Aires–La Plata. The city consists of a rectangular grid with regularly distributed plazas, but the connecting diagonals (which run north–south and east–west) can make the layout disorienting—a slight wrong turn can send you far out of your way. Its streets and avenues are numbered rather than named; locations are commonly described by their intersections and cross streets rather than building numbers.

THE PAMPAS

LA PLATA AND VICINITY

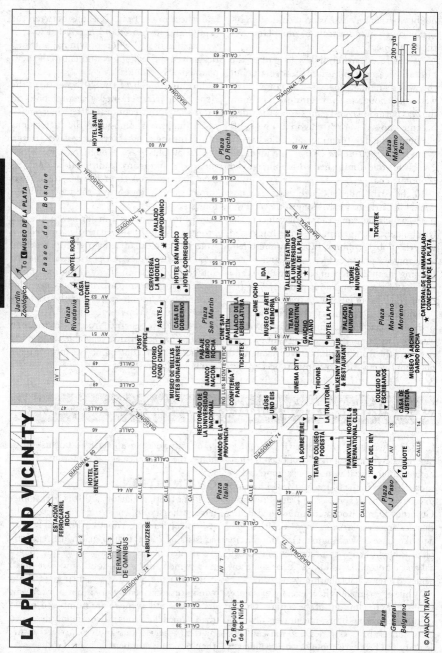

© AVALON TRAVEL

SIGHTS

Governor Rocha laid La Plata's **Piedra Fundacional** (Foundation Stone, 1882) in the center of sprawling **Plaza Mariano Moreno,** which fills four full blocks bounded by Calle 12, Calle 14, Calle 50, and Calle 54. Along with architects Ernesto Meyer and Emilio Coutaret, Benoit designed the French neo-Gothic **Catedral de la Inmaculada Concepción de la Plata** at the southwest corner.

Rocha resided in what is now the **Museo y Archivo Dardo Rocha** (Calle 50 No. 933, tel. 0221/427-5631, 3–6 P.M. Sat. only). Two blocks west, the French-style **Casa de Justicia** fills an entire block bounded by Avenida 13, Calle 47, Calle 48, and Calle 14.

On the northeast side, fronting on Calle 12, Hanover architect Hubert Stiers built the German Renaissance **Palacio Municipal** (1886), where marble staircases, imported oak floors, stained-glass windows, and bronze chandeliers adorn its **Salón Dorado.** Two blocks away, bounded by Calle 9, Calle 10, Avenida 51, and Avenida 53, the **Teatro Argentino** replaced a dignified performing arts center that burned to the ground in 1977.

Two blocks northeast, facing Plaza San Martín on Avenida 7, Hanoverian architects Gustav Heine and Georg Hagemann designed the **Palacio de la Legislatura** in the German Renaissance style. Across the plaza, fronting on Calle 6, Belgian architect Julio Doral created the Flemish Renaissance **Casa de Gobierno,** home to the executive branch and, seemingly, a challenge to the federal capital's nondescript Casa Rosada.

At the northwest corner, La Plata's first railroad station is now the **Pasaje Dardo Rocha** (1887), home to several museums and other cultural institutions. Across Avenida 51, the **Museo Provincial de Bellas Artes** (Avenida 51 No. 525, tel. 0221/421-8629, 10 A.M.–7 P.M. Tues.–Sat., 2–9 P.M. Sun., free) is a contemporary art museum.

To the southeast, the **Museo de Arte y Memoria** (Calle 9 No. 984, tel. 0221/483-5590, www.comisionporlamemoria.org.ar, free) deals with human rights themes in the aftermath of the "Dirty War," but the emphasis is more on art than on propaganda.

Several blocks northeast, facing Plaza Rivadavia and dating from 1948, the **Casa Curutchet** (Calle 53 No. 320, tel. 0221/482-2631, www.capba.org.ar, 10 A.M.–2 P.M. weekdays, US$2.50 for Argentines, US$10 for foreigners) was designed by the famed Swiss architect Le Corbusier as a private residence and office for Dr. Pedro Curutchet. It's one of just two Le Corbusier works in the western hemisphere (the other is Harvard University's Carpenter Center for the Visual Arts).

Across Avenida 1, the 60-hectare **Paseo del Bosque** is a forested park whose facilities include the **Anfiteatro Martín Fierro,** an outdoor theater; the exceptional natural sciences **Museo de La Plata;** the **Observatorio Astronómico** (Astronomical Observatory); and the **Jardín de la Paz** (Peace Garden), with small pavilions for each country with diplomatic representation in Argentina.

The park's **Jardín Zoológico y Botánico** (Paseo del Bosque s/n, tel. 0221/427-3925, www.jardinzoologico.laplata.gov.ar, US$1.25 ages 12 and up) is a 14-hectare Victorian-style zoo with more than 180 native and exotic species, including giraffes, elephants, lions, monkeys, and rhinoceroses. Hours are 10 A.M.–6 P.M. Tuesday–Sunday.

Catedral de la Inmaculada Concepción de la Plata

Construction of La Plata's cathedral is a story in itself, even by the standards of Argentine public-works projects. Begun in 1885, it did not open officially until 1932, and its three crowning towers went unfinished until 1999. Construction took so long, in fact, that the building underwent its first restoration (1997) even before its completion!

Overlooking Plaza Moreno, the cathedral contains a subterranean **Museo de la Catedral** (Calle 14 between 51 and 53, tel. 0221/427-3504, 9 A.M.–7 P.M. daily, US$2.50 pp), which contains the tombs of provincial governor Dardo Rocha and his wife; a gallery also offers special exhibitions.

Miradores (overlooks) at the 42-meter and 63-meter levels, reached by elevator, offer fine city views, but most of the rest will interest only the truly devout. For more info, contact the Fundación Catedral (tel. 0221/422-3931, www.catedraldelaplata.com).

Museo de La Plata

Patagonian explorer Francisco Pascasio Moreno donated his personal anthropological, archaeological, and paleontological collections to Argentina's premier natural history museum, which opened in 1888 under his own lifetime directorship. Today, more than 400,000 visitors per annum view at least some of the 2.5 million items in its 21 exhibition halls, which also deal with botany, geology, zoology, and other fields.

The four-story building is a monument to its era, its exterior a hybrid of Greek regional styles with indigenous American—Aztec and Incaic—flourishes. Home to the Universidad Nacional de La Plata's natural sciences department, it has upgraded its displays on earth sciences (especially geology and paleontology, with an emphasis on Argentine biomes), life sciences (botany and zoology), and anthropology (physical anthropology, archaeology, and ethnography, including a fine exhibit on Mesopotamia's Jesuit missions). There are also temporary displays on special topics such as herpetology.

The Museo de La Plata (Paseo del Bosque s/n, tel. 0221/425-7744, www.fcnym.unlp.edu.ar/museo) is open 10 A.M.–6 P.M. Tuesday–Sunday and closed January 1, May 1, and December 25; when other holidays fall on Monday, it is open. Admission costs US$1.50 pp for those over 12 years of age; the official price for foreigners is US$4.50 pp, but enforcement is lax. There are guided tours at 4 P.M. Tuesday–Friday, and at 10:30 A.M. and 2:30, 3:30, and 4:30 P.M. on weekends.

Pasaje Dardo Rocha

Formerly the Estación 19 de Noviembre, La Plata's first major railroad station, the French classic Pasaje Dardo Rocha has undergone an adaptive reuse into a major cultural center with several museums, plus cinemas, auditoriums, conference rooms, cafés, and other features. It's a handsome building, but its full restoration has been a slow process.

Opened in 1999, the **Museo de Arte Contemporáneo Latinoamericano** (Calle 50 between Calles 6 and 7, tel. 0221/427-1843, www.macla.laplata.gov.ar, 10 A.M.–8 P.M. Tues.–Fri., 2–9 P.M. weekends except in summer, when hours are 4–10 P.M., free) features modern Latin American art. There are guided tours by advance arrangements only.

The **Museo Municipal de Arte** (tel. 0221/425-1990, 10 A.M.–10 P.M. Tues.–Sun.) is a painting and sculpture museum focused on local artists.

Teatro Argentino

Rebuilt after its destruction by fire in 1977, the homely Teatro Argentino reopened in October 2000 with a presentation of *Tosca*. With all the elegance of a multistory car park, this 60,000-square-meter concrete structure mirrors the military dictatorship that approved it—a fortified bunker that (had it been complete) might have bought the generals and admirals extra time in power after their 1982 Falklands debacle.

Still, the facility looks and sounds better within than without and remains one of the country's top performing arts venues, with its own orchestra, chorus, ballet, and children's chorus. Its principal hall is the Sala Alberto Ginastera, seating more than 2,000 spectators; smaller halls seat 300–700. Past performers include Arthur Rubinstein, Anna Pavlova, Andrés Segovia, and Richard Strauss.

The Teatro Argentino (Avenida 51 between Calle 9 and Calle 10, tel. 221/429-1700, www.teatroargentino.ic.gba.gov.ar) offers free guided tours (9 and 10:30 A.M., noon, and 2 P.M. Tues.–Fri., 11:30 A.M. and 2:30 P.M. Sat.).

República de los Niños

According to some accounts, Walt Disney took the inspiration for Disneyland from República de los Niños, a 50-hectare children's

© WAYNE BERNHARDSON

La Plata's massive Teatro Argentino replaced a historical structure destroyed by fire.

amusement park on what was once a golf course built for the English meatpacker Swift in La Plata's northern suburbs. Disney, though, visited Argentina in 1941—a decade before the Argentine park opened.

Conceived by Evita Perón, officially opened by Juan Perón himself, República de los Niños had a strong political subtext that's less obvious today. In the Peronist context, its origins as an expropriated property and its role as a destination for underprivileged working-class children are significant.

República de los Niños displays a mélange of architectural miniatures from around the world, ranging from the medieval Europe of Grimm's fairy tales to Islamic mosques and the Taj Mahal, but most notably replicas of the Argentine presidential palace, legislature, and courts—with the obvious implication that its youthful public could aspire to office (and perhaps graft, as there's also a jail). A steam train makes the rounds of the park.

República de los Niños (tel. 0221/484-1409, www.republica.laplata.gov.ar, 10 A.M.–6 P.M. weekdays, 9 A.M.–7 P.M. weekends, US$1.25 pp, children under 8 free) is at Camino General Belgrano and 501 in the suburb of Manuel Gonnet. Some secondary attractions, such as the train, have small additional charges.

From Avenida 7 in downtown La Plata, buses No. 518 and 273 go to República de los Niños, but not all No. 273s go all the way—ask before boarding.

ARTS AND ENTERTAINMENT

For event tickets, visit **Ticketek** (Calle 50 No. 612, tel. 021/447-7200, www.ticketek.com.ar).

Cinema

La Plata has three downtown movie theaters: the six-screen **Cine Ocho** (Calle 8 No. 981, between 51 and 53, tel. 0221/482-5554); the four-screen **Cine San Martín** (Calle 7 No. 923, between 50 and 51, tel. 0221/483-9947); and the three-screen **Cinema City** (Calle 50 No. 723, between 9 and 10, tel. 0221/423-5456). All share a common website (www.cinemalaplata.com).

Performing Arts

La Plata's major venue is, of course, the **Centro de las Artes Teatro Argentino** (Avenida 51 between 9 and 10, tel. 0800/666-5151 toll-free, www.teatroargentino.ic.gba.gov.ar). Its box office (tel. 0221/429-1733) is open 10 A.M.–8 P.M. Tuesday–Sunday. The Teatro Argentino provides free transportation from Buenos Aires for ticket holders.

Another important locale is the **Teatro Coliseo Podestá** (Calle 10, between 46 and 47, tel. 0221/424-8457, www.coliseopodesta. laplata.gov.ar).

ACCOMMODATIONS

For budget travelers and backpackers, La Plata finally has a hostel in the centrally located HI affiliate **Frankville Hostel & International Club** (Calle 46 No. 781, tel. 011/428-3100, www.frankville.com.ar, US$12–17 pp dorm, US$34–62 d), whose name plays on La Plata's Francophile origins. Rates vary according to the number of beds in the room and whether or not it has private bath.

Friendly but no-frills **Hotel Saint James** (Avenida 60 No. 377, tel. 221/421-8089, www. hotelsj.com.ar, US$24 s, US$35 d, with private bath) is best for the truly budget-conscious, but it's often full. Cable TV and parking cost extra.

At the intersection of Avenidas 13 and 44, **Hotel del Rey** (Plaza Paso 180, tel. 0221/427-0177, www.hoteldelrey.com.ar, US$33 s, US$40 d, US$78 s or d suites) is a 10-story tower with well-kept midsize rooms and suites with modern conveniences.

On a quiet block near the Paseo del Bosque, **Hotel Roga** (Calle 54 No. 334, tel. 0221/427-4070, www.hotelroga.com.ar, US$40–45 s, US$53–62 d, with private bath) is modern, friendly, and comfortable. There's a surcharge, though, for credit-card payments, and the cheaper rooms lack air-conditioning.

Expanding **Hotel del Sol** (Calle 10 No. 1061, tel. 0221/427-2049, www.hoteldel-sol-laplata.com.ar, US$44–70 s, US$66–70 d), really a recycled older building, has mostly midsize rooms plus a handful of slightly dearer "executives" and amenities such as Wi-Fi.

The restored **Hotel Benevento** (Calle 2 No. 645, corner of Diagonal 80, tel. 0221/423-7721, www.hotelbenevento.com.ar, US$42–54 s, US$54–64 d) occupies a century-old building that once housed the provincial labor ministry. Its rooms have high ceilings, traditional balconies, and modernized baths (showers only), but some of the singles, though comfortable, are truly Lilliputian.

Rates at centrally located, 70-room **Hotel La Plata** (Avenida 51 No. 783, tel./fax 0221/422-9090, www.weblaplatahotel.com.ar, US$47 s, US$66 d) include breakfast *and* dinner, with air-conditioning, cable TV, and similar amenities, but prices have risen significantly.

The 110-room high-rise **Hotel Corregidor** (Calle 6 No. 1026, tel. 0221/425-6800, www. hotelcorregidor.com.ar, US$88 s or d) is La Plata's only four-star facility, though the Benevento has more style.

FOOD

For breakfast, coffee, or pastries, the best option is tobacco-free **Confitería París** (Avenida 7 and Calle 49, tel. 0221/482-8840).

The **Colegio de Escribanos** (Avenida 13 No. 770, tel. 0221/412-1915) is a lunchtime favorite for lawyers and judges from the nearby Tribunales. Plaza Paso's **El Quijote** (Avenida 13 and Avenida 44, tel. 0221/483-3653) specializes in seafood.

La Trattoría (Calle 47 and Diagonal 74, tel. 0221/422-6135) is a casual Italian restaurant with sidewalk seating, while **Abruzzese** (Calle 42 No. 457, tel. 0221/421-9869) is more formal. Open for dinner only, **Gaucho Italiano** (Calle 50 No. 724, between 9 and 10, tel. 0221/483-2817) serves 50 varieties of pizzas, meat and cheese *tablas,* and pastas with a hybrid pampas touch. There's a tobacco-free area, but the background music is dreadful.

New on the scene, 🅘 **Ida** (Calle 54 No. 684, tel. 0221/482-5875, idateawine@gmail. com, US$10) is a modern combination of deli, teahouse, and wine bar, with excellent cheap lunches—perhaps the best in town—and dinners Tuesday–Saturday. The music, with endless repeats of Muzak versions of Stevie Wonder and other English-speaking artists, could use some rethinking.

Even in midwinter, La Plata's Cervecería La Modelo is the place for a cold brew.

THE PAMPAS

© WAYNE BERNHARDSON

The line between places to eat and places to drink is not always obvious here, but the best blend of the two is the classic **⟨ Cervecería La Modelo** (Calle 5 and Calle 54, tel. 0221/421-1321, US$10), which prepares terrific sandwiches, plus draft beer and hard cider with free unshelled and unsalted peanuts. The pizza, though, is substandard and the service can be spotty.

Another option is the **Wilkenny Irish Pub & Restaurant** (Calle 50 No. 797, tel. 0221/483-1772, www.wilkenny.com.ar), whose menu includes pub grub like lamb stew in the US$5–7 range (though most plates are Argentine and there are even a couple of Chinese dishes). Irish beers (Guinness, Harp, and Kilkenny) are on tap by the pint and half-pint, along with a larger selection of bottle brews, plus Irish and specialty coffees.

Beer also shares the bill with the food at **La Bartola** (Avenida 44 No. 599), which has inexpensive lunch specials and fine pastas.

For ice cream, try **La Sorbetière** (Calle 47 and Calle 10) or nearby **Thionis** (Diagonal 74 No. 1578, tel. 0221/423-2030).

INFORMATION AND SERVICES

In the Pasaje Dardo Rocha, the **Información Turística La Plata** (Calles 6 and 50, tel. 0221/427-1535, www.laplata.gov.ar, 9 A.M.–5 P.M. daily) is the municipal tourist office. It distributes far better city maps, informational brochures, and bus schedules than in the past, and the staff is more accommodating. It works under the **Dirección de Turismo** (Diagonal 79 at Calle 8, tel. 0221/422-9764, 9 A.M.–5 P.M. weekdays) in the historic Palacio Campodónico.

In the high-rise Torre Municipal, the **Dirección Provincial de Turismo** (Calle 12 and Avenida 53, 13th floor, tel. 0221/429-5553, www.styd.gba.gov.ar, 9 A.M.–3 P.M. weekdays) can be bureaucratic but also surprisingly helpful for out-of-town sights.

ATMs are numerous, such as **Banco Nación** (Avenida 7 and Calle 49). **Correo Argentino** (Avenida 51 and Calle 4) is the post office and **Locutorio Fono Cinco** (Avenida 51 and Calle 5) provides long-distance phone and Internet services.

Asatej (Avenida 5 No. 990, at Avenida 53, tel. 0221/483-8673, laplata@asatej.com.ar) is a branch of Argentina's student- and youth-oriented travel agency.

GETTING THERE
Air

La Plata has no commercial airport, but **Manuel Tienda León** (tel. 0810/888-5366) provides door-to-door service to Buenos Aires's Ezeiza and Aeroparque.

Bus

The **Terminal de Omnibus** is at Calle 42 and Calle 4 (tel. 0221/421-2182); **Costera Metropolitana** (tel. 0800/222-6798) and **Empresa Plaza** (tel. 0800/333-1970) operate frequent buses to and from Retiro (1 hour–plus,

US$2.50), but also pick up and drop off passengers along the capital's Avenida 9 de Julio or Avenida Alem.

Train

Unless you're a committed train-spotter or desperately poor, bus service is far better than trains to and from the century-old **Estación Ferrocarril General Roca** (Avenida 1 and Avenida 44, tel. 0221/423-2575). **Transportes Metropolitana** (tel. 011/4304-0021, www. ugofe.com.ar) operates around 50 weekday trains from Constitución (Buenos Aires) to La Plata (1.5 hours); the number drops to around 35 or 40 trains on weekends and holidays. The last train returns to Constitución around 10:30 P.M., but it starts up again around 3 A.M.

The Pampa Gaucha

Beyond the outskirts of Buenos Aires, the relentlessly flat pampas are still, symbolically at least, *tierra de gauchos*. To the west, the city of Luján is a major religious destination, but it's also home to a museum complex that brings Argentine history alive. The best place to see the living vestiges of gaucho life is San Antonio de Areco, whose historic *estancias* have acquired an international reputation for get-away-from-it-all holidays.

In the province's southwestern corner, the low mountain ranges of Tandilia and Ventania are exceptions to an otherwise almost featureless relief. The city of Tandil and the village of Sierra de la Ventana are popular with Argentines, but they get relatively few foreign visitors despite their attractiveness—Tandil, in particular, is an oasis with a fascinating history. Several other important *estancias* lie in the vicinity of the triangle formed by Tandil, Sierra de la Ventana, and the city of Olavarría.

LUJÁN

History and legend blend in Luján, Argentina's most important devotional center. Modern Luján, though, is an incongruous potpourri

of piety and the profane, where pilgrims purchase shoddy souvenirs and, after making their obligatory visit to the landmark basilica, party until dawn.

Luján merits a visit for the truly devout and those with an intellectual interest in orthodox Catholicism, but what really shines is its complex of historical museums in handsome colonial buildings. As a sacred symbol, it gets at least 4 million visitors per year, mostly on weekends and for religious holidays like Easter and May 8 (the Virgin's day). Also important are events like October's Peregrinación de la Juventud (Youth Pilgrimage), a 62-kilometer walk from Once that acquired a semipolitical character during the Dirty War but has since returned to its devotional origins. For most foreigners it makes a better day trip, unless *estancia* accommodations are an option.

On the right bank of its eponymous river, Luján (pop. about 87,000) is about 65 kilometers west of Buenos Aires via RN 7. Most points of interest are on and around Avenida Nuestra Señora de Luján, the broad avenue that enters town from the north.

History

Legend says that in 1630 an oxcart bearing a terra-cotta image of the Virgin Mary stuck in the mud, unable to move until gauchos removed the statue. Its devout owner took this as a sign that the Virgin should remain at the spot, and he built her a chapel. Apparently, though, Argentina's patron saint was not totally immovable—she now occupies more opulent quarters in the French Gothic basilica, five kilometers from her initial abode.

Basílica Nacional Nuestra Señora de Luján

Glazed in silver to protect her from deterioration, clothed in white and blue robes, the ceramic Virgin is a diminutive 38-centimeter image that was baked in Brazil. In the 1880s, on a trip to Europe, the French Lazarist missionary Jorge Salvaire created her elaborate crown; apparently deciding that was not enough, he worked tirelessly to build the Gothic basilica whose pointed spires now soar 106 meters above the pampas. Not completed until 1937, its facade has undergone a recent restoration. Pope John Paul II said Mass here in 1982, only a few days before Argentina's Falklands War surrender.

Twice removed from the world outside, the Virgencita (little virgin) inhabits a separate *camarín* (chamber) behind the main altar; begging her help, pilgrims proceed at a snail's pace past plaques left by their grateful predecessors.

The Basílica Nacional Nuestra Señora de Luján (San Martín 50, tel. 02323/41-2070, www.basilicadelujan.org.ar, 7 A.M.–8 P.M. daily) overlooks the barren Plaza Belgrano. Immediately west of the basilica, the **Museo Devocional** (San Martín 51, tel. 02323/42-0058, 2–5:15 P.M. Sundays only) holds larger *ex-votos* (gifts left in thanks for her help).

C Complejo Museográfico Enrique Udaondo

On the west side of Avenida Nuestra Señora de Luján, immediately north of the basilica, the former *cabildo* (colonial town council, 1797) and the **Casa del Virrey** (House of the Viceroy, 1803) hold one of the country's finest museum assemblages. No viceroy every lived in Luján, by the way, but the Marqués de Sobremonte once spent a few hours here.

Porteño architect Martín S. Noel's 1918 restoration of the *cabildo* took some liberties with the original unadorned facade and a few other features. Still, the three hectares of buildings and well-kept grounds, bounded by Lezica y Torrezuri, Lavalle, San Martín, and Parque Ameghino, are distinguished for their contents as well.

Within the *cabildo* and the Casa del Virrey, the **Museo Histórico** has a thorough display on Argentine history, with a dazzling assortment of maps, portraits, and artifacts (such as caudillo Facundo Quiroga's bloodstained vicuña poncho) that bring history to life.

Immediately north, the **Museo de Transporte** houses a remarkable assortment of horse carriages in mint condition, including hearses, a carriage that belonged to General Mitre, and the stuffed carcasses of Gato and Mancha, the hardy criollo horses that 1930s adventurer A. F. Tschiffely rode from Buenos Aires to Washington, D.C. There is also a Dornier seaplane, cobuilt by Spaniards and Argentines, and the country's first-ever locomotive, from the Ferrocarril Oeste. The main showroom's upper level contains an elaborate exhibit on *mate* and its ritual, from colonial times to the present.

The Complejo Museográfico (tel. 02323/42-0245, noon–6 P.M. Wed.–Fri., 10:15 A.M.–6:30 P.M. weekends and holidays, US$0.35) has a box office (Avenida Nuestra Señora de Luján and Lavalle) with a salon for special exhibits; admission is valid for all museum facilities.

Events

For most visitors, entertainment consists of spontaneous barbecues in Parque Ameghino or, when campgrounds are really crowded, on the median strip of Avenida Nuestra Señora de Luján. In February, though, there's the annual **Encuentro de la Fe y la Historia** (Encounter

THE PAMPAS

of Faith and History), a four-day festival that blocks off Avenida Nuestra Señora de Luján for folkloric music by the likes of Antonio Tarragó Ros and Soledad Pastorutti (who goes by her first name only).

Accommodations and Food

Across from the bus terminal, **Hotel Royal** (9 de Julio 696, tel. 02323/42-1295, US$35 s or d) has smallish but otherwise adequate rooms with TV; it has a restaurant, but a modest breakfast costs US$2.25 more. On the basilica's east side, the well-managed **Hotel de la Paz** (9 de Julio 1054, tel. 02323/42-8742, www.hoteldelapaz. com.ar, US$50 d with private bath) is a dignified inn that has been around nearly a century. Weekday rates fall about 20 percent.

The 45-room **Hotel Hoxón** (9 de Julio 769, tel. 02323/42-9970, www.hotelhoxon.com.ar, US$36–46 s, US$58–73 d) is a major step up, and the only place in town with its own pool.

For breakfast and dessert, the best choice is **Berlín** (San Martín 135, tel. 02323/44-0780), half a block east of the basilica.

The exposed bricks in its 18th-century adobe exterior sag like a syncline and weeds may be sprouting on the roof, but that gives the **1800 Restaurant** (Rivadavia and Almirante Brown, tel. 02323/43-3080) part of its charm. That wouldn't mean much, though, if their moderately priced menu of meat, pasta, fish, and seafood were not so good, the service so agreeable, and the *pulpería* interior equally charming.

Befitting Luján's ecclesiastical importance, the traditional choice for a family lunch or dinner is the across-town Carmelite-run **L'eau Vive** (Constitución 2112, tel. 02323/42-1774, noon–2:15 P.M. Tues.–Sun. and 8:30–10 P.M. Tues.–Sat.). Served by nuns, fixed-price lunches or dinners lean toward French specialties.

Information and Services

At the west end of Lavalle, the municipal **Dirección de Turismo** (Parque Ameghino s/n, tel. 02323/42-7082, 8 A.M.–5 P.M. weekdays, noon–6 P.M. weekends) occupies offices in the Edificio La Cúpula.

Getting There

The **Estación Terminal de Ómnibus** (Avenida Nuestra Señora del Rosario between Almirante Brown and Dr. Reat, tel. 02323/42-0044) is three blocks north of the basilica. **Transportes Atlántida** (Línea 57, tel. 02323/42-0032) connects Luján with Palermo's Plaza Italia (1.5 hours, US$2.60).

TBA's **Línea Sarmiento** (Avenida España and Belgrano, tel. 02323/42-1312, www.tbanet. com.ar) goes to and from the capital's Estación Once (Subte: Plaza Miserere, Línea A), but it's necessary to change trains in Moreno. The fare is negligible, but it takes at least two hours.

◖ SAN ANTONIO DE ARECO

Bidding for UNESCO World Heritage Site status, the 18th-century town of San Antonio de Areco is Argentina's unofficial gaucho capital, host to its biggest gaucho festivities, and home to a critical mass of traditional craftspeople and artists unequalled in any other town its size. Ironically, many of those most closely associated with gaucho tradition have Italian-immigrant surnames.

San Antonio was the home of *gauchesco* novelist Ricardo Güiraldes, who wrote *Don Segundo Sombra* (1926) here. It was also the location for director Manuel Antín's 1969 movie version, which featured the author's now-deceased nephew Adolfo Güiraldes in the title role of a dignified rustic whose practical wisdom leaves a lasting imprint on a landowner's son.

While some small pampas towns struggled after the 2002 economic crisis, San Antonio continued to emit an air of tidy prosperity, with many of its Italianate houses and other buildings restored or recycled. The local real-estate market is booming with an influx of *porteño* refugees from big-city bustle.

The biggest annual event is November's **Día de la Tradición,** celebrating the gaucho heritage, but weekends are busy all year. The pace is relaxed, though, with greater deference to pedestrians and cyclists than anywhere else in the country. Many Arequeños, in fact, get around on bicycles, and hotels often provide their guests free *bicis.*

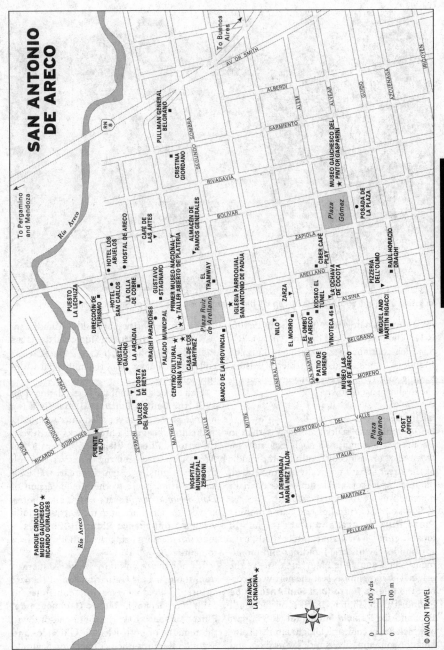

SAN ANTONIO DE ARECO

THE PAMPAS

To Pergamino and Mendoza

To Buenos Aires

Río Areco

RN 8

AV. DR. SMITH

ALBERDI

ALEM

ALVEAR

GUIDO

IBIGOYEN

AZCUENAGA

SARMIENTO

RIVADAVIA

BOLIVAR

ZAPIOLA

ARELLANO

ALSINA

BELGRANO

MORENO

ARISTOBULO DEL VALLE

ITALIA

MARTINEZ

PELLEGRINI

SEGUNDO SOMBRA

PULLMAN GENERAL BELGRANO

CRISTINA GIORDANO

MUSEO GAUCHESCO DEL PINTOR GASPARINI ★

Plaza Gómez

POSADA DE LA PLAZA

CAFÉ DE LAS ARTES

HOTEL LOS ABUELOS

HOSTAL DE ARECO

ALMACÉN DE RAMOS GENERALES

CIBER CAFÉ PLAY

RAÚL HORACIO DRAGHI

PUESTO LA LECHUZA

DIRECCIÓN DE TURISMO

HOTEL SAN CARLOS

LA OLLA DE COBRE

GUSTAVO STAGNARO

EL TRAMWAY

PRIMER MUSEO NACIONAL Y TALLER ABIERTO DE PLATERÍA ★

IGLESIA PARROQUIAL SAN ANTONIO DE PADUA ★

ZARZA

PIZZERIA DELL'OLMO

LA OCHAVA DE COCOTA

Río Areco

LÓPEZ

HOSTAL GAUCHO

LA ARCADIA

DRAGHI PARADORES

PALACIO MUNICIPAL ★

Plaza Ruiz de Arellano

EL MORRO

NILO

KIOSKO EL TUNEL

EL OMBÚ DE ARECO

VINOTECA 45

MIGUEL AND MARTIN RIGACCI

LA COSTA DE REYES

DULCES DEL PAGO

CENTRO CULTURAL USINA VIEJA ★

CASA DE LOS MARTÍNEZ ★

BANCO DE LA PROVINCIA

PATIO DE MORENO

SAN MARTIN

MUSEO LAS LILAS DE ARECO

GENERAL PAZ

ZERBONI

MATHEU

LAVALLE

MITRE

PUENTE VIEJO ★

RICARDO GÜIRALDES

SOSA

NOGUERA

PARQUE CRIOLLO Y MUSEO GAUCHESCO RICARDO GÜIRALDES ★

HOSPITAL MUNICIPAL ZERBONI

LA DEMORADA/ MARIA INEZ TALÓN

POST OFFICE

Plaza Belgrano

ESTANCIA LA CINACINA ★

0   100 yds
0   100 m

© AVALON TRAVEL

© WAYNE BERNHARDSON

In late 2009, the Río Areco overran its banks and flooded parts of San Antonio.

San Antonio de Areco (pop. about 25,000) is 113 kilometers west of Buenos Aires via RN 8, which continues west toward San Luis and Mendoza. The commercial street of Alsina, leading south from Plaza Ruiz de Arellano, is the liveliest part of town.

Sights

San Antonio is so pedestrian-friendly that, in a country where motorists rarely even slow for crosswalks, townsfolk often stroll in the middle of the street. That's not really recommended, but its compact core and leisurely pace do make it attractive to walkers and cyclists.

Unlike most central plazas, San Antonio's **Plaza Ruiz de Arellano** is not the hub of local life, but it's an appealingly shady park surrounded by historic buildings and monuments: the **Casa de los Martínez,** site of the original *estancia* house, is at the northwest corner; the **Iglesia Parroquial San Antonio de Padua** (Parish Church, 1869) is on the south side; and the **Palacio Municipal** (1885), part of which has become the Draghi family's combination museum, silversmith's workshop, and

art gallery, is on the north side. An adjacent part now holds the **Museo Municipal de Artes Plásticas** (Lavalle 373, 8 A.M.–7:45 P.M. weekends and holidays, free), the municipal sculpture museum.

Half a block north of the Plaza, dating from 1901, the **Centro Cultural Usina Vieja** is a former power plant recycled into a museum and cultural center. Three blocks northwest, the restored **Puente Viejo** (1857) over the Río Areco may have been the country's first toll bridge; originally designed for cart traffic, it lent its atmosphere to the movie version of *Don Segundo Sombra*. It's now a bike, horse, and pedestrian shortcut to the **Parque Criollo y Museo Gauchesco Ricardo Güiraldes,** a museum memorializing the author's *gauchesco* romanticism.

It's not the town's only *gauchesco* institution, though: Luis Gasparini, son of the late painter Osvaldo Gasparini, continues to paint and operate the **Museo Gauchesco del Pintor Gasparini.** At the south end of town, the remains of both Ricardo Güiraldes and Segundo Ramírez (the fictional Don Segundo

Sombra's role model) repose in the **Cementerio Municipal** (RN 8 and Soldado Argentino).

CENTRO CULTURAL USINA VIEJA

Handsomely recycled as a museum and events center, San Antonio's century-old power plant holds permanent collections of odds and ends, such as an experimental biplane built here, and sample works by local artisans. It has also managed impressive exhibits that re-create overlooked everyday institutions, like the simple barbershop and *botica* (apothecary), while the garden holds an array of antique farm machinery.

While it has plenty of good artifacts, the Centro Cultural Usina Vieja (Alsina 66, tel. 02326/45-2021, 11 A.M.–5 P.M. daily except nonholiday Mondays, US$0.50) presents little historical and cultural interpretation.

MUSEO GAUCHESCO DEL PINTOR GASPARINI

Since his father's death, Luis Gasparini continues to live in and operate this *gauchesco* art museum, which has half a dozen rooms devoted to gaucho-themed sculpture, silverwork, and painting (including works by Benito Quinquela Martín and Lino Spilimbergo, among others). There is also a chapel, an atelier with the family's own *gauchesco* works, and a library; appropriately enough, there's a hitching post outside for those who arrive on horseback.

The Museo Gauchesco (Alvear 521, tel. 02326/45-3930, gaspa@arecoonline.com.ar, 8 A.M.–7 P.M. daily year-round, free) is just off Plaza Gómez.

PARQUE CRIOLLO Y MUSEO GAUCHESCO RICARDO GÜIRALDES

Set on 97 hectares of parkland, San Antonio's gaucho museum is a romantic idealization of the already romantic *gauchesco* literature of Ricardo Güiraldes, whose family lived on the nearby Estancia La Porteña. Created by the provincial government in the 1930s, the museum lacks the *estancia*'s authenticity, but it does offer ironic insights into the way Argentines—even *porteños*—have internalized the gaucho heritage.

The irony, of course, was that the landowning Güiraldes, however sincere, presumed to speak for the illiterate gaucho—a defiantly independent figure who became a humble dependent laborer on the oligarchy's *estancias*. Nowhere is this clearer than in the principal **Casa del Museo,** a 20th-century replica of an 18th-century *casco* (big house): It devotes two rooms to Güiraldes himself; another to his wife Adelina del Carril; another to his painter cousin Alberto; a **Sala de los Escritores** to *gauchesco* literature, including Walter Owen's English-language translation of José Hernández's epic poem *Martín Fierro;* a **Sala Pieza de Estanciero** that includes the bed of the tyrant landowner Juan Manuel de Rosas (who exploited gauchos with a ruthless opportunism but counted them as enthusiastic allies); and, finally, a **Sala del Gaucho** that stresses horse gear and *gauchesco* art, but not the gaucho's marginal status.

The Casa del Museo gives only a partial account of the gaucho; the surrounding park contains the **Pulpería La Blanqueada,** a real 19th-century roadhouse with a life-size gaucho diorama. Nearby are three other aging structures, **La Ermita de San Antonio,** an adobe chapel with an image of its patron saint; the **La Tahona** flour mill (1848); and the **Galpón y Cuarto de Sogas,** a carriage house.

Reached by the Puente Viejo shortcut, the Museo Gauchesco (Camino Ricardo Güiraldes s/n, tel. 02326/45-5839, 11 A.M.–4:45 P.M. Wed.–Mon.) costs US$1 pp except for retired persons, who pay US$0.35, and children under age 12, who get in free. A late 2009 flood has damaged some of the exhibits.

PRIMER MUSEO NACIONAL Y TALLER ABIERTO DE PLATERÍA

Recycling a century-old residence that was in near ruin, silversmith Juan José Draghi has enriched the moribund Plaza Ruiz de Arellano with his new museum-shop and adjacent bed-and-breakfast. Besides the opportunity to see a master craftsman and his protégés at work, there are museum-quality displays of gaucho gear that reflect their regions of origin. *Facones* (gaucho knives) and spurs from the featureless pampas are unadorned, for instance, while their ornamented counterparts from Mesopotamian provinces, such as Entre Ríos and Corrientes, reflect the exuberant natural environment of riverside gallery forests.

Some items in the shop—such as ceremonial silver bridles that take a year to produce and cost up to US$20,000—are commissioned jobs awaiting shipment. Others, such as cutlery with intricately threaded leather handles and ritual silver *mates,* may be available for over-the-counter purchase.

The museum (Lavalle 387, tel. 02326/45-4219, www.draghiplaterosorfebres.com, US$2.50) is open 9 A.M.–1 P.M. and 3:30–8:30 P.M. daily Monday–Saturday, and 10 A.M.–1:30 P.M. and 4–8 P.M. Sunday. It offers guided visits on the half-hour from 10:30 A.M., in Spanish or very good English.

MUSEO LAS LILAS DE ARECO

New in 2009, this museum, which showcases the art of *gauchesco* caricaturist Florencio Molinas Campos, ran into trouble with Molina Campos's heirs and had to change its name, even though it continues its prominent displays of many of the artist's originals. Sited in a transformed former smithy and workshops, it also offers occasional lectures, concerts, and other cultural events.

The Museo Las Lilas (Moreno 279, tel. 02326/45-6425, www.museolaslilas.org, US$5.50) is open 10 A.M.–8 P.M. Friday–Sunday and holidays mid-September–May 25; the rest of the year it closes two hours earlier.

FIESTA DE LA TRADICIÓN

Since 1934, November's Fiesta de la Tradición has feted San Antonio's gaucho heritage with guided visits to historic sites, lectures by folklorists, crafts fairs, and folk music and dance—plus flamboyant horsemanship on Plaza Ruiz de Arellano. While the principal **Día de la Tradición** is November 10, the festivities normally stretch over two weekends, climaxing on the final Sunday. Reservations are critical for anyone wanting to stay here rather than

in the surrounding countryside or neighboring towns.

Shopping

San Antonio's silversmiths are the country's finest, so don't expect to find any giveaways—a silver *mate* can cost up to US$1,500, though there are, of course, cheaper versions. Other typical silver dress items include the long-bladed *facón* (gaucho knife), *rastra* (coin-studded belt), and *espuelas* (spurs).

Juan José Draghi's magnificent museum-shop is a major contributor to San Antonio's appeal. Other silversmiths include **Raúl Horacio Draghi** (Guido 391, tel. 02326/45-4207), who also works in leather; **Gustavo Stagnaro** (Arellano 59, tel. 02326/45-4801, www.stagnaro.com.ar), who specializes in religious imagery; and **Miguel and Martín Rigacci** (Belgrano 381, tel. 02326/45-6049). **Cristina Giordano** (Sarmiento 112, tel. 02326/45-2829, www.telarcriolloypampa.com.ar) is a weaver, as is **María Inés Talón** (General Paz 115, tel. 02326/45-6360), at the new La Demorada B&B.

El Moro (Alsina and San Martín, tel. 02326/45-5443) is a commercial dealer in leather, silver, ropes, and crafts and is good for an overview of what's available.

El Tramway (Segundo Sombra 411, tel. 02326/45-5561) is a spacious, entertainingly cluttered antiques dealer.

La Olla de Cobre (Matheu 433, tel. 02326/45-3105, www.laolladecobre.com.ar) produces artisanal chocolates and other sweets, while **Dulces del Pago** (Zerboni 136, tel. 02326/45-4751, www.delpagodeareco.com.ar) specializes in fruit preserves. **Vinoteca 45** (Alsina and Alem, tel. 02326/45-6296) has the best wine selection.

Accommodations

Until recently, San Antonio proper has had only limited (if decent) accommodations; in recent years some hotels have expanded and services have improved, as even some moderately priced accommodations have added swimming pools and air-conditioning.

Many silversmiths have hung out their shingle in San Antonio de Areco.

During November's Fiesta de la Tradición, when reservations are imperative, visitors lodge in communities for miles around. Prices may rise on weekends, when reservations are advisable, but informal bed-and-breakfast accommodations may also be available—ask at the tourist office.

With good-natured management, the **Hostel Gaucho** (Zerboni 308, tel. 02326/45-3625, www.hostelgaucho.com.ar, US$13 pp dorm, US$34–40 s or d) is the first of its kind in San Antonio, with both dorms and private rooms (all with private baths). The higher rates are for weekends.

Though not quite pristine, the **Hostal de Areco** (Zapiola 25, tel. 02326/45-6118, www.hostaldeareco.com.ar, US$42 d) has large to huge rooms, ample and inviting common spaces in classic San Antonio style, and a spacious, woodsy, and pool-less garden that ensures quiet during the siesta hours.

Expanding **Hotel San Carlos** (Zapiola and Zerboni, tel. 02326/45-3106, www.

hotel-sancarlos.com.ar, US$37 s, US$47 d, US$53–66 s or d weekends and summer with a two-night minimum) provides cable TV, a pair of smallish pools (one with a whirlpool tub), and other amenities, including free bicycles. It can get a little noisy, though, when kids play around the pool. A few cozy rooms have what might be called micro-closets, but the more expensive ones are more like small apartments.

Next door, the smallish rooms at modern **Hotel Los Abuelos** (Zapiola and Zerboni, tel. 02326/45-6390, www.sanantoniodeareco.com/losabuelos, US$24 s and US$38 d weekdays, US$42 s or d weekends and summer) are comfortable enough, but what might have been a secluded central garden has instead become a dreary driveway and parking lot. Rates include private baths, high ceilings with fans, telephones, cable TV, a swimming pool, and breakfast.

New in 2009, ◖ **La Demorada** (General Paz 115, tel. 02326/45-6360, lademorada@gmail.com, US$58–63 s or d) is a custom-built B&B, though most of the doors and windows are salvage classics and the exposed brick exterior conforms to San Antonio's classic style. Co-owner Inés Talón's weavings add a personalized touch to the decoration. With just two spacious rooms, reservations are essential.

Until recently, Areco proper lacked stylish accommodations, but ◖ **Draghi Paradores** (Lavalle 387, tel. 02326/45-4219, paradores@sanantoniodeareco.com, US$79 s or d) has filled that niche nicely. Entered from Matheu, immediately behind the Draghi museum on Plaza Ruiz de Arellano, this converted garage (combined with new construction) emulates traditional style on fountain-studded grounds that also have a pool. Furnished with antiques, the spacious rooms have high ceilings, kitchenettes, and distinctive design flourishes that suggest a skilled silversmith's attention to detail; some but not all have whirlpool tubs. Museum admission and tours are free for guests, as are bicycles.

Opposite Plaza Gómez, the ◖ **Posada de la Plaza** (Alvear 480, tel. 02326/45-2955, www.posadadelaplaza.com, US$79 s or d) is a

THE *ESTANCIAS* OF ARECO

Just off RP 41, northbound from San Antonio, several historic *estancias* grow soybeans and raise livestock, but tourism helps pay the bills. All take overnight guests and even offer "day in the country" excursions, including a lunchtime *asado* as well as rural activities like horseback riding.

ESTANCIA LA CINACINA

The most self-consciously tourist-oriented of all Areco's *estancias*, the 50-hectare La Cinacina's "Fiesta Gaucha" mimics a day in the country without actually leaving town – the former dairy farm is only six blocks west of Plaza Ruiz de Arellano. It can accommodate up to 400 visitors for visits (Tues. and Thurs.-Sun., US$31 pp) that include snacks, a city tour, lunch, and folkloric music and dance; from Buenos Aires, with transportation, it costs about US$48 pp.

Effectively isolated from the day-trippers, a nearby cluster of recycled buildings at La Cinacina (Lavalle 1, tel. 02326/45-2045, www.lacinacina.com.ar, US$160-200 s or d with breakfast) now operates as a hotel. There are 16 rooms and two suites of "rustic luxury" so that travelers can spend the night. Bicycles are free; horseback rides cost extra.

ESTANCIA LA PORTEÑA

San Antonio's most emblematic *estancia*, La Porteña has belonged to the Güiraldes family since the early 19th century. Of all the area's farms, it has the finest grounds; French landscape architect Carlos Thays, who created major public parks like Palermo's Jardín Botánico and Mendoza's Parque General San Martín, designed the plan, including the stately avenue of elm-like hackberries that leads to the main house.

La Porteña has only a few guest rooms, so reservations are essential. Beef is the standard menu, but the kitchen will happily accommodate vegetarians with pasta and other meatless dishes, served in a dining room filled with French and British antiques. La Porteña eschews television, but there's a large swimming pool and a library. English is spoken.

Recently reopened after a lengthy closure due to a family dispute, Estancia La Porteña (tel. 011/15-5626-7347, www.laportenadeareco.com) is about six kilometers northeast of San Antonio via RP 8 and RN 41. Accommodations cost US$155 pp with full board, pool access, and use of horses; day-in-the-country excursions cost US$85 pp, with horseback rides extra.

---

new four-room boutique-style B&B in a 19th-century residence that includes original furniture but also contemporary amenities such as air-conditioning. It also features an attractive central patio that leads to even more spacious grounds, where it plans an expansion.

New in late 2007, **Patio de Moreno** (Moreno 251, tel. 02326/45-5197, www.patiodemoreno.com, US$111–166 s or d) is a former warehouse recycled into an 11-room boutique "hotel with personality." That description might be self-serving, but the spacious bedrooms, some with whirlpool tubs, are accented with hand-woven blankets and cowhide rugs. A luminous high-ceilinged wine bar is open to the public, while the interior patio has an ample-sized swimming pool.

Food

Pizzería Dell'Olmo (Alsina 365, tel. 02326/45-2506) is a passable pizzeria. **La Costa de Reyes** (Belgrano and Zerboni, tel. 02326/45-2481) serves primarily *parrillada* but also pasta, with friendly service and moderate prices. The best fast-food choice, though, is the pizza and empanadas at **La Ochava de Cocota** (Alsina and Alem, tel. 02326/45-1176).

Zarza (San Martín 361, tel. 02326/45-3948) is a middling option, with decent pasta including seafood ravioli with shrimp and saffron sauce (US$8), pleasant decor with high ceilings, and exposed brick walls.

In a cozy bar environment with historic style, **La Vieja Sodería** (Bolívar 196, tel. 02326/45-6376) has fine cheap sandwiches and desserts.

ESTANCIA EL OMBÚ DE ARECO

Named for Argentina's wide-crowned national tree, set among four hectares of formal gardens on a 300-hectare property, El Ombú is the area's most lavish *estancia* in terms of furnishings, facilities, and activities. It once belonged to General Pablo Ricchieri, who first inflicted military conscription on Argentina's youth.

Rooms include six impeccable doubles and three triples; vegetarians should verify the menu, which leans heavily toward beef. Amenities and activities include a pool, satellite TV and video, telephone, horseback and bicycle riding, and games.

Estancia El Ombú de Areco (tel. 02326/49-2080 or 02325/15-68-2598, www.estanciaelombu.com, US$200 s, US$320 d, with full board) is about 11 kilometers northeast of San Antonio via RN 8, paved RP 41, and graveled RP 31. It also offers "day in the country" visits (US$70 pp) and arranges transportation from the capital and its airports for overnighters. It also has a Gran Buenos Aires contact (Avenida Argentina 2162, Boulogne, Buenos Aires Province, tel. 011/4737-0436).

ESTANCIA EL ROSARIO DE ARECO

Only six kilometers southwest of San Anto-nio, El Rosario raises polo ponies and offers a polo school with two full playing fields on about 80 hectares of land. Nonplayers and even nonriders, though, will appreciate the design ingenuity that has turned the former stables into 16 comfortable, spacious, and tasteful suites.

In addition to the accommodations, part of a complex that includes a main house dating from the 1890s, owner Francisco Guevara has built a conical open-sided *quincho* (a covered shelter) for *asados*. There are also living and dining areas just far enough from the sleeping quarters to ensure peace and quiet, as well as a pool for guests.

Rates at El Rosario de Areco (tel. 02326/45-1000, tel. 914/220-7883 in the U.S., www.rosariodeareco.com.ar) are US$195 pp with full board and activities included. "Day in the country" visits cost around US$75 pp depending on the number of guests, with a full bar option extra. Guevara tries not to mix overnight guests and day-trippers, nor unrelated groups, so reservations are essential – preferably as far in advance as possible. El Rosario also hosts business groups on retreat and has Wi-Fi access and a dedicated conference room.

Plaza Ruiz Arellano's **La Esquina de Merti** (Arellano 149, tel. 02326/45-6705, www.esquinademerti.com.ar) serves pretty good fixed-price lunches in a stylishly restored building, but the service continues to be erratic.

In new quarters near the river, **Puesto La Lechuza** (Arellano s/n, tel. 02326/45-2351) serves home-cooked Argentine food—your basic *bife de chorizo* and salad, but also appetizers of homemade salami, cheese, bread, and *empanadas,* in a *pulpería* atmosphere. There's usually live music on weekends; if not, ask owner Marcelo Zaldívar to play "Whiter Shade of Pale" on the antique Parisian organ.

In a charmingly recycled house whose original brickwork shows through the plaster, the ◖ **Almacén de Ramos Generales** (Zapiola 143, tel. 02326/45-6376, www.ramosgeneralesareco.com.ar, US$10–20) is primarily a *parrilla* but also has fine pastas and the occasional oddity, such as the Basque seafood casserole *txan gurro,* with king crab, tuna, red peppers, and tomatoes. Its cozy walls festooned with bottles, ladles, padlocks, paintings, posters, and photographs, it also makes particularly good desserts and sells homemade salami and cheeses.

Loaded with antiques and artworks, another good choice is **Café de las Artes** (Bolívar 70, tel. 02362/15-51-1684), which is very strong on pastas, including homemade gnocchi with a beet sauce.

◖ **La Arcadia** (Alsina 6, tel. 02326/45-4271, US$10–20) serves the usual *parrilla* but is more diverse and sophisticated than most Areco restaurants, though not everything works—the bondiola in a Malbec sauce does, for instance, but the accompanying fried sweet potatoes are too dry. It's reasonably quiet, but the service is a little slow or occasionally inattentive.

The stylishly urban decor and wok-fried menu at **Ara** (San Martín 326, tel. 02326/45-3872, www.aracocinadisco.com) stand out from San Antonio's tradition, but the execution (with items such as sweet-and-sour chicken breast) is above average. It also offers sushi and exotic meats such as caiman, wild boar, and venison. Prices start around US$21 for large portions intended to be shared, but they'll halve the price for single diners. Wine, however, gets a high markup.

Nilo (Alsina 234, tel. 02326/45-2341) is the best ice creamery.

Information

The municipal **Dirección de Turismo** (Zerboni and Ruiz de Arellano, tel. 02326/45-3165, www.pagosdeareco.com.ar, 8 A.M.–8 P.M. daily) distributes an excellent town map that includes a list of tourist-oriented services and local artisans.

Services

Correo Argentino (Alvear and Aristóbulo del Valle) is the post office. **Kiosko El Túnel** (Alsina 264) provides long-distance phone service, while **Ciber Café Play** (Arellano 285-A) has reliable Internet access. Money is available through several ATMs, including **Banco de la Provincia** (Mitre and Alsina).

For medical emergencies, there's the **Hospital Municipal Zerboni** (Moreno and Lavalle, tel. 02326/45-2759).

Getting There

Just off the highway, on the east side of town, San Antonio's **Parador Chevallier** (Avenida Dr. Smith and General Paz, tel. 02326/45-3904 or 011/4000-5255 in Retiro) has up to 14 buses daily to Retiro (1.5–2 hours, US$6). Just to the north, **Pullman General Belgrano**

(Avenida Dr. Smith and Segundo Sombra, tel. 02326/45-4059) has four buses daily except Sunday, when it has only three.

TANDIL

Surrounded by the rounded slopes of its namesake Sierras, Tandil offers literal relief from the flatness of southern Buenos Aires Province—even though its Precambrian granite summits top out at Cerro Albión, only 502 meters above sea level. Still, its irregular terrain, with the illusion of alpine fell fields, has helped make charmingly cobblestoned Tandil one of southern Buenos Aires Province's top recreational destinations.

Tandil is also an Easter pilgrimage site, when tens of thousands converge at cross-topped Monte Calvario, so named for its supposed resemblance to Golgotha. The city is also known for its gaucho souvenirs and for delectable homemade hams, salamis, and cheeses.

Tandil (pop. about 150,000) is 360 kilometers south of Buenos Aires via RN 3 and RN 226, and 160 kilometers northwest of Mar del Plata via RN 226. Plaza Independencia sits precisely in the center of the compact original grid.

History

Placid Tandil has had a colorful but violent past ever since its origins as Fuerte Independencia, a military outpost established in 1823, during Argentina's campaign against its native peoples. When dictator Juan Manuel de Rosas assumed power in 1829, the conflict intensified, and between 1820 and 1870, Pampas Indians may have rustled 11 million cattle, 2 million horses, and 2 million sheep; killed 50,000 people; and destroyed 3,000 houses.

The frontier had receded by 1872, but violence did not vanish. On New Year's Day of that year, the messianic healer Gerónimo de Solané, popularly known as Tata Dios (literally, "God the Father") or Médico Dios ("God the Healer") inspired a brief reign of throat-slitting xenophobia. Some 35 European settlers—British, French, Italian, and Spanish—died at the hands of Solané's gaucho

© WAYNE BERNHARDSON

Tandil's legendary "Movediza" boulder tumbled to the ground in 1912, but a few years ago local authorites erected a replica in its place.

followers; the sole Argentine death was apparently a case of mistaken identity.

In part, the gauchos' resentment of their own marginal status spurred the massacres, but landowners and corrupt local officials, in an area where Buenos Aires's authority was tenuous, also played a part. Solané, though he did not participate in the killings, died unaccountably of gunshot wounds while detained in the Tandil jail.

These massacres were not unique, but the seemingly unprovoked violence had broader repercussions. The perception grew, particularly among British observers in Buenos Aires and overseas, that the federal government could not guarantee settlers' lives and livelihoods. Immigration subsided and investment withdrew, at least temporarily; historians have argued that this set a pattern of mistrust that continues to the present.

Sights

Densely wooded and dotted with neoclassical statuary and fountains, **Plaza Independencia** occupies two full blocks; a central obelisk marks the **Piedra Fundamental,** Tandil's founding stone.

On the former site of Fuerte Independencia (which was demolished in 1864), on the plaza's south side, the stunningly Tuscan-styled **Palacio Municipal** (1920) stands alongside the former **Banco Hipotecario Nacional,** a Greco-Roman structure that also contains municipal offices. Around the corner is the **Museo de Bellas Artes** (Fine Arts Museum, Chacabuco 367, tel. 02293/43-2067, 9 A.M.–noon Mon.–Fri., 4–8 P.M. daily, free).

Across from the Municipalidad, the neo-Gothic **Templo de la Inmaculada Concepción** (1878) includes stones from Fuerte Independencia, but the triple towers are a late (1969) addition. Its **campanario** (bell tower, 1931) came from Bochum, Germany.

The **C Museo Histórico Fuerte Independencia** (4 de Abril 845, tel. 02293/43-5573, 4–8 P.M. Tues.–Sun., US$1.25) is a kitchen-sink museum that seems to try to display everything with anything to do with Tandil.

It's rather like visiting a thrift shop—hundreds of photographs, works by local artists, a replica *pulpería* (rural bar), dozens of horse carriages, and even a 1940s fighter plane, in 17 cavernous exhibit halls.

Tandil proper is mostly level, but the Sierras start barely six blocks southwest of the plaza in Parque Independencia, whose main entrance is at Avenida Avellaneda and Rondeau. To the northwest, at the end of Avenida Monseñor de Andrea, Easter rites take place at **Monte Calvario.**

In 1872, Tata Dios's followers gathered at **Cerro La Movediza,** about three kilometers northwest of the plaza, where a 300-ton boulder wobbled in the wind for centuries. According to legend, the so-called **Piedra Movediza** even resisted the efforts of General Rosas's draft animals to pull it down, but it finally tumbled on its own in 1912. In 2007, authorities placed a hollow 12-ton replica, created by engineers at the Universidad Nacional del Centro de la Provincia de Buenos Aires, in its stead, but many locals deride it is as the "Movediza Trucha" (Bogus Movediza). Bus No. 503 (blue) goes directly to the base of the small park where it's located.

Entertainment

The **Teatro Cervantes** (Rodríguez 551, tel. 02293/44-9607) is a major performing arts venue and a historical monument—tango legend Carlos Gardel performed here five times. For movies, try the **Cinecenter** (Panamá 351, tel. 02293/42-2332).

Tandil enjoys a lively bar scene at places like the **Bar Tolomé** (Rodríguez and Mitre, tel. 02293/42-2951), which also has live music; the punning name derives from the street named for president Bartolomé Mitre. **Cerveza Antares** (9 de Julio 760, tel. 02293/44-6636) is a brewpub with several other branches around the country.

Shopping

Along with San Antonio de Areco, Tandil is one of the best places to shop for gaucho souvenirs such as horse gear, leather, and silver. **El Desván** (14 de Julio 585, tel. 02293/42-5159) has a representative selection.

The other local specialties are dairy products and cured meats, such as ham and salami, at **Época de Quesos** (San Martín and 14 de Julio, tel. 02293/44-8750, www.epocadequesos.com, US$10–20), which is also a fine restaurant.

Sports and Recreation

Tandil is also a major site for mountain biking and for rock climbing thanks to its steep granite faces (though the summits themselves are walk-ups). **Kumbre** (Avenida Alvear 121, tel. 02293/43-4313) rents bikes and does tours.

For horseback riding, trekking, and other activities, try **Gabriel Barletta Cabalgatas** (Avellaneda 673, tel. 02293/42-7725 or 02293/15-50-9609, cabalgatasbarletta@yahoo.com.ar), who charges premium prices to foreigners but is the most reliable.

Accommodations

Reservations are advisable on weekends and especially during Semana Santa, when Tandil is mobbed and many Tandilenses rent out spare rooms.

The location may be less than central, but the immaculate bed-and-breakfast–style **Lo de Olga** (Chacabuco 977, tel. 02293/44-0258, www.lodeolgagandolfi.com.ar, US$40 s or d) occupies a vintage 1918 house. Rooms are on the small side, however, and there's a three-night minimum in the summer high season.

Past its prime, **Hotel Austral** (9 de Julio 725, tel. 02293/43-6942, www.hotelaustraltandil.com.ar, US$20 s, US$50 d) is still passable, but singles are few and small. Under the same management, in a rehabbed older building, friendly **Hotel Torino** (Sarmiento 502, tel. 02293/42-3454, www.hoteltorinotandil.com.ar, US$27s, US$48 d) is comparable but charges extra for breakfast.

B&B Belgrano (Belgrano 39, tel. 02293/42-6989, cell 02293/15-60-7076, hutton@speedy.com.ar, US$40–53 s, US$74 d) is an English-run bed-and-breakfast that, at the time of its construction, was the *casco* of an *estancia* on Tandil's outskirts. There are only two rooms with private baths—one sleeps up to five people without feeling crowded—but it is quiet, with spacious grounds, a pool, parking, and everything within easy walking distance. Rates include a self-serve breakfast with homemade yogurt.

Ask for a 7th-floor balcony room overlooking Plaza Independencia at **Hotel Dior** (Rodríguez 471, tel. 02293/43-1901, www.hoteldior.com, US$60 s, US$84 d, with buffet breakfast and Wi-Fi). The view from the well-kept rooms extends to the southern Sierras.

In a 1970s building, the **Plaza Hotel** (General Pinto 438, tel. 02293/42-7160, www.plazahoteldetandil.com.ar, US$50–84 s, US$74–84 d) has decent well-furnished rooms, mostly with showers rather than tubs. Rates include breakfast and parking, but vary to the higher end on weekends and in summer.

The high-rise (**Hotel Libertador** (Mitre 545, tel. 02293/42-2127, www.hotel-libertador.com.ar, US$74 s, US$87 d, with buffet breakfast) is one of few small-town hotels that truly deserves its four-star rating—by any standard, the rooms are comfortable and spacious, and service is exemplary.

On Tandil's southern outskirts, the Anglo-Mexican **Chacra Bliss** (Paraje La Porteña s/n, tel. 02293/15-62-0202, www.cybertandil.com.ar/chacrabliss, US$80–104 s or d) occupies a large lot on rolling terrain, with two large double rooms in a Mexican motif. Rates vary from weekdays to weekends; it also has a large pool.

Across the road from Chacra Bliss, (**Hostería Ave María** (Avenida Colón 1440, tel. 02293/42-2843, www.avemariatandil.com.ar, US$160–187 s, US$239–258 d) is a Normandy-style farmhouse surrounded by 40 hectares of conifers, magnolias, and oaks. Part of what was once a much larger *estancia,* it has eight guest rooms, all with fireplaces and private baths. Activities include horseback riding and carriage excursions, cycling, carriage rides, swimming, and massages; the area beyond the *estancia* offers many more activities. Rates include half board; meals include *asados* and homegrown vegetables.

Food

The **Grill Argentino** (Rodríguez 560, tel. 02293/44-8666)—known to locals simply as the "Grill"—is a *parrilla* and pizzeria that unfortunately suffers from a high decibel level. Still, its popularity is undeniable for decent quality at modest prices.

El Estribo (San Martín 750, tel. 02293/42-5943) is a *parrilla* that specializes in pork. For chicken, there's **El Nuevo Don José** (Monseñor de Andrea 269, tel. 02293/42-4970). Hotel Libertador's **Les Oranges** (Irigoyen 787, tel. 02293/42-2127) is a formal Mediterranean-style restaurant.

In addition to its cheese-and-salami retail outlet—a sight in itself— (**Época de Quesos** (San Martín and 14 de Julio, tel. 02293/44-8750, www.epocadequesos.com) is also a restaurant that specializes in *tablas* (platters) of those same cold cuts, generally for two or more people (single diners can take the surplus home). With delightful traditional decor and a huge shady patio, it's open 9 A.M.–midnight daily.

(**Azafrán** (Fuerte Independencia and Constitución, tel. 02293/43-6800, lunch and dinner daily, closed Tues.) has a young talented chef using locally acquired ingredients in a creative new *arrocería* that specializes in risottos and paella, but try also the chicken in mushroom sauce (US$7). With spare but pleasant decor, this small restaurant—reservations are advisable—is a little noisy because of bad acoustics. The price and quality are high, with a limited selection of wine by the glass.

Tandil's gourmet pioneer, however, is **Trauun** (Fuerte Independencia 26, tel. 02293/43-4212, dinner Wed.–Sat. only), which serves nouvelle cuisine dishes such as suckling pig with a spicy puree (US$13), plus creative appetizers, but it's nearly twice as expensive as Azafrán.

For breakfast, try **Café y Confitería Renzo** (Rodríguez 792, tel. 02293/44-3078), which also serves ice cream and desserts. However, the newly opened **Figlio** (Avenida Colón 1140, tel. 02293/43-0101) has been gaining adherents for its ice cream. **La Sorbetiere** (Belgrano and General Rodríguez, tel. 02293/42-9298), at the

THE PAMPAS

corner of Plaza Independencia, serves equally fine ice cream.

Information

Providing a good city map and brochures, the main office of the **Dirección Municipal de Turismo** (Espora 1120, tel. 02293/43-2225, www.tandil.gov.ar, 8 A.M.–7 P.M. Mon.–Fri., 10 A.M.–6 P.M. Sat., 9 A.M.–1 P.M. Sun.) is about 20 blocks north of Plaza Independencia. The office at the bus terminal (Avenida Buzón 650, tel. 02293/43-2092, 8 A.M.–2 P.M. and 3–8 P.M. Mon.–Sat.) is also helpful. A new downtown office on General Rodríguez is due to replace the tiny kiosk on Plaza, which is open 8 A.M.–8 P.M. weekdays.

For motorists, **ACA** is at General Rodríguez 399 (tel. 02293/42-5463).

Services

Jonestur (San Martín 698, tel. 02293/43-4838) is the only exchange house. There are numerous ATMs, including **Standard Bank** (formerly BankBoston; Pinto 745).

Correo Argentino is at Pinto 623; the postal code is 7000. Plaza Independencia's **Tecoop** (Pinto 462) is one of many long-distance phone and Internet centers.

Hospital Municipal Ramón Santamarina is at General Paz 1430 (tel. 02293/42-2010). The private **CAMI** (Pinto 846, tel. 02293/42-5107) has 24-hour emergency services.

Barbini Turismo (Rodríguez 40, tel. 02293/42-8912) is a reliable agency for tours and activities.

Getting There and Around

The Terminal de Buses (Avenida Buzón 650, tel. 02293/43-2092) has frequent services to Buenos Aires (5 hours, US$23–25) and several more to Mar del Plata (2.5 hours, US$8.50). There are better connections elsewhere in the country from the city of Azul, 90 kilometers northwest.

SIERRA DE LA VENTANA

Rising sharply more than 1,200 meters above sea level, the Sierra de la Ventana's abrupt topography is a startling contrast to most of the pampas region—even more so than the lower, rounded Sierra de Tandil. Its rugged terrain has made the range, also known as Ventania, a draw for outdoor recreation, centered on its namesake village—a sort of hill station for weekenders from Bahía Blanca and interior provincial towns like Olavarría.

Even in peak season, Sierra de la Ventana (pop. about 4,500) seems a sleepy village, especially during the midday siesta, but the surrounding sierras offer camping, hiking, climbing, cycling, horseback riding, and fishing. Cycling is particularly important, as automobile traffic seems to move slower than elsewhere in the country, but there are also conventional tourist attractions like swimming pools and golf courses.

The village of Sierra de la Ventana is 550 kilometers southwest of Buenos Aires via RN 3 to Azul, RN 226 to Olavarría, and RP 76. It is 125 kilometers north of Bahía Blanca via RN 33 to Tornquist, and then RP 76.

Most services are on or near Avenida San Martín in the southerly Villa Tivoli sector; Villa Arcadia, north of the Río Sauce Grande, is mostly residential.

Accommodations

Some accommodations are past their prime, but others are improving, and new ones are appearing; in summer, though, single travelers usually have to pay double for a room, and reservations are advisable, especially on weekends. Villa Arcadia's dusty streets are quieter than Villa Tivoli, which gets more through traffic.

Villa Arcadia's **Residencial Carlitos** (Coronel Suárez and Punta Alta, tel. 0291/491-5285, US$48 pp) has added a large swimming pool to what were already pretty good accommodations.

Arcadia's best value, though, is the **La Flor Azul** (Coronel Suárez 287, tel. 0291/491-5507, US$42 d), a friendly bed-and-breakfast in flawless new facilities. Almost equally good, though more like a conventional hotel, the eight-room **Hostería Amosba** (Punta Alta 276, tel. 0291/491-5071, US$32 s, US$40 d)

THE *ESTANCIAS* OF OLAVARRÍA

Best known as Buenos Aires Province's Capital del Cemento (Cement Capital), about 400 kilometers southwest of the federal capital, the city of Olavarría is no great destination in its own right – even the former Festival del Cemento with its Reina del Cemento (Cement Queen) has fallen by the wayside. It's close, however, to the tourist *estancias* La Isolina and Sumain.

ESTANCIA LA ISOLINA

In the course of shooting *Imagining Argentina* with Antonio Banderas, British actress Emma Thompson relaxed at Estancia La Isolina, just outside the Olavarría suburb of Hinojo. On the banks of the slow-flowing Arroyo Tapalqué, La Isolina's English-style *casco* (1920) sits among five hectares of manicured grounds on a 1,130-hectare property and offers horseback and carriage rides, fishing, canoeing, tennis, and swimming in a giant pool. Owners Jorge and María Louge are the successors of French founder Esteban J. Louge, whose family arrived in 1854.

La Isolina can accommodate up to a dozen guests in nine rooms furnished, but not cluttered, with antiques. English and French are spoken.

Rates are US$150 s and US$200 d with full board, with a discount for children; dinners are more formal than breakfast or lunch. Their *día*

de campo (day in the country) program, which lasts 11 A.M.–5 P.M., costs US$90 pp and includes a lunchtime *asado* and late-afternoon tea.

Estancia La Isolina (tel. 02284/15-47-7043, www.laisolina.com.ar) will also pick up passengers at the Olavarría bus terminal (there are no commercial flights, but comfortable buses take five hours from Retiro).

ESTANCIA SUMAIN

Closer to the city of Bolívar than to Olavarría, Estancia Sumain has a modern *casco* dating from the 1970s, sheltered by conifers on 17 grassy hectares. Like La Isolina, it offers horseback and carriage rides, walks on the farm, and fishing in a nearby arroyo, as well as bicycle rides. Also like La Isolina, it's a working farm, where the French-Basque Inçaurgarat family employs several gauchos and participates actively in farm activities.

There are seven double rooms with private baths, a huge dining room, and an attractive sunken bar. Estancia Sumain (Rivadavia 1378, Olavarría, tel. 02314/49-3013, www.estancia-sumain.com.ar) also has a Buenos Aires contact (Libertad 844, 11-B, tel. 011/4816-8634). Rates are around US$66 pp per night, including four meals and all activities, but not drinks or IVA. Sumain will pick up or drop off passengers at the Bolívar bus terminal for a small additional charge.

is one of few places that doesn't charge solo travelers for a double, even in high season. On wooded grounds, all the rooms have TV and ceiling fans but no other luxuries.

Recently leased to private interests, Tivoli's aging **Hotel Provincial Sierra de la Ventana** (Drago s/n, tel. 0291/491-5024, hotelprovincialmun@hotmail.com, US$25 s, US$34 d) is supposed to undergo five-star renovation, and in truth it badly needs the investment. That said, it has some outstanding features—the town's biggest swimming pool (pushing Olympic-size), extensive grounds, and decent rooms with, on the upper floor at least, balcony views of the Sierras.

Just across the railroad tracks from Villa Tivoli, **Hotel Silver Golf** (Barrio Parque Golf, tel. 0291/491-5079, www.hotelsilvergolf.com, US$24 pp) is less exclusive than its links-side location implies, with large and comfortable but somewhat dark rooms. There is also a large pool, but it is not as large as others around town.

Arcadia's **Hotel Pillahuincó** (Avenida Rayces 161, tel. 0291/491-5423, www.hotelpillahuinco.com.ar, US$47–58 pp) has expansive wooded grounds, a large pool, and considerable character. It has had its share of deferred maintenance but has recently spruced up, and rates with half board make it a good value. The rooms, in four different buildings, vary in size and amenities; some are spacious with enormous baths, others less so, but the main reason for price differences is the presence (or absence) of air-conditioning.

Food
Sol y Luna (Avenida San Martín and Tornquist, tel. 0291/491-5316) is a combination restaurant, pizzeria, and teahouse whose specialty is trout, which comes in a delicately spiced sauce of rosemary and shredded almonds. For single diners, they will also make half-pizzas, but the pasta sauces are mediocre.

Eneas (Avenida San Martín 412, tel. 0291/491-5144) has outstanding pizza, pasta, and calzone, with efficient and friendly service in appealing surroundings. Other good pizzerias include **El Establo** (San Martín between Islas Malvinas and Avenida Roca) and **Sher** (Güemes and San Martín, tel. 0291/491-5055), which also has fine pasta. **Rali-Hue** (Avenida San Martín 307) is a conventional *parrilla.*

Arcadia's **La Angelita** (Avenida Pillahuincó 383) is a Welsh-style teahouse in a handsome old building that looks as if it were meant to be a teahouse. There's a wide choice of teas and even specialty beers, but some pastries may be a little too sugary for some palates.

Information and Services
In nearby Hotel Silver Golf, just over the railroad tracks in Villa Arcadia, the **Oficina Municipal de Turismo Municipal** (Avenida del Golf s/n, tel. 0291/491-5303, www.sierradelaventana.org.ar) distributes maps and brochures, and they will phone around to help locate accommodations. Hours are 8 A.M.–8 P.M. daily, but in summer it may stay open until 10 P.M.

Banco de la Provincia (San Martín 260) has the only ATM.

Correo Argentino is at Avenida Roca 195; the postal code is 8168.

Telefónica (Avenida San Martín 193) has phone and fax. **Intersierras** (Avenida San Martín 403) provides Internet access.

Lavadero El Molino (Avenida Roca 100) does laundry.

Getting There and Around
La Estrella (Avenida San Martín and Namuncurá, tel. 0291/491-5091) has bus service to Retiro (Buenos Aires) daily except Saturday (8 hours, US$33). Both La Estrella and **Expreso Cabildo** (Avenida San Martín between Avenida Roca and Malvinas, tel. 0291/15-649-8867) serve Bahía Blanca (2 hours, US$6.50).

Ferrobaires trains from Buenos Aires to Bahía Blanca pass through Sierra de la Ventana, stopping at the Ferrocarril UPCP station (Avenida Roca and Avenida San Martín, tel. 0291/491-5164). Southbound trains leave Constitución at 7:35 P.M. Tuesday and Thursday, arriving here at 5:30 A.M.; northbound trains leave Sierra de la Ventana at 9 P.M. Wednesday and Friday, arriving at Constitución at 7:50 A.M.

Transporte Silver (Avenida San Martín 156, tel. 0291/491-5533) links Sierra de la Ventana with surrounding communities including Saldungaray, Villa Ventana, Cerro de la Ventana, and Tornquist. Schedules change seasonally, but there are usually four buses daily in each direction between 7 A.M. and 6 P.M.

Ciclismo El Tornillo (Avenida Roca 142) rents mountain bikes.

VICINITY OF SIERRA DE LA VENTANA
Most sights and activities are not in the village of Sierra de la Ventana but in the surrounding mountains. **Geotur** (Avenida San Martín and Iguazú, tel. 0291/491-5355, sergiorodriguezturismo@infovia.com.ar) arranges excursions.

Estancia Cerro de la Cruz
One of the province's elite *estancias,* four kilometers north of Sierra de la Ventana, Cerro de la Cruz features a Normandy-style *casco* by famed architect Alejandro Bustillo on sprawling formal gardens surrounded by 6,000 hectares of farmland and ranchland. Conspicuous

© WAYNE BERNHARDSON

Bodega Saldungaray is the first commercial winery in the Sierra de la Ventana area.

hunting and fishing trophies, displayed between magnificent ceiling beams and burnished *caldén* floors, make the living and dining areas reminders of the lifestyle that oligarchic families like the Bunges, who still own the property, enjoyed before even they felt the brunt of hard times.

Oriented toward the international market, Estancia Cerro de la Cruz (RP 72 Km 9, tel. 0291/15-746-5601, www.estanciacerrodelacruz. com) has seven well-furnished rooms with fireplaces for US$71 pp with half board, US$82 pp with full board; reservations are essential. This includes activities such as horseback riding, and there is a large swimming pool as well as easy river access for fishing. The proprietors speak excellent English.

Bodega Saldungaray

Nine kilometers south of Sierra de la Ventana, just before the railroad tracks in the village of Saldungaray, a dirt road leads southwest for two kilometers to Bodega Salgundary, the area's first commercial winery. With only nine hectares of recent plantings, it produces a surprising diversity of varietals, including cabernet franc, cabernet sauvignon, malbec, pinot noir,

chardonnay, and sauvignon blanc, and a blend of tempranillo, merlot, and pinot noir.

Because the vines are so young, this is a winery that hasn't yet found its direction, but it's an interesting experiment in an area where late spring frosts can be problematic for the grapes. The cabernet franc is probably the most fully realized of the varietals.

Bodega Saldungaray (Camino a Santo Tomás de la Sierra s/n, tel. 0291/15-412-5261, www. bodegasalgundaray) is open for free guided tours on the hour 11 A.M.–6 P.M. Friday–Sunday, but in January and February these tours are given daily except Tuesday. It also has sommelier-hosted evening tastings, with food to match, for US$8, the second weekend of every month. Its wines are for sale at its restaurant, **El Silo** (11 A.M.–midnight Fri.–Sun. year-round, 11 A.M.–midnight Wed.–Mon. Jan.–Feb.), which offers tastings on request.

Villa Ventana

With its oval design, sandy streets, and incongruous chalets 17 kilometers northwest of Sierra de la Ventana via RP 76, Villa Ventana exudes a borderline kitschy charm that is lacking in its more established but now somewhat ragged neighbor. Its **Oficina de Turismo** (tel. 0291/491-0095), at the entrance to town from the highway, is more than helpful.

The best accommodations are at the rustically luxurious **Posada Agua Pampas** (Las Piedras s/n, tel. 0291/491-0210, www.agua-pampas.com.ar, US$64–82 s or d).

Parque Provincial Ernesto Tornquist

Perhaps Argentina's most frequently climbed summit, 1,136-meter **Cerro de la Ventana** is the literal high point of this 6,700-hectare provincial park, with vast panoramas of the nearby Sierras and outlying pampas. It's not Buenos Aires Province's highest point, though—that honor goes to Cerro Tres Picos.

Cerro de la Ventana is a simple if occasionally steep hike that takes about two hours for anyone in average condition, but rangers (who appear to think every potential trekker is a three-packs-a-day *porteño*) restrict access after around 11 A.M.–noon, even though summer sunlight lasts until almost 9 P.M. Truly resolute hikers may persuade them to grant permission, which costs US$2.50 pp, for an afternoon ascent, but only by signing a waiver. Rangers are on-site 8 A.M.–5:30 P.M. daily.

From the park's main entrance, about midway between Villa Ventana and the Campamento Base trailhead for Cerro de la Ventana, the impressive wrought-iron gates date from the days of the Tornquists, a German-immigrant

banking family that donated the parkland to the province. Here there's a well-organized **Centro de Visitantes** (tel. 0291/491-0039), open 8 A.M.–5:30 P.M. Monday–Thursday, 7 A.M.–5:30 P.M. Friday–Sunday; winter hours are 9 A.M.–5 P.M. daily. Rangers here sometimes lead guided walks to parts of the park not normally open to the public.

At the Cerro de la Ventana trailhead, **Campamento Base** (tel. 0291/15-649-5304, US$4 pp plus US$1.50 per tent the first day) offers wooded campsites with clean baths and hot showers. Toward the west is **Hotel El Mirador** (RP 76 Km 226, tel. 0291/494-1338, www.complejoelmirador.com.ar, US$54 s, US$71 d).

Transporte Silver buses from Sierra de la Ventana to the trailhead cost US$3.50.

Cerro Tres Picos

Some 11 kilometers west of Sierra de la Ventana, but reached from the Tornquist side of the summit, 1,239-meter Cerro Tres Picos is Buenos Aires Province's highest point and thus a favorite climb for visitors. Unlike the more frequently climbed Cerro de la Ventana, the summit is on private property and requires permission from Mónica Silva at Estancia Funke (tel. 0291/494-0058, www.funketurismo.com), which charges US$4 for day trips, US$8 with overnight camping; since the approach is lengthy, this is often done as an overnight backpack.

The Atlantic Shore

The Atlantic shore is Argentina's summer playground, whose broad sandy beaches bring families from the federal capital and around the country for traditional summer vacations. That said, destinations along the coast vary dramatically in their offerings. Mar del Plata is a large diverse city with an active cultural life; upper-middle-class to upper-class resorts like Villa Gesell and Pinamar have frenetic nightlife and are widely perceived as elitist. Those south of

Mar del Plata, from Chapadmalal to Necochea and beyond, draw working-class vacationers. The port city of Bahía Blanca is a gateway to Patagonia and home to one of the country's most interesting museums.

MAR DEL PLATA

In January and February, sun-seekers search for a spot on the sand beyond the colorful canvas tents of the countless *balnearios* that line

© WAYNE BERNHARDSON

THE PAMPAS

In January, beachgoers are almost elbow-to-elbow on Mar del Plata's Playa Popular.

the beaches of Mar del Plata, Argentina's premier seaside resort. On Buenos Aires Province's southern coast, less exclusive than it was when the Argentine counterpart to Britain's Bloomsbury group dominated the social scene, "Mardel" has become *the* affordable destination for working- and middle-class holidaymakers. After Buenos Aires it's the country's major destination for congresses and conventions as well as being a major arts and entertainment center.

Mar del Plata's popularity can make it suffocatingly crowded in summer. Foreign visitors may enjoy the spring and autumn shoulder seasons, when the weather is often better, prices fall, and lines are shorter for the major attractions.

History

In 1581, Juan de Garay, the founder of Buenos Aires, was probably the first European to see the *costa galana* (elegant coast, a term still used today), but it took nearly two centuries for Jesuit missionaries to establish an inland presence at Laguna de los Padres. It took another century-plus for Portuguese investors to build a *saladero* (meat- and hide-salting plant) and the

port that became Mar del Plata, after they sold out to Patricio Peralta Ramos, in 1874.

Peralta Ramos promoted Mar del Plata as an industrial center and later a beach resort where the *porteño* elite built summer chalets in Barrio los Troncos. Victoria Ocampo, daughter of an elite family and founder of the literary magazine *Sur,* put Mardel on the cultural map in the 1920s and 1930s by bringing famous writers from around Latin America and the world to her own summer house, now a cultural center and museum.

Many Ocampo-era families have since departed for other provincial beach resorts like Villa Gesell and Pinamar, and even the Uruguayan resort of Punta del Este. Mar del Plata's declining exclusivity is reflected in the number of hotels that belong to labor unions, dating from the Perón period. Since then, working- and middle-class families have deluged the city in summer, despite the survival of some elite barrios. In other barrios, though, generic high-rises have blocked the sun and blighted the neighborhoods.

Orientation

Mar del Plata (pop. about 625,000) stretches along eight kilometers of sandy Atlantic

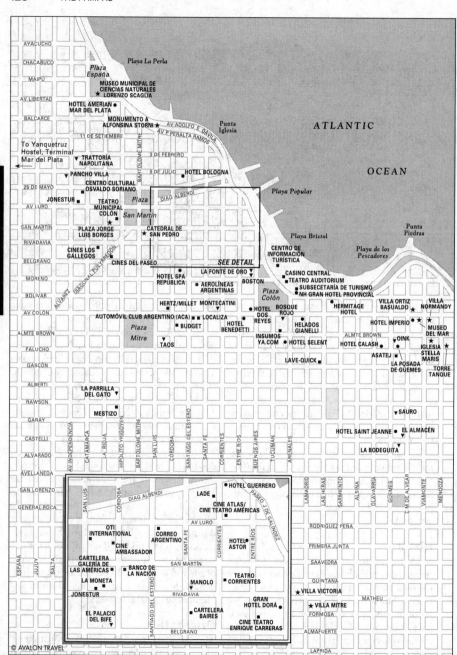

AYACUCHO

CHACABUCO

MAIPÚ

AV LIBERTAD

BALCARCE

25 DE MAYO

AV LURO

SAN MARTÍN

RIVADAVIA

BELGRANO

MORENO

BOLÍVAR

AV COLÓN

ALMTE BROWN

FALUCHO

GASCÓN

ALBERTI

RAWSON

GARAY

CASTELLI

ALVARADO

AVELLANEDA

SAN LORENZO

GENERAL ROCA

Playa La Perla

Plaza España

MUSEO MUNICIPAL DE CIENCIAS NATURALES ★ LORENZO SCAGLIA

HOTEL AMERIAN MAR DEL PLATA ●

MONUMENTO A ALFONSINA STORNI ★

AV ADOLFO E. DÁVILA

AV P. PERALTA RAMOS

Punta Iglesia

ATLANTIC

11 DE SETIEMBRE

To Yanquetruz Hostel, Terminal Mar del Plata

3 DE FEBRERO

▼ TRATTORÍA NAPOLITANA

9 DE JULIO   HOTEL BOLOGNA ■

OCEAN

▼ PANCHO VILLA

CENTRO CULTURAL ■ OSVALDO SORIANO

DIAG ALBERDI   *Playa Popular*

JONESTUR ■   TEATRO MUNICIPAL COLÓN   *Plaza*

San Martín

CATEDRAL DE ★ SAN PEDRO

Playa Bristol

Punta Piedras

PLAZA JORGE LUIS BORGES ■

CINES LOS GALLEGOS ■

CINES DEL PASEO ■

SEE DETAIL

CENTRO DE INFORMACIÓN TURÍSTICA

Playa de los Pescadores

LA FONTE DE ORO ▼

HOTEL SPA ● REPÚBLICA   ■ AEROLÍNEAS ARGENTINAS

BOSTON ■

CASINO CENTRAL ■ TEATRO AUDITORIUM SUBSECRETARÍA DE TURISMO ● NH GRAN HOTEL PROVINCIAL

Plaza Colón

HERTZ/MILLET MONTECATINI ▼

AUTOMÓVIL CLUB ARGENTINO (ACA) ■ ■ LOCALIZA

HOTEL DOS REYES ●

BOSQUE ROJO

HERMITAGE HOTEL ■

VILLA ORTIZ BASUALDO ★

VILLA NORMANDY

HELADOS ● GIANELLI

Plaza Mitre

■ BUDGET

HOTEL BENEDETTI ●

HOTEL IMPERIO ● ● ★ ★ ★

MUSEO DEL MAR

INSUMOS YA.COM ● HOTEL SELENT ■

ALMTE BROWN

HOTEL CALASH ■

● OINK ▼

IGLESIA ★ STELLA MARIS

▼ TAOS

LAVE-QUICK ■

ASATEJ ■

LA POSADA DE GÜEMES

TORRE TANQUE

LA PARRILLA DEL GATO ▼

▼ SAURO

MESTIZO ■

HOTEL SAINT JEANNE ● EL ALMACÉN ▼

LA BODEGUITA ■

AV INDEPENDENCIA
CATAMARCA
LA RIOJA
HIPÓLITO YRIGOYEN
BARTOLOMÉ MITRE
SAN LUIS
CÓRDOBA
SANTIAGO DEL ESTERO
SANTA FE
CORRIENTES
ENTRE RÍOS
BUENOS AIRES
TUCUMÁN
ARENALES

LAMADRID
LAS HERAS
SARMIENTO
ALSINA
OLAVARRÍA
GÜEMES
C.M DE ALVEAR
VIAMONTE
MENDOZA

Detail:

● HOTEL GUERRERO

SAN LUIS
CÓRDOBA
DIAG ALBERDI

LADE ■

CINE ATLAS/ CINE TEATRO AMÉRICAS ■

PASEO J. DE GAINZA

AV LURO

RODRÍGUEZ PEÑA

OTI INTERNATIONAL ■

CORREO ■ ARGENTINO

SANTA FE

CORRIENTES

HOTEL ■ ASTOR

CINE AMBASSADOR ■

PRIMERA JUNTA

SAN MARTÍN

SAAVEDRA

CARTELERA GALERÍA DE LAS AMÉRICAS ■

● BANCO DE LA NACIÓN

TEATRO CORRIENTES ■

QUINTANA

LA MONETA ■

MANOLO ●

★ VILLA VICTORIA

JONESTUR ■

RIVADAVIA

GRAN HOTEL DORÁ ●

★ VILLA MITRE

MATHEU

EL PALACIO DEL BIFE ■

ESPAÑA
JUJUY
SALTA

SANTIAGO DEL ESTERO

CARTELERA BAIRES ●

CINE TEATRO ENRIQUE CARRERAS ●

FORMOSA

ALMAFUERTE

BELGRANO

LAPRIDA

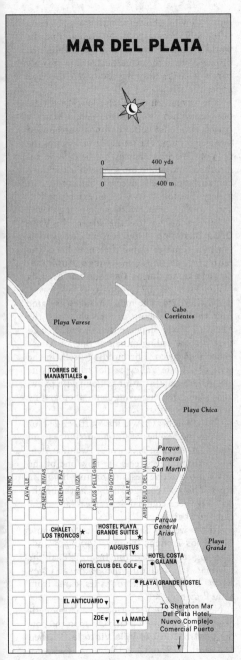

MAR DEL PLATA

0   400 yds

0   400 m

Playa Varese

Cabo Corrientes

TORRES DE MANANTIALES

Playa Chica

Parque General San Martín

PAUNERO
LAVALLE
GENERAL RIVAS
GENERAL PAZ
URDUIZA
CARLOS PELLEGRINI
B DE IRIGOYEN
N ALEM
ARISTÓBULO DEL VALLE

Parque General Arias

CHALET LOS TRONCOS ★
HOSTEL PLAYA GRANDE SUITES ★

Playa Grande

AUGUSTUS ▼

HOTEL COSTA GALANA

HOTEL CLUB DEL GOLF ●

● PLAYA GRANDE HOSTEL

EL ANTICUARIO ▼

ZOE ▼   ▼ LA MARCA

To Sheraton Mar Del Plata Hotel, Nuevo Complejo Comercial Puerto

THE PAMPAS

beaches, 404 kilometers south of Buenos Aires via RP 2, a four-lane toll road. Most sights lie within the area bounded by the curving coastline, Avenida Independencia (which runs northeast–southwest), and Avenida Juan B. Justo (which leads northwest from the port). The coastal road, popularly known as Bulevar Marítimo, is called Avenida Peralta Ramos in the downtown area but changes names to the north (Avenida Félix U. Camet) and south (Avenida de los Trabajadores, formerly Martínez de Hoz).

Sights

From mid-December through February, Mardel's municipal tourist authority, Emtur, offers free Spanish-only tours known as **Paseos para Gente Inquieta** (Excursions for Restless People), which require advance registration at their office (Bulevar Marítimo 2270, Local 51). Among sights visited are Villa Victoria (home of Victoria Ocampo and now a major cultural center), the impressive Museo del Mar (Museum of the Sea), and Villa Mitre (now the municipal history museum).

The densely built downtown has only a handful of sights, such as the century-old neo-Gothic **Catedral de San Pedro,** on **Plaza San Martín**'s south side. A block northwest, the much smaller **Plaza Jorge Luis Borges** (San Martín and La Rioja) features Miguel Repiso's tiled mural of Argentina's great literary figure.

Several blocks east, the **Playa Popular** (People's Beach) holds the most closely packed concentration of summer rental tents. To the north, just beyond Punta Iglesia, the **Monumento a Alfonsina Storni** marks the point where, in 1938, the Argentine poet drowned herself by walking into the South Atlantic.

A few blocks farther north, Plaza España is home to the **Museo Municipal de Ciencias Naturales Lorenzo Scaglia** (Libertad 3099, tel. 0223/473-8791, 9 A.M.–4:30 P.M. Mon. and Wed.–Fri., 3–6:30 P.M. Sat.–Sun. Mar.–Dec., 5 P.M.–midnight daily Jan.–Feb., US$1 adults, US$0.50 children, free Wed.), Mardel's outstanding natural sciences museum. With paleontological, archaeological, geological, and zoological exhibits, it also has a ground-floor aquarium that highlights oceangoing and freshwater local species.

Mar del Plata may be more democratic than it once was, but Barrio Stella Maris and Barrio los Troncos, southeast of **Plaza Colón,** still shine with the patina of a patrician past. Rising 88 meters above sea level at Falucho and Mendoza, the terrace of the 1943 **Torre Tanque** waterworks (Falucho 93, tel. 0223/451-4681, 8 A.M.–2:45 P.M. weekdays, free) provides a panoramic perspective on the city's most exclusive residential neighborhoods. The seemingly endless blocks of tile-roofed chalets to the south show that Mardel retains its upper-middle-class status, at least (photographers can ask personnel to open windows and balcony doors, which are closed for safety reasons). Designed by architect Cornelio Lange, this unusual tower on the Stella Maris hill was the solution to a water-distribution problem—Mardel gets all its water from wells—with an elevated 500,000-liter tank above a two-cistern 13-million-liter reservoir. The Torre Tanque has an elevator that carries visitors to the terrace, but there's also a spiral staircase for either ascending or descending.

Immediately northwest, the neo-Gothic **Iglesia Stella Maris** (Brown 1054), which dates from 1910, is a reminder that Mar del Plata remains a fishing port—its namesake virgin, sculpted by a disciple of Rodin, is the fleet's patron saint. One block north, dating from 1920, **Villa Normandy** (Viamonte 2213) is a Francophile residence that until recently housed the Italian consulate.

Across the block, the **Museo del Mar** (Avenida Colón 1114, tel. 0223/451-9779, www.museodelmar.org, 9:30 A.M.–midnight daily in summer, 10 A.M.–9 P.M. daily the rest of the year, US$5 adults, US$4 children) is one of the city's most impressive attractions. Integrated with a house dating from Mardel's aristocratic heyday, this sparkling multilevel facility presents collector Benjamín Sisterna's impressive assortment of 30,000 seashells far better than an earlier downtown museum ever

did. Following a boyhood enthusiasm, Sisterna (1914–1995) collected shells from around the world for over 60 years, and the well-lighted display cases in the cylindrical atrium are only part of what is a stunning addition to the city's appeal.

The new museum features a lower-level tidal pool set within its Confitería Gloria Maris, a perfect choice for coffee or lunch, surrounded by an aquarium. The second level contains the bulk of Cisterna's seashells, a cybercafé, an auditorium, and a museum shop, while the third contains more shells, a lecture hall, and an art gallery. The fourth level has an exhibition hall and a rooftop terrace with outstanding views.

Immediately across the street, the **Villa Ortiz Basualdo** (1909) was an elite *porteño* family's summer home that now hosts the municipal art museum, **Museo Municipal de Arte Juan Carlos Castagnino** (Avenida Colón 1189, tel. 0223/486-1636, 5–10 P.M. daily, US$1.25). The museum takes its name from the Mardel-born painter who, with the Mexican David Siqueiros and others, created the awesome ceiling murals at Buenos Aires's Galerías Pacífico. The building itself, in the style of a Loire Valley castle, still sports its original Belgian furnishings along with paintings, sculptures, engravings, and photography by Argentine artists.

To the southeast, Avenida Martínez de Hoz leads to the beaches of **Cabo Corrientes** and **Playa Grande,** an area whose Avenida Alem and surrounding streets are now one of the city's most active restaurant and nightlife areas. This may change, though, as the neighbors have been complaining, at least about the clubs and bars.

To the west is Barrio los Troncos, whose **Chalet los Troncos** (Urquiza 3440) is a landmark log-style house dating from 1938; all the raw materials, including the *lapacho* and *quebracho* hardwoods and roof tiles, came from Salta Province.

Nearby is **Villa Victoria,** the onetime residence of writer-muse Victoria Ocampo and now the **Centro Cultural Villa Victoria** (Matheu 1851, tel. 0223/492-0569, 10 A.M.–1 P.M.

and 5–9 P.M. daily, US$1). In the 1920s and 1930s, Ocampo's Mardel residence was the gathering place for a diversity of artists and intellectuals from around the world, among them her countryman Jorge Luis Borges, Chilean poet Gabriela Mistral, Indian novelist Rabindranath Tagore, and Russian composer Igor Stravinsky—not to mention her sister and poet Silvina and Silvina's husband, novelist Adolfo Bioy Casares. Founder and editor of the literary journal *Sur,* Ocampo donated the building to UNESCO in 1973, but it later reverted to municipal control as a museum and cultural center.

Nearby is **Villa Emilio Mitre** (1930), one of the Argentine oligarchy's classic residences, now home to the **Museo Archivo Histórico Municipal Roberto T. Barili** (Lamadrid 3870, tel. 0223/495-1200, archivohistoricomdp@ yahoo.com.ar, 9 A.M.–8 P.M. weekdays, 5–9 P.M. weekends, US$1 adults, US$0.60 children). The municipal history museum documents the city's history—the good, the bad, and even the ugly high-rises that now dominate the city—through photographs, posters, and a documentary archive.

South of downtown, beyond Playa Grande and the Mar del Plata Golf Club, the **Banquina de Pescadores** is a working fishing wharf whose docks double as a magnet for tourists. Thanks to its rainbow fleet, the maned male sea lions that gather for scraps at the end of the day, and the cluster of nearby seafood restaurants, it's more entertaining than a day sunning on the beach.

Male sea lions can be aggressive toward humans, but here, at least, a fence safely separates them from their two-legged admirers. Along with the multicolored fishing boats, they are ideal photographic subjects.

Named for a local painter, the **Museo del Hombre del Puerto Cleto Ciocchini** (Centro Comercial del Puerto, Local 8, tel. 0223/480-1228, 6 P.M.–midnight Tues.–Sun., US$0.75) occupies new quarters at the port entrance. It features maritime-themed art and historical artifacts.

The Centro Comercial is also home to numerous seafood restaurants where you can order delicacies fresh off the boat. From downtown, local buses Nos. 221 and 581 drop passengers right at the entrance, only a short walk from the port proper.

From the port, there are also 11:30 A.M. and 4 P.M. harbor excursions (US$12 adults, US$5 kids) on the 30-meter *Crucero Anamora* (tel. 0223/484-0103, www.anamoracrucero. com.ar). In summer there are also 2 and 4 P.M. sailings.

Entertainment

In summer, Mar del Plata is Argentina's entertainment capital, even surpassing Buenos Aires for live theater and musical events. Like the capital, it has *carteleras* that sell discount tickets to movies, live theater, and live music events; try **Cartelera Baires** (Santa Fe 1851) or **Cartelera Galería de las Américas** (Córdoba 1737, tel. 0223/494-5252).

Some venues are difficult to categorize. For instance, the **Centro Cultural Osvaldo Soriano** (25 de Mayo 3108, tel. 0223/499-7893, programacion@cultura.mardelplata. gov.ar) offers a broad calendar of events that include theater, music, film, and lectures.

Befitting a city with a cinema festival, Mar del Plata is a big moviegoers' town; some cinemas are *cine teatros* that double as live theater venues. The main locales are the **Cine Ambassador** (Córdoba 1673, tel. 0223/499-9200); the **Cine Teatro Enrique Carreras** (Entre Ríos 1828, tel. 0223/494-2753); the multiscreen **Cines del Paseo** (Diagonal Pueyrredón 3058, tel. 0223/499-9299); and the two-screen **Cines Shopping Los Gallegos** (Rivadavia 3050, tel. 0223/499-6977).

With several separate salons, the **Teatro Auditorium** (Bulevar Marítimo 2280, tel. 0223/493-6001) features summer musical theater imported from Buenos Aires. Similar locales include the the **Teatro Atlas** (Avenida Luro 2289, tel. 0223/494-3240), the **Teatro América** (also at Avenida Luro 2289, tel. 0223/494-3240), **Teatro Municipal Colón** (Yrigoyen 1665, tel. 0223/494-8571), and the **Teatro Corrientes** (Corrientes 1766, tel.

0223/493-7918). Several of these share a common website (www.multiteatro.com.ar). For those with money to burn, the **Casino Central** (Bulevar Marítimo 2100, tel. 0223/495-7011) is the place to start the fire. Nightlife spots **Roxy Mar del Plata** (San Luis 1750, tel. 0223/494-2950), **Taos** (Brown 2660, tel. 0223/15-600-4514), and **Mestizo** (Irigoyen and Rawson) all offer live rock and electronic music. **Sauro** (Güemes 2782, tel. 0223/486-0113) is the place for predancing drinks, though it also has live music most nights and DJs on weekends.

Events

February 10 is **Fundación de la Ciudad,** celebrating the city's 1874 founding.

Argentina's cinematic revival has helped restore the prestige of November's **Festival Internacional de Cine.** It's not Cannes, but that's a good thing, and there are plenty of quality offerings from Argentina, the rest of Latin America, and the rest of the world.

Shopping

The **Diagonal de los Artesanos** is an open-air crafts market that lines Pueyrredón between San Martín and Rivadavia. Plaza Rocha's **Mercado de Pulgas,** seven blocks northwest on 20 de Septiembre between Avenida Luro and San Martín, is a wide-ranging flea market.

Mardel's traditional signature products are sweaters and jackets from Avenida Juan B. Justo, the so-called "Avenida del Pullover," reached by buses Nos. 561 and 562. The center for designer clothing, though, is the Avenida Güemes corridor south of Avenida Colón.

Sports and Recreation

Most activities center on the beach, ranging from sedentary sunbathing to more active pastimes like swimming, diving, and fishing; even pursuits like parasailing (which seems to go dangerously close to coastal high-rises) take place in the vicinity. There is also cycling, horseback riding, and even skydiving. For a thorough list of offerings, see Emtur's free pamphlet *Guía de Actividades,* which is updated monthly.

Accommodations

One of Argentina's major domestic destinations, Mar del Plata boasts about 600 hotels with a total of 60,000 beds. Many are union-built and operated, dating from the Peronist heyday of the 1940s and 1950s, and have failed to modernize. Nearly all the establishments below are on or near the beach, though many visitors rent beach tents that may be some distance from where they're staying.

Prices listed below are for the summer peak, when rates can rise and fluctuate dramatically and singles are hard to find. Even then there are often bargains, and off-season prices can fall by half or more. Many *marplatenses* also rent out their apartments and houses in summer. You can get information on rentals from the tourist office, though sometimes people stand around at bus and train stations with signs advertising them.

Under US$25: In summer, at least, the only true shoestring accommodations are at the HI affiliate **Yanquetruz Hostel** (9 de Julio 3634, tel. 0223/473-8098, www.yanquetruz.com.ar, US$8–17 pp dorm, US$19–41 s or d), but it's fairly distant from the beach.

Also an HI affiliate, the **Hostel Playa Grande** (Quintana 168, tel. 0223/451-2396, www.hostelplayagrande.com.ar, US$12–20 pp dorm, US$42–64 s or d) enjoys a better location near its namesake beach and the Alem restaurant and nightlife district. It's open only in the peak summer season, but its nearby **Hostel Playa Grande Suites** (Alem 3495, tel. 0223/451-2396, US$12–25 pp dorm, US$42–68 d) stays open all year.

US$25-50: The family-run **La Posada de Güemes** (Falucho 1285, tel. 0223/451-4287, posadadeguemes@infovia.com.ar, US$50 s or d) attracts plenty of foreign visitors to an appealing chalet-style building whose rooms come with breakfast, cable TV, and similar amenities. **Hotel Bologna** (9 de Julio 2542, tel. 0223/494-3369, www.hotelbologna.com.ar, US$50 s or d) has smallish rooms, though some have balconies.

US$50-100: Family-operated **Hotel Calash** (Falucho 1355, tel. 0223/451-6115, www.

© WAYNE BERNHARDSON

Though its exterior hasn't changed, the Spanish NH chain has renovated and reopened Mar del Plata's historic Gran Hotel Provincial.

calashmdp.com.ar, US$63 d) has attractive comfortable rooms with rates that include parking.

The 30 simple but well-kept rooms at quiet (**Hotel Selent** (Arenales 2347, tel. 0223/494-0878, www.hotelselent.com.ar, US$55 s, US$74 d) enjoy a substantial setback from the street. This well-maintained older building offers an above-average breakfast and has ample parking (uncommon in this part of town) for a small extra charge, the staff can manage English and French, and it has Wi-Fi. Some singles, though, resemble tunnels—long and narrow.

In its three-star category, the gracefully aging (**Hotel Imperio** (Avenida Colón 1186, tel./fax 0223/486-3993, www.imperiohotel.com. ar, US$70–84 s or d) is a standout for its location, natural light, and spacious rooms, some with balconies.

Rates at the reliable Argentine chain hotel **Hotel Amerian Mar del Plata** (Libertad 2996, tel. 0223/491-2300, www.amerian.com, US$85–95 s or d) vary according to whether they have a city or ocean view. It charges extra for amenities such as Wi-Fi, however.

The three-star **Hotel Benedetti** (Colón 2198, tel. 0223/493-0032, www.hotel-benedetti.com.ar, US$100 d) gets high marks for service and 97 only slightly-less-than-sumptuous rooms with a buffet breakfast, Wi-Fi in common areas, and parking.

US$100-200: Hotel Club del Golf (Aristóbulo del Valle 3641, tel. 0223/451-3456, www.hotelclubdelgolf.com.ar, US$111 s or d) has relatively small but modern and attractive rooms and fine service.

Reservations are always advisable at the popular, efficiently run **Hotel Guerrero** (Diagonal Juan B. Alberdi 2288, tel. 0223/495-8851, www.hotelguerrero.com.ar, US$111–127 s or d); the higher rates correspond to seaview rooms. Amenities include free Internet access, a gym, a swimming pool, parking, and a strongbox in every room; there's a 5 percent discount for cash.

Hotel Astor (Entre Ríos 1649, tel./fax 0223/492-1616, www.hotelastor.com.ar, US$121 d with buffet breakfast) offers free airport transfers, free beach transfers, sauna, and similar amenities.

Under the same management as the Astor, **Gran Hotel Dorá** (Buenos Aires 1841, tel./ fax 0223/491-0033, www.hoteldora.com.ar, US$126–140 s or d) is a 1930s landmark that has improved thanks to recent renovations; the higher rates correspond to ocean views. According to locals, though, it has a reputation for below-average service in its category.

The 330-room **Hermitage Hotel** (Bulevar Pedro Peralta Ramos 2657, tel. 0223/451-9081, www.hermitagehotel.com.ar, US$144–162 s or d) is a classic 1940s hotel that has undergone an overdue renovation and modernization along with the addition of a new wing. The higher rates correspond to ocean views. Outside the front door, its "Walk of Fame" features handprints from figures in the Argentine entertainment world and also international figures such as Jeremy Irons and Jacqueline Bisset.

Rooms at four-star **Hotel Dos Reyes** (Avenida Colón 2129, tel. 0223/491-2174, www.dosreyes.com.ar, US$128–144 s, US$136–151 d) come with parking as well as transfers to, and a shared shade tent at, the *balneario* at Punta Mogotes.

Built for the 1978 World Cup, the well-managed **Hotel Spa República** (Córdoba 1968, tel. 0223/492-1142, www.hotelsparepublica.com. ar, US$156 s or d) still hosts visiting soccer teams, but even the smallish standard rooms have had contemporary upgrades; all have kitchenettes. In 1992 it added a five-story spa, but use of the pool, Jacuzzis, saunas, steam baths, and the like costs extra; there are also packages that include half board, and a beach tent at Punta Mogotes.

After sitting empty for over a decade before its reopening in 2008, the **NH Gran Hotel Provincial** (Blvd. Patricio Peralta Ramos 2502, tel. 0223/499-5900, www.nh-hoteles.com, US$145–218 s or d) is a 500-room labyrinth undergoing restoration by the Spanish chain that specializes in rehabbing classic hotels. Designed by the famous Alejandro Bustillo, the landmark structure features its own theater, various salons, a gym, and allegorical murals by the architect's son César. The renovated rooms have double-paned windows that even

eliminate the sound of the surf. Access to its pool and beach tents cost extra.

Over US$200: Overlooking the Playa Grande, ⬛ **Hotel Costa Galana** (Bulevar Marítimo 5725, tel. 0223/486-0000, www. hotelcostagalana.com, US$222–292 s or d) is a five-star facility that lives up to its luxury billing.

Overlooking Cabo Corrientes, the high-rise **Torres de Manantiales** (Alberti 453, tel. 0223/486-1999, www.manantiales.com. ar, US$253 s or d) is a luxury apartment-hotel where amenities including a sauna, gym, pool, and a 28th-floor restaurant with the city's most panoramic views. Off-season rates can fall to half.

Near Playa Grande and the Alem dining-nightlife district, the 191-room **Sheraton Mar del Plata Hotel** (Alem 4221, tel. 0223/414-0000, www.sheratonmardelplata.com.ar, US$285–1,695 s or d) boasts a large luminous atrium, two restaurants, two bars, and business center among its amenities.

New in late 2009, the **Hotel Sainte Jeanne** (Güemes 2850, tel. 0223/420-9200, www.hotel-saintjeanne.com, US$315–475 s or d) is a self-styled boutique hotel that could be called an over-the-top "Paris of the South" theme park for its classic Parisian style and decor; it's a love-it-or-hate-it choice. Cheaper "classic" rooms faces noisy Güemes but double-paned windows keep it quiet. What's distinctively modern is an indoor spa pool with Jacuzzi seating along the sides, and even underwater chaises longues, plus a sauna and other spa services.

Food

For breakfast, sandwiches, and pastries, the best choices are two classic *confiterías*: **La Fonte d'Oro** (Belgrano 2102, tel. 0223/495-1677, www.lafontedoro.com) and **Boston** (Buenos Aires 1927, tel. 0223/495-4040, www. confiteriaboston.com.ar), virtually alongside it. La Fonte has especially fine pastries; both have several other branches around town.

Family favorite **Montecatini** (Avenida Colón 2309, tel. 0223/491-2505) offers a conventional Argentine menu throughout the day.

© WAYNE BERNHARDSON

The new Terminal Mar del Plata fills up with summer beachgoers.

Italo-Argentine fast food, pizza, and the like are available at **Manolo** (Rivadavia 2371, tel. 0223/410-3633). For more elaborate (and expensive) Italian entrées, try **Trattoría Napolitana** (3 de Febrero 3154, tel. 0223/495-3850).

Parrillas of interest include **El Palacio del Bife** (Córdoba 1857, tel. 0223/494-7727) and **La Parrilla del Gato** (Yrigoyen 2699, tel. 0223/495-5309). The comparable **La Marca** (Almafuerte 253, tel. 0223/451-8072) is popular enough that reservations are advisable.

At the popular, informal **❰ La Bodeguita** (Castelli 1252, tel. 0223/486-3096, www.labodeguitamdq.com) the kitchen is quick with good-quality pub food that includes some Cuban specialties—for example, pork ribs with a strawberry sauce and fried bananas (US$12)—in a *cubanísimo* environment of books, photographs, and posters. Many dishes are meant to be shared, but not the minty mojitos (there's a two-for-one happy hour from 7–9 P.M. Sun.–Thurs., except in Jan.–Feb.). The service is excellent and candid, and English is spoken; tobacco (including cigars) is still permitted in part of the building.

Other ethnic food is uncommon here, but **Pancho Villa** (9 de Julio 3204, tel. 0223/493-2324) serves Mexican dishes.

Specializing in pasta and seafood, **El Almacén** (Carlos 2889, tel. 0223/486-3076) is a cozy corner restaurant with traditional style and natural wood decor whose pastas include king crab ravioli with squid ink (US$9). With friendly service, it's a reliable if unexceptional choice for fish dishes, such as flounder with a garlic sauce, and a limited by-the-glass wine selection.

Reservations are advisable at the innovative **❰ El Anticuario** (Bernardo de Irigoyen 3819, tel. 0223/451-6309, www.elanticuarioonline.com.ar), which has a large and diverse menu of pastas, beef, and especially fish in the US$13 range and up. There's a good wine list and excellent service.

Down the block, with a new sushi section, **Zoe Sushi Club** (Bernardo de Irigoyen 3947, tel. 0223/486-5355) has exceptional homemade pastas, though more elaborate fish and beef dishes are more expensive (around US$10 and up). The service is friendly and attentive, but it can get noisy.

In addition to its hypermodern decor and friendly service, ◖ **Oink** (Güemes 2364, tel. 0223/486-5251, www.oinkrestaurant.com) is bidding to become a landmark for its creative cuisine—the Spanish-style *montaditos*, with pork slices and quail eggs on bruschetta, could be a main course instead of an appetizer. The house specialty lasagna, though, needs a better balance among the abundant spinach, tender lamb, and minimal pasta, though the individual flavors are good. It needs to improve the wine offerings in some categories—there is nothing by the glass, and only a mediocre Malbec in half-bottle size.

On the seaside south of downtown, the Nuevo Complejo Comercial Puerto (Avenida Martínez de Hoz 200) offers several seafood venues. For more elaborate meals, try **Chichilo** (Local 17, tel. 0223/489-6317) or **Piedra Buena** (Local 7, tel. 0223/480-4682), a very good traditional seafood restaurant.

Helados Gianelli (Avenida Colón 1802) has fine ice cream, but **Bosque Rojo** (Colón 1934) is mounting a challenge in the premium ice cream sweepstakes. Playa Grande's **Augustus** (Alem 3570, tel. 0223/451-1065) has an exceptional raspberry mousse.

Information

The Ente Municipal de Turismo (Emtur) operates the **Centro de Información Turística** (Rambla Casino, Bulevar Marítimo 2270, Local 51, tel. 0223/495-1777, www.turismomardelplata.gov.ar), which is open 8 A.M.–8 P.M. daily, except in summer, when it closes around 10 P.M. It has abundant maps, brochures, and a useful activities calendar, but can be almost industrially impersonal. There's a satellite branch at San Luis 1949 (tel. 0223/494-4140, ext. 131, 8 A.M.–8 P.M. daily).

Just down the block, the provincial **Subsecretaría de Turismo** (Rambla del Hotel Provincial, Bulevar Marítimo 2500, Local 48, tel. 0223/494-0134) is open 8 A.M.–7 P.M. weekdays most of the year, but stays open until 9 P.M. in summer.

For motorists, **ACA** is at Avenida Colón 1450 (tel. 0223/491-2096).

Services

ATMs, such as the one at **Banco de la Nación** (San Martín 2594), are numerous. Exchange houses include **La Moneta** (Rivadavia 2623, tel. 0223/494-5769) and **Jonestur** (San Martín 2574, tel. 0223/495-0762, www.jonestur.com.ar; Avenida Luro 3181, tel. 0223/494-9103).

Correo Argentino is at Avenida Luro 2460; the postal code is 7600.

Long-distance call centers and Internet locales such as **Insumos Ya.com** (Brown 1975) are abundant.

Oti International (San Luis 1632, 2nd floor, tel. 0223/494-5414, www.otiviajes.com) is the Amex affiliate. **Asatej** (Güemes 2416, Oficina 4, tel./fax 0223/486-4975, rcantaloube@asatej.com.ar) is a student- and youth-oriented travel agency.

Lave-Quick (Las Heras 2471, tel. 0223/495-1431) will pick up and drop off the washing at no extra charge.

The **Hospital Regional** (J. B. Justo 6700, tel. 0223/477-0030) is less central. For emergencies, dial 107.

Getting There

Aerolíneas Argentinas (Moreno 2442, tel. 0223/496-0101) flies several times daily to Buenos Aires's Aeroparque.

LADE (Corrientes 1537, tel. 0223/491-1484) flies north to Aeroparque and south to Bahía Blanca and Patagonian destinations, but schedules are infrequent and erratic.

Sol Líneas Aéreas (tel. 0810/444-4765) flies to Aeroparque and Rosario. **Líneas Aéreas Entre Ríos** (tel. 0810/777-5237) flies to Aeroparque and Paraná.

More than 50 bus companies operate out of the sparkling new **Terminal Mar del Plata** (25 de Mayo and San Juan, www.terminaldemicrosmdp.com.ar), immediately behind the railroad station, to destinations around the country. In the peak summer season and on holiday weekends, fares may rise and reservations are advisable.

Typical destinations, times, and fares include Villa Gesell (1.5 hours, US$5), Tandil (3 hours, US$7), La Plata (5 hours, US$25–28), Buenos

Aires (5.5 hours, US$28), Rosario (10 hours, US$45), Neuquén (14 hours, US$53–64), Bariloche (19 hours, US$86), Puerto Madryn (16 hours, US$58), and Mendoza (18 hours, US$61–71).

Ferrobaires (Avenida Luro 4500, tel. 0223/455-6076, www.ferrobaires.gba.gov. ar), the provincially run rail service, has offices at the **Estación Terminal de Ferrocarril,** some 17 blocks northwest of Plaza San Martín. Ferrobaires operates two or three trains daily to Buenos Aires; the trip takes six to seven hours, and standard one-way fares range from US$15 (in stiff-backed *clase única*) to US$19 (in reclining Pullman seats). The summer Expreso del Atlántico (US$24) and the weekend El Marplatense (US$24) have more creature comforts.

Getting Around

Mardel has an extensive bus system that requires an inexpensive rechargeable magnetic card; most fares are around US$0.40. Emtur's brochure *Actividades Recreativas* lists the appropriate bus lines for sights and activities in the vicinity.

Aeropuerto Astor Piazzola (RN 2 Km 396, tel. 0223/478-3990) is 10 kilometers north of town. City bus No. 542 goes directly there from the corner of Bulevar Marítimo and Belgrano. Taxis and *remises* charge around US$8.

For car rentals, try **Hertz/Millet** (Córdoba 2149, tel. 0223/496-2772, hertzmardelplata@ sinectis.com.ar); **Budget** (Córdoba 2270, tel. 0223/495-2935, mardelplata@budgetargentina.com); or **Localiza** (Avenida Colón 2450, tel. 0223/491-0091).

Rental bicycles are available at Plaza Mitre's **Bicicletería Madrid** (Hipólito Yrigoyen 2249, tel. 0223/494-1932).

◖ Museo del Automovilismo Juan Manuel Fangio

Fortunately, the Fangio Automotive Museum, named for racing legend Juan Manuel Fangio and located in his Balcarce birthplace near Mar del Plata, is not just for fossil-fuel fanatics.

While it focuses on the five-time world champion's exploits, it also credits his competition and, more significantly, places racing in a context of evolving transportation technology.

Fangio (1911–1995) won a Formula One world title in 1951 and then annually from 1954 through 1957. Three films have chronicled his life: exploitation producer Armando Bó's *Fangio, the Devil of the Racetrack;* the documentary *Fangio* (1976) by Oscar-winning director Hugh Hudson (*Chariots of Fire*); and director Alberto Lecchi's *Operación: Fangio* (1999), about the racer's kidnapping by Cuban guerrillas in 1958. Fangio played himself in John Frankenheimer's *Grand Prix* (1966), and is also the subject of the tribute *Fangio: A Pirelli Album* (Motorbooks International, 1991), by Fangio's rival Sterling Moss and Doug Nye.

The building housing the museum is a recycled century-old structure with a spiral ramp that climbs through eight levels of exhibits on everything from Fangio's childhood through his championships and retirement (though it ignores incidents like his kidnapping). At the same time, it integrates his biography with world events through photographs and a time line. There's an extraordinary collection of classic automobiles—not just his racing cars—along with a souvenir shop and a café.

One conspicuously absent topic is highway safety, a critical matter in Argentina, a culture that apparently idolizes high-speed driving. Fangio himself, for instance, killed his navigator Daniel Urrutia when he rolled his Chevrolet during a Peruvian road race in 1948, yet authorities have named the Buenos Aires–Mar del Plata freeway in his honor. The YPF oil company's highest-octane fuel also bears his name.

On retirement in 1958, Fangio spoke of being a role model: "If my efforts have had any value, if racing automobiles has been useful to my homeland, time will tell. I have only one wish, which is that if my conduct in the world can be useful to youth; for that, I will also await the answer of time." Argentina's high highway death tolls may be part of that answer.

The Museo Fangio (Dardo Rocha 639,

Balcarce, tel. 02266/43-0758, www.museo-fangio.com, 10 A.M.–5 P.M. daily, winter hours slightly shorter, US$7 adults, US$4 children above age 6) is 60 kilometers northwest of Mar del Plata via RN 226. From the Mar del Plata terminal, frequent El Rápido buses to Balcarce charge about US$2.50.

VILLA GESELL

Turning barren dunes into a botanical garden of ecological exotics traversed by tree-shaded crisscross streets, Carlos Idaho Gesell's transformation of the town that bears his name resembles what William Hammond Hall and John McLaren did in San Francisco's Golden Gate Park. Gesell's vision fashioned one of the province's most appealing coastal resorts, less exclusive than many people believe. Its irregular plan and sandy streets favor pedestrians and cyclists over automobile traffic, except on its cluttered commercial strip—which would likely appall its creator.

Villa Gesell (pop. about 44,000) is about 110 kilometers northeast of Mar del Plata via the coastal highway RP 11, and 360 kilometers south of Buenos Aires via RN 2, RP 11, and a couple of shortcuts. Parallel to the beach, Avenida 3 is the only paved street—with wall-to-wall restaurants, souvenir shops, and video-game parlors. Most hotels are on quieter side streets known as *paseos*.

Sights

For a quick orientation to local attractions and activities, a good option is the **Trencito Histórico de Villa Gesell** (Avenida 3 and Paseo 110 bis, tel. 02255/46-8920). Despite the name, it's a bus whose two-hour outings (US$5 pp, children in arms free) visit Gesell's houses (now a museum and an exhibition hall), the surrounding Parque Cultural Pinar del Norte, early pioneer houses, and the fishing pier.

Farther afield, **Turismo Aventura** (tel. 02255/46-3118 or 02255/46-6797) offers four-hour 4WD excursions (US$13 pp, children slightly cheaper) to **Faro Querandí,** a landmark lighthouse separated from Gesell by dunes.

Parque Cultural Pinar del Norte

Gesell's vision for his town is clearest in these car-free woodlands only a block north of Avenida 3 and Avenida Buenos Aires, the access road from RP 11. Within the reserve, really a large city park, the **Museo Histórico Municipal** (Alameda 201 and Calle 303, tel. 02255/46-8624, 10 A.M.–8 P.M. daily, US$0.75) was his modest original residence (1931). Containing photographs, maps, and other artifacts associated with the project, it offers guided tours; English-speaking guides are available.

Gesell's later residence, the **Centro Cultural Chalet de Don Carlos** (tel. 02255/45-0530, 10 A.M.–8 P.M. daily, US$0.75), dating from 1952, is now an exhibition center.

Entertainment and Events

In summer especially, Villa Gesell has many cultural activities and an active nightlife.

Since 1969 the **Anfiteatro del Pinar** (Avenida 10 and Paseo 102) has hosted summer's **Encuentros Corales de Verano** (www.encuentroscorales.com.ar), a national choral competition that lasts from early January to early March.

The **Casa de la Cultura** (Avenida 3 No. 874, tel. 02255/46-2513) hosts live summer theater. Cinemas include the **Cine Atlantic** (Paseo 105 between Avenida 2 and Avenida 3, tel. 02255/46-2323) and the **Cine Teatro Atlas** (Paseo 108 between Avenida 3 and Avenida 4, tel. 02255/46-2969).

At the northern approach to town, **Pueblo Límite** (Avenida Buenos Aires 2600, tel. 02255/45-2845, www.pueblolimite.com) is a complex of various dance clubs with food as an afterthought. In summer it's open nightly; the rest of the year on Saturday only.

Shopping

Gesell's crafts workers display their wares at the **Feria Artesanal, Regional y Artística** (Avenida 3, between Paseos 112 and 113). From mid-December through mid-March, it happens daily, but the rest of the year it takes place weekends and holidays only.

Sports and Recreation

Both rental horses and guided excursions are available from the **Escuela de Equitación San Jorge** (Circunvalación and Paseo 102, tel. 02255/45-4464). Local fishing enthusiasts crowd the **Muelle de Pesca** (Playa and Paseo 129), a pier extending 15 meters into the South Atlantic. Rental bicycles are available at **Bicigesell** (Avenida 3 and Paseo 141, tel. 02255/47-6820).

Accommodations

Gesell's accommodations range from campgrounds to simple *hospedajes* and four-star hotels, but many are open only in summer. Those listed here are open all year.

Gesell has its first hostel in the small but attractive **La Deseada** (Avenida 6 No. 1883, tel. 02255/47-3276, www.ladeseadahostel.com.ar, US$20 pp), which has only six rooms.

For family-run *hospedajes,* all near the beach and charging from US$26 d, try **Hospedaje Villa Gesell** (Avenida 3 No. 812, tel. 02255/46-6368, hospedajevillagesell.8k.com) and **Hospedaje Viya** (Avenida 5 No. 582, tel. 02255/46-2757, www.gesell.com.ar/viya). One-star hotels, such as **Hotel Villa del Sol** (Avenida 3 No. 1469, tel. 02255/46-7781, www.villagesell.com.ar/hotelvilladelsol), are only slightly dearer, starting around US$32 d.

Two-star hotels, starting in the US$45 d range, include **Hotel Posada de la Villa** (Paseo 125 No. 182, tel. 02255/46-4855, www.gesell.com.ar/posadavg) and the upgraded **Hotel Bellavista** (Paseo 114 No. 256, tel. 02255/46-2293, www.hotelspileon.com.ar).

The three-star seven-story **Hotel Castilla** (Avenida Buenos Aires 76, tel./fax 02255/46-4100, www.gesell.com.ar/hotelcastilla) charges US$75 d. The spa-style **Hotel Bahía Club** (Avenida 1 No. 855, tel. 02255/46-2838, www.hotelbahiavg.com.ar, US$135–174 d), a beachfront high-rise, is the only prestige hotel that remains open all year.

Food

A Gesell stalwart, **La Jirafa Azul** (Avenida 3 between Paseo 102 and Avenida Buenos Aires, tel. 02255/46-8968) has been serving a standard Argentine menu for nearly 40 years; it has a second branch at Avenida 3 and Paseo 140 (tel. 02255/47-6171).

La Taberna de Don Ramón (Avenida 3 and Paseo 124, tel. 02255/46-3299) is good for Galician-style seafood, with excellent service and entrées in the US$7–10 range except for pastas, which are cheaper. Try the chocolate mousse for dessert.

Cantina Arturito (Avenida 3 No. 186, tel. 02255/46-3037) also specializes in pasta and seafood, plus appetizers such as homemade ham.

Fríos (Avenida 3 and Paseo 108) has fine ice cream.

Information and Services

At the northern entrance to town, the conscientious **Secretaría de Turismo y Cultura** (Avenida Buenos Aires 1921, tel. 02255/45-8596 or 02255/45-7255, www.gesell.gov.ar) stays open 8 A.M.–10 P.M. daily in summer, 8 A.M.–8 P.M. weekdays and 10 A.M.–6 P.M. weekends the rest of the year. Its Oficina Terminal (tel. 02255/47-7253) is open 6 A.M.–2 P.M. and 5 P.M.–1 A.M. daily.

Correo Argentino is on Avenida 3 between Paseo 108 and Paseo 109; Gesell's postal code is 7165. **Cyber Time** (Avenida 3 and Paseo 105) has Internet services.

Hospital Municipal Arturo Illia is at Paseo 123 and Avenida 8 (tel. 02255/46-2618).

Getting There and Around

Sol Líneas Aéreas (tel. 0810/444-4765, www.sol.com.ar) is a budget carrier serving Buenos Aires's Aeroparque, Rosario, and Santa Fe.

The Terminal de Ómnibus (Avenida 3 and Paseo 140, tel. 02255/47-6058) has direct buses to Buenos Aires (5 hours, US$26–30) and to Mar del Plata (1.5 hours, US$4–5). From 5:45 A.M. to 1:05 A.M. there are hourly-plus buses to Pinamar (US$1.50) from the bus terminal via Bulevar Silvio Gesell.

PINAMAR

Exclusive Pinamar bears the stamp of architect Jorge Bunge, one of the Argentine oligarchy's

vista from the fisherman's wharf towards the north

biggest names. Apparently following Carlos Gesell's precedent, Bunge turned the dunes behind its long sandy beaches into the province's most select beach resort. It's home to the usual beach activities: swimming, sunbathing, surfing, and fishing, as well as cycling and horseback riding.

Pinamar (pop. about 40,000) is 127 kilometers north of Mar del Plata via RP 11 and 340 kilometers southeast of Buenos Aires via RN 2, RP 11, and shorter interconnected roads. Avenida Libertador, parallel to the beach, and Avenida Bunge, perpendicular to Avenida Libertador, are the main thoroughfares, but Bunge's otherwise fan-shaped city plan often confuses first-time visitors. The tourist office distributes an excellent town map.

Sights

Dunes are encroaching on **La Elenita,** the modest beachfront cabin of former President Arturo Frondizi. Curious beachgoers can see this national historical monument's exterior, but tours are not offered.

Entertainment

Pinamar has three cinemas: the **Cine-Teatro Oasis** (Avenida Shaw and Lenguado, tel. 02254/48-3334), **Cine Bahía** (Avenida Bunge and De la Sirena, tel. 02254/48-2747), and **Cine Pinamar** (also at Avenida Bunge and De la Sirena, tel. 02254/48-1012). In summer there's lots of open-air live music on stages set up along Avenida Bunge and at the beach.

Accommodations

Like Gesell, Pinamar has abundant accommodations—more than 200 venues—but lacks the cheapest alternatives. The municipal tourist office does an exemplary job of helping find accommodations when occupancy is high. All of those listed below are on or near the beach.

One of Pinamar's best bargains is Italian-run **Hotel Gaviota** (Del Cangrejo 1332, tel. 02254/48-2079, US$32 s, US$58 d), a one-star gem with no frills (it's TV-free, for instance). Rooms are small but impeccable and comfortably furnished, with private baths and breakfast. **Hotel Berlín** (Rivadavia 326, tel. 02254/48-2320, www.hotelberlinpinamar.com.ar, US$55–74 d) is comparable but slightly more expensive in its newer wing, though it has some cheaper backpacker rooms.

On a woodsy block, the three-star **Hostería Bora Bora** (Del Tuyú 441, tel. 02254/48-0164 or 02254/48-2394, www.boraborapinamar.com.ar, US$69–87 d with breakfast) has good midsize rooms; the higher-priced rooms enjoy air-conditioning and more contemporary baths.

Adjacent Ostende's **Hotel Nitra** (Avenida Juan de Garay 299, tel. 02254/48-6680, www.hotelesnitra.com.ar, US$87 s, US$98 d) is a nearly new 50-room hotel in a quiet area near the beach. Though older, the comparable **Hotel Las Araucarias** (Avenida Bunge 1411, tel. 02254/48-0812, www.hotelaraucarias.com.ar, US$107 d) is a 30-room chalet-style facility that offers 5 percent discounts for cash payments.

Food

Primarily a pizzeria, **Vadinho** (Avenida Bunge 766, tel. 02254/40-4435) also serves decent seafood in the US$6–10 range; in a town where seasonal workers are the rule, the service is enthusiastic but amateur. It's more comfortably spacious than many Argentine restaurants.

Directly on the beach, **Viejo Lobo** (Avenida Bunge and Avenida del Mar, tel. 02254/48-3218) serves a pretty good shrimp risotto (US$8) and has attentive service, but the kitchen's so quick as to suggest that they're reheating instead of cooking.

Il Garda (Avenida Shaw 136, tel. 02254/48-2582) is good for pastas. **Estilo Criollo** (Avenida Bunge 768, tel. 02254/49-5246) is known for beef, pork, and especially *chivito* (grilled kid goat).

For breakfast, savor the succulent croissants and coffee at **Confitería La Reina** (Avenida Shaw 135, tel. 02254/48-4727), which also serves snacks and sweets in the afternoon. **Heladería El Piave** (Avenida Bunge 449) has excellent ice cream.

Information and Services

Pinamar's **Dirección de Turismo** (Avenida Shaw 18, tel. 02254/49-1680, www.pinamar.gov.ar) is open 8 A.M.–10 P.M. daily in summer, 8 A.M.–8 P.M. weekdays and 10 A.M.–6 P.M. weekends the rest of the year. It's the place to stop for help in seeking a room, especially in high season—they'll phone to check availability in your price range.

Correo Argentino is at Jasón 75; the postal code is 7167. The **Centro Telefónico Pinamar** (Avenida Shaw 157) has long-distance and Internet services.

For medical emergencies, Pinamar's **Hospital Comunitario** is at Avenida Shaw 250 (tel. 02254/48-2390).

Getting There and Around

From the Terminal de Ómnibus (Jasón 2250, tel. 02254/40-3500), near the entrance to town, several companies go to Mar del Plata (2 hours, US$5) and Buenos Aires (4.5 hours, US$25–29). From 6:35 A.M. to 11:35 P.M., hourly shuttles go to Villa Gesell (US$1).

Pinamar enjoys rail service to Constitución (Buenos Aires) Sunday night at 11:40 P.M. (US$15–19). The local stop is **Estación Divisadero** (RP 74 Km 4, tel. 02267/49-7973).

BAHÍA BLANCA

Home to the unique Museo del Puerto—reason enough for a visit—the southern Buenos Aires Province port of Bahía Blanca is a frequent stopover for Patagonia-bound travelers, especially motorists. It's also a major port for petrochemicals, grains from the pampas, and produce from Patagonia's Río Negro Valley, and is home to South America's largest naval base.

In addition to its commercial and military importance, Bahía Blanca is the site of Universidad Nacional del Sur. The main reason to visit, though, is the suburb of Puerto Ingeniero White—its museum, a self-effacing tribute to immigrants, is a welcome antidote to the pompously nationalistic institutions that pass for historical museums elsewhere in the country.

Bahía Blanca grew around the site of Colonel Ramón Estomba's Fortaleza Protectora Argentina, established in 1828 to enforce an Argentine presence in what, at the time, was an insecure area because of indigenous resistance to the European invaders. Arrival of the railroad from Buenos Aires in 1884 opened the way for it to become southern Buenos Aires Province's key port. Both the bay and the city take their name from the shoreline's dry white salt.

Bahía Blanca (pop. about 320,000) is 687 kilometers southwest of Buenos Aires via RN 3, 278 kilometers north of Viedma via RN 3, and 530 kilometers east of Neuquén via RN 22. Most points of interest and services are within a few blocks of the central Plaza Rivadavia. Street names change on either side of the plaza.

◖ Museo del Puerto

On Bahía Blanca's eastern edge, the 19th-century docks of Puerto Ingeniero White were—and still are—Argentina's most important port outside Buenos Aires. Nearly half the country's grain exports leave from here. It was also a thriving multiethnic community with a vigorous street life, and one of Argentina's most engaging museums still carries the torch for White's immigrant heritage.

The Museo del Puerto occupies the former customs house (1907), which sits inconspicuously atop pilings. Built by Ferrocarriles del Sud, the English-owned southern railway, the rehabbed building houses "a museum of local lifestyles" as reflected in institutions such as barbershops (each immigrant community had its own, represented here by caricature mannequins). Other exhibits include bars, classrooms, and shops.

Dating from 1885, named for an Anglo-Argentine engineer by former president Julio A. Roca in 1901, Puerto Ingeniero White first went by the name "Nueva Liverpool." At the time, the Argentine government actively promoted immigration, with certain restrictions (one official announcement said "Workers required: if English, French or German, good. No weaklings, sick or anarchists accepted").

Today, though, some of White's inhabitants—who prefer to call themselves *whitenses* rather than *bahienses*—consider the port something of a ghost town, with the decline of its ethnic bars, barbershops, and clubs. Every November, though, they gather to honor San Silverio, the patron saint of fishermen from Ponza, Italy (in Italy, San Silverio puts to sea in June, but here the event occurs in November because the seasons are reversed).

The Museo del Puerto (Guillermo Torres 4180, tel. 0291/457-3006, mpuerto@bb.mun.gba.gov.ar) is open 8:30 A.M.–12:30 P.M. weekdays and 3:30–7:30 P.M. weekends, but closes the entire month of January. Admission is free, but they request a small donation.

In addition to the permanent exhibits, the museum has an archive with documents, photographs, and recorded oral histories. A planned expansion will include information on the railroad.

When the museum is open, the kitchen offers meals based on immigrant cookbooks. From downtown Bahía Blanca, bus Nos. 500 and 501 go nearly to the front door.

Other Sights

Bahía Blanca's neoclassical **Teatro Municipal** (1913) at Alsina and Dorrego is a notable historical monument. The surrounding neighborhood, especially around the corner of Zeballos and Portugal, boasts a cluster of deco-style houses and apartments.

In the theater's basement, the **Museo Histórico Municipal** (Dorrego 116, tel. 0291/456-3117, http://mhistorico.bahiablanca.gov.ar, 8 A.M.–1 P.M. and 4–8 P.M. weekdays) is more like a quality antiques shop—lots of interesting objects, in good to excellent condition, all well arranged, but not particularly enlightening. The focus is on Colonel Estomba and the city's founding, along with European immigration, but this is covered better and more entertainingly at Puerto Ingeniero White.

The **Museo de Arte Contemporáneo** (Sarmiento 450, tel. 0291/459-4006, http://mbamac.bahiablanca.gov.ar) is the first provincial Argentine museum to specialize in contemporary art. Housed in a rehabbed 1920s building, it's open 2–8 P.M. weekdays and 4–8 P.M. weekends.

Entertainment

The main high-culture performing arts venue is the **Teatro Municipal** (Alsina 425, tel. 0291/456-3973, www.bahiablanca.gov.ar/teatro).

There are several downtown cinemas: the **Cine Plaza** (Alsina 166, tel. 0291/453-3289), **Cine Visión** (Belgrano 137, tel. 0291/451-8503), and **Cine Visual** (Chiclana 452, tel. 0291/451-8503); the latter two share a website as well (www.cinesdelcentrobb.com.ar).

Accommodations

In a well-maintained 75-year-old French-style building, **Hotel Victoria** (General Paz 84, tel. 0291/452-0522, www.hotelvictoriabb.com.ar, US$34 s, US$48 d) offers rooms with private baths, high ceilings, and fans. All rooms now have private baths at cheerful, recently modernized **Hotel Chiclana** (Chiclana 366, tel. 0291/453-0436, www.hotelchiclana.com.ar, US$38 s, US$54 d), where rates include parking (uncommon in this part of town).

Hotel Santa Rosa (Sarmiento 373, tel. 0291/452-0012, www.bvconline.com.ar/hotelsantarosa, US$31 s, US$44 d) is a small but friendly spot that, unlike most downtown hotels, has its own parking.

Bahía Blanca's finest value may be **Hotel Italia** (Brown 181, tel./fax 0291/456-2700, www.hotelitaliasa.com.ar, US$37 s, US$50 d), a handsome building with a mansard roof and rehabbed interior. Rooms are compact but well furnished, the baths glisteningly modern; interior rooms and those facing the Arribeños alleyway are quieter than those fronting on Brown.

Friendly, well-kept **Bahía Hotel** (Chiclana 251, tel. 0291/455-3050, www.bahia-hotel.com.ar, US$38 s, US$61 d) has plain but sizeable rooms, and sometimes offers a 10 percent discount for cash payments.

Four-star **Hotel Argos** (España 149, tel. 0291/455-0404, www.hotelargos.com, US$66 s, US$79 d) is widely considered Bahía's best, but it lacks the Italia's personality.

Food

La Cibeles (Alsina 301) is good for breakfast or coffee.

More like a Spanish *tasca* than the trattoria its name implies, **Pavarotti** (Belgrano 272, tel. 0291/450-0700) serves a fine *jamón serrano,* squash ravioli, and a decent pesto. The diverse menu also includes beef, seafood, and fish.

Packed with people relishing Germanic specialties and washing it down with draft beer, **Gambrinus** (Arribeños 164, tel. 0291/452-2380) is a Bahía Blanca institution dating from 1897. Unfortunately, smokers light up with impunity, even in the ostensible nonsmoking section.

El Mundo de la Parrilla (Avenida Colón 379, tel. 0291/454-6646) is popular for grilled beef. **Víctor** (Chiclana 83, tel. 0291/452-3814) is a *parrilla* that also offers fine seafood. Other seafood options include the Basque-style **Taberna Baska** (Lavalle 284, tel. 0291/452-1788, www.taberna-baska.com.ar) and **Bizkaia** (Soler 783, tel. 0291/452-0191).

For pizza, try **Il Pirata** (Lamadrid 360, tel. 0291/454-8829). **El Mago de la Empanada** (Undiano 26, tel. 0291/456-5393) has the best and widest choice of empanadas.

Information

The **Oficina de Información Turística** (Alsina 65, tel. 0291/459-4000, ext. 2393, www.bahiablanca.gov.ar, 8 A.M.–7 P.M. weekdays and 9 A.M.–7 P.M. Sat.) is directly across from the central Plaza Rivadavia, but in the basement; it has some English-speaking personnel.

Motorists will find **ACA** at Chiclana 305 (tel. 0291/455-0076).

Services

There are numerous ATMs near Plaza Rivadavia, such as at **Banco de la Nación** (Estomba 52). The travel agency **Pullman Turismo** (San Martín 171, tel. 0291/455-3344, www.pullman.com.ar) is also an exchange house.

Correo Argentino is at Moreno 34; the postal code is 8000.

Webhouse (Alsina and San Martín) has both phone and Internet service.

For laundry, try **Laverap** (Avenida Colón 197).

The **Hospital Municipal de Agudos** is at Estomba 968 (tel. 0291/459-8484, www. hmabb.gov.ar). The **Hospital Privado del Sur** is at Las Heras 164 (tel. 0291/455-0270, www. hps.com.ar).

Getting There

Bahía Blanca has air, bus, and limited rail services.

Aerolíneas Argentinas (San Martín 298, tel. 0291/456-0561) averages two flights daily to Buenos Aires's Aeroparque.

LADE (Darregueira 21, tel. 0291/452-1063) flies shifting schedules north to Mar del Plata and Aeroparque, and south to Patagonian destinations.

In new quarters barely two blocks from its old location, the **Terminal de Ómnibus San Francisco de Asís** (Drago 1800, tel. 0291/481-9615) is about two kilometers east of Plaza Rivadavia. It's a major hub for overland transportation in southern Buenos Aires Province and long-distance buses north and south.

Typical destinations, times, and fares include Sierra de la Ventana (2 hours, US$6.50), Mar del Plata (7 hours, US$28), La Plata (9 hours, US$26), Buenos Aires (8 hours, US$38–48), Viedma (3.5 hours, US$15), Bariloche (14 hours, US$45), Trelew (12 hours, US$45), Comodoro Rivadavia (15 hours, US$55), and Río Gallegos (26 hours, US$86).

Ferrobaires trains still go to Constitución from the landmark **Estación Ferrocarril Roca** (Avenida Cerri 750, tel. 0291/452-9196). Departures via Sierra de la Ventana and Coronel Pringles take place at 7:35 P.M. Tuesday and Friday; departures via Lamadrid are at 7:40 P.M. Tuesday, Thursday, and Sunday. Fares to Constitución are US$10 *turista*, US$13 *primera*, and US$18 Pullman.

Getting Around

Aeropuerto Comandante Espora (RN 3 Norte, Km 674, tel. 0291/486-1456) is 15 kilometers east of town on the naval base. AM Viajes (tel. 0291/488-2180) offers minivan transfers for US$4 pp.

City buses use magnetic *tarjebús* cards, available from downtown kiosks. Bus Nos. 505, 512, 514, 516, and 517 reach the bus terminal from downtown; No. 504 goes to Ingeniero White; and No. 505 goes to Balneario Maldonado via Avenida Colón.

Localiza (Avenida Colón 194, tel. 0291/456-2526) rents cars.

La Pampa Province

More people seem to travel around thinly populated La Pampa Province than through it, which is a pity. Immediately west of Buenos Aires Province, La Pampa has one substantial city—the capital, Santa Rosa—but a diversity of environments that range from lush grasslands to dense *caldén* forests, broad saline lakes with hordes of migratory birds (including flamingos), and rounded pink-granite mountains whose canyons sheltered the indigenous resistance to General Roca's 19th-century "Conquest of the Desert." Its top attraction is wildlife-rich Parque Nacional Lihué Calel, a worthwhile stopover for travelers to or from Patagonia.

SANTA ROSA AND VICINITY

One of Argentina's newest cities, Santa Rosa de Toay is the gateway to Parque Nacional Lihué Calel and one of the gateways to Patagonia. Before its founding in 1892, this was a dangerous frontier zone, but today it's a modern provincial capital and agricultural service center.

Santa Rosa (pop. about 115,000) is 607 kilometers west of Buenos Aires via RN 5, 641 kilometers south of Córdoba via RN 35, and

327 kilometers northwest of Bahía Blanca via RN 35. Plaza San Martín is the commercial and administrative center of its regular grid, but the Centro Cívico, seven blocks east, is the seat of provincial government.

Sights

The **Museo Provincial de Historia Natural** (Pellegrini 180, tel. 02954/42-2693, cultura-museodehistorianatural@lapampa.gov.ar, 8 A.M.–noon and 2–6 P.M. weekdays, 6–9 P.M. Sun., free) specializes in provincial paleontology, geology, and flora and fauna.

Housed in a handsome building at 9 de Julio and Villegas, the **Museo Provincial de Artes** (tel. 02954/42-7332, 8 A.M.–1 P.M. and 2–8:30 P.M. weekdays, 6:30–8:30 P.M. weekends) deals with provincial and Argentine artists, including works by Antonio Berni, Benito Quinquela Martín, and Juan Carlos Castagnino, but also has special exhibitions.

One of Santa Rosa's most distinguished constructions, the baroque **Teatro Español** (Hilario Lagos 54, tel. 02954/42-4520) dates from 1908 but is open for events only.

Reserva Provincial Parque Luro

In the early 20th century, Argentines acquired an international reputation for ostentatious excess thanks to figures like Dr. Pedro Luro (1860–1927), a businessman, politician, and sport hunter who created his own private hunting reserve, with Carpathian deer and European boar, 35 kilometers south of Santa Rosa. Then known as Estancia San Huberto, Luro's property featured an extravagant French-style lodge on 20,000 hectares of *caldén* forests and grasslands.

Now reduced to 7,500 hectares and under provincial stewardship, Parque Luro is open to the public, and Luro's lodge is a museum—like many other wealthy Argentines whose unrestrained tastes exceeded their resources, Luro, his heirs, and even subsequent purchasers were unable to hold onto the deteriorating property. Today, it's holding its own, with hiking trails, bicycle paths, and a **Centro de Interpretación** that focuses on the park's environmental and

THE OCTOPUS ON LA PAMPA

In pioneer days – which lasted into the 20th century in La Pampa Province – the *pulpería* of Chacharramendi was one of the frontier's most isolated outposts. Built of wood with exterior metal cladding, it held a local monopoly as the only general store in a vast and desolate area. It was a combination grocery, hardware store, pharmacy, shoe store, smithy, saddlery, and even justice of the peace – and sold almost anything essential for isolated homesteads.

Though it's now only 200 kilometers southwest of Santa Rosa by a smooth paved highway, this was indigenous territory when Fernando Seijó established himself in 1865; long after José Feito acquired the property in 1901, it was still insecure. The architectural details of the restored **Parador Histórico Chacharramendi** show that it could be a dangerous area: There remain several peepholes for pointing pistols or rifles in self-defense, and the main store had a basement hatch leading to an escape tunnel. All the goods were kept behind bars (though this was not an unusual practice on the frontier) and clients pointed out what products interested them.

Also known as the Boliche de Feito and El Viejo Almacén, the *pulpería* served as a hotel, bar, and general gathering place – one of the frontier's few social institutions (according to legend, one of its guests was the famous bandit Juan Bairoletto). It operated until 1975, when the Feito family donated it to the province; from the surviving account books alone, it would probably be possible to reconstruct the hamlet's history.

For Neuquén-bound motorists on RN 143, Chacharramendi makes an ideal breather and even a stopover for gas, food, and lodging, though its sole hotel and restaurant offer no luxury. As the solitary establishment offering a range of services, to a degree Chacharramendi still operates on the principle of the *pulpería* – a Spanish-American term that derives from the word for "octopus."

cultural history. There are also a small zoo, places to picnic, and a **Sala de Carruajes** with a collection of classic horse carriages.

Guided tours of the **Castillo Luro** (RN 35, Km 292, tel. 02954/49-9000, www.parqueluro.gov.ar) and grounds are available on request for US$2; park admission costs an additional US$1. Hours are 9 A.M.–7 P.M. daily in summer, 10 A.M.–6 P.M. daily the rest of the year.

Meals are available at the restaurant **El Quincho** (tel. 02954/42-0071).

Entertainment

The **Teatro Español** (Hilario Lagos 54, tel. 02954/42-4520) hosts the biggest performing arts events. For movies, try **Cine Don Bosco** (Avenida Uruguay 795, tel. 02954/43-9935) or **Cine Amadeus** (Coronel Gil 31, tel. 02954/41-4490).

Shopping

Santa Rosa deserves a stop for souvenir-seekers after gaucho gear. Sharing quarters with the provincial tourist office, the **Mercado Artesanal** (Avenida Luro 400) displays quality goods from throughout the province. Other outlets include down-the-block **Artesanías Argentinas** (Avenida Luro 616, tel. 02954/41-4150) and **El Matrero** (Pellegrini 86, tel. 02954/42-2076).

Accommodations

Only a block from the bus terminal, **Hostería Santa Rosa** (Hipólito Yrigoyen 696, tel. 02954/42-3868, US$17 s, US$26 d) is a good budget choice. Friendly **Residencial Atuel** (Avenida Pedro Luro 356, tel. 02954/42-2597, www.atuel.aehglp.org.ar, US$26 s, US$32 d) is directly across from the terminal. **Hotel San Martín** (Alsina 101, tel. 02954/42-2549, www.hsanmartin.com.ar, US$32 s, US$48 d) is more central.

The high-rise **Hotel Calfucurá** (Avenida San Martín 695, tel. 02954/42-3612, www.hotelcalfucura.com, US$50–74 s, US$68–74 d) is more conspicuous than luxurious, thanks to its high-climbing mural of the cacique Calfucurá,

who led the resistance to Roca's invaders. For a couple, the larger higher-priced rooms are worth the difference.

On eight hectares east of town, Santa Rosa's best is the **La Campiña Club Hotel** (RN 5 Km 604, tel. 02954/42-6714, www.lacampina.com, US$55 s, US$86 d). In addition to a sauna, a gym, a hot tub, and other recreational facilities, this Spanish colonial–style hotel has its own restaurant.

Food

At the northwest corner of Plaza San Martín, **La Recova** (Hipólito Yrigoyen and Avellaneda, tel. 02954/42-4444) is the best breakfast choice.

Don Pepe (Pellegrini 115, tel. 02954/43-0095) serves inexpensive *tenedor libre* beef and pasta. There are several decent pizzerias, including **Pizza Quatro** (Sarmiento and Pellegrini, tel. 02954/43-4457) and particularly **La Ochava** (Avenida San Martín and Urquiza, tel. 02954/43-4240), which has sidewalk seating.

Cantina Rumi (Pueyrredón 9, tel. 02954/41-1666) gets lots of families, but it has a more sophisticated menu of homemade pastas, with about a dozen options for sauces, than that usually suggests. Bright and cheerful, with excellent service, it also offers *parrillada* and pizza.

Heladería Robert (Avenida Luro 424, tel. 02954/43-7170) has outstanding ice cream.

Information

Directly across from the bus terminal, the provincial **Subsecretaría de Turismo** (Avenida Pedro Luro 400, tel. 02954/42-5060, www.turismolapampa.gov.ar) is open 8:30 A.M.–8:30 P.M. daily, though this can vary somewhat throughout the year. Well-stocked with maps and brochures, it also has English-speaking staff.

At the terminal, the municipal **Centro de Informes** (Avenida Pedro Luro 365, tel. 02954/42-2952, www.santarosa.gov.ar/turismo.htm) stays open 24 hours.

For motorists, **ACA** (Avenida San Martín

102, tel. 02954/42-2435) is at the southeast corner of Plaza San Martín.

Services
Several banks near Plaza San Martín have ATMs, including **Banco de la Nación** (Avenida Roca 1).

Correo Argentino is at Rivadavia 202; the postal code is 6300.

Telefónica Centro (Avellaneda 190) has phone and fax services. For Internet, try **CTS,** on the north side of Plaza San Martín.

Swiss Travel (Pellegrini 219, tel. 02954/42-7507) is a full-service agency.

Burbujas (Rivadavia 253) does the laundry.

Hospital Lucio Molas (Raúl P. Diaz and Pilcomayo, tel. 02954/45-5000) is two kilometers north of downtown.

Getting There and Around
Aeropuerto Santa Rosa (tel. 02954/43-2915), about three kilometers north of town, is easily reached by taxi or *remise* (about US$3).

Aerolíneas Argentinas (tel. 02954/43-3076 at the airport) flies three times weekly to Aeroparque (Buenos Aires) via Bahía Blanca.

Santa Rosa is a key crossroads for bus services throughout the republic. The **Estación Terminal de Ómnibus** (Avenida Pedro Luro 365, tel. 02954/42-0183) is at the Centro Cívico.

Sample destinations and fares include Bahía Blanca (4.5 hours, US$20), Neuquén (six hours, US$30), Buenos Aires (9 hours, US$35–45), Córdoba (9 hours, US$35–45), Mar del Plata (9 hours, US$35), Mendoza (12 hours, US$45–55), and Bariloche (13 hours, US$35–55).

【 PARQUE NACIONAL LIHUÉ CALEL
Rising gently but perceptibly above the arid flats of southern La Pampa Province, Lihué Calel's landscape stands out not just for its topography, flora, and fauna but also for its archaeological and historical importance. Its topography has created niches for its surprisingly abundant plant and animal life, but it also supported the lifestyle of pre-Columbian hunter-gatherers—still visible in several rock-art sites—and sheltered the indigenous resistance against invasions by Spain and, later, the Argentine state.

After the Mapuche cacique Namuncurá finally surrendered to General Roca's invaders in 1885, Lihué Calel (whose Pehuenche name means "The Range of Life") fell into private hands as Estancia Santa María. Following decades of exploitation for agriculture, ranching, and even copper mining, it was expropriated by the province in 1964. Later donated to the APN for a national park, it has become a regular stop on the itineraries of some international overland expedition companies but is still undervisited.

Reaching a maximum elevation of 589 meters above sea level, Lihué Calel comprises 32,000 hectares of varied terrain, 226 kilometers southwest of Santa Rosa via RN 35 and RN 152. Its northerly slopes are gentle, but the southerly approach is steeper. The incorporation of the Salitral Levalle salt flats, to the north, constitutes a major expansion.

Flora and Fauna
Lihué Calel is arid, with only about 400 millimeters of precipitation per annum, but that precipitation supports nearly 350 plant species in a variety of associations and microenvironments. In a sense, Lihué Calel's mountains are an archipelago surrounded by desert rather than water.

Water, though, contributes to its biodiversity. Rain may be infrequent, but it collects and remains more easily in some areas than others, and can support surprisingly lush vegetation. The main plant association is the dry scrub known as *monte,* but more humid spots support denser groves of *caldén,* a relative of the common mesquite. In shadier areas, ferns may even grow within rocky cracks, while cacti colonize more exposed areas. Lichens form circular patterns on the more exposed rocks.

Thanks both to forest cover and wide-open spaces, wildlife is more abundant and conspicuous than in the densely settled areas of Buenos Aires Province. Rare pumas have been seen, but smaller predators like Geoffroy's cat, the jaguarundi, and the Patagonian fox also live here. Hundreds of guanacos graze the open grasslands; other common mammals include the *mara* (Patagonian hare) and viscacha, related to the chinchilla.

Birds are also plentiful, ranging from the flightless rhea or *ñandú* to predators that include the common *carancho* (crested caracara) and the rare crowned eagle. When the *caldén* fruits, there are many *loros barranqueros* (parakeets).

Harmless lizards are common, but beware the rare but venomous pit vipers commonly known as *yarará*.

Sights and Recreation

A visitors center, at the park campground, provides a sophisticated and well-illustrated account of the park's natural and cultural history.

One of the best areas to view wildlife is the *caldén* forest near the campground and park headquarters—at dawn and dusk, foxes scurry among the campsites, and countless birds call from the shade trees. The campground is also the starting point for the **Sendero El Huitru,** a well-marked nature trail through the *monte* that leads to some sadly vandalized petroglyphs.

Another trail leads to the park's highest point, the 589-meter **Cerro de la Sociedad Científica Argentina,** but the open granite slopes provide numerous alternative routes. The summit panorama includes the entire Lihué Calel range, the arid pampas, the Salitral Levalle to the north, and shallow marshes like Laguna Urre Lauquen to the southwest.

Well west of the visitors center, the ruined **Viejo Casco** was headquarters for the former Estancia Santa María; with a vehicle, it's possible to loop through the **Valle de las Pinturas,** whose unblemished petroglyphs are about 2,000 years old.

Practicalities

Near the visitors center, the APN operates a free, shady **campground** with fire pits, picnic tables, electricity until 11 P.M., and clean bathrooms with flush toilets and hot showers.

The Administración de Parques Nacionales has a **Centro de Informes** about two kilometers west of the well-marked park entrance on RN 152. Official hours are 8 A.M.–noon and 3–6 P.M. in summer, 9 A.M.–noon and 2–6 P.M. the rest of the year, but in practice the rangers are accessible at almost any reasonable hour. There is no park admission fee. Its main office is in the town of General Acha (tel. 02952/43-6595, lihuecalel@apn.gov.ar).

Leaving Santa Rosa four times between 12:30 and 5:30 A.M., **El Valle** (tel. 02954/43-2694 in Santa Rosa) passes the park entrance (US$10) en route to Puelches. Neuquén-bound buses with **TAC** (tel. 02954/43-7779) and **TUS** (tel. 02954/43-2140) pass the park entrance as well, also leaving in the early A.M. hours.

MESOPOTAMIA AND THE PARANÁ

North of Buenos Aires, the Río Paraná is one of the world's great rivers. In South America, only the Amazon is longer; from its source in tropical Brazil to its mouth at the temperate Atlantic, its 3,998 kilometers make it the world's 13th-longest river and longer than the Mississippi. Draining more than 1 million square kilometers, it flows south from Brazil, forms much of the border between Argentina and Paraguay, and finally meets the Río Uruguay north of Buenos Aires to form the Río de la Plata.

For the northeastern Argentine provinces, the Paraná and the Uruguay are a great part of their visitor appeal. In the area between the rivers, known collectively as Mesopotamia, the provinces of Entre Ríos, Corrientes, and Misiones boast natural attractions like the rolling palm savannas of Parque Nacional El Palmar; the wildlife-rich wetlands of Esteros del Iberá, and the thunderous Iguazú Falls.

They also have cultural allure: the Entre Ríos city of Gualeguaychú hosts Argentina's liveliest Carnaval, though the provincial capital of Corrientes comes a close second. Misiones takes its name from the colonial Jesuit outposts, now in ruins, that inspired the film *The Mission*.

On the Paraná's western banks, the port of Rosario and its agricultural hinterland make Santa Fe Province an economic powerhouse. Rosario, for its part, is a city of monuments and a vigorous cultural life that challenges Córdoba's claim as the republic's second city. North of Santa Fe, Chaco and Formosa Provinces are hot, subtropical lowlands whose national parks

MESOPOTAMIA

HIGHLIGHTS

◖ Gualeguaychú: Home to Argentina's liveliest Carnaval for a few late-summer weekends, this is the country's biggest party town. Situated on the Río Uruguay, it's a popular riverside beach resort year-round (page 153).

◖ Parque Nacional El Palmar: This nearly undeveloped palm savanna on the Río Uruguay offers a glimpse of Argentine Mesopotamia before the arrival of the Spaniards. Its unique environment harbors many kinds of mammals and birds (page 157).

◖ Esteros del Iberá: The masses throng to thunderous Iguazú, but those in the know prefer the silent, wildlife-rich marshes of central Corrientes Province. This unique environment is at risk, though, from exotic forestry projects and rising water levels caused by the Yacyretá dam (page 164).

◖ San Ignacio Miní: History lives in the vivid red ruins of Argentina's best-preserved Jesuit mission, among many in the upper Paraná. The details were sculpted by Guaraní artisans under the tutelage of South America's most intriguing missionary order (page 177).

◖ Parque Nacional Iguazú: One of the continent's greatest natural sights, Iguazú Falls makes Niagara look like a leaky faucet. For a unique perspective, avoiding the crowds, schedule your visit for the full moon – it's more magical under moonlight (page 179).

◖ Monumento Nacional a la Bandera: In Rosario (perhaps Argentina's most underrated city), this huge monument pays tribute to the Argentine flag and its designer, Manuel Belgrano (page 191).

◖ Parque Nacional Chaco: If crossing the Chaco to or from Salta, take a detour to sample the flora and fauna of the humid eastern region in this haven of forest and wetlands (page 203).

◖ Parque Nacional Río Pilcomayo: In little-visited Formosa Province, this park of shallow, shimmering waters along the Paraguayan border is an overlooked gem (page 206).

LOOK FOR ◖ TO FIND RECOMMENDED SIGHTS, ACTIVITIES, DINING, AND LODGING.

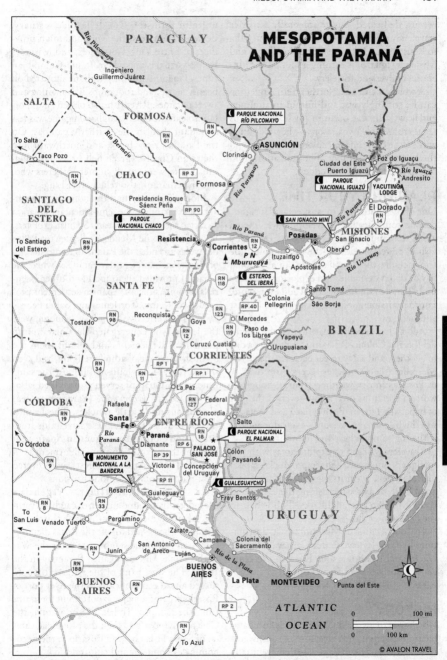

MESOPOTAMIA AND
THE PARANÁ

PARAGUAY

SALTA

FORMOSA

Río Pilcomayo

Ingeniero
Guillermo Juárez

Parque Nacional
Río Pilcomayo

RN
86

RN
81

RP 3

ASUNCIÓN

Clorinda

Ciudad del Este
Puerto Iguazú

Foz do Iguaçu

Río Iguazú
Andresito

To Salta

Taco Pozo

Río Bermejo

CHACO

Formosa

Río Paraguay

Parque
Nacional Iguazú

YACUTINGA
LODGE

RN
16

SANTIAGO
DEL
ESTERO

Presidencia Roque
Sáenz Peña

RP 90

El Dorado

RN
14

Parque Nacional Chaco

Río Paraná

San Ignacio Miní

MISIONES

RN
89

Resistencia

Corrientes

RN
12

Posadas

San Ignacio

To Santiago
del Estero

P N
Mburucuyá

Ituzaingó

Oberá

Apóstoles

Río Uruguay

SANTA FE

RN
118

Esteros
del Iberá

Santo Tomé

Colonia
Pellegrini

São Borja

RP 40

BRAZIL

Tostado

RN
98

Reconquista

RN
123

Goya

RN
12

Mercedes

RN
119

Paso de
los Libres

Yapeyú

Uruguaiana

RN
34

Curuzú Cuatiá

CORRIENTES

RP 1

RN
11

RP 1

La Paz

CÓRDOBA

Rafaela

RN
127

Federal

RN
19

Santa
Fe

Concordia

Río
Paraná

Paraná

ENTRE RÍOS

Salto

To Córdoba

Diamante

RN
18

Parque Nacional
El Palmar

RP 6

RN
9

MONUMENTO
NACIONAL A LA
BANDERA

RP 39

PALACIO
SAN JOSÉ

Colón

Paysandú

Victoria

Concepción
del Uruguay

RP 11

GUALEGUAYCHÚ

To
San Luis

Rosario

RN
33

Gualeguay

Fray Bentos

RN
8

Venado Tuerto

Pergamino

URUGUAY

RN
7

Junín

San Antonio
de Areco

Zárate

Luján

Campana

Colonia del
Sacramento

RN
188

BUENOS
AIRES

RN
5

BUENOS
AIRES

Río de la Plata

La Plata

MONTEVIDEO

Punta del Este

RP 2

ATLANTIC
OCEAN

RN
3

To Azul

0   100 mi

0   100 km

© AVALON TRAVEL

MESOPOTAMIA

reward dedicated, environmentally sensitive travelers; and the trans-Chaco route from Salta to Resistencia, Corrientes (including Iberá), and Misiones (Iguazú) is earning a spot on the itineraries of overland travelers.

A word on climate: Northeastern Argentina can be stiflingly hot and humid in summer, and heavy rains can occur in any season. Locals say there are only two seasons—the mild sunny winter (the best time to explore the region) and the hot muggy summer. The transition from one to the other can be sudden.

PLANNING YOUR TIME

One of the continent's most spectacular sights, despite some negative developments, Iguazú alone demands at least three days from any visitor, preferably during the full moon; if the trip includes the Brazilian side, an additional day or two is desirable, and exploring the area's more remote rain forests could add even more. For the mission at San Ignacio, figure at least another day.

Add no less than three days to tour the Esteros del Iberá at Colonia Pellegrini, and figure a day to get there and a day to get back via the city of Mercedes (there's quicker access from the city of Posadas in dry weather). Iberá, though, is worth a trip in its own right—even at the cost of bypassing Iguazú. Both Iguazú and Iberá are worthwhile at any season—even during the withering summer heat and humidity.

Travelers wishing to explore areas with few foreigners can use the Chaco provincial capital of Resistencia, with its vigorous cultural and artistic life, as a base for visiting the Chaco and Río Pilcomayo National Parks. This is best in the cool winter, however.

In southernmost Mesopotamia, destinations like Gualeguaychú (for Carnaval), Parque Nacional El Palmar, and Rosario are close enough for weekend excursions from Buenos Aires.

HISTORY

Northeastern Argentina's history is inseparable from the two great rivers—the southward-flowing Uruguay and Paraná—that eventually unite to form the Río de la Plata estuary. Between the rivers, the Mesopotamian provinces of Entre Ríos, Corrientes, and Misiones form a virtual island where, in pre-Columbian times, Guaraní-speaking Indians subsisted on beans, maize, and root crops like manioc and sweet potatoes. River fish also played an important role in the diet, though wild game was less abundant than in the southerly pampas. On the Paraná's right bank, and northward into the Gran Chaco's "green hell," the aboriginal inhabitants were mostly hunter-gatherers who, like the Guaraní, also relied on fishing.

More numerous than the nomadic inhabitants of the pampas, the semi-sedentary Guaraní attracted the attention of early Spanish explorers. In 1537, Pedro de Mendoza's lieutenant Pedro de Ayolas ascended the Paraná to found the city of Asunción, in present-day Paraguay, where the Guaraní provided them food and other essentials. From Asunción, Spanish settlement proceeded south into Corrientes and Santa Fe.

The most effective colonizers, though, were the Jesuits who congregated the Guaraní into permanent settlements and taught them the Spanish language, Catholic religion, and even skilled trades like violin-making. At the same time, many Guaraní served as unskilled labor on the Jesuits' *yerba mate* (Paraguayan tea) plantations and cattle ranches. The Jesuits' success provoked Portuguese slave raids from Brazil and political intrigues in Spain that brought their expulsion from the Americas in 1767, and lush subtropical forests soon covered their monumental sandstone missions.

In postcolonial times, Argentine Mesopotamia became an area of caudillos (provincial strongmen)—most notably Justo José Urquiza, who helped topple the Rosas dictatorship—and then the staging point for the War of the Triple Alliance against Paraguay in the 1870s. The west bank of the Paraná, though, surged ahead economically as the river port of Rosario became a major export point for grains from the pampas. Today, Mesopotamia, the Chaco provinces, and even the provincial capital of Santa Fe lag behind Rosario in their economic development and cultural life.

Entre Ríos Province

After Buenos Aires's unrelentingly level pampas, the lush rolling hills of Entre Ríos can be a pleasure. As befits its name ("between the rivers"), the province's great natural asset is its enormous southbound rivers, the Paraná and the Uruguay, that unite to form the Río de la Plata (often glossed into English as "River Plate"). Gualeguaychú's summer Carnaval is the biggest event, while the palm savannas of Parque Nacional El Palmar preserve a truly unique environment.

◖ GUALEGUAYCHÚ

Entre Ríos's biggest party town, Gualeguaychú hosts Argentina's top Carnaval celebration—not quite Rio, but worthwhile if you're in Buenos Aires instead of Brazil. Dating from 1783, it has a smattering of colonial constructions, but it is most popular with Argentines for access to its namesake river.

To the east, the Puente Internacional General Libertador San Martín offers the southernmost bridge access into Uruguay, to the city of Fray Bentos. In recent years, though, anger over a proposed pulp mill on the Uruguayan side has brought roadblock demonstrations by Argentine environmental activists and less savory opportunists.

Gualeguaychú (pop. about 100,000) is 220 kilometers north of Buenos Aires via RN 14 and an eastbound lateral road that leads directly to the central Plaza San Martín, a square occupying four full blocks. To the east, the Río Gualeguaychú, a tributary of the larger Uruguay, meanders southward.

Sights and Recreation

Dating from 1914, the city's only national historical monument is the **Teatro Gualeguaychú** (Urquiza 705). It's still the principal high-culture venue, with theater, music, and dance performances.

the towers of the cathedral of Gualeguaychú

At the northeast corner of Plaza San Martín, Gualeguaychú's oldest construction (1800) is the **Solar de los Haedo** (San José 105, 9 A.M.–11:45 A.M. and 5–8 P.M. Wed.–Sat., 9 A.M.–11:45 A.M. Sun., free), which Italian patriot Giuseppe Garibaldi used as his headquarters during the Uruguayan struggle against Rosas.

José S. Álvarez, better known by his pen name Fray Mocho, resided at the **Casa de Fray Mocho** (Fray Mocho 135), which awaits restoration as a museum. Álvarez founded the early-20th-century satirical magazine *Caras y Caretas,* the counterpart of England's *Punch.*

On the grounds of the former **Estación Ferrocarril Urquiza** (railroad station, Avenida Rocamora and Avenida Irazusta), the enclosed **Corsódromo** is the main site for the midsummer Carnaval parades. The station also contains the open-air **Museo Ferroviario,** with antique steam locomotives, dining cars, and other rolling stock.

Entertainment and Events

The landmark **Teatro Municipal** (Urquiza 705, tel. 03446/42-7989) remains the principal performing arts locale.

Oriented toward visitors from Buenos Aires, Gualeguaychú's **Carnaval del País** (www.carnavaldelpais.com.ar) celebrations take place weekends in mid to late summer, depending on the Lenten calendar. If bad weather intervenes, though, the final weekend may even be pushed back in Lent. Admission to the Corsódromo costs around US$16 pp, with the best reserved seats an additional US$10 pp.

Accommodations

Gualeguaychú is always a popular summer destination, but on Carnaval weekends accommodations are at a premium, reservations almost imperative, and prices rise. Most choices are central, but lower-end places lack air-conditioning.

Residencial Amalfi (25 de Mayo 571, tel. 03446/42-6818, amalfi@hotmail.com, US$16 s, US$27 d) is in an attractive older building but is otherwise plain. On summer weekends, though, prices more than double.

Its Bavarian exterior looks utterly out of place in subtropical Entre Ríos, but the simple **Hotel Alemán** (Bolívar 535, tel. 03446/42-6153, www.hotelaleman.com.ar, US$ 53 s or d) offers good value.

Hotel Puerto Sol (San Lorenzo 477, tel. 03446/43-4017, www.hotelpuertosol.com.ar, US$68 s or d) is a solid midsize hotel with midsize rooms, some with balconies and others whose windows face the interior gardens. The service is outstanding in its price range.

Other possibilities include **Hotel Berlín** (Bolívar 733, tel. 03446/42-5111, www.hotel-berlin.com.ar, US$73 s or d), which has improved services, but the rooms are still on the small side. **Hotel Embajador** (3 de Febrero 115, tel. 03446/42-4414, www.hotel-embajador.com, US$85 s or d) is a more modern construction.

Hotel Aguay (Costanera 138, tel. 03446/42-2099, www.hotelaguay.com.ar, US$79 s, US$111 d), a four-star entry overlooking the river, has become the best in town.

Food

For fish fresh from the river, don't miss **Dacal** (Costanera and Andrade, tel. 03446/42-7602), and there are several others along the waterfront, including **Lo de Carlitos** (San Martín 206, tel. 03446/43-2582).

One block west of the Costanera, authorities have turned Calle Alem into a shady cobbled street with planter boxes and wide sidewalks where a number of restaurants, mostly pizzerias, have taken hold. The most popular are **Águila Club** (3 de Caballería 300, corner of Alem), which also has live music, and **El Galpón de Mi Viejo** (Alem 377, tel. 03446/42-7252).

For ice cream, the best choice is the riverfront **Bahillo** (Costanera and San Lorenzo, tel. 03446/42-6240); it also has a downtown branch (25 de Mayo and Italia, tel. 03446/42-7349).

Information and Services

Gualeguaychú's main **Oficina de Información Turística Puerto** (Tiscornia and Goldaracena, tel. 03446/42-3668, www.

PALACIO SAN JOSÉ

In a symbolic challenge to his Buenos Aires rival Juan Manuel de Rosas, Entre Ríos caudillo Justo José Urquiza (1801–1870) began this improvised yet imposing palace in 1848, under the supervision of contractor Jacinto Dellepiane. Italian-born architect Pedro Fossati, though, brought out its full Italianate grandeur in completing it between 1857 and 1860.

Twin towers mark the location of Urquiza's 38-room residence, still isolated in the middle of the *entrerriano* countryside, surrounded by an outer ring of native forest and an inner ring of elegant gardens. The palace itself surrounds two major patios, built of Carrara marble, while outbuildings include a private chapel, a carriage house, a bakery, a smithy, an aviary, and a *pulpería* (store).

The furnishings include Urquiza's 8.5-meter dining room table, suitable for hosting prestigious guests like Bartolomé Mitre and Urquiza's onetime critic Domingo F. Sarmiento, who eventually reconciled with the caudillo. The kitchen includes an equally impressive octagonal stove, while other sections are decorated with French tiles and distinctive wrought iron.

The chapel contains notable religious images, while marble statuary graces the gardens – though some of it was stolen in 1991. Declared a national monument in 1935, the complex had one of Argentina's first modern plumbing systems, bringing water nearly two kilometers from the Río Gualeguaychú by pumps and pipes. In fact, Urquiza even built an artificial lake for recreational sailing.

Urquiza, who earned his fame by defeating Rosas at the battle of Caseros in 1852, did not live to enjoy his retirement here. On April 11, 1870, agents of his political rival Ricardo López Jordán assassinated the caudillo in his own bedroom; Urquiza's wife, 25 years younger than he, made the room into a memorial shrine.

The Palacio San José (tel. 03442/43-2620, www.palaciosanjose.com.ar) is 30 kilometers west of Concepción del Uruguay via RP 39. Hours are 8 A.M.-7 P.M. weekdays, 9 A.M.-6 P.M. weekends and holidays, with four or five guided tours per day. There are occasional nighttime tours, for which visitors should consult the excellent website (in Spanish only). Admission costs US$1.25.

ACCOMMODATIONS AND FOOD

The nearest accommodations are in Concepción del Uruguay, where the three-star **Hotel Carlos 1°** (Eva Perón 115, tel. 03442/42-6776, US$50 s, US$66 d) is a good value. The palace's restaurant **La Posta de San José** (tel. 03442/49-2196) serves lunch Thursday–Sunday and dinner Friday–Saturday only, but there are also many options in Concepción.

GETTING THERE AND AWAY

There's no direct public transportation to Palacio San José, but Basavilbaso- and Paraná-bound buses on RP 39 from Concepción del Uruguay pass within a half-hour's walk of the grounds. There are also tours from Concepción, and the cost of a *remise* is not excessive – about US$15-20 including a two-hour wait at the site.

MESOPOTAMIA

---

gualeguaychuturismo.com) is on the riverfront Paseo del Puerto. At the bus station, it also has a convenient **Oficina de Información Turística** (Avenida Artigas and Bulevar Jurado, tel. 03446/44-0706). Both have helpful personnel, thorough information that includes accommodation details, and improved maps. Hours are 8 A.M.–10 P.M. daily in summer, 8 A.M.–8 P.M. the rest of the year.

For motorists, **ACA** is at Urquiza 1001 (tel. 03446/42-6088).

Half a dozen banks along Avenida 25 de Mayo have **ATMs**, but there are no exchange houses.

Correo Argentino (Urquiza and Angel Elías) is the post office; the postal code is 2820. There are **Telecentros** at the bus terminal and at 25 de Mayo 562. **Cibernet** (25 de Mayo 874) has fast Internet access.

For medical services, **Hospital Centenario** (25 de Mayo and Pasteur, tel. 03446/42-7831) is west of downtown.

Getting There and Around

Gualeguaychú's shiny new **Terminal de Ómnibus** (Avenida Artigas and Bulevar Jurado, tel. 03446/44-0688) is at the southwest approach to town. Buses to Fray Bentos and other Uruguayan destinations are suspended until further notice because of the pulp mill controversy.

Otherwise, sample destinations, times, and fares include Buenos Aires (3 hours, US$11); Paraná (5 hours, US$12); and Córdoba (11 hours, US$40).

COLÓN

Of all the towns along the Río Uruguay, Colón possesses the most charm. Founded in 1863, it lacks even Gualeguaychú's limited colonial character, but its small-town intimacy, 19th-century architecture, and tree-lined streets and riverfront join to make it an ideal stopover for north- or southbound travelers along RN 14. It's also a border crossing, linked to the larger Uruguayan city of Paysandú via the Puente Internacional General Artigas, the bridge over the river.

On the Uruguay's west bank, Colón (pop. about 21,000) is 104 kilometers north of Gualeguaychú and 330 kilometers north of Buenos Aires. It is 50 kilometers south of Parque Nacional El Palmar and 101 kilometers south of Concordia, the next major Uruguayan border crossing.

Sights and Recreation

The parklike waterfront along **Avenida Costanera Gobernador Quirós** is the main attraction, while the **Parque Doctor Herminio Quirós,** at its south end, is the site of mid-February's Fiesta Nacional de la Artesanía, an annual crafts fair that also showcases live folkloric music.

General Urquiza himself decreed construction of the 1860s **Aduana de Colón** (Avenida Costanera and Emilio Gouchón), a customs house for the export of farm products from nearby Colonia San José. The distinctive building now serves as the municipal tourist office.

Four kilometers northwest of town, the

Molino Forclaz (9 A.M.–noon and 4–7 P.M. Tues.–Sun., US$0.50), Colón's first flour mill, is a national historical monument. Eight kilometers west, the **Museo Histórico Regional Colonia San José** (Urquiza 1127, tel. 03447/47-0088, www.museosanjose.com. ar, 9 A.M.–noon and 3–6 P.M. Tues.–Sun., US$0.50) chronicles the history of the province's second major agricultural colony.

For excursions into the gallery forests and onto the sandbanks of the Uruguay, contact English-speaking **Itaicorá** (San Martín 97, tel. 03447/42-3360, www.itaicora.com). Itaicorá also visits nearby overland destinations like Liebig, site of a now-abandoned meat-extract plant.

The **Cine Chaplin** (J. J. Paso 122, tel. 03447/42-3723) shows recent movies.

Accommodations and Food

For budget lodgings, try the basic **Hospedaje Bolívar** (Bolívar 577, tel. 03447/42-2721, US$2 d).

In a handsome 1880s building exuding real character, the misleadingly named **⟨ Hostería Restaurant del Puerto** (Peyret 158, tel. 03447/42-2698, www.hosteriadecolon.com.ar, US$58 s or d) has, after several years, added a restaurant to live up to its name. Built on a slope, its centerpiece is an attractive sunken patio, while the surrounding rooms all have antique furniture and tile floors. A new wing contains more contemporary rooms, and it has added a pool as well.

Impressively modernized, the **Hotel Plaza** (Belgrano and 12 de Abril, tel. 03447/42-1043, www.hotel-plaza.com.ar, US$73–121 s or d) has reclaimed a spot at the top of the accommodations pyramid.

Its brick walls decorated with photographs of Colón's historic downtown, **⟨ El Viejo Almacén** (Urquiza and J. J. Paso, tel. 03447/42-2216) serves a surprisingly spicy *boga a la cerveza* (river fish in beer sauce) for US$8, with most other entrées slightly more expensive. There are also pastas and *parrillada,* plus fine empanadas and salads. For accommodations, it operates the

Hostería Viejo Almacén (Urquiza 106, tel. 03447/42-2216, jgermanier@argentina.com, US$53 d).

The best new eatery is **Chiva Chiva** (Urquiza and Almirante Brown, tel. 03447/42-4815, www.chivachiva.com.ar), a combination restaurant-bar and art space, where friendly personnel (including one fluent English-speaker) serve mixed drinks, river fish, pastas, and meat dishes in the US$6–10 range.

La Cosquilla del Ángel (Peyret 180, tel. 03447/42-2371) serves three-course meals in the US$8 range, including starters like pâté, and entrées like fish and ravioli, plus homemade bread. Down the block, **Campo Adentro** (Peyret and Chacabuco, tel. 03447/42-2003) is a cavernous *parrilla* that, in addition to beef, also has a good selection of grilled river fish—but avoid their heavy sauces in order to concentrate on the fish itself.

Heladería Italia (12 de Abril 173, tel. 03447/42-1191) has exceptional ice cream.

Information and Services

The helpful municipal **Secretaría de Turismo y Ambiente Humano** (Costanera and Gouchón, tel. 03447/42-1996 or 03447/42-1233, www.colon.gov.ar, 7 A.M.–9 P.M. daily) occupies the historic customs headquarters. It distributes decent maps and brochures on Colón and vicinity.

Banco Nación (12 de Abril 151) has an ATM. **Correo Argentino** is at Artigas and 12 de Abril; the postal code is 3280. **Telecentro Shopping Colón** (12 de Abril 338) provides phone service. **Barnet** (Lavalle 32) offers fast Internet access.

Getting There and Around

The **Terminal de Ómnibus** (Rocamora and 9 de Julio, tel. 03447/42-1716) is a stop for long-distance buses on north–south RN 14; northbound buses pass the entrance to Parque Nacional El Palmar.

Copay and Río Uruguay alternate bus service to Paysandú, Uruguay (1 hour, US$3) at 12:45 A.M., and 12:15, 1:45, and 6:30 P.M. except Sunday, when there's an 8:45 P.M. bus only.

PARQUE NACIONAL EL PALMAR

Midway between the cities of Colón and Concordia, 8,500-hectare Parque Nacional El Palmar offers a backward glimpse of what Entre Ríos and adjacent areas of Uruguay and Brazil looked like before 19th-century farming, forestry, and cattle altered the ecology of the native *yatay*-palm savannas. Although *Syagrus yatay* remains in substantial numbers here and its reproduction has improved since the park's establishment in 1966, its population structure is uneven—some individuals are more than 200 years old, but "middle-aged" trees are few.

The unnatural clusters of older specimens caused by grazing livestock give real character to the park's surviving savannas, but they are not its only attraction. Along with the gallery forests along the Río Uruguay and its tributary creeks, they provide ample habitat for mammals, birds, and other wildlife.

There is also unwelcome animal life: About 3,000 European boar, introduced for hunting in the 1930s, inhibit the *yatay*'s reproduction by consuming fallen seeds (there is now a program to reduce the boar population by hunting). Introduced for similar reasons, the axis deer (native to India) competes with native cervids.

El Palmar is an 8,500-hectare unit 360 kilometers north of Buenos Aires and 50 kilometers north of Colón via RN 14; it is 50 kilometers south of Concordia via the same highway. Except for a small information center at the highway turnoff, all services are 11 kilometers east.

Flora and Fauna

The park takes its name from the *yatay*, which grows up to 18 meters in height with a diameter of 40 centimeters. The most conspicuous mammals are the innocuous semiaquatic *carpincho* (capybara, the world's largest rodent, weighing up to 60 kg), and the chinchilla relative viscacha, once abundant but now reduced in numbers. Wild boar (a European introduction responsible for habitat damage), foxes, and raccoons are also common.

The ostrich-like *ñandú* or rhea races across

MESOPOTAMIA

the savannas, but the wetlands and gallery forests are also home to cormorants, egrets, herons, storks, caracaras, kingfishers, parakeets, and woodpeckers. The most conspicuous reptiles are the large nocturnal toads that invade the campground showers and toilets; bites from the highly venomous *yarará,* a pit viper that reaches upward of two meters, are rare, but it deserves respect in its savanna habitat.

Sights and Recreation

Near the Los Loros campground, beaches along the **Río Uruguay** draw swimmers and boaters, but hikers and cyclists can enjoy **Paseo Arroyo los Loros,** a better wildlife-watching area northwest of the campground (rental canoes and bicycles are available at the campground store).

Five kilometers southwest of Los Loros, a gravel road leads across the savanna to **Arroyo El Palmar,** a Río Uruguay tributary that's also one of the best areas to see the *yatay* palms that give the park its name. There's a fine swimming hole here.

Accommodations and Food

The nearest hotels are in the cities of Colón and Concordia. El Palmar's only accommodations are at shady **Camping El Palmar** (tel. 03447/42-3378), which has showers, a grocery, and a *confitería* for simple meals. Campers pay a one-time fee of US$2.50 per tent plus US$2.50 pp per day.

Information

At the park entrance, immediately east of RN 14, rangers collect an admission fee (US$2 for Argentines, US$4.50 for foreigners).

Across from the campground, the APN operates a **Centro de Interpretación** (tel. 03447/49-3053, elpalmar@apn.gov.ar, 8 A.M.–6 P.M. daily). In addition to permanent natural history displays, it offers videos on park attractions and ecology.

Getting There and Around

RN 14 goes directly past the park entrance, so any north- or southbound bus between Colón

and Concordia will drop passengers there, and even long-distance buses may do so. There is, however, no public transport over the 11 kilometers from the park entrance to the visitors center and camping area. Hitching is feasible, as are *remises* from Colón or Concordia.

PARANÁ

Capital of Entre Ríos Province, across its namesake river from Santa Fe, Paraná is one of the best access points to the upper Paraná Delta's islands and gallery forests, including little-visited Parque Nacional Pre-Delta. It's arguably more livable than its sweltering neighbor, thanks to shady streets, lush riverside parks, and better river access. In the city center, authorities have even widened sidewalks to create "slow streets" in a country where motorists usually consider that might makes right.

Paraná was briefly Argentina's capital, after native son General Urquiza defeated the Buenos Aires dictator Rosas, but it wasn't even the provincial capital until the late 1880s. It has maintained a high political profile, even hosting a 1994 convention that revised Argentina's constitution to lift presidential term limits—benefiting the now-disgraced Carlos Menem.

Paraná (pop. about 300,000) is 470 kilometers northwest of Buenos Aires via RN 12 and RP 11 through Gualeguay, Victoria, and Diamante; the distance is 500 kilometers via RN 9 to Rosario and A-008 to Santa Fe, which are better and faster highways. Unlike the low-lying cities along the Río Uruguay, most of Paraná occupies a hilly site above the Río Paraná; on the floodplain, Parque Urquiza stretches over a kilometer of mostly open riverfront.

Sights

Paraná lacks colonial monuments but has no shortage of handsome 19th-century buildings near Plaza 1 de Mayo. On the plaza's east side, dating from 1885, the neoclassical **Iglesia Catedral** (cathedral) is a national historical monument distinguished by its columnar facade, twin bell towers, and a gracefully arched central dome.

Two blocks west, the **Museo y Mercado Provincial de Artesanías** (Avenida Urquiza 1239, tel. 0343/420-8891, 9 A.M.–12:30 P.M. and 4–8 P.M. Mon.–Fri., 9 A.M.–12:30 P.M. Sat., free) is a hybrid institution displaying classic crafts from around the province—wood carvings, ceramics, leather goods, and metalwork—and selling comparable pieces. One block north, dating from 1908, the **Teatro Municipal 3 de Febrero** (25 de Junio 60) is Paraná's prime performing arts venue, distinguished by its horseshoe-shaped auditorium and ceiling frescos.

The San Martín pedestrian mall, popular for Saturday-morning outings, ends two blocks north at **Plaza Alvear,** the site of three key museums. The **Museo Histórico Provincial Martiniano Leguizamón** (Buenos Aires 286, tel. 0343/420-7869, US$2) highlights—and sometimes exaggerates—the province's role in Argentina's mid-19th-century political history. Hours are 8 A.M.–12:30 P.M. Tuesday–Friday, but if the budget permits, it may open in the afternoon and on weekends.

On the west side of Plaza Alvear, the **Museo de Bellas Artes Pedro E. Martínez** (Buenos Aires 355, tel. 0343/420-7868, museobellasartes@yahoo.com.ar, 7 A.M.–1 P.M. and 3–7 P.M. Tues.–Fri., 10 A.M.–2 P.M. and 5–8 P.M. Sat., 4–7 P.M. Sun., free) showcases provincial painters, sculptors, and illustrators.

In new quarters, the **Museo de la Ciudad** (Buenos Aires 226, tel. 0343/421-1884, 8 A.M.–noon and 4–8 P.M. Tues.–Fri., 9 A.M.–noon and 4–8 P.M. Sat., 4–8 P.M. Sun., free), details Paraná's urban development.

On the north side of the plaza, the **Museo de Ciencias Naturales y Antropológicas Doctor Antonio Serrano** (Carlos Gardel 62, tel. 0343/420-8894, museoserrano@hotmail.com, 8 A.M.–12:30 P.M. and 2–6 P.M. Tues.–Sat., 9 A.M.–noon Sun., free, donations accepted) specializes in natural history and archaeology.

One block west of Plaza Alvear, Swiss architect Bernardo Rigoli designed the **Casa de Gobierno** (1887), which became the site of the executive, legislative, and judicial branches when the provincial government relocated

from Concepción del Uruguay; the courts have since moved to a newer building immediately south. Four blocks north, **Parque Urquiza** is the city's signature open space, along the Paraná riverfront.

At the Santa Fe approach to town, the **Túnel Subfluvial Uranga Silvestre Begnis** (1969) is a civil engineering monument, a three-kilometer toll tunnel beneath the river that's the only one of its kind in the country. It's also a political monument, representing cooperation with Santa Fe at a time when the federal government refused to permit the two provinces to build a bridge. Free guided tours (tel. 0343/420-0400) take place 7 A.M.–7 P.M. daily.

Entertainment and Events

The municipal **Teatro 3 de Febrero** (25 de Junio 60, tel. 0343/423-5701) has offerings ranging from live theater and film to art exhibits. For current commercial movies, try the **Cine Rex** (Monte Caseros 266, tel. 0343/423-3222).

The sight of teenagers in Little League uniforms seems incongruous in soccer-mad Argentina, but for decades the diamond at **Estadio Ingeniero Nafaldo Cargnel,** near the Santa Fe tunnel entrance, has hosted slow-pitch and fast-pitch softball tournaments, including the 1995 Pan American Games. Adult leagues also play here and at the city's seven other fields.

Sports and Recreation

Fishing for river species like *boga, sábalo, dorado,* and *surubí* requires a license from the **Dirección de Flora y Fauna** (España 33, tel. 0343/420-7870).

Hour-long river excursions (US$5.50 pp) leave from the Puerto Nuevo (Costanera and Vélez Sarsfield) with the **Catamarán Río Missie** (tel. 0343/15-448-1294) at 10:30 A.M. and 3 P.M. daily.

Accommodations

Even nonbackpackers may want to consider the private rooms at the **Paraná Hostel** (Andrés Pazos 159, tel. 0343/455-0847,

MESOPOTAMIA

www.paranahostel.com.ar, US$11 pp dorm, US$25–30 s or d), a handsome new facility just a block off the plaza. The charming **Hotel San Jorge** (Belgrano 368, tel. 0343/422-1685, www.sanjorgehotel.com.ar, US$26 s, US$37 d) occupies a handsome early-20th-century building with a luxuriant patio and stylishly modernized rooms with air-conditioning and cable TV.

New in 2008, in an ideal neighborhood near Parque Urquiza, the (C **Posada del Rosedal** (Santiago del Estero 656, tel. 0343/422-3148, www.posadadelrosedal.com.ar, US$36–45 s, US$50–59 d) is a tobacco-free three-room B&B with an abundant breakfast and reliable Wi-Fi. Parking costs extra, however.

On the *peatonal,* **Gran Alvear Hotel** (San Martín 637, tel. 0343/422-0000, www.granhotelalvear.com.ar, US$40 s, US$55 d) is a decent value. Rates include parking and air-conditioning.

The facade of the **Paraná Hotel** (9 de Julio 60, tel./fax 0343/423-1700, www.hotelesparana.com.ar, US$34–52 s, US$42–60 d) is deceptive, as its interior is more modern and most of its rooms smaller—compact, one might generously say—than the exterior suggests. Several original rooms that surround the interior patio are used only when the hotel is full, because of heavy foot traffic.

Facing Plaza 1 de Mayo, **Gran Hotel Paraná** (Urquiza 976, tel. 0343/422-3900, www.hotelesparana.com.ar, US$40–74 s, US$53–92 d) is a mixed bag—rooms on the lower floors, which generally go to tour groups, are utilitarian, but those on the upper floors live up to its four-star billing.

Towering over the riverside, the **Howard Johnson Mayorazgo Plaza Resort** (Etchevere and Miranda, tel. 0343/420-6800, www.hjmayorazgo.com.ar, US$115 s or d) is the new casino hotel.

Food

Giovani (Avenida Urquiza 1045, tel. 0343/423-0527) is a reliable *parrilla.* The Gran Hotel Paraná's **La Fourchette** (Urquiza 976, tel. 0343/422-3900) serves good river fish like *pacú*

and *surubí,* but it is expensive by local standards, including high markups on the wine list.

At **Lola Valentina** (Mitre 302, tel. 0343/423-5234) the specialty is river fish, but while the ingredients are good, it comes smothered in spuds—huge portions of them. Packed with locals, who consider it good value, it has well-meaning but erratic service. The wine list is huge, but not everything may be available. Cash-only is the rule here—no credit cards.

Heladería Bahíllo (San Martín 722), part of a small Entre Ríos chain, serves good ice cream.

Information

The **Dirección Municipal de Turismo** (Buenos Aires 132, tel. 0343/423-0183, www.turismoparana.gov.ar) is open 8 A.M.–8 P.M. daily. Its riverfront **Oficina Parque** (Avenida Laurencena and Juan de San Martín, tel. 0343/420-1837) keeps identical hours, as does another at the bus terminal (Ramírez 2300, tel. 0343/420-1862).

Open 7 A.M.–1 P.M. weekdays only, the **Secretaría Provincial de Turismo** (Laprida 5, tel. 0343/420-7989, www.entrerios.gov.ar/turismo) has helpful personnel and keeps another **Oficina del Túnel** (tel. 0343/420-1803) at the mouth of the tunnel from Santa Fe.

For motorists, **ACA** is at Buenos Aires 333 (tel. 0343/431-1319).

Services

Paraná has no exchange houses but numerous ATMs, such as the one at **Banco Francés** (San Martín 763), near Plaza 1 de Mayo.

Correo Argentino (25 de Mayo and Monte Caseros) is the post office; the postal code is 3100. The **Telecentro** on San Martín between Uruguay and Pazos has both long-distance and Internet access.

For medical services, try **Hospital San Martín** (Presidente Perón 450, tel. 0343/431-2222).

Lavadero Belgrano (Belgrano 306, tel. 0343/431-1556) does the laundry.

Getting There and Around

Paraná has a small airport, but nearly all commercial flights leave from neighboring Santa

Fe. The exception is the regional airline **Laersa** (San Martín 918, tel. 0810/777-5237, www.laersa.com.ar), which flies weekday mornings to Buenos Aires, and also to Mar del Plata.

Paraná's **Terminal de Ómnibus** (Avenida Ramírez 2300, tel. 0343/422-1282) is opposite Plaza Martín Fierro, about 10 blocks southeast of Plaza 1 de Mayo. There are frequent buses to Santa Fe (45 minutes, US$1.25).

Long-distance destinations, times, and fares resemble those from Santa Fe, but there are more departures from Santa Fe. Among the possibilities here are Rosario (2.5 hours, US$10), Córdoba (6.5 hours, US$19), Corrientes (8 hours, US$29), Resistencia (7.5 hours, US$27), Buenos Aires (6 hours, US$23), Posadas (10 hours, US$42), Puerto Iguazú (14 hours, US$42–60), and Mendoza (15 hours, US$48).

PARQUE NACIONAL PRE-DELTA

Toward the northern end of the Paraná Delta, this little-visited park protects 2,458 hectares of wetlands and gallery forest just south of the city of Diamante, less than an hour south of the provincial capital. Dating from 1992, it features forested natural levees that become islands when the river rises, and interior depressions that support wildlife-rich marshes and lagoons. It offers a pair of short nature trails, but visitors will see more by hiring a launch to explore its islands and watercourses.

Flora and Fauna

Pre-Delta's most conspicuous flora are gallery forests of large trees like willows and alders, where the *espinero rojizo* (common thornbird) builds conspicuous hanging nests of sticks.

Twisted *ceibos* and the cedar-like *timbó* grow on islands, while mammals like the capybara make their way among floating islands of water hyacinths with violet flowers. Reeds cover lower-lying areas, where there are also nutria and river otters, as well as *yacaré* (caiman). Other birds include ducks, swans, egrets, and the kingfisher (the park's symbol).

Practicalities

The ranger station at Paraje La Jaula, at the end of the road from Diamante, has a small **campground,** free of charge, with fire pits for barbecues. There's a small **shop** at Paraje La Azotea, immediately before the park entrance, but it's better to bring supplies from Diamante or Paraná.

There is a **ranger station** right at Paraje La Jaula, where the road from Diamante dead-ends; there's a small shop at Paraje La Azotea. The park also has a **Diamante** office (25 de Mayo 389, tel. 0343/498-3535, predelta@apn.gov.ar). Park admission is free.

Parque Pre-Delta is only six kilometers south of Diamante, where it's easy to hire a *remise* to the park entrance at Paraje La Jaula. There, **Excursiones Fluviales Ave Fénix** (tel. 0343/15-47-68525) provides launches to explore the intricate waterways. The nearest big city, Paraná, has frequent bus service to Diamante.

Corrientes Province

For travelers continuing up the Río Uruguay littoral through Corrientes Province, there are only minor points of interest en route to Misiones Province and its world-famous Iguazú Falls. The capital city of Corrientes, in the northwest corner of the province, has its strong points, including one of the country's best Carnaval celebrations.

What should be Corrientes's biggest attraction is Esteros del Iberá, a wildlife-rich wetland equal (if not superior) to Brazil's better-known Pantanal and even Amazonia—but it remains almost unknown because of relative isolation and the fact that both provincial and national authorities seem clueless as to its environmental wealth and traveler appeal. Still, anyone pressed for time but eager for a more intimate experience should consider writing off heavily touristed Iguazú to see Iberá, which is worth a trip to the province—or even to Argentina—in its own right. It's accessible from the western provincial city of Mercedes or, with more difficulty, from the Misiones provincial capital of Posadas.

YAPEYÚ

For foreign travelers, southeastern Corrientes is primarily a transit route, with several Brazilian border crossings. To Argentines of all political persuasions, though, the sleepy village of Yapeyú occupies a special status as the birthplace of José de San Martín (1778–1850), the country's most prominent—and romanticized—national hero. Many feel a patriotic obligation to visit his humble house, virtually preserved under glass, though there's little else to see.

Barely a decade before his birth, Yapeyú had been the southernmost Jesuit mission in the upper Paraná-Uruguay drainage. After Spanish king Carlos III expelled the order from the Americas in 1767, San Martín's father administered what remained of the mission (founded 1627), which once housed 8,000 Guaraní neophytes with up to 80,000 cattle.

Only the red sandstone foundations remain of the original Jesuit church and school, which burned to the ground in 1800; in 1817, Brazilian troops sacked the town. There is a small but worthwhile Jesuit museum in situ.

Yapeyú is 690 kilometers north of Buenos Aires and 395 kilometers southeast of the provincial capital. It is six kilometers southeast of RN 14 via the Avenida del Libertador turnoff. All sights and services are within easy walking distance of Plaza San Martín, on high ground above the river.

Sights

At the east end of Plaza San Martín, its interior adorned with tributary plaques, the **Templete Sanmartiniano** protecting the excavated remains of San Martín's birthplace is a textbook example of chauvinistic hero worship. Interestingly, though, the controversial plaque on which Proceso dictator General Jorge Rafael Videla professed his "most profound faith" in San Martín's ideals of liberty no longer disgraces the Liberator's memory. The official explanation is that all other such plaques are from institutions rather than individuals, but the aging Videla's nonperson status (he remains under house arrest in Buenos Aires for kidnapping children during the 1976–1983 "Dirty War") is evident.

Two blocks west, several small contemporary pavilions sit atop Jesuit foundations at the **Museo de Cultura Jesuítica Guillermo Furlong** (Sargento Cabral and Obispo Romero), an open-air museum that is always open to the public. Each pavilion has a good photographic display of the missions and their history, while a handful of mission artifacts (most notably a sundial) surround them.

At the south end of Avenida del Libertador, at the army's Granaderos regimental headquarters, the **Museo Sanmartiniano** (free) intensifies the hero worship with San Martín family artifacts and documents. Hours vary, so good luck.

Accommodations and Food

Yapeyú has its charms, but accommodations and food are few and ordinary at best. On Plaza San Martín, **Hotel San Martín** (Sargento Cabral 712, tel. 03772/49-3120, US$37 d) has large rooms surrounding a barren courtyard, but some lack exterior windows. Rooms have decent beds and private baths, plus air-conditioning, but no breakfast is available.

More visually appealing than the San Martín, **Complejo El Paraíso** (José de San Martín s/n, tel. 03772/42-4102, www.termas-deyapeyu.com.ar, US$42–74 d) has reinvented itself as a hot-springs spa. Each motel-style bungalow has two bedrooms, one with a double bed and the other with four singles, but the rooms are dark. It now has a restaurant.

There are two other places to eat, both utilitarian with limited menus: Hotel San Martín's own basic restaurant and **Comedor El Paraíso** (Gregoria Matorras s/n, tel. 03772/49-3053), around the corner.

Getting There

Three blocks northwest of the plaza, Yapeyú's tiny **bus station** (Avenida del Libertador

THE ROBIN HOOD OF CORRIENTES

Gateway to the Esteros del Iberá, Mercedes is also the home base of Argentina's fastest-spreading religious cult, the shrine to the Gaucho Antonio Gil. Second only to San Juan's Difunta Correa as a popular religious phenomenon, the Gauchito (the faithful use the affectionate diminutive) is rapidly gaining adherents.

Unlike the improbable Difunta, Gil really existed, even if the details of his legend get romanticized. In the 1850s, so the story goes, Gil was an army deserter who spent years on the run as he took from the rich and gave to the poor. When he was finally apprehended, the police hanged him from an *espinillo* tree; before dying, Gil warned that the sergeant in command would find his own son gravely ill, and the boy would recover only if the sergeant prayed for Gil's soul.

When the boy recovered, the repentant sergeant carved a cross of *espinillo* and placed it at the site of Gil's death. Every January 8 – the anniversary of his death – up to 100,000 believers swarm to a site of chapels, *comedores,* and campgrounds decorated with hundreds upon hundreds of bright-red flags. So numerous as to close the highway, the pilgrims bring prized possessions to the Gauchito, whom they credit with miracles and life-changing experiences. In the process, they take away souvenirs, ranging from tiny red banners to near-life-size statues of Gil – a Christ in gaucho regalia – from a swarm of stands that make a major contribution to the local economy.

Over the past several years, the red flags that mark the Mercedes shrine have spread rapidly to roadside sites from Jujuy to Tierra del Fuego. Argentina's economy may have rebounded, but the results have been uneven. Nearly a decade later, the perceived injustices of Argentina's economic meltdown still seem to require a Robin Hood.

and Chacabuco) has services to Buenos Aires, Posadas, and intermediate points.

MERCEDES

There's a *correntino* gaucho on every corner in Mercedes, which is also the gateway to the world-class wetlands of the Esteros del Iberá, an ecological jewel that occupies much of the province's geographical center. Because of bus schedules to the marshes, travelers without their own vehicles often have to spend a night here.

Still, it's worth a stay to appreciate one of Argentina's most popular pilgrimage sites. The spontaneously colorful shrine to the gaucho Antonio Gil, a 19th-century Robin Hood (and popular saint) unjustly executed by provincial authorities, is nine kilometers west of town. A newer attraction is the **Centro de Interpretación de la Ciudad de Mercedes** (Caá Guazú and José María Gómez), a small museum complex that's open 8 A.M.–noon and 2–6 P.M. Monday–Friday and 2–6 P.M. Saturday–Sunday.

Mercedes (pop. about 41,000) is 710 kilometers from Buenos Aires via RN 14 and RN 119. Gravel RP 40 leads 120 kilometers northeast to Colonia Pellegrini, the most convenient access point for Iberá.

Accommodations and Food

In new quarters, the HI affiliate **Hospedaje Delicias del Iberá** (Dr. Rivas 688, tel. 03773/42-3167, deliciasdelibera@yahoo.com.ar, US$10 pp, US$26 d) has become a backpacker's fixture on the trans-Chaco route from Salta to Iberá. The maintenance of the crumbling adobe is imperfect, though, and it lacks attention to detail.

Hotel El Sol (San Martín 519, tel. 03773/42-0283, US$21 s, US$32 d) has drawn raves for impeccable rooms in a 19th-century building with a family-run atmosphere.

The pick of accommodations is the Anglo-Argentine bed-and-breakfast **La Casita de Ana** (Mitre 924, tel. 03773/42-2671, manoscorrentinas@hotmail.com, US$26 s, US$48 d). Set among lush subtropical gardens in a handsome adobe whose interior looks airlifted from England, rates include an abundant breakfast with muesli, fruit, and other goodies.

Food here is nothing special, but **La Casa de Chirola** (Avenida San Martín 2191, tel. 03773/42-0869) is a decent *parrilla*. **Sabor Único** (San Martín 1240, tel. 03773/42-0314) has above-average pastas and meats, with excellent service, and makes an effort at creating an innovative menu and an inviting atmosphere.

Information

The municipal **Dirección de Turismo Mercedes** (Caá Guazú and José María Gómez, tel. 03773/15-41-4384, munimer-turismo@ hotmail.com, 9 A.M.–1 P.M. and 3–9 P.M. Mon.–Fri., 9 A.M.–1 P.M. and 2–8 P.M. Sat., 2–8 P.M. Sun.) is part of the new Centro de Interpretación.

Other Practicalities

Correo Argentino (Rivadavia and Martínez) is the post office; the postal code is 3470. **Banco de la Nación** (Rivadavia 602) has an ATM; load up with cash before visiting Esteros del Iberá, as Colonia Pellegrini has no exchange facilities.

From **Terminal Hipólito Yrigoyen** (San Martín and Alfredo Perreyra) numerous **buses** pass through town en route to the provincial capital of Corrientes (3.5 hours, US$10) and to Buenos Aires (9 hours, US$30–43).

El Rayo (Pujol 1166, tel. 03773/42-0184) and **Itatí II** (tel. 03773/42-1932) operate buses to Colonia Pellegrini (3 hours, US$9), in the Esteros del Iberá. Both depart around 11:30 A.M.–noon.

◖ ESTEROS DEL IBERÁ

Argentina's biggest unsung attraction, Esteros del Iberá is a breathtaking wetland covering up to 13,000 square kilometers (estimates vary), nearly 15 percent of the province. Recharged almost exclusively by rainwater, it's really a broad shallow river covered by semisubmerged marsh grasses, reeds, and other water-loving plants; it flows almost imperceptibly northeast

A *yacaré* lurks in the Esteros del Iberá.

© WAYNE BERNHARDSON

CALLING FOR SOCORRO

For nearly two decades, environmental philanthropist Douglas Tompkins struggled to get authorization for a privately administered national park in Chile's southern rain forests. In 2005 his highly publicized efforts finally succeeded, but similar projects in Argentina went almost unnoticed until recently.

In 2004 Tompkins and his wife, Kris McDivitt, donated parts of the former Estancia Monte León, in Santa Cruz Province, to Argentina's national park service through the Patagonia Land Trust. Another conservation challenge, though, has been the Esteros del Iberá, where he has purchased several *estancias* open to the public and sponsored research into reintroducing the giant anteater. He now spends the southern winter at Estancia Rincón del Socorro, a prime destination for environmentally oriented tourists on the south side of the marshes.

In late 2006, though, Tompkins's Argentine efforts earned unwanted publicity when *piquetero* demagogue Luis D'Elía – then a federal government official – falsely claimed that Tompkins had blocked a rural road through Estancia El Tránsito in another part of the marshes. In a blatant publicity stunt, D'Elía staged an invasion of Tompkins's property with ostensible *campesinos* in support.

D'Elía and a handful of congressional xenophobes called for expropriation, but he badly misjudged his own position. Tompkins's donation of Monte León had benefited President Néstor Kirchner's home province of Santa Cruz, and combined with the fact that other Corrientes landowners united behind Tompkins, D'Elía soon found himself jobless.

That has not been Tompkins's only challenge, though. The latest villain is Forestal Andina, a timber company that's built unauthorized earthworks to drain parts of the marshes for grazing cattle. Such a project would disrupt water flow elsewhere, with unpredictable but almost certainly negative consequences.

Meanwhile, wild capybaras and rheas still stroll the lawns at Tompkins's **Hostería Rincón del Socorro** (tel. 03782/49-7073, www.rincondelsocorro.com, US$220-300 s, US$360-520 d, with full board and excursions). Managed by Anglo-Argentine Leslie Cook and his wife, Valeria Verdaguer, it has six impeccably decorated guest rooms with high ceilings and fans, plus three separate bungalows, along with a restaurant open to nonguests by reservation only. Much of the food, including spectacular tomatoes, comes from their own organic gardens. Children ages 3-6 pay 25 percent, and 50 percent for children ages 6-10.

Additional amenities include a *quincho* for barbecues, a game room with a DVD player (though the guest rooms are TV-free), a library, and even satellite-based Wi-Fi.

Besides accommodations, Rincón del Socorro organizes boat excursions into the marshes from Colonia Pellegrini, 35 kilometers east, plus horseback rides and catch-and-release fly-fishing (in certain seasons). Guests also have access to mountain bikes.

Rincón del Socorro is one of three Tompkins properties open to guests; the others are Estancia San Alonso (US$170 s, US$260 d), reached only by private plane, and Estancia Batel, west of Mercedes. Because of Socorro's isolation, some guests arrive by plane; there is a one-kilometer airstrip 800 meters from the *hostería*.

to southwest, where the Río Corrientes enters the middle Paraná. There are also open-water stretches, however, like Laguna Iberá, a 24,550-hectare lagoon that's protected under the Ramsar convention on wetlands of international importance.

In terms of wildlife, Iberá is an American Serengeti—while it may lack the faunal biomass of Africa's famous plain, the variety of species and the sheer numbers of birds, mammals, and reptiles is still awesome. For these reasons, it has attracted the attention of international conservationists such as former Esprit clothing magnate Douglas Tompkins, who has purchased several area *estancias* to help preserve their natural wealth.

MESOPOTAMIA

And Iberá needs defenders, as the marshes have a fragile ecology imperiled by mega-hydroelectric developments of the Yacyretá dam, north of the city of Ituzaingó. As runoff from Yacyretá's rising reservoir seeps into Iberá, deepening waters threaten to break the link between the marsh vegetation and the dissolved sediments from which the plants derive their nutrients. Additional threats have included land invasions and forestry projects.

Orientation

Esteros del Iberá stretches over an enormous area, but the most convenient access point is **Colonia Pellegrini** (pop. about 800), a hamlet of wide dirt roads on a peninsula jutting into Laguna Iberá, 120 kilometers northeast of Mercedes via RP 40. Technically, Pellegrini has formal street names, but it's hard to find signs and, on occasion, even people to ask for directions.

Passable under most conditions, though sections of it are bumpy, RP 40 can be muddy and difficult for conventional vehicles in wet weather. It requires caution and moderate speeds at all times. Eastbound RP 40 to the junction with paved RN 14 is impassable except for 4WD vehicles, and it is especially difficult in wet weather.

Note that Pellegrini has no bank or other exchange facilities. Some hotels may accept U.S. dollars, but it's better to bring enough money for your stay.

Flora and Fauna

Iberá is a wonderland of biodiversity. Scattered open-water lagoons lie within an endless horizon of marshland grasses, aquatic plants, and *embalsados* ("floating islands"), which some ecologists have likened to tropical peat bogs. Even relatively large trees like the *ceibo* and laurel flourish here and in gallery forests along faster-flowing waters.

Biologists have catalogued over 40 species of mammals, 35 species of amphibians, 80 species of fish, and 250–300 species of birds. The most readily seen mammals are the *carpincho* (capybara), marsh deer, pampas deer, and *mono*

carayá (howler monkey). Less easily seen are the *lobito de río* (Paraná otter) and the nocturnal *aguará guazú* (maned wolf).

Among the reptiles are two species of caimans, the rare *yacaré overo* and the more common *yacaré negro*. Australians take note: These skinny two-meter creatures are not Queensland's massive crocodiles and do not pounce out of the swamps in search of human nourishment, though attempting to pet them is not advisable. The endangered water *curiyú* (water boa) is also present.

Birds species are too numerous to mention more than a sampling, but the signature species include the *chajá* (crested screamer), *mbiguá común* (olive cormorant), several species of storks, herons, and egrets as well as many waterfowl, including the endangered *pato crestudo* (comb duck).

Sights and Recreation

Iberá is a year-round destination, but the summer months can be brutally hot and humid, and rain can fall at any time. Activities include wildlife-watching, hiking on a gallery-forest nature trail, and horseback riding.

Launch tours on **Arroyo Corrientes,** which involve poling through floating islands where an outboard motor is useless, are available through all the hotels and private guides as well. **Canal Miriñay** is an alternative that offers better wildlife viewing when the waters rise and wildlife may retreat to the interior of the *embalsados*.

Two-hour excursions, which cover a lot, begin in the US$18 pp range for one or two people, slightly less for larger groups. As some animals are nocturnal, nighttime tours are also available, especially under the full moon.

Rental canoes and kayaks are available, but kayaks are unsuitable for exploring the marshes, whose dense vegetation makes visibility poor—other than Pellegrini's cell phone tower, this nearly featureless terrain has few landmarks, and you can't stand up in a kayak to get your bearings. José Martín's **Iberá Expediciones** (tel. 03773/15-40-1405, www.iberaexpediciones.

A capybara and her pup relax on dry land at the Esteros del Iberá.

com) does after-dark and full-moon safaris along the Mercedes highway to view nocturnal wildlife.

Pellegrini now has a small museum, the **Museo Yjára** (Yangapiry and Yaguareté, 4–8 P.M. daily except Tues., free).

Accommodations and Food

Pellegrini may be small, but it offers a diversity of quality accommodations and food for all budgets. In general, most places offer packages that include two or more nights of accommodation, full board, and at least an excursion per day. Most of the mid to top-end places are adding Wi-Fi, which has been late to reach here.

Except for hotel dining rooms, it lacks good restaurants; in fact, most of the local *comedores* are pretty dire. To eat where you're not staying, make advance arrangements, as drop-ins are uncommon. Limited supplies are available; locals stock up during shopping trips to Mercedes.

Shoestring backpackers will find a growing number of *hospedajes* such as **Posada San Cayetano** (Aguapé and Yacaré, tel. 03773/15-62-8763, US$13 pp) with tidy but basic multi-bed rooms. It has even added air-conditioning and a pool.

The accommodations at **Rancho Inambú Hostel** (tel. 03773/43-6159, Yerutí between Aguapé and Pehuajó, www.ranchoinambu.com.ar, US$16 pp) occupy a typical *rancho correntino* with adobe walls and mud roof, but the large common areas, in a separate building, include pool tables and a bar-restaurant that serves as a pub on weekends. Prices are likely to rise as it adds private baths.

Hospedaje Jabirú (Caraguata and Yaguareté, tel. 03773/15-41-3750, US$32 d with fan, US$37 d with a/c) is a friendly and tidy place that only suffers by having too many beds in some rooms. Its next-door restaurant **Jacarú Porá** has a more diverse menu than the basic *comedores,* and the dishes are prepared with a little more care. It has especially choice empanadas—try the cheese and onion.

The best value is underpriced **(Posada Rancho Ypa Sapukai** (Yacaré and Mburucuyá, tel. 03773/42-0155 or 03773/15-62-9536, www.ypasapukai.com.ar, US$75 pp with half board and excursions) for elegantly simple rooms with private baths, ceiling fans, and air-conditioning on request. On beautifully maintained grounds along the lagoon, it has attractive common areas good enough for just relaxing if bad weather delays excursions, as well as above-average food.

On densely wooded grounds, **Hostería Ñandé Retá** (Guasú Virá and Caraguatá, tel. 03773/49-9411 or 03773/15-62-9109, tel./fax 03773/42-0155 in Mercedes, www.nandereta.com, US$90 pp with full board and excursions) has a jungle-lodge feeling despite its midst-of-the-village location. The rooms, though, are a bit smaller than those at other, newer places.

Irupé Lodge (Capivara and Irupé, tel. 03773/15-40-2193, www.irupelodge.com.ar, US$125 pp with full board and one excursion per day) is not bad, but less appealing than other places and arguably overpriced. At handsomely designed **Rancho de los Esteros** (Yacaré and Yangapiry, tel. 03773/15-49-3041, www.ranchodelosesteros.com.ar, US$125 pp), a so-called *rancho boutique*, the price includes full board and excursions.

⊂ Posada de la Laguna (Guasú Virá and Timbó, tel. 03773/49-9413 or 03773/15-62-9827, tel. 011/4797-7449 in Buenos Aires, www.posadadelalaguna.com, US$198 s, US$290 d, with full board and excursions) has six spacious rooms with high ceilings and comfortably stylish furnishings set on sprawling gardens along the lagoon; it also features a swimming pool and a separate bar-restaurant. The owner is Elsa Güiraldes, a niece of Ricardo Güiraldes, author of the classic *gauchesco* novel *Don Segundo Sombra*.

The largest accommodation is the colonial-style **⊂ Posada Aguapé** (Yacaré and Timbó, tel./fax 03773/49-9412, www.iberaesteros.com.ar, US$106–137 pp with full board and two excursions per day), which sprawls along the lagoon in two wings with overhanging galleries for protection from both sun and rain, along with a large pool. Decorated with high-quality but rustically styled furniture, the 12 suites are substantial and appealing; there is also a bar

and a dining room. Rates include several excursions; children under 10 pay half, children under three are free. Its Buenos Aires contact is María Paz Galmarini (Coronel Obarrio 1038, 1642 San Isidro, Provincia de Buenos Aires, tel./fax 011/4742-3015).

Other Practicalities

At the approach to Colonia Pellegrini, immediately before the Bayley bridge that crosses Laguna Iberá, former poachers staff the provincial **Centro de Intepretación,** the reserve's visitors center. On the other side of the bridge, Pellegrini's **Oficina de Información Turística** (7:30 A.M.–7:30 P.M. daily except Tues.) has good maps and lists of services, with helpful personnel. Hotel staff and guides are also excellent sources of information.

Daily except Sunday, **El Rayo** (tel. 03773/42-0184) and **Itatí II** (tel. 03773/42-1722) operate bus services from Colonia Pellegrini back to Mercedes (3 hours, US$8). The El Rayo bus leaves around 4–5 P.M., but Itatí II departs around 4 A.M. This allows locals to make shopping trips and return in the same day, but it's not so great for travelers who want a full night's sleep. They will pick you up at your accommodations in Pellegrini, however.

From the Posadas airport, it's possible to arrange direct transfers for four to six people in a 4WD vehicle for about US$200–225 with **Anamatours** (tel. 03752/42-0199). From Pellegrini, **Trans-Beto** (tel. 03757/15-51-5862) and **Hugo Boccalandro** (tel. 03773/15-40-0929) offer similar services.

CORRIENTES

Capital of its namesake province, settled by Spaniards from Asunción in the late 16th century, Vera de las Siete Corrientes took its name from founder Juan Torres de Vera y Aragón and the irregular Paraná currents just below its confluence with the Río Paraguay. Its appeal lies in its colonial core and its riverside location—the views across the Paraná toward the seemingly endless Chaco are soothing, especially at sunset.

Indigenous resistance made the city precarious in its early years. Graham Greene set his semisatirical novel *The Honorary Consul* in Corrientes's *villas miserias,* its peripheral slums.

Corrientes (pop. about 400,000) is 927 kilometers north of Buenos Aires via RN 12 and RN 14. It is 324 kilometers west of Posadas via RN 12, and only 19 kilometers east of Resistencia, the capital of Chaco Province across the Paraná. Avenida 3 de Abril leads west to Puente General Manuel Belgrano, the Resistencia bridge, and east toward Ituzaingó and Posadas.

Sights

Corrientes's compact colonial core makes it a good walker's city, at least in winter or during the cool morning hours. In practice, the best walk is an evening stroll along the riverfront **Avenida Costanera General San Martín,** which enjoys spectacular sunsets across the slow-flowing Paraná's glassy surface. On the Costanera at the west end of Junín, the **Jardín Zoológico** (Avenida Costanera 99, tel. 03783/15-34-1356, 9 A.M.–6 P.M. Tues.–Sun., free) focuses on regional fauna, such as caimans, Geoffrey's cat, the puma, and birds like the toucan; there is also a serpentarium.

One block south of the Costanera, bounded by Quintana, Buenos Aires, Salta, and 25 de Mayo, the civic center is **Plaza 25 de Mayo;** it's home to the **Casa de Gobierno** (governor's palace), the legislature, and the **Iglesia de la Merced,** a landmark 19th-century church.

Where the Costanera becomes Plácido Martínez, at Juan Torres de Vera y Aragón, it's a short walk to Calle San Juan's **Paseo Italia,** a monumental tribute to the Italian community, but there's a more impressive feature in the vivid **Murales Históricos,** a series of murals that turns the corner at Quintana and depicts the city's history since colonial times.

Immediately east, dating from the late 16th century, the **Convento de San Francisco** (Mendoza 450) underwent an impressive restoration in 1939. Two blocks south, the **Museo Histórico de Corrientes** (9 de Julio 1044, tel. 03783/47-5946, 8 A.M.–noon and 5–8 P.M. Mon.–Fri., free) focuses on colonial art, antique weapons and furniture, and numismatics.

Bearing the name of Alexander von Humboldt's 19th-century travel companion, the **Museo de Ciencias Naturales Amado Bonpland** (San Martín 850, tel. 03783/47-5944, 9 A.M.–noon and 4–8 P.M. Mon.–Sat., free) is a sprawling facility focusing on entomology and vertebrates, but it also has a good fossil collection.

In the 16th century, according to legend, insurrectionary Indians attempted but failed to burn a wooden cross that survives in the **Iglesia de la Cruz,** on the south side of its namesake plaza, bounded by Bolívar, Salta, Buenos Aires, and Belgrano.

Entertainment

Occupying a large tent with long tables, the informal *parrilla* **El Quincho** (Avenida Pujol and Pampir) is less notable for its food than for its live *chamamé,* the accordion-based Mesopotamian music that resembles Tex-Mex *conjunto.* The menu is not for single diners or drinkers, or vegetarians—beef slabs only, no half bottles of wine, and beer by the liter. Still, prices are more than reasonable. It's open Friday–Sunday only.

Named for the city's founder, the **Teatro Oficial Juan de Vera** (San Juan 637, tel. 03783/42-7743, www.teatrovera.gov.ar) is the site for high-culture events such as classical music concerts and live theater.

Events

Huge crowds, including performing *comparsas* (troupes) from nearby provinces—and even from Brazil and Paraguay—descend on Corrientes for the **Carnaval Correntino,** whose celebrations take place Friday, Saturday, and Sunday in the summer carnival season.

At the confluence of the Paraná and Paraguay Rivers, 35 kilometers northeast of Corrientes, the town of Paso de la Patria draws an international sportfishing crowd to mid-August's **Fiesta Internacional del Dorado,** with prizes for capturing the largest specimen of the Paraná's favorite fighting fish. Peak season is July–September; closed season runs early October–early March. For details, contact Paso de la Patria's **Dirección de Turismo** (25 de Mayo 450, tel. 03783/49-4993).

Shopping

Something of a hybrid institution, the **Museo de Artesanía Folklórica** (Quintana 905, tel. 03783/47-5945, 8 A.M.–7 P.M. Mon. and Wed.–Sat.) displays classic crafts from around the province but also sells souvenir versions, sometimes directly from the artisans themselves.

Accommodations

Accommodations are few for a city its size, and budget options are scarce. For summer Carnaval, the provincial tourist office keeps a list of inexpensive *casas de familia,* local families who rent out spare rooms.

Spacious wooded grounds, a large pool, and proximity to the Costanera are the strengths of the Peronist-vintage **Gran Hotel Turismo** (Entre Ríos 650, tel. 03783/42-9112, www.ghturismo.com.ar, US$48 s, US$55 d), which has preserved more charm than comfort. Still, it has undergone a rehab, and prices are fair enough.

Impeccably modernized **Orly Hotel** (San Juan 867, tel. 03783/42-7248, www.hotelorlycorrientes.com.ar, US$37 s, US$44 d) is probably the best value for money. Prices have risen faster than improvements have taken place at the renamed high-rise **Costanera Hotel & Resort** (Plácido Martínez 1098, tel. 03783/43-6100, www.costaneraryh.com.ar, US$32 s, US$40 d), overlooking the Costanera.

On the north side of Plaza Cabral, the 110-room **Corrientes Plaza Hotel** (Junín 1549, tel./fax 03783/46-6500, www.hotel-corrientes.com.ar, US$42 s, US$58 d) may not quite live up to its four-star billing, but it has at least three-star comfort at suitable prices. There's also a secluded pool, a gym, secure on-site parking, and a 10 percent discount for cash payments.

Business-oriented **Gran Hotel Guaraní** (Mendoza 970, tel. 03783/43-3800, www.hotelguarani.com, US$50–82 s, US$57–92 d) has both standard, superior, and VIP rooms, plus some other more expensive suites. Likewise, there's a 10 percent discount for cash.

New in 2009, **❰ La Rozada Suites** (Plácido Martínez 1223, tel. 03783/43-3001, US$101–158 s or d) has transformed a 19th-century general store into a shiny new boutique hotel with 20 spacious rooms or suites, most of which have river-view balconies.

Also new in 2009, **La Alondra** (Avenida 3 de Abril 827, tel. 03783/43-0555, www.laalondra.com.ar, US$143–191 s or d) is an elegantly furnished boutique hotel that suffers, by comparison, from a less-than-optimal location—rather than enjoying river views, it sits on the main highway through town. The rooms are large, though, at around 50 square meters.

Food

For breakfast, sandwiches, afternoon tea, and sweets, the best choice is **Marta de Bianchetti** (9 de Julio 1198, tel. 03783/42-3008), which even hosts occasional tango performances.

Pizzería Los Pinos (San Lorenzo 1191, tel. 03783/46-2025) is a decent pizzeria with varied toppings and moderate prices. The **Eco Pizza Pub** (Hipólito Yrigoyen 1108, tel. 03783/42-5900) is slightly more upmarket. For river fish, try **El Mirador** (Avenida Costanera and Edison, tel. 03783/46-1806) or **Las Brasas** (Avenida Costanera and San Martín, tel. 03783/43-5106), both of which have given up their riverside locations to move to new facilities across the avenue.

Heladería La Terraza (Hipólito Yrigoyen 1135, tel. 03783/42-3219) sets the standard for ice cream.

Information

The provincial **Subsecretaría de Turismo** (25 de Mayo 1330, tel. 03783/42-7200, www.corrientes.gov.ar) is open 7 A.M.–1 P.M. and 3–9 P.M. weekdays, but its website is weak. The **Subsecretaría Municipal de Turismo** (tel. 03783/47-4702, 7 A.M.–9 P.M. daily) maintains a riverfront office at Punta Tacura, where 9 de Julio and Junín intersect the Costanera, and even stays open later on weekends.

For motorist services, try **ACA** (25 de Mayo and Mendoza, tel. 03783/42-2844).

Services

Cambio El Dorado (9 de Julio 1341) is the only exchange house. **Banco de Corrientes** (9 de Julio 1092) has one of many downtown ATMs.

Correo Argentino (San Juan and Avenida San Martín) is the post office; the postal code is 3400. The **Telecentro** (Pellegrini 1239) is one of many *locutorios*. **El Paseo Cybercafé** (San Juan 531) has Internet access.

Quo Vadis (Pellegrini 1140, tel. 03783/42-3096) is the Amex representative.

The **Hospital Escuela San Martín** (Avenida 3 de Abril 1251, tel. 03783/42-0697) is the public hospital.

Getting There

Aerolíneas Argentinas/Austral (Junín 1301, tel. 03783/42-8678) flies most days to Aeroparque (Buenos Aires). Nearby Resistencia also has flights to and from the capital.

From the foot of Calle Salta, Ticsa and Ataco Norte buses link Corrientes to Resistencia (30 minutes, US$1), where long-distance connections are better for western and northwestern Argentina.

Corrientes's **Terminal de Ómnibus** (Avenida Maipú s/n, tel. 03783/45-5600), at the southeast edge of town, occupies the former train station. Typical destinations, times, and fares include Posadas (4.5 hours, US$18), Rosario (9 hours, US$33), Puerto Iguazú (8 hours, US$28), and Buenos Aires (15 hours, US$46–58). Buses to Mercedes, transfer point for the Iberá marshes, cost about US$6 (3.5 hours).

Getting Around

From the Costanera at the north end of Salta, local bus No. 105 goes directly to Aeropuerto Doctor Fernando Piragine Niveyro (tel. 03783/45-8332), about 10 kilometers east of town on RN 12. Aerolíneas provides minibus transfers for flights from Resistencia.

Bus No. 103 goes to the long-distance bus terminal on Avenida Maipú.

PARQUE NACIONAL MBURUCUYÁ

On the north side of the Esteros del Iberá, 147 kilometers southeast of Corrientes via RN 12 and the paved lateral RP 13, the small town of Mburucuyá is the gateway to its namesake national park, preserving 17,660 hectares of wetlands and palm savannas. Once a Danish-owned *estancia,* the park offers similar habitat and wildlife to those of Esteros del Iberá, with short nature trails among its marshes, gallery forests, and groves of *yatay* palms.

The town of Mburucuyá has a couple of simple accommodations, and the park has a basic campground. There is regular bus service from Corrientes, but the park itself lies 11 kilometers east via a dirt road.

For more details, contact Parque Nacional Mburucuyá (Casilla de Correo 1, 3427 Mburucuyá, Corrientes, tel. 03782/49-8907, informesmburucuya@apn.gov.ar).

MESOPOTAMIA

Misiones Province

Almost surrounded by Brazil and Paraguay, mountainous Misiones has the highest-profile sights of any Mesopotamian province. In the upper Paraná drainage, shared with Brazil, the Cataratas del Iguazú (Iguazú Falls) pull visitors from around the globe. The Jesuit-mission ruins of San Ignacio across the border in Paraguay are additional reasons to visit.

Averaging about 500 meters above sea level, once covered with subtropical forest, Misiones's mountains are fast giving way to plantations of tea, *yerba mate,* and northern hemisphere pines.

In a few areas, coniferous native araucarias still dominate the natural vegetation.

HISTORY

Along with its diverse ecology, Misiones has an epically rich history thanks to its dense Guaraní population and the Jesuits who proselytized among them. In the early 17th century, the Jesuits abandoned their efforts among the Chaco's nomadic hunter-gatherers for the semisedentary Guaraní, shifting cultivators who were better candidates for missionization.

SLEEPING IN THE SELVA: THE FOREST LODGES OF MISIONES

The Amazonian countries of Brazil, Venezuela, Colombian, Ecuador, Perú, and Bolivia are replete with so-called "jungle lodges" in their dense tropical rain forests, but the forests of Misiones haves a couple of similar accommodations barely an hour from Puerto Iguazú. Coincidentally, both of them are forest reserves in their own right.

POSADA PUERTO BEMBERG

Barely half an hour south of Puerto Iguazú, Posada Puerto Bemberg is a 400-hectare property with a hotel originally built for that purpose – at a time when the easiest means of visiting the famous falls was to take a steamer up the Paraná and its tributaries. In addition to the recently expanded hotel, a rustically stylish luxury accommodation better than anything in and around the town or the park itself, Puerto Bemberg boasts substantial stands of native selva, with some areas undergoing forest restoration. Other parts of the land are dedicated to growing the hotel's own organic produce.

Expropriated during the Perón years, this onetime *yerba mate* plantation was repurchased by the Bembergs, whose fortune is synonymous with the Quilmes brewing empire, a few years ago. One of its landmarks is a chapel, overlooking the Paraná, by the famous architect Alejandro Bustillo; at one time the Paraguayan faithful used to gather on the opposite bank to hear Sunday mass broadcast over loudspeakers. The family's most famous member, though, is probably film director María Luisa Bemberg, whose historical drama *Camila* earned an Oscar nomination as best foreign film in 1984.

Activities at Puerto Bemberg include hiking (in some cases, with obligatory guides), cycling, excursions on the river and to Iguazú, and swimming (in the pool rather than the river). The hotel's common areas include a huge library in several languages, with some of the books for sale, and an exceptional bar-restaurant with exquisite caipirinhas. The 13 rooms and single suite also include small libraries, but TV is available only by special request (though Wi-Fi is available).

Posada Puerto Bemberg (Fundadores Bemberg s/n, Puerto Libertad, tel. 03757/49-6500, www.puertobemberg.com, US$250-360 s, US$280-360 d, for bed and breakfast; US$320-440 s, US$360-520 d, with full board and activities) is about 30 kilometers south of Aeropuerto Internacional Iguazú by smoothly paved RN 12. Transfers to and from the airport cost extra.

YACUTINGA LODGE

Set in a 570-hectare private reserve about an hour east of Parque Nacional Iguazú, Yacutinga Lodge is far smaller than the park,

In all, they founded 30 *reducciones,* populated with perhaps 100,000 Guaraní, in a territory that now comprises parts of Argentina, Brazil, and Paraguay.

Hollywood rarely depicts history with any accuracy, but director Roland Joffe got it mostly right in his 1986 film *The Mission,* starring Robert De Niro and Jeremy Irons. Joffe portrayed the Jesuit experiment in organizing indigenous peoples and educating them not just as farmers but also as craftspeople and even performing artists. He also deftly explained the political and economic intrigues of the time, as Portuguese *malocas* (slavers) and other Spanish settlers coveted the Jesuits' productive *yerba mate* plantations and labor monopoly.

Eventually, under pressure from these interests, Spanish king Carlos III expelled the Jesuits from the Americas in 1767. After the expulsion, many indigenes fled to the forest, and the missions fell into ruins, their walls pried apart by strangler figs and their Guaraní-carved sandstone statuary toppled.

After the South American states gained independence in the early 19th century,

but its remaining (and recovering) subtropical rain forest provides a more up-close-and-personal view of the natural environment in accommodations that far surpass the Sheraton in style.

For bird-watchers, Yacutinga offers a list of more than 300 species, plus many mammals, reptiles, and butterflies; with technical assistance from Fundación Vida Silvestre Argentina, it has created its own biological research station supported by profits from the lodge. Eight separate nature trails, one self-guided and the rest open with local guides, range from 500 meters to six kilometers (round-trip). There is also a short but fascinating catwalk through the forest canopy, six meters above ground level, leading to a platform that's ideal for observing birds and other flora.

The lodge proper deserves special mention. Using the maximum possible materials salvaged from the forest, the Argentine owners have created a Gaudí-esque combination of tranquility, comfort, and style that amounts to five-star rusticity. The main building is an idiosyncratic masterpiece, with a large living room, dining room, and bar. Twenty tasteful rooms can sleep two or three people each in five secluded units, but except during major holidays such as Holy Week, the proprietors prefer to host only a small percentage of their capacity to ensure a quality experience. Accommodations are available on a full-board basis only (drinks extra); day excursions are not offered. There is electricity from sundown to 8 A.M.

Yacutinga also meets many standards for appropriate development as 70 percent of the staff, including native Guaraní, come from the nearby community of Andresito, and most supplies are purchased locally, except for beverages such as beer, wine, and soft drinks. In the off-season, Yacutinga offers complimentary environmental education programs to neighboring schools.

Yacutinga's food is good, though if you stayed longer than a week it might seem repetitive. Unlike in Argentina's pampas heartland, the beef comes from chewy (though tasty) Zebu cattle. Vegetarian menus are available on request, though sometimes the main dish is vegetarian for everyone. Breakfast's homemade bread deserves special mention.

Yacutinga makes accommodations arrangements and quotes prices through travel agencies only. For additional information and travel assistance, contact Yacutinga (www.yacutinga .com) through their website.

Guests get picked up at Raíces Argentinas, a handicrafts store on RN 12 at Avenida Juan Domingo Perón, in modern vans that travel through Parque Provincial Urugua-í and plantations of *yerba mate*. After 45 kilometers of paved road, they transfer to a 4WD Mercedes truck for the last 12 kilometers.

Misiones was the object of contention among various countries in an area where it took time to fix international borders. After the megalomaniacal Paraguayan dictator Francisco Solano López blundered into the hopeless War of the Triple Alliance (1865–1870) against Argentina, Brazil, and Uruguay, his catastrophic loss left Misiones in Argentine hands.

Administratively, Misiones became part of Corrientes Province, but as colonization proceeded from the west, Misiones became a separate territory with Posadas as its capital. The Urquiza railway's 1912 arrival at Posadas provided a way for farmers to get their products to market.

Yerba mate remained the major product of enormous properties acquired under questionable circumstances. By the early 20th century, the federal government expropriated some properties and turned them over to agricultural colonists from many countries, including Argentina, Brazil, Denmark, France, Germany, Greece, Italy, Paraguay, Spain, Sweden, Switzerland, the Ukraine, the United States, and even Asia and the Middle East.

POSADAS

After the war with Paraguay, the growing city of Posadas became the territorial capital when Buenos Aires separated Misiones from Corrientes Province. Now a commercial center and border crossing, it's also the access point to the upper Paraná's Jesuit missions on both the Argentine and Paraguayan sides as well as to Parque Nacional Iguazú.

Now capital of its province, Posadas is reclaiming part of its waterfront above the encroaching waters of the downstream Yacyretá hydroelectric project. Densely planted street trees help offset the summer heat and humidity.

On the Paraná's south bank, opposite the smaller Paraguayan city of Encarnación, Posadas (pop. about 330,000) is 1,007 kilometers north of Buenos Aires via RN 14 and RN 105, 324 kilometers east of Corrientes via RN 12, and 302 kilometers southwest of Puerto Iguazú, also via RN 12. Avenida Mitre leads east to the graceful suspension bridge that crosses the river to Encarnación.

Posadas's awkward street numeration continues to confuse nonresidents, as locals continue to prefer the old numbers to the new. Addresses listed below use the new system but in some cases they indicate the old numbers as well, and occasionally refer to precise locations—some buildings lack numbers from either system.

Sights

On the east side of Plaza 9 de Julio, the Francophile **Casa de Gobierno** (1883) was actually the work of an Italian, engineer Juan Col. On the plaza's north side, famed architect Alejandro Bustillo designed the twin-towered **Catedral** (1937).

Posadas's waterfront **Museo Ferrobarcos,** at the east end of Avenida Guacurarí, is where trains between Buenos Aires and Asunción once shuttled across the river. Built in Glasgow in 1911, this rail ferry transported up to four passenger cars or eight cargo units at a time across the river from 1913 until 1990, when train service between the two countries ceased. Now staffed by retired railroad workers, it's

open 6 P.M.–midnight weekdays, 6 P.M.–2 A.M. weekends and holidays; admission is free.

Accommodations

Prices have risen considerably at **Hotel Colonial** (Barrufaldi 2419, tel. 03752/43-6149, US$26 s, US$42 d, with a/c and cable TV), a former shoestring favorite that has been upgraded.

The rooms are a little makeshift but the mattresses are firm at friendly **Le Petit Hotel** (Santiago del Estero 1630, tel. 03752/43-6031, www.hotellepetit.com.ar, US$32 s, US$45 d, with cable TV, telephones, and Wi-Fi). The rates fit the service, though parking is two blocks away.

The utilitarian **Hotel Libertador** (San Lorenzo 2208, tel. 03752/43-6901, www.libertadorposadas.com.ar, US$36 s, US$58 d, with a/c) has spacious but styleless rooms and responsive personnel.

Near the riverfront, unusual in Posadas, **Flor House** (Avenida Gobernador Roca 962, tel. 03752/43-8053, www.florhouse.com.ar, US$56 s, US$60 d) is a three-room B&B with a pool, extensive gardens, and other amenities unusual in Posadas.

Overlooking Plaza 9 de Julio, the highrise **Hotel Continental** (Bolívar 1879, tel. 03752/44-0990, www.hoteleramisiones.com.ar, US$51–66 s, US$63–82 d) is mostly business-oriented. The nearby **Posadas Hotel** (Bolívar 1949, tel. 03752/44-0888, www.hotelposadas.com.ar, US$53–63 s, US$65–72 d) has recast itself as a boutique facility. That's probably an exaggeration, but it has definitely improved.

The four-star 94-room **Hotel Julio César** (Entre Ríos 1951, tel. 03752/42-7930, www.juliocesarhotel.com.ar, US$66–75 s, US$79–88 d) is the city's best. It's the only one with a pool, gym, and similar executive amenities, as well as more expensive suites.

Food

On Plaza 9 de Julio, **Nouvelle Vitrage** (Bolívar and Colón) is best for breakfast, coffee, and snacks, including desserts. **Los Pinos** (Sarmiento and Buenos Aires, tel. 03752/42-

A MONUMENT TO CORRUPTION

Near the Corrientes town of Ituzaingó, the massive Yacyretá-Apipé dam has submerged the Río Paraná to form a 1,600-square-kilometer reservoir that reaches 80 kilometers east to Posadas and beyond. In 1973 the scandal-plagued project was Juan Perón's last-gasp legacy to Argentina's unsavory public works history, helping raise Argentina's foreign-debt burden to unsustainable levels. Even former president Carlos Menem called the continent's biggest hydroelectric project "a monument to corruption," and he knows one when he sees one.

It takes two to tango, and two countries created the Argentine-Paraguayan Entidad Binacional Yacyretá (EBY), which has displaced some 40,000 upstream residents, mostly Paraguayans. It also threatens the Esteros del Iberá, where southwesterly seepage from the dam could raise the marshes' shallow water and sever "floating" islands from their underwater anchorages.

Despite a reputation for secrecy, EBY's **Ofi-** **cina de Relaciones Públicas** (Avenida 3 de Abril and Ingeniero Mermoz, Ituzaingó, tel. 03786/42-1543, www.eby.org.ar) offers well-organized guided tours, free of charge, at 9 and 11 A.M. and 12:30 and 2 P.M. A visitors center museum (8 A.M.–4 P.M. daily) shows artifacts discovered during construction as well as a scale model of the project.

In academic circles, Yacyretá has spawned its own cottage industry. Readers interested in more details can consult Gustavo Lins Ribeiro's *Transnational Capitalism and Hydropolitics in Argentina: The Yacyretá High Dam* (Gainesville, FL: University Press of Florida, 1994), and Carmen A. Ferradás's *Power in the Southern Cone Borderlands* (Westbrook, CT: Bergin & Garvey, 1998), dealing primarily with the displacement of local communities.

There are regular **bus services** to and from Posadas (1 hour, US$3) with several companies, including Vía Uruguay and Crucero del Norte.

7252) is the place for pizza and cold beer on tap. For river fish, try the basic takeaway **El Doradito** (Avenida Corrientes and La Rioja), which has only a couple of sit-down tables amidst the simplest decor.

Posadas's finest dining is at 🇨 **Cavas** (Bolívar 1729, tel. 03752/43-5514), with a fusion-style menu; most entrées, such as their excellent gnocchi, are in the US$5–8 range. It's open for lunch and dinner daily except Saturday, when it's dinner only. Facing Plaza 9 de Julio, the *parrilla* **La Querencia** (Bolívar 1849, tel. 03752/43-7117) is an outstanding backup choice.

Via Chero (San Lorenzo 1808) has good ice cream.

Information

The provincial **Secretaría de Turismo** (Colón 1985, tel. 03752/44-7540, www.turismo.misiones.gov.ar, 7 A.M.–8 P.M. weekdays, 8 A.M.–noon and 4–8 P.M. weekends and holidays) offers a selection of maps and brochures for Posadas and the entire province.

For motorists, **ACA** is at Córdoba and Colón (tel. 03752/43-6955).

Services

Cambios Mazza (Bolívar 1932) changes travelers checks. **Banco Nazionale del Lavoro** (Bolívar and Félix de Azara) is one of many downtown ATMs.

Correo Argentino (Bolívar and Ayacucho) is the post office; the postal code is 3300. There are many *locutorios* and Internet outlets.

Express Travel (Félix de Azara 2097, tel. 03752/43-7687) is the Amex representative.

Hospital General R. Madariaga (Avenida López Torres 1177, tel. 03752/44-7775) is about one kilometer south of downtown.

Getting There

Posadas enjoys pretty good air connections to Buenos Aires, and it's a hub for provincial and long-distance buses, but rail service to Buenos Aires is suitable only for fanatical rail fans. There are also buses and launches across the border to Encarnación, Paraguay.

MESOPOTAMIA

Aerolíneas Argentina (Ayacucho 1728, tel. 03752/43-7110) flies once or twice daily to Buenos Aires's Aeroparque.

Distant from downtown, Posadas's **Terminal de Ómnibus** (Avenida Quaranta and Avenida Santa Catalina, tel. 03752/45-4888) is 44 blocks south and 14 blocks west of Plaza 9 de Julio. Buses to San Ignacio Miní (1 hour, US$2) leave roughly hourly starting around 5:30 A.M.

Sample destinations, times, and fares include Corrientes (4.5 hours, US$18), Resistencia (5 hours, US$20), Puerto Iguazú (4 hours, US$12), Buenos Aires (12 hours, US$46–60), and Salta (18 hours, US$53). There are also international services to Asunción, Paraguay (5.5 hours, US$18), and to the Brazilian cities of Porto Alegre (12 hours, US$40) and São Paulo (24 hours, US$80).

Between 7 A.M. and 10 P.M., international shuttle buses to Encarnación, Paraguay (US$1.25), pass along Entre Ríos en route to the international bridge. With border formalities the crossing can take up to an hour but is usually faster.

Trenes del Litoral (Avenida Córdoba s/n, tel. 03752/43-6076, www.trenesdellitoral.com.ar) offers cheap, slow, and erratic rail service on the Urquiza line to Buenos Aires's Estación Federico Lacroze. Scheduled departures are 10 A.M. Wednesday and 11 P.M. Sunday for the 26-hour trip.

Getting Around

From San Lorenzo between La Rioja and Entre Ríos, city bus No. 8 goes to **Aeropuerto Internacional General San Martín**, 12 kilometers southwest of town via RN 12. A *remise* will cost about US$6.

City buses No. 8, 15, 21, and 24 all go to the long-distance bus terminal.

For car rental, try **Avis** (Félix de Azara 1908, Local 12, tel. 03752/43-0050, www.avis.com.ar).

VICINITY OF POSADAS

The most worthwhile sights near Posadas are the Jesuit mission ruins across the border in Paraguay and en route to San Ignacio de Miní and Puerto Iguazú.

Trinidad and Jesús (Paraguay)

Immediately across the Paraná via the international bridge, the Paraguayan city of **Encarnación** barely merits a visit in its own right (though it's morbidly fascinating to see the Yacyretá's rising waters slowly submerge its historic downtown). It's well worth crossing the border, though, to see the nearby Paraguayan Jesuit missions of Trinidad and Jesús de Tavarangue.

Both Trinidad and Jesús were relative latecomers in the Jesuit empire—Jesús, in fact, was still under construction when Carlos III expelled the Jesuits in 1767. Trinidad dates from 1706, but took more than five decades to its completion in 1760—only seven years before the Jesuits' departure.

Trinidad, where more than 4,000 Guaraní once resided, sprawls across a grassy hilltop site, 28 kilometers northeast of Encarnación via Paraguay's paved Ruta 6. Its pride was architect Juan Bautista Prímoli's well-preserved red sandstone church, with equally well-preserved details like its intricately sculpted pulpit and statuary (Trinidad's Guaraní were known for their statuary but also for finely made musical instruments that included bells, harps, and organs). On a more materialist level, the mission supported itself with plantations of *yerba mate* and sugar (which they milled here), and three cattle *estancias*.

Jesús occupies a similar hilltop site, 11 kilometers north of Trinidad via a dirt road that can become impassable with heavy rain. While it lacks Trinidad's architectural details—after all, Jesús was never finished—it's the only one of 30 Jesuit missions with a surviving bell tower.

Together with the older mission, Jesús makes an ideal half-day-plus excursion from Posadas. Schedules vary seasonally, but both generally stay open during daylight hours; each collects a token admission charge.

Buses from Encarnación's central terminal (Avenida Estigarribia and General Cabañas) pass within a kilometer of Trinidad and also go several times daily to Jesús. These are cheap, but the trip can be done more efficiently (if more expensively) by hiring a taxi at the terminal.

U.S., Canadian, Australian, and Mexican citizens need visas (US$45 single entry, US$65 multiple entry, three photos required) to enter Paraguay. Paraguay's Posadas consulate (San Lorenzo and Sarmiento, tel. 03752/42-3858, 7 A.M.–2 P.M. weekdays only) provides same-day service.

Santa Ana and Loreto

From Posadas, undulating RN 12 climbs and dips northeast over leached red earth past several Jesuit mission ruins, the best-preserved of which is San Ignacio Miní. Though less well-preserved, Santa Ana and Loreto both have their assets, but progress in restoration has nearly ceased. Both are national historical monuments.

Founded in 1637, Santa Ana once sustained a Guaraní population of more than 4,000, though more than half departed within two decades after the Jesuits' expulsion. Only the mission walls remain, some still covered by strangler figs and with other aggressive vegetation wedged between the cracks. Immediately alongside it, the disconcertingly open crypts and coffins of an abandoned 20th-century cemetery are a reminder that the Jesuit experiment was only the first failed settlement here.

Santa Ana is 43 kilometers east of Posadas and one kilometer southeast of RN 12 via a dirt road that can get muddy; the junction is clearly marked, and buses from Posadas will drop passengers here. Hours are 7 A.M.–6 P.M. daily; the US$7 admission charge is valid for 15 days and applicable to the province's other Jesuit ruins.

Work at Loreto, which dates from 1632 but moved here only in 1660, has lagged behind that of Santa Ana, but plaques with descriptive quotations from Jesuit priests help visitors imagine what the site might have been. In 1700, *Martirologio Romano* (Roman Martyrology), the first book ever published within what is now Argentina, was printed here. It later appeared in Guaraní.

The Loreto turnoff is at Km 48, five kilometers beyond that to Santa Ana, but the site itself is three kilometers farther south of RN 12. Both sites have small museums and cafés.

SAN IGNACIO

Home to Argentina's best-kept Jesuit-mission ruins, the village of San Ignacio is an essential stopover on the overland route to or from Iguazú's famous falls. It also enjoys literary celebrity as the home of writer Horacio Quiroga, who produced some of his finest fiction in a residence that still survives here.

San Ignacio (pop. about 7,000) is 56 kilometers northeast of Posadas via RN 12. From the highway junction, Avenida Sarmiento leads to Calle Rivadavia, which leads six blocks north to the ruins.

◖ San Ignacio Miní

In terms of preservation, including the architectural and sculptural details that typify "Guaraní baroque," San Ignacio Miní is one of the best surviving examples of the 30 Jesuit missions in the region. It's a tourist favorite for its accessibility in the midst of the present-day village of San Ignacio.

San Ignacio's centerpiece was Italian architect Juan Brasanelli's monumental church, 74 meters long and 24 meters wide, with red sandstone walls two meters thick and ceramic-tile floors. Overlooking the plaza, decorated by Guaraní artisans, it's arguably the finest remaining structure of its kind; the adjacent compound included a kitchen, dining room, classrooms, and workshops. The priests' quarters and the cemetery were also here, while more than 200 Guaraní residences—whose inhabitants numbered 4,000 at the mission's zenith in 1733—surrounded the plaza.

Founded in 1609 in present-day Paraguay, San Ignacio Guazú moved to the Río Yabebiry in 1632 and to its present location in 1697, but it declined rapidly with the Jesuits' expulsion in 1767. In 1817, Paraguayan troops under paranoid dictator Gaspar Rodríguez de Francia razed what remained.

Rediscovered in 1897, San Ignacio gained some notoriety after poet Leopoldo Lugones

© WAYNE BERNHARDSON

San Ignacio Miní is the best preserved of Argentina's colonial Jesuit missions.

led an expedition here in 1903, but restoration had to wait until the 1940s. Parts of the ruins are still precarious, supported by sore-thumb scaffolding that obscures the complex's essential harmony but does not affect individual features.

Visitors enter the grounds through the **Centro de Interpretación Regional,** a mission museum (Alberdi between Rivadavia and Bolívar, 7 A.M.–7 P.M. daily, US$7, valid for other Jesuit sites in the province). A nightly light-and-sound show, lasting 50 minutes, costs an additional US$7. Outside the exit, on Rivadavia, eyesore souvenir stands detract from the mission's impact.

Casa de Horacio Quiroga

One of the first Latin American writers to reject the city for the frontier, novelist, storyteller, and poet Horacio Quiroga (1878–1937) spent the prime of life in his self-built house overlooking the Paraná just southwest of downtown San Ignacio. While he made writing his career, Quiroga also worked as a cotton farmer and charcoal maker. He took notable photographs

of San Ignacio's Jesuit ruins, incorporating his outside interests into his writing.

His life plagued by violence—Quiroga accidentally shot a youthful friend to death, and his stepfather and first wife both committed suicide—the writer lived here from 1910 to 1917, and again from 1931 until his own cyanide-induced death. The home is now a museum with 1930s furniture, photographs of his life, and personal belongings. This was not Quiroga's first house; a replica of that, built for director Nemesio Juárez's film *Historias de Amor, de Locura y de Muerte* (Stories of Love, Madness and Death, 1996), stands nearby.

The grounds of Quiroga's house (Avenida Quiroga s/n, US$0.50) are open 7 A.M.–dusk daily.

Accommodations and Food

San Ignacio's accommodations and food are improving but lag well behind Puerto Iguazú and even Posadas. Some distance south of the ruins, **Hospedaje El Descanso** (Pellegrini 270, tel. 03752/47-0207, US$8 pp) has earned high marks for cleanliness and basic comforts. It also has camping spaces.

There are no extravagances at **Hotel San Ignacio** (Sarmiento 823, tel. 03752/47-0047, hotelsanignacio@arnet.com.ar, US$19 s, US$24 d), but it has fairly complete services.

On sprawling woodsy grounds, the best new option is the **Adventure Hostel San Ignacio** (Independencia 469, tel. 3752/47-0955, www. sihostel.com, US$10 pp dorm, US$26 s, $US37 d, with private baths). It occupies the former Automóvil Club motel, which, though it's stylistically superannuated, makes it a great hostel, with sleeping areas well separated from the pool, bar, pool table, Ping-Pong, and foosball facilities. Some rooms have air-conditioning.

Opposite the ruins, **Hotel Portal del Sol** (Rivadavia 1105, tel. 03752/47-0005, www. portaldelsolhotel.com, US$22 s, US$32 d) has upgraded its facilities to include luxuries (by local standards) such as flat-screen TVs; there is also a pool. Its restaurant, **La Misionerita** (Rivadavia 1105, tel. 03752/15-57-8895), is reasonably priced for river fish.

Three blocks south of the ruins, **Pizzería la Aldea** (Rivadavia s/n, tel. 03752/47-0567) serves fine pizza with varied toppings and has attractive sidewalk seating to boot.

Restaurants near the ruins may be assembly-line operations geared toward large tour groups, but the standard Argentine menus are by no means bad if you can tolerate the crowds and swarms of urchins who want to wash your car and drag you to their kickback restaurant of choice. Opposite the entrance to the ruins, try **Don Valentín** (Alberdi 444, tel. 03752/47-0284). Opposite the exit, there's **Liana Bert** (Rivadavia 1133, tel. 03752/47-0151) or **La Carpa Azul** (Rivadavia 1295, tel. 03752/47-0096) just to the north.

Other Practicalities

At the junction of RN 12 and Avenida Sarmiento, the helpful **Oficina de Información Turística** is open 7:30 A.M.–12:30 P.M. and 1 P.M.–6 P.M. daily. **Banco Macro** (San Martín and Sarmiento) has an ATM.

Buses arrive and leave from the new **Terminal de Ómnibus** across the highway from the tourist office. The main destinations are Posadas (1 hour, US$3) and Puerto Iguazú (3 hours, US$9). Milk-run buses are considerably slower than express services.

◖ PARQUE NACIONAL IGUAZÚ

In the Guaraní language, *iguazú* means "big waters," and the good news is that the thunderous surge of Iguazú Falls—perhaps the planet's greatest chain of cascades—continues to plunge over an ancient lava flow some 20 kilometers east of the town of Puerto Iguazú. Its overwhelming natural assets, including the surrounding subtropical rain forest, have earned it recognition as a UNESCO World Heritage Site.

The bad news is that Argentina's APN, the state entity charged with preserving and protecting this natural heritage, has buckled to rampant Disneyfication. The falls, its core attraction, have become a mass-tourism destination that might more accurately be called Parque Temático Iguazú—Iguazú Theme Park.

They've done something right in limiting automobile access—cars must park in a guarded lot, and visitors enter the park on foot—but the concessionaire has turned the area surrounding the falls into an area of manicured lawns, fast-food eateries, and souvenir stands connected by a cheesy narrow-gauge train. Maintenance crews use leaf-blowers to clean the concrete trails near the visitors center every morning.

Around the falls proper, clean-cut youths with walkie-talkies shunt hikers out by 6 P.M.—the perfect closing hour for a theme park—unless you're a privileged guest at the Sheraton, the park's only accommodations. The exception to the rule is the monthly full-moon tour, which is well worthwhile.

That's not to say commercial greed has completely overrun nature—the park still has extensive subtropical rain forests, with colorfully abundant birdlife along with less conspicuous mammals and reptiles. All of these animals demand respect, but some more so than others—in 1997 a jaguar killed a park ranger's infant son; pumas are even more common, and poisonous snakes are also present.

In 1541 Alvar Núñez Cabeza de Vaca, one of colonial America's most intrepid Spaniards, was the first European to see the falls. But in an area populated by tens of thousands of Guaraní Indians prior to the European invasion, he can hardly have discovered them, despite the assertions of a commemorative plaque.

The Natural Landscape

According to Guaraní legend, a jealous serpent-god created Iguazú Falls by collapsing the riverbed in front of fleeing lovers Naipi and Caroba; Naipi plunged over the ensuing falls to become a rock at their base, while her lover Caroba became a tree condemned to see, but unable to touch, his beloved.

A less fanciful explanation is that the languid Río Iguazú streams over a basalt plateau that ends where an ancient lava flow finally cooled; before reaching the lava's end, small islands, large rocks, and unseen reefs split the river into multiple channels that become the individual waterfalls that, in sum, form the celebrated *cataratas,* some more than 70 meters in height.

At this point, in an area stretching more than two kilometers across the Argentine-Brazilian border, at least 1,500 cubic meters of water per second roar over the edge onto an older sedimentary landscape, but the volume can be far greater in flood. With the water's unstoppable force, the falls are slowly but inexorably receding toward the east.

About 18 kilometers southeast of the town of Puerto Iguazú, and 1,280 kilometers north of Buenos Aires via RN 12, Parque Nacional Iguazú is a 67,000-hectare unit with a roughly 6,000-hectare Reserva Nacional—whose presence has led to rampant commercial development in the vicinity of the falls.

Flora and Fauna

Misiones's high rainfall (about 2,000 mm per annum) and subtropical temperatures create a luxuriant forest flora on relatively poor soils.

Unlike the midlatitudes, where fallen leaves and other plant litter become part of the soil, here they are almost immediately recycled to support a dense, multilevel flora with diverse faunal habitats. The roughly 2,000 identified plant species are home to almost innumerable insects, 448 bird species, 80 mammal species, and many reptiles and fish.

The tallest trees, such as the *lapacho* and *palo rosa,* reach 30 meters above the forest floor, while the *guapoy* (the appropriately named "strangler fig") uses the larger trees for support and eventually kills them by asphyxiation. A variety of orchids use the large trees for support only.

Lesser trees and shrubs grow in the shade of the canopy, such as *yerba mate,* the holly relative that Argentines, Uruguayans, Paraguayans, and Brazilians consume as tea (grown mostly on plantations in Misiones and Corrientes). Ferns are also abundant in the shade thrown by the large trees.

For most visitors, the most conspicuous fauna will be colorful birds such as parakeets and parrots, the piping guan, the red-breasted toucan, and the lineated woodpecker in the trees, while tinamous scurry along the forest floor. The tufted capuchin monkey is a fruit-eating tree-dweller.

The most commonly seen mammal, though, is the coatimundi, a raccoon relative that thrives around humans (do not feed it); the largest is the rarely seen tapir, distantly related to the horse. Like the tapir, the puma and *ya-guareté* (jaguar) avoid human contact, preferring the forest's denser, more remote areas; barely a dozen-plus jaguars remain.

The most common reptile is the innocuous iguana; venomous snakes, while they generally avoid humans, deserve respect in their forest habitat.

Sights

The earliest written record came from Cabeza de Vaca, who saw the falls as an obstacle to his downstream progress and reported, with apparent irritation, that "It was necessary…to take the canoes out of the water and carry them by hand past the cataract for half a league with great labor." Still, he could not help but be impressed by the noise and mist:

> The current of the Yguazú was so strong that the canoes were carried furiously down the river, for near this spot there is a considerable fall, and the noise made by the water leaping down some high rocks into a chasm may be heard a great distance off, and the spray rises two spears high and more over the fall.

Most visitors come to see the falls, and rightly so, but try to arrive early to avoid the crush of tour buses from Puerto Iguazú and Brazil. The sole exception to the Disneyland entry hours are the monthly full-moon hikes, guided by park rangers.

Visitors pay the entrance fee at the Portal Cataratas, the gate to the slickly managed complex of fast-food restaurants, souvenir stands, and tour operators. The most worthwhile sight here is the park service's **Centro de Interpretación.**

Traditionally, park visitors walk along three major circuits on mostly paved trails and *pasarelas* (catwalks) that zigzag among the islands and outcrops to make their way to overlooks of the falls. The **Circuito Superior** (Upper Circuit) is a 650-meter route with the best panoramas of the Argentine side of the falls, while the 1,700-meter **Circuito Inferior** (Lower Circuit) offers better views of individual falls and also provides launch access to **Isla San Martín** for exceptional perspectives on the amphitheatrical **Garganta del Diablo** (Devil's Throat), Iguazú's single most breathtaking cataract.

Most visitors take the **Tren de la Selva,** the narrow-gauge railway, to reach the trailhead for the 1,130-meter catwalk to the overlook for the Garganta del Diablo; this means an unavoidable soaking while watching the *vencejo de tormenta* (ashy-tailed swift) dart through the booming waters to and from nesting sites beneath the falls. The view almost defies description, though the spray can obscure the base of the falls and even on the hottest days can chill sightseers—bring light raingear, plastic bags to protect cameras and other valuables, and perhaps even a small towel.

Far fewer visitors explore forest trails than the *pasarelas,* except for the 20-minute **Sendero Verde,** a short forest walk leading to a small wetland that's home to birds and butterflies. The six-kilometer **Sendero Macuco,** a nature trail that starts near the train station, is the likeliest place to spot or hear the tufted capuchin monkey. Mostly level, it drops to the **Salto Arrechea,** a small waterfall, via a steep, muddy, and slippery segment. Mosquito repellent is desirable.

Sports and Recreation

Above the falls, the Río Iguazú itself is suitable for canoeing, kayaking, and other water sports; it should go without saying that there's serious danger in getting too close to the falls. Below the falls there are additional opportunities.

The principal tour operator is **Iguazú Jungle Explorer** (tel. 03757/42-1600, ext. 582, tel./fax 03757/42-1696, www.iguazu-junglexplorer.com), which has an office in the Sheraton and kiosks at the Portal Cataratas and at the Garganta del Diablo trailhead. Offerings include a 30-minute *Paseo Ecológico* (US$9) through the gallery forests and islands above the falls; a 15-minute *Aventura Naútica* (US$20) that approaches the Garganta del Diablo from below; and the *Gran Aventura* (US$40) that includes an eight-kilometer forest excursion by 4WD vehicle, a motorized descent of the lower Iguazú including two kilometers of rapids; and visits to the various falls.

Explorador Expediciones (Perito Moreno 217, Puerto Iguazú, tel. 03757/42-1632, www.rainforestevt.com.ar) has similar excursions and some more active offerings, such as whitewater rafting and rappelling. It also has offices at the Sheraton (tel. 03757/42-1922) and a kiosk near the park entrance.

Accommodations and Food

By default, almost everyone will stay in or near Puerto Iguazú—the park's only option

MESOPOTAMIA

is the behemoth **Sheraton Iguazú Resort & Spa** (tel. 03757/49-1800, www.sheraton.com/iguazu, US$265–455 s or d), an incongruously sited building whose ungainly exterior has a certain Soviet-style presence (in fairness, Sheraton took over an existing hotel here). The more expensive rooms have views of the falls.

The hotel has several restaurants, but anyone not eating there will have to settle for the fast-food clones, a pizzeria, and the odd *parrilla* on the park grounds. Better food is available in Puerto Iguazú.

Other Practicalities

Panels at the APN's **Centro de Interpretación** (tel. 03757/49-1444, 7:30 A.M.–6:15 P.M. daily spring and summer, 8 A.M.–5:45 P.M. daily the rest of the year) give vivid explanations of the park's environment, ecology, ethnology, and history; there are also helpful personnel on duty.

For foreigners, the admission charge of US$16, payable in Argentine pesos only, is one of the most expensive to any Argentine national park; if you return the next day, your ticket is half price. Provincial residents pay US$2, other Argentines US$5, and residents of other Mercosur countries US$8. Entry fees include the Tren de la Selva and launch access to Isla San Martín. The concessionaire Iguazú Argentina has a useful website (www.iguazuargentina.com) in Spanish, Portuguese, and English.

From the Puerto Iguazú bus terminal, **El Práctico** buses (US$1.50) operate frequently between 7:15 A.M. and 8 P.M., taking 45 minutes to or from the park.

PUERTO IGUAZÚ

At the confluence of the Paraná and the Iguazú Rivers, Puerto Iguazú lives partly from a thriving tourist trade, thanks to its proximity to the famous Iguazú Falls. Visitors from all over the globe pass through or stay in town, though fewer cross the border to Brazil's own national park and the city of Foz do Iguaçu than in the past because of Brazil's punitive visa fees.

As part of the Tres Fronteras (Three Borders) area that includes Foz and the Paraguayan city of Ciudad del Este, Puerto Iguazú has a dark side as well; on the entire continent, Tres Fronteras' only challenger in corruption is the tripartite Amazonian border of Brazil, Colombia, and Perú. Here, linked by bridges, residents of the three countries pass freely, sustaining plenty of legitimate commerce, but at more furtive crossings, they move contraband weapons, drugs, and money. Money is a particularly contentious point, as Brazil- and Paraguay-based merchants of Middle Eastern origins reportedly have financial links to groups like Hamas and Hezbollah, though there have been no terrorist incidents here.

This does not mean Puerto Iguazú is unsafe—most travelers consider it positively placid. Foz, though, has serious street-crime problems.

Puerto Iguazú (pop. about 60,000) is about 300 kilometers northeast of Posadas via RN 12, a paved toll road that's gradually being widened; it is 1,287 kilometers north of Buenos Aires. Because of widespread smuggling, there are thorough Gendarmería (Border Guard) inspections about 30 kilometers south of town.

Sights

At the west end of Avenida Tres Fronteras, the **Hito Argentino** is an obelisk that triangulates the Paraná-Iguazú confluence with similar markers in Brazil and Paraguay, both of which are visible from here.

On the west side of Plaza San Martín, the **Casa del Pionero** (Santa María 890, 7 A.M.–1 P.M. and 4–8 P.M. daily) tells Puerto Iguazú's story through family photographs— literally so, as almost no text accompanies them. Opposite the plaza, across Avenida Victoria Aguirre, the **Paseo de la Identidad** is a series of sculptural murals that portray scenes of regional ecology, ethnology, and history.

The **Jardín de los Picaflores** (Fray Luis Beltrán 150, US$2) is a lush subtropical garden, with bird feeders, that claims to have a greater diversity of hummingbirds than the national park. Outside town, just north of the highway, **La Aripuca** (RN 12 Km 4.5, tel. 03757/42-3488, www.aripuca.com.ar, mainly

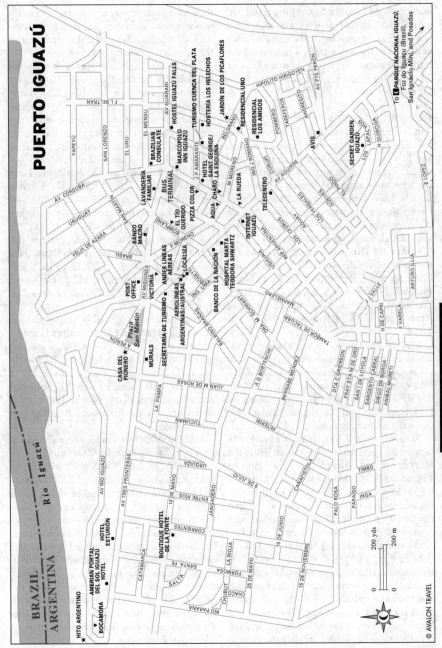

PUERTO IGUAZÚ

BRAZIL

ARGENTINA

Rio Iguazú

★ HITO ARGENTINO

▲ BOCAMÓRA

■ AMERIAN PORTAL DEL SOL IGUAZÚ HOTEL

■ HOTEL ESTURIÓN

AV RIO IGUAZÚ

AV TRES FRONTERAS

■ BOUTIQUE HOTEL DE LA FONTE

CATAMARCA

SANTA FE

SALTA

CHACO

CHUBUT

RIO PARANÁ

CORRIENTES

LA RIOJA

FORMOSA

25 DE MAYO

15 DE NOVIEMBRE

10 DE JUNIO

ENTRE RIOS

10 DE MAYO

JANGADERO

URQUIZA

9 DE JULIO

CAÑARISTOLA

PALO ROSA

PARAISO

INGA

TIMBÓ

E LÓPEZ

ARTURO ILLIA

CASA DEL PIONERO ★

★ Plaza San Martin

PEÑÓN

LA PAMPA

TUCUMÁN

JUAN M DE ROSAS

PETERIBI

BERNABÉ MÉNDEZ

A. G BORTENICHI

DÍA. M. SCHWARZ

TAMBOR DE TACUARÍ

MARMELERO

DÍA C CRINERSON

FRAY STA N DE ORO

SAN I DE LOYOLA

SARGENTO CABRAL

DIEGO DE BOROA

ANIBAL MORETI

J VALLE

H DE CAPRI

H SCHWART

F VARELA

POST OFFICE ■

AV MISIONES

VICTORIA ■

SECRETARÍA DE TURISMO ■

■ MURALS

ANDES LÍNEAS AÉREAS ■

AEROLÍNEAS ARGENTINAS/AUSTRAL ■

BANCO MACRO ■

BRASIL

FÉLIX DE AZARA

URUGUAY

SAN MATÍAS

AV CÓRDOBA

YAPEYÚ

SAN LORENZO

EL URÚ

F.L. BELTRÁN

P. MORENO

ING UMÁ

ING BÓSETTI

BABINO BRAÑAS

■ LOCALIZA

■ BANCO DE LA NACIÓN

■ HOSPITAL MARTA TEODORA SHWARTZ

RÍO QUERIDO ■

■ BONPLAND

PIZZA COLOR ▲

AQUA ▲

CHARO ▲

LA ESQUINA ▼

LA RUEDA ▼

J P AMARANTE

M MORENO

ING J ROMANO

CURUPÍ

TELECENTRO ■

AV AGUIRRE

INTERNET IGUAZÚ ■

USHUAIA

RÍA ARGENTINA

LOS CEDROS

GÜEMES

AGUAY

LOS YERBALES

EL INDIO

LAVANDERÍA FAMILIAR ■

BUS TERMINAL ■

EL MENSÚ

■ BRAZILIAN CONSULATE

AV GUARANÍ

● HOSTEL IGUAZÚ FALLS

MARCOPOLO INN IGUAZÚ ●

■ TURISMO CUENCA DEL PLATA

HOTEL SAINT GEORGE/ ●

● HOSTERÍA LOS HELECHOS

★ JARDÍN DE LOS PICAFLORES

● RESIDENCIAL UNO

RESIDENCIAL LOS AMIGOS ●

BELGRANO

HIPÓLITO HIRIGOYEN

POMBERO

AV PTE PERÓN

TAREFEROS

ANDRESITO

■ AVIS

SECRET GARDEN IGUAZÚ ●

SOL

LOS LAPAC

H QUIROGA

To ◀ **PARQUE NACIONAL IGUAZÚ,**
Foz do Iguaçu (Brazil),
San Ignacio Miní, and Posadas

MESOPOTAMIA

0   200 yds
0   200 m

© AVALON TRAVEL

open daylight hours, US$1.50) is a forest and ethnological museum that takes its name from the clever traps used by the Guaraní to catch game. Its main structure is a macro-*aripuca* built of massive logs salvaged from the *selva*. There's a small snack bar, and a restaurant is due to open soon.

Accommodations

While Puerto Iguazú gets visitors all year round, demand is highest during Semana Santa and July's patriotic holidays, when prices tend to rise. Recent new luxury constructions, plus the renovation of existing hotels into shining hostels, have improved the accommodations scene. Most of the best places are on the outskirts, on the road to the park, but there are some delightful places in town as well.

Under US$10: Two campgrounds on the park road offer decent facilities for around US$4 pp plus US$2.50 per tent: **Camping El Pindó** (RN 12 Km 3.5, tel. 03757/42-1795, lisandro_lozina@hotmail.com) and **Camping Americano** (RN 12 Km 5, tel. 03757/42-0190).

US$10-25: Puerto Iguazú has several HI affiliates and other hostels that offer excellent value. Only a block from the bus terminal, the **Hostel Iguazú Falls** (Avenida Guaraní 70, tel. 03757/42-1295, www.hosteliguazufalls.com.ar, US$10 pp, US$28 d) has the standard amenities and a swimming pool.

Across from the bus terminal, under the same management as the Hostel Inn, the **Marcopolo Inn Iguazú** (Avenida Córdoba 158, tel. 03757/42-0434, www.hostel-inn.com, US$9-10 pp dorm, US$32-37 s or d) has remade a conventional family-run hostelry into downtown's most appealing budget option, with manicured gardens and even a small pool.

On the park road, **(Hostel Inn Iguazú** (RN 12 Km 5, tel. 03757/42-0156, www.hostel-inn.com, US$10-12 pp dorm, US$38-44 s or d) occupies sprawling but well-kept grounds and has more elaborate amenities, including a giant pool with its own bar, Wi-Fi, pool and Ping-Pong tables, and some hotel-style doubles. It's also one of the livelier hostels here, though

the sleeping quarters are well-separated from the bar-restaurant and other common areas. Rates vary according to HI membership, and whether the room has air-conditioning or not.

New in late 2009, the **Marcopolo Suites Iguazú** (RN 12 Km 3.5, tel. 03757/42-2440, www.hostel-inn.com, US$10-12 pp dorm, US$38-45 s or d) is a renovated hotel whose clientele leans more toward slightly older travelers who prefer a bit more quiet and greater amenities than its sister Hostel Inn, which is just a few hundred meters down the road.

US$25-50: Once a hostel, **Residencial Uno** (Fray Luis Beltrán 116, tel. 03757/42-0529, residencialuno@gmail.com, US$26-32 s, US$32-40 d) is now a more conventional accommodation, though it still has a friendly feel.

On a quiet block, on sprawling grounds with a new pool, **Residencial Los Amigos** (Fray Luis Beltrán 82, tel. 03757/42-0756, www.residencialamigos.com, US$37 d) has simple rooms with private baths. Off-season rates drop by a third.

Reservations are advisable for popular, efficient **(Hostería Los Helechos** (Paulino Amarante 76, tel. 03757/42-0338, www.hosterialoshelechos.com.ar, US$34 s, US$44 d), an excellent value that's often crowded even off-season. The rooms enjoy a delightful garden setting, with a large pool and other amenities, but rooms with air-conditioning cost slightly more.

US$50-100: No longer the only one of its kind, **(Secret Garden Iguazú** (Los Lapachos 623, tel. 03757/42-3099, www.secretgardeniguazu.com, US$90 s, US$100 d) may still be Iguazú's best bed-and-breakfast and is virtually the only thing in its price range. Host John Fernandes, a Portuguese-Indian photographer from Mumbai by way of Buenos Aires, has created an intimate secluded hostelry in a quiet residential neighborhood where the liveliest presence is Roxy, his energetic Jack Russell terrier. Separated from the main house, the guest rooms are cheerful and luminous, with breakfast served on the main deck (where late-afternoon caipirinhas and conversation are an additional attraction).

Hostel Inn Iguazú is enormously popular with backpackers and other budget travelers.

US$100-200: On five hectares of lush grounds along the Iguazú highway, the **Orquídeas Palace Hotel** (RN 12 Km 5, tel. 03757/42-0472, www.orquideashotel.com, US$101–174 s or d) has darkish but comfortable standard rooms. Only a little more luminous, the more expensive superior rooms are substantially larger. In addition to its grounds, the hotel has a restaurant and a swimming pool with a bar.

The best downtown hotel in its price range is the tastefully modernized **C Hotel Saint George** (Avenida Córdoba 148, tel. 03757/42-0633, www.hotelsaintgeorge.com, US$86–112 s, US$105–129 d), which offers very good contemporary lodgings with gardens and a pool.

At the west end of town, overlooking the confluence, upgraded **Hotel Esturión** (Avenida Tres Fronteras 650, tel. 03757/42-0100, www.hotelesturion.com, US$109–158 s or d) has both garden- and river-view rooms.

New in 2009, the Italian-run **Boutique Hotel de la Fonte** (1e de Mayo and Corrientes, tel. 03757/42-0625, www.bhfboutiquehotel.com, US$120–190 s or d) consists of a central reception, dining room, and other shared areas surrounded by eight freestanding rooms with a fairly nondescript brick exterior, but the interiors boast fine design touches and amenities such as flat-screen TVs. Gourmet meals are available for guests only, though the owners may open a separate restaurant.

East of town, **Hotel Cataratas** (RN 11 Km 4.5, tel. 03757/42-1100, www.hotelcataratas.com, US$183–290 s or d) will win no truth-in-labeling awards—it's far closer to town than to the world-famous cascades, and its only falls are the bogus ones that tumble into its oversize swimming pool. Still, the rooms are large and well-equipped, and the rates are commensurate with its amenities.

Over US$200: West of the Esturión, new in 2008, the 102-room **Amerian Portal del Sol Iguazú Hotel** (Avenida Tres Fronteras 780, tel. 03757/49-8200, www.portaldeliguazu.com, US$250–275 s or d) is a modern multistory hotel with views across to Brazil and Paraguay, but it is part of a business-oriented chain that doesn't really fit in here. Still, it probably has the most complete services of any in-town hotel.

CROSSING TO BRAZIL

Many visitors to Misiones also cross to the Brazilian side of Iguazú Falls, which involves a different set of immigration rules and travel conditions. Given the nuisance of obtaining a visa for a short visit, many visitors to Argentina are now bypassing the Brazilian side, but for those who decide to cross, here are some pointers.

FOZ DO IGUAÇU

Compared with pastoral Puerto Iguazú, the Brazilian city of Foz do Iguaçu is a frantic, fast-moving center of commerce and construction that has grown uncontrollably as a result of the Itaipú dam, a joint Brazilian-Paraguayan effort that's the Iguazú of hydroelectric projects. Foz has a broader range of services than Puerto Iguazú – with a capacity of 22,000 hotel beds – but lacks the Argentine town's greenery.

Foz's unbridled growth has also focused Brazil's serious social problems here – its downtown streets can be unsafe at night, and its riverside *favelas* (shantytowns) should be avoided at any hour.

VISAS AND OFFICIALDOM

In the controversial Triple Frontier area, border-crossing regulations change frequently.

Traditionally, visitors entering Brazil for less than 24 hours simply to visit the other side of the falls have crossed freely even when their nationality should require them to obtain an advance visa. According to San Francisco's Brazilian consulate, the Policía Federal (which enforces the country's immigration laws at the border) can be flexible, but it falls into a gray area for nationalities that normally need visas. If in doubt, get the proper visa.

If at all possible, get the visa in your home country, where consulates normally issue five-year multiple-entry visas; if you apply elsewhere, you may get only a 90-day multiple-entry visa. In the past, the first entry to Brazil *had to* take place within 90 days of issue or the visa became invalid, but authorities have apparently dispensed with this requirement. Depending on the applicant's nationality, Brazilian consulates require a variable processing fee, which is refunded if the visa is not granted.

Open 8 A.M.-1 P.M. weekdays only, Puerto Iguazú's Brazilian Consulate (Avenida Córdoba 264, tel. 03757/42-1273) is only half a block from the bus terminal. Visa processing, requiring one passport-sized photograph, takes about an hour. It accepts only Argentine pesos, however, and because of volatile exchange rates, it

On the shores of the river, which is barely visible for the dense rain forest, the **Loi Suites Iguazú Hotel** (Selva Iryapú s/n, tel. 03757/49-8300, www.loisuites.com.ar, US$242–550 s or d) is the first hotel in a newly developing area east of the road to Foz. Part of a design hotel chain that also has branches in Recoleta, Bariloche, and El Calafate, this newest branch is large—120 rooms—with the common areas in a central building and the accommodations divided among several others, sometimes connected by suspension bridges. The best values are the upper-story suites (US$345), which have outdoor Jacuzzis with river views. Despite the hotel's size, its visual impact is surprisingly light.

Food

Alfresco eating is the norm in Puerto Iguazú, at least in the morning or after the sun sets, and every place has at least some outdoor seating. At midday, when many if not most visitors are at the falls, indoor air-conditioning is more than welcome.

Its patio particularly packed at dinnertime, **Pizza Color** (Avenida Córdoba 135, tel. 03757/42-0206) serves a diversity of pizzas. Puerto Iguazú has a pair of pretty good *parrillas:* **Charo** (Avenida Córdoba 106, tel. 03757/42-1529) and **El Tío Querido** (Bonpland s/n, tel. 03757/42-0750).

The Hotel St. George's **(La Esquina** (Avenida Córdoba 148, tel. 03757/42-1597) serves some of the best food, with starters like

builds itself a cushion against devaluation: The fee for U.S. citizens is theoretically US$131, but because the consulate fixes the rate higher than Argentine banks and exchange houses, in practice the fee may be 50 percent higher. Other nationalities requiring visas include Canadians (US$65), Japanese (US$50), Australians (US$35), and Mexicans (US$30). Other nationalities needing advance visas pay US$20.

Argentine authorities have been checking the documents of border crossers carefully; the Brazilians less so. While crossing to Brazil for the day without an advance visa *may* be possible, if you have a valid visa, you *must* get a Brazilian stamp in your passport. Buses wait on the Argentine side but not on the Brazilian side; if you need a Brazilian stamp, you may have to wait for the next bus. In this instance, the driver will provide you with a chit to continue on the following one.

HEALTH AND SAFETY

Public health conditions are not dramatically different on the Brazilian side of the river, but travelers continuing north into Brazil may want to consider prophylaxis for malaria and other tropical diseases.

Note that auto theft is common in the Triple Frontier area, carjackings have taken place on the Brazilian side, and street crime is more common in Foz than in Puerto Iguazú. It's better to leave your vehicle in secure parking on the Argentine side and take a bus or hire a taxi or *remise* to the Brazilian side of the falls.

MONEY AND PRICES

The Brazilian currency is the *real* (plural *reis*), which is stronger than the Argentine peso at about 1.82 per U.S. dollar. In practice, the two currencies circulate almost interchangeably, while the Paraguayan *guaraní* (about 4,765 per U.S. dollar) is also acceptable tender. Most businesses, such as hotels and restaurants, also accept U.S. dollars.

Because of the stronger currency, Brazilian prices are higher for comparable services than in Argentina.

MISCELLANEOUS

Brazilians speak Portuguese rather than Spanish. Travelers with a command of Spanish may be able to read Portuguese, but speaking and understanding Brazilians is more problematic.

At certain times of the year, Argentina is an hour behind Brazil so that, for example, 7 A.M. in Brazil may be 6 A.M. in Argentina.

MESOPOTAMIA

jamón crudo (prosciutto) for around US$4 and entrées like grilled *surubí* (river fish) in the US$7–10 range. The service, however, can be erratic and even absent-minded. **La Rueda** (Avenida Córdoba 28, tel. 03757/42-2531) also serves fine grilled fish.

Victoria (Avenida Brasil 39, tel. 03757/42-0441) prepares large, lightly grilled portions of not just *surubí* but also *dorado* and *pacú*, which are harder to find on river-fish menus. For around US$10, this is an excellent value, with good-natured service and equally good desserts.

C Aqua (Avenida Córdoba and Carlos Thays, tel. 03757/42-2064, US$10–20) is an ambitious restaurant with local river fish and twists on traditional dishes such as *ñoquis*

(gnocchi) made with manioc. With improved service and the town's most diverse menu, it's easily the best in town.

There are views of three countries and the Paraná-Iguazú confluence from **Bocamora** (Avenida Costanera s/n, tel. 03757/42-0550, www.bocamora.com), which has a menu of regional specialties, such as grilled surubí and manioc gnocchi, and standard Argentine dishes at a similarly high level. New in late 2009, it needs to work out some kinks—the service is well-meaning but a little overbearing—but it has the potential to match Aqua's standards.

Information

The provincial **Secretaría de Turismo**

(Avenida Victoria Aguirre 311, tel. 03757/42-0800) is open 8 A.M.–noon and 4–8 P.M. weekdays, 7 A.M.–1 P.M. and 2–9 P.M. weekends. The local **Ente Municipal de Turismo** (Avenida Córdoba and Avenida Misiones, tel. 03757/42-2938, www.iguazuturismo.gov.ar, 8 A.M.–8 P.M. daily) is downstairs at the bus terminal.

For motorists, **ACA** (tel. 03757/42-0165) is on the southeastern outskirts of town, just beyond Camping El Pindó.

Services

Banco de la Nación (Avenida Victoria Aguirre 179) has an ATM, as does **Banco Macro** (Avenida Misiones and Bonpland).

Correo Argentino is at Avenida San Martín 780; the postal code is 3370.

The downtown **Telecentro** (Avenida Victoria Aguirre and Los Cedros) has long-distance phone connections. **Internet Iguazú** (Avenida Victoria Aguirre 552, tel. 03757/42-4034) has Internet services.

For tours on both the Argentine and Brazilian sides, and into nearby Paraguay as well, try **Turismo Cuenca del Plata** (Paulino Amarante 76, tel. 03757/42-1062).

The **Lavandería Familiar** (Avenida Misiones 42, tel. 03757/42-1096) does the washing.

Hospital Marta Teodora Shwartz (Avenida Victoria Aguirre and Ushuaia, tel. 03757/42-0288) is the public hospital.

Getting There

Aerolíneas Argentinas (Avenida Victoria Aguirre 295, tel. 03757/42-0237) flies several times daily to Aeroparque (Buenos Aires), but no longer operates international flights from here. **LAN** (tel. 03757/42-4296) also flies to Aeroparque; its local representative is **Turismo Dick** (Avenida Victoria Aguirre 379, tel. 03757/42-0380).

Andes Líneas Aéreas (Avenida Victoria Aguirre 279, tel. 03757/42-5566) now flies Monday and Friday to Salta and Córdoba, making it possible to reach the Andean northwest without backtracking to Buenos Aires.

Puerto Iguazú's **Terminal de Ómnibus**

(Avenida Córdoba and Avenida Misiones, tel. 03757/42-3006) has long-distance services throughout Argentina and is also the terminal for local buses to Foz do Iguaçu (Brazil) and Ciudad del Este (Paraguay).

Sample destinations, times, and fares include Posadas (4.5 hours, US$12), Corrientes (9 hours, US$29), Resistencia (9.5 hours, US$31), Buenos Aires (16 hours, US$52–84), and Salta (23 hours, US$65–75).

Getting Around

Aeropuerto Internacional Iguazú is about 10 kilometers southeast of town. Several local agencies have combined their services to offer airport transfers as Four Tourist Travel (tel. 03757/42-0681), for US$4 pp. A *remise* costs about US$16 for up to four people.

El Práctico and Crucero del Norte **buses** to Parque Nacional Iguazú (US$1.35) operate between 7:30 A.M. and 8 P.M., taking 45 minutes to the park. To Foz do Iguaçu (US$1.25), there are frequent buses with Tres Fronteras, Risa, and El Práctico; travelers going through border formalities must usually disembark on the Brazilian side and wait for the succeeding bus (of any company) at no additional charge.

Rental **bicycles** are available from **Iguazú Internet** (Avenida Victoria Aguirre 552, tel. 03757/42-4034).

For car rental, try **Alamo** (Avenida Victoria Aguirre 271, tel. 03757/42-3780) or **Avis** (Avenida Victoria Aguirre 1149, tel. 03757/42-2395, iguazu@avis.com.ar).

PARQUE NACIONAL DO IGUAÇU (BRAZIL)

By consensus, the Brazilian side of the border offers the best panoramas of the falls, even if the Argentine side provides better close-ups. Fauna, flora, and services are similar on both sides, but the Brazilian side has fewer easily accessible areas for roaming. The best views are available along the trail leading from Hotel Tropical das Cataratas down to the riverside overlook.

Like the Argentine side, its infrastructure has undergone considerable changes in recent years, with private vehicles consigned to parking lots and shuttle buses carrying passengers to the falls. One unchanged feature is the noisy 10-minute helicopter overflights, which Argentine authorities complain disrupt nesting birds and other wildlife.

The park's only accommodations are at the **(Hotel Tropical das Cataratas** (tel. 55/45/2102-7000, www.hoteldascataratas.com, US$275–915 s or d), oozing a tasteful tropicality that Argentina's concrete Sheraton bunker can hardly match.

Payable in Brazilian, Argentine, or U.S. currency, the admission charge is equivalent to US$3.50 for local residents, US$10 for other Brazilians, US$15 for residents of other Mercosur countries, and US$18 for all other foreigners. Park hours are 9 A.M.–6 P.M. daily October–March, 9 A.M.–5 P.M. daily April–September.

From Puerto Iguazú's terminal, take any Tres Fronteras, Risa, or El Práctico **bus** over the Puente Internacional Tancredo Neves, the bridge over the Río Iguazú. These buses go to downtown Foz do Iguaçu's local bus terminal, at Avenida Juscelino Kubitschek and Rua Mem de Sá, where Transbalan city buses leave directly for the park. Park-bound passengers from Argentina, though, can disembark at the Avenida das Cataratas junction, just north of the bridge, and take the Transbalan bus to the park entrance.

Nationalities needing visas can get same-day service at Puerto Iguazú's Brazilian consulate (Avenida Córdoba 264, tel. 03757/42-1348) by providing one photograph and paying approximately US$170 (in Argentine pesos only, refunded if the visa is not granted). The consulate is open 7 A.M.–1 P.M. weekdays only; the staff speak only Portuguese.

Santa Fe Province

Historian Ezequiel Gallo has called wealthy Santa Fe Province the *pampa gringa* for its transformation, through European immigration, from humid grasslands into one of the world's great granaries. Its attractions are primarily urban, in the cities of Rosario and the provincial capital of Santa Fe, but the middle Paraná Delta remains to be explored.

ROSARIO

Possibly Argentina's most underrated city, the economic powerhouse of Rosario is an industrial city and a major port for grains from the *pampa gringa,* but it also boasts one of the country's liveliest cultural scenes, with first-rate museums, art, theater, and live music. Among its many creative artists have been comedian Alberto Olmedo, actress Libertad Lamarque, actor Darío Grandinetti, and pop musician Fito Páez.

For nationalists, Rosario is the "Cuna de la Bandera" (Cradle of the Flag), where General Manuel Belgrano designed and first displayed

Rosario is a city of riverside parks.

MESOPOTAMIA

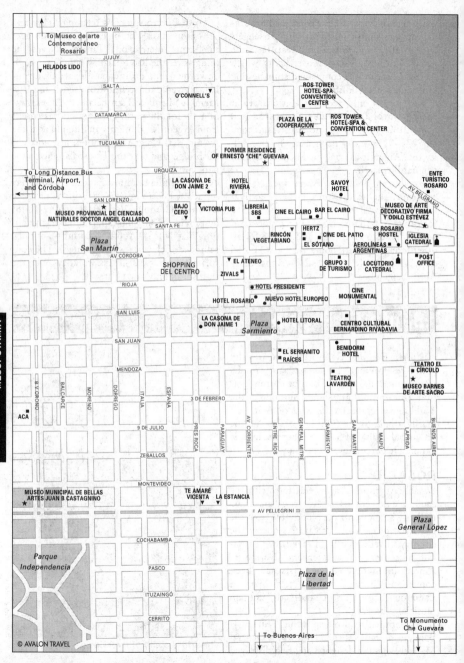

ROSARIO

Río

Paraná

MONUMENTO
NACIONAL A LA
BANDERA

Plaza
Belgrano

ESTACIÓN
FLUVIAL

Plaza de
Andrea

★ MUELLE 1

*Parque Nacional
de la Bandera*

LA CHERNIA/
ELCUCHO Y LA CHOLGA

DE MAYO

L N ALEM

AVACUCHO

COLÓN

NECOCHEA

CHACABUCO

DOS
RUEDAS

PUERTO GABOTO

*Parque
Urquiza*

OBSERVATORIO ★
VICTOR
CAPOLONGO

ESMERALDA

BERUTI

J. M DE ROSAS

0   300 yds

0   300 m

the colors that still wave over the republic today. For Rosarinos themselves, it's the country's "second city," though they have to argue the point with residents of Córdoba.

Sensibly sited Rosario mostly occupies high ground above the Paraná floodplain; when it rains heavily, though, many intersections and even sidewalks can flood, and residents remove their shoes and roll up their trouser legs to get around. Beyond the densely built downtown, tree-lined streets and open spaces like Parque Independencia are the rule. On the floodplain itself, most structures are port facilities or recycled port facilities set among open green spaces.

History

The first Europeans settled around 1720, moving southward from the city of Santa Fe. Following the mid-19th-century civil wars, the railroad to Córdoba made Rosario a major port and spurred agricultural colonization through the Central Argentine Land Company. New European settlers arrived directly from Europe rather than through Buenos Aires, and by the early 20th century Rosario's population of more than 200,000 exceeded Santa Fe's. Because of its late growth, the best parts of Rosario's cityscape reflect that era's Francophile preferences—or pretensions.

Orientation

On the Paraná's west bank, Rosario (pop. about 960,000) is 320 kilometers northwest of Buenos Aires via RN 9, a four-lane toll road that also leads west to Córdoba (as a two-lane highway). It is 167 kilometers south of Santa Fe via A-008, another four-lane toll road, and now linked to the nearby city of Victoria, Entre Ríos, via a 57-kilometer series of bridges and causeways across the Paraná Delta.

Monumento Nacional a la Bandera

It's tempting to call Rosario's most overwhelming monument, which pays tribute to the Argentine flag and its designer Manuel

THE TRACKS OF CHE GUEVARA

Revolutionary Rosarinos like to claim Ernesto "Che" Guevara as one of their own – as an infant he lived in the **Edificio La Rosario** (Urquiza and Entre Ríos), an apartment building in a middle-class neighborhood.

Che's father, Ernesto Guevara Lynch, and his mother, Celia de la Serna, probably pushed their son's stroller around the nearby **Plaza de la Cooperación** (Tucumán and Mitre), where a mural of Che's face, illuminated at night, glares intensely at local dog walkers and their companions, for whom it serves as toilet facilities.

Rosario's biggest Che monument, oddly enough, is even less distinguished. Fifteen blocks south of the Monumento a la Bandera, **Plaza Che Guevara** (Buenos Aires and 27 de Febrero) boasts a surprisingly unimposing larger-than-life bronze of the guerrilla leader, erected here on the 80th anniversary of his official birth. Its isolation in the sprawling, indifferently maintained plaza seems to diminish, rather than accentuate, Guevara's charisma. In fact, his pedestal seems more like a diving board from which he's about to jump, fully clothed, into the ocean.

Belgrano, a colossal failure or even a shrine to kitsch—the outline of architect Angel Guido's design represents a ship whose symbolic mast is a 78-meter tower on its bow. Alfredo Bigatti and José Fioravanti sculpted the patriotic statues that adorn it, while Eduardo Barnes carved bas-reliefs depicting the country's diverse geography.

Fioravanti expected that the remains of General Manuel Belgrano, who designed the flag and first hoisted it here, would lie in a crypt at the tower's base, but Belgrano remains at Buenos Aires's Iglesia de Santo Domingo. In any event, the monument's pseudo-grandeur overwhelms Belgrano's own unpretentious achievement. Catalina de Vidal actually sewed the original flag, now preserved in the museum. Every June, Rosario observes **La Semana de la Bandera** (Flag Week), which culminates with ceremonies on June 20, the anniversary of Belgrano's death.

For panoramic views of the Paraná waterfront, it's possible to take the elevator (US$0.50) to the top of the Monumento Nacional a la Bandera (Santa Fe 581, tel. 0341/480-2238, www.monumentoalabandera.gov.ar, 9 A.M.–7 P.M. Tues.–Sun., 2–7 P.M. Mon.), which is bounded by Santa Fe, Rosas, Córdoba, and Avenida Belgrano. A military color guard raises the flag at 8:15 A.M. daily and lowers it at 7 P.M.

Other Sights and Recreation

Rosario is a city of monuments and museums, ranging from utterly unassuming to pompously patriotic. Most are in and around several attractive parks, both along the waterfront and its bluffs, and farther inland. A handful of sights are scattered elsewhere downtown.

Across Avenida Belgrano, the **Parque Nacional de la Bandera** stretches several blocks along the floodplain in an area that still houses part of Rosario's port facilities. Sailing from its own pier opposite the flag monument, the *Ciudad de Rosario* (Avenida Belgrano s/n, tel. 0341/449-8688) offers two-hour river excursions (US$5.50 pp) at 2:30 and 5 P.M. weekends and holidays. For a more intimate look at Rosario and its surroundings, **Dos Ruedas** (Zeballos 327, tel. 0341/15-571-3812, www.bikerosario.com.ar) offers city tours on bikes and kayak tours on the river.

Continuing its policy of waterfront improvement, Rosario has dramatically upgraded its **Estación Fluvial,** Avenida Belgrano's passenger terminal for the delta islands. It also holds the **Museo del Paraná y las Islas** (Avenida Belgrano and Rioja, tel. 0341/440-0751, 7–7:30 P.M. weekends only, US$0.75), the site of Rosarino painter Raúl Domínguez's straightforward murals of delta lifestyles.

Like the best muralists, Domínguez ("the painter of the river") deals with everyday themes rather than heroic deeds. Among his subjects are the environmental setting in *Creciente* (In Flood) and *Bajante* (In Drought), travels through the delta in *Recorrido del Paraná* (Exploring the Paraná), folklore in *El Paraná y Sus Leyendas* (The Paraná and Its Legends), and settlers' livelihoods in *Cortador de Paja* (Thatch Cutter) and *El Nutriero* (The Otter Trapper).

Several blocks southeast, **Parque Urquiza** is the site of the **Complejo Astronómico Municipal** (Municipal Observatory, tel. 0341/480-2533, US$0.75). Although light pollution may make a large city like Rosario less than ideal for viewing the southern skies through the telescopes at its **Observatorio Víctor Capolongo,** visitors can stargaze free of additional charge 8–10:30 P.M. Wednesday–Sunday, weather permitting.

In the basement of the Teatro Círculo, the **Museo Barnes de Arte Sacro** (Laprida 1235, tel. 0341/448-3784, www.teatro-elcirculo.com.ar, US$1.50 as part of a theater tour) exhibits its Bible-themed sculptures from one of the contributors to the Monumento a la Bandera. Actually seeing them, though, can be problematic; it's open for guided tours, by reservation only, at 10:30 A.M. Monday, Wednesday, Friday, and Saturday. For a more diverse collection of European art and artifacts (and more flexible hours), check the **Museo de Arte Decorativo Firma y Odilo Estévez** (Santa Fe 748, tel. 0341/480-2547, www.museoestevez.gov.ar, 3–8 P.M. Wed.–Fri., 10 A.M.–8 P.M. weekends, free), occupying a distinguished Italianate residence.

Reopened after a devastating fire in which it lost 70 percent of its collections, the **Museo Provincial de Ciencias Naturales Doctor Angel Gallardo** (San Lorenzo 1949, tel. 0341/472-1449, www.museogallardo.org.ar, free) is strongest on taxidermy, with its outstanding specimen of the rare maned wolf (a nocturnal beast found mostly in the Corrientes wetlands of Esteros del Iberá). It also offers special exhibitions, such as a tribute to Charles Darwin, stressing his South American travels, in 2009, the bicentennial of his birth. Hours

are 9 A.M.–6 P.M. weekdays and 2–7 P.M. weekends, but in summer it's closed on weekends.

The **Museo Municipal de Bellas Artes Juan B. Castagnino** (Avenida Pellegrini 2202, tel. 0341/480-2542, www.museocastagnino.org.ar, 2–8 P.M. Mon.–Wed. and Fri., 1–7 P.M. weekends, US$1) is the top fine arts museum. Housed in a spacious building dating from 1937, it boasts a diverse collection starting with a small assortment of European masters through 19th-century and later landscapes (both European and South American). Its strength, though, is modern Argentine art both figurative and abstract, much of it by Rosarinos. Among the prominent artists on display are Prilidiano Pueyrredón, Benito Quinquela Martín, Antonio Berni, and Eduardo Schiavoni.

At beautifully designed **Parque Independencia,** throngs of joggers and cyclists lope and pedal along footpaths and trails while families float on paddleboats in this urban sanctuary that gets heavier recreational use than any other public park. Having celebrated its centennial in 2002, it offers 112 hectares of verdant open space with museums, a small zoo, a rose garden, tennis courts and other athletic fields, a hippodrome, and an important soccer stadium.

Covered with bright-red bougainvillea, a neoclassical pergola follows the lakeshore on Bulevar Oroño where, nightly at 8:30 P.M., colored lights illuminate a fountain of **Aguas Danzantes** ("dancing waters"). Farther south, the **Museo de la Ciudad** (Bulevar Oroño 2350, tel. 0341/480-8665, www.museodelaciudad.org.ar, 9 A.M.–6 P.M. Tues.–Fri., 2–8 P.M. weekends, free) focuses on Rosario's history.

Immediately west of the lake, the **Museo Histórico Provincial Doctor Julio Marc** (tel. 0341/472-1457, 9 A.M.–5 P.M. Tues.–Fri., 3–7 P.M. weekends and holidays, free) traces regional development from the earliest cultures through the Spanish invasion and evangelization on the frontier, but its focus is the postindependence period.

Immediately west of the museum, the Newell's Old Boys soccer stadium is colloquially known as **El Coloso** (The Colossus). To its south, the park's largest single construction is the **Hipódromo Independencia,** the racetrack.

Creatively built into abandoned grain silos, Rosario's newest museum is the **Museo de Arte Contemporáneo Rosario** (Blvd. Oroño and Río Paraná, tel. 0341/480-4981, www.museomacro.com.ar, 3–9 P.M. daily except Wed., US$1). Overlooking the river at the north end of Blvd. Oroño, it has frequently changing shows by contemporary artists and traveling exhibitions.

Entertainment

Rosario has a diversity of entertainment offerings. The "Cartelera" page of *Rosario/12,* the local edition of the left-of-center *porteño* daily *Página/12,* has the most complete listings. For purchasing seats, try **Ticketek** (Córdoba 1643, Local 133, tel. 0341/527-7200) in the Shopping del Siglo.

The four-screen **Cine Monumental** (San Martín 999, tel. 0341/421-6289) shows recent films. Other cinemas include the multiscreen **Cines del Siglo** (Córdoba and Roca, tel. 0341/425-0761), **Cine del Patio** (Sarmiento 778, tel. 0341/448-9842), and the restored repertory **Cine El Cairo** (Santa Fe 1120, tel. 0341/421-9180).

The **Centro Cultural Bernardino Rivadavia** (San Martín 1080, tel. 0341/480-2401, www.ccbr.gov.ar) sponsors theater and dance events, along with films; a large gallery showcases local artists.

Teatro El Círculo (Laprida and Mendoza, tel. 0341/424-5349, www.teatro-elcirculo.com.ar) is the city's top traditional live theater and music venue. **Teatro Lavardén** (Mendoza and Sarmiento, tel. 0341/472-1462, www.lavarden.com) is another prestigious facility.

For the latest updates on live music acts and venues in town, visit the website Rosario Rock (www.rosariorock.com). **El Sótano** (Mitre 785, tel. 0341/15-642-8411, www.elsotanoclubdemusica.blogspot.com) showcases live local music, normally on weekends.

The Irish-style **O'Connell's** (Paraguay 212,

Rosario's Museo de Arte Contemporáneo Rosario occupies the former Davis silos.

tel. 0341/440-0512) serves imported beers, plus pub grub for lunch and dinner. There's a 7–9 P.M. happy hour. Occupying a corner building with high brick ceilings and a polished wooden bar, the **Victoria Pub** (San Lorenzo and Roca) has less elaborate decor— primarily rock photos on the walls—but more gregarious service and above-average food in substantial portions.

Buy tickets for Newell's Old Boys, the first-division soccer team, at **Estadio Parque Independencia** (Avenida Las Palmeras s/n, tel. 0341/411-7725, www.nob.com.ar). At the north end of town, the city's other favorite plays at its namesake **Estadio Club Atlético Rosario Central** (Bulevar Avellaneda and Avenida Génova, tel. 0341/472-4071, www.rosariocentral.com).

Shopping

On weekends and holidays, antiques and bric-a-brac fill the stalls at the **Mercado de Pulgas**

del Bajo, a flea market at Avenida Belgrano and Buenos Aires.

For gaucho gear and other souvenirs, try **Raíces** (Entre Ríos 1191, tel. 0341/426-0330) or **El Serranito** (Entre Ríos 1147).

Librería SBS (Santa Fe 1340, tel. 0341/426-1276) sells English-language books. **Zivals** (Corrientes 826, tel. 0341/527-2722) has a fine selection of tango CDs and DVDs.

Accommodations

The HI affiliate is **La Casona de Don Jaime 1** (Roca 1051, tel. 0341/527-9964, www.youth-hostelrosario.com.ar, US$8–12 pp dorm, US$23–36 s or d), which has mostly dorms but a couple of private rooms as well. Its expanded **La Casona de don Jaime 2** (San Lorenzo 1530, tel. 0341/530-2020, US$9–16 pp dorm, US$29–42 s or d) is more spacious and has more private rooms with updated baths. Weekend rates tend toward the upper end of the scale.

The friendly **83 Rosario Hostel** (Córdoba 824, tel. 0341/424-3587, www.83rosariohostel.com.ar, US$9–13 pp) occupies an old attractive house directly on the pedestrian mall, but this location is as dead as a cemetery at night—good if you want to sleep, but not so good for walking to the action.

Hotel Litoral (Entre Ríos 1043, tel. 0341/421-1426, www.hotellitoralrosario.com.ar, US$21 s, US$34 d) is a friendly, no-frills but clean budget option, with air-conditioning and Wi-Fi. Some of its 60 rooms boast balconies, but that's a mixed blessing, given the proximity of busy Plaza Sarmiento.

Neither new (though it has upgraded in recent years) nor European (despite its deco-ish exterior), **Nuevo Hotel Europeo** (San Luis 1364, tel. 0341/424-0382, www.nuevohoteleuropeo.com, US$36 s, US$49 d) has 90 spacious, well-lighted rooms with air-conditioning, phones, and TV. **Hotel Benidorm** (San Juan 1049, tel. 0341/421-9368, www.hotelbenidorm.com.ar, US$40 s, US$56 d) is a good mid-range choice with parking.

On a short block with little traffic, **(Hotel Rosario** (Ricardone 1365, tel. 0341/424-2170, www.hotelrosario.com.ar, US$52 s, US$60 d)

is no longer a giveaway, but its rooms are ample and well maintained with air-conditioning, cable TV, and parking; even better rooms cost just a little more.

Hotel Presidente (Corrientes 919, tel./fax 0341/424-2545, www.solans.com, US$64 s, US$70 d) is part of a chain of not-quite-luxurious business-oriented hotels with excellent service and amenities. Try negotiating a lower rate, especially for longer stays. Under the same management, **Hotel Riviera** (San Lorenzo 1486, tel. 0341/424-2058, www.solans.com, US$70 s, US$86 d, US$95–101 s or d) is a step up, especially in its suites.

For decades a favorite for low-cost grand hotel nostalgia, the century-old 84-room **(Hotel Esplendor Savoy Rosario** (San Lorenzo 1022, tel. 0341/429-6000, www.esplendorsavoyrosario.com, US$75–179 s or d) has undergone a major restoration and modernization that has taken it well out of the shoestring category. It's still good value in the summer low season, though, even if prices rise slightly on weekends.

With 139 rooms, the still-sparkling **(Hotel Plaza Real** (Santa Fe 1632, tel./fax 0341/440-8800, www.plazarealhotel.com, US$95–198 s or d with buffet breakfast) is a legitimate four-star facility. Amenities include a pool and sauna, but parking costs US$10 extra.

Rosario's first five-star facility, the 139-room **(Ros Tower Hotel-Spa & Convention Center** (Mitre 299, tel. 0341/529-9000, www.rostowerhotel.com.ar, US$218–342 s or d) has ample standard rooms and more spacious suites (with Jacuzzis), plus amenities such as a buffet breakfast and a surprisingly large rooftop pool. Its Aguaterra Spa offers saunas, massages, and Jacuzzis as well; there are occasional substantial discounts off the rack rates.

Food

For the most part, Rosario's cuisine lags behind the city's other cultural resources. Rosario a la Carta (www.rosarioalacarta.com.ar) is a good general information site on local restaurants.

The bookstore **El Ateneo** (Córdoba 1473, tel. 0341/425-9306) has an outstanding café for sandwiches and desserts, but it closes early, around 9 P.M. **Rincón Vegetariano** (Mitre 720, tel. 0341/411-0833) is a longstanding vegetarian favorite.

La Chernia, El Chucho y la Cholga (Mendoza and Rosas, tel. 0341/421-2253) specializes in seafood, but their selection of river fish is limited. Some sauces are a little heavy, but it's busy even on Mondays and has fine service. Most entrées are in the US$8–12 range.

Highly regarded **Puerto Gaboto** (Pellegrini 590, tel. 0341/447-1024) specializes in river fish such as *boga, dorado, pacú,* and *surubí.*

At the north end of Avenida Oroño, **Davis** (Avenida Brigadier López 2550, tel. 0341/435-7142), is the restaurant-bar of the Museo de Arte Contemporáneo, and its upstairs is a lively night spot on weekends.

At **Bajada España** (España and Riberas del Río, tel. 0341/449-6801), container ships float by so close that it almost seems possible to leap aboard, but those who stay seated will be rewarded with grilled river fish—the half-portion is big enough for two hungry diners—at modest prices. At the north end of Avenida España, cross the road and look for the inconspicuous elevator, beyond the former train station, that drops to the riverside location.

Themed after the life of outlaw Juan Moreira, **Te Amaré Vicenta** (Roca 1677, tel. 0341/411-2505, www.teamarevicenta.com) is a *parrilla* whose attentive waiters, in subdued gaucho garb, deliver fine grilled meats. There are also some more complex plates, such as the *lomo Pachamama,* served with a sauce of white wine and herbs and accompanied by a risotto in a light crust and country fried potatoes. Nearby **La Estancia** (Avenida Pellegrini 1510, tel. 0341/449-8052) also has its adherents.

Part of the Puerto España complex in the old Rosario Central railroad station, **Don Ferro** (España and Río Paraná, tel. 0341/421-1927) serves beef and more beef, but also river fish and more complex dishes such as stuffed

Named for the grain silos that now house the Museo de Arte Contemporáneo Rosario, Davis is the museum's riverside restaurant/café/wine bar.

© WAYNE BERNHARDSON

Patagonian lamb (US$12) with grilled potatoes. The service is assiduous, and the river views memorable.

For a formal meal in attractive surroundings alongside the Estación Fluvial, try 🅲 **Muelle 1** (Avenida de los Inmigrantes 410, tel. 0341/426-3509, www.muelle-1.com.ar). Entrées such as *surubí* start around US$8–10; service is highly professional.

Adjacent to its eponymous cinema, the restored 🅲 **Bar El Cairo** (Santa Fe 1102, tel. 0341/449-0714, www.barelcairo.com, US$10–20) is a place for drinks but also has a gourmet menu at dinnertime. A favorite with the late cartoonist Roberto Fontanarrosa, with cavernous brick ceilings, it showcases live music and gets many other figures from the Argentine sports and entertainment world.

Rosario's ice cream is not Argentina's finest, but **Bajo Cero** (Santa Fe and Roca, tel. 0341/425-1538) is a respectable choice. **Lido** (Blvd. Oroño 117, tel. 0341/440-0029) is also reliable.

Information and Services

The riverfront **Ente Turístico Rosario** (Etur, Avenida Belgrano and Buenos Aires, tel. 0341/480-2230, www.rosarioturismo.com, 9 A.M.–7 P.M. Mon.–Sat., 9 A.M.–6 P.M. Sun.) has fine maps, obliging English-speaking staff, and a helpful Spanish-only website. Its separate office at the bus terminal is open 8 A.M.–8 P.M. daily.

For motorists, **ACA** (tel. 0341/440-1278) is at Bulevar Oroño and 3 de Febrero.

Downtown ATMs are abundant, but there are no specialized exchange houses.

Correo Argentino is at Córdoba 721; the postal code is 2000.

There are numerous phone and Internet offices, such as **Locutorio Catedral** (Córdoba 801).

In the Shopping del Siglo, **Asatej** (Córdoba 1643, Local 224, tel. 0341/425-6002, rosario@asatej.com.ar) is a student- and budget-oriented travel agency. **Grupo 3 de Turismo** (Córdoba 1015, 3rd floor, tel. 0341/410-5800) is the Amex representative.

In new quarters, the **Hospital Clemente Alvarez** (Avenida Pellegrini 3205, tel. 0341/480-8111) is about six blocks west of Parque Independencia.

Getting There

Rosario has air connections to Buenos Aires, other northern Argentine destinations, and Santiago, Chile; bus connections almost everywhere; and cheap but slow trains to BA, Córdoba, and Tucumán.

Aerolíneas Argentinas (Córdoba 852, tel. 0341/420-8138) flies frequently to Aeroparque (Buenos Aires). **Sol Líneas Aéreas** (tel. 0341/452-0526 at the airport, www.sol.com.ar) is a budget carrier serving Buenos Aires, Santa Fe, Córdoba, Villa Gesell, and Punta del Este (Uruguay). **Gol** (Santa Fe 1515, tel. 0341/530-1150, www.voegol.com) serves Brazilian destinations.

Rosario is a major overland transport hub from the **Estación Terminal de Ómnibus Mariano Moreno** (Cafferata 702, tel. 0341/437-2384, www.terminalrosario.com.ar), about 15 blocks west of Plaza San Martín.

Typical domestic destinations, times, and fares include Santa Fe (2 hours, US$6), Buenos Aires (4 hours, US$15–20), Córdoba (6 hours, US$23–29), Mendoza (11–14 hours, US$47–55), Salta (15 hours, US$57–69), Puerto Iguazú (17 hours, US$58–71), and Bariloche (22 hours, US$81).

Ferrocentral trains to Buenos Aires (5.5 hours, US$5.50–14) leave Monday at 12:46 A.M. and Wednesday at 5:38 P.M. from **Estación Rosario Norte** (Avenida del Valle and Avenida Ovidio Lagos, tel. 0341/436-1661). Trains from Buenos Aires continue to Córdoba or Tucumán, passing Rosario Norte at 2:53 A.M. Monday and Friday. There are also trains north to Tucumán, but this long trip is far less comfortable than comparable buses.

Getting Around

Aeropuerto Rosario Islas Malvinas (Avenida Jorge Newbery s/n, tel. 0341/451-1226, www.aeropuertorosario.com) is eight kilometers west of town in the suburb of Fisherton; from Plaza

Sarmiento, Monticas and Las Rosas buses drop passengers at the airport entrance for about US$1. **Manuel Tienda León** (San Lorenzo 935, tel. 0341/409-8000, www.miguelcanton.com.ar) offers *remise* (US$11) connections to the airport.

Plaza Sarmiento is the hub of the public **Rosario Bus** system (www.rosariobus.com.ar), which now uses magnetic cards rather than coins. Bus No. 101 goes to the long-distance bus terminal.

For car rental, try **Hertz** (Mitre 747, tel. 0341/426-3400).

SANTA FE

Capital of its province, the city of Santa Fe plays second fiddle to youthful Rosario in economics and culture, but it has a core of colonial monuments that no other nearby place can match. It also enjoys easy access to the middle Paraná islands, thanks to a series of bridges across the river's tributaries to the city of Paraná, Entre Ríos.

The river, though, is a mixed blessing, as Santa Fe is vulnerable to floods—in May 2003 an inundation by the Río Salado killed dozens and displaced thousands, causing millions of dollars in damage—and even to desiccation, as shallow Laguna Setúbal nearly evaporated in 1964 for lack of rainfall in the upper Paraná. The summer heat and humidity can make Santa Fe a sweat lodge of a city.

Sited 10 kilometers east of the Paraná's main channel, Santa Fe (pop. about 500,000) is 167 kilometers north of Rosario and 475 kilometers north of Buenos Aires via RN 11 and the *autopista* A-008. It is 25 kilometers west of the Entre Ríos provincial capital of Paraná via RN 168 and a subfluvial tunnel, and 544 kilometers south of Resistencia via RN 11.

History

In 1573, southbound from Asunción in present-day Paraguay, Juan de Garay founded Santa Fe de la Vera Cruz on the Río San Javier, a Paraná tributary about 80 kilometers northwest of Santa Fe's present site. The first Santa Fe, though, proved insecure because its isolation exposed it to indigenous raiders, and the location was even more flood-prone than it is now. The ruling *cabildo* (town council) moved and rebuilt the city on the original plan; significant colonial architecture remains, but some of it fell to the wrecking ball in a 19th-century Francophile construction boom and 20th-century redevelopment.

Sights

The river and its tributaries are a palpable presence. One of Santa Fe's most offbeat sights, crossing Laguna Setúbal at the east end of Bulevar Gálvez, is the **Puente Colgante** (1928), the suspension bridge that linked the city to the islands and the city of Paraná until a 1983 flood damaged it beyond usability until just a couple years ago, when it underwent a major retrofit (it still doesn't handle big trucks, but normal passenger vehicles, as well as bicycles and pedestrians, can use it).

Four blocks west of the river, **Plaza 25 de Mayo** is the city's colonial, and contemporary, civic center. On its east side, the lavish interior of the Jesuit **Iglesia de la Compañía** (San Martín and Estanislao López), dating from 1697, contrasts with its unadorned exterior. Returned to the Jesuits in 1862, almost a century after their expulsion from the Americas, it's a national historical monument.

On the plaza's north side, the twin-towered **Catedral Metropolitana** (Estanislao López and San Gerónimo), dating from 1751, is also a national monument. The south side underwent a major transformation, however, when the mansard-topped French Renaissance **Casa de Gobierno** (government house) replaced the colonial *cabildo* in the early 20th century.

Immediately southeast, **Parque General Belgrano** contains a cluster of colonial structures that are historical monuments and museums. In a musty 18th-century residence, distinguished by an impressive sample of religious carvings from colonial missions, the **Museo Histórico Provincial Brigadier General Estanislao López** (San Martín 1490, tel. 0342/457-3529, muhistsf@ceride.gov.ar, free) contains silverwork, pottery, period furniture, and material on the province's chaotic postcolonial political history, plus paintings from colonial Perú. Summer hours are 8:30 A.M.–noon and 4–8:30 P.M. weekdays, 5:30–8:30 P.M. weekends and holidays. The rest of the year, afternoon hours are slightly shorter; it's closed January 1, May 1, Good Friday, the first Friday of December, and December 25.

The **Museo Etnográfico y Colonial Juan de Garay** (25 de Mayo 1470, tel. 0342/457-3550, www.ceride.gov.ar/etnografico, free but donations encouraged) focuses on Santa Fe la Vieja, including the area's indigenous heritage and a scale model of the city's original site near present-day Cayastá. Spanish-colonial relics include ceramics and coins. Summer hours are 8:30 A.M.–noon and 3:30–8:30 P.M. Tuesday–Friday, 5–8 P.M. weekends and holidays. Afternoon hours are shorter and slightly earlier the rest of the year; it's closed January 1, May 1, Good Friday, the first Friday of December, and December 25.

Begun in 1673 and finished in 1688, the **Iglesia y Convento de San Francisco** (Amenábar 2257, tel. 0342/459-3303) is Santa Fe's most significant remaining colonial landmark. Damaged by lightning in 1824, it slowly deteriorated, suffered several instances of ill-advised remodeling over more than a century, and finally survived thanks to thoughtful restoration between 1938 and the early 1950s.

What survived, thanks to the efforts of architects Angel Guido and Mario Buschiazzo, were the original facade, thick adobe walls, and a red-tile ceiling supported by beams of hardwoods and cedar, held together by leather and dowels rather than nails. Its hand-carved exterior doors lead to a nave with a gold-laminated pulpit.

As elsewhere in the city, the church bears witness to the force of the river—oddly enough, in the tomb of Padre Magallanes, who was attacked by a jaguar that entered the church while fleeing an 1825 flood. Provincial caudillo Estanislao López and his wife also repose here.

In one wing of the cloisters, the **Museo Histórico San Francisco** (8 A.M.–noon and 4–7 P.M. Mon.–Sat., free) deals with both religious and secular history in colonial and early-independence years. Among the exhibits are ceramics, furniture, silverwork, weapons, religious artifacts from various eras, and sacred and secular art. Its Sala de los Constituyentes displays wax figures of the representatives to the assembly that wrote the Argentine Constitution of 1853.

One block west of the plaza, also a national monument, the late colonial **Templo de Santo Domingo** (3 de Febrero and 9 de Julio) is a neoclassical hodgepodge dating from 1805 that took a century to complete. Two blocks farther west, **Plaza Italia** is the setting for the **Palacio Legislativo** (provincial legislature); immediately east, the outstanding **Museo Provincial de Bellas Artes Rosa Galisteo de Rodríguez** (4 de Enero 1510, tel. 0342/457-3577, free), the provincial fine arts museum, holds 2,200 paintings, sculptures, and engravings. Hours are 9 A.M.–1 P.M. and 2–6 P.M. Tuesday–Friday, 10 A.M.–1 P.M. and 3–7 P.M. weekends and holidays; it is closed January 1, May 1, Good Friday, the first Friday of December, and December 25.

Four blocks north of the plaza, the San Martín pedestrian mall is home to the **Museo Municipal de Artes Visuales Sor Josefa Díaz y Clucellas** (San Martín 2068, tel. 0342/457-1886, free) showcasing contemporary art; it's open 8:30 A.M.–12:30 P.M. and 4–8 P.M. Tuesday–Friday, 5–8 P.M. weekends and holidays.

Entertainment

Santa Fe's major performing arts locale is the French Renaissance **Teatro Municipal Primero de Mayo** (Avenida San Martín 2020, tel. 0342/457-1883), whose restoration has earned architectural prizes. **Cine América** (25 de Mayo 3075, tel. 0342/452-2246) shows recent movies.

Accommodations

In Santa Fe's sweltering summer, ceiling fans are essential, and even budget travelers may wish to splurge for air-conditioning. Every place listed here has air-conditioning unless otherwise indicated.

Nuevo Hotel California (25 de Mayo 2190, tel. 0342/452-3988, US$26 s, US$34 d) helps compensate for drab architecture with amiability.

A deco-era classic, the **(Castelar Hotel** (25 de Mayo 2349, tel. 0342/456-0999, www. castelarsantafe.com.ar, US$34 s, US$52 d, small discount for cash) has a graceful exterior, an inviting burnished wood lobby, and friendly staff. The rehabbed rooms are smaller and simpler than one might expect; some have tiny showers but others have tubs.

It's worn around the edges, but the family-run **Emperatriz Hotel** (Irigoyen Freire 2440, tel./fax 0342/453-0061, emperatrizhotel@ arnet.com.ar, US$39 s, US$59 d) evokes the style of a bygone colonial era. It has added contemporary touches such as Wi-Fi.

One of the best values is the comfortable **Meridien Suites Apart Hotel** (25 de Mayo 2620, tel. 0342/452-8966, www.meridiensantafe.com.ar, US$42 s, US$52 d). Rates include a private bath and kitchenette, cable TV, and telephone.

At the traditional **Gran Hotel España** (25 de Mayo 2647, tel. 0342/400-8834, www. lineaverdedehoteles.com.ar, US$39–47 s, US$50–60 d), the newer executive wing is worth the relatively small price difference.

Under the same management, just across the street, the business-oriented **Conquistador Hotel** (25 de Mayo 2676, tel. 0342/400-1195, www.lineaverdedehoteles.com.ar, US$59 s, US$70 d) has 70 good rooms.

At high-rise **Hostal Santa Fe de la Vera Cruz** (Avenida San Martín 2954, tel./fax 0342/455-1740, www.hostalsf.com, US$45–62 s, US$71–76 d), the common areas are more impressive than the rooms themselves (which are OK). More spacious rooms are only a little more expensive.

Food

For breakfast, lunch, or coffee, the classic is **Confitería las Delicias** (San Martín 2898, tel. 0342/453-2126), alongside Hostal Santa Fe;

the juices deserve special mention. **Cafetería La Citi** (La Rioja 2609, tel. 0342/455-4764) is another good option.

The **Círculo Italiano** (Hipólito Yrigoyen 2457, tel. 0342/452-0628) specializes in pastas. **Triferto** (San Martín 3301, tel. 0342/453-7070) features a diverse pizza menu.

Across from its namesake hotel, **España** (San Martín 2644, tel. 0342/400-8834) serves an outstanding garlic *surubí* (Paraná catfish), plus an exceptional *arroz con leche* (rice pudding) for dessert. The **Centro Español** (San Martín 2219, tel. 0342/456-9968) is more elaborate but not that much better.

For fresh fish, the riverfront **(El Quincho de Chiquito** (Brown and Obispo Vieytes, tel. 0342/460-2608) is a Santa Fe institution. Beneath a cavernous thatched roof, waiters serve large portions of grilled specialties like *boga, sábalo,* and *surubí* for about US$7–8; take bus No. 16 from Avenida Gálvez in the northern downtown area.

Via Verona (San Martín 2585, tel. 0342/455-4575) is the place for ice cream (a virtual staple in the steamy summer).

Information

Downstairs at the bus terminal, the municipal **Subsecretaría de Turismo de la Ciudad** (Belgrano 2910, tel. 0342/457-4124, www. santafeturismo.gov.ar, 7 A.M.–8 P.M. weekdays, 8 A.M.–8 P.M. weekends) has decent maps and helpful personnel, but technologically it's behind the times. There are additional offices at Boca del Tigre (tel. 0342/457-1862), at the city's southern approach; on the north side at the Paseo del Restaurador (Bulevar Pellegrini and Pedro Vittori, tel. 0342/457-1881); and at the riverfront Terminal de Catamarán (Dique No. 1). All are open 8 A.M.–8 P.M. daily.

For motorists, **ACA** is at Avenida Rivadavia 3101 (tel. 0342/455-3862) and at Pellegrini and Avenida San Martín (tel. 0342/455-4142).

Services

Tourfe (San Martín 2500, tel. 0342/455-0157) is a full-service travel agency that also serves as an exchange house. There are numerous ATMs along the San Martín pedestrian mall.

Correo Argentino is at Mendoza 2430; the postal code is 3000.

Telecom long-distance telephones are upstairs at the bus terminal, but there are numerous other *locutorios*. **Santa Fe Computación** (La Rioja 2489) has both phones and Internet connections.

Hospital Provincial José María Cullen (Avenida Freire 2150, tel. 0342/459-9719) is west of downtown.

Getting There

Santa Fe has air links to Buenos Aires and bus connections around the country.

Aerolíneas Argentinas (25 de Mayo 2287, tel. 0342/452-5959) flies daily to Buenos Aires's Aeroparque, in early morning or early evening. **Sol Líneas Aéreas** (tel. 0810/444-4765, www. sol.com.ar) is a budget carrier serving Rosario and Aeroparque.

The **Estación Terminal de Ómnibus** (Belgrano 2940) is four blocks west of San Martín. Its Oficina de Informes (tel. 0342/454-7124, www.terminalsantafe.com) conspicuously lists destinations and updated fares.

Typical domestic destinations, times, and fares include Paraná (45 minutes, US$1), Rosario (2 hours, US$9), Córdoba (5 hours, US$19), Corrientes (7.5 hours, US$29), Resistencia (7 hours, US$26), Buenos Aires (6 hours, US$23), Posadas (11 hours, US$41), Mendoza (12 hours, US$48), and Puerto Iguazú (15 hours, US$60).

Getting Around

Aeropuerto Sauce Viejo (tel. 0342/499-5061) is seven kilometers south of town on RN 11. From the corner of Hipólito Yrigoyen and San Luis, Línea Continental buses go to the airport cheaply.

Alamo (Corrientes 2538, tel. 0342/400-8000) has rental cars.

Chaco and Formosa Provinces

Together, the provinces of Chaco and Formosa form the Gran Chaco, a hot, humid lowland stretching from the banks of the Paraná and Paraguay to the Andean foothills, and across international borders into Paraguay and Bolivia. While the Argentine Chaco has a low international profile, the Chaco provincial capital of Resistencia is a magnet for the visual arts and the region's backcountry national parks are treasure troves of wildlife. The trans-Chaco route from Resistencia to Salta has become popular with travelers from the Esteros del Iberá to Salta, and vice versa.

RESISTENCIA

Named for its defiance of indigenous assaults after its settlement as the Jesuit mission of San Fernando del Río Negro in 1750, Resistencia owes its growth to the tannin industry and the westward-advancing agricultural frontier that spurred construction of a trans-Chaco railroad

to Salta. The "city of sculptures" has a rich cultural life, though, reflected in its abundant but original public art—plus a major university, several significant museums, and a smattering of cultural centers.

Resistencia (pop. about 350,000), with nearly 500,000 in a metropolitan area that includes the port of Barranqueras, is 995 kilometers north of Buenos Aires via RN 11 through Rosario and Santa Fe, 810 kilometers east of Salta via RN 16, and only 19 kilometers west of Corrientes via the Belgrano bridge over the Paraná. Filling four entire blocks, palm-studded Plaza 25 de Mayo is the city's geographical center.

Sights

Resistencia prides itself on the hundreds of sculptures in and on its parks, plazas, sidewalks, and boulevards. The highest concentration is found in the **Parque de las Esculturas**

Aldo y Efraín Boglietti (Avenida Laprida and Sarmiento), an open-air display at the former **Estación Ferrocarril Santa Fe** (1907), the city's only national historical monument. The **Museo Provincial de Bellas Artes René Bruseau** (Mitre 163, tel. 03722/45-3007, 8 A.M.–12:30 P.M. and 3:30–8:30 P.M. weekdays, free) focuses on sculpture but also hosts traveling exhibitions.

Much of the momentum behind Resistencia's reputation as a visual-arts mecca comes from **El Fogón de los Arrieros** (Brown 350, tel. 03722/42-6418, elfogondelosarrieros@hotmail. com, 8 A.M.–noon and 9–11 P.M. Mon.–Fri., 8 A.M.–noon Sat., US$1.25), a local institution that blends artistic miscellanea from the province, the country, and the globe into a casual, bar-style atmosphere. The trustees—a nonprofit foundation runs El Fogón—go out of their way to make visitors feel welcome, but the exterior is worth a look even outside the operating hours, when there may be tango lessons.

In new quarters, the **Museo del Hombre Chaqueño Profesor Ertivio Acosta** (J. B. Justo 280, tel. 03722/45-3145, cultura@ecom-chaco.com.ar, 8 A.M.–noon and 5–8 P.M. weekdays, 5–8 P.M. Sat., free) recounts the Chaco's settlement and transformation from the perspective of its aboriginal Toba, Mocoví, and Wichí peoples, the development of criollo culture, and early-20th-century European immigration.

Entertainment and Events

In even-numbered years, in the last fortnight of July, on Plaza de Mayo, the **Fundación Urunday** (Avenida de los Inmigrantes 1001, tel. 03722/41-5020, www.bienaldelchaco.com) sponsors the competitive **Concurso Nacional e Internacional de Escultura y Madera,** in which contestants sculpt the reddish tree trunk of the native *urunday* into a work of art.

The **Peña Nativa Martín Fierro** (Avenida 9 de Julio 695, tel. 03772/42-3167) showcases folk music such as Mesopotamian *chamamé,* as well as the occasional tango, in the context of a *parrilla* restaurant.

The **Complejo Cultural Provincial Guido**

Miranda (Colón 164, tel. 03722/42-5421) seats more than 500 spectators for current movies, theater productions, and concerts.

Alfonso (Avenida Sarmiento 408, tel. 03722/44-4000) is a popular bar.

Shopping

For indigenous crafts from throughout the province, visit the **Centro Cultural y Artesanal Leopoldo Marechal** (Pellegrini 272, tel. 03722/44-8427). **Chac Cueros** (Güemes 186) specializes in leather goods.

Accommodations

Dating from 1927 but now modernized, **Hotel Marconi** (Perón 352, tel. 03722/42-1978, hotel-marconi@yahoo.com.ar, US$27 s, US$34 d) is one of Resistencia's better values. **Hotel Colón** (Santa María de Oro 143, tel. 03722/42-2863, hotelcolon@gigared.com, US$28 s, US$41 d) is another respectable no-frills choice.

Undergoing an expansion, the **Gran Hotel Royal** (José M. Paz 297, tel. 03722/44-4466, www.granhotelroyal.com.ar, US$30 s, US$42 d) has been showing wear and tear, but when the work is completed it will be worth a look again. At present, Wi-Fi is available only in the noisy café.

The nearly new, business-oriented **Atrium Hotel** (Hernandarias 249, tel. 03722/42-9094, www.hotelatrium.com.ar, US$37 s, US$45 d) adds some much-needed contemporary style to the scene. Its more-than-reasonable rates include access to gym facilities and a tennis court.

Just a block off Plaza 25 de Mayo, the renovated **Hotel Covadonga** (Güemes 200, tel. 03722/44-4444, www.hotelcovadonga.com. ar, US$63 s, US$67 d) offers amenities including a pool and Wi-Fi, with one drawback: On weekends, the pub scene along Güemes can get noisy. In this case, choose an interior room or turn up the air-conditioning.

Food

Café de la Ciudad (Pellegrini 109, tel. 03722/42-0214), one of the best examples of the new wave *confiterías,* is an exceptional breakfast choice but also keeps late pub hours, especially on weekends. **Barrilito** (Avenida Lavalle 289, tel. 03722/44-4081) is a beer-garden restaurant.

At the expanded 🄲 **Kebón** (Don Bosco 120, tel. 03722/42-2385), whose menu includes upscale versions of Argentine standards, the kitchen seems to have its ups and downs. If the prices seem over the top, try its adjacent (but more economical) *rotisería* for food to go.

Helados San José (Pellegrini 582, tel. 03722/42-7008) produces Resistencia's best ice cream.

Information

In new quarters, the **Dirección Provincial de Turismo** (Avenida Sarmiento 1675, tel. 03722/43-8880, www.chaco.gov.ar/turismo) is open 7 A.M.–8 P.M. weekdays, 10 A.M.–12:30 P.M. and 5–7:30 P.M. weekends. Facing Plaza 25 de Mayo, the *municipal information office* (Avenida Roca 20, tel. 03722/45-8289) is open 7 A.M.–12:30 P.M. and 2–8 P.M. weekdays, 8 A.M.–noon and 3–8 P.M. Saturday, and 6–8:30 P.M. Sunday.

For motorists, **ACA** is at Avenida 9 de Julio and Avenida Italia (tel. 03722/43-1184).

Services

Cambio El Dorado (Jose María Paz 36) changes travelers checks. There are several ATMs around Plaza 25 de Mayo.

Correo Argentino (Avenida Sarmiento 102) is opposite Plaza 25 de Mayo; the postal code is 3500. There are **Telecentros** at J. B. Justo 136 and at Arturo Illia and Colón; **C-Net** (Perón 299) has fast Internet and large monitors.

Laverap (Vedia 23, tel. 03722/42-4223) has laundry service.

For medical aid, there's **Hospital Julio C. Perrando** (Avenida 9 de Julio 1101, tel. 03722/42-7233).

Getting There

Aerolíneas Argentinas (J. B. Justo 184, tel. 03722/44-5550) flies frequently to Aeroparque (Buenos Aires), but there are also flights from nearby Corrientes. **Aerochaco** (Avenida

Sarmiento 615, tel. 03722/43-2772, www.aero-chaco.net) flies to Buenos Aires and Córdoba.

A hub for provincial and long-distance buses, the spacious, gleaming **Estación Terminal de Ómnibus** (Avenida MacLean and Islas Malvinas, tel. 03772/46-1098) is about four kilometers west of Plaza 25 de Mayo.

Sample destinations, fares, and times include Posadas (5 hours, US$20), Puerto Iguazú (9 hours, US$32), Rosario (9 hours, US$33), Buenos Aires (12 hours, US$44–55), and Salta (12 hours, US$33).

Getting Around

Ataco Norte and Ticsa buses shuttle between Corrientes and Resistencia. The trip takes about half an hour.

Aeropuerto Internacional Resistencia (tel. 03722/43-6280) is six kilometers south of town on RN 11; from the post office on Plaza 25 de Mayo, take city bus No. 8.

To the bus terminal from the Casa de Gobierno (near the post office) on Plaza 25 de Mayo, take city bus Nos. 8 or 10.

🄲 PARQUE NACIONAL CHACO

West of Resistencia, but not quite to the mid-Chaco's "Impenetrable," Parque Nacional Chaco is a little-visited mosaic of dense forest and bird-rich wetlands. Most of the park avoided deforestation during the heyday of the tannin trade; some parts are recuperating.

Though not the equal of the magnificent Esteros del Iberá in Corrientes Province, the park's verdant woodland footpaths can justify a detour for trans-Chaco travelers. Because mosquitoes are abundant, the dry and relatively cool winter is the best time for a visit.

In the humid eastern Chaco, 15,000-hectare Parque Nacional Chaco is 115 kilometers northwest of Resistencia via RN 16 and paved RP 9 to the village of Capitán Solari; to the park entrance, it's another five kilometers on a dusty (in dry weather) or muddy (in wet weather) road. After heavy rain, low-clearance vehicles may not be able to reach the park, but it's possible to hike in or rent horses in Capitán Solari.

Flora and Fauna

At first glance, the Chaco's limited relief—it rises almost imperceptibly from east to west—seems to offer little environmental diversity. Minor variations, though, mean dramatically different habitats.

As part of the Gran Chaco, extending north into Paraguay and Bolivia, the park comprises part of the "estuarine and gallery forest" subregion, but its biologically rich marshes and gallery forests are but a fraction of the total area. Where the winding Río Negro has shifted course, aquatic plants cover shallow oxbow lakes that are becoming meadows and will eventually be forest.

Away from the watercourses, relatively large trees like the thorny *algarrobo, lapacho,* and *quebracho* ("ax-breaker") form the forest canopy of the *monte fuerte*. In their shade grow smaller specimens of the same species that, when an older tree dies and topples, exploit the ensuing light gap to claim their place in the canopy.

Sparser scrub forests alternate with fan palm savannas of *caranday* and *pindó*. Human-induced fires and grazing have helped create savannas, but fire suppression and livestock restrictions are permitting more forest species to expand their habitat.

In the dense forests, mammals are likelier heard than seen—especially the howler monkey. The 340 or so bird species include the *ñandú* (rhea, endangered in this area), jabirú stork, roseate spoonbill, various cormorants, the common caracara, kingfishers, and the like. The Chaco is an entomologist's wonderland—research scientists from the Smithsonian have ongoing projects here—but the common mosquito unavoidably attracts the most attention. Bring repellent, especially in summer and shortly thereafter.

Sights and Recreation

Hiking and bird-watching are the main activities, preferably in early morning or around sunset. There's a 1.5-kilometer nature trail near the campground, but the narrow grassy road that leads northwest gets so little automobile traffic that it might as well be a footpath.

A short distance before the road ends, the signed **Sendero Laguna Carpincho** is a three-kilometer forest loop that also leads to **Laguna Yacaré** (both these marshy lakes are prime wildlife areas, with raised and shaded platforms that permit better viewing) before returning to the road.

In Capitán Solari, Ñato Mendoza rents horses for about US$1.50 per hour. This is the best alternative for visiting soggier areas, where slogging through the muck on foot is less appealing.

Practicalities

Camping, free of charge, is the only option. There are clean toilets, hot showers, fire pits, and firewood; a tent is necessary to keep out of the rain and insects, particularly the mosquitoes. There are simple accommodations only, plus limited supplies, at Capitán Solari; it's better to bring everything from Resistencia. Bicycles may be available.

The **APN** (in Capitán Solari, tel. 03725/49-9161, chaco@apn.gov.ar) no longer collects an admission charge, but rangers are happy to provide information.

From Resistencia, La Estrella has five buses daily (6:30 A.M. and 12:30, 3:30, 5:30, and 8 P.M.) to Capitán Solari (2.5 hours, US$4); return buses leave at 5:25, 5:30, and 11:30 A.M. and 4:50 and 6:45 P.M.

PRESIDENCIA ROQUE SÁENZ PEÑA

Settled by a mosaic of European agricultural immigrants less than a century ago, this barren but hospitable cotton town draws Argentine visitors to its thermal baths, currently undergoing modernization. Its other attraction is an outstanding zoo focused on species from the Chaco itself.

Presidencia Roque Sáenz Peña owes its awkward official moniker not to the Argentine president who brought about universal male suffrage but to his term of office (1910–1913); most Argentines, though, simply call it Sáenz Peña. Its thermal baths date from 1937, when drillers seeking potable water struck hot mineral springs instead. Still, it's hard to imagine anyone living here in summer until the advent of air-conditioning.

Roque Sáenz Peña (pop. about 100,000) is 165 kilometers northwest of Resistencia and 685 kilometers southeast of Salta via the trans-Chaco RN 16. Willow-shaded Plaza San Martín is the civic center, and north–south Avenida San Martín is the main commercial thoroughfare, but it's liveliest around the baths.

Sights and Events

The **Complejo Termal Municipal** (Brown 545, tel. 03732/43-0030, 6 A.M.–12:30 P.M. and 2:30–8 P.M. daily) is a complex of hot mineral baths and saunas that also offers massages and physical therapy. Thermal soaks and saunas cost about US$6 each pp, while a half-hour massage from a professional kinesthesiologist costs barely US$10.

On the eastern outskirts, on the south side of RN 16, the **Complejo Ecológico Municipal** (tel. 03732/42-4284, 7 A.M.–7 P.M. daily, US$0.75) features native regional fauna like tapirs and jaguars in spacious enclosures, plus artificial lakes that attract migratory wildfowl. City bus No. 2 goes directly to the zoo.

Accommodations and Food

The prosaically named **Hotel Familiar** (Moreno 488, tel. 03732/42-9906, juliobojanich@yahoo.com.ar, US$21 s, US$32 d) has medium-sized but immaculate rooms with smallish baths, cable TV, air-conditioning, and parking.

The best new accommodation, though, is the **Hotel Aconcagua** (Azcuénaga and Julio A. Roca, tel. 03732/42-8111, www.hotelacon-caguachaco.com.ar, US$26 s, US$44 d), which has far more complete services.

Across from the bath complex, shaded by palms and awnings, **Sky Blue** (Brown and Moreno) is an outdoor beer garden, pizzeria, and sandwich place that draws evening crowds. In addition to the pizzas, there are welcome appetizers of potato salad, popcorn, and peanuts (which tend to increase beer consumption).

Helados Ama Nalec (Moreno 613, tel. 03732/42-4303) serves the best ice cream.

Information and Services

In the thermal-bath complex, the **Dirección de Promoción Turística** (Brown 545, tel. 03732/43-0030, dirdeturismosp@hotmail.com, www.ciudadtermal.com.ar, 6 A.M.–12:30 P.M. and 2:30–8 P.M. daily) keeps identical hours to the baths.

ACA (Rivadavia and 25 de Mayo, tel. 03732/42-0471) has motorist services and free Wi-Fi.

Banco de la Nación (Avenida San Martín 301) has an ATM.

Correo Argentino (Belgrano 602) is the post office; the postal code is 3700.

Try **Telecentro Chaco** (San Martín 1016) for telephone services and Internet access.

Hospital 4 de Junio (tel. 03732/42-4568) is at Las Malvinas 1350.

Getting There and Around

City bus No. 1 goes from the baths to the **Terminal de Ómnibus** (Canteros between Avellaneda and López y Planes, tel. 103—a free local call), east of downtown.

The main destination is Resistencia (2 hours, US$7), but there are also direct services to Buenos Aires (14 hours, US$53–66). Trans-Chaco services from Resistencia to Salta also stop here.

FORMOSA

Except for an abundance of public art that falls short of Resistencia's, sultry Formosa has little to recommend it as a destination, but visitors bound for Parque Nacional Río Pilcomayo may have to spend a night here.

Formosa (pop. about 220,000) is 175 kilometers north of Resistencia and 113 kilometers south of Clorinda, on the border with Paraguay, via RN 11.

Museo Histórico Municipal

The municipal history museum (Avenida 25 de Mayo 84, free) occupies the **Casa Fotheringham** (1885), built as a private

MESOPOTAMIA

residence by the first territorial governor, a general with the quintessentially Argentine name of Ignacio Hamilton Fotheringham. The city's only national historical monument, it chronicles the province's history and political development, particularly after Argentina grabbed this part of the Chaco from Paraguay during the War of the Triple Alliance (1864–1870).

Accommodations and Food

Formosa has decent if unspectacular accommodations, such as **Hotel Colón** (Belgrano 1068, tel. 03717/42-0719, www.hotelcolonformosa. com, US$26 s, US$36 d), which has a plain exterior but a pleasant interior, with rooms on the small side. **Hotel Plaza** (Uriburu 920, tel. 03717/42-6767, plaza_formosa@hotmail.com, US$37 s, US$42 d) has the most complete services, including air-conditioning, a pool, covered parking, and Wi-Fi.

Near the river, the Spanish bar–style **El Tano Marino** (Avenida 25 de Mayo 63, tel. 03717/42-0628) stresses freshly caught local fish but also serve meats and pastas.

Information and Services

The provincial **Ministerio de Turismo** (Uriburu 820, tel. 03717/43-6120, www.formosa.gob.ar) is open 7:30 A.M.–1 P.M. and 4–9 P.M. daily.

Banco de Galicia (Avenida 25 de Mayo 160) has an ATM.

Correo Argentino (Avenida 9 de Julio 930) is opposite Plaza San Martín; the postal code is 3600. The **Telefónica** *locutorio* (Avenida 25 de Mayo 251) also has Internet access.

The **Hospital Central** is at Salta 545 (tel. 03717/42-6194).

Getting There and Around

Aerolíneas Argentinas (Avenida 25 de Mayo 601, tel. 03717/42-9314) flies daily to Buenos Aires's Aeroparque (usually via Corrientes) from Aeropuerto El Pucú, four kilometers south of town along RN 11.

The modern **Estación Terminal de Ómnibus Formosa** (ETOF, Avenida Gutñiski

and Antártida Argentina, tel. 03717/45-1766) is 15 blocks west of Plaza San Martín.

Godoy SRL (tel. 03717/45-8148) goes three times daily to Laguna Naick-Neck (US$6.50), the closest settlement to Parque Nacional Río Pilcomayo, via the border-post city of Clorinda; the first departure is 10 A.M., the second at noon, and the last at 7:30 P.M.

Other sample destinations, times, and fares include Resistencia (2 hours, US$7) and Buenos Aires (13 hours, US$51).

◖ PARQUE NACIONAL RÍO PILCOMAYO

Nudging the Paraguayan border in the humid eastern Chaco, 47,754-hectare Parque Nacional Río Pilcomayo is an internationally recognized Ramsar Convention wetland whose centerpiece is shallow Laguna Blanca, but there are also marshes, gallery forests, and grasslands.

Parque Nacional Río Pilcomayo is about 45 kilometers west of Clorinda via paved RN 86 and a dirt road that leads to Seccional Laguna Blanca (do not confuse this with the park's administrative headquarters at the town of Laguna Blanca, another 11 kilometers west on the paved highway).

Río Pilcomayo's flora and fauna resemble those of Parque Nacional Chaco, though the distribution of the various environments differs—Pilcomayo has larger stretches of open water, for instance. Still, visitors will see many of the same birds, mammals, and reptiles that are so abundant to the south.

From the Laguna Blanca campground, the **Sendero Laguna Blanca** is an elevated *pasarela* (boardwalk) leading over marshy ground to an even higher *mirador* (overlook) with panoramic views across the lake; there are also three shoreline platforms for sunbathing and swimming (the smallish *yacarés,* while they may float ominously on the lake surface, do not attack humans). Capybaras wallow in the marshes along and beneath the boardwalk.

Practicalities

At the park's **Camping Laguna Blanca,** free

facilities include picnic tables, fire pits, toilets, and cold showers. The campground is closed to motor vehicles; campers must carry their tents and supplies from the parking lot. Limited supplies are available just outside the park, but it's better to purchase them in Laguna Blanca, Clorinda, or Formosa.

Rangers at Seccional Laguna Blanca, near the campground, provide information and advice. The APN's **Intendencia Parque** **Nacional Pilcomayo** (Pueyrredón s/n, tel./fax 03718/47-0045, riopilcomayo@apn.gov.ar) is in the town of Laguna Blanca.

At Laguna Naick-Neck, on RN 86, Godoy buses from Formosa and Clorinda pass a well-marked turnoff to Seccional Laguna Blanca. From the turnoff, though, it's necessary to hike, hitch, or hail a *remise* for the last five kilometers over a dirt road. Minibuses from Clorinda also pass through here.

CUYO AND CÓRDOBA

On the eastern slope of the Andes, comprising the provinces of Mendoza, San Juan, San Luis, and La Rioja, the Cuyo region can claim two world-class features: mountains and wine. At 6,962 meters, Cerro Aconcagua's soaring summit is the highest of countless peaks that trap the snowfall in winter whose spring thaw irrigates the sandy soils of three-quarters of Argentina's underrated—but rapidly advancing—vineyards. Under bright desert sun, the same snowmelt fills the rivers where rafters and kayakers battle white-water waves and rapids, and the reservoirs where windsurfers race across the surface and fishers troll for trout.

Cuyo is a year-round destination. As the western hemisphere's highest peak, Aconcagua draws climbers from around the world, but exploring the Andes on foot or saddle is not just for peak-baggers. The provincial capital of Mendoza, for its part, is one of Argentina's most livable cities, its numerous wineries and fine food a bonus. In winter, skiers frequent international resorts such as Las Leñas, and others explore fossil-filled desert parks like San Juan Province's Ischigualasto and La Rioja's Parque Nacional Talampaya (both UNESCO World Heritage Sites) and San Luis's Las Quijadas. All of these have seen major paleontological discoveries but can be deadly hot in summer.

To the east, San Luis Province shares Argentina's central sierras with Córdoba Province, whose namesake capital is arguably Argentina's "second city." Relatively few foreigners stop here, but overland explorers will enjoy the province's Jesuit ruins, as well as

HIGHLIGHTS

◖ **Cerro Aconcagua:** At 6,962 meters, the "Roof of the Americas" is literally the high point of anyone's trip to the continent. Only a handful of people attempt the summit, but many more make it to base camp, and just about anyone can catch a glimpse of the summit. Other nearby points, like the Cristo Redentor statue on the Chilean border, offer the views without the exertion (page 234).

◖ **Las Leñas:** West of Malargüe, one of Argentina's top ski resorts is expanding its activities for summer vacationers (page 243).

◖ **Difunta Correa Shrine:** In the desert 60 kilometers east of San Juan, this sprawling shrine to a popular "saint" will impress skeptics as much as it does the hundreds of thousands of pilgrims who visit every year (page 250).

◖ **Parque Provincial Ischigualasto:** In northern San Juan Province, the "Valley of the Moon" badlands are part of a triangle of parks fast becoming stops on the international dinosaur-fossil circuit (page 253).

◖ **Parque Nacional Talampaya:** Reminiscent of Utah and Arizona, the thinly settled western desert of La Rioja Province is rich in scenery, fossils, and pre-Columbian rock paintings and petroglyphs (page 260).

◖ **Parque Nacional Sierra de las Quijadas:** In northern San Luis Province, Las Quijadas's sandstone canyons are a scenic maze that recall the canyon country of Utah or New Mexico, and its dinosaur fossils are the source of endless material for Argentina's growing community of paleontologists (page 263).

◖ **Iglesia Catedral:** In Argentina's historic second city, this 17th-century church features a richly decorated interior and is the resting place of several notable locals (page 270).

◖ **Manzana Jesuítica:** This site in Córdoba, featuring the Iglesia de La Compañía, is just one of many examples of Jesuit heritage in the province. The urban legacy and rural *estancias* of the Jesuit order became a UNESCO World Heritage site in 2000 (page 271).

◖ **Alta Gracia:** This gracious colonial town features notable Jesuit monuments, well worth a day trip from the capital. It was also the boyhood home of Ernesto "Che" Guevara; one of his family's former rental homes is now a museum dedicated to the Cuban revolution's charismatic icon (page 278).

◖ **Parque Nacional Quebrada del Condorito:** The trail through Córdoba's high steppe is the best way to experience the area's open skies and peek at the Andean condor's nesting sites on rocky outcroppings over the Río Condorito Canyon (page 282).

LOOK FOR ◖ TO FIND RECOMMENDED SIGHTS, ACTIVITIES, DINING, AND LODGING.

CUYO AND CÓRDOBA

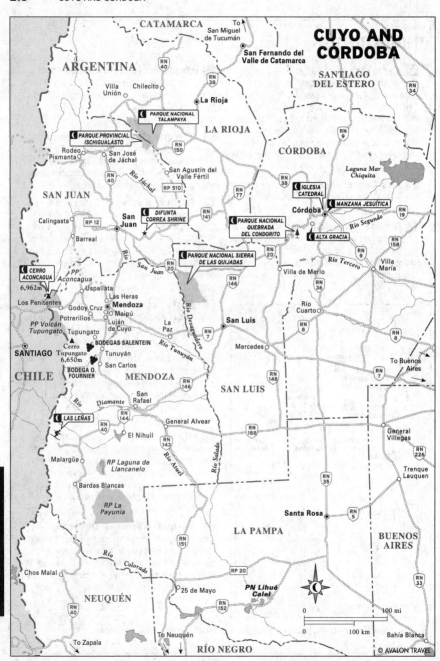

CUYO AND CÓRDOBA

CATAMARCA

To San Miguel de Tucumán

San Fernando del Valle de Catamarca

ARGENTINA

SANTIAGO DEL ESTERO

RN 40

RN 38

Villa Unión   Chilecito

La Rioja

LA RIOJA

CÓRDOBA

RN 34

RN 9

PARQUE NACIONAL TALAMPAYA

PARQUE PROVINCIAL ISCHIGUALASTO

Rodeo Pismanta

San José de Jáchal

RN 150

Laguna Mar Chiquita

San Agustín del Valle Fértil

RN 38

RN 40

Río Jáchal

RP 510

RN 77

IGLESIA CATEDRAL

MANZANA JESUÍTICA

SAN JUAN

RN 141

Córdoba

RN 19

Calingasta

RP 12

San Juan

DIFUNTA CORREA SHRINE

PARQUE NACIONAL QUEBRADA DEL CONDORITO

Río Segundo

ALTA GRACIA

RN 9

RN 158

Barreal

Río

San Juan

RN 20

PARQUE NACIONAL SIERRA DE LAS QUIJADAS

RN 20

Río Tercero

Villa María

CERRO ACONCAGUA 6,962m

PP Aconcagua

Villa de Merlo

RN 146

Los Penitentes

Uspallata

Las Heras

Río Desaguadero

RN 36

Godoy Cruz   **Mendoza**

Río Cuarto

PP Volcán Tupungato

Potrerillos   Maipú

Luján de Cuyo

La Paz

RN 7

San Luis

RN 8

RN 8

Tupungato

Cerro Tupungato 6,650m

BODEGAS SALENTIN

Tunuyán

Río Tunuyán

Mercedes

To Buènos Aires

RN 7

SANTIAGO

BODEGA O. FOURNIER

San Carlos

MENDOZA

RN 146

SAN LUIS

RN 148

CHILE

Río Diamante

San Rafael

General Villegas

LAS LEÑAS

RN 144

General Alvear

RN 188

RN 226

RN 40

El Nihuil

RN 143

Río Atuel

Río Salado

Trenque Lauquen

Malargüe

RP Laguna de Llancanelo

RN 35

Bardas Blancas

RP La Payunia

Santa Rosa

RN 5

LA PAMPA

BUENOS AIRES

Río Colorado

RN 151

RP 20

PN Lihué Calel

RN 33

Chos Malal

25 de Mayo

0   100 mi

0   100 km

NEUQUÉN

RN 40

RN 152

To Zapala

To Neuquén

RÍO NEGRO

Bahía Blanca

© AVALON TRAVEL

© WAYNE BERNHARDSON

Bodega O. Fournier, one of the Uco Valley's state-of-the-art wineries

off-the-beaten-path places like Parque Nacional Quebrada del Condorito.

PLANNING YOUR TIME

For wine lovers, Mendoza alone merits at least a week; even those with only a passing interest in the vine should spend a few days, ideally during the March *Vendimia* (harvest festival, when reservations are almost obligatory). The upper Río Mendoza valley, en route to Chile, is close enough for recreational activities like white-water rafting and even winter skiing, though there are also accommodations at the slopes of Los Penitentes. Wine aficionados can extend their stay to Uco and San Rafael vineyards to the south.

Whether hiking or climbing, Aconcagua is a trip in its own right. A three-day hike is possible, but the trek to and from base camp is a 10-day commitment, and climbers should budget three weeks for a summit assault—whether successful or not.

Visiting the desert parks of San Juan and San Luis, plus La Rioja's Talampaya, would ideally require a week because of the distances between them, even given only a day at each unit (plus a recommended detour to the Difunta Correa shrine). It's best to avoid these areas in summer's heat, when rare storms can cause flash floods.

Córdoba's urban attractions are independent of the seasons, and its Sierras are popular throughout the year (but crowded in summer). Many visitors cross back and forth between Córdoba and the Sierras of San Luis.

HISTORY

In pre-Columbian times, present-day Cuyo was peripheral to the central Andean empire of the Inkas, but the indigenous Huarpe did pay tribute to the lords of Cusco. As settled agriculturalists, the Huarpe were numerous enough that Spaniards crossed the cordillera from Chile to establish *encomiendas*. Because impassable Andean snowfields separated it from Santiago for much of the year and because Buenos Aires was so distant, Cuyo developed a distinctive and persistent regional identity.

By the 17th century, vintners were carting casks of wine to Córdoba and even Buenos

CUYO AND CÓRDOBA

Aires. Still, it took nearly two centuries to reorient the economy after the creation of a viceroyalty at Buenos Aires and then Argentine independence closed Chilean markets. In 1835 Charles Darwin contrasted Mendoza's agricultural bounty with its economic stagnation: "Nothing could appear more flourishing than the vineyards and the orchards of figs, peaches and olives," he wrote, but "the prosperity of the place has much declined of late years."

In 1884 the railroad brought Mendoza into Buenos Aires's orbit and spurred the expansion of grapevines and olive orchards, thanks largely to Italian immigrants. Between 1890 and 1910, the province's vineyards grew sevenfold to 45,000 hectares; growth slowed in the next six decades, but they still quintupled. Many vineyards and bodegas are still small owner-operated businesses, but since the mid-1970s foreign investors—American, Chilean, Dutch, French, and others—have acquired and expanded properties. Mendoza still serves the domestic table-wine market, but there is an increasing focus on premium varietals and blends for both national consumption and export.

Mendoza Province

At one end of the Andes' busiest highway crossing, Mendoza gets a steady stream of international visitors but also has a flourishing domestic travel industry. Its biggest attraction, literally, is the formidable Andean range—symbolized by the hemisphere's highest mountain, 6,962-meter Cerro Aconcagua. Many visitors find the provincial capital of Mendoza and its surrounding wine country so appealing that they stay longer than they expected.

Economically, tourism is a major contributor to the economy, but provincial oil and gas fields supply a quarter of Argentina's fossil fuels. Augmented by hydroelectric power from Andean reservoirs, abundant energy resources have promoted industrial growth.

MENDOZA

In the shadow of the arid central Andes, modern Mendoza lacks Salta's colonial charm or Bariloche's scenic immediacy, but the provincial capital delights Argentines and foreigners alike as one of the country's most livable cities. Its dearth of distinctive historic architecture stems from its seismic vulnerability, but Mendocinos have compensated by creating sycamore-shaded streets, irrigated by ancient acequias, with broad sidewalks and verdant open spaces. In the words of Mexican novelist Carlos Fuentes, it's "protected by a roof of leaves woven together like the fingers of a huge circle of inseparable lovers."

On top of that, it has an active cultural life, thanks to its university, museums, and performing arts venues, and there's a vigorous nightlife district between downtown and the green expanses of Parque General San Martín. Much of Mendoza's prosperity depends on the petroleum industry, but dozens of bodegas, open for tours and tasting, draw many visitors. That makes it an ideal place to organize activities like a white-water descent of the Río Mendoza or an icy ascent of Aconcagua and to celebrate them afterward.

History

Named for colonial Chilean Governor García Hurtado de Mendoza, the city dates from 1561. Its early history was one of isolation—for much of the year, Andean snows made travel to Santiago impossible, and even under the best conditions it was time-consuming. The early 17th-century Spanish chronicler Vásquez de Espinosa reported only 40 Spaniards and 1,500 Indians under a Mendoza-based *corregidor* (magistrate) and various missionary orders. In the late 18th century, though, it came under the administration of the Buenos Aires–based Virreinato del Río de la Plata (Viceroyalty of the River Plate) through the Intendencia de Córdoba.

© WAYNE BERNHARDSON

Cheeses and snacks complement a flight at Vines of Mendoza's wine bar.

Peripheral throughout colonial times, Mendoza became central when General José de San Martín trained his Ejército de los Andes (Army of the Andes) here before crossing the cordillera to liberate Chile from Spain. After independence, though, it struggled (Darwin unfavorably contrasted its "stupid, forlorn aspect" with the Chilean capital of Santiago), but the railroad's arrival linked the burgeoning wine industry to Buenos Aires.

As the city has grown and earthquakes have forced reconstruction, the city center shifted from the colonial Ciudad Vieja (Old City) at the north end of Parque O'Higgins to contemporary Plaza Independencia in 1861. Earthquakes are a constant, most recently in 1968, 1985, and 1997, but they've only stalled rather than stopped Mendoza's growth.

Wine has also remained a constant—Mendoza and vicinity account for more than three-quarters of the country's production—but nearby petroleum reserves have also encouraged industrial development. Meanwhile, tourism has taken off because of wine, access to the Andes, and most recently, proximity to Chile, as bargain-seekers from across the Andes have flocked here since the 2002 devaluation.

Orientation

On the eastern Andean piedmont, 761 meters above sea level, Mendoza (pop. about 112,000, but roughly 1 million when adjacent municipalities are included) is 1,073 kilometers west of Buenos Aires via RN 7 and 340 kilometers northwest of Santiago, Chile, via RN 7 to the Los Libertadores border complex. It is 168 kilometers south of San Juan via RN 40, 665 kilometers southwest of Córdoba via San Luis, and 825 kilometers north of Neuquén via a series of paved highways.

Filling four full blocks, Plaza Independencia is the literal city center, around which four satellites—Plaza Chile, Plaza San Martín, Plaza España, and Plaza Italia—symbolically revolve. Three blocks east of Plaza Independencia, north–south Avenida San Martín (also known as the Alameda) is the axis of the daily bustle, while three blocks north, Avenida General Las Heras is the downtown shopping area. Five

CUYO AND CÓRDOBA

WINERIES IN MAIPÚ

East of downtown Mendoza, Maipú department has a huge concentration of wineries, many of them open for tours and tasting. Weekday tours are the rule, but several are open Saturday morning and a handful on Saturday afternoon and Sunday. The Grupo 10 No. 182 *colectivos* reach several of these from Mendoza's main bus terminal; they are arranged according to distance from the capital. Public transportation is cheapest, but guided tours or hired *remises* can make logistics simpler – and safer than driving.

BODEGAS LÓPEZ

One of Mendoza's largest wineries, dating from 1898, López is an industrial facility that grows 95 percent of its own grapes on 1,060 hectares near the Uco Valley town of Tupungato; 90 percent of its output is for domestic consumption, while 10 percent goes for export. Its diverse line includes cabernet sauvignon, malbec, merlot, Sangiovese, pinot noir, chardonnay, chenin blanc, and semillón.

Hour-long guided tours, with fluent English-speaking guides, begin with a video and then cover the entire production process, from the arrival of the grapes to bottling and packaging, and end with a liberal tasting. On 48 hours' advance notice, López arranges lunches or dinners for a minimum of four people, with unlimited wine. A new building, specifically for tours and tasting, has been under construction.

Bodegas López (Ozamis 375, General Gutiérrez, Maipú, tel. 0261/497-2406, www. bodegaslopez.com.ar) is 13.5 kilometers from downtown Mendoza. Free of charge, tours take place hourly 9 A.M.-5 P.M. weekdays, hourly 9:30 A.M.-12:30 P.M. Saturday and holidays, and at other times by appointment only. English-language tours take place at 11:30 A.M. and 3:30 P.M. weekdays and Saturday morning only.

MUSEO NACIONAL DEL VINO Y LA VENDIMIA

Seven blocks south of Bodegas López, the former Bodega Giol (Ozamis 1040) was once a major winery that has fallen into disrepair and awaits a major building project. Meanwhile, across the street to the south, the founding Gargantini-Giol family's French Classic mansion is now the Museo Nacional del Vino y la Vendimia (Ozamis 914, tel. 0261/497-7763, casasgiolgargantini@gmail.com), offering a good historical summary of Maipú's winemaking industry (guided tours US$0.25).

Unfortunately, when the province took over the winery for offices in the 1960s, it sold off most of the classic furnishings and painted over the original woodwork and zinc ceilings, but it has recently undergone a major renovation. Guided tours, with wine tasting, take place 9 A.M.-7 P.M. Monday-Saturday, 9 A.M.-3 P.M. Sunday.

BODEGA LA RURAL

One of Mendoza's largest wineries, with a capacity of 10.7 million liters and four vineyards scattered around the province, La Rural produces some of the country's finest premium vintages in its Rutini line. On only 10 hectares (though it has vineyards elsewhere

blocks south of Plaza Independencia, the Barrio Cívico is official Mendoza's nucleus.

Mendoza's relatively small population is misleading in that the provincial capital's compact grid borders on several adjacent and nearby municipalities—Guaymallén (to the east), Godoy Cruz (to the south), Las Heras (to the north), Maipú (to the southwest), and Luján de Cuyo (south of Godoy Cruz). In a sense, Gran Mendoza's large population is also misleading in that some municipalities include fairly distant rural communities and sprawling wild areas that are almost unpopulated—Luján de Cuyo, for instance, is an area of 4,847 square kilometers that extends west all the way to the Chilean border.

Sights

Mendoza makes a great walker's city; to get the lay of the town, take the elevator to the rooftop **Terraza Mirador** at the Municipalidad (9 de Julio 500, tel. 0261/429-6500), two

as well), its Maipú facility turns out red varietals including cabernet sauvignon, malbec,
merlot, and Syrah, as well as chardonnay and
gewürztraminer. It is now owned by the Catena
Zapata group but operates autonomously.

Dating from 1885, La Rural is also one of the
most popular wineries for guided tours, partly
because of its remarkable **Museo del Vino,** a
wide-ranging collection of antique winemaking technology. The museum includes vehicles
like tractors and trucks, plus horse carriages
of many kinds, and also has a well-integrated
first-rate tasting room and an art gallery.

Despite capable guides, tours can be disap-
pointing – and excruciatingly slow – because
La Rural's popularity means groups as large
as 50 people. Avoid holidays, in particular, and
try to go early in the morning in hopes of join-
ing a smaller group.

Bodega La Rural (Montecaseros 2625, Coquimbito, tel. 0261/497-2013, www.bodegalar-
ural.com.ar) is open 9 A.M.-1 P.M. and 2-5 P.M.
Monday-Saturday, closed Sunday and holidays.

BODEGA VIÑA EL CERNO

It's tempting to call Viña El Cerno the anti-La
Rural, as this tiny boutique winery's annual
production is fewer than 10,000 bottles each
of malbec, cabernet sauvignon, Syrah, merlot,
and chardonnay, plus some sparkling wines.
Genuinely charming, its aged brick *cavas* hold
barely a dozen visitors, but the guides are gracious and its ample tasting facility – guides also
instruct guests *how* to go about it – is ideal.

Viña El Cerno (Moreno 631, Coquimbito,

Maipú, tel. 0261/481-1567, www.elcerno.com.
ar) is about seven kilometers south of La Rural
on the same bus line. It's open 10 A.M.-7 P.M.
Monday-Saturday.

BODEGA FAMILIA ZUCCARDI

One of Mendoza's biggest wineries, Zuccardi
is a mass producer of fine wines for export as
well as table wines for the domestic market.
Well-organized tours allow visitors to taste
its standards and even test varietals, such as
pinot grigio and marselan, being produced in
small batches only. English-speaking guides
are readily available. If there's any criticism,
it's that the winery itself is less architecturally
striking than some newer competitors.

Zuccardi also hosts one of the local industry's biggest events, mid-November's **De-
gustación Anual,** where the company sets up
a series of tents showcasing its diverse wines,
including some of their experiments. For a
modest fee, public admission gains the right to
almost unlimited sampling, to the accompaniment of live music and other entertainment.

Bodega Familia Zuccardi (RP 36, Fray Luis
Beltrán, Maipú, tel. 0261/421-0000, www.fa-
miliazuccardi.com) offers guided tours (US$4
pp) on a drop-in basis 9:30 A.M.-5 P.M. Monday-
Saturday and 9:30 A.M.-3 P.M. Sunday. There
are also specialized tours, such as a Wednesday cycling and tasting excursion through
vineyards, and hot-air ballooning. As it's one
of the farthest wineries from downtown Mendoza, public transport is awkward, and a taxi
costs around US$40 round-trip.

blocks south of Plaza España. Hours are
8:30 A.M.-1:30 P.M. and 5-8 P.M. weekdays,
10 A.M.-1 P.M. weekends.

The best place to start a walk, though, is
the broad **Plaza Independencia,** bounded
by Espejo, Chile, Rivadavia, and Patricias
Mendocinas. Crossed by diagonal, perpendicular, and curving pathways, embellished
by trees and fountains, it's a major site for
civic events, outdoor concerts, and a weekend
crafts fair. It also features the subterranean

Teatro Quintanilla and the contemporary
Museo Municipal de Arte Moderno (tel.
0261/425-7279, 9 A.M.-8 P.M. Tues.-Sun.,
US$1, free Wed.).

Immediately east of Plaza Independencia,
under a forest-dense canopy, the pedestrian
Paseo Sarmiento is home to the **Legislatura
Provincial** (provincial legislature), detailed in
Argentina's national colors of *celeste* (sky blue)
and white. Sarmiento's sidewalk cafés and
benches make it ideal for people-watching; take

CUYO AND CÓRDOBA

WINERIES IN LUJÁN DE CUYO

South of Mendoza proper, Luján de Cuyo is one of two key wine districts in the greater metropolitan area. It's possible to get around by public transportation, but the best option would be to contract a tour or to assemble a small group and hire a *remise* – thus reducing the risk of becoming a drunk-driving accident victim. Because several wineries are close to Chacras de Coria's gourmet ghetto, a lunch break there is an attractive prospect. It's worth verifying hours before visiting any winery, especially if you need an English-speaking guide, but drop-ins are often welcome.

BODEGA Y CAVAS DE WEINERT

In Chacras de Coria, owned by Brazilians of German descent since 1975, Weinert is a premium industrial winery producing 3 million liters per annum. While the production facilities are state-of-the-art, the historic subterranean *cavas*, with their classic French oak casks, date from the 1890s. A tasting (US$2.50 for 3 wines) can include cabernet, chardonnay, sauvignon blanc, rosé, and some blends, from an ample selection in the bodega shop.

Bodega y Cavas de Weinert (Avenida San Martín 5923, Chacras de Coria, tel. 0261/496-0409, www.bodegaweinert.com) is open 9 A.M.-12:30 P.M. and 2:30-4:30 P.M. Monday-Friday, 10 A.M.-12:30 P.M. and 2:30-3:30 P.M. Saturday. Guides speak English, German, and French. Bus No. 19 (Grupo 1) passes nearby.

BODEGA NIETO SENETINER

In the Vistalba area just south of Chacras de Coria, entered by an alameda of ancient olive trees with the Andean front range as a backdrop, Nieto Senetiner's immaculate grounds surround one of the area's most pleasant wineries. The bodega dates from 1904, but the production facilities have undergone modernization; the informative tours conclude with a tasting of malbec, the main varietal produced here.

Tours at Bodega Nieto Senetiner (Guardia Vieja s/n, Vistalba, tel. 0261/498-0315, www.nietosenetiner.com.ar) take place daily at 10 and 11 A.M. and 12:30 and 4 P.M. (3 P.M. in winter), but if guides are available, other times

are possible. Some guides speak English. With 24 hours' notice, garden lunches are also possible, and there are many other activities, including evening tastings with cheeses as well as horseback riding. From downtown Mendoza, *colectivo* No. 206 (Grupo 1) goes directly to the portal.

BODEGA VISTALBA

One of Mendoza's most imposing wineries, on 53 hectares planted with bonarda, cabernet sauvignon, malbec, and merlot, Vistalba produces fine wines in an almost intimidating atmosphere that includes a luxurious two-room guesthouse and a landmark French restaurant. The exception is the casual subterranean tasting room, where visitors can sample its Tomero line of varietals (including a torrontés from Salta grapes), and the more sophisticated Vistalba line of red blends.

Tours and a surprisingly generous tasting (US$6.50, including chocolates and snacks) at Bodega Vistalba (Sáenz Peña 3531, Vistalba, tel. 0261/498-9400, www.carlospulentawines.com) are by appointment only. Those for whom money is no issue can lodge at Pulenta's **La Posada** (US$194 s, US$363 d), one of whose 70-square-meter suites faces the Andes; the other faces the bodega. Anybody with the cash (or credit) can lunch at celebrity chef Jean-Paul Bondoux's **La Bourgogne** (tel. 0261/498-9421), which has a pretentious menu in French followed by Spanish and imperfect English; it also has branches at Mendoza's Diplomatic Park Suites and at Buenos Aires's Alvear Palace Hotel.

BODEGA LAGARDE

Ideally combined with a visit to the nearby Museo Provincial de Bellas Artes Emiliano Guiñazú, the Lagarde winery comprises 250 hectares of vineyards with an annual production capacity of about 1.6 million liters. Its diverse varietals, for both domestic consumption and export, include chardonnay, sauvignon blanc, cabernet sauvignon, malbec, merlot, and Syrah.

Dating from 1897, its original bodega and big house intact, Bodega Lagarde (San Martín

1745, Mayor Drummond, tel. 0261/498-3330, ext. 27, www.lagarde.com.ar) offers guided tours (US$5 pp with tasting) from 10 A.M.–4 P.M. Monday–Friday, 10 A.M.–noon Saturday, by reservation. There are English- and Portuguese-speaking guides. Its restaurant is open for lunch, also by reservation, Monday–Saturday.

BODEGA CABRINI

Dating from 1918, under four generations of the same family, Cabrini is a small unpretentious Italo-Argentine winery that produces quantities of *vino licoroso*, a blend of malbec, tempranillo, lambrusco, and bonarda grapes, in demijohns for Catholic masses. Commercially it produces malbec, merlot, Syrah, bonarda, cabernet sauvignon, chardonnay, and chenin from its own Perdriel and Agrelo vineyards and farther south at Ugarteche and Tupungato. It also makes a rosé – not too good, in all honesty – out of malbec grapes.

Tours, which include a generous tasting, are a low-key pleasure. Bodega Cabrini (RP 15 Km 22, Perdriel, tel. 0261/488-0218, www.cabrini.com.ar) is open 9 A.M.–noon and 2–6 P.M. Monday–Friday and 9 A.M.–noon Saturday. Phone ahead for English-language guides.

BODEGA LUIGI BOSCA

One of Argentina's best-known industrial bodegas, Luigi Bosca has just one small vineyard in the Mayor Drummond suburb of Luján de Cuyo, where it has converted its oldest facilities into a stylish visitors center where guided tours of the production process conclude with a generous tasting in relaxing surroundings. One distinctive feature is the portrait-sized series of three-dimensional murals, created from cement, by local artist and winemaker Hugo Leytes, that depict the winemaking process.

Bosca's varietals comprise a wide range of reds that include malbec, pinot noir, and Syrah, and whites that include chardonnay, sauvignon blanc, and gewürztraminer.

Luigi Bosca (San Martín 2044, Mayor Drummond, Luján de Cuyo, tel. 0261/498-0347, www.luigibosca.com.ar) offers tours at 10 A.M., noon, and 2 P.M. Monday–Friday, and at noon

on Saturday. Make reservations and confirm whether the tour is in Spanish or English.

EL LAGAR CARMELO PATTI

One of Mendoza's least pretentious wineries, this is a boutique facility not in terms of technology but in terms of quality wines produced with minute attention from the winemaker, a local legend. It's so unpretentious, in fact, that it's easy to miss – there's no sign, and Carmelo Patti seems to lack the ego to promote himself. That may be unnecessary, though, given the word-of-mouth reputation that the wines of this family-run business – his son also works here – enjoy. The production is only 65,000 bottles per annum of malbec and cabernet sauvignon, sometimes blended with cabernet franc and/or merlot, and a sparkling wine based on chardonnay and pinot noir.

Tours of El Lagar Carmelo Patti (San Martín 2614, Mayor Drummond, Luján de Cuyo, tel. 0261/498-1379) take place on request (phone ahead) 10 A.M.–5 P.M. weekdays only.

BODEGA MELIPAL

Like other nearby wineries along the international highway to Chile, including Séptima and Ruca Malén, Melipal is a state-of-the-art facility, with stainless steel vats and gleaming presses, on 62 hectares of drip-fed vines of cabernet sauvignon, merlot, and cabernet franc. It has another 25 hectares of malbec (used also for a rosé) in the Valle de Uco, an hour-plus to the south. It makes no whites.

New in 2005, though some of the vines are nearly a century old, Bodega Melipal (RN 7 Km 1056, Agrelo, Luján de Cuyo, tel. 0261/524-8040, www.bodegamelipal.com) offers tours and tasting by reservation only. Its luminous modern restaurant, facing the vineyards and the Andes, offers a four-course menu, paired with Melipal wines, for US$48 pp. Both the food and service are excellent.

BODEGA SÉPTIMA

Also on the highway to Chile, set among 300 hectares of vineyards with unobstructed Andean views, Séptima's imposing winery re-

(continued on next page)

WINERIES IN LUJÁN DE CUYO (continued)

sembles a pre-Columbian Huarpe-style *pirca* (fortress) of stones set one atop another. Modern seismic safety concerns, though, led the architects of this high-tech facility to reinforce the walls to avoid the fate of most Huarpe fortresses, which lie in ruins throughout the central Argentine Andes.

Dating from 1999, built by the Spanish Codorniu group, Séptima produces a limited assortment of white and red varietals, as well as a notable cabernet-malbec blend. About 60 percent is exported, while the rest goes to the Argentine market.

Bodega Séptima (RN 7 Km 6.5, Agrelo, tel. 0261/498-5164, www.bodegaseptima.com.ar) offers guided tours with tasting (US$6 pp, with more expensive options), by reservation, at 10 A.M. and 3 P.M. weekdays in English, and 11:30 and 4:30 P.M. weekdays in Spanish. In addition, there are 12:30 and 1 P.M. tours (no charge) for those who lunch at its restaurant, **María,** recently reopened under the former chef of Mendoza's landmark restaurant La Sal. Séptima may accommodate drop-ins if schedules permit, but it's better to make reservations.

BODEGA RUCA MALÉN

Immediately east of Séptima, dating from 1998, Ruca Malén is one of Mendoza's most hospitable wineries. Its creator, Jean-Pierre Thibaud, served 10 years as Chandon's chairman before building this expanding boutique winery that sits on 27 hectares of chardonnay, cabernet, and malbec vines.

With Andean views from its grounds, terraces, and restaurant, it offers thorough tours with a generous tasting, accompanied by finger food and perhaps a quinoa salad, from its budget line through its more complex vintages. Many visitors opt for lunch, which includes additional wines paired with each course, before or after the tour.

Bodega Ruca Malén (RN 7 Km 1059, Agrelo, tel. 0261/410-6214, www.bodegarucamalen. com) is open for free guided tours, by reservation, at 10 and 11 A.M. and 3 P.M. Monday–Friday, and at 10 and 11 A.M. Saturday. It's open Sunday for tours only with lunch (US$40), also by reservation. The restaurant is also open by reservation Monday–Saturday, but if tables are available, it may be possible to eat on the spot.

BODEGA CATENA ZAPATA

Argentina's most architecturally startling winery, Catena Zapata is a Mayan-style pyramid that rises above its Agrelo vineyards south of RN 7, the highway to Chile. With stunning views of its vineyards and the Andes, its terrace is almost unmatchable.

Inspired by California's Napa Valley, Catena Zapata produces a diversity of white and red varietals, but its top-end specialties are

---

a detour into the *vitraux*-studded galleries of its **Pasaje San Martín.**

Two blocks south of Sarmiento, **Plaza España**'s intricate tile work makes it the city's most interesting; four blocks west, **Plaza Italia** honors the city's Italian community. Four blocks north of Plaza Italia, rehabbed **Plaza Chile** honors Argentina's western neighbor. Once part of colonial Chile, Cuyo feels closer to the adjacent republic than any other part of Argentina—so close that, since the 2002 devaluation, Mendoza officials have encouraged Chileans to celebrate Chile's September patriotic holidays here.

One block north of Plaza Chile, on Avenida Las Heras between Avenida Perú and 25 de Mayo, the inventive **Museo Popular Callejero** is a series of historical dioramas in metal and glass cases on the sidewalk. They depict typical activities on what was once a dry streambed but became one of Mendoza's major shopping streets.

Four blocks west of Plaza Chile, **Plaza San Martín** aspires to honor Argentina's icon but wallows in hero worship. At its northwest corner, dating from 1875, the **Basílica de San Francisco** (Necochea and España) is the oldest church in the new city. It holds the image of Nuestra Señora del Carmen de Cuyo, the

chardonnay, cabernet sauvignon, and malbec. One of Argentina's most important wine conglomerates, it owns several other wine producers, including Maipú's La Rural, but they continue to operate autonomously with their own traditions.

Led by some of the industry's most proficient guides, Catena Zapata's tours include a glass of white on arrival and red on departure; more elaborate tastings of premium wines are available for an additional (but reasonable) charge.

Catena Zapata (Cobos s/n, Agrelo, Luján de Cuyo, tel. 0261/490-0214, www.catenawines.com) is open for tours and tasting by reservation only.

BODEGA BRESSIA

Set in an inconspicuous vineyard not far from Melipal, Ruca Malén, and Séptima, Bressia is a tiny new winery making premium wines – primarily malbec and blends with cabernet sauvignon, merlot and Syrah – that have drawn national and international attention. There's also a bit of sparkling wine, and a grappa from merlot and sauvignon blanc skins.

Intended to resemble a railroad station, the building itself is a modern facility with stainless steel vats and similar contemporary technology. As a business, it's family-run – literally, as every employee is a family member.

Bodega Bressia (Cochabamba 7752, Agrelo, Luján de Cuyo, tel. 0261/439-3860, www.bressiabodega.com) is open for tours and tasting (US$18 pp, with a *tabla* of cheeses and cured meats) on weekdays by reservation only. Tours are for individuals or small groups and do not mix individuals who do not already know each other.

BODEGA DOLIUM

South of the RP 7 highway to Chile, Dolium is Argentina's only totally subterranean bodega, having ramped the earth to create a naturally air-conditioned production area; only the business offices and tasting room stand above soil level. It produces the usual malbec but also a rosé from malbec as well as less common red varietals such as tempranillo and even a torrontés with grapes from La Rioja Province, several hundred kilometers north.

Less than one kilometer south of Chandon, Bodega Dolium (RP 15 Km 30, Agrelo, Luján de Cuyo, tel. 0261/490-0190, www.dolium.com) is open for guided tours and tastings 9 A.M.–5 P.M. Monday–Friday, but by reservations only. It's one of few Mendoza wineries to charge (US$9 pp) for the privilege, but the staff handle English well, and visitors may even get to sample from the barrels with owner Ricardo Giadorou.

patron of San Martín's army, while its mausoleum is the final resting place of the Liberator's daughter, son-in-law, and granddaughter (the patriarch himself remains in Buenos Aires).

To the north, the **Museo Histórico General San Martín** (Remedios Escalada de San Martín 1843, tel. 0261/425-7947, 9:30 A.M.–1 P.M. and 3:30–7 P.M. Mon.–Fri., 9:30 A.M.–1 P.M. Sat., US$1.25) is a kitchen-sink clutter of sanmartiniana that still needs a professional makeover.

Seven blocks east of Plaza San Martín, the south end of **Parque Bernardo O'Higgins** holds the **Acuario Municipal** (Ituzaingó and Buenos Aires, tel. 0261/425-3824, 7 A.M.–7 P.M. daily, US$1). The municipal aquarium has small tanks with mostly small to midsized subtropical and tropical species, primarily from the Río Paraná but also elsewhere in the Americas along with a few from Asia and Africa. The standout exception is an enormous loggerhead turtle named Jorge, caught off Bahía Blanca in 1985 but not returned to the ocean because of an injury.

At the park's north end, the so-called **Ruinas de San Francisco** are the seismic remains of a 17th-century Jesuit church and school, but the Franciscans claimed the site after the Jesuits' 1767 expulsion from the Americas.

CUYO AND CÓRDOBA

Museo del Area Fundacional

Dating from 1749, the colonial Cabildo stood on Mendoza's Plaza Mayor until 1861, but that year's devastating earthquake made authorities rebuild the city center at present-day Plaza Independencia. Renamed **Plaza Pedro de Castillo,** the plaza now holds the Museo del Area Fundacional, a spacious modern structure that shelters the excavated foundations of the adobe Cabildo (and the subsequent slaughterhouse).

As a museum, it's a thoughtful account of Mendoza's development since pre-Columbian times, with ethnographic, historical, and contemporary detail. Its strengths are Huarpe Indian artifacts as well as historical dioramas and photographs; loaner booklets with English descriptions of the exhibits are available. There's a pleasant café and a souvenir shop.

As an archaeological site, its strength is the subterranean remains of the fountain where 19th-century Mendocinos came to collect potable water brought from the Andes by an underground aqueduct. Guided tours of the site cost an additional US$0.50.

The Museo del Area Fundacional (Alberdi 571, tel. 0261/425-6927, US$1.50 adults, free Wed.) is open 8:30 A.M.–8 P.M. Tuesday–Saturday and 3–8 P.M. Sunday.

Bodega Escorihuela

One of Mendoza's most convenient wineries is Godoy Cruz's Bodega Escorihuela, about a half-hour walk or a short bus or cab ride from downtown. At Escorihuela's founding in 1884, Godoy Cruz was the boonies, but Gran Mendoza gradually surrounded this full-block facility, whose vineyards are scattered throughout the province.

Escorihuela produces the dry but fruity white viognier and reds including malbec, Syrah, and a cabernet-malbec blend. Its courtyard is also home to celebrity chef Francis Mallman's renowned restaurant **1884,** one of Argentina's top dining experiences.

In late 2008, however, Bodega Escorihuela (Belgrano 1188, Godoy Cruz, tel. 0261/424-2744, www.escorihuela.com.ar) suffered a major fire; reconstruction is underway, but tours are on hold as of press time.

Parque San Martín

At the west end of downtown Mendoza, across Avenida Boulogne Sur Mer, famed French architect Carlos Thays designed this 420-hectare park on property donated by governor (later senator) Emilio Civit. Planted with pines and eucalyptus, its literal high point is the **Cerro de la Gloria,** topped by Uruguayan sculptor Juan Manuel Ferrari's **Monumento al Ejército Libertador,** an equestrian tribute to San Martín's army (interestingly, one of its mounted soldiers is Afro-Argentine).

At the west end of Avenida Emilio Civit (an extension of Sarmiento), the park's stunning iron-filigree gates are a story—or different stories—in themselves. Legend says they were originally forged for Turkish Sultan Abdul Hamid and crowned by Islam's crescent moon, but Civit opportunistically purchased them in Paris after Hamid's overthrow. When they were planted at the park's entrance, though, the provincial coat of arms and a condor with wings spread replaced the moon of Muhammad. An alternative, less romantic version is that Civit ordered the gates directly from Glasgow's McFarlane Ironworks.

Parque San Martín is also home to **Estadio Islas Malvinas** (a soccer venue built for the 1978 World Cup), the hillside **Jardín Zoológico** (zoo, tel. 0261/428-1700, 9 A.M.–6 P.M. Tues.–Sun., US$1), and the **Anfiteatro Frank Romero Day** (site of outdoor concerts and festival events). Under unified administration, the history-anthropology **Museo de Ciencias Naturales y Antropológicas Juan Cornelio Moyano** (tel. 0261/428-7666) and the **Museo Arqueológico Salvador Canals Frau** are both open 8 A.M.–1 P.M. and 2–7 P.M. Tuesday–Friday, 8 A.M.–1 P.M. and 3–7 P.M. weekends. Admission costs US$1.

The park is an easy 1.5-kilometer walk from Plaza Independencia. *Bateas* (open-air buses) shuttle passengers from the gates to Cerro de la Gloria.

© WAYNE BERNHARDSON

Bodega Escorihuela

Entertainment

Mendoza has plenty to do at night. The liveliest nightlife area is the barhoppers' row of Arístides Villanueva, where there's a lot of turnover; **El Abasto** (Arístides Villanueva 308), which hosts live rock and roll, has lasted a while, however.

Most Mendoza **cinemas** are suburban multiplexes, but there are irregular programs downtown at the **Microcine Municipal Davíd Eisenchlas** (9 de Julio 500, tel. 0261/449-5180), in the basement of the Municipalidad. The **Cine Teatro Universidad Nacional de Cuyo** (Lavalle 55, tel. 0261/420-4549) also shows occasional films.

Dating from 1925, Mendoza's major performing arts venue is the remodeled neoclassical **Teatro Independencia** (Chile 1187, tel. 0261/438-0644, www.teatroindependencia.com. ar). The subterranean **Teatro Quintanilla** (tel. 0261/423-2310) is part of Plaza Independencia's modern art museum complex.

For live folklore and tango on weekends, along with regional cuisine, try **El Retortuño** (Dorrego 123, Guaymallén, tel. 0264/431-6300, www.intertournet.com.ar/elretortuno), a few blocks south of the bus terminal.

Vines of Mendoza (Espejo 567, tel. 0264/438-1031, www.vinesofmendoza.com) is a contemporary tasting room in a private patio location around the corner from the Park Hyatt that specializes in vintages from local boutiques and also serves appropriate snacks to complement the wines. Open 3–10 P.M. Monday–Saturday, it also host events such as Wednesday's "Meet the Winemaker" that features one local specialist every week.

At the nearby Park Hyatt, its **Vines Wine Bar & Vinoteca** (Chile 1124) hosts Friday night social gatherings (US$10) that include three glasses of wine from a highlight bodega, accompanied by tapas or other finger food.

Events

Mendoza's biggest single festival is March's moveable **Fiesta Nacional de la Vendimia** (www.vendimia.mendoza.gov.ar), celebrating the autumn wine harvest over a four-day weekend that starts on Friday. Filled with concerts and parades, it ends with the queen's coronation in Parque San Martín's amphitheater.

Mid-February's **Vuelta Ciclística de Mendoza** is a major road race for bicyclists. August's **Festival de la Nieve** marks the ski season.

Shopping

Plaza Independencia is the site of the **Plaza de las Artes** outdoor crafts fair, which takes place every Friday, Saturday, and Sunday. The downtown **Mercado Artesanal** (Avenida San Martín 1143, tel. 0261/420-4239, 8 A.M.–1 P.M. Mon.–Thurs.) offers the opportunity to purchase handicrafts from around and beyond the province, including weavings, horse gear, and basketry.

More than its name would suggest, **Las Viñas** (Avenida Las Heras 399, tel. 0261/425-1520, www.lasvinas.com.ar) has plenty of wines but also a bundle of crafts ranging from ceramics and silverwork to leather, hides, ponchos, weavings, and even dried fruits. It has occupied the same site since 1950.

Mendoza also has specialty wine shops such as **La Casa del Vino** (Arístides Villanueva 160, tel. 0261/423-5862), with a large selection and tastings as well, and **Vines of Mendoza** (Chile 1124, www.vinesofmendoza.com), which also has a stylish wine bar in the Park Hyatt.

García Santos Libros (San Martín 921, tel. 0261/429-2287) has a sophisticated choice of books on Argentina and Spanish-language literature. **Librería SBS** (Gutiérrez 54, tel. 0261/425-2917) has English-language books.

Sports and Recreation

Mendoza Province is a prime outdoor recreation area, offering climbing and hiking, cycling and mountain biking, skiing, and white-water rafting and kayaking. It's possible to organize many (though not all) activities through city agencies listed below, but other providers have on-site services in the Andes along RN 7 (the main route to Chile) and the Río Mendoza. Most operators handle more than one activity.

For specific information on climbing Cerro Aconcagua and support services, see the *Parque Provincial Aconcagua* section later in this chapter.

The **Club Andinista Mendoza** (Fray Luis Beltrán 357, Guaymallén, tel. 0261/431-9870) is a general information source for climbing and hiking. **Orviz** (Avenida J. B. Justo 532, tel. 0261/425-1281) rents and sells climbing and hiking gear.

Several places in town rent or sell ski gear, including **Esquí Mendoza Competición** (Avenida Las Heras 583, tel. 0261/429-7544) and **Rezagos de Ejército** (Avenida Mitre 2002, tel. 0261/423-3791).

Betancourt Rafting (Lavalle 35, Local 8, tel. 0261/429-9665, www.betancourt.com.ar) does the Río Mendoza's lower stretches from its Cacheuta base (25 kilometers south of town); Cacheuta is, in a sense, a dead-end destination since the Panamericana's rerouting.

The other white-water operators, **Ríos Andinos** (Sarmiento 721, tel. 0261/429-5030, www.riosandinos.com) and **Argentina Rafting** (Primitivo de la Reta 992, Local 4, tel. 0261/429-6325, www.argentinarafting.com), are based near Potrerillos, on the upper Río Mendoza.

Accommodations

Mendoza has abundant accommodations, including a growing number of quality hostels, but the area's popularity occasionally puts pressure on available resources in all categories. Reservations are essential for March's Fiesta de la Vendimia and advisable for Semana Santa and other long weekends—including mid-September's Chilean patriotic holidays (since the 2002 Argentine devaluation, Chileans have swarmed Mendoza at every opportunity). Tourist offices at the bus terminal and downtown are helpful in locating accommodations.

US$10-25: Hostel Puertas del Sol (Espejo 751, tel. 0351/425-7983, www.hostelpuertas-delsol.com.ar, US$9 pp dorm, US$21–35 d) is a slightly cramped but well-located garden hostel that also organizes abundant excursions.

Occupying a large rehabbed house on Plaza Independencia, congenial 🍷 **Hostel Independencia** (Mitre 1237, tel. 0261/423-1806, www.hostelindependencia.com.ar, US$10 pp dor m, US$25 d) has cramped sleeping quarters—the dorms average eight beds to a room—but it has great common areas, including a wine bar, and offers some unique excursions.

For many years, the **Savigliano Hostel** (Pedro Palacios 944, tel. 0261/423-7746, www.savigliano.com.ar, US$8–10 pp dorm, US$23–29 s or d with private bath, breakfast included) was *the* top budget choice; it's still the best near the bus terminal, at least, but better-located hostels have usurped much of its clientele. It's easily accessible by the pedestrian tunnel beneath Avenida Videla.

Traditionally popular with climbers and trekkers, just off Plaza Independencia, the HI-affiliated 34-bed **Hostel Campo Base** (Avenida Mitre 946, tel./fax 0261/429-0707, www.hostelcampobase.com.ar, US$10–11 pp dorm, US$29–31 s or d) is popular enough that reservations are advisable all year. Most rooms are dorms, but there are a couple of doubles with private baths. There's also a bar as well as Wednesday- and Saturday-night *asados.*

Another HI affiliate, now under Campo Base ownership, the capacious **Hostel Internacional Mendoza** (Avenida España 343, tel./fax 0261/424-0018 or 0261/424-8432, www.hostelmendoza.net, US$10–11 pp dorm, US$29–32 s or d, with breakfast) has kitchen facilities, a restaurant, and the *El Carajo* bar with occasional live music. It also picks up guests at the bus terminal and arranges excursions in and around town.

Don't expect to get to sleep early at **Hostel Mendoza Inn** (Arístides Villanueva 470, tel. 0261/420-2486, www.mendozahostel.com, US$10–12 pp dorm, US$29–32 s or d)—that's not why people visit Mendoza's burgeoning restaurant and nightlife district. The building is an enormous family house with sprawling gardens, a small pool, and a variety of rooms that range from quadruples to more spacious rooms with private bath.

Friendly **Hotel Zamora** (Perú 1156, tel. 0261/425-7537, www.hotelzamora.netfirms. com, US$22 s, US$32 d) has no luxuries, and some of the singles are small, but all rooms have private baths, and rates include cable TV and parking. Pancho, the resident Old English sheepdog, provides entertainment.

US$25-50: Austere but otherwise outstanding in its range, the well-kept and well-placed **City Hotel** (General Paz 95, tel. 0261/425-1343, http://cityhotelmendoza.tripod.com, US$24 s, US$36 d, with private bath, breakfast, and a/c) is friendly and helpful.

On a placid downtown cul-de-sac, **Hotel Milena** (Pasaje Babilonia 17, tel. 0261/420-2490, www.milenahotel.com.ar, US$34 s, US$44 d, with breakfast) has smallish but well-maintained rooms and parking.

Down the block from the Mendoza Inn, the 🍷 **Damajuana Hostel** (Arístides Villanueva 282, tel./fax 0261/425-5858, www.damajuanahostel.com.ar, US$16 pp dorm, US$45 d) has mostly dorms. Its common areas include spacious gardens, a large pool, and a bar-restaurant that's worth considering even for nonguests. Like Mendoza Inn, it's best for nightlifers.

US$50-100: The glisteningly modernized, conveniently central 🍷 **Hotel Puerta del Sol** (Garibaldi 82, tel. 0261/420-4820, www.hotelpuertadelsol.com.ar, US$46–50 s, US$59–65 d) is overtaking some of the more established downtown hotels and offers breakfast, cable TV, and similar amenities.

The three-star **Hotel Carollo** (25 de Mayo 1184, tel. 0261/423-5666 or 0261/423-5667, www.hotelcarollo.com, US$58 s, US$65 d, with breakfast and free airport transfers) is a remodeled business-oriented building.

Despite a misleadingly modern facade, the Carollo's adjacent and slightly more expensive sister, **Hotel Princess** (25 de Mayo 1168, tel./fax 0261/423-5669, www.hotelprincess.com.ar, US$65 s, US$74 d), is not dramatically better.

Rooms at the immaculate, highly recommended **Hotel Provincial** (Belgrano 1259, tel. 0261/425-8284, www.hotelprovincialmza.com,

US$50 s, US$67 d) are an excellent value in its price range, and for a government-run place it's surprising cheerful and efficient. Electronic amenities include Wi-Fi, magnetic locks, and strongboxes, and there are also a pool with a Jacuzzi as well as a sauna.

Dating from the 1940s, **Grand Hotel Balbi** (Avenida Las Heras 340, tel. 0261/423-3500, www.hotelbalbi.com.ar, US$66 s, US$79 d) may be a four-star anachronism, but it's still good value, with a spacious lobby and other common areas, plus a modest swimming pool and contemporary amenities such as Wi-Fi. Some rooms have Jacuzzis.

From its formal furnishings, **B&B Plaza Italia** (Montevideo 685, tel. 0261/423-4219, www.plazaitalia.net, US$90 s or d) looks like an idealized museum of upper-middle-class domesticity from the 1920s. The reality, though, is a gracious but informal reception by outgoing hosts who have created an oasis of tranquility in what can be a bustling downtown.

US$100-200: Arguably Mendoza's best when it opened for the 1978 World Cup, **Hotel Huentala** (Primitivo de la Reta 1007, tel. 0261/420-0766, www.huentala.com, from US$120 s or d with buffet breakfast) has reinvented itself as a boutique hotel under the Sheraton umbrella, but that's been a gradual process. With 81 rooms, it's a little large for a boutique, but the accommodations are up to snuff, with a minimalist decor, and there are nice touches like a subterranean wine bar in the model of a traditional cellar. Some of the common areas, though, have lagged behind, and the facade—due for a makeover in the near future—still suffers from a kitschy pseudo-Islamic style.

Also a World Cup legacy, the high-rise **Hotel Aconcagua** (San Lorenzo 545, tel. 0261/520-0500, www.hotelaconcagua.com, US$86–143 s or d) has undergone a major restoration that has left its uniformly midsized rooms in primo condition; the common areas, including a pool, restaurant, and relandscaped grounds, are equally appealing. The higher prices correspond to a handful of suites.

Over US$200: Only the facade remains of the landmark Hotel Plaza, which has been gutted, partially demolished, and replaced by a multistory five-star structure that nevertheless has managed to blend into a traditional neighborhood as the new 【 **Park Hyatt Mendoza** (Chile 1124, tel. 0261/441-1234, www.mendoza.park.hyatt.com, $193–441 s or d). Once again Mendoza's prestige hotel, it has a restaurant, a café, a spa, a wine bar, a casino, a sports bar, and frequent events and entertainment.

New in early 2009, the **Diplomatic Park Suites** (Belgrano 1041, tel. 0261/405-1900, US$236–300) is a 19-story structure that, with its Francophile decor, seemingly aspires to emulate Buenos Aires's venerable Alvear Palace—in fact, it even boasts a branch of the Alvear Palace's La Bourgogne restaurant. In reality, in the global economic crisis, the upper five floors are unlikely to be ready for several more years, but some of the finished floors are thematic wine floors sponsored by the likes of Catena Zapata and Zuccardi. Rates vary according to city view (cheaper) and mountain view (dearer), and for corner rooms (dearer yet). The presidential suite goes for more than US$3,600 per night.

New in late 2008, the **Sheraton Mendoza** (Primitivo de la Reta 989, tel. 0261/441-5500, www.sheraton.com.ar, US$205–381 s or d) is a 17-story 180-room high-rise integrated into the new casino.

Food

Mendoza's restaurant scene has always been dispersed. Some places are both food and entertainment venues, so check the *Entertainment* section as well. There are also fine restaurants in Chacras de Coria, which has a separate listing below, and in many vineyards (covered in sidebars on *Luján de Cuyo* and *Maipú*).

For lunch on a budget or for picnic fixin's, the best and most diverse option is **Mercado Central** (Avenida Las Heras and Patricias Mendocinas), dating from 1883; a warren of stalls sell groceries and first-class fast food, including empanadas, pizza, and sandwiches.

For a sandwich on downtown's shaded

sidewalks, along with cold draft beer, try **La Cervecería** (Sarmiento 63) or any of several others nearby.

Tasca La Plaza (Montevideo 117, tel. 0261/423-3466) is a small, informal Spanish-style restaurant with youthful energy, decent lunch specials, and very fine desserts. **El Mesón Español** (Montevideo 244, tel. 0261/429-6175) is a more traditional Spanish locale. **Praga** (Leonidas Aguirre 413, tel. 0261/425-9585, dinner daily Sun.–Fri.) has earned a reputation for its seafood specialties. The Damajuana hostel's **Chano** (Arístides Villanueva 282, tel. 0261/425-5858) is remarkably stylish and lively, with variations on standard Argentine dishes.

Parrillas are numerous. Among the good choices for beef-eaters are **Boccadoro** (Mitre 1976, tel. 0261/425-5056); **Arturito** (Chile 1515, tel. 0261/425-1489); and the more upmarket **Facundo** (Avenida Sarmiento 641, tel. 0261/420-2866), which has attractive outdoor seating.

Relocated from Chacras de Coria, down the block from the Diplomatic Suites, **Flora** (Belgrano 1069, tel. 0261/420-4322) serves a diverse menu ranging from light but filling salads to hearty dishes like lamb-stuffed *sorrentinos* in a Malbec sauce (US$9); the bread and accompanying pâté, embellished with almonds and raisins, merits special mention. Beware the desserts, which are good but too big for most single diners.

Open daily for lunch and dinner, **La Albahaca** (Espejo 659, tel. 0261/438-0041) has an excellent kitchen for both magnificently presented antipasti and specialties such as ravioli with a shrimp sauce (US$10), risotto, and trout. The dessert menu lacks imagination, though.

Reincarnated on its original site, years after a fire forced its temporary relocation, the once-modest **❰ La Marchigiana** (Patricias Mendocinas 1550, tel. 0261/423-0751, www.marchigiana.com.ar) has become a contemporary-design restaurant with high ceilings, recessed lighting, and modern furnishings. The style changes, though, haven't altered its unpretentious Italian kitchen, unexpectedly

democratic ambience, and outstanding service. It's pricier than the standard Italo-Argentine fare, but well worth the small difference.

In Godoy Cruz's Escorihuela winery courtyard, celebrity chef Francis Mallman's **❰ 1884** (Belgrano 1188, tel. 0261/424-2698, francism@nysnet.com.ar) is Mendoza's prestige dining experience, with gourmet versions of regional dishes such as kid goat from Malargüe as well as a diversity of tapas-style appetizers. Diners sit in contemporary high-backed chairs or on long sofas with pillows for support in a room with high ceilings and burned-reddish walls. It's expensive by Argentine standards, with entrées in the US$15–25 range, but food of this quality would cost triple that in North America or Europe. Unaffected by the Escorihuela fire that destroyed much of the winery, it has a diverse wine list from many area wineries, ranging from cheap to extravagant. The service is unobtrusively impeccable, and reservations are advisable; it's open for lunch and dinner daily except in January, when it is open for lunch only.

Information

The municipal **Centro de Información Turística** (CIT, Garibaldi and San Martín, tel. 0261/420-1333, 9 A.M.–9 P.M. daily) has maps, brochures, and capable personnel that usually includes an English speaker. Their parent office, the **Dirección Municipal de Turismo** (9 de Julio 500, tel. 0261/449-5185, www.ciudaddemendoza.gov.ar), is open 8 A.M.–1 P.M. weekdays only.

At the Guaymallén bus terminal, there's a separate and very efficient **Oficina de Informes** (Alberdi and Reconquista, tel. 0261/431-3001, 7 A.M.–11 P.M. daily).

The provincial **Secretaría de Turismo** (Avenida San Martín 1143, tel. 0261/420-2800, www.turismo.mendoza.gov.ar, 8 A.M.–9 P.M. weekdays, 9 A.M.–10 P.M. weekends) has good information on the entire province, but only a techie could love the organization of its new website.

ACA (Avenida San Martín 985, tel. 0261/420-2900) has road maps and other motorist services.

Services

At one end of a key border crossing, Mendoza has the most complete services of any provincial city.

Mendoza is one of the easiest places to cash travelers checks in the entire country, thanks to efficient exchange houses like **Cambio Santiago** (Avenida San Martín 1199), which is open late Saturdays; it charges a 2 percent commission, however.

Downtown ATMs are abundant, including the ones at **Citibank** (Sarmiento 20) and **Banco de la Nación** (Necochea and 9 de Julio).

Correo Argentino (Avenida San Martín and Avenida Colón) is the post office; central Mendoza's postal code is 5500.

There are countless downtown *locutorios* with Internet access, and the Sarmiento pedestrian mall is a public Wi-Fi hotspot.

Student- and budget-oriented **Asatej** (Sarmiento 223, tel./fax 0261/429-0029, mendoza@asatej.com.ar) will seek out the best airfares. **ISC Viajes** (Avenida España 1016, tel. 0261/425-9259, www.iscviajes.com) is the Amex affiliate.

Many agencies offer excursions ranging from simple city and wine tours to river rafting, climbing, and trekking. Among adventure operators, try **Campo Base Travel & Adventure** (Sarmiento 231, tel. 0261/425-5511, www.cerroaconcagua.com), specifically for climbing and trekking; and **Aymará Turismo** (9 de Julio 1023, tel. 0261/420-2064, www.aymara.com.ar) for mule trips, trekking, rafting, and winery visits.

Two bordering countries have consulates: Chile (Belgrano 1080, tel. 0261/425-4844, www.congechilemendoza.com.ar) and Bolivia (Garibaldi 380, 1st floor, tel. 0261/429-2458).

For visa extensions (US$100), visit the **Dirección Nacional de Migraciones** (Avenida San Martín 1859, Godoy Cruz, tel. 0261/424-3512), but it's nearly as cheap to cross into Chile and return.

For Spanish-language instruction, try the **Instituto Intercultural de Lenguas Extranjeras** (República de Siria 241, tel. 0261/429-0269, www.intercultural.com.ar). It's best at one-on-one.

The **Asociación Mendocina de Intercambio Cultural Argentino Norteamerica** (Chile 987, tel. 0261/423-6367, www.amicana.com) has an English-language lending library.

For laundry service, try **La Lavandería** (San Lorenzo 338, tel. 0261/429-4782).

The **Hospital Central** is at Salta and Alem (tel. 0261/420-0600). For ambulance service, contact the **Servicio Coordinado de Emergencia** (tel. 107 or 0261/428-0000).

Getting There

Mendoza has both domestic and international connections by air and road. There is talk of reviving rail service to Chile, but this is unlikely for the near future.

Aerolíneas Argentinas (Sarmiento 82, tel. 0261/420-4100) and close affiliate Austral fly several times daily to Buenos Aires's Aeroparque, sometimes via Córdoba.

Mendoza's only international connections are with **LAN** (Avenida España 1002, tel. 0261/425-7900), which flies at least twice daily to Santiago, Chile. LAN also flies to Córdoba and Buenos Aires.

Mendoza's gigantic bus station, **Terminal del Sol** (Avenida Gobernador Videla and Avenida Acceso Este, Guaymallén, tel. 0261/431-3001 or 0261/431-0500, www.mendozaterminal.com.ar), is just over the departmental line. Provincial, regional, long-distance, and international services (frequently to Chile, less frequently to Perú, seasonally to Uruguay, and no service to Bolivia) are available. There are also restaurants, shops, and even showers.

To the upper Río Mendoza Valley destinations of Uspallata and Los Penitentes (for Parque Provincial Aconcagua), there are three or four buses daily with **Expreso Uspallata** (tel. 0261/431-3309).

Vallecito (tel. 0261/432-4456) goes daily to San Agustín del Valle Fértil via the provincial capital of San Juan and the Difunta Correa shrine, while several other companies go to San Juan only. There are also services to Barreal and Calingasta, in western San Juan Province, and to Jáchal, north of San Juan.

In ski season, several companies go directly

to Las Leñas, including Turismo Mendoza and Expreso Uspallata, but the rest of the year it's necessary to change in San Rafael or Malargüe.

Typical destinations, times, and fares include San Rafael (3 hours, US$6), San Juan (2 hours, US$6), Uspallata (2.5 hours, US$5), Los Penitentes (3.5 hours, US$8), San Agustín del Valle Fértil (6 hours, US$13), and Malargüe (5 hours, US$12).

Mendoza is a hub for long-distance buses, with frequent departures in almost every direction except perhaps the Mesopotamian littoral (Puerto Iguazú, for instance, has just a few buses each week).

Typical destinations, times, and fares include Córdoba (9 hours, US$25–33), Neuquén (13 hours, US$30–40), Tucumán (15 hours, US$35–50), Buenos Aires (14 hours, US$42–66), Mar del Plata (19 hours, US$63–75), Salta (19 hours, US$57–73), Bariloche (18 hours, US$50), Puerto Madryn (21 hours, US$65), Corrientes (20 hours, US$60), Puerto Iguazú (26 hours, US$80), and Río Gallegos (37 hours, US$110).

Numerous companies cross the Andes to the Chilean capital of Santiago (7 hours, US$15–18) and the beach resort of Viña del Mar, but shared *minibuses* like **Coitram** (tel. 0261/431-1999) and **Chiar Autos** (tel. 0261/432-3112) to Santiago are faster and only a little more expensive (6 hours, US$21). **Empresa General Artigas** (EGA, tel. 0261/431-7758) and **El Rápido** (tel. 0261/431-4093) go to Montevideo, Uruguay (22 hours, US$80), with onward service to Punta del Este and Brazil.

Getting Around

Getting around compact central Mendoza is fairly straightforward on foot, but reaching wineries and other suburban sites requires using taxis (not extravagantly expensive) or buses. The bus system has undergone a major rerouting project; riders need a rechargeable Redbus card or, alternatively, they can pay with coins (but get no change).

Aeropuerto Internacional El Plumerillo (tel. 0261/520-6000) is six kilometers north of downtown along RN 40. From downtown's Calle Salta, bus No. 60 (Grupo 6) goes directly to the terminal, or a *remise* costs about US$6.50.

Just across the departmental line in Guaymallén, the Terminal del Sol is easily accessible via a pedestrian underpass from Avenida Alem.

Rental agencies include **Avis** (Primitivo de la Reta 914, tel. 0261/420-3178), **Dollar** (Primitivo de la Reta 936, Local 6, tel. 0261/429-9939), **Hertz** (Espejo 591, tel. 0261/420-3313), and **Localiza** (Primitivo de la Reta 936, Local 4, tel. 0261/429-6800).

CHACRAS DE CORIA AND VICINITY

Thirty years ago, the Luján de Cuyo suburb of Chacras de Coria was an area of vineyards and orchards on Mendoza's southern outskirts. Some vintners and growers hang on, but trophy houses on giant lots have displaced much of this former fruit bowl. The surviving poplar windbreaks and sycamore-lined streets hide many of the worst offenders, though, and Chacras's stylish and diverse restaurants have made it popular for evenings out—or lunch between vineyard visits.

Baccus Vineyards Biking (Loria 5727, tel. 0261/496-1975, www.baccusbiking.com.ar) offers cycling tours of vineyards in the vicinity.

Sights

In and around Chacras, the biggest attractions are the wineries; for details and visiting hours, see the sidebar *Wineries in Luján de Cuyo.*

The **Museo Provincial de Bellas Artes Emiliano Guiñazú** (San Martín 3651, Mayor Drummond, Luján de Cuyo, tel. 0261/496-0224, 8 A.M.–7 P.M. Tues.–Fri., 3–8 P.M. weekends, free) takes its official name from its owner, but its popular name, **Casa de Fader,** comes from Fernando Fader, the artist hired to decorate this summer residence. Set among expansive gardens, the building is an attraction in itself, with the artist's own peeling murals and remarkable tiled indoor pools. It also holds collections of Fader's landscapes and portraits, plus exhibitions of contemporary art, some of it very imaginative. From downtown Mendoza, take bus No. 10 (Grupo 1).

Entertainment

Directly on the plaza, **Cacano Bar** (Aguinaga 1120, tel. 0261/496-2018) has scheduled live music but also enjoys performances by drop-in talents like local guitarist David Lebón and, on occasion, his buddy Charly García. There's ample space except for really big draws, but the bar food menu is only so-so.

Accommodations

Chacras has a growing number of accommodations, and the ones it has offer real quality. About the only drawback is the nighttime barking of street dogs and the occasional muffler-free moped, but that's no worse than Mendoza's traffic.

The once-deteriorated 40-room **Hotel San Francisco** (Pueyrredón 2265, tel. 0261/496-0110, www.nuevohotelsanfrancisco.com, US$74–87 s or d) has undergone a major restoration; it has a pool and spacious wooded grounds.

Posada Borravino (Medrano 2658, tel. 0261/496-4445, www.posadaborravino.com, US$76–102 s or d) is an eight-room boutique hotel in a quiet neighborhood, with a pool, air-conditioning, and similar amenities. It's less convenient than its competitors, though, in terms of walking distance to restaurants and other businesses.

New in 2006, set among artfully landscaped grounds barely a block from the plaza, parts of ❰ **Parador del Angel** (Newbery 5418, tel. 0261/496-2201, www.paradordelangel.com.ar, US$130–150 s or d with breakfast) occupy a century-old adobe. The accommodations proper, though, are contemporary dwellings that replicate the traditional style to create impeccable unity even with modern touches that include a swimming pool, a video and games room, and Wi-Fi. For mountaineers, owner Daniel Alessio also has extensive Aconcagua experience.

Set on two hectares of lush orchards and vineyards worked by mules, ❰ **Finca**

the gate to Mendoza's Club Tapiz, a hotel-vineyard-winery-restaurant complex

© WAYNE BERNHARDSON

Adalgisa (Pueyrredón 2222, tel. 0261/496-0713 or 0261/15-654-3134, www.fincaadalgisa.com.ar, US$235–390 s or d) has eleven rooms plus a pool, fish and duck ponds, and even a small wine bar featuring its homegrown malbec (made with assistance from nearby master Carmelo Patti). A finished product just a few years after its founding, this self-described "rural hotel" features large and comfortable rooms with colorful interiors, fine vineyard views toward the Andes (at least from the upper floor), and amenities such as Wi-Fi.

Also new in 2006, **Lares de Chacras** (Larrea 1266, tel. 0261/496-1061, www.lares-dechacras.com, US$175–195 s or d) is a comfortable ten-room suburban hotel that's easy walking distance from the plaza and restaurants. While the spacious rooms have balconies and the maturing landscape design is a strong point, its fusion of contemporary and rustic elements is a little odd.

Under the same ownership, new in late 2009, across the highway from Chacras, **Lares en Finca Terrada** (Terrada 5998, Carrodilla,

Luján de Cuyo, tel. 0261/496-1061, www.fin-caterrada.com, US$150–170 s or d) is a new vineyard hotel whose disadvantage—or advantage to some—is its relatively isolated location. Presently it has five rooms with designer touches, such as central circular showers in the baths of three rooms; the larger suites also have tubs. While it lacks a full-fledged restaurant, it does prepare light meals and occasional dinners for guests, and has a small wine bar that serves its own malbec.

New in 2008, a few blocks north of the plaza, **Casa Margot** (Italian 6016, tel. 0261/496-1877, www.casamargot.com.ar, US$250–350 s or d) is a unique two-suite guest house with vaulted brick ceilings, built for local sculptor Eliana Molinelli before her untimely death, that's favored by honeymooners and other romantics. Its owners also operate a Valle de Uco winery and serve their own sparkling wines and varietals (malbec, sauvignon blanc) in the sprawling gardens.

Across the highway from Chacras, **Club Tapiz** (Pedro Molina s/n, Ruta 60 Km 2.5, Russell, Maipú, tel. 0261/496-3433, www.tapiz.com.ar, US$170 s or d) is a cozy seven-room vineyard hotel in a former winery—its present winery is a short distance south, in Agrelo—that's also known for its elite restaurant. **El Terruño** (tel. 0261/496-0131) serves a weekday three-course lunchtime special (US$21) that includes a glass of wine, but on weekends it's an à la carte menu that includes items such as kid goat in a white wine sauce (US$16).

In a category of its own, south of the highway to Chile near the Ruca Malén winery turnoff, ◖ **Cavas Wine Lodge** (Costa Flores s/n, tel. 0261/479-0200, www.cavas-winelodge.com, US$605–762 s or d) consists of a main building with bright common areas (decorated with contemporary art), a restaurant with both indoor and patio seating, a Moorish spa, and 14 spacious freestanding Taos-style accommodations surrounded by vineyards. Designed for privacy, each building has its own plunge pool and rooftop terrace for sunset views of the Andes. Nonguests can dine by reservation only.

Food

Chacras is becoming Mendoza's gourmet ghetto, but there are both economical and upscale dining choices. Since buses stop running around midnight, consider taking a cab or a *remise* back into town.

Bianco y Nero (Mitre 1495, tel. 0261/496-5093, www.bianca-nero.com.ar) is a design shop that also operates as a Wi-Fi café 9 A.M.–9 P.M. It specializes in handmade chocolates, but also has coffees and tea.

For Mexican semi–fast food and respectable margaritas, try the **Taco Bar** (Viamonte s/n), serving a variety of Mexican dishes beyond its name, including good guacamole. It's also cheap, even by current Argentine standards.

New in early 2010, **Nadia O.F.** (Italia 6055, tel. 0261/15-553-1550, ww.nadiaof.com) is an outgrowth of the Urban restaurant at the O. Fournier winery in the Uco Valley. Chef Nadia Harón offers a weekly tasting menu (US$25), matched with Fournier's own wines with each course (price varies depending on the line). Diners here, though, are welcome to bring their own wine for a modest corkage fee.

El Palenque (Mitre 1541) is a casual Argentine restaurant with a diverse menu and patio dining that falls somewhere between a scene and a dining experience, though it partakes of both. Its unique feature is that it lacks a wine list per se—rather, diners choose their own bottle off the racks and take it to the table. The service, though, can be inconsistent.

Chilean-owned ◖ **Mar y Monte** (Darragueira 765, tel. 0261/496-5164, www.marymonte.com.ar) is a thematic restaurant whose menu combines upmarket versions of Chilean standards (mostly fish and seafood) with Cuyo-tinged variations on Argentine standards and wild game dishes (viscacha, for instance). Because it's ambitious and even experimental, not everything works, but when it does the results can be spectacular. Most entrées fall in the US$10 range.

Maceratta (Viamonte 4734, tel. 0261/496-0152, dinner Tues.–Sat., lunch Sun.) is a sprawling trattoria with multiple dining rooms and garden seating, with a diverse pasta menu plus pizza and some other Italianate dishes. Try the smoked salmon ravioli with king crab sauce (US$10).

THE RÍO MENDOZA VALLEY

For locals, the upper Río Mendoza valley makes a nearby getaway, but almost everyone finds it a diverse recreational destination.

Cacheuta

Since the realignment of RN 7 (the Panamericana to Chile) for expansion of a hydroelectric and irrigation reservoir on the Río Mendoza, Cacheuta has become an end-of-the-road destination for its hot springs hotel—other places that depended on through traffic have closed—and the rafting company on the river's lower reaches. At 1,237 meters above sea level, Cacheuta is 36 kilometers southwest of Mendoza.

Betancourt Rafting (Lavalle 35, Local 8, Mendoza, tel. 0261/429-9665 or 0261/15-559-1329, www.betancourt.com.ar) descends the river below the dam for about US$18–58 pp, depending on difficulty and time on the water; it also does trekking, mountain biking, and horseback riding in Potrerillos. Its base address is Ruta Panamericana Km 26, Blanco Encalada, Luján de Cuyo.

Cacheuta's only permanent accommodations, **Hotel Termas Cacheuta** (RP 82 Km 39, tel. 02624/49-0153, www.termascacheuta.com, US$150 s, US$255 d, with full board, some drinks extra) is an all-inclusive resort offering thermal baths, massage, and various recreational programs including hiking and mountain biking. Nonguests may use the facilities for US$45–50 pp, but lunch and transportation from Mendoza are extra.

Next to the police station, **Mi Montaña** serves fine pasta at reasonable prices. Nearby **El Coirón** has also drawn praise.

Potrerillos

Since RN 7's southerly realignment, it's longer (in distance) but shorter (in time) to Potrerillos, the upper Río Mendoza's whitewater rafting, kayaking, and river-boarding

center. Now 53 kilometers from the provincial capital—about eight kilometers farther than it used to be—Potrerillos (pop. about 300, elev. 1,351 meters) is growing because the Embalse de Potrerillos, a hydroelectric project, has relocated displaced people in sharp new houses with fine views and finer conveniences than they've ever had before. Whether once-isolated rural people will prosper in their new village environment on an international highway is another issue entirely.

Windsurfing is gaining popularity on the reservoir, but water sports are not the only recreational option. Winding RP 89, which leads south to the wine country of Tupungato, is a scenically spectacular and little-traveled mountain bike route—though this stiff climb would be easier from the other side. It's also close to the modest ski area of Vallecitos; for more details, see the sidebar *Skiing in Mendoza*.

Raging with runoff from the snowmelt of the high Andes, the Class III-plus Río Mendoza reaches its peak of about 2,000 cubic meters per second in the late spring and summer months of December and January. At this volume, the water is high enough that there aren't many rapids, but it's fast enough and the waves large enough to provide an enthralling rafting or kayaking experience.

There are now three main Potrerillos-based operators: **Argentina Rafting Expediciones** (Perilago s/n, tel./fax 02624/48-2037; Primitivo de la Reta 992, Local 4, Mendoza, tel. 0261/429-6325, www.argentinarafting.com), directly on the old highway; **Mendoza Rafting** (RN 7 Km 555, www.mendozarafting.com.ar); and nearby **Ríos Andinos** (RN 7 Km 55, tel. 0261/429-5030 in Mendoza, www.riosandinos.com.ar). Ríos Andinos has a bar-restaurant and may add accommodations in the future.

Rafting excursions come in various lengths, ranging from one-hour trips (US$18–23) starting nearby to three-hour descents (US$55–65) from Cerro Negro and even overnighters from Uspallata. Companies also arrange hiking, horseback riding, and other activities. See the *Mendoza* section for their city offices.

SKIING IN MENDOZA

In winter, Pacific storms drop prodigious amounts of snow on the western slopes of the Andes, where Chilean resorts like Valle Nevado and Portillo draw skiers from around the continent and the world. Some of this snow crosses the Andean crest – southerly Las Leñas is Mendoza Province's biggest and best winter resort – but Vallecitos and Los Penitentes are more convenient to the provincial capital.

Area ski resorts generally open in July and close by early October, but in poor snow years they may shut down in early September.

VALLECITOS

About 80 kilometers from Mendoza and 15 kilometers west of Potrerillos in the Cordón del Plata, Vallecitos is a modest 100-hectare ski area at a base of 2,900 meters ranging up to 3,350 meters. Most visitors are day-trippers from Mendoza who pay US$19 per day for lift access; the resort provides its own transport from the capital for US$11 round-trip.

Shoestring travelers can share dorm space at the **Refugio Ski y Montaña** for US$13 pp with breakfast (but without sheets); at the **Refugio Hostería Valle Nevado,** quadruples cost US$80 (US$20 pp), also with breakfast. Half board and full board packages are also available.

The season runs from July to early October, but accommodations remain open the entire year; for more details, contact **Valles del Plata** (Perú 1523, Mendoza, tel. 0261/429-7338, cell 0261/15-415-0751, www.skivallecitos.com).

LOS PENITENTES

The summer gateway to Aconcagua, 165 kilometers from the city of Mendoza, Los Penitentes is an accessible winter resort at a base altitude of 2,580 meters. It has better infrastructure and snow cover than Vallecitos, but in dry years the season can still be short.

Covering 300 hectares, Los Penitentes has 28 separate runs totaling 25.5 kilometers; lift tickets range US$27–41 per day, depending on the time of the season. Many people, however, buy multiday tickets and contract full packages at the resort or other hotels in town. For more details, contact **Los Penitentes** (tel. 0261/428-3601, www.penitentes.com).

Uspallata

From the west, the long lines of Lombardy poplars flanking RN 7 offer a dramatic approach to Uspallata, a crossroads village in an area that, thanks to its resemblance to the central-Asian highlands, enjoyed 131 minutes of cinematic fame as the base for French director Jean-Jacques Annaud's movie (and Brad Pitt vehicle) of Heinrich Harrer's memoir *Seven Years in Tibet*. Annaud airlifted in yak extras from Montana for the filming, which journalist Orville Schell chronicled in his *Virtual Tibet* (New York: Metropolitan Books, 2000).

Since losing out to Luján de Cuyo as a *zona franca* (duty-free zone) for exports to Valparaíso, Chile, Uspallata (pop. 3,284) has returned to its pre-Hollywood tranquility. In a broad valley surrounded by colorful Andean peaks, 1,751 meters above sea level, it is 52 kilometers northwest of Potrerillos.

While westbound RN 7 continues to Parque Provincial Aconcagua and the Chilean border, RP 39 leads north into remote parts of San Juan Province; RP 52 makes a 102-kilometer loop back to Mendoza via the **Villavicencio** hot springs on a route followed by San Martín's army in crossing the Andes to liberate Chile, and later by Charles Darwin in crossing the Andes from Santiago. The RP 52 loop is probably a safer route for cyclists than RN 7, which has several tunnels and heavy truck traffic.

There's little to see in Uspallata proper, which is primarily a service center along RN 7, but several nearby sights form a collective, loosely defined museum with erratic hours and a small admission fee. About two kilometers north of the highway junction, the **Bóvedas Históricas Uspallata** contains a series of conical kilns used for metallurgy during the 17th century, but even

CUYO AND CÓRDOBA

before the Spanish invasion the local Huarpe population processed local ores here. The kilns themselves are a museum that contains a series of dioramas on General Gregorio de Las Heras's trans-Andean campaign in support of San Martín (several key battles took place nearby), but also includes exhibits on mineralogy and the indigenous Huarpe. Descriptions are in Spanish and fractured English.

On the Calingasta road, the **Comunidad Huarpe Guaytamari** (RP 149 Km 12, San Alberto) is a llama farm and crafts center run by a handful of Huarpe Indians. About seven kilometers northeast of town, on RP 52 to Villavicencio, volcanic **Cerro Tunduqueral** offers a fading series of pre-Columbian petroglyphs. Nearby is a monument to Ceferino Namuncurá, a Mapuche Indian who succumbed to pulmonary disease while studying and tending to patients in Italy; promoted as a saint in Argentina, he has not yet cracked the Catholic hierarchy due to a lack of any miracles attributed to him.

Beyond Cerro Tunduqueral, the **Caracoles de Villavicencio** is a zigzag gravel road that leads to the now-closed hot springs hotel of the same name, where it becomes a straight-as-an-arrow paved highway into Mendoza. En route the road passes a plaque to Darwin, who found fossil araucaria trees here, and reaches the scenic heights of the 3,800-meter **Cruz del Paramillo.** A warning sign at Uspallata's northern outskirts indicates regulated hours for ascending and descending the Caracoles, but its presence owes more to bureaucratic inertia than current reality.

In summer, two adventure travel operators maintain offices at the highway junction for outdoor activities such as rafting, mountain biking, and trekking: **Pizarro Expediciones** (tel. 02624/42-0003, www.pizarroexpediciones. com.ar) and **Desnivel Aventura** (tel. 02624/42-0275, www.desnivelaventura.com.ar).

Half a kilometer north of the highway junction, the wooded **Camping Municipal** (US$3 pp) has picnic tables and barbecue pits; the bathrooms have wood-fired showers, so the availability of hot water can vary.

At the eastern approach to town, the HI-affiliated **Hostel Uspallata** (RN 7 Km 1141.5, tel. 0261/15-466-7240, www.hosteluspallata. com.ar, US$12 pp dorm, US$42 d) is, incongruously enough, a remodeled slaughterhouse with both dorms and private rooms. The common areas include a bar that offers simple meals and a cavernous hall where the cattle once hit the floor (it has been long enough that there are no bloodstains).

East of the junction, **Hotel Viena** (Avenida Las Heras 240, tel. 02624/42-0046, US$36 d) has utilitarian rooms with private baths and cable TV. Directly at the junction, the more spacious **Los Cóndores Hotel** (tel./fax 02624/42-0002, www.loscondoreshotel.com. ar, US$40 s, US$59 d) has a restaurant.

Built for a labor union during the 1940s Peronist heyday, on RN 7 about one kilometer west of the highway junction, **Hotel Uspallata** (tel./fax 02624/42-0066, www. granhoteluspallata.com.ar, US$70 s, US$82 d, with breakfast) has improved considerably since coming under management of the Cadena del Sol chain. It's notable for its spacious and manicured grounds, which include a large swimming pool, but the rooms are comfortable enough, and it's clearly the best value in town.

On the same grounds, Cadena del Sol has also opened the **Gran Hostel Uspallata** (tel. 02624/42-0367, US$12 pp), an 85-bed facility with its own amenities and access to the hotel pool. Most rooms are triples with shared baths.

On the highway at the south end of town, appealing **Hotel Valle Andino** (tel. 02624/42-0095, www.hotelvalleandino.com, US$49 s, US$78 d, with breakfast) has amenities that include an indoor pool.

In a strip mall at the highway junction, **Café Tibet** (tel. 0261/15-512-0971) opened during the cinema boom, but it has managed to outlast the Brad Pitt blip with a menu of inexpensive but good-quality pizza and sandwiches.

Other offerings are almost exclusively *parrillas*, including **San Cayetano** (tel. 02624/42-0049), behind the YPF station; **La Estancia**

de Elías (tel. 02624/42-0165) at the southern approach to town; and **El Rancho de Don Olmedo** (RN 7 and Cerro Chacay, tel. 02624/42-0109).

At the highway junction, the new **Informador Turístico** (RN 7 and RP 52, tel. 02624/42-0410, turismolasheras@hotmail.com) is open 8 A.M.–10 P.M. daily. Uspallata also has a post office (postal code 5545) and an ATM at Banco de la Nación. Within 50 meters of the junction are several *locutorios* and Internet outlets.

In the same strip mall as Café Tibet, just north of the highway junction, Expreso Uspallata operates three or four **buses** daily to and from Mendoza (2.5 hours, US$5); westbound services continue to Puente del Inka. If continuing to Chile, buy a ticket in Mendoza and pick up your bus here or at Penitentes; through buses are often full.

Los Penitentes

Westbound RN 7 splits the settlement of Penitentes, the main base for Aconcagua-bound trekkers and climbers in summer, and for skiers in winter.

Affiliated with Mendoza's Campo Base Hostel, the **Hostel Refugio Penitentes** (tel. 0261/429-0707, www.penitentes.com.ar), just west of the YPF gas station, is open all year; summer rates range US$9–11 pp dorm, but ski season rates with half board are the best value in town.

Penitentes's best accommodations, the 50-room **Hotel Ayelén** (RN 7 Km 165, tel. 02624/42-0229, www.ayelenpenitentes.com.ar, summer US$80 s, US$97 d) also has a restaurant, but the spacious rooms have limited views. Accommodations include shuttle service to and from the park entrance, and they also offer other excursions in the vicinity.

Nearby, under the same management, **Hostería Ayelén** (tel. 0261/427-1123 or 0261/427-1283, US$28–38 pp) is a cheaper but still very good alternative with accommodations in doubles, quadruples, and sextuples with private baths; it also has an inexpensive pizzeria.

Puente del Inka

Seven kilometers west of Penitentes, also split by RN 7, Puente del Inka takes its name from the natural bridge over the Río Mendoza that once held a rustic hot springs. Since detection of a fissure in the bridge, though, it's closed to the public except for photographs—from a distance, for safety reasons.

It's also notable for the **Cementerio de los Andinistas,** the climbers' cemetery that reminds visitors that Cerro Aconcagua demands the respect—and sometimes the lives—of intending summiteers (not all those buried here died on the mountain, though—some chose this as their final resting place). At 2,720 meters above sea level and 177 kilometers west of Mendoza, it's the closest settlement to the Horcones entrance to Parque Provincial Aconcagua, but Penitentes has more abundant and better accommodations and food.

Puente del Inka enjoys spectacular panoramas of the mountains surrounding Aconcagua and south to the 6,650-meter massif of **Cerro Tupungato,** also part of a provincial park; most easily accessible from Tunuyán, its summit route is a technical climb suitable for accomplished snow-and-ice mountaineers only.

Chile-bound travelers, especially those in private vehicles, should note that all border formalities—immigration and customs—take place on the Chilean side; those coming from Chile complete formalities at Los Horcones, immediately west of Penitentes on the Argentine side. Penitentes has the last gas station before the border; the next one is some 50 kilometers west at Río Blanco, Chile.

Shoestring travelers can pitch their tents at **Camping Los Puquios,** on the north side of the highway, but it's a barren, exposed site.

Built for the climate, with smallish bedroom windows that minimize heat loss in winter but also reduce the natural light, **Hostería Puente del Inka** (RN 7 Km 175, tel. 02624/42-0266, US$38 s, US$45 d, with breakfast) is a mountain lodge with multibed rooms. Its so-so restaurant serves lunch and dinner.

Cristo Redentor

From Las Cuevas, the last Argentine outpost before the tunnel into Chile, a zigzag dirt road barely wide enough for a single vehicle in some spots, climbs eight kilometers to a blustery border ridge where Uruguayan sculptor Mateo Alonso's eight-meter, six-ton statue **Cristo Redentor** marks the border between Chile and Argentina. Taken by train to Uspallata in 1904, it went the rest of the way by mule; it commemorates the peaceful conclusion, in 1902, of a territorial dispute between the two countries.

Reaching 4,200 meters above sea level, this forbidding road was the main route between the two countries until the three-kilometer Cristo Redentor tunnel opened in 1980; today it's the province of tourists and tour buses. Upward-bound vehicles have the right-of-way, but not every Argentine driver appears to appreciate this, so be on guard. It's still possible to continue to the Chilean border post at Los Libertadores by foot or bicycle, but the road is not open to motor vehicles beyond the ridge.

At the pass, there are two *refugios,* one Argentine and one Chilean: The former sells cheap sandwiches and coffee, while the latter gives away hot chocolate (tips appreciated). Befitting a monument devoted to peace between peoples, Cristo Redentor has its own binational website (www.cristoredentorchiar.galeon.com).

PARQUE PROVINCIAL ACONCAGUA

Approaching the Chilean border, Parque Provincial Aconcagua is the site of the province's most prominent attraction—literally so, as the bulky 6,962-meter Cerro Aconcagua is the "The Roof of the Americas," the highest peak on two continents.

Parque Provincial Aconcagua, encompassing 71,000 hectares, lies entirely north of RN 7. The main entry point is Laguna Horcones, four kilometers northwest of Puente del Inka, but there's also access via Punta de Vacas, 20 kilometers east.

◀ Cerro Aconcagua

An irresistible magnet for climbers (and aspiring climbers) from around the world,

Aconcagua also draws casual visitors in private motor vehicles and tour buses, as well as day-hikers and long-distance trekkers, to enjoy the big-sky views of the Andean high country.

Of the world's highest summits, Aconcagua probably draws the most climbers because the main route requires no technical expertise—simply good conditioning (and willingness to acknowledge physical limitations), suitable equipment, and the readiness to recognize when conditions become dangerous. The extreme and changeable weather, in particular, has claimed the lives of even experienced mountaineers: over 100 have died on the mountain, and there are fatalities almost every year, including five in the 2008–2009 season.

In 1897, Swiss climber Matthias Zurbriggen made Aconcagua's first confirmed ascent, but the 1985 discovery of an Inka mummy on the southwest face, at an altitude of 5,300 meters, demonstrated that pre-Columbian civilizations explored the wild high country of the central Andes. There is disagreement over the etymology of *aconcagua*—some claim the word comes from the Quechua language, and others from the Mapuche—but everyone recognizes its indigenous genesis. Geologically, the mountain consists of uplifted marine sediments covered by volcanic andesite.

Flora and Fauna

Discussions of Aconcagua rarely mention flora and fauna, partly because the mountain's sheer size and altitude overwhelm most other considerations, and partly because of the focus on climbing. Another reason is that, in the rain shadow of the Andean crest, the park is one of the most barren parts of the Andes, with only a discontinuous cover of prostrate shrubs and grasses. At the highest altitudes, it is almost pure scree and snow.

That doesn't mean it lacks wildlife, as the Andean condor soars above the ridges and summits, and lesser birds are also present along the watercourses that descend from its glaciers and snowfields. Mammals like guanacos and red foxes may be conspicuous, along with smaller rodents.

Clouds cover the summit of Cerro Aconcagua, "The Roof of the Americas."

Hiking and Climbing

The main sight is Aconcagua itself, which is visible from RN 7, but there are better views from **Laguna Horcones,** about two kilometers north of the highway and about 20 minutes from the ranger station (though probably a bit farther than the 400 meters the trail sign suggests).

For day-hikers, the best outing is **Confluencia,** about eight kilometers from the ranger station, at an elevation of 3,368 meters. For a three-day camping trip, the best option is to **Plaza Francia,** another 13 kilometers to the north, at an elevation of 4,500 meters. This is the base camp for the highly difficult and technical **Pared Sur** (South Face), first ascended by a French group in 1954.

Most climbers take the longer but technically simpler **Ruta Noroeste** (Northwest Route) to Plaza de Mulas, 4,230 meters above sea level, where there is camping and even a hotel, and then try for the summit. Hikers can go as far as Plaza de Mulas, for which it makes sense to have a seven-day permit.

An alternative approach, longer than the Ruta Noroeste but less technical than the Pared Sur, is the **Ruta Glaciar de los Polacos** (Polish Glacier route), pioneered by Polish nationals in 1934. Starting at Punta de Vacas, 15 kilometers southeast of Puente del Inka, this route is less crowded than the others but more time-consuming and expensive.

Note that there are variations on all these routes. By whatever route, Aconcagua is a serious mountain that requires excellent physical conditioning, time to adapt to the great altitude, and proper gear for snow, ice, wet, and cold. People have done the summit in as little as seven days from Puente del Inka, but at least an additional week is desirable.

Accommodations and Food

Independent camping is possible at the base camps and along the trails, but tour operators and climbing guides monopolize the best sites during the season. It's also possible to stay and eat at the provincial **Hotel Plaza de Mulas** (tel. 0261/425-0871 in Mendoza, cell 0261/15-569-4652, www.aconcaguahut.com), which also

CUYO AND CÓRDOBA

ACONCAGUA TOUR OPERATORS

Seasoned mountaineers can and have climbed Aconcagua with only their backpacks and boots for support, but less-experienced travelers with the yen (or dollars or pesos) to stand atop the Roof of the Americas usually contract overseas package tours or make logistical support arrangements with local guides and muleteers. Most local operators are based at Penitentes in summer, but also have offices in Mendoza proper or nearby suburbs like Godoy Cruz or Guaymallén. Aconcagua Express, however, has its main office in Santiago, Chile.

All of the following operators have substantial experience on the mountain and either have or can arrange pack mules. For suggestions on overseas operators, who usually subcontract with one of those listed here.

ACONCAGUA EXPRESS
Augusto Mira Fernández 14248, Las Condes,
    Santiago, Chile
tel. 56/32-217-9101
fax 56/32-247-0430
www.aconcagua-express.com

ACONCAGUA TREK
Barcala 484, Mendoza
tel./fax 0261/429-5007
www.rudyparra.com

ANDESPORT
Olascoaga 2273, Mendoza
tel. 0261/423-9653
www.andesport.com

CAMPO BASE
Sarmiento 231, Mendoza
tel. 0261/425-5511
www.campo-base.com.ar
www.cerroaconcagua.com

EXPEDICIONES ACONCAGUA ATMIR
Vicente Gil 471, Mendoza
tel. 0261/420-2536
www.aconcaguatmir.com.ar

FERNANDO GRAJALES EXPEDICIONES
25 de Mayo 2985, Villa Nueva,
    Guaymallén, Mendoza
tel./fax 0261/428-3157, cell 0261/15-500-7718,
    tel. 800/516-6962 in the U.S.
www.grajales.net

INKA EXPEDICIONES
Juan B. Justo 345, Mendoza
tel./fax 0261/425-0871
www.inka.com.ar

MALLKU EXPEDICIONES
Perú 1499, Mendoza
tel. 0261/420-4811, cell 0261/15-509-4147
www.mallkuexpediciones.com.ar

---

features electricity, hot showers, telephones, and luggage deposit.

Because of the difficult logistics, though, prices are higher than for comparable services elsewhere. Rates for "Cuervo" dorm rooms are US$40 pp with breakfast, US$72 pp with half board, and US$102 pp with full board. More comfortable "Bonete" rooms cost US$50 pp with breakfast, US$82 pp with half board, and US$112 pp with full board; for "Aconcagua" rooms with private baths, the corresponding rates are US$70 pp, US$102 pp, and US$132 pp.

Other Practicalities
The main information post is at **Los Horcones,** where the rangers have good information and suggestions as well as supplying trash bags for climbers and trekkers; it's open 8 A.M.–9 P.M. weekdays, 8 A.M.–8 P.M. Saturday. There are also rangers at Confluencia, Plaza de Mulas, Las Leñas on the Polish route up the Río de las Vacas, and at Plaza Argentina, the last major base camp along the Polish route.

Both hikers and climbers must have permits; those with hiking permits may not continue beyond the base camps. In Mendoza, for most of the year, get permits from the provincial **Dirección de Recursos Naturales Renovables** (Avenida de los Plátanos s/n, tel. 0261/425-2090, www.recursosnaturales. mendoza.gov.ar, 8 A.M.–6 P.M. weekdays, 9 A.M.–1 P.M. weekends), just inside the gates of Parque San Martín. In summer only, though, permits are available from the nearby Edificio Cuba, and in winter, hiking permits are available at Los Horcones itself (though climbing permits are not). In past years, however, permits have been available through the provincial Subsecretaría de Turismo in Mendoza, and this could change again. For the most up-to-date information, check the park's website (www. aconcagua.mendoza.gov.ar), in Spanish and very readable English as well. Climbers must present proof of their experience and show their equipment.

Permit prices depend on season and nationality (there is now a differential pricing system for Argentines and resident foreigners and for non-Argentines). Low season runs November 15–30 and February 21–March 15, midseason is December 1–14 and February 1–20, and high season is December 15–January 31. Outside these seasons, fees are reduced.

Rangers collect a US$5 fee for the short walk to Laguna Horcones, and a US$20 fee for the day hike to Confluencia. For non-Argentines, three-day hiking permits cost US$47 except in high season, when they cost US$55. Seven-day permits (more desirable for their greater flexibility) cost US$68 in low and mid-season, US$105 in high season; climbers pay US$158 in low season, US$316 in mid-season, and US$474 in high season. Argentines and resident foreigners pay around one-third of these prices.

For more detail on hiking in the park and climbing Aconcagua, look for the improved fifth edition of Tim Burford's *Chile and Argentina: The Bradt Trekking Guide* (Chalfont St Peter, UK: Bradt Travel Guides, 2001), and for the second edition of R. J. Secor's climbing guide *Aconcagua* (Seattle: The Mountaineers, 1999).

Buses from Mendoza to Uspallata continue to Penitentes, where most hikers and climbers stay. From Penitentes, it's necessary to walk or hire a car to the trailhead at Horcones.

SAN RAFAEL

Irrigated by the Atuel and Diamante Rivers, vineyards and orchards still survive within San Rafael's city limits, heart of a prosperous wine- and fruit-producing area southeast of the city of Mendoza. Recreationally, the city can be a base for rafting on the Atuel and Diamante as well as for other activities in the nearby Andean foothills.

Dormant during the afternoon siesta, when there is little or no traffic on its sycamore-shaded avenues, San Rafael comes alive in the evening, when locals fill the café tables that occupy its broad clean sidewalks. Most of the local wine route, a good enough reason to visit in its own right, is negotiable on foot, but many locals get around on bicycles—which seem as numerous as automobiles except Sunday evenings, when Avenida Hipólito Yrigoyen becomes a slow-moving see-and-be-seen car cruising scene.

San Rafael (pop. 104,782) is 236 kilometers southeast of the provincial capital via paved RN 40 and RN 143, and 186 kilometers northeast of Malargüe via RN 144 and RN 40. It is 996 kilometers west of Buenos Aires via RN 7 to Junín (Buenos Aires Province), RN 188 to General Alvear, and RN 143.

Museo Integral del Pasado Histórico de San Rafael

For aficionados of kitchen-sink regional museums, San Rafael's can be an amusing place to wander half an hour or so through its natural history and historical collections. The former include a small but pretty good sample of minerals and a few ragged taxidermy specimens (guanacos, rheas, and viscachas). The latter include photographs (some outstanding, others that wouldn't find a place in most family albums), literary and cultural items including classic Argentine movie posters, and a mezzanine dedicated almost

WINERIES IN THE VALLE DE UCO

About an hour southwest of Mendoza, near the towns of Tupungato and Tunuyán, the Uco Valley is increasingly important, but its wineries are more scattered than those around Mendoza. That may well change, as it's the site of some ambitious wine development and real-estate projects.

BODEGAS Y VIÑEDOS FAMILIA GIAQUINTA

West of RN 40, near the town of Tupungato, Giaquinta is a cluttered but cozy family winery that won't quite drop everything to accommodate visitors, but they'll do their best to keep the wait short. While it lacks the slick professionalism of many Mendoza wineries, the Spanish-only tours, led by family members and regular employees, communicate their enthusiasm for wine and the winemaking process, with a generous tasting on top of that.

Bodegas y Viñedos Familia Giaquinta (Carril Zapata s/n, La Arboleda, Tupungato, tel. 02622/48-8090, www.familiagiaquinta.com. ar) is open for tours Monday–Saturday during normal business hours.

BODEGA Y VIÑEDOS O. FOURNIER

On the plains at the edge of the Andes, O. Fournier is a sprawling vineyard-winery complex with a gourmet restaurant just a few kilometers west of RN 40 at 1,100 meters above sea level. Landscaped with drought-tolerant plants and gravel that mimics a stream bed, built of reinforced concrete, the winery proper employs the latest technology – sleek presses and stainless steel vats – but produces finely tuned premium Syrah, malbec, and cabernet aged in French and American oak. Its Urban line, however, has excellent affordable varietals such as tempranillo and torrontés as well as some blends, and the barrel-filled cellars also contain a fine contemporary art collection.

O. Fournier (Calle Los Indios, La Consulta, San Carlos, tel. 02622/45-1088, www. ofournier.com), 130 kilometers south of Mendoza by smoothly paved RN 40, is open for guided tours (US$4, with a sample from the Urban line) by reservation only 9:30 A.M.– 4:30 P.M. daily. More elaborate tastings, at prices ranging US$10-20, are also available.

Five-course lunches and dinners at Fournier's sophisticated Urban restaurant, which faces a pond where wildfowl take a breather, range US$23-47, depending on the wines (or lack of) that accompany the meal; the vineyards and the Andean front range are also part of the

entirely to wine festival queens (with little on the local industry itself).

The Museo Integral (25 de Mayo 250, tel. 02627/42-2127, ext. 367, US$0.50) is open 7:30 A.M.–noon and 2–7 P.M. weekdays, 10 A.M.–7 P.M. weekends.

Wineries

San Rafael grew around its wineries, and while some have moved to the outskirts, others are central. On foot or by public transportation, it's possible to visit four or five in a single day.

In 1883, two decades before the city's founding, French immigrant Rodolfo Iselín planted the first vines at what is now **Bodega La Abeja** (Avenida Hipólito Yrigoyen 1900, tel. 02627/43-9804, www.bodegalaabeja.com. ar). Set back from the road, a distinctive tower atop an aging adobe overlooks what seems at first glance more a wine museum than a modern winery. Nearly all La Abeja's vintage equipment, such as wooden presses, is still in use, and only in the last few years has it expanded beyond jug wines into fine reds such as cabernet sauvignon, malbec, merlot, tempranillo, a tempranillo-bonarda blend, and chenin blanc. Informative tours and tasting are available 9:30 A.M.–1 P.M. and 3–7 P.M. Monday–Saturday.

Just a few blocks west, founded by a Franco-Swiss family in 1956, is **Bodega Jean Rivier e Hijos** (Avenida Hipólito Yrigoyen 2385, tel. 02627/43-2676, www.jeanrivier. com, 8–11 A.M. and 3–6 P.M. Mon.–Fri.,

view. Fournier also offers morning horseback rides (US$37) that include breakfast, but lunch is extra, depending on the option chosen.

BODEGAS SALENTEIN

Built by Dutch capital near the Andean foothill town of Tunuyán, Bodegas Salentein (RP 89 s/n, Los Arboles, Tunuyán, tel. 02622/42-9500, www.bodegasalentein.com) is a futuristic – one might even say New Age – winery with a contemporary aesthetic sensibility. At ground level, stainless-steel tanks hold the wine in four separate wings, each of which operates autonomously; eight meters below ground level, forming the an equilateral cross, the four wings meet in a subterranean central amphitheater where the subdued light on circular rows of oak barrels creates a cathedral atmosphere. It is, in fact, a temple of wine.

On top of that, Salentein has created a separate structure as the **Galería Killka,** with collections of late-19th-century and early-20th-century Dutch art (mostly landscapes) and more innovative contemporary works by regional artists. In the same building, its new restaurant, with magnificent Andean and vineyard views, as well as a wine shop, are making Salentein an international destination.

At 33° south latitude, Salentein's vineyards enjoy sunny days and cool nights (the annual average temperature is 14°C) on rocky alluvial soils at a mean elevation of 1,250 meters. Ranging 1,050–1,500 meters above sea level, the vineyards are up to 30 years old, but new plantings are also underway.

Guided tours, which cost US$2.50 pp in Spanish or English (usually less crowded), take place hourly 10 A.M.-4 P.M. Monday–Saturday. Rates include admission to the gallery and a tasting of one red and one white.

Bodegas Salentein can be most easily reached by private car or by *remise* from Tunuyán, 82 kilometers south of Mendoza via RN 40. Tunuyán is 17 kilometers east of Salentein.

There are 16 double rooms available at **Posada Salentein** (Emilio Civit 778, Mendoza, tel. 0261/441-1000, www.salenteintourism.com), in several buildings in an isolated part of the vineyard that has a trout-stocked reservoir. Rates are US$260-327 s or US$303-363 d with half board, including wine and some activities like hiking and horseback riding, along with tours of the bodega. Lunch costs an extra US$40. Argentine residents pay about one-third less for accommodations.

8–11 A.M. Sat.). Still a small-scale family affair, its spontaneous tours (one-on-one if necessary, in Spanish, or French on request) and generous tasting include its specialty *tocai friulano,* a varietal of Italo-Hungarian origin. There are also malbec-bonarda and torrontés-chenin blends.

Now a partnership rather than a family business, the Swiss-founded **Bodegas Suter** (Avenida Hipólito Yrigoyen 2850, tel. 02627/42-1076, www.bodegasuter.com) is a more industrial winery, with large stainless-steel tanks in lieu of epoxy-lined concrete vats. In addition to reds and whites, they are also producing champagne (employees wear eye protection to avoid accidental damage by high-speed corks). Hourly tours (English-speaking guides

available) take place at 9:30 A.M. and at 12:30, 1:30, 4:30 and 6 P.M. Monday–Saturday.

Having moved operations to the western outskirts of town, the venerable **Bodega Valentín Bianchi** (RN 143 and Valentín Bianchi, Las Paredes, tel. 02627/43-5353, www.vbianchi.com) offers guided tours (Spanish, English, and Italian) with tasting 9 A.M.–noon and 2–6 P.M. Monday–Saturday. The facilities, which include a champagne plant, house a state-of-the-art operation—even the rack on which the champagne bottles are rotated to concentrate their sediments is automated—that contrasts dramatically with its original downtown bodega. Something's been lost in the move, though, as the classic original had a traditional integrity that the neoclassical kitsch of the new winery will never equal—even if the latter's tasting facilities and grounds, in particular, are far superior.

Also on the city's outskirts, **Algodón Wine Estates** (RN 44, Km 674, Cuadro Benegas, tel. 02627/42-9020, www.algodonwineestates. com, US$150–200 s or d) is a vineyard wine lodge and restaurant with a nine-holf golf course (due to expand to 18). The winery itself is small but produces boutique amounts of pinot noir and others with modern technology; the lodge consists of a renovated 1920s house and a newer wing with more spacious air-conditioned rooms.

Entertainment

Holiday Cinemas (San Martín 153, tel. 02627/42-0850) shows recent movies.

Accommodations

Six kilometers west of downtown via RN 143 is Isla Río Diamante's **Camping El Parador** (tel. 02627/42-0492, complejoelparador@infovia.com.ar, US$2 pp plus US$4 per tent). There are also cabañas sleeping up to four for US$27.

Amiable **Hotel Residencial La Esperanza** (Avellaneda 263, tel. 02627/42-7978, www.laesperanzaresidencial.com, US$10 pp dorm, US$21 s, US$29 d) has spacious, well-lighted garden rooms with either shared or private baths, breakfast included. The cheapest rooms are hostel dorms; it's quiet, but some baths are small.

Opposite the cathedral, half a block off Plaza San Martín, **Hotel Tonín** (Pellegrini 330, tel. 02627/42-2499, www.sanrafael-tour. com/tonin, US$19 s, US$32 d) is good value with cable TV, air-conditioning, parking, and breakfast. Some beds are soft, however, and a few rooms are very dark.

It's right on the main drag, but the slightly worn **Hotel Cerro Nevado** (Avenida Hipólito Yrigoyen 378, tel. 02627/42-3993, www.cerronevadohotel.com.ar, US$36 d) is surprisingly quiet as well as tidy and friendly. In the aging plumbing, the hot water is slow to arrive, but the water pressure is steady.

Although it's on a busy street, the spotless rooms at **Hotel Jardín** (Avenida Hipólito Yrigoyen 283, tel. 02627/43-4621, www.hoteljardinhotel.com.ar, US$30 s, US$50 d) are quiet—nearly silent, really—because of the Mediterranean-garden setback. The pseudoclassical statuary, though, is a kitschy distraction.

Rising 10 stories above low-rise San Rafael, new in 2001, the 97-room **Tower Inn & Suites** (Avenida Hipólito Yrigoyen 774, tel. 02627/42-7190, www.towersanrafael.com, US$96 s, US$108 d) is, ironically, a hotel with a history. The province's tallest hotel until recently, its white-elephant skeleton stood empty 35 years before opening. Maybe the results weren't worth the wait, but they're good enough to make it the city's best.

Food

El Pancho (Avenida Hipólito Yrigoyen 1110, tel. 02767/42-5085) is an open-flame *parrilla* whose specialty is *chivito* (grilled goat). **El Romancero** (Belgrano 338, tel. 02627/42-2336), the Jockey Club restaurant, has a standard Argentine menu in agreeable surroundings.

Other options include the Italian **La Gringa** (Chile 26, tel. 02627/43-6500) and the *parrilla* **La Fusta** (Avenida Hipólito Yrigoyen 538, tel. 02627/42-9726), whose US$10 dinner includes a diverse salad bar, an entrée, and dessert. Its wine list focuses on local vintages.

The star of the scene, though, is **El Restauro** (Comandante Salas and Day, tel. 02627/44-5482), with a sophisticated regional menu in surroundings that invite you to linger over the food. The service is impeccable, and the prices are reasonable for what it offers.

Las Delicias (Avenida Hipólito Yrigoyen 597), a very good ice creamery, also has Wi-Fi, but it's often overrun with noisy children.

Information

The **Dirección Municipal de Turismo** (Avenida Hipólito Yrigoyen 745, tel. 02627/43-7860, www.sanrafaelturismo.gov.ar) has good maps but printed matter is otherwise limited. Hours are 7 A.M.–10 P.M. daily in summer, 8 A.M.–9 P.M. the rest of the year.

Services

Banco Regional de Cuyo (Avenida Hipólito Yrigoyen 124) has one of several ATMs in the downtown area.

Correo Argentino is at San Lorenzo 35; the postal code is 5600. There are numerous telephone and Internet outlets along Avenida Hipólito Yrigoyen.

For medical services, contact **Hospital Teodor J. Schestakow** (Comandante Torres 150, tel. 02627/42-4290).

Getting There and Around

In the winter ski season, **Aerolíneas Argentinas** (Avenida Hipólito Yrigoyen 395, tel. 02627/43-8808) flies every weekday.

San Rafael's **Terminal de Ómnibus** (Coronel Suárez between Avellaneda and Almafuerte) is one block south of Avenida Hipólito Yrigoyen. Sample destinations, times, and fares include Malargüe (3 hours, US$9), Mendoza (3 hours, US$9), Buenos Aires (13 hours, US$38–60), Mar del Plata (15 hours, US$42), Neuquén (8 hours, US$25), and Bariloche (13 hours, US$40).

Hertz (25 de Mayo 450, tel. 02627/43-6959, hertzsanrafael@speedy.com.ar) has rental cars.

VICINITY OF SAN RAFAEL

Most things to see and do are in the vicinity of San Rafael rather than in the town itself. Six kilometers west of town, the **Museo de Historia Natural** (tel. 02627/42-2121, ext. 290, 7 A.M.–7:30 P.M. weekdays, 8 A.M.–7:30 P.M. weekends, US$1.25) occupies a site at Isla Diamante's Parque Mariano Moreno. Regionally focused, it has sectors on anthropology and archaeology, botany and zoology, paleontology and geology, and astronomy.

En route to Malargüe, southwest-bound RP 144 zigzags for 32 kilometers up the **Cuesta de los Terneros**, where the **Parque Sierra Pintada**, a 5,000-hectare private reserve, contains pre-Columbian rock-art sites and indigenous fauna like the guanaco. Inexplicably it has also introduced nonnative fauna like the Indian water buffalo.

South of San Rafael, despite three hydroelectric dams, the **Cañón del Atuel** retains enough water for Class II–III descents of its namesake river. **Turismo Aventura Raffeish** (RP 173 Km 35, tel./fax 02627/43-6996, www.raffeish.com.ar) is the most popular rafting and kayaking operator on the Río Atuel and will also organize descents of the Class IV Diamante, in rugged country west of San Rafael.

MALARGÜE

West of San Rafael, the isolated massifs of 5,189-meter El Sosneado, 4,589-meter Cerro Paraguay, and other summits soar above the plains west of RN 40. At the foot of the Andes, the town of Malargüe is a winter sports destination that depends on tourism, especially to the upscale ski resort of Las Leñas.

Otherwise, it's a truly out-of-the-way place despite volcanic badlands at Payunia, waterfowl-rich Laguna Llancanelo, caves at Caverna de las Brujas and Pozo de las Ánimas, archaeological and paleontological sites, and access to an adventurous summer route across the Andes to Talca, Chile. Visitors to Payunia, in particular, should try to book excursions ahead of time to avoid delays; Patagonia-bound travelers on RN 40 still need to return to San Rafael unless they are, by bicycle or motorized transport, self-propelled, but there may soon be bus service south to Neuquén Province.

In colonial times, Malargüe and its surroundings were Pehuenche territory, and it takes its name from a Mapudungun (Mapuche) word meaning "Place of Rocky Mesas." Today, the Pehuenche are largely a memory, and the regional economy lives by ranching and mining in addition to tourism.

Malargüe (pop. 17,710) is 186 kilometers southwest of San Rafael via RN 144 and RN 40. At 1,402 meters above sea level, it's 151 kilometers from the Chilean border at the 2,553-meter Paso Pehuenche via paved RN 40 and gravel RP 224; on the Chilean side, the excitingly narrow Ruta 115 (currently being paved) continues another 180 kilometers to Talca.

Sights

Immediately south of the tourist office, antique farming implements embellish the landscaped spaces of the 10-hectare **Parque del Ayer**, a handsome city park. At the north end of the park, the improved **Museo Regional Malargüe** (tel. 02627/47-0154, 9 A.M.–1 P.M. and 5–9 P.M. daily, free) has professionalized its displays on natural and regional history.

At the south end of the park, Malargüe's founder built the **Molino de Rufino Ortega**, a historic flour mill dating from 1876 that's undergoing restoration.

Malargüe has also acquired an astronomical reputation thanks to the presence of the multinational **Observatorio Pierre Auger** (Avenida San Martín Norte 304, tel. 02627/47-1556, www.auger.org), which offers tours at 5 P.M. weekdays. Its specialty is ultra-high-energy cosmic rays.

A complement to the Auger, the new **Planetario Malargüe** (Aldao and Rodríguez, tel. 02627/47-2116, planetario@malargue.gov. ar, free) is Argentina's first digital observatory. Primarily didactic, it offers weekday visits for school children except on Tuesday. There are afternoon programs for adults 5–8 P.M. weekdays, 3–8 P.M. weekends.

Events

Every town needs a festival, and Malargüe's is the **Fiesta Nacional del Chivo** (National Goat Festival), a fixture fiesta since 1986. For a week in early January, hotels fill and major folkloric figures like Antonio Tarragó Ros and Suna Rocha perform before substantial crowds.

November 16's **Día de Malargüe** is a local holiday honoring the town's foundation in 1950. The following Saturday, runners from around the region compete in the **Maratón Nocturno** (nighttime marathon).

Accommodations and Food

Malargüe's accommodations are improving, but still, for many of them, their primary goal is to cram the maximum number of shoestring skiers (who can't afford ritzy Las Leñas) into each room (the average is about three beds each). Peak rates are in winter; summer is substantially cheaper, and the shoulder seasons are almost giveaways. The following are summer rates.

Unquestionably cheapest is the **Camping Municipal Malargüe** (Alfonso Capdevila s/n, tel. 02627/47-0691, US$5 per tent for up to five people), at the north end of town.

In quiet farm-style surroundings four kilometers south of town, the HI affiliate **Hostel Internacional Malargüe** (tel. 02627/15-40-2439, www.hostelmalargue.net, US$8–10 pp dorm, US$20–26 s, US$23–32 d) has dorm quadruples with radiant floor heating and a country-style breakfast included; the toilet and shower are conveniently separate in the private baths. It has also added singles and doubles with private baths and has expanded common areas, including a new bar. Transport to and from the bus terminal is free, as are loaner bikes.

Under the same management, the former Hotel Andysol is now the **Hostel City** (Rufino Ortega 158, tel. 02627/47-0391, www.hostel-malargue.net, US$8–10 pp dorm, US$23–29 s, US$28–35 d). It will need some work to live up to its parent hostel's facilities, but the prognosis is good.

Hotel Rioma (Fray Inalicán 68, tel. 02627/47-1065, hotelrioma@rucared.com.ar, US$41 s, US$48 d) has greater amenities but is not dramatically better than the hostel. For the same price, **El Cisne Hotel** (General Villegas and Emilio Civit, tel. 02627/47-1350, hotelelcisne@hotmail.com, US$41 s, US$48 d) is a better value, but it fills up quickly.

On the northern outskirts of town, the **Río Grande Hotel** (RN 40 s/n, tel. 02627/47-1589, hotelriogrande@infovia.com.ar, US$42 s, US$55 d) has ample rooms with comfortable beds, but the hot water takes a while to reach the showers at the back of the building. Breakfast and cable TV are available.

Malargüe's best new choice is the **Maggio Hotel** (Álvarez and Ruibal, tel. 02624/42-7496, www.maggiohotel.com, US$47 s, US$62 d), a minimalist design-style hotel that's a bargain compared with its counterparts in other, more touristed areas.

La Posta (Avenida Roca 374, tel. 02627/47-1306) has an extensive Argentine menu; its specialties are trout and *chivito* (grilled goat), but the latter is not always available. It has recently added accommodations at **Hostería La Posta** (Avenida San Martín 646, tel. 02627/47-2079, laposta_malargue@yahoo.com.ar, US$16 s, US$22 d).

Decorated with a sophisticated rusticity, **El Bodegón de María** (Rufino Ortega and Villegas, tel. 02627/47-1655) serves light-crusted empanadas with several vegetarian options, with entrées (meats, trout, and pastas) in the range of US$8 or less. Directly across the street, **La Rotisería del Bodegón** has much of the same menu in takeaway form.

Information

At the northern approach to town is the well-organized **Dirección de Turismo** (RN 40 s/n, tel./fax 02627/47-1659, www.malargue.gov.ar, 8 A.M.–9 P.M. daily). It has an excellent selection of printed material, and its personnel are friendly, thorough, and knowledgeable, but there's only a single English speaker.

Services

Banco de la Nación (Avenida San Martín and Fray Inalicán) has an ATM.

Correo Argentino is at Adolfo Puebla and Saturnino Torres; the postal code is 5613. Several *locutorios* along Avenida San Martín have long-distance phone service but slow Internet connections.

Karen Travel (Avenida San Martín 1054, tel. 02627/47-0342, www.karentravel.com.ar), which has English-speaking personnel, can arrange excursions in the vicinity.

Hostel Internacional Malargüe's travel agency, **Choique Turismo Alternativo** (San Martín and Rodríguez, tel. 02627/47-0391, www.choique.net), arranges excursions in the vicinity and activities like horseback riding and mountain biking. A Payunia day tour costs around US$50 pp.

For medical attention, **Hospital Malargüe** is at Avenida Roca and Esquivel Aldao (tel. 02627/47-1048).

Getting There and Around

In ski season, Aerolíneas Argentinas sometimes flies charters between Buenos Aires's Aeroparque and nearby **Aeródromo Malargüe** (tel. 02627/47-1600), with tickets available from travel agencies.

Malargüe's improved **Terminal de Ómnibus** (Avenida General Roca and Aldao) has frequent service to San Rafael (3 hours, US$9), where it's usually but not always necessary to transfer for Mendoza (6 hours, US$15). **Transporte Viento Sur** (tel. 02727/47-0455) has direct services to Mendoza, while Andesmar goes directly to Buenos Aires.

In ski season, travel agencies shuttle skiers to Las Leñas.

VICINITY OF MALARGÜE
Los Molles

For those who can't afford to stay at high-powered, high-altitude Las Leñas, Los Molles is a budget alternative that's closer to the slopes than Malargüe. Here, 55 kilometers northwest of Malargüe and 1,900 meters above sea level, it's only 15 kilometers east of the more elaborate and prestigious resort.

On the south side of the river, the **Hotel Termas Lahuen-có** (tel. 02627/49-9700 in Los Molles, www.hotellahuenco.com, US$40 pp with half board, US$48 pp with full board) has modernized, at least within the context of its architectural limitations—the south-facing rooms have small windows, for instance—but for those prices it's hard to complain. Its thermal baths are open to hotel guests for no additional charge; nonguests pay US$4 pp.

The nearby **Los Molles Hotel** (RP 222 Km 30, tel. 02627/49-9712, www.losmolleshotel.com.ar, US$32 pp with half board in summer) is a pretty comfortable alternative; parts are worn, but the rooms have good views and the price is right. It has a bar with satellite TV, a restaurant, and other spacious common areas.

◖ Las Leñas

Near the end of a winding mountain highway, 2,240 meters above sea level, self-contained Las Leñas is Argentina's most exclusive ski resort.

THE POWER OF EL ZONDA

Everybody gripes about the weather, but nobody suffers it like the Cuyanos when "El Zonda" is blowing. In many parts of the world, similar hot dry winds descend the easterly slopes of longitudinal mountain ranges, but for sheer human impact, El Zonda far surpasses the Foehn of the Alps, the Chinook of the Rockies, and other powerful airstreams.

El Zonda is a katabatic wind, a sinking air mass that gusts up to 40 knots or more, raises temperatures 10-15°C in just a few minutes, stirs up clouds of dust and pollen, blows over signs, breaks branches, and even knocks down trees, strips off roofing, and shrivels crops. When falling branches clog irrigation channels, it can even cause flooding despite the absence of rain. Starting around midday and lasting up to 10 hours, Zonda episodes usually take place between May and October, but they can happen in any season.

But it's the impact on humans that's really striking. When the Zonda hits, atmospheric pressure plummets, humidity drops to nearly zero, and the few folks on the streets all seem hypoglycemic or hungover, rubbing their eyes red against their better judgment. The rest stay home with low blood pressure or migraines.

Some might argue that this is no different than similar occurrences in the Alps or the Rockies, but that's not necessarily so because of the Andes' sheer height. Research has suggested that if the Andes were lower, Zonda events would be more frequent but less extreme.

Because of its isolation, most visitors come on week-long package tours. That said, it's close enough to Malargüe and Los Molles that even some shoestring skiers can afford to spend the day—especially when the resort offers half-price lift tickets to those lodging in nearby towns during ski season.

Open mid-June to early October, Las Leñas claims 40 separate runs, the longest of which exceeds four kilometers, with a maximum elevation of 3,430 meters; there are seven chairlifts, the steepest of which gains 786 meters, and four other lifts. Slopes range from easy to very difficult, and there is even one sector with restricted access where helmets are obligatory. Some of the runs are lighted for night skiing, and there is a ski school with instruction in Spanish, English, French, German, Italian, and Portuguese.

In addition, Las Leñas enjoys an active nightlife, with pubs, discos, cinemas, and casinos, and it even has its own radio station (specializing in bland Anglo-pop). It's trying to make itself into a year-round destination as well, offering nonwinter activities like rafting, hiking, climbing, mountain biking, tennis, paddleball, volleyball, and basketball.

Las Leñas is 445 kilometers south of Mendoza via RN 40, RN 143, RN 144, and RP 222 (note that the rough unpaved segment of RN 40 south of Pareditas makes the longer paved detour via RN 143 and RN 144 more desirable, especially in winter). It is 204 kilometers southwest of San Rafael via RN 144, RN 40, and RP 222, and also 70 kilometers northwest of Malargüe, also via RN 40 and RP 222.

Prices for **lift tickets** vary throughout the ski season, which runs from mid-June to early October. For the most current figures, see the Las Leñas website (www.laslenas.com). Children and seniors get a roughly 30 percent discount, while skiers lodged in Malargüe get a 50 percent discount.

Lifts operate 9 A.M.–5 P.M. daily and sometimes at night when lighting is available. Rental equipment, including snowboards, is readily available.

Las Leñas has five four-star **luxury hotels** (tel. 02627/47-1100 for all) with capacity for 740 skiers, plus apart-hotel accommodations for another 2,219. Since it's oriented toward package tours in ski season, this is obviously not a drop-in situation, but when things are slow in summer it's possible to stay at places like **Hotel Géminis** and **Aparthotel Delphos** (www.maxisol.com.ar) for as little as US$25 pp.

Las Leñas's five hotels all have restaurants, but there are also **Johnny's Restaurant** and **Innsbruck** (tel. 02627/47-1100, ext. 1205), which also delivers from a menu that's primarily pasta and sandwiches.

Las Leñas's on-site **Oficina de Informes** (tel. 02627/47-1100, ext. 1241 or 1243) is open 9 A.M.–8 P.M. daily. Its Buenos Aires contact is **Ski Leñas** (Cerrito 1186, 8th floor, tel. 011/4816-6999, www.laslenas.com).

In season, **Aerolíneas Argentinas** operates charters from Buenos Aires to Malargüe, including transfers to and from Las Leñas. There is seasonal **bus** service from Mendoza and San Rafael, and year-round service from Malargüe.

Provincial Reserves

Thinly populated southern Mendoza Province can pride itself on several important and diverse reserves of various sizes and accessibility. For the most complete information, visit the website for the provincial **Dirección de Recursos Naturales Renovables** (www.recursosnaturales.mendoza.gov.ar).

Immediately west of Malargüe, a 28-kilometer gravel road leads toward the Andes and the 650-hectare **Reserva Natural Castillos de Pincheira,** a series of volcanic sedimentary landforms resembling castles that were a hideout for caudillo-bandit José Antonio Pincheira.

About 65 kilometers southeast of Malargüe via RN 40 and RP 186, the most significant feature of the 40,000-hectare **Reserva Natural Laguna de Llancanelo** is a shallow wetland that's home to 220 bird species, many of them migratory, including three species of flamingos. While it's ostensibly open for guided visits only, matters are much more flexible for those with their own transportation.

Immediately south of Laguna de Llancanelo, Mendoza Province's largest reserve is the 442,996-hectare **Reserva Natural La Payunia,** a volcano-studded landscape whose high point is 3,680-meter Cerro Payún (it is only one of 800 volcanoes within the reserve, however). It has abundant wildlife, including more than 10,000 guanacos as well as pumas, condors, and rheas. Accommodations are available through Malargüe's **Kiñe Turismo Rural Ecológico** (tel. 02627/47-1344, tel. 011/4524-2993 in Buenos Aires, www.kinie.com.ar).

On the southwestern slopes of Cerro Moncol, 80 kilometers from Malargüe via paved southbound RN 40 and an eight-kilometer dirt lateral, the 450-hectare **Reserva Natural Caverna de las Brujas** (8 A.M.–5 P.M. daily, US$5 adults, US$2.50 children) is a limestone cave open for guided tours. Reservations are not required—just visit the tourist office during open hours.

San Juan Province

North of Mendoza, San Juan Province stands in the shadow of its more populous and prosperous southern neighbor, but its tidy namesake capital city has a progressive wine district, the offbeat Difunta Correa shrine is a popular phenomenon, and its desert and mountain backcountry—including fossil-rich Parque Provincial Ischigualasto—offers almost unlimited adventure travel choices. To the west, the 4,779-meter Agua Negra pass, the highest between Argentina and Chile, is an exhilarating alternative to the usual crossing from Mendoza to Santiago.

SAN JUAN

San Juan de la Frontera dates from 1562, but its modern aspect stems from repeated earthquakes. The event with the greatest impact—and not just seismically—was the 1944 temblor that brought Juan Domingo Perón, then a minor political figure, to prominence for his disaster-relief efforts. Perón used this role as a springboard to found the controversial political movement known formally as Justicialism but more commonly as Peronism.

Though smaller, poorer, drier, and hotter

than Mendoza, San Juan has much in common with the larger city: wide tree-shaded avenues, sidewalk cafés, a wine industry that's lifting the local economy, and a work schedule that starts early but shuts down for several hours in the smothering summer heat. It has been less successful in diversifying its economy, which is largely administrative and agricultural.

San Juan was the birthplace and home of statesman, educator, and author Domingo F. Sarmiento, who wrote the famous polemic *Civilization and Barbarism* about the excesses of provincial caudillos.

Orientation

San Juan (pop. 115,556, elev. 650 meters) is 168 kilometers north of Mendoza via RN 40, and 1,138 kilometers northwest of Buenos Aires; the Avenida Circunvalación ring road keeps through traffic out of the city center. Its relatively small population is misleading as, like Mendoza, it's the center of a larger metropolitan area (which exceeds 400,000).

Occupying a full block, Plaza 25 de Mayo is the civic center; north–south Calle Mendoza and east–west Avenida San Martín divide the grid into quadrants. Street addresses all have cardinal points to simplify orientation, but the outskirts are more irregular.

Sights

Lushly landscaped **Plaza 25 de Mayo** is a handsome central plaza, with its palms, fountains, and statuary, but buildings like its brutalist **Iglesia Catedral** (Mendoza and Rivadavia) seem to have been designed primarily to withstand earthquakes, despite some appealing details. For a panorama of the area, take the elevator (US$1) to the top of its 53-meter clock tower.

One block west and one block north, the **Celda Histórica de San Martín** (Laprida 57 Oeste, 4–7 P.M. Mon.–Sat., US$0.50), where the general stayed while raising funds and shoring up support for his daring Chilean campaign, is the only part of the colonial **Convento de Santo Domingo** to survive the 1944 earthquake.

Barely a block farther west, the **Casa Natal de Sarmiento** (Sarmiento 21 Sur, tel. 0264/422-4603, www.casanatalsarmiento. gov.ar, 8:30 A.M.–1:30 P.M. and 5–9:30 P.M. Tues.–Fri. and Sun., 8:30 A.M.–1:30 P.M. Sat., US$1.35), Domingo F. Sarmiento's boyhood home, was the first building ever declared an Argentine national monument. Despite provincial origins that might have made him a caudillo, Domingo Faustino Sarmiento (1811–1888) became a renaissance man with a distinguished public career as an educator, journalist, diplomat, and the first president from Argentina's interior provinces. While exiled in Chile during the Rosas dictatorship, he wrote the anti-caudillo polemic *Civilization and Barbarism,* often subtitled *Life in the Argentine Republic in the Days of the Tyrants* and still in print in many languages.

Dating from 1801, built by Sarmiento's mother Paula Albarracín, Sarmiento's birthplace grew in time from the original one-room adobe to a 12-room brick house with two patios and a fig tree that appears prominently in his memoir, *Recuerdos de Provincia.* It suffered earthquake damage in 1944 but underwent a successful restoration.

Where Laprida meets Avenida España, at Plaza Julieta Sarmiento, covering 2.5 blocks, the **Centro Cívico** structure was a decades-long corruption-plagued project that was finally finished in time for Argentina's 2010 bicentennial, and the result is not too bad.

Two blocks north of the Centro Cívico, beyond Plaza España, the former **Estación Belgrano** (railway station) is now home to the **Centro Cultural María Eva Duarte de Perón** (Avenida España and San Luis). One block farther north, the most worthwhile item at the **Museo de Ciencias Naturales** (Avenida España 400 Norte, tel. 0264/421-6774, 9 A.M.–1 P.M. weekdays, free) is the reconstructed *Herrerasaurus* skeleton from Parque Provincial Ischigualasto. One block east and two blocks north, the **Antigua Bodega Chirino** (Salta 782 Norte, tel. 0264/421-4327, 11 A.M.–1 P.M. and 6–9 P.M. Tues.–Sat., 11 A.M.–1 P.M. Sun.–Mon.) is no longer a

A symbol of San Juan, mobile orange juice carts offer welcome relief from the city's torrid temperatures.

working winery—that moved out of town—but parts of the old facilities are a museum, and there is a tasting room.

One block south of the Centro Cívico, the **Museo de la Memoria Urbana** (Avenida España and Mitre, 9 A.M.–1 P.M. and 4–9 P.M. Tues.–Sun.) covers San Juan's urban evolution, with special emphasis on the 1944 earthquake.

About one kilometer southeast of Plaza 25 de Mayo, two museums share a building at Avenida Rawson and General Paz, though both are due to move before press time. The **Museo de Bellas Artes Franklin Rawson** (Avenida Rawson 621 Sur, tel. 0264/422-9638, 8:30 A.M.–1 P.M. Mon.–Wed. and Fri., 8:30 A.M.–1 P.M. and 6–9 P.M. Thurs., 9 A.M.–1 P.M. Sat., free) boasts an impressive roster of works by 19th-century Argentine artists, including Rawson himself and Prilidiano Pueyrredón, plus modern figures like Antonio Berni, Raquel Forner, Lino Spilimbergo, and others.

The same building holds the **Museo Histórico Provincial Agustín Gnecco**

(Avenida Rawson 621 Sur, tel. 0264/422-9638, 8:30 A.M.–1 P.M. Mon.–Wed. and Fri., 8:30 A.M.–1 P.M. and 6–9 P.M. Thurs., 9 A.M.–1 P.M. Sat., free), which traces San Juan's history from prehistory through the 19th century via archaeological artifacts and items like silverwork, furniture, wine technology, and coins.

Under the auspices of the Universidad Nacional de San Juan, the **Museo Arqueológico Mariano Gambier** (Calle 5 and Progreso, Rawson, tel. 0264/424-1424, 8 A.M.–8 P.M. weekdays, 10 A.M.–6 P.M. weekends, US$1.25) chronicles 8,000 years of pre-Columbian peoples in what is now San Juan Province. Relocated from the countryside to Rawson, the exhibits explore the region's cultural evolution in depth through artifacts that include tools, ceramics, basketry, and mummies—well-preserved in San Juan's hot dry climate.

Entertainment and Events

On the south side of Plaza 25 de Mayo, the two-screen **Cine San Juan** (Mitre 41 Este, tel. 0264/423-3503) shows recent films. For live theater and music, there's the **Teatro Sarmiento** (Avenida Alem Norte 34, tel. 0264/421-7363).

Shopping

Immediately south of the tourist office, **El Carrascal** (Sarmiento 40 Sur, tel. 0264/422-6733) focuses on items like weavings and basketry.

Accommodations

In spacious new quarters that could use a little more maintenance, the HI affiliate is the **Zonda Hostel** (Caseros 486 Sur, tel. 0264/420-1009, www.zondahostel.com.ar, US$8–10 pp dorm, US$19 s, US$24 d), which now has private rooms as well as semi-basement dorms (which, in San Juan, have the advantage of being cooler than the rest of the house). All the baths are shared, however, and the small backyard needs tidying up.

Once a geriatric home, in a quiet neighborhood northeast of Plaza 25 de Mayo, the sprawling **Triásico Hostel** (Pedro Echagüe 520 Este, tel. 0264/421-9528, www.triasico-hostel.com.ar, US$8–13 pp dorm, US$24–27 s or d) has dorms with either shared or private baths as well as private rooms with and without air-conditioning. It also arranges excursions, but the Wi-Fi has limited reach.

Half a block north of the tourist office, **Hostel Argentia** (Sarmiento 57 Norte, tel. 0264/421-4206, www.hostelargentia.com, US$9–11 pp dorm, US$12–18 s, US$21–26 d, with breakfast) has the usual dorm rooms in the spacious main house but also private garden rooms (even a suite that sleeps four) that are quiet unless an evening *asado* is in progress. A large swimming pool separates the main house from the back.

Though it stands in dreary surroundings five blocks north of the bus terminal, **Petit Hotel Dibú** (Avenida San Martín and Patricias Sanjuaninas, tel. 0264/420-1034, hoteldibu@yahoo.com.ar, US$26 s, US$31 d, with breakfast) has clean, sizeable rooms.

Another good basic choice is friendly **Hotel Bristol** (Entre Ríos 368 Sur, tel. 0264/421-4629, bristolhotel@yahoo.com.ar, US$24 s, US$33 d, with breakfast), which has 45 decent rooms with repellent wallpaper. Well-kept **⟨ Hotel Nuevo San Francisco** (Avenida España 284 Sur, tel. 0264/427-2821, www.nuevo-sanfrancisco.com.ar, US$33 s or d with private bath and breakfast) offers firm beds plus bright and spacious common areas as well as arranging excursions.

The tiny reception area at **Hotel Selby** (Avenida Rioja 183 Sur, tel. 0264/422-4766, www.hotelselby.com.ar, US$33 s, US$39 d, with breakfast) is a misleading approach to an aging but well-maintained hotel with smallish but otherwise good rooms with private baths.

The traditional elite hotels are **Gran Hotel Provincial** (formerly Hotel Nogaró, Ignacio de la Roza 132 Este, tel. 0264/422-7501, www.granhotelprovincial.com, US$57 s, US$70 d) and **Hotel Alkázar** (Laprida 82 Este, tel. 0264/421-4965, www.alkazarhotel.com.ar, US$73 s, US$82 d, with breakfast).

They've been overshadowed, though, by the new **Del Bono Park Hotel, Spa & Casino** (José Ignacio de la Roza Oeste 1946, tel. 0264/426-2300, www.hoteldelbono.com.ar, US$121 s or d), whose modernistic architecture and garish casino stand out in an otherwise conservative provincial capital. In services, though, it has gone far ahead of anything else in town.

Food

Traditionally, Avenida San Martín Oeste, about two kilometers west of downtown, is San Juan's gastronomic axis, but some new downtown options are worth exploring.

San Juan's greatest simple pleasure is the fresh-squeezed orange juice from the mobile carts around and near Plaza 25 de Mayo—only about US$0.25 for a paper cup of sweet chilled refreshment.

For specialty sandwiches—large enough to be a meal in their own right—the best choice is **Pirandello** (San Martín 3105 Oeste, tel. 0264/426-0260), which has indoor and outdoor seating. For pastas, pizzas, and draft beer, the cavernous **Un Rincón de Napoli** (Rivadavia

175 Oeste) has zero atmosphere but prices that aren't much higher than that.

The classic 🄲 **Club Sirio Libanés** (Entre Ríos 33 Sur, tel. 0264/422-3841) has genuine Middle Eastern ambience and hospitality; the diverse US$10 buffet includes items like kibbe, tabbouleh, and stuffed grape leaves, but the à la carte menu is also good value.

Under the same ownership, **Hostal de Palito** (Avenida Circunvalación 278 Sur, tel. 0264/423-0105) serves some of the same dishes but offers a more diverse meat and seafood menu, with a particularly good wine list of local vintages. Portions are abundant, and prices reasonable (around US$8 for entrées).

Remolacha (Avenida Jose I de la Roza 199 Oeste, tel. 0264/427-7070) is a popular downtown *parrilla* that is almost impossibly full on Sunday afternoons. **Soychú** (Ignacio de la Roza 223 Oeste, tel. 0264/422-1939) is a tradition in vegetarian *tenedor libre.*

🄲 **Il Duomo** (Avenida Libertador San Martín 1802 Oeste, tel. 0264/420-1827, US$10–20) is a *parrilla* that also has a superb Italian menu—or an Italian restaurant with superb *parrillada*—that serves upscale versions of beef, stuffed gnocchi, and Spanish desserts like *natillas,* with both indoor and outdoor seating.

Over the last few years, **De Sánchez** (Rivadavia 61 Oeste, tel. 0264/420-3670) has carved out a gourmet niche for its meats, seafood, and pastas. It's simultaneously a classy book and CD shop, embellished with larger-than-life photo portraits of classic actresses Zully Moreno and Tita Merello, smaller representations of literary figures like Julio Cortázar and Ernesto Sábato, and even photos of Elvis and Frank Zappa. It's fairly pricey, with entrées in the US$10–15 range, but the kitchen is outstanding and there's a fine local wine list.

Alongside De Sánchez, the same owners run the simpler and cheaper **Bar Ó** (Rivadavia 55 Oeste, tel. 0264/422-3066), which specializes in pastas and standards such as *milanesa* but prepares some uncommon variations such as *agnolotti* stuffed with venison or smoked chicken (US$5).

Information

The provincial **Subsecretaría de Turismo** (Sarmiento 24 Sur, tel. 0264/421-0004, www. turismo.sanjuan.gov.ar, 7:30 A.M.–8 P.M. daily winter, 7 A.M.–9 P.M. daily the rest of the year) has up-to-date hotel information and distributes a good city map plus brochures on destinations elsewhere in the province. An airport office is open for arriving flights only.

For motorists, **ACA** is at 9 de Julio 802 Este (tel. 0264/421-4245).

Services

Cambio Santiago (General Acha 52 Sur) changes money; **Banco de San Juan** (José Ignacio de la Roza 85 Oeste) has one of many downtown ATMs.

Correo Argentino is at José Ignacio de la Roza 259 Este; the postal code is 5400. *Locutorios* and Internet outlets are on almost every block in the vicinity of Plaza 25 de Mayo.

Several agencies arrange excursions to destinations like Ischigualasto and Talampaya (La Rioja), including **Mario Agüero Turismo** (General Acha 17 Norte, tel. 0264/427-7278, agueroturismo@speedy.com.ar).

Laverap (Rivadavia 493 Oeste, tel. 0264/421-5747) handles the laundry.

Hospital Rawson (General Paz and Estados Unidos, tel. 0264/422-2272 for emergencies) is the public hospital.

Getting There and Around

Aerolíneas Argentinas (Avenida San Martín 215 Oeste, tel. 0264/422-5049) flies daily to Buenos Aires's Aeroparque. LAN has begun flights here from Aeroparque on a trial basis.

San Juan's **Terminal de Ómnibus** (Estados Unidos 492 Sur, tel. 0264/422-1604) has provincial, long-distance, and international services (though it's usually necessary to change in Mendoza for Santiago or Viña del Mar/Valparaíso).

Sample destinations, times, and fares include Mendoza (2 hours, US$6), San Agustín del Valle Fértil (3.5 hours, US$10), Córdoba (8 hours, US$22), Santiago (Chile) or Valparaíso/Viña (9 hours, US$22), Tucumán

(13 hours, US$39–45), Buenos Aires (16 hours, US$40–65), and Salta (17 hours, US$50–65).

A cab or *remise* to **Aeropuerto Domingo F. Sarmiento** (tel. 0264/425-0487), about 13 kilometers southeast of town via RN 20, costs about US$5–7.

For rental cars, contact **Avis** (Laprida 82 Este, tel. 0264/420-0571), at the Hotel Alkázar.

VICINITY OF SAN JUAN

Local operators arrange excursions to some of the province's better but less easily accessible sights, including the Jáchal/Pismanta area and Parque Provincial Ischigualasto (sometimes combined, in a long day trip, with La Rioja's Parque Nacional Talampaya). In addition to those listed above, try **Money Tur** (Santa Fe 202 Oeste, tel. 0264/420-1010, www.moneytur.com.ar) or Raphael Joliat at Swiss-run **Fascinatur** (tel. 0264/15-504-3933, fascinatur@ingamasrl.com or raphaeljoliat@speedy.com.ar), where English and French are spoken.

Ruta del Vino San Juan (Pocito)

On San Juan's southern outskirts, the locality of Pocito is home to a cluster of wineries that are worth sampling, even if they can't match Mendoza's size and diversity. All are on or near RN 40, the paved highway from Mendoza.

Closest to town is **Champañera Miguel Más** (Calle 11 s/n, tel. 0264/422-5807, miguelmas@infovia.com.ar), 300 meters east of RN 40. A family-run bodega with only 2.5 hectares of organic grapes, it produces fewer than 10,000 bottles of sparkling wine per annum. It also makes some cabernet sauvignon and malbec, a small amount of muscatel, and quantities of jam and honey. At this mom-and-pop operation, tours and tasting are about as personal as can be; hours are 9 A.M.–6 P.M. weekdays, 9 A.M.–1 P.M. Saturday.

About two kilometers farther south, fronting the west side of the highway, **Fabril Alto Verde** (RN 40 between Calle 13 and Calle 14, tel. 0264/421-2683, www.fabril-altoverde.com.ar) is an organic winery with a more high-tech and diverse production that includes varietals like Chablis, chardonnay, malbec, and Syrah, plus some sparkling wines. The winery and its contemporary tasting room are open for tours (make advance arrangements for English) 9 A.M.–1 P.M. and 3:30–7:30 P.M. Monday–Friday, 9 A.M.–1 P.M. Saturday.

In sheer tourist appeal, the best choice is **Viñas de Segisa** (Aberastain y Calle 15, tel. 0264/492-2000, www.saxsegisa.com.ar, 10 A.M.–7 P.M. Mon.–Sat., 10 A.M.–2 P.M. Sun.), a boutique winery that has conserved its century-old facilities and adapted them to individualized guided tours—which include tastings directly from their cellar casks. It is nevertheless a contemporary bodega producing cabernet sauvignon, Syrah, malbec, chardonnay, and a torrontés-chardonnay blend, plus a premium line that includes tempranillo.

Dique Ullum

In San Juan's hot, arid climate, the vineyards thrive on water from 3,200-hectare Dique Ullum, 18 kilometers west of town via RP 60; it's also the place where Sanjuaninos go to beat the heat by swimming, sailing, windsurfing, and fishing. From the bus terminal, take bus No. 23 to Zonda; for schedules, contact **Empresa Ullum** (tel. 0264/422-1910).

If the heat relents, hike from the dam outlet to the top of 1,800-meter **Cerro Tres Marías.** This waterless walk traces the crest of the southwest-trending Serranía de Marquesado and takes two hours one-way. The conspicuous zigzag trail begins at the Stations of the Cross; carry plenty of liquids and high-energy snacks.

◖ Difunta Correa Shrine

Until very recently, Roman Catholicism was Argentina's official faith, and it still permeates daily life. When the shepherd fails the flock, though, the people seek help from popular saints like the Difunta Correa—whose shrine draws upwards of 100,000 Semana Santa pilgrims to the desert hamlet of **Vallecito,** about 60 kilometers east of San Juan. More than a religious experience, it's an economic force, and even nonbelievers will find plenty to contemplate in the contradictions between the sacred and the profane.

According to legend, María Antonia Deolinda Correa died of thirst in the desert while following her conscript husband—a small landowner—during the mid-19th-century civil wars. When passing muleteers found her body, though, her baby son was still at her breast. While it seems far-fetched that any infant could survive on milk from a lifeless body, the legend had such resonance that the waterless site became a spontaneous shrine. The Difunta ("Defunct," as dead people are known in the countryside) became a popular "saint," despite uncertainty that she even existed.

In the 150-plus years since the Difunta first colonized the consciousness of poor Sanjuaninos, millions of other Argentines have come to regard her as a miracle worker. She is *not* a saint, though—the official church regards her as a superstition (at best) or contrary to dogma (at worst). It has even installed its own priest and built its own church to combat the heresy.

Church efforts have been futile. From negligible origins as a solitary cross atop a knoll, the shrine has grown into a complex that includes a hotel, a campground, restaurants, a police station, a post office, a school, souvenir shops, and even its own tourist office. There is also the Fundación Vallecito, the nonprofit bureaucracy that administers the site.

For queues of pilgrims, though, the goal is the grotto with a prostrate image of the Difunta and her baby. To fulfill pledges they have made and to thank her for favors granted, some crawl the concrete steps backwards like crabs. They leave an astonishing assortment of license plates, model cars and houses, photographs, and other personal items that signify their gratitude; the foundation, for its part, "recycles" many items to finance its activities (which include delivery of 2,000 liters of water daily from the town of Caucete).

Pilgrims visit the shrine all year. It's most impressive at Easter, May Day, and Christmas, but events like mid-April's *gauchesco* **Cabalgata de la Fe** (Ride of Faith) from San Juan and December's **Festival del Camionero** (Trucker's Festival) are increasingly important.

Writing in the 19th century, Domingo F. Sarmiento—himself a Sanjuanino—expressed what the official church still privately believes about rural religious practices like the Difunta Correa: "Christianity exists...as a tradition which is perpetuated, but corrupted; colored by gross superstitions and unaided by instruction, rites, or convictions."

Believers, for their part, see no contradiction between their formal faith and devotion to the Difunta. That devotion has spread throughout the republic, as shown in roadside shrines—some astonishingly elaborate—from the Bolivian border to Tierra del Fuego. Their marker is the water-filled bottles left to slake her thirst, but there are also banknotes (from the hyperinflationary past), low-value coins, and miscellaneous vehicle parts (truckers are among her most committed adherents).

The Difunta may be the most widespread of popular religious figures, as measured by roadside shrines, but she's not the only one. Sites devoted to the Gaucho Antonio Gil, an unjustly executed "Robin Hood" figure from Corrientes Province, are proliferating alongside the Difunta since Argentina's 2001 economic and political implosion.

The shrine has its own branch of the provincial tourist office; there is also an ostensibly official website (www.visitedifuntacorrea.com.ar).

Informally, pilgrims camp almost anywhere they like, but the shrine's own **Hotel Difunta Correa** (tel. 0264/496-1018 in Caucete, US$37 d) has Spartan rooms with private baths (electric showers) and breakfast; it's presumably undergoing an upgrade, which may amount to little more than fresh paint. There's plenty of *parrillada* plus empanadas and similar snacks at any of several street-side *comedores*.

From San Juan, **Empresa Vallecito** (tel. 0264/422-1181) has direct service to the shrine (1 hour, US$5 round-trip) at 8:30 A.M. and 4 P.M., returning at 11:15 A.M. and 6:45 P.M. Other eastbound buses, toward cities like La Rioja or Córdoba, will stop at the shrine on request.

Jáchal and Vicinity

From San Juan, paved RN 40 leads 156 kilometers north to the vineyards and olive orchards of San José de Jáchal (pop. 10,901), a town renowned for its gaucho customs and its handmade blankets and ponchos. Mid-November's weekend **Fiesta de la Tradición** highlights this reputation, while its most notable sight is the **Iglesia San José** (1878), a national historical monument blemished by a new and incongruous freestanding bell tower. Also notable is the church's **Cristo Negro** (Black Christ) or **Señor de la Agonía** (Lord of Agony), a grisly 18th-century image imported from Bolivia.

East of Jáchal, the scenic graveled RP 491 links up with RN 40 to the village of **Huaco,** the birthplace and gravesite of poet and musician Buenaventura Luna (a lacquered cement guitar lies atop his adobe tomb). Huaco is also home to the **Viejo Molino,** a magnificently restored late-colonial flour mill.

To the west, narrow RN 150 leads through madly folded landforms over the pass known as the **Cuesta del Viento** to the town of **Rodeo,** where **Rafting San Juan** (Paoli s/n, tel. 0264/427-6143, 0264/433-2352, or 0264/15-436-6439) descends the Class III Río Jáchal, a good starter river with one exciting slot canyon.

Jáchal has numerous **campgrounds.** A block-plus north of the plaza, **Hotel San Martín** (Echegaray 367, tel. 02647/42-0431, www.jachalhotelsanmartin.com, US$20 s, US$27 d) has commodious rooms with amenities such as air-conditioning, cable TV, and private baths; it has made an impressive effort to improve common areas as well. Half a block east of the plaza, moribund **Hotel Plaza** (San Juan 546, tel. 02647/42-0256, US$10–12 s, US$15–20 d) has rooms with either shared or private baths. For dining, try **Nicco y Pascual** (San Martín and Echegaray), at the southwest corner of the plaza.

On the plaza's north side, the obliging **Casa de la Cultura y Turismo** (tel. 02647/42-0003, ext. 311, www.jachal.gov.ar) is open 24-7 (the night watchman does his best in the early hours).

Jáchal's **Terminal de Ómnibus** (Presidente Perón and Laprida) is six blocks east and three blocks south of the plaza. From San Juan, the main carriers are **Clasur** (tel. 0264/421-4108) and **TAC** (also tel. 0264/421-4108).

Pismanta and Vicinity

From Rodeo, paved RN 150 leads southwest to the foothill hot springs of Pismanta, where **Hotel Termas de Pismanta** (tel. 02647/49-7091, www.pismantaspa.com.ar, US$40 s, US$71 d, with breakfast, up to US$55 s, US$103 d, with full board) attracts mostly middle-aged and aging Argentines to its enormous hot baths and a decent restaurant that are both open to nonguests.

From Pismanta, RN 150 climbs 92 kilometers through the upper Jáchal drainage to the Chilean border at 4,779-meter **Paso de Agua Negra,** the highest pass between the two countries. Open at least December–March, it features an impressive glacier and the snowmelt pinnacles known as *penitentes* along the narrow highway, which continues to the scenic Elqui Valley and the beach resort of La Serena in Chile. San Juan authorities envision keeping it open all year—highly unlikely without expensive tunneling.

SAN AGUSTÍN DEL VALLE FÉRTIL

It has taken time, but San Agustín del Valle Fértil seems finally poised to make its mark with international travelers. For weekend visitors from the searingly hot provincial capital, it has long been a refreshingly tranquil and hospitable "hill station," but improved services and better roads have made it an almost ideal base for visiting Parque Provincial Ischigualasto and La Rioja's adjacent Parque Nacional Talampaya.

On San Juan's eastern edge, San Agustín's mountainous microclimate helps create a well-watered enclave of lush hills and valleys that seems a mirror image of the rest of this desert province. Founded in 1788, the town commemorates its anniversary on April 4.

On the eastern slopes of the sedimentary

Sierras Pampeanas, San Agustín (pop. 4,000-plus) is 247 kilometers northeast of San Juan via paved RN 141 and freshly paved RP 510, which continues to Baldecitos (the Ischigualasto turnoff), beyond which it meets paved RP 26 to Parque Nacional Talampaya and RN 150 toward La Rioja. Locals generally ignore street names, but it's small and regular enough to make orientation easy.

Sights

San Agustín's main sights are archaeological: the petroglyphs of **Piedra Pintada,** about 300 meters over the Río Seco; the **Morteros Indígenas** (Indian Mortars) another 500 meters on; and the **Meseta Ritual** (Ritual Mesa), on the grounds of the Escuela Agrotécnica. Known for its fresh dairy products, the nearby farming village of **La Majadita,** a seven-kilometer hike or ride in the dry winter, is even calmer than San Agustín.

Accommodations and Food

Many visitors stay at campgrounds, such as the riverside **Camping Municipal** (Rivadavia s/n, tel. 02646/42-0104, US$5 per two-person tent). The woodsy **Camping Valle Fértil** (Rivadavia s/n, tel. 02646/42-0015, US$2.50 pp) has better infrastructure.

As Valle Fértil's appeal grows, it should draw a younger crowd to the dorms-only **Hostel Campo Base Valle Fértil** (Tucumán s/n, tel. 02646/42-5511, www.hostelvalledelaluna.com. ar, US$7–9 pp). Amenities include kitchen facilities, a bar, and a small backyard pool.

In a converted disco that can't completely disguise its origins, rates at the **Fatme Hotel** (Rivadavia s/n, hotelfatme@hotmail.com, tel. 02646/42-0014, US$25–30 d) rise for winter holidays, Semana Santa, and some other weekends. It's quiet, the rooms are spacious with private baths and cable TV, and some have air-conditioning; all the windows are small, though, and a couple of downstairs rooms lack exterior windows.

San Agustín's best remains the hilltop **Hostería Valle Fértil** (Rivadavia 1510, tel. 02646/42-0015, vallefertil@alkazarhotel.com.

ar, US$45 s, US$52 d, with breakfast). Under the same management as San Juan's Hotel Alkázar, it also offers half or full-board options at its restaurant-*confitería*.

The food scene is improving. In addition to the *hostería* and the established **Parrilla de Zulma** (Tucumán s/n), **La Cocina de Zulma** (Rivadavia s/n, opposite a plaza) and especially **Rinco's Restó** (Rivadavia s/n), a couple of blocks west, offer a greater diversity of Italo-Argentine food and atmosphere.

Other Practicalities

Open 7 A.M.–11:30 P.M. daily, directly across from the plaza, the **Dirección de Turismo** (General Acha s/n, tel. 02646/42-0104) is quick to offer suggestions. There's a satellite office with irregular hours at the bus terminal.

The post office is at Laprida and Mendoza. **Telefónica** has a *locutorio* on Tucumán between Mitre and Santa Fe, and Internet service has finally arrived through **Cemafe** (Mitre and General Acha).

Patricio Viajes (Mitre s/n, tel. 02646/42-0143) and **Paula Tour** (Tucumán s/n, tel. 02646/42-0096, www.paula-tour.com.ar) offer excursions to Ischigualasto and Talampaya.

San Agustín's **Terminal de Ómnibus** is at Entre Ríos and Mitre. **Empresa Vallecito** (tel. 02646/42-0427) links the town with San Juan (4 hours, US$10) daily, and with La Rioja (US$6) Monday, Wednesday, and Friday, passing the Ischigualasto turnoff at the inconvenient hour of 4 A.M.

◖ PARQUE PROVINCIAL ISCHIGUALASTO

Nicknamed "Valle de la Luna" for the lunar landscapes formed from its colorless clay, reddish sandstone, and black volcanic ash, Parque Provincial Ischigualasto also deserves to be called "Triassic Park" for fossil-rich sediments that have yielded dinosaur skeletons 228 million years old. Finds like the early predator *Eoraptor lunensis,* the *Tyrannosaurus*-like *Herrerasaurus,* and the herbivorous *Riojasaurus* have made Ischigualasto, together with nearby Parque Nacional Talampaya, a UNESCO World Heritage Site.

About 80 kilometers northwest of San Agustín via newly paved RP 510 and smoothly paved RN 150, Ischigualasto encompasses 63,000 hectares of eroded sedimentary badlands between the easterly Cerros Colorados and the westerly Quebrada de los Jachalleros. RP 150 dead-ends about 15 kilometers to the west, and it's likely to be some time before it reaches the last 35 kilometers or so to the junction with RN 40 and Jáchal.

Flora and Fauna

Rather than plants and animals, most visitors come to see whatever the sparse vegetation of hillside cacti and streambed shrubs and *algarrobos* doesn't cover. In the withering summer heat, most wildlife is nocturnal, but there are guanacos, foxes, hares, rheas, and pumas as well as rodents, snakes, and other reptiles.

Sights and Recreation

All visits now begin with a tour of the outstanding **Museo de Ciencias Naturales,** a branch of the Universidad Nacional de San Juan with first-rate paleontology and dinosaur exhibits with well-trained guides from the university. Unfortunately, neither the guides nor the explanatory panels can handle English.

From the visitors center, museum guides accompany private vehicles and operators on the **Circuito Vehicular,** an unpaved 40-kilometer loop that covers most of the top sights. Most visitors without their own vehicles now contract day tours, which also take in Parque Nacional Talampaya, from San Agustín del Valle Fértil.

Here the two-hour excursion passes distinctive landforms such as the **Cancha de Bochas** (The Ball Court), **El Esfinge** (The Sphinx), **El Gusano** (The Worm), **El Hongo** (The Mushroom), and **El Submarino** (The Submarine)—all of which bear some resemblance to the objects from which they take their names. There are also bicycle and full-moon tours.

For alternative excursions such as the three-hour climb of the 1,748-meter **Cerro Morado** (US$5.50 pp), which gains about 800 meters en route to the solitary summit, local guides are obligatory.

Parque Provincial Ischigualasto (tel. 02646/49-1100, www.ischigualasto.org) is open 9 A.M.–4 P.M. daily April 1–September 30, 8 A.M.–5 P.M. daily October 1–March 31.

Practicalities

Camping (US$1 pp) is permitted behind the museum, but there is no shade whatsoever; sparkling new bathrooms, built mainly to accommodate tour buses, include flush toilets, hot showers, and even disabled access, but that doesn't necessarily mean there's water to wash and flush—that arrives on trucks.

The **Confitería Dinosaurios** provides above-average meals, cold beer, wine, and sodas, and regional products like olives and dried fruit. Alongside the ranger station, there are outdoor crafts stands.

Foreign visitors pay a US$10.50 entrance fee at the park's **Centro de Visitantes,** which includes the museum and vehicular circuit; Argentines and other residents get a small discount.

The Thursday and Sunday Empresa Vallecito **buses** from San Juan to La Rioja stop at the Los Baldecitos checkpoint on RP 510, but that still leaves 17 kilometers to the visitors center and raises the question of getting around the circuit (which could be dangerous for hikers and cyclists in the unrelenting summer heat).

Visiting Ischigualasto without a vehicle may be possible, but a rental car or a tour certainly simplifies things. San Agustín's **Paula Tour** (Tucumán s/n, tel. 02646/42-0096, www.paula-tour.com.ar) and **Turismo Veza** (Mitre s/n, tel. 02646/42-0143) offer tours from Valle Fértil to both Ischigualasto and nearby Talampaya.

La Rioja Province

La Rioja's highest-profile destination is Parque Nacional Talampaya, a series of fossil-rich desert canyons so near San Juan's Ischigualasto that the two parks are often visited in the same day. That said, the provincial capital is a major devotional center, and the historic mountain town of Chilecito—high enough to offer some relief from the capital's oppressively hot summer—is also part of a small but significant wine district that produces some of the country's best torrontés.

LA RIOJA

Dating from 1591, Todos los Santos de la Nueva Rioja has managed to maintain a colonial ambience in a city that has somehow survived repeated political conflicts and natural disasters since its founding by governor and *encomendero* Juan Ramírez de Velasco. Missionaries of several orders defused the earliest conflicts between the Spanish invaders and the indigenous Diaguita, while caudillos like Facundo Quiroga and his present-day counterparts have kept the city under their thumbs. In the meantime, earthquakes have leveled much of the city's historical heritage, but the rebuilding effort has managed to preserve the feeling, if not every feature, of the Andean past.

At the foot of the eastern face of the Sierra de Velasco, 498 meters above sea level with a climate resembling that of Phoenix, La Rioja (pop. 143,921) is 1,153 kilometers northwest of Buenos Aires via RN 9 and RN 38. It is 456 kilometers northwest of Córdoba and 154 kilometers southwest of Catamarca via RN 38, and 452 kilometers northeast of San Juan via a series of national and provincial highways.

Sights

Earthquake-prone La Rioja has few buildings of any real antiquity, but most of those are on or around Plaza 25 de Mayo.

© JOSÉ PORRAS

Iglesia Catedral

CUYO AND CÓRDOBA

On the south side of the Plaza, the Byzantine **Iglesia Catedral** (1899) holds the venerated image of the city's patron San Nicolás de Bari. The provincial **Casa de Gobierno** (25 de Mayo 10) faces the west side of the plaza.

Franciscans were the first order to establish themselves in La Rioja, in the **Convento de San Francisco** (25 de Mayo 218) one block north of the plaza. An image of the Niño Alcalde, a Christ Child figure acknowledged as the city's symbolic mayor, resides here.

One block east of the plaza, the **Convento de Santo Domingo** (Pelagio Luna and Lamadrid, open after 6 P.M.) is Argentina's oldest convent, built by Diaguita labor from the *encomienda* of Juan Ramírez de Velasco. The carved *algarrobo* door frame bears the original date of 1623, though only the stone exterior church walls survived the earthquake of 1894.

Two blocks west of the plaza, in renovated quarters, the misleadingly named **Museo Folklórico** (Pelagio Luna 811, tel. 03822/42-8500, 8 A.M.–12:30 P.M. and 5–9 P.M. Tues.–Fri., 8 A.M.–12:30 P.M. Sat.–Sun., free) is more and better than its prosaic name suggests. Stressing local customs, beliefs, and artifacts, it places them in a historic household context rather than in glass-case isolation; it offers many of these same items for sale (appropriately enough, given their economic significance in everyday life). Among the items on display are ponchos, wood carvings, and silver and leather work. The museum occupies a handsome 19th-century house with a shady central patio that's suitable for a breather.

Half a block west of Plaza 9 de Julio, the turreted **Casa de Joaquín V. González** (Rivadavia 952, tel. 03822/42-6863, 9 A.M.–noon and 5–8:30 P.M. Mon.–Fri.) was the Gothic-style residence of a true renaissance man: He founded the Universidad de La Plata, his written works totaled 25 volumes, and he also served as a legislator and diplomat.

Events

La Chaya, an indigenous version of Carnaval, takes place in February or March and can get raucously wet with water balloons—the Diaguita-derived deity known as Pujllay appears, according to popular belief, as a rain cloud in the Andes before dying on the celebration's final Sunday.

December 31's midday **El Tinkunako** also has indigenous origins in San Francisco Solano's 1593 mediation between the Spanish invaders and the Diaguitas, who insisted on replacing the Spanish *alcalde* (mayor) with the Niño Alcalde, a Christ Child image that still resides in the Franciscan church. In a procession that ends in front of Plaza 25 de Mayo's government house, the indigenous patron saint San Nicolás de Bari bows three times to acknowledge the image's authority.

Shopping

The **Mercado Artesanal de La Rioja** (Pelagio Luna 792, tel. 03822/46-8433) displays and sells provincial crafts such as weavings, ceramics, and silver and leather work. A virtual crafts museum, its hours are 8 A.M.–noon and 4–8 P.M. Tuesday–Friday, 9 A.M.–1 P.M. weekends.

Paseo del Aljibe (Rivadavia 537, tel. 03822/43-5074) is a wine bar that also stocks regional sweets like dried fruit and jams as well as crafts like basketry, ceramics, and weavings.

Accommodations

Cozy family-run **Residencial Anita** (Lagos 476, tel. 03822/42-4836, US$20 s, US$31 d) is one of La Rioja's best bargains.

Facing a narrow alleyway on downtown's western edge, **Hotel Savoy** (San Nicolás de Bari 1100, tel. 03822/42-6894, hotelsavoy@arnet.com.ar, US$32–40 s, US$40–48 d, with a buffet breakfast) has rooms with cable TV and effective but aging and noisy air-conditioning units. The cheaper downstairs rooms vary in size, so don't hesitate to ask for a larger upstairs room.

As the once rundown Parque Yacampis, northwest of downtown, recovers some of its former luster, ACA's adjacent rehabbed **Motel Yacampis** (Avenida Ramírez de Velasco s/n, tel. 03822/42-5216, US$34 s, US$53 d) has become a more attractive option.

One of the better values in its price range,

King's Hotel (Avenida Quiroga 1070, tel. 03822/42-2122, US$42 s, US$74 d, www.k-hotellarioja.com.ar) has tacky decor but also a large pool.

Its boxy interior limits its curb appeal, but **Hotel Plaza** (San Nicolás de Bari Oeste 502, tel. 03822/42-5215, www.plazahotel-larioja.com.ar, US$60–75 s, US$69–84 d) has comfortable midsized rooms with balconies. It also has a swimming pool and bar.

La Rioja finally has luxury hotel accommodations in the business-oriented high-rise **Naindo Park Hotel** (San Nicolás de Bari 475, tel. 03822/47-0700, www.naindoparkhotel.com, US$99 s, US$114 d), which opened in 2005. Just off Plaza 25 de Mayo, its 133 rooms are far superior to anything else in town, and it has held its prices fairly steady.

Food

Café del Paseo (Pelagio Luna and 25 de Mayo, tel. 03822/42-2069) is good for breakfast, coffee, and sandwiches.

La Vieja Casona (Rivadavia 427, tel. 03822/42-5996) serves the usual *parrillada* but also regional specialties like *locro* and tangy empanadas. **Cavadini** (Avenida Quiroga 1131, tel. 03822/42-2183) is Italo-Argentine.

A new gastronomic quarter is developing in the vicinity of the old railroad station at the east end of Rivadavia. One good choice is the smartly stylish **Open Piazza** (Avenida Gordillo and Rivadavia, tel. 03822/42-5390), serving Italo-Argentine fare. The most ambitious menu, though, is the diverse pasta and sauces at 【 **L'Stanzza** (Dorrego 64, tel. 03822/43-0809, US$10–20), which boasts a strong provincial wine list, imaginative deserts, and attentive service.

Heladería Islas Malvinas (Buenos Aires 257) has excellent ice cream.

Information

The **Dirección Municipal de Turismo** (Dimutur, San Nicolás de Bari and Buenos Aires, tel. 03822/47-4031, 8 A.M.–1 P.M. and 5–9 P.M. daily) has fewer maps and brochures than in the past, but the personnel do their best.

The efficient **Agencia Provincial de Turismo** (Pelagio B. Luna 345, tel. 03822/42-6345, www.turismolarioja.gov.ar, 8 A.M.–10 P.M. daily) has a better supply of printed material and an occasional English speaker.

For motorists, **ACA** is at Vélez Sarsfield and Copiapó (tel. 03822/42-5381).

Services

Several banks have ATMs, including **Nuevo Banco de la Rioja** (Rivadavia 702).

Correo Argentino is at Avenida Perón 764; the postal code is 5300. On the south side of Plaza 25 de Mayo, **Telefónica** (San Nicolás de Bari 531) has both long-distance service and Internet access.

There are two convenient laundries: **Mamá Espuma** (Avenida Perón 324, tel. 03822/15-66-4474) and **Lavadero Rocío** (Avenida Perón 946).

For medical attention, try **Hospital Vera Barros** (San Nicolás de Bari Este 97, tel. 03822/42-7814).

Getting There and Around

Aerolíneas Argentinas (Belgrano 63, tel. 03822/42-6307) flies daily except Saturday to Buenos Aires's Aeroparque.

From Plaza 9 de Julio, city bus No. 3 goes to **Aeropuerto Vicente Almonacid** (tel. 03822/43-9211), seven kilometers east of town on RP 5. A *remise* costs around US$4.

La Rioja's **Estación Terminal de Ómnibus** (Avenida Ortiz de Ocampo and Gobernador Félix de La Colina, tel. 03822/42-7991) is now on the southern outskirts of town. Sample destinations, times, and fares include Catamarca (2 hours, US$5), Chilecito (2.5 hours, US$5), Tucumán (5 hours, US$13), Córdoba (5.5 hours, US$14–19), Mendoza (8.5 hours, US$27–33), Salta (11 hours, US$38–44), and Buenos Aires (16 hours, US$41–63).

La Riojana (Buenos Aires 154, tel. 03822/43-5279) operates faster minibuses to Chilecito (2 hours, US$7). **El Zonda** (Dorrego 79, tel. 03822/42-1930) goes to Villa Unión, in the province's western cordillera, for connections to Parque Nacional Talampaya.

Winner Rent A Car (Hipólito Yrigoyen 412, tel. 03822/43-1318, www.winner-rentacar.com) has rental vehicles.

ANILLACO

Nobody at Anillaco, at an elevation of 1,800 meters in the mountains north of La Rioja, apologizes for the widely despised former president Carlos Menem—it's his home town, and his late father's winery (no longer open for visits) is one of its main employers (it overoptimistically produced wines to be uncorked on Menem's anticipated third inauguration after the 2003 presidential elections, but he withdrew from a runoff in the face of a certain crushing defeat by Néstor Kirchner).

Thanks to Menem, this village of fewer than 1,000 residents, 93 kilometers from the provincial capital via RP 75, also has an airport built to international standards (it acquired the sarcastic nickname *la pista de las aceitunas* after the former president suggested it was built to export olives). On top of that, it has an 18-hole golf course that raised more than a few eyebrows during and since his tenure. He has been investigated for illegal enrichment, though no charges have yet been brought, and campaigned again for the presidency in 2007 despite being widely loathed by the electorate.

Visitors can stay at the ACA's **Hostería Anillaco** (Coronel Barros s/n, tel. 03827/49-4064, US$14–19 s, US$22–31 d).

CHILECITO

In the longitudinal valley between the eastern Sierra de Velasco and the western Sierra de Famatina, Chilecito is a onetime mining town that's now the center of a wine-producing area that also grows olives and walnuts. Founded in 1715 as Santa Rita de Casia, it acquired its present name from the Chilean miners who worked the Famatina gold deposits for most of the 19th century. When caudillo Facundo Quiroga occupied La Rioja in the 1820s, it briefly served as the de facto provincial capital.

With its refreshing climate, at an altitude of 1,100 meters, Chilecito (pop. about 42,000) is the province's most appealing town and a gateway to Parque Nacional Talampaya, the province's number-one attraction. At the base of 6,250-meter Nevado de Famatina, the town is directly west of the provincial capital, but reaching it requires a detour around the southern Sierra de Velasco via RN 38 and RN 74, a distance of 192 kilometers.

Sights

In the late 19th century, the Famatina mines were so important that Chilecito became the site of the second branch of **Banco de la Nación** (Joaquín V. González and 19 de Febrero), at the northwest corner of **Plaza Caudillos Federales,** formerly the Plaza Sarmiento: Although it is impressive, the current building is not the original.

One block west, the **Centro Cultural Gonzaleano** (Joaquín V. González and Santiago Bazán) is a period house recycled as an art space. Three blocks farther west, Chilecito founder Domingo de Castro y Bazán built and owned the **Molino de San Francisco** (Ocampo 63, 8 A.M.–noon and 3–7:30 P.M. daily, free), a well-restored colonial flour mill that's now a museum displaying local minerals, pre-Columbian tools, colonial documents, and historic weapons; leather work and wood carvings; and weavings and paintings.

One block farther west, **Bodega La Riojana** (La Plata 646, tel. 03825/42-3150, www.lariojana.com.ar) is a cooperative specializing in torrontés *riojano* but also producing malbec, cabernet, and others, as well as dried fruit. Free guided tours, with tasting, take place four times between 10:30 A.M. and 3 P.M. each weekday, and at 9:30 and 11 A.M. Saturday.

At the southern approach to town, the **Cablecarril La Mejicana** (Avenida Presidente Perón s/n) is a Leipzig-built aerial tramway that connected the railway station with the Santa Florentina smelter and the La Mejicana mine from 1904 until 1929. Replacing an obsolete mule-back system, it carried laborers and materials 34 kilometers to and from the mine, gaining 3,500 meters in elevation. The longest of its kind in the Americas and the second-longest in the world, it consisted of nine stations, each of which had dormitories for the laborers, linked by 262 towers; the 450 ore carts and passenger carts traveled at speeds up to 28 kilometers per hour.

Now a museum, the Cablecarril's base station is open 8 A.M.–1 P.M. and 2–8 P.M. weekdays, 8 A.M.–8 P.M. weekends, with tours (US$1.25) led by municipal guides. In addition to the tower platform and carts, the ground-level offices hold a variety of tools, minerals, and other items. The entire system is a national historical monument.

Chilecito has also opened **Estación No. 2,** the Cablecarril's second station on a promontory above nearby Santa Florentina. Its century-old German-built steam power station remains in working condition, and the slowly rusting facilities are a photographer's dream; in addition, the site offers spectacular panoramas of the Famatina Valley and its cordillera. It's about eight kilometers west of downtown Chilecito; the best transport option is to hire a *remise*, as it's a hot, steep climb from Santa Florentina.

About three kilometers east of town via RP 12, **Samay Huasi** (tel. 03825/42-2629, 9 A.M.–7 P.M. daily, US$0.50) was educator Joaquín V. González's country house, and the Universidad Nacional de La Plata, which he founded, administers the building as a natural sciences museum and research base; there is also a collection of Argentine art.

Accommodations

The HI affiliate **Hostel del Paimán** (Maestro 198, tel. 03825/42-5102, www.hotelruta40.com.ar, US$9 pp dorm; US$14 s, US$21 d, with private bath) occupies a handsome old adobe, with rooms arranged along a gallery that extends the depth of the lot; it also has large gardens. Under the same ownership, **Hotel Ruta 40** (Libertad 68, tel. 03825/42-2804, www.hotelruta40.com.ar, US$9 pp dorm with shared bath; US$14 s, US$23 d, with private bath) has plain but immaculately clean rooms with firm beds and small amenities such as writing desks.

Downtown's best choice may be family-run **Hostal Mary Pérez** (Florencio Dávila 280,

tel./fax 03825/42-3156, hostal_mp@hotmail.com, US$26 s, US$31 d), which offers large comfy rooms with good beds, cable TV, and a decent breakfast. It's normally quiet, but the walls are a little thin.

On ample shaded grounds, ACA's **Hotel Chilecito** (Timoteo Gordillo 101, tel. 03825/42-2201, US$37–47 s, US$47–67 d) is architecturally drab but has upgraded the interior. Prices, though, have more than doubled.

Food

Opposite the plaza **Oh! Santino** (25 de Mayo and Joaquín V. González) is an upgraded bar-*confitería* that aspires to be a full-scale *restó*, and at least the decor is there.

Having moved from the now defunct Club Árabe, **Jaime y Alicia** (Avenida Presidente Perón s/n) still produces tasty versions of Middle Eastern specialties like *niños envueltos* (stuffed grape leaves) at low prices.

For *parrillada,* the best option is **La Posta** (19 de Febrero and Roque Lanús, tel. 03825/42-5988). The most diverse menu is at **La Rosa** (Alberto G. Ocampo 149, tel. 03825/42-4693), which serves an above-average Argentine menu and good pizza in attractive surroundings, but service can be inconsistent.

For the biggest menu, and best service, try the local institution **El Rancho de Ferrito** (Pelagio B. Luna 647, tel. 03825/42-2481), a cavernous *parrilla* and restaurant with high ceilings, tremendous regional atmosphere, and affordable prices—few entrées exceed US$6. The English menu translation also provides entertainment, at least for those who appreciate "Crowing of Chicken to the Switzerland."

Helados Vanesa (Joaquín V. González 50) has the best ice cream.

Information and Services

The competent, helpful **Ente Municipal de Turismo** (Castro y Bazán 52, tel. 03825/42-2688, www.emutur.com.ar, 8 A.M.–8 or 9 P.M. daily) also has satellite offices on Plaza Caudillos Federales and at the bus terminal.

Several banks with ATMs have branches facing the central Plaza Caudillos Federales.

Correo Argentino is at Joaquín V. González and Pelagio B. Luna; the postal code is 5360. **Cabinas Telefónicas** (Córdoba and Dávila) has long-distance phone services. Internet service, including Wi-Fi, is available at **Link** (Santiago Bazán between Castro Barros and Joaquín González), one block south of the plaza.

Getting There and Around

At the south end of town, Chilecito's shiny new **Estación Terminal de Ómnibus** (Avenida Presidente Perón s/n and Formosa) is a big improvement on the old one, but it's less central. Sample destinations, times, and fares include La Rioja (2.5 hours, US$5), Córdoba (8 hours, US$21), and Buenos Aires (17 hours, US$65).

La Riojana (El Maestro 61, tel. 03825/42-4710) provides minibus service to the provincial capital (US$7). **Facundo** (tel. 03825/42-9171) offers minibus service to Villa Unión (2 hours, US$6.50), for Parque Nacional Talampaya, at 3 P.M. Monday, Wednesday, and Friday.

◖ PARQUE NACIONAL TALAMPAYA

On the waterless western slopes of the Sierra de Sañogasta, Talampaya's colorful canyon country is a jumble of wildly eroded landscapes that draws more overseas visitors than any other part of La Rioja. Many combine it with a trip to San Juan Province's Parque Provincial Ischigualasto, colloquially known as the Valle de la Luna (Valley of the Moon).

Talampaya takes its name from a Quechua term with sacred allusions, meaning "Dry Riverbed of the Tala," where the *tala* tree once grew. While the riverbed may be dry, running water has played the key role in creating its sheer-sided sandstone canyons and silhouette landforms from an enormous lakebed that covered the Talampaya basin during Permian and Triassic times.

One of ex-President Carlos Menem's least controversial decisions was to grant this deserving area, which along with Ischigualasto is a UNESCO World Heritage Site, its national park status in 1997 (it was previously a provincial park). Besides its natural appeal, it boasts archaeological and rock-art sites (both

figurative and abstract) that date from around A.D. 100–1200.

From a junction 15 kilometers south of Chilecito, westbound RN 40 becomes a gravel road as it climbs the hairpin turns of the scenic Río Miranda gorge to the 2,020-meter **Cuesta de Miranda,** before descending to Villa La Unión or alternatively, via RP 18, to the village of Pagancillo. From Pagancillo, RN 76 leads south to Talampaya for a total distance of about 140 kilometers.

Sprawling over 215,000 hectares of desert, the park is 217 kilometers from La Rioja on a roundabout route via southbound RN 38, westbound RN 150, and northbound RN 76. Midway between Villa La Unión and Los Baldecitos, a paved turnoff leads a few hundred meters east to the park entrance.

Flora and Fauna

Talampaya's sparse vegetation consists largely of shrubs, including the nearly leafless *retamo* and the resinous *jarilla,* as well as cacti that include the *cardón*. In some areas, subterranean water supports larger trees like the *algarrobo* and pepper (*Schinus molle*).

The most conspicuous mammal is the common gray fox, but the *chinchillón* (vizcacha) and the armadillo are also present. Birds include scavengers like the Andean condor and turkey vulture, and raptors including the peregrine falcon.

Talampaya's most dramatic fauna, such as the dinosaur-like *Lagosuchus talampayensis* and the turtle *Palaeocheris talampayensis,* have been extinct since the early Triassic, 250 million years ago.

Sights and Recreation

Visitors may no longer use their own vehicles, but must hire guided tours through park concessionaires. Winter hours are 8:30 A.M.–5:30 P.M. daily; summer hours are 8 A.M.–6 P.M. daily, but the relatively cool mornings are better than the hot afternoons.

The main concessionaire, for the traditional excursions starting at the canyon's **Puerta de Talampaya** (Gate of Talampaya) entrance, is Córdoba's Rolling Travel (tel. 03825/47-0397,

© GINO LUCAS T.

Parque Nacional Talampaya

tel. 0351/570-9909 in Córdoba, www.talam-paya.com). Based at the Parador Turístico near the highway, it does its main 2.5-hour excursion (US$17 pp) on demand with a maximum 45-minute wait, even for a single client; it has added a new roofless vehicle for better sightseeing. That excursion does a short but informative hike to the **Petroglifos** rock-art and mortar site (explanatory panels include a competent English translation); another short hike through the so-called **Jardín Botánico,** which arrives at the **Chimenea del Eco,** a natural echo chamber; stops at the sheer-sided sandstone cliffs of **La Catedral;** and finishes at **El Monje,** a freestanding landform that resembles a Spanish friar. A 4.5-hour excursion that takes in the canyon of **Las Cajones** costs US$25 pp.

At a roadside office a few kilometers south of the Parador Turístico, a local cooperative named Turismo Talampaya (tel. 03825/15-51-2367, www.turismoentalampaya.com.ar) does the five-hour excursion to the **Ciudad Perdida** (Lost City, so named because its landforms resemble ruined buildings). Including a 2.5-hour hike, this costs US$32 for one or two persons; each additional person costs an extra US$13.

Practicalities

Visitors can crash at the Parador Turístico's new **campground** (US$2 pp), which has some shaded picnic tables, and shower at its **Resto Bar Naturaleza Mística**'s new bathrooms. Otherwise, the nearest accommodations are at Pagancillo, 27 kilometers north. Despite its pretentious name, the restaurant serves basic short orders and sandwiches, and cold drinks at reasonable prices.

At the RN 76 junction for Puerta de Talampaya, a toll booth collects park-entrance fees (US$7 pp for foreigners, US$2 pp for Argentine residents).

Most visitors without their own vehicles now contract tours at San Agustín del Valle Fértil, but it's possible to arrange a tour, or hire a *remise,* from either La Rioja or Chilecito, or a *remise* from the town of Villa Unión. From La Rioja, **El Zonda** (Dorrego 79, El Zonda, tel. 03822/42-1930) goes to Villa Unión for connections to the park. From Chilecito, **Facundo** (tel. 03825/42-9171) minibuses leave for Villa Unión (2 hours, US$6.50) at 3 P.M. Monday, Wednesday, and Friday, which means they arrive too late for same-day tours.

CUYO AND CÓRDOBA

San Luis Province

San Luis is a contradiction: a tiny province with a small population that has gained and maintained notoriety through the Rodríguez Saá political dynasty. Its most prominent figure, erratic populist Adolfo Rodríguez Saá ("El Adolfo"), proudly declared Argentina's 2001 debt default in a brief term as caretaker president. Ironically, the province remained solvent despite widespread corruption in what opponents of El Adolfo and brother Alberto punningly call a *dictadura Saátanica*.

San Luis prefers to be called *Portal de Cuyo* (The Gateway to Cuyo); its roads are among the country's best, its namesake city is a tidy provincial capital, and there's open access Wi-Fi throughout the province. For foreigners, its most worthwhile sight is the fossil-rich canyon country of Parque Nacional Sierra de las Quijadas; for Puntanos (provincial natives) and other Argentines, it's the underrated Sierras on the border of Córdoba Province.

SAN LUIS

Capital of its province, San Luis itself has no international attractions, but it's the best place to arrange excursions to Parque Nacional Sierra de las Quijadas, and overland travelers to Mendoza may stop over here. It's also a backdoor approach to Córdoba Province and its Sierras.

San Luis (pop. about 180,000) is 820 kilometers west of Buenos Aires via RN 7, 257 kilometers east of Mendoza via RN 7, and 405 kilometers southwest of Córdoba via RN 148. Most sights lie between Plaza Pringles, at the north end of the commercial axis formed by the parallel streets Rivadavia and San Martín, and Plaza Independencia, four blocks south.

Sights

Most sights lie on or between the city's two principal plazas. Distinguished by an imposing sculptured pediment, the neoclassic **Iglesia Catedral** (started in 1883 but not finished until 1944) faces lushly landscaped **Plaza Pringles** from Rivadavia, while the Art Nouveau **Colegio Nacional Juan Crisóstomo Lafinur** (1869), across the plaza, is the province's most prestigious school.

The provincial **Casa de Gobierno** (1913) overlooks the equally well-landscaped **Plaza Independencia** from Calle 9 de Julio. On the opposite side, the city's oldest building is the 17th-century **Iglesia de Santo Domingo** (25 de Mayo s/n), but most of this Moorish-style church is a 1930s reconstruction; its outstanding original feature is the carved but weathering *algarrobo* doors.

Entertainment and Events

Barhoppers will find a flourishing pub scene on Avenida Arturo Illia, running northwest from Plaza Pringles; several double as restaurants. Among them are **Baco's Bar** (Avenida Arturo Illia 180), which also has live music, and **The Movie** (Avenida Arturo Illia 187, tel. 02652/44-1470), immediately across the avenue. **Morrison** (Pringles 830, tel. 02652/44-0818), as in Jim, is a rock-and-roll theme bar with above-average food.

Accommodations

Often full, the best budget option is **Residencial María Eugenia** (25 de Mayo 741, tel. 02652/43-0361, US$20 s, US$37 d, with private bath), near Plaza Independencia. Nearby, some of the large rooms at friendly, family-run **Hotel Buenos Aires** (Buenos Aires 834, tel. 02652/42-4062, US$22 s, US$40 d) have air-conditioning; all offer cable TV and parking.

Friendly, well-kept **Hotel Castelmonte** (Chacabuco 769, tel. 02652/42-4963, US$30 s, US$40 d) is more central. Its midsize rooms have firm beds and opaque windows that open onto interior patios.

Also often full, the **Inka Hotel** (Bolívar 943, tel. 02652/42-4923, www.inca-hotel.com.ar, US$32 s, US$47 d) has decent midsize rooms, but some mattresses are on the soft side.

One of the highlights at **Hotel Aiello** (Avenida Arturo Illia 431, tel. 02652/42-5609, www.hotelaiello.com.ar, US$65 s, US$80 d, with buffet breakfast) is the good-humored staff, but its sizeable rooms are impeccable even if relatively small windows limit the natural light.

The four-star **Hotel Quintana** (Avenida Arturo Illia 546, tel. 02652/43-8400, www. hotelquintana.com.ar, US$77 s, US$104 d) is a sparkling seven-story hotel with impeccable service and more-contemporary amenities than others in town. Though it has been the class of town, it's getting competition from the **Vista Suites & Spa** (Avenida Arturo Illia 546, tel. 02652/42-5794, www.vistasuites.com.ar, from US$114 s, US$126 d).

Food

For breakfast, the bus terminal's **Confitería La Terminal** (Avenida España s/n) is better than most of its kind, with fresh croissants and espresso drinks.

An institution since 1945, **La Porteña** (Junín 696, tel. 02652/43-1722 or 02652/42-3807) has plain decor but an excellent menu with unusual (for Argentina) items such as pineapple chicken. **Kopito's** (Avenida Illia 364) is the place for ice cream.

Information

The staff at the provincial **Ministerio de Turismo, Cultura y Deporte** (Avenida Arturo Illia and Junín, tel. 02652/42-3957, www.turismosanluis.gov.ar, 8 A.M.–8 P.M. Mon.–Fri., 7 A.M.–8 P.M. Sat.–Sun.) vary in helpfulness. Its maps and service listings are useful, but the glossy flyers are more notable for their photography.

For motorists, **ACA** (tel. 02652/42-3188) is at Avenida Arturo Illia 401.

Services

Banco de la Nación has an ATM at San Martín 695, at the southwest corner of Plaza Pringles.

Correo Argentino is at Arturo Illia and San Martín; the postal code is 5700.

Locutorio San Luis (Avenida Arturo Illia 305) has both phone and Internet access. **Internauta** (Junín 1135) is another Internet outlet, but free Wi-Fi is ubiquitous in town.

Dasso Viajes (Rivadavia 444, Local A, tel. 02652/42-1017) does excursions to provincial destinations like Las Quijadas and Merlo.

The **Hospital Regional** is at Avenida República Oriental del Uruguay 150 (tel. 02652/42-2627).

Getting There and Around

Aerolíneas Argentinas (Avenida Arturo Illia 468, tel. 02652/42-5671) flies to Buenos Aires's Aeroparque Monday–Saturday. **Aerolíneas Sol** (tel. 0810/444-4765, www.sol.com.ar) has recently commenced flights from Aeroparque but keeps no offices here.

San Luis's **Terminal de Ómnibus** (Avenida España between Francia and Estado de Israel, tel. 02652/42-4021), six blocks north of Plaza Pringles, has frequent provincial and long-distance services as well as direct connections to Chile.

Typical destinations, times, and fares include San Juan (4 hours, US$13), Mendoza (3 hours, US$10), Merlo (3 hours, US$6), Córdoba (5 hours, US$18–21) and Buenos Aires (13 hours, US$38–45).

Aeropuerto Brigadier Mayor César R. Ojeda (tel. 02652/42-2457) is only about three kilometers north of town on RN 146, so a cab or *remise* is inexpensive.

For rental cars, try **Hertz** (Avenida Arturo Illia 300, tel. 02652/42-2820).

◖ PARQUE NACIONAL SIERRA DE LAS QUIJADAS

Evoking the red sandstone ravines of Utah's Bryce Canyon, Parque Nacional Sierra de las Quijadas is rich in scenery, fossils, and pre-Columbian archaeological sites. In Lower Cretaceous times, about 120 million years ago, pterosaurs and their contemporaries left tracks in a semiarid landscape that has since become a jumble of barren cliffs, cornices, terraces, and desiccated lakebeds. Far later, the Huarpe and their predecessors left evidence of their camps and settlements.

Comprising 74,000 hectares in northwestern San Luis Province, the park is the subject of ongoing paleontological research by Universidad

Nacional de San Luis and New York's Museum of Natural History as well as excavations of early Huarpe sites. Badly in need of its own interpretive center, it's open all year, but the mild spring and autumn months are best for visits; in the suffocating summer, thunderstorms can cause dangerous flash floods. The provincial government has initiated a request for UNESCO World Heritage Site status as part of a paleontology circuit with Ischigualasto (San Juan) and Talampaya (La Rioja).

Las Quijadas is about 120 kilometers northwest of San Luis via paved RN 147 and a signed six-kilometer westbound gravel lateral. Most of the enormous park, though, is accessible only on foot.

Flora and Fauna

When the pterosaurs roamed here, Las Quijadas was a mostly level marshland, but climate changes over 100 million years have left it a desert where summer temperatures often exceed 40°C, and plants and animals have adapted to this regime. Typical of the flora is the endemic *chica,* a small slow-growing tree whose hard, dense wood forms a twisted trunk. Truncated shrubs like the *jarilla* and several species of cacti are also typical.

The most notable mammals are the collared peccary, guanaco, puma, and red fox; the endangered Argentine land turtle is also present here. Peregrine falcons and other raptors dive for small prey, while the Andean condor soars in search of carrion.

Sights and Recreation

Las Quijadas's most unforgettable sight is the natural amphitheater of **Potrero de la Aguada,** where the last 25 million years of runoff—from precipitation that now averages only 300 millimeters per annum—has eroded ancient sediments to expose bright sandstone beds and conglomerates to the west. An easy trail follows the Aguada's rim toward the south for about half an hour, but hikers should refrain from descending into the intricate canyons without plenty of water, high-energy snacks, and an obligatory local guide.

Along the gravel road to Potrero de la Aguada, stop at the recently excavated **Hornillos Huarpes,** the ovens where the park's pre-Columbian inhabitants prepared their meals and fired their ceramics. These have been carbon-14 dated at about A.D. 1000.

Practicalities

About one kilometer east of the Potrero de la Aguada overlook, there's a free APN campground with clean flush toilets as well as a small grocery with snacks and cold drinks.

There's still no formal visitors center, but rangers at the park entrance (who collect a US$7 admission for foreigners, US$2 for Argentine residents) provide maps and can answer questions. At the campground, local guides offer several reasonably priced (around US$7–10 pp) 3–4-hour hikes into the badlands, though none of them can manage English.

Spanish-speaking visitors to San Luis should look for the self-published guidebook *El Parque Nacional Sierra de las Quijadas y Sus Recursos Naturales* by English-speaking geologist **David Rivarola** (tel. 02652/15-54-3629, rivarola@ unsl.edu.ar, www.lasquijadas.com), who offers the most informative park tours, but because of time demands only does so for large groups and for foreigners in particular.

Buses between San Luis and San Juan can drop passengers on the access road just north of the hamlet of Hualtarán. Travel agencies in San Luis sometimes organize day tours.

VILLA DE MERLO

Fast-growing Merlo, a traditional Puntano hill station on the western slope of the Sierras de Comenchingones, claims to have the world's third-best microclimate after Lenk, Switzerland, and an unidentified California site. Despite an admittedly refreshing climate and recreational opportunities, foreign travelers are few. Like towns in the nearby Sierras de Córdoba, it's busiest in summer, during holiday periods like Semana Santa, and on weekends.

Merlo (pop. about 22,000), 900 meters above sea level, is 194 kilometers northeast of San Luis via RP 20 to La Toma, an eight-kilometer detour via RP 10 and RN 148 to Santa Rosa del Conlara, where eastbound RP 5 goes to Merlo. Plaza Márques de Sobremonte is the town center, but most services are on or near Avenida del Sol, two blocks south, which climbs steeply east to the barrio of El Rincón.

Sports and Recreation

Adventure sports such as hiking, climbing, rappelling, and even paragliding are possible at **Mirador de los Cóndores** (tel. 02656/47-9257 or cell 02652/15-31-8964, orejarodriguez@hotmail.com). At 2,100 meters in the Comenchingones immediately east of town by a steep road that's paved until the last three kilometers, it also operates a comfortably scenic *confitería* with a short-order menu and particularly choice desserts.

Accommodations

Space prohibits mention of more than a handful of Merlo's countless accommodations. Prices are highest in summer and during Semana Santa and winter holidays, when singles are few; at other times rates may be as much as 30 percent lower.

On woodsy grounds, **Hotel Aguada del Zorro** (Avenida Dos Venados 1277, tel. 02656/47-5740, aguadadelzorro@merlo–sl.com.ar, US$21 pp) is a friendly motel-style place with flaky management and slightly dark but well-kept rooms. Amenities include a pool, parking, and Wi-Fi in common areas that reaches some of the rooms.

In a quiet location just off Avenida del Sol, the only frills at the handsome, nearly new **Hostería Cerro Azul** (Saturno y Jupiter, tel. 02656/47-8648, www.hosteriacerroazul.com.ar, US$50 s or d) are cable TV and a good-sized swimming pool.

The rooms are good but the management a little grumpy at **Hostería Argentina** (Los Almendros 102, tel. 02656/47-5825, www.hosteriargentina.com.ar, US$30 s, US$53 d).

Posada del Valle (Poeta Lugones and Neptuno, tel./fax 02656/47-6103, posadadelvalle@merlo-sl.com.ar, US$58 s or d) is a fine place with six double rooms in a recycled older house; rates include a large homemade breakfast. It does not accept children younger than 14.

In a quiet neighborhood, the new and immaculately kept **Hostería Sueños Dorados** (Avenida del Deporte Sur and El Trapiche, tel. 02656/47-4440, www.sueniosdorados.com.ar, US$58–63) has comfortable if slightly dark rooms, a pool, and friendly ownership. The Windows-friendly Wi-Fi, though, doesn't work with Macs or iPods.

Hotel Parque y Sol (Avenida del Sol 715, tel. 02656/47-5150, www.parqueysol.com.ar, US$69 s or d) has motel-style units on spacious grounds.

Hotel Mirasierras (Avenida del Sol and Pedernera, tel. 02656/47-5045, www.hotelmirasierras.com.ar, US$71 s or d) has good but plain and decent-sized rooms, as well as a pool.

Apart Hotel Piscú Yaco (Pasaje los Teros 235, tel. 02656/47-5127, www.aparthotelpiscuyaco.com.ar, US$50–84 s or d) enjoys a great location on a quiet alleyway, with ample grounds and a pool. The midsized rooms are simply furnished.

Food

The **Montana Café** (Avenida del Sol 25) is a good breakfast spot with exceptionally succulent croissants. **Heladería Michelangelo** (Avenida del Sol 100, tel. 02656/47-7418) has outstanding ice cream.

Cirano (Avenida del Sol 280, tel. 02656/47-5638, www.ciranomerlo.com.ar) is a large but cheerful and efficient *parrillada* and pasta place, with reasonable prices and above-average desserts. The wine list is conventional, from Mendoza's biggest bodegas only.

Giorgio (Avenida del Sol 558, tel. 02656/47-6555) and **Reina Mora** (Avenida Dos Venados 740, tel. 02656/47-6637) have more sophisticated menus, including both Argentine and international dishes.

Information and Services

At the traffic circle where RP 1 and RP 5 intersect, the delegation of the **Dirección Provincial**

CUYO AND CÓRDOBA

de Turismo (tel. 02656/47-6079) is open 8 A.M.–8 P.M. daily except in summer, when it may stay open as late as 10 P.M. It has an excellent city map and brochures; in the same office, the Asociación Hotelera will phone to find suitable accommodations in your price range.

The municipal **Oficina de Informes** (Coronel Mercau 605, tel. 02656/47-6078, www.villademerlo.gov.ar, 8 A.M.–9 P.M. daily) is also helpful but less encyclopedic in its information, though the website is useful.

There are ATMs in the vicinity of Plaza Mercau. **Correo Argentino** is at Coronel Mercau 579; the postal code is 5881. The **Cooperativa Telefónica** is at Poeta Agüero

770; **Merlo Digital** (Presbítero Becerra 624), facing Plaza Mercau, has Internet access, but Wi-Fi is ubiquitous in town.

Lavandería Marva (Avenida del Sol 202, tel. 92656/47-6173) does the washing.

Getting There and Around

Merlo's **Terminal de Ómnibus** (RP 1 and Independencia) is about 500 meters south of the Rotonda junction. Typical destinations, times, and fares include Buenos Aires (11 hours, US$32–40), San Luis (3 hours, US$6), and Mendoza (6 hours, US$20). There are also services northeast across the Sierras to the city of Córdoba (5 hours, US$12–14).

Córdoba Province

Geographically, historically, politically, and culturally, Córdoba's key feature is its centrality. Bordering every major region except Patagonia, it shares the pampas with Santa Fe and Buenos Aires Provinces and the Gran Chaco with Santiago del Estero, and borders the northwestern Andean provinces of La Rioja and Catamarca. Most significantly for travelers, it shares its central sierras—a major vacation land for Argentines—with the Cuyo province of San Luis, so it's easy to travel back and forth between the two on the dense road network.

The Sierras' main gateway, though, is the vibrant capital city of Córdoba. When Buenos Aires was a colonial backwater, this was a center of learning thanks to the Jesuit order; their imprint is tangible in both the city and the countryside—including nearby Alta Gracia, where revolutionary Ernesto "Che" Guevara spent his formative years.

In the Sierras, small towns like Villa Carlos Paz and La Falda are weekend getaways for locals and vacation destinations for middle-class *porteños* and other Argentines. The backcountry is not so wild as Patagonia, but the rolling steppes of Parque Nacional Quebrada del Condorito offer broad vistas and ample wildlife, including condors and guanacos.

HISTORY

Córdoba's aboriginal inhabitants were the Comechingones, settled agriculturalists who also herded llamas, collected wild fruit—and failed to stop the Spanish invasion with guerrilla tactics. After Jerónimo Luis de Cabrera founded the city of Córdoba (1573), Dominican, Franciscan, and Jesuit missionaries streamed into the province, but they and other Spaniards introduced diseases that wiped out the remaining indigenes within a century.

For more than two centuries, linked overland to the viceregal capital of Lima, Perú, Córdoba was the most important city in what is now Argentina. From the late 18th century, though, it suffered a literal reversal of fortune—Buenos Aires's enhanced status as capital of the Viceroyalty of the River Plate made Córdoba second fiddle to the up-and-coming port city. This in turn spurred resentment among traditionalist political and religious elites—royalists opposed independence, and after independence, fanatical Federalists opposed Buenos Aires's secular Unitarists with the slogan "Religion or Death."

From the late 19th century, though, European immigration, agricultural

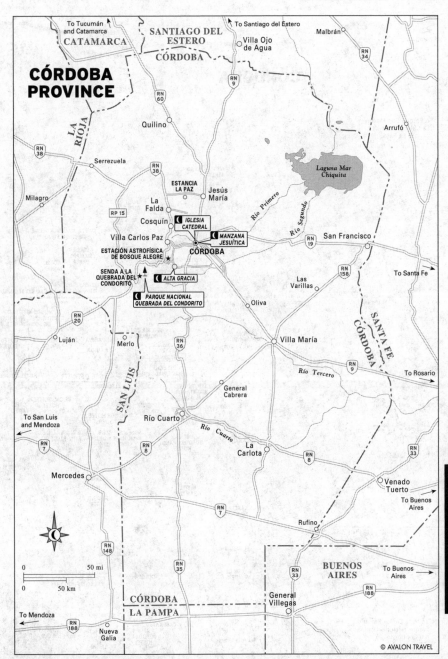

CÓRDOBA PROVINCE

To Tucumán and Catamarca

CATAMARCA

SANTIAGO DEL ESTERO

Villa Ojo de Agua

To Santiago del Estero

Malbrán

RN 34

CÓRDOBA

RN 60

RN 9

Quilino

LA RIOJA

RN 38

Serrezuela

Arrufó

Laguna Mar Chiquita

RN 38

ESTANCIA LA PAZ

Jesús María

Milagro

La Falda

RP 15

Cosquín

IGLESIA CATEDRAL

Río Primero

Río Segundo

Villa Carlos Paz

MANZANA JESUÍTICA

RN 19

San Francisco

ESTACIÓN ASTROFÍSICA DE BOSQUE ALEGRE

CÓRDOBA

RN 158

To Santa Fe

SENDA A LA QUEBRADA DEL CONDORITO

ALTA GRACIA

Las Varillas

SANTA FE

PARQUE NACIONAL QUEBRADA DEL CONDORITO

Oliva

RN 20

Luján

Merlo

SAN LUIS

RN 36

Villa María

RN 9

To Rosario

Río Tercero

To San Luis and Mendoza

General Cabrera

RN 7

Río Cuarto

Río Cuarto

La Carlota

RN 8

RN 8

RN 33

Mercedes

Venado Tuerto

To Buenos Aires

RN 7

RN 148

BUENOS AIRES

RN 33

Rufino

To Buenos Aires

0   50 mi

0   50 km

CÓRDOBA

LA PAMPA

General Villegas

RN 188

To Mendoza

RN 188

Nueva Galia

RN 35

© AVALON TRAVEL

CUYO AND CÓRDOBA

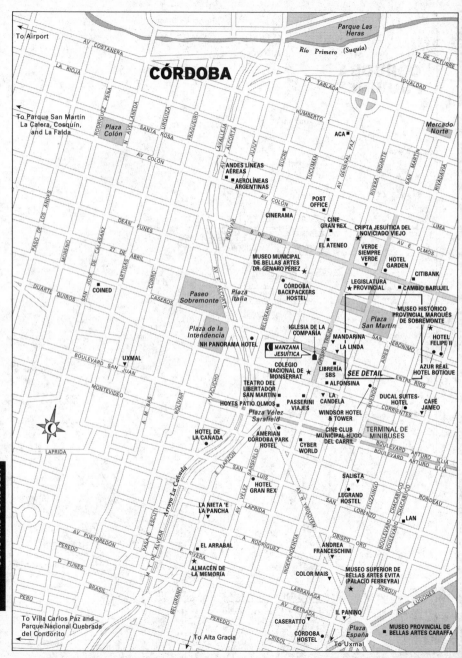

CÓRDOBA

Parque Las Heras

Río Primero (Suquía)

To Airport

AV COSTANERA

LA RIOJA

12 DE OCTUBRE

IGUALDAD

LA TABLADA

HUMBERTO I

To Parque San Martín La Calera, Cosquín, and La Falda

RODRIGUEZ PEÑA

N. AVELLANEDA

SANTA ROSA

URQUIZA

FRAGUEIRO

LAVALLEJA

ALCORTA

JUJUY

SUCRE

TUCUMÁN

AV GENERAL PAZ

RIVERA INDARTE

SAN MARTÍN

RIVADAVIA

Mercado Norte

Plaza Colón

AV COLÓN

ACA ■

AV COLÓN

ANDES LÍNEAS AÉREAS ■

■ AEROLÍNEAS ARGENTINAS

BOLÍVAR

8 DE JULIO

POST OFFICE ■

CINERAMA ■

CINE GRAN REX ■

EL ATENEO ■

LIMA

CRIPTA JESUÍTICA DEL NOVICIADO VIEJO

AV E OLMOS

CITIBANK ■

VERDE SIEMPRE VERDE ■

HOTEL GARDEN ■

PASEO DE LOS ANDES

DEAN FUNES

MORENO

27 DE ABRIL

SAN JOSÉ DE CALASANZ

ARTIGAS

CORRO

CASEROS

AV F. ALCORTA

BELGRANO

MUSEO MUNICIPAL DE BELLAS ARTES DR. GENARO PÉREZ ★

CÓRDOBA BACKPACKERS HOSTEL ■

LEGISLATURA ★ PROVINCIAL

■ CAMBIO BARUJEL

MUSEO HISTÓRICO PROVINCIAL MARQUÉS DE SOBREMONTE ★

DUARTE QUIRÓS

■ COINED

Paseo Sobremonte

Plaza Italia

Plaza de la Intendencia

IGLESIA DE LA COMPAÑÍA ■

OBISPO TREJO

Plaza San Martín

MANDARINA ■ LA LINDA

SAN JERÓNIMO

HOTEL FELIPE II ■

UXMAL ▼

NH PANORAMA HOTEL ■

☾ MANZANA JESUÍTICA ■

BUENOS AIRES

ENTRE RÍOS

AZUR REAL HOTEL BOTIQUE ■

SEE DETAIL

BOULEVARD SAN JUAN

AYACUCHO

BOLÍVAR

A. M. BAS

COLÉGIO NACIONAL DE MONSERRAT ★

LIBRERÍA SBS ■

▼ ALFONSINA

MONTEVIDEO

TEATRO DEL LIBERTADOR SAN MARTÍN ■

HOYTS PATIO OLMOS ■

PASSERINI VIAJES ■

▼ LA CANDELA

WINDSOR HOTEL & TOWER ■

DUCAL SUITES HOTEL ■

CORRIENTES

CAFÉ JAMEO ■

LAPRIDA

☾

HOTEL DE LA CAÑADA ■

Plaza Vélez Sarsfield

AMERIAN CÓRDOBA PARK HOTEL ■

CYBER WORLD ■

CINE CLUB MUNICIPAL HUGO DEL CARRIL ■

TERMINAL DE MINIBUSES

BOULEVARD ARTURO ILLIA

BOULEVARD ARTURO ILLIA

Arroyo La Cañada

E. GARZÓN

SAN

SARSFIELD

AV VÉLEZ

SALISTA ▼

TUCUZINGO

CHACABUCO

BOULEVARD CHACABUCO

RONDEAU

HOTEL GRAN REX ●

SAN LUIS

LAPRIDA

LEGRAND HOSTEL ■

SAN LORENZO

LAN ■

LA NIETA 'E LA PANCHA ▼

AV PUEYRREDÓN

PEREDO

D FUNES

PERÚ

M. T. DE ALVEAR

PASAJE ESCUTI

F. RIVERA

A. RODRIGUEZ

INDEPENDENCIA

EL ARRABAL ▼

ALMACÉN DE LA MEMORIA ★

COLOR MAIS ▼

ANDREA FRANCESCHINI ▼

OBISPO ORO

BOULEVARD CHACABUCO

MUSEO SUPERIOR DE BELLAS ARTES EVITA (PALACIO FERREYRA) ★

DERQUI

BRASIL

BELGRANO

PEREDO

LARRAÑAGA

AV ESTRADA

CASERATTO ▼

CRISOL

IL PANINO ▼

CÓRDOBA HOSTEL ●

Plaza España

AV L. LUGONES

MUSEO PROVINCIAL DE ■ BELLAS ARTES CARAFFA

To Villa Carlos Paz and Parque Nacional Quebrada del Condorito

To Alta Gracia

To Uxmal

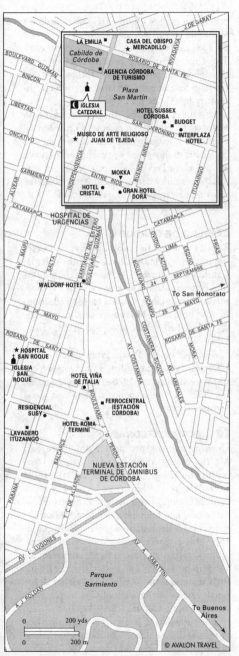

colonization, railroad expansion, and industrialization reinforced Buenos Aires's primacy and eclipsed Córdoba's conservatism. Ironically enough, the province's political revival started when student radicals and labor activists helped bring down General Juan Carlos Onganía's 1960s dictatorship in the so-called *cordobazo* uprising, which had repercussions throughout the country.

CÓRDOBA

Córdoba preserves the most impressive colonial remains of any large Argentine city, and that architectural heritage embodies its tradition as an educational and cultural center. Though much of the mid-1950s *microcentro* is insipidly utilitarian, and the area is nearly treeless, the creation of several pedestrian malls, the widening of sidewalks, and the restriction of automobile traffic are hopeful signs. Another encouraging development is the renascent Nueva Córdoba neighborhood, full of popular restaurants and bars, fronting on Parque Sarmiento's open spaces.

Orientation

Sprawling Córdoba (pop. about 1.4 million), 400 meters above sea level on the eastern piedmont of its namesake Sierras, is 701 kilometers northwest of Buenos Aires via RN 9, and about 400 kilometers northeast of San Luis via paved routes either over or around the Sierras de Córdoba. There are another 100,000 people in the metropolitan area.

The eastward-flowing Río Primero (or Suquía) meanders around downtown, whose Plaza San Martín is the heart of a compact area bounded by the northern Avenida Olmos, the eastern Avenida Chacabuco, the southern Bulevar Illia, and the western Avenida General Paz. Many businesses line the perpendicular pedestrian malls 25 de Mayo and Rivera Indarte to the northwest.

All these avenues have extensions that together form the *microcentro;* south of Bulevar Illia, fashionable Nueva Córdoba is less densely built, with many upgraded houses, restaurants and pubs, and Parque Sarmiento.

CUYO AND CÓRDOBA

Sights

On and around **Plaza San Martín**, Córdoba's compact center lends itself to walking. For US$13 pp, the **Servicio de Guías de Turismo** (Rosario de Santa Fe 39, tel. 0351/428-5600, guiasdecordoba@gmail.com) conducts two-hour city tours, including the city's Jesuit heritage, at 4:30 P.M. Tuesday–Sunday and at 9:30 A.M. Sunday and holidays, as well as a subterranean tour at 9:30 A.M. Tuesday–Friday; foreign-language tours cost US$5 more. Another option is a London bus excursion (US$3.50 pp) with **Córdoba City Tour** (Chacabuco 325, tel. 0351/424-6605, www.cordobacitytour.com.ar), leaving from the cathedral once or twice daily.

On the plaza's west side, the colonial **Cabildo de Córdoba** (Independencia 30) dates from 1775. Immediately south, several architects needed more than a century to complete the **Iglesia Catedral** (1758). On the north side, dating from 1700, the **Casa del Obispo Mercadillo** (Rosario de Santa Fe 39) was home to the bishop who transferred the episcopate from Tucumán to Córdoba, reinforcing Córdoba's religious primacy; note the baroque facade and forged-iron balcony.

Two blocks east, the **Museo Histórico Provincial Marqués de Sobremonte** (Rosario de Santa Fe 218) is the provincial history museum, in an 18th-century house distinguished by its balcony and corner pillar. One block farther east, dating from 1763, the **Hospital San Roque** (Rosario de Santa Fe and Salguero) stands alongside the better-preserved **Iglesia San Roque** (1764).

Half a block south of the plaza, the 18th-century **Iglesia de Santa Teresa y Convento de Carmelitas Descalzas de San José** houses the **Museo de Arte Religioso Juan de Tejeda** (Independencia 122, tel. 0351/570-2545, 9:30 A.M.–12:30 P.M. Wed.–Sat., US$2.50). One block west is the **Legislatura Provincial** (Provincial Legislature, Rivera Indarte and Rosario de Santa Fe).

Two blocks north, beneath Avenida Colón, neophyte priests studied at the **Cripta Jesuítica del Noviciado Viejo**. To the south, the pedestrian mall of Obispo Trejo was Córdoba's **Manzana Jesuítica**, also known as **Manzana de las Luces** (Block of Enlightenment). Together with other Jesuit establishments throughout the province, it's a UNESCO World Heritage Site; its standout landmark is the 17th-century **Iglesia de La Compañía**.

In Nueva Córdoba, the **Almacén de la Memoria** (Rivera 287) is a former general store recycled as a space for young (and talented) provincial artists to show their work. Popularly known as the Casa de Pepino for its original owner, José Tucci, its quirky corner balcony resembles the prow of a steamship. Hours are 9 A.M.–7 P.M. Tuesday–Sunday; admission is free.

CABILDO DE CÓRDOBA

Replacing an earlier building that had deteriorated over a century and a half, the colonial Cabildo dates from 1775. Its outstanding feature is the ground-floor gallery, with 15 graceful arches; the clock tower is an 1885 addition. It now holds the **Museo de la Ciudad** (tel. 0351/434-1202, 10 A.M.–7 P.M. Tues.–Sun., US$0.50).

A plaque on the Pasaje Santa Catalina side acknowledges the building's unsavory recent history—during the 1976–1983 dictatorship, the "D2" provincial police station here was a torture center.

◖ IGLESIA CATEDRAL

Dominating the prospect from Plaza San Martín, one of Argentina's few notable 17th-century buildings, Córdoba's cathedral was the work of several architects, most notably Jesuit Andrés Blanqui (who designed the neoclassical facade) and Franciscan Vicente Muñoz (responsible for the Romanesque dome). Begun in 1677, this extended project resulted in contradictory styles—the towers were the work of an anonymous architect and postdated the building's inauguration in 1758. The richly decorated interior is the work of Catamarca-born painter Emilio Caraffa (1863–1939).

The cathedral is also the final resting place of several distinguished Cordobeses, including priest-politician Gregorio Funes (1749–1829), a key independence figure, and General José María Paz (1791–1854), whose career spanned the wars of independence and the civil wars against Rosas. The most offbeat presence is the literally heartless Fray Mamerto Esquiú (1826–1883)—following his sudden death and an autopsy, the Franciscan bishop left his heart in his Catamarca birthplace (where the pickled-in-alcohol organ was on display in the order's landmark church before being stolen a few years ago).

MUSEO HISTÓRICO PROVINCIAL MARQUÉS DE SOBREMONTE

With its corner pillar, flanked by separate entrances on perpendicular streets and a balcony that looks onto both, the residence of colonial governor (later viceroy) Rafael Núñez adds a touch of architectural distinction. Ecclesiastical artwork, musical instruments, gaucho gear, and elaborate furniture fill its 26 rooms and five courtyards, but the lack of interpretation means that the building is the real star here.

The Museo Histórico Provincial Marqués de Sobremonte (Rosario de Santa Fe 218, tel. 0351/433-1661, US$0.50) is open 8:30 A.M.–2 P.M. weekdays only.

◖ MANZANA JESUÍTICA

Córdoba owes much of its intellectual heritage to the Jesuits, whose Belgian architect Philippe Lemaire solved the problem of roofing the **Iglesia de La Compañía** (Obispo Trejos and Caseros) by adapting shipbuilding techniques from French architect Philibert de l'Orme. Cedar beams, imported from the Paraguayan missions, sit atop the austere stone walls—more than 1.5 meters thick—while solid wooden doors provide access to the elaborately carved baroque altarpiece.

Immediately south, the **Rectorado de la Universidad Nacional de Córdoba** (Obispo Trejo 242) is a direct descendent of the Seminario Convictorio de San Javier, the continent's second university (the first was in Lima, Perú). The walls and vaults date from Jesuit times, but the rest of the building has undergone tasteful modification over the centuries. Immediately south, dating from 1782,

the Spanish Renaissance **Colegio Nacional de Monserrat** (Obispo Trejo 294) is a prestigious high school whose alumni include three Argentine presidents.

CRIPTA JESUÍTICA DEL NOVICIADO VIEJO

Uncovered in 1989, this subterranean Jesuit chapel dates from the early 18th century, when it was part of a more extravagant project terminated on orders from Rome. After the Jesuits' 1767 expulsion, the Bethlemites used it as a hospital, but soon abandoned it for Hospital San Roque. It was later used for burials, but the creation of Avenida Colón in the 1920s filled it with rubble.

Thick but unfinished stone walls separate its three naves. In its restored state, it hosts exhibits, small theater presentations, and concerts. The Cripta Jesuítica (Rivera Indarte and Avenida Colón, tel. 0351/428-4500, cryptaje-suitica@hotmail.com, US$0.50) is open 10 A.M.–3 P.M. weekdays only.

MUSEO MUNICIPAL DE BELLAS ARTES DR. GENARO PÉREZ

Focusing on Argentine art, with paintings by 20th-century figures like Antonio Berni, Juan Carlos Castagnino, Benito Quinquela Martín, Lino Spilimbergo, and Raúl Soldi, the municipal fine arts museum also includes illustrations, engravings, and sculptures among its 800-plus works. Built in 1905 for then vicegovernor (later governor) Félix Garzón, the building has a Louis XVI facade and a sweeping ceremonial staircase; details by Catamarca-born Emilio Caraffa adorn the rooms. Don't overlook the modern patio sculptures around the corner from the main entrance.

The Museo de Bellas Artes (Avenida General Paz 33, tel. 0351/428-5905, museo-genaroperez@cordoba.gov.ar, free) is open 10 A.M.–8 P.M. Tuesday–Sunday.

MUSEO SUPERIOR DE BELLAS ARTES EVITA (PALACIO FERREYRA)

New in 2007, Córdoba's provincial fine arts museum focuses on local artists in landscape, portraiture, and modern art, including abstract and neo-figurative art. Parts of the latter exhibitions were sponsored by Kaiser Argentina, which located a plant here in the mid-1950s after Oakland-based Henry Kaiser of California. The beaux arts building itself is a gem, dating from 1916, and so are its collections. Famed landscape architect Charles Thays designed the gardens.

The Museo Superior de Bellas Artes Evita (Hipólito Yrigoyen 511, tel. 0351/434-3629, 10 A.M.–8 P.M. Tues.–Sun., US$0.75, free Wed.) has four guided tours in Spanish and one in English at noon Tuesday–Friday.

MUSEO PROVINCIAL DE BELLAS ARTES CARAFFA

Yet another provincial fine arts museum, the Caraffa dates from 1911 but has undergone a major expansion and modernization to become a multilevel state-of-the-art facility showcasing contemporary Argentine artists along with well-established figures.

The Museo Caraffa (Poeta Lugones 411, tel. 0351/433-3414, www.museocaraffa. org.ar, US$0.75) is open 10 A.M.–8 P.M. Tuesday–Sunday.

Entertainment and Events

July 6 is **Fundación de la Ciudad,** the anniversary of Córdoba's 1572 founding. From early to mid-September, the **Feria del Libro** reinforces the city's intellectual history and status as a regional publishing center.

Theater and Music: Córdoba's primary high-culture performing arts center is the **Teatro del Libertador San Martín** (Avenida Vélez Sarsfield 365, tel. 0351/433-2320, www. teatrodellibertador.com).

Cinema: Commercial cinemas include the multiscreen **Hoyts Patio Olmos** (Avenida Vélez Sarsfield 361, tel. 0351/446-2444), **Cine Gran Rex** (Avenida General Paz 174, tel. 0351/424-8709), and the three-screen **Cinerama** (Avenida Colón 345, tel. 0351/422-0866). The **Cine Club Municipal Hugo del**

Córdoba's Museo Caraffa has undergone a major expansion and modernization to display contemporary Argentine art, including special exhibitions.

© WAYNE BERNHARDSON

Carril (Bulevar San Juan 49, tel. 0351/433-2463, www.cineclubmunicipal.org.ar), which reprises older films, occupies the Sociedad Italiana's former headquarters.

Nightlife: Most but not all of the bar scene is in and around the Nueva Córdoba area. There are exceptions, though, like El Ateneo's literary wine bar **La Imprenta** (Avenida General Paz 156, tel. 0351/428-4371, www.cafeyletras.com.ar), and the less pretentious, highly popular **Alfonsina** (Duarte Quirós 66, 0351/427-2847), which is also a good spot for simple regional cuisine.

El Arrabal (Belgrano 899, tel. 0351/460-2990, www.elarrabal.com.ar) showcases tango in a nightclub ambience with a long wooden bar and a small elevated stage. There's a live orchestra Thursday, Friday, and Saturday nights, followed by a participatory *milonga* (which also takes place, following classes, every night except Sunday). It's also a pretty good place for lunch or dinner, with a diverse regional menu, moderate prices, and exceptional service.

Shopping

For leather goods and other souvenirs, try **La Emilia** (Deán Funes 18, tel. 0351/423-8402) or **Regionales La Fama** (9 de Julio 336, tel. 0351/422-8354), whose specialty is woolens.

El Ateneo (General Paz 156, tel. 0351/423-4718) is a branch of Buenos Aires's outstanding bookstore. **Librería SBS** (Caseros 79, tel. 0351/423-6448) sells English-language books.

Sports and Recreation

Hiking and climbing in the nearby Sierras are popular with locals. The **Club Andino de Córdoba** (7 de Abril 2050, tel. 0351/480-5126, www.clubandinocordoba.com.ar) is the best information source.

Accommodations

Córdoba has abundant accommodations ranging from hostels and simple *hospedajes* to five-star hotels, with good values in all categories. At peak seasons, like Semana Santa and winter holidays, reservations are advisable.

US$10–25: The best nonhostel shoestring selection is frills-free but friendly **Residencial Susy** (Entre Ríos 528, tel. 0351/421-0819, US$16 s, US$24 d).

In a sprawling but worn Nueva Córdoba house with a secluded shady garden, the HI-affiliate **Córdoba Hostel** (Ituzaingó 1070, tel. 0351/468-7359, www.cordobahostel.com.ar, US$8–10 pp dorm, US$13–15 s, US$23–27 d, plus US$1 with breakfast) has amenities including kitchen and laundry facilities, lockers, Internet access, and a barbecue. Guests must pay a small extra charge for towels, however.

The **Córdoba Backpackers Hostel** (Deán Funes 285, tel. 0351/422-0593, www.cordobabackpackers.com.ar, US$8–13 pp dorm, US$26–32 s or d) is also an HI affiliate. It is comparable to Córdoba Hostel but more centrally located. **Hotel Roma Termini** (Entre Ríos 687, tel. 0351/421-8721, US$15 s, US$23 d, with private bath but without breakfast) is adequate.

In a neighborhood full of bars, it's nevertheless surprisingly easy to sleep at **Hostel Le Grand** (Buenos Aires 547, tel. 0351/422-7115, www.legrandhostel.com, US$9–15 pp dorm, US$30–32 s or d), a large hostel with big rooms, some painted with multicolored murals, and excellent private baths (though some dorms have shared baths). There's a big central patio for socializing and barbecues, and Wi-Fi reaches the rooms, but the breakfast is forgettable, some staff are clueless, and a couple are surly.

US$25-50: By current standards, Nueva Córdoba's **Hotel Gran Rex** (Avenida Vélez Sarsfield 601, tel. 0351/423-8659, www.granrexhotel.com.ar, US$21 s, US$32 d, with breakfast) is an excellent value for its location and simple amenities such as cable TV and air-conditioning (US$3 extra).

On the pedestrian mall a block north of Plaza San Martín, improved **Hotel Garden** (25 de Mayo 35, tel. 0351/421-4729, US$25–36 s, US$29–40 d) has rooms with private baths and TVs and some rooms with air-conditioning.

In an upgraded deco-style building near the old railroad station, friendly **Hotel Viña**

de Italia (San Jerónimo 611, tel. 0351/422-6589, www.hotelvinadeitalia.com.ar, US$29 s, US$41 d) has decent but smallish rooms with oddly decorative balconies (only windows, not doors, provide access). Its restaurant includes a wine bar.

US$50-100: Well-worn but also well-kept—some original wallpaper survives in surprisingly good shape—the deco-style **Waldorf Hotel** (Avenida Olmos 513, tel./fax 0351/422-8051, www.waldorfhotelcba.com.ar, US$40 s, US$55 d) has some rooms with balconies. They are also surprisingly spacious.

Hotel Felipe II (San Jerónimo 279, tel. 0351/425-5500, www.hotelfelipe.com.ar, US$52 s, US$66 d) is a popular three-star choice, though the common areas are more appealing than the retro-style rooms.

Half a block from Plaza San Martín, west-facing upper floors at the 110-room **Hotel Sussex Córdoba** (San Jerónimo 125, tel. 0351/422-9070, www.hotelsussexcba.com.ar, US$52 s, US$66 d) have the best views of any hotel in town. Its shadowy lobby is a misleading approach to a well-maintained, if aging, 1950s building.

A block south of Plaza San Martín, **Hotel Cristal** (Entre Ríos 56, tel. 0351/424-5000, www.hotelcristal.com.ar, US$38 s, US$49 d, with buffet breakfast) has fairly small but otherwise acceptable rooms. The single beds, though, are narrow.

Though the standard rooms are a bit cluttered, **Gran Hotel Dorá** (Entre Ríos 70, tel. 0351/421-2031, www.hoteldora.com, US$80 s, US$86 d, with buffet breakfast) is still a decent option. Executive rooms, which have terraces, are far more spacious.

West of downtown, **Hotel de la Cañada** (Marcelo T. de Alvear 580, tel. 0351/421-4649, www.hoteldelacaniada.com.ar, US$62-70 s, US$78-90 d, with breakfast) projects a progressive stylishness in materials—wood and brick—that's lacking in most other Córdoba hotels. There's a pool, a sauna, and other amenities.

Rooms at the professionally run **Ducal Suites-Hotel** (Corrientes 207, tel. 0351/570-8888, www.hotelducal.com.ar, US$67-83 s,

US$83-102 d, with breakfast) are spacious and good. As it's primarily business-oriented, management discounts prices by about 20 percent on weekends.

Over US$100: The Spanish-chain affiliate (**◖ NH Panorama Hotel** (Marcelo T. de Alvear 251, tel. 0351/420-4000, nhpanorama@nh-hotels.com, US$101 s, US$119 d) has contemporary rooms with buffet breakfast and access to amenities like the pool, gym, and sauna. There are also more elaborate suites at higher prices.

The **Windsor Hotel & Tower** (Buenos Aires 214, tel./fax 0351/422-4012, www.windsor-tower.com, US$120-136 s or d) has adequate standard rooms in its older hotel sector, but the king-size beds in the more ample and comfortable 1998 addition are worth the additional cost. Guests in both sectors get the buffet breakfast and use of the pool, sauna, and gym.

The business-oriented **Amerian Córdoba Park Hotel** (Bulevar San Juan 165, tel. 0351/420-7000, www.amerian.com, US$132-150 s or d) is a full-service hotel with pool, sauna, gym, and buffet breakfast.

Rates at the **◖ Interplaza Hotel** (San Jerónimo 137, tel. 0351/426-9800, www.corplaza.com, US$120 s, US$165 d) are an outstanding value for a five-star facility, but multinight discounts are an even better deal. Included are breakfast buffet, pool, gym, and similar amenities.

Córdoba's first boutique hotel, the recycled **◖ Azur Real Hotel Boutique** (San Jerónimo 243/257, tel. 0351/424-7133, www.azurrealhotel.com, US$169-254 s or d) was once a dormitory annex of the Colegio Dean Funes: Che Guevara literally slept here when he was not commuting from nearby Alta Gracia. The spacious interior rooms are virtually silent, but the smaller standard rooms facing the street get some noise despite the double glazing.

Food

For cheap eats, especially at lunchtime, try the empanadas and pizza at the municipal **Mercado Norte** (La Tablada and San Martín), a 1927 landmark that's also a lively wholesale and

ESTANCIA LA PAZ

Many hotels claim, at least figuratively, to treat you like a king. Few claim to treat you like a president, but Estancia La Paz, near the village of Ascochinga about 45 minutes north of the provincial capital, is one of them.

Estancia La Paz once belonged to Julio Argentino Roca, the military man responsible for the so-called Conquista del Desierto (Conquest of the Desert) that drove southern Buenos Aires Province's native population into Patagonia in the late 19th century. Roca also served two terms as Argentina's president, and Estancia La Paz was where he went to get away from it all.

No longer in the Roca family, the former *casco* (big house, dating from 1830) is now a 20-room hotel on sprawling grounds that include an artificial lake (which attracts many birds), polo grounds, a stable (for nonpolo riders as well), a spa, and a fine restaurant that's open to nonguests by reservation. In 1994 the Alvears, descendents of the Rocas, sold it to Italian interests who neglected the *casco* and sold off many of the original furnishings. The Scarafia family of Córdoba, who purchased it in 1998, have managed to assemble a credible collection of antique furnishings that at least recreate the feeling of Roca's heyday.

In addition to the *estancia*, local attractions include the nearby Sierras, where hiking and other outdoor activities are possible, and the Jesuit monuments near the town of Jesús María (which is home to January's Festival de Doma y Folklore, a nationally televised festival where gauchos engage in bronco-busting and the country's top folk musicians play).

For all this, Estancia La Paz (RP E-66 Km 14, tel. 03525/49-2073, www.estancialapaz. com, US$130 pp) is surprisingly affordable for bed and breakfast, with lunch or dinner for about US$20 (with a sophisticated menu that changes daily). Roca's "Camp David" comes cheap, at least for anyone with frustrated presidential ambitions.

---

retail grocery market. For coffee and snacks, try **Café Jameo** (Avenida Chacabuco 294), **Mokka** (Entre Ríos 85), or **Il Panino** (Hipólito Yrigoyen 584), which also has reliable Wi-Fi.

In the university district, **Mandarina** (Obispo Trejo 171, tel. 0351/426-4909) is a student hangout for fixed-price lunches. Downtown's **Verde Siempre Verde** (9 de Julio 36, tel. 0351/421-8820) has over a decade's credibility in vegetarian cuisine. Nueva Córdoba's **Salsita** (Rondeau 124, tel. 0351/422-0366) serves pizza and especially choice empanadas at bargain prices.

For regional versions of empanadas and *locro*, there's nothing better than **La Candela** (Duarte Quirós 69, tel. 0351/428-1517). It gets loud and crowded, though, and its informality has a cost: The motto is "he who knows how to eat knows how to wait." Either that reflects its philosophy of service, the kitchen's failure to work on several dishes simultaneously, or the staff's inability to walk and wait tables at the same time.

La Linda (Caseros 84, tel. 0351/429-0045, www.lalindarestaurant.com, US$5–20) serves genuinely spicy *salteña*-style beef empanadas, with a variety of other flavors and regional dishes that include tamales (resembling their Mexican counterparts) and *humitas*, plus a variety of more standard Argentine dishes including beef and pasta. The service is exceptional and welcoming.

In the gentrifying Barrio General Paz, a few blocks east of the river via the Olmos bridge, **San Honorato** (25 de Mayo and Pringles, tel. 0351/453-5252, www.sanhonorato.com.ar, US$10–20) is a Spanish tapas restaurant named for the patron saint of bakers, as it occupies a recycled bakery. One of its highlights is the wine cellar, where patrons can sample (free of charge) the wines they might like to have with their lunch or dinner as they snack on bread, cold cuts, and vegetables.

Genuine Mexican food is hard to find in Buenos Aires, let alone the provinces, but Mexican-run **Uxmal** (Bulevar San Juan 700, tel. 0351/426-5649) has been an exception.

Primarily producing *antojitos* (short orders) such as green enchiladas (US$5), it offers options far spicier than the average Argentine palate can handle, but its recent sale to local ownership is cause for at least a little skepticism.

Nueva Córdoba's **La Nieta 'e la Pancha** (Belgrano 783, tel. 0351/468-1920) produces regional versions of empanadas (sweetish but slightly spicy), lamb stew, pork chops, and pastas, with most entrées around US$7–8. The service can be erratic, though, and folkloric music would be more appropriate than symphonic versions of Queen's greatest hits.

Good for a relaxed or romantic dinner, **Color Mais** (Hipólito Yrigoyen 464, tel. 0351/468-4628, colormais@gmail.com) has river fish such as surubí (Paraná catfish) with sautéed vegetables (US$10), good wines by the glass (US$2.50), good service, and a kitchen willing to correct mistakes.

Also in Nueva Córdoba, **Caseratto** (Buenos Aires 1001, tel. 0351/468-2060) has good ice cream, but **Andrea Franceschini** (Hipólito Yrigoyen 413, tel. 0351/469-1118) has taken it a step further.

Information

The quantity and quality of information available varies, but on balance it's below average.

In the colonial Cabildo, staff at the municipal **Dirección de Turismo de la Ciudad de Córdoba** (tel. 0351/434-1200, munturis@cordoba.gov.ar, www.cordoba.gov.ar, 8 A.M.–8 P.M. daily) do the minimum necessary. The bus terminal branch (Bulevar Perón 380, tel. 0351/433-1982, 7 A.M.–9 P.M. daily) is most useful for hotel information. The airport branch (Camino Pajas Blancas Km 11, tel. 0351/434-8390) is open 8 A.M.–8 P.M. weekdays.

For motorists, **ACA** (tel. 0351/421-4713) is at Avenida General Paz 499.

Services

Citibank (Rivadavia 104) has one of many downtown ATMs. Nearby **Cambio Barujel** (Rivadavia 97) changes travelers checks.

Correo Argentino (Avenida Colón 210) is the post office.

Locutorios are numerous, including a **Telecentro** at the bus terminal. **Cyber World** (Obispo Trejos 443) keeps long hours for Internet access, but there are many others.

The student- and budget-oriented travel agency **Asatej** is in Shopping Patio Olmos (Avenida Vélez Sarsfield 361, Local 349, tel./fax 0351/422-9453). The Amex rep is **Passerini Viajes** (Obispo Trejo 324, tel. 0351/422-6269).

The highly regarded language school **Coined** (Caseros 873, tel. 0351/422-6260, www.coined.com.ar) operates a branch here.

For clean clothes, try **Lavadero Ituzaingó** (Paraná 290).

The **Hospital de Urgencias** is at Catamarca 441 (tel. 0351/427-6200).

Getting There

Córdoba has better air connections than any other Argentine city but Buenos Aires, extensive bus services, and limited rail service.

Air: Aerolíneas Argentinas (Avenida Colón 520, tel. 0351/410-7676) flies frequently to Buenos Aires's Aeroparque, twice daily to Mendoza, and less frequently to Tucumán, Salta, Jujuy, Puerto Iguazú, and Bariloche.

LAN (San Lorenzo 309, tel. 0351/425-3030) flies daily to Santiago, Chile, while **Gol** (tel. 0351/475-3027 at the airport only) flies to Brazilian destinations.

Andes Líneas Aéreas (Avenida Colón 532, tel. 351/426-5809) now flies Monday and Friday to Salta and Puerto Iguazú, making it possible to visit the Andean northwest and the famous falls without backtracking to Buenos Aires.

Sol Líneas Aéreas (tel. 0810/444-4765, www.sol.com.ar) is a budget carrier serving Rosario and Punta del Este (Uruguay).

Bus: Facilities at the **Nueva Estación Terminal de Ómnibus de Córdoba** (NETOC, Bulevar Perón 300, tel. 0351/423-4199, www.terminalcordoba.com) include a tourist information office, ATMs, restaurants, newsstands, toilets, and hot showers as well as postal, telephone, and Internet services. Since Córdoba is a hub for overland travel throughout the country, it has dozens of bus companies traveling just about everywhere, and even some international connections.

Sample destinations, times, and fares include Catamarca (5.5 hours, US$19), Santa Fe (5 hours, US$17), Rosario (6 hours, US$20), Tucumán (8 hours, US$28), Salta (11 hours, US$42–48), Buenos Aires (9 hours, US$27–40), Mendoza (9 hours, US$37), Posadas (16 hours, US$62–70), Puerto Iguazú (21 hours, US$78–82), and Bariloche (21 hours, US$82).

For provincial destinations like Alta Gracia, Jesús María, Cosquín, La Falda, and Mina Clavero, there are frequent services from the **Terminal de Minibuses** at the Mercado Sud, on Bulevar Illia between Buenos Aires and Ituzaingó; buses park in a passageway on the market's north side.

Train: Opposite the bus station, **Ferrocentral** (Bulevar Perón 101, tel. 0351/426-3565, www.ferrocentralsa.com.ar) goes to Retiro (Buenos Aires) at 9:13 P.M. Wednesday and 4:21 P.M. Sunday from Estación Córdoba, on the former Mitre line. The trip takes 14.5 hours and costs US$8–24 pp, depending on the class of travel, with *camarote* sleepers for US$79 d.

Getting Around

Popularly known as "Pajas Blancas," **Aeropuerto Internacional Ingeniero A. L. Taravella** (Avenida La Voz del Interior 8500, tel. 0351/475-0874) is about 11 kilometers north of town via RP 38. The A5 city bus goes directly to the airport from the NETOC terminal, but a *remise* costs only about US$6–7.

City buses require *cospeles* (tokens), available for US$0.40 from kiosks, or rechargeable magnetic cards.

Localiza (Entre Ríos 70, tel. 0351/422-4867), in an office alongside Gran Hotel Dorá, rents cars.

VICINITY OF CÓRDOBA

From downtown Córdoba, Avenida Colón leads northwest to **La Calera,** one of the city's closest getaways. It's most notable for its restored early-18th-century **Capilla Jesuítica** (Jesuit chapel); rubble from other Jesuit constructions surrounds the site. It's also noteworthy for the roadside stands selling *salame casero* (homemade salami) and fresh bread. The road continues west to Lago San Roque, an alternative route to Villa Carlos Paz.

In a secluded wooded canyon at the foot of the Sierra Chica, about 40 kilometers northwest of Córdoba via the hamlet of El Manzano, the **Capilla del Rosario de Candonga** is a Jesuit chapel dating from 1730. With its rounded archway entrance and red-tiled roof, it remains an 18th-century vision, surrounded by ruined walls and foundations of the Jesuit Estancia Santa Gertrudis.

Some 48 kilometers north of the capital via RN 9, the former *estancia*—now a small city—of Jesús María is the site of the **Museo Jesuítico Nacional de Jesús María** (Pedro de Oñate s/n, tel. 03525/42-0126, 8 A.M.–7 P.M. Tues.–Fri., 10 A.M.–noon and 3–7 P.M. Sat.–Sun., US$1.25), the church and convent of an enterprise whose vineyards, orchards, and pastures helped the Jesuits finance their other activities. On nine hectares of beautifully landscaped grounds, the museum holds collections of Comechingones archaeology and colonial art.

Five kilometers north of Jesús María, independence figures such as Manuel Belgrano and Juan Lavalle slept at the **Museo de la Posta Rural de Sinsacate** (Camino Real s/n, tel. 03525/40-2240, postadesinsacate@gmail.com, 2:30–7 P.M. Tues.–Fri., 3–7 P.M. Sat.–Sun., US$1), a post house on the colonial route between Alto Perú and Córdoba. Its most famous visitor, though, may have been caudillo Facundo Quiroga, whose wake took place here after his 1835 assassination.

SIERRAS DE CÓRDOBA

Between the Andes and the pampas, the Sierras de Córdoba comprise several parallel mountain ranges, including the Sierras Chicas immediately west of the capital and the higher Sierra de Comechingones toward San Luis, separated by longitudinal valleys. Most Argentine visitors flock to Villa Carlos Paz, a middle-class casinos-and-discos resort, but the region's real pleasures are historic hill towns like Alta Gracia (boy-hood home of revolutionary icon Ernesto "Che" Guevara) and La Falda, and the backcountry of Parque Nacional Quebrada del Condorito.

January, February, Semana Santa, and July are the peak seasons, but weekends are always busy. Because the Sierras do not exceed 2,800 meters, most of the high country is accessible even in midwinter, and the dense road system makes it a cycling favorite. The roads, how-ever, are narrow, and the many unpaved sur-faces make a mountain bike desirable.

Alta Gracia

On the Sierra Chica's gentle western slopes, Alta Gracia was a major Jesuit *estancia* that became a town, and the place where Che Guevara's parents relocated to relieve their son's chronic asthma. Jesuit monuments in excellent repair grace the main plaza, and the historic Hotel Sierras, once *the* destination of choice for the socially prominent from around the coun-try, has reopened as a casino.

Alta Gracia was also the residence of Viceroy Santiago Liniers, a resistance hero during the British invasions of Buenos Aires whose royalist convictions led to his execution during the inde-pendence wars, and Spanish composer Manuel de Falla, who fled the Franco dictatorship after the Spanish Civil War. It's an easy day trip from the capital, but worth an overnight.

Only 35 kilometers southwest of Córdoba via paved RP 5, Alta Gracia (pop. about 50,000) has a compact center based on Plaza Manuel Solares. The northwestern road over the Sierra Chica offers an alternative route to Villa Carlos Paz and the high country to the west.

Sights: Overlooking Plaza Solares, Alta Gracia's Jesuit monuments are the main rea-son to visit. Finished only five years before the Jesuits' expulsion, the **Iglesia Parroquial Nuestra Señora de la Merced** stands along-side the **Museo de la Estancia Jesuítica de Alta Gracia** (tel. 03547/42-1303, www.mu-seoliniers.org.ar, US$1.25). Also known as the Casa del Virrey Liniers because the vice-roy resided here for a few months in 1810, it has 17 permanent exhibit rooms on topics

ranging from Comechingones ethnology to daily provincial life and customs. Hours are 9 A.M.–8 P.M. Tuesday–Friday, 9:30 A.M.–8 P.M. weekends and holidays in summer; the rest of the year, it's open 9 A.M.–1 P.M. and 3–7 P.M. Tuesday–Friday, 9:30 A.M.–12:30 P.M. and 3:30–6:30 P.M. weekends and holidays.

Other Jesuit constructions flank the church and museum: To the south, the workshops known as **El Obraje** (1643) survive as a public school; to the north, the **Tajamar** (1659) diked a field to create a reservoir for irrigating their vineyards and orchards. It's now a city park.

Several blocks northwest, the Guevaras frequented the recently restored **Sierras Hotel** (Avenida Vélez Sarsfield 198), though their diminished economic standing under-cut their social position. Spanish composer Manuel de Falla lived seven years in the house known as **Chalet Los Espinillos,** now home to **Museo Manuel de Falla** (Avenida Pellegrini 1011, tel. 03547/42-1592, US$0.50, free Wed.). It still contains the composer's Eavestaff mini-piano and other personal items. Summer hours are 9 A.M.–8 P.M. Monday–Friday, 9 A.M.–7 P.M. weekends; the rest of the year 9 A.M.–7 P.M. Monday–Friday, 9 A.M.–6 P.M. weekends.

Immediately opposite Falla's house, Che fre-quented the **Club de Golf,** acquiring a taste for the game that lasted into his Cuban years. His family moved from house to rented house, but their principal residence was **Villa Nydia** (also known as Villa Beatriz), a solid, spacious, middle-class residence—despite financial set-backs, the Guevaras were not poor.

Villa Nydia is now home to **Museo Ernesto Che Guevara,** a memorial to Che's Alta Gracia period, which gained enormous publicity when Fidel Castro and Hugo Chávez made a joint visit in 2006. While it does a good job of re-constructing Che's boyhood—through a pho-tographic history of Ernesto and his family in Alta Gracia society, his school report cards, and memories by his classmates, cook Rosario González, and others—it doesn't really place it in any greater context. This may not be the place for a full biography, but from its contents, one would hardly know that Che was a controversial figure, nor have any idea why it was converted into a museum, nor why so many neighbors opposed the conversion—nor even why Castro and Chávez visited in 2006.

Exhibits in the museum include a video of interviews of Che's neighbors and boyhood friends, with imperfect but useful English subtitles. There are also a bicycle and a motorcycle of the same models that the youthful Che used in his trips around South America. The museum has recently added a light-and-sound show (US$2.50) at 8:30 P.M. Thursday–Sunday.

In summer, the Museo Ernesto Che Guevara (Avellaneda 501, tel. 03547/42-8579, museochealtagracia@hotmail.com, US$1.25, free Wed.) is open 9 A.M.–8 P.M. weekdays, 9:30 A.M.–8 P.M. weekends and holidays. The rest of the year, hours are 9 A.M.–7 P.M. weekdays, 9:30 A.M.–7 P.M. weekends and holidays.

Accommodations and Food: The only one of its kind in town, friendly **Alta Gracia Hostel** (Paraguay 218, tel. 03547/42-8810, www.altagraciahostel.com.ar, US$10–11 pp dorm, with breakfast) is a cozy, immaculate facility with eighteen bunks and individual lockers in three rooms with private baths. Rates include kitchen access, but towels cost US$1 extra.

Hostería Asturias (Vélez Sarsfield 147, tel. 03547/42-3668, US$21 s, US$29 d, with private bath) occupies a handsome building dating from Argentina's railroad heyday. More utilitarian in style, **Hotel Covadonga** (Presidente Quintana 285, tel. 03547/42-3456, hospedaje_covadonga@hotmail.com, US$36 d) is comfortable enough.

Immediately west of the plaza, **Apart Hotel La Posada** (Avenida Padre Viera 95, tel. 03547/42-2809, www.laposadaaparthotel.com.ar, US$55 s or d) has huge comfortable rooms. To live like the Guevaras's social set, though, you'll have to stay at the renovated **Sierras Hotel Casino** (Vélez Sarsfield 198, tel. 03547/43-1200, reservasag@cetsa.com.ar, US$130 s or d, with promotional rates for longer stays). Its otherwise stylish restaurant offers a fairly conservative but moderately priced Argentine menu.

On the south side of Plaza Solares, **Trattoria Oro** (España 18, tel. 03547/42-5619) has a diverse menu focused on regional dishes. In a comfortable colonial-style house with beamed ceilings and porticos, **Morena** (Avenida Sarmiento 413, tel. 03547/42-6365) serves "contemporary Argentine food" that takes some chances, such as their black ravioli stuffed with a shrimp mousse (US$8). The kitchen is quick, the service attentive, and the bread homemade.

La Merced (Belgrano 45) has fine ice cream.

Information and Services: The municipal **Secretaría de Turismo** (Avenida del Tajamar 1, tel. 03547/42-8128, www.altagracia.gov.ar) is on the ground floor of the Reloj Público, the clock tower at the northwest corner of Plaza Manuel Solares. It's normally open 7 A.M.–9 P.M. daily, but may keep even longer hours in summer, winter holidays, and on long weekends.

Banco de Córdoba (Belgrano and Lozada) has an ATM.

Correo Argentino is at Avenida Libertador 577; the postal code is 5186. **Stuttgart Cyber** (Belgrano 137) has telephone and Internet services.

Getting There and Around: The new long-distance **Terminal de Ómnibus** (Butori and Costanera) has direct service to Buenos Aires (11 hours, US$36–57). Opposite Plaza Solares, **Sarmiento Diferencial de Pasajeros** (Belgrano 71, tel. 03547/42-6001) goes to Córdoba every 15 minutes or so and operates 6–8 buses daily to Villa Carlos Paz.

Estación Astrofísica de Bosque Alegre

Midway between Alta Gracia and Villa Carlos Paz via a winding mountain road, protruding above the pines on a 1,250-meter hilltop, the Estación Astrofísica de Bosque Alegre is one of the main resources for Argentina's small community of about 100 professional astronomers. Begun in 1928 but not opened until 1942, the observatory building measures 20 meters in diameter and 25 meters in height.

Within, it rotates a Pittsburgh-built 60-inch, 28-ton Warner & Swasey reflector telescope that dates from 1922; the instrument itself has undergone continual upgrades to the latest electronic instrumentation. Part of the provincial capital's **Observatorio Astronómico de Córdoba** (Laprida 854, tel. 0351/433-1064, www.oac.uncor.edu, US$1.25), the Bosque Alegre facility is open for grad student–guided tours 10 A.M.–1 P.M. and 4–7 P.M. daily in summer, during Semana Santa and July winter holidays, and on three-day weekends. The rest of the year, hours are 10 A.M.–1 P.M. and 3–6 P.M. daily.

Villa Carlos Paz

Half a century ago, Villa Carlos Paz was a bucolic hill town in the Sierra Chica at the outlet of the Río Suquía. Development around sailboat-studded Lago San Roque—the result of a dam project originally built to store drinking water for the provincial capital in the 1890s—made it a summer madhouse for tourists from all over Argentina, as well as a popular weekend destination for Cordobeses.

More recently, a four-lane toll road has turned it into a bedroom community for capital commuters. Packed with upwards of 10,000 hotel beds, receiving 850,000 visitors per year, it has become a small-scale freshwater Mar del Plata—but without the cultural resources of Argentina's premier beach resort.

Crawling up and down the south arm of Lago San Roque, 640 meters above sea level, fast-growing Carlos Paz (pop. about 70,000) is 36 kilometers west of Córdoba via four-lane RN 20. Two-lane RN 38 continues north to the resorts of Cosquín and La Falda, while RN 20 continues southwest past Parque Nacional Quebrada del Condorito to Mina Clavero and San Luis Province.

Sights: Carlos Paz looks better at a distance, from the 953-meter summit of **Cerro de la Cruz,** reached by footpath or chairlift from the **Complejo Turístico Aerosilla** (Florencio Sánchez s/n, tel. 03541/42-2254, www.aerosilla.com). Since opening in 1955, the chairlift has been a traditional activity for Argentine families—nearly all of whom seem to have purchased photos from its lurking shooters. The chairlift charges US$5 pp

round-trip, but many mountain bikers now use it just to get up the hill.

At the summit, a passenger monorail (US$2.50 pp more) loops past grazing goats on other parts of the hillside. Soft drinks, beer, and sandwiches at the hilltop *confitería,* which offers panoramas of the higher Sierras to the west, are reasonably priced.

Accommodations and Food: Many visitors stay at campgrounds such as ACA's waterfront **Centro Turístico Villa Carlos Paz** (Avenida San Martín and Nahuel Huapi, tel. 03541/42-2132, US$5 pp plus US$2 per tent).

Typical of two-star accommodations is the very decent **Hotel Alpre** (Avenida San Martín 1035, tel. 03541/42-6012, www.hotelalpre.com.ar, US$52–63 s or d with breakfast), where the higher price includes air-conditioning. It also has a pool, a restaurant, and Wi-Fi.

The four-star resort **Hotel Portal del Lago** (Avenida Gobernador Alvarez and Gobernador Carrera, tel. 03541/42-4931, www.portal-del-lago.com, US$110 s or d) has first-rate accommodations.

The cinema-themed **Villapaz** (General Paz 152, tel. 03541/43-3230) is primarily but not exclusively a *parrilla,* with excellent *bife de chorizo,* outstanding *provoletta* for a starter, and superb desserts.

Information and Services: At the bus terminal, the central office of the **Secretaría de Turismo** (Avenida San Martín 400, tel. 0351/42-1624, www.villacarlospaz.gov.ar/turismo) is open 7 A.M.–11 P.M. daily in summer, 7 A.M.–9 P.M. daily the rest of the year. On a traffic island at the north end of town, its **Oficina de Informes Caminera** (San Martín 1000, tel. 03541/43-5597) is also helpful.

ATMs, Telecentros, and Internet outlets are abundant along Avenida San Martín.

Correo Argentino is at Avenida San Martín 198; the postal code is 5152.

Getting There and Around: Fonobus and Carcor minibuses to Córdoba leave every 15 minutes from the **Estación Terminal de Ómnibus** (San Martín 400); **Sarmiento Diferencial de Pasajeros** (tel. 03541/42-1571) has half a dozen buses daily to Alta Gracia.

Some long-distance companies from Buenos Aires start and end their Córdoba routes here, and there are also westward routes toward San Luis and Mendoza. Fares and times resemble those from the provincial capital.

Cosquín

Nearly as cluttered as Carlos Paz with hotels and *parrillas,* Cosquín is the events center of the Valle de Punilla, which rises gradually north toward and beyond La Falda. It has few sights, but major folk and rock festivals take place here in summer.

At 700 meters above sea level, Cosquín (pop. about 20,000) is 52 kilometers from Córdoba via La Calera, and 63 kilometers from the provincial capital via Villa Carlos Paz. RN 38 goes directly through the middle of town as Avenida San Martín, passing the central Plaza San Martín and, four blocks farther north, the Plaza Próspero Molino, site of the biggest musical events.

Sights: After straggling out of bed around midday, Argentine tourists head for the 1,260-meter summit of **Cerro Pan de Azúcar,** about seven kilometers east of town, for views of the Sierras to the west and the city of Córdoba to the east. A gravel road goes most of the way, but there is no scheduled public transport; from the parking area, the peak is a half-hour climb or a US$5 chairlift ride away. At the foot of the chairlift, souvenirs and simple meals are available from a pair of *confiterías;* at one of these, owner Luis de Giacomo has built a museum-shrine to Carlos Gardel, including a larger-than-life monument to the great *tanguero.*

Events: Traditionally, Cosquín's biggest draw is the **Festival Nacional del Folklore** (national folklore festival, www.aquicosquin.org); held the last week of January for more than 30 years, it lasts around 10 days and brings in artists like Horacio Guarany, Mercedes Sosa, and Soledad (who normally omits her surname Pastorutti).

The festival normally fills the 8,100-seat open-air theater on Plaza Próspero Molino, where hanging advertisements on the chain-link fence block the views of non–ticket holders (who can still hear the music). Events start around 10 P.M. and finish about 3–4 A.M.

Early February's three-day **Cosquín Rock** (www.cosquinrock.com), which draws performers of the stature of Attaque 77, Babasónicos, and Las Pelotas, now takes place at San Roque, about 10 kilometers south of Cosquín.

Accommodations and Food: Cosquín has an enormous roster of hotels and other accommodations, but many are open in summer only or, perhaps, as late as Semana Santa; off-season, rates can drop dramatically. Visitors seeking peace and quiet, but still wishing to attend the festivals, should consider staying nearby in La Falda.

The simple but impeccable and modern **Hotel del Valle** (San Martín 330, tel. 03541/45-2802, US$19 s, US$26 d) has the drawback of being on the main drag. The inviting **Petit Hotel** (Sabattini 730, tel. 03541/45-1311, US$79 s or d, petithotel@infocosquin.com.ar) has kept high standards for many years.

Parrillada is the standard at places like **San Marino** (Avenida San Martín 715, tel. 03541/45-2927), whose specialty is *chivito* (grilled goat). Pizza and pasta are also popular, as at **Pizzería Riviera** (Avenida San Martín and Sabattini, tel. 03541/45-1152).

Information: The **Dirección Municipal de Turismo** (San Martín 560, tel. 03541/45-4644, turismocosquin@gmail.com) is open 7 A.M.–9 P.M. daily.

Getting There and Around: Cosquín's Terminal de Ómnibus (Perón and Salta) is one block west of Plaza San Martín. There are frequent buses to Córdoba, and up and down the Valle de Punilla.

La Falda

Forested La Falda owes its origins to the Cruz del Eje railroad, which arrived here in 1892, and the grand Hotel Edén—now in ruins—that opened six years later. For much of the first half of the 20th century, it was *the* place for socialites summering in the Sierras—though its later history had a dark side. La Falda has become a more democratic destination, but its quiet tree-lined streets are still a contrast to raucously populist Carlos Paz and Cosquín.

At the foot of Sierra Chica's steeper western slope, 934 meters above sea level, La Falda (pop. about 17,000) is 19 kilometers north of Cosquín and 45 kilometers north of Villa Carlos Paz via RN 38. Most businesses are on or near Avenida Edén, which leads east off the highway.

In its heyday, 1898 to about 1945, **Hotel Edén** hosted figures of the stature of president Julio A. Roca, Nicaraguan poet Rubén Darío, Albert Einstein, and the Prince of Wales. Its second set of German owners, though, were Nazi sympathizers, and the Argentine government expropriated the property after declaring war on Germany on March 28, 1945.

After closing in 1965 and being ransacked by locals—including its supposed custodians—in the 1970s and 1980s, today it's a ghostly grand hotel offering only hints of what it once was. Some locals, though, take pride in at least part of its history and dream of the day that it might reopen—many years and millions of dollars in the future, if ever. Partly restored, Hotel Edén (Avenida Edén s/n, tel. 03548/42-6643) is open for guided tours 9 A.M.–8 P.M. weekdays, 10 A.M.–6 P.M. weekends. Admission costs US$5.50.

Accommodations and Food: La Falda has abundant accommodations that offer, in general, more spacious grounds and greater quiet than those in Cosquín or Carlos Paz. Few accommodations in its price range can boast a pool, but the shoestring **Hostería Marina** (Güemes 134, tel. 03548/42-2640, US$12 pp) can.

Well-landscaped **Hotel Old Garden** (Capital Federal 28, tel. 03548/42-2842, oldgarden@arnetbiz.com.ar, US$34 s, US$47 d) also has a pool and exceptionally friendly management that also handles English and German.

With its lush grounds and huge pool, **Hotel Scala** (Avenida Edén 450, tel. 03548/42-3072, www.scalahotel.com.ar, US$52 d) is a contradiction—well past its 1960s prime even though the rooms are large and functional. It's suffering deferred maintenance, but if you can look past chipped plaster and faded wallpaper, it's a good value, at least in the off-season.

The standard for excellence, though, is

Hotel Tomaso di Savoia (Avenida Edén 732, tel. 03548/42-3013, hotel@tomasodisavoiahotel.com.ar, US$50 s, US$63 d), which also has an outstanding restaurant.

La Parrilla de Raúl (Avenida Edén 1002, tel. 03548/42-3001) is a cavernous *parrilla* that's cool in winter even when the embers are smoldering, but the huge buffet is an exceptional value.

Lo de Nedda (Avenida Edén 124, tel. 03548/42-7101) serves fine *chivito* (roast goat) in large portions (US$10), with appetizer extras and a pretty good wine list. Service is well above average, and the kitchen makes an extra effort to accommodate its clients.

San Cayetano (Avenida Edén 213) has the best ice cream.

Information and Services: Occupying the former train station, La Falda's **Secretaría de Turismo, Cultura y Deporte** (Avenida España 50, tel. 03548/42-3007, www.lafalda.gov.ar) is open 8 A.M. to 10 P.M. daily in summer, 8 A.M. to 9 P.M. daily the rest of the year.

Banco de Córdoba (Avenida Edén 402) has an ATM.

Correo Argentino is at Avenida Argentina 199; the postal code is 5172.

Getting There and Around: From La Falda's **Estación Terminal de Ómnibus** (RN 38 and Chubut), there are frequent buses up and down the Valle de Punilla and to Córdoba, and long-distance services to the Cuyo cities of San Juan and Mendoza as well as to Buenos Aires and intermediates.

◖ PARQUE NACIONAL QUEBRADA DEL CONDORITO

The world's most famous carrion carnivore, the majestic Andean condor, reaches its easternmost range in the Altas Cumbres (High Summits) of the Sierras de Córdoba, where it lends its name to the area's only national park. Because of its year-round accessibility, the park makes an ideal excursion from Villa Carlos Paz or even the provincial capital, or a stopover en route to or from San Luis Province.

Quebrada del Condorito is 55 kilometers

southwest of Villa Carlos Paz and 90 kilometers southwest of Córdoba via RP 20, the Camino Altas Cumbres, which continues west to Mina Clavero and San Luis. Comprising some 37,000 hectares of rolling high terrain cut by eastward-draining streams on the Pampa de Achala, up to 2,300 meters above sea level, the park lies mostly south of the highway.

The average annual temperature is about 8°C, but at these altitudes winter temperatures can fall to -25°C. Most precipitation falls in spring and summer (Nov.–Mar.), so it snows only three to five times per year.

Flora and Fauna

Most of the park consists of high-altitude grasslands where high evaporation discourages trees and even shrubs. The slopes of its sheltered, well-watered canyons, though, support dwarf forests of *tabaquillo* and *maitén,* along with ferns and a host of endemics.

Its signature animal, of course, is the condor, which soars overhead and breeds on rocky outcrops in the canyon that bears its name. It is also home to mammals like the puma and red fox and a host of other birds including the red-and-black-headed turkey vultures. If hiking, watch carefully for the highly venomous pit viper *yarará ñata;* fortunately, most reptiles are harmless lizards.

Senda a La Quebrada del Condorito

The most accessible sight/activity is the nine-kilometer hike, a signed trail from Paraje La Pampilla, on the highway, to Balcón Norte, the Río Condorito Canyon's northern overlook. Unlike most mountain trails, this one starts high and descends gradually, over undulating terrain, to the Quebrada's edge.

The Quebrada itself is a V-shaped canyon, 800 meters deep, 1.5 kilometers wide, and about 12 kilometers long; a short lateral descends through scrub forest and ferns to an overlook for the condor nesting site—colloquially known as the **Escuela de Vuelo** (Flight School)—on the nearly vertical south-side walls.

Hiking the trail—really an abandoned road for most of its length—takes about 2–2.5 hours

one-way; carry water and snacks. While the trail is well-signed and the weather is normally clear, fog banks can disrupt visibility. Bicycles are permitted in dry weather only.

Accommodations and Food

The nearest hotels are in Villa Carlos Paz and Mina Clavero, both some distance from the park. Park rangers, though, will grant permission to camp at Cañada del Hospital, near the new visitors center; Pampa Pajosa, near Balcón Norte; and at Puesto Condorito, about 20 minutes across the Río Condorito. The latter involves a steep descent and river ford.

About nine kilometers before Paraje La Pampilla, the **Fundación Cóndor** has a respectable restaurant with standard Argentine food and regional specialties like *locro.* Campers must bring camp stoves—no fires are allowed within the park.

Information

About two kilometers south of Paraje La Pampilla, rangers staff the new **Centro de Visitantes,** open 7 A.M.–8 P.M. daily. Nine kilometers east of La Pampilla, the **Fundación Cóndor** is a private foundation that also has a Córdoba office (José J. Díaz 1036, tel. 0351/464-6537, ramallotr@arnet.com.ar or mldepi@yahoo.com.ar).

The **APN** has its Intendencia in Villa Carlos Paz (Resistencia 30, tel. 03541/43-3371, quebradadelcondorito@apn.gov.ar). There is still no entry fee, but this may change.

Getting There

Contact travel agencies in Córdoba or the Fundación Cóndor for guided excursions. Otherwise, it's possible to take **Ciudad de Córdoba** buses (tel. 0351/428-2811) from Córdoba to La Pampilla (about 1.5 hours) at 8:30 and 10:30 A.M. and 1:15, 4:45, 7:30, and 11:30 P.M.; return buses from Mina Clavero pass La Pampilla at 4:45 A.M. and 12:45, 4, 6:35, and 8:35 P.M. Schedules can change, though, so visitors should verify times. Buses from Córdoba can be caught about 50 minutes later in Villa Carlos Paz.

THE ANDEAN NORTHWEST

In their dramatic landscapes, rich pre-Columbian culture, and gripping history, the northwestern Andean provinces resemble the southwestern U.S. states of Arizona, New Mexico, and Utah. Once part of the Inka empire, the region of Argentina with the largest indigenous population still shares the central Andean heritage. Set among brightly colored sedimentary strata, its hillside fortresses and terraced fields recall highland Perú and Bolivia rather than the urban jumble of Buenos Aires or the vast open spaces of the pampas, and the indigenous Quechua language is still widely spoken.

Unlike Buenos Aires, the Northwest boasts a palpable colonial legacy in the adobe churches and other monuments of the city of Salta, the Valles Calchaquíes, and the Quebrada de Humahuaca. Because of its rich history, the Quebrada de Humahuaca became a UNESCO World Heritage Site in 2003, while the Calchaquíes are also one of the world's most distinctive wine regions—lesser known than Cuyo, but well worth exploring for their unique high-altitude vintages.

Comprising the provinces of Jujuy, Salta, Tucumán, Catamarca, and Santiago del Estero, the northwest is also a geographical extravaganza of natural landscapes and ecosystems, many protected by national parks and other reserves. One unique environment is the *yungas,* a discontinuous longitudinal strip of subtropical cloud forest along the easternmost Andes.

There are also vivid deserts and desolately scenic high-altitude steppes, punctuated by volcanoes soaring above vast dry salt pans

HIGHLIGHTS

(Museo de Antropología y Arqueología de Alta Montaña: Facing the central plaza of Salta, northwestern Argentina's best-kept colonial city, this new museum offers a remarkable account of high Andean archaeology in cultural and historical context (page 293).

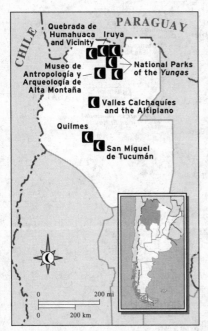

(Valles Calchaquíes and the Altiplano: West and south of Salta, explore the polychrome Quebrada de Cafayate and its nearby wine country, the vertiginous mountain road to remote Cachi, and the scenic "Train to the Clouds" (page 297).

(Quebrada de Humahuaca and Vicinity: The deep canyon's stunning landscapes, archaeological monuments, and settlements have preserved so much indigenous integrity that the valley received UNESCO World Heritage Site designation in 2003 (page 313).

(Iruya: Reached via the Quebrada de Humahuaca, the "lost valley of the Inkas" deserves recognition in its own right (page 322).

(National Parks of the *Yungas:* In this strip of eastern Andean cloud forest, several national parks display some of Argentina's greatest biodiversity. **Calilegua** and **El Rey** are easier to visit, while access to **Baritú** is difficult (page 325).

(San Miguel de Tucumán: This capital of a poverty-stricken province takes pride in its historical role as the cradle of Argentine independence (page 327).

(Quilmes: At the south end of the Valles Calchaquíes in Tucumán Province, but also easily reached from Cafayate, these hillside ruins of a pre-Columbian fortress may be the country's most impressive archaeological site (page 336).

LOOK FOR **(** TO FIND RECOMMENDED SIGHTS, ACTIVITIES, DINING, AND LODGING.

and shallow lakes teeming with migratory birds. Salta's Tren a las Nubes (Train to the Clouds) traverses part of this literally breathtaking landscape, which rises well above 4,000 meters.

PLANNING YOUR TIME

In terms of logistics and services, Salta is the best base for visiting the region. Strategically central, it's almost equidistant from sights

such as the Quebrada de Humahuaca, the national parks of the *yungas,* the altiplano heights toward the Chilean border, and the Valles Calchaquíes. Many of these may be done as day trips or multiday loops.

To see the key attractions, at least a week is essential; two weeks are desirable; and a month would be worthwhile. Its subtropical latitudes are agreeable most of the year, though the highest altitudes above 4,000 meters get cold

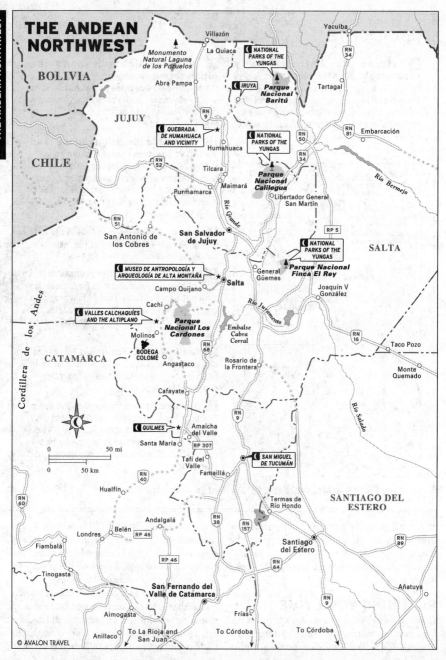

THE ANDEAN NORTHWEST

BOLIVIA

CHILE

JUJUY

SALTA

CATAMARCA

SANTIAGO DEL ESTERO

Cordillera de los Andes

Yacuiba

Villazón

La Quiaca

Monumento Natural Laguna de los Pozuelos

NATIONAL PARKS OF THE YUNGAS

Abra Pampa

Tartagal

☾ IRUYA

Parque Nacional Baritú

RN 34

RN 9

QUEBRADA DE HUMAHUACA AND VICINITY ★

Humahuaca

NATIONAL PARKS OF THE YUNGAS

RN 50

Embarcación

RN 81

RN 52

Tilcara

RN 34

Maimará

Parque Nacional Calilegua

Purmamarca

Río Bermejo

RN 51

Río Grande

Libertador General San Martín

San Antonio de los Cobres

San Salvador de Jujuy

RP 5

NATIONAL PARKS OF THE YUNGAS

SALTA

MUSEO DE ANTROPOLOGÍA Y ARQUEOLOGÍA DE ALTA MONTAÑA

General Güemes

⚑ *Parque Nacional Finca El Rey*

Campo Quijano

Salta

Joaquín V González

Cachi

Río Juramento

VALLES CALCHAQUÍES AND THE ALTIPLANO ★

Parque Nacional Los Cardones

Embalse Cabra Corral

RN 16

Taco Pozo

Molinos

BODEGA COLOMÉ

RN 68

Rosario de la Frontera

Monte Quemado

Angastaco

Cafayate

Río Salado

RN 9

☾ QUILMES ★

Amaicha del Valle

Santa María

RP 307

Tafí del Valle

⚑ SAN MIGUEL DE TUCUMÁN

Famaillá

SANTIAGO DEL ESTERO

RN 40

Hualfín

Termas de Río Hondo

RN 60

Andalgalá

RN 38

RN 157

RN 89

Londres

Belén

RP 46

Santiago del Estero

Fiambalá

RP 46

RN 64

Tinogasta

San Fernando del Valle de Catamarca

RN 9

Añatuya

Aimogasta

Frías

Anillaco

To La Rioja and San Juan

To Córdoba

To Córdoba

0   50 mi

0   50 km

© AVALON TRAVEL

in winter (June–August), especially at night. Many visitors, though, prefer the dry winter to the wet summer, when desert flash floods can occur and roads into the humid *yungas* are impassable. Ironically enough, summer snowstorms can make the altiplano harder to reach than in winter.

Because Argentines often head north during winter holidays (the last two weeks of July), demands on services can be high and reservations desirable for the best-value accommodations, rental cars, and the Tren a las Nubes (which does not operate in summer).

HISTORY

For travelers who see Europeanized Buenos Aires before visiting the mountainous Andean provinces, the northwest can seem a historical relic that's failed to keep pace with the megalopolis of the pampas. What's happened is a reversal of fortune—in immediate pre-Columbian times, the pampas were a peripheral backwater peopled with hunter-gatherers, while today's northwestern highland valleys were part of a sophisticated civilization. It may seem marginal now, but when the Spaniards first saw South America, this region held about two-thirds of the population of what is now Argentine territory.

Until the mid-15th century A.D., indigenous groups like the Diaguita, Omaguaca, and Lules lived in more or less autonomous communities in the well-watered canyons, where they could grow corn, beans, and squash, and on the eastern Andean slopes. At higher altitudes they grew potatoes and quinoa (a native grain); military fortifications, agricultural terraces, and complex irrigation systems recall their political and technological sophistication.

Around A.D. 1480, the expanding Inka state brought ever more distant regions, including the northwest, under Cusco's control. While the Inkas were a military juggernaut when necessary, they only required that subject peoples acknowledge the Inka Viracocha as their deity and pay tribute to the Inka state.

In the early 16th century, Spanish invasion and exploration proceeded from Perú and Alto Perú (present-day Bolivia). In 1535, Diego de Almagro became the first Spaniard to set foot in the region—a year before Pedro de Mendoza's initial landing in Buenos Aires. Almagro's massive expedition, with 500 Spaniards and thousands of Indians, traveled south through what is now Jujuy and Salta but endured severe hardship crossing to Chile via the brutally cold Puna de Atacama; consequently, he returned to Perú by a different route.

In the 1550s, after subjecting the central Andean peoples to labor and tribute obligations under the *encomienda,* the Spaniards moved into what is now northwestern Argentina, but the sparser population of this area never rewarded its *encomenderos* with the same riches. Over the next century-plus, introduced European diseases devastated the indigenous populations and made *encomiendas* worthless.

Still, the Spaniards founded a string of cities along the Andean front range and beyond, starting with Santiago del Estero (1553) and followed by San Miguel de Tucumán (1565), Córdoba (1573), Salta (1582), La Rioja (1591), and San Salvador de Jujuy (1592). Catamarca's first settlement was Belén (1555), but Diaguita resistance destroyed it and delayed permanent Spanish presence in the province for more than a century.

In colonial times, the entire northwest went by the name "Tucumán." Economically, it supplied mules, cotton, cloth, and eventually sugar to Alto Perú's bonanza silver mine at Potosí. In 1776, with formation of the Buenos Aires–based Virreinato del Río de la Plata (Viceroyalty of the River Plate) and the opening of Buenos Aires to foreign commerce, Tucumán reversed its political and economic orientation. Argentine independence reinforced this trend but also left Salta and Jujuy out of the loop, as routes to Alto Perú and Lima fell into disuse. The late-19th-century arrival of the railroad from Buenos Aires–Córdoba to San Miguel completed the process.

In the meantime, political progress lagged behind economic growth, as caudillos like Catamarca's Felipe Varela (1821–1870) set a precedent for modern provincial strongmen such as Vicente Saadi (1913–1988). Economic decline, particularly in the sugar industry, has left the population vulnerable to demagogues like Tucumán's Antonio Domingo Bussi, a

"Dirty War" general elected mayor by the slimmest majority in 2003 but later impeached, and Peronist union leader Luis Barrionuevo, whose followers disrupted Catamarca's provincial gubernatorial election that same year.

Salta and Jujuy Provinces

Between them, Salta and Jujuy Provinces provide the best reasons for visiting northwestern Argentina. Except for an easterly plain that grades into the low-lying Gran Chaco, this is a mountainous area whose westernmost peaks, on the Bolivian and Chilean borders, reach upwards of 5,000 meters. Beneath those summits, domestic llamas and wild vicuñas graze the grasses of the Andean steppe (puna or altiplano), where migratory birds frequent enormous shallow lakes and blindingly white *salares* (salt pans) open onto the horizon.

East and south of the altiplano, rivers have cut deep canyons and valleys like the Quebrada de Humahuaca, the Quebrada del Toro, and the Valles Calchaquíes, where most of the pre-Columbian population lived; there are still archaeological sites but also colonial villages and modern vineyards. Where the rivers leave their canyons, the provincial capitals of Salta and San Salvador de Jujuy are contemporary urban centers that still show their colonial origins. Where the Andes meet the Chaco, east of Salta and San Salvador, the *yungas* comprise a longitudinal strip of cloud forest that has given the region several national parks.

In one sense, though, Salta is the country's most backward province. At the moment, at least, the country's biggest tobacco-producing region is a free-fire zone for cigarette junkies, even in restaurants and bus stations (but not, fortunately, in the buses themselves, where federal law prevails). In both provinces, though, antitobacco legislation is advancing.

SALTA
Experiencing a tourist boom from within and beyond Argentina's borders, the colonial

city of Salta is the northwest's urban gateway, thanks to its picturesque plazas, impressive architecture, and cultural life. It also offers the region's best accommodations, food, and other services. Nearly surrounded by mountains, it also enjoys one of the most scenic settings of any Argentine city, making it an ideal base for Andean excursions in any of several directions. Suitably enough, it is nicknamed *Salta la Linda* (Salta the Beautiful).

Salta dates from 1582, when tyrannical Tucumán governor Hernando de Lerma led colonists to the fertile alluvial valley that now bears his name. Its mild climate and rich soils were ideal for raising crops and fattening animals for the high-altitude silver miners of Potosí, in Alto Perú (present-day Bolivia). After independence, Salta briefly declined but soon reoriented itself toward Buenos Aires and other Pampas cities that, thanks to the railroad's arrival, became the primary destinations for sugar and other subtropical crops.

Orientation
In the sheltered Lerma Valley, 1,200 meters above sea level, Salta (pop. about 550,000) is 1,495 kilometers northwest of Buenos Aires via RN 9, which turns abruptly west at General Güemes before dropping into town. It is 92 kilometers south of San Salvador de Jujuy via RN 9, a paved but narrow mountain road not suitable for buses or trucks; it is 120 kilometers from San Salvador via RN 34 and RN 66, the safer but more roundabout route taken by buses. It is 813 kilometers northwest of Resistencia via the trans-Chaco RN 16 and RN 9.

Plaza 9 de Julio is the centerpiece of Salta's

grid, from which most points of interest are within a few blocks. North–south streets change names on either side of Caseros, but east–west streets are continuous. Toward the east, across Avenida Virrey Toledo, the grid gives way to streets that follow the contours of Cerro 20 de Febrero and Cerro San Bernardo.

Sights

For an overview, take the *teleférico* (gondola, tel. 0387/431-0641, 10 A.M.–7 P.M. daily, US$5 adults, US$2.50 children 6–12, US$2.50 one-way) from Parque San Martín to the top of 1,454-meter **Cerro San Bernardo.** From the summit, a zigzag footpath descends to the **Monumento a Güemes,** the memorial to Salta's favorite caudillo.

Salta's palm-studded **Plaza 9 de Julio** is the best starting point for exploring the compact center on foot. Nearly all the surrounding buildings feature *recovas* (porticos), beneath which hotels, cafés, and small businesses have their entrances.

On the west side, dating from 1913, the Francophile eclectic **Centro Cultural América** (Mitre 23) was a private club until 1950, when it became the provincial **Casa de Gobierno;** in 1987, when executive offices moved to the suburbs, it became a cultural center. Immediately north, occupying a former girls school dating from 1860, the **Museo de Antropología y Arqueología de Alta Montaña,** described in more detail below, specializes in high-altitude archaeology.

On the north side, the ornate 19th-century **Iglesia Catedral** (España 596) replaced an earlier cathedral destroyed by an earthquake; it holds the remains of independence hero and salteño caudillo General Martín Miguel de Güemes.

On the south side, the asymmetrical colonial **Cabildo** (1780, restored 1945) replaced a series of precarious earlier buildings. It now serves as the **Museo Histórico del Norte** (Caseros 549, tel. 0387/421-5340, www.museonor.gov. ar, 9 A.M.–6 P.M. Tues.–Fri., 9 A.M.–1:30 P.M. Sat.–Sun., US$1.25), whose collections include antique furniture, ecclesiastical and

© WAYNE BERNHARDSON

Salta's Teleférico Cerro San Bernardo offers aerial panoramas of the city.

SALTA

RÍO BERMEJO

ESTACIÓN FERROCARRIL BELGRANO

B FIGUEROA

HOTEL PATIOS DE LERMA
JOSÉ BALCARCE

MUSEO PAJCHA ★
LA VIEJA ESTACIÓN ●
BONNIE & CLYDE

HOSTEL PRISAMATA ●
▼ LA LEÑITA

ADOLFO ALSINA

LA TORRE

LAVANDERÍA SOL DE MAYO ■

AV ENTRE RÍOS

POSADA DE LAS NUBES ●

LEGADO MÍTICO DE SALTA
■ ACA

RIVADAVIA

Plaza Güemes

FIAMBRERÍA LA CORDOBESA ▼

LEGUIZAMÓN

25 DE MAYO

20 DE FEBRERO

BALCARCE

HOTEL SOLAR DE LA PLAZA ●

FACUNDO DE ZUVIRIA

J TODD

M ALVEAR

A GÜEMES

AV SARMIENTO

HOTEL DEL VIRREY ●

HOTEL RESIDENCIAL BALCARCE

SANTIAGO DEL ESTERO

CHILEAN CONSULATE ■

B MITRE

MAIPÚ

IBAZETA

MARTÍN CORNEJO

GUILLERMO BROWN

GENERAL SIMÓN BOLÍVAR

GENERAL GÜEMES

HELADERÍA FILI ▼

ECLECTIC HOSTAL ■

M CASTRO

Plaza Belgrano

HOTEL ALEJANDRO 1 ●

ARTEAGA

AV BELGRANO

ESPAÑA

BANCO DE LA NACIÓN ■

■ MIGRACIONES

FALCON CALCHAQUÍ

HOTEL PROVINCIAL PLAZA ●

Plaza 9 de Julio

JULIO CASEROS

MUSEO DE BELLAS ARTES ★

GENERAL ALVARADO

SANTA ROSA

SEE DETAIL

FERRO TURISMO ■

PJE RUIZ DE LOS LLANOS

JUSTO J DE URQUIZA

ESTECO

MERCADO CENTRAL ▼

RESIDENCIAL ELENA ●

EL BOLICHE DE BALDERRAMA ■

CARLOS PELLEGRINI

AV SAN MARTÍN

HELADOS GIANNI ▼

MIRAMAR ▼
ALVAREZ ▼

LAPRIDA

10 DE OCTUBRE

GENERAL LAMADRID

GENERAL J M PAZ

GENERAL J GORRITI

MENDOZA

JUJUY

ITUZAINGÓ

LA FLORIDA

JUAN BAUTISTA ALBERDI

BUENOS AIRES

SAN JUAN

CLUB AMIGOS DE LA MONTAÑA ●

SAN LUIS

© AVALON TRAVEL

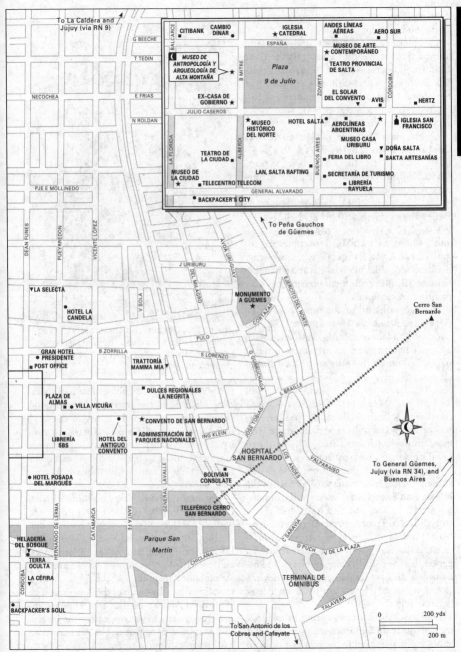

contemporary art, and animal-powered transportation technology.

One block east of the plaza, under the same administration, the 18th-century **Museo Casa Uriburu** (Caseros 417, tel. 0387/421-5340, 9 A.M.–6 P.M. Tues.–Fri., 9 A.M.–1:30 P.M. Sat.–Sun., US$1.25) was the residence of José Evaristo Uriburu (1831–1914), who twice served as Argentina's president.

On the plaza's east side, the **Museo de Arte Contemporáneo** (Zuviria 90, tel. 0387/437-0498, 9 A.M.–8 P.M. Tues.–Sat., 4–8 P.M. Sun., US$0.50) displays rotating exhibits of cutting-edge Argentine art.

One block west of the plaza, the **Museo de Bellas Artes** (Florida 20, tel. 0387/421-4714, 9 A.M.–1:30 P.M. Mon.–Fri., 10 A.M.–1 P.M. and 5–8 P.M. Sat., US$0.50) occupies the colonial **Casa Arias Rengel** (1752), a two-story mansion with thick adobe walls and a hanging balcony. Its collections focus on contemporary painting and sculpture.

At the south end of the same pedestrian street, the **Casa de Hernández** (1780) is another handsome colonial residence with a corner balcony and an attractive interior patio. It houses the **Museo de la Ciudad** (Florida 97, tel. 0387/437-3352, www.museociudadsalta.gov.ar, 9 A.M.–1 P.M. and 4–8:30 P.M. Mon.–Fri., 5–8:30 P.M. Sat., free), which deals with municipal government history and objects of daily usage. The most imposing item, though, is Lorenzo Gigli's historical oil painting.

Immediately east, dating from 1796 and lit at night, Salta's most outlandish church is the **Iglesia San Francisco** (Caseros and Córdoba, 9 A.M.–12:30 P.M. and 5–8 P.M. Mon.–Sat.), embellished by Franciscan architect Luis Giorgi from 1868 to 1872; the four-story tower—terraced like a ziggurat—also dates from this period. It's the reddish color, gilt trim, and ornamental details that really grab the viewer's attention, but until it gets new paint it will look better at night.

One block farther east, dating from 1582, the **Convento de San Bernardo** (Caseros and Santa Fe) is a Carmelite convent not open to

© WAYNE BERNHARDSON

The colonial facade and elaborately carved doors at Salta's Convento de San Bernardo are as much as visitors can see at this closed convent.

the public, though its cobblestone patio, dazzling adobe walls, and intricate *algarrobo* doors (1762) impart a colonial dignity to the city's oldest surviving religious landmark. In reality, it has served other functions—it was once a hospital, for example—and has undergone modifications because of earthquake damage and changing uses.

Just west of the Balcarce nightlife district, the **Museo Pajcha** (20 de Febrero 838, tel. 0387/422-9417, www.museodearteetnico.com.ar, 10 A.M.–1 P.M. and 4–8 P.M. Mon.–Sat., US$2) is a private, professionally organized and presented collection of ethnic art from throughout Argentina and the Andes, with a sampling from elsewhere in the Americas. The focus is on Andean textiles and religious imagery, ceramics and weavings from the Chaco, and Mapuche silverwork. The museum also has a small café and a store.

◖ Museo de Antropología y Arqueología de Alta Montaña

Salta's most professional museum chronicles the recovery of the mummies of Inka children from atop the Andean summit of Llullaillaco, on the Chilean border. With video and explanatory panels, including good English translations, it details the expedition that retrieved the mummies, the challenges of extreme archaeology, and the cold dry conditions that permitted the bodies' near-perfect preservation.

Further exhibits put the findings in context by explaining the significance of high Andean peaks in Inka cosmology, the importance of textiles and other everyday products, and subsequent research into the life and death of the mummies in question. As a cautionary tale, there's also an extensive account of an earlier mummy, removed by climbers from Cerro Chuscha near Cafayate in the 1920s, that underwent a long odyssey to Buenos Aires and back, being sold several times before finally going on display here (the Llullaillaco mummies, not having suffered the same indignities and deterioration, are kept in research facilities).

The Museo de Antropología y Arqueología de Alta Montaña (Mitre 77, tel. 0387/437-0499, www.maam.org.ar, US$2.50 for Argentines, US$8 for foreigners) is open 11 A.M.–7:30 P.M. Tuesday–Sunday. There are also a museum shop and a café.

Entertainment

The line between entertainment and dining is not always clear in Salta, especially when it comes to the well-established folkloric venues scattered around town and the newer, more fashionable locales along Balcarce. In some instances, especially along Balcarce, the same performers may work at several different places on the same night.

Some 20 blocks west of Plaza 9 de Julio, the participatory **La Casona del Molino** (Luis Burela 1, tel. 0387/434-2835) has adapted itself to the traditional layout of a sprawling residence to offer live folkloric music in intimate surroundings. There's also a prime regional menu of *locro, humitas,* empanadas, and wines.

On the lower slopes of Cerro San Bernardo, east of downtown, the **Peña Gauchos de Güemes** (Avenida Uruguay 750, tel. 0387/492-1621, www.gauchosdesalta.com.ar) has regular dinner-and-show packages. Reservations are essential at **El Boliche de Balderrama** (San Martín 1126, tel. 0387/421-1542), in the same location for more than 40 years. Its dinner-and-show package is comparably priced (about US$20) to that of Gauchos de Güemes.

In the former Cine Victoria, the **Teatro Provincial de Salta** (Zuviría 70, tel. 0387/422-4515, www.culturasalta.gov.ar) has become the city's prime performing-arts venue. Occupying the former Gran Cine Alberdi, the **Teatro de la Ciudad** (Alberdi 56, tel. 0387/431-3330) also offers live theater and concerts.

Shopping

Sakta Artesanías (Córdoba 32, tel. 0387/15-683-3720) sells woodcarvings, pottery, silverwork, handmade clothing, regional sweets, and the like. **Dulces Regionales La Negrita** (España 79, tel. 0387/421-1833) also sells homemade sweets.

Salta has an outstanding selection of bookstores, including **Librería Rayuela** (Alvarado 570, tel. 0387/431-2066 or 0387/431-8886, rayuela@arnet.com.ar) and **Feria del Libro** (Buenos Aires 83, tel. 0387/421-0359). **Librería SBS** (Lerma 45, tel. 0387/431-8868) carries English-language books.

It's hard to categorize **Plaza de Almas** (Pueyrredón 6, tel. 0387/422-8933, www.plazadealmas.com), a café-bar with pub grub at modest prices, but its strength is the diversity of regional crafts, as well as books and music, that make it a seamless cultural institution. There's a larger and even livelier branch in Tucumán.

Accommodations

Thanks to its increasing tourist appeal and traditional commercial importance, Salta has a wide variety of accommodations in many categories, ranging from backpackers' favorites to business-oriented hostelries and sophisticated boutique hotels.

US$10-25: Lodged in an older house near the Balcarce entertainment district, the casual **Hostal Prisamata** (Mitre 833, tel. 0387/431-3900, www.hostalprisamata.com, US$9 pp dorm, US$15 s, US$27 d) provides amenities like a climbing wall, hammocks, a mini-gym, and rental bikes.

With mostly dorms but a few doubles, the **Terra Oculta Youth Hostel** (Córdoba 361, tel. 0387/421-8769, www.terraoculta.com, US$10 pp, US$24-27 s or d) is a friendly and lively hostel with a great rooftop bar for *asados*. Across Avenida San Martín it has a separate house that has the only double, with a private bath.

Rooms at the simple but clean and friendly **Hotel Residencial Balcarce** (Balcarce 460, tel. 0387/431-8135, www.residencialbalcarce.com.ar, US$9 s, US$16 d, with shared bath; US$16 s, US$25 d, with private bath and TV) surround a shady grape arbor. Rates at this well-located place, close (but not too close) to the main restaurant and nightlife district, are a bargain, but do not include breakfast.

US$25-50: Two-plus blocks south of Plaza 9 de Julio, the 18-room **Residencial Elena** (Buenos Aires 256, tel. 0387/421-1529, www.elenaresidencial.com.ar, US$19 s, US$32 d) occupies an enormous deep lot with several shady patios and gets surprisingly little street noise. The large rooms—some of which are multibed rooms—have high ceilings, and there's a pretty good book exchange.

The most established hostel is HI affiliate **(Backpacker's Home** (Buenos Aires 930, tel. 0387/423-5910, www.backpackers-salta.com, US$13-16 pp dorm, US$30-36 s, US$41-49 d), 10 blocks south of Plaza 9 de Julio. In addition to accommodations, it organizes tours, has weekly barbecues on its rooftop terrace, and arranges outings to local restaurants and clubs. The same management runs the nearby **Backpacker's Soul** (San Juan 413, tel. 0387/431-8944, US$13-16 pp dorm, US$30-36 s, US$41-49 d), which offers larger rooms closer to downtown, as well as downtown's **Backpacker's City** (Alvarado 751, tel. 0387/431-6476, US$13-16 pp dorm,

US$30-36 s, US$41-49 d), in a handsome colonial-style house on a deep lot.

The **Eclectic Hostal** (25 de Mayo 333, tel. 0387/421-2243, www.eclectichostal.com.ar, US$29 s, US$34 d) isn't quite what it sounds—the style is definitely colonial—but the rooms are large and immaculate, the baths large to huge, and there's a quiet rear garden with barbecue access. At these prices, it's an exceptional value.

Well-located **Posada de las Nubes** (Balcarce 639, tel. 0387/432-1776, www.posadadelasnubes.com.ar, US$40-45 d) has large well-kept rooms and basic amenities that include Wi-Fi. The higher rates correspond to rooms with cable TV.

The only drawback at **Villa Vicuña** (Caseros 266, tel. 0387/421-7816, www.villavicuna.com.ar, US$37 s, US$50 d) is that most rooms in this restored colonial house lack exterior windows and thus can be dark. They are large and beautifully furnished, and there's plenty of fresh air and sunlight in the rear garden of this deep lot.

US$50-100: In the up-and-coming area south of Plaza 9 de Julio, **Hotel Posada del Marqués** (Córdoba 195, tel. 0387/431-7741, www.posadadelmarques.com.ar, US$47 s, US$52 d) is a cozy colonial-style place with only 19 rooms, so it fills up fast.

Upgraded in recent years, business-oriented **Hotel Provincial Plaza** (Caseros 786, tel. 0387/432-2000, www.provincialplaza.com.ar, US$40-58 s or d) is a good value in its price range.

The **(Hotel del Antiguo Convento** (Caseros 113, tel. 0387/422-7267, www.hoteldelconvento.com.ar, US$53-61 s or d) remains an outstanding value. All the smartly furnished rooms enjoy a quiet setback from the street, and there's also a small pool, a gym, and Wi-Fi.

Around the corner from the Balcarce dining-and-nightlife zone, across from the train station in an area once crowded with flophouses, **Hotel Patios de Lerma** (Ameghino 653, tel. 0387/432-0500, www.patiosdelerma.com.ar, US$69 s, US$77 d) is a handsome new business-and-boutique hotel that includes a small spa.

Furnished with style, the boutiquish **⟨C Hotel del Virrey** (20 de Febrero 420, tel./ fax 0387/422-8000, www.hoteldelvirrey.com. ar, US$74 s, US$82 d) is an eight-room colonial-style accommodation that's an excellent value. Its pool is for wading or soaking only, but it has all other amenities.

At recycled **Hotel La Candela** (Pueyrredón 346, tel. 0387/422-4473, www.hotellacandela. com.ar, US$63–100 s or d), the cheaper rooms are smallish but still very good, with access to amenities that include a large garden and almost equally large pool.

Gran Hotel Presidente (Avenida Belgrano 353, tel./fax 0387/431-2022, www.granhotel-presidente.com, $60–75 s, $90–108 d) is a four-star facility with average- to plus-sized rooms that lack tubs but otherwise have everything.

Aging gracefully, **Hotel Salta** (Buenos Aires 1, tel. 0387/431-0740, www.hotelsalta.com, $65–119 s, $92–158 d) is a 1940s colonial-style hotel with magnificent tile work, but the rooms have updated baths and modern conveniences such as broadband connections.

Over US$100: Facing Plaza Güemes, Salta's most stylish new hotel is business-oriented **⟨C Hotel Solar de la Plaza** (J. M. Leguizamón 669, tel./fax 0387/431-5111, www. solardelaplaza.com.ar, US$136–225 s or d), a magnificently retrofitted family house. Rates include parking, taxes, pool, gym, sauna, air-conditioning, and safe deposit boxes.

More institutional, **Hotel Alejandro 1** (Balcarce 252, tel. 0387/400-0000, www. alejandro1hotel.com.ar, US$123–442 s or d) is a glistening new high-rise with every contemporary convenience, but it lacks the Solar's ambience.

In a recycled early 20th-century house, **⟨C Legado Mítico** (Mitre 647, tel. 0387/422-8786, www.legadomitico.com, US$170–210 s or d) is a thematic boutique hotel with handsomely designed, spacious suites that, in contrast to its Buenos Aires branch, stress *regional* historical figures. One measure of the service is that at check-in, each guest is given a form to request a custom breakfast the following morning.

Food

There are plenty of good places to eat scattered around downtown and other areas, but the focus of Salta's gastronomic scene has shifted north to Calle Balcarce, between Plaza Güemes and the old railroad station. In style, if not in scale, the area resembles Buenos Aires's Palermo Soho, with inventive restaurants occupying recycled premises. Unfortunately, in this tobacco-producing province, most of them don't even offer a nonsmoking section, so consider an early dinner to avoid the worst offenders, or a table on the sidewalk.

Part of the new anthropology museum, Wi-Fi–equipped **Bar 77** (Mitre 77, tel. 0387/422-1175) is ideal for a quiet breakfast or snack, as it's more subdued than other nearby cafés. Try the llama empanadas and the fresh coca-leaf tea.

La Selecta (Santiago del Estero and Deán Funes, tel. 0387/421-3724) is good for sandwiches, pizza, empanadas, and good mixed drinks at reasonable prices. The no-smoking section, though, is almost laughably small.

Among sit-down restaurants, **Alvarez** (Buenos Aires 302, tel. 0387/421-4523) is one of the most economical Argentine choices, and it offers live tango Saturday nights. Quiet with fine service, downtown's best *parrilla* is **⟨C El Solar del Convento** (Caseros 444, tel. 0387/421-5124, US$10–20), with an outstanding *bife de chorizo* and regional specialties like empanadas and *humitas*.

Doña Salta (Córdoba 46, tel. 0387/432-1921) is stereotypically *gauchesco*, but its empanadas are among Salta's best. Meat dishes are a better option than its pastas, whereas **Trattoría Mamma Mia** (Pasaje Zorrilla 1, tel. 0387/422-5061) has wider selection.

With wines stacked from floor to ceiling and cured hams twirling on strings, out-of-the-way **⟨C Fiambrería La Cordobesa** (J. M. Leguizamón 1502, tel. 0387/422-2794, US$10) is a delightfully informal deli that also serves early-evening tapas at a handful of tables. It gets crowded and the service is erratic, but it's well worth any wait.

Just walking the length of Balcarce between

Plaza Güemes and the train station can offer any number of choices, but one of the most popular is **❨ La Vieja Estación** (Balcarce 885, tel. 0387/421-7727, US$10–20). With *locro* and *chivito* (grilled goat) on the menu and live folkloric entertainment on the stage, it's open until 5 A.M.

Unable to decide whether it's a restaurant or a theme pub, **Bonnie & Clyde** (Balcarce 813, tel. 0387/15-453-6183) prepares some uncommon dishes, such as goat-cheese ravioli, but it also serves mixed drinks, wine by the glass, and pop videos.

La Leñita (Balcarce and Alsina, tel. 0387/421-4865) is an appealing *parrilla* with great service and talented singer-guitarist waiters, but it is on the expensive side with most entrées in the US$10 range. Two other nearby entries, more restaurants than nightspots per se, deserve a look: **Don Cosme** (Balcarce 585, tel. 0387/421-2806, www.milrosemusiccafe. com) and especially **Antigua** (Balcarce 525, tel. 0387/422-8498).

A block from the frenzy in an atmospheric 19th-century building with its walls uncovered to reveal its brick superstructure, **❨ José Balcarce** (Mitre 912, tel. 0387/421-1628, www.cocinadealtura.com.ar) carries the *cocina de altura* (high-altitude cooking) flag, with dishes such as llama steak with a sunflower seed sauce accompanied by guacamole-stuffed chili peppers (US$13) as well as a fine regional wine list supplemented by Mendoza vintages. Another good choice is the *sorrentinos* (US$8), stuffed with maize and goat cheese in a basil sauce.

In the unfashionable area south of Parque San Martín, **La Céfira** (Córdoba 481, tel. 0387/421-4922, lacefira@arnet.com.ar) specializes in fine fresh pastas, but dishes such as boneless chicken breast stuffed with shrimp in a lightly creamy asparagus sauce (US$8) also stand out. The ambiance is attractive, but the service a little anxiously amateur.

Salta boasts an abundance of ice creameries, but **Heladería Fili** (General Güemes 1009, tel. 0387/422-3355) has flourished for over half a century. **Heladería del Bosque** (Córdoba 353,

tel. 0387/421-2424) and **Helados Gianni** (San Martín 595) are good backups.

Information

The provincial **Secretaría de Turismo** (Buenos Aires 93, tel. 0387/431-0950, www. turismosalta.gov.ar, 8 A.M.–9 P.M. weekdays, 9 A.M.–8 P.M. weekends and holidays) distributes brochures and maps, and it usually has English-speaking personnel.

In new downtown quarters, the **Dirección Municipal de Turismo** (Caseros 711, tel. 0387/437-3341) is open 9 A.M.–9 P.M. daily; in high season, at the bus terminal, it maintains a smaller office open 1–4 P.M. daily.

For motorists, **ACA** is at Rivadavia and Mitre, tel. 0387/431-0229.

For national parks information, visit the **Administración de Parques Nacionales** (APN, Santa Fe 23, tel. 0387/422-7093, drnoa@apn.gov.ar, 10 A.M.–noon and 3–5 P.M. daily).

For information on mountaineering, try the **Club Amigos de la Montaña** (San Luis 510, cam1956@hotmail.com), which meets Tuesday, Wednesday, and Thursday at 8 P.M.

Services

Cambio Dinar (Mitre 101), at the northwest corner of Plaza 9 de Julio, changes cash and travelers checks (with a commission). Numerous banks have ATMs, such as **Banco de la Nación** (Mitre 151) and Citibank (Balcarce and España).

Correo Argentino is at Deán Funes 170; the postal code is 4400.

For visa renewals, **Migraciones** (Maipú 35, tel. 0387/422-0438) is 11 blocks west of Plaza 9 de Julio.

Argentina's neighbors Chile (Santiago del Estero 965, tel. 0387/431-1857) and Bolivia (Mariano Boedo 34, tel. 0387/421-1040) have consulates here.

Telecentro Telecom (Alvarado 686) is one of many call centers. Downtown Internet outlets are abundant, and many cafés around Plaza 9 de Julio have Wi-Fi.

Laundry pickup and delivery are free from

Lavandería Sol de Mayo (25 de Mayo 755, tel. 0387/431-9718).

Hospital San Bernardo (Boedo 69, tel. 0387/432-0300) is the public hospital.

Getting There and Around

Salta has the most complete transportation options in northwestern Argentina.

Aerolíneas Argentinas (Caseros 475, tel. 0387/431-1331) flies frequently to Aeroparque (Buenos Aires), sometimes via Córdoba; some flights from Aeroparque continue to Jujuy. **LAN Argentina** (Buenos Aires 92, Local 1, tel. 0387/432-9436) also flies to Aeroparque.

Andes Líneas Aéreas (España 478, tel. 0387/416-2600, www.andesonline.com.ar) flies to Aeroparque and Puerto Madryn, and twice weekly to Puerto Iguazú. Return flights from Puerto Iguazú continue to Córdoba.

The Bolivian carrier **AeroSur** (España 414, tel. 0387/432-0043) flies north to Santa Cruz de la Sierra, with connections to Miami. Southbound from Bolivia, it continues to Tucumán.

Aeropuerto Internacional Martín Miguel de Güemes (tel. 0387/424-7356) is nine kilometers southwest of town on RP 51; for transfers, contact Airbus (tel. 0387/431-5327).

At the east end of Parque San Martín, the renovated **Terminal de Ómnibus** (Avenida Hipólito Yrigoyen s/n, tel. 0387/401-1143) has provincial, long-distance, and even international services to Chile.

Several times weekly, **Pullman Bus** (tel. 0387/422-1366) or **Géminis** (tel. 0387/431-7778), and **Andesmar** (tel. 0387/431-0263) cross the Andes to San Pedro de Atacama (11 hours, US$48–53) and Calama, Chile (13 hours, US$50–55). At Calama, there are connections to Antofagasta, Iquique, and the border city of Arica.

At least a score of bus companies offer long-distance runs. Typical destinations, times, and fares include Jujuy (2 hours, US$6), Tucumán (4.5 hours, US$15–17), Resistencia (12 hours, US$33), Córdoba (12 hours, US$45–48), Mendoza (16 hours, US$58–70), and Buenos Aires (18–20 hours, US$60–73).

El Indio (tel. 0387/431-4389) goes three times daily to Cafayate (3 hours, US$9), as does **Saeta** (tel. 0387/422-8228), which leaves from the base of the Teleférico. **Ale Hermanos** (tel. 0387/423-2226) climbs to San Antonio de los Cobres (5 hours, US$8) at 7:30 A.M. daily except Tuesday and Thursday.

Empresa Marcos Rueda (tel. 0387/421-4447) goes to Cachi (4.5 hours, US$10) at 7 A.M. every day as well as at 1:30 P.M. Tuesday and Saturday, at 3:30 P.M. Thursday, and at 6 P.M. Sunday; and to Molinos (6.5 hours, US$14) at 7 A.M. Monday, Wednesday, Friday, and Sunday as well as at 1:30 P.M. Saturday (with a change in Cachi).

While the **Ferrocarril Belgrano** (Ameghino 690, tel. 0387/431-0809) has no regular passenger services, it is still the departure point for the legendary **Tren a las Nubes** (Train to the Clouds), a tourist train that goes beyond San Antonio de los Cobres to a spectacular viaduct before returning to Salta. For more details, contact **Ferro Turismo** (Buenos Aires 191, tel. 0387/431-5314, www.ferroturismo.todoweb-salta.com.ar).

Hertz (Caseros 374, tel. 0387/421-6785) and **Avis** (Caseros 420, tel. 0387/421-2181) are the main car rental agencies.

◖ VALLES CALCHAQUÍES AND THE ALTIPLANO

West and south of Salta, the Andean canyon lands bear the collective name of the Valles Calchaquíes, after the indigenous Calchaquí or Diaguita peoples who inhabited the area before the Spanish invasion; the altiplano uplands are a high, thinly populated steppe. Rich in scenery and archaeological heritage, its highlights are the Quebrada del Toro, through which the Tren a las Nubes chugs northwest to the Chilean border; the polychrome Quebrada de Cafayate and its wine country; and the picturesque towns of the Río Calchaquí proper.

Several Salta operators offer excursions in the area. **Tastil Viajes** (Caseros 468, tel. 0387/431-1223, www.movitrack.com.ar) does a one-day "MoviTrack" Safari a las Nubes (US$138 pp) to San Antonio de los Cobres, Salinas Grandes, and Purmamarca; a two-day excursion that also includes the Quebrada de Humahuaca (US$232 pp); and a two-day version that also includes Quilmes and Cafayate (US$250).

Another reliable operator, specializing in natural history and bird-watching in particular, is **Clark Expediciones** (Mariano Moreno 1950, tel. 0387/497-1024, www.clarkexpediciones. com), which focuses on the *yungas* but also travels to the altiplano and other remote areas of the northwest. English-speaking operator-conservationist Ricardo Clark has written several bird-watching guides.

Quebrada del Toro

West of Salta, graveled RP 51 parallels the railroad as it climbs the Quebrada del Toro canyon

---

A TRAIN TO THE CLOUDS

One of South America's most impressive engineering achievements, from an economic standpoint, has been one of its most useless. From its base at Salta, 1,187 meters above sea level, a 571-kilometer westbound rail line climbs the vividly colorful Quebrada del Toro and traverses the monochrome puna beneath intense blue Andean skies to Socompa, at 3,858 meters, on the Chilean border. At Abra Chorrillos, its highest point, it scrapes 4,575 meters.

Its greatest feature is the **Viaducto La Polvorilla,** the turnaround point for excursions on the popular Tren a las Nubes (Train to the Clouds) excursion. Sixty-four meters above the desert floor, at an altitude of 4,220 meters, the 224-meter viaduct straddles a scenic desert canyon. En route to La Polvorilla, the line passes through more than 20 tunnels and 19 stations, zigzagging up hillsides at El Alisal (1,806 meters) and Chorrillos (2,111 meters), and literally spiraling twice between Tacuara (3,036 meters) and Diego de Almagro (3,503 meters).

In conception, this was an international railway that linked Salta to the Chilean port of Antofagasta; in practice it still is, but not in the way its founders envisaged. In the first instance, it took 60 years to complete a line first proposed in 1888 to supply Chile's nitrate mines with fresh produce, by which time the nitrate boom had fizzled.

After opening in 1948, it failed as a passenger line because demand was too small and the 38-hour trip, which required changing trains at Socompa, was simply too exhausting. In 1973, when Chile used the link to freight a trial load of copper to the Brazilian port of Santos, it took more than two weeks to reach

the Atlantic; only recently has the shipment of motor vehicles across the Andes to Paraguay justified keeping the line open. According to British rail historian Ian Thomson, "It's a superlative railroad both in terms of its technical achievements and of the expenses to keep it in service."

After several years' suspension, the Tren a las Nubes reopened in 2008 for trips to the La Polvorilla viaduct. It leaves Salta's aging railroad station (Ameghino and Balcarce, tel. 0387/422-3033), which has no regular passenger services, at 7 A.M. every Saturday; rates are US$140 pp in high season (Semana Santa and July's winter holidays) and US$120 pp in low season. Services shut down December–March, the altiplano rainy season; for more details, contact the local representative **Ferroturismo** (Buenos Aires 191, tel. 0387/431-5314, www .ferroturismo.todowebsalta.com.ar) or the Buenos Aires office of **Tren a las Nubes** (Cerrito 844, tel. 011/5246-6666, www.ecotren.com).

For those who want to live the entire experience, it has been possible to reach the border on the infrequent freights, but according to a reliable source, the last foreigner to wrangle a spot, in 2002, needed nearly three weeks to convince the engineer. Anyone lucky enough to reach Socompa can try to switch to the run-down Chilean freight, which continues to the town of Baquedano on Ruta 5, Chile's main north-south highway. Through wild, high scenery that's about as far off the beaten track as you can get, this uncertain trip requires language skills, patience, and lots of time. Carry Chilean pesos from Salta to meet expenses until you can reach a city.

en route to the mining town of San Antonio de los Cobres, the largest settlement in the provincial altiplano, and the stunning viaduct at La Polvorilla. While many people enjoy the Tren a las Nubes, the "Train to the Clouds," the highway has its own appeal and is usually open in summer, when the train may not run.

Before the train, which dates from the 1940s, and even before the road, the Quebrada del Toro was the route by which stockmen drove cattle and mules over the Andean altiplano to the nitrate mines of Chile's Atacama desert. By the time the animals arrived in Chile, they were usually scrawnier than when they had left Salta (on Diego de Almagro's 16th-century expedition, both men and horses froze to death with the cold, and subsequent Spaniards scavenged meat from the preserved animal carcasses).

About 55 kilometers from Salta, the train and the highway intersect at **Estación Chorrillos,** 2,111 meters above sea level, where there's a small campground suitable for cyclists and other travelers. **Santa Rosa de Tastil,** 3,110 meters above sea level and 110 kilometers from Salta, is the site of pre-Inka ruins; while tour buses cannot easily approach the ruins, smaller operators do. In any event, the modest **Museo Regional Moisés Zerpa** (10 A.M.–6 P.M. weekdays, 10 A.M.–2 P.M. weekends, US$1) holds regional artifacts, and there is also an indigenous crafts market.

Befitting its name, **San Antonio de los Cobres** (pop. about 5,000) relies on a nearby copper mine for its economy, but for most visitors it's the last station on the Tren a las Nubes before the La Polvorilla viaduct, where the train turns around and returns to Salta. At 3,775 meters above sea level, 168 kilometers from Salta, it's also a stop for loop tours to the Salinas Grandes salt flats along RN 40, to the north, which return to Salta via Purmamarca and the Quebrada de Humahuaca. In dry weather, this route is passable for any vehicle, but in rainy weather it can be treacherous.

Note that even when the train is not running, volunteer guides from the San Antonio's Instituto Terciario del Turismo will take

visitors to the viaduct for the cost of gasoline (a tip, though, would be appropriate).

San Antonio's best accommodation is the well-heated **Hostería de las Nubes** (RN 51 s/n, tel. 0387/490-9059, reservas@maresdelsur.com, US$42–53 s, US$53–63 d), which offers large but simply furnished rooms with private baths and TVs. It also has a large crafts shop, and its restaurant has a decent but limited lunch and dinner menu.

Ale Hermanos (tel. 0387/423-2226) operates five buses weekly to Salta (5 hours, US$8).

Quebrada de Escoipe

South of Salta, RN 68 rises slowly out of the Lerma Valley past the westbound RP 33 turnoff through the Quebrada de Escoipe, a mostly gravel road that is one of Argentina's most spectacular mountain highways, to Parque Nacional Los Cardones and the picturesque town of Cachi.

Where the paved road ends and the gravel section begins, RP 33 snakes through a gorge so narrow that there's barely room for a single lane of traffic, and washouts are possible in wet weather. That said, it does not require 4WD. Cyclists interested in making the strenuous 520-kilometer loop trip from Salta, though, should take the more gradual climb via Cafayate and Cachi rather than the very steep ascent from here to the 3,600-meter **Cuesta del Obispo.** Looking back east toward Salta, the views—and the descent—are vertiginous.

Located mostly on the high plateau west of the Cuesta del Obispo, the 65,000-hectare **Parque Nacional Los Cardones** also occupies arid canyons and summits ranging from 2,700 to 5,000 meters above sea level. About 100 kilometers from Salta, its emblematic species is the columnar *cardón* or candelabra cactus (*Trichocereus pasacana*), which forms imposing stands at altitudes up to 3,400 meters. In the otherwise treeless aridity of the puna, the *cardón* was the only available construction wood for the pre-Columbian population, and colonial Spaniards adapted it to their own

© WAYNE BERNHARDSON

At lower elevations, fog often obscures the cacti at Parque Nacional Los Cardones.

houses and churches. Now paved, the straight-as-an-arrow **Recta de Tin Tin** parallels an Inka road to the village of Payogasta.

The park itself lacks infrastructure, though many Salta travel agencies offer excursions here. There is a ranger at Piedra del Molino, near the Cuesta del Obispo, while the park headquarters is at Payogasta (San Martín s/n, tel. 03868/49-6005, loscardones@apn.gov.ar), 11 kilometers north of Cachi.

Quebrada de Cafayate and Vicinity

About 50 kilometers south of Salta, paved RP 47 leads east to **Embalse Cabra Corral**, a hydroelectric reservoir whose carefully timed releases permit year-round white-water rafting through the scenic Río Juramento canyon.

Based at Cabra Corral, **Salta Rafting** (RP 47 Km 34, tel. 0387/401-0301; Buenos Aires 88, Local 13, Salta, tel. 0387/421-4114, www.saltarafting.com) offers two-hour, 12-kilometer descents of the Class-III river, sometimes under a full moon, for US$40 pp plus US$16 pp for round-trip transport from Salta; they

also organize other activities such as kayaking, rappelling, and mountain biking. Try also **Norte Rafting** (RP 47 Km 18, tel. 0387/424-8474, www.norterafting.com).

Another 50 kilometers south, beyond the hamlet of Alemania, the landscape changes abruptly from the lush upper Lerma to the arid canyon of the north-flowing Río de las Conchas, popularly known as the Quebrada de Cafayate. At the foot of the Sierra de Carahuasi, the river has eroded the range's sedimentary strata into uniquely shaped and colorful landforms reminiscent of the southwestern United States.

On the southbound bus from Salta to Cafayate, grab a left-side window seat for the best views of landforms like the **Garganta del Diablo** (Devil's Throat), **El Anfiteatro** (The Amphitheatre), **El Sapo** (The Toad), **El Fraile** (The Friar), **El Obelisco** (The Obelisk), **Los Castillos** (The Castles), and the **Los Médanos** dunes, on the outskirts of the town. From Cafayate to Salta, sit on the right side of the bus.

For more in-depth explorations of these landmarks and box canyons, which are mostly concentrated in the last 58 kilometers before Cafayate, it's possible to disembark and continue on a subsequent bus, while hiking between the closer sights. It's also possible to rent a bicycle in Cafayate and ride through the canyon, returning on the bus if you don't care to ride back. Whether walking or riding, carry high-energy snacks and plenty of water.

Cafayate

Thanks to its sandy soils, mild dry climate, and high altitude, the town of Cafayate is the hub of a key wine region, with producers ranging from tiny family bodegas and boutiques to full-scale industrial operations. Though it lacks Mendoza's reputation and critical mass of wineries, it has begun to make the most of the Argentine wine boom; its signature varietal is the dry but fruity white torrontés, long since disappeared from its Spanish origins, which one French grower likens to "eating the grape."

With the bonus of its scenic surroundings, Cafayate is southwestern Salta Province's top destination, but it has been underappreciated by foreigners until recently. One negative, though, is the new "wine and golf" resort going up on Cafayate's southern outskirts—vintners can conserve water by using drip irrigation, but golf courses cannot.

At 1,660 meters above sea level, Cafayate (pop. 10,729) is 236 kilometers south of Salta via paved RN 68; RN 40 leads northwest toward Molinos and Cachi, and south toward the ruins of Quilmes (Tucumán Province). The town itself has a compact grid whose main drag is north–south Avenida Güemes (RN 40). Addresses on Güemes are known directionally, depending on whether they are north (Norte) or south (Sur) of the central Plaza San Martín.

SIGHTS

For most visitors, Cafayate's wineries are its primary appeal. At the same time, it's one of the centers for northwestern Argentine artisans, particularly weavers, and the plaza is full of quality items.

© WAYNE BERNHARDSON

the tasting room at Cafayate's Bodega El Tránsito

THE ANDEAN NORTHWEST

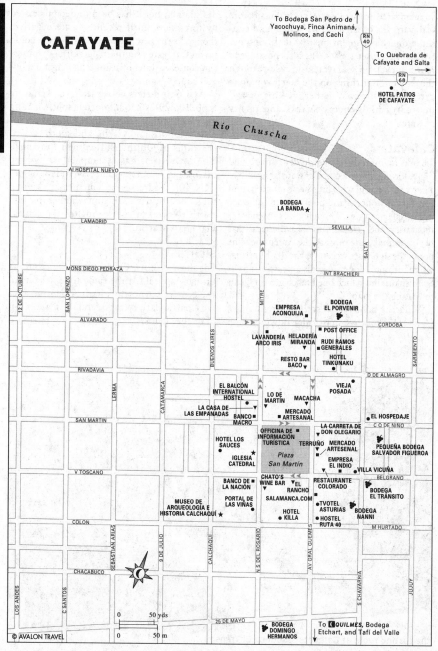

CAFAYATE

To Bodega San Pedro de
Yacochuya, Finca Animaná,
Molinos, and Cachi

RN 40

To Quebrada de
Cafayate and Salta

RN 68

HOTEL PATIOS
DE CAFAYATE

Río Chuscha

AL HOSPITAL NUEVO

LAMADRID

BODEGA
LA BANDA

SEVILLA

MONS DIEGO PEDRAZA

INT BRACHIERI

12 DE OCTUBRE

SAN LORENZO

ALVARADO

EMPRESA
ACONQUIJA

BODEGA
EL PORVENIR

POST OFFICE

CORDOBA

SARMIENTO

MITRE

BUENOS AIRES

SALTA

LAVANDERÍA
ARCO IRIS

HELADERÍA
MIRANDA

RUDI RAMOS
GENERALES

RESTO BAR
BACO

HOTEL
TINKUNAKU

RIVADAVIA

LERMA

CATAMARCA

EL BALCÓN
INTERNATIONAL
HOSTEL

LO DE
MARTÍN

MACACHA

VIEJA
POSADA

D DE ALMAGRO

LA CASA DE
LAS EMPANADAS

BANCO
MACRO

MERCADO
ARTESANAL

EL HOSPEDAJE

SAN MARTIN

C Q DE NINO

HOTEL LOS
SAUCES

OFFICINA DE
INFORMACIÓN
TURÍSTICA

LA CARRETA DE
DON OLEGARIO

TERRUÑO

MERCADO
ARTESANAL

PEQUEÑA BODEGA
SALVADOR FIGUEROA

IGLESIA
CATEDRAL

*Plaza
San Martín*

EMPRESA
EL INDIO

VILLA VICUÑA

V TOSCANO

BELGRANO

BANCO DE
LA NACIÓN

CHATO'S
WINE BAR

EL
RANCHO

RESTAURANTE
COLORADO

BODEGA
EL TRÁNSITO

MUSEO DE
ARQUEOLOGÍA E
HISTORIA CALCHAQUÍ

PORTAL DE
LAS VIÑAS

SALAMANCA.COM

TVOTEL
ASTURIAS

BODEGA
NANNI

COLON

HOTEL
KILLA

HOSTEL
RUTA 40

M HURTADO

SEBASTIAN ARIAS

9 DE JULIO

CALCHAQUÍ

N S DEL ROSARIO

AV GRAL GUEMES

S CHAVARRIA

JUJUY

CHACABUCO

LOS ANDES

C SANTOS

0   50 yds

0   50 m

25 DE MAYO

BODEGA
DOMINGO
HERMANOS

To **QUILMES**, Bodega
Etchart, and Tafí del Valle

Founded by the late historian-archaeologist Rodolfo Bravo, the private **Museo de Arqueología e Historia Calchaquí** (Colón 191, tel. 03868/42-1054, 11 A.M.–9 P.M. weekdays, 11 A.M.–3 P.M. Sat., free) comprises an enormous assortment of pre-Columbian arrow and spear points, ceramics, textiles, and funerary urns, plus colonial and postcolonial weapons, horse gear, musical instruments, and leather goods. Bravo, an autodidact, undertook research in the archives of Salta and Tucumán Provinces as well as those of local farms and ranches.

ENTERTAINMENT AND EVENTS
The misleadingly named **Semana de Cafayate** is really a three-day folklore celebration based around February 20. The annual **Fiesta de la Virgen** takes place October 7.

At the Quebrada de Cafayate's appropriately named canyon El Anfiteatro, the musical **Concierto en la Montaña** takes place the last Sunday in July.

SHOPPING
Cafayate's **Mercado Artesanal,** on Güemes across from Plaza San Martín, has been the main handicrafts outlet, but there are several others on three sides of the plaza.

ACCOMMODATIONS
Except for the rundown campground, Cafayate's accommodations have increased and improved in all categories, from hostels to country inns. It often gets crowded with visitors from the provincial capital on weekends, when hotel reservations are advisable.

HI affiliate **Hostel Ruta 40** (Avenida Güemes Sur 178, tel. 03868/42-1689, www.hostel-ruta40.com, US$8.50–10 pp dorm, US$32–38 d) is a cozy but orderly place with mostly dorms but also a couple of doubles with private baths. The independent **El Balcón International Hostel** (Pasaje 20 de Febrero 110, tel. 03868/42-1739, www.elbalconhostel.com.ar, US$11 pp dorm, US$13–18 d) runs its own tours, including some difficult-to-reach sites.

No longer a hostel, the expanded **El Hospedaje de Martín** (Salta 13, tel. 03868/42-1680, elhospedaje@gmail.com, US$24–27 s, US$32–40 d) has style as well as substance, not to mention amenities such as a pool and its own café. All rooms now have private baths, but some have ceiling fans in lieu of air-conditioning.

A bargain for the price, **Vieja Posada** (Diego de Almagro 87, tel. 03868/42-2251, www.viejaposada.com.ar, US$27–40) is a charming colonial-style bed-and-breakfast. Nicely appointed rooms vary in size, with small but functional baths except for one larger, more expensive suite. Amenities include Wi-Fi and off-street parking.

Renovated and expanded, **Hotel Asturias** (Güemes Sur 154, tel. 03868/42-1328, www.hotel-asturias.com.ar, US$42–100 s, US$66–130 d) continues to improve, but its size—some 130 rooms—makes it more institutional than other Cafayate hotels, but it also means there's usually something available. It boasts a large swimming pool and ample parking.

Friendly, family-run **Portal de las Viñas** (Nuestra Señora del Rosario 165, tel. 03868/42-1098, www.portalvinas.com.ar, US$48 s, US$60 d) has tidy multibed rooms with private baths on a deep lot with vine- and walnut-shaded patios. The common areas, though, are substantially more appealing than the rooms themselves.

On a quiet block west of the plaza, comfortable **Hotel los Sauces** (Calchaquí 62, tel. 03868/42-1158, www.hotellossaucessa.com, US$64 s, US$83 d, suites US$85 s, US$102 d) is steadily improving, but prices are also steadily rising. The roomy upstairs suites come with large balconies as well.

◖ **Villa Vicuña** (Belgrano 76, tel. 03868/42-2145, www.villavicuna.com.ar, US$66–112 s or d) is a restoration of a colonial house with period furnishings. The major departure from the traditional is the three-dimensional patio mural of regional folkloric figures by local artists Jorge del Pozo and Tito Cruz.

Within town, the best choice is the innovative ◖ **Hotel Killa** (Colón 47, tel. 03868/42-2254,

WINES AND WINERIES OF CAFAYATE

Cafayate is one of South America's most elevated wine regions, whose signature varietal is the fruity but dry white torrontés. Seven wineries are within staggering distance of the plaza, three others within weaving distance on a bicycle. For the moment, though, there's no historical perspective, as the former **Museo de Vitivinicultura** (Güemes Sur and Colón), Cafayate's wine museum, has been closed for an overhaul that involves major construction.

South of the plaza, **Domingo Hermanos** (Nuestra Señora del Rosario and 25 de Mayo, tel. 03868/42-1225, www.domingohermanos.com) offers the most professional tours, where a generous tasting in appealing surroundings includes malbec, torrontés, and their own goat cheese (which can be purchased separately). Guided tours take place in Spanish only, 9 A.M.-12:30 P.M. and 2:30-6:30 P.M. weekdays, 9 A.M.-12:30 P.M. Saturday, and 10:30 A.M.-12:30 P.M. Sunday and holidays. The vineyards stand above 2,000 meters in nearby Yacochuya.

East of the plaza, the organically certified **Bodega Nanni** (Chavarría 151, tel. 03868/42-1527, www.bodegananni.com) is an informal family business with barely 10 hectares of vines and a handful of employees. In addition to torrontés, it produces cabernet sauvignon, malbec, and tannat; hours are 9 A.M.-1 P.M. and 2-6 P.M. Monday-Saturday.

Just up the block, **Bodega El Tránsito** (Belgrano 102, tel. 03868/42-2385, www.bodegaeltransito.com) is a new boutique winery with a longtime presence in the area. Having upgraded its malbec, cabernet, and torrontés, as well as blends of cabernet with either Syrah or malbec, it produces about 350,000 bottles per annum. Tours of its modern facility, with a free-of-charge tasting, take place 9 A.M.-1 P.M. and 3:30-8 P.M. daily.

Less than a block to the northeast, in a narrow alleyway, the **Pequeña Bodega Salvador Figueroa** (Pasaje 20 de Junio 25, tel. 03868/42-1289, gualiama@gmail.com) is one of Argentina's smallest bodegas, a Lilliputian locale producing only 2,500 bottles of classic malbec, 2,500 of oaked malbec roble, and 600 bottles of torrontés per annum.

Brief tours, with an inexpensive tasting (about US$1.25 pp) that belies the quality of a vintner who has worked for decades in other area wineries, take place 8:30 A.M.-12:30 P.M. and 2:30-7:30 P.M. Monday-Saturday, 9:30 A.M.-12:30 P.M. Sunday.

About two blocks farther north, **Bodega El Porvenir** (Córdoba 32, tel. 03868/42-2007, www.bodegaselporvenir.com) produces the Amauta line of young varietals and the more elite Laborum line, with a greater diversity of varietals and blends, including Syrah and tannat. Individualized tours and tasting, in a handsome lounge, cost US$8-16 pp, with a *picada* of cheese and cold cuts, depending on which line of wines you choose to taste. Hours

www.killacafayate.com.ar, US$103–137 s or d), a bed-and-breakfast whose hospitality exceeds even the ample size of its Wi-Fi–equipped rooms and the design-conscious sophistication of its *algarrobo* furnishings. Some upstairs rooms have mountain views, the subtropical gardens are soothing, and the diverse buffet breakfast includes abundant fresh fruit.

In the scenic Quebrada de las Conchas, just west of the highway to Salta, **La Casa de la Bodega** (RN 68 Km 18, tel. 03868/42-1888, www.lacasadelabodega.com.ar, US$85–218 s or d) is a self-styled wine boutique hotel with its own vines and state-of-the-art winery. Its restaurant is the only place to sample its organic torrontés and cabernet-malbec blend, which are otherwise exported. Unfortunately, it sometimes enforces discriminatory rates against foreigners.

About 15 kilometers south of town, **Altalaluna** (RN 40 Km 4326, tel. 03868/42-2501, www.altalaluna.com, US$120 s, US$180 d) is a 20-room boutique hotel whose common areas are a recycled 19th-century landmark, but the accommodations themselves are a modern wing in colonial style, with spacious and

are 10 A.M.-6 P.M. daily, but it's best to make advance arrangements.

Occupying a mid-19th-century structure at the north edge of town, the 800-hectare **Bodega la Banda** (Avenida Güemes Norte s/n, tel. 03868/42-1850, www.vasijasecreta.com) conducts individualized tours and tasting 9 A.M.-7 P.M. daily. Varietals include the usual cabernet, merlot, and torrontés, but there's also burgundy and a cabernet-merlot blend.

Just south of town, dating from 1850, **Bodega Etchart** (RN 40 Km 1047, tel. 03868/42-1310, www.bodegasetchart.com) devotes half its 300 hectares on Finca La Florida to whites, including torrontés (the inexpensive Etchart Cafayate is one of the country's best values), chardonnay, and sauvignon blanc, and the rest to reds, including cabernet franc, cabernet sauvignon, malbec, merlot, pinot noir, Syrah, and tannat. Total production is around 5 million liters per annum at this industrial winery. Slightly disorderly 45-minute tours include tasting; for English-languages guides, it's best to phone ahead. Hours are 9 A.M.-5 P.M. Monday-Friday, 9 A.M.-noon Saturday.

Tucked into a mountainside about five kilometers southwest of town, **Bodega Mounier** (El Divisadero s/n, tel. 03868/42-2129, www.bodegamounier.com) is the anti-Etchart, a boutique winery making only about 40,000 bottles of torrontés, rosé, and a malbec-cabernet-tannat blend per annum. So small

that the *vendimia* (harvest) takes just a single day, it encourages friends, family, and even tourists to participate in the work to be rewarded by lunch, dinner, and a party. It sells much of the production out of the bodega itself, where it offers attentive tours and tasting (US$4, which can be applied to purchases); with a day or two's notice it can provide lunch with a view. Hours are 9:30 A.M.-1:30 P.M. Monday-Friday, 9:30 A.M.-2 P.M. Saturday, but can fluctuate throughout the year.

Co-owned and operated by Etchart and French interests, **Bodega San Pedro de Yacochuya** (tel. 03868/40-0890, www.sanpedrodeyacochuya.com.ar) lies eight kilometers northwest of town at an elevation of 2,035 meters. On only 14 hectares, it produces especially outstanding torrontés and malbec; hours are 10 A.M.-5 P.M. Monday-Friday, 10 A.M.-1 P.M. Saturday, closed Sunday. Tours and tasting at its visitors center normally require one day's notice.

For a different sort of experience, there's **Finca Animaná** (RN 40 Km 1064, tel. 03868/49-2019, bodegaanimana@arnet.com.ar), an industrial facility that produces for the regional market only, on 200 hectares of its own vineyards 15 kilometers north of Cafayate. A commercial winery since the early 20th century, it's the only one in the province to produce cheap, boxed table wines, though it's making forays into finer wines. Dating from 1797-1806, the handsome *casco* alongside the offices features a colonnade with Moorish arches.

attractive rooms that look onto vineyards and the Andes. A spa is under construction, and in a few years it'll have its own boutique winery.

About three kilometers southwest of town via 25 de Mayo, **Wine Resort Viñas de Cafayate** (Finca Calchaquí s/n, tel. 03868/42-2272, www.cafayatewineresort.com, US$112–194 s, US$190–340 d) has a dozen rooms, including two suites, surrounding a central courtyard with a fountain; all have exterior galleries with mountain or vineyard views. There's a pool and Wi-Fi, but its restaurant has lots of kinks to be worked out—especially the slow kitchen and amateur service.

At the north-end highway junction, on the grounds of Bodega El Esteco, the Sheraton-owned **Hotel Patios de Cafayate** (RP 68 and RN 40, tel. 03868/42-2229, www.luxurycollection.com/cafayate, US$285–430 s or d) is a 19th-century mansion with five huge comfortable rooms furnished with antiques and 25 identically styled rooms in an even more luxurious newer sector. In addition, it's a wine spa where you can indulge in a cabernet barrel bath or a torrontés whirlpool bath. The restaurant is open to nonguests for lunch and dinner, by reservation.

THE ANDEAN NORTHWEST

FOOD

Like its accommodations, Cafayate's gastronomic options are increasing and improving. In addition to hotel restaurants, don't hesitate to sample regionally oriented eateries in town.

It's not exactly a restaurant, but **Chato's Wine Bar** (Nuestra Señora del Rosario 132, chatoswinebar@yahoo.com.ar) is an ideal predinner stop, serving *picadas* of local cheeses, cured meats, and olives to accompany a wide selection of local by-the-glass wines at modest prices. With friendly English-speaking ownership, it's open 6–10 P.M. daily.

On the east side of Plaza San Martín, **La Carreta de Don Olegario** (Avenida Güemes Sur 2, tel. 03868/42-1004) serves regional dishes. At **El Rancho** (Toscano 10, tel. 03868/42-1256), on the plaza's south side, the beef is only so-so but the rest of the diverse menu is more appealing, and the service is outstanding. **Lo de Martín** (Mitre 25) is an above-average *parrilla* with assiduous service.

Across the street, **La Casa de las Empanadas** (Mitre 24, tel. 03868/15-45-4111) is a welcoming family-run place where visitors use the walls to scrawl their praise for the varied empanadas and other regional dishes. Extremely cheap, it's an ideal lunch stop.

The informal **Resto Bar Baco** (Avenida Güemes Norte and Rivadavia) is a step above routine Argentine and regional food, with particularly good pizza. Its casual design and youthfulness set it apart from the more traditional places.

Macacha (Avenida Güemes Norte 28, tel. 03868/42-2319) dedicates each of several appealing dining rooms to a local bodega as the kitchen prepares savory dishes such as llama in cabernet sauce (US$10) with quinoa on the side. The wine list, of course, stresses local vintages, and the gravel patio makes for perfect alfresco dining.

Run by U.S. expats, **C Restaurante Colorado** (Belgrano 28, tel. 03868/42-1280, www.restaurantecolorado.com, US$10–15)

Diners decorate the walls at La Casa de las Empanadas.

© WAYNE BERNHARDSON

has the most innovative menu, with items such as Thai curries and Mexican specialties but also regional dishes. Their stuffed pastas, with grilled vegetables enhancing the sauce, deserve special attention. It's open evenings and occasionally for lunch.

◖ Terruño (Güemes Sur 28, tel. 03868/42-2460) delivers a savory *entraña* (skirt steak, US$9), quinoa flan for dessert, and a good wine list that includes a decent by-the-glass selection. The service is a little erratic, but sidewalk seating—with ample space between tables—helps avoid the Abba/Queen soundtrack.

Heladería Miranda (Güemes Norte near Córdoba) has earned a reputation for its inventive wine-flavored sorbets—the fruity white torrontés is tastier than the red cabernet.

INFORMATION AND SERVICES

Plaza San Martín's helpful **Oficina de Información Turística** (Güemes and San Martín, 03868/42-2442) is open 8 A.M.–9 P.M. or even later daily.

Banco de la Nación and **Banco Macro**, both facing Plaza San Martín, have ATMs; the latter is more reliable.

Correo Argentino (Güemes Norte 197) is the post office; the postal code is 4427. Internet connections have improved; try **Salamanca. com** (Güemes Sur 138), half a block south of Plaza San Martín, which also has long-distance telephone service.

Lavandería Arcos Iris (Mitre 189) does the laundry.

GETTING THERE AND AROUND

El Indio (Belgrano 34, tel. 03868/42-1002) operates three buses daily to Salta (4 hours, US$9). It also has one bus daily to Angastaco (2 hours, US$4), but there are no onward connections to Molinos, Cachi, and back to Salta. From the plaza, **Saeta** has services to Salta at 6 A.M. and 2 and 7 P.M. daily.

El Aconquija (Avenida Güemes and Córdoba, tel. 03868/42-2175) goes twice daily to San Miguel de Tucumán (6.5 hours, US$15) via Tafí del Valle (4 hours, US$8.50) and Santa María (2 hours, US$4). These buses are the

best option to visit the pre-Columbian ruins of Quilmes, just over the provincial border.

Rudi Ramos Generales (Güemes Norte 175) rents mountain bikes for visiting nearby wineries or riding the Quebrada de Cafayate (take the El Indio bus to El Anfiteatro and ride back downhill to town).

Valle Calchaquí

The Valle Calchaquí proper begins at its namesake river's headwaters, just south of the 4,895-meter Andean pass known as the Abra del Acay, about 30 kilometers south of San Antonio de los Cobres. Dusty RN 40 parallels the river south through picturesque hamlets and villages that include La Poma, Payogasta, Cachi, Seclantás, Molinos, Angastaco, and San Carlos, and beyond Cafayate to the pre-Columbian fortress of Quilmes.

Until the mid-17th century, the region's Quilmes Indians held off the Spanish invasion before finally suffering a forced march to the Buenos Aires suburb that now bears their name. Their irrigated lands fell to Spanish landowners, while the Quilmes themselves either scattered or died out in the century-plus before Argentina became an independent country. In colonial times the valley was one of the main routes across the Andes to Chile and Perú.

Set among the vividly colored sedimentary canyons and high summits of the Andes, ruins like Quilmes and other archaeological sites are the legacy of the valley's native peoples. The autumn sight of red peppers drying on the hillsides adds another intense hue to a distinctive cultural landscape, many of whose rural adobes display flourishes like Doric columns and Moorish arches.

Fifty kilometers south of Cafayate via paved RN 40, the restored fortress of **Quilmes** is the area's most important archaeological site. Frequently visited from Cafayate, it lies within Tucumán Province and appears in more detail later in this chapter.

North of San Carlos, 22 kilometers from Cafayate, paved RN 40 becomes a dusty washboard that parallels the Río Calchaquí

ESTANCIA COLOMÉ

In the Andes southwest of Molinos, Swiss winemaker Donald Hess has created perhaps his most audacious experiment yet, a high-altitude (2,300 meters) state-of-the-art winery and hotel complex in isolation from any other in the region. Dating from 1831, its vineyards ranging 2,200-3,015 meters above sea level, Bodega Colomé may be Argentina's oldest working winery, but its aging malbec and cabernet sauvignon vines are still flourishing.

Among other interests, the Hess Group has vineyards in Australia, South Africa, and California's Napa Valley. Here it produces a limited line of premium wines that includes a Colomé Reserva malbec blend from old vines, a Colomé Estate malbec blend, and torrontés.

In addition to its winery, Colomé is now home to the **Museo James Turrell,** housing the paintings and especially the elaborate light-and-space constructions of the California-born artist (born 1943), who now lives in Arizona. The interactive museum, visited in small groups by guided tours only, is a disorienting experience with a loss of depth perception for many visitors. Hours are 10:30 A.M.-6 P.M. daily.

For accommodations, Estancia Colomé (RP 53 Km 20, Molinos, tel. 03868/49-4044, www.estanciacolome.com, US$292-340 s or d) has seven spacious junior suites and two larger master suites with radiant floor heat for cool winter nights. Amenities include a dining room and bar, a library, a TV room, a hotel shop, a large swimming pool, tennis courts, hiking trails, a putting green, and satellite Internet service. Rates also include a glass of wine on arrival, a buffet breakfast, an *estancia* tour, and loaner bicycles. Lunch and dinner are extra, as are massages and horseback rides.

Open for guided tours 10:30 A.M.-6 P.M. daily (US$8-13 pp, depending on wines tasted), the winery is 18 kilometers from Molinos by a winding gravel road. Because of its isolation, it's better to phone ahead than to drop in. Nonguests can lunch or dine at the hotel restaurant by reservation only, but the winery proper offers a menu of light meals all day. It's four hours overland from Salta, but only 30 minutes by helicopter.

---

as it passes through a geological wonderland of folded Tertiary sediments that resemble the Quebrada de Cafayate but for their more subdued colors.

At the 70-kilometer point, a short turnoff leads west to the village of **Angastaco,** home to pepper fields, vineyards, a modest archaeological museum, and nearby pre-Columbian ruins. There is also an increasing number of weekend and summer homes, with some offbeat architecture.

For accommodations, there's the slowly declining **Hostería Angastaco** (Avenida Libertador s/n, tel. 03868/49-7700, US$13 s, US$19 d), which has a restaurant and swimming pool (but not always water to fill it). El Indio has one bus daily to Cafayate, but there is no scheduled transport north to Molinos.

Founded in the 17th century as the administrative base for Diego Díaz Gómez's

encomiendas (labor and tribute grants) on the upper Calchaquí, **Molinos** preserves the setting of a slow-moving colonial village with its namesake flour mill, landmark church, and a magnificent historical residence converted into a hotel. At 2,020 meters above sea level, it's 39 kilometers north of Angastaco and 39 kilometers south of Cachi via RN 40.

Molinos's **Iglesia de San Pedro de Nolasco** was Díaz Gómez's original chapel, enlarged by his son-in-law Domingo de Isasmendi, but the current church is a late-18th-century construction that's also the burial site of *encomendero* Nicolás Severo de Isasmendi, Salta's last royalist governor. Its twin bell towers, linked by a semicircular arch that shades the main entrance, rise above the thick adobe wall and red-tiled roof.

Nicolás Isasmendi (1753–1837) also built and occupied the **Casa de Isasmendi,** immediately across from the church. It's now the provincial tourist hotel, but rejuvenated under a private concession. About 1.5 kilometers west of town via a good dirt road, the **Criadero Coquera** is a captive breeding site for the endangered vicuña, at a relatively low elevation (around 1,900 meters) for this high-puna camelid. Part of the former Estancia Luracatao, now belonging to the state agricultural extension service INTA, the **Casa de Entre Ríos** contains a little-visited but excellent artisans' market, including the characteristic red-striped *ponchos de Güemes*, woven from alpaca wool.

The cheapest accommodations option is **Camping Municipal** (tel. 0387/15-483-9305, US$4 per tent plus US$1.25 pp), with access to hot showers and use of the nearby swimming pool, though the shade trees have been slow to grow. The adjacent, spotless **Cabañas Municipales** has a dozen double rooms with shared baths charging US$6.50–8 pp.

Across from the church, new concessionaires have dramatically improved the 18 colonially stylish rooms and amenities at █ **Hacienda de Molinos** (Abraham Cornejo s/n, tel. 03868/49-4094, www.haciendademolinos. com.ar, US$110–150 s or d), which surrounds a pepper-shaded patio and features a restaurant open to the public, a pool, a small archaeological museum, an artisans' shop, and Wi-Fi in common areas. It now offers excursions and horseback riding as well.

Marcos Rueda buses via Cachi to Salta (6.5 hours, US$14) leave at 7 A.M. Monday, Tuesday, Thursday, and Saturday and at 1 P.M. Sunday.

Nineteen kilometers north of Molinos, an eastbound bridge crosses the Río Calchaquí to **Seclantás**, a hillside hamlet with a shady plaza, the early-19th-century **Iglesia de Nuestra Señora del Carmen,** and an atmospheric cemetery with a ruined chapel. For accommodations, try **Hostería La Rueda** (Cornejo s/n, tel. 03868/49-8041, US$13–19 s, US$21–27 d), where the more expensive rooms have private baths.

Eleven kilometers north of Cachi, **Payogasta** is a quiet village that's the headquarters of

Parque Nacional Los Cardones (San Martín s/n, tel. 03868/49-1066). There's a fine crafts shop here, and good new accommodations at the **Sala de Payogasta** (RN 40 Km 4509, tel. 03868/49-6052, www.saladepayogasta.com, US$63–88 s, US$69–88 d), a reconditioned century-old adobe that has a restaurant across the road.

Cachi

Scenic Cachi dates from an 18th-century *encomienda* that, as the indigenous population declined, became the Aramburu family's hacienda and then the picturesque village it is today. Easily reached from Salta, less so from Cafayate, it makes an ideal stopover on the scenic 520-kilometer loop that connects the three localities. At 2,280 meters above sea level, with narrow cobbled streets, Cachi (pop. 2,235) enjoys a spectacular setting at the base of the imposing 6,380-meter Nevado de Cachi.

SIGHTS

Immediately east of shady **Plaza 9 de Julio,** the colonial **Iglesia San José** (1796) has an unadorned facade with three bells facing south, in a line, over the entrance. Craftsmen fashioned many of its interior features, including the ceiling and confessional, from *cardón*-cactus wood.

Immediately south of the church, the **Museo Arqueológico Pío Pablo Díaz** (Juan Calchaquí s/n, tel. 03868/49-1080, 10 A.M.–7 P.M. Mon.–Sat., 10 A.M.–1 P.M. Sun.) provides a sophisticated account of the area's cultural development from its hunter-gatherer origins to the Inka conquest and the Spanish invasion. Well-arranged and illustrated, the exhibits have good explanatory text (in Spanish only). The admission charge of US$1.25–2.50 is voluntary.

EVENTS AND SHOPPING

The **Festival de la Tradición,** taking place the third weekend of January, is a folkloric happening. March 19's **Día de San José** honors Cachi's patron saint.

Half a block off Plaza 9 de Julio, Cachi's

Centro de Artesanías (Ruiz de Los Llanos s/n) sells regional crafts.

ACCOMMODATIONS

The central Hotel Nevado de Cachi (Ruiz de los Llanos and Federico Suárez, tel. 03868/49-1063, US$8 pp shared bath; US$16 s, US$19 d, private bath) is the cheapest option. On a quiet block full of adobes, about 100 meters south of Plaza 9 de Julio, Hospedaje Don Arturo (Bustamante s/n, tel. 03868/49-1087, hospedajedonarturo@infonoa.com.ar, US$10–13 pp) is simple but comfy and friendly; it offers terraces for sunbathing, excursions, and even a little wine-tasting.

Converted to a B&B with rooms that are more like apartments, with several internal patios, Tampu Bed & Breakfast (Avenida Güemes s/n, tel. 03868/49-1092, www.tampucachi.com, US$26 s, US$29 d) was until recently a colonial-style family house. An excellent value, it's quiet and friendly, with Wi-Fi and attractive common areas including a parrilla for barbecues, but the baths are tiny.

Opened in 2005, Hostal Llaqta Mawk'a (Ruiz de los Llanos s/n, tel. 03868/49-1016, www.puebloantiguo.com.ar, US$37 s, US$48 d) is a fine family-oriented place with a pool and even a separate playground for kids. Some rooms are on the small side.

One of the country's best values, ACA's ◖ Hostería de Cachi (Automóvil Club Argentino s/n, tel. 03868/49-1105, www.hosteriacachi.com.ar, US$41–53 s, US$67–96 d) sits on immaculate grounds; its rooms surround an expansive courtyard, in one corner of which rises and spreads a gigantic pepper tree. It also has Cachi's most sophisticated restaurant and a pool; the higher rates are for nonmembers, but those who belong to foreign automobile clubs are eligible for the lower ones.

Immediately across the street, offering friendly family attention, the 15-room ◖ Hostal el Cortijo (Automóvil Club Argentino s/n, tel. 03868/49-1034, www.hostalelcortijo.com.ar, US$58 s, US$71 d) is even better. An elegantly transformed colonial farmhouse, it boasts a central patio sculpted

with a fountain and running water to mimic the sounds of the acequias (canals) that irrigate local vineyards. Thematically decorated rooms ("Andean Angels" with colonial-style statuary, for instance) include antique furniture but modern baths and heating; rates, which may be negotiable, include an above-average breakfast.

On Cachi's outskirts, on a prominent hillside site, La Merced del Alto Hotel & Spa (Fuerte Alto s/n, tel. 03868/49-0030, www.lamerceddelalto.com, US$140–150 s, US$163–175 d) is a new 14-room spa hotel in a self-conscious but well-executed colonial style. Amenities include a restaurant, a wine bar, a pool, and a spa with a Jacuzzi; massages are also available.

There are also two country inns nearby. Six kilometers west of town, furnished partly with antiques and enjoying spectacular views of the Nevado de Cachi, Samay Huasi (tel. 03868/49-1194, samayhuasi@ciudad.com.ar, US$53 d) was once the casco of an estancia.

Eight kilometers south of town, en route to Molinos, the French-run Hostería La Paya (tel. 03868/49-1139, US$43 s, US$48 d) is a country inn dating from 1878. All rooms have fireplaces, and there is also a pool.

FOOD

In addition to ACA and other hotel restaurants, there are several good but less elaborate and less expensive eateries focusing on regional food. Among them are Confitería del Sol (Ruiz de los Llanos s/n, tel. 03868/49-1103), on the north side of Plaza 9 de Julio; the Oliver Café (Ruiz de los Llanos s/n, tel. 03868/49-1052), immediately to the west; and moderately priced Platos y Diseño (Güemes s/n, tel. 0387/15-513-3861), two blocks south of the plaza, with innovations such as a goat cheese provoletta. Just downhill from the church, Bodega Cachi (Pasaje Borja s/n) is a new wine bar that also prepares snacks.

INFORMATION AND SERVICES

On the west side of Plaza 9 de Julio, the helpful Oficina de Turismo (Güemes s/n, tel. 03868/49-1053, www.salnet.com.ar/cachi) is open 8:30 A.M.–2 P.M. and 3–9 P.M. Monday–Saturday, 9 A.M.–3 P.M. and 5–9 P.M. Sunday.

On the west side of the plaza, **Banco Macro** (Güemes s/n) has an ATM around the corner on Ruiz de los Llanos.

For postal services, **Correo Argentino** (Güemes s/n) is one block south of the plaza. Long-distance phone and Internet providers are within a block of the plaza.

Try the **Hospital Regional** (Benjamín Zorrilla s/n, tel. 03868/49-1085) for medical services.

GETTING THERE

Marcos Rueda (tel. 03868/49-1063) buses to Molinos (1.5 hours, US$4) go at 11:30 A.M. Monday, Wednesday, Friday, and Sunday and at 6 P.M. Saturday. There is service to Seclantás at 11:30 A.M. daily. Buses back to Salta (4.5 hours, US$9) leave at 9:05 P.M. Monday–Saturday, 3 P.M. Monday, Thursday, and Friday, and at 3:30 and 3:45 P.M. Sunday.

For about the same price, given a full complement of four passengers, **Remises Interurbanos San José** (tel. 03868/49-1907, tel. 0387/424-3077 in Salta) and other taxi companies also take passengers to and from Salta. This would more easily permit photo ops along the spectacular Cuesta del Obispo and the Quebrada de Escoipe.

SAN SALVADOR DE JUJUY

Settled from Perú in 1592, San Salvador de Jujuy (commonly called "Jujuy") was then the northernmost Spanish settlement in what is now Argentina. Despite a handful of colonial monuments, it's mainly the gateway to the Quebrada de Humahuaca, the scenic and culturally rich Río Grande canyon that slopes southward from the altiplano, the high Andean plateau extending into Chile, Bolivia, and Perú.

At 1,200 meters elevation, Jujuy's spring-like climate and rich alluvial soils made it agriculturally productive from its earliest days: According to Spanish chronicler Vásquez de Espinosa, early-17th-century Jujuy had about "100 Spanish residents, mostly muleteers, who freight flour, corn, cheese, and other foodstuffs

to the Chichas and Lipes mines; they have mule and cattle ranches, and drive their stock to Potosí."

During the early-19th-century independence struggle, General Manuel Belgrano ordered Jujuy's evacuation to prevent the population's falling into Spanish hands. In postindependence times, sugar has dominated the economy.

Orientation

On high ground between the Río Grande and the smaller Río Xibi Xibi, just above the two rivers' confluence, Jujuy (pop. About 300,000) is 1,523 kilometers northwest of Buenos Aires via RN 9, RN 34, and RN 66; RN 9 continues north through the Quebrada de Humahuaca to the Bolivian border. Salta is 88 kilometers south via RN 9, a narrow road unsuitable for bus traffic, which must take a more roundabout route of 115 kilometers.

Sights

Most sights are on or within a few blocks of **Plaza Belgrano,** whose outstanding feature is the west-side **Iglesia Catedral** (1763, but with an Italianate facade dating from the early 20th century); its baroque gold-laminated pulpit is one of the country's finest. On the north side of the plaza, housing the police station, the colonnaded **Cabildo** (1864) replaced an earlier building destroyed by an earthquake. Across the plaza, fronting on San Martín, the **Casa de Gobierno** (1920) reflects the early 20th century's Francophile fashionability.

Two blocks west of the plaza, the **Museo Histórico Provincial** (Lavalle 256, tel. 0388/422-1355, 9 A.M.–8 P.M. daily, US$0.75) occupies the 19th-century Casa Alvarado. The house witnessed history before it chronicled it—during the post-independence civil wars, Unitarist General Juan Lavalle died here from a gunshot that, according to an aide, pierced the bulky wooden door. The museum details this incident, but also the Alvarado family, colonial art, the independence wars and Belgrano's evacuation, and provincial political history.

Two blocks north, the impressive **Museo**

Arqueológico Provincial (Lavalle 434, tel. 0388/422-1315, 9 A.M.–8 P.M. daily, US$0.75) chronicles pre-Columbian cultural sequences from the Quebrada de Humahuaca, the altiplano, and elsewhere in the province.

Recently reopened, part of the Basílica San Francisco, the **Museo de Arte Sacro** (Belgrano 677, 9 A.M.–1 P.M. and 4–7 P.M. daily, US$0.50) holds an impressive collection of colonial religious art.

Of Argentina's major cities, Jujuy has the largest indigenous population; the best place to appreciate that fact is the **Mercado del Sur** (Avenida Dorrego and Leandro Alem), opposite the old long-distance bus terminal. Here Quechua merchants market products from the countryside and neighboring countries (some items, like fresh coca leaves, are semi-illicit) to their city-bound clients.

Entertainment

The elegant **Teatro Mitre** (Alvear 1009, tel. 0388/422-1342), an architectural and cultural landmark dating from 1901, hosts live theater and concerts. For recent movies, try the two-screen **Cine Opera** (Alvear 1125, tel. 0388/422-2234) or the **Cine Teatro Alfa** (Patricias Argentinas 360, tel. 0388/423-0426).

Events

Jujeños take a week to celebrate August's **Éxodo Jujeño,** Belgrano's evacuation of the city. There are several other major events, but one of the most colorful is September's **Fiesta Nacional de los Estudiantes** (www.fne.org.ar), a student festival known for its spontaneity and colorful floats.

Shopping

For provincial crafts, visit the various booths at the **Paseo de los Artesanos** (Sarmiento 240), immediately south of the cathedral.

Rayuela Libros (Belgrano 638, tel. 0388/423-0658) is the best bookstore.

Accommodations

Engagingly decorated in Andean pictograph motifs, **Hostal Casa de Barro** (Otero 294, tel. 0388/422-9578, www.casadebarro.com.ar, US$9 pp dorm, US$12 s, US$21 d) is a hostel-style facility in a distinctive colonial-style building, with both dorms and private rooms as well as kitchen privileges.

Also for shoestring travelers, the HI affiliate **Club Hostel** (San Martín 132, tel. 0388/423-7565, www.noroestevirtual.com.ar/club/hostel/htm, US$9–11 pp dorm, US$32–37 d) has moved to new quarters across the street from its old location. The dorms are a bit crowded, but there are private rooms, and the common areas include a small pool.

Rooms vary in size at the expanded **Hostería Munay** (Alvear 1222, tel. 0388/422-8435, www.munayhotel.com.ar, US$27 s, US$36 d), an inviting bed-and-breakfast–style place, but all of them are comfortable, and the service is gracious.

Hotel Alvear (Senador Pérez 398, tel. 0388/424-4580, www.hotelalvearjujuy.com.ar, US$35 s, US$49 d) is a comfortable midsize hotel. Providing a measure of boutique style at moderate prices, **Hostería Terraza Balcarce** (Balcarce 354, tel. 0388/431-0030, www.terrazabalcarce.com.ar, US$45–50) is well worth the small price difference.

The 800-pound gorilla of Jujuy hotels is the **Howard Johnson Plaza Hotel** (Güemes 864, tel. 0388/424-9800, www.hjjujuy.com.ar, US$93 s or d), which also has spa facilities.

Food

Regional food is the best choice here. **Ruta 9** (Belgrano 750, tel. 0388/423-7043) is a classic for spicy specialties like *locro,* while **Viracocha** (Independencia and Lamadrid, tel. 0388/423-3554) is also highly regarded for llama, lamb, trout, and regional wines in attractive surroundings. **Cacao** (Sarmiento 330, tel. 0388/423-2037) is a new tapas bar (lunch and dinner) and gourmet restaurant (dinner only).

In pleasant quarters, **◖ Manos Jujeñas** (Avenida Senador Pérez 379, tel. 0388/15-682-2087) has become a Jujuy institution for its exceptional regional cuisine—and this is one place where you can get legitimately spicy food like *picante de pollo* (US$6) along with outstanding empanadas. Smothered in sautéed onions and garnished with maize and potatoes, the llama steak (US$7) is another outstanding choice.

For fish, the best is the **Sociedad Española** (Belgrano 1102, tel. 0388/423-5065). The well-established **Madre Tierra** (Belgrano 619, tel. 0388/422-9578) is a reliable vegetarian alternative to the standard Argentine menu.

Helados Pingüino (Belgrano near Lavalle) has better-than-average ice cream.

Information

The genial, improved **Secretaría de Turismo y Cultura de la Provincia** (Gorriti 295, tel. 0388/422-1326, www.turismo.jujuy.gov.ar) is open 8 A.M.–10 P.M. daily.

For motorists, **ACA** (tel. 0388/422-3865) is at Senador Pérez and Alvear.

Services

Graffiti Turismo (Belgrano 601, tel. 0388/423-4033) changes U.S. dollars and travelers checks.

Banco de la Nación (Alvear 801) has an ATM, but there are several others along both Belgrano and Lamadrid.

Correo Argentino (Belgrano 877) is the post office; the postal code is 4600.

The **Bolivian consulate** (Independencia 1098, tel. 0388/424-0501) is open 8 A.M.–1 P.M. weekdays.

There's a convenient **Telecentro** at Belgrano and Lavalle. For Internet, **Zona Cyber** (Belgrano 574) keeps long hours.

Tea Turismo (Belgrano 775, Oficina 4, tel. 0388/423-6270) is a well-established travel agency.

For laundry, try **Laverap** (Belgrano 1214).

Hospital Pablo Soria (tel. 0388/422-2025, or tel. 107 for emergencies) is at Güemes and General Paz.

Getting There and Around

Aerolíneas Argentinas (Senador Pérez 345, tel. 0388/422-7198) flies daily to Aeroparque (Buenos Aires). **Andes Líneas Aéreas** (San Martín 1283, tel. 0388/431-0279) flies to Aeroparque via Salta daily except Sunday.

Aeropuerto Internacional Dr. Horacio Guzmán (tel. 0388/491-1106) is 32 kilometers southeast of town via RP 66. Aerolíneas does its own minibus transfers.

By the time this book sees print, the new **Terminal de Ómnibus** (Acceso Sur and RP 66) should have replaced the grimy, congested terminal at Avenida Dorrego and Iguazú, but it will be less conveniently central. Like its predecessor, it will have provincial, long-distance, and international services to Chile. There are frequent buses up the Quebrada de Humahuaca to La Quiaca, on the Bolivian border, via Purmamarca, Tilcara, and Humahuaca, and additional services to western altiplano destinations like Susques. Buses also go to Libertador General San Martín (for Parque Nacional Calilegua).

Typical destinations, times, and fares include Purmamarca (1 hour, US$2.50), Salta (2 hours, US$6), Tucumán (5 hours, US$19), La Quiaca (4 hours, US$10), Susques (6.5 hours, US$12), Córdoba (12 hours, US$51), Mendoza (17 hours, US$50–63), Resistencia (14 hours, US$38), and Buenos Aires (22 hours, US$60–73).

Chile-bound buses from Salta stop here before crossing the Paso de Jama to San Pedro de Atacama (11 hours, US$53) and Calama (12.5 hours, US$55), with onward connections to Antofagasta, Iquique, and Arica; make reservations as far in advance as possible at **Géminis** (tel. 0388/422-7330), **Pullman** (0388/424-2943), and **Andesmar** (0388/424-3733). Frequencies vary, depending on time of year.

◖ QUEBRADA DE HUMAHUACA AND VICINITY

Declared a UNESCO World Heritage Site for its cultural and historical riches—not to mention its stunning scenery—the Quebrada de Humahuaca is becoming the attraction for foreign visitors that it long has been for Argentines. Linked to the pre-Columbian highland Andean civilizations, the route includes some 200 archaeological sites, plus major colonial monuments and ecological treasures, as well as the intangible legacy of its indigenous musical, linguistic, and religious heritage.

West of San Salvador, RN 9 climbs slowly northwest past the Termas de Reyes hot springs turnoff, and then steadily north toward and up the Quebrada to the Bolivian border at La Quiaca. At the hamlet of Volcán, the former railroad station is now the **Centro de Visitantes Quebrada de Humahuaca,** a tourist information center for the entire canyon that also includes sophisticated exhibits on geography, geomorphology, history, and archaeology. It's open 8 A.M.–8 P.M. daily.

Past Humahuaca, the highway rises higher yet to the barren altiplano at Abra Pampa on a smoothly paved surface that has cut travel times. If driving, watch for livestock, including cattle, sheep, goats, and, at higher elevations, llamas.

Purmamarca

At the base of the vivid Cerro de los Siete Colores, peaceful Purmamarca's adobe ambience is ironically making it one of the Quebrada de Humahuaca's fastest-growing settlements. While the arrival of town-dwellers

to these Andean foothills could undermine the colonial character of a village with only a few hundred inhabitants, newcomers have so far respected Purmamarca's captivating style, despite a growing abundance of tourist-oriented services.

In the long run, a likelier villain is heavy truck traffic along the paved international highway that stretches from Pacific Chile to Purmamarca as part of the so-called *Corredor Bi-Oceánico* (Bi-Coastal Corridor) to Atlantic Brazil. For the present, though, Purmamarca remains one of the Quebrada's most pleasing points, and a planned highway bypass may reduce the noise and other nuisances.

Purmamarca (elev. 2,190 meters, pop. about 800) is 65 kilometers northwest of San Salvador de Jujuy via RN 9 and RN 52, which climbs west to the Chilean border for access to San Pedro de Atacama, Calama, and Antofagasta.

Purmamarca is a sight in itself, what with its pepper-shaded plaza and, at its south end, the colonial **Iglesia Santa Rosa de Lima**. The church itself dates from 1778 or 1779; a

Craft shops fill the streets of Purmamarca.

© WAYNE BERNHARDSON

lintel dated 1648 probably came from an earlier construction.

Starting from and returning to the plaza, the **Paseo de los Colores** is a cactus-studded three-kilometer loop that winds around its namesake hill behind town. While it's fine for automobiles, it makes an equally good or even better hike, but take water, snacks, and sunscreen.

The **Mercado Artesanal,** having grown with increasing numbers of tourist buses from Salta and Jujuy, now nearly surrounds the plaza.

ACCOMMODATIONS

Both accommodations and food are remarkably good for a village of Purmamarca's size, and prices are reasonable. Just off the plaza, **Hostal El Pequeño Inti** (Florida s/n, tel. 0388/490-8089, elintidepurmamarca@hotmail.com, US$20 s, US$29 d, with private bath) offers excellent value for money.

Immediately behind the church, **El Viejo Algarrobo** (Salta s/n, tel. 0388/490-8286, elviejoalgarrobo@hotmail.com, US$40–53 d) exudes all the style of the striking wood from which it takes its name, but the upstairs rooms have far better light. The cheaper rooms have shared baths.

On a dead-end street, with views of the town and plaza below, **Hostería Viltipoco** (Sarmiento s/n, tel. 0388/490-8023, www.viltipocohosteria.com.ar, US$26 pp with private bath) is remarkable not just for its above-average rooms but for several patios and spectacular terraced gardens that include a cactarium.

◖ Hostería La Posta de Purmamarca (Pantaleón Cruz s/n, tel. 0388/490-8029, www.postadepurmamarca.com.ar, US$56 s, US$64 d) is a lovely but simple hotel, in local style, with friendly staff. It has a separate eponymous restaurant on Rivadavia, on the east side of the plaza.

In a neo-Incaic style, the nine-room **Hostería del Amauta** (Salta s/n, tel. 0388/490-8043, www.hosteriadelamauta.com.ar, US$83 s, US$94 d) has been among Purmamarca's best, but the competition is making it tougher here.

Across the highway to Susques and Chile, built to mimic an Andean village with a central plaza surrounded by buildings and houses, **La Comarca** (RN 52 Km 4, tel. 0388/490-8001, www.lacomarcahotel.com.ar, US$98 s or d), has 13 standard doubles, four quadruple cabañas, two houses for larger family groups, and a presidential suite (US$186) with a loft bedroom. The standard baths are small but efficiently designed, and all rooms have either balconies or patios. Like other hotels along the highway, it enjoys a scenic setting; amenities include a mini-spa, a swimming pool, balky Wi-Fi that should be corrected soon, and a restaurant with an inventive menu and especially good desserts.

Across from La Comarca, the **Casa de Adobe Hotel Spa** (RN 52 Km 4.5, tel. 0388/490-8003, www.casadeadobe.com.ar, US$71–103 s or d) has attractive standard rooms and even better ones with in-room saunas, as well as an impressive restaurant and views. The grass-covered roofs eliminate the need for air-conditioning, and it has other design innovations as well.

The best new place right in town is the **◖ Marqués de Tojo** (Pasaje Santa Rosa 4, tel. 0388/411-6001, www.marquesdetojo.com.ar, US$113–139 s or d), a regionally styled ten-suite design masterpiece with a gourmet restaurant, a fine wine cellar, and convivial English-speaking staff. All rooms have Jacuzzis, satellite TV, and many other amenities.

A short distance east of La Comarca, set among orchards, **◖ Hotel El Manantial del Silencio** (RN 52 Km 3.5, tel. 0388/490-8080, www.hotelmanantial.com.ar, US$120 s, US$150 d) is a colonial-style country inn featuring large rooms with tiled floors, modern baths, and a large pool.

FOOD

For sophisticated food, or sophisticated versions of regional food, the best choices are the upscale hotel restaurants. Other choices, however, like **El Rincón de Claudia Vilte** (Libertad s/n, tel. 0388/490-8088), have similar menus that include llama steaks, plus *charqui* and quinoa empanadas, at substantially lower prices. On weekends it has live folkloric entertainment. Next door to Hostería del Amauta, **Los Morteros** (Salta s/n) has an ambitious menu and decor.

OTHER PRACTICALITIES

Just off the plaza, Purmamarca's helpful **Oficina de Información Turística** (Florida and Rivadavia, tel. 0388/490-8442) is open 8 A.M.–6 P.M. daily, but at peak times it may stay open later in the evening.

Macro Bansud has an ATM on the plaza.

There are many **buses** to San Salvador de Jujuy (US$2.50) and up the Quebrada to Maimará, Tilcara (US$1), and Humahuaca (US$2.25).

Susques

From Purmamarca, RN 52 zigzags west up the spectacular Cuesta de Lipán, reaching 4,170 meters at Altos del Morado before dropping onto the altiplano at the blindingly white salt flats of **Salinas Grandes**. It then climbs less precipitously before descending into Quebrada Mal Paso and the Quechua village of Susques (3,675 meters), 139 kilometers from Purmamarca, notable for its **Iglesia Nuestra Señora de Belén** (1598). The paintings of saints and other religious figures on its walls are equally noteworthy.

From Susques, the undulating highway continues to the 4,425-meter **Paso de Jama**, which marks the Chilean border, and San Pedro de Atacama, but the only through buses start in Salta.

About four kilometers west of the village, the **Complejo Turístico Pastos Chicos** (RN 52, Casas Quemadas, tel. 03887/49-0267, www.pastoschicos.com.ar, US$19–24 s, US$29–42 d, with an abundant but mediocre breakfast) has excellent motel-style accommodations. Pastos Chicos also has a decent bar-restaurant with attentive service, satellite TV, and the last gas pump until San Pedro.

For those arriving from Chile without Argentine cash, **Macro Bansud** has an ATM in the village. There's also an **Oficina de Información Turística** (9 A.M.–7 P.M. daily).

Empresa Purmamarca and Bus Andes alternate bus service Sunday–Friday to and from San Salvador de Jujuy (3 hours, US$10).

La Posta de Hornillos

In late colonial times, when the Quebrada de Humahuaca was the main route between Buenos Aires and Lima, the Posta de Hornillos was one of a chain of way stations connecting the two viceregal capitals, although the original structure was built earlier than this restored structure. During the independence wars, General Manuel Belgrano slept here.

In mid-2003, President Néstor Kirchner presided over the Quebrada's dedication as a UNESCO World Heritage Site here. The museum contents and presentation, including archaeological and historical materials, have undergone a major upgrade. Knowledgeable guides offer tours in Spanish only.

The Posta de Hornillos (RN 9 Km 73, 8 A.M.–6 P.M. Wed.–Mon., US$0.75) is 11 kilometers north of the Purmamarca junction. Buses up and down the Quebrada will deposit visitors at the gate.

Maimará

Maimará's most memorable view, only a few kilometers north of Hornillos, may be the dazzling hillside cemetery seen from RN 9 as the highway passes through the Quebrada. Then again, it may simply be its scintillating setting beneath the polychrome La Paleta del Pintor (Painter's Palette), comparable to Purmamarca's Cerro de los Siete Colores. In any case, this dusty farming village (elev. 2,320 meters) is something to look at.

Across the river from the village, inaccessible when the river is high, the province's only winery is **Bodega Fernando Dupont** (tel. 0388/15-473-1918, www.bodegafernandodupont.com). On rocky and sandy soils, it produces only about 5,000 bottles per annum of drip-irrigated malbec, blended with small amounts of cabernet sauvignon and Syrah. It's open 9 A.M.–5 P.M. daily but, in case of rain, phone ahead to verify accessibility.

New in 2009, the friendly Brazilian-run

© WAYNE BERNHARDSON

Bodega Fernando Dupont is the Quebrada de Humahuaca's first commercial winery.

Hostel Flor de Maimará (San Martín and Padilla, tel. 0388/499-7380, www.flordemaimara.com.ar, US$9–11 pp dorm, US$24–28 s or d, with breakfast) has plain but comfortable rooms with either shared or private baths. It has a bar but not a restaurant and also rents bicycles.

The attractive **Hostería Posta del Sol** (Martín Rodríguez and San Martín, tel. 0388/499-7156, www.postadelsol.com, from US$34 s, US$46 d) offers spacious rooms with stylish *algarrobo* furniture and views. There is also a pool and a restaurant.

Buses up the Quebrada pass through town en route to Tilcara and Humahuaca.

Tilcara

Thanks to its Andean archaeological heritage, living indigenous presence, artist-colony atmosphere, and scenery to match the rest of the Quebrada de Humahuaca, many visitors enjoy Tilcara more than any other settlement along the route. In the sheltered Río Grande Valley, it's becoming an all-year destination, closer to Jujuy and warmer than Humahuaca, with far better services.

Tilcara (pop. about 6,000) is 86 kilometers north of San Salvador de Jujuy and 2,461 meters above sea level via RN 9, which passes west of the Río Grande; a bridge connects the town to the highway. Plaza Prado is its civic center, but beyond it the streets are irregular. It is small enough, though, that orientation is easy despite uneven terrain and the absence of street signs.

SIGHTS

On Plaza Prado's south side, specializing in regional archaeology in general and the Quebrada de Humahuaca in particular, the **Museo Arqueológico Doctor Eduardo Casanova** (Belgrano 445, tel. 0388/495-5006, 9 A.M.–6 P.M. Wed.–Mon., US$2.50) showcases many of its 5,000 pieces in this colonial-style house; six of its eight rooms host permanent displays while the other two usually have special exhibitions. Admission is also valid for the Pucará de Tilcara.

Immediately west of the archaeological museum, the **Museo Ernesto Soto Avendaño** (Belgrano s/n, tel. 0388/495-5354,

10 A.M.–7 P.M. Wed.–Mon., US$0.50) displays some of the more modest efforts of the sculptor of Humahuaca's hubris-laden monument to the heroes of Argentine independence, of which there is a scale model here. The colonial building once belonged to gaucho colonel Manuel Alvarez Prado, to whom one room is dedicated.

Half a block west of Plaza Prado, the five-room **Museo Irureta de Bellas Artes** (Belgrano and Bolívar, tel. 0388/495-5124, 10 A.M.–1 P.M. and 4–7 P.M. Tues.–Sun., US$0.75) presents some 150 paintings, illustrations, engravings, and sculptures by modern Argentine artists, including its founder, sculptor Hugo Irureta.

On the east side of Plaza Prado, the **Museo José Antonio Terry** (Rivadavia 459, tel. 0388/495-5005, 8 A.M.–noon and 3–7 P.M. daily, US$1.25) honors a *porteño* painter whose oils chronicled local and regional traditions and landscapes as he lived in Tilcara (1910–1953).

Before the Spaniards, the Quebrada de Humahuaca was an outlier of the Inka empire, but at least five centuries earlier the region's peoples had built hilltop fortifications like the **Pucará de Tilcara** to detect invaders—such as the Inka latecomers—and defend their settlements. About one kilometer south of Plaza Prado, this reconstructed archaeological site appears to have some Inka features. Admission (valid also for the Plaza Prado archaeological museum) costs about US$2.50, well worth it for the panoramas that the site's defenders were probably unable to appreciate; there is also a native-plant botanical garden.

About 10 kilometers north of Tilcara, just before the hamlet of Huacalera, a monolith on the west side of RN 9 marks the **Tropic of Capricorn.**

EVENTS AND SHOPPING

Tilcara's most specifically local event is January's **Enero Tilcareño,** a month-long celebration that encompasses many individual cultural activities, including music and sports. Both February's **Carnaval Norteño** and April's **Semana Santa** are observed throughout the Quebrada. The indigenous **Festival de Pachamama** (Mother Earth Festival) takes place in August.

Plaza Prado is sinking beneath the weight of its souvenir stalls. For distinctively decorative and functional calabashes, visit the **Taller Artesanal** (tel. 0388/495-5169) in Quebrada Sarahuaico, directly across the highway from the YPF gas station.

ACCOMMODATIONS

Tilcara's popularity has meant rising prices. With some exceptions, it's possible to find accommodations that are cheap or good, but not both. The **Tilcara Hostel** (Bolívar 166, tel. 0388/495-5105, www.tilcarahostel.com, US$10 pp dorm, US$40 s or d) is the cheapest choice and not without appeal.

Hospedaje El Pucará (Padilla s/n, tel. 0388/495-5050, c_marquez@cootepal.com.ar, US$13 s, US$20 d, with shared bath; US$25–37 d with private bath) enjoys a delightful garden setting but is otherwise so-so.

Around the corner and uphill from the bus terminal, **Hostería La Morada** (Debenedetti s/n, tel. 0388/495-5118, www.lamoradatilcara.com.ar, US$32 d) is a cozy adobe guesthouse with spacious, well-furnished, and nicely decorated rooms. While there's no breakfast, each room has a kitchenette stocked with tea and coffee, and there's also off-street parking.

New in 2009, downhill from the church, the six-room **La Posada de Uriel** (Alverro 276, tel. 0388/495-5154, www.posadadeuriel.com, US$26 s, US$45 d) is a friendly family-run place whose accommodations occupy a modern addition to an older building. It's quiet and has nearby parking, but the breakfast is ordinary and the Wi-Fi balky.

Perched on landscaped hillside grounds several blocks north of Plaza Prado (follow the signs), **☾ Hostel Malka** (San Martín s/n, tel. 0388/495-5197, www.malkahostel.com.ar, US$12–14 pp dorm, US$32–35 s, US$37–40 d) has dorm accommodations for shoestring travelers but also much finer private rooms for individuals or couples. The buffet breakfast includes fresh bread, fruit, yogurt, and other treats.

Exuding an institutional character that contrasts with Tilcara's indigenous ambience, the municipal **Hotel de Turismo** (Belgrano 590, tel. 0388/495-5002, tilcahot@imagine.com.ar, US$42 s, US$52 d, with private bath) has one renovated floor, but the others sometimes get noisy school groups.

Hostería Uwa Wasi (Lavalle 564, tel. 0388/495-5368, www.uwawasi.com.ar, US$37 s, US$53 d) is a family-run place whose new private patio rooms are small to midsize but exquisitely designed and decorated. Rooms with a shared bath in the main house are half the price, but small children make it noisy at times.

In a contemporary southwestern style, the **Posada de Luz** (Ambrosetti and Alberro, tel. 0388/495-5017, www.posadadeluz.com.ar, US$58 s, US$66 d) is a handsome six-room boutique hotel that has drawn highly favorable commentary. Its extensive grounds include a swimming pool.

Just outside the town center, **La Posada del Río** (Avenida Costanera 625, tel. 0388/15-524-5829, www.tanpumayu.com.ar, US$40 s, US$69 d) is a handsome new 10-room hotel at a bargain price, with finely adapted Andean stylistic elements. The largest room, which goes for a bit more, has a huge Jacuzzi.

One of Tilcara's gems is **(Quinta La Paceña** (Padilla s/n, tel. 0388/495-5098, www. quintalapacena.com.ar, US$48–63 s, US$76–90 d), where small but private and romantic garden rooms come with personalized service; the breakfast takes place in the main house, which has inviting common areas in a style similar to the Posada de Luz.

West of the bus terminal, **Posada con los Ángeles** (Gorriti 156, tel. 0388/495-5153, www.posadaconlosangeles.com.ar, US$66–82 s or d) has 11 garden rooms that vary in size but all are exquisitely styled and furnished. The management is accommodating, and it has a fine restaurant.

Aimed at a sophisticated public, the attractively designed **Hotel Viento Norte** (Jujuy 536, tel. 0388/495-5605, US$71–104 s, US$82–104 d) offers ample rooms with either balconies or patios facing the pool and garden. The personnel are gracious, and it's worth serious consideration.

At the new boutique hotel **Las Terrazas** (San Martín and La Sorpresa, tel. 0388/495-5589, www.lasterrazastilcara.com.ar, US$71–111 s, US$90–111 d), every standard or premium room has its own terrace in a striking building that climbs the hillside. The rooms are large, especially the premiums, but the windows lack double panes.

FOOD

Alongside the Hotel de Turismo, popular **Pachamama** (Belgrano 590, tel. 0388/495-5293) offers *salteñas* (spicier than mainstream empanadas), the spicy stew *locro,* and *parrillada.* Nearby **Sirviñacu** (Belgrano and Padilla, tel. 0388/495-5569) is a small but cheerful wine bar that serves regional food, pizza, and snacks, with occasional live music; it also has outdoor seating.

Across from the tourist office, **Los Puestos** (Belgrano and Padilla, tel. 0388/495-5100) has upscale versions of regional staples, such as empanadas, and an interesting llama steak with an onion and orange sauce (US$6). The soothing surroundings include Andean murals and glass-top tables decorated with Andean crops.

Even more upmarket, in both price and aspirations, the kitchen at **La Chacana** (Belgrano 472, tel. 0388/15-414-0833) prepares items such as a llama carpaccio starter (US$3) and inventive pastas such as *sorrentinos* stuffed with smoked pumpkin (US$6). With wine, it's easy to spend upwards of US$20 pp—high by Tilcara standards.

Occupying a classic early-20th-century building decorated with works by local artists, **El Nuevo Progreso** (Lavalle 351, tel. 0388/495-5237, www.elnuevoprogresoweb. com.ar) is also a live music locale with occasional folk, jazz, and tango. Some dishes, such as the llama pepper steak in a malbec sauce (US$9), are better in conception than execution, and the service can be distracted.

With a diversity of llama dishes, and cozier decor than El Nuevo Progreso, **El Patio**

(Belgrano 352, tel. 0388/495-5044) gets high marks from local residents. The menu may be less ambitious, but the cook-owner (also an anthropologist) executes to perfection.

OTHER PRACTICALITIES

Alongside the Hotel de Turismo, the municipal **Centro de Informes** (Belgrano s/n, turismo@tilcaranet.com.ar, 8 A.M.–9 P.M. daily) has improved significantly. At the western approach to town, the private **Asociación de Turismo de la Quebrada y Puna Jujeña** (Avenida Villafañe s/n) is only open 4–8 P.M. Tuesday–Friday. They have a useful website, www.tilcara.com.ar.

Correo Argentino (Belgrano and Rivadavia) is directly on Plaza Prado. Just off the plaza, **Macro Bansud** (Lavalle 542) has an ATM. **Telecentro Tilcara** (Lavalle 448) has long-distance phone service, while **Cyber Tilcara** (Belgrano s/n) has decent Internet service.

From the **Terminal de Ómnibus,** at the west end of Belgrano, at least two dozen buses daily go to Jujuy, some continuing to Salta, while an equivalent number head north to Humahuaca and occasionally to La Quiaca. There are also several daily to Purmamarca.

Uquía

Only a few kilometers south of Humahuaca, straddling RN 9, the hamlet of Uquía is notable for its **Capilla de San Francisco de Paula,** a colonial chapel dating from 1691. It's also notable for the chapel's restored Cusco-school paintings featuring the *ángeles arcabuceros,* nine angels armed with 15th-century European matchlock guns, and for its baroque altarpiece, possibly the work of a Potosí craftsman. The church is open 10 A.M.–noon and 2–4 P.M. daily.

Alongside the church, the tidy **Hostal de Uquía** (tel. 03887/49-0523, hostaluquia@yahoo.com.ar, US$24 s, US$29 d) has comfortable rooms with private baths as well as a bar-restaurant.

Humahuaca and Vicinity

North of Tilcara, Humahuaca's higher, colder climate has discouraged the influx of lowlanders who have built weekend houses in Purmamarca and Tilcara, and the village has remained more visibly indigenous and more typically Andean in its narrow, cobbled, adobe-lined streets. Services, although not as good as those in Tilcara, are improving, and it's a popular stop for budget travelers.

Beyond Uquía, RN 9 climbs steeply toward and then bypasses Humahuaca (pop. about 10,000), which straddles the Río Grande to the east; in a more exposed location than Tilcara, it sits 2,939 meters above sea level. Most but not all sights and services are west of the river; some are across the bridge in the neighborhood known as La Banda. The key archaeological site of Coctaca is 10 kilometers northeast via the La Banda bridge.

SIGHTS

Humahuaca's cobbled colonial streets can barely accommodate automobiles, and motorcycles would have problems passing through some narrow alleyways. Facing the central Plaza Sargento Gómez from the west, the 17th-century **Iglesia de la Candelaria y San Antonio** is a national historical monument that has needed frequent repairs because of earthquake damage and underwent an almost total rehab between 1926 and 1938. The twin bell towers are an 1880 addition, but the rococo altarpiece dates from around 1680. The Cusco school's Marcos Sapaca created *Los Doce Profetas* (The Twelve Prophets), an 18th-century series of paintings decorating the church's walls.

Immediately north of the church, a broad flight of stone steps rises to Tilcara sculptor Ernesto Soto Avendaño's pompous **Monumento a la Independencia** (Monument to Independence, 1950), which took 10 years to complete. Out of place in a town whose populace is largely indigenous, it's also out of proportion to its surroundings.

On the plaza's south side, at noon daily, a full-size replica of San Francisco Solano emerges from the clock tower at the **Cabildo de Humahuaca.** Thanks to clock repairs, it's now fairly reliable.

The privately run **Museo Folklórico**

Regional (Buenos Aires 447, tel. 03887/42-1064, US$1.25) is the work of author and activist Sixto Vázquez Zuleta, also known by his Quechua name of Toqo. Hours are 8 A.M.–8 P.M. daily for guided tours only.

Across the bridge and about 10 kilometers north, the bench terraces of **Coctaca** cover about 40 hectares of what were once intensively cultivated lands, irrigated by canals and sluices, on an alluvial fan. Now almost uncultivated, they suggest that the area once supported many more people. Visitors must hire local guides through the tourist office.

EVENTS AND SHOPPING

Humahuaca celebrates February 2 as the **Fiesta de la Virgen de Candelaria** in honor of its patron saint. February is also the month of the **Carnaval Norteño,** which takes place in many communities along the Quebrada.

The old train station, just west of the river, is the site of Humahuaca's **Mercado Artesanal;** woolens are the pick of the crafts.

ACCOMMODATIONS AND FOOD

Dramatically improved, the 60-bed **Hostal Humahuaca** (Buenos Aires 447, tel. 03887/42-1064, www.humahuacahostal.com.ar, US$10 pp dorm, US$37 d) has both dorms (some with too many beds) and rooms with private baths. The gardens, patios, and breakfast room are also far more appealing than in the past.

Across the river bridge, in Barrio Medalla Milagrosa about one kilometer east of the tracks, HI affiliate **Posada El Sol** (tel. 03887/42-1466, www.posadaelsol.com.ar, US$9 pp dorm, US$25 s, US$32 d) is an improving hostel on spacious grounds. Prices rise about 15 percent during February's Carnaval.

Just east of the tracks and two blocks from the bus terminal, the quiet, immaculate **Hostal La Soñada** (San Martín and Río Negro, tel. 03887/42-1228, hostallasoniada@yahoo.com.ar, US$15 pp with private bath) is not luxurious, and the windows are small (conserving heat at this altitude), but it's the best value in town. It has also put serious effort into its Andean decor as well as the practicalities.

At the northern edge of downtown, the simple but tidy **Hostal La Vasija** (San Luis 97, 03887/42-1397, www.hostallavasija.com.ar, US$13 pp with shared bath, US$37 d with private bath), enjoys a quiet location at the northern edge of downtown, but it's easy walk to the sights and restaurants.

Also across the bridge, ◖ **Hostal Azul** (tel. 03887/42-1107, www.hostalazulhumahuaca.com.ar, US$48 s or d) may have Humahuaca's finest facilities—a cozy living room with a fireplace, central heating, a breakfast nook with homemade bread in the morning, and eight attractive rooms surrounding a delightful interior patio. Rates are more than fair, though it has imperfections: The single beds are narrow, the service is a little erratic, and the garish exterior (it is, after all, the "blue house") is not really appropriate to a desert setting.

New in 2009, **Los Airampos** (Belgrano and Canal del Norte, tel. 03887/15-62-9084, www.losairampos.com.ar, US$27–54 s or d), is an adobe constructions that only looks old—thanks to its recycled doors. It has very good downstairs rooms with nice furnishings and shared baths, better upstairs rooms with private baths, attractive common areas, and eager-to-please management.

Just across the bridge, opposite the municipal campground, **Hostería Camino del Inka** (Ejército del Norte s/n, tel. 03887/42-1136, www.noroestevirtual.com.ar, US$66 d) has attractive common areas and friendly management, but the rooms are unexpectedly small.

FOOD

Part of its popular namesake hostel, **El Portillo** (Tucumán 69, tel. 03887/42-1288) has a limited regional menu that does, however, include llama dishes. **La Casa Vieja** (Buenos Aires and Salta) makes more effort than most to create a pleasing decor and has live music, but it often runs out of signature dishes such as llama steaks (US$6).

La Cacharpaya (Jujuy 295, tel. 03887/42-1016) seats large numbers of diners for regional specialties like *locro, salteñas,* and tamales. **El Fortín** (Buenos Aires 200, tel. 03887/42-1178) has similar fare.

Mikunayoc (Tucumán and Corrientes, tel. 03887/42-1163) offers an interesting menu that includes a vegetarian quinoa risotto (US$6.50), plus quinoa and goat-cheese empanadas.

Unique in the Quebrada, open evenings only in peak season (January–February and July), **La Chichería** (Buenos Aires 435, tel. 03887/42-1064, toqohumahuaca@yahoo.com) specializes not in regional food but in *etnocomidas,* of Andean origin.

OTHER PRACTICALITIES

Humahuaca's municipal **tourist office,** in the Cabildo at Tucumán and Jujuy, is presumably open 9 A.M.–1 P.M. and 2–6 P.M. weekdays only. At the highway turnoff, the provincial **Oficina de Información Turística** has been closed recently.

Correo Argentino (Buenos Aires s/n) is across from the plaza; the postal code is 4630. There's a **Telecentro** at Jujuy 399, behind the Municipalidad.

For medical services, **Hospital Belgrano** (Santa Fe 34) is now open 24 hours.

All northbound and southbound buses, between Jujuy (2 hours, US$5) and La Quiaca (2.5 hours, US$5), stop at the **Terminal de Ómnibus** (Belgrano and Entre Ríos). Transportes Iruya (tel. 03887/42-1174) and the more comfortable **Panamericano** go several times daily to the remote Andean village of Iruya (3 hours, US$3.50–4.50), which is in Salta Province but only accessible via a lateral highway that leads northeast from RN 9. Buses leave Humahuaca at 8:30 and 10:30 A.M. daily, and at 6 P.M. Sunday–Friday. Panamericano goes at 8:30 A.M. daily.

[Iruya

Perched on a hillside above its namesake river, Iruya is a settlement of steep cobbled streets where a handful of automobiles can go no faster than the far more numerous burros. Its colonial **Iglesia de Nuestra Señora del Rosario y San Roque** rises above the squat adobes that conserve their heat at 2,780 meters above sea level.

Iruya is also the terminus of RP 13, a stunningly scenic gravel road that passes through

Nestled in a remote corner of the Andes, Iruya feels like the lost valley of the Inkas.

© WAYNE BERNHARDSON

several hamlets to an altitude of 4,000 meters at the Abra del Cóndor. At this point, entering Salta Province, it begins a vertiginous descent through terrain that evokes the most remote Peruvian highlands, with pre-Columbian agricultural terraces clinging to nearly sheer hillsides fast being undercut by the river.

Iruya (pop. about 1,200) is about 80 kilometers northeast of Humahuaca via RN 9 and RP 13, which is open all year, but a couple of stream crossings can be tricky for passenger cars in the wet summer. This would be an exhilarating mountain bike ride on arrival, as the climb from Humahuaca makes a strenuous but relatively gradual workout, but the return trip from Iruya would be exhausting, as the climb is much steeper.

Hostal Tacacho (Plaza La Tablada s/n, tel. 03887/15-62-9350, www.iruyahostaltacacho.com, US$13 pp, US$37 d) has upgraded its rooms substantially and offers food service. Nearby **Hostería Federico Tercero** (tel. 03887/15-62-9152, www.complejofederico.com, US$40–53 d), which also has a restaurant, continues to upgrade as well.

Were it not beyond and above the village proper, the sore-thumb **Hostería de Iruya** (tel. 0387/15-407-0909, www.hosteriadeiruya.com.ar, US$53–64 s, US$62–73 d, with an outstanding breakfast) would stick out even more, as it's larger than any other building in town. In its own right, the spacious provincial hotel boasts bright, cheerful, well-furnished rooms; a well-decorated, airy lobby and restaurant; and attentive service. Rates vary for hillside rooms (which lack views) and for rooms with valley views; if business is slow, the staff may upgrade you at the lower rate. Entrées on the restaurant menu, which includes locally grown Andean tubers, run US$6–10.

Opposite the Telecentro (San Martín s/n), **K-meca** offers Internet access and maintains a useful website (www.iruyaonline.com).

Buses are more frequent than in the recent past. Transporte Iruya returns to Humahuaca at 2, 3:15, and 4 P.M. daily, and at 6 A.M. Monday–Saturday. Panamericano does so at 2 P.M. daily.

Abra Pampa

Ninety kilometers north of Humahuaca, paved RN 9 emerges onto the altiplano at windswept Abra Pampa, a low-slung treeless town nearly 3,500 meters above sea level. Though it's often cold and cloudy, when the sky clears and the wind drops, the vast landscape can be enthralling.

Most of Abra Pampa's 7,495 inhabitants are Quechua Indians who live off their herds of goats, sheep, llamas (watch for llama-crossing signs on the highway!), and a handful of cattle. Otherwise, there's little to see or do, but southbound travelers from Bolivia, especially those descending the Quebrada de Humahuaca on bicycles, may have to stay here. The best accommodation option is probably **Residencial La Coyita** (Gobernador Fascio 123, tel. 0388/749-1052, US$8 s, US$13 d); breakfast costs US$1 extra.

La Quiaca

Where RN 9 ends at the Bolivian border, the altiplano town of La Quiaca is often an obligatory stopover for international travelers. Neither La Quiaca nor Bolivia's border town of Villazón has much to see, but the nearby village of Yavi is worth a detour and preferably an overnight stay.

La Quiaca (pop. about 15,000) is 280 kilometers north of San Salvador de Jujuy. Most services are west of the inoperative Belgrano railroad, but the border crossing (open 24 hours) is east of the tracks via a bridge over the Río Villazón. Smuggling is rampant, so Argentine Gendarmería (border guards) may search your person or belongings on demand, but they are usually polite and professional.

Hostería Munay (Belgrano 51, tel. 03885/42-3924, www.munayhotel.com.ar, US$26 s, US$36 d) is a branch of its excellent San Salvador de Jujuy namesake. The comfortable, spick-and-span **Hotel de Turismo** (San Martín and Árabe Siria, tel. 03885/42-2243, hotelmun@laquiaca.com.ar, US$37 s, US$45 d, with private bath) has a heated swimming pool.

East of the tracks, the **ACA** service station

has maps for sale, but there is no tourist office. The ATM at **Banco de Jujuy** (Árabe Siria 445) offers currency exchange for those crossing the border at odd hours.

Buses south to Jujuy (4 hours, US$10), Salta, and intermediate points leave roughly hourly from the **Terminal de Ómnibus** (25 de Mayo and Avenida España).

Yavi

Only a short drive east of La Quiaca, where the Río Yavi has cut into the altiplano to create a sheltered valley, out-of-the-way Yavi has a colonial charisma that's utterly lacking in its dowdy neighboring border town. Southbound travelers should spend at least an afternoon here, and increasing numbers of visitors are choosing to stay a night or more.

Yavi dates from the late 17th century, when Juan Fernández Campero y Herrera married into the family of the area's original *encomendero;* the settlement became the *encomienda's* administrative base and, later, the base of the family's extensive landholdings.

SIGHTS AND EVENTS

When Juan Fernández Campero y Herrera laid the cornerstone of Yavi's **Iglesia de San Francisco** in 1682, it was only a modest chapel. Today's austere but handsome church is the result of various improvements during colonial times; it's the ornate interior, though, that makes the trip worthwhile. From the forged ironwork of its doors to the wooden choir and the laminated gold altarpiece and pulpit, this is a colonial treasure. Ostensibly, hours are 9 A.M.–noon and 3–6 P.M. Tuesday–Friday, 9 A.M.–noon Saturday, but it's sometimes necessary to track down the custodian elsewhere in the village.

Immediately across from the church, the crumbling **Casa del Marqués Campero** was the *encomendero's* residence and is now a hybrid museum-library, though its eclectic exhibits include none of the family's personal effects. It has no fixed hours; ask around for the custodian (who may or may not be the same as the church's). Two blocks south of the house is a ruined *molino,* a water-powered flour mill.

Immediately north of town, the reddish **Cerros Colorados** contain pre-Columbian rock-art sites at **Las Cuevas.** About five kilometers northeast via an undulating gravel road, the terrain near the village of **Yavi Chico** resembles a scale-model cutaway of the Grand Canyon.

Toward the end of March, the **Encuentro de la Comida Regional y la Música Popular** offers regional cooking and live folkloric music in the campground at the riverside park. Dishes include tamales, *humitas,* and the like.

PRACTICALITIES

Hospedaje Aborígen (Senador Pérez s/n, tel. 03387/49-1138, lapachos@jujuytel.com.ar, US$13 s, US$21 d) is stylistically simple but remarkably inviting. The casual **Hostal la Casona** (Senador Pérez and San Martín, tel. 03885/42-2316 in La Quiaca, mccalizaya@laquiaca.com.ar, US$16–21 s or d) is a hostel-style adobe with rooms surrounding a sheltered courtyard; it also has a small restaurant.

From La Quiaca, Flota La Quinqueña offers public transport to Yavi, but there's also a frequent pickup truck from the Mercado Municipal on Avenida Hipólito Yrigoyen, east of the railroad tracks.

Monumento Natural Laguna de los Pozuelos

In the altiplano's azure clarity, northwest of Abra Pampa and southwest of La Quiaca, Laguna de los Pozuelos is a shallow but biologically bountiful wetland that's a breeding site for coots, ducks, geese, and three flamingo species, along with many other migratory and resident species like plovers and avocets. Because of this rich but sensitive habitat, it's a designated critical wetland under the international Ramsar convention; in all, there are 44 breeding bird species.

The biggest attention-getters, though, are the 25,000 flamingos, which build conical mud nests on the shoreline. The lake itself is seven level kilometers north of the Río Cincel ranger station on RP 7.

Laguna de los Pozuelos (elev. about 3,600

meters) covers some 15,000 hectares about 50 kilometers northwest of Abra Pampa via RP 7 or 85 kilometers southwest of La Quiaca via RP 5 and RP 69. All of these are unpaved routes that can be impassable in wet summer weather.

There is basic camping at the Río Cincel ranger station, on RP 7 at the south end of the reserve, but no other services or supplies. The village of Rinconada, 11 kilometers west, has basic accommodations and food.

Locally, ask for information at the Río Cincel ranger station; in Abra Pampa, try the offices of the Monumento Natural Laguna de los Pozuelos (Macedonio Graz 141, tel. 03887/49-1349, raulangerami@hotmail.com).

From Abra Pampa, midmorning buses to Rinconada pass the Río Cincel ranger station at the south end of the reserve. A car provides more flexibility, but carry extra fuel—none is available beyond Abra Pampa.

◖ NATIONAL PARKS OF THE *YUNGAS*

In subtropical northwestern Argentina, most storms come out of the east and, as they lose their power, drop their moisture on the slopes of the eastern Andes. The fragmented terrain creates multiple microclimates, including the narrow longitudinal strip of cloud forest known as the *yungas,* stretching from the Bolivian border through Jujuy and Salta south into Tucumán and even a spot of northernmost Catamarca.

Within Jujuy and Salta, three national parks preserve remnants of the rare ecosystem: Calilegua, Baritú, and El Rey. As public transportation is limited and access is especially difficult in the wet summer, rental cars (preferably 4WD) or guided tours (normally from Salta) are the best options for visiting them.

Parque Nacional Calilegua

Most of Jujuy Province is high-altitude desert. The major exception is the area along the province's eastern limits, where the verdant subtropical *yungas* cover the slopes of the Serranía de Calilegua, the most accessible of the parks that preserve this ecosystem in Jujuy and Salta. Its dense woodlands and deeply incised canyons

provide one of the last Argentine refuges of the endangered *yaguareté* (jaguar).

In recent years, the area between Calilegua and Parque Nacional Baritú, to the north, has been the subject of a contentious dispute between environmental organizations and indigenous communities of the altiplano on the one hand, and commercial interests on the other, over construction of a gas pipeline from the Chaco to Chile. According to the Fundación Vida Silvestre Argentina, the controversy reached a satisfactory conclusion, with environmental mitigation on the part of gas and construction interests, plus the provision of natural gas to the indigenous altiplano communities. Greenpeace, on the other hand, split with Vida Silvestre over the issue, and it's unclear that either mitigation or community assistance has worked.

Encompassing 76,306 hectares of rugged terrain, Parque Nacional Calilegua is about 110 kilometers northeast of San Salvador via a roundabout route on eastbound RP 56 and northbound RN 34 to Libertador General San Martín and westbound RP 8. It is 170 kilometers from Salta via RN 34.

FLORA AND FAUNA

One of Argentina's greatest biodiversity centers, Calilegua boasts a variety of ecological zones that depend partly on altitude and partly on the microclimates created by its rugged topography. Annual rainfall varies between 800 and 1,800 millimeters, but winter is almost invariably dry.

At lower elevations, between 350 and 500 meters, the *selva de transición* (transitional forest) resembles the arid Chaco, with deciduous trees like *lapacho* and *palo amarillo.* Between 500 and 1,800 meters, though, the *selva montana* comprises dense cloud forest with clusters of epiphytes, verdant ferns, and climbing lianas. Above 1,800 meters, the *bosque montano* consists mainly of the coniferous *Podocarpus* and deciduous *aliso.* Above 2,600 meters, puna grasslands take over.

Rare mammals like the jaguar, tapir, and otter inhabit the densest low-elevations forests, where there are also fruit-eating bats. The grayish deerlike *taruca* (northern *huemul*) grazes the higher elevations. There are hundreds of bird species, among them the toucan, torrent duck, solitary eagle, and condor (at the highest elevations).

SIGHTS AND RECREATION

There are several trails in the vicinity of the Aguas Negras and Mesada de las Colmenas, all of which offer opportunities for wildlife sightings, though birds are easier to spot than mammals in this densely wooded country. At Aguas Negras, the **Sendero Pié de Montaña** leads to an overlook of the Río San Lorenzo. The longer **Sendero a la Junta** leads through the forest to the confluence of the Arroyo Negro and Arroyo Toldos. **Sendero La Herradura** is an easy nature trail.

At Mesada de las Colmenas, it's possible to climb 3,600-meter **Cerro Hermoso** for spectacular panoramas toward the east, but this is cross-country walking.

From Valle Grande, west of the park, it's possible to hike through the Sierra de Zenta to Humahuaca. For details, see Tim Burford's *Chile and Argentina: The Bradt Trekking Guide* (Chalfont St Peter, UK: Bradt Travel Guides, 2001).

PRACTICALITIES

Near the park entrance, **Camping Aguas Negras** has picnic tables, barbecue pits, and latrines, but also mosquitoes—don't forget repellent. Basic camping is permitted at **Mesada de las Colmenas** near the ranger station.

Libertador General San Martín's **Hotel Los Lapachos** (Entre Ríos 400, tel. 03886/42-3790) charges US$21 s, US$26 d. The leisurely **Hostería Posada del Sol** (Los Ceibos and Pucará, Barrio La Loma, tel. 03886/42-4900, www.posadadelsoljujuy.com.ar, US$61 s, US$76 d) has a swimming pool, a restaurant, and Internet access, and also offers excursions to the park and other areas of interest.

Bequeathed by the Ledesma sugar mill, the park's Intendencia at the town of Calilegua, immediately north of Libertador General San Martín, includes a **Centro de Visitantes** (San Lorenzo s/n, tel. 03886/42-2046, calilegua@ apn.gov.ar, 8 A.M.–noon weekdays). The visitors center provides information on all the area's national parks, including those in neighboring Salta Province such as Baritú and El Rey, and current road conditions. Information is also available at ranger stations at Aguas Negras and Mesada de las Colmenas.

From Libertador General San Martín, daily except Wednesday, 8:30 A.M. buses to the village of Valle Grande travel through the park on RP 83, passing the Aguas Negras ranger station and campground, and the Mesada de las Colmenas ranger station. Schedules are subject to change, so travelers should confirm services at the visitors center.

Parque Nacional Baritú

Along with Calilegua, Parque Nacional Baritú is one of Argentina's only two truly tropical parks, lying north of the Tropic of Capricorn on the border with Bolivia (Calilegua is just south of the line). Like Calilegua, it preserves a substantial sector of *yungas* cloud forest; like the isolated village of Iruya, the 72,000-hectare unit belongs to Salta Province, but access is even more difficult because the only road passes through Bolivian territory via the border post of Aguas Blancas, at the northern terminus of RN 50.

There is, however, access via westbound RP 19 from Aguas Blancas and a northbound footpath that follows the course of the Río Lipeo—in winter only, as the rising and fast-moving river can be dangerous in the wet summer. Thanks to its inaccessibility, the park is a refuge for rare mammals like the Brazilian tapir, jaguar, capuchin and howler monkeys, and the southern river otter. It also offers habitat for the harpy eagle, the world's largest eagle.

That habitat is in danger, though, from a proposed hydroelectric project that would drown the Río Bermejo and flood the easterly sector of Baritú, as well as the new highway from Bermejo to Tarija on the Bolivian side. It could also foment tropical diseases such as leishmaniasis, yellow fever, and dengue.

While the park proper has no tourist infrastructure, the nearby **Portal del Baritú** (tel. 0388/422-6998 or 0338/15-685-4357, www.portaldelbaritu.com.ar, US$100 pp with full board, two-night minimum) offers half a dozen forest *cabañas*. For more park information, contact Salta's APN office or the visitors center at Parque Nacional Calilegua (tel. 03886/42-2046) in the village of Calilegua, Jujuy Province.

Parque Nacional El Rey

Created in 1948 by expropriating private land, Parque Nacional El Rey protects 44,162 hectares of *yungas* forest and similarly diverse environments on Salta Province's eastern edge. Given its proximity to Salta, it's probably the most visited of several similar parks in the region.

Directly east of Salta, Parque Nacional El Rey is 200 kilometers from the provincial capital by paved RN 9 and RP 5, and dusty (in winter) or muddy (in summer) RP 20.

El Rey's flora and fauna resemble those of Calilegua and Baritú, the other *yungas* parks, though it does not reach the same high altitudes. El Rey is a particularly good bird-watching destination, however, as evidenced by its emblematic toucan. In the wet summer, though, mosquitoes are the most abundant fauna.

From the visitors center, there are several short footpaths and one main vehicular trail, the 10-kilometer **Senda Río Popayán** on the drier Chaco side. Of the footpaths, the best is the 12-kilometer **Senda Pozo Verde,** a bird-rich trail climbing through dense forest to a small lake; the first part follows an abandoned road. Another worth consideration is the 10-kilometer **Sendero Chorro de los Loros,** which climbs the watershed of its namesake creek.

Except for basic free campgrounds with running water and pit toilets near park headquarters, El Rey lacks infrastructure. Bring food and other supplies from Salta.

Prior to going, consult with Salta's APN office; at the park itself, rangers staff the **Centro de Visitas,** which has a small museum.

Except for tours from Salta, there is public transportation only to the intersection of RN 9 and RP 5. Hitching is difficult because there is almost no traffic along the 46 kilometers of RP 20 to park headquarters. For motorists, RP 20 has new bridges and an improved surface, but 4WD may still be advisable in wet weather.

Tucumán Province

Traditionally known as the Jardín de la República (Garden of the Republic), Tucumán is the cradle of Argentine independence, declared in the provincial capital of San Miguel in 1816. Its garden reputation stems from the subtropical fertility that made it the Southern Cone's post-independence sugar bowl, but its witheringly hot and humid summers can make it La Sauna de la República.

Since the 2001 crisis, when things got so desperate that even some Argentines began to call Tucumán "the Ethiopia of Argentina" for its rural poverty and high child mortality, devaluation has reinvigorated the sugar industry by lowering costs. Commerce and fruit cultivation, especially citrus, have led the province's recovery, however.

◖ SAN MIGUEL DE TUCUMÁN

For patriotic Argentines, San Miguel de Tucumán is a pilgrimage site, the place where delegates declared the country's independence on July 9, 1816. Its historical legacy, which also includes several colonial monuments plus its access to the nearby Sierra de Aconquija, have been drawing more foreign visitors, mostly Europeans.

In 2003, Tucumán became a politically divided city when former dirty warrior General Antonio Domingo Bussi won a closely contested mayoral election before being jailed for 1970s human-rights violations on the request of Spanish judge Baltasar Garzón. Federal intervention also threw out Bussi's son as governor, and politics have become more sedate since.

THE ANDEAN NORTHWEST

SAN MIGUEL DE TUCUMÁN

To Aeropuerto Internacional Benjamín Matienzo

AV. GOB. DEL CAMPO

CASA OBISPO COLOMBRES

Parque 9 de Julio

To Córdoba

AUTOPISTA W. POSSE

AV. BENJAMÍN ARÁOZ

ESTACIÓN DE ÓMNIBUS

To Tafí del Valle, Córdoba, and Buenos Aires

500 yds
500 m

AV. DE LOS PRÓCERES
AV. SOLDATI
AV. BRÍGIDO TERÁN

GARCÍA
PRÓSPERO
HONDURAS
HAITÍ
GUATEMALA
CUBA

HOTEL CATALINAS PARK
HOTEL GARDEN PARK SUITES

AV. AVELLANEDA
BALCARCE
MONTEAGUDO
RIVADAVIA
LAPRIDA

CÓRDOBA
ALVAREZ
LORENZO
CRISÓSTOMO
SAN
AV. SÁENZ PEÑA
M. MORENO
ENTRE RÍOS
LAVALLE
HERAS
BOLÍVAR

TELLO HELADOS PREMIUM

LA CORZUELA

MARCOS PAZ
25 DE MAYO

Plaza Urquiza

SETIMIO

PAZ
LAS
MADRID
LA

AV. SARMIENTO
SANTA FE
LA BERNASCONI
JUNÍN
KLÓ & KLÓ
SANTIAGO
SAN JUAN

MUÑECAS
MAIPÚ

CINE ATLAS
LAVADERO LAPRIDA
CENTRO CULTURAL EUGENIO FLAVIO VIRLA
MI NUEVA ESTANCIA
BACKPACKERS TUCUMÁN
IL POSTINO
POST OFFICE
CAFÉ 25

AEROSUR
MUSEO IRAMAIN
DUPORT TRUISMO
MOVIL RENTA
CONGRESO
GRAL.
9 DE JULIO
Plaza Yrigayen
AQUA LAV

Plaza Independencia

24 DE SETIEMBRE

CASA DE LA INDEPENDENCIA

BUENOS AIRES
EMPANADAS BUENOS AIRES
LOS LEÑOS
GUANABARA JAZZ CLUB
TUCUMÁN HOSTEL

Plaza San Martín
Plaza Rivadavia

MUSEO FOLKLÓRICO
PASTA TURISMO
CHACABUCO
AVACUCHO
LAS PIEDRAS

SEE DETAIL

AV. SALTA
JUJUY

HOSTEL OH
CATAMARCA
HOTEL AMÉRICA
J. COLOMBRES
MARCO AVELLANEDA

MENDOZA
ASATEJ
CITIBANK
MAXICAMBIO
AV. MATE DE LUNA
ACA
LA ROJA
ALBERDI

HOSPITAL ANGEL C. PADILLA

Plaza Belgrano

FERROCENTRAL
Plaza Alberdi

SUIPACHA

AV. MITRE
12 DE OCTUBRE
LUCAS CÓRDOBA
ASUNCIÓN
SAN MIGUEL
PASEO DE LOS ANDES

CORRIENTES
CÓRDOBA
MENDOZA
SAN MARTÍN

MUSEO DE LA UNIVERSIDAD NACIONAL DE TUCUMÁN

Parque N. Avellaneda

TEMPLO Y CONVENTO DE SAN FRANCISCO
JOCKEY CLUB
HOTEL DEL SOL
CENTRO CULTURAL A. ROUGÉS
EL PORTAL
HOTEL MEDITERRÁNEO
MUSEO HISTÓRICO DE LA PROVINCIA (CASA AVELLANEDA)

Plaza Independencia
INFORMATION
IGLESIA CATEDRAL
HOTEL VERSAILLES
HOTEL FRANCIA
LAN ARGENTINA

CASA DE GOBIERNO
MUSEO CASA PADILLA
BLUE BELL
24 DE SETIEMBRE
HOTEL METROPOL
MUSEO TIMOTEO NAVARRO
GRAN HOTEL PREMIER

© AVALON TRAVEL

While Tucumán remains one of Argentina's noisiest cities—and that's saying something—it's cleaning up its act with renovated hotels, new pedestrian malls, and other improved public spaces. The Barrio Norte neighborhood around Plaza Urquiza is becoming an important restaurant and nightlife district, but at the same time, it's still full of scavengers who scrounge recyclables after the sun has fallen.

History

San Miguel de Tucumán dates from 1565, when it was a highway hub linking the highlands of Alto Perú (present-day Bolivia) and the city of Salta, to the north, with Córdoba to the south and Santa Fe and Rosario to the southeast. By the early 17th century, wrote Spanish chronicler Vásquez de Espinosa, the region had begun to acquire a reputation for its fertile soils, plentiful water, and abundant livestock, making it the region's wealthiest city.

Following independence, declared by a mainly Unitarist congress of clergy, lawyers, merchants, and military (Federalist forces boycotted the gathering), Tucumán soon adapted to the changed economic and political circumstances. With its frost-free subtropical climate, the province was well positioned to supply the burgeoning Buenos Aires market with sugar, and arrival of the railroad from Córdoba lowered transportation costs.

In recent decades, though, falling world sugar prices, obsolete equipment, and low levels of reinvestment caused many sugar mills to close, and more capital-intensive farming for crops like cotton, grains, soybeans, and fruit has superseded labor-intensive cane. This in turn has increased rural unemployment and fomented migration to the capital.

Between the steep, densely wooded Sierra de Aconquija to the west and the Río Salí to the east, San Miguel de Tucumán (pop. about 580,000) is 1,191 kilometers northwest of Buenos Aires via RN 9, and 303 kilometers south of Salta via the same highway. Street names change on either side of 24 de Septiembre. The largest open space is the wooded 100-hectare Parque 9 de Julio, six blocks east of the plaza.

Sights

Tucumán's civic center is **Plaza Independencia,** whose provincial **Casa de Gobierno** (1912) has been the site of frequent demonstrations, thanks to the province's perpetual financial plight and contentious history. Across the street to the north, the **Templo y Convento de San Francisco** (1879) is a rebuilt version of a colonial church that passed into Franciscan hands after the Jesuits' expulsion from the Americas in 1767; the convent sits atop Jesuit foundations.

Immediately south of government house, the mid-19th-century **Casa Padilla** (25 de Mayo 36, 9 A.M.–1 P.M. Tues.–Sun., free), built by provincial governor José Frías and furnished in the fashion of its time, is now a museum of European art (taking its name from Frías's son-in-law, a city mayor).

On the plaza's south side, its twin bell towers topped by cupolas, the neoclassical **Iglesia Catedral** (1847–1856) is a national historical monument. Half a block south, dating from 1836, the **Museo Histórico de la Provincia** (Congreso 56, tel. 0381/431-1039, 9 A.M.–12:30 P.M. and 3–8 P.M. Tues.–Sun., US$0.75) was President Nicolás Avellaneda's birthplace; a pleasant surprise, this well-organized museum holds some exceptional colonial items, including finely carved religious imagery as well as paintings, coins, and the like.

One block farther south, Tucumán's key historical landmark is the colonial **Casa de la Independencia** (Congreso 151), described in more detail below. Two blocks east of the historical museum, the **Museo Iramain** (Entre Ríos 27, tel. 0381/421-1874, 10 A.M.–1 P.M. weekdays as well as 7–10 P.M. Tues. and Sat., free) showcases Argentine painting and sculpture.

Half a block south of the plaza, the **Museo de Bellas Artes Timoteo Navarro** (9 de Julio 44, tel. 0381/422-7300, 9:30 A.M.–12:30 P.M. and 5–9 P.M. Tues.–Fri., 10 A.M.–1 P.M. and 5–9 P.M. Sat.–Sun., US$0.75, free Sun.) offers rotating art exhibits.

Beyond the city center there is a pair of other notable museums. The **Museo de la Universidad Nacional de Tucumán** (MUNT,

San Martín 1545, tel. 0381/452-7550, 9 A.M.–1 P.M. and 5–9 P.M. Mon.–Fri., free) is a multidisciplinary facility focused on geology, paleontology, and archaeology. On the west side of Parque 9 de Julio, the **Casa del Obispo Colombres** (Avenida Capitán Casares s/n, free) was the bishop's 19th-century residence and site of the local sugar industry's first ox-driven *trapiche,* a mill that's still in working condition. Hours are 8:20 A.M.–6 P.M. daily, with informative guided tours in Spanish only.

Casa de la Independencia

Now fronted by an attractive pedestrian mall, the late-colonial Casa de la Independencia is where the signatories to the country's definitive declaration of independence met to approve the final document on July 9, 1816. Though the congress itself moved to Buenos Aires the following year, the heirs sold the building to the federal government in 1872, when it became the site of judicial and postal offices.

Much of the building was demolished in 1903, except the renovated facade and the restored salon in which the declaration was signed; in 1943, though, architect Mario Buschiazzo rebuilt the structure based on documents and photographs predating the demolition. From the walls, portraits of the signatories face the table at which the declaration was signed.

Unfortunately, despite some impressive holdings, the museum within needs professional help to clarify its mission not just to foreigners—English translations would help—but also to interpret them to Argentines.

The **Museo de la Independencia** (Congreso 151, tel. 0381/431-0826, 10 A.M.–6 P.M. daily, US$1.25) has a light-and-sound show (US$2.50) at 8 or 8:30 P.M. nightly except Thursday; the Friday and Saturday events (US$5) are more elaborate, with costumed actors.

Entertainment and Events

July 9's **Día de la Independencia** (Independence Day) is the single biggest celebration, but September 24's anniversary of the **Batalla de Tucumán** (Battle of Tucumán) is also important.

The Universidad Nacional de Tucumán's **Centro Cultural Eugenio Flavio Virla** (25 de Mayo 265, tel. 0381/422-1692) holds theater and music events along with art exhibits, and also has a crafts shop.

Plaza Independencia's **Centro Cultural Doctor Alberto Rougués** (Laprida 31, tel. 0381/427-7976, 8:30 A.M.–12:30 P.M. and 5–9 P.M. Mon.–Fri., 10:30 A.M.–12:30 P.M. and 6:30–8:30 P.M. Sat.) is a fine-arts facility.

Better for drinking than eating, Barrio Norte's casual **Plaza de Almas** (Maipú 791, tel. 0381/430-6067, www.plazadealmas.com) is a lively cultural café-bar (open from 8:30 P.M.), exhibition center, and native-art shop (open 10 A.M.–1 P.M. only). The menu is pub grub—pizza, sandwiches, and few more complex dishes—but it's a major gathering place.

For live music, try also the **Guanabara Jazz Club** (Lavalle 652), in Barrio Sur south of Plaza Independencia.

Tucumán's only remaining downtown movie theater is the **Cine Atlas** (Monteagudo 250, tel. 0381/422-0825).

Shopping

Housed in a colonial construction that belonged to the family of independence figure and sugar pioneer Bishop José Eusebio Colombres, the misnamed **Museo Folklórico Manuel Belgrano** (24 de Setiembre 565, tel. 0381/421-8250, 10 A.M.–1 P.M. and 3–8 P.M. Tues.–Fri., 10 A.M.–1 P.M. Sun., 3–8 P.M. Mon.) has nothing to do with General Belgrano. Rather, it's a hybrid institution that displays and sells museum-quality versions of indigenous carvings, weavings, and ceramics, leather goods and horse gear, and the intricately woven lace known as *randa,* from the provincial village of Monteros.

Plaza de Almas (Maipú 791, tel. 0381/430-6067, www.plazadealmas.com) is the crafts outlet of the popular bar-restaurant and cultural center.

Accommodations

With up-and-coming hostels, renovated midrange places, and traditional upscale choices,

Tucumán's hotel scene is improving. Rates often rise here in the winter months, July through September.

US$10-25: Occupying a handsome older house with five-meter ceilings, on a deep lot with a plunge pool in the back, 🄲 **Tucumán Hostel** (Buenos Aires 669, tel. 0381/420-1584, www.tucumanhostel.com, US$9 pp dorm, US$23–27 s or d) has mostly dorms but also a few private rooms, some with private baths, an attractive patio and bar with hammocks, and amenities such as Wi-Fi. From the bus terminal, Centro Taxi provides free transportation.

Recently acquired by the Salta hostel chain, in similar quarters but with smaller gardens and common areas, **Backpackers Tucumán** (Laprida 456, tel. 0381/430-2716, www.backpackerstucuman.com, US$10–12 pp dorm, US$17–24 s, US$27–34 d) is more central and closer to Barrio Norte restaurants and nightlife.

In a lime-green deco-style building, Barrio Norte's **Hostel Oh** (Santa Fe 993, tel. 0381/430-8849, www.hosteloh.com.ar, US$10 pp dorm, US$24 s or d) is ideally placed for enjoying the nearby pub and restaurant scene, but it has plenty of attractions and amenities in its own right, such as a pool, a bar, and occasional live music.

US$25-50: Amiable **Hotel Versailles** (Crisóstomo Alvarez 481, tel. 0381/422-9760, www.hotelversaillestuc.com.ar, US$34 s, US$40 d) has smallish rooms with narrow beds but is adequate in this price range.

Upgraded **Hotel América** (Santiago del Estero 1064, tel. 0381/430-0810, www.hotelamerica.com.ar, US$34 s, US$40 d) has 72 rooms with air-conditioning, strongboxes, Wi-Fi, and other amenities; it also has a restaurant.

US$50-100: Like the América, **Hotel Francia** (Crisóstomo Alvarez 467, tel. 0381/431-0781, www.franciahotel.com, US$45 s, US$57 d) has upgraded its 42 rooms and its amenities.

Opposite Plaza Independencia, **Hotel Mediterráneo** (24 de Setiembre 364, tel. 0381/431-0025, www.hotelmediterraneo.com.ar, US$59 s or d) is a business-oriented place.

Once worn, the 110 rooms at the deco-style **Gran Hotel Premier** (Crisóstomo Alvarez 502, tel. 0381/431-0381, www.redcarlosv.com.ar, US$50 s, US$62 d) have undergone a major rehab to become a recommended choice. Facing Plaza Independencia, **Hotel del Sol** (Laprida 35, tel. 0381/431-0393, US$71 s, US$92 d) is a contemporary high-rise with the usual amenities in its range.

Over US$100: Opposite Parque 9 de Julio, the **Hotel Garden Park Suites** (Avenida Soldati 330, tel. 0381/431-0700, www.gardenparkhotel.com.ar, US$87 s, US$100 d) is a legitimate four-star facility.

One of Tucumán's finest, the **Hotel Metropol** (24 de Setiembre 524, tel. 0381/431-1180, www.swisshotelmetropol.com.ar, US$91 s, US$115 d) traditionally offers 20 percent discounts for the asking, at times at least. Its outstanding amenity is a rooftop pool.

Nearly next door to the Garden Park, **Hotel Catalinas Park** (Avenida Soldati 380, tel. 0381/450-2250, www.catalinaspark.com, US$110–130 s, US$126–145 d) is the only five-star choice.

Food

Il Postino (Córdoba 501) is good for croissants, coffee, and breakfast, but has expanded its menu to more sophisticated fare. **Café 25** (Mendoza 502, tel. 0381/422-8688) serves a mostly standard Argentine menu with a few surprises, most notably decent fajitas and other Tex-Mex dishes, and has good service.

More a snack bar than a restaurant, **El Portal** (24 de Septiembre between Laprida and Rivadavia) is a worthwhile stop for regional delicacies like *humitas,* empanadas, and *locro.* **Empanadas Buenos Aires** (Buenos Aires 598, tel. 0381/420-5246) is highly regarded for beef and chicken empanadas.

It's hard to spend more than US$10 for a good meal at **Los Leños** (Buenos Aires 668, tel. 0381/420-0216), which features *parrillada* and a diversity of regional menu dishes including *humitas,* tamales, and a variety of empanadas including beef, chicken, *sfija* (*árabe*), and *mondongo* (tripe).

The **Jockey Club** (San Martín 451, tel. 0381/421-3946) is a traditional favorite for *parrillada* and other Argentine specialties. **Mi Nueva Estancia** (Córdoba and Laprida, tel. 0381/430-7049) is a newer upscale *parrilla*. **Kló & Kló** (Junín 663, tel. 0381/422-3340) provides a diverse menu of pasta and seafood.

When they finish their lunches, local businessmen chew fresh coca leaves at **[** **La Corzuela** (Laprida 866, tel. 0381/421-6402), which boasts a large, diverse menu that includes the usual *parrillada* and pasta along with regional dishes, fish (fresh trout), seafood, poultry, and salads. Its high brick walls are covered with weavings, paintings, and gaucho gear; it also offers great service, a small but fine wine list, an exquisitely refreshing lemonade (more than welcome in this climate), and entrées in the US$4–7 range.

Emblematic of Barrio Norte improvements, **[** **Setimio** (Santa Fe 512, tel. 0381/431-2792) is a soothing wine bar and restaurant in a neighborhood that's undergoing major gentrification. *Cordero al ajillo* (roast lamb flavored with garlic, US$10) is a weekend specialty but may be available at other times. As it also sells wine, the list is enormous, but more limited for by-the-glass selections unless there's a bottle already open.

The nearby **[** **La Bernasconi** (Santa Fe 562, tel. 0381/431-2059) is a stylish restaurant with fine pastas and a diversity of other dishes in the US$6–8 range, with a Wednesday-night fondue special. The service is attentive but unobtrusive, and the wine list is fine if not quite so impressive as Setimio's.

Plaza Independencia's **Blue Bell** (25 de Mayo 26, tel. 0381/422-8343) offers above-average ice cream, but **Tello Helados Premium** (Santa Fe 202, tel. 0381/430-8118) is taking over.

Information

On the south side of Plaza Independencia, Tucumán's provincial **Ente Autárquico Tucumán Turismo** (24 de Setiembre 484, tel. 0381/430-3644, www.tucumanturismo.gov. ar, 8 A.M.–10 P.M. weekdays, 9 A.M.–9 P.M. weekends) has an improved selection of printed matter, including an outstanding city map. There is also a bus terminal office (8 A.M.–1 P.M. and 5–10 P.M. daily).

For motorists, **ACA** (tel. 0381/430-3384) is at Crisóstomo Alvarez 901.

Services

As a provincial capital, San Miguel has a full complement of services.

Maxicambio (San Martín 779) is a convenient exchange house. Several downtown banks have ATMs, including **Citibank** (San Martín 859).

Correo Argentino is at 25 de Mayo and Córdoba; the postal code is 4000. *Locutorios* and Internet outlets are on almost every downtown block.

Patsa Turismo (Chacabuco 38, tel. 0381/421-6806) is the Amex affiliate. **Duport Turismo** (Congreso 160, tel. 0381/422-0000) organizes half-day city tours and full-day excursions to Tafí del Valle (with a possible extension to the ruins at Quilmes). **Asatej** (Mendoza 916, tel. 0381/430-3034, tucuman@ asatej.com.ar) is the local branch of the student-oriented travel agency.

Lavadero Laprida (Laprida 325, tel. 0381/421-6573) does the laundry inexpensively, as does **Aqua Lav** (9 de Julio 689, tel. 0381/424-9557).

Hospital Angel C. Padilla is at Alberdi 550 (tel. 0381/424-8008).

Getting There

Tucumán enjoys air, road, and even rail connections to Buenos Aires and much of the rest of the republic.

Aerolíneas Argentinas (9 de Julio 112, tel. 0381/431-1030) flies to Buenos Aires's Aeroparque, occasionally stopping in Córdoba or Santiago del Estero. **LAN Argentina** (Laprida 176, tel. 0381/497-7362) flies several nonstops daily to Aeroparque, while **Sol Líneas Aéreas** (tel. 0810/444-4765) has weekday flights to Rosario and Córdoba. **AeroSur** (Rivadavia 137, tel. 0381/452-2300) flies four times weekly to Santa Cruz de la Sierra (Bolivia) via Salta.

Six blocks east of Plaza Independencia, Tucumán's **Estación de Ómnibus** (Avenida Brígido Terán 350, tel. 0381/430-4696) also contains a post office, a supermarket, restaurants, and a major shopping center.

Within the province, Aconquija (tel. 0381/422-7620) goes at least four times daily to Tafí del Valle (2.5 hours, US$6), Amaicha del Valle (4 hours, US$9), and to Cafayate at 6 A.M. and 2 P.M. daily, with a transfer at Santa María.

Typical destinations, times, and fares include Termas de Río Hondo (1.5 hours, US$3), Santiago del Estero (2 hours, US$6), Salta (4 hours, US$15), La Rioja (6 hours, US$20), Cafayate (7 hours, US$14), Córdoba (8 hours, US$26–30), Corrientes (13 hours, US$35), Mendoza (11 hours, US$35–45), Posadas (18.5 hours, US$55–65), and Buenos Aires (16 hours, US$46–60).

Ferrocentral, at the Estación Mitre (Corrientes 1045, tel. 0381/430-9220) operates a slow (25-hour) **train** to Retiro (Buenos Aires) at 6:05 P.M. Wednesday and at 8:50 P.M. Saturday. Rates are US$12 *turista,* US$19 *primera,* US$35 Pullman with air-conditioning and reclining seats, and US$105 d (with breakfast) in *camarote* sleepers. The ticket office is open 9 A.M.–8 P.M. Monday–Saturday.

Getting Around
Aeropuerto Internacional Benjamín Matienzo (tel. 0381/426-4906) is eight kilometers east of downtown via Avenida Gobernador del Campo, which runs along the northern edge of Parque 9 de Julio. **Viajes Especiales** (tel. 0381/678-3248) provides door-to-door transfers (US$8 for up to 3 passengers).

City buses use inexpensive *cospeles* (tokens), available from downtown kiosks, but also accept coins.

Móvil Renta (San Lorenzo 370, tel. 0381/431-0550, www.movilrenta.com.ar) rents out cars.

TAFÍ DEL VALLE AND VICINITY
When subtropical San Miguel becomes a summer sauna, the capital's residents flee to the hill station of Tafí del Valle, 107 kilometers west via a highway that's a highlight in itself. At an elevation of 1,976 meters, Tafí's permanent population is only a few thousand, but when every bed in its hotels and weekend houses is occupied, those numbers can double or triple.

Unlike steamy San Miguel, Tafí's microclimate is subject to fogs and drizzle that can require sweaters, jackets, and mufflers even in midsummer, but when the weather clears the scenery is dazzling. There's a certain tension between rural residents and weekenders, as the former often ignore the numerous street signs that prohibit horses in the center, where road apples often cover the pavement. In addition to tourism, the economy depends on cool-weather crops like potatoes and temperate fruits like apples, pears, and blueberries. Farther afield, farmers pasture cattle, sheep, and even llamas at the highest elevations.

From Acheral, 42 kilometers southwest of the provincial capital via RN 38, paved RP 307 meanders up the narrow Río de los Sosa canyon until, at roughly the 100-kilometer mark, the landscape widens into Tafí's open valley where, when the fog clears, the 4,000-meter-plus summits of the Nevados de Aconquija tower toward the north. The highway continues over the 3,050-meter Abra del Infiernillo to Amaicha del Valle (55 kilometers), Quilmes (77 kilometers), and Cafayate (123 kilometers, in Salta Province).

History
In pre-Columbian times, Calchaquí farmers and llama herders lived in scattered settlements in and around Tafí, but the Spanish invasion brought them under the *encomienda*'s labor and tribute obligations. As the population declined and the *encomienda* lost value, Jesuit missionaries gained control, and under their relatively benevolent philosophy of self-sufficiency, the economy rebounded. After the Jesuits' expulsion from the Americas in 1767 and Argentine independence half a century later, the valley faltered in isolation. Completion of a new highway, however,

brought improved access to San Miguel's markets and brought the tourist trade to Tafí.

Sights

Most points of interest are not in Tafí proper but nearby and en route from Tucumán and beyond toward Quilmes and Cafayate.

Built in the early 18th century, across the Río Tafí bridge at the south end of Perón, the **Capilla La Banda** was part of the Jesuit *estancia* that dates from their takeover of the 17th-century *encomienda*. Restored in the 1970s after multiple postindependence modifications, it is now Tafí's **Museo Histórico y Arqueológico** (Avenida Gobernador Silva s/n, tel. 0387/421-685, 10 A.M.–6 P.M. daily, US$1.25), with collections of pre-Columbian funerary urns and colonial religious art and ecclesiastical items, along with typical 19th-century furnishings and an escape tunnel.

About 10 kilometers south of Tafí, a paved lateral leads to the village of El Mollar, where authorities have moved the **Parque de los Menhires** (8 A.M.–6 P.M. daily, US$0.75), a collection of some 80 pre-Columbian granite monuments gathered in the vicinity. The monuments themselves, carved with representations of humans and animals, are intriguing, but they've been wrenched out of geographical context more than once.

Events

Tafí's major annual event is mid-February's **Festival del Queso,** celebrating the local cheese industry.

Shopping

Try **Los Artesanos** (Avenida Perón 252, tel. 03867/42-1758) for souvenirs.

Sports and Recreation

Local guides lead hikes to nearby summits, including 2,650-meter Cerro El Pelao (4 hours, US$20 pp), 4,437-meter Cerro Muñoz (4 hours, US$20 pp), and 4,660-meter Cerro Negrito (a full day, US$30 pp), with discounts for groups of up to five people. For details, ask

at the Casa del Turista, the nearby private information office, or Hostel La Cumbre.

Accommodations

Hostel La Cumbre (Perón 120, tel. 03867/42-1758, www.lacumbretafidelvalle.com, US$10 pp) has reinvented itself as a hostel facility, with a couple private rooms as well, and also offers excursions and guide services.

Just south of the river bridge and down the hill a few hundred meters, the HI affiliate is **Hostel Nómade** (José Félix Sosa s/n, tel. 03867/421-378, nomadehostel@hotmail.com, US$10 pp, US$20 d), a large and comfortable house where the sleeping quarters are well isolated from the bar, barbecue, kitchen, and other common areas. It's mostly dorms but has a couple of private rooms as well.

The placid **Hotel Tafí** (Avenida Belgrano 177, tel. 03867/421-007, www.hoteltafiweb.com.ar, US$40 s, US$50 d) offers simply furnished, midsize rooms, some with views; it also enjoys sprawling gardens and large common areas with high ceilings.

Up the street, the stylishly modern and spacious **Hostería La Rosada** (Avenida Belgrano 322, tel. 03867/42-1323, hotellarosada@uolsinectis.com.ar, US$40 s, US$60 d, with buffet breakfast) retains some appeal, but prices have risen steeply, and some mattresses are on the soft side.

Easily the pick of the standard accommodations, 🄲 **Hostería Lunahuaná** (Avenida Gobernador Critto 540, tel./fax 03867/42-1360, www.lunahuana.com.ar, US$70 s, US$90 d) offers a mix of contemporary comforts and traditional design; some rooms even have lofts.

For colonial style in a rehabbed *estancia* house, try any of the half-dozen rooms at the intimate 🄲 **Posada las Tacanas** (Perón 372, tel. 03867/42-1821, www.estancialastacanas.com, US$92 s, US$102 d).

Food

Tafí's restaurant scene is by no means bad, but it does lack variety. Most eateries are on Avenida Perón within a block or two of each other.

Regional specialties like *humitas* and *locro,* along with pizza, are the items at **El Rancho de Félix** (Perón and Belgrano, tel. 03867/42-1022).

Under new ownership, **(€ El Portal de las Valles** (Avenida Perón s/n, tel. 03867/42-1834) still serves great *cabrito* (kid goat) at reasonable prices; it also offers good empanadas and *humitas.* The **Resto Pub Kkechuwa** (Perón s/n) serves empanadas and other regional dishes, plus its own microbrew beer. **El Patio de las Empanadas** (Perón s/n) is also worth consideration.

Directly on the highway, **El Blanquito** (RP 307 Km 61) is an outstanding teahouse with desserts crafted from locally grown blueberries, raspberries, and other fruits.

Information and Services

On the south side of Plaza Estéves is Tafí's helpful **Casa del Turista** (Los Faroles s/n, tel. 03867/42-1880, ext. 11, 8 A.M.–10 P.M. daily).

In the Centro Cívico, **Banco de Tucumán** (Gobernador Critto 311) has an ATM. For postal services, **Correo Argentino** is at San Martín s/n, half a block north of Plaza Estéves; the postal code is 4137. **Telecom** (Perón and Gobernador Critto) has long-distance phone booths, while **Internet Los Arcos** (Perón s/n) provides online services.

Getting There and Around

From Tafí's handsome new bus terminal, **Empresa Aconquija** (Avenida Gobernador Critto s/n, tel. 03867/42-1035) has seven or eight buses daily to the provincial capital of San Miguel (2 hours, US$6). Two buses from San Miguel (8:30 A.M. and 8:30 P.M.) continue to Amaicha del Valle, Santa María (Catamarca), and Cafayate (Salta), passing the major ruins at Quilmes.

AMAICHA DEL VALLE

From Tafí del Valle, RP 307 climbs steeply northwest over the curiously named Abra del Infiernillo (literally "Little Hell"), a fog-shrouded 3,050-meter pass that marks the transition to the western desert. As the highway descends into the Valles Calchaquíes basin, at an elevation of 2,560 meters, it passes the **Observatorio Astronómico Ampimpa** (RP 307 Km 107, tel. 0381/15-609-2286, ampimpa@turismoentucuman.com), a small teaching-oriented observatory that offers both day and night astronomical programs along with simple accommodations and a restaurant.

Another 10 kilometers west, in the village of Amaicha del Valle, Héctor Cruz's **Museo Pachamama** or Casa de Piedra (RP 307 Km 118, tel. 03892/42-1004, US$2.50) is a stunning, sprawling juxtaposition of indigenously themed sculptures by Cruz and other regional artists set among cactus gardens and fountains. It's also a series of museums with informative thematic exhibits on geology, mining, natural history, archaeology, and Cruz's own art. Well worth a detour from either Tafí del Valle or Cafayate, it offers informative guided tours (in Spanish only) 8 A.M.–1 P.M. and 2–6 P.M. weekdays, 9 A.M.–1 P.M. and 2–5 P.M. Sunday. There's a large museum shop and a small café, but hotel construction is stalled because of a lawsuit.

Accommodations and Food

Directly on the plaza, **Hostal L'Apacheta** (tel. 03892/42-1173, www.hostalapacheta.com.ar, US$11 pp) has ample and immaculate rooms with private baths, balconies, and ceiling fans, though the shower design is faulty. It's frills-free but, peso for peso, perhaps the country's best value.

West of Amaicha, just south of the highway, **Altos de Amaicha** (RP 307 Km 117, tel. 03892/42-1430, www.altosdeamaicha.com.ar, US$42 s, US$69 d) is a mini-casino masquerading as a boutique hotel and restaurant. Only two years old, the rooms are decent but already showing signs of wear.

In the same building as L'Apacheta, but operated separately, **La Termena** serves pizza and regional specialties such as empanadas, *humitas,* and tamales.

Getting There

Buses from Tucumán and Tafí drop and pick up passengers here.

◖ QUILMES

Arguably northwestern Argentina's most impressive pre-Columbian ruins, the fortified settlement of Quilmes ascends the arid eastern slope of the Cerro Alto del Rey, 77 kilometers northwest of Tafí del Valle and 55 kilometers south of Cafayate. Covering about 30 hectares, the city supported a population upwards of 5,000 in terraced buildings with thick defensive walls overlooking irrigated farmlands.

Dating from about A.D. 1000, Quilmes developed autonomously as part of the regional Diaguita/Calchaquí culture, but fell under Inka influence in the late 15th century. The Quilmes Indians fiercely resisted the Spaniards, who, when they defeated them in 1667, deported the last 2,000 survivors to Buenos Aires, where their legacy is an industrial southern suburb known for its namesake brewery.

Climbing and exploring the ruins is a rewarding experience that justifies at least half a day; the ideal would be to spend the night at its low-impact hotel. Admission to the ruins, which are open 8 A.M.–7 P.M. daily, costs US$1.25.

Because of a lawsuit by Calchaquí Indians, who are now offering guided tours as well, the on-site hotel is closed for the foreseeable future. Bring food and drinks.

Getting There and Around

Empresa Aconquija buses from San Miguel de Tucumán and Tafí del Valle to Cafayate will drop passengers at the junction, as will return services from Cafayate to Santa María or Tafí. From the junction, though, it's hike or hitch to the ruins, which are five kilometers west of the highway.

Catamarca Province

Like neighboring La Rioja, Catamarca is an Andean desert province that reminds some visitors of the Middle East, and many settlers came from that part of the world. Like La Rioja, it boasts wild, high, and rarely visited country near the Chilean border that will reward adventurous travelers; it is also a major pilgrimage site for Argentine Catholics. Unfortunately, it shares the region's corruption problem thanks to figures such as labor leader Luis Barrionuevo, who once remarked that "nobody in Argentina ever got rich by working" and that Argentina's foreign-debt problems could be resolved "if we just stop stealing for a couple of years."

SAN FERNANDO DEL VALLE DE CATAMARCA

Home to the revered image of the Virgen del Valle, one of Argentina's most important pilgrimage sites, San Fernando del Valle de Catamarca—more simply known as Catamarca—lives by faith and faith-based tourism. Images of the virgin are ubiquitous,

and religious holidays like December 8 bring masses to the city.

Catamarca's founding date of 1683 is relatively late for a capital in the colonial northwest—because indigenous resistance to the Spaniards prevented any permanent presence until then. As capital of a province with perhaps the most dysfunctional politics of any in Argentina, it's tempting to say that Catamarca needs that faith to survive the poverty and political backwardness imposed by its caudillos.

In the valley of the Río del Valle, between the western Sierra del Colorado and the eastern Sierra Graciana, Catamarca (pop. 140,556) is 1,131 kilometers northwest of Buenos Aires via RN 9 to Córdoba, northbound RN 60, and RP 33. It is 154 kilometers northeast of La Rioja and 230 kilometers from Tucumán via RN 38, and 209 kilometers from Santiago del Estero via RN 64.

Sights

City authorities have upgraded long-neglected public spaces such as French landscape architect Carlos Thays's shady **Plaza 25 de Mayo,** which blends almost seamlessly with the pedestrian mall that provides access to Italian architect Luis Caravati's landmark **Catedral Basílica de Nuestra Señora del Valle** (Sarmiento 653), immediately west. Most visitors here are pilgrims who come to visit the basilica to see its 17th-century image of the **Virgen del Valle,** the city's patron saint (appropriately enough, she's also the Patrona Nacional de Turismo, the national patron saint of tourism). Most pilgrims time their visits for and following Semana Santa and December 8, her patronal day, the only times her diamond-studded crown is on display.

Dating from 1859–1869, with a recent exterior restoration, the Italianate building rises impressively above Thays's landmark plaza design; the interior boasts a decorative baroque pulpit and an equally impressive carved altar. Immediately north of the basilica, Caravati also created the provincial **Casa de Gobierno** (1859).

One block–plus north, the **Museo Arqueológico Adán Quiroga** (Sarmiento 450, tel. 03833/43-7413, 8 a.m.–1 p.m. and 3–8 p.m. weekdays, 10 a.m.–7 p.m. weekends, US$1) is both more and less than it suggests: In addition to extensive artifacts from regional prehistory, it also showcases materials from colonial and religious history (including the belongings of Franciscan priest and constitutionalist politician Fray Mamerto Esquiú), but the presentation is uninspired.

One block immediately east, architect Luis Giorgi's Italianate **Iglesia y Convento de San Francisco** (Esquiú 550), dating from 1882–1905, is the third in a series of Franciscan churches to occupy the site; it still contains remnants of the original colonial cloisters and the cell of Padre Esquiú, whose heart, in a bizarre incident, once ended up in a crystal urn on the church's roof. Even more strangely, in early 2008, a young man—apparently mentally ill—shattered a glass case that held the heart and apparently dumped the organ into a trash bin. It has never been found.

For the area's finest views, take a tour or a *remise* up the narrow, zigzag **Cuesta de El Portezuelo,** a paved 17-kilometer portion of RP 2 that climbs the steep western face of the Sierras de Ancasti, where it connects with RP 42 toward Santiago del Estero. The panoramas of the valley and the high westerly Sierra del Ambato, which separates the provincial capital from its western deserts and altiplano, are stupendous.

Entertainment and Events

The multiscreen **Cinemacenter** (Avenida Güemes 856, tel. 03833/42-3040) is at the bus terminal. The **Cine Teatro Catamarca** (San Martín 555, tel. 03833/43-7565) has occasional classic films and live performances.

For two weeks after Semana Santa, pilgrims from Catamarca and other Andean provinces celebrate the **Fiesta de Nuestra Señora del Valle,** which includes a *novena* (nine days of prayer) after which they parade the Virgen del Valle out of her chamber in the cathedral and around Plaza 25 de Mayo.

July 5's **Fundación de Catamarca** recalls the city's 1863 founding. During winter holidays, the last two weeks of July, the **Fiesta Nacional del Poncho** honors traditional weavers with folkloric music and dance— including performances from high-profile performers from around the country—and traditional cuisine.

Throngs of pilgrims from around Argentina overrun all available accommodations, campgrounds, and all other services for December 8's **Día de la Virgen,** honoring the city's patron saint.

Shopping

Catamarca's biggest crafts outlet is the **Mercado Artesanal Permanente y Fábrica de Alfombras** (Avenida Virgen del Valle 945, tel. 03833/43-7862), which showcases the province's traditional handmade rugs, blankets, and ponchos as well as jewelry and similar items.

La Yunta (Sarmiento 489, tel. 03833/42-8101) sells regional products such as leather goods and woolens, *mate* paraphernalia, and sweets such as sugared walnuts.

Accommodations

The **San Pedro Hostel Bar** (Sarmiento 341, tel. 03833/45-4708, www.hostelsanpedro.com.ar, US$8 pp, US$27 d) is not the place for an early night's sleep, but this independent hostel has casual style and amenities that include kitchen privileges, a library, a TV/DVD room, a bar, and even a plunge pool set among deep sunny gardens.

Opposite the bus terminal, the **Coral Hotel** (Tucumán 1179, tel. 03833/45-4674, www.catamarcacoral.com.ar, US$32 s, US$48 d) is a modern well-kept hotel with Wi-Fi, ample parking, and friendly staff. Ask for a room facing away from the terminal, although double-paned windows do reduce the ruckus.

No longer the bargain it once was, often-understaffed **Hotel Pucará** (Caseros 501, tel. 03833/43-0688, www.hotelpucara.com.ar, US$36 s, US$48 d) has lost ground to other, slightly more expensive places. It has plain but comfortable furnishings and cable TV; there's a surcharge for credit-card payments.

Worn but with bright rooms in a contemporary style, the respectable **Hotel Suma Huasi** (Sarmiento 541, tel. 03833/43-5699, hotelescatamarca@hotmail.com, US$43 s, US$52 d), has air-conditioning, cable TV, and the like, but the beds are a little soft.

Rooms at **Hotel Arenales** (Sarmiento 542, tel. 03833/43-0307, www.hotel-arenales.com.ar, US$58 s, US$70 d) are larger than those at the more prestigious Hotel Ancasti. It also has a gym and a pool.

Claiming to be business-oriented, **Hotel Ancasti** (Sarmiento 520, tel. 03833/43-5951, www.hotelancasti.com.ar, US$54 s, US$68 d) has only one public computer, but it offers good, decent-sized rooms with desks; the bathrooms lack tubs, though. There's some bargaining room if business is slow.

Amerian Catamarca Park Hotel (República 347, tel. 03833/42-5444, www.amerian.com, US$91 s or d with buffet breakfast) is a marble-and-travertine tower that seems out of place in Catamarca, but it is impressive.

Food

Nobody visits Catamarca for its cuisine, but it's possible to find passable food. Penurious pilgrims eat cheaply at **Comedor El Peregrino** (San Martín s/n), in the gallery immediately behind the cathedral, where basic pasta and *parrillada* are the rule.

The **Bar Richmond** (República 534, tel. 03833/42-3123) has a larger, more diverse menu, but it's hit-and-miss as to what they've got and whether it's good or not—though it's worth a look. **Las Tinajas** (Sarmiento 533, tel. 03833/43-5853) is a pasta specialist, while **Los Maestros** (Rivadavia 973, tel. 03833/43-2357) is for pizza. **Los Troncos** (Mota Botello 33, tel. 03833/45-4944) is a local favorite with a large *parrilla* menu and assiduous service, but the food quality can vary.

Coppo di Sabore (Rivadavia 620) has Catamarca's finest ice cream, but **Heladería Venecia** (Avenida Virgen del Valle 730) ain't bad.

Information

The helpful **Centro de Cultural y Turismo Municipal** (República 525, tel. 03833/45-5385, www.sfvcatamarca.gov.ar, 9 A.M.–1 P.M. and 5–9 P.M. weekdays, 8 A.M.–1 P.M. and 5–9:30 P.M. weekends) answers questions and helps find accommodations.

The provincial **Secretaría de Turismo y Cultura** (República 446, tel. 03833/43-7791, www.turismocatamarca.gov.ar, 7 A.M.–9 P.M. weekdays, 8 A.M.–9 P.M. weekends) is better stocked with maps and brochures.

For motorists, **ACA** (tel. 03833/42-4513) is at República 102.

Services

Several downtown banks have ATMs, including **Banco de Galicia** (Rivadavia 554) and **Banco de la Nación** (San Martín 632).

Correo Argentino is at San Martín 753; the postal code is 4700. **Telecentro Plaza** (Rivadavia 758) has long-distance; for Internet access, try **Cyberia** (Esquiú and Sarmiento), a block north of the plaza.

Yokavil Turismo (Rivadavia 916, tel. 03833/43-0066, www.yokavilturismo.com.ar) arranges tours in the vicinity.

Espumitas (Mota Botello 343, tel. 03833/42-4504) does the laundry.

For medical emergencies, try **Hospital San Juan Bautista** (Avenida Illia 200, tel. 03833/43-7654).

Getting There and Around
Aerolíneas Argentinas (Sarmiento 589, tel. 03833/42-4460) flies most days to Buenos Aires's Aeroparque via La Rioja.

Aeropuerto Felipe Varela (tel. 03833/43-0080) is 22 kilometers east of Catamarca on RP 33; Aerolíneas's Servicios Diferenciales minibus charges US$5 pp to or from the airport.

Catamarca's state-of-the-art **Terminal de Ómnibus** (Avenida Güemes 850, tel. 03833/43-7578) offers services throughout the province and the country. Sample destinations, times, and fares include La Rioja (2 hours, US$5), Tucumán (3.5 hours, US$8), Córdoba (7.5 hours, US$19–23), Salta (9 hours, US$26–31), Mendoza (11 hours, US$33–38), and Buenos Aires (15 hours, US$46–69).

BELÉN
Convenient to a number of worthwhile but underappreciated sights, including Inka ruins, and popular for its woolen ponchos, the western highlands town of Belén is one of Catamarca's oldest settlements. The Inkas themselves had a tenuous presence in the area, which was inhabited by native Calchaquí peoples until the Spaniards established an almost equally tenuous presence in the mid-16th century. It was ultimately settled from La Rioja, to the south.

Where RN 40 meets the westbound road from Andalgalá, 89 kilometers to the east, Belén (pop. 11,281) is the best place to stay between Chilecito (221 kilometers to the south, in La Rioja Province) and Santa María (180 kilometers to the north).

Sights
Belén's main gathering place is the pine- and pepper-studded **Plaza Olmos y Aguilera,** the site of its **Iglesia Nuestra Señora de Belén** (1907), a brick construction that's unusual in this part of Argentina. At the southeast corner of the plaza, the provincial **Museo Arqueológico Cóndor Huasi** (San Martín 310, 1st floor, 8 A.M.–1 P.M. and 3–7 P.M. Tues.–Sun.) is a small but well-organized facility specializing in regional cultural evolution.

Three blocks west of the plaza, a 1,900-meter footpath climbs steeply to far-larger-than-life-size statues of the Virgin Mary and Jesus on the **Cerro de la Virgen.** The base of the mountain is the site of preparatory activities for December 20's **Día de la Fundación,** which start up to a week earlier.

Accommodations and Food
The cheapest choice, by no means bad for the price, is **Hotel Gómez** (Calchaquí 213, tel. 03835/46-1388, US$11 s, US$16 d), one block west of the plaza. **Hotel Samay** (Urquiza 349, tel. 03835/46-1320, US$21 s, US$27 d) has adequate but small and darkish rooms.

In the style of an Andean *pirca,* the renovated **Complejo Turístico Belén** (Belgrano and Cubas, tel. 03835/46-1501, www.belencat.com.ar, US$27 s, US$50 d, with buffet breakfast) is the best in town. Nearly a full block of gardens surrounds its 17 reconditioned rooms, which have air-conditioning, and there are ample common spaces.

Parrillada is the dining standard, best sampled at **El Único** (General Roca and Sarmiento), which serves a fine *lomo a la pimienta* (pepper steak) for around US$6.

Other Practicalities
For woolens, especially ponchos, try **Regionales Los Antonitos** (Lavalle 418, tel. 03835/46-1940) or **El Collita** (Belgrano 267, tel. 03835/46-1712).

Belén's **Oficina Municipal de Turismo** (tel. 03835/46-1304) is at the foot of Cerro de la Virgen, three blocks west of the plaza.

Southwest of the plaza, Belén's **Terminal de Ómnibus** (Sarmiento and Rivadavia) has eastbound provincial services to and from Andalgalá (1.5 hours, US$4) and to Catamarca (4.5 hours, US$8), northbound to Hualfín and Santa María (2.5 hours, US$5.50), and southbound to La Rioja (4.5 hours, US$10) and Córdoba (9 hours, US$21).

Vicinity of Belén

From Belén, paved RN 40 leads south 15 kilometers through Londres (pop. 2,128), named by founder Juan Pérez de Zurita in 1558 for the marriage of Mary Tudor to the Spanish King Felipe II. The area's oldest Spanish settlement, repeatedly abandoned and resettled for political and military reasons, it holds the **Festival Provincial de la Nuez** (Provincial Walnut Festival) the first two weeks of February.

About six kilometers west of Londres, at the base of the Sierra de Quimivil, the Inka fortress of **El Shinkal** is a 21-hectare site where the lords of Cusco maintained a presence from around A.D. 1470 to 1536. While it's no Machu Picchu, Shinkal contains more than 100 constructions, including ceremonial platforms, depositories, staircases, and roads.

From Belén, there are seven buses daily to Londres, where a westbound dirt road from Plaza Eusebio Colombres leads to the ruins; at the sign that says "La Toma," turn right. Admission to the site costs US$1.

SANTA MARÍA

About 60 kilometers north of Belén, following the old Inka route, RN 40 enters the village of **Hualfín**, whose simple **Capilla de Nuestra Señora del Rosario** is a national historical monument dating from 1770. Another 120 kilometers northeast, the paved highway arrives at Santa María de Yokavil, a Valles Calchaquíes settlement more often visited from Cafayate (Salta) or Tafí del Valle (Tucumán).

Santa María (pop. 10,794) is known for its **Museo Arqueológico Provincial Eric Boman** (Belgrano and Sarmiento, tel. 03838/42-1282, 8:30 A.M.–1 P.M. and 5–9 P.M. daily). Named for an early-20th-century French archaeologist who did substantial field research in the vicinity, it focuses on early hunter-gatherers but also contains a substantial collection of Diaguita/Calchaquí ceramics.

Practicalities

Residencial Inti Huayco (Belgrano 146, tel. 03838/42-0476, US$21–27 pp) provides good value, as does **Hotel Cielos del Oeste** (San Martín 450, tel. 0838/42-0240, US$24 s, US$37 d). The unusual Moorish adobe **Complejo Arquitectónico Artesanal Santa María** (Avenida 9 de Julio s/n, tel. 03838/42-1627, www.hotelcaasama.com.ar, US$33 s, US$40 d) has 24 rooms with private baths and also has a pool.

Santa María has several *parrillas;* for regional cuisine, try **Rancho El Cardón** (Abel Acosta 158, tel. 03838/42-0172).

Some but not all **buses** to and from Cafayate and Tucumán via Tafí del Valle pass through Santa María. There are also southbound buses to Hualfín and Belén.

Santiago del Estero Province

The province of Santiago del Estero, whose namesake capital is the country's oldest city, attracts more Argentine than foreign travelers. Its main draw is the hot springs resort of Termas de Río Hondo, mainly a winter destination in a subtropical lowland province that suffers brutally hot summers. Like Tucumán it is poverty-stricken, thanks largely to the legacy of a provincial caudillo, ex-governor Carlos Juárez.

SANTIAGO DEL ESTERO

Capital of a province that sometimes seems a semifeudal fiefdom, Santiago del Estero has failed to sustain its birthright as the colonial "Madre de Ciudades" (Mother of Cities) and has become more a stopover than a destination. That said, a night spent here need not be a wasted one.

In 1553, Francisco de Aguirre founded the first city in what is now Argentina on the meandering flood-prone Río Dulce, a transitional site between the arid Chaco and the Andes. Since independence, though, it has suffered some of the worst politicians ever in a country notorious for misgovernment; in the 1990s, political discontent resulted in arson attacks on government offices, partly in response to official impunity, but the dynasty of former governor Carlos Juárez and his wife, Mercedes Aragonés (who succeeded him), survived any efforts to reduce their influence until a high-profile murder case brought federal intervention.

Santiago del Estero (pop. about 250,000) is 1,045 kilometers northwest of Buenos Aires and 440 kilometers north of Córdoba by RN 9; it's 170 kilometers southeast of Tucumán. Street names change on each side of Avenida Belgrano and Avenida Libertad, which runs southwest–northeast along Plaza Libertad.

Sights

As Argentina's oldest city, Santiago has retained a handful of colonial construction and a representative sample of museums, along with some more-contemporary landmarks. Most but not all are northwest of Plaza Libertad.

Fronting on Plaza Libertad, the neoclassical **Iglesia Catedral** (1868–1877) is the fifth of a series of successors to the country's first cathedral, which dated from 1578. Striking bas-reliefs decorate the triangular facade above its Corinthian columns, flanked by twin bell towers.

Santiago's best museum is the **Museo Wagner de Ciencias Antropológicas y Naturales** (Avellaneda 355, tel. 0385/421-1380, 7 A.M.–1 P.M. and 2–8 P.M. Mon.–Fri., 7 A.M.–1 P.M. Sat., free). Specializing in natural history, archaeology, and ethnography of the Chaco, it's one of the country's most orderly museums, with informative guided tours (Spanish only).

Two blocks southeast, the **Museo Histórico Provincial Dr. Oreste di Lullo** (Urquiza 354, tel. 0385/421-2893, 7 A.M.–8 P.M. Tues.–Fri., 10 A.M.–6 P.M. Sat.–Sun., free) occupies a colonial architectural landmark but stresses postcolonial history as viewed through sacred and secular art, the province's first families, and numismatics. It is due to move to the new **Complejo Cultural Santiago del Estero,** presently under construction facing Plaza Libertad.

Just beyond the Museo Wagner, the **Palacio Legislativo** is home to the provincial legislature and also the performing arts **Teatro 25 de Mayo.** Two blocks beyond the Museo Wagner, Spanish missionary San Francisco Solano occupied a 16th-century cell in the **Convento de San Francisco** (Avellaneda between Avenida Roca and Olaechea), an 18th-century reconstruction; its namesake neo-Gothic church dates from 1895. Both are national historical monuments; their **Museo de Arte Sacro** (Museum of Sacred Art, tel. 0385/421-1548, free) is open 9 A.M.–noon and 6–9 P.M. daily.

Beyond Olaechea, offering relief from Santiago's torrid summers, densely wooded **Parque Aguirre** features a small zoo, a swimming pool (the water supply is unpredictable), a municipal campground, and other simple attractions.

Entertainment and Events

In the same building as the provincial legislature, **Teatro 25 de Mayo** (Avellaneda and 25 de Mayo, tel. 0385/21-4141) is the main performing arts facility.

Santiago celebrates a raucous **Carnaval** in February. Late July's weeklong **Fundación de Santiago** commemorates the city's founding.

Accommodations

Near the former bus terminal, the five-room **Residencial Emaus** (Moreno Sur 673, tel. 0385/421-5893, US$15 s, US$24 d) is a tidy and friendly shoestring choice.

The large rooms—some very large—at **Nuevo Hotel Santiago** (Buenos Aires 60, tel. 0385/421-4949, nuevosantiago@radar.com.ar, US$38 s, US$45 d) are excellent values; luxuries are few, but it has a snack bar and room service.

Sweeping marble staircases climb to well-kept rooms at the 80-year-old **Hotel Savoy**

(Tucumán 39, tel. 0385/421-1234, www.savoysantiago.com.ar, US$40 s, US$55 d), which has hung onto some of its historical charm while undergoing renovation.

Business-oriented **Hotel Centro** (9 de Julio 131, tel./fax 0385/421-9502, ly@ocanet.com. ar, US$49 s, US$62 d) is modern and well-maintained, though the single beds are soft and narrow; the double beds are firmer.

In a quiet neighborhood opposite a triangular plaza, the inconspicuous **Libertador Hotel** (Catamarca 47, tel./fax 0385/421-9252, www. hotellibertadorsrl.com.ar, US$49 s, US$65 d, with a buffet breakfast) offers cash discounts. The staff is friendly, and the rooms are spacious; there's a pool and ample parking among the extensive gardens.

The newest entry here is the 30-room **Hotel Ciudad** (Avenida Moreno and Sáenz Peña, tel. 0385/421-6395, www.hotelciudad.com.ar, US$55 s, US$74 d). The multistory 【 **Hotel Carlos V** (Independencia 110, tel. 0385/424-0303, www.carlosvhotel.com.ar, US$66 s, US$90 d), a legitimate four-star facility, serves a sumptuous buffet breakfast; amenities include a pool, a sauna, a gym, and Internet connections in every room.

Food

Santiago's dining scene is only adequate. For fresh produce and the cheapest *comedores,* try the **Mercado Armonía,** fronting on Pellegrini between the Tucumán and Rojas pedestrian malls.

One of the standbys is the Italo-Argentine **Mía Mamma** (24 de Setiembre 15, tel. 0385/421-9715), which serves a wide assortment of pastas, *parrillada,* and salads. The **Jockey Club** (Independencia 68, tel. 0385/421-4722) is a standard Argentine eatery in what has been an elite Argentine institution.

Parque Aguirre's **La Casa del Folclorista** (Pozo de Vargas s/n) is a *parrilla* that also offers folkloric entertainment, as its name suggests.

Information

Facing Plaza Libertad, the **Subsecretaría de Turismo de la Provincia** (Avenida Libertad 417, tel. 0385/421-4243, www.turismosantiago. gov.ar) is open 7 A.M.–1 P.M. and 3–9 P.M. weekdays, 10 A.M.–1 P.M. and 3–6 P.M. weekends.

For motorists, **ACA** is at Avenida Sáenz Peña and Avenida Belgrano Norte, tel. 0385/421-8899.

Services

Citibank (Avellaneda 41) has an ATM.

Correo Argentino is at Buenos Aires 250; the postal code is 4200.

Telefónica (24 de Septiembre 220) has long-distance services.

Laverap (Independencia 265) does the washing.

Getting There and Around

Aerolíneas Argentinas (24 de Septiembre 547, tel. 0385/422-4335) flies daily except Friday and Sunday to Buenos Aires's Aeroparque via Tucumán. City bus No. 19 goes to **Aeropuerto Vicecomodoro Ángel Aragonés** (Avenida Madre de Ciudades s/n, tel. 0385/422-2386), six kilometers northwest of downtown via Avenida Belgrano Norte.

About eight blocks northwest of Plaza Libertad, the new **Terminal de Ómnibus Santiago del Estero** (Perú and Chacabuco, tel. 0385/422-7091, www.tosde.com.ar) is a huge improvement on the decrepit facility it replaced.

Sample destinations, times, and fares include Termas de Río Hondo (1 hour, US$3), Catamarca (3 hours, US$8), Tucumán (2 hours, US$6), Córdoba (5.5 hours, US$20–23), Puerto Iguazú (12 hours, US$40), and Buenos Aires (13 hours, US$40–52).

TERMAS DE RÍO HONDO

Roughly midway between the provincial capitals of San Miguel de Tucumán and Santiago del Estero via RN 9, Termas de Río Hondo draws crowds to its thermal springs in the cooler winter months. Otherwise, it mainly belongs to its 37,000-plus permanent inhabitants, and most of its 150-plus hotels and other services shut down. The whole year, though, it's a cheerful place that welcomes travelers of any sort.

In addition to its thermal waters, Río Hondo's main attraction is the **Dique Frontal,** a sprawling reservoir used for water sports such as swimming, boating, *dorado* fishing, and windsurfing. Most services are on or near Avenida Alberdi (RN 9), the main thoroughfare.

Accommodations

Many visitors prefer campgrounds, such as the secluded and wooded **Camping del ACA** (tel. 03858/42-1648), on the road to the Dique Frontal.

While many hotels close in summer, prices for those remaining open can be real bargains; even modest places have huge sunken tubs for hot mineral baths, and many have pools. The prices that follow are from summer.

Shoestring travelers can try the simple **Hotel Mon Petit** (Alberdi 602, tel. 03858/42-1822, US$13–15 pp). **Hotel Provincial** (Sarmiento 127, tel. 03858/42-3037, US$32 d) is plain but extraordinarily hospitable, with state-of-the-art air-conditioning and cable TV.

A step up is three-star **Hotel Termal Los Felipe** (San Francisco Solano 230, tel. 03858/42-1484, US$40 d). Though its facade is unimpressive, the **Casino Center Hotel** (Caseros 126, tel. 03858/42-1346, www.hotelcasinocenter.com.ar, US$27 pp) has a renovated and upgraded interior; it's directly across from, but not part of, the garish casino.

Food

La Casa de Rubén (Sarmiento 35, tel. 03858/42-1147) is a traditionally outstanding *parrilla* that sometimes closes when business is slow. **San Cayetano** (Caseros 204, tel.

03858/42-1878) grills a tasty *chivito* (grilled goat) and has first-rate service.

Game fish, particularly the feisty *dorado,* are the forte at **La Cabaña de Lucía** (Avenida Alberdi and Libertad). **Massimo** (Rivadavia 146) has the best ice cream.

Information and Services

Hours at the **Secretaría Municipal de Turismo** (Caseros 132, tel. 03858/42-2143, www.lastermasderiohondo.com) are 7 A.M.–11 P.M. daily in the winter peak, 7 A.M.–1 P.M. and 4–10 P.M. daily the rest of the year. Its website is useful for the entire province.

Banco de la Nación (Caseros 56) has an ATM.

Correo Argentino is on Avenida Alberdi 766; the postal code is 4220. There are abundant *locutorios* and Internet outlets.

Laverap (Hipólito Yrigoyen and Avenida San Martín) does the washing.

The **Hospital Zonal** (Antonino Taboada s/n, tel. 03858/42-1578) provides medical services.

Getting There and Around

Termas de Río Hondo has no commercial airport, but Tucumán is barely an hour away (Santiago del Estero is even closer, but has few flights).

Buses to and from Buenos Aires (15 hours, US$43–55) stop at Río Hondo's Terminal de Ómnibus (Las Heras between España and 12 de Octubre, tel. 03858/42-1768), six blocks west of the triangular Plaza San Martín and two blocks north of Avenida Alberdi. Long-distance services resemble those to and from Santiago del Estero and Tucumán.

NORTHERN PATAGONIA

On a bridge over the Río Colorado in southern Buenos Aires Province, midway between Bahía Blanca and the Río Negro, a roadside sign reading "Patagonia Starts Here" marks the boundary of southernmost South America's vast, legendary region. No other part of the continent—not even Amazonia—so stimulates the imagination. Ever since Magellan's chronicler Antonio Pigafetta concocted encounters with a giant "so tall that the tallest among us reached only to his waist," the remote southern latitudes have projected a mystique that has been a mixture of anticipation and apprehension.

Geographically, Patagonia is more diverse, with its long Atlantic coastline, boundless steppes, and Andean lakes, forests, and peaks, than simple statistics would suggest. Many of the country's finest wildlife sites and national parks draw visitors from around the globe, but several towns and cities are also worth a visit. Though they vary in quality, increasing numbers of *estancias* (ranches) have become enticing getaways.

In Argentina, Patagonia comprises the area south of the Río Colorado, primarily the provinces of Neuquén, Río Negro, Chubut, and Santa Cruz. While the four provinces' roughly 1.9 million residents are less than five percent of the country's 40.5 million, they cover more than 27 percent of Argentine territory, an area roughly equivalent to Texas or the United Kingdom.

Between them, Neuquén and Río Negro Provinces, the overland gateways to Patagonia, contain most of the Argentine lakes district,

HIGHLIGHTS

◖ **Volcán Lanín:** In the northernmost sector of Argentina's fabled lakes district, this snowcapped centerpiece of Parque Nacional Lanín is perhaps the region's most recognizable summit (page 371).

CHILE

Volcán Lanín

Parque Nacional Los Arrayanes

Lago Nahuel Huapi

Centro Cívico

Feria Artesanal

Cerro Piltriquitrón

Circuito Lacustre

PACIFIC OCEAN

0   200 mi

0   200 km

LOOK FOR ◖ TO FIND RECOMMENDED SIGHTS, ACTIVITIES, DINING, AND LODGING.

◖ **Parque Nacional Los Arrayanes:** *Arrayán* forests are the highlight of this park on the shore of Lago Nahuel Huapi. The town of Villa la Angostura provides easy access (page 374).

◖ **Centro Cívico:** The buildings surrounding the central square of San Carlos de Bariloche represent the best of Argentine Patagonia's architecture, setting a standard for the entire lakes district with their steep roofs and arched *recovas* (page 380).

◖ **Lago Nahuel Huapi:** From the alluring shoreline of this glacial finger lake, the terrain of Parque Nacional Nahuel Huapi, one of Argentina's most-visited national parks, rises to the forests, pinnacles, and ice fields of the Andes (page 390).

◖ **Feria Artesanal:** This three-times-a-week market surrounding El Bolsón's Plaza Pagano is the perfect place to find local crafts and sample regional food and drink (page 394).

◖ **Cerro Piltriquitrón:** This 2,284-meter granite summit rises east of Bolsón, where a clear day reveals snow-covered peaks along the Chilean border. There's a parking area at 1,200 meters with a forest of chainsaw stump sculptures nearby (page 399).

◖ **Circuito Lacustre:** The most popular excursion in Parque Nacional Los Alerces is this lake circuit, by boat and by foot, starting at Puerto Limonao, on Lago Futalaufquen's south end, and ending at Puerto Sagrario (page 409).

NORTHERN PATAGONIA

the traditionally popular vacation area on the eastern Andean slopes. Along the Chilean border, its alpine peaks and glaciers, indigo finger lakes, and dense forests have long been a prime destination; if Patagonia were a country, its logical capital might be the Río Negro resort of San Carlos de Bariloche.

Together, though, the two provinces extend from the Andes to the Atlantic, and the coastal zone features the colonial city of Carmen de Patagones and the Río Negro

provincial capital of Viedma, plus a scattering of wildlife reserves and beach resorts. An energy storehouse for its petroleum reserves and hydroelectric resources, the intervening steppe is the site of some of the world's most momentous dinosaur discoveries.

In addition to Río Negro and Neuquén, this chapter includes parts of Chubut Province, most notably the city of Esquel and vicinity, including Parque Nacional Los Alerces, which are most frequently visited from southern Río

NORTHERN PATAGONIA

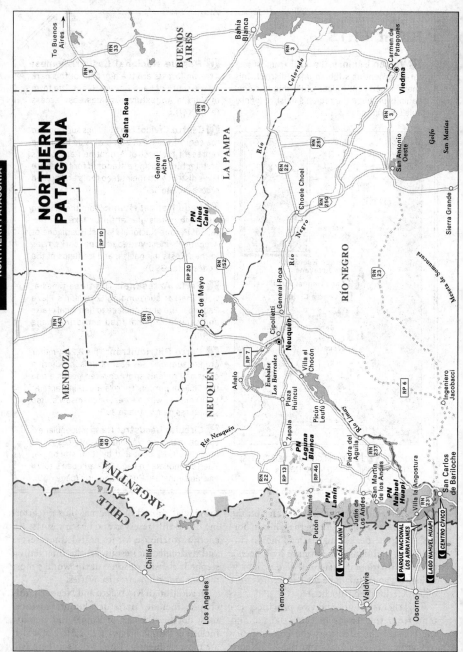

NORTHERN PATAGONIA

To Buenos Aires

BUENOS AIRES

Bahía Blanca

Carmen de Patagones
Viedma

Golfo San Matías

Santa Rosa

LA PAMPA

San Antonio Oeste

Sierra Grande

General Acha

PN Lihué Calel

RÍO NEGRO

Choele Choel

General Roca
Cipolletti
Neuquén

Río Negro

25 de Mayo

Meseta de Somuncurá

MENDOZA

NEUQUÉN

Anelo
Embalse Los Barreales
Villa el Chocón
Plaza Huincul
Picún Leufú

Ingeniero Jacobacci

CHILE
ARGENTINA

Río Neuquén

Zapala
PN Laguna Blanca

Piedra del Aguila

Río Limay

Chillán

Aluminé
PN Lanín
Pucón

Junín de Los Andes
San Martín de Los Andes
PN Nahuel Huapi
Villa la Angostura

San Carlos de Bariloche

Los Angeles

Temuco

Valdivia

Osorno

◀ **VOLCÁN LANÍN**

◀ **PARQUE NACIONAL LOS ARRAYANES**

◀ **LAGO NAHUEL HUAPI**

◀ **CENTRO CÍVICO**

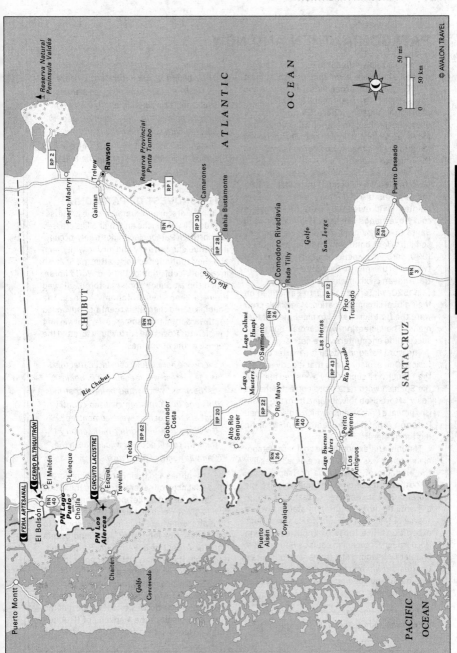

PATAGONIA, THEN AND NOW

For such a thinly populated territory, Patagonia has a complex, even epic history. At least 11,000 years ago, probably several thousand years earlier, the first inhabitants arrived as aboriginal hunter-gatherers who subsisted on guanaco, rhea, and other wild game. They may even have contributed to the extinction of megafauna like the *Mylodon* ground sloth and the American horse.

In cave sites ranging from present-day Neuquén to Tierra del Fuego, they left clues as to the peopling of Patagonia. Their successors painted vivid evidence of their life ways in rocky overhangs like Cueva de las Manos in Santa Cruz Province. These were essentially self-sufficient bands; much later, around A.D. 1000, ceramic evidence suggests contact between northernmost Patagonia and the central Andean civilizations.

In 1520, wintering at Puerto San Julián on their global circumnavigation, Magellan's crew were the first Europeans to meet the Patagonians. Their meeting was cordial, but many succeeding encounters were not.

The word *Patagonia* itself is a matter of confusion. One explanation is that it derived from the Tehuelches' supposedly oversized feet, but the Spanish word *pata* more correctly means "paw." More probably, it came from the Spanish romance *Primaleón*, in which a giant named Patagón inhabits an island of fur-wearing hunter-gatherers.

Though little-explored, the northern Patagonian interior was also a source of tall tales like the kingdom of Trapalanda or Trapananda, a southern city of gold (real marvels like the Moreno Glacier remained unseen by Europeans until the 19th century). If Patagonia was a source of tall tales, though, it also saw serious expeditions, like those of Englishman John Narborough, Frenchman Louis de Bougainville, Spaniard Alejandro Malaspina, and of course, Charles Darwin on the *Beagle*. It was Darwin who debunked the lingering legends of "Patagonian giants":

We had an interview at Cape Gregory with the famous so-called gigantic Patagonians, who gave us cordial reception. Their height appears greater than it really is, from their large guanaco mantles, their long flowing hair, and general figure; on an average their height is about six feet, with some men taller and only a few shorter; and the women are also tall; altogether they are certainly the tallest race which we anywhere saw.

THE CONQUEST OF PATAGONIA

In immediate pre-Columbian times, the semisedentary Mapuche and their allies crossed the northern Patagonian Andes freely, occupying Tehuelche territory and mixing with them, and they continued to do so after the Spanish invasion. Acquisition of the Old World horse, which the Mapuche soon mastered, allowed them to keep their autonomy even as the Spaniards and then the Argentines advanced southward from the pampas. After Darwin met the dictator Rosas, he sorrowfully foretold the demise of the aborigines:

Every one here is fully convinced that this is the justest war, because it is against barbarians. Who would believe that in this age in a Christian civilised country that such atrocities were committed?... Great as it is, in another half century I think there will not be a wild Indian in the Pampas north of Río Negro.

The Argentines and their European immigrant allies advanced on several fronts. In the 1860s foreign minister Guillermo Rawson struck a deal to grant Welsh dissidents farms in coastal Chubut, from where they moved westward to the Andes. Not long after, with land grants from the Argentine government, Scottish settlers from the Falkland Islands began to conquer Santa Cruz with sheep.

In 1879 – proving Darwin's prescience – General Julio Argentino Roca began his so-called Conquista del Desierto (Conquest of the Desert) to displace the Mapuche of Neuquén and Río Negro in favor of settlers' cattle and sheep. The railway's arrival from the coast opened the fertile Río Negro Valley to agricultural development.

PATAGONIA TODAY

Today, thanks to fishing, industrial preferences, and tourism, Patagonia (including Tierra del Fuego) is Argentina's fastest-growing region, with the most positive demographic indicators. Since 1980, all the Patagonian provinces had experienced rapid population growth – in the case of Tierra del Fuego, almost exponential growth.

Patagonia now has the highest employment rates outside of Buenos Aires, the highest mean monthly income, the lowest poverty rates, the lowest mortality rate, the lowest rate of death by heart disease and infection, and the lowest infant mortality. It has the highest percentage rate of access to potable water and sewer service, and the highest literacy rates.

Ironically, the Argentine economic implosion of 2001-2002 revived the wool industry, as the new exchange rate made Argentine wool more competitive internationally. At the former one-to-one rate with the U.S. dollar, production costs were impossibly high, but costs have begun to rise again.

Many beneficiaries of the new boom have been foreign companies who bought the best properties at bargain prices. In Santa Cruz, sheep still outnumber humans 10 to one, and Patagonia's largest wool producer, the Italian conglomerate Benetton, owns flagship ranches like Estancia El Cóndor near Río Gallegos.

Devaluation also made tourism competitive. For much of the 1990s, Argentines took their vacations in Chile or other "inexpensive" countries like the United States, but the exchange rate trend then reversed, and Chileans and other foreigners flocked to Patagonia. Recently exchange rate adjustments have slowed this growth, and prices have risen, but Patagonia remains a brand with global notoriety.

Negro. Coastal sections of Chubut, and all of Santa Cruz Province, appear in the *Southern Patagonia* chapter.

PLANNING YOUR TIME

Patagonia's highlights could consume a lifetime, so even repeat visitors usually have to make decisions on what to see and do. Because distances are so great, it's often necessary to fly, especially if visiting widely separated areas like the northerly lakes of Neuquén and Río Negro, and southern Patagonia's coastal wildlife areas and massive Andean glaciers.

Unlike the coast, where sights and settlements are often far apart, the Andean lake district of Neuquén, Río Negro, and northwestern Chubut is a more compact area with dense infrastructure and easy accessibility. A week here can be rewarding for special-interest visitors like fly-fishing aficionados, but general-interest travelers would easily enjoy two weeks or more, and dedicated sports-oriented travelers like climbers could spend a month or an entire summer.

San Carlos de Bariloche makes an ideal hub for excursions in and around the lakes, but towns like San Martín de los Andes, Villa la Angostura, El Bolsón, and Esquel are also good choices—not to mention rural lodges and *estancias*.

In Patagonia's southerly latitudes, January and February are the main vacation months, but they are also the most expensive. The shoulder months of November–December and March–April have less crowding, lower prices, and almost equally good (sometimes better) weather. By April, days are getting shorter, but the region becomes a winter destination thanks to skiing in Bariloche, San Martín de los Andes, and a few less developed areas.

Note that throughout Patagonia, overland transportation schedules change from season to season and year to year and may be disrupted by weather.

Coastal Río Negro Province

CARMEN DE PATAGONES

On the Río Negro's north bank, founded in 1779, Carmen de Patagones was once Spain's farthest outpost in what is now Argentina, and it's the only Patagonian city with a genuine colonial feel. "Patagones" is also Buenos Aires Province's most southerly city, but the south bank Río Negro capital of Viedma has a greater variety of hotels, restaurants, and other services.

Befitting its dual heritage, the city's name is a hybrid of the indigenous (Patagones, after the aborigines) and the European (after its patron, the Virgen del Carmen). The original colonists came from Maragatería, in the province of León; in 1827, in a conflict over the buffer state of Uruguay, their descendents fended off Brazilian invaders. Locals still use the nickname *maragatos.*

Carmen de Patagones (pop. 18,095) is 279 kilometers south of Bahía Blanca and 915 kilometers south of Buenos Aires via coastal RN 3, which continues west and then south to Chubut, Santa Cruz, and Tierra del Fuego. Two bridges connect it to Viedma, but most locals shuttle across the river on motor launches.

Sights

Patagones's most conspicuous landmark, the twin towers of the Salesian-built **Iglesia Parroquial Nuestra Señora del Carmen** (1883) rise above the **Plaza 7 de Marzo,** which commemorates the victory over Brazil in 1827. Immediately west, the **Torre del Fuerte** (1780) is the sole remnant of Patagones's frontier fortifications.

Immediately south of the tower, between a set of antique cannons, the broad staircase of **Pasaje San José de Mayo** descends to the adobe **Rancho de Rial** (1820), home of Carmen's first elected mayor. One block east, dating from 1823, the restored **Casa de la Cultura** (Mitre 27) was once a flour mill. Across the street, fitted with period furniture, the 19th-century **Casona La Carlota** (Bynon and Mitre) offers guided tours; contact the Museo Histórico for details.

To the south, the waterfront **Mazzini & Giraudini** was a thriving merchant house in the early 20th century. Naval hero and Patagonian explorer Luis Piedra Buena once lived in adjacent **Parque Piedra Buena;** a block west, the **Casa Histórica del Banco de la Provincia** (J. J. Biedma 64), the former provincial bank, now houses the regional history museum.

Immediately opposite the dock for launches to and from Viedma, the **Museo Histórico Regional Emma Nozzi** (J. J. Biedma 64, tel. 02920/46-2729, 10:30–11:30 A.M. and 7–8:30 P.M. Mon.–Sat., free) evinces a stereotypically ethnocentric attitude—the clear if unspoken notion that General Roca's 19th-century "Conquest of the Desert" was a greater good that justified a genocidal war against Patagonia's native peoples—that undercuts the quality of its pre-Columbian artifacts. In context, its most interesting exhibit is the **Cueva Maragata,** one of several excavations that sheltered the first Spanish colonists.

The building itself has served several roles, including a naval-stores depot, a girls school, bank branches, and retail. Banco de la Provincia restored the structure, which suffered serious flood damage in 1899, as a museum; a series of historical photographs displays the flood's devastation, which caused the evacuation of lower-lying Viedma.

Entertainment and Events

The **Cine Garibaldi** (España 206) shows recent films.

The weeklong **Fiesta del 7 de Marzo** in early March commemorates the victory over Brazilian forces. Most festivities take place on Plaza Villarino, four blocks north of Plaza 7 de Marzo.

Accommodations and Food

Carmen has decent shoestring accommodations, with private baths, at **Residencial Reggiani** (Bynon 422, tel. 02920/46-1065, residencialreggiani@hotmail.com, US$37 d), which has recently added a restaurant; there's a 5 percent discount for cash. The tidy, Francophile-style **Hotel Percaz** (Comodoro Rivadavia 384, tel. 02920/46-4104, www.hotelpercaz.com.ar, US$32 s, US$45 d) offers 10 percent discounts for cash payments.

Confitería Sabbatella (Rivadavia 218) is fine for breakfast, coffee, or sandwiches. **Pizzería Neptuno** (Comodoro Rivadavia 310) sells its namesake.

Information and Services

Well-stocked with maps and brochures, including suggested walking tours, the helpful **Dirección Municipal de Turismo** (Bynon 186, tel. 02920/46-1777, ext. 253, www.patagones.gov.ar, turismopatagones@speedy.com.ar) is open 7 A.M.–1 P.M. and 3–9 P.M. weekdays, 10 A.M.–1 P.M. and 5–8 P.M. weekends in summer; in other seasons, hours are 7 A.M.–7 P.M. weekdays.

Banco de la Nación (Paraguay 2) has an ATM on Plaza 7 de Marzo. **Correo Argentino** (Paraguay 38) is immediately east; the postal code is 8504. **Locutorio Patagones** (Olivera 9) is on the south side of Plaza 7 de Mayo.

Getting There and Around

Services to and from Patagones's **Terminal de Ómnibus** (Barbieri and Méjico, tel. 02920/46-2666), two blocks north and three blocks east of Plaza 7 de Marzo, are less frequent than Viedma's; many long-distance buses stop at both, however.

From Estación Carmen de Patagones (Bulevar Juan de la Piedra and Italia), **Ferrobaires** (tel. 02920/46-1048, www.ferrobaires.gba.gov.ar) runs a Sunday train (11:40 A.M.) to Buenos Aires (23 hours, US$18–21). Nearby Viedma has an airport.

Lanchas (passenger launches) cross the river to Viedma every few minutes during daylight hours.

VIEDMA

While it lacks Patagones's colonial character, Viedma long ago surpassed its neighbor in services and significance—it is even Río Negro's capital despite its distance from other cities in this Atlantic-to-the-Andes province. Locals swim and kayak along the willow-shaded riverfront with its *parrilla* restaurants and sailing school.

Founded simultaneously with Patagones in 1779, Viedma became Patagonia's de facto capital exactly a century later and then, following the "Conquest of the Desert," capital of Río Negro territory. In 1955, it became capital of the new Río Negro Province. In the 1980s, President Raúl Alfonsín tried to move the federal capital here from Buenos Aires—a foolishly visionary boondoggle that, fortunately, never came to be.

Viedma (pop. 46,767) is 280 kilometers south of Bahía Blanca and 439 kilometers north of Puerto Madryn via coastal RN 3. It's 982 kilometers east of Bariloche, Río Negro's largest city, via the Río Negro Valley and Neuquén.

Sights

On **Plaza Alsina's** southwest side, the entire block bounded by Yrigoyen, Colón, Rivadavia, and Alvaro Barros is a national historical monument dating from the 1880s, when the Salesian order installed itself here. Among its works were the **Vicariato Apostólico de la Patagonia Septentrional** (Vicarage of Southern Patagonia, 1883–1897), with its neo-Renaissance brick facade and tower.

For many years, the structure served as the **Colegio San Francisco de Sales** (a boys' school) and an orphanage. Since 1975, it has been the **Centro Histórico Cultural Salesiano,** comprising two separate museums: the **Museo Salesiano Cardenal Cagliero** (Rivadavia 34, tel. 02920/15-30-8671, 9 A.M.–1 P.M. and 7–9 P.M. Tues.–Thurs., free), presenting the Salesian viewpoint on Patagonian evangelization, and the **Museo Tecnológico del Agua y del Suelo** (Colón 498, 1st floor, tel. 02920/42-6096, www.museo-dpa.blogspot.com, 8:30 A.M.–6 P.M. Mon.–Tues. and Fri., 10 A.M.–noon and 2–6 P.M. Wed.–Thurs., free), focusing on irrigation.

Part of the same complex but facing Plaza Alsina, the **Catedral de la Merced** (1912) replaced an earlier church that came down after the 1899 flood; alongside it, the neoclassical **Obispado de Viedma** (Bishopric of Viedma, 1945) replaced the **Hospital de San José.**

Key public buildings cluster around Plaza San Martín, including the **Casa de Gobierno** (Government House) and the dignified **Residencia del Gobernador** (Governor's Residence). On the north side, the **Museo Gobernador Eugenio Tello** (San Martín 262, tel. 0290/42-5900, 8:30 A.M.–4:30 P.M. Mon.–Fri., 4–6 P.M. Sat. winter, 9:30 A.M.–1 P.M. and 5–7 P.M. Mon.–Fri., 5–7 P.M. Sat. the rest of the year, free) stresses archaeology and secular history.

At 5 P.M. Thursday–Sunday (Sunday only May–December) the catamaran *Curru Leuvu II* (tel. 02920/15-40-8599) offers 1.5-hour river excursions (US$8 adults, US$1.50 children age 12 and under) from the **Muelle de Lanchas** at the foot of 25 de Mayo.

Events

Viedma's biggest event is January's **Regata del Río Negro** (www.regatadelrionegro.com.ar). Its highlight is "the world's longest regatta," a 500-kilometer kayak race from Neuquén.

Shopping

Craftsworkers populate an informal **Mercado Artesanal** on Plaza Alsina. For wines, try the large selection at **La Bodega de Marzio** (San Martín 319, tel. 02920/42-2087).

Accommodations

Carmen de Patagones actually has more shoe-string options, but **Residencial Río Mar** (Rivadavia and Santa Rosa, tel. 02920/42-4188, US$23 s, US$33 d) is good enough.

Under new ownership, **Hotel El Vasco** (25 de Mayo 174, tel. 02920/43-0459, www.elvascohotel.com.ar, US$30 s, US$45 d) is no longer a spa hotel, but both the rooms (some of them small) and the common areas have been spruced up, and prices are reasonable.

Overlooking Plaza Alsina, no-frills **Hotel Peumayén** (Buenos Aires 334, tel. 02920/42-5222, www.hotelpeumayen.com.ar, US$32 s, US$47 d) is a decent choice with carpeted

rooms, air-conditioning, parking, and TV, with cash discounts.

Friendly **Hotel Nijar** (Mitre 490, tel. 02920/42-2833, www.hotelnijar.com, US$37 s, US$55 d) is a modern hotel with good service, parking, and other amenities, including Wi-Fi that reaches some upstairs rooms. Over the last few years it has suffered a bit of wear, but it's still a good value.

Overlooking the river, there's **Hotel Austral** (Avenida Villarino 292, tel. 02920/42-2615, www.hotelesaustral.com.ar, US$51–60 s, US$66–75 d), which has similar amenities but a better location than the Nijar.

Food

Camila's Café (Buenos Aires and Saavedra) is good for coffee and desserts.

Sahara Pizza & Pasta (Saavedra 326, tel. 02920/15-60-7790, lunch and dinner daily) is the most popular pizzeria, but **Los Tíos** (Belgrano 387, tel. 02920/42-2790, lunch and dinner daily) runs a close second. For *parrillada,* try **El Tío** (Avenida Zatti and Colón, tel. 02920/42-0757, lunch and dinner daily) or the waterside **De Carne Somos** (Avenida Villarino 207, tel. 02920/43-0086, lunch and dinner daily).

Ideal for lunch beneath the riverside willows, **Sal y Fuego** (Avenida Villarino 55, tel. 02920/43-1259, lunch and dinner daily) specializes in fish and seafood.

The ambitious ◖ **Capriasca** (Alvaro Barros 685, tel. 02920/42-6754, lunch and dinner daily) has diverse entrées (US$6–10) including pastas, Patagonian lamb, beef, and seafood; the bittersweet chocolate mousse is a good dessert choice. The kitchen is prompt, and the rehabbed period house, its walls partly opened to reveal its structure and the rest painted in pastels, is a plus.

Fiore Helados (Buenos Aires and Aguiar, tel. 02920/42-1600) serves fine ice cream.

Information

The riverfront **Oficina de Informes Turísticos** (Villarino 51, tel. 02920/42-7171, www.viedma.gov.ar) is open 8 A.M.–8 P.M. weekdays, 11 A.M.–7 P.M. weekends.

The **Ministerio de Turismo** (Avenida Caseros 1425, tel. 02920/42-2150) provides information and printed matter for the entire province.

For motorists, **ACA** (tel. 02920/42-2441) is at RN 3 Km 692.

Services

Banco Patagonia (Buenos Aires 184) has one of many ATMs. **Tritón Turismo** (Namuncurá 78, tel. 02920/43-1131, tritonturismo@hotmail.com) changes money, rents cars, and arranges excursions.

Correo Argentino is at 25 de Mayo 457; the postal code is 8500. **Locutorio Zattitel** (Zatti and Ameghino, tel. 011/43-1540) has both long-distance phone and Internet access.

Lavandería Automática Siglo XXI (Mitre 343, tel. 02920/15-62-3946) does the laundry.

Hospital Artémides Zatti (Avenida Rivadavia 351, tel. 02920/42-2333) is the public hospital.

Getting There

Aerolíneas Argentinas (Colón 246, tel. 02920/42-2018) flies two or three weekly nonstops to Buenos Aires's Aeroparque, and sometimes via Bahía Blanca. **LADE** (Saavedra 576, tel. 02920/42-4420) flies south to Puerto Madryn and Trelew and north to Bahía Blanca, Mar del Plata, and Aeroparque.

Sefepa (Cagliero s/n, tel. 02920/42-2130, www.trenpatagonico-sa.com.ar) connects Estación Viedma, on the southeast edge of town, with Bariloche by rail at 6 P.M. Friday. The 15-hour trip costs US$15 in hard-backed *económica*, US$32 in reclining Pullman, or US$60 in *camarote* sleepers; children ages 5–12 pay half.

Viedma's **Terminal Patagonia** (Guido 1580, tel. 02920/42-6850. www.terminalpatagonia.com.ar) is 13 blocks south of downtown. Sample destinations, times, and fares include Las Grutas (2.5 hours, US$4.50), Puerto Madryn (6 hours, US$19–24), Trelew (7 hours, US$22–26), Neuquén (8 hours, US$25), Comodoro Rivadavia (11 hours,

US$40–48), Buenos Aires (12 hours, US$41–57), Bariloche (14 hours, US$30), and Río Gallegos (20 hours, US$65).

Getting Around

Taxis or *remises* to **Aeropuerto Gobernador Castello** (tel. 02920/42-5311), five kilometers south of town on RP 51, cost only about US$3.

On-demand *lanchas* cross the river to Carmen de Patagones (7 A.M.–8 P.M. weekdays, US$0.40) from the Muelle de Lanchas at the foot of 25 de Mayo. **Tritón Turismo** (Namuncurá 78, tel. 02920/43-1131) has rental cars.

GOLFO SAN MATÍAS AND VICINITY

From Viedma, RN 3 turns west and slightly inland toward the port of San Antonio Oeste, paralleling the Golfo San Matías shoreline, but day-trippers and visitors with their own vehicles should consider a detour along coastal RP 1. Here, about 30 kilometers east of Viedma at the mouth of the Río Negro, **Balneario El Cóndor** draws beachgoers from the provincial capital; from Viedma's Plaza Alsina, Empresa Ceferino (Schieroni 383, tel. 02920/42-4542) has six buses daily (US$1.50).

RP 1 and some buses continue another 30 kilometers to **La Lobería,** where the **Reserva Faunística Provincial Punta Bermeja** protects some 4,000 southern sea lions; the scenic coastline is also a prime bird-watching area.

West of La Lobería, the pavement ends but RP 1's scenery improves to include massive dunes at **Bahía Creek** and another sea lion colony at **Reserva Provincial Caleta de los Loros,** where nesting parakeets burrow into the headlands from September to January. At Punta Mejillón, the highway swerves inland, where it's possible to return to RN 3 via unpaved RP 52, or else continue west toward San Antonio Este, where paved RN 251 also turns north to RN 3.

Some 187 kilometers west of Viedma but east of RN 3, summer and weekend visitors swarm the beaches of **Las Grutas** (permanent pop. 2,708), named for the wave-cut grottoes that have penetrated the sedimentary headlands. Because of a wide tidal range, the beachfront can recede to just tens of meters, suitable for only the most gregarious beachgoers. There are nearly 100 hotels, *hospedajes,* and campgrounds; for suggestions, visit the **Secretaría Municipal de Turismo** (Avenida Río Negro 715, tel. 02934/49-7470). Las Grutas has frequent bus links to San Antonio Oeste, 12 kilometers northeast.

About 125 kilometers south of San Antonio Oeste and 140 kilometers north of Puerto Madryn, RN 3 passes through **Sierra Grande** (pop. 6,768), an iron-mining town that's the northernmost point to purchase gasoline at Patagonian prices—at least a third cheaper than in Las Grutas or San Antonio Oeste. Southbound drivers should nurse their fuel to get here, while the northbound should top off the tank.

NEUQUÉN AND VICINITY

Capital of its namesake province, Neuquén is a gateway to the northern Patagonian lakes, but also an ideal base for visiting a triangle of nearby dinosaur sites and a cluster of new wineries. At the confluence of two major rivers, it's a clean modern city that benefits from abundant energy resources, its productive financial sector, and the upper Río Negro valley's agricultural plenty. It also has an active cultural life, best exemplified by its new fine arts museum.

Where the Río Neuquén and the Río Limay meet, Neuquén (pop. 201,729) is 537 kilometers east of Bahía Blanca via RN 22, 559 kilometers southwest of Santa Rosa via several paved highways, and 429 kilometers northeast of San Carlos de Bariloche via RN 237. RN 22 through the upper Río Negro Valley and west toward Zapala is a narrow highway with heavy truck traffic and dangerously impatient drivers.

Sights

Nearly all the sights are in the **Parque Central,** the recycled rail yard bounded by Avenida San Martín/Avenida Independencia, and the streets of Salta/Manuel Láinez,

Tucumán/Tierra del Fuego, and Sarmiento/Mitre on the south.

The most important is **Museo Nacional de Bellas Artes.** Just north of the old bus terminal, the **Sala de Arte Emilio Saraco** (Avenida Olascoaga s/n, tel. 0299/449-1200, ext. 4390, 10 A.M.–8 P.M. weekdays, 4–10 P.M. weekends and holidays, free) occupies the railroad station's former cargo terminal, with exhibits of contemporary art. Across the tracks, **Juntarte en el Andén** is an outdoor art space at the former passenger terminal.

Two blocks east, the **Museo de la Ciudad Paraje Confluencia** (Avenida Independencia and Córdoba, tel. 0299/15-555-3082, 10 A.M.–8 P.M. weekdays, 6–10 P.M. weekends and holidays, free) traces Neuquén's cultural evolution and history from early pre-Columbian times through the first European contact, the development of the Mapuche nation, and their resistance to General Roca's "Conquest of the Desert."

Museo Nacional de Bellas Artes

In luminous new quarters in the Parque Central, this is the first provincial branch of the national fine arts museum, with permanent collections of European and Argentine art complemented by rotating exhibits. Mobile walls-on-wheels separate its 2,000-square-meter interior into manageable spaces as needed, but the shabby gravel parking lot still needs new landscaping commensurate with the building's aspirations.

The Museo Nacional de Bellas Artes (Mitre and Santa Cruz, tel. 0299/443-6268, www.mnbaneuquen.com.ar, free) is open 8 A.M.–9 P.M. Monday–Saturday, 6–10 P.M. Sunday and holidays.

Entertainment and Events

La Casona (Alvear 59) is a bar with occasional live music. For current films, there's the **Cine Teatro Español** (Avenida Argentina 271, tel. 0299/442-2048).

January's **Regata del Río Negro** (www.regatadelrionegro.com.ar) is a 500-kilometer kayak marathon that starts here and ends a week later in Viedma.

Shopping

Near Avenida Independencia and Avenida Argentina lies the Parque Central's **Paseo de los Artesanos** (Vuelta de Obligado s/n, 10 A.M.–9 P.M. Fri.–Sun.), an artisans' market.

The province of Neuquén sponsors **Artesanías Neuquinas** (Almirante Brown 280, tel. 0299/442-3806, www.artesanias-neuquinas.com), with a diverse crafts selection at reasonable prices. **Cardón** (Ministro González 54, tel. 0299/448-0155) sells leather goods, *mates,* and silverwork. **Artesanías Mapuches** (Roca 151, tel. 0299/443-2155) focuses on indigenous silverwork.

El Lagar (Félix San Martín 106, tel. 0299/447-1239) stocks a sound selection of Patagonian wines.

Accommodations

Nearly all accommodations lie in the scruffy but not unsafe retail area between RN 22 and the bus terminal. Right on the highway, **Hotel Inglés** (Félix San Martín 534, tel. 0299/442-2252, US$18 s, US$28 d, without breakfast) is quiet, clean, and family-run.

Rooms at friendly, centrally located **Hostería Belgrano** (Rivadavia 283, tel. 0299/448-0612, www.hosteriabelgrano.com, US$26 s, US$33 d) are small—some claustrophobic—but also immaculate. Under the same management, modernized **Hotel Alcorta** (Ministro Alcorta 84, tel. 0299/442-2652, alcortahotel@infovia.com.ar, US$23 s, US$34 d) has most contemporary conveniences.

Hotel Ideal (Avenida Olascoaga 243, tel. 0299/442-2431, www.interpatagonia.com/hotelideal, US$39 s, US$53 d, with breakfast) has clean, comfortable rooms with modern amenities but lacks parking.

Under the same management as Hotel Royal, **Hotel Huemul** (Tierra del Fuego 335, tel. 0299/442-2344, www.royalhotel.com.ar, US$28 s, US$40 d) could use renovation—the shower fixtures are antediluvian and the metal door frames are starting to rust, but everything still works well. The beds are firm, it's quiet, and the good-humored staff is a big plus.

The local classic **Hotel Iberia** (Avenida Olascoaga 294, tel. 0299/442-2372, luislo@neunet.com.ar, US$52 s, US$76 d) has tidy, ample rooms with standard conveniences.

Tobacco-free **Hotel Royal** (Avenida Argentina 145, tel. 0299/442-2408, www.royalhotel.com.ar, US$60 s, US$78 d) has large rooms and baths, cable TV, and Wi-Fi in common areas; there's also a 10 percent cash discount.

Though showing some wear, **◖ Hotel El Prado** (Perito Moreno 484, tel. 0299/448-6000, www.hotel-elprado.com.ar, US$45–75 s, US$68–118 d) remains one of the city's better values. The large well-furnished rooms have private baths, air-conditioning, cable TV, telephones, key cards, and Wi-Fi). In addition, there's an abundant buffet breakfast and superb service.

Downtown's four-star **Hotel del Comahue** (Avenida Argentina 387, tel. 0299/442-2439, www.hoteldelcomahue.com, US$123 s, US$145 d) is the pick of the litter, sometimes offering 10 percent cash discounts.

Food

Neuquén is strong on pizza and pasta at places like the traditional **La Mamma** (9 de Julio 56, tel. 0299/442-5291, lunch and dinner daily), **El Sótano** (Brown 162, tel. 0299/443-1122, lunch and dinner daily), and **La Tartaruga** (Roca 193, tel. 0299/443-6880, lunch and dinner daily). **Franz y Peppone** (9 de Julio and Belgrano, tel. 0299/448-2299, lunch and dinner daily) blends the Teutonic and the Mediterranean.

Pasty (Félix San Martín 246, tel. 0299/443-5860, lunch and dinner daily) serves fine, fairly priced pasta and chicken dishes, with well-intentioned but inconsistent service; the sidewalk seating is a mixed blessing, as the highway runs almost alongside it.

◖ La Birra (Santa Fe 19, tel. 0299/443-4344, labirra_nqn@hotmail.com) is a popular, casual pub-restaurant with an Italo-Argentine menu that includes items such pizza, pasta, and the like in the US$8 range in a congenial atmosphere with outstanding service. Oddly for its name, it has a limited beer selection.

THE WINERIES OF PATAGONIA

When foreigners think of Patagonia, their first thoughts are usually of a remote region in the antipodes, where the winds blow and the snow falls. Few think of grapes and even fewer of wine grapes, but in reality, grapes grow as far south as Punta Arenas (Chile), Estancia Sara (in Argentine Tierra del Fuego), and even the Falkland Islands.

That's a little misleading, because in all of these destinations the vines grow indoors, as they do in the winter garden at Punta Arenas's Hotel José Nogueira, and produce table grapes. Nevertheless, wine grapes have grown, with commercial success, for more than a century in Argentine Patagonia – Bodega Humberto Canale, half an hour east of the city of Neuquén, celebrated its centennial in 2009.

In fact, the Patagonian wine industry is expanding rapidly with the new San Patricio del Chañar district, less than an hour northwest of Neuquén. Having made the *New York Times* list of "31 Places to Go in 2010," Chañar figures to grab even more attention in the coming years, thanks to wineries such as Bodega del Fin del Mundo, Bodega NQN, and Bodega Familiar Schroeder.

Neuquén Province is also a hotbed for field-based paleontology research and especially dinosaur discoveries, so some visitors might want to combine the two activities.

BODEGA HUMBERTO CANALE

In both Neuquén and Río Negro Provinces, the upper Río Negro Valley is becoming a trendy zone of boutique wineries, but the Canale winery is no newcomer. In anticipation of its centennial, the family-owned enterprise sold off outside interests to concentrate on its 150 hectares of vineyards and 350 more of orchards.

Canale is a sizable winery, producing more than 1 million bottles per annum of reds from cabernet sauvignon, pinot noir, merlot, malbec, and cabernet franc, and whites from sauvignon blanc, semillón, torrontés, and viognier grapes. In addition, it makes blends of some of its reds.

Open for free tours, which can be slow-paced when crowds are large, Canale has a small but well-presented wine museum that also serves

as a tasting room. It's remodeling older parts of the winery for larger events and groups to help promote its "Patagonian" wines.

About eight kilometers west of the city of General Roca and 29 kilometers east of Neuquén via RN 22, Bodega Humberto Canale (Chacra 186, General Roca, tel. 02941/43-0415, www.bodegahcanale.com) offers Spanish-only tours at 10:30 A.M. Thursday and Saturday. Public transportation is frequent to General Roca, but the winery itself is about three kilometers south of the highway junction (which is opposite a conspicuous cement factory).

BODEGA DEL FIN DEL MUNDO

Surrounded by irrigated fields in rocky to sandy soils, in an area that gets little rain, Fin del Mundo is a modern industrial-style winery whose vineyards depend on drip irrigation from the Río Neuquén; trellised vines help prevent wind erosion. Relying on stainless steel tanks for maceration and fermentation, and oaken casks for aging, it produces about 85 percent reds (mostly malbec, with some blends) and 15 percent whites (including a sparkling white and Late Harvest Semillón). The harvest starts in February and ends by mid-April.

Tours, which include a free tasting, take place 10 A.M.-4 P.M. Tuesday-Friday, 10 A.M.-5 P.M. Saturday and holidays. Bodega del Fin del Mundo (RP 8 Km 9, San Patricio de Chañar, tel. 0299/15-580-0414, www.bodegadelfindelmundo.com) is a short distance north of RP 7, the main highway through the Chañar district. Wines are for sale onsite.

BODEGA NQN

Though its ecology resembles that of Fin del Mundo, NQN is a smaller bodega with about 135 hectares under cultivation, nearly half of those in malbec. Merlot comprises nearly a quarter, with the rest devoted to cabernet sauvignon, pinot noir, sauvignon blanc, and chardonnay. Built into a banked hillside, the winery itself is modern and handsome.

Visits to NQN begin with an overview through a model of the bodega, followed by a walk through the platform above the stain-

© WAYNE BERNHARDSON

Bodega del Fin del Mundo is one of the Chañar district's new wineries.

less steel tanks to the reception area for the grapes, followed by a descent into the cellars and a view of the oaken barrels. There, a tasting is free of charge.

Bodega NQN (RP 7, Picada 15, tel. 0299/489-7500, www.bodeganqn.com.ar) is open for hourly guided tours 10 A.M.–5 P.M. weekdays, 10:30 A.M.–4:30 P.M. weekends. Its **Malma Resto Bar** (tel. 0299/489-7600, reservas@bodeganqn.com.ar) is open for lunch daily with a fixed-price menu and an à la carte menu, but on weekends it's à la carte only. The food tends toward sophisticated versions of Patagonian standards, such as lamb, along with pork, pastas, and trout – accompanied, of course, by its own wines.

BODEGA FAMILIA SCHROEDER

The most easterly of Chañar's wineries, Schroeder is more of a boutique locale that boasts something no other winery can – an in situ fossil of the herbivorous *Aeololsaurus*

reonegrinus, a 12-meter, Upper Cretaceous dinosaur uncovered during construction excavations and incorporated into the cellars. That, in fact, led Schroeder to apply the name Saurus to one of its lines, which includes varietals such as cabernet sauvignon, chardonnay, malbec, merlot, pinot noir and sauvignon blanc.

The tour itself starts in vineyards and continues within, stopping first at the reception area (where an elevated walkway permits an aerial view of the facilities, even during harvest time, without getting in the way of operations). It continues to the cellars and the visitors center, where tasting takes place.

Tours of Famila Schroeder (RP 7, Picada 7, tel. 0299/489-9600, www.familiaschroeder.com, 9 A.M.–5 P.M. weekdays, 10:30 A.M.–5:30 P.M. weekends), cost US$4, which can be applied to purchases of wine. Its restaurant, **Saurus,** (tel. 0299/15-409-1754), comparable to NQN's, is open noon-4 P.M. daily.

NEUQUÉN'S DINOSAUR TRIANGLE

Where there's oil, there are dinosaurs, and Neuquén's sedimentary steppe is one of Argentina's late-Cretaceous hot spots. By rental car, a triangle of sites northwest, west, and southwest of the provincial capital makes an ideal (if long) full-day excursion, though one of these, Lago Barreales, is more difficult to reach and is best in fall and winter. The other two, Plaza Huincul and Villa El Chocón, are easily accessible by public transportation.

YACIMIENTO PALEONTOLÓGICO LAGO LOS BARREALES

The best place to see an on-site excavation is this reservoir northwest of Neuquén, where paleontologists demonstrate the separation and rescue of fossil deposits as well as the cleaning and extraction of the fossils themselves. Beasts in the sediments here include the sauropod *Futalognkosaurus* (a long-tailed quadruped with a long neck and small head), teropods (bipedal carnivores with huge claws such as *Megaraptor*), and ornithopods (small bipedal herbivores), along with bivalves, crocodiles, turtles, and pterosaurs.

Only when the water level falls in autumn, usually in early April, can the Museo de Geología y Paleontología de la Universidad Nacional del Comahue, under Jorge Calvo, resume its work, so this is the ideal time to go. There is now an interpretive trail with some fossils in situ, and an improvised museum in a Nissen hut.

On Barreales's north shore, the Yacimiento Paleontológico Lago Los Barreales (Avenida Megaraptor 1450, RP 1 Km 65, tel. 0299/15-404-8614, www.proyectodino.com.ar) is open 9 A.M.-7 P.M. daily. Guided tours cost US$6 pp for Argentines, US$12.50 pp for foreigners, and US$4 for children under 12. Foreign university students can hire on to participate in the digs (for a price).

Actually reaching the site can be complicated, but the simplest route is to take RP 7 from Cipolletti almost to Añelo, about 100 kilometers northwest of Neuquén, and then turn south on a gravel road to the north shore of Barreales. It's now well-signed but still re-

quires close attention, and there are plenty of heavy trucks kicking up dust.

MUSEO MUNICIPAL CARMEN FUNES (PLAZA HUINCUL)

At the oil town of Plaza Huincul, about midway between Neuquén and Zapala, the municipal museum's prize exhibit is a replica skeleton of *Argentinosaurus huinculensis,* the world's largest dinosaur at 35 meters long and 18 meters high. So large is the herbivore *A. huinculensis* that an adult male human barely reaches its knee, and one of its dorsal vertebrae measures 1.6 meters.

Former oil worker Guillermo Heredia found the fossil only three kilometers away, along the highway, in 1987. In addition to the imposing skeleton, there are models of the carnivorous *Mapusaurus* and several smaller dinosaurs, a clutch of dinosaur eggs some 80 million years old, and remains of crocodiles found in Picún Leufú, about 75 kilometers to the south.

In expanded quarters along the highway, the Museo Municipal Carmen Funes (Avenida Córdoba 55, tel. 0299/496-5486, museocarmenfunes@copelnet.com.ar, US$1) is open 9 A.M.-7 P.M. Monday-Friday, 9:30 A.M.-6:30 P.M. weekends and holidays.

Plaza Huincul, 110 kilometers west of Neuquén via RN 237 and RN 22, has an **Oficina de Informes** (RN 22 s/n, tel. 0299/496-7637) directly on the highway. Buses from Neuquén are frequent and comfortable.

MUSEO PALEONTOLÓGICO MUNICIPAL ERNESTO BACHMANN (VILLA EL CHOCÓN)

Plaza Huincul boasts the world's largest herbivore, but Villa El Chocón claims its carnivorous counterpart in *Giganotosaurus carolinii.* Above the Embalse Exequiel Ramos Mexía, an enormous hydroelectric reservoir southwest of Neuquén, the municipal museum also features models of *Carnotaurus* and the smaller *Pianitzkysaurus.* There are also dinosaur tracks in the vicinity.

G. carolinii takes its name from amateur paleontologist Rubén Carolini, who discovered the fossil; Rodolfo Coria, Leonardo Salgado, and Jorge Calvo first identified it. Measuring 14 meters in length and 4.65 meters high at the hip, it weighed up to eight tons.

Unfortunately, because the massive hydroelectric dam drowned the Río Limay's sedimentary canyon here, many probable paleontological sites have disappeared beneath the water. The Museo Paleontológico Municipal Ernesto Bachmann (8 A.M.–7 P.M. daily, US$1.25) also offers exhibits on the area's archaeology and a whitewashed history of the dam and former *estancia* owner Manuel Bustigorry.

Villa El Chocón, 136 kilometers southwest of Neuquén via RN 237, originated as a company town during the dam's construction. The **Dirección Municipal de Turismo** (tel. 0299/490-1223), at the northern approach to town off RN 22, is open 8 A.M.–7 P.M. daily; there's a paleontological excavation site within easy walking distance.

On the shoreline, **La Posada del Dinosaurio** (tel. 0299/490-1200, www.posadadinosaurio. com.ar, US$68 d) offers excellent accommodations, with a good, reasonably priced restaurant and outstanding service. Camping also exists nearby.

Cuore di Panna (Brown and Belgrano, tel. 0299/443-5000) surpasses Neuquén's other ice creameries.

Information

Directly on RN 22, the **Subsecretaría de Turismo** (Félix San Martín 182, tel. 0299/442-4089, www.neuquentur.gov.ar) is open 7 A.M.–11 P.M. daily. In content, accuracy, and usefulness, their maps and brochures are among the country's best.

For motorists, **ACA** is at Rivadavia and the diagonal 25 de Mayo (tel. 0299/442-4860).

Services

Banco de la Provincia de Neuquén (Avenida Argentina 13) has one of many ATMs. **Cambio Olano** (J. B. Justo 107, tel. 0299/442-6192) and **Cambio Pullman** (Ministro Alcorta 144, tel. 0299/442-2438) are exchange houses.

Correo Argentino is at Rivadavia and Santa Fe; the postal code is 8300.

Arlequín I (Avenida Olascoaga 222) has both telephone and Internet access.

Neighboring Chile has a **consulate** (tel. 0299/442-2727) at La Rioja 241. **Migraciones** (tel. 0299/442-2061) is at Santiago del Estero 466.

Zanellato Viajes (Avenida Independencia 366, tel. 0299/443-0105) is the Amex representative.

Lava Ya (Avenida Independencia 326, tel. 0299/443-4318) does the washing.

The **Hospital Regional** (Buenos Aires 421, tel. 0299/449-0800) can handle emergencies or routine care.

Getting There

Aerolíneas Argentinas (Santa Fe 52, tel. 0299/442-2409) averages three or four flights daily to Buenos Aires's Aeroparque. Travel agencies can handle ticketing for **American Jet** (tel. 0810/345-9876, www.americanjet. com.ar), which has recently begun air taxi service to San Martín de los Andes (five times weekly). **LADE** (Brown 163, tel. 0299/443-1153) has infrequent Patagonian flights.

About five kilometers west of downtown, Neuquén's shiny new **Terminal de Ómnibus** (Planas and Solalique, tel. 0299/445-2300) is a hub for provincial, national, and some international bus services (to the Chilean city of Temuco, reservations are advisable). Southbound arrivals can get to town quicker by disembarking at **Terminal Cipolletti** (Pacheco 390, tel. 0299/478-4757), just across the river in Río Negro Province.

Sample provincial and long-distance destinations, times, and fares include Zapala (2.5 hours, US$5), Bariloche (5 hours, US$16–20), San Martín de los Andes (6.5 hours, US$15–23), Villa La Angostura (6.5 hours, US$18–20),

Puerto Madryn (9.5 hours, US$26–32), El Bolsón (7.5 hours, US$21), Mendoza (11 hours, US$32–40), Esquel (10 hours, US$28–32), Buenos Aires (13 hours, US$45–59), Comodoro Rivadavia (14 hours, US$45–55), and Río Gallegos (25 hours, US$80).

Chile-bound buses normally leave around 7–9 A.M. or 11 P.M. for Temuco via Zapala and the Pino Hachado pass (9.5 hours, US$30–35). Carriers include **Narbus/Igi Llaima** (tel. 0299/442-3661), **El Valle** (tel. 0299/446-4412), **Centenario** (tel. 0299/445-2520), and **Grupo Plaza** (tel. 0800/333-1970). **Andesmar** (tel. 0299/445-2493) goes to Santiago, Chile, via Mendoza.

Getting Around
Aeropuerto Internacional J. D. Perón (tel. 0299/444-0244) is seven kilometers west of town via RN 22 (despite its name, there are no international services at present). A taxi or *remise* costs US$5, while the local Indalo bus No. 11 is a cheaper option. For the new bus terminal, take Indalo bus No. 9 or 10 from downtown.

Car rental agencies include **Alamo** (Perticone 735, tel. 0299/443-8714, neuquen@alamoargentina.com.ar); **Avis** (Lastra 1196, tel. 0299/444-1297, avisneuquen@arnet.com.ar); and **Dollar** (Carlos Rodríguez 518, tel. 0299/442-0875, dollarneuquen@speedy.com.ar).

ZAPALA
Argentine backpackers once used forlorn Zapala, the erstwhile end of the line for the Ferrocarril Roca's northern spur, as a takeoff point to the lakes district's least-visited parts. Since the railroad shut down, the town and the bleak surrounding steppe is mainly a convenient stopover en route to San Martín de los Andes, though it has good access to bird-rich Parque Nacional Laguna Blanca.

Zapala (pop. 31,265) is 189 kilometers west of Neuquén via RP 22, which continues northwest toward Las Lajas and the Chilean border at Pino Hachado, and 244 kilometers northeast of San Martín de los Andes via RN 40 and RN 234. The main drag is Avenida San Martín, which leads south from the traffic-circle intersection of RN 22 and RN 40.

Museo Olsacher
Zapala's modernized mineralogical museum fills a recycled warehouse with minerals from around the world and paleontological exhibits from Neuquén. Its prize exhibit is the remains of the herbivorous dinosaur *Zapalasaurus bonapartei*, but there are also displays on marine reptiles, paleobotany, systematic mineralogy, Argentine economic minerals, and invertebrate and vertebrate paleontology, along with a specialized library.

Alongside the bus terminal, the Museo Olsacher (Etcheluz and Ejército Argentino, tel. 02942/42-2713, free) is open 8 A.M.–2 P.M. and 6–9 P.M. Tues.–Fri., 5–9 P.M. weekends and holidays.

Shopping
Zapala's **Escuela de Cerámica** (Luis Monti 240, tel. 02942/42-4166) has a long tradition in artisanal pottery.

Accommodations and Food
While accommodations and dining are limited, the quality is good. The cheapest are **Residencial Coliqueo** (Etcheluz 165, tel. 02942/42-1308, US$20 s, US$35 d) and the immaculate **Pehuén Hotel** (Etcheluz and Elena de la Vega, tel. 02942/42-3135, US$23 s, US$40 d). **Hotel Hue Melén** (Almirante Brown 929, tel. 02942/42-2391, hotelhuemelen@hotmail.com, US$48 s, US$73 d) also has a restaurant.

For breakfast, coffee, and snacks, there's **El Chancho Rengo** (Avenida San Martín and Etcheluz, tel. 02942/42-2795). Directly on RN 22 near the rotary, **El Fogón** (Houssay and Bolivia, tel. 02942/15-66-4781) is a good *parrilla*. **Helados Don Héctor** (Etcheluz 527) is only so-so compared with ice creameries elsewhere, but it's not a desperation choice.

Information
Providing information on the province's northernmost lakes district, the **Centro de Informes Turísticos Portal del Pehuén** (RN 22 Km 1398, tel. 02942/42-4296, turismozapala@yahoo.com.ar) occupies new quarters near the ACA gas station on the eastern approach to town.

Summer hours are 7 A.M.–10 P.M. daily; the rest of the year, it's open 7 A.M.–9 P.M. daily. An office at the bus terminal is open 8 A.M.–8 P.M. daily.

The **Administración de Parques Nacionales (APN)** (Ejército Argentino 260, tel. 02942/43-1982, lagunablanca@zapala. com.ar) provides information on Parque Nacional Laguna Blanca.

Services

Banco de la Provincia del Neuquén (Cháneton 460) has an ATM.

Correo Argentino is at Avenida San Martín 324; the postal code is 8340. **Telefónica** (Etcheluz 527) has long-distance telephones and improved Internet.

For medical needs, try the **Hospital Regional** (Luis Monti 155, tel. 02924/43-1555).

Getting There and Around

A new terminal at the junction of RN 22 and RN 40 is due to replace downtown's **Terminal de Ómnibus** (Etcheluz and Uriburu, tel. 02924/42-3191), which has provincial and long-distance services; some Chile-bound carriers will pick up passengers here.

Sample destinations, times, and fares include Neuquén (2.5 hours, US$8), San Martín de los Andes (3.5 hours, US$10), Bariloche (5 hours, US$15), and Buenos Aires (18 hours, US$67). Most often, for Buenos Aires, it's easiest to transfer in Neuquén.

Several companies now pass Parque Nacional Laguna Blanca (1 hour, US$2.50) en route to Aluminé.

PARQUE NACIONAL LAGUNA BLANCA

In the stark volcanic steppe southwest of Zapala, alkaline Laguna Blanca is a shallow, plankton-rich interior drainage lake with breeding populations of the striking black-necked swan. Designated a major international wetland under the Ramsar convention, it's also the place to spot coots, ducks, grebes, gulls, upland geese, and the occasional flamingo. Even the flightless *choike* (rhea) scurries along the barren shoreline for a drink.

From a junction 10 kilometers south of Zapala via RN 40, paved RP 46 leads 20 kilometers southwest to the park, which comprises 11,250 hectares of undulating terrain 1,276 meters above sea level; the lake itself covers 1,700 hectares to a depth of 10 meters.

Sights

From the roadside visitors center, a short nature trail leads across the steppe to the shoreline for glimpses of the swans, which are always here, but birdlife is most abundant November–March. A roofed shelter, open on the leeward side, holds a 1915 Zeiss telescope that still awaits repair, so carry lightweight binoculars.

Practicalities

On the north side of RP 46, about one kilometer east of the visitors center, a free APN campground offers shade and shelter from the westerlies that gust across the steppe, but Laguna Blanca really makes a better day trip than an overnight. There's no food available—bring everything you'll need.

Directly on RP 46, the steadily improving **Centro de Visitantes** has helpful rangers, informative exhibits, clean toilets, and a crafts outlet. It's open 9 A.M.–6 P.M. daily mid-December–March; the rest of the year it's open weekends and holidays only.

Public transportation is limited; from Zapala (1 hour, US$2.50), several bus companies now pass the park en route to Aluminé. If schedules are inconvenient, considering hiring a *remise*.

NORTHERN PATAGONIA

The Lakes District

JUNÍN DE LOS ANDES

Where the steppe meets the sierra, the Río Chimehuin gushes from the base of 3,776-meter Volcán Lanín to become one of Argentina's top trout streams near Junín de los Andes. Styling itself Neuquén's "trout capital," Junín also provides the best access to the central sector of Parque Nacional Lanín, which takes its name from the symmetrical cone along the Chilean border.

In addition to its natural attractions, Junín promotes itself as a pilgrimage site for links to the recently beatified Chilean Laura Vicuña, a young girl who (legend says) willed her own death to protest her widowed mother's affair with an Argentine landowner, and for the ostensible blend of Catholic and Mapuche traditions here. Founded in 1883, during General Roca's so-called "Conquista del Desierto" (Conquest of the Desert), it's Neuquén's oldest city.

At the confluence of the Chimehuin and its Curruhué tributary, Junín (pop. 10,243) is 402 kilometers southwest of Neuquén via RN 22, RN 40, and RN 234, and 41 kilometers northeast of San Martín de los Andes via RN 234. It's 218 kilometers north of San Carlos de Bariloche via RN 234, RN 40, and RN 237.

The main thoroughfare is north–south RN 234; the compact city center, a regular grid around Plaza San Martín, lies east between the highway and the river.

Sights

The **Museo Mapuche** (Ginés Ponte 540, 9 A.M.–noon and 2–7 P.M. Mon.–Fri., 9 A.M.–noon Sat., free) focuses on indigenous artifacts and historical exhibits, but it also displays fossils.

Recent developments reflect Junín's promotion of religious tourism. The recently modernized **Santuario Nuestra Señora de las Nieves y Beata Laura Vicuña** (Ginés Ponte and Don Bosco) has become an airy, luminous structure incorporating Mapuche elements; it also holds an urn with one of Laura Vicuña's vertebrae. It's open for guided tours 9 A.M.–7 P.M. daily.

In the western foothills, the **Vía Cristi** is a Stations of the Cross footpath climbing two kilometers to the summit of **Cerro de la Cruz.**

Entertainment and Events

Late January's **Feria y Exposición Ganadera** is the landowners' extravaganza of blue-ribbon cattle, horses, and sheep as well as rabbits and poultry. Gauchos also show off their skills, but they take center stage at mid-February's **Festival del Puestero.**

The pre-Lenten **Carnaval del Pehuén** fills the streets with parades, costumed celebrants, water balloons, and confetti. Mid-July's **Semana de Artesanía Aborígen** lets the Mapuche showcase their crafts.

Shopping

Junín's **Paseo Artesanal** (Padre Milanesio 568) houses a cluster of artisans working in ceramics, leather, wood, and wool.

Sports and Recreation

Both Argentines and foreigners flock here for fishing on the Chimehuín, the Aluminé, their tributaries, and Parque Nacional Lanín's glacial lakes. Catch-and-release is the norm; for licenses and suggested guides, visit the tourist office on Plaza San Martín. For nonresidents of the province, licenses cost US$20 per day, US$66 per week, or US$92 for the season; the national parks have separate licenses.

The **Club Andino Junín de los Andes** in the Paseo Artesanal (Padre Milanesio 568) provides information on hiking and climbing Volcán Lanín and other excursions, as does **Parques Nacionales** (Padre Milanesio 570, tel. 02972/49-2748, www.parquenacionallanin.gov.ar).

Estancia Huechahue

On the Río Aluminé, about 30 kilometers east of Junín via RN 234, the 15,000-hectare

Anglo-Argentine Estancia Huechahue is a forested cattle ranch that doubles as a recreational getaway for serious gaucho-style riders, or those who want to become serious riders. November–April, Jane Williams's well-trained horses carry a maximum of 12 guests at a time over the mountainous terrain into Parque Nacional Lanín or undertake a circuit of various nearby *estancias.*

For accompanying nonriders, or for a change of pace, there's hiking, birding, fishing, swimming, and even tennis. Huechahue also features volcanic caves, Tehuelche rock-art sites, and wildlife that includes Andean condor nesting sites (not to mention deer and feral boar).

Most visitors arrange packages from overseas; drop-ins are not possible, but with at least a few days' notice it may be possible to arrange a stay (three-day minimum). The basic rate of US$375 pp, in twin-bed rooms, includes full board (traditional Patagonian fare rather than the European-style cuisine of some *estancias*), drinks (beer, wine, and spirits), hot tub and sauna, and activities (fishing guides and massages are extra). It also includes transportation between Huechahue and San Martín de los Andes's Aeropuerto Chapelco; transportation to or from Bariloche is possible for an additional charge. For details, contact Jane Williams at Estancia Huechahue (www.huechahue.com).

Accommodations

The riverside municipal **Camping La Isla** (Ginés Ponte s/n, tel. 02972/49-1461, US$4 pp) has good facilities but collects a small additional charge for showers, which have limited hours: 8–10 A.M. and 8–10 P.M.

The roadside **Residencial Marisa** (Bulevar Juan Manuel de Rosas 360, tel. 02972/49-1175, residencialmarisa@jdeandes.com.ar, US$21–28 s, US$27–39 d) has both doubles and bunks; breakfast is an inexpensive extra. Plaza San Martín's basic **Hostería del Montañés** (San Martín 555, tel. 02972/49-1155, US$28 s, US$39 d) is a basic budget choice.

Aging but agreeable, the riverside **Hostería Chimehuín** (Coronel Suárez and 25 de Mayo, tel. 02972/49-1132, hosteriachimehuin@

fronteradigital.net.ar, US$47 s, US$55 d) has 23 comfortable rooms, including a few slightly cheaper ones with shared baths, and a restaurant. Breakfast includes homemade scones and other specialties.

On Junín's northern outskirts, **Hotel Alejandro Primero** (Bulevar Juan Manuel de Rosas and Chubut, tel. 02972/49-1182, hotelalejandro1@fronteradigital.net.ar, US$40 s, US$55 d) also has a restaurant, but the hotel staff are not well-trained.

Junín's only four-star accommodations, the self-consciously rustic **Río Dorado Lodge** (Pedro Illera 448, tel. 02972/49-1548, www.riodorado.com.ar, US$98 s, US$160 d, with buffet breakfast; US$133 s, US$230 d, with half board, including wine and beer) has become the default option for foreign tour groups, especially but not exclusively for fly-fishing.

Food

For pizza and pasta, plus sandwiches and empanadas, the traditional favorite is **Roble Bar** (Ginés Ponte 331, tel. 02972/49-1111, lunch and dinner daily). It has a credible challenger, though, in **Pizzería Offa** (Padre Milanesio 520, tel. 02972/49-2577, lunch and dinner daily).

Primarily a *parrilla,* the cavernous ◖ **Ruca Hueney** (Padre Milanesio 641, tel. 02972/49-1113, lunch and dinner daily) has a more diverse menu (try the *pollo al ajillo,* garlic chicken, US$6), good service even with large numbers of diners, and is now tobacco-free.

In an attractive building styled after Bariloche's landmark civic center, the awkwardly named **Centro de Turismo** (Padre Milanesio 586, tel. 02972/49-2555, lunch and dinner daily) has a mostly standard Argentine menu; the standout item is the butter-grilled trout (US$7).

Across the plaza, **Tío Tom** (Lamadrid and San Martín, tel. 02972/49-2510) has Junín's best ice cream.

Information

Facing Plaza San Martín, the **Subsecretaría de Turismo y Cultura** (Padre Milanesio 596, tel. 02972/49-1160, www.junindelosandes.gov.ar, 8 A.M.–9 P.M. daily) answers questions and sells fishing permits.

Immediately north, the **APN** (Padre Milanesio 570, tel. 02972/49-2748, www.parquenacionallanin.gov.ar, 9 A.M.–8:30 P.M. Mon.–Fri., 2:30–8:30 P.M. Sat.–Sun.) provides information and entry permits (US$8) for Parque Nacional Lanín.

Services

Banco de la Provincia del Neuquén (Avenida San Martín and Lamadrid) has an ATM.

Correo Argentino is at Suárez and Don Bosco; the postal code is 8371. For long-distance phone service, use the *locutorio* at Padre Milanesio 530, half a block north of the tourist office. **Arroba Computación** (Lamadrid 342) has Internet access.

Laverap Pehuén (Ginés Ponte 340) does the washing.

For medical emergencies, contact the **Hospital de Area** (Avenida Antártida Argentina and Pasaje 2 de Abril, tel. 02972/49-1107).

Getting There and Around

Aeropuerto Aviador Carlos Campos-Chapelco (RN 234 Km 24, tel. 02972/42-8388) lies midway between Junín and San Martín de los Andes. Air schedules change frequently, especially in ski season. **Aerolíneas Argentinas** (Belgrano 949, tel. 02972/41-0588) flies regularly to Buenos Aires, usually to Aeroparque but sometimes to Ezeiza. **LADE** (Villegas 231, San Martín, tel. 02972/42-7672) flies occasionally to Aeroparque and to other Patagonian destinations. **American Jet** (tel. 0810/345-9876, www.americanjet.com.ar) has just begun weekday flights to Neuquén.

Services at Junín's **Terminal de Ómnibus** (Olavarría and Félix San Martín, tel. 02972/49-2038) resemble those at San Martín de los Andes, including trans-Andean buses to Chile.

SAN MARTÍN DE LOS ANDES

Barely a century since its founding as a frontier fortress, San Martín de los Andes has become one of the lakes district's most fashionable resorts. Nestled in the hills near Lago Lácar, it owes its appeal to its surrounding scenery, the trout that thrash in Parque Nacional Lanín's lakes and streams, and the ski boom that began at nearby Chapelco in the 1940s.

San Martín itself is picturesque enough, thanks to the legacy of architect Alejandro Bustillo, whose rustically styled Centro Cívico builds on his designs at Bariloche. Unlike Bariloche, San Martín has shunned the high-rise horrors that have degraded Bustillo's legacy there; its biggest blight is the increasingly aggressive marketing of timeshares. The height limit has its own downside in promoting San Martín's perceived exclusivity—in a sense, it's Argentina's version of Jackson Hole, Wyoming, where fashion often trumps nature.

At Lago Lácar's east end, 642 meters above sea level, San Martín (pop. 22,269) is 189 kilometers north of Bariloche via RN 237, RN 231, and RN 234; it's 109 kilometers north of Villa la Angostura via RN 234. It's 259 kilometers from Bariloche via the roundabout route, but a faster alternative is via Junín.

Sights

Lavishly landscaped **Plaza San Martín's** masterpiece is Bustillo's former **Intendencia Parque Nacional Lanín,** which matches the style of its Bariloche counterpart and has influenced architects and designers throughout the region. The exterior consists of roughly hewn blocks, rustically carved beams, attic windows that jut out from the main structure, and wooden roof shingles. Now combining a museum on the park's origins and natural history with its traditional information center, the **Museo del Parque Nacional Lanín** (Emilio Frey 749, tel. 02972/42-0664, free) is open 9 A.M.–6 P.M. Monday–Friday.

Across the plaza, the **Museo Primeros Pobladores** (Rosas 758, 02972/42-8676, ext. 2, museoprimerospobladores@yahoo.com.ar, 10 A.M.–3 P.M. and 4–6 P.M. Mon.–Tues. and Thurs.–Fri., 3–10 P.M. Sat.–Sun., US$0.35) is a modest effort at acknowledging all the area's cultural influences, from pre-Columbian hunter-gatherers to settled Mapuche

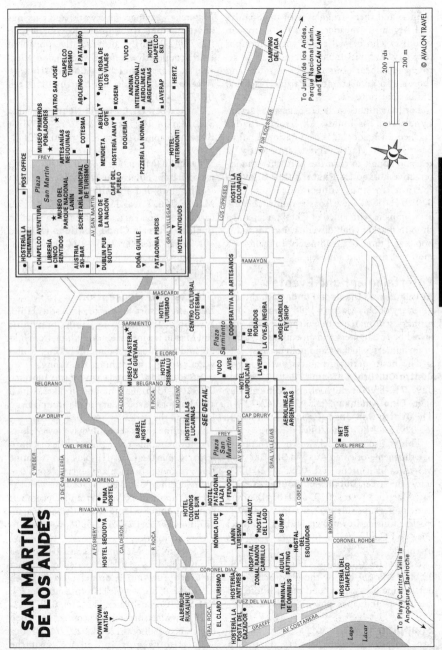

SAN MARTÍN DE LOS ANDES

NORTHERN PATAGONIA

© AVALON TRAVEL

200 yds

200 m

To Junín de los Andes,
Parque Nacional Lanín,
and **VOLCÁN LANÍN**

CAMPING DEL ACA

AV DR KOESSLER

Detail inset labels:

HOSTERÍA LA CHEMINEE
POST OFFICE
MUSEO PRIMEROS POBLADORES
TEATRO SAN JOSÉ
CHAPELCO TURISMO
PATALIBRO
HOTEL ROSA DE LOS VIAJES
YUCO
HOTEL CHAPELCO SKI
CHAPELCO AVENTURA
Plaza San Martín
ARTESANÍAS NEUQUINAS
FREY
ABOLENGO
ANDINA INTERNACIONAL/ AEROLÍNEAS ARGENTINAS
HERTZ
LIBRERÍA CHINO SENTIDOS
MUSEO DEL PARQUE NACIONAL LANÍN
COTESMA
MENDIETA
HOSTERÍA ANAY
ABUELA GOYE
KOSEM
SECRETARÍA MUNICIPAL DE TURISMO
BOQUERÍA
LAVERAP
AUSTRIA SKI-BAR
CAFÉ DEL PUEBLO
PIZZERÍA LA NONNA
HOTEL INTERMONTI
AV SAN MARTÍN
BANCO DE LA NACIÓN
DUBLIN PUB SOUTH
DOÑA GUILLE
GRAL VILLEGAS
PATAGONIA PISCIS
HOTEL ANTIGUOS

Main map labels:

DOWNTOWN MATÍAS
A FOSBERY
HOSTEL SEQUOYA
C WEBER
3 DE CABALLERÍA
PUMA HOSTEL
CALDERÓN
R ROCA
BELGRANO
CAP DRURY
CNEL PEREZ
MARIANO MORENO
RIVADAVIA
CORONEL DÍAZ
JUEZ DEL VALLE
GRAEFF
GRAL ROCA
ALBERGUE RUKALHUE
EL CLARO TURISMO
HOSTERÍA ANTARES
HOSTERÍA LA POSTA DEL CAZADOR
AV COSTANERA

HOTEL COLONOS DEL SUR
MÓNICA DUE
LANÍN TURISMO
HOSPITAL ZONAL RAMÓN CARRILLO
ÁGUILA RAFTING
TERMINAL DE ÓMNIBUS
HOSTERÍA DEL CHAPELCO

MASCARDI
HOTEL TURISMO
CENTRO CULTURAL COTESMA
COTESMA
SARMIENTO
MUSEO LA PASTERA CHE GUEVARA
HOTEL CRISMALÚ
E ELORDI
BELGRANO
R ROCA
P MORENO
BABEL HOSTEL
HOSTERÍA LAS LUCARNAS
SEE DETAIL
FREY
Plaza San Martín
AV SAN MARTÍN
HOTEL PATAGONIA PLAZA
FENOGLIO
CHARLOT
HOSTAL DEL LAGO
BUMPS
HOSTAL DEL ESQUIADOR

COOPERATIVA DE ARTESANOS
RAMAYÓN
Plaza Sarmiento
HG RODADOS
LA OVEJA NEGRA
JORGE CARDILLO FLY SHOP
YUCO
AVIS
HOTEL CAUPOLICÁN
LAVERAP
CAP DRURY
AEROLÍNEAS ARGENTINAS
GRAL VILLEGAS
NET SUR
CNEL PEREZ
M MORENO
G OBEID
BROWN
CORONEL ROHDE

LOS CIPRESES
HOSTEL LA COLORADA

To Playa Catritre, Villa La
Angostura, Bariloche

Lago Lácar

farmers and their struggles with the Spanish and Argentine invaders, and the European colonists who helped create the contemporary city. Exhibits include items such as arrowheads, spear points, and ceramics, and there's also an account of Parque Nacional Lanín's creation.

For four nights in 1952, Ernesto Guevara Lynch and his buddy Alberto Granados crashed on hay bales in the national park's barn in San Martín. That, apparently, is reason enough to turn the barn into the interactive **Museo La Pastera Che Guevara** (Sarmiento and Rudecindo Roca, tel. 02972/41-1994, www.lapasteramuseoche.org.ar), complete with video of Che's career and a shop to market Che souvenirs, including his books and those of his admirers. In reality, it's more a shrine than a museum.

Entertainment and Events

At February 4's **Día de la Fundación,** the anniversary of San Martín's 1898 founding, the military still marches down the avenues, followed by fire fighters and an equestrian array of foxhunters, gauchos, and polo players.

The main performing-arts outlet is the **Centro Cultural Cotesma** (Roca 1154, tel. 02972/42-8399), which offers recent movies at its **Cine Amankay** (tel. 02972/42-7274). The **Teatro San José** (Capitán Drury 743, tel. 02972/42-8676) hosts live theater.

This is also a bar-goer's town, with places like the theme-oriented **Austria Ski-Bar** (San Martín and Moreno, tel. 02972/42-7071); across the street, **Dublin Pub South** (Avenida San Martín 599, tel. 02972/41-0141) offers beer, pub grub, sidewalk seating, and Wi-Fi. The hillside **Downtown Matías** (Coronel Díaz and Calderón, tel. 02972/42-1699) has live music.

Boquería (Capitán Drury 857, tel. 02972/42-5663) is a by-the-glass or by-the-bottle wine bar, with a food menu limited to sandwiches and tapas, plus nightly specials.

Shopping

San Martín's souvenir outlets start with Mapuche weavings, silverwork, and carvings at **Artesanías Neuquinas** (Rosas 790, tel. 02972/42-8396), a provincially sponsored crafts cooperative. There's also a good selection at Plaza Sarmiento's **Cooperativa de Artesanos** (Avenida San Martín 1050, tel. 02972/42-9097).

For textiles, try **La Oveja Negra** (Avenida San Martín 1025, tel. 02972/42-8039) or **Kosem** (Capitán Drury 838, tel. 02972/42-7269).

Fenoglio (Moreno 743, tel. 02972/42-7515) is popular for homemade-style chocolates.

The cramped **Patalibro** (Avenida San Martín 866, Local 11, tel. 02972/42-1532) carries books on Patagonia, including some in English. **Librería Cinco Sentidos** (Moreno 701, Local 5, tel. 02972/41-0160) is a gleaming and spacious bookstore that doubles as a Wi-Fi café.

Sports and Recreation

Like the resort town of Jackson Hole, Wyoming, and thanks to Lanín's proximity, San Martín is a mecca for everything from hiking and climbing to mountain biking, whitewater rafting, trout fishing, and skiing.

HG Rodados (Avenida San Martín 1061, tel. 02972/42-7345) rents mountain bikes, which are ideal for the secondary roads around Lago Lácar and the park.

Argentine rivers generally have lower flows and fewer rapids than their Chilean counterparts, but the Class III–plus Río Aluminé flows through spectacular scenery a couple of hours north of San Martín. It's best with the spring runoff in November and December; contact **Lanín Turismo** (Avenida San Martín 437, Local 7, tel. 02972/42-5808, www.laninturismo.com.ar).

Closer to San Martín, the Class II Río Hua Hum provides a gentler experience. Contact **El Claro Turismo** (Coronel Díaz 751, tel. 02972/42-8786, www.elclaroturismo.com.ar); **Net Sur** (Coronel Pérez 1124, tel. 02972/42-7929, www.netsurpatagonia.com.ar); or **Yuco** (Belgrano 845, Local 12, tel. 02972/42-3150).

For fishing gear and advice, visit the

THE SLOPES OF CHAPELCO

Overlooking San Martín de los Andes, at a maximum elevation of 1,920 meters, Cerro Chapelco draws enthusiastic winter crowds to 29 different runs, the longest combination of which is about 5.3 kilometers. The diversity of conditions means it's suitable for both experienced skiers and novices. The **Fiesta Nacional del Montañes,** the annual ski festival, takes place in August, when there are also provincial skiing championships.

Chapelco Aventura (Mariano Moreno 701, tel. 02972/42-7845, www.cerro-chapelco.com) is the resort office in San Martín. Rental equipment is available onsite but also in town at **Bumps** (Villegas 465, tel. 02972/42-8491) and **La Colina** (San Martín 532, tel. 02972/42-7414).

Lift-ticket prices depend on timing; the season runs mid-June–mid-October but is subdivided into low, mid, or peak season. For current rates, check Chapelco's website.

Jorge Cardillo Fly Shop (Villegas 1061, tel. 02972/42-8372).

Accommodations

Accommodations are abundant, but the best values go fast. Reservations are advisable—and single occupants usually have to pay double rates—in summer, during Semana Santa, and throughout ski season. The municipal tourist office will make every effort to help find the best accommodations in your price range.

US$10-25

On the Junín highway, the wooded **Camping del ACA** (Avenida Koessler 2176, tel. 02972/42-9430, US$3 pp off-season, US$20 per site in summer) is spacious and shady, but the best sites go early. There are other campgrounds north and south of town in Parque Nacional Lanín.

In an attractive house with sparkling common areas, the 21-bed **Hostel La Colorada** (Avenida Koessler 1614, tel. 02972/41-1041, www.lacoloradahostel.com.ar, US$12–14 pp dorm, US$34 d) is an independent hostel that has mostly dorms but also one double with shared bath. Its main drawback is its location along a busy avenue.

US$25-50

Named for the giant redwood in its garden, the HI affiliate **Hostel Secuoya** (Rivadavia 411, tel. 02972/42-4485, www.hostelsecuoya.com.ar, US$14 pp dorm, US$35 d) isn't up to Puma's standards, with only two downstairs bathrooms and most of the beds upstairs in rooms with thin walls. Still, it's friendly, well located, and has Wi-Fi; breakfast is a voucher to a downtown *confitería*.

Albergue Rukalhue (Juez del Valle 682, tel. 02972/42-7431, www.rukalhue.com.ar, US$15 pp dorm, US$48 d) offers respectable hostel accommodations as well as inexpensive dinners.

Babel Hostel (Rudecindo Roca 720, tel. 011/41-2120, www.babelhostel.com.ar, US$15 pp dorm) is a cozy new garden hostel. Peak-season reservations are imperative at HI-affiliated **(Puma Hostel** (Fosbery 535, tel. 02972/42-2443, www.pumahostel.com.ar, US$17 pp dorm, US$47 d), an attractive and well-run 50-bed facility north of the arroyo.

Belonging to another era, **Hotel Turismo** (Mascardi 501, tel. 02972/42-7592, hotelturismo@smandes.com.ar, US$26 s, US$36 d) still has an impressive exterior, but the rooms are small and dark compared with the city's newer accommodations. The baths have been upgraded, though, and for a budget choice it's by no means bad.

With responsive management, **Hostería Las Lucarnas** (Coronel Pérez 632, tel. 02972/42-7085, hosterialaslucarnas@gmail.com, US$34 s, US$39 d) is a decent budget choice with amenities that include cable TV, Wi-Fi, strongboxes, and parking.

Near the lake, **Hostería del Chapelco** (Brown 297, tel. 02972/42-7610, hcchapelco@smandes.com.ar, US$42 s, US$48 d) has the best location of any hotel in its range; some second-story rooms have balconies with lake or mountain views.

US$50-100

At the east end of town, on the road toward Junín, **Hostería Parque Los Andes** (RN 234, Km 2, tel. 02972/42-8211, hosteriaparquelosandes@smandes.com.ar, US$53 s or d) retains its classic style but has brightened and improved its rooms. After Chilean poet Pablo Neruda fled over the Andes on horseback to avoid political persecution in 1949, he may have shared drinks with Juan Perón in the gallery bar.

Central **Hotel Chapelco Ski** (Belgrano 869, tel. 02972/42-7480, www.chapelcoskihotel. com.ar, US$48 s, US$55 d) is a little worn and has limited parking but is otherwise OK.

The handsome classic **Hotel Crismalú** (Rudecindo Roca 975, tel. 02972/42-7283, crismalu@smandes.com.ar, US$48 s, US$58 d) is showing its age but is still reasonable for what it offers.

Hotel Rosa de los Viajes (Avenida San Martín 821, tel. 02972/42-7484, rosahotel@smandes.com.ar, US$52 s, US$58 d) is small (20 rooms) and homey, but both foot and auto traffic are heavy in this part of town.

Just far enough off the main drag to ensure some quiet, **Hotel Colonos del Sur** (Rivadavia 686, tel. 02972/42-7224, www.colonosdelsur.com.ar, US$58 s or d) has smallish rooms with bathtubs in a category where showers are the rule.

Set among attractive gardens, **Hostería Anay** (Capitán Drury 841, tel. 02972/42-7514, anay@smandes.com.ar, US$48 s, US$61 d) has 10 cozy rooms and enjoys a welcome site setback from the street in a bustling area.

Run by relocated *porteño* shrinks, cozy **Hostal del Lago** (Rohde 854, tel. 02972/42-7598, hostaldellagosma@yahoo.com.ar, US$66 d) has six reasonably spacious rooms with good beds, desks, and cable TV, but it could use a color consultant.

Try also **Hostal del Esquiador** (Coronel Rohde 975, tel. 02972/42-7674, www.

hostaldelesquiador.com.ar, UD$58 s, US$68 d), a block from the bus terminal, which has clean pleasant rooms with appealing designer touches.

Upstairs rooms are better at **Hostería La Posta del Cazador** (Avenida San Martín 175, tel. 02972/42-7501, www.postadelcazador.com.ar, US$77 s or d), a Middle European–style place on a quiet block near the lake. The credit-card surcharge is high—pay cash.

Sedate **Hotel Intermonti** (Villegas 717, tel./fax 02972/42-7454, www.hotelintermonti.com.ar, US$70 s, US$84 d) has 24 well-furnished midsize rooms, plus attractive common areas.

US$100-200

Hotel Antiguos (Coronel Díaz 753, tel. 02972/41-1876, www.hotelantiguos.com.ar, US$102 s or d) is a luminous new 12-room hotel with natural wood details and some luxuries, including Jacuzzis in every bathroom. While the rooms are on the small side, they are stylish.

Four-star **Hotel Patagonia Plaza** (San Martín and Rivadavia, tel./fax 02972/42-2280, www.hotelpatagoniaplaza.com.ar, from US$167 s and US$185 d) has become one of the city's premier accommodations, with 90 rooms ranging from relatively simple doubles to sprawling suites.

OVER US$200

Hostería La Cheminee (Avenida Roca and Mariano Moreno, tel. 02972/42-7617, www.hosterialacheminee.com.ar, US$208 s or d), which has upgraded into one of the town's most stylish hotels, has managed to raise its prices despite the down economy. It features an indoor pool, sauna, wine bar, art gallery, and many other distinctive features.

San Martín's latest luxury option, **Hostería Antares Patagonia** (Avenida San Martín 251, tel. 02972/42-7670, www.antarespatagonia.com.ar, US$208 s or d) is a recycled and expanded family mansion on a large lot with 10 spacious (75-square-meter) suites, a heated pool, a sauna and a Jacuzzi, a business center, and other spacious common areas.

NORTHERN PATAGONIA

Food

Try **Plaza Pueblo** (Avenida San Martín and Coronel Pérez) for coffee, croissants, sandwiches, and desserts. Cozy, comfortable **Abolengo** (Avenida San Martín 806, tel. 02972/42-7732) is ideal for rich hot chocolate on a cool night.

Pizzería La Nonna (Capitán Drury 857, tel. 02972/42-2223) serves about 30 varieties of pizza, including wild boar, trout, and venison, plus calzones and empanadas. It gets noisy, though—either take earplugs, go early or late, or consider takeout.

Reservations are advisable for the mom-and-pop 【 **Mónica Due** (Rivadavia 759, tel. 02972/42-3643), which has only seven tables but authentic Italian pastas, from Bologna by way of Costa Rica, served with genuine warmth. Mediocre pesto may be the main shortcoming of Italo-Argentine cuisine, but here it's the real thing. Prices are reasonable, around US$7–9 per entrée.

Similarly small and popular, **Doña Guille** (Mariano Moreno 885, tel. 02972/42-3378) specializes in trout, venison (with a sweet and sour raspberry sauce, US$12), and pastas. The kitchen can be slow, but the results indicate attention to detail.

New in 2008, **Dama Juana** (Coronel Pérez 860, tel. 02972/41-1941, nightly from 6 P.M. Mon.–Sat.) is a combination restaurant–wine bar with a good regional menu and fine service.

Dinner lines form early outside popular *parrillas* like **Mendieta** (San Martín 713, tel. 02972/42-9301) and **Patagonia Piscis** (Villegas 598, tel. 02972/42-3247), which also serves fish and game. The service can be erratic, though.

For a romantic dinner, try the understated 【 **La Reserva** (Belgrano 940, tel. 02972/42-8734, www.lareservarestaurant.com.ar), serving moderately priced (from US$10) Patagonian tapas, salads, and entrées like squash *panzotti*. It also offers Tuesday-night dinners (US$16) where each of three courses is paired with wines from a different bodega.

For ice cream, try **Charlot** (Avenida San Martín 467, tel. 02972/42-8561), with dozens of imaginative flavors. **Abuela Goye** (Capitán Drury 812, tel. 02972/42-9409) is also outstanding and has superb chocolate confections.

Information

At Plaza San Martín's east end, the **Secretaría Municipal de Turismo** (Avenida San Martín and Rosas, tel. 02972/42-7347, informes.turismo@smandes.gov.ar, www.smandes.gov.ar, 8 A.M.–10 P.M. daily summer, 8 A.M.–9 P.M. daily the rest of the year) provides advice, maps, and brochures plus an up-to-the-minute database of accommodations and rates; in peak season, though, high demand can test its resources.

The APN's **Centro de Visitantes de Parque Nacional Lanín** (Emilio Frey 749, tel. 02972/42-0664, www.parquenacionallanin.com.ar, 9 A.M.–4 P.M. Mon.–Fri.) provides park information and has a selection of maps and brochures.

Services

Banco de la Nación (Avenida San Martín 687) and several others have ATMs. **Andina Internacional** (Capitán Drury 876) is the only currency-exchange house.

Correo Argentino (General Roca and Coronel Pérez) is the post office. **Cotesma** (Capitán Drury 761) has telephone, fax, and Internet services.

Chapelco Turismo (Avenida San Martín 876, tel. 02972/42-7550) offers conventional excursions to Parque Nacional Lanín, Villa la Angostura, and other destinations.

For laundry, **Laverap** (tel. 02972/42-8820) has two locations: Capitán Drury 880 and Villegas 972.

Hospital Zonal Ramón Carrillo (Avenida San Martín and Coronel Rohde, tel. 02972/42-7211) is central.

Getting There

Air and bus schedules change frequently, especially in ski season. **Aerolíneas Argentinas** (Belgrano 949, tel. 02972/41-0588) flies regularly to Buenos Aires, usually to Aeroparque but sometimes to Ezeiza. Occupying a booth in the bus terminal, **LADE** (Villegas 231, tel. 02972/42-7672) flies occasionally to Aeroparque and to other Patagonian destinations. **American Jet** (tel. 0810/345-9876, www.americanjet.com.ar) has just begun weekday flights to Neuquén.

San Martín's **Terminal de Ómnibus** (Villegas 231, tel. 02972/42-7044) has regional, long-distance, and Chilean connections.

Transportes Ko Ko (tel. 02972/42-7422) goes to Villa la Angostura (3 hours, US$9) via the scenic Siete Lagos route, sometimes continuing to Bariloche, but most services to Bariloche (4.5 hours, US$13) use the longer but smoother Rinconada route. **Albús** (tel. 02972/42-8100) also goes to Villa la Angostura three times daily via the Siete Lagos route and twice to Bariloche, while **La Araucana Viajes** (tel. 02972/42-1330) goes twice daily via the Siete Lagos route.

In summer, Ko Ko goes to the Chilean border at Paso Hua Hum (US$3) at 9 A.M. and 6:30 P.M. daily. Monday–Saturday, **Igi-Llaima** (tel. 02972/42-8100) and **Empresa San Martín** (tel. 02972/42-7294) alternate service to Pucón (6.5 hours, US$17) and Temuco, Chile (8 hours, US$20); Empresa San Martín continues to Valdivia. In summer, **Buses Lafit** (tel. 02972/42-7422) goes Wednesday and Sunday to the Chilean border post of Pirehueico (2 hours, US$8) and on to Panguipulli (4.5 hours, US$20).

Other typical destinations include Junín de los Andes (45 minutes, US$2), Neuquén (5.5 hours, US$14–26), and Buenos Aires (21 hours, US$65–96).

Getting Around

Aeropuerto Aviador Carlos Campos-Chapelco (RN 234 Km 24, tel. 02972/42-8388) lies midway between San Martín and Junín de los Andes. Patanor (tel. 02944/42-5688) provides airport transfers.

In summer only, **Transportes Ko Ko** (tel. 02972/42-7422) runs several buses daily (US$1) to Lago Lolog.

At the foot of Obeid, **Naviera Lacar y Nonthue** (Avenida Costanera s/n, tel. 02972/42-7380) sails six to eight times daily to Quila Quina (US$10 round-trip) on Lago Lácar's south shore, and daily to Hua Hum (US$37 round-trip).

For rental cars, try **Alamo/National** (Avenida San Martín 836, 1st floor, tel. 02972/41-0811) or **Hertz** (Avenida San Martín 831, 1st floor, tel. 02972/42-0280).

PARQUE NACIONAL LANÍN

In westernmost Neuquén, stretching from Lago Ñorquinco in the north to a diagonal that runs between Lago Nonthué on the Chilean border and Confluencia on RN 237, Parque Nacional Lanín comprises 412,000 hectares of arid steppe, mid-altitude forests ringing glacial lakes and streams, alpine highlands, and volcanic summits. From Aluminé in the north to San Martín de los Andes in the south, several longitudinal highways intersect graveled westbound access roads.

When the eastward-flowing Pleistocene glaciers receded, they left a series of deep finger lakes draining into the Río Limay's upper and lower tributaries. Unlike Parque Nacional Nahuel Huapi to the south, these lakes and the Valdivian forests surrounding them have suffered less commercial development, but they are recovering from timber exploitation and livestock grazing that persist in some areas.

Most park visitors use either Junín or San Martín as their base.

Flora and Fauna

Up to 3,000 millimeters of precipitation per annum supports dense humid Valdivian woodlands. Lanín's signature species is the coniferous *pehuén* or monkey puzzle tree (*Araucaria araucana*), for centuries a subsistence resource for the Mapuches and Pehuenches (a subgroup whose name stresses their dependence on the tree's edible nuts). Along with the broadleaf deciduous southern beech *raulí*, the *pehuén* forms part of a transitional forest overlapping southern beech species that dominate the more southerly Patagonian forests, such as the *coihue*, *lenga*, and *ñire*. In places, the solid bamboo *colihue* forms almost impenetrable thickets.

At higher elevations, above 1,600 meters, cold and wind reduce the vegetative cover to shrubs and grasses. At lower elevations the drier climate supports shrubs and steppe grasses.

Except for its trout, Lanín is less celebrated for its wildlife than for its landscapes. Fortunate visitors may see the secretive spaniel-size deer known as the *pudú* or the larger *huemul* (Andean deer). The major predator is the puma, present on the steppes and in the forest, while the torrent duck frequents the faster streams and the Andean condor glides on the heights. The lakes and rivers attract many other birds.

Volcán Lanín

Looming above the landscape, straddling the Chilean border at 3,776 meters above sea level, lopsided Lanín is the literal and metaphorical center of its namesake park. Covered by permanent snow, rising 1,500 meters above any other nearby peak, its irregular cone is a beacon for hundreds of kilometers to the east and, where the rugged terrain permits, to the north and south.

Sector Lago Tromen

From a junction 11 kilometers north of Junín, northwesterly RP 60 leads to the Chilean border at Paso Mamuil Malal, where Lago Tromen marks the most convenient approach to the summit of **Volcán Lanín.** Because of the northeasterly exposure, hiking and climbing routes open earlier here than on the southern side, which lies partly in Chile.

Before climbing Lanín, obtain permission from the APN in San Martín, which will ask to inspect your gear, which should contain crampons, an ice ax, plastic tools, and appropriate clothing and peripherals (gloves, hats, insulated jackets, sunglasses, and sunscreen).

From the trailhead at the Argentine border, the **Camino de Mulas** route takes 5–7 hours to the **Refugio Club Andino Junín de los Andes** (altitude 2,600 meters; capacity 10 people); beyond this point, snow gear is essential. The shorter but steeper **Espina del Pescado** route starts at the Argentine army's

Refugio Regimiento Infantería de Montaña (elevation 2,350 meters; capacity 15 people); it's possible to approach either route from the Lago Huechulafquen side as well. Both *refugios* are unfortunately dirty, and construction of a new one is still on the back burner; there is an improvised tent camp, with some services, in season.

Sector Lago Huechulafquen

About four kilometers north of Junín, RP 61 leads northwest along the Río Chimehuín and Lago Huechulafquen's north shore for 52 kilometers to Puerto Canoas and **Lago Paimún** (at road's end). En route, several trailheads lead north; the most interesting is the **Cara Sur** (Southern Face) approach to Volcán Lanín along the wooded Arroyo Rucu Leufú, which meets the trail coming south from Lago Tromen. Hikers not wishing to continue to Lanín's base, about a four-hour walk, or the seven hours to the Regimiento de Infantería de Montaña (RIM) *refugio* can still stroll through the araucaria woodland; climbers should obtain permission from the APN ranger here.

From the Piedra Mala campground at Lago Paimún, a 30-minute hike goes to **Cascada El Saltillo,** a 20-meter waterfall. It's no longer possible to walk around Lago Paimún, most of whose north shore is closed for environmental reasons, but for US$1 summer hikers can cross the La Unión narrows that separates Huechulafquen and Paimún on a *balsa* (cable platform). The rest of the year, it's possible to hire a rowboat to get across; on the north shore a Mapuche family runs the basic **Camping Ecufén.**

From La Unión, the trail continues through *coihue* and *pehuén* forest for about five hours to a Mapuche-run campground at **Aila,** and another eight hours to the rustic **Termas de Epulafquen.** From Epulafquen, RP 62 returns to Junín de los Andes.

For nonhikers, the **Catamarán José Julián** (Avenida San Martín 643, San Martín de los Andes, tel. 02972/42-9264, www.catamaranjosejulian.com.ar) offers a 90-minute lake excursion from Puerto Canoa over Huechulafquen,

Paimún, and Epulafquen (US$15 pp) four or five times daily in summer, less frequently the rest of the year.

Lago Lolog and Lago Lácar

About 15 kilometers north of San Martín, Lago Lolog has several campgrounds and regular summer transportation; it's particularly popular with windsurfers.

San Martín's own Lago Lácar is wilder toward the Chilean border, where there is camping, hiking, and white-water rafting at the outlet of the Río Hua Hum.

In summer only, **Transportes Ko Ko** (tel. 02972/42-7422) runs several buses daily (US$1) to Lago Lolog from San Martín.

At the foot of Obeid in San Martín, **Naviera Lacar y Nonthue** (Avenida Costanera s/n, San Martín, tel. 02972/42-7380) sails six to eight times daily to Quila Quina (US$10 round-trip) on Lago Lácar's south shore, and daily to Hua Hum (US$37 round-trip).

Accommodations and Food

Except in nearby towns, accommodations and food are few. Organized campgrounds with hot showers and other services charge slightly more than so-called *agreste* (wild) sites, which cost around US$2 pp.

Sector Lago Tromen: Alongside the Gendarmería post, facilities at **Camping Lanín** (tel. 02972/49-1355) recently suffered a fire that has left its immediate future in doubt.

Reservations are essential for the six twin rooms at **Hostería San Huberto** (RP 60 Km 28, tel. 02972/42-1875, www.sanhubertolodge. com.ar, US$300–375 s, US$440–560 d, with full board), which appeals chiefly to fly-fishing fanatics.

Sector Lago Huechulafquen: Free rustic campgrounds line the shores of Lago Huechulafquen and Lago Paimún, but the community-oriented sites that charge a fee are better maintained and have better services.

Camping Bahía Cañicul (RP 61 Km 48, US$4 pp) has a small store, but supplies are cheaper and more diverse in Junín. **Camping Raquithué** (RP 61 Km 54) costs US$3 pp for

anyone over age 6. Only those older than 10 pay at attractive **Camping Piedra Mala** (RP 61 Km 60, US$4 pp); campers age 10 and under pay only a small charge for showers.

A few kilometers before Lago Paimún, **Hostería Huechulafquen** (RP 61 Km 55, tel. 02972/42-6075, www.hosteriahuechulafquen. com, US$105 pp with half board) is pleasant enough. **Hostería Paimún** (RP 61 Km 58, tel. 02972/49-1758, hosteriapaimun@jdeandes. com.ar, US$92 pp with half board, US$105 pp full board) is primarily a fishing lodge.

Lago Lolog: Basic **Camping Puerto Arturo** is free of charge.

Hua Hum: Westbound from San Martín, gravel RP 48 follows Lago Lácar's north shore to the Chilean border at Hua Hum. En route, open mid-December through Semana Santa, **Estancia Quechuquina** (RP 48 Km 30, tel. 02972/42-5340) is a rustic teahouse with exceptional cakes and cookies; hours are noon–7:30 P.M. daily for lunch and tea. Though lacking accommodations, it enjoys lake access and makes an ideal day trip.

Other Practicalities

In addition to the APN visitors center at San Martín, there are ranger stations at all major lakes and some other points. While the rangers are helpful, they do not generally have maps or other printed matter. The US$8 pp admission fee, valid for one week, must be paid at APN and local tourist offices outside the park rather than at the park entrance.

San Martín de los Andes and Junín de los Andes are the main gateways, but public transportation is limited. On international buses to Chile, via the southerly Hua Hum and the northerly Tromen passes, through passengers have priority.

VILLA LA ANGOSTURA AND VICINITY

On Lago Nahuel Huapi's north shore, Villa la Angostura lies within Bariloche's economic orbit. Its proximity to less developed parts of the lake, to Parque Nacional Los Arrayanes, and to the Cerro Bayo winter-sports center, though,

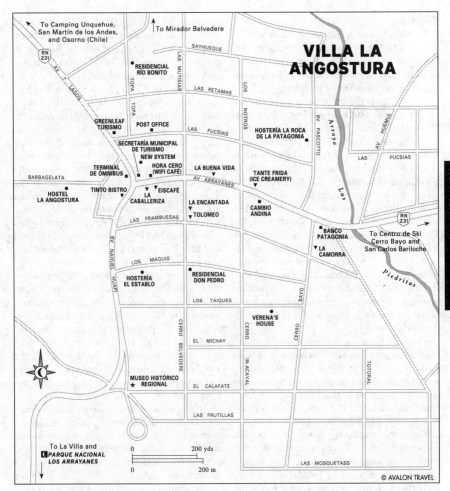

have helped established its own identity—with an air of exclusivity—for both Argentines and foreigners. It has excellent accommodations and restaurants with prices on the high side because it gets hordes of Chilean visitors thanks to the paved international highway.

Villa la Angostura (pop. 7,311) is 80 kilometers northwest of Bariloche via RN 237 and RN 231 (the highway to Osorno, Chile) and 109 kilometers south of San Martín de los Andes via RN 234, the scenic Siete Lagos (Seven Lakes) route that's now being paved. It's 870 meters above sea level, but the mountains rise sharply from the lakeshore.

Many services line both sides of RN 231 (Avenida Los Arrayanes and its westward extension Avenida Los Lagos) as it passes directly through El Cruce. Three kilometers south, residential La Villa also has a cluster of hotels and restaurants; Parque Nacional Los Arrayanes occupies all of Península Quetrihué, the southward-jutting peninsula linked to La Villa by the isthmus that gives Villa la Angostura its name (The Narrows).

Sights

Foot, bicycle, and kayak are the best ways to see Villa la Angostura and nearby sights. For hiking in the mountains, where the trails are too steep and narrow for bicycles, consider hiring a taxi or *remise* to the trailhead.

At El Cruce, four blocks south of the bus terminal, the **Museo Histórico Regional** (Bulevar Nahuel Huapi and El Calafate, 02944/49-4476, ext. 21, free) deals primarily with pioneer timber cutting, the agriculture that followed it, the families who established themselves here, and the binational Mapuche legacy. It has recently been closed for repairs.

From June–September, nine kilometers southeast of El Cruce, the **Centro de Ski Cerro Bayo** (Las Fucsias 121, Oficina 3, tel. 02944/49-4189 in town, www.cerrobayoweb. com) operates 26 kilometers of runs ranging from 1,050 to 1,782 meters above sea level with five chairlifts and five tow bars. Cerro Bayo also has accommodations, restaurants, and rental equipment on-site; for lift ticket prices, consult the website.

From El Cruce, a narrow four-kilometer road zigzags to **Mirador Belvedere,** a wide parking area and overlook with views along Lago Correntoso to the north, the implausibly short Río Correntoso that connects it to Lago Nahuel Huapi, and the hoary western peaks that mark the Chilean border.

About midway up the route, an eastbound forest trail leads to **Cascada Inacayal,** a 50-meter waterfall. From the parking area, a three-kilometer trail to 1,992-meter **Cerro Belvedere** climbs through *coihue* forest before dipping into a saddle and then ascending steeply over Cerro Falso Belvedere before continuing to the summit. The road, with several blind curves, can be difficult in wet weather.

◖ Parque Nacional Los Arrayanes

Local folklore says Walt Disney's cartoon feature *Bambi* modeled its forest after the *arrayán* woodland at the tip of Península Quetrihué, a former *estancia* that became a national park in 1971. With their bright white flowers, the eye-catching red-barked forests of *Myrceugenella apiculata* do bear a resemblance, but a Disney archivist has pointed out that *Bambi* was in production before Walt's 1941 trip to Argentina and that he never visited the area.

So close to La Villa that it feels more like a sprawling city park—it's larger than the town itself—Los Arrayanes occupies Quetrihué's entire 1,753 hectares, which stretch south into Lago Nahuel Huapi. Its namesake forest covers only about 20 hectares, but the rest of the peninsula bristles with trees like the *maitén* and the southern beeches *coihue, lenga,* and *ñire* as well as colorful shrubs like the *notro* and *chilco* and dense bamboo thickets of *colihue.*

The park's floral standout is the *arrayán,* whose individual specimens reach 25 meters and 650 years of age, but it's also ideal for hiking and mountain biking—the undulating 12-kilometer trail to or from the peninsula's tip is a perfect half-day excursion (on a bicycle or doing one-way by boat and the other on foot) or a full day by hiking in both directions. Argentine rangers often exaggerate the time needed on certain trails, but the three hours they suggest is about right for this walk in the woods, which passes a pair of lakes. Only at the park portal, near La Villa, are there any steep segments.

At the portal, rangers collect a US$8 admission charge (US$2 for Argentine residents); even those whose only goal is the 20-minute stroll to the panoramic **Mirador Arrayán** must pay the fee. Near the dock at the peninsula's southern tip, a *confitería* with a cozy fireplace serves sandwiches, coffee, and hot chocolate.

From the Bahía Mansa dock near park headquarters, nonhikers can reach the *arrayán* forest in about 30 minutes on the *Catamarán Futaleufú,* run by El Cruce's **Greenleaf Turismo** (Avenida Siete Lagos 118, 1st floor, tel. 02944/49-4405, www.bosquelosarrayanes.com.ar), at 10:30 A.M., 2 P.M., and 5 P.M.; the cost is US$16 one-way, US$31 round-trip, plus a small boarding tax. Cyclists can rent bikes in La Villa, but hikers and bikers must leave the park by 4 P.M.

From the Bahía Brava dock across the isthmus, the newer *Catamarán Patagonia Argentina* (tel. 02944/49-4463) runs a slightly cheaper service (US$13 one-way, US$25 round-trip) at 10:30 A.M., 2:45 P.M., and 5:30 P.M.

Shopping and Events

Locals and parachutists peddle their wares at El Cruce's **Feria de Artesanos** (Belvedere between Avenida Los Arrayanes and Las Fucsias, daily in summer).

For four days, early February's provincial **Fiesta de los Jardines** (Garden Festival) occupies center stage.

Sports and Recreation

English-speaking Anthony Hawes operates **Alma Sur Eco Trips** (tel. 02944/15-56-4724, www.almasur.com), with activities ranging from hiking and riding to mountain biking, fly-fishing, and white-water rafting and kayaking.

Accommodations

In the recent past, Villa la Angostura was almost exclusively upscale, but recent developments include some fine budget options.

Some 500 meters west of the tourist office, the **Camping Unquehue** (Avenida Los Lagos s/n, tel. 02944/49-4922, unquehue@ciudad.com.ar, US$5.50 pp plus US$2 per tent) offers wooded sites with hot showers in the communal baths.

The next cheapest are the HI-affiliates **Hostel la Angostura** (Barbagelata 157, tel. 02944/49-4834, www.hostellaangostura.com.ar, US$15 pp dorm, US$48 d), an imposing alpine-style building on spacious grounds, and **Bajo Cero Hostel** (Río Caleufú 88, tel. 02944/49-5454, www.bajocerohostel.com, US$16 pp dorm, US$52 d).

Two blocks north of the bus terminal, the private rooms at **Residencial Río Bonito** (Topa Topa 260, tel. 02944/49-4110, riobonito@ciudad.com.ar, US$42 d) enjoy a quiet garden setting. El Cruce's **Residencial Don Pedro** (Belvedere and Los Maquis, tel. 02944/49-4269, US$48 d) is comparable.

With friendly management and traditional Euro-Andean style, on a large lot in a quiet area, **Hostería La Roca de la Patagonia** (Bulevar Pascotto 155, tel. 02944/49-4497, www.larocadelapatagonia.com, US$39 s, US$53 d) offers half a dozen rooms on its upper floor, with the common areas on street level.

El Cruce's **Hostería Verena's Haus** (Los Taiques 268, tel. 02944/49-4467, www.verenas-haus.com.ar, US$66 s or d) is a German-Argentine B&B with tacky wallpaper but comfortable beds and small but functional baths. It also has off-street parking in a large garden, Wi-Fi through most of the building, and an exceptional breakfast.

About one kilometer west of El Cruce, **Hostería Las Cumbres** (Avenida Siete Lagos s/n, tel. 02944/49-4945, www.hosterialascumbres.com, US$66 d) is an eight-room owner-operated hotel that's a fine value. Home-cooked dinners are also available.

Dating from 1938, originally built for the APN, La Villa's lakeside classic **Hotel Angostura** (Nahuel Huapi 1911, tel. 02944/49-4224, www.hotelangostura.com, US$74 d) has 20 rooms, some with lake views, and three separate bungalows sleeping up to six people. While its aged floors are creaky and the hot water slinks slowly through the pipes for the morning's first shower, this once-romantic hotel still has style, personality, good beds, no TVs or phones in the rooms, and friendly service.

In Puerto Manzano, about six kilometers southeast of El Cruce, the eight-room **Hosteria Naranjo en Flor** (Chucao 62, tel. 02944/47-5363, www.naranjoenflor.com.ar, US$74 d) occupies a forested lot with views of Lago Nahuel Huapi and the Andes. It also has a pool, and a restaurant that pulls in nonguests as well, so the slightly more expensive half-board option is worth consideration.

Set among large lush gardens, **Hostería El Establo** (Los Maquis 56, tel. 02944/49-4142, www.hosteriaelestablo.com.ar, US$71 s, US$95 d) is an Andean lodge that offers 14 comfortable rooms with individualized decor plus engaging common areas and an excellent buffet breakfast. It's one of the town's best values.

Across the Río Correntoso, three kilometers northwest of El Cruce, the historic **Hotel Correntoso** (tel. 02944/15-61-9728, tel.

011/4803-0030 in Buenos Aires, www.correntoso.com, US$220–320 s or d) started as a fishing lodge in 1917 and became a major attraction before burning down. Once nearly abandoned, it has undergone a rehab that has restored its former glory and more. There's a lakeside fishing bar, a wine bar, and an outstanding restaurant as well.

A short distance west of town, the **Sol Arrayan Hotel & Spa** (RN 231 Km 64.5, tel. 02944/48-8000, www.solarrayan.com, US$194–293 s or d) benefits from a sloping lot that insulates it from highway noise. It benefits even more from assiduous service and 42 luminous lake-view rooms with balconies, plus common areas that include a restaurant, a wine bar, and a spa that includes an indoor-outdoor pool.

The area's standout is the Relais & Chateaux affiliate **(Hostería Las Balsas** (tel. 02944/49-4308, www.lasbalsas.com, from US$480 d), a 12-room, three-suite Bustillo classic south of El Cruce. All rooms have lake views; rates include unlimited spa access and breakfast, and there's a highly regarded hybrid restaurant with French and traditional Argentine dishes.

Food

In addition to hotel restaurants, Villa la Angostura offers a diversity of dining options at moderate to upmarket prices.

La Buena Vida (Avenida Arrayanes 167, Local 4, tel. 02944/49-5200) is a small homey place that serves a fine risotto. **La Camorra** (Avenida Cerro Bayo 65, Local 3, tel. 02944/49-5554) offers a blend of Italian, Spanish, and criollo cuisine with dishes such as stews, pot roast, polenta, focaccia, and especially risotto.

Not necessarily the area's best, but conceivably its best value, moderately priced **(La Encantada** (Cerro Belvedere 69, tel. 02944/49-5515, US$10–15) serves exceptional *ahumados* (smoked appetizers), exquisite trout empanadas, and fine pizzas and pastas, with attentive service (including savvy wine recommendations).

In the same building, **Tolomeo** (Cerro Belvedere 69, tel. 02944/48-8083) gets enthusiastic recommendations from locals for its European-style cuisine and intimate bar.

Set on wooded grounds, Puerto Manzano's **(Waldhaus** (Avenida Arrayanes 6431, tel. 02944/49-5123, www.saboresdelneuquen.com.ar) serves Continental-style dishes like carpaccio, fondue, goulash, and raclette with a Patagonian touch. With entrées well upwards of US$10, chef Leo Morsella's restaurant is open for lunch and for dinner (when reservations are obligatory) and has a fine wine list.

Under the same ownership as Waldhaus, **La Caballeriza** (Avenida Arrayanes 44, tel. 02944/49-4248, www.lacaballeriza-argentina.com) is a *parrilla* that has several branches in Buenos Aires, but this is the first in Patagonia. It has kept the pastas and desserts of Morsella's previous restaurant, La Macarena.

Reservations are critical at the star of the cuisine scene, the **(Tinto Bistro** (Bulevar Nahuel Huapi 34, tel. 02944/49-4924). Run by brother-to-royalty Martín Zorreguieta (sister Máxima married Holland's Crown Prince William in 2002), it offers Asian-Patagonian fusion food, with entrées in the US$8–11 range. Typical dishes include appetizers like Patagonian roll with lamb dipped in honey–soy sauce and Thai-flavored pastas with shrimp and crayfish (spicy by Argentine standards). Open for dinner only, it offers the area's finest wine list (including very expensive vintages).

Tante Frida (Avenida Arrayanes 209) is a teahouse with fine ice cream. Still the best, though, is **Eiscafé** (Avenida Arrayanes 40, tel. 02944/49-5671), which carries a selection of premium ice cream flavors from El Bolsón's Jauja.

Information and Services

The **Secretaría Municipal de Turismo** (Avenida Arrayanes 9, El Cruce, tel. 02944/49-4124, www.villalaangostura.gov.ar) is open 8:30 A.M.–9 P.M. daily in summer, 8:30 A.M.–8 P.M. daily in winter.

The APN's **Seccional Villa la Angostura** (Nahuel Huapi s/n, tel. 02944/49-4152) is in La Villa.

Virtually all services are in El Cruce, where **Banco Patagonia** (Avenida Arrayanes 275) has an ATM. **Cambio Andina** (Avenida Arrayanes 256) is a currency exchange house. **Correo Argentino** is at Las Fucsias 121; the postal code is 8407. **New System** (Avenida Arrayanes 21, Local 2) has long-distance phones and Internet connections. **Hora Cero** (Avenida Arrayanes 45) is a Wi-Fi café.

Getting There

El Cruce's convenient **Terminal de Ómnibus** (Avenida Siete Lagos and Avenida Arrayanes, tel. 02944/49-4961) has frequent connections to Bariloche, several buses daily to San Martín de los Andes via the scenic Siete Lagos route, and long-distance services to Neuquén. Chile-bound buses from Bariloche stop here, but reservations are advisable because they often run full.

Sample destinations include Bariloche (1.5 hours, US$4.50), San Martín de los Andes (3 hours, US$9), and Neuquén (6 hours, US$20).

SAN CARLOS DE BARILOCHE AND VICINITY

If Patagonia ever became independent, its logical capital might be San Carlos de Bariloche, the highest-profile destination in an area explorer Francisco P. Moreno once called "this beautiful piece of Argentine Switzerland." It's not just that Bariloche, with its incomparable Nahuel Huapi setting, is the lakes district's largest city, transportation hub, and gateway to Argentina's first national park; in the 1930s the carved granite blocks and rough-hewn polished timbers of its landmark Centro Cívico set a promising precedent for harmonizing urban expansion with wilder surroundings.

Dating from 1902, Bariloche was slow to grow—when former U.S. President Theodore Roosevelt visited in 1913, he observed:

> Bariloche is a real frontier village…. It was like one of our frontier towns in the old-time West as regards the diversity in ethnic type and nationality among the citizens. The little houses stood well away

© WAYNE BERNHARDSON

For nearly eight decades, the Club Andino Bariloche has promoted mountain recreation in the area.

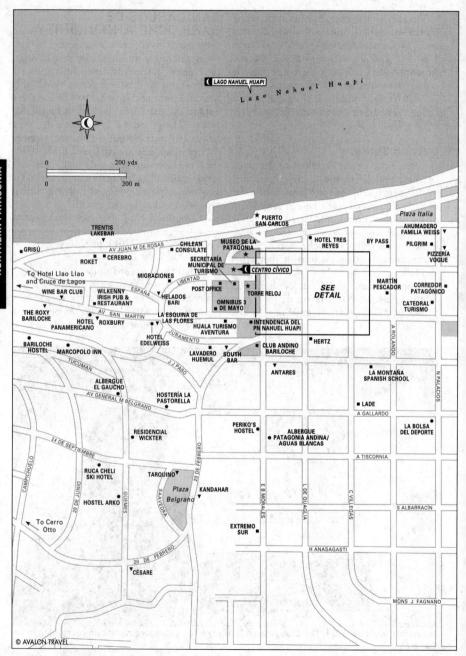

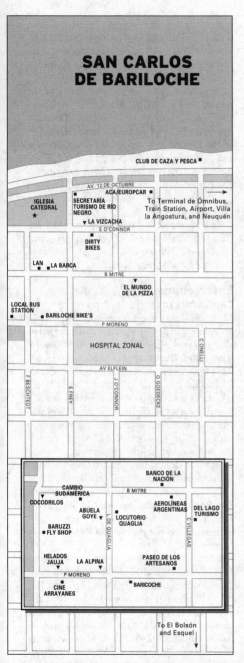

SAN CARLOS DE BARILOCHE

NORTHERN PATAGONIA

from one another on the broad, rough, faintly marked streets.

When Roosevelt crossed the Andes from Chile, Bariloche was more than 700 kilometers from the nearest railroad, but it boomed after completion of the Ferrocarril Roca's southern branch in 1934. Its rustically sophisticated style has spread throughout the region—even to phone booths—but unrelenting growth, promoted by unscrupulous politicians and developers, has detracted from its Euro-Andean charm. For much of the day, for instance, the Bariloche Center, a multistory monstrosity authorized by the brief and irregular repeal of height-limit legislation, literally overshadows the Centro Cívico.

As the population has grown from about 60,000 to 90,000 in the past 25 years, its congested *microcentro* has become a clutter of chocolate shops, hotels, and time-shares, and notorious for high-school graduation bashes that leave hotel rooms in ruins. Student tourism is declining, in relative terms at least, but Bariloche still lags behind aspirations that were once higher than Cerro Catedral's ski areas. Like other Patagonian destinations, it booms in the summer months of December, January, and February.

Bariloche holds a unique place in Argentine cinema as the location for Emilio Vieyra's *Sangre de Vírgenes* (Blood of the Virgins), a Hammer-style vampire flick that was ahead of its time when shot in 1967 (it's available on DVD). Perhaps Vieyra envisaged the unsavory things to come, but Bariloche's bloodsuckers are only part of the story—the city and its surroundings still have much to offer, at reasonable cost. Many of the best accommodations, restaurants, and other services lie along or near Avenida Bustillo between Bariloche proper and Llao Llao, about 25 kilometers west.

Orientation

On Lago Nahuel Huapi's southeastern shore, 764 meters above sea level, Bariloche (pop. 89,475) is 1,596 kilometers from Buenos Aires and 429 kilometers southwest of Neuquén via

RN 237, but 982 kilometers west of Viedma, Río Negro Province's coastal capital. It is 123 kilometers north of El Bolsón via RN 258.

As RN 237 enters Bariloche from the east, it becomes Costanera Avenida 12 de Octubre, Avenida Juan Manuel de Rosas, and then Avenida Bustillo, continuing west to Llao Llao. En route, it skirts the landmark Centro Cívico; one block south, the parallel Avenida Bartolomé Mitre is the main commercial street in the densely built downtown. North–south streets—some of them staircases—climb steeply from the lakeshore.

◖ Centro Cívico

Even with the kitsch merchants who pervade the plaza with Siberian huskies and Saint Bernards for photographic poses and the graffiti that often deface General Roca's equestrian statue, the array of buildings that border it would be the pride of many cities around the globe. The view to Lago Nahuel Huapi is a bonus, even when the boxy Bariloche Center blocks the sun.

The Centro Cívico was a team effort, envisioned by architect Ernesto de Estrada in 1936 and executed under APN director Exequiel Bustillo until its inauguration in 1940. When the Municipalidad's **Torre Reloj** (Clock Tower) sounds at noon, figures from Patagonian history appear to mark the hour. Other buildings of interest, with steep-pitched roofs and arched arcades that offer shelter from inclement weather, include the former **Correo** (post office, but now the tourism office) and the **Museo de la Patagonia.**

Exequiel Bustillo's brother, architect Alejandro Bustillo, designed the **Intendencia de Parques Nacionales** (National Park Headquarters, San Martín 24), one block north, to harmonize with the Centro Cívico. As a collective national monument, they represent Argentine Patagonia's best.

Museo de la Patagonia Francisco P. Moreno

At the Centro Cívico's northeast corner, Bariloche's Patagonian museum admirably attempts to place the region (and more) in ecological, cultural, and historical context. Its multiple halls touch on natural history through taxidermy (better than most of its kind); insects (inexplicably including subtropical Iguazú); Patagonia's population from antiquity to the present; the aboriginal Mapuche, Tehuelche, and Fuegian peoples; caudillo Juan Manuel de Rosas; the "Conquista del Desierto" (Conquest of the Desert) that displaced the aboriginals; and Bariloche's own urban development. There is even material on Stanford University geologist Bailey Willis, a visionary consultant who did the region's first systematic surveys in the early 20th century.

The Museo de la Patagonia (Centro Cívico s/n, tel. 02944/42-2309, US$1) is open 10 A.M.–12:30 P.M. and 2–7 P.M. Tuesday–Friday, 10 A.M.–5 P.M. Saturday.

Entertainment

Cine Arrayanes (Perito Moreno 39, tel. 02944/42-2860) shows recent movies.

A cluster of downtown bars also offer palatable pub grub. Choices include the **Wilkenny Irish Pub & Restaurant** (San Martín 435, tel. 02944/42-4444, www.wilkennybariloche.com.ar) and the comparable **Pilgrim** (Palacios 167, tel. 02944/42-1686, www.pilgrim.com.ar). Popular **Antares** (Elflein 47, tel. 02944/43-1454, www.cervezaantares.com) is a brewpub with a decent food menu of German specialties and sandwiches to complement the suds. **South Bar** (Juramento 30, tel. 02944/52-2001) is also popular with the pub-crawlers.

For live music, there are two good choices: **The Roxy Bariloche** (San Martín 580), a bar-restaurant that's a branch of its Buenos Aires namesake, and the nearby **The Roxbury** (San Martín 490).

Bariloche nightspots open late—around 1 A.M.—and close around daybreak. The most central is the youthful **By Pass** (Rolando 157, tel. 02944/42-0549, www.bypass.com.ar). Several others lie a few blocks west of the Centro Cívico: **Cerebro** (Juan Manuel de Rosas 406, tel. 02944/42-4948, www.cerebro.com.ar), **Roket** (Juan Manuel de Rosas

424, tel. 02944/43-1940, www.roket.com), and **Grisú** (Juan Manuel de Rosas 574, tel. 02944/42-2269, www.grisu.com).

Events

More than just a pretty landscape, Nahuel Huapi has an active cultural life. Llao Llao's Camping Musical Bariloche (www.camping-musicalbche.org.ar) sponsors chamber music and brass concerts at the **Festival de Música de Verano** in January and February.

March's **Muestra Floral de Otoño** is an end-of-summer flower show. May 3 marks the **Fiesta Nacional de la Rosa Mosqueta,** when local bakers and confectioners make the most of the wild rose hips, a European introduction that has become an ecological pest. July's **Fiesta Nacional de la Nieve** (National Snow Festival) marks the start of ski season.

Gardeners again get their turn at October's **Fiesta del Tulipán** (Tulip Festival) and the **Muestra Floral de Primavera** (Spring Flower Show). Late December brings the **Navidad Coral** (Christmas Chorus).

Shopping

Local artisans live off souvenir hunters who frequent the **Paseo de los Artesanos** (Villegas and Perito Moreno, 10 A.M.–9 P.M. daily).

The **Wine Bar Club** (Avenida San Martín 597, tel. 02944/43-6300) carries a wide selection of reds and whites. Chocoholics flock to **Abuela Goye** (Quaglia 221, tel. 02944/42-3311), and similar locales.

La Barca (Mitre 534, Local 3, tel. 02944/43-6744) has a good selection of books and maps.

Sports and Recreation

Because of Parque Nacional Nahuel Huapi, Bariloche is the base for outdoor activities ranging from fishing, hiking, and climbing to mountain biking, horseback riding, white-water rafting and kayaking, and skiing.

Mid-November–mid-April, the entire region is a **fishing** enthusiast's paradise for its lakes (where trolling is the rule) and streams (for fly-fishing). The **Club de Caza y Pesca** (Costanera

12 de Octubre and Onelli, tel. 02944/42-1515, www.apcnh.com) is a good information source. For rental gear, try **Baruzzi Fly Shop** (Urquiza 250, tel. 02944/42-4922) or **Martín Pescador** (Rolando 257, tel. 02944/42-2275, martinpescador@bariloche.com.ar).

Non-Argentines can purchase licenses at the APN's Intendencia on the Centro Cívico for US$20 per day, US$66 per week, or US$92 per season; there are additional charges for trolling permits.

The APN can provide hiking and climbing information, but the best source is the **Club Andino Bariloche** (20 de Febrero 30, tel. 02944/42-2266, www.clubandino.org), which also organizes excursions and sells trail maps.

Bariloche's roads, both paved and gravel, and many wide trails make **cycling** an attractive option. Mountain-bike rental, with gloves and helmet, costs about US$15 per day. **Dirty Bikes** (Eduardo O'Connor 681, tel. 02944/42-5616, www.dirtybikes.com.ar) rents bikes and also offers half-day to multiday excursions that include other activities as well. **Bariloche Bike's** (Moreno 520, tel. 02944/42-4657) also rents bikes and gear. **Bike Cordillera** (Avenida Bustillo Km 18.6, tel. 02944/53-4828, www.cordillerabike.com) starts its tours beyond the busiest, narrowest sector of the Circuito Chico. **Bike Way** (Moreno 237, tel. 02944/45-6571, www.bikeway.com.ar) has similar offerings and longer trips.

Local **horseback-riding** trips can last from two hours (about US$15) to a full day (US$35–50 with lunch), with mult-day excursions also possible. The main operators are **Cabalgatas Carol Jones** (Modesta Victoria 5600, tel. 02944/42-6508, www.caroljones.com.ar) and **Estancia Fortín Chacabuco** (tel. 02944/55-4148, www.estanciaspatagonicas.com).

For **rafting and kayaking,** the Río Limay is a half-day Class II float through agreeable scenery east of Bariloche. The more challenging Río Manso, midway between Bariloche and El Bolsón to the south, is a full-day, mostly Class III descent (around US$70 pp) with some taxing Class IV rapids on multi-day trips.

River operators include **Aguas Blancas** (Morales 564, tel. 02944/43-2799, www.aguas-blancas.com.ar), **Extremo Sur** (Morales 765, tel. 02944/42-7301, www.extremosur.com), and **Huala Turismo Aventura** (San Martín 66, tel. 02944/52-2438, www.patagoniarafting.com).

Accommodations

Bariloche has plentiful accommodations options in all categories, from camping to hostels, B&Bs, hotels, and luxury lodges. Hostels in particular have proliferated. The finest hotels are west of the city proper, on and along the Llao Llao road.

The municipal tourist office keeps a thorough accommodations database and, when summer demand is high, they're an excellent resource. Since many low-priced to midrange hotels cater to high school graduation trips, it's better to avoid them toward the end of December.

UNDER US$10

The lakefront **Camping Petunia** (Avenida Bustillo 13500, tel. 02944/46-1969, www.campingpetunia.com, US$6 pp for adults, US$4 pp for kids) is one of numerous campgrounds west of town.

US$10-25

Most places in this range are hostels that have dorms as well as private rooms that are only slightly more expensive on a per-person basis, with the quality of an above-average hotel. They also offer amenities such as Wi-Fi and sometimes even include dinner in their rates.

On wooded grounds in a quiet barrio west of town, **Alaska Hostel** (Lilinquén 326, tel. 02944/46-1564, www.alaska-hostel.com, US$12 pp dorm, US$32–37 d) is walking distance from Avenida Bustillo Km 7.5. Several buses, including Nos. 10, 20, and 21, will drop passengers here.

Under the same management, **(** **Periko's Hostel** (Morales 555, tel. 02944/52-2326, www.perikos.com, US$12 pp dorm, US$35–42 d) has mostly dorm rooms but also some new

stylish doubles (the cheaper ones have shared baths) on the upper floors. The secluded garden is uncommon in this part of town.

La Bolsa del Deporte (Palacios 405, tel. 02944/42-3529, www.labolsadeldeporte.com.ar, US$12 pp dorm, US$42 d) is cheap but well-established.

Only 500 meters west of the bus terminal, the HI affiliate **Tango Inn Soho** (12 de Octubre 1915, tel. 02944/43-0707, www.tangoinn.com, US$12 pp dorm, US$40–45 s or d) has a restaurant, a cafeteria, and a bar.

Also good is the **Albergue El Gaucho** (Belgrano 209, tel. 02944/52-2464, www.hostelelgaucho.com, US$12 pp dorm, US$45 d), which has mostly dorms but also a handful of doubles, all with private baths. It also rents bicycles, and the staff can manage English, German, and Italian.

New in 2008, Barrio Belgrano's **(** **Hostel Arko** (Güemes 685, tel. 02944/42-3109, www.eco-family.com, US$13 pp dorm, US$46 d) is, as the URL suggests, a family-run place with a long history in the area and the neighborhood—when space is short here, hostellers can hop next door to one of Bariloche's oldest, most hospitable B&Bs and still enjoy services such as the kitchen, laundry, Wi-Fi, and great advice from the mountaineering staff.

US$25-50

Several hostels with private rooms, mentioned above, are at least as good as standard accommodations in this range.

In the hostel-with-a-view category, it's tough to top friendly **Bariloche Hostel** (Salta 528, tel. 02944/42-5460, www.barilochehostel.com.ar, US$15 pp dorm, US$45 d), a converted residence where both dorms and doubles have private baths. The lake panoramas are even better from the deck on the slope behind the house, where there's a magnificently productive pear tree and other fruit trees.

The HI affiliate **Marcopolo Inn** (Salta 422, tel. 02944/40-0105, www.marcopoloinn.com.ar, US$15 pp dorm, US$52 d) is a converted hotel whose rooms, all with private baths, are more spacious than most hostels. Rates include not just breakfast but also dinner (9–10 P.M. in the bar) and free Internet and Wi-Fi. There is also low-cost laundry service.

Well-located places include Barrio Belgrano's **Residencial Wikter** (Güemes 566, tel. 02944/42-3248, hospedajewikter@gmail.com. ar, US$35 d) and **Hostería Güemes** (Güemes 715, tel. 02944/42-4785, US$50 d).

US$50-100

On the Llao Llao road, cozy ❰ **Hostería Pájaro Azul** (Avenida Bustillo 10800, tel. 02944/46-1025, www.hosteriapajaroazul.com. ar, US$50 s, US$56 d) has eight pine-paneled rooms with mountain views through relatively small windows.

Some of the 13 rooms at **Hostería La Pastorella** (Avenida Belgrano 127, tel. 02944/42-4656, www.lapastorella.com.ar, US$41 s, US$58 d) are a little too cozy for comfort, but it does offer a diverse breakfast and amenities including a sauna.

Built in an Austrian style, Barrio Belgrano's **Hostería Las Marianas** (24 de Septiembre 218, tel. 02944/43-9876, www.hosterialasmarianas.com.ar, US$64–74 s or d) is a friendly, family-run inn with only 16 rooms—each named for a nearby Andean peak.

Barrio Belgrano's upgraded **Ruca Cheli Village Ski Hotel** (24 de Setiembre 275, tel./ fax 02944/42-4528, www.rucacheli.com. ar, US$70 s, US$86 d, with buffet breakfast) has reasonably large rooms and obliging management.

US$100-200

Surprisingly, there's not much in this price range. The lakefront ❰ **Hotel Tres Reyes** (Avenida 12 de Octubre 135, tel. 02944/42-6121, www.hoteltresreyes.com, US$89–100 s, US$95–109 d), a stylishly rehabbed classic dating from 1951, is a reliable downtown hotel whose higher rates correspond to lake views. Some rooms are smallish, but even these can rise in price in ski season.

It's past its prime, but **La Posada del Angel** (Avenida Bustillo Km 12.5, tel. 02944/46-1263, www.posadadelangel.com.ar, US$90

s, US$110 d) does enjoy friendly family service, a large pool, and five pine-sheltered hectares. The rooms are ample and comfortable, but small windows limit the light and alpine views.

Highly regarded **Hostería Los Juncos** (Avenida Bustillo Km 20, tel. 02944/44-8485, www.visitlosjuncos.com, US$130 d) is a seven-room B&B on Bahía Campanario.

OVER US$200

Downtown's most prestigious option is **Hotel Panamericano** (San Martín 536, tel. 02944/42-5846, www.panamericanobariloche. com, US$206–230 s or d), a sprawling complex on both sides of the avenue, linked by glassed-in elevated bridges. It also holds a casino and a spa, but it's not up to the standards—not to mention the style or location—of places like the Llao Llao. Rates vary according to the view (none or lake).

Hotel Edelweiss (San Martín 202, tel. 02944/44-5500, www.edelweiss.com.ar, US$235–255 s or d) has 100 spacious standard to superior rooms, plus more elaborate suites. Price can rise by half in ski season.

Llao Llao's ❰ **Hotel Tunquelén** (Avenida Bustillo Km 24, tel. 02944/44-8600, www. tunquelen.com, US$240–510 s or d) might be the area's top choice were it not for the nearby Hotel Llao Llao. Unlike some hotels here, it has managed to stabilize its rates.

Part of a golf development near Lago Gutiérrez, the 23-room **Arelauquen Lodge** (RP 82 Km 4.5, tel. 02944/47-6110, www. arelauquenlodge.com, US$278–575 d) is the latest entry in the local luxury-lodge sweepstakes. Rates vary according to whether the rooms have mountain or golf-course views.

Part of a six-hotel chain scattered between Salta and Ushuaia, informal despite its exclusivity, ❰ **Design Suites Bariloche** (Avenida Bustillo Km 2.5, tel. 02944/45-7000, www. designsuites.com, US$333–610 s or d) differs from all of its kin in setting and architecture. In this case, the common areas consist of a luminous clubhouse with cathedral ceilings and views over Nahuel Huapi as well as an

NORTHERN PATAGONIA

indoor-outdoor pool, a gym, and sauna facilities. The accommodations proper occupy three separate buildings with greater setbacks from the busy avenue; all rooms enjoy lake views (and whirlpool tubs, some of them with views as well).

Not just a hotel but a landmark in its own right, **Hotel Llao Llao** (Avenida Bustillo Km 25, tel. 02944/44-8530, www.llaollao. com, US$240–2,360 s or d) is an Alejandro Bustillo classic dating from 1940, its interior completely renovated in the 1990s. Rates depend on the room's size, views, and amenities as well as the season.

New in 2005, built into the slopes of Península San Pedro, the **Aldebarán Hotel & Spa** (Avenida Bustillo 20400, Península San Pedro, tel. 02944/44-8678, www.aldebaranpatagonia. com, US$254–356 s or d plus taxes) is a strikingly modern view hotel with panoramas to Cerro Campanario, Cerro López, and beyond. The rustically stylish rooms are enormous, 35–45 square meters plus huge baths, with balconies overlooking the lake. It also boasts a good restaurant and enjoys contemporary spa facilities.

Food

For breakfast, coffee, sandwiches, and sweets, try *confiterías* like **La Alpina** (Perito Moreno 98, tel. 02944/42-5693).

Bariloche abounds in pizzerias, starting with the inexpensive, unpretentious, and excellent **Cocodrilos** (Mitre 5, tel. 02944/42-6640, lunch and dinner daily), although **El Mundo de la Pizza** (Mitre 759, tel. 02944/42-3461, lunch and dinner daily) has greater variety. In addition to pizza, **Césare** (20 de Febrero 788, tel. 02944/43-2060, lunch and dinner daily) prepares around 20 kinds of empanadas.

Even the staff seem to be enjoying themselves at the informal **Trentis Lakebar** (Juan Manuel de Rosas 435, tel. 02944/42-2350, lunch and dinner daily), with a menu of inexpensive sandwiches, the occasional oddity (for Argentina) such as quesadillas (probably unrecognizable to most Californians, but not bad), and good vibes. Lake views and Wi-Fi are bonuses, but it gets crowded.

On the Llao Llao road, the **Berlina Brew House & Restaurante** (Avenida Bustillo 11750, tel. 02944/52-3336, www.

Few accommodations enjoy a more spectacular setting than the historic Hotel Llao Llao.

© WAYNE BERNHARDSON

cervezaberlina.com) offers beer samplers and excellent sandwiches plus pizzas, pastas, and a few standard Argentine dishes such as bife de chorizo. Open from 1 P.M., it has an outdoor beer garden and a 5–7 P.M. happy hour.

Only a short distance west, **Bahía Serena** (Avenida Bustillo 12275, tel. 02944/52-4614, lunch and dinner daily) specializes in pastas and is one of few Bariloche restaurants to enjoy a lakefront location and even an adjacent small sandy beach. Game dishes are also on the menu, but pastas remain the best choice (though some stuffed pastas feature wild game).

For smoked *ciervo* (venison), *jabalí* (wild boar), and *trucha* (trout), visit expanded **Ahumadero Familia Weiss** (Palacios and V. A. O'Connor, tel. 02944/43-5789, www.restauranteweiss.com, lunch and dinner daily), a tourist-oriented *parrilla* and beer garden that also packages these items for takeaway. Specialties include pork loin with raspberry sauce and applesauce with a side of spaetzle (US$11).

In new tobacco-free quarters, **La Vizcacha** (Eduardo O'Connor 630, tel. 02944/42-2109, lunch and dinner daily) is a venerable downtown *parrilla*. The full-sized *bife de chorizo* at ◖ **El Boliche de Alberto** (Avenida Bustillo Km 8.8, tel. 02944/46-2285, www.elbolichedealberto.com, lunch and dinner daily) will challenge all but the most ravenous adolescents; even the half-portion (US$9) may be too large for a single diner and some couples.

Primarily a *parrilla* but also serving excellent trout, ◖ **Tarquino** (24 de Septiembre and Saavedra, tel. 02944/42-1601, www.virtuosoytarquino.com.ar, lunch and dinner daily) is a Hansel-and-Gretel construction with high ceilings that has been erected around living trees. Most entrées, including venison ravioli and *ñoquis,* cost around US$8–9, but a handful are dearer.

Despite the name, ◖ **Kandahar** (20 de Febrero 698, tel. 02944/42-4702, www.kandahar.com.ar, dinner only) does not serve Afghan food but rather Patagonian game dishes such as a venison casserole garnished with applesauce and red cabbage (US$12) in intimate

surroundings with a Sinatra soundtrack. The service is excellent, the kitchen involved, but the dessert menu is weak.

Camouflaged in residential Barrio Belgrano, ◖ **Naan** (Campichuelo 568, tel. 02944/42-1785, naan@restaurante.com.ar, dinner only) produces a truly cosmopolitan menu of local dishes with creative touches, complemented by French, Italian, Mexican, and even Vietnamese entrées in moderately sized and flavorful portions. Entrées start around US$10, the service is highly individual, and two huge picture windows offer panoramas of Bariloche, Nahuel Huapi, and the cordillera behind the lake.

Relocated to Lago Gutiérrez, **Cassis** (Peñon de Arelauquen, RP 82, tel. 02944/47-6167, www.cassis.com.ar, dinner only) is a gourmet-style Patagonian restaurant specializing in game dishes.

For *picadas,* pizzas, and draft beer, don't miss ◖ **Cervecería Blest** (Avenida Bustillo 11600, tel. 02944/46-1026, lunch and dinner daily, US$10); it closes relatively early, at midnight.

Despite its intimidating size, cavernous ◖ **El Patacón** (Avenida Bustillo Km 7, tel. 02944/44-2898, www.elpatacon.com, lunch and dinner daily, US$20) has personalized service and meticulously prepared food. Former U.S. President Bill Clinton dined on dishes such as the *provoletta* appetizer and venison ravioli, whose prices are rapidly rising.

Bariloche has exceptional ice creameries, starting with **Abuela Goye** (Quaglia 221, tel. 02944/42-2311). The real standout, though, is **Helados Jauja** (Perito Moreno 18, tel. 02944/43-7888; Palacios 156), whose dizzying diversity includes unconventional wild fruit flavors, half a dozen or more kinds of chocolate, and the remarkable *mate cocido.* (There's even greater variety at its home base in El Bolsón.)

Information
The **Secretaría Municipal de Turismo** (Centro Cívico s/n, tel. 02944/42-9850 or 02944/42-9896, www.barilochepatagonia.info) is open 8 A.M.–9 P.M. daily, but in peak season it's overrun with visitors seeking accommodations and other information. There are

satellite offices at the bus terminal (Avenida 12 de Octubre 2400) and at the airport.

The APN's **Intendencia del Parque Nacional Nahuel Huapi** (San Martín 24, tel. 02944/42-3111, www.nahuelhuapi.gov.ar) is one block south of the Centro Cívico. Another block south, the **Club Andino Bariloche** (20 de Febrero 30, tel. 02944/42-4531, www.clubandino.org) provides information and park hiking permits; it's open 9:30 A.M.–1 P.M. and 4:30–8:30 P.M. Monday–Saturday.

For motorists, **ACA** (tel. 02944/42-2611) is at 12 de Octubre 785.

Services

Cambio Sudamérica (Mitre 63) changes foreign cash and traveler's checks. **Banco de la Nación** (Mitre 180) is one of many downtown banks with ATMs.

Correo Argentino (Moreno 175), the post office, has moved from the Centro Cívico; the postal code is 8400.

Locutorio Quaglia (Quaglia 220) has phone, fax, and Internet, but there are also countless others.

Del Lago Turismo (Villegas 222, tel. 02944/43-0056, www.dellagoturismo.com.ar) is a full-service agency that will arrange a variety of excursions around the area.

Another option is **Chaltén Travel** (Moreno 126, Local 3, tel. 02944/45-6005, www.chaltentravel.com), which offers transportation and tours along both RN 40 (to El Chaltén and El Calafate) and Chile's Carretera Austral (reentering Argentina at Los Antiguos). They also offer trips near Bariloche and as far afield as Ushuaia.

La Montaña Spanish School (Elflein 251, tel. 02944/52-4212, www.lamontana.com) charges US$160 per week for 20 hours of instruction.

Chile has a **consulate** (tel. 02944/42-2842) at Avenida Juan Manuel de Rosas 180. For visa matters, visit the **Dirección Nacional de Migraciones** (Libertad 191, tel. 02944/42-3043).

Lavadero Huemul (Juramento 37, tel. 02944/52-2067) is one of many laundries.

The **Hospital Zonal** (tel. 02944/42-6119) is at Perito Moreno 601.

Getting There

Bariloche is northern Argentine Patagonia's transportation hub and has regional and international connections.

LAN (Mitre 534, Local 1, tel. 02944/43-1043) now flies between Santiago (Chile) and Bariloche Fridays and Sundays, sometimes via the southern Chilean city of Puerto Montt, and has added domestic flights to Buenos Aires.

Aerolíneas Argentinas (Mitre 185, tel. 02944/42-2425) flights to Buenos Aires normally go to Aeroparque, but a few flights make international connections at Ezeiza; a handful go to El Calafate, and there's the occasional connection to Esquel and Trelew.

Bariloche is something of a hub for **LADE** (Villegas 480, tel. 02944/42-3562), with cheap flights to Buenos Aires and to other Patagonian destinations, but most of these are only weekly, and schedules often change.

On the eastern outskirts of town, across the Río Ñireco, Bariloche's **Terminal de Ómnibus** (Avenida 12 de Octubre s/n, tel. 02944/43-2860) is immediately east of the train station. There are international services (to Osorno and Puerto Montt, Chile), long-distance buses throughout the republic, and provincial and regional routes.

Chaltén Travel (Moreno 126, Local 3, tel. 02944/42-3809, www.chaltentravel.com) offers bus services along southbound RN 40 to El Chaltén and El Calafate (31 hours, US$116) via the town of Perito Moreno, with overnights (at additional cost) in Perito Moreno. In peak summer season, southbound departures are at 7 A.M. on odd-numbered days.

Four companies cross the Andes to the Chilean cities of Osorno (5.5 hours) and Puerto Montt (6.5 hours, US$21): **Andesmar** (tel. 02944/43-0211), **Bus Norte** (tel. 02944/43-0303), **Tas Choapa** (tel. 02944/42-2288), and **Cruz del Sur** (tel. 02944/42-2818). Most leave by 10 A.M.

Sample domestic destinations include Villa La Angostura (1.5 hours, US$4.50), El Bolsón

(2 hours, US$7), San Martín de los Andes (3.5 hours, US$12), Esquel (4 hours, US$12–16), Neuquén (5.5 hours, US$16–23), Viedma (14 hours, US$40), Trelew (13 hours, US$38–53), Puerto Madryn (14 hours, US$40–55), Comodoro Rivadavia (12 hours, US$38–50), Buenos Aires (19–20 hours, US$61–96), and Río Gallegos (24 hours, US$70).

Immediately west of the bus terminal, **Sefepa** (Avenida 12 de Octubre s/n, tel. 02944/43-1777, www.trenpatagonico-sa.com.ar) connects Bariloche with Viedma via **train** at 6 P.M. Monday and Friday. The 15-hour trip costs US$15 in hard-backed *económica,* US$32 in reclining Pullman, or US$60 in *camarote* sleepers; children ages 5–12 pay half.

Cruce Andino (www.cruceandino.com) operates the bus-boat shuttle over the Andes to Puerto Montt, Chile (US$230 pp without lunch), via Puerto Pañuelo, Puerto Blest, Puerto Frías, Peulla (Chile), Petrohué, and Puerto Varas. With an overnight at Peulla, the trip costs US$350–378 pp, depending on the hotel. For bookings, contact **Catedral Turismo** (Palacios 263, tel. 02944/42-5444). Foreigners pay an additional US$4.50 in national park entry fees; it's possible to do this trip in segments or as a round-trip, for example from Puerto Pañuelo to Puerto Blest and back.

Getting Around

Aeropuerto Teniente Candelaria (tel. 02944/42-2767) is 15 kilometers east of Bariloche via RN 237 and RP 80. Micro Ómnibus 3 de Mayo's No. 72 bus goes directly there (US$1), while cabs and *remises* cost about US$5.

From the corner of San Martín and Pagano, **Ómnibus 3 de Mayo** (tel. 02944/42-5648) goes to Cerro Catedral (US$1.50) hourly 7:15 A.M.–7:15 P.M., sometimes via Avenida de los Pioneros and others via Avenida Bustillo.

For most of the day, Ómnibus 3 de Mayo's No. 20 bus goes every 20 minutes to Llao Llao and Puerto Pañuelo, which is also the final destination of some of its seven Nos. 10 and 11 buses via Colonia Suiza on the Circuito Chico route through Parque Nacional Nahuel Huapi, but through the night it's only every hour or so.

Ómnibus 3 de Mayo's Nos. 50 and 51 buses go to Lago Gutiérrez (US$1.50) every 30 minutes, while in summer its Línea Mascardi goes to Villa Mascardi (US$2.50) and Puente Los Rápidos (US$3) at 9:10 A.M., 1:10 P.M., and 6:10 P.M. daily. Their Línea Manso goes twice on Friday to Río Villegas and El Manso (US$4), on Parque Nacional Nahuel Huapi's southwestern edge.

Bariloche has several car-rental agencies, including **Baricoche** (Moreno 115, 1st floor, tel. 02944/42-7638), **Budget** (Mitre 106, 1st floor, Oficina 4, tel. 02944/42-2482), **Europcar** (12 de Octubre 785, tel. 02944/45-6594), and **Hertz** (Quaglia 352, tel. 02944/42-3457).

PARQUE NACIONAL NAHUEL HUAPI

In 1903, Patagonian explorer Francisco Pascasio Moreno donated three square leagues of "the most beautiful scenery my eyes had ever seen," at Lago Nahuel Huapi's west end near the Chilean border, to "be conserved as a natural public park." Citing the United States' example in creating large public reserves, Moreno's burst of idealism returned part of a personal land grant to the Argentine state. First known as Parque Nacional del Sur, the property became today's Parque Nacional Nahuel Huapi.

Since then, countless Argentine and foreign visitors have benefited from Moreno's civic generosity in a reserve that now encompasses a far larger area of glacial lakes and limpid rivers, forested moraines and mountains, and snow-topped Andean peaks that mark the border. So many have done so, in fact, that it's debatable whether authorities have complied with Moreno's wish that "the current features of their perimeter not be altered, and that there be no additional constructions other than those that facilitate the comforts of the cultured visitor."

Prior to the "Conquest of the Desert," Araucanian peoples freely crossed the Andes via the Paso de los Vuriloches south of 3,554-meter Cerro Tronador. The pass lent its name to Bariloche, which, over a century since its 1903 founding, has morphed from lakeside hamlet to a sprawling city whose wastes imperil the air, water, and surrounding woodlands.

For all that, Nahuel Huapi remains a beauty spot that connects two countries via a series of scenic roads and waterways. In 1979, Argentine and Chilean military dictatorships fortified the borders and mined the approaches because of a territorial dispute elsewhere, but a papal intervention cleared the air and perhaps reflected Moreno's aspirations:

This land of beauty in the Andes is home to a colossal peak shared by two nations: Monte Tronador unites both of them.... Together, they could rest and share ideas there; they could find solutions to problems unsolved by diplomacy. Visitors from around the world would mingle and share with one another at this international crossroads.

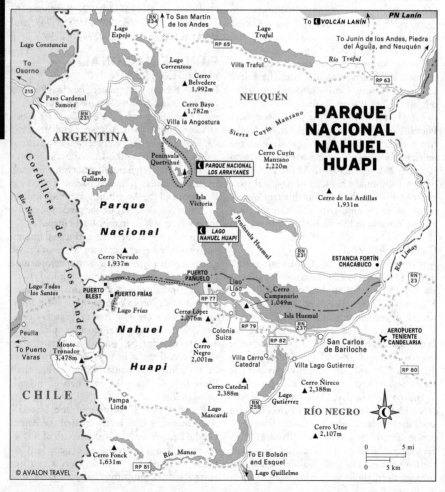

HONORING THE EXPERT: THE LEGACY OF PERITO MORENO

The career of Francisco Pascasio Moreno (1852–1919) began improbably at his father's Buenos Aires insurance agency, but by age 20, the inquisitive Moreno had founded the Sociedad Científica Argentina (Argentine Scientific Society). From 1875, when much of Patagonia was still hostile and unknown territory, he explored the Río Negro and Limay valleys up to Lago Nahuel Huapi (twice), and the Río Santa Cruz to its source at Lago San Martín. On his 1879–1880 Nahuel Huapi expedition, he fell prisoner to previously friendly Manzanero Indians – for whom he evinced a sympathy that was unfashionable during General Roca's Conquista del Desierto (Conquest of the Desert) – and escaped down the Limay on a precarious log raft.

In 1884, dedicated to the public good, Moreno donated his natural history collections to the Museo Antropológico y Etnológico de Buenos Aires, which became the Museo de Historia Natural de La Plata, which U.S. surveyor Bailey Willis compared with the Smithsonian Institution. In 1897, recognizing Moreno's knowledge of the region, the government named the *perito* (expert) its delegate to a commission settling border differences with Chile; five years later, he oversaw the placement of permanent boundary markers.

The following year, honoring his services, the government granted him a Nahuel Huapi property near the Chilean border, which the altruistic Moreno gave back on the stipulation that it become the cornerstone of a national park system. Five years later, in 1908, he founded the Argentine Boy Scouts; in 1913 he hosted former U.S. President Theodore Roosevelt at Bariloche.

Only a few years later, dismayed by changes in a country that ignored his ideas, and feeling betrayed and bitter like San Martín a century earlier, Moreno died in near poverty in Buenos Aires. In Patagonia, his public legacy is a few frequently confused place-names – a street in Bariloche, his namesake lake to the west, the dusty provincial town of Perito Moreno, Parque Nacional Perito Moreno, and the famous Glaciar Perito Moreno.

Yet according to Bailey Willis (whose own name graces a peak near Bariloche), Moreno was the first to grasp Patagonia's potential as a "national asset" that needed impartial research to be properly unlocked: "Among men of Moreno's nationality, personal ambition is more often than not the ruling motive. But he was selfless where knowledge of the truth was his objective."

Orientation

Now stretching from the northerly Lago Queñi, west of San Martín de los Andes, to the southerly Río Manso, midway between Bariloche and El Bolsón, the park now covers 750,000 hectares in southwestern Neuquén and western Río Negro. Together with Parque Nacional Lanín to the north, it forms an uninterrupted stretch of well over 1 million hectares, but part of that is a *reserva nacional* that permits commercial development. At the park's western edge, Tronador is the highest of a phalanx of snow-covered border peaks.

Flora and Fauna

The park's flora and fauna resemble those of Lanín to the north and Los Alerces to the south, but differ in some respects. There are three principal ecosystems: the easterly Patagonian steppe, the Andean-Patagonian forest, and the high Andes above 1,600 meters, which consists of low shrubs and sparse grasses adapted to cold, wind, and snow.

Guanacos graze the semiarid steppe grasslands, stalked by foxes and even pumas, while raptors like the cinereous harrier and American kestrel patrol the skies. Toward the west, open woodlands of coniferous cypress, *ñire* (southern false beech), and *maitén* stand among rocky soils.

Farther west, at slightly higher altitudes, dense false beech forests of *coihue, lenga,* and *ñire* cover the slopes, while the shoreline and stream banks burst with a flowering understory of *notro* and climbing vines like *mutisia* with clusters of the cinnamon-barked *arrayán.*

Near Puerto Blest, rainfall up to 4,000 millimeters per annum supports a humid Valdivian forest of Guaiteca cypress, *Podocarpus,* and tree ferns. Nahuel Huapi, though, lacks Lanín's monkey puzzle forests, and the more southerly *alerce* tree is less abundant than in Chubut Province.

Sightings of the *huemul* (Andean deer) and the *pudú* miniature deer are rare here. Other mammals include the carnivorous *huillín* (otter) and the *tuco-tuco,* an endemic ground squirrel–like rodent.

Normally oceangoing, the king cormorant has a colony along Lago Nahuel Huapi, where the kelp gull often trails the boats that sail the lake. Nahuel Huapi, its tributary streams, and other lakes teem with trout and other fish.

Lago Nahuel Huapi

Nahuel Huapi's focal point is its namesake lake, whose fingerlike channels converge near the Llao Llao peninsula to form the main part of its 560-square-kilometer surface. With a maximum depth of 454 meters, it drains eastward into the Río Limay, a Río Negro tributary.

In the middle of Nahuel Huapi's northern arm, **Isla Victoria** once housed the APN's park ranger school (since relocated to Tucumán), which trained rangers from throughout the Americas. From Puerto Pañuelo, Turisur's *Modesta Victoria* (Mitre 219, tel. 02944/42-6109, www.turisur.com.ar) sails to the island (US$35 plus US$7 national park entry fee) at 12:15 A.M. while the *Cau Cau* (Mitre 139, tel. 02944/43-1372, www.islavictoriayarrayanes. com, US$36 plus US$7 national park entry fee) goes at 2 P.M.; both continue to Parque Nacional Los Arrayanes (which is more accessible from Villa la Angostura on the north shore). *Bioceánica Turismo* (Avenida San Martín 484, tel. 02944/43-6240, www.bioceanicaturismo. com.ar, US$32) sails at 9 A.M. and 1:30 P.M.

Circuito Chico

Bariloche's single most popular excursion leads west on Avenida Bustillo to Península Llao Llao

the Llao Llao peninsula, with Lago Nahuel Huapi and the Chilean border in the background

© WAYNE BERNHARDSON

and returns via the hamlet of Colonia Suiza, at the foot of Cerro López. En route, it passes or touches several points of interest; public buses will pick up and drop off passengers almost anywhere, and it's also popular with cyclists.

For exceptional panoramas of Nahuel Huapi and surroundings, take the **Aerosilla Campanario** (Avenida Bustillo Km 17.5, tel. 02944/42-7274, US$7 pp) to the 1,050-meter summit of **Cerro Campanario.** The chairlift operates 9 A.M.–5:30 P.M. daily, as does the restaurant-*confitería* at the summit.

The bus-boat "Cruce de Lagos" to Chile starts at **Puerto Pañuelo,** but excursions to Isla Victoria and Parque Nacional Los Arrayanes (across the lake) also leave from here. The outstanding cultural landmark is the **Hotel Llao Llao** (Avenida Bustillo Km 25, tel. 02944/44-8530, www.llaollao.com), a Bustillo creation open to nonguests for guided tours (free of charge, except for parking).

Almost immediately west of Puerto Pañuelo, a level footpath from the parking area leads southwest to an *arrayán* forest in **Parque Municipal Llao Llao;** the trail rejoins the paved road at **Lago Escondido.** The road itself passes a trailhead for **Cerro Llao Llao,** a short but stiff climb that offers fine panoramas of Nahuel Huapi and the Andean crest. On the descent, the trail joins a gravel road that rejoins the paved road from Puerto Pañuelo, which leads south before looping northeast toward Bariloche; a gravel alternative heads east to **Colonia Suiza,** known for its Sunday crafts fair (in summer also on Wednesday). There is also a regular Sunday *curanto* (a mixture of beef, lamb, pork, chicken, sausage, potatoes, sweet potatoes, and other vegetables, baked on heated earth-covered stones) and a spectacular assortment of sweets and desserts. On any day, try the regional menu at **Fundo Colonia Suizo** (tel. 02944/15-63-7539, www.fundocoloniasuiza.com.ar), which is open noon–7:30 P.M. daily. The individual *tabla* of smoked venison, pork, trout, salami, and cheese (US$9) is an unusual practice—most restaurants have a two-person minimum—and one that's very welcome.

THE SLOPES OF BARILOCHE

After decades of decline and eclipse by resorts like Las Leñas (Mendoza), Bariloche is reestablishing itself as a ski destination with new investment and technological improvements at **Catedral Alta Patagonia** (Base Cerro Catedral, tel. 02944/42-3776, www.catedralaltapatagonia.com), only a short hop west of town. It's still more popular with Argentines and Brazilians than intercontinental travelers, but new snow-making and grooming gear have complemented the blend of 15 beginner-to-advanced runs, and lift capacities have also improved. From a base of 950 meters, the skiable slopes rise another 1,000 meters.

As elsewhere, ticket prices depend on timing; the season runs mid-June–mid-October but is subdivided into low, mid, and peak season. For prices, check the area's website.

Basic rental equipment is cheap, but quality gear is more expensive. In addition to on-site facilities, try downtown's **Baruzzi Fly Shop** (Urquiza 250, tel. 02944/42-4922) or **Martín Pescador** (Rolando 257, tel. 02944/42-2275) for ski equipment rentals.

In addition to downhill skiing, there are also cross-country opportunities at close-in Cerro Otto.

From Colonia Suiza, a zigzag dirt road suitable for mountain bikes climbs toward the Club Andino's **Refugio López,** 1,620 meters above sea level; near the junction of the paved and gravel roads, a steep footpath climbs 2.5 hours to the *refugio,* open mid-December–mid-April.

For most of the way, the route is obvious, but where it seems to disappear into a grove of *lengas* it actually climbs steeply to the left, brushing the dirt road, before continuing toward the *refugio.* In fact, it's much simpler if a little longer to walk the upper sections along the private 4WD road (in any event, the last kilometer or so is on the road itself).

From Refugio López, a good place to take a break and a beer, the route climbs to **Cerro Turista,** a strenuous scramble over rugged volcanic terrain. With an early start, it's possible to reach the 2,076-meter summit of **Cerro López.**

Many Bariloche agencies offer the Circuito Chico as a half-day tour (about US$10 pp), but it's also possible (and cheaper) on public transportation: For most of the day, from the corner of San Martín and Pagano in Bariloche, **Ómnibus 3 de Mayo**'s (tel. 02944/42-5648) No. 20 bus goes every 20 minutes to Llao Llao and Puerto Pañuelo, which is also the final destination of some of its seven Nos. 10 and 11 buses via Colonia Suiza on the Circuito Chico route through Parque Nacional Nahuel Huapi, but through the night it's only every hour or so.

From Bariloche, Ómnibus 3 de Mayo's Línea Manso goes twice on Friday to Río Villegas and El Manso (US$4), on Parque Nacional Nahuel Huapi's southwestern edge.

Cerro Otto

From Bariloche's Barrio Belgrano, Avenida de los Pioneros intersects a gravel road that climbs gently and then steeply west to Cerro Otto's 1,405-meter summit. While it's a feasible eight-kilometer hike or mountain-bike ride, it's easier via the gondolas of **Teleférico Cerro Otto** (Avenida de los Pioneros Km 5, tel. 02944/44-1035, www.telefericobariloche.com.ar, 10 A.M.–6 P.M. daily, US$15 pp, US$6 children ages 6–12); city buses Nos. 50 and 51 go directly to the base station.

On the summit road, at 1,240 meters, the Club Andino's **Refugio Berghof** has 40 bunks and serves meals and drinks. Its **Museo de Montaña Otto Meiling,** with cheap guided tours, honors an early mountaineer who built his residence here.

Cerro Catedral

About 20 kilometers southwest of Bariloche, Cerro Catedral's 2,388-meter summit overlooks **Villa Catedral,** the area's major winter-sports complex. From Villa Catedral, the **Cablecarril y Silla Lynch** (10 A.M.–5 P.M.

daily, US$13 pp) carries visitors to **Confitería Punta Nevada** and **Refugio Lynch,** which also has a *confitería.* Hikers can continue along the ridgetop to the Club Andino's 40-bed **Refugio Emilio Frey** (tel. 02944/35-5222, www.refugiofrey.com, US$9 pp), 1,700-meters above sea level and open all year; the spire-like summits nearby are a magnet for rock climbers.

Monte Tronador

Its inner fire died long ago, but the ice-clad volcanic summit of Tronador still merits its name (the "Thunderer") when frozen blocks plunge off its face into the valley below. The peak that surveyor Bailey Willis called "majestic in savage ruggedness" has impressed everyone from Jesuit explorer Miguel de Olivares to Perito Moreno, Theodore Roosevelt, and the hordes that view it every summer. Its ascent, though, is for skilled snow-and-ice climbers only.

Source of the Río Manso, Tronador's icy eastern face gives birth to the **Ventisquero Negro** (Black Glacier), a jumble of ice, sand, and rocky detritus, and countless waterfalls. Passing Pampa Linda, at the end of the Lago Mascardi road, whistle-blowing rangers prevent hikers from approaching too closely to the **Garganta del Diablo,** the area's largest accessible waterfall.

From Pampa Linda, hikers can visit the Club Andino's basic **Refugio Viejo Tronador,** a kiln-shaped structure that sleeps a maximum of 10 climbers in bivouac conditions, via a trail on the road's south side. On the north side, another trail leads to the 60-bed **Refugio Meiling,** 2,000 meters above sea level. Well-equipped backpackers can continue north to Laguna Frías via the 1,335-meter Paso de las Nubes and return to Bariloche on the bus-boat shuttle via Puerto Blest and Puerto Pañuelo; it's also possible to do this route from Bariloche or Puerto Pañuelo.

Reaching the Tronador area requires a roundabout drive via southbound RN 258 to Lago Mascardi's south end, where westbound RP 81 follows the Río Manso's south bank; at Km 9, a northbound lateral crosses the river and becomes a single-lane dirt road to Pampa

© WAYNE BERNHARDSON

Cyclists take a breather along the Circuito Chico, just west of Bariloche.

Linda and Tronador's base. Because it's narrow, morning traffic is one-way inbound (until 2 P.M.) and afternoon traffic outbound (after 4 P.M.). At other hours, it's open to cautious two-way traffic. From mid-November, **Active Patagonia** (tel. 02944/52-7966, www.active-patagonia.com.ar) provides transportation from the Club Andino's Bariloche headquarters to Pampa Linda at 9 A.M. daily, returning at 5 P.M. (2 hours, US$20 round-trip).

Accommodations and Food

Campgrounds are numerous, especially in areas accessible by road. Club Andino *refugios* charge around US$12–14 pp for overnight stays, US$4–6 for breakfast, US$10–15 for lunch or dinner, and US$2 for kitchen use. Make reservations for bunks, which are limited, but day-hikers can buy simple meals and cold drinks.

Hotels and other accommodations are scattered around various park sectors. At Lago Mascardi's northwest end, on the Pampa Linda road, **Hotel Tronador** (tel. 02944/44-1062, www.hoteltronador.com, US$99–119

pp with full board) is a lakes-district classic in the Bustillo tradition. It's open November 1–mid-April.

Near road's end, **Hostería Pampa Linda** (tel. 02944/49-0517, www.hosteriapampalinda. com.ar, US$115 s, US$146 d, with half board; US$166 s, US$246 d, with full board) is a rustically contemporary inn that also organizes hikes and horseback rides (at additional cost).

Information

For detailed park information and hiking permits, contact the APN (San Martín 24, tel. 02944/42-3111) or Bariloche's Club Andino (20 de Febrero 30, tel. 02944/42-2266, www. clubandino.org, 9:30 A.M.–1 P.M. and 4:30–8:30 P.M. Mon.–Sat.). The *refugios* are good sources of information within the park.

The Club Andino's improved trail map, *Refugios, Sendas y Picadas,* at a scale of 1:100,000 with more detailed versions covering smaller areas at a scale of 1:50,000, is a worthwhile acquisition, but Aonek'er GIS Solutions publishes more sophisticated versions of some areas. The fifth edition of Tim Burford's *Chile* and *Argentina: The Bradt Trekking Guide* (Chalfont St Peter, UK: Bradt Travel Guides, 2001) covers several trails in detail, but its maps are suitable for orientation only.

EL BOLSÓN

El Bolsón, Argentine Patagonia's counterculture capital, may be the place to replace your faded tie-dyes, but it's also a beauty spot in a fertile valley between stunning longitudinal mountain ranges that provide fine hiking. So far, despite completion of the paved highway from Bariloche, this self-styled "ecological municipality" and outspoken nonnuclear zone has managed to stymie five-star hotels and ski areas in favor of simpler—earthier, even—services and activities.

El Bolsón's alternative lifestyle, which began in the 1960s, grew as an island of tolerance and tranquility even during the Dirty War dictatorship. More affordable than Bariloche, it embraces visitors, turns its agricultural bounty—apples, cherries, pears, raspberries, strawberries—into delectable edibles, and makes local hops into a distinctive brew. Motorists appreciate that it's the northernmost place to buy gasoline at Patagonian discount prices.

Río Negro's southernmost city, El Bolsón (pop. 13,845, elevation 300 meters) is 123 kilometers south of Bariloche via RN 258 and 167 kilometers north of Esquel via RN 258 and RN 40. West of the south-flowing Río Quemquemtreu, the Cordón Nevado's snowy ridge marks the Chilean border, while Cerro Piltriquitrón's knife-edge crest rises steeply to the east. Surrounding an artificial lake, the elliptical Plaza Pagano is the town's civic center and the site of its popular street fair.

◖ Feria Artesanal

Nearly encircling Plaza Pagano, buskers, bakers, candle-makers, flower arrangers, and other crafts workers have transformed Bolsón's street fair from a once-a-week gathering to a Tuesday, Thursday, and Saturday event (and in summer there is a smaller version on Sunday). Forgo a restaurant lunch and snack to the max on the Belgian waffles, empanadas, sandwiches,

sausages, and sweets, and wash them all down with fresh-brewed draft beer. It starts around 10 A.M. and winds down around 3 P.M. or so.

Other Shopping

The Mapuche-oriented **Centro Artesanal Cumey Antú** (Avenida San Martín 2020) sells indigenous textiles. **Cabaña Micó** (Islas Malvinas 2753, tel. 02944/49-2691) sells fresh fruit from its own vines in season, and homemade preserves the rest of the year.

Entertainment and Events

Founded in 1926, the city celebrates its **Aniversario** on January 28. Local brewers take center stage in mid-February's four-day **Festival Nacional del Lúpulo** (National Hops Festival).

Sports and Recreation

Several travel agencies arrange excursions such as boating on Lago Puelo, hiking and climbing, horseback riding, mountain biking, rafting on the Río Azul and the more distant Río Manso, and parasailing. Where logistics are complex, as in reaching some trailheads, these can be a good option.

Operators include **Grado 42** (Avenida Belgrano 406, Local 2, tel. 02944/49-3124, www.grado42.com) and **Patagonia Adventure** (Pablo Hube 418, tel. 02944/49-2513, www.argentinachileflyfishing.com).

Accommodations

El Bolsón has quality accommodations for every budget except the luxury category (though what lacks in luxury often compensates with character). Some of the best values are not in town but scattered around the outskirts.

At the north end, directly on the Bariloche highway, **Camping El Bolsón** (RN 258 s/n, tel. 02944/49-2595, cervezaselbolson@elbolson.com, US$4–5 pp) operates its own brewery and beer garden and has a pool as well; it's open November–April.

Hospedaje Piltri (Saavedra 2729, tel. 02944/45-5305, lucas_breidel7@hotmail.com, US$26 d) is a quiet family-run place whose spacious but sparsely furnished rooms have

NORTHERN PATAGONIA

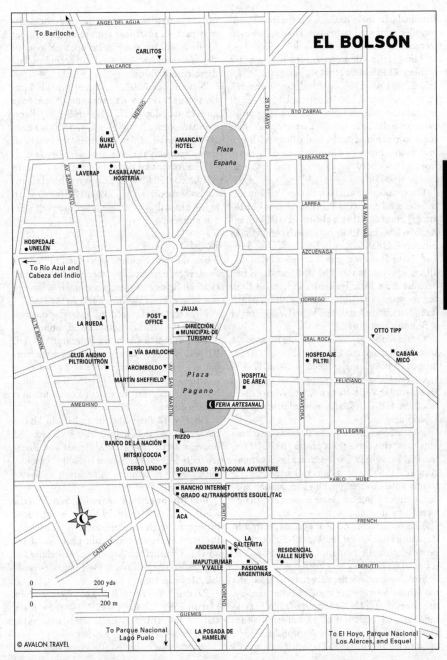

EL BOLSÓN

To Bariloche

ANGEL DEL AGUA
CARLITOS
BALCARCE
MERINO
25 DE MAYO
STO CABRAL
ÑUKE MAPU
AMANCAY HOTEL
Plaza España
HERNANDEZ
AV. SARMIENTO
LAVERAP
CASABLANCA HOSTERÍA
LARREA
ISLAS MALVINAS
AZCUENAGA
HOSPEDAJE UNELÉN
To Río Azul and Cabeza del Indio
DORREGO
ALTE BROWN
POST OFFICE
JAUJA
DIRECCIÓN MUNICIPAL DE TURISMO
GRAL ROCA
OTTO TIPP
LA RUEDA
VÍA BARILOCHE
CABAÑA MICÓ
CLUB ANDINO PILTRIQUITRÓN
ARCIMBOLDO
Plaza Pagano
HOSPEDAJE PILTRI
MARTÍN SHEFFIELD
AV. SAN MARTÍN
HOSPITAL DE ÁREA
FELICIANO
AMEGHINO
FERIA ARTESANAL
SAAVEDRA
PELLEGRINI
IL RIZZO
BANCO DE LA NACIÓN
MITSKI COCOA
CERRO LINDO
BOULEVARD
PATAGONIA ADVENTURE
PABLO HUBE
RANCHO INTERNET
GRADO 42/TRANSPORTES ESQUEL/TAC
PERITO
ACA
FRENCH
CASTELLI
LA SALTEÑITA
ANDESMAR
RESIDENCIAL VALLE NUEVO
MAPUTUR/MAR Y VALLE
PASIONES ARGENTINAS
BERUTTI
MORENO
0   200 yds
0   200 m
GUEMES
To Parque Nacional Lago Puelo
LA POSADA DE HAMELIN
To El Hoyo, Parque Nacional Los Alerces, and Esquel
© AVALON TRAVEL

firm beds. Its main drawback is the insufficient number of shared baths (which are, however, immaculate) when it's crowded.

About four kilometers north of town, HI affiliate **El Pueblito Hostel** (Barrio Luján s/n, tel. 02944/49-3560, www.elpueblitohostel. com.ar, US$10–13 pp in dorms, US$26–32 d) is a comfortable, sociable place on a large property, with 40 beds but also separate cabañas, some with shared baths and others with private baths. From downtown Bolsón there are hourly buses between 7:45 A.M. and 8:45 P.M. except at 7:45 P.M.

On secluded grounds in Barrio Turismo just off the road to Cerro Piltriquitrón, HI affiliate (**Hostal Altos del Sur** (tel. 02944/49-8730, www.altosdelsur.bolsonweb.com, US$13 pp dorm, US$46 d, with breakfast) has four- and six-beds dorms, plus a couple of doubles, all with private baths. The first transfer is free because it's a little isolated and hard to find, but its pristine facilities and amenities, which include a library, satellite TV, and Wi-Fi, make it Bolsón's best hostel.

Other moderate choices include **Hospedaje Unelén** (Azcuénaga 134, tel. 02944/48-3728, hospedaje-hostel-unelen@hotmail.com, US$40 s, US$50 d), which stays open all year, and **Residencial Valle Nuevo** (25 de Mayo 2329, tel. 02944/49-2087, albahube@hotmail.com, US$55 d).

West of the highway on Bolsón's northern outskirts, **Hostería del Campo** (RN 258 s/n, tel. 02944/49-2297, www.cabaniasdelcampo. com.ar, US$53 s or d) has quiet motel-style rooms with covered parking, set among spacious gardens, but breakfast is extra and there's a credit-card surcharge.

The four-room **La Posada de Hamelin** (Granollers 2179, tel. 02944/49-2030, www. posadadehamelin.com.ar, US$41 s, US$61 d) is one of El Bolsón's best B&Bs.

Six kilometers north of town, by a signed dirt road that diverges from the Bariloche highway, the riverside (**La Casona de Odile** (Barrio Luján s/n, tel. 02944/49-2753, odile@elbolson. com, www.interpatagonia.com/odile, US$32 pp with breakfast, US$53 pp with half board)

offers home-cooked French dinners (nonguests may partake of dinner with reservations), but Odile is a heavy smoker. It's open October or November to late April and can accommodate disabled individuals.

New in late 2008, in a quiet eastside location, **Hostería La Escampada** (Azcuénaga and 25 de Mayo, tel. 02944/48-3905, laescampada.com.ar, US$37 s, US$66 d) is a cozy B&B with friendly management and regional style—possibly the best new place in town.

The **Amancay Hotel** (Avenida San Martín 3217, tel. 02944/49-2222, www.hotelamancaybolson.com.ar, US$39 s, US$66 d) is an aging but still serviceable hotel showing wear but not tear.

Food

Given the fresh fruit and vegetables, El Bolsón's food exceeds expectations, though it lacks sophistication. Be sure to give up one lunch in favor of snacking at Plaza Pagano's **Feria Artesanal.**

Note that most places in Bolsón stay open all day, serving breakfast, lunch, and dinner.

La Salteñita (Avenida Belgrano 515, tel. 02944/49-3749) serves spicy northern empanadas for takeaway. **Mitski Cocoa** (San Martín 2526, tel. 02944/49-1878) is an ideal breakfast spot for succulent croissants and hot chocolate.

Boulevard (San Martín and Pablo Hube) has morphed into a hybrid Irish-style pub and pizzeria. **Otto Tipp** (Isla Malvinas and Roca, tel. 02944/49-3700) is more stylishly Teutonic, with free beer samples in addition to pastas and pizzas.

Martín Sheffield (Avenida San Martín 2740, tel. 02944/49-1920) is a welcome presence, with cooked-to-order chicken, Patagonian trout, and lamb, plus local beer on tap. Unusual for Argentina, especially for this part of Argentina, it even prepares credible Mexican tacos.

Packed for dinner, **Il Rizzo** (Avenida San Martín 2599, tel. 02944/49-1380) is for pizza and pasta. **Carlitos** (Avenida San Martín 3410, tel. 02944/45-5654) is a *parrilla.*

Several places have failed in its location,

but **Pasiones Argentinas** (Avenida Belgrano and Beruti, tel. 02944/48-3616) seems off to a good start with a diversity of pizzas (including game toppings such as venison and wild boar), and more elaborate versions of standards such as *bife de chorizo*. Most entrées fall in the US$6–10 range. It has occasional live jazz or rock bands on weekends.

(**Jauja** (San Martín 2867, tel. 02944/49-2448, US$10–20) may have slipped a notch, but it's still the best in town. Vivid flower arrangements set the stage for succulent pastas such as gnocchi with a garlic cream sauce, vegetarian dishes such as *milanesa de soja* (breaded soybean steak), trout with a creamy almond sauce, outstanding homemade bread, and local brews. It's tobacco-free noon–4 P.M. and 8 P.M.–midnight only.

Ignore Jauja's in-house desserts, and step just outside to (**Helados Jauja,** one of the country's top ice creameries, with an almost paralyzing choice of nearly 60 inventive flavors. The author's longstanding favorite is *mate cocido con tres de azúcar* (boiled and slightly sweetened *mate*), though even some Argentines blanch at consuming their favorite bitter infusion in frozen form. *Chocolate profundo,* a bittersweet chocolate mousse, is also interesting.

Information

At Plaza Pagano's north end, the **Dirección Municipal de Turismo** (Avenida San Martín and Roca, tel./fax 02944/49-2604, www.bolsonturistico.com.ar) provides decent maps of accommodations and other services; it even employs an accommodations specialist who makes suggestions and books hotels. Summer hours are 9 A.M.–11 P.M. Monday–Friday, 9 A.M.–11 P.M. Saturday, and 10 A.M.–10 P.M. Sunday; the rest of the year, hours are 9 A.M.–9 P.M., sometimes a little later, daily.

For hiking and climbing suggestions, visit the **Club Andino Piltriquitrón** (Sarmiento between Roca and Feliciano, tel. 02944/49-2600, www.capiltriquitron.com.ar), which also rents bikes.

For motorists, **ACA** (tel. 02944/49-2260) is at Avenida Belgrano and San Martín.

Services

Banco de la Nación (Avenida San Martín 2598) has an ATM.

Correo Argentino is at Avenida San Martín 2806; the postal code is 8430. **Rancho Internet** (Avenida San Martín and Pablo Hube) has the best Internet connections.

Laverap (José Hernández 223, tel. 02944/49-3243) does the washing.

The **Hospital de Area** (Perito Moreno s/n, tel. 02944/49-2240) is behind Plaza Pagano.

Getting There

In new quarters, **LADE** (Avenida Sarmiento 3238, tel. 02944/49-2206) flies throughout Patagonia on erratic schedules. Flights leave from the Aeroclub El Bolsón (tel. 02944/49-1125) at the north end of Avenida San Martín.

El Bolsón lacks a central **bus** terminal, but most companies are within a few blocks of each other.

Andesmar (Belgrano and Perito Moreno, tel. 02944/49-2178) goes to Bariloche and Buenos Aires, usually with a change in Neuquén, and south to Esquel. **Vía Bariloche** (Sarmiento and Roca, tel. 02972/45-5554) goes to Esquel, Bariloche, and Buenos Aires; **Transportes Esquel** (Belgrano 406, tel. 02944/49-3124) also goes to Esquel via Parque Nacional Los Alerces.

Grado 42 (Belgrano 406, tel. 02944/49-3124) represents TAC, which goes to El Maitén and Esquel, and to Bariloche, and makes connections in Neuquén for Mendoza and other northern destinations. **Don Otto** (Belgrano and Berutti, Local 3, tel. 02944/49-3910) goes to Bariloche and Comodoro Rivadavia, with connections in Esquel for Trelew and Puerto Madryn. **Maputur/Mar y Valle** (Perito Moreno 2331, tel. 02944/49-1440) goes directly to Puerto Madryn.

The usual destinations are Bariloche (2 hours, US$6–8) and Esquel (2.5 hours, US$7–9), Trelew (11 hours, US$36–57), and Puerto Madryn (12 hours, US$39–60). Fares to other northbound destinations are slightly more expensive than those from Bariloche; fares to southbound destinations are slightly cheaper.

Getting Around

For a small town, El Bolsón has fine public transportation for excursions to places like Cerro Piltriquitrón and Lago Puelo. There are also abundant radio taxis and *remises*.

For rental bikes, try **La Rueda** (Avenida Sarmiento 2972, tel. 02944/49-2465) or **Ñuke Mapu** (Azcona 3236, tel. 02944/49-8934).

VICINITY OF EL BOLSÓN

One of El Bolsón's virtues is its convenience to trailheads for hiking and secondary roads for mountain biking. Most are just far enough away, though, to require an early start for those without their own vehicle; consider hiring a *remise* to the trailheads. Spanish-speaking hikers should look for Gabriel Bevacqua's inexpensive local hiking guide *Montañas de la Comarca*, for sale in Bolsón's tourist office. Its orientation map is adequate for initial planning.

Both east and west of town, there are backcountry *refugios* where hikers can either camp or rent a bunk or floor space as well as cook or purchase meals. These are fairly basic, but inexpensive and comfortable enough, and the *refugieros* who run them are building a series of connector trails to supplement the access points and create a hikers circuit. Some of these are already operating.

Two blocks north of Plaza Pagano, westbound Azcuénaga crosses the Quemquemtreu and continues six kilometers to a footpath overlooking its southerly confluence with the Río Azul and Lago Puelo in the distance; the short but precipitous northbound trail leads to the natural metamorphic silhouette colloquially known as the **Cabeza del Indio** (Indian's Head). There's now a token admission charge; the local Mapuche sometimes hold ceremonies here.

About six kilometers north of town via the Bariloche road, a northwesterly gravel road leads to a signed southeasterly turnoff to the municipal **Reserva Forestal Loma de Medio-Río Azul** (token admission). Its main attraction is an 800-meter loop trail to the **Cascada Escondida,** where the river follows a fault before tumbling down in a classic bridal veil. It is best during spring runoff, when the volume of water turns the single falls into two or three larger ones.

About 10 kilometers north of town by the same main road, but via a northeasterly lateral, the **Cascada Mallín Ahogado** is a 20-meter waterfall on the Quemquemtreu tributary of the Arroyo del Medio. Diverted for agriculture, it's also best in early spring. The caretaker has carved scale models of traditional oxcarts, wheelbarrows, and the like.

A parallel main road continues 15 kilometers northwest to Club Andino's 70-bunk **Refugio Perito Moreno** (tel. 02944/49-3912, US$4–10 pp); a small ski area, at a base elevation of 1,000 meters, has a T-bar lift to 1,450 meters. From the *refugio,* the 2,206-meter summit of **Cerro Perito Moreno** is about a three-hour hike. The *refugio* is busiest in summer, when it gets lots of schoolkids; meals are also available here.

Cajón del Azul

Immediately west of Mallín Ahogado, 15 kilometers northwest of El Bolsón, a signed gravel road suitable only for 4WD vehicles drops steeply into the canyon of the Río Azul, which flows eastward out of the Andes before turning sharply south at the confluence with the Río Blanco. Beyond the Arco Iris campground, where the road ends, two precarious *pasarelas* (pedestrian bridges) cross the rivers before the trail becomes an up-and-down hike that leads to a sheer-sided gorge. Here, beneath a sturdy log bridge, the spring runoff explodes like a cannon shot.

Just across the bridge, about 2.5 hours from the confluence, **Refugio Cajón del Azul** is open all year. Run by an English-speaking semi-hermit named Atilio who offers a free coffee, tea, or *mate* to every arrival, the *refugio* also offers camping (US$2.50 pp) and mattresses for overnighters (US$9 pp) in a communal dormitory. Though dark, the rustically comfortable *refugio* even has a water-driven turbine for electricity. Most supplies arrive on horseback, though in summer and fall Atilio's irrigated *chacra* provides fresh apples, cherries, peaches, plums, raspberries, and the like. The westbound trail continues another hour or more to

Refugio El Retamal (elretamal@gmail.com, US$9 pp).

An alternative northwesterly trail from the Arco Iris trailhead dead-ends at **Refugio Dedo Gordo** (US$7 pp), providing access to the summit of its namesake 2,065-meter summit. Before the final climb to Refugio Cajón del Azul, a new but poorly signed trail climbs steeply southward and then drops into the drainage of the Arroyo Teno and to **Refugio Hielo Azul** (hieloazul@elbolson.com, US$10 pp bunks, US$4 pp camping) This route allows overnight hikers to loop back to El Bolsón.

◖ Cerro Piltriquitrón

East of Bolsón, the piedmont rises steadily and then sharply to 2,284-meter Piltriquitrón's granite summit, where a clear day reveals the snow-covered phalanx of peaks along the Chilean border, from Tronador and beyond in the north to Lago Puelo and beyond the Cordón Esperanza in the south. When the clouds clear, Volcán Osorno's Fuji-perfect cone, in Chile, appears almost immediately west of Tronador.

From Bolsón, a winding dirt road climbs 13 kilometers to a parking area at the 1,200-meter level, where a steep footpath leads to the **Bosque Tallado** (US$1 pp). Here, chainsaw carvers have transformed trunks from a scorched *lenga* forest into 25 memorable sculptures.

Beyond the Bosque Tallado, the trail climbs to the Club Andino's **Refugio Piltriquitrón** (tel. 02944/15-69-0044) at 1,400 meters. Bunks cost US$6.50 pp, but you need your own sleeping bag; meals are also available. This was once a ski area, and the path climbs even more steeply along the rusty T-bar cable before leveling off and rounding Piltriquitrón; marked by paint blazes, it then climbs steeply over loose talus to the summit. From the *refugio*, it takes about two hours; carry water and high-energy snacks.

In summer, **Grado 42** (Avenida Belgrano 406, Local 2, tel. 02944/49-3124) goes to the parking area at 8:30 A.M. daily, returning two hours later. The fare is US$12 round-trip, while a *remise* costs US$20.

Interior Chubut Province

PARQUE NACIONAL LAGO PUELO

Fed by four rivers and numerous arroyos, nearly surrounded by forested peaks, Lago Puelo is the turquoise showpiece of its namesake national park. In addition to its scenery, it's popular for camping, swimming, boating, and hiking, and it offers a little-used option for crossing into Chile (unlike most Argentine lakes, Lago Puelo drains toward the Pacific).

Just 15 kilometers south of El Bolsón, Lago Puelo lies across the Chubut provincial line. It encompasses 27,675 hectares of mostly mountainous forested land, except for the Río Azul's lakeshore deltas in the north, and the Río Turbio, across the lake to the south. The lake lies only 200 meters above sea level, but the summits rise above 1,500 meters.

Flora and Fauna

Lago Puelo's flora and fauna closely resemble those of Nahuel Huapi to the north and Los Alerces to the south. Its relatively low elevations and exposure to Pacific storms, though, create a mild lakeshore microclimate that permits the growth of tree species like the *ulmo*, with its showy white flowers, and the *lingue*. The *huemul* (Andean deer) and *pudú* (miniature deer) are present but rarely seen.

Sports and Recreation

Several trailheads start near the Centro de Informes. The most popular is the **Sendero al Mirador del Lago,** to the east, which climbs 130 meters to an overlook.

To the west, the **Senda Los Hitos** fords the Río Azul and leads five kilometers to Arroyo Las Lágrimas, where Chile-bound hikers can complete Argentine border formalities. Five kilometers farther west, Chilean Carabineros finish the paperwork; from there, continue to the Chilean town of Puelo, with onward connections to Puerto Montt.

For most visitors, though, sailing the lake is the main attraction. The *Juana de Arco* (tel. 02944/49-8946 in El Bolsón) and *Popeye 2000* carry passengers on half-hour excursions (US$8 pp) after 2:30 P.M.; they also offer 11 A.M. departures to the Chilean frontier (US$25 pp), stopping for paperwork at the Argentine border post.

Practicalities

Immediately east of the visitors center, **Camping Lago Puelo** (tel. 02944/15-31-4020, US$8 pp) has a small *confitería,* and limited supplies are available.

In addition, there's a free site at Arroyo Las Lágrimas, about five kilometers west on the footpath to the border, and other free sites at Río Turbio, at the lake's south end.

Near the park entrance, where rangers collect US$1 pp for Argentine residents, US$2.50 pp for foreigners, the helpful **Oficina de Informes** (tel. 02944/49-9232, lagopuelo@ apn.gov.ar, 9 A.M.–7 P.M. daily in summer only) provides practical information on attractions and activities.

From El Bolsón, Transporte La Golondrina **buses** shuttle down Avenida San Martín to the park and back 16 times between 6:45 A.M. and 10:30 P.M. Monday–Friday, but they start a little later, at 7 A.M., on weekends. Return times are 30–45 minutes later.

EL MAITÉN

In 1979, Paul Theroux's overrated opus *The Old Patagonian Express* made the dying narrow-gauge railway that ran south from Ingeniero Jacobacci to Esquel a global household word. Its antique steam locomotives no longer traverse the entire 402-kilometer route, but the dusty township of El Maitén, with its rusting rails, weathered workshops, and twirling turntables, is the best place to savor this picturesque economic folly. Like Esquel, it retains enough

rolling stock that committed train-spotters can board this living anachronism and fill their photo albums in the process.

El Maitén (pop. 3,399) is 70 kilometers southeast of El Bolsón via RN 258 and newly paved RP 70. It's 130 kilometers north of Esquel via RN 40 and a spur with a 20-kilometer unpaved segment.

La Trochita

Gringos may cite the Gospel of Theroux, but Argentines know the train as *La Trochita* (a diminutive for "gauge") or *El Trencito* (Little Train). The yards are still open, though only a couple of locomotives (an American Baldwin and a 1922 German Henschel) are in running order; the mostly Belgian cars date from 1922 to about 1960.

February's combined **Fiesta Provincial del Trencito** and **Fiesta Nacional del Tren a Vapor** (National Steam Train Festival) fill the handful of hotels and campgrounds. Celebrating the railroad, it also features live music on a new custom-built stage, horseback races, bronco-busting, and regional delicacies.

In summer, by reservation only, the train does a 2.5-hour excursion to Thomae (the first station south of Maitén) and back (US$20 pp) four or five times weekly in January and February; the rest of the year, it's only once or twice weekly. For reservations, contact Grado 42 (Avenida Belgrano 406, El Bolsón, tel. 02944/49-3124, latrochita@elbolson.org).

For current schedules, contact El Maitén's **Secretaría de Turismo** (Avenida San Martín s/n, tel. 02945/49-5016, www.elmaiten.com. ar), near the railroad tracks, or **Estación El Maitén** (Carlos Pellegrini 841, tel. 02945/49-5190). The new platform is a welcome addition, and the old station has added a small but interesting museum (9 A.M.–7 P.M. daily, US$0.50). The nearby workshops are open 8 A.M.–2 P.M. daily.

Practicalities

The **Camping Municipal** (tel. 02945/49-5189, US$2 pp) is on the nearby Río Chubut.

Hostería Refugio Andino (Avenida San Martín 1317, tel. 02945/49-5007, refugioandino@epuyen.net.ar, US$10 pp) has accommodations, a restaurant, and long-distance phones.

Grado 42 (Avenida San Martín 1136, tel. 02944/49-4955) goes to El Bolsón (US$5) at 7:30 A.M. daily. **Vía Bariloche** (Avenida San Martín 1317, tel. 02945/15-68-1121) goes to Esquel (2 hours, US$5) at 4 P.M. Tuesday, Thursday, and Saturday.

ESQUEL

Across the Chubut border, the gateway to Parque Nacional Los Alerces and the end of the line for the "The Old Patagonian Express," Esquel is a deceptively tranquil town of wide avenues divided by densely planted medians. It's also a city recently divided by a plebiscite that rejected a nearby gold mine that would have used toxic cyanide to leech the valuable mineral. What's more, it's a place where Mapuche militancy is palpable, in graffiti that says "Neither Argentine nor Chilean, but Mapuche."

Esquel (pop. 28,117) is 167 kilometers south of El Bolsón via RN 258, RN 40, and RN 259, all of them smoothly paved. Alternatively, many visitors take the graveled RP 71, south of the town of Epuyén, directly to Parque Nacional Los Alerces. Esquel is also 608 kilometers west of Trelew via several paved highways across the Patagonian steppe, and 581 kilometers northwest of Comodoro Rivadavia via equally good roads.

The city itself is a compact grid on the north bank of the Arroyo Esquel. Southbound RN 259 leads to a junction to Parque Nacional Los Alerces, the Welsh-settled town of Trevelin, and the Chilean border at Futaleufú.

La Trochita

From the old Roca railway station, now a museum, La Trochita still makes entertaining excursions to the Mapuche hamlet of Nahuel Pan. Its wooden passenger wagons, with salamander stoves and hard-backed benches, are classics of their era, and the entire line is a national historical monument.

As the train departs the new station, opened

NORTHERN PATAGONIA

Esquel houses La Trochita, northern Patagonia's legendary steam train.

NORTHERN PATAGONIA

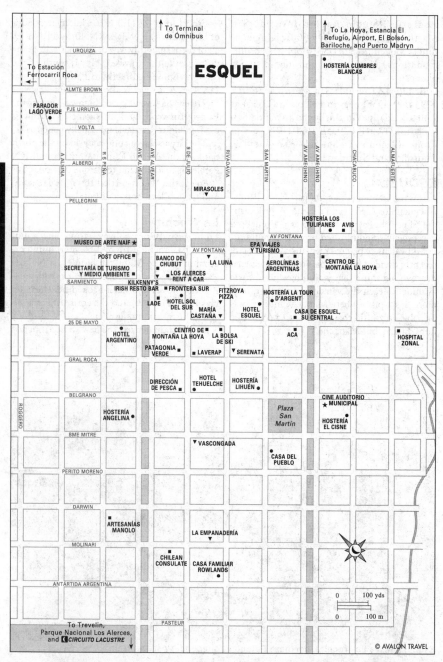

To Terminal de Ómnibus

To La Hoya, Estancia El Refugio, Airport, El Bolsón, Bariloche, and Puerto Madryn

URQUIZA

To Estación Ferrocarril Roca

ESQUEL

HOSTERÍA CUMBRES BLANCAS

ALMTE BROWN

PARADOR LAGO VERDE

PJE URRUTIA

VOLTA

A ALSINA

R S PEÑA

AVE ALVEAR

AVE ALVEAR

9 DE JULIO

RIVADAVIA

SAN MARTIN

AV AMEGHINO

AV AMEGHINO

CHACABUCO

ALMAFUERTE

ALBERDI

MIRASOLES

PELLEGRINI

HOSTERÍA LOS TULIPANES   AVIS

AV FONTANA

MUSEO DE ARTE NAIF ★

AV FONTANA

EPA VIAJES Y TURISMO

POST OFFICE

BANCO DEL CHUBUT

LA LUNA

AEROLÍNEAS ARGENTINAS

CENTRO DE MONTAÑA LA HOYA

SECRETARÍA DE TURISMO Y MEDIO AMBIENTE

LOS ALERCES RENT A CAR

SARMIENTO

KILKENNY'S IRISH RESTO BAR

FRONTERA SUR

FITZROYA PIZZA

HOSTERÍA LA TOUR D'ARGENT

LADE

HOTEL SOL DEL SUR

MARÍA CASTAÑA

HOTEL ESQUEL

CASA DE ESQUEL, SU CENTRAL

25 DE MAYO

HOTEL ARGENTINO

CENTRO DE MONTAÑA LA HOYA

LA BOLSA DE SKI

ACA

HOSPITAL ZONAL

PATAGONIA VERDE

LAVERAP

SERENATA

GRAL ROCA

ROGGERO

DIRECCIÓN DE PESCA

HOTEL TEHUELCHE

HOSTERÍA LIHUÉN

CINE AUDITORIO MUNICIPAL ★

BELGRANO

HOSTERÍA ANGELINA

Plaza San Martín

HOSTERÍA EL CISNE

BME MITRE

VASCONGADA

PERITO MORENO

CASA DEL PUEBLO

DARWIN

ARTESANÍAS MANOLO

LA EMPANADERÍA

MOLINARI

CHILEAN CONSULATE

CASA FAMILIAR ROWLANDS

ANTÁRTIDA ARGENTINA

0   100 yds

0   100 m

To Trevelin, Parque Nacional Los Alerces, and CIRCUITO LACUSTRE

PASTEUR

© AVALON TRAVEL

in late 2008, residents leave their houses and cars to wave as it chugs past their backyards and crosses the highway. Each passenger coach has a guide, but the rolling stock is so noisy that understanding the narration is difficult.

Taking about an hour to reach Nahuel Pan, La Trochita remains there an hour before returning to Esquel. In the meantime, there are good oven-baked empanadas, drinks, and Mapuche crafts as well as short horseback rides. The **Museo de Culturas Originarias Patagónicas** (9 A.M.–noon Mon., Wed., and Fri., 9 A.M.–noon and 5–7 P.M. Tues., Thurs., and Sat., free) has moved here from downtown Esquel.

In summer, the train leaves at 10 A.M. and 2 P.M. daily, but excursions are less frequent in other seasons. The fare is US$13 pp, cash only; you can usually buy a ticket without a reservation. For details, contact La Trochita (Roggero and Urquiza, tel. 02945/45-1403, www.latrochita.org.ar).

Events and Entertainment
Late February's **Semana de Esquel** marks the city's 1906 founding.

Hotel Argentino (25 de Mayo 862) has a great bar with a classic kitchen-sink collection of memorabilia and junk as well as friendly staff, but don't expect to get to get to sleep early if you're staying upstairs.

In the utterly transformed old bus terminal, the new **Centro Cultural de Esquel Melipal** (Avenida Fontana and Avenida Alvear) encompasses a variety of art and performing arts spaces. The renovated **Cine Auditorio Municipal** (Belgrano 330, tel. 02945/45-1929) shows first-run movies.

Shopping
In summer, the Asociación de Artesanos de Esquel sponsors Plaza San Martín's **Feria Artesanal Permanente;** hours are 6–11:30 P.M. Thursday–Sunday.

For wood carvings, try **Artesanías Manolo** (Alsina 483). **Casa de Esquel** (25 de Mayo 415, tel. 02945/45-2544) is a bookstore and crafts outlet.

Sports and Recreation
Hiking, climbing, fishing, horseback riding, rafting, and kayaking are all on the docket. Argentina's Río Corcovado is a Class II–III starter river, but the Class V Futaleufú, across the Chilean border, has world-class white-water.

Patagonia Verde (9 de Julio 926, tel. 02945/45-4396, www.patagonia-verde.com. ar) arranges activities like hiking, climbing, and riding. **Frontera Sur** (Sarmiento 784, tel. 02945/45-0505, www.fronterasur.net) organizes water sports like rafting (US$46 for a full day) and kayaking on the Corcovado, as well as hiking, riding, and mountain biking. **Epa Expediciones** (Avenida Fontana 482, tel. 02945/45-7015, www.grupoepa.com) also does rafting and other activities.

For fishing licenses, contact the **Dirección de Pesca** (Belgrano 722, tel. 0297/45-1063); the season runs November–mid-April. **Andrés Müller** (Sarmiento 120, tel. 02945/45-4572, framumi@ar.inter.net) is a reliable independent fishing guide, while **Rincón Andino** (Miguens 40, tel. 02945/45-2185, www.rinconandino. com.ar) is a specialist operator.

Accommodations
Esquel has abundant budget accommodations but little in the upper categories, and things can get tight in summer and in ski season. Standards in general, though, are good.

Casa Familiar Rowlands (Rivadavia 330, tel. 02945/45-2578, gales01@hotmail.com, US$11 pp) has expanded from a simple family house; breakfast costs US$1 more. **Hostería El Cisne** (Chacabuco 778, tel. 02945/45-2256, hosteria.el.cisne@gmail.com, US$19 s, US$26 d) is comparable.

Backpackers can try **Parador Lago Verde** (Volta 1081, tel. 02945/45-2251, www.patagonia-verde.com.ar, US$11 pp), which, though no longer an HI affiliate, still offers good value. **Casa del Pueblo** (San Martín 661, tel. 02945/45-0581, www.esquelcasadelpueblo.com.ar, US$12 pp, US$32 d) is now the HI affiliate. The 10-room **Hostería Lihuén** (San Martín 822, tel. 02945/45-2589, f_ejarque@speedy.com.ar, US$26 s, US$30

d) is a friendly no-frills place where breakfast costs US$2 pp extra.

Renovated **Hotel Esquel** (San Martín 1044, tel. 02945/45-2534, hotelesquel@ hotmail.com, US$40 s, US$48 d) has improved, but the similarly priced ◖ **Hostería los Tulipanes** (Avenida Fontana 365, tel. 02945/45-2748, US$32 s, US$39 d) is a real find—the decor may be tacky, but the beds are firm, the baths spacious, and the breakfast abundant and diverse. There's also warmth in the details, like bedside chocolates, in this family-run hostelry.

A commonplace facade conceals the spacious well-furnished rooms at ◖ **Hostería Angelina** (Avenida Alvear 758, tel./fax 02945/45-2763, hosteriaangelina@argentina.com, US$45–47 s, US$50–66 d), whose gregarious owner goes out of his way to make guests feel welcome. Rates include telephone, cable TV, parking, and central heating; the buffet breakfast (US$2 pp) includes croissants, ham, cheese, bread, cereal, fruit and fruit salad, coffee, and tea.

Other options include **Hotel Sol del Sur** (9 de Julio 1086, tel. 02945/45-2189, www. hsoldelsur.com.ar, US$32–44 s, US$40–66 d), alpine-styled **Hostería La Tour D'Argent** (San Martín 1063, tel. 02945/45-4612, www. latourdargent.com.ar, US$42 s, US$58 d), and spacious **Hotel Tehuelche** (9 de Julio 825, tel. 02945/45-2420, www.cadenarayentray.com.ar, US$51–57 s, US$64–70 d).

In the Villa Ayelén neighborhood, opposite the racetrack just south of the town center, ◖ **Hostería Canela** (Los Notros and Los Radales, tel. 02945/45-3890, www.canelaesquel.com, US$115 s or d) is a former teahouse turned bed-and-breakfast with six spacious rooms on immaculate grounds. Hosts Jorge Miglioni and Verónica Ayling speak fluent English, provide an ample breakfast, and offer dining and excursions suggestions.

The 20 midsize-plus rooms at **Hostería Cumbres Blancas** (Avenida Ameghino 1683, tel. 02945/45-5100, www.cumbresblancas. com.ar, US$150 s, US$216 d) look as good as the day they opened a decade ago, and some are nonsmoking. It also has Wi-Fi, a sauna, a highly regarded restaurant, and grounds that include its own mini-golf course and a duck pond. If business is slow, try asking for the lower Argentine rates.

Food

María Castaña (25 de Mayo 605, tel. 02945/45-1752) serves breakfast, coffee, and good sandwiches. **Empanadería Molinari** (Molinari 619) bakes a variety of takeaway empanadas.

In attractive new quarters, **La Luna** (Avenida Fontana 656, tel. 02945/45-3800, www.lalunarestobar.com.ar) has improved and diversified its menu as well, and now offers patio seating; the midday lunches are a bargain for around US$7. Reliable but unremarkable, the traditional **Vascongada** (9 de Julio and Mitre, tel. 02945/45-2229) serves Patagonian specialties.

◖ **Fitzroya Pizza** (Rivadavia 1048, tel. 02945/45-0512, US$10) is a first-rate pizzeria with an enormous variety of toppings; solo diners can order half portions. Irish-style pubs are a staple in Argentina, but **Killarney's Irish Resto Bar** (Avenida Alvear and Ameghino, tel. 02945/45-7041) is the first of its kind here.

In new quarters, open for dinner only, the bistro-style ◖ **Mirasoles** (Pellegrini 643, tel. 02945/45-6390) is best for Italo-Argentine entrées like *ñoquis* and appetizers like *mozzarella caprese.*

Las Piedras (Avenida Ameghino 1683, tel. 02945/45-5100) is Hostería Altas Cumbre's upmarket restaurant. It has an abbreviated midday menu of pastas and Argentine standards such as *bife de chorizo* and a more elaborate dinner menu.

Take a taxi to slightly hard-to-find **Mapuche** (Las Lengas y Los Cipreses, tel. 02945/45-2440), in quiet Villa Ayelén just south of town on the Trevelin road—it's worth the effort for their delicately grilled lamb (US$10) or trout, the *ensalada caprese* (US$5) of tomato, cheese, and basil, and a fine wine list. The high-ceilinged quarters are attractive, and the service is attentive.

Serenata (Rivadavia 939, tel. 02945/45-5999) has Esquel's finest ice cream.

Information

Open 8 A.M.–10 P.M. daily, the **Secretaría de Turismo** (Avenida Alvear 1120, tel. 02945/45-1927, www.esquel.gov.ar) maintains a thorough database on accommodations and other services here and in Parque Nacional Los Alerces. In peak season, a satellite office at the bus terminal is open 6–8 A.M. and 7–11 P.M. daily.

For motorists, **ACA** (tel. 02965/45-2382) is at 25 de Mayo and Ameghino.

Services

Banco del Chubut (Alvear 1131) has one of several downtown ATMs.

Correo Argentino is at Alvear 1192; the postal code is 9200. **Su Central** (25 de Mayo 415) has both phone and Internet access.

Chile's honorary **consulate** (Molinari 754, tel. 02945/45-1189) is open 8:30 A.M.–1:30 P.M. weekdays.

For laundry (about US$4 per load), try **Laverap** (9 de Julio and Roca, tel. 02945/45-5959).

For medical services, contact the **Hospital Zonal** (25 de Mayo 150, tel. 02945/45-0222).

Getting There

Esquel has limited air services, better bus connections, and rail fantasies.

Aerolíneas Argentinas (Avenida Fontana 406, tel. 0297/45-3614) flies three times a week to Buenos Aires via Bariloche, and occasionally to Trelew. **LADE** (Alvear 1085, tel. 02945/45-2124) usually flies twice weekly to Bariloche and Buenos Aires, and weekly to El Calafate, but schedules change frequently.

The **Terminal de Ómnibus** (Avenida Alvear 1871, tel. 02945/45-1566, terminalesq@ciudad.com.ar) is a contemporary facility four blocks northeast of downtown. It has good local and regional services, but long-distance links are better in Bariloche.

Transportes Jacobsen/Vía Bariloche (tel. 02945/45-3528) connects Esquel with El Maitén at 1:30 P.M. Tuesday, Thursday, and Saturday.

Jacobsen also serves nearby Trevelin (frequently) and La Balsa/Futaleufú (8 A.M.

Mon.–Fri. summer, 8 A.M. Mon., Wed., and Fri. the rest of the year).

In summer, **Transportes Esquel** (tel. 02945/45-3529) goes to Parque Nacional Los Alerces and Lago Puelo at 8 A.M. (connecting with lake excursions) and 2 P.M. daily. Fares are US$4 to La Villa, US$5.50 to Bahía Rosales, US$6.50 to Lago Verde, US$8 to Lago Rivadavia, US$10 to Cholila, and US$13 to Puelo, where there are easy connections to El Bolsón, but the afternoon bus goes only as far as Lago Verde. Puelo-bound passengers with through tickets can stop anywhere en route and continue on any succeeding bus. Winter schedules may differ.

Typical destinations, times, and fares include Trevelin (30 minutes, US$1.50), La Balsa/Futaleufú (1.5 hours, US$5), El Maitén (2 hours, US$5), El Bolsón (2.5 hours, US$7), Bariloche (4 hours, US$12), Trelew (8 hours, US$29), Puerto Madryn (9 hours, US$32), Comodoro Rivadavia (9 hours, US$21–30), and Buenos Aires (24 hours, US$70–89).

Getting Around

Aeropuerto Esquel is 20 kilometers east of town on RN 40; a taxi or *remise* is the only option.

Los Alerces Rent a Car (Sarmiento 763, tel. 02945/45-6008, losalercesrentacar@ciudad.com.ar) and **Avis** (Avenida Fontana 331, tel. 02945/15-699-0580) have rental cars.

VICINITY OF ESQUEL

In addition to Parque Nacional Los Alerces (covered separately below), Esquel has many other points of interest within an hour or two.

Cerro La Hoya

Only 13 kilometers north of Esquel, La Hoya is a modest ski area that gets fine powder thanks to its location on the Andes' drier eastern side, which compensates for its relatively small size. It's substantially cheaper than Bariloche, and the infrastructure is improving, but limited capacity can mean long lift lines.

Ranging 1,200–2,500 meters above sea level, La Hoya has 25 runs totaling about 22

NORTHERN PATAGONIA

kilometers on 60 hectares. Its modern lifts include the 1,100-meter Telesilla del Bosque, which also carries hikers to high-country trailheads in summer (US$2.50), and the 1,018-meter Telesilla del Cañadón. In season it also has a ski school; the **Fiesta Nacional del Esquí** (National Ski Festival) takes place the second week of September.

Equipment can be rented on-site or in Esquel at **La Bolsa del Ski** (Rivadavia and 25 de Mayo, tel. 02945/45-2379, www.bolsadeski. com.ar). For other details, contact concessionaire **Frontera Sur** (Avenida Ameghino and Avenida Fontana, tel. 02945/45-3018, www. cerrolahoya.com).

Museo Leleque

Midway between Esquel and El Bolsón, on what was one of Argentina's largest *estancias,* the Museo Leleque (RN 40 Km 1440, museoleleque@ciudad.com.ar, www.latrochita. com.ar/museo.htm, 11 A.M.–5 P.M. Wed.–Mon. July–Apr., US$1) covers Patagonia from prehistory to the present. Funded by fashion icon Carlo Benetton, who purchased the Argentine Southern Land Company and several other Patagonian properties, it houses the collections of Ukrainian immigrant Pablo S. Korschenewski, who left Buenos Aires half a century ago to explore the Patagonian countryside on foot and by horseback.

In the process, Korschenewski amassed over 14,000 artifacts, including arrowheads, bone drills, ceremonial axes, grinding stones, and pottery shards. Striking a chord with Benetton, he persuaded the Italian to turn Leleque's historic buildings, once a general store, hotel, and school, into a contemporary museum that now gets 8,500 visitors, mostly Argentines, every year. Not just archaeological, the exhibits stress contact and postcontact history of the region's first peoples, regional and oral histories, photographs, and documents. One prize is a receipt signed by Butch Cassidy, who lived in nearby Cholila from 1901 to 1905 under the alias Santiago Ryan.

Administered by the Fundación Ameghino, the Museo Leleque is 90 kilometers north of Esquel. The museum has a souvenir shop and a *confitería* for snacks and coffee.

Cholila

Though it's barely a wide spot in the road, Cholila has become an offbeat pilgrimage site ever since U.S. author Anne Meadows pinpointed the house of *yanqui* outlaws Robert Leroy Parker and Harry Longabaugh in her historical travelogue *Digging Up Butch and Sundance* (Lincoln, NE: Bison Books, 2003). Bruce Chatwin also told of the Cholila cabin—perhaps taking literary license—in his classic *In Patagonia.*

Butch and Sundance presumably tried to go straight here, but fled to Chile in 1905 when accused of a robbery in Río Gallegos and the Pinkertons got on their scent. After the 1999 death of its elderly occupant Aladín Sepúlveda, souvenir hunters targeted the unoccupied and crumbling cabin, but the municipality has restored the buildings—in fact, they look livable enough that you almost expect to see cardboard cutouts of Paul Newman and Robert Redford—but there are no exhibits within. In theory, a caretaker collects a small admission charge.

Near Parque Nacional Los Alerces's northeastern entrance, a few kilometers north of Cholila at Km 21 of RP 71 near the signed junction to the Casa de Piedra teahouse, the cabin is visible on the west side of the highway; Transportes Esquel buses between Puelo and Esquel via Los Alerces pass within sight of it.

Beyond the entrance, a westbound lateral leads to the **Casa de Piedra** (tel. 02945/49-8056, US$53 d), a hybrid B&B-teahouse that's open from December through Semana Santa. It makes an ideal detour even for day-trippers.

TREVELIN AND VICINITY

Few settlements in Chubut's Andean interior retain the Welsh imprint, but tranquil Trevelin, with historic houses and teahouses to rival Gaiman, is the exception. Only half an hour from Esquel, it owes its name to a Welsh compound meaning "mill town" after its first flour mill, now a history museum.

Trevelin (pop. 4,849), south of Esquel 24 kilometers via RN 259, is also unique for its disorienting octagonal Plaza Coronel Fontana, from which the highway continues south as Avenida San Martín; it's the main commercial street and thoroughfare to Corcovado and the Chilean border post of Futaleufú. Other streets fan out from the plaza.

Chile-bound motorists should fill the tank here, as Futaleufú has no gas station and Chilean prices are substantially higher than those in Argentine Patagonia.

Sights

In 1922, Welsh immigrants founded the Molino Harinero de la Compañía Andes, the flour mill that's now the **Museo Molino Viejo** (Molino Viejo 488, tel. 02945/48-0189, 9 A.M.–9 P.M. daily Jan.–Feb. and July, 11 A.M.–7 P.M. the rest of the year, US$1 adults, US$0.50 children under age 12). Commercially closed in 1953, it was then used for wool storage; a fire gutted the interior in 1972, but its solid brick walls survived to become the city's historical museum. Contents include period clothing, furniture, carriages, and agricultural machinery as well as photographs, maps, and documents. It also devotes space to the Mapuche and Tehuelche and notes an early-20th-century banditry crackdown by the army that was tough on honest settlers.

Two blocks northeast of the plaza, the offbeat **Museo Cartref Taid** (Malacara s/n, tel. 02945/48-0108, 10 A.M.–noon and 3:30–8 P.M. daily summer and July, 3:30–8 P.M. daily the rest of the year, US$2) holds the **Tumba de Malacara,** the final resting place of a horse that helped its rider, Trevelin founder John D. Evans, flee an Araucanian raid during the Argentine army's 1880s war against the indigenes.

At the south end of town, built of brick, the **Capilla Bethel** (Ap Iwan and Laprida) is a Welsh chapel dating from 1897; it has also served as a school.

About 19 kilometers south of Trevelin via RN 259 and a short southbound lateral, **Reserva Provincial Nant-y-Fall** is a provincial park with a 400-meter footpath to a string of waterfalls, the highest of which is 67 meters. Nant-y-Fall's source is **Lago Rosario,** a subalpine lake on a Mapuche reservation 24 kilometers southwest of Trevelin via RP 17 and a short eastbound lateral.

Six kilometers west of Nant-y-Fall, the provincial **Estación de Salmonicultura** (salmon hatchery) offers guided tours 10 A.M.–noon and 2–8 P.M. weekdays. There are several campgrounds and *cabañas* along RN 259, which leads to the Chilean border.

In the Valle 16 de Octubre, about five kilometers east of Trevelin via gravel road, the historic **Escuela No. 18** stands near the site of a 1902 plebiscite that determined that Trevelin would stay on the Argentine side of the border (the original adobe building no longer exists). The onetime school now holds the **Museo del Plebiscito 1902** (11 A.M.–8:30 P.M. Thurs.–Sun. summer, 10 A.M.–6 P.M. Thurs.–Sun. the rest of the year, free), an outlier of Trevelin's regional museum that commemorates the 1902 events.

In summer, Plaza Coronel Fontana hosts a weekend **crafts market** that also takes place on holidays. The rest of the year, it takes place every other Sunday.

Accommodations

Except for *cabañas,* which are primarily for family groups, accommodations are few. On high ground a few blocks east of the plaza, the HI affiliate ◖ **Casaverde Hostel** (Los Alerces s/n, tel. 02945/48-0091, www.casaverdehostel.com.ar, US$10–13 pp dorm, US$35–42 d) is a prize: comfortable rooms, a bar, and extensive grounds with views of the Andes. It's small, though, so reservations—or good timing—are essential. It also rents bicycles, but breakfast costs extra.

Other options include **Residencial Pezzi** (Sarmiento 353, tel. 02945/48-0146, hpezzi@intramed.com.ar, summer only, US$42 d) and **Residencial Estefanía** (Perito Moreno and Sarmiento, tel. 02945/48-0148, santidoc@ciudad.com.ar, US$42 d), which has petulant ownership.

New in 2008, Trevelin's best new option **Hostería Casa de Piedra** (Brown 244, tel. 02945/48-0357, www.casadepiedratrevelin. com, US$66 s or d), a 10-room two-story B&B of stone and polished natural wood that offers king-size beds, continental or buffet breakfast, and amenities that include Wi-Fi.

Food

Welsh teahouses are fewer here than in Gaiman, but the quality is still outstanding. The traditional favorite, in modern quarters, is ◖ **Nain Maggie** (Perito Moreno 179, tel. 02945/48-0232), but there's nothing wrong with **Las Mutisias** (Avenida San Martín 170, tel. 02945/48-0165). Very filling late-afternoon teas cost about US$10 pp.

Reservations are advisable at ◖ **Patagonia Celta** (25 de Mayo s/n, tel. 02945/48-0722, lunch and dinner daily), which has a diverse menu of Argentine regional specialties in agreeable surroundings as well as excellent service. Despite the name, it has no direct Welsh connections.

Decer (Almirante Brown 398) has outstanding ice cream.

Information

The erratic **Dirección de Turismo** (Plaza Coronel Fontana s/n, tel. 02945/48-0120, www.trevelin.org) is open 8 A.M.–9 P.M. daily December–March; the rest of the year, hours are 8 A.M.–8 P.M. daily.

Services

Banco del Chubut (Avenida San Martín and Brown) has an ATM.

Correo Argentino (Avenida San Martín and Brown) is across from the bank; the postal code is 9203.

Gales al Sur (Avenida Patagonia 186, tel. 02965/48-0427) organizes excursions and activities in and around town, and also has Wi-Fi.

Lavitrev (Avenida San Martín 559, tel. 02945/48-0393) does the washing.

Hospital Trevelin (Avenida San Martín and Primera Junta, tel. 02945/48-0132) is nine blocks south of Plaza Coronel Fontana.

Getting There and Around

In daylight hours, **Transportes Jacobsen/ Vía Trevelin** shuttles between Esquel and Trevelin frequently; some buses continue to the Chilean border crossing at La Balsa/Futaleufú (8:30 A.M. and 6:30 P.M. Mon., Wed., and Fri., US$8). Long-distance travelers have to return to Esquel.

PARQUE NACIONAL LOS ALERCES

Parque Nacional Los Alerces owes its existence and name to *Fitzroya cupressoides,* the coniferous monarch of the humid Valdivian forests, also known as false larch or Patagonian cypress. Easily western Chubut's most popular attraction, the park draws campers and fishing aficionados to its forests and finger lakes. Despite a magnificent setting, with snowy Andean summits to the west, hikers find it frustrating because the scant trail network often forces them to walk the shoulders of dusty roads with heavy auto traffic.

Geography and Climate

About 45 kilometers west of Esquel via RN 259 and RP 71, Los Alerces is a 263,000-hectare unit on the eastern Andean slope. Its highest point is 2,253-meter Cerro Torrecillas, but Pacific storms that penetrate the lower cordillera here make it wetter than most of Argentine Patagonia.

Past glaciations have left navigable finger lakes that provide access to some of the park's finest sights. Summers are mild, with temperatures reaching 24°C with cool nights, but winters average barely 2°C and see ample snowfall.

Most destinations within the park are described with reference to La Villa, the village-like cluster of services at Lago Futalaufquen's south end.

Flora and Fauna

Besides the *alerce,* the park's other conifers include the Chilean incense cedar and the Guaiteca cypress, both with limited geographical distribution. Most of the rest of the forest consists of the broadleaf southern beeches

THE REDWOOD OF THE SOUTH

Like California's redwoods, the coniferous alerce (*Fitzroya cupressoides*) is long-lived (up to 4,000 years), tall (up to 70 meters, though most top out around 40), and makes an attractive, easily worked, water- and insect-resistant lumber. It's more abundant on the Chilean side, where its native habitat ranges from coastal Valdivia south to archipelagic and continental Chiloé. In Argentina it's found from Lago Nahuel Huapi south to Parque Nacional Los Alerces.

While it grows mostly between 400 and 700 meters above sea level, the alerce also thrives in poorly drained marshlands at lower altitudes. The branches of younger specimens touch the ground, but the reddish-barked lower trunks of mature trees are barren. The Mapuche know it as the *lawen*, but Charles Darwin gave the tree its botanical name, after the famous commanding officer of his equally famous vessel. Still, history's greatest scientist offers just a few descriptive remarks in his *The Voyage of the Beagle.*

coihue, lenga, and *ñire.* The *arrayán* nears the southern limit of its range here.

For hikers, one of the worst plagues is the *colihue,* a solid bamboo that forms impassable thickets. The aggressive exotic *Rosa moschata,* a European introduction, is displacing native plants.

In this dense forest, Los Alerces's fauna is less conspicuous, but the *huemul* (Andean deer) is present, along with its miniature distant relative the *pudú.* Birds include the *chucao* (a common songbird), the austral parakeet, and the Patagonian woodpecker.

Sights and Recreation

On the Río Desaguadero, east of RP 71 at the south end of Lago Futalaufquen, the **Sendero del Poblamiento Prehistórico** is an easy 500-meter nature trail that passes a natural overhang with fading pre-Columbian rock art, some of it clearly geometrical; it then climbs through forest to an overlook with expansive panoramas to the north.

Register with rangers to hike the steep route to the 1,916-meter summit of **Cerro Alto El Dedal,** reached by a trailhead from Puerto Bustillo, two kilometers north of La Villa; figure about six hours round-trip to complete the hike. From the same trailhead, **Cinco Saltos** is a shorter and easier hike to a series of waterfalls.

From Puerto Limonao, four kilometers north of La Villa, the 25-kilometer **Sendero Lago Krüger** follows Lago Futalaufquen's south shore to the smaller Lago Krüger, which has a campground and a lodge; register with rangers before beginning the hike, which has only one authorized campsite, at Playa Blanca, between the trailhead and the lodge. Daily boat service to Lago Krüger costs about US$20 pp.

Circuito Lacustre

Los Alerces' traditional excursion is the "lake circuit" from Puerto Limonao, at Lago Futalaufquen's south end, to the Río Arrayanes outlet of Lago Verde; at **Puerto Mermoud,** a catwalk crosses to Lago Menéndez's **Puerto Chucao,** where another boat continues to **Puerto Sagrario.**

From Puerto Sagrario, passing blue-green **Lago Cisne,** a looping nature trail goes to the **El Alerzal** grove and the landmark **El Abuelo,** the oldest and most impressive *alerce* specimen. While there are guides on the hike to and from El Abuelo, it's possible to separate from the group; it's not possible, though, to hike elsewhere in an area that's mostly limited-access *zona intangible.*

It's possible to start the excursion at either Puerto Limonao (US$42 pp) or Puerto Chucao (US$29 pp), though low water often eliminates the Limonao–Chucao segment. Scheduled departures are at 9:30 A.M. from Limonao, returning by 6 P.M., and 11:30 A.M. from Chucao, returning by 4:15 P.M. Any Esquel travel agency can make reservations, but it's possible to purchase tickets here on a space-available basis.

Accommodations and Food

Los Alerces has numerous campgrounds and other accommodations, mostly near Lago Futalaufquen. In addition to organized campgrounds, formerly free *agreste* ("wild") campgrounds now charge for limited services but are much cleaner than in the past.

Accessible by road, organized campgrounds all have picnic tables, fire pits, toilets, hot showers, and access to groceries and restaurants; some have electrical outlets. Among them are **Camping Los Maitenes** (tel. 02945/45-1003, US$5 pp), only 200 meters from the Intendencia at Futalaufquen's south end; **Camping Bahía Rosales** (tel. 02945/47-1004, US$6 pp), 14 kilometers from La Villa on the eastern lakeshore; **Camping Lago Verde** (tel. 02945/45-4421, US$7 pp), 36 kilometers north of La Villa on the eponymous lake; and **Camping Lago Rivadavia** (tel. 02945/45-4381, US$5 pp), 42 kilometers north of La Villa at the south end of its namesake lake.

Reached only by a 25-kilometer footpath or launch from Puerto Limonao, **Camping & Hostería Lago Krüger** (tel. 02945/45-3718 in Esquel) is the only backcountry campsite and hotel. Having undergone a major renovation, it charges about US$6 pp for camping, US$87 pp with full board in the *hostería*.

For groups of any size, the cheapest noncamping options are places like **Cabañas Tejas Negras** (RP 71, tel. 02945/47-1046, tejasnegras@ciudad.com.ar, US$79 d), about 12 kilometers north of La Villa.

About six kilometers north of La Villa, **Hostería Quimé-Quipán** (RP 71 s/n, tel./fax 02945/47-1021, US$61–66 s, US$68–100 d, with half board) has simple but comfortable rooms, some with lake views; the restaurant is adequate.

Four kilometers north of La Villa, the park's prestige accommodation is the Bustillo-built **⟨** **Hostería Futalaufquen** (tel. 02945/15-46-5941, www.brazosur.com.ar, US$159–242 s or d with half board, depending on view, in high season). With only nine rooms, it enjoys a privileged end-of-the-road location on Lago Futalaufquen's western shore; distinctive features include beamed Tudor-style ceilings, a walk-in granite fireplace, copper chandeliers, and a polished wooden bar. The restaurant is open to nonguests (reservations required for dinner).

Other Practicalities

Colloquially known as La Villa, Villa Futalaufquen is the park headquarters. The APN's **Museo y Centro de Informes** (tel. 02945/47-1015, ext. 14, infoalerces@apn.gov.ar, 8 A.M.–9 P.M. daily mid-Dec.–Apr., 9 A.M.–8 P.M. daily the rest of the year) is both a museum, with history and natural history exhibits, and a helpful ranger information center.

At both the northern Lago Rivadavia and eastern La Portada entrances, rangers collect a US$7 pp admission charge, which is valid for a week and includes other area parks. After 9 P.M., when the tollbooths close, there's no one to collect the charge, but they check on the way out.

In addition to the APN headquarters, La Villa also has a grocery, public telephones, and a first-aid station.

Transportes Esquel **buses** between Esquel and Lago Puelo pick up and drop off passengers along RP 71 within the park; some northbound buses go only to Lago Rivadavia before returning to Esquel. Puelo-bound passengers can disembark and reboard another day as long as they do not reverse direction.

GOBERNADOR COSTA

Some 153 kilometers south of Esquel, Gobernador Costa is a cow town with the best services on the long haul between Esquel and Río Mayo on RN 40 (south of here, the paved route becomes RP 20, while graveled RN 40 veers west through Alto Río Senguer). **Lago General Vintter,** on the Chilean border via graveled westbound RP 19, is popular for fishing.

Accommodations and Food

North of the highway, the **Camping Municipal** (US$1 pp) has hot water (US$1 per shower) and electricity. **Hostería y Parrilla Mi Refugio** (Avenida Roca s/n, tel. 02945/49-1097, US$37 d) has firm, comfortable beds but is ragged around the edges. Its restaurant serves pretty good versions of Argentine standards.

Across from the tourist office, **El Petiso** (Avenida Roca s/n) is best for beef.

Other Practicalities

The helpful new **Oficina de Informes** (Avenida Roca s/n, tel. 02945/49-1004) is open 9 A.M.–8 P.M. daily.

Banco del Chubut (Sarmiento and San Martín) has an ATM.

The bus terminal has services northbound to Esquel, eastbound to Trelew, and southbound to Sarmiento and Comodoro Rivadavia.

RÍO MAYO

Because public transportation is almost nonexistent on RN 40 between Gobernador Costa and Perito Moreno, only self-propelled southbound travelers normally see the crossroads town of Río Mayo; in fact, few vehicles of any kind use the dull but spine-jarring gravel section that intersects RP 43, the paved route between Comodoro Rivadavia and the Chilean border, 124 kilometers to the south. Despite having little to see, it's a stopover for cyclists, bikers, and motorists as well as southbound safaris from Bariloche.

Living primarily off the wool trade, though petroleum is making a comeback, Río Mayo (pop. 2,940) is 224 kilometers south of Gobernador Costa, and 274 kilometers west of Comodoro Rivadavia via paved RN 26 and RP 20. There is westbound public transportation on RN 26 to Coyhaique, Chile; some buses take the slightly longer route via RP 55.

Sights and Events

The modest **Museo Regional Federico Escalada** (Avenida Ejército Argentino s/n, tel. 02903/42-0400) is open 8 A.M.–1 P.M. and 4–7 P.M. Monday–Friday.

Featuring sheep-shearing contests and horseback races, early January's **Festival Nacional de la Esquila** is the principal festival.

Accommodations and Food

Camping El Labrador (Belgrano and Sarmiento) charges US$3 per vehicle. Modernized **Hotel Aka-ta** (San Martín 640, tel. 02903/42-0054, hotelakata@yahoo.com. ar, US$27 s, US$47 d) has rooms with private baths and an improved but cramped restaurant with Internet access.

Reservations are advisable for **Hotel El Viejo Covadonga** (San Martín 573, tel. 02903/42-0020, covadonga_hotel@yahoo.com.ar, US$15 pp, US$22 s, US$40 d), which fills with safari passengers on the RN 40 circuit between Bariloche and El Calafate. Though the previous owners absconded with its classic Old West–style bar, this spruced-up hotel has gracious management and is also the best place to eat.

Information and Services

At the eastern approach to town, the **Oficina de Informes** (Avenida Ejército Argentino s/n, tel. 02903/42-0400, culturayturismorio@yahoo.com.ar, 9:30 A.M.–1 P.M. and 2:30–7 P.M. Mon.–Fri., 10 A.M.–1 P.M. and 2–7 P.M. Sat., 10 A.M.–12:30 P.M. Sun.) currently occupies quarters in the museum, but it may move to a freestanding kiosk on the nearby median strip.

Banco del Chubut (Yrigoyen and Antártida Argentina) has an ATM. The **Cooperativa Eléctrica** (9 de Julio 409) has long-distance telephones and Internet access, and also arranges burials (seriously!).

Hospital Río Mayo (Sarmiento 637, tel. 02903/42-0022) provides medical services.

Getting There

Schedules are subject to change from Río Mayo's **Terminal de Ómnibus** (Fontana and Irigoyen). **Transaustral** (tel. 02903/42-0167) has daily eastbound services to Comodoro Rivadavia (4 hours, US$8), and westbound buses to Coyhaique, Chile (6 hours, US$26), leave at noon Wednesday and Saturday (reservations are essential as these often fill up in Comodoro).

SOUTHERN PATAGONIA

Argentina's second- and third-largest provinces, stretching from the Atlantic to the Andes, Santa Cruz and Chubut might be considered Argentina's "Deep South," whose vast open spaces and scattered population lend themselves to Patagonia's "wild and remote" stereotype. That said, there are substantial cities and towns with hotels and other services, many good roads (plus others not so good), and decent public transportation.

Southern Patagonia's most dramatic sight (and sound) is the Moreno Glacier at Parque Nacional Los Glaciares—along with Buenos Aires and Iguazú, it's one of the top reasons people travel to Argentina. Many spend entire days gazing upon and listening to this relentless river of ice. More active visitors take the bus to the hamlet of El Chaltén, where a cluster of trailheads offer access to wild backcountry and, for climbers, some of the continent's most challenging technical peaks. Even day hikers, though, will appreciate its striking Andean scenery.

Even then, the barren coastline draws many visitors to Península Valdés and other sites where packs of penguins waddle ashore in the southern spring, elephant seals give birth in summer, and the great right whales breed and birth in sheltered shallows in winter and spring. The coast and steppe also feature picturesque towns such as the Welsh settlement of Gaiman and the historic ports of Puerto Deseado and Puerto San Julián. On the Santa Cruz steppe, there are several petrified forests and the landmark rock art of Cueva de las Manos, a UNESCO World Heritage Site.

© JAVARMAN/123RF.COM

HIGHLIGHTS

Ecocentro Puerto Madryn: Home to living tidepools, gardens, a research library, and more, this environmental center is a testament to the ecological commitment of Puerto Madryn, coastal Patagonia's largest beach resort (page 419).

Reserva Provincial Península Valdés: It's hard to choose among coastal Patagonia's countless wildlife reserves, but Península Valdés has everything: guanacos, rheas, penguins, elephant seals, sea lions, orcas, and the great right whales. It doesn't have everything at the same time, though, so every season's a different experience (page 423).

Reserva Provincial Every austral spring, nearly Magellanic penguins waddle this remote spot, where there are also plenty of other seabirds and shorebirds (page 437).

Parque Nacional Monte León: Where the tides strike the headlands, the South Atlantic has gouged deep kelp-filled caverns in this recently created coastal park. In addition, there's plenty of wildlife, including penguins and guanacos (page 450).

Estancia Monte Dinero: On the coastal steppe southeast of Río Gallegos, Monte Dinero is a model working ranch that also provides homey accommodations and access to the giant penguin colony and other sights at Cabo Vírgenes (page 455).

Eolo Lodge: Southwest of El Calafate, this new country lodge re-creates the style of the original Patagonia *estancias*, with vast panoramas and modern luxuries (page 465).

Parque Nacional Los Glaciares: The constantly calving 60-meter face of groaning Glaciar Moreno, west of El Calafate, is one of the continent's most awesome sights (and sounds). Sector Fitz Roy, near the hamlet of El Chaltén, offers some of the Andes' most exhilarating scenery, hiking, and climbing (page 466).

Parque Nacional Perito Moreno: West of RN 40, Argentina's loneliest highway, what may be Patagonia's wildest park offers endless vistas and varied terrain – ranging from sub-Antarctic forest to high Andean pastures (page 483).

Cueva de las Manos: East of RN 40, where the Río Pinturas has carved a canyon into the steppe, this UNESCO World Heritage Site's rock art includes hundreds of human hands and other more abstract designs nearly 10,000 years old (page 485).

LOOK FOR **(** TO FIND RECOMMENDED SIGHTS, ACTIVITIES, DINING, AND LODGING.

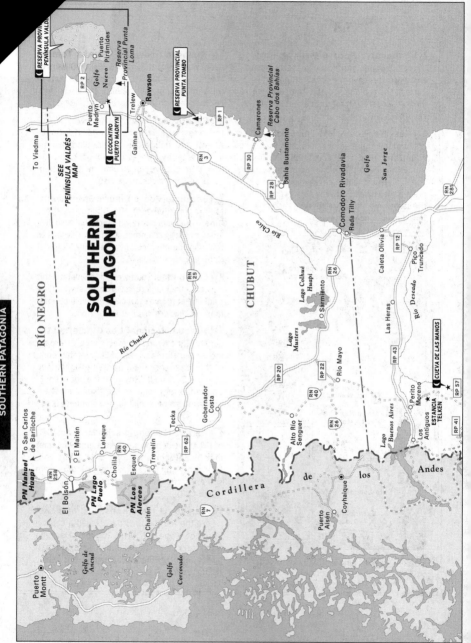

SOUTHERN PATAGONIA

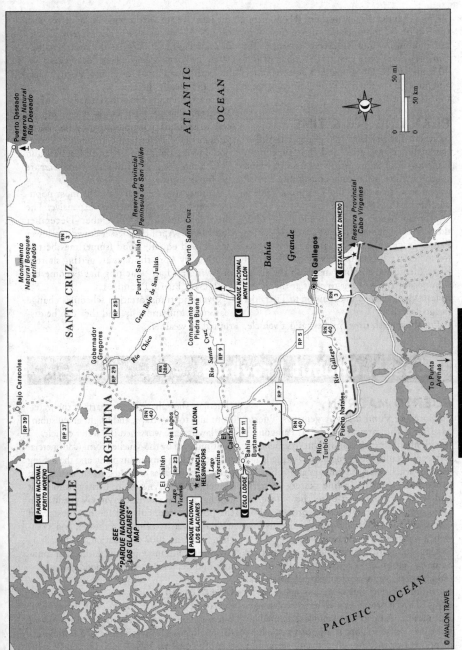

SOUTHERN PATAGONIA

© AVALON TRAVEL

Note that details on northern RN 40, from the Río Negro provincial border to the southern Chubut town of Río Mayo, appear in the *Northern Patagonia* chapter. Sections of RN 40 from Río Turbio, along the Chilean border, and north to the town of Perito Moreno appear in this chapter.

PLANNING YOUR TIME

Southern Patagonia's highlights are limitless, but distances are great and flying is almost imperative for short-term visitors—overland transportation is too time-consuming to visit widely separated sights like Península Valdés's wildlife and the Moreno Glacier.

Moreno Glacier visitors should make additional time—perhaps at least a week—to hike Parque Nacional Los Glaciares's Fitz Roy sector and even Chile's Parque Nacional Torres del Paine (dedicated climbers may wait the entire summer for the weather to clear at these latitudes). Many choose an extension to Tierra del Fuego as well.

For those with time, money, and a vehicle, the ideal way to see the region is to drive south on RN 3—all the way to the Moreno Glacier or even Tierra del Fuego—and return via RN 40 to Bariloche or beyond. Besides a sturdy vehicle, this requires at least a month, preferably two, and ideally three.

Coastal Patagonia's best base is Puerto Madryn, which has the best services, and access to secondary attractions like the Welsh settlements of Trelew and Gaiman. For the national parks along the Andes, El Calafate and El Chaltén along with full-service *estancias* are the top options.

January and February are the most popular months, but also the most expensive. The shoulder months of November–December and March–April have lesser crowding, lower prices, and equally good (sometimes better) weather. By April the days are getting shorter, but winter whale-watching has become big business at Puerto Pirámides.

Overland transportation schedules change seasonally and annually, and they can be disrupted by weather.

Coastal Chubut Province

PUERTO MADRYN

For foreigners and many Argentines, Puerto Madryn is the gateway to coastal Patagonia's wealth of wildlife; the Golfo Nuevo's sheltered waters and sandy shoreline have also made it a premier beach resort. In January and February, sunbathers, cyclists, in-line skaters, joggers, and windsurfers irrupt onto the *balnearios* along the Costanera Avenida Brown, while divers seek out reefs and wrecks as the shallow waters warm with the season.

Madryn's tourist season only weakens after Semana Santa until July, when Península Valdés's great right whales help fill hotels and restaurants. Conscious of its ecological birthright, Madryn promotes itself as an ecofriendly destination; its Ecocentro complex, focused on maritime conservation, is a positive development. Meanwhile, though, souvenir stores and chocolate shops have turned parts of the waterfront into tourist traps, and bright green suburban lawns have worsened the water deficit.

Stimulated by the Muelle Storni (commercial pier), the Aluar aluminum plant, and the fishing fleet, three decades of rapid growth have almost obliterated Madryn's Welsh heritage (though it still has a sister city in Nefyn, Gwynedd). On the positive side, cultural life has blossomed with a university campus, a theater, and a cinema. Since the 2002 devaluation, many visitors have been Chileans, especially during that country's mid-September patriotic holidays.

Orientation

Puerto Madryn is 1,308 kilometers south of Buenos Aires and 1,219 kilometers north of Río Gallegos via RN 3. It is 673 kilometers east of Esquel via RN 3, RN 25, and RN 40;

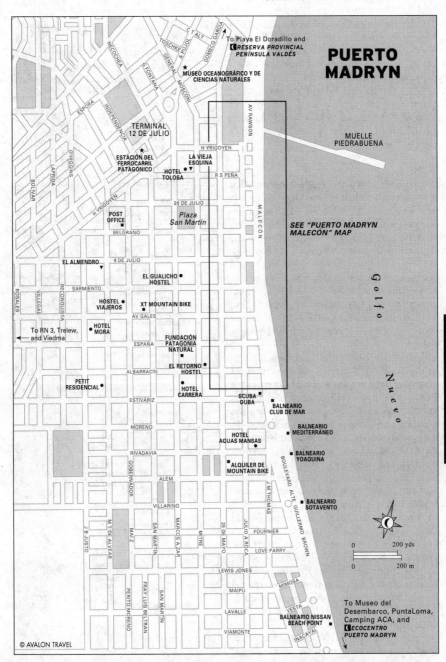

PUERTO MADRYN

To Playa El Doradillo and
⦗ RESERVA PROVINCIAL
PENÍNSULA VALDÉS

★ **MUSEO OCEANOGRÁFICO Y DE**
CIENCIAS NATURALES

MUELLE
PIEDRABUENA

TERMINAL
12 DE JULIO

ESTACIÓN DEL
★ FERROCARRIL
PATAGÓNICO

LA VIEJA
ESQUINA

HOTEL
TOLOSA

SEE "PUERTO MADRYN
MALECÓN" MAP

POST
OFFICE

Plaza
San Martín

EL ALMENDRO

EL GUALICHO
HOSTEL

HOSTEL
VIAJEROS

XT MOUNTAIN BIKE

To RN 3, Trelew,
and Viedma

HOTEL
MORA

FUNDACIÓN
PATAGONIA
NATURAL

EL RETORNO
HOSTEL

PETIT
RESIDENCIAL

HOTEL
CARRERA

SCUBA
DUBA

BALNEARIO
CLUB DE MAR

G o l f o

N u e v o

HOTEL
AGUAS MANSAS

BALNEARIO
MEDITERRÁNEO

BALNEARIO
YOAQUINA

ALQUILER DE
MOUNTAIN BIKE

BALNEARIO
SOTAVENTO

0	200 yds

0	200 m

BALNEARIO NISSAN
BEACH POINT

To Museo del
Desembarco, PuntaLoma,
Camping ACA, and
⦗ ECOCENTRO
PUERTO MADRYN

Street names: C T ALT, TOSCHKE, DOMECQ GARCÍA, NECOCHEA, G FONTANA, GENERAL MOSCONI, ESPORA, INDEPENDENCIA, O'HIGGINS, LAPRIDA, BOLÍVAR, H YRIGOYEN, R S PEÑA, 28 DE JULIO, BELGRANO, 9 DE JULIO, SARMIENTO, ROSALES, VILLEGAS, RECONQUISTA, AV GALES, ESPAÑA, ALBARRACÍN, ESTIVÁRIZ, MORENO, RIVADAVIA, GOBERNADOR, ALEM, VILLARINO, M T DE ALVEAR, J B JUSTO, MAÍZ, SAN MARTÍN, MARCOS A ZAR, MITRE, 25 DE MAYO, JULIO A ROCA, FOURNIER, LOVE PARRY, LEWIS JONES, MAIPU, PERITO MORENO, FRAY LUIS BELTRAN, SAN MARTIN, LAVALLE, VIAMONTE, MIMOSA, VESTA, INACAYAL, J M THOMAS, BOULEVARD ALTE GUILLERMO BROWN, AV RAWSON, MALECÓN

SOUTHERN PATAGONIA

© AVALON TRAVEL

719 kilometers southeast of Neuquén; and 896 kilometers from Bariloche. It is 65 kilometers north of Trelew. By the census of 2002, the population is 57,571, but it may now be approaching 100,000.

Most services are within a few blocks of the waterfront Avenida Roca and Avenida Brown, with their sandy beaches and *balnearios,* which are the main points of interest in the city itself.

Sights

North of downtown, the **Museo Oceanográfico y de Ciencias Naturales** (Domecq García and Menéndez, tel. 02965/45-1139, www.hostar.com.ar/museo, 9 A.M.–8 P.M. Mon.–Fri., 4–8 P.M. Sat., US$1.50, free Tues.) stresses the regional environment, wildlife, and history, including geology and paleontology, botany and oceanography, invertebrates, marine mammals, fish, birds, and the Welsh colonization. It occupies the neoclassical **Chalet Pujol** (1915), built by businessman and Madryn mayor Agustín Pujol and topped by a domed hexagonal tower.

Immediately in front of the new bus terminal, one of Madryn's oldest structures (1889), the former **Estación del Ferrocarril Patagónico** (train station, Hipólito Yrigoyen and Independencia) previously served as a bus terminal and is due to become a museum. On the waterfront, the modest **Museo Municipal de Arte** (Municipal Art Museum, Avenida Roca 444, tel. 02965/45-3204, museodearte@madryn.gov.ar, free but donations encouraged) is open 10 A.M.–1 P.M. and 6–9 P.M. Monday–Friday, 6–9 P.M. Saturday.

Where the first Welshmen came ashore in 1865, about three kilometers southeast of town via Bulevar Brown, the **Parque Histórico Punta Cuevas** preserves remnants of the shelters whose foundations they dug into the bluff above the high-tide mark. Its **Museo del Desembarco** (puntacuevas@madryn.com, 3–7 P.M. Wed.–Mon., US$1.25), provides more details.

For Puerto Madryn's 1965 centennial, *porteño* artist Luis Perlotti created two monumental

sculptures: downtown's **Monumento a La Gesta Galesa** (Avenida Roca and Belgrano), to honor the Welsh contribution to the area, and Punta Cuevas's **Monumento al Indio Tehuelche,** a tribute to the province's aboriginal inhabitants.

◉ Ecocentro Puerto Madryn

In season, southern right whales approach the promontory of this luminous "Magellanic" structure, crowned by a tower that yields views of distant Península Valdés across the Golfo Nuevo. It's the work of a nonprofit institution striving to bring environmental education, research, and the arts under the same roof.

As a maritime-life educational center, the Ecocentro has superb displays of South Atlantic fauna, including birds, seals, and especially whales; one of the finest is a living tidal pool. Even the surrounding gardens serve a didactic purpose—in lieu of residential Madryn's water-hungry lawns, the directors have chosen to preserve the native coastal desert flora.

Reached by a spiral staircase, the three-level tower holds a library, an exhibition room for local artists and authors, and a reading room. Painting, photography, and sculpture are all on display; the ground-floor atrium accommodates the largest works. There are also a 150-seat theater for concerts and lectures, a crafts and souvenir shop, and a café.

Reached by Bulevar Almirante Brown, about five minutes from downtown by taxi, 15 minutes by bicycle, and 40 minutes on foot, the Ecocentro (Julio Verne 3784, tel. 02965/45-7470, www.ecocentro.org.ar, US$8 adults, US$5 children ages 6–12) is open 5–9 P.M. daily January–February, plus 10 A.M.–1 P.M. when cruise ships are in port. Hours are 3–7 P.M. Tuesday–Sunday in March and July–September, 3–7 P.M. Wednesday–Sunday April–June, and 3–8 P.M. daily October–December.

Entertainment and Events

Madryn has an active cultural calendar, starting with the **Teatro del Muelle** (Rawson 60, tel. 02965/45-7966), which offers theater programs, usually on weekends. The **Casa de la Cultura** (Roque Sáenz Peña 86, tel. 02965/47-2060) hosts a variety of events.

The **Cine Teatro Auditorium** (28 de Julio 129, tel. 02965/45-5653) shows current movies and also offers live theater. The **Teatro La Escalera** (Estivariz and San Martín, tel. 02965/45-7707) is a newer theater company with a good reputation.

For occasional live music and Wi-Fi from next door, try the **Margarita Bar** (Roque Sáenz Peña 15), which has pub grub (rock-bottom cheap, with a diversity of outstanding midday specials) and costlier drinks. **La Oveja Negra** (Hipólito Yrigoyen 144) is another popular bar, with live music on weekends and occasional tango during the week.

July 28's **Fundación de la Ciudad** celebrates the initial Welsh landing at Punta Cuevas. Festivities continue for several days.

Shopping

The waterfront avenues are full of souvenir shops, but the best option remains **Manos del Sur** (Avenida Roca 516, tel. 02965/47-2539). **Recreo** (Roque Sáenz Peña 101, tel. 02965/47-2971) carries a fine selection of books on Patagonia, some in English. **Barrika** (Avenida Roca 109, tel. 02965/45-0454) has the best wine selection.

Sports and Recreation

Water sports are the attraction on the crescent of sandy beaches stretching from Muelle Storni in the north almost to Punta Cuevas in the south. In these sheltered waters, hazards like rip currents are nonexistent, but at low tide the water retreats hundreds of meters on the gently sloping beach.

At the beaches along Bulevar Almirante Brown, several *balnearios* rent water-sports equipment and have snack bars and restaurants. From north to south, they are **Balneario Vernardino Club de Mar** (Bulevar Brown 860, tel. 02965/47-4289, www.vernardinoclubde-mar.com.ar), **Balneario Yoaquina** (Bulevar Brown 1050, tel. 02965/45-6058), **Balneario Mediterráneo** (Bulevar Brown 1070, tel.

02965/45-8145), **Balneario Sotavento** (Bulevar Brown 1300, tel. 02965/45-3002), and **Balneario Nissan Beach Point** (Bulevar Brown and Inacayal, tel. 02965/45-7403).

Balnearios also rent items like in-line skates and mountain bikes. Some operators who arrange diving excursions and other activities have space here; others are scattered around town.

Divers favor Madryn because of its clear waters, natural and artificial reefs, and shipwrecks; most operators do initial dives for novices, PADI certification courses, and underwater photography. Operators working out of the *balnearios* include **Ocean Divers** (Balneario Yoaquina, tel. 02965/47-2569, www.oceandivers.com.ar), **Patagonia Buceo** (Balneario Maminas, Bulevar Brown and Castelli, tel. 02965/45-2278, www.patagoniabuceo.com), and **Puerto Madryn Buceo** (Balneario Nissan Beach Point, tel. 02965/15-56-4422, www.madrynbuceo.com). Operators elsewhere include **Aquatours** (Avenida Roca 550, tel. 02965/45-1954, www.aquatours.com.ar), **Lobo Larsen** (Avenida Roca 885, tel. 02965/47-0277, www.lobolarsen.com), and **Scuba Duba** (Bulevar Brown 893, tel. 02965/45-2699, www.scubaduba.com.ar).

Accommodations

In addition to current hotel prices, the Secretaría de Turismo keeps a register of rental apartments on a daily, weekly, or monthly basis. In peak season, most hotels charge double rates even for a single guest. Hotel occupancy is high, but the summer trend is toward apartment complexes, as people come here to spend two weeks on the beach.

In addition to these options, Madryn has a number of reasonably priced hostels for shoestring travelers.

US$25-50

On the Punta Cuevas road, the wooded 800-site **Camping ACA** (tel. 02965/45-2952, www.acamadryn.com.ar, US$13 for 2 persons) offers discounts to members and affiliates.

Most accommodations in this range are

hostels, with simple exceptions such as **Hotel del Centro** (28 de Julio 149, tel. 02965/47-3742, US$13–17 s, US$22–24 d), **Hotel Vaskonia** (25 de Mayo 43, tel. 02965/47-2581, mariaandrade@infovia.com.ar, US$21 s, US$26 d), and **Hotel Mora** (Juan B. Justo 654, tel. 02965/47-1424, www.morahotel.com.ar, US$40 d).

Only half a block from the beach, Israeli favorite **Chepatagonia Hostel** (Alfonsina Storni 16, tel. 02965/45-5783, www.chepatagoniahostel.com.ar, US$11 pp dorm, US$34–39 d) is an independent hostel with mostly dorm accommodations, but it's spotless and pleasant.

Though a little farther from the beach, **El Retorno Hostel** (Mitre 798, tel. 02965/45-6044, www.elretornohostel.com.ar, US$10–16 pp dorm, US$34 d) has more private rooms in a beautifully appointed place.

The Spartan **Petit Residencial** (Marcelo T. de Alvear 845, tel. 02965/45-1460, hotelpetit@arnet.com.ar, US$33 s, US$39 d) is a friendly place with small motel-style rooms and ample parking; breakfast costs US$2 more.

Freshly modernized, set among pleasing gardens, the motel-style **Hostel Viajeros** (Gobernador Maíz 545, tel. 02965/45-6457, www.hostelviajeros.com, US$13 pp dorm, US$29 s, US$42 d) is an amiable place with dorms, legitimate single rooms, and doubles with private baths.

Madryn's HI affiliate is the exceptional **€ El Gualicho Hostel** (Marcos A. Zar 480, tel. 02965/45-4163, www.elgualichohostel.com.ar, US$13 pp dorm, US$58 d with private bath). Comfortably furnished and attractively decorated, it also has a shady patio that encourages socializing.

Set back from the busy avenue, centrally located **Residencial Manolo's** (Avenida Roca 763, tel. 02965/47-2390, manolos@speedy.com.ar, US$37 s, US$45 d) has firm beds but slightly cramped rooms.

US$50-100

Rates have stabilized at tranquil **Hotel Aguas Mansas** (José Hernández 51, tel. 02965/47-3103, www.aguasmansas.com, US$58 s, US$63 d), a pleasant contemporary place on a residential block but still close to the beach.

Though its smallish rooms don't get many style points, the homey, well-kept **Hotel Carrera** (Marcos A. Zar 844, tel. 02965/45-0759, www.hotelcarrera.com.ar, US$53 s, US$68 d) offers personalized service in a quiet neighborhood, with a very decent breakfast to boot. The well-located **Hotel Gran Madryn** (Lugones 40, tel. 02965/47-2205, www.gran-madryn.com, US$46–51 s, US$57–69 d) is comparable.

Re-creating the style of Madryn's early Welsh houses, but with contemporary comforts, ◖ **Hotel Bahía Nueva** (Avenida Roca 67, tel./fax 02965/45-1677, www.bahianueva.com.ar, US$57 s, US$73 d) also has spacious gardens and ample parking in a central beachfront location.

While it may have improved, prices at the **Costanera Hotel** (Almirante Brown 759, tel. 02965/45-3000, www.patagoniaargentina.com.ar, US$82–92 s, US$92–106 d) have risen even more, and it primarily relies on its convenient beachfront location.

OVER US$100

All of Madryn's top-end hotel follow the unfortunate policy of charging foreigners more, often substantially more, than they do Argentines.

Hotel Playa (Avenida Roca 181, tel. 02965/45-1446, www.playahotel.com.ar, 102 s or d) draws its character from its age. **Hotel Península Valdés** (Avenida Roca 155, tel. 02965/47-1292, www.hotelpeninsula.com.ar, US$70–134 s or d) has fine standard rooms, but spectacular ocean views make the larger panoramic rooms worth consideration.

Though well-established and central, **Hotel Tolosa** (Roque Sáenz Peña 253, tel. 02965/47-1850, www.hoteltolosa.com.ar, US$135–155 s or d) is not as good as some cheaper places.

Facing the beach, **Hotel Yenehue** (Avenida Roca 33, tel. 02965/47-1496, yenehue@austra-lis.com.ar, www.australiset.com.ar, US$140–190 s, US$156–212 d) is a spa hotel with high-rise ocean views from the rooms that front on the avenue. In addition to saunas,

massage, and other treatments (which are open to nonguests), amenities include a restaurant, Wi-Fi, and good disabled access.

Food

Puerto Madryn's dining scene is mostly uninspired, with diminished creativity and innovation, but there are exceptions.

Good choices for breakfast, snacks, and coffee include **Café Mar y Tiempo** (Roque Sáenz Peña 112) and the **Lizard Café** (Avenida Roca and Gales, tel. 02965/45-5306), also a decent pizzeria. The **Havanna Café** (Avenida Roca and 9 de Julio, tel. 02965/47-3373), though, is probably the best *confitería*.

Madryn's only Welsh teahouse, **Del Chubut** (Avenida Roca 369, tel. 02965/45-1311) also sells takeaway *alfajores* (cookies sandwiched around sweet fillings like *dulce de leche*) and *torta galesa* (a dense black cake).

La Barra (Bulevar Brown and Lugones, tel. 02965/45-5550, lunch and dinner daily) is one of several moderately priced pizzerias. Reinvented as a sports bar, **Ambigú** (Avenida Roca 97, tel. 02965/47-2541, lunch and dinner daily) has eight TVs and Wi-Fi, but pizza is still the best bet here (although the scallops aren't bad).

Part of its namesake *balneario,* **Vernardino** (Bulevar Brown 860, tel. 02965/47-4289, lunch and dinner daily) has stuffed pastas (around US$6–8) and house wine by the glass, but it's a little *too* family-friendly for a quiet dinner. Down the block, the comparable **Yoaquina** (Bulevar Brown 1050, tel. 02965/45-6058, lunch and dinner daily) has good lasagna (US$7) and raspberries with cream for dessert.

Cantina El Náutico (Avenida Roca 790, tel. 02965/47-1404, lunch and dinner daily) and **Puerto Marisko** (Avenida Rawson 7, tel. 02965/45-0752, lunch and dinner daily) are traditional seafood choices. The former is especially popular; the latter has its seaside location to recommend it, but service is erratic and the kitchen slow.

Made in the metal-clad Magellanic style, with Georgian flourishes and a brick interior adorned with artifacts from the early days of settlement, **La Vieja Esquina** (Mitre and Roque Sáenz Peña, tel. 02965/47-5601, lunch and dinner daily) has a varied menu of meat, fish, seafood, and pasta. For warm nights, there's outdoor seating and a play area for kids, but an illuminated soft-drink sign scars the historic exterior.

In new quarters, ◖ **Mar y Meseta** (Avenida Gales 32, tel. 02965/45-8740, www.marymeseta.com.ar, lunch and dinner daily, US$10–20) boasts intriguing dishes like gnocchi with lamb, prawn ravioli, and crab cannelloni in a shrimp sauce, but not everything is available every night. Consider the lamb skewers with onion, bacon, and peppers, or the *abadejo* (pollock) in a honey sauce.

Named for the almond tree that shades its entrance, ◖ **El Almendro** (Alvear and 9 de Julio, tel. 02965/47-0525) is one of few Madryn restaurants that provides quiet dining in sophisticated surroundings at reasonable prices, with items such as ravioli stuffed with Patagonian lamb along with a pesto of almonds, basil, garlic, and mint (US$8), plus simple well-executed dishes such as *lomo tres pimientas* (three-pepper steak). With good desserts, a decent wine list, and attentive service, this is one of the city's top choices.

The kitchen can be creative at **Plácido** (Avenida Roca 506, tel. 02965/45-5991, www.placido.com.ar, lunch and dinner daily), but the appetizers, desserts and drinks are unconscionably expensive by Argentine standards—a modest malbec by the glass, for instance, costs almost as much as an entire bottle of pretty good wine in some other places.

Madryn has superb ice creameries, including the 40-plus flavors at **Vía Roca** (Lugones 51, tel. 02965/45-0704), and **Kebom** (Avenida Roca 540).

Information

The exemplary and tireless **Secretaría de Turismo** (Avenida Roca 223, tel. 02965/45-3504 or 02965/45-6067, www.madryn.gov.ar) provides information in Spanish, English, French, and German and helps find accommodations when beds are scarce. Hours are

7 A.M.–11 P.M. January–March; in other seasons, hours are 7 A.M.–9 P.M. weekdays, 8 A.M.–9 P.M. weekends and holidays.

For motorists, **ACA** (tel. 02965/45-6684) is at Belgrano 19.

The **Fundación Patagonia Natural** (Marcos A. Zar 760, tel. 02965/47-4363, www.patagonianatural.org) is an NGO working to preserve Patagonia's natural wealth.

Services

Banco del Chubut (25 de Mayo 154) has one of many ATMs. The only currency exchange house is **Cambio Thaler** (Avenida Roca 497).

Correo Argentino is at Belgrano and Gobernador Maíz; the postal code is 9120.

Telefónica Roca (Avenida Roca and 9 de Julio) has phone, fax, and Internet services. Madryn now has free public Wi-Fi.

Nievemar (Avenida Roca 493, tel. 02965/45-5544) is the Amex affiliate.

Presto-Lav (Avenida Brown 605, tel. 02965/45-1526) can do the washing.

The **Hospital Subzonal** (tel. 02965/45-1240) is at Pujol 247.

Getting There

Commercial flights traditionally land at Trelew, 65 kilometers south, but Puerto Madryn's **Aeródromo El Tehuelche** (tel. 02965/45-6774) gets some commercial flights. **Andes Líneas Aéreas** (Avenida Roca 624, tel. 02965/45-2355, www.andesonline.com) flies to and from Buenos Aires's Aeroparque with connections to Córdoba, Puerto Iguazú, Salta, and Jujuy. **LADE** (Avenida Roca 119, tel. 02965/45-2355) has sporadic southbound flights to Comodoro Rivadavia and northbound flights to Neuquén and to Aeroparque.

Aerolíneas Argentinas (Avenida Roca 427, tel. 02965/45-1998) flies out of Trelew once or twice daily to Aeroparque, and occasionally to El Calafate, Río Gallegos, and Ushuaia.

Madryn's bus terminal, **Terminal 12 de Julio** (Dr. Avila s/n, tel. 02965/45-1789), stands directly behind the old terminal (and former railroad station). It has frequent service to Trelew with **Línea 28 de Julio** (tel. 02965/47-2056)

plus extensive regional and long-distance connections. **Mar y Valle** (tel. 02965/45-0600) goes to Puerto Pirámides at 8:55 A.M. daily; in summer and during whale-watching season it adds departures at 5 and 6:45 P.M.

Sample destinations, times, and fares include Trelew (1 hour, US$2.50), Puerto Pirámides (1.5 hours, US$4.50), Comodoro Rivadavia (6 hours, US$20–24), Esquel (10 hours, US$29–40), Neuquén (10 hours, US$27–37), Bariloche (12 hours, US$43–51), Río Gallegos (18 hours, US$51–65), and Buenos Aires (20 hours, US$60–91).

Getting Around

For flights from Madryn's Aeródromo El Tehuelche, **Transporte Aitué** (Avenida Roca 331, tel. 02965/15-27-2444) provides shuttle service for US$4 pp. A taxi or *remise* costs US$6.50.

For flights to and from Trelew, **Transportes Eben-Ezer** (tel. 02965/47-2474, 02965/15-66-0463) charges US$6.50 pp for door-to-door shuttle service, but a taxi or *remise* costs around US$37.

Bicycle-rental outlets include **XT Mountain Bike** (Avenida Gales 439, tel. 02965/47-2232), which also leads guided tours, and **Alquiler de Mountain Bike** (25 de Mayo 1136, tel. 02965/47-4426).

Because the area's attractions are spread out and the roads are decent, renting a car is a good option. Agencies include **Avis** (Avenida Roca 493, tel. 02965/47-5422), **Hertz** (Avenida Roca 115, tel. 02965/47-5247), **Puerto Madryn Turismo** (Avenida Roca 624, tel. 02965/45-2355), and **Rent A Car Patagonia** (Avenida Roca 293, Local 8, tel. 02965/45-2095).

VICINITY OF PUERTO MADRYN

Madryn's tour agencies go farther afield as well, to Trelew, Gaiman, Punta Tombo, and, of course, Península Valdés. Operators include **Cuyun-Co** (Avenida Roca 165, tel. 02965/45-1845, www.cuyunco.com.ar), **Huinca Travel** (Belgrano 198, Oficinas 1 and 2, tel. 02965/45-0720, www.huincatravel.com),

Puerto Madryn Turismo (Avenida Roca 624, tel. 02965/45-4411, www.madrynturismo.com), and **Turismo Puma** (28 de Julio 46, tel. 02965/45-1063, www.turismopuma.com). Full-day excursions run in the US$35–40 range, not including meals or park admission fees; whale-watching is extra, even on full-day tours to Península Valdés.

Reserva Provincial Punta Loma

Close enough to Madryn for a mountain-bike excursion, Punta Loma lacks the sheer wildlife numbers and diversity of Península Valdés, but its ample sea lion colonies, along with cormorants, giant petrels, gulls, terns, and snowy sheathbills are reason enough to visit. Only 15 kilometers southwest of Madryn via an undulating gravel road, it gets far fewer visitors than Valdés.

Near the sea lion colony, there's a visitors center and an overlook that permits good views of the animals. Hours are 8 A.M.–8 P.M. daily; admission costs US$7 for foreigners, US$2 for Argentine residents, and US$0.75 for Chubut residents. There's no scheduled transportation, but Madryn operators will arrange excursions, or a small group can go cheaply by *remise*.

Playa El Doradillo

From Playa El Doradillo's headlands, 17 kilometers northeast of Madryn via RP 42, deep water lets whales approach the shore—the next best choice to an in-the-water view at Península Valdés. Like Punta Loma, this is close enough for a bike ride or a shared taxi.

◖ RESERVA PROVINCIAL PENÍNSULA VALDÉS

Coastal Patagonia's top destination, the World Biosphere Reserve of Península Valdés is the place where the great southern right whale arrives to breed and birth in the winter months. Protected since 1935, the *ballena franca* occupies a nearly unique position as a "natural monument"—a designation normally reserved for territorial ecosystems—within the Argentine national park system.

Península Valdés itself, a provincial reserve

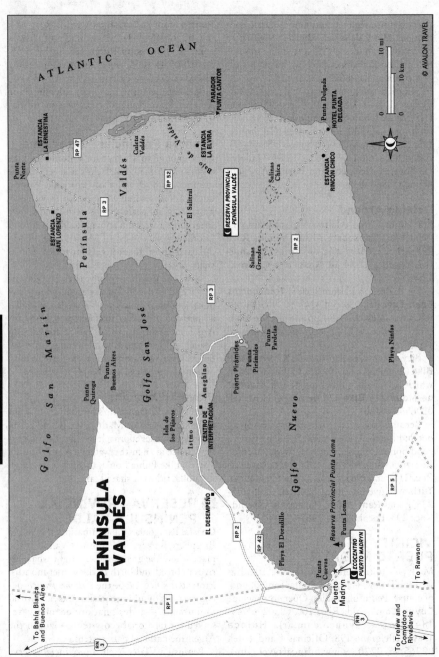

PENÍNSULA VALDÉS

© AVALON TRAVEL

rather than a national park, has more to offer than just whales. Some marine mammal species—ranging from sea lions to elephant seals and orcas—cover the beaches or gather in the Golfo San José, Golfo Nuevo, or the open South Atlantic all year. There are also concentrations of burrowing Magellanic penguins and flocks of other seabirds, plus herds of grazing guanacos and groups of sprinting rheas in the interior grasslands.

The main activity center is the hamlet of Puerto Pirámides, which, like Puerto Madryn enjoys a longer tourist season because of the whale- and orca-watching periods. Once the export point for salt from the Salina Grande depression, it has grown haphazardly, and water continues to be a problem in this desert environment.

Sometimes called Puerto Pirámide, the village has since reasserted its plurality. According to local accounts, when the Argentine navy used the area as a firing range, they destroyed two of the three pyramidal promontories that gave the settlement its original moniker.

Geography and Climate

Connected to the mainland by the narrow Istmo de Ameghino, Península Valdés is 56 kilometers northeast of Puerto Madryn via RP 2, but visiting the major wildlife sites involves a circuit of roughly 400 kilometers to Puerto Pirámides and Punta Delgada via RP 2, Caleta Valdés and Punta Norte via RP 47, and RP 3 back to Puerto Pirámides. Beyond Puerto Pirámides, loose gravel and dirt can be hazardous to inexperienced drivers, especially with low-clearance vehicles.

Broad sandy beaches line much of the coast, but unconsolidated sediments make the steep headlands that rise above them dangerous to descend. Sheep *estancias* occupy most of the interior, whose Salina Grande depression (42 meters below sea level) is one of the world's lowest points. The climate is dry, with high evaporation due to long hours of sunlight and perpetual winds.

Flora and Fauna

Most of Peninsula Valdés consists of rolling *monte* (scrubland) with patches of pasture that expand in wet years. The stocking rate for sheep is low, permitting guanacos and rheas to thrive alongside them.

Marine mammals—whales, orcas, elephant seals, and sea lions—are the big draw, along with Magellanic penguin colonies. In addition to penguins, there are breeding populations of Dominican gulls, white herons, black-crowned night herons, olivaceous and black cormorants, steamer ducks, Patagonian crested ducks, and Magellanic and black oystercatchers. Several species of gulls, terns, and plovers are visitors, along with the Chilean flamingo and the snowy sheathbill.

Whales: From June to December, the breeding, breaching, blowing, and birthing of *Eubalaena australis* brings whale-watchers to the warm shallow waters of the Golfo Nuevo and Golfo San José. Since the first census in 1971, the population has grown from 580 to over 3,000.

Inhabiting the South Atlantic at latitudes from about 20° to 55° south, the southern right whale reaches 17 meters in length and weighs up to 100 tons; females are larger than males. They are baleen whales, filtering krill and plankton as seawater passes through sieves in their jaws.

Right whales acquired their English name from whalers who sought them out because dead specimens, instead of sinking, floated to the surface; hence, they were the "right whales" for hunting. Identifiable by keratin calluses on their heads, about 1,300 of Valdés's population have names; this has allowed researchers to follow their movements and even trace their kinship.

After the cows give birth, their calves get closest to the catamarans that do commercial whale-watching from Puerto Pirámides. Over the season, though, it's possible to see all stages of the mating and breeding cycle.

Orcas: For much of the year, *Orcinus orca* swims the South Atlantic in search of squid, fish, penguins, and dolphins, but October–April, pods of these "killer whales" prowl the Punta Norte shoreline for sea lion pups—a nine-meter orca can consume up to eight pups per day. The largest of the dolphin family, the

950-kilogram animal is conspicuous for its sleek black body, white underbelly, and menacing dorsal fin, which can rise two meters above the water.

Elephant seals: Valdés's sandy beaches are the only continental breeding site for *Mirounga leonina,* though there are also breeding colonies on sub-Antarctic islands in Chile, the Falkland (Malvinas) Islands, and at South Georgia. Largest of the pinnipeds, it's a true seal with no external ear, but its distinguishing characteristic is the male's inflatable proboscis, which truly resembles an elephant's trunk.

Ungainly on land, 2,500–4,000-kilogram "beachmaster" males come ashore in spring to dominate harems that number up to 100 females (who weigh only about 500 kilograms). Reaching seven meters in length, the beachmasters defend their harems in fights with younger bachelors that leave all parties bloody, scarred, and even disfigured.

Females spend most of their pregnancy at sea, giving birth on returning to land in spring. Pups spend only a few weeks nursing, gaining weight quickly, before the mother abandons them (some die crushed beneath battling males). At sea, the elephant can plunge up to 600 vertical meters in search of squid before surfacing for air half an hour later.

Sea lions: Present all year on the beaches and reefs beneath the peninsula's headlands, *Otaria flavescens* is common from southern Brazil and Uruguay all the way around the tip of South America and north to Perú. With its thick mane, the 300-kilogram 2.3-meter male resembles an African lion, but Spanish speakers call it *lobo marino* (sea wolf). The female, about 1.8 meters long, weighs only about 100 kilograms.

Unlike the larger elephant seal, the sea lion has external ears. Also unlike the elephant seal, it propels itself on land with both front and rear flippers, and the male is quick enough to drag away elephant pups. More often, though, it feeds on krill and the odd penguin.

For Spanish speakers, by the way, this is the *lobo marino de un pelo;* the *lobo marino de dos pelos,* or southern fur seal (*Arctocephalos*

A *pichi* (armadillo) stands its ground at Península Valdés.

© WAYNE BERNHARDSON

australis), whose pelt was more valuable to commercial sealers, is found farther south.

Penguins: *Spheniscus magellanicus,* the braying and burrowing jackass, is the only penguin species here. From September to March or April, it breeds and raises its young at isolated Caleta Valdés and Punta Norte, but summer swimmers have had close encounters at Puerto Pirámides.

Sights and Recreation

Many visitors book excursions in Madryn, but day trips are too brief for more than a glimpse of the best—especially if the operators spend too much time at lunch. Staying at Puerto Pirámides and contracting tours there is ideal for whale-watching, as you have the flexibility to pick the best time to go out.

Five Pirámides operators, some with offices in Madryn as well, offer whale-watching in semirigid rafts (which get closer to the animals) or larger catamarans: **Tito Bottazzi** (Primera Bajada, tel. 02965/49-5050, www.titobottazzi.com), **Hydrosport** (Primera Bajada, tel. 02965/49-5065, www.hydrosport.com.ar), **Pinino Aquatours** (Primera Bajada, tel. 02965/49-5015, www.whalesargentina.com.ar), **Punta Ballena** (Segunda Bajada, tel. 02965/49-5112, www.puntaballena.com.ar), and **Peke Sosa** (Segunda Bajada, tel. 02965/49-5010, www.pekesosa.com.ar). Prices start around US$30 but can cost more, depending on the vessel and the tour's duration.

In Golfo San José, 800 meters north of the isthmus, penguins, gulls, cormorants, and herons all nest on **Isla de los Pájaros,** an off-shore bird sanctuary; it's off-limits to humans, but a stationary shoreline telescope magnifies the breeding birds. Near the telescope is a replica chapel of Fuerte San José, the area's first Spanish settlement (1779, but destroyed by Tehuelches in 1810).

Puerto Pirámides has the major concentration of services, including its most affordable accommodations and food. June–December, whales are the main attraction, but beachgoers take over in January and February. Carless visitors can hike or bike to the southern sea

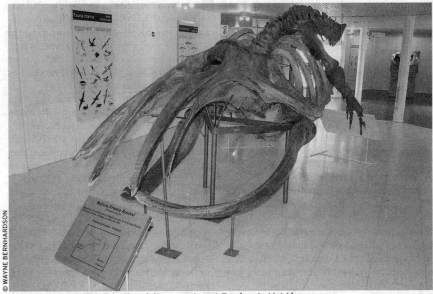

a right whale skeleton in the visitors center at Península Valdés

lion colony at Punto Pirámide, four kilometers west, for vast panoramas and sunsets over the Golfo Nuevo.

Beneath the headlands at the peninsula's southeastern tip, **Punta Delgada** is home to elephant seal and sea lion colonies, reached by trail from the lighthouse at the former naval station (now a hotel-restaurant). Hotel concessionaires provide English-speaking guides to lead tour groups and individuals, but they collect a small charge for those who do not eat at the restaurant. They have also turned the lighthouse into a museum and offer horseback tours of the area.

On the peninsula's eastern shore, about midway between Punta Delgada and Punta Norte, **Caleta Valdés** is a sheltered bay that's fast becoming a lagoon as its ocean outlet fills with sediment. Meanwhile, though, Magellanic penguins swim north to a breeding colony and elephant seals haul up onto shore in the mating season. Even guanacos may be seen along the beach.

Where RP 47 and RP 3 meet at the peninsula's northern tip, **Punta Norte** features a mixed colony of southern elephant seals and sea lions, but October–April this is also the best place to see orcas that lunge onto the beach to grab unwary pups. Punta Norte also has a museum that places marine mammals in both natural and cultural context, thanks to exhibits on the aboriginal Tehuelche and a historical account of the sealing industry.

Near Punta Norte, reached by a northwesterly road off RP 3, **Estancia San Lorenzo** conducts tours of its own Magellanic penguin colony but does not offer accommodations.

Accommodations and Food

Puerto Pirámides has sprouted many more places to stay, eat, and recreate than ever before, but demand is high. In summer and in the whale-watching season, reservations are advisable. There are *estancia* accommodations scattered around Punta Delgada, Caleta Valdés, and Punta Norte, but no camping is permitted beyond Puerto Pirámides.

Immediately behind the dunes, the shoreline **Camping Municipal** (tel. 02965/15-38-3874, US$8 pp) charges separately for showers (water is limited and the showers timed). The bathrooms are clean, and a store carries basic supplies, but few sites have shade.

The next cheapest option is **Hospedaje El Español** (Avenida de las Ballenas s/n, tel. 02965/49-5025, US$9 pp dorm, US$37 s or d), which can accommodate up to 36 people in Spartan accommodations with shared baths. On the approach to town, **Hostería ACA** (tel. 02965/49-5004, www.motelacapiramides.com, US$40 s, US$63 d, for members; US$50 s, US$78 d, for nonmembers) was once Piramides's top choice and has recently been spruced up. At the member price, which members of foreign affiliates can take advantage of, it's an excellent value.

At **Hostería La Estancia del Sol** (Avenida de las Ballenas s/n, tel. 02965/49-5007, hosteria_estanciadelsol@hotmail.com, US$66 d) plain but reasonably spacious rooms, immaculately clean, are the rule.

Its handsome brick superstructure mimicking Chubut's Welsh heritage, the inviting ◖ **Hostería Paradise** (Avenida de las Ballenas s/n, tel./fax 02965/49-5003, www.hosteriaparadise.com.ar, US$180–218 s or d) is a substantial improvement on the usual utilitarian choices. Fixed-price lunches or dinners cost slightly more for foreigners than for Argentines; there's a sandwich and pizza menu as well.

New in late 2008, set back from the main drag, the **Hostería Ecológica del Nómade** (Avenida de las Ballenas s/n, tel. 02965/49-5044, www.ecohosteria.com.ar, US$145–170 s or d) is a new eight-room accommodation designed to minimize its carbon footprint and water consumption in this desert area; it does so without sacrificing style.

In a casual ambience blending traditional artifacts and artwork with pop music, **La Estación** (Avenida de la Ballenas s/n, tel. 02965/49-5047) serves excellent fresh fish and salads, but the kitchen is slow and the service amateurish.

On the bluffs overlooking Punta Delgada, alongside the lighthouse at RP 2's east end, ◖ **Hotel Punta Delgada** (tel. 02965/15-

40-6304, www.puntadelgada.com) is an upgraded property on lease from the navy. It offers a lovely location and good access to wildlife, including penguins and elephant seals. With 30 comfortable doubles, its high-season (September 1–January 1) rates are US$180 s or US$220 d with breakfast, US$228 s or US$316 d with half board, and US$273 s or US$406 d with full board; low-season rates, January 1–April 15, are about 10 percent less. Tour buses often stop at its restaurant, which is open to nonguests.

Near Punta Delgada, run by a young Madryn couple, the best tourist-oriented *estancia* is **C Estancia Rincón Chico** (Almirante Brown 1783, Puerto Madryn, tel. 02965/15-68-8302 or 02965/47-1733, www.rinconchico.com.ar, US$333 s, US$474 d). Five kilometers south of RP 2, its purpose-built hotel has eight well-furnished doubles plus a *quincho* for barbecues. Three months of the year, they host elephant-seal researchers from the University of California, Santa Cruz, as the seals frequent their long coastal frontage. Rates are all-inclusive, with all meals and activities but not drinks; they normally close in May and June.

In a sheltered depression west of Caleta Valdés, along RP 47, **Estancia La Elvira** (Hipólito Yrigoyen 257, Local 2, Puerto Madryn, tel. 02965/15-66-9153 or 02965/47-4248, www.laelvira.com.ar) lacks Rincón Chico's mature landscaping, but the rooms and common areas are attractive enough. Rates are US$190 s or US$280 d with half board, and US$215 s or US$330 d with full board. Near the elephant seal colony, they also operate the roadside **Parador Punta Cantor** (tel. 02965/15-40-6183), which gets lunchtime tour buses.

Toward Punta Norte, just west of RP 47, the amiable six-room **Estancia la Ernestina** (tel. 02965/15-66-1079, tel. 02965/45-8061 in Puerto Madryn, www.laernestina.com) offers easy access to Estancia San Lorenzo's large penguin colony. Three of the rooms have only two baths among them. Rates are US$240 s or US$390 d with full board, drinks, and excursions.

Information

At El Desempeño, at the west end of the Istmo de Ameghino, a provincial toll booth collects an admission fee of US$13 for most foreigners, US$4 for Argentines and nationals of neighboring countries. Immediately east, the **Centro de Interpretación** (8 A.M.–8 P.M. daily) exhibits a complete right whale skeleton but also historical materials ranging from Tehuelche times to Spanish colonization and Argentine settlement for salt mining and sheep ranching. An observation tower offers panoramas across the northerly Golfo San José to the southerly Golfo Nuevo, and east across the peninsula's interior.

Turismo Puerto Pirámides (Avenida de las Ballenas s/n, tel. 02965/49-5048, www.puertopiramides.gov.ar), the municipal tourist office, serves visitors from 8 A.M.–6 P.M. daily.

Getting There and Around

In summer, from Puerto Madryn, **Mar y Valle** (tel. 02965/45-0600) has daily buses to Puerto Pirámides (1.5 hours, US$4.50) at 8:55 A.M. and 6 P.M.; return buses leave at 11 A.M. and 7 P.M. In winter, there may be morning departures only, but in summer there is an additional evening bus.

On a space-available basis, tour buses may allow passengers to disembark at Pirámides and return another day, but make advance arrangements.

Distances from Pirámides to other peninsula destinations are too great for nonmotorized transport, so it's worth considering a **rental car** in Puerto Madryn. Many consider day trips from Madryn too rushed.

TRELEW

Less obviously tourist-oriented than Puerto Madryn, the Río Chubut city of Trelew retains more visible remnants of its Welsh birthright than its ocean-side sister city. It also offers access to the lower Chubut Welsh communities of Gaiman and Dolavon, the dolphin-watching beach resort of Playa Unión, and the massive penguin colonies at Punta Tombo. Its own attraction, though, is the state-of-the-art paleontological museum that documents

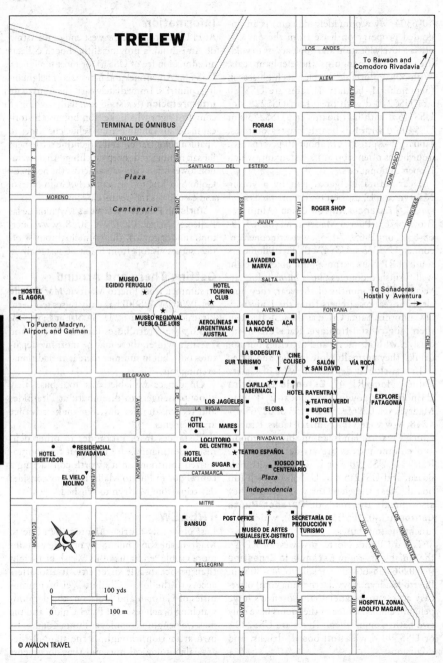

TRELEW

To Rawson and
Comodoro Rivadavia

LOS ANDES

ALÉM

ALBERDI

R. J. BERWIN

A. MATHEWS

TERMINAL DE ÓMNIBUS

URQUIZA

LEWIS

SANTIAGO   DEL

ESTERO

FIORASI ■

DON BOSCO

Plaza

MORENO

Centenario

JONES

ESPAÑA

JUJUY

ITALIA

ROGER SHOP ■

HONDURAS

LAVADERO ■   NIEVEMAR ■
MARVA

SALTA

HOSTEL
● EL AGORA

MUSEO
EGIDIO FERUGLIO ★

HOTEL
TOURING
CLUB ★

To Soñadoras
Hostel y Aventura →

To Puerto Madryn,
Airport, and Gaiman

MUSEO REGIONAL
PUEBLO DE LUIS ★

★

AVENIDA

AEROLÍNEAS ■
ARGENTINAS/
AUSTRAL

FONTANA

BANCO DE   ACA ■
LA NACIÓN ■

MENDOZA

CHILE

TUCUMÁN

LA BODEGUITA ■
SUR TURISMO ■

CINE
COLISEO

SALÓN ■
★ SAN DAVID

VÍA ROCA ▼

BELGRANO

9 DE JULIO

AVENIDA

CAPILLA ★★■▼
TABERNACL

HOTEL RAYENTRAY ●

LA RIOJA

LOS JAGÜELES ■

ELOISA ■

★ TEATRO VERDI

EXPLORE ■
PATAGONIA

CITY
HOTEL ●

MARES ▼

■ BUDGET

● HOTEL CENTENARIO

LOCUTORIO ■
DEL CENTRO ●

RIVADAVIA

HOTEL
LIBERTADOR ●

● RESIDENCIAL
RIVADAVIA

RAWSON

AVENIDA

HOTEL
GALICIA ■

SUGAR ▼

★ TEATRO ESPAÑOL

KIOSCO DEL ■
CENTENARIO

EL VIELO ▼
MOLINO

CATAMARCA

Plaza

Independencia

MITRE

ECUADOR

GALES

BANSUD ■

POST OFFICE ■

★

MUSEO DE ARTES
VISUALES/EX-DISTRITO
MILITAR

SECRETARÍA DE
PRODUCCIÓN Y
TURISMO

LOS INMIGRANTES

JULIO A. ROCA

PELLEGRINI

25 DE MAYO

SAN MARTIN

28 DE JULIO

HOSPITAL ZONAL ■
ADOLFO MAGARA

0   100 yds

0   100 m

© AVALON TRAVEL

Argentina's dramatic dinosaur discoveries of recent decades.

Dating from 1886, when the railroad united Puerto Madryn with the lower Chubut's farm towns, Trelew takes its name from Welsh colonist and railroad promoter Lewis Jones (in Welsh, *tre* means town, while *lew* was an abbreviation of Lewis). It has since absorbed several waves of immigration—Italians and Spaniards, as well as Argentines from elsewhere in the country—and boom-and-bust cycles thanks to the wool industry, customs preferences, and industrial promotion.

Despite the changes, Trelew has retained its Welsh identity in events like the Eisteddfod (a poetry and music festival) and other cultural activities.

On the Río Chubut's north bank, Trelew (pop. 88,397) is 65 kilometers south of Puerto Madryn and 377 kilometers northeast of Comodoro Rivadavia via RN 3. It is 608 kilometers west of Esquel via paved RN 25, RP 62, and RN 40.

Sights

On the pleasingly landscaped **Plaza Independencia,** the Victorian-style **Kiosco del Centenario** (1910) marked the centennial of Argentine independence. To the south, once isolated by walls and gates, the former **Distrito Militar** (army headquarters), dating from 1900, now houses the **Museo de Artes Visuales** (Mitre 351, tel. 02965/43-3774, 8 A.M.–8 P.M. Mon.–Fri., 2–8 P.M. Sat.–Sun., free), exhibiting historical photos as well as modern photography, painting, and sculpture. The tourist office occupies its adjacent **Anexo** (Annex, Mitre 387).

In 1920, Trelew's Spaniards built the **Teatro Español** (25 de Mayo 237), on the plaza's west side. Half a block east of the plaza, dating from 1914, the **Teatro Verdi** (San Martín 128) served the Italian community; at San Martín and Belgrano, the **Salón San David** (1913) still hosts the Eisteddfod festival. Half a block northwest, the Welsh **Capilla Tabernacl** (1889) is Trelew's oldest surviving building.

Two blocks northeast of the plaza, early Patagonian tourists stayed at the **Hotel Touring Club** (formerly the Hotel Martino, dating from 1906), which underwent a major 1920s upgrade but now seems frozen in time (the moribund Touring Club Argentino once rivaled the Automóvil Club Argentino). It is still a popular meeting place for *trelewenses,* however.

Half a block northwest, dating from 1889, the **Antigua Estación del Ferrocarril** (Fontana and Lewis Jones) was the city's second railway station and is now the regional history museum; immediately north, the **Museo Egidio Feruglio** (Avenida Fontana 140) is a state-of-the-art paleontology museum.

Museo Regional Pueblo de Luis

An antique steam locomotive and other equipment still stand outside Trelew's former train station, where, from 1889 to 1961, the Ferrocarril Central Chubut delivered passengers and freight from Puerto Madryn. Now housing the regional museum, packed with Welsh memorabilia, including historical photographs, furnishings, and clothing, the interior is short on interpretation; this remains to be remedied as it becomes an "Ecomuseo" documenting the landscape's transformation by aboriginal peoples and European settlers.

The Museo Regional (Avenida Fontana and Lewis Jones, tel. 02965/42-4062, US$0.50) is open 8 A.M.–8 P.M. weekdays and 2–8 P.M. weekends.

Museo Egidio Feruglio

West of Trelew, the central Patagonian steppe is a prime dinosaur dig, and the city's paleontological museum is reason enough to visit the city. Its main appeal is the magnificently mounted models of Argentine dinosaurs like the carnivorous *Pianitzkysaurus floresi* and *Carnotaurus sastrei,* but there are also dinosaur eggs, a genuine touchable dinosaur femur, and a working lab visible to the public.

At the same time, the museum acknowledges the achievements of pioneering Patagonian researchers like Florentino Ameghino, George Gaylord Simpson, and Alejandro Pianitzky in its hall of fame. It owes its name to an Italian paleontologist who came to Argentina in 1925 as a petroleum geologist for the state company YPF.

The Museo Egidio Feruglio (Avenida Fontana 140, tel. 02965/42-0012, www.mef.org.ar, 10 A.M.–6 P.M. weekdays, 10 A.M.–8 P.M. weekends, US$6 adults, US$3 children age 12 and under) has a small café (with Wi-Fi) and a souvenir shop. It also arranges excursions to Geoparque Bryn Gwyn, near Gaiman.

Entertainment and Events

The **Cine Coliseo** (Belgrano 371, tel. 02965/42-5300) shows recent films, while the **Teatro Verdi** (San Martín 128, tel. 02965/43-1398) provides live theater and music.

In odd-numbered years only, mid-September's **Certámen Internacional de Coros** draws on the Welsh choral tradition. Later in the spring, the **Fiesta Provincial del Pingüino** celebrates the arrival of Punta Tombo's penguins.

October 20's **Aniversario de la Ciudad** marks Trelew's 1886 founding. Late October's **Eisteddfod de Chubut** festival focuses on the lower Chubut valley's Welsh traditions, particularly folk music and poetry.

Shopping

For souvenirs and clothing, including horse gear, leather, and woolens, visit **Los Jagüeles** (25 de Mayo 144, tel. 02965/42-2949).

Accommodations

For backpackers, Trelew now has two serviceable hostels: **Hostel El Agora** (Edwin Roberts 33, tel. 02965/42-6899, www.hostelelagora.jimdo.com, hostelagora@hotmail.com, US$12 pp) and **Soñadores Hostel y Aventura** (Pasaje Lamadrid 1312, tel. 02965/43-6505, hosteltrelew@speedy.com.ar, www.poex.com.ar, US$13 pp). Both are dorms-only facilities.

Upstairs rooms at **Hotel Rivadavia** (Rivadavia 55, tel. 02965/43-4472, hotelriv@infovia.com.ar, www.cpatagonia.com/rivadavia, US$25–30 s, US$30–32 d) have better beds and bathrooms, in addition to cable TV, than the more economical downstairs rooms. Breakfast costs about US$3 extra.

For a touch of old Patagonia—perhaps because it's well past its prime—try the landmark **Hotel Touring Club** (Avenida Fontana 240, tel. 02965/43-3998, www.touringpatagonia.com.ar, US$32 s, US$50 d). Rates include breakfast and parking.

Rooms at the 1970s-era **City Hotel** (Rivadavia 254, tel./fax 02965/43-3951, www.hotelcitypatagonia.com.ar, US$32 s, US$53 d) are smallish but bright, cheerful, and tidy. **Hotel Centenario** (San Martín 150, tel. 02965/42-0542, hotelcentenario@yahoo.com.ar, US$48 s, US$55 d) is also OK, with Wi-Fi and covered parking.

Four-star in designation, the 90-room **Hotel Libertador** (Rivadavia 31, tel./fax 02965/42-0220, www.hotellibertadortw.com, US$59 s, US$74 d) is a less-than-exceptional hostelry with friendly personnel and a buffet breakfast but rather dull rooms.

Rehabbed ◀ **Hotel Galicia** (9 de Julio 214, tel. 02965/43-3802, www.hotelgalicia.com.ar, US$90 s, US$100 d) has impressive public areas—note the elegant marble staircase—if slightly less impressive rooms; still, this is the best choice among Trelew's accommodations. Prices have risen substantially, though it does offer significant cash discounts.

The central 110-room **Hotel Rayentray** (San Martín 101, tel. 02965/43-4702, www.cadenarayentray.com.ar, US$92 s, US$153 d) has amenities including a restaurant, a gym, a sauna, and a swimming pool. Still, for the price, it's hard to say it's demonstrably better than the Galicia.

Food

Even those who don't stay at the hotel should take breakfast or coffee at the **Confitería Touring Club** (Avenida Fontana 240, tel. 02965/43-3998) to partake of its timeless ambience. **Sugar** (25 de Mayo 247, tel. 02965/43-5978) is a sandwich and short-order option.

La Bodeguita (Belgrano 374, tel. 02965/43-6276, lunch and dinner daily) serves good pasta (particularly cannelloni) and pizza, with decent service.

© WAYNE BERNHARDSON

The bar at Trelew's Hotel Touring Club is a Patagonian classic.

The best new choice on the scene is **Eloisa** (Belgrano 351, tel. 02965/43-1606, www.eloisa.com.ar, US$10–15), a *parrilla*-restaurant with Patagonian flair in its meats, seafood, and even the wine list.

About three blocks north of Plaza Independencia, in an elegantly recycled flour mill dating from 1910, **El Viejo Molino** (Avenida Gales 250, tel. 02965/42-8019, lunch and dinner daily, US$10–20) is Trelew's most ambitious restaurant; its best dishes are variations on the traditional *parrillada* as well as pastas.

For ice cream, try **Mares** (25 de Mayo 195), and **Vía Roca** (Belgrano and Roca).

Roger Shop (Moreno 463, tel. 02965/43-0690), Trelew's only Welsh teahouse, is the place to purchase traditional black cake.

Information

At Plaza Independencia's southwest corner, the well-organized municipal **Secretaría de Producción y Turismo** (Mitre 387, tel. 02965/42-0139, www.trelewpatagonia.gov.ar, 8 A.M.–8 P.M. weekdays and 9 A.M.–9 P.M. weekends summer, 9 A.M.–1 P.M. and 3–8 P.M. daily the rest of the year) usually has an English speaker on hand. There are also offices at the bus terminal (8:30 A.M.–8:30 P.M. weekdays) and the airport (for arriving flights only).

For motorists, **ACA** (tel. 02965/43-5197) is at Avenida Fontana and San Martín.

Services

Many visitors stay in Puerto Madryn, but Trelew agencies also do excursions to destinations like Rawson and Playa Unión, the lower Chubut valley's Welsh villages, Punta Tombo, and even Península Valdés.

Several banks have ATMs, including **Banco de la Nación** (Avenida Fontana and 25 de Mayo).

Correo Argentino is at Calle 25 de Mayo and Mitre; the postal code is 9100. **Locutorio del Centro** (25 de Mayo 219), at Plaza Independencia's northwest side, has telephone, fax, and Internet services.

Nievemar (Italia 98, tel. 02965/43-4114, www.nievemartours.com.ar), the Amex representative, also arranges excursions to the Welsh settlements and Punta Tombo. **Explore**

SOUTHERN PATAGONIA

Patagonia (Julio A. Roca 94, tel. 02965/43-7860, www.explore-patagonia.com.ar) also offers a variety of tours.

Lavadero Marva (Sarmiento 363, tel. 02965/43-4233) washes clothes.

For medical needs, contact the **Hospital Zonal Adolfo Margara** (28 de Julio 160, tel. 02965/42-7542).

Getting There

Aerolíneas Argentinas (25 de Mayo 33, tel. 02965/42-0222) flies once or twice daily to Buenos Aires's Aeroparque and occasionally to El Calafate, Río Gallegos, and Ushuaia.

With offices in the bus terminal, **LADE** (Urquiza 150, tel. 02965/43-5740) flies sporadically to Aeroparque as well as southern and western Patagonian destinations.

The **Terminal de Ómnibus** (Urquiza 150, tel. 02965/42-0121) is six blocks northeast of Plaza Independencia.

Mar y Valle (tel. 02965/43-2429) has regular service to Puerto Pirámides, leaving Trelew at 7:45 A.M., with additional summer service; from Puerto Madryn, Mar y Valle goes to Puerto Pirámides at 8:55 A.M. daily, with added departures at 5 and 6:45 P.M. in summer and during whale-watching season. **El Ñandú** (tel. 02965/42-7499) goes to the coastal town of Camarones at 8 A.M. Monday, Wednesday, and Friday.

Typical destinations, times, and fares include Camarones (3.5 hours, US$7), Puerto Pirámides (3 hours, US$5.50), Comodoro Rivadavia (5 hours, US$18–21), Esquel (9 hours, US$25–38), Neuquén (10 hours, US$29–40), Río Gallegos (16 hours, US$48–62), Bariloche (11 hours, US$49–68), and Buenos Aires (21 hours, US$62–92).

Getting Around

Aeropuerto Internacional Marcos A. Zar (RN 3 s/n, tel. 02965/43-3443) is five kilometers north of town on the east side of the Puerto Madryn highway. Cabs or *remises* cost about US$4.50.

Línea 28 de Julio (tel. 02965/43-2429) has frequent buses to Puerto Madryn (US$2.50) and to Gaiman (US$1.50) and Dolavon (US$2), though weekend services are fewer.

Empresa Rawson goes to Rawson (US$1) and Playa Unión every 15 minutes, starting at 5:30 A.M.

Car-rental agencies include **Budget** (San Martín 146, tel. 02965/43-4634) and **Fiorasi** (Urquiza 310, tel. 02965/43-5344).

RAWSON AND PLAYA UNIÓN

Rawson (pop. 22,355) is Chubut's low-profile capital, and in truth there's little to see in this nondescript bureaucratic outpost. Its suburb of Playa Unión, though, is an ecotourism destination for the glossy black-and-white Commerson's dolphins that dart around and under launches that motor through the waters fronting its long sandy beach.

To see the dolphins (which are common in other coastal destinations), contact **Toninas Adventure** (Avenida Marcelino González s/n, tel. 02965/49-8372, toninasadventure@msn.com) or **Estación Marítima Commerson's** (Avenida Marcelino González s/n, tel. 02965/49-8508); excursions cost about US$25 pp. While waiting, or afterward, try a seafood lunch at a dockside cantina such as **Cantina Marcelino** (tel. 02965/49-6960).

Playa Unión also has decent accommodations at **Hostería Le Bon** (Rifleros 68, tel. 02965/49-6638, US$50 s, US$57 d).

Rawson's **Secretaría de Turismo y Areas Protegidas de la Provincia del Chubut** (Moreno and Avenida Maíz, tel. 02965/48-1113, www.chubutur.gov.ar) has information on the entire province. Playa Unión has its own **Centro de Atención al Turista** (Avenida Rawson and Centenario, tel. 02965/449-6887, 8 A.M.–6 P.M. Mon.–Sat., 10 A.M.–6 P.M. Sun.).

Trelew to Rawson buses run every 15 minutes; from the Rawson terminal, it's necessary to catch another local bus or taxi to Playa Unión.

GAIMAN AND VICINITY

More than any other lower Chubut settlement, Gaiman has sustained and capitalized on its Welsh heritage. Though it's known for tourist teahouses, sturdy stone buildings, and community events like the Eisteddfod, several new B&Bs have made it a destination rather than just an excursion.

Gaiman (pop. 4,300), 17 kilometers east of Trelew via RN 25, dates from 1874, when Welsh farmers first harnessed the river to irrigate their fields and orchards. The aboriginal Tehuelche gave it the name Gaiman (Stony Point).

Sights

The best starting point is the **Amgueddfa Hanesyddol** (Sarmiento and 28 de Julio, tel. 02965/49-1007, 3–7 P.M. Tues.–Sun., US$0.50), the regional historical museum in the former train station. Staffed by Welsh- and English-speaking volunteers, it holds documents, photographs, and possessions of early immigrants.

Two blocks northwest, Dolavon-bound trains no longer chug through the **Twnnel yr Hen Reilfford,** a 300-meter brick tunnel that's now open to pedestrians only. A block west of the tunnel exit, dating from 1899, the **Coleg Camwy** (Bouchard and Michael D. Jones) may have been Patagonia's first secondary school. At the east end of 28 de Julio, historic headstones, many of them in Welsh, dot the **Mynwent** (cemetery).

Parque El Desafío

Turning everyone else's trash into lighthearted objets d'art, Joaquín Alonso's magnum opus is a whimsical labor of love by a man seemingly incapable of throwing anything away. In the process, he's created credible mural replicas of works by Florencio Molina Campos, Benito Quinquela Martín, and even Pablo Picasso (*Guernica*). The most amusing single item may be the *palo borracho* (a pun on northern Argentina's spiny *Chorisia speciosa* tree, colloquially known as "drunken stick" because of its water-swollen trunk). The leaves of this drunken stick, though, are beer and wine bottles.

According to the *Guinness Book of Records,* Alonso's one-hectare property contains 50,000 wine and beer bottles, 30,000 aluminum cans, 25,000 spools of thread, 12,000 bottle caps, and 5,000 plastic bottles, along with automobiles, TVs, refrigerators, washing machines, and 200-liter water tanks. It's easy to amuse yourself for an hour or so just looking at the odds and ends, and even easier if your Spanish is good enough to appreciate the aphorisms on scattered plaques.

Parque El Desafío (Avenida Almirante Brown s/n, tel. 02965/49-1340, US$2 adults, US$1 children) is open 9 P.M.–1 P.M. and 3–8 P.M. Thursday–Monday, 3–7 P.M. Tuesday–Wednesday. The elderly Alonso, who turned 90 in early 2009, is only occasionally around, but his family continues the tradition.

Geoparque Paleontológico Bryn Gwyn

Exposed by meanderings of the Río Chubut after an earlier subtropical sea evaporated, Bryn Gwyn's sedimentary badlands are an open book of Tertiary fossils. The oldest beds are too recent for dinosaur bones, but there is evidence of marine mammals such as seals, dolphins, and whales along with penguins, giant anteaters, and ungulates from times when this was savanna.

Visitors to the park, eight kilometers south of Gaiman via RP 5, can hike the well-organized trail, which climbs gradually and then steeply up the cliffs from the south-side *confitería*. There are at least a dozen excavations, with some fossils in the open and others preserved in glass cases.

Affiliated with Trelew's Museo Feruglio, Bryn Gwyn charges US$2.50 admission for adults, US$1 for children; groups larger than 20 can arrange guided visits. Hours are 9 A.M.–6 P.M. Tuesday–Sunday. There's no scheduled transportation, but *remises* from Gaiman are not unreasonable.

Shopping

For crafts, visit the **Paseo Artesanal Crefft Werin** (Avenida Eugenio Tello and Michael D. Jones, tel. 02965/49-1134), opposite Plaza Roca.

Accommodations

The quality of accommodations is high, as top teahouses now offer B&B. Options are still limited, though, so reservations are advisable.

Gaiman's only purpose-built hotel, the aging **Hotel Unelem** (Avenida Eugenio Tello and 9 de Julio, tel. 02965/49-1663, www.unelem. com, US$22 s, US$30 d) has large rooms with private baths, some with fireplaces.

The Welsh name is misleading at **Hostería Dyffryn Gwyrdd** (Avenida Eugenio Tello 103, tel. 02965/49-1777, www.dwhosteria.com.ar, US$25–30 s, US$35–38 d), which is not one of those teahouses, but it's a decent place run by Italo-Argentines.

Rooms vary and some have shared baths at **Hostería Yr Hen Ffordd** (Michael D. Jones 342, tel. 02965/49-1394, www.yrhenffordd. com.ar, US$31 s, US$36 d, with breakfast), but it's friendly and helpful.

◖ **Hostería Gwesty Plas y Coed** (Yrigoyen 320, tel. 02965/49-1133, www.plasycoed.com. ar, US$35 s, US$48 d) is a B&B annex of Gaiman's landmark teahouse.

◖ **Hostería Ty Gwyn** (9 de Julio 147, tel. 02965/49-1009, www.tygwyn.com.ar, US$48 s, US$61 d) is a quality teahouse with several stylishly furnished rooms—the beds are handsome, and antique sewing machines serve as desks. Some rooms have balconies facing the river—a mixed blessing, as they also face a playground where families with children play until midnight or even later, and the mosquitoes are ferocious. Breakfast is a delicious reprise of the previous afternoon's tea.

Food

Gaiman may be picturesque, but it's pointless to come here without indulging yourself on cakes, jams, scones, pies, and a bottomless teapot. Since tea starts around 2:30–3 P.M., either skip lunch or go later and then skip dinner; for about US$10 pp, it's a de facto all-you-can-eat. When tour buses are parked outside, slow service is almost certain.

Gaiman's oldest teahouse is **Plas y Coed** (Yrigoyen 320, tel. 02965/49-1133, www.plasy-coed.com.ar), which wins points for exceptional

sweets and personalized service. Ivy-covered **Ty Nain** (Hipólito Yrigoyen 283, tel. 02965/49-1126) is the most stylish, but **Ty Gwyn** (9 de Julio 111, tel. 02965/49-1009, www.tygwyn. com.ar) is also appealing. The newest teahouse, **Ty Cymraeg** (Mathews 74, tel. 02965/49-1010, www.gaimantea.com) blends a traditional style but lacks the historical patina of, say, Plas y Coed; still, its scones, grape jam, and lemon pie are outstanding.

Across the river, reached by a roundabout route over the bridge at the south end of J. C. Evans, **Ty Caerdydd** (tel. 02965/49-1053) is an enormous teahouse set among its own irrigated fields, which produce fresh fruits and berries for its own products, and elaborate flower gardens. Lady Diana, as Princess of Wales, was once a celebrity guest.

Overnighters can't gorge themselves on Welsh teas every day. Other restaurants include **Pizzería Gustos** (Avenida Eugenio Tello 156, tel. 02965/49-1453, lunch and dinner daily) and the more ambitious **El Angel** (Rivadavia 241, tel. 02965/49-1460, reservations essential), which keeps limited days and hours.

Other Practicalities

In the Casa de Cultura (Belgrano 235, tel. 02965/49-1571, www.gaiman.gov.ar), the municipal **Oficina de Informes** is open 9 A.M.–8 P.M. Monday–Saturday, 11 A.M.–8 P.M. Sunday.

Correo Argentino is at Juan Evans and Hipólito Yrigoyen, just north of the bridge over the river; the postal code is 9105. There's a *locutorio* on Avenida Tello between 25 de Mayo and 9 de Julio.

Empresa 28 de Julio's **buses** between Trelew and Dolavon stop on Plaza Roca's south side.

DOLAVON

Unlike Gaiman, sleepy Dolavon (pop. 2,481) has never become a tourist town, but the brick buildings along its silent streets evince a greater architectural harmony than its larger neighbor—even though, founded in 1919, it's much newer. Its major landmark, the **Molino Harinero** (1930), is a former grain mill that now houses a museum

THE WILDLIFE ROUTES OF COASTAL CHUBUT

For Patagonia travelers, arrow-straight RN 3 is the quickest ticket south, but visitors with their own wheels – whether two or four – should explore coastal Chubut's dusty back roads. It's common enough to rent a car for Península Valdés, where a bicycle is awkward because camping is prohibited, but the loop from Rawson south to Punta Tombo and Camarones, returning via RN 3, is an intriguing alternative for automobiles, motorbikes, and bicycles.

Along southbound RP 1, the big attraction is Punta Tombo's penguins, but most visitors see them on a tour. Rather than returning to Puerto Madryn or Trelew, the self-propelled can get an *estanciero*'s view of the thinly set-tled area by following the dusty, narrow, but smooth gravel road south past desolate Cabo Raso, with its steep gravel beach, and on to picturesque Camarones.

From Camarones, the provincial wildlife reserve at Cabo Dos Bahías makes an ideal excursion before returning to RN 3 via a paved lateral and heading back north – perhaps for tea in Gaiman – or continuing south toward Bahía Bustamante, the kelp-gathering community that's part of the new Parque Nacional Patagonia Austral along the Atlantic shoreline, and Comodoro Rivadavia. With an early start, the Punta Tombo-Camarones-Gaiman circuit could be a day trip, but an overnight in Camarones is a better option.

and the restaurant **La Molienda** (Maipú 61, tel. 02965/49-2290). *Norias* (waterwheels) in nearby canals still distribute Río Chubut water to the fields and orchards.

From the Trelew terminal, Empresa 28 de Julio runs 10 buses daily to and from Dolavon via Gaiman.

◖ RESERVA PROVINCIAL PUNTA TOMBO

On barren South Atlantic shores, 107 kilometers southeast of Trelew, more than 200,000 pairs of Magellanic penguins waddle ashore every austral spring to nest on only 210 hectares at Punta Tombo. Despite its isolation, more than 100,000 visitors a year—and up 2,500 in a single day—find their way down RN 3 and a new shortcut to a dusty southeasterly lateral and the continent's largest single penguin colony. Besides penguins, there are giant petrels, kelp and dolphin gulls, king and rock cormorants, and shorebirds including oystercatchers and flightless steamer ducks—not to mention offshore whales.

Despite their numbers, penguin populations here and at Península Valdés may be in trouble. A late 2006 article in *Science* concluded that continued overfishing of the Patagonian anchovy, which constitutes half the penguins' diet (and also sustains elephant seals, dolphins, and other South Atlantic species) could cause a population collapse.

Tours from Trelew (around US$40 pp) arrive around 11 A.M., but the birds are so dispersed that it rarely seems crowded. Authorities have marked off the nesting grounds, and human visitors must stay on marked trails and boardwalks; visitors must now walk in rather than drive on the roads. Still, since penguins do not respect fences, it's possible to get up-close-and-personal photos while respecting the birds' space (their beaks can inflict a nasty gash).

Tombo's infrastructure remains limited, though a visitors center is ostensibly in the works. Still, the simple *confitería* has fresh-baked lamb empanadas and clean modern-ized toilets.

At the entrance, provincial authorities collect US$9 pp for adult foreigners, US$3.20 for Argentine residents and citizens of neighboring countries. No camping is permitted.

While it's also possible for a group to hire a taxi for a day trip to the reserve, renting a car in Trelew or Puerto Madryn would make it possible to follow the scenic desert coastline south past the ghost town of Cabo Raso to the picturesque fishing port of Camarones and Cabo Dos Bahías, a reserve with both penguins and sea lions. From Camarones it's possible to return to Trelew or Puerto Madryn via paved RN 3.

CAMARONES AND VICINITY

Toward the south end of its namesake bay, Camarones is a sleepy fishing port with just two paved streets but so many wide gravel roads that it seems to be waiting for something to happen. Its citizens may wait a while, but Camarones is just picturesque enough, close enough to the wildlife reserve at Cabo Dos Bahías, and an interesting enough jaunt from Punta Tombo via the Cabo Raso route that it's an ideal off-the-beaten-road loop for anyone with a vehicle. Its new museum also deserves a look.

Alternatively, there's public transportation via southbound RN 3 from Trelew and eastbound RP 30, a distance of about 250 kilometers. The town holds a **Fiesta Nacional del Salmón** (National Salmon Festival) the second weekend of February.

Museo de la Familia Perón

Camarones's Perón family museum occupies a shiny new replica of Juan Domingo Perón's boyhood home—the caudillo's father, Tomás Perón, ran a sheep estancia on the town's western outskirts in the early years of the 20th century (Juan Domingo was born in 1895). It differs from other Perón museums not in that it's professionally organized—so is Buenos Aires's Evita museum—but in that it admits that Perón was a controversial and contradictory figure whose loyalists even engaged each other in firefights in the 1970s (right- and left-wing factions were each convinced the general was on their side).

While the museum leans toward the interpretations of Argentina's current left-of-center Peronists, it avoids the polemics so common in Argentine politics. Not only that, the English translations that accompany the exhibits are well above average.

The Museo de la Familia Perón (Estrada 467, 0297/496-3013, free) is open 9 A.M.–8 P.M. daily.

Reserva Provincial Cabo Dos Bahías

Only 30 kilometers southeast of Camarones, the 12,000-strong Magellanic penguin colony Dos Bahías is smaller than Punta Tombo's, but Dos Bahías's open terrain makes it easier to appreciate the colony's extent. In addition to penguins, it boasts a southern sea lion colony on offshore **Isla Moreno,** though they're hard to see without binoculars. Besides many of the same seabirds that frequent Punta Tombo, terrestrial wildlife includes armadillos, foxes, guanacos, and rheas.

Unlike Punta Tombo, it's possible to camp at beaches en route to Dos Bahías and at the reserve itself, though there are no other services. There is no scheduled transportation either, though it's possible to hire a car with driver in Camarones (try Hotel Viejo Torino). At the reserve's entrance, provincial authorities collect a US$5 admission fee from adult foreigners, US$2.50 for Argentines.

Accommodations and Food

Open all year, the waterfront **Camping Camarones** (Espora s/n, tel. 02965/15-32-2906, US$2 per site) has sheltered sites with electricity and clean bathrooms with hot showers.

Totally remodeled, the **Indalo Inn** (Sarmiento and Roca, tel. 0297/496-3004, www.indaloinn.com.ar, US$42 s, US$50 d) has a reliable restaurant. Once a hotel, **Viejo Torino** (Brown 100, tel. 0297/496-3003) is an attractive seafood and pasta restaurant that was once also a hotel, but since it's now lodging commercial fishermen, the food may suffer.

Information and Practicalities

Near the shoreline at the foot of Calle Roca, Camarones's **Oficina de Turismo** (Espora s/n, turismo.cultura.municamarones@gmail.com) is open 7:30 A.M.–8 P.M. daily.

Correo Argentino is at Roca and Estrada. **Banco Chubut** (San Martín and 25 de Mayo) has an ATM.

Getting There

From the terminal at 9 de Julio and Rivadavia,

El **Ñandú** buses go to Trelew (3 hours, US$8) at 4 P.M. Monday, Wednesday, and Friday.

BAHÍA BUSTAMANTE (PARQUE NACIONAL PATAGONIA AUSTRAL)

Recently declared along the Chubut shoreline south Camarones and Reserva Provincial Cabo Dos Bahías, Parque Nacional Patagonia Austral comprises only a strip of Argentina's South Atlantic coastline, exactly one nautical mile out to sea and 1.5 kilometers (nearly one statute mile) inland. Its easiest access point is the unique Bahía Bustamante, a sort of company town based not on mining but on seaweed! Dating from about 1952, it once had 500 residents—most of them employees—but now has only about 40 or so. Many of them gather seaweed along the shoreline; it is then dried in the sun and trucked to Gaiman, where a factory processes it into food additives.

All Bahía Bustamante's streets are named for species of seaweed; only a handful of the houses are occupied, but some of those—the former administrators' houses—have been transformed into stylishly retrofitted guesthouses at premium prices. At the same time, there are rather cheaper accommodations with private baths and kitchens, and even some hostel facilities. In fact, it's even possible to camp nearby, and Bustamante's restaurant serves intriguing meals that often use seaweed as a condiment.

From Bahía Bustamante, it's possible to take multiple excursions, including one to offshore islands that are part of the new national park and home to thousands of Magellanic penguins, cormorants, dolphin gulls, and steamer ducks as well as large colonies of southern sea lions. This is possible only at high tide, though, as the five-meter tidal range makes it impossible for the flat bottom launch to navigate at low tide.

At low tide, there are other options: Beyond the limits of the new national park, Bustamante possesses a remarkable badlands that features a sprawling petrified forest equivalent to Santa Cruz Province's Parque Nacional Bosques Petrificados and Chubut's own Reserva Provincial Bosque Petrificado José Ormachea.

Accommodations in the guesthouses at **Bahía Bustamante** (RN 3 Km 1674, tel. 0297/15-625-7500, www.bahiabustamante. com, US$360 s, US$430 d, with full board) are all-inclusive; in the less elaborate **Casas de la Estepa** (www.casasdeestepa.blogspot.

© WAYNE BERNHARDSON

About 30 km inland from Bahía Bustamante, the petrified forest is a popular attraction.

com), rates are US$120 for up to three people, with kitchen facilities. Hostel-style *refugio* accommodations, with external baths, cost US$20 pp. Those staying at the cheaper accommodations pay extra for tours to the offshore islands and the petrified forest, on a space-available basis. Bahía Bustamante is 30 kilometers east of the main highway turnoff by a good gravel road.

COMODORO RIVADAVIA AND VICINITY

Comodoro Rivadavia's motto is "a city with energy," and Chubut's southernmost city is really Houston by the Sea. For nearly a century, ever since water-seeking drillers hit a crude gusher instead, it has been the locus of Argentina's petroleum industry. Thanks to the former state oil company Yacimientos Petrolíferos Fiscales (YPF), it has an outstanding petroleum museum.

On the surrounding hills, the landscape remains a jumble of drilling rigs, pipelines, storage tanks, and seismic survey markers. Ironically, though, Cerro Chenque's high-tech windmills herald alternative energy.

A frequent stopover for southbound motorists, hilly Comodoro (pop. 135,813) is 369 kilometers south of Trelew and 780 kilometers north of Río Gallegos via RN 3; most services are on or near east–west Avenida San Martín, within a few blocks of the ocean. It's 581 kilometers southeast of Esquel via paved RN 26, RP 20, and RN 40.

Sights

For a panorama of Golfo San Jorge's curving coastline, climb the footpath to **Cerro Chenque,** immediately north of downtown. Nearly barren, prone to landslides that have covered RN 3, it's now the site of **Parque Eólico Antonio Morán,** South America's largest windmill farm.

On the Avenida Rivadavia median strip, a stiff climb from downtown, the orderly but uninspiring **Museo Patagónico Antonio Garcés** (Rivadavia and Chacabuco, tel. 0297/447-7101, 9 A.M.–5 P.M. weekdays, free) chronicles

Comodoro's development through fossils, aboriginal artifacts, and photographs.

In Comodoro's old railway station, the **Museo Ferroportuario** (Avenida Rivadavia and 9 de Julio, tel. 0297/447-3330, ext. 345, 9 A.M.–5 P.M. weekdays, free) chronicles the train that hauled wool and produce from the city of Sarmiento, 149 kilometers west; intended to reach Lago Buenos Aires, it never went beyond Sarmiento, though it also carried crude from nearby oilfields to the port.

About three kilometers north of downtown, the Universidad Nacional de Patagonia's **Museo Nacional del Petróleo** (San Lorenzo 250, tel. 0297/455-9558, museodelpetroleo@speedy.com.ar, 9 A.M.–5 P.M. Mon.–Sat., US$4 foreigners, slightly less for Argentines) is a YPF legacy. On the grounds of Comodoro's initial gusher, it presents a professional account of Argentina's oil industry, from the natural and cultural environment to petroleum technology and its social and historical consequences. From the Comodoro bus terminal, take the No. 4 Saavedra or No. 5 Universidad bus.

Nearby, on sprawling shoreline grounds, dating from 1923, the **Museo Chalet Huergo** (tel. 0299/455-0225, 9 A.M.–5 P.M. weekdays, free) was the residence of YPF administrators and during the oil-boom years hosted guests like the Shah of Iran. Today, though, it's the centerpiece of a public park and home to special events and exhibitions.

Entertainment

A classic of its era, the **Cine Teatro Español** (Avenida San Martín 664, tel. 0297/447-7700) offers recent movies and theater productions. There's also the **Cine Coliseo** (San Martín 570, tel. 0297/444-5500).

Accommodations

Because Comodoro is the largest city in almost 1,000 kilometers of highway, hotels can fill up fast, and reservations are advisable. Prices have risen substantially.

Hotel del Mar (Ameghino 750, tel. 0299/447-2025, hoteldelmar@hotmail.com, US$25 s, US$40 d) is one of several plain but acceptable accommodations, along with **Hostería Rua Marina** (Belgrano 738, tel. 0297/446-8777, US$27 s, US$49 d) and **Hotel Español** (9 de Julio 850, tel. 0297/446-0116, US$34 s, US$58 d, without breakfast).

Rehabbed **Hotel Azul** (Sarmiento 724, tel./fax 0297/447-4628, www.hotelazul.com.ar, US$61 s, US$66 d) always had pretty good rooms, but the common areas are now more presentable. **Residencial Comodoro** (España 919, tel. 0297/446-2582, US$49 s, US$68 d) is comparable.

The traditional **Hotel Comodoro** (9 de Julio 770, tel. 0297/447-2300, www.comodorohotel. com.ar, US$76–91 s, US$86–105 d) continues to lag behind some newer options.

Really two hotels in one, the **Austral Hotel** (Rivadavia 190, US$79 s, US$91 d) and the recent addition [**Hotel Austral Plaza** (Moreno 725, tel. 0297/447-2200, www.australhotel.com.ar, US$155 s, US$167 d) share a reception area, telephones, bar, *confitería,* and restaurant. The Austral's rooms are comfy enough, if a little small, but they're less extravagant than the Plaza's. Rates have risen substantially at both; guests at both enjoy the same buffet breakfast.

Hotel Lucania Palazzo (Moreno 676, tel. 0297/449-9300, www.lucania-palazzo.com, US$162 s, US$181 d) is a four-star high-rise with all the amenities and skyrocketing rates.

Food
Comodoro has several quality *parrillas,* including **Bom Bife** (España 789, tel. 0297/446-8412, lunch and dinner daily) and **La Rastra** (Rivadavia 348, tel. 0297/444-3623, lunch and dinner daily).

Pizzería Giulietta (Belgrano 851, tel. 02965/446-1201, lunch and dinner daily) serves fine pasta as well; in the same vein, there's **Cayo Coco** (Rivadavia 102, tel. 0297/447-3033, lunch and dinner daily).

Waterfront **Puerto Cangrejo** (Avenida Costanera s/n, tel. 0297/444-4590, lunch and dinner daily) serves ample portions of similar fare in the US$10–13 range.

The Hotel Austral Plaza's [**Tunet** (Rivadavia 190, tel. 0297/447-2200, lunch and dinner daily, US$10–25) is Comodoro's top restaurant, with an elaborate fish and seafood menu that also includes tapas.

Chocolate's (San Martín 231, tel. 0297/446-4488) serves Comodoro's best ice cream.

Information
The municipal **Dirección de Turismo** (Rivadavia 430, tel. 0297/444-0664, turismo@comodoro.gov.ar, www.comodoro.gov. ar) is open 8 A.M.–3 P.M. weekdays only. A bus terminal branch is open 9 A.M.–9 P.M. daily.

For motorists, **ACA** (tel. 0297/446-4036) is at Dorrego and Alvear.

Services
Banco de la Nación (San Martín 102) has one of several ATMs along the avenue. **Cambio Thaler** (Mitre 943) is the only currency exchange house.

Correo Argentino is at Avenida San Martín and Moreno; the postal code is 9000. There are many *locutorios* with phone, fax, and Internet services.

Turismo Ceferino (9 de Julio 880, 1st floor, tel. 0297/447-3805) is the Amex representative.

The **Chilean consulate** (tel. 0297/446-2414) is at Almirante Brown 456, Oficina 3.

For medical assistance, try the **Hospital Regional** (Hipólito Yrigoyen 950, tel. 0297/444-2287).

Laverap (Rivadavia 287) does the laundry.

Getting There
Aerolíneas Argentinas (Rivadavia 154, tel. 0297/454-8190) flies two or three times daily to Buenos Aires's Aeroparque. LAN Argentina (tel. 0297/454-8171 at the airport) also flies to Buenos Aires.

Comodoro is a hub for **LADE** (Rivadavia 360, tel. 0297/447-0585), which flies northbound to Aeroparque and intermediate towns, westbound to Gobernador Gregores and other towns, and southbound to El Calafate, Río Gallegos, and intermediate towns.

Comodoro's **Terminal de Ómnibus**

Teniente General Angel Solari (Pellegrini 730, tel. 0297/446-7305) has regional, long-distance, and limited international service to Coyhaique, Chile.

At 8 A.M. Wednesday and Saturday, **ETAP** (tel. 0297/447-4841) departs for Coyhaique (9 hours, US$25); these buses usually run full and schedules can vary, so reservations are essential.

Other sample destinations, times, and fares include Caleta Olivia (1 hour, US$3), San Julián (5.5 hours, US$12), Trelew (5 hours, US$18–21), Puerto Deseado (4.5 hours, US$15), Puerto Madryn (6 hours, US$20–25), Los Antiguos (6 hours, US$30), Esquel (10 hours, US$28–40), Río Gallegos (11 hours, US$35–50), Bariloche (14 hours, US$38–50), and Buenos Aires (25 hours, US$75–108).

Getting Around
Opposite the bus terminal, the No. 8 Patagonia Argentina (Directo Palazzo) bus goes to **Aeropuerto General Mosconi** (RN 3, tel. 0297/454-8093), which is nine kilometers north of town.

Car-rental agencies include **Budget** (Moreno 864, tel. 0297/444-0008, comodoro@budgetargentina.com) and **Dubrovnik** (Moreno 855, tel./fax 0297/444-1844, Dubrovnik@infovia.com.ar).

Coastal Santa Cruz Province

CALETA OLIVIA
South of Comodoro Rivadavia, there's heavy truck traffic and plenty of reckless drivers on winding RN 3 before arriving at the oil port of Caleta Olivia. Its forlorn appearance gradually improving, Caleta (pop. 36,323), south of Comodoro 79 kilometers, is a crossroads for westbound traffic to Lago Buenos Aires and the Chilean border. It's 346 kilometers north of Puerto San Julián but only 216 kilometers northwest of Puerto Deseado, an underrated wildlife destination.

The only conspicuous sight, dominating a rotary that marks the town center, is the **Monumento al Obrero Petrolero** (1969), popularly known as "El Gorosito." Facing north, Pablo Daniel Sánchez's 10-meter sculpture of a muscular shirtless worker turning an oil valve symbolizes thinly peopled Patagonia's contribution to (or exploitation by) the populous heartland. It's also an oblique reference to authoritarian president Juan Domingo Perón, whose most devoted followers were working-class *descamisados* ("shirtless ones").

Accommodations and Food
Hotel Capri (José Hernández 1145, tel. 0297/485-1132, US$19–27 s, US$27–35 d) has rooms with shared bath or private bath; breakfast is extra. **Hospedaje Rodas** (Matheu 12, tel. 0297/485-1880, US$22 s, US$31 d) offers good value with private baths. **Posada Don David** (Hipólito Yrigoyen 2385, tel. 0297/485-7661, posadadondavid@hotmail.com, US$33 s, US$38 d) has similar offerings.

Expanding **Hotel Robert** (Avenida San Martín 2151, tel. 0297/485-1452, www.hotelrobert.com.ar, US$45–54 s, US$50–59 d, with small discounts for cash payment) is the top hotel here; its restaurant, **La Rosa,** comes recommended.

Buonna Pizza (Independencia 52, tel. 0297/485-2653, lunch and dinner daily) also has a variety of takeaway empanadas. Down the block, **El Puerto** (Avenida Independencia 1060, tel. 0297/485-1313, lunch and dinner daily) is best for seafood and *parrillada.*

Heladería Centro (Independencia 1175, tel. 0297/485-3721) has fine ice cream.

Information and Services
The municipal **Centro de Informes** (Avenida San Martín and Güemes, tel. 0297/485-0988, turismo@caletaolivia.gov.ar) is open 8 A.M.–9 P.M. daily.

Banco de la Nación (Avenida Eva Perón 135) has one of several ATMs.

Correo Argentino is at Hipólito Yrigoyen 2194. **Telefonía Caleta** (San Martín 5) has long-distance services, while **Cyber Centro** (Avenida Independencia and Fagnano) has Internet connections.

Getting There

From the **Terminal de Ómnibus** (Avenida Tierra del Fuego 850), 15 blocks northwest of the Gorosito sculpture, there are northbound and southbound services along RN 3, plus westbound connections to Los Antiguos and Chile Chico via paved RP 43.

Typical destinations, times, and fares include Comodoro Rivadavia (1 hour, US$3), Puerto Deseado (3.5 hours, US$12), Río Gallegos (10 hours, US$32–48), Los Antiguos (5 hours, US$27), and Buenos Aires (26 hours, US$75–110).

PUERTO DESEADO AND VICINITY

Bypassed by RN 3—but not by nature or history—Puerto Deseado is one of Patagonia's underrated pleasures. Visited by Magellan, settled by Spanish whalers, explored by Charles Darwin in 1833, and resettled half a century later, it clings to its pioneer ambience in what Francisco P. Moreno called "the most picturesque place on the eastern Patagonian coast." The star, though, is the Ría Deseado, where strong tides rush up the estuary to create a wildlife-rich environment that supports a growing ecotourism sector. At the same time, Deseado has become a homeport for the South Atlantic shrimp fishery, and some businesses keep signs in Spanish, English, and Russian.

On the Ría Deseado's north shore, Puerto Deseado (pop. 10,252) is 216 kilometers southeast of Caleta Olivia and 295 kilometers from Comodoro Rivadavia via RN 3 and paved RN 281 (but 125 kilometers from the RN 3 junction).

Sights

For a small town, Deseado has plenty to see. The big draw is the **Reserva Provincial Ría Deseado,** but various historical monuments all have good stories behind them.

By the late 19th century, Deseado seemed

SOUTHERN PATAGONIA

© WAYNE BERNHARDSON

A moulting rockhopper penguin at Isla de los Pingüinos, off Puerto Deseado.

DEATH RODE THE RAILS

The handsome wooden railcar now at the corner of San Martín and Almirante Brown in Puerto Deseado is more than an object of train-spotter nostalgia. During the Santa Cruz Anarchist rebellion of 1921 (a struggle dramatized in Osvaldo Bayer's film *La Patagonia Rebelde*), it was the mobile command center for Colonel Héctor Benigno Varela, who led government forces against striking farm workers throughout the territory. At Jaramillo station, near the present-day junction of RN 281 and RN 3, Varela personally executed gaucho insurgent José Font (known as "Facón Grande" or "Big Knife") under false pretenses (appropriately enough, Varela died from a bomb and bullets by German Anarchist Kurt Gustav Wilckens in Buenos Aires in 1923).

As a symbol of military brutality – in total, some 1,500 people died at the hands of Varela's forces – the car is an enduring monument. Nearly six decades later, in December 1980, in a defiant demonstration against Argentina's fiercest dictatorship ever, Deseado residents encircled the historic railcar with 40 private automobiles to prevent its removal by truck. Not only did the demonstrators challenge armed authority – in a town with a tank regiment – but they bravely signed their names and ID card numbers in a petition to Santa Cruz's military governor. Astonishingly, the de facto government backed down.

destined to become a rail port, as authorities planned a northwesterly freight-and-passenger line to Bariloche. It never advanced beyond Las Heras, 283 kilometers northwest, and closed in 1977, leaving the stately **Estación del Ferrocarril Patagónico** (Eufrasia Arias s/n, 4–7 P.M. Mon.–Sat., free) as a surprisingly good museum staffed by former railroad workers.

Several monuments date from this era, most notably the railroad's **Vagón Histórico** (1898), an historic railcar in a small plaza at San Martín and Almirante Brown. Immediately across the street, **Banco de la Nación** has preserved its classic lava-block style, but the supermarket that occupies the former **Compañía Argentina del Sud** (1919) has concealed its vintage details with hideous painted signs on all sides (pointlessly, as it has no competition in town). One block west stands the **Sociedad Española** (1915).

Along the waterfront, the **Museo Regional Mario Brozoski** (Brown and Colón, tel. 0297/487-0673, 8 A.M.–5 P.M. weekdays, 3–7 P.M. weekends, free) holds artifacts from the English corvette *Swift*, sunk nearby in 1770 and rediscovered in 1982. Several kilometers northeast, **Balneario Las Piletas** is a volcanic beach area where retreating tides leave pools warm enough for swimming, at least in summer.

At the north end of Almirante Zar, after passing beneath a railroad bridge, the road leads five kilometers into the isolated **Cañadon Quitapenas** and excellent camping sites (no services). Ten kilometers west of town, a southbound lateral leads to the **Gruta de Lourdes,** a secluded pilgrimage site where the faithful have left devotional plaques. Rare rainstorms produce ephemeral waterfalls here.

Reserva Natural Ría Deseado

One of coastal Patagonia's primo wildlife sites, the Ría Deseado submerges a long narrow valley that once carried more freshwater. As the freshwater flow diminished, seawater penetrated farther and farther inland, creating new islands and other fauna-rich habitats. Offshore islands also form part of the reserve.

Several operators organize wildlife-watching excursions in and around the Ría to locations such as the Magellanic penguin colony at **Isla Chaffers** and cliff-side colonies of rock cormorants and gray or red-legged cormorants at **Banca Cormorán,** where deep water permits close approach to the nests. On any excursion, swiftly swimming *toninas overas* (Commerson's dolphins) breach and dive around and under the outboard launches; in mating season, they leap out of the water.

At **Isla de los Pingüinos,** 30 kilometers offshore, there are breeding elephant seals, sea lions, and the world's northernmost colonies of the tireless rockhopper penguin, which braves crashing waves up steep stone faces to reach its nesting sites. Some operators also follow Darwin's route up the Ría where, wrote the great naturalist, "I do not think I ever saw a spot which appeared more secluded from the rest of the world, than this rocky crevice in the wild plain."

In handsome new quarters that include a sea-view *confitería,* **Darwin Expediciones** (Avenida España s/n, tel. 0297/15-624-7554, www.darwin-expeditions.com) has extensive experience here and also does sea kayaking. Half-day trips to Isla Chaffers cost about US$37 pp; full-day trips, following Darwin's estuary route, cost about US$92 pp. A full-day excursion to the rockhopper colony at Isla de los Pingüinos runs about US$84 pp with an eight-passenger minimum.

Turismo Aventura Los Vikingos (Estrada 1275, tel. 0297/487-0020, tel. 0297/487-0020, www.losvikingos.com.ar) does similar maritime itineraries.

Accommodations and Food

Reservations are advisable in summer for the limited accommodations.

At the western approach to town, the sheltered **Camping Cañadón Giménez** (tel. 0297/15-466-3815, US$2.50 pp) also charges US$5 per tent.

Some of the singles are tiny at labyrinthine **Residencial Los Olmos** (Gregores 849, tel. 0297/487-0077, US$27 s, US$38 d), but the management is friendly, with (balky) Wi-Fi and closed parking. At **Hotel Oneto** (Oneto 1401, tel. 0297/487-0455, hoteloneto@infovia.com.ar, US$18 pp, US$32 s, US$48 d), the cheaper rooms with shared baths are small and inferior to the larger rooms with private baths.

Hotel Isla Chaffers (San Martín and Moreno, www.hotelislachaffers.com.ar, tel. 0297/487-2246, US$50 s, US$60 d) is a notable upgrade.

At **Hotel los Acantilados** (España and Pueyrredón, tel. 0297/487-2167, acantour@pdeseado.com.ar, US$42–60 s, US$50–69 d), downstairs rooms come with small but serviceable baths; upstairs rooms have sea views and better furniture, but the baths are equally small. Its bar is one of the best places to watch the sunset.

El Pingüino (Piedrabuena 958, tel. 0297/487-2105, lunch and dinner daily) is a *parrilla.* **Puerto Cristal** (España 1698, tel. 0297/487-0387, lunch and dinner daily) has decent seafood, excellent pastas, exceptional service, and bad pop music. **Lo de Armando** (San Martín and Sarmiento, tel. 0297/15-430-6443), though, is the only place in town that makes an effort at creativity in both its menu and decor. The shrimp *sorrentinos* (US$10) are excellent, but stay away from the house wine.

Information and Services

The **Dirección Municipal de Turismo** (Avenida San Martín 1525, tel. 0297/487-0220, www.turismo.deseado.gov.ar) is open 8 A.M.–8 P.M. daily in summer, 9 A.M.–6 P.M. daily the rest of the year.

Banco de la Nación (San Martín 1001) has an ATM.

Correo Argentino (San Martín 1075) is the post office; the postal code is 9050. **Telefonía Deseado** (Almirante Brown 544) has telephones and Internet connections.

For medical services, try the **Hospital Distrital** (Brown and Colón, tel. 0297/487-0200).

Getting There and Around

From the **Terminal de Ómnibus** (Sargento Cabral 1302), about 10 blocks northeast of downtown, there are buses to Caleta Olivia (3.5 hours, US$12) and Comodoro Rivadavia (4.5 hours, US$15) with **Transporte La Unión** (tel. 0297/15-592-8598, 3 buses daily) and **Sportman** (tel. 0297/487-0013, 2 buses daily).

SOUTHERN PATAGONIA

MONUMENTO NATURAL BOSQUES PETRIFICADOS

One of RN 3's most desolate stretches is the 350 kilometers between Caleta Olivia and Puerto San Julián, but just north of the halfway point there's an incomparable detour to this 13,700-hectare badlands. In Jurassic times, before the Andes rose in the west, this was a humid region of coniferous *Proaraucaria* woodlands. After volcanic eruptions flattened the forests and buried them in ash 130 million years ago, water and wind gradually uncovered the now-petrified trunks.

Measuring up to three meters in diameter and 35 meters in length, *Proaraucaria* was a forerunner of the Andean araucaria. Until 1954, when the area became a natural monument (meriting Argentina's highest possible level of protection), the best and biggest specimens were regularly looted. Proposed additions would increase the protected area to 60,000 hectares.

Solitary Bosques Petrificados, 50 kilometers west of RN 3 via graveled RP 49, gets only a few thousand visitors per year, mostly in summer. In addition to its petrified forests,

it has desert steppe vegetation and wildlife including guanacos and rheas. It has no water, and there is no public transportation, but Puerto Deseado operators will organize excursions to the site. For camping, try Estancia La Paloma, roughly midway between RN 3 and the forest.

For more information, contact Caleta Olivia's APN office (Hipólito Irigoyen 2044, tel. 0297/485-1000, bosquespetrificados@apn.gov.ar).

PUERTO SAN JULIÁN AND VICINITY

Coastal Patagonia's single most important historical site, windswept San Julián was where Magellan's crew wintered in 1520 during the first circumnavigation of the globe. Both Magellan and Sir Francis Drake (half a century later) faced mutinies that they repressed ruthlessly, while Antonio de Viedma founded a short-lived Spanish colony at nearby Floridablanca—southern Patagonia's first European settlement—in 1780. Darwin, who found the countryside "more sterile" than Deseado, uncovered a llama-like fossil with an elephantine trunk here.

Rheas, or *ñandúes*, are a common sight on the Patagonian steppe.

© WAYNE BERNHARDSON

These flags at Puerto San Julián reflect the origins of its early settlers.

In the 1890s, British settlers from the Falkland Islands and Scotland finally established a permanent presence through the powerful San Julián Sheep Farming Company. Even in the late 1930s, according to John Locke Blake, "English was spoken freely round town," and the company's extensive holdings—175,000 hectares of pastureland—dominated life into the 1960s. Today, it's a secondary ecotourism destination for its dolphins and penguins, and a common stopover between Caleta Olivia and Río Gallegos.

San Julián (pop. 6,152) is 351 kilometers south of Caleta Olivia and 355 kilometers north of Río Gallegos via RN 3. Avenida San Martín, the main thoroughfare, is an extension of the eastward lateral than connects the town with the highway.

Sights

In the bay just north of town, **Isla Cormorán** has a Magellanic penguin colony; there's a king cormorant colony nearby at the sardonically named **Isla Justicia,** where Magellan stopped a mutiny by decapitating one rebel, quartering another, and leaving two others to starve. Headquartered in an adapted shed, **Pinocho Excursiones** (Avenida Costanera and Mitre, tel. 02962/45-4600, www.pinochoexcursiones.com.ar) takes visitors on harbor tours (US$25 pp), with English-speaking guides, that include dolphin- and penguin-watching; when winds are too strong, the rigid inflatables may not sail.

At the foot of Avenida San Martín, San Julián's most conspicuous waterfront attraction is a Disneyish scale model of Magellan's ship that holds the **Museo Temático Nao Victoria.** It's tempting to describe this as "Pirates of the South Atlantic," but it makes an effort to cover local history. Admission costs US$1 for kids, US$2 for Argentine adults, and US$3 for foreigners; and it's open from 8 A.M–10 P.M. or dark, whichever is earlier.

The archaeological and historical **Museo Regional y de Arte Marino Rosa Novak** (Avenida Hernando de Magallanes s/n) continues to occupy temporary quarters on the waterfront as it awaits the remodel and expansion of its permanent quarters in an archetypal Patagonian house at Vieytes and Rivadavia. Summer hours are 9 A.M.–noon and 3–7 P.M. weekdays, 10 A.M.–1 P.M. and 4–9 P.M. weekends. Even these are kept inconsistently, and winter hours (weekdays only) are shorter.

Immediately across from the museum's permanent site, the memorial **Plazoleta Albino Argüelles** commemorates one of the army's victims in the 1921 Anarchist rebellion. From here, the coastal Avenida Hernán de Magallanes leads north past the marked grave of *Beagle* crewman Robert Sholl, who died on the voyage prior to Darwin's. The road continues to the **Frigorífico Swift,** a mutton freezer that operated from 1912 to 1967; its crumbling shell and pier appeal to postindustrial photographers.

Accommodations and Food

The waterfront **Autocamping Municipal** (Avenida Hernán de Magallanes 650, tel. 02962/45-2806, US$1.25 pp plus US$2.50 per vehicle) has well-sheltered sites with picnic tables and fire pits, clean bathrooms, hot showers, laundry facilities, and even a playground.

◖ **Hospedaje La Casona** (Avenida Hernando de Magallanes 650, tel. 02962/45-2434, US$29 s, US$39 d) is a B&B in a recycled waterfront house—the most distinctively Patagonian lodgings in town. It has comfortable beds, spacious and attractive common areas, and a kitchen for a basic self-serve breakfast.

Under the same ownership, the 12-room **Hostería Miramar** (Avenida San Martín 210, tel. 02962/45-4626, miramar146@speedy.com.ar, US$34 s, US$40 d) looks better on the surface, but the interior workmanship shows some shortcomings, even if it's not a desperation choice.

Under new management, **Hotel Sada** (Avenida San Martín 1112, tel. 02962/45-2013, www.hotelsada.com.ar, US$34 s, US$46 d) has 18 rooms with private baths, but it's their new **Posada Drake** (Mitre and Rivadavia, tel. 02962/45-2523, www.

posadadedrake.com.ar, US$34 s, US$40 d) that deserves attention for immaculate new quarters that include a teahouse.

Government-run hotels are notorious for shoddy service and maintenance, but the **Hostería Municipal de Turismo** (25 de Mayo 917, tel. 02962/45-2300, www.costanerahotel.com, US$47 s, US$55 d) is an exception. Its renovated rooms are simple but comfortable and spotless, and the staff are proud of it, but those renovations have meant higher prices.

Hotel Bahía (Avenida San Martín 1075, tel. 02962/45-4028, www.hotelbahiasanjulian.com.ar, US$58–65 s, US$62–71 d) is an attractive new hotel that fills up fast. Its only drawback is its location on the main avenue.

Crowded even on weekdays, ◖ **La Rural** (Ameghino 811, tel. 02962/45-4066, lunch and dinner daily) specializes in beef and lamb, but its own factory produces fine pastas (particularly *sorrentinos*). It has expanded its fish and seafood offerings and also prepares outstanding salads. Prices are reasonable and service excellent.

Right on the waterfront, **Naos** (9 de Julio 1106, tel. 02962/45-2714, lunch and dinner daily) has a new name and new ownership, but it's still a quality fish and seafood restaurant. **La Juliana** (Zeballos 1134, tel. 02962/45-2074, lunch and dinner daily) has made good impressions with relatively expensive homestyle cooking. **Popeye** (Moreno 1070, tel. 02962/45-2045, lunch and dinner daily) has the best pizza.

M&M (Avenida San Martín 387, tel. 02962/45-4419) has superb ice cream.

Information and Services

A **municipal information office** (10 A.M.–10 P.M. daily mid-Dec.–Mar.) occupies an office in the Hotel Alamo at the highway junction. On the main avenue median, the municipal **Centro de Informes** (Avenida San Martín s/n, between Moreno and Rivadavia, tel. 02962/45-2301, www.sanjulian.gov.ar) is open 7 A.M.–midnight weekdays and 9:30 A.M.–9:30 P.M. weekends in summer, 7 A.M.–2 P.M. weekdays only the rest of the year.

Banco de la Nación (Mitre 101) has an ATM.

Correo Argentino is at Avenida San Martín 155; the postal code is 9310. For telecommunications, try **Portal Patagonia** (Avenida San Martín and Rivadavia). **CTO.com** (San Martín 614) has fast Internet access, but it's also the rowdy home-away-from-home for adolescent computer gamers.

Lavandería Arco Iris (Roca 1077, tel. 02962/45-2171) does the washing.

For medical services, try the **Hospital Distrital Miguel Lombardich** (9 de Julio s/n, tel. 02962/45-2020) or the private **Clínica Austral** (San Martín 979, tel. 02962/45-2044).

Getting There

LADE (tel. 02962/45-2137) occupies an office in the Terminal de Ómnibus (Avenida San Martín 1552), with occasional flights to Comodoro Rivadavia, Gobernador Gregores, and Río Gallegos; flights leave from the airfield near the highway junction.

On a highway the length of RN 3, somebody has to draw the short straw, and nearly all San Julián buses arrive and leave between midnight and 6 A.M., mostly between 1:30 and 4 A.M. There are several services to Buenos Aires and intermediate towns, and also south to Río Gallegos.

Cerro San Lorenzo (Berutti 970, tel. 02962/45-2403) goes to Gobernador Gregores (US$15) at 7:30 A.M. Monday–Saturday.

COMANDANTE LUIS PIEDRA BUENA

When Charles Darwin and the *Beagle* crew ascended the Río Santa Cruz in 1834, swift currents beyond Isla Pavón obliged them to walk the shore and drag their boats on lines, limiting their progress to about 10 miles per day. Twenty-five years later, naval explorer Luis Piedra Buena first raised the Argentine flag where his namesake town now stands; Perito Moreno ascended partway in 1879, and territorial governor Ramon Lista made the first arduous steamer ascent in 1890, all the way to Lago Argentino and Lago Viedma.

Piedra Buena (pop. 4,175) has little to see, but its services makes it worth a lunch break or even an overnight stay before seeing Parque Nacional Monte León. On the Río Santa Cruz's north bank, it's 127 kilometers south of Puerto San Julián and 235 kilometers north of Río Gallegos via RN 3. About 45 kilometers south, westbound RP 9 provides a bumpy motorist's or cyclist's shortcut along the Río Santa Cruz valley to El Calafate.

While the town is nondescript, **Isla Pavón,** reached by a turnoff from the bridge over the Río Santa Cruz about three kilometers south of the highway junction, is a wooded beauty spot that's popular for fishing; a small museum honors Piedra Buena's efforts.

Accommodations and Food

On the island, the **Camping Vial Isla Pavón** (tel. 02962/15-53-9168, US$3 per site) has electricity, clean toilets, and hot showers (US$0.65).

Despite its unappealing and unimaginative name, the spacious motel-style rooms at ⟨ **Hotel Sur Atlantic Oil** (RN 3 Km 2404, tel. 02962/49-7008, US$37 s or d), part of the YPF gas station complex, fill up early (and it does not take reservations). Popular with southbound travelers, it also has a remarkable restaurant with particularly choice pastas (take lunch in the restaurant proper, rather than the adjacent *confitería*).

Across the highway, the new **Hotel Río Santa Cruz** (tel. 02962/49-7245, h_riosantacruz@yahoo.com.ar, US$43 s or d) is a good backup choice. Isla Pavón's municipal *hostería*, usually the best option here, has been closed for renovation.

Getting There and Around

Northbound and southbound services along RN 3 use the **Terminal de Ómnibus** (Ibáñez Norte 130), but it's also possible to flag down buses on the highway.

In summer, **Transporte Las Lengas** (tel. 02962/49-3023, laslengaselchalten@yahoo.com.ar) offers a daily 2 P.M. service to the El Chaltén sector of Parque Nacional Los Glaciares (6 hours, US$29).

◖ PARQUE NACIONAL MONTE LEÓN

Donated to the APN by the Fundación Vida Silvestre and the Patagonia Land Trust by environmental philanthropists Doug Tompkins and Kris McDivitt, 62,000-hectare Monte León's 30-kilometer shoreline and headlands are an ecological wonderland of copious wildlife and uncommon landscapes. Little known and less visited, this former *estancia* is Argentina's second coastal national park, after Parque Nacional Tierra del Fuego (similar reserves in Río Negro, Chubut, and Santa Cruz are provincial parks).

Flora and Fauna

Monte León's coastline is home to some 60,000 Magellanic penguins, as well as gray and king cormorants, snowy sheathbills, Patagonian crested and steamer ducks, Dominican gulls, and sea lions, while its interior grazes guanacos and rheas and shelters armadillos and *liebres* (Patagonian hares). The vegetation is primarily grasses and prostrate shrubs of the Patagonian steppe. There are also pumas as well as red and gray foxes.

Sights and Recreation

Wildlife-watching is the principal activity, but the landscape is special: Where the tides meet the headlands, the sea has eroded deep caverns. Seen from the steppe above, **La Olla** (The Kettle) took its name from its almost perfectly circular opening, but heavy rains and seas caused it to collapse in October 2006.

Unlike much of the South Atlantic, the coastline here abounds with offshore rocks and stacks. Guano collectors worked one of these, **Isla Monte León,** by stringing a still-existing cable tram from the headland. At low tide, exploring La Olla's remnants and Isla Monte León's base is possible, but be aware of the tides to avoid being stranded in a dangerous situation—the route is slippery, and the tide comes in fast. Try to descend about an hour before low tide—the RN 3 visitors center can advise on times.

Accommodations and Food

Camping is possible at Monte León proper, but there are better accommodations at ◖ **Hostería**

Monte León (RN 3 Km 2385, tel. 011/4621-4780 in Buenos Aires, www.monteleon-patagonia.com, US$210 s, US$320 d, with half board), the former *estancia's casco,* which also arranges excursions to the shoreline.

While donating the *estancia* to the park service through their Patagonia Land Trust, Tompkins and McDivitt have retained about 330 hectares and left the *hostería's* management to former owner Silvia Braun and her Swiss-Argentine husband, Juan Kuriger. The *casco* itself is a spacious, high-ceilinged beauty with four guest rooms and a small museum; much of the produce comes from Silvia Braun's organic garden.

Other Practicalities

For information, especially on the tides and the state of the washout-prone road, ask at Hostería Monte León, where there are rangers stationed nearby (tel. 02962/49-8184 in Puerto Santa Cruz, monteleon@apn.gov.ar).

There is no public transportation to Monte León, which is 58 kilometers south of Piedra Buena via paved RN 3 and graveled RP 63; if road conditions are bad, the gate will be locked.

RÍO GALLEGOS

Travelers often dismiss windy Río Gallegos as merely a port and service center for Anglo-Argentine wool *estancias* and, more recently, the petroleum industry. Dating from 1885, near continental Argentina's southern tip, it has a handful of museums, historical landmarks, and other distinctive Magellanic buildings as well as a handsomely redeveloped waterfront; it's also the gateway to one of the continent's largest penguin colonies and several historic *estancias* open to visitors. It's no longer the main gateway to El Calafate since construction of the new international airport there, but travelers bound for Punta Arenas (Chile) and Tierra del Fuego may have to spend the night here.

Río Gallegos (pop. about 90,000) is 696 kilometers south of Comodoro Rivadavia and 351 kilometers south of Puerto San Julián via RN 3, and 67 kilometers north of the Chilean border post of Monte Aymond. From

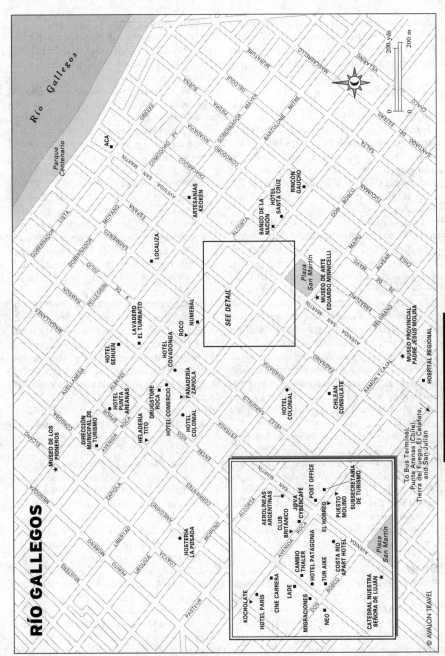

RÍO GALLEGOS

Río Gallegos

Río Gallegos

Parque Centenario

SOUTHERN PATAGONIA

ACA

ARTESANÍAS KEOKEN

BANCO DE LA NACIÓN

HOTEL SANTA CRUZ

RINCÓN GAUCHO

LOCALIZA

NUMERAL

ROCO

SEE DETAIL

Plaza San Martín

MUSEO DE ARTE EDUARDO MINNICELLI

MUSEO PROVINCIAL PADRE JESÚS MOLINA

HOSPITAL REGIONAL

LAVADERO EL TUMBAITO

HOTEL SEHUEN

HOTEL COVADONGA

PANADERÍA ZAPIOLA

HOTEL PUNTA ARENAS

DRUGSTORE ROCA

HOTEL COMERCIO

HELADERÍA TITO

HOTEL COLONIAL

DIRECCIÓN MUNICIPAL DE TURISMO

HOTEL COLONIAL

CHILEAN CONSULATE

MUSEO DE LOS PIONEROS

HOSTERÍA LA POSADA

To Bus Terminal, Punta Arenas (Chile), Tierra del Fuego, El Calafate, and San Julián

Detail

AEROLÍNEAS ARGENTINAS

CLUB BRITÁNICO

J@VA CYBERCAFÉ

POST OFFICE

SUBSECRETARÍA DE TURISMO

PUESTO MOLINO

EL HORREO

Plaza San Martín

KOCHOLATE

HOTEL PARIS

CINE CARRERA

LADE

CAMBIO THALER

MIGRACIONES

HOTEL PATAGONIA

TUR AIKE

NEO

COSTA RÍO APART HOTEL

CATEDRAL NUESTRA SEÑORA DE LUJÁN

© AVALON TRAVEL

200 yds

200 m

Monte Aymond it's another 196 kilometers to Punta Arenas or, alternatively, 571 kilometers to Ushuaia, Tierra del Fuego (including a ferry crossing at Primera Angostura). It's 305 kilometers southeast of El Calafate via paved RP 5.

Sights

Opposite Plaza San Martín, the **Catedral Nuestra Señora de Luján** (1899) was the work of Salesian priest Juan Bernabé, who was also responsible for the cathedrals of Punta Arenas and Ushuaia. Like other pioneer buildings, it reflects the wood-framed metal-clad Magellanic style.

On the plaza's south side, the **Museo de Arte Eduardo Minnicelli** (Maipú 13, tel. 02966/43-6323, www.museominnicelli.com.ar, 8 A.M.–7 P.M. Tues.–Fri., 3–7 P.M. Sat.–Sun. and holidays, closed Dec. 20–Feb. 10, free) showcases provincial artists such as its namesake sculptor.

Three blocks south, the comprehensive **Museo Provincial Padre Jesús Molina** (Ramón y Cajal 51, tel. 02966/42-3290, museopadremolina@yahoo.com.ar, 10 A.M.–7 P.M. weekdays, 11 A.M.–7 P.M. weekends and holidays, free) holds material on geology, paleontology, natural history, ethnology, and local history, including a good photographic collection.

In a pioneer house that belonged to Arthur and Victor Fenton, the city's first physicians, the **Museo de los Pioneros** (Elcano and Alberdi, tel. 02966/43-7763, pioneros@riogallegos.gov.ar, 10 A.M.–7:30 P.M. daily, but in winter may close as early as 6 P.M., free) documents southern Patagonia's early settlers. Aging Scots-Argentine volunteers greet visitors and explain the details in English.

Shopping

Rincón Gaucho (Avenida Roca 619, tel. 02966/42-0669) specializes in horse gear and the like. **Artesanías Keokén** (Avenida San Martín 336, tel. 02966/42-0335) specializes in woolens but also sells leather goods and food items (preserves and candies).

Accommodations

Traditionally, accommodations are scarce, prices high, and quality mediocre, but things are improving. Demand is also high, so reservations are advisable.

With gracious and conscientious ownership, **Hotel Colonial** (Rivadavia and Urquiza, tel. 02966/42-2329, US$21 s, US$31 d, with shared bath and without breakfast) is the best shoestring choice, but the rooms are small. Rates include kitchen access.

Undergoing a major renovation, friendly **Hotel Punta Arenas** (Federico Sphur 55, tel. 02966/443-1924, US$21–40 s, US$29–42 d) looks to improve considerably, though some rooms are still a little rough around the edges. The renovation will probably eliminate its budget rooms, however, which have shared baths. Breakfast takes place in its adjacent Something Café, which has Wi-Fi and a small but tasty snack menu.

Ill-planned remodeling has cost **Hotel París** (Avenida Roca 1040, tel. 02966/42-2432, US$31 s, US$37 d) most of its original charm, but it's still respectable though rough around the edges. Modern motel-style rooms at the back have high ceilings and firm single beds.

Aging but reliable **Hotel Covadonga** (Avenida Roca 1244, tel. 02966/42-0190, hotelcovadongargl@hotmail.com, US$20–27 s, US$34–38 d, with breakfast) has rooms with both shared and private baths as well as sheltered parking.

Amiable **Hostería La Posada** (Ameghino 331, tel. 02966/43-6445, marianobertinat@hotmail.com, US$38 s, US$46 d) is a major step up for comfortable rooms with private baths (including tubs) and cable TV, and popular enough that reservations are advisable. Meals are available in its small restaurant.

Reservations are almost essential for spacious, friendly, and well-kept **Hotel Sehuen** (Rawson 160, tel. 02966/42-5683, www.hotelsehuen.com, US$40 s, US$50 d).

Better than its lackluster exterior implies, the large, spotless rooms at aging **Hotel Comercio** (Avenida Roca 1302, tel. 02966/42-0209, hotelcomercio@informacionrgl.com.ar, US$58 s, US$81 d, with a so-so breakfast) are worn around the edges with dim lighting and insufficient electrical outlets. Still, the private baths have tubs, there's phone service and satellite TV, and the common areas are excellent. There's a 10 percent discount for cash.

Nondescript **Hotel Santa Cruz** (Avenida Roca 701, tel. 02966/42-0601, htlscruz@infovia.com.ar, US$58–71 s, US$75–94 d) has undergone a remodel, but it's not clear than the improvements have been dramatic enough to justify its rising prices.

It took 20 years to finish, and the 80-room **Hotel Patagonia** (Fagnano 54, tel. 02966/44-4969, www.hotel-patagonia.com, US$95–161 s, US$106–171 d) still needs to tidy up some details. Still, under the same ownership as El Calafate's Hotel Los Alamos, it has established itself as the city's best, with a gym, a spa, a business center, and Wi-Fi throughout. The higher rates correspond to five larger suites.

Food

As with accommodations, the restaurant scene is improving, but unfortunately none of Gallegos's restaurants even include a nonsmoking section.

Puesto Molino (Avenida Roca 854, tel. 02966/42-9836, lunch and dinner daily) serves a particularly fine *fugazzeta,* but also has *parrillada.* For a diverse menu of specialties like salmon ravioli with pesto (US$8), in enormous portions, popular **RoCo** (Avenida Roca 1157, tel. 02966/42-0203, lunch and dinner daily) is worth consideration.

Anyone who's ever been, or aspired to be, an Anglo-Argentine wool baron will want to dine at the classic **Club Británico** (Avenida Roca 935, tel. 02966/42-5223, lunch and dinner daily). The atmosphere (which includes live jazz some nights) still trumps the food, though.

Although they'll mislead you about tobacco-free areas—there are none—the most sophisticated menu belongs to **(El Horreo** (Roca 862, tel. 02966/42-6462, lunch and dinner daily). Local lamb (about US$10) is the specialty, but the empanada gallega makes an ideal appetizer.

For ice cream, **Kocholate** (Avenida Roca 1084, tel. 02966/42-0249) has an edge on traditional favorite **Heladería Tito** (Zapiola and Corrientes, tel. 02966/42-2008), but the latter is not a desperation choice.

Information

The well-organized **Subsecretaría de Turismo de la Provincia** (Avenida Roca 863, tel. 02966/43-8725, www.epatagonia.gov.ar, 9 A.M.–4 P.M. Mon.–Fri.) has maps and details on accommodations, excursions, and transportation.

The **Dirección Municipal de Turismo** (Avenida Roca 1587, tel. 02966/43-6920, www.turismo.riogallegos.gov.ar) is open 8 A.M.–5 P.M. weekdays only; another office (tel. 02966/42-2365, ext. 1138, 9 A.M.–8 P.M. weekdays) occupies an old railcar at Roca and San Martín. It also maintains a **Centro de Informes** (tel. 02966/44-2159, 7 A.M.–8 P.M. weekdays, 7 A.M.–noon and 6–8 P.M. weekends and holidays) at the bus terminal.

For motorists, **ACA** (Orkeke 10, tel. 02966/42-0477) is at the north end of Avenida San Martín.

Services

Cambio Luis Lopetegui (Zapiola 469, tel. 02966/42-1202) and **Cambio Thaler** (Monseñor Fagnano 20, tel. 02966/43-6052) exchanges U.S. dollars, Chilean pesos, and travelers checks. **Banco de la Nación** (Avenida Roca 799) has one of many ATMs.

Correo Argentino (Avenida Julio Roca 893) occupies a historic building; the postal code is 9400. **Numeral** (Avenida Roca 1113) is one of many *locutorios,* while **Neo** (Zapiola 104) is a convenient Internet outlet (but has rowdy gamers as well).

Macatobiano (Avenida Roca 998, tel. 02966/42-2466, www.macatobiano.com) is the American Express representative.

For visa matters, **Migraciones** (Monseñor Fagnano 95, tel. 02966/42-0205) is open 8 A.M.–4 P.M. weekdays only. The **Chilean consulate** (Mariano Moreno 148, tel. 02966/42-2364) is open 9 A.M.–2 P.M. Monday–Friday.

SOUTHERN PATAGONIA

Lavadero El Tumbaito (Alberdi 397, tel. 02966/42-2452) handles the laundry.

For medical attention, try the **Hospital Regional** (José Ingenieros 98, tel. 02966/42-0025).

Getting There

Air services are fewer since El Calafate's airport opened. Overland, there are westbound bus connections to El Calafate and Parque Nacional Los Glaciares as well as the coal town of Río Turbio, and to Chile's Puerto Natales and Parque Nacional Torres del Paine; southbound links are to Punta Arenas, Chile, and to Argentine Tierra del Fuego.

Aerolíneas Argentinas (Avenida San Martín 545, tel. 02966/42-2020) flies daily to Buenos Aires's Aeroparque and to Ushuaia. **LADE** (Fagnano 53, tel. 02966/42-2316) flies northbound to Buenos Aires and intermediate towns; westbound to interior Santa Cruz Province; and southbound to Río Grande and Ushuaia.

LAN Argentina (tel. 02966/45-7189) flies to Aeroparque Sunday and Monday; for details, contact travel agencies. Once a month, Saturday **LAN** flights between Punta Arenas and the Falkland Islands pick up passengers here and drop them off the following week.

About two kilometers west of downtown, Río Gallegos's **Terminal de Omnibus Manuel Alvarez** (Charlotte Fairchild s/n, tel. 02966/44-2159) fronts on RN 3 near Avenida Eva Perón. There are provincial, long-distance, and international services to Chile.

Daily in high season, there's direct service to Río Grande (8 hours, US$33) and Ushuaia (12 hours, US$48), in Argentine Tierra del Fuego, with **Tecni-Austral** (tel. 02966/44-2447) and **Transportes Marga** (tel. 02966/44-2671).

El Pulgarcito (tel. 02966/44-2687, emulcebrogg@hotmail.com) goes at 7 A.M. daily to Gobernador Gregores (5.5 hours, US$20), the quasi-gateway to Parque Nacional Perito Moreno (*not* the famous Moreno Glacier).

Other typical destinations, times, and fares include San Julián (5 hours, US$16), Río Turbio (5 hours, US$12), El Calafate (4 hours, US$12), Comodoro Rivadavia (11 hours, US$29–37), Trelew (16 hours, US$47–57), Puerto Madryn (17 hours, US$50–60), and Buenos Aires (36 hours, US$101–126).

Several carriers go to Punta Arenas, Chile (4 hours, US$10), including **El Pingüino** (tel. 02966/44-2169), **Buses Ghisoni** (tel. 02966/45-7047), **Magallanes Tour** (tel. 02966/44-2765), and **Pacheco** (also tel. 02966/44-2765). El Pingüino goes Tuesday and Saturday to Puerto Natales (6 hours, US$11), the gateway to Torres del Paine, but it's also possible to bus to Río Turbio, where there are frequent shuttles to Natales.

Getting Around

Taxis and *remises* (about US$5) are the only public transport to **Aeropuerto Internacional Pilot Civil Norberto Fernández** (tel. 02966/44-2340), about five kilometers west of town on RN 3.

From downtown Avenida Roca, city buses Nos. 1 and 12 ("Terminal") go directly to the Terminal de Ómnibus, on the southwestern outskirts of town, but cabs are also reasonable.

Car-rental agencies include **Localiza** (Sarmiento 245, tel. 02966/43-6717) and **Riestra** (Avenida San Martín 1504, tel. 02966/42-1321, www.riestrarentacar.com), near the traffic circle junction with RN 3.

VICINITY OF RÍO GALLEGOS

Given its proximity to historic *estancias* and wildlife sites, most notably the Cabo Vírgenes penguin colony, Río Gallegos is earning a newfound respect even though it's not a major destination itself. Gallegos travel agencies such as **Macatobiano** (Avenida Roca 998, tel. 02966/42-2466, www.macatobiano.com) can arrange excursions to outlying attractions such as Cabo Vírgenes (US$38–48 pp depending on whether it's high season).

Returning from Cabo Vírgenes, Chile-bound travelers with their own vehicles can take the RP 51 shortcut to the Monte Aymond border post but should ask directions before doing so, as it's not always obvious or clearly signed.

◖ Estancia Monte Dinero

From a junction about 15 kilometers south of Río Gallegos, RP 1 swerves southeast through rolling pasturelands where gas-and-oil derricks remind you that Santa Cruz is an energy storehouse. The gravel road is smooth to the picture-postcard settlement of **Estancia Cóndor** (neighboring farmers consider the Benetton empire, which now owns Cóndor, to be indifferent to its neighbors, who traditionally help each other out).

Beyond Cóndor, the road deteriorates toward **Estancia Monte Dinero,** a pioneer sheep farm open to overnighters and day-trippers. Some 120 kilometers from Río Gallegos, 26,000-hectare Monte Dinero benefits from proximity to the Cabo Vírgenes penguin colony, but it's also interesting as a ranch that, unlike most others in the area, has subdivided its fragile pastures into smaller paddocks to manage its 19,500 sheep more intensively. Also unlike other *estancias,* it trains its contract shearers to use manual rather than electric shears, pays them a premium to do so, and shears ewes before lambing to ensure a higher lambing rate.

Founded by the Fentons, another pioneer Patagonian family, **Hostería Monte Dinero** has four downstairs bedrooms (three with private baths) and two upstairs (with a shared bath), plus satellite TV; the *casco*'s former sun porch has been expanded into an attractive and spacious, but not extravagant, bar and dining room. A small museum holds family keepsakes (including a perfect puma skull), and there's also a billiard table (*not* a pool table).

Estancia Monte Dinero (tel./fax 02966/42-8922, www.montedinero.com.ar) is open October–April. Rates are US$130 pp with half board, US$150 pp with full board (excluding drinks), and include a variety of farm activities such as dog trials, sheep shearing, and hiking.

For nonguests, there's a *día de campo* (US$90 pp) that includes farm activities and lunch but not drinks. Neither accommodations nor day-trip prices include the 21 percent IVA.

Reserva Provincial Cabo Vírgenes

Beyond Monte Dinero, the road improves as it approaches Cabo Vírgenes, second only to Punta Tombo among Argentina's Magellanic penguin colonies. With more than 120,000 breeding pairs, the rapidly growing colony has increased by at least a third in a decade-plus.

The abundance of brush here means the birds are less visible than at Dos Bahías, and there's no direct beach access. A 1,500-meter nature trail, though, permits close approach to the birds, and there's an interpretive brochure in good English. There's an admission fee of US$5 for foreigners, less for Argentine and Santa Cruz residents.

At the reserve's northeast corner, the rehabbed hilltop **Faro Cabo Vírgenes,** the historic Argentine lighthouse, includes a small museum. Outside, facing the ocean, there remain foxholes dug to repel British commandos who might have landed here during the 1982 Falklands war (Britain conducted operations in Argentine Patagonia and Tierra del Fuego, escaping into Chile with collusion from the Pinochet dictatorship, which feared an Argentine attack if the Brits lost).

At the so-called **Cementerio Histórico,** the only truly legitimate tomb may be that of Conrado Assinbom, a hermit who lived in the shack beneath the lighthouse. One older cross is almost illegible, and it's not certain anyone's buried there.

At the reserve's southern edge, visitors can cross the border—technically illegally—to see **Faro Punta Dungeness** (1897), the lighthouse at the east end of Chile's narrow latitudinal strip along the Strait of Magellan. When duties permit, Chilean navy personnel show visitors around the facility.

Estancia Monte Dinero has the nearest accommodations, and its sparkling *confitería* **Al Fin y al Cabo** has become the place to stop for lunch and sweets—try the rhubarb cake with *calafate* sauce. While it's fairly expensive, the quality is excellent and the building has magnificent shoreline views south to Cabo Dungeness.

SOUTHERN PATAGONIA

Interior Santa Cruz Province

EL CALAFATE

Spreading along the south shore of Lago Argentino, a giant glacial trough fed by meltwater from the Campo de Hielo Sur, fast-growing El Calafate is the poster child for Argentina's tourism boom. The gateway to Parque Nacional Los Glaciares and its spectacular Moreno Glacier, it has few points of interest in itself. Still, it has increasing and improving services, including hotels and restaurants, and it is southwestern Santa Cruz's transport hub.

Calafate owes its growth to (1) a new international airport that has nearly eliminated the overland route from Río Gallegos for long-distance passengers; (2) the competitive Argentine peso; (3) the fact that former Argentine president Néstor Kirchner, a Santa Cruz native, built a home here and invited high-profile international figures, such as Brazilian president Luis Inácio Lula da Silva and former Chilean president Ricardo Lagos, to admire the Moreno Glacier with him.

The boom has had drawbacks, though. As the population has more than doubled in a decade, real-estate prices have skyrocketed. Unfortunately, a prime downtown location that once housed the old power plant—admittedly a noisy eyesore—has become the site of a hideous casino.

Orientation

El Calafate (official pop. 6,439) is 320 kilometers northwest of Río Gallegos and 32 kilometers west of northbound RP 40, which leads to the wilder El Chaltén sector of Parque Nacional Los Glaciares and an adventurous overland to Chile. While only about 50–60 kilometers from Torres del Paine as the crow flies, the town is 215 kilometers from the Cerro Castillo border crossing and about 305 kilometers from Puerto Natales via Argentine highways RN 40, RP 5, and RP 11, plus a small additional distance on the Chilean side.

A former stage stop, El Calafate has an elongated city plan that has spread barely a few blocks north and south of its main east-west thoroughfare, the pompously named Avenida del Libertador General José de San Martín (for Argentina's independence hero). Most services and points of interest are close to "Avenida Libertador" or "San Martín," as the street is variously called, but explosive hotel growth is taking place to the east, on and near the former airfield.

Sights

After years of near abandonment, the **Museo Regional El Calafate** (Avenida Libertador 575, tel. 02902/49-1924, 10 A.M.–5 P.M. weekdays, free) has reopened, but it's hard to say that the sparse and poorly presented exhibits on paleontology, natural history, geology, and ethnology were worth the wait. The pioneer families' photographic histories show promise, but it still lacks an explanation of the 1920s labor unrest that led to several shooting deaths on the *estancias*.

More promising is the **Centro de Interpretación Histórica** (Almirante Brown and Bonarelli, tel. 02902/49-2799, calafate-centro@cotecal.com.ar, 10 A.M.–8 P.M. daily Sept.–Semana Santa, 10 A.M.–6 P.M. the rest of the year, US$5.50), whose sophisticated timeline puts southern Patagonia's natural, cultural, and historical events in context; it has many photographs, good English translations, and a quality library. Admission includes *remise* transportation from downtown.

At the north edge of town, a onetime sewage pond is now **Reserva Municipal Laguna Nimez,** a freshwater body now frequented by more than 100 bird species. It is fenced, but locals and others often squeeze through gaps for a walk through the wetlands and along the lakeshore.

One sight that locals know but few foreigners recognize is the **Casa Kirchner** (Los Gauchos and Namuncurá), the home of Argentina's first couple, ex-president Néstor Kirchner and current president Cristina Fernández de Kirchner.

Entertainment

El Calafate is surprisingly light on nightlife, which consists mostly of dining out and drinking at venues such as **Don Diego de la Noche** (Avenida Libertador 1603, tel. 02902/49-3270). On Calafate's western outskirts, the best place for drinks is the **Shackleton Lounge** (Avenida Libertador 3287, tel. 02902/49-3516), which has lake views but suffers excesses of electronica.

Tradiciones Argentinas (Avenida del Libertador 351, tel. 02902/49-1281) is a folkloric music venue.

Shopping

Downtown Avenida del Libertador is lined with souvenir shops such as **Open Calafate** (Avenida Libertador 996, tel. 02902/49-1254), which also sells books and maps. **Keokén** (Avenida Libertador 1311, keoken@cotecal.com.ar) has a more representative selection of Patagonian crafts.

Boutique del Libro (Avenida Libertador 1033, tel. 02902/49-1363) carries a broad selection of books (many in English) on Antarctica, Argentina, and Patagonia, including Moon handbooks and novels.

For premium homemade chocolates, try **Ovejitas de la Patagonia** (Avenida Libertador 1118, tel. 02902/49-1736), **Laguna Negra** (Avenida Libertador 1250, tel. 02902/49-2423), or any of several similar locales.

Recently, trendy Buenos Aires design and fashion shops have installed themselves here. **Cardón** (Emilio Amado 835, tel. 02902/49-2074), for instance, is a casual clothing counterpart to Esprit or Patagonia. **Pampa** (Avenida Libertador 1179, tel. 02902/49-1305) and **Pueblo Indio** (Avenida Libertador and 9 de Julio, tel. 02902/49-1965, www.puebloindio.com.ar) carry high-end crafts from around the country, including ceramics, silverwork, and tapestries.

Accommodations

El Calafate has diverse high-standard accommodations ranging from camping to five-star extravagance. Its custom-built hostels, with stylish architecture, engaging common areas with stunning views, and even restaurants and bars, far surpass the dingy no-frills reputation that the word sometimes implies. In addition to dorms, several have excellent private rooms that shame some hotels.

Occupancy rates are at all-time highs, and places that once stayed open only in summer now stay open all year. Unless otherwise indicated, prices listed below are for high season, usually October–April, but dates vary, and if business is slow, rates can be negotiable. Every place in categories over US$50 includes breakfast; less expensive places may or may not provide it. Argentine hotels, unlike those in Chile, do not discount IVA to foreign visitors.

CAMPING

Flanking the Arroyo Calafate, the municipal **Camping El Ovejero** (José Pantín s/n, tel. 02902/49-3422, campingelovejero@hotmail.com, US$4 pp) has reopened under a private concessionaire. Fenced and forested, it has good common toilets and hot showers, and each site has its own fire pit; areas east of the creek are for walk-in campers only.

On the grounds of its namesake *hospedaje,* **Camping Jorgito** (Moyano 943, tel. 02902/49-1323, US$4 pp) is decent enough. **Camping Los Dos Pinos** (9 de Julio 218, tel. 02902/49-1271, www.losdospinos.com, US$4 pp plus US$2 per car) has improved and expanded.

US$10-25

Friendly **Hospedaje Jorgito** (Moyano 943, tel. 02902/49-1323, hospedajejorgito@cotecal.com.ar, US$12–16 pp) has decent multibed rooms with shared or private baths, best for small groups of friends.

Expanded **Hospedaje los dos Pinos** (9 de Julio 358, tel./fax 02902/49-1271, www.losdospinos.com, US$10–12 pp dorm, US$52 d) provides a variety of plain but spacious and immaculate rooms—ranging from hostel dorms to private doubles and *cabañas* (its tours, though, have drawn some criticism). Breakfast costs extra.

Custom-built **Che Lagarto** (25 de Mayo 311, tel. 02902/49-6670, www.chelagarto.com, US$12 pp dorm, US$42 d) is a hostel

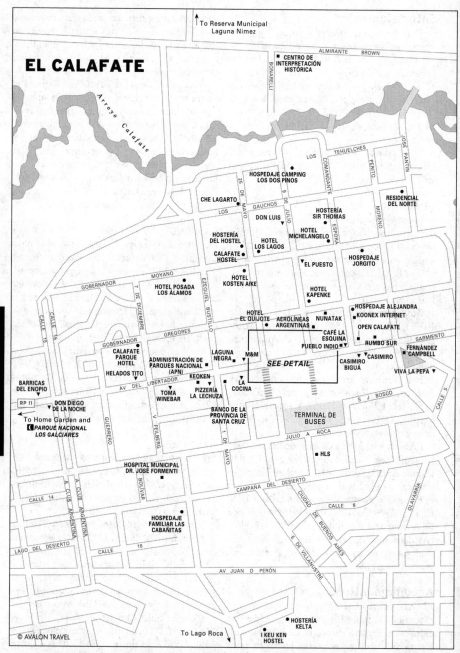

EL CALAFATE

SOUTHERN PATAGONIA

© AVALON TRAVEL

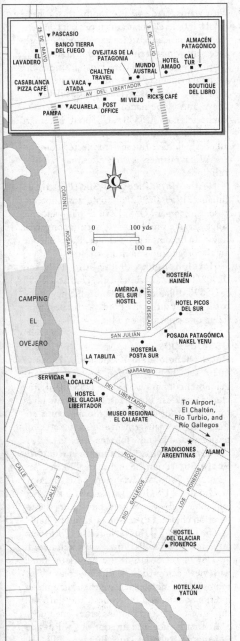

with large and luminous common areas, but some of the dorms are cramped with up to a dozen beds. Even some of the dorms have balconies, though, which add a touch of style to its amenities.

The **I Keu Ken Hostel** (Pontoriero 171, tel. 02902/49-5175, www.patagoniaikeuken.com. ar, US$13 pp, US$37 d) is a purpose-built hostel in the Magellanic style, with truly inviting common areas. All rooms are quadruple dorms with lockers and shared baths; rates include breakfast. It's a bit uphill from downtown, but there are free transfers from the bus terminal.

Among the best in its nonhostel class, family-run **Hospedaje Alejandra** (Espora 60, tel. 02902/49-1328, US$19 s, US$24 d) has small but spotless rooms with twin beds and shared baths, but serves no breakfast.

"Think big" seems to be the motto at **Calafate Hostel** (Gobernador Moyano 1296, tel. 02902/49-2450, www.calafatehostels. com, US$12 pp dorm), which has dorms with shared baths and balconies in a stylish building with vast common areas; it also has better rooms with private baths (US$40 s, US$51 d, with breakfast).

East of the arroyo, open October–mid-April, the HI affiliate **Hostel del Glaciar Pioneros** (Los Pioneros 251, tel./fax 02902/49-1243, www.glaciar.com, US$12–14 pp dorm, US$36–53 s, US$45–58 d) has extensive common spaces, including a large lounge with Wi-Fi, kitchen space, and laundry facilities. The higher rates are for larger and comfortable but no-frills hotel-style rooms with breakfast; it also offers its own Moreno Glacier excursions.

Under the same management, the nearly new **Hostel del Glaciar Libertador** (Avenida Libertador 587, tel./fax 02902/49-1792, www. glaciar.com, US$12–14 pp dorm, US$40–66 s, US$49–72 d) has 22 rooms with private baths; some are four-bed dorms, while others are twins or doubles. Both hostels offer roughly 15 percent discounts for HI members, and 30 percent low-season discounts in October and April (except for Semana Santa).

Near the old airfield, a short walk from América del Sur, the **Marco Polo Inn** (Calle

SOUTHERN PATAGONIA

405 No. 82, tel. 02902/49-3899, www.marcopoloinncalafate.com, US$12–14 pp dorm, US$57–63 d, with breakfast) has opened a new hostel here to complement its others in Puerto Iguazú and Bariloche. Amenities include a kitchen, a bar, and a restaurant, and there are half a dozen private rooms in addition to the dorms.

US$25-50

Several hostels in the previous category also have private accommodations that are excellent values in this price range, which otherwise has few options.

On the hilltop immediately east of the municipal campground, custom-built (**América del Sur Hostel** (Puerto Deseado s/n, tel. 02902/49-3525, www.americahostel.com.ar, US$13 pp dorm, US$57 d) has friendly management, spectacular common spaces with panoramic views, and well-designed rooms in which the toilet and shower are separate and the vanity is outside of both. Rates include breakfast and free transfers from the bus terminal; off-season rates are about 20 percent less.

Hostería Sir Thomas (Espora 257, tel. 02902/49-2220, www.sirthomas.com.ar, US$41 s, US$48 d) is reliable; breakfast costs US$2.50 more. Reservations are advisable at the chalet-style **Hospedaje Familiar Las Cabañitas** (Valentín Feilberg 218, tel. 02902/49-1118, lascabanitas@cotecal.com.ar, US$40 s, US$48 d), which offers some of Calafate's most *simpático* management, taking a personal interest in and responsibility for their guests.

US$50-100

Tidy, well-regarded **Hotel Los Lagos** (25 de Mayo 220, tel. 02902/49-1170, www.loslagoshotel.com.ar, US$60 d with breakfast) has come up in the world—as have its rates, which also include free Internet and Wi-Fi. The rooms, though, are on the small side.

Directly across from the América del Sur hostel, **Hostería Hainén** (Puerto Deseado 118, tel. 02902/49-3874, www.hosteriahainen.com, US$61 s or d) is a handsome wooden structure

with wainscoted midsize rooms in soothing colors. It lacks elaborate amenities but compensates with peace and quiet (except for the nearly incessant winds at this exposed location).

Alongside the Calafate Hostel, under the same management but with a separate reception area, the **Hostería del Hostel** (25 de Mayo and Gobernador Moyano, www.calafatehostels.com, US$50 s, US$66 d) is a smart new building with immaculate midsize rooms, all of which have Internet-connected computers. When business is slow, rates may fall by a third or so.

Nearby **Hotel Picos del Sur** (Puerto San Julián 271, tel. 02902/49-3650, www.hotelpicosdelsur.com.ar, US$71 s or d) has overcome some service problems—it's truly congenial now—to become a good choice. Rates include an airport pickup and drop-off.

Hotel Kapenke (9 de Julio 112, tel. 02902/49-1093, www.kapenke.com.ar, US$95 s, US$98 d) has added a handsome new wing to an already attractive hotel, with rates stabilizing or even dropping a bit.

US$100-200

Hotel Michelangelo (Gobernador Moyano 1020, tel. 02902/49-1045, www.michelangelohotel.com.ar, US$87 s, US$100 d) includes breakfast, but its restaurant draws raves for lunch or dinner as well. Some rooms are small, but the management and service are professional, and it's now tobacco-free.

Near the old airfield, the rooms at **Hostería Posta Sur** (Puerto San Julián 490, tel./fax 02902/49-2406, www.hosteriapostasur.com.ar, US$100 s, US$105 d) are small for the price and some lack even closets, but it's not a desperation choice. Off-season rates fall by half.

The hillside (**Hostería Kelta** (Portoriero 109, tel. 02902/49-1966, www.kelta.com.ar, US$94 s, US$116 d) is a handsome hotel with views across the lake; the larger lake-view rooms are no more expensive than the smaller interior rooms, and on request, the staff will shift guests to better rooms as they open up.

At first glance, the interior of (**Posada Patagonia Rebelde** (José R. Haro 442, tel.

02902/49-4495, www.patagoniarebelde.com, US$94–132 s, US$118–132 d) seems more a well-stocked antiques shop than a boutique hotel in a distinctive Patagonian style. Ironically, much of the recycled material that built the building came from the Buenos Aires barrio of La Boca, and its own rustic sophistication contrasts dramatically with the sophisticated design hotels elsewhere in town. Though it's not for everyone, everyone who's read *In Patagonia* is likely to love it.

Its exterior handsomely rehabbed in wood and glass, the pastel rooms at **Hotel El Quijote** (Gregores 1191, tel. 02902/49-1017, www.quijotehotel.com.ar, US$126 s, US$153 d) make it one of El Calafate's most stylish hotels. A recent remodel enlarged the rooms and made them more comfortable, but it has also meant thinner walls that conduct noise more easily.

Hotel Mirador del Lago (Avenida Libertador 2047, tel. 02902/49-3176, www.miradordellago.com.ar, US$117–167 s, US$126–176 d) is two decades old, but a recent rehab and expansion have left it looking like new. Rooms in the newer wing are slightly larger and more expansive, but even the older rooms are good, and from its knoll on the east side of the road, it has fine lake views. The staff often anticipates (rather than reacts to) its guests' needs.

New in late 2007, **Patagonia Queen** (Avenida Padre Agostini 49, tel. 02902/49-6701, www.patagoniaqueen.com.ar, US$165–186 s or d) is a 20-room boutique hotel done in stunning natural wood with earnest Korean-Argentine management. The rooms are only midsize, but all the baths have whirlpool tubs, and it's tobacco-free throughout.

When El Calafate was smaller, ☕ **Hotel Kau Yatún** (tel. 02902/49-1259, www.kauyatun.com, US$145–260 s, US$170–260 d, with breakfast) was part of Estancia 25 de Mayo; the older part was the *casco,* whose suites have whirlpool tubs, fireplaces, and other amenities, including a full buffet breakfast. Note that its business address, Avenida Libertador 1190, is not the same as the property itself; the hotel is east of the arroyo and up the hill from the Albergue del Glaciar.

The 60-room **Hotel Kosten Aike** (Gobernador Moyano 1243, tel. 02902/49-2424, www.kostenaike.com.ar, US$184 s or d) is an impressive four-star facility with every modern convenience, including a gym and a spa, modem access, and even facilities for disabled guests. The large and comfy quarters have drawn uniformly positive comments.

OVER US$200

Upping the stakes in Calafate's competitive hotel scene, the architecturally audacious ☕ **Design Suites Calafate** (Calle 94 No. 190, tel. 02902/49-4525, www.designsuites.com, US$210–275 s or d plus taxes) enjoys spectacular panoramas from a blustery bluff north of the old airfield. The higher-priced suites have lake views, while slightly smaller standard rooms face the steppe, but all rates are discriminatory against foreign visitors.

Hotel Posada Los Álamos (Gobernador Moyano 1355, tel. 02902/49-1144, www.posadalosalamos.com, from US$222–484 s, US$242–484 d) may be Calafate's most complete hotel, with a pool, a spa, and a convention center. Breakfast takes place in the restaurant across the street, where it also operates the compact nine-hole (three holes with three different tees each) Campo de Golf Pinar.

It has drawn some attention, but it's questionable whether the midsize rooms at the **Calafate Parque Hotel** (7 de Diciembre and Gobernador Gregores, tel. 02902/49-2970, www.calafateparquehotel.com.ar, US$236–472 s or d) justify the rack rates. The facilities, including a third-floor gym and spa as well as a fairly elaborate restaurant, are good enough, but does it justify more than double the price of, say, the Hainén (admittedly with fewer amenities)? Discounted rates may be possible through its website.

New in 2005, atop a hill near the eastern approach to town, the upper-midsize rooms at **Hotel Alto Calafate** (RP 11 s/n, tel. 02902/49-4110, www.hotelaltocalafate.com.ar, US$247 s or d) command views of the entire Lago Argentino basin and the Andes to the southwest, or of the "Balcón de Calafate" that rises immediately behind it. The service is exemplary, and its bar-restaurant precludes the need to dine or drink in town (though a free hourly shuttle is available). There are no neighbors to make any noise, but the wind can wail at this exposed location.

In a sense, every room is a presidential suite at **Casa Los Sauces** (Los Gauchos 1352, tel. 2902/49-5854, www.casalossauces.com, from US$1,200 d), as it's the property of President Cristina Fernández and her husband, ex-President Néstor Kirchner. It 36 rooms, in several buildings over three willow-studded hectares, adjoin the presidential weekend house, and the rates seem more suitable for kings.

Food

El Calafate has the province's best restaurants, and in southernmost Argentine Patagonia, only Ushuaia can match it for quality. Prices have risen considerably, although the quality remains high.

Unfortunately, unlike Ushuaia, it has not yet banished tobacco from the food scene; some individual restaurants have done so, and others have tobacco-free areas, though some of those are merely symbolic.

The best breakfast spot is **Cafetería Don Luis** (9 de Julio 265, tel. 02902/49-1550), with the best coffee, the most succulent croissants, and many other treats to try throughout the day.

Several decent *confiterías* offer short orders, sandwiches, coffee, and the like. Among them are **Café La Esquina** (Avenida Libertador 1000, tel. 02902/49-2334) and the tobacco-heavy Wi-Fi–equipped **Casablanca Pizza Café** (Avenida Libertador 1202, tel. 02902/49-1402).

(Pizzería La Lechuza (Avenida Libertador and 1° de Mayo, tel. 02902/49-1610, lunch and dinner daily, US$10) deserves special mention for its *super cebolla y jamón crudo* (onion and prosciutto), and its empanadas. The pastas-only **La Cocina** (Avenida Libertador 1245, tel. 02902/49-1758, lunch and dinner daily) has slipped a notch but still has its public. New on the scene, **Mirábile** (Avenida del

Libertador 1329, tel. 02902/49-2230, closed Mon.) has plenty of tough competition in the pastas category, but has moderate prices (most entrées under US$10) and excellent service.

(Viva la Pepa (Emilio Amado 833, Local 1, tel. 02902/49-1880, lunch and dinner daily) offers a variety of outstanding sweet and savory crepes (US$7–12) that are an ideal antidote for anyone who's overdosed on beef, lamb, or other Patagonian staples. The small wine list stresses Patagonian vintages.

In one of Calafate's oldest buildings (1957), **El Puesto** (Gobernador Moyano and 9 de Julio, tel. 02902/49-1620, lunch and dinner daily) has three snug little dining rooms, one glassed in to enjoy garden views, with decor that reflects the theme of a outside house on a sheep *estancia*. The Patagonian lamb dishes are the most sophisticated, but there are also fine pizzas and pasta as well as a variety of baked empanadas. The posted sentiment "Enjoy our aromas and flavors—don't smoke" is a welcome one, but they don't enforce it strictly.

La Vaca Atada (Avenida Libertador 1176, tel. 02902/49-1227, lunch and dinner daily) is a popular *parrilla* that also has fine soups and pasta at moderate prices. Remodeled **Rick's Café** (Avenida Libertador 1105, tel. 02902/49-2148, lunch and dinner daily) and **La Tablita** (Coronel Rosales 28, tel. 02902/49-1065, lunch and dinner daily) are both well-regarded *parrillas*. The best of the bunch, though, is **(Mi Viejo** (Avenida Libertador 1111, tel. 02902/49-1691, lunch and dinner daily, US$10–20), which is worth the difference in price.

(Casimiro (Avenida Libertador 963, tel. 02902/49-2590, www.casimirobigua.com, lunch and dinner daily) would be a good choice almost anywhere in the world; the plate of smoked Patagonian appetizers is exquisite. Other entrées, in the US$9–15 range, are close behind but less interesting, though portions are large in pastas, trout, and lamb. It's also a by-the-glass wine bar, with an imposing list reaching upwards of US$600 per bottle (though there are other more affordable, and more than palatable, choices).

A few doors west, under the same ownership,

Casimiro Biguá (Avenida del Libertador 993, tel. 02902/49-3993, www.casimirobigua.com, lunch and dinner daily) has an overlapping menu, but it's best to stick with its *parrilla* specialties of grilled beef and lamb.

In the same vein as Casimiro, **([** **Pascasio** (25 de Mayo 52, tel. 2902/49-2055, lunch and dinner daily) is a gourmet restaurant with starters such as lamb carpaccio (US$8), pastas with a regional touch, a lamb risotto (US$16), and occasional game dishes such as Patagonian hare.

A spinoff from its near namesakes, new in late 2007, **Casimiro Biguá Trattoria** (Avenida Libertador 1359, tel. 02962/49-2993, lunch and dinner daily) specializes in Patagonian-inspired pastas such as lamb ravioli (US$15). The flavors are rich, the portions generous, and the wine list diverse, but the service can border on indifferent or inattentive.

Often accommodating tour groups, **Las Barricas** (Avenida Libertador 1610, tel. 02902/49-3414, www.barricasdeenopio.com.ar, lunch and dinner daily) prepares a variety of meat, fish, and game dishes, plus smoked meats. Desserts are only so-so, but there's a big list of premium wines in the US$20–50 range; decent by-the-glass house wines are moderately priced.

Two blocks west of Barricas, **([** **Pura Vida** (Avenida Libertador 1876, tel. 02902/49-3356, lunch and dinner daily) gets few foreigners for quality versions of traditional Argentine and Patagonian dishes such as gnocchi (US$8) with a saffron sauce, *carbonada* (a motley stew large enough for two hungry diners, US$13), and *cazuela de cordero* (a lamb casserole, US$16). Self-consciously casual—no two chairs nor menu cards are alike—it has mezzanine seating with views over Laguna Nimes and, in the distance, Lago Argentino; the main floor, though, is cozier. The menu rarely changes, and the wine list is modest (with nothing by the glass).

El Calafate went nearly a decade without a quality ice creamery, but now it has three outstanding ones. **Acuarela** (Avenida Libertador 1177, tel. 02902/49-1315) can aspire toward Buenos Aires's best, but **Sabores** (Avenida Libertador 1222, tel. 02902/49-2422) and **Tito** (Espora 65) are also fine. For a local treat, try Sabores's fresh *calafate* flavor, slightly better than Acuarela's.

Information
At the bus terminal, the **Secretaría de Turismo de la Municipalidad de El Calafate** (Avenida Roca 1004, tel. 02902/49-1090, www.elcalafate.gov.ar, 10 A.M.–10 P.M. daily) maintains a database of hotels and other services; it has English-speaking personnel, maps, brochures, and a message board.

The **Administración de Parques Nacionales** (APN, Avenida Libertador 1302, tel. 02902/49-1755 or 02902/49-1545, losglaciares@apn.gov.ar) is open 7 A.M.–2 P.M. weekdays only.

There is a useful private website, www.losglaciares.com, with considerable information on El Calafate and surroundings.

Services
Cambio Thaler (Avenida del Libertador 963, tel. 02902/49-3245) is the only currency exchange house. Both **Banco Santa Cruz** (Avenida Libertador 1285) and **Banco Tierra del Fuego** (25 de Mayo 40) have ATMs.

Correo Argentino (Avenida Libertador 1133) is the post office.

The **Cooperativa Telefónica de Calafate** (Cotecal, Avenida Libertador 1486, tel. 02902/49-1900) has the best and cheapest Internet service; there are no collect phone calls, though. **Open Calafate** (Avenida Libertador 996, tel. 02902/49-1254) provides some competition in both telephone and Internet service, but its connections are slower.

El Lavadero (25 de Mayo 43, tel. 02902/49-2182) charges around US$5 per laundry load.

The **Hospital Municipal Dr. José Formenti** (Avenida Roca 1487, tel. 02902/49-1001 or 02902/49-1173) handles medical matters.

Getting There
El Calafate is the transport hub for western Santa Cruz thanks to its new airport, road connections to Río Gallegos, and improving links north and south along RN 40.

AIR

Aerolíneas Argentinas (9 de Julio 57, tel. 02902/49-2815) normally flies north to Trelew and Buenos Aires's Aeroparque, and south to Ushuaia, but it sometimes has service to or from Bariloche as well. **LAN Argentina** has an increasing number of flights; travel agencies such as **Rumbo Sur** (9 de Julio 81, tel. 02902/49-2155, rumbosur@cotecal.com.ar) can arrange seats.

LADE (tel. 02902/49-1262, ladecalafate@cotecal.com.ar) keeps an office at the bus terminal (Avenida Roca 1004). It flies northbound to Comodoro Rivadavia and Buenos Aires, and southbound to Río Gallegos, Río Grande, and Ushuaia.

BUS

El Calafate's **Terminal de Ómnibus** overlooks the town from its perch at Avenida Roca 1004; for pedestrians, the easiest approach is a staircase from the corner of Avenida Libertador and 9 de Julio. There has been little progress on plans to move it to the former airfield terminal just west of the bridge over the arroyo so that buses would no longer enter town. For long-distance connections to most of the rest of the country, it's necessary to backtrack to Río Gallegos, but there are services to Puerto Natales and Torres del Paine, Chile.

Interlagos (tel. 02902/49-1179), **Taqsa** (tel. 02902/49-1843, www.taqsa.com.ar), and **Sportman** (tel. 02902/44-2595) shuttle between El Calafate and the Santa Cruz provincial capital of Río Gallegos (4 hours, US$13), where there are northbound connections to Buenos Aires and intermediate towns, and southbound connections to Punta Arenas (Chile). These buses will also drop passengers at the Río Gallegos airport.

Three carriers connect El Calafate with El Chaltén (4.5 hours, US$18–20) in the Fitz Roy sector of Parque Nacional Los Glaciares: **Cal Tur** (tel. 02902/49-1842), **Chaltén Travel** (tel. 02902/49-2480), and Taqsa. Most services leave around 7:30–8 A.M., though there are sometimes afternoon buses around 5–6 P.M. Winter services are fewer, but normally go at least daily among the three companies.

From September to April, Taqsa now has a daily afternoon service to Perito Moreno (the town, not the glacier) and Los Antiguos (16 hours, US$52), along desolate RN 40, for connections to Chile Chico. While this is more expensive than comparable distances elsewhere, it's also more direct, quicker, and even cheaper than the roundabout routes via coastal RN 3, especially if you factor in accommodations.

December–April or so, Chaltén Travel also provides alternate-day bus service from El Calafate to Perito Moreno and Los Antiguos (14 hours, US$75). Passengers from El Chaltén can board the northbound bus from El Calafate at the junction of RN 40 and RP 23 without having to return to El Calafate. Buses depart Calafate on odd-numbered days and return from Los Antiguos on even-numbered days.

In summer, **Turismo Zaahj/Bus Sur** (tel. 02902/49-1631, www.turismozaahj.co.cl) and **Cootra** (tel. 02902/49-1444) alternate daily services to Puerto Natales, Chile (4.5 hours, US$15); occasionally there are direct services to Parque Nacional Torres del Paine. In winter, these services may operate only weekly.

Getting Around

For US$7.50 pp, **Ves Patagonia** (tel. 02902/49-4355, www.vespatagonia.com.ar) provides door-to-door shuttles to **Aeropuerto Internacional El Calafate** (tel. 02902/49-1220, aerocal@cotecal.com.ar), 23 kilometers east of town and just north of RP 11. A *remise* costs about US$23 for up to four passengers.

Car-rental agencies include **Alamo** (Avenida Libertador 290, tel. 02902/49-3707, calafate@alamoargentina.com.ar), **Hertz** (Avenida Libertador 1822, tel. 02902/49-2525), **Localiza** (Avenida Libertador 687, tel. 02902/49-1398, localizacalafate@hotmail.com), **Nunatak** (Gobernador Gregores 1075, tel. 02902/49-1987, nunatakrentacar@cotecal.com.ar), and **Servicar** (Avenida del Libertador 695, tel. 02902/49-2301, servicar@cotecal.com.ar).

Half a block south of the bus terminal, **HLS** (Buenos Aires 173, tel. 02902/49-3806) rents bicycles.

VICINITY OF EL CALAFATE

Tours and transport to the Moreno Glacier and other nearby attractions are possible with a variety of competent operators. In alphabetical order, they include **Aventura Andina** (Avenida del Libertador 761, Local 4, tel. 02902/49-1726, andina@cotecal.com.ar), **Cal Tur** (Avenida Libertador 1080, tel. 02902/49-2217, www.caltur.com.ar), **Cordillera del Sol** (25 de Mayo 43, tel. 02902/49-2822, www.cordilleradelsol.com), **Eurotur** (Avenida del Libertador 1025, tel. 02902/49-2190, www.eurotur.com.ar), **Mundo Austral** (Avenida Libertador 1114, tel. 02902/49-2365, mundoaustral@cotecal.com.ar), and **Rumbo Sur** (9 de Julio 81, Local 2, tel. 02902/49-2155, www.rumbosur.com.ar).

El Galpón del Glaciar

Formerly the *casco* (big house) of Estancia Alice, west of El Calafate en route to the Moreno glacier, El Galpón del Glaciar (RP 11 Km 22) is open for day tours that may include activities such as birding and horseback riding, as well as exhibitions of sheep herding and shearing, afternoon tea, and a barbecued-lamb dinner. Rates are around US$53 pp with transportation to and from the farm; horseback rides (US$20 per hour) are extra.

El Galpón also offers accommodations (US$410 s, US$460 d, 2-night minimum, with limited activities included). For details, contact Agroturismo El Galpón (Avenida Libertador 761, El Calafate, tel. 02902/49-1793, www.elgalpondelglaciar.com.ar).

◖ EOLO LODGE

On the 4,000-hectare Estancia Alice, Eolo is an exclusive mountainside lodge with 17 spacious suites and equally spacious common areas, all with "big sky" views that include either Lago Argentino to the east, the Valle de Anita immediately south, the Brazo Rico to the west, or a combination of them. On a clear day, there are even glimpses across the border to Torres del Paine.

Eolo owes its style to the *cascos* of the great Patagonian wool *estancias,* with corrugated metal

SOUTHERN PATAGONIA

© WAYNE BERNHARDSON

Perched on a hillside, Eolo Lodge offers views over the vast steppes and, on a clear day, the spires of Chile's Torres del Paine.

siding, antique furnishings, and English tea settings. Contemporary technology such as double-paned windows, though, allows far greater natural light and better views than the poorly insulated buildings of the late 19th and early 20th centuries. The baths are also modern.

Like those houses, though, the suites at Eolo lack modern conveniences such as television and Internet (though there's a satellite TV and DVD lounge, as well as Wi-Fi in common areas). There's a sheltered interior patio studded with Technicolor lupines in summer, a small indoor pool, and a restaurant (also open to nonguests, by reservation only).

Open mid-September through April, Eolo (RP 11 Km 23, tel. 2902/49-2042, www.eolo. com.ar, US$995 s, US$1,420 d, 2-night minimum) also has a Gran Buenos Aires contact (Laprida 3278, Oficina 39, San Isidro, tel. 011/4700-0705). Eolo helps arrange excursions to the Moreno Glacier and other nearby sights but does not organize them itself.

Hostería Alta Vista

Once a separate *estancia,* since absorbed by adjacent Estancia Anita, Hostería Alta Vista (RP 15 Km 35, tel./fax 02902/49-9902, www. hosteriaaltavista.com.ar, US$366 s, US$483 d) is an outpost of the Braun-Menéndez dynasty that dominated the Patagonian wool industry of Chile and Argentina. As such, its seven-room *casco* is the place to be spoiled; surrounded by luxuriant gardens in a sheltered location at the foot of 1,294-meter Cerro Freile, it has a guests-only bar-restaurant, a separate *quincho* for lamb *asados,* and flawless service from its English-speaking staff.

Alta Vista also offers excursions that include horseback riding in the nearby hills, offering a small lagoon full of wildfowl with condors soaring above, and distant views of the Moreno glacier. Two-night packages that include excursions to the glacier and other more remote sights are slightly more expensive.

Accommodations are all-inclusive except for incidentals such as telephone charges and laundry. Alta Vista also offers activities-oriented packages at rather higher prices.

◖ PARQUE NACIONAL LOS GLACIARES

On the eastern Andean slopes, Parque Nacional Los Glaciares comprises over 750,000 hectares where slowly flowing ice gives birth to clear frigid rivers and vast lakes, interspersed with Magellanic forests, along the Chilean border west and north of El Calafate. A UNESCO World Heritage Site, it's famous for the Moreno glacier, which draws thousands of sedentary visitors for day trips but also pulls in scientists absorbed in glaciology and climate studies. The northern sector—a 3.5-hour bus trip from El Calafate—attracts those seeking to spend several days in vigorous exercise, either trekking or the far more demanding and dangerous technical climbing. Wildlife includes the rare endangered Andean *huemul.*

Geography and Climate

As the Pleistocene ended and the Campo de Hielo Sur receded, it left behind the two huge glacial troughs that are now Lago Argentino and, to the north, the roughly parallel Lago Viedma. While these lakes lie only about 250 meters above sea level, the Andean summits along the border rise to 3,375 meters on Cerro Fitz Roy and nearly as high on pinnacles such as 3,102-meter Cerro Torre, which match Chile's Torres del Paine for sheer majesty.

Most of these bodies of water lie beyond park boundaries, but the eastern Andean slopes still contain their remnants, some of the world's most impressive, and accessible, glaciers. Thirteen major glaciers flow toward the Argentine side, including the benchmark Moreno glacier; ice covers 30 percent of the park's surface.

Despite its accumulated snow and ice, the Argentine side is drier than the Chilean, receiving only about 400 millimeters of precipitation on the eastern steppe, rising to about 900 millimeters at its forested western elevations. The warmest month is February, with an average maximum temperature of 22°C and a minimum of 9°C; the coolest is August, when the maximum averages only 5°C and the minimum is -1°C. As elsewhere in Patagonia, it gets ferocious winds, strongest in spring and summer.

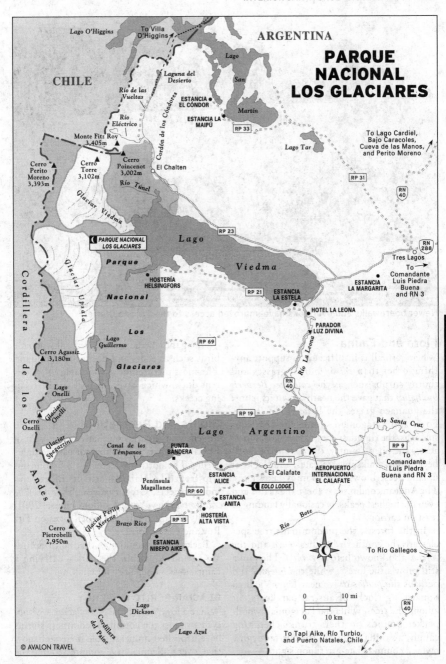

PARQUE NACIONAL LOS GLACIARES

© AVALON TRAVEL

© WAYNE BERNHARDSON

Newer boardwalks and overlooks have improved access to the Moreno Glacier.

Flora and Fauna

Where rainfall is insufficient to support anything other than *coirón* bunch grasses and thorny shrubs such as the *calafate (Berberis buxifolia)* that gave the nearby town its name, the guanaco grazes the Patagonian steppe. Foxes and Patagonian skunks are also conspicuous, the flightless rhea or *ñandú* scampers across the open country, the *bandurria* (buff-necked ibis) stalks invertebrates, and flocks of upland geese browse the swampy lakeshores. The Andean condor soars above the plains and even the highest peaks, occasionally landing to feast on carrion.

In the forests, the predominant tree species are the southern beeches *lenga* and the *coigüe,* also known here as *guindo.* The puma still prowls the forest, while the *huemul* and perhaps the *pudú* survive near Lago Viedma. Squawking flocks of austral parakeets flit among the trees, while the Patagonian woodpecker pounds on their trunks. Perching calmly, awaiting nightfall, the austral pygmy owl is a common late-afternoon sight.

Along the lakeshores and riverbanks, aquatic birds such as coots and ducks are abundant. The most picturesque is the Patagonian torrent duck, which dives for prey in the rushing creeks.

Sights and Recreation

In general, the park's southerly sector, west of El Calafate, gets day visitors for passive sightseeing. The northerly sector—a 3.5-hour bus trip from El Calafate—attracts hikers and mountaineers. Gregory Crouch's *Enduring Patagonia* (New York: Random House, 2001) details one mountaineer's experiences on Fitz Roy and Cerro Torre.

Backpackers should note that no campfires are permitted within the park—carrying a camp stove is obligatory for cooking.

GLACIAR PERITO MORENO

Where a low Andean pass lets Pacific weather systems cross the cordillera, countless storms have deposited immeasurable meters of snow that, over millennia, have compressed into the

Moreno Glacier, the groaning, rasping river of ice that's one of the continent's greatest sights and sounds. Fifteen times during the 20th century, the advancing glacier blocked Lago Argentino's **Brazo Rico** (Rico Arm) to form a rising body of water that eventually, when the weight became too great for the natural dam, triggered an eruption of ice and water toward the lake's main glacial trough.

No such event took place from 1988 until March 14, 2004, when the avalanche of ice and water could have been a metaphor for the flood of tourists that invaded El Calafate in anticipation. On any given day, though, massive icebergs still calve off the glacier's 60-meter face and crash into the **Canal de los Témpanos** (Iceberg Channel) with astonishing frequency. Perched on newly modernized catwalks and overlooks, many visitors spend entire days either gazing at or, eyes closed, simply listening to this rumbling river of ice. Descending to lake level is prohibited because of the danger of backwash and flying ice chunks; it's possible, though, to contract full-day "minitrekking" excursions onto the ice (US$129 pp with transport from El Calafate) with **Hielo y Aventura** (Avenida Libertador 935, El Calafate, tel. 02902/49-1053, www.hieloyaventura.com). Hielo y Aventura also offers a more strenuous "Big Ice" trip (US$150 pp) and a passive "Safari Náutico" boat trip (1 hour, US$10 pp) that approaches the glacier's face.

Organized tours to the glacier, 80 kilometers southwest of El Calafate via RP 11, leave every day, as does scheduled transport; transport is usually extra for everything except bus tours.

GLACIAR UPSALA

Even larger than the Moreno Glacier, 50 kilometers long and 10 kilometers wide at its foot, the Upsala glacier is accessible only by crowded catamaran trips from Puerto Bandera via Lago Argentino's Brazo Norte (North Arm). Impressive for its sheer extent, the sizeable bergs that have calved off it, and their shapes and colors, it's the trip's outstanding sight.

At midday the boat anchors at Bahía Onelli, but bring a bag lunch (skipping the restaurant) to hike to ice-clogged **Lago Onelli.** The land portion of this excursion is regimented, and the guide-suggested pace—30 minutes from dock to lakeshore—is suitable for those on crutches. Smoking is prohibited on the forest trail.

Visitors should realize that this is a mass-tourism excursion that may frustrate hikers accustomed to freedom of the hills. If you take it, choose the biggest available ship, which offers the most deck space to see the Spegazzini and Upsala glaciers. On board, the freshest air is within the cabin of the *ALM,* whose seats are cramped but where smoking is prohibited; on deck, desperate smokers congregate even in freezing rain. Reasonably priced cakes, sandwiches, coffee, tea, and hot chocolate are available on board.

Puerto Bandera is 45 kilometers west of Calafate via RP 11 and RP 8. For information and reservations, contact concessionaire Fernández Campbell (Avenida Libertador 867, El Calafate, tel. 02902/49-1155 or 02902/49-1428, www.fernandezcampbell.com.ar). The full-day trip costs about US$85 pp; this now includes transfers to Puerto Bandera but not the US$17 park fee for non-Argentines.

A new alternative is an overnight trip, with onboard accommodations and meals, through **Cruceros Marpatag** (9 de Julio 57, Local 10, El Calafate, tel. 02902/49-2118, www.crucerosmarpatag.com), which visits the Upsala and Spegazzini glaciers the first day and the Moreno glacier on the second before returning to Puerto Bandera. Rates are US$625 pp, double occupancy.

LAGO ROCA

Also known as La Jerónima, the park's little-visited southwesterly sector along Lago Roca's Brazo Sur (South Arm) offers camping and cross-country hiking—there are no formal trails, only routes such as the one from the campground to the summit of **Cerro Cristal,** 55 kilometers from El Calafate. The landscape's most striking feature is the high shoreline—dry from the days when the lake backs up behind the advancing Moreno glacier. Unlike other sectors, Lago Roca charges no admission fee.

SECTOR FITZ ROY

In the park's most northerly sector, the Fitz Roy Range has sheer spires to match Torres del Paine, but even if you're not a top technical climber, trails from the village of El Chaltén to the base of summits such as Fitz Roy and Cerro Torre make for exhilarating hikes. It's even possible to traverse the southern Patagonian ice fields, but visitors seeking a sedate outdoor experience will find a handful of former sheep *estancias,* onetime Patagonian wool producers that have reinvented themselves as tourist accommodations.

From a signposted trailhead at El Chaltén's north end, just south of the former Camping Madsen, the **Sendero Laguna Torre** is an 11-kilometer track gaining about 200 meters in elevation as it winds through southern beech forests to the climbers' base camp for Cerro Torre; figure about 3–3.5 hours. At the lake, in clear weather, there are extraordinary views of Cerro Torre's 3,102-meter summit, crowned by the so-called ice-and-snow "mushroom" that technical climbers must surmount. While Italian Cesare

Maestri claimed that he and Austrian Toni Egger reached the summit in 1959 (Egger died in an avalanche, taking the expedition's camera with him), Italian Casimiro Ferrari made the first undisputed ascent in 1974.

From the Madsen pack station, the more demanding **Sendero Río Blanco** trail rises steeply at the outset before leveling out through boggy beech forest and continuing to the Fitz Roy base camp, climbing about 350 meters in 10 kilometers. About midway to Río Blanco, a signed lateral leads south to **Laguna Capri,** which has backcountry campsites.

From Río Blanco, a vertiginous zigzag trail ascends 400 meters in just 2.5 kilometers to **Laguna de los Tres,** a glacial tarn whose name commemorates three members of the French expedition—René Ferlet, Lionel Terray, and Guido Magnone—who summited Fitz Roy in 1952. Truly a top-of-the-world experience, Laguna de los Tres offers some of Patagonia's finest Andean panoramas.

From the Río Blanco campground (reserved for climbers), a northbound trail follows the

© WAYNE BERNHARDSON

The trail to Loma de Pliegue Tumbado offers fine views of Fitz Roy and other peaks at Parque Nacional Los Glaciares.

river's west bank north to **Laguna Piedras Blancas,** whose namesake glacier continually calves small icebergs. The trail continues north to the Río Eléctrico, beyond the park boundaries, where a westbound trail climbs the river to Piedra del Fraile and a possible circuit of the Campo de Hielo Sur, only for experienced snow-and-ice trekkers. At the Río Eléctrico, it's also possible to rejoin the road from El Chaltén to Lago del Desierto.

From the park visitors center, a short ascent (about 45 minutes) leads to the **Mirador de los Cóndores,** for good views of El Chaltén and the confluence of the Río de las Vueltas and the Río Fitz Roy.

From the same trailhead, the hike to **Loma del Pliegue Tumbado** is a 500-meter elevation gain that yields some of the area's views—weather permitting, the panorama takes in Fitz Roy, Cerro Torre, Cerro Solo, Glaciar Torre, and Lago Torre, but the wind at the overlook can be overpowering. Four hours is about right for an average hiker, but the truly fit can do it three; the descent takes about 2.5 hours.

GLACIAR VIEDMA

From Lago Viedma's north shore, south of El Chaltén, the park's best lake excursion is the *Viedma Discovery's* full-day catamaran voyage to the Viedma glacier, which includes an ice-climbing component.

Sailing from Bahía Túnel, the vessel rounds the ironically named **Cabo de Hornos** (Cape Horn) to enter an iceberg-cluttered area before anchoring in a rocky cove. After disembarking, visitors hike to an overlook (the glacier is Argentina's largest, though its lakeside face is small) with additional views of 2,677-meter Cerro Huemul. Those who want to can strap on crampons and continue onto the glacier for about 2.5 hours (even some sedentary city dwellers do so).

The bilingual guides know glaciology and provide more personalized service than the Fernández Campbell excursion from Puerto Bandera. While the price here does not include lunch, they do provide an aperitif on the glacial rocks.

Departure time from El Chaltén is 8:30 A.M., while the boat sails from Bahía Túnel at 9 A.M.; the cost is US$105 pp including transportation from El Chaltén. For details, contact **Patagonia Aventura** (Güemes s/n, tel. 02962/49-3110, El Chaltén, www.patagonia-aventura.com).

LAGO DEL DESIERTO

Elongated Lago del Desierto, 37 kilometers north of El Chaltén, is a scenic end-of-the-road destination with hiking trails, boat excursions, and even a challenging border crossing to the Chilean settlement of Villa O'Higgins.

From the lake's south end, a short trail winds west through dense southern beech forest to a vista point and the hanging glacier at **Laguna Huemul;** a longer route follows the eastern shore to the border, a 20-kilometer trek over gentle terrain. Every year a few hundred people cross the Argentine-Chilean border in a zone that was once so contentious that a Chilean Carabinero even lost his life in a firefight with Argentine border guards in 1965.

Despite objections by a handful of Chilean nationalists, the matter is resolved, the border is peaceable, and determined hikers or even mountain bikers can readily reach Villa O'Higgins. Before attempting it, though, verify the latest details with Argentina's Gendarmería (Border Patrol) in El Chaltén.

From El Chaltén, **Transporte Las Lengas** (Viedma 95, tel. 02962/49-3023, laslengaselchalten@yahoo.com.ar) minibuses go to El Pilar (US$10 pp) and Río Eléctrico (US$13) at 7 and 8:30 A.M. and 3 P.M. daily; the later two runs continue to Lago del Desierto (US$21 one-way or round-trip), returning at 2:30 and 8:30 P.M. Hitching is feasible, but vehicles are few and often full. At the lake itself, the *Viedma 1* carries passengers to the north end and back (US$24 pp).

Accommodations and Food

Since most Moreno Glacier visitors stay at El Calafate, the park's southern sector has only limited accommodations, but they're increasingly abundant in and around El Chaltén in the Fitz Roy sector.

SOUTHERN PATAGONIA

Hikers should note that campfires are prohibited—camp stoves are obligatory for cooking. Rangers assert that park water is potable throughout.

GLACIAR MORENO
The only accommodations near the glacier, multiday packages with full board and excursions are the rule at the lavish **❚ Hostería Los Notros** (tel. 02902/49-9510). It rivals Torres del Paine's Hotel Salto Chico in the "room with a view" competition; all 32 rooms face the ice. Minimum two-night packages start at US$1,826 s, US$2,574 d; for details, contact Hostería Los Notros (Arenales 1457, 7th floor, Buenos Aires, tel. 011/4814-3934, www.losnotros.com).

Also at the glacier, **Nativos de la Patagonia** operates both a snack bar (sandwiches for US$5–7, plus coffee and desserts) and a separate restaurant with set meals (around US$20); there's also an à la carte menu. A couple kilometers east of the park entrance, highly recommended by Calafate-based guides, **Los Ventisqueros** serves a limited lunchtime menu of pasta, chicken, lamb, or beef.

LAGO ROCA
La Jerónima's **Camping Lago Roca** (tel. 02902/49-9500, lagoroca@yahoo.com.ar, US$6 pp) also has four-bed dorm-style *cabañas* (US$37 d, US$48 quadruple) with exterior baths. Hot showers are available, and its *confitería* serves decent meals.

At the terminus of RP 15, southwest of El Calafate 56 kilometers, the *casco* at Croatian-founded **Estancia Nibepo Aike** (tel./fax 02966/42-2626 in El Calafate, www.nibepoaike.com.ar) preserves its original rustic style but is now a five-room guesthouse with contemporary conveniences. Rates are US$389 s, US$510 d, with half board, for a minimum two-night stay. Open October 1–April 30, it also has a newer **Quincho Don Juan** for day-trippers to lunch or dine; overnight guests can choose to dine there or in the main house's dining room. "Day in the country" excursions cost around US$45 pp with either lunch or dinner and transportation.

Information
At the Río Mitre entrance, the main Moreno Glacier approach, the Administración de Parques Nacionales (APN) collects a US$17 admission fee (payable in pesos only) for non-residents of Argentina. At present, the Lago Roca and El Chaltén sectors continue to be fee-free.

At the southern approach to El Chaltén, the **APN** (tel. 02962/49-3004, 9 A.M.–8 P.M. daily) has turned a former *hostería* into a visitors center. In addition to natural history exhibits, it provides a decent trail map (scale 1:75,000) and also issues climbing permits (free).

Hikers may want to consult Tim Burford's *Chile and Argentina: The Bradt Trekking Guide* (Chalfont St Peter, UK: Bradt Travel Guides, 2005) or Clem Lindenmayer's and Nick Tapp's *Trekking in the Patagonian Andes* (Melbourne: Lonely Planet, 2003). Both are overdue for updates; the former has thorough text, but the latter has better maps. There is also Miguel A. Alonso's locally available, bilingual *Trekking en Chaltén y Lago del Desierto* (Los Glaciares, 2003), which covers numerous hikes in the vicinity. Alonso has also written *Lago Argentino & Glaciar Perito Moreno Handbook* (Buenos Aires: Zagier & Urruty, 1997), a more general guide that's available in English, Italian, German, and French.

For an informed guide who leads back-country trips in the El Chaltén sector, contact retired ranger Adrián Falcone (tel. 02962/49-3064, aefalcone@gmail.com), who speaks English and even a smattering of Japanese.

Getting There and Around
The Moreno Glacier is about 80 kilometers west of El Calafate by RP 11, which is now completely paved; the trip takes slightly over an hour. Both **Cal Tur** (tel. 02902/49-1842) and **Taqsa** (tel. 02902/49-1843, www.taqsa.com.ar) at El Calafate's bus terminal have scheduled services at 9 A.M. daily (US$23 round-trip), returning in the afternoon.

In addition to regularly scheduled services, guided bus tours are frequent, but both are less frequent in winter. Competent operators include **Aventura Andina** (Avenida del Libertador 761, Local 4, tel. 02902/49-1726, andina@cotecal.com.ar), **Cal Tur** (Avenida Libertador 1080, tel. 02902/49-2217, www. caltur.com.ar), **Cordillera del Sol** (25 de Mayo 43, tel. 02902/49-2822, www.cordilleradelsol.com), **Eurotur** (Avenida del Libertador 1025, tel. 02902/49-2190, www. eurotur.com.ar), **Mundo Austral** (Avenida Libertador 1114, tel. 02902/49-2365, mundoaustral@cotecal.com.ar), and **Rumbo Sur** (9 de Julio 81, Local 2, tel. 02902/49-2155, www.rumbosur.com.ar).

El Calafate's **Albergue del Glaciar** runs its own guided minivan excursions (US$50 pp), leaving about 8:30 A.M. and returning about 5 P.M. These include more hiking and a navigation for a waterside view of the lake.

EL CHALTÉN

Billing itself as "Capital Nacional del Trekking," Argentina's national trekking capital, El Chaltén has become popular for easy access to Fitz Roy range trailheads in Parque Nacional Los Glaciares. Many trails are suitable for overnight backpack trips, but access is so easy that day hikers can cover nearly as much ground.

Exposed to fierce westerly winds and to potential floods from the Río de las Vueltas, El Chaltén has somehow managed to achieve a sense of permanence in what, just a few years back, seemed a bleak outpost of government offices aimed to uphold Argentina's presence in a disputed border zone (the last of many Chilean-Argentine territorial quarrels, over Lago del Desierto to the north, was finalized a few years ago). With the highway from the RN 40 junction recently paved, it's growing so rapidly that some fear it will become the next El Calafate, where real estate development (and speculation) are rampant.

When the last 17 kilometers of the RN 40 link are paved, travel time from El Calafate will fall to about three hours. Meanwhile, the town is enjoying improvements as the streets are paved to keep down the dust, and a new bus terminal is under construction.

El Chaltén (pop. about 500) is 220 kilometers northwest of El Calafate via eastbound RP 11 to the Río Bote junction, northbound RN 40, and westbound RP 23 along Lago Viedma's north shore. It's worth mentioning that, while street addresses are increasingly common, locals pay little attention to them.

Events

El Chaltén celebrates several events, including October 12's **Aniversario de El Chaltén,** marking its formal founding in 1985; November 10's **Día de la Tradición,** celebrating the gaucho heritage; and early February's weeklong **Fiesta Nacional del Trekking.**

Shopping

Marco Polo (Andreas Madsen 12, tel. 02962/49-3122) sells books, maps, and CDs, with English-language titles including current Moon handbooks and novels.

Recreation

There are extensive hiking and climbing opportunities in nearby Parque Nacional Los Glaciares.

From here, it's possible to arrange a one-day trek and ice climb on Glaciar Torre (US$85 pp) with **Fitz Roy Expediciones** (Avenida San Martín 56, tel. 02962/49-3017, www. fitzroyexpediciones.com.ar), which also offers lengthier guided hikes—nine-day expeditions, really—on the Campo de Hielo Sur, the Southern Continental Ice Field. **Oscar Pandolfi Expediciones** (Calle 2 No. 23, tel. 02962/49-3043, www.caminoabierto.com) and **Alta Montaña** (Lionel Terray 55, tel. 02962/49-3018, altamont@infovia.com.ar) are also guides.

NYCA Adventure (Cabo García 122, tel. 02962/49-3185, www.nyca.com.ar) offers half-day excursions that include activities such as climbing, hiking, mountain biking, rafting, and rappelling. **Lago San Martín** (Avenida San Martín 275, tel. 02962/49-3045) arranges excursions to and from Lago San Martín, across the mountains to the northeast, with *estancia* accommodations. The **Casa de Guías** (Avenida

SOUTHERN PATAGONIA

SOUTHERN PATAGONIA

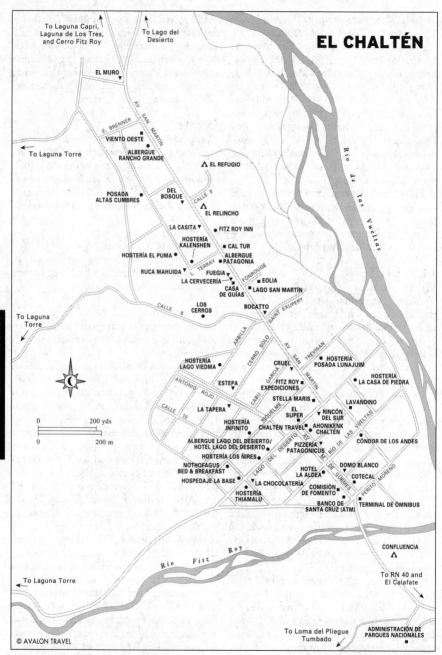

EL CHALTÉN

To Laguna Capri, Laguna de Los Tres, and Cerro Fitz Roy

To Lago del Desierto

EL MURO ▼

AV. SAN MARTIN

E. BRENNER
VIENTO OESTE ■

ALBERGUE
RANCHO GRANDE ▼

To Laguna Torre

△ EL REFUGIO

POSADA
ALTAS CUMBRES ●

DEL
BOSQUE ▼

CALLE 3

△ EL RELINCHO

LA CASITA ▼   ● FITZ ROY INN

HOSTERÍA
KALENSHEN ▼   ■ CAL TUR

HOSTERÍA EL PUMA ●   ALBERGUE
■ PATAGONIA

L. TERRAY

RUCA MAHUIDA ▼   FUEGIA ▼
LA CERVECERÍA ▼   ● EOLIA

FONROUGE

CASA
DE GUÍAS ■   ■ LAGO SAN MARTÍN

CALLE 8   LOS
CERROS ■   BOCATTO ▼

SAINT EXUPERY

To Laguna
Torre

ARBILLA

CERRO SOLO

GARCÍA

AV. SAN MARTIN

TREVISAN

HOSTERÍA
LAGO VIEDMA ●

CRUEL ■   ● HOSTERÍA
POSADA LUNAJUIM

HOSTERÍA
● LA CASA DE PIEDRA

ANTONIO ROJO

ESTEPA ▼

FITZ ROY
EXPEDICIONES ■

CABU

RIQUELME

STELLA MARIS ■

LAVANDINO

CALLE 10

LA TAPERA ▼

HOSTERÍA
INFINITO ●

EL
SUPER ▼

CHALTÉN TRAVEL ■

▼ RINCÓN
DEL SUR

AHONIKENK
CHALTÉN ▼

AV. M. DE GÜEMES

CÓNDOR DE LOS ANDES ●

ALBERGUE LAGO DEL DESIERTO/
HOTEL LAGO DEL DESIERTO ■

HOSTERÍA LOS ÑIRES ●

PIZZERÍA ▼
PATAGÓNICUS

LAGO DEL DESIERTO

RÍO DE LAS VUELTAS

NOTHOFAGUS
BED & BREAKFAST ●

HOSPEDAJE LA BASE ●

HOTEL
LA ALDEA ■

▼ LA CHOCOLATERÍA

DOMO BLANCO ▼

COTECAL ●

PERITO MORENO

HOSTERÍA
THIAMALU ●

COMISIÓN
DE FOMENTO ■

BANCO DE
SANTA CRUZ (ATM) ■

TERMINAL DE ÓMNIBUS ■

Río de las Vueltas

CONFLUENCIA
△

To RN 40 and
El Calafate

Río Fitz Roy

To Laguna Torre

To Loma del Pliegue
Tumbado

ADMINISTRACIÓN DE
PARQUES NACIONALES ■

0   200 yds
0   200 m

© AVALON TRAVEL

San Martín 310, tel. 02962/49-3118, www.cas-adeguias.com.ar) is another possibility.

Just north of Albergue Rancho Grande, **Viento Oeste** (San Martín 898, tel. 02962/49-3200, vientooeste@infovia.com.ar) rents and sells climbing, camping, and wet-weather gear, as does **La Brecha** (Costanera Sur 246, tel. 02962/49-3151). **Eolia** (Pasaje Fonrouge 45, tel. 02962/49-3066, www.patagoniamagica.com) also rents gear and provides guide service.

Accommodations

El Chaltén has a reasonable selection of accom-modations, some of them very good, but high summer demand makes reservations advisable. Many places close in winter, but there's usually something available.

CAMPING

Directly across from the APN office, on the Río Fitz Roy's banks, **Camping Confluencia** is free, but sheltered sites are few here, and toilet facilities are rustic.

Commercial campgrounds, which offer hot showers and shelter for cooking, in-clude **Camping El Refugio** (Calle 3 s/n, tel. 02962/49-3221, US$6 pp) and **Camping El Relincho** (San Martín 505, tel. 02962/49-3007, elrelincho@cotecal.com.ar, US$6 pp).

US$10-25

Having more than doubled its capacity by adding a second floor, the 90-bed HI affiliate **Albergue Rancho Grande** (San Martín 635, tel./fax 02962/49-3005, www.ranchogran-dehostel.com, US$12 pp dorm, US$57 s or d) has drawn some flak for failing to insu-late the between-floors gap for sound. It does offer B&B packages with transportation from El Calafate; for reservations, contact Chaltén Travel (Avenida Libertador 1174, El Calafate, tel. 02902/49-2212, www.chalten-travel.com).

Comparably priced hostels include **Ahonikenk Chaltén** (Güemes 23, tel. 02962/49-3070, ahonikenkchalten23@yahoo.com.ar, US$12 pp dorm, US$40 d) and **Albergue Lago del Desierto** (Lago del Desierto 135, tel. 02962/49-3010, hos-teldellago_elchalten@yahoo.com.ar, US$12 pp dorm).

US$25-50

Like El Calafate, El Chaltén has little or noth-ing exclusive to this range, but several hostels also offer private rooms that are excellent val-ues for around the same price or a little more.

Open all year except June, the HI affiliate **《 Albergue Patagonia** (San Martín 493, tel. 02962/49-3019, www.elchalten.com/patagonia, US$12 pp dorm, US$36–58 s or d) provides utilitarian dorms—four beds per room—but also has shared-bath doubles and a separate wing of more spacious and comfortable dou-bles and twins with private baths; the latter include continental breakfast. On the hostel side, it also provides cooking facilities, laun-dry service, meals, a book exchange, and bike rentals, and it organizes excursions. Its main drawback is that the hostel toilet and shower facilities, while good enough, are arguably too few. English and Dutch are spoken.

Cóndor de los Andes (Avenida Río de las Vueltas and Halvorsen, tel. 02962/49-3101, www.condordelosandes.com, US$12–14 pp dorm, US$48 d) has four- and six-bed dorms, each with its own bath, kitchen facilities, and spacious common areas with exceptional views. It has also added private rooms.

US$50-100

Family-run **Hospedaje La Base** (Lago del Desierto 97, tel./fax 02962/49-3031, labase@elchaltenpatagonia.com.ar, US$52 s or d) has two firm beds per room, which are two-bed-room *cabañas* that share a kitchen but have pri-vate baths. Like many other places, it closes June–November.

Cozy, friendly, and tobacco-free, **《 Nothofagus Bed & Breakfast** (Calle 10 No. 40, tel. 02962/49-3087, www.nothofa-gusbb.com.ar, US$37–53 s, US$40–55 d, with breakfast) has seven rooms in a handsome house with convivial common areas; rates vary according to whether the room has a shared or private bath.

The no-frills **Hostería Los Ñires** (Lago del Desierto 120, tel. 02962/49-3009, www. losnireschalten.com.ar, US$45 s, US$50–57 s or d with a middling breakfast) has tiny but functional singles (some with thin walls), larger but awkwardly shaped doubles that lack closet space, and more standard rooms with traditional amenities. All have private baths. Separated from its bar-restaurant by a long corridor, the sleeping quarters are normally quiet.

Friendly **Hostería Thiamalu** (Lago del Desierto 99, tel. 02962/49-3736, www.thiamalu.com.ar, US$60 s, US$70 d, with breakfast) isn't up to the level of the Nothofagus, though all its rooms do have private baths.

Recently expanded **Posada Altas Cumbres** (Lionel Terray 342, tel. 02962/49-3060, altas_cumbres@hotmail.com, www.elchalten.com/altascumbres, US$66–70 s or d) has a dozen spacious new rooms and a restaurant.

Open November–April, **Hotel Lago del Desierto** (Lago del Desierto 137, tel. 02962/49-3010, hotellagodeldesierto@yahoo.com.ar, US$71 s or d with breakfast) also rents six-bed *cabañas* with kitchen facilities for US$130, and has camping facilities (US$6 pp).

Open October–March, **Hostería Lago Viedma** (Arbilla 71, tel. 02962/49-3089, hosterialagoviedma@hotmail.com, US$74 s or d) has just four small but well-designed rooms with private baths and breakfast; it may add more rooms.

US$100-200

At the southern approach to town, **Hotel La Aldea** (Avenida Güemes 95, tel. 02962/49-3040, www.hotellaaldea.com.ar, US$77–93 s, US$87–108 d, with breakfast) is more a motel-style complex, with the rooms separate from a two-story reception area that includes a restaurant and bar.

Rates at the venerable (by Chaltén standards) **Fitz Roy Inn** (San Martín 520, tel. 02962/49-3062, hosteriafitzroyinn@elchalten.net.ar, US$100 s, US$105 d) drop considerably outside the November–March high season; it also has multiday packages with half or full board,

but the full-board option would preclude eating at other good places.

New in late 2008, **Hostería Infinito Sur** (Riquelme 208, tel. 02962/49-3325, www. infinitosurelchalten.com, US$110 s or d) is a boutique-style hotel with just nine rooms in a building of quarried stone and rough-hewn wood. Only the bar–breakfast room, though, enjoys views of Fitz Roy. Rates fall by about 20–25 percent outside January–February.

Hostería Kalenshen (Lionel Terray 30, tel. 02962/49-3108, www.kalenshen.com, US$100–140 s, US$110–140 d, with breakfast) has 17 rooms with handmade furniture and another six *cabañas* (US$225, for up to four people).

Rates have risen at **Hostería La Casa de Piedra** (Lago del Desierto 423, tel./fax 02962/49-3015, hosterialacasadepiedra@yahoo.com.ar, US$112–290 s, US$120–330 d), which provides large and comfy but tackily decorated rooms with private baths. It has well-tended grounds and is quiet, though the nearby power plant might bother some guests.

North of town, in an out-of-the-way location bordering the Lago del Desierto road, ◖ **Hostería El Pilar** (tel./fax 02962/49-3002, tel. 011/5031-0755 in Buenos Aires, www.hosteriaelpilar.com.ar, US$120 s, US$143 d, with breakfast) has the classic style of a Patagonian *casco,* but it's really a recent construction (1996). Reservations are essential for this cozy and increasingly popular place, open October–April, but it's possible to dine in the restaurant without being a guest, although reservations are advisable. Shuttle transportation from El Chaltén is free for guests.

With improved landscaping, ◖ **Hostería Posada Lunajuim** (Trevisan 45, tel. 02962/49-3047, www.posadalunajuim.com.ar, US$121 s, US$148 d) continues to make a good impression with appealing common areas (including a bar-restaurant) and rooms with private baths, central heating, and breakfast.

The eight-room ◖ **Hostería El Puma** (Lionel Terray 212, tel. 02962/49-3095, www. hosteriaelpuma.com.ar, US$130 s, US$160 d) and its Terray restaurant make another impressive addition to Chaltén's accommodations scene. Prices with half board are an additional US$30 pp.

OVER US$200

Atop a hillock with panoramic views of the Río de la Vueltas, under the same ownership as Hostería Los Notros, **Los Cerros** (tel. 02962/49-3182, tel. 011/4814-3934 in Buenos Aires, www.loscerrosdelchalten.com, from US$362 s, US$452 d) works mainly with multiday packages but takes other guests on a space-available basis. Spacious and luminous, with baths all featuring whirlpool tubs, the rooms have massive picture windows; the common areas, many of them decorated with historic maps, have soaring cathedral ceilings that flood them with natural light.

Food

Hikers and climbers stock up on supplies at **El Super** (Lago del Desierto 248), **El Gringuito** (Cerro Solo 108), and **Stella Maris** (Avenida San Martín 36). For its size, though, El Chaltén offers a fine and improving restaurant selection.

La Chocolatería (Lago del Desierto 105, tel. 02962/49-3008) is more than it sounds—the desserts are good enough, but the breakfasts and pizzas are also excellent, and the Bailey's-spiked hot chocolate is comforting on a cold night. **La Senyera del Torre** (Lago del Desierto 240, tel. 02962/49-3063) prepares Argentine comfort food such as the *locro* (a hearty stew) and excellent desserts.

Domo Blanco (Avenida Güemes 71, tel. 02962/49-3036) serves exceptional ice cream, with local ingredients such as raspberries and strawberries, and will also deliver to your hotel. **Bocatto** (Avenida San Martín s/n) makes the best takeaway empanadas, in several varieties, all a little larger than the Argentine standard. **Cruel** (San Martín 84, tel. 02962/49-3167) is best for a quick sandwich. New in late 2008, **Rincón del Sur** (Lago del Desierto 265) is Chaltén's first wine bar, with sandwiches

and platters of cheeses, cold cuts, and smoked Patagonian meats—not to mention great cycling advice.

In new quarters, (**La Tapera** (Antonio Rojo 76, tel. 02962/49-3138, lunch and dinner daily) is an exceptionally friendly restaurant–tapas bar with a small but excellent menu of fixed-price dinners (US$13) that includes soup and a choice among four entrées—one of the best values in town.

Del Bosque (San Martín 591) is a combination teahouse and ice cream parlor. **La Cervecería** (San Martín 320, tel. 02962/49-3109, lunch and dinner daily) is a pizza pub with its own microbrew beer (US$2 per pint); it also prepares an outstanding *locro* (US$5.50), a meal-in-itself northwestern Argentine stew that's ideal for a cool Chaltén evening.

Open in summer only, (**Ruca Mahuida** (Lionel Terray 55, tel. 02962/49-3018, lunch and dinner daily) is one of Chaltén's most imaginative eateries—try the lamb ravioli in mint sauce (US$12)—with improved service. With only four (big) tables, it's open for lunch but most people come at dinnertime after their hikes. There are fine appetizers in the US$5–7 range, but most entrées cost nearly US$20 and up.

Lamb is the specialty at **La Casita** (San Martín 430, tel. 02962/49-3042, lunch and dinner daily), which otherwise serves a standard Argentine menu—beef, pizza, pasta, and the like. Its major downside is the cramped and tobacco-heavy atmosphere. In midsummer it can be hard to get a table at popular **Pizzería Patagonicus** (Güemes 57, tel. 02962/49-3025, lunch and dinner daily), one of few Argentine eateries to have lamb on the pizza menu; the decor, with natural wood and mountaineering photos, embodies Chaltén's evolving style. **Pangaea** (Lago del Desierto 330, tel. 02962/49-3084) has decent pizza and a really excellent wine list.

Reservations are advisable for (**Fuegia** (San Martín 342, tel. 02962/49-3019, lunch and dinner daily), Albergue Patagonia's bistro-style restaurant, though it's expanded to accommodate demand for dishes like rack of lamb and

Patagonian trout (US$15). Likewise, plan ahead for the unpretentious **(Estepa** (Cerro Solo 86, tel. 02962/49-3069, lunch and dinner daily), a snug, tobacco-free, six-booth place with views of Fitz Roy. Offering home-style cooking at a high level, its enduring specialty is the *cordero estepa* (US$16) lamb with *calafate* sauce, but there are also pizzas and empanadas, with most other entrées in the US$8–15 range.

Also tobacco-free, at the north end of town, tiny **El Muro** (San Martín 912, tel. 02962/49-3248, lunch and dinner daily) is a bistro-style restaurant where the kitchen pays minute attention to diners' tastes, but the service can be distracted when it gets busy. Dishes such as lamb loin with a fresh raspberry-and-cherry sauce (US$15), though, are well worth minor inconveniences. Special mention goes to the light-crusted empanadas, including lamb and beef.

Information and Services

El Chaltén's **Comisión de Fomento** (Avenida Güemes 21, tel. 02962/49-3011, www.el-chalten.com, 8 A.M.–8 P.M. daily in summer, 9 A.M.–5 P.M. weekdays only the rest of the year), just north of the bridge across the Río Fitz Roy, has maps and other information.

Correo Argentino is due to open a new post office on Madsen between Güemes and Halvorsen. **Cotecal** (Güemes 109) has long-distance phone and fax service. **Chaltén Travel** (Avenida Güemes 7) has relatively but not outrageously expensive Internet connections, but they're agonizingly slow.

There are no formal exchange houses, but **Banco de Santa Cruz** now operates an ATM at the corner of Avenida Güemes and Perito Moreno; still, it's better to bring as much cash as feasible. Some businesses will accept U.S. dollars or euros in exchange for services, but few handle credit cards.

Lavandino (Halvorsen 41) handles the washing, though many accommodations also do so at reasonable prices.

Getting There

Several bus companies connect El Chaltén with El Calafate (3.5 hours, US$18–20): **Cal Tur** (San Martín 451, tel. 02962/49-3062), **Chaltén Travel** (San Martín 724, tel. 02962/49-3005), and **Taqsa** (Antonio Rojo 88, tel. 02962/49-3294). Departures are usually in the late afternoon around 5–6 P.M. There are several buses daily in summer, but this falls to about one daily in winter.

With Chaltén Travel, it's possible to travel north on gravel RN 40 to the towns of Perito Moreno and Los Antiguos in Chubut Province (13 hours, US$57). Chaltén Travel leaves Chaltén on alternate days in summer; passengers from El Calafate can board the bus at the RN 40 junction. The rest of the year, there may be only one bus weekly. **Corredor Patagónico** also does this route.

Transporte Las Lengas (Viedma 95, tel. 02962/49-3023, laslengaselchalten@yahoo.com.ar) goes to Comandante Luis Piedra Buena (6 hours, US$29) at 5:30 A.M. daily in summer. It has also started a new service to Aeropuerto Internacional El Calafate (3.5 hours, US$21) at 6:30 and 10:30 A.M. daily, returning at 1:30 and 7 P.M.

Also in summer, at 5 A.M. Monday, Thursday, and Saturday, **Transpatagonia Servicios** (Cerro Solo 95, tel. 02962/49-3160) provides door-to-door service to Río Gallegos (5 hours, US$36), which makes it feasible to connect with buses to Argentine Tierra del Fuego and to Punta Arenas, Chile.

Getting Around

When the national park shuttles don't meet your needs, consider a meterless taxi service such as Remises Chaltén Móvil (tel. 02962/49-3061), an economical option if shared by several riders.

RN 40 SOUTH

Southeast of El Calafate, RN 40 and RP 5 are contiguous as far as El Cerrito, where RN 40 forks southwest toward the Chilean border. At the junction of RN 40 and east–west RP 7, about halfway to Puerto Natales, Tapi Aike is a wide spot in the road where there's a gas station, a convenience store, and accommodations at nearby Estancia Tapi Aike.

From here, the road continues southwest to the border crossing at **Cancha Carrera,** the easiest access to Torres del Paine, with occasional direct summer bus connections. Most travelers, though, enter Chile at Río Turbio, an otherwise bleak coal town with a historic narrow-gauge railway and a modern ski resort.

Estancia Tapi Aike

Historically part of the Braun empire, the Tapi Aike sheep ranch sprawls over 60,000 hectares of steppe, but the settlement is a compact one near the RN 40 junction with RP 7. Open November–April, the comfortable *casco,* reinvented as Posada Tapi Aike (San Martín 255, tel. 02966/42-0092 in Río Gallegos, bvdesign@fibertel.com.ar, US$60 pp), offers bed-and-breakfast accommodations between Calafate and the border; some visitors stay here and make Torres del Paine a day trip.

Besides accommodations, Tapi Aike offers simple but well-made lunches and dinners (US$15 pp), including a main dish, salad, soda, wine, and dessert. The Viel family, descendents of the Brauns, speak English and Spanish. Estancia Tapi Aike also has a Buenos Aires contact (tel. 011/4812-3428, fax 011/4784-4360).

Estancia Rupai Pacha

From Tapi Aike, RN 40 leads southwest past the **Hotel Fuentes del Coyle,** a bare-bones country inn that's a local landmark; about 22 kilometers southwest via a detour from the new route, the Sturtzenbaum family's Estancia Rupai Pacha (Piedra Buena 129, Río Gallegos, tel. 02966/49-4057, www.rupai-pacha.com, US$100 s, US$120 d, with breakfast) provides organic produce for El Calafate and raises sheep on 26,000 hectares of rolling steppe. With views of Torres del Paine to the southwest, it also offers congenial farm-stay accommodations, plus hiking, riding, and especially bird-watching on its marshy lowlands. Founded in 1973, it's not a historic *estancia,* but the gardens are a treasure, with delectable raspberries and other fresh fruits in season, and there's also a handicrafts shop.

About 180 kilometers south of El Calafate and 70 kilometers north of Río Turbio, Rupai Pacha is about 10 kilometers west of the new RN 40 from a signed junction. Rates include breakfast, while additional meals cost US$32 pp; there is also a sheltered campground (US$15 d). English and German are spoken.

Río Turbio

In one of Argentina's remotest corners, the gritty coal town of Río Turbio had been declining as its underground seams neared exhaustion, but it got an ironic shot in the arm with the 2002 peso meltdown—as locals could no longer afford to shop in Chile, supermarkets and other businesses here opened and even expanded during the country's worst economic crisis ever. Even Chileans began to cross the border for cheaper Argentine goods.

Even the mines recovered as national fuel shortages made the local mineral a competitive energy source, but this had a downside as well. In mid-2004 an underground fire killed 14 miners, plunging the community into mourning and raising questions about cost-cutting measures by the private concessionaire.

Though it's no beauty spot, Río Turbio holds some interest for its aging locomotives and railcars—the narrow-gauge railway still carries coal to Punta Loyola, near Río Gallegos—and for its modest winter-sports center.

Río Turbio (pop. 6,652) is 270 kilometers west of Río Gallegos via RN 40, and 30 kilometers north of Puerto Natales, Chile. It's 242 kilometers south of El Calafate via RN 40 and RP 11.

Near the Villa Dorotea border post, about four kilometers south of town, the **Centro de Deportes de Invierno Valdelén** (tel. 02902/42-1900, angeli@oyikil.com.ar) is a modest but lighted ski area, with elevations ranging 180–690 meters; there are about 12 hectares of downhill slopes and 160 suitable for cross-country. Hours are 10 A.M.–10 P.M. daily when snow is sufficient, usually June–August.

Whatever its shortcomings as a hometown, Río Turbio has decent accommodations, starting

GET YOUR FLATS ON LA CUARENTA

From the Bolivian border near La Quiaca to its terminus near Río Gallegos, RN 40 is Argentina's great unfinished interior highway. Some segments of "La Cuarenta" in the central Cuyo provinces are smoothly paved, while others in the Andean northwest are rough and rugged. None of those, though, enjoys the notoriety of the segment between the El Calafate junction and the town of Perito Moreno, on the cusp between the Patagonian steppe and the icy southern Andes.

It may not be Argentina's loneliest road – some of the cul-de-sac tracks that spin off it seem simply *abandoned* – but for Argentines and foreigners alike it has become the standard for adventurous driving and cycling thanks to its secluded Andean lakes, isolated *estancias*, plentiful wildlife, and rare sights like the pre-Columbian rock art of Cueva de las Manos. Even the advent of (infrequent) public transportation has not diminished its mystique.

When the author first drove the 594 kilometers in early 1991, he saw only three other vehicles in four days, and services were almost nil. Since then, traffic has not exactly burgeoned, but the summer season sees a small but steady procession of motorists, motorcyclists, and bicyclists. It's as if a selective bunch has absorbed Charles Darwin's insight that the appeal of the bleak Patagonian plains was "the free scope given to the imagination."

It's clearly not for everyone, though, and a trip up or down La Cuarenta requires planning. With accommodations and supplies few and far between, bicyclists and motorcyclists *must* carry tents and cold-weather gear, even in midsummer, and plenty of food. Detailed maps, like ACA's newest regional sheets, are essential. Preferably, automobiles should carry at least two spare tires.

Also carry extra fuel – between El Calafate and Perito Moreno, the only dependable supplies are

with **Hospedaje Yenu** (2 de Abril 170, Barrio Islas Malvinas, tel. 02902/42-1694, US$25 s, US$37 d). Another good option is **Hotel Nazo** (Gobernador Moyano 464, tel. 02902/42-1800, nazo@oyikil.com.ar, US$47 s, US$53 d).

Don Pablo I (Pellegrini and Roque Sáenz Peña, tel. 02902/42-1220) is a pizzeria that also serves inexpensive *minutas* (short orders). Hotel Nazo's **Fond du Cave** (Gobernador Moyano 474, tel. 02902/42-1800) is the best full-service restaurant.

Río Turbio's helpful **Centro de Información Turística** (Plazoleta Agustín del Castillo s/n, tel. 02902/42-1950, rioturbio@rioturbio.gov.ar) is presumably open 8 A.M.–9 P.M. weekdays and 9 A.M.–9 P.M. weekends; in practice it keeps irregular hours.

Banco de Santa Cruz (Gobernador Lista s/n) has an ATM. For postal services, **Correo Argentino** is at Avenida de los Mineros and Roque Sáenz Peña.

LADE (Avenida de los Mineros 375, tel. 02902/42-1224) flies sporadically to Río Gallegos and Río Grande (Tierra del Fuego).

Río Turbio has no central bus terminal, but all the companies are fairly close to each other. **Cootra** (Teniente del Castillo 01, tel. 02902/42-1448) operates 5–7 buses daily to Puerto Natales (1 hour, US$5.50) except on weekends, when there are only two or three. **Bus Sur** (Avenida de los Mineros 262) goes once or twice daily.

Taqsa (Teniente del Castillo 130, tel. 02902/42-1422) goes to Río Gallegos (4.5 hours, US$12) at 2:30 and 11:30 A.M. and 4 P.M. daily.

RN 40 NORTH

About 30 kilometers east of El Calafate, northbound RN 40 covers 596 kilometers of rugged gravel road—scheduled to be completely paved within four years or so—in the Andes' arid eastern foothills, before arriving at the cow town of Perito Moreno near Lago Buenos Aires, the oasis of Los Antiguos, and the Chilean border town of Chile Chico. In recent years, this desolate highway has seen more and more overland travelers, but mixed

at El Chaltén (a 90-kilometer detour), Tres Lagos, Gobernador Gregores (a 70-kilometer detour, but it sometimes runs out), and Bajo Caracoles (which also sometimes runs out). Some tourist *estancias* will sell gasoline to their clients or in an emergency, but don't count on it.

Road hazards are numerous. Bicyclists and motorcyclists must contend with powerful Patagonian winds that can knock them down in an instant, and deep gravel adds to the danger. Even high-clearance vehicles are vulnerable to flipping on loose gravel, especially when braking suddenly, and 50-knot gusts make things worse. Though four-wheel drive is not essential, some drivers prefer it to avoid fishtailing on gravel.

Chipped, cracked, and even shattered windshields are par for the course on RN 40 and other graveled roads. Normally, rental-car insurance policies do *not* cover such damage, and replacements are expensive in Argentina (though fairly cheap in Punta Arenas, Chile).

Approaching vehicles usually brake to minimize the possibility of such damage, but some drivers find they need to play chicken to slow down an onrushing pickup truck or SUV.

The big news is that within a few years, thanks to former Santa Cruz governor and former president Néstor Kirchner, this segment of RN 40 will be paved and may be rerouted to pass through Gobernador Gregores. Hearing that RN 40 will be paved evokes enough nostalgia for a tango, but there will remain plenty of gravel roads to last the lifetime of most of this book's readers.

If driving or cycling doesn't appeal to you, but you still want to see the loneliest highway, summer bus and minivan services now connect El Calafate and El Chaltén, at the south end, with Perito Moreno and Los Antiguos at the north end of the province, and with Bariloche; for details, see the appropriate destination sections.

reviews indicate it's not for everyone: The unrelenting westerlies bowl over cyclists and bikers alike, sharp rocks blow tires and shatter windshields, and vehicles can break down in the middle of nowhere.

Still, this segment of "La Cuarenta"—running from Río Gallegos almost to the Bolivian border, RN 40 is Argentina's longest interior highway—has a mystique all its own. Some love it, some loathe it, and others are ambivalent, but no one forgets it.

La Leona and Vicinity

Since 1916, the landmark **Hotel de Campo La Leona** (tel. 011/5032-3415 in Buenos Aires, www.hoteldecampolaleona.com.ar) has been a rural roadhouse where today's travelers brake for chocolate and lemon pie, banana bread, and tea and coffee. Though the exterior looks much as it did a century ago, a Buenos Aires investor has totally transformed the interior, with a small souvenir shop in addition to a more spacious and cheerful dining room (with equally cheerful personnel).

Little more than a wide turnout alongside the road, at junction of RN 40 and westbound RP 21, it's a useful stop for cyclists, either northbound or southbound, who don't care to set up the tent; the four remodeled rooms, with private baths, cost US$80 d, US$90 triple, US$100 quadruple, with breakfast. Camping costs US$10 pp, without breakfast.

Under the same ownership, west of the highway, the more luxurious **Estancia La Estela** (www.estancialaestela.com.ar, US$130 d) offers custom-built accommodations with views of Lago Viedma and the Fitz Roy range, plus activities that include rafting, riding, and even archery. An entire house, sleeping six, is available for US$330.

Nearby, the recently discovered **Bosque Petrificado La Leona** is a badlands reserve of petrified forests and dinosaur fossils on nearby Estancia Santa Teresita, visited by guided tour only. For details on this full-day excursion (US$45), contact any El Calafate travel agency.

SOUTHERN PATAGONIA

Once a simple roadhouse, Hotel de Campo La Leona has undergone major improvements.

Tres Lagos and Vicinity

Beyond La Margarita, RN 40 climbs over the volcanic Meseta Escorial before dropping into the enigmatically named hamlet of Tres Lagos (Three Lakes; the only nearby water is the humble Río Shehuen). Northbound motorists *must* fill up at the YPF station, which has the only gasoline until Bajo Caracoles, 338 kilometers north.

Tres Lagos has few other services, though there is a pretty good municipal **Camping Comunal** (tel. 02962/49-5031, US$2.50 per tent plus US$1 per vehicle) with hot showers (US$0.50). Very good fresh-baked empanadas and lesser snacks are available at the YPF station.

To the northwest, gravel RP 31 and RP 33 lead 100 kilometers to **Lago San Martín,** but unfortunately the landmark Estancia La Maipú, which used to offer accommodations, is presently closed.

Lago Cardiel and Vicinity

North of Tres Lagos, RN 40 winds north over the Meseta Cascajosa before coming within sight of Lago Cardiel, a deep interior drainage lake that's a bellwether for ongoing climate-change studies. It also enjoys a certain popularity for fishing, but it's so remote that there's little competition.

On the west side of the highway, 22 kilometers south of the RP 29 junction to Gobernador Gregores, **Estancia La Siberia** (tel. 02966/42-6972 in Río Gallegos, www.lasiberia.8k.com) is the casual doppelgänger of the stereotypical tourist *estancia*. With little livestock, set among an aging orchard of apricot, cherry, pear, and plum trees, it's open October–mid-April and rents rooms for US$19 pp in hostel-style accommodations, US$40–66 pp with private baths and hot showers; inexpensive camping (US$5.50 pp) makes it popular with cyclists.

Estancia La Angostura and Vicinity

About 60 kilometers northwest of La Siberia on RN 40, midway between RP 29 and RP 25, an eastbound dirt road drops into the Río Chico marshlands, dotted with birds that include upland geese, coots, and lapwings. Sheltered

© WAYNE BERNHARDSON

by densely planted trees, La Angostura has seven comfortable guest rooms (US$90 s or d with breakfast), but also a decent campground (US$10 pp) on a farm that leans toward the rustic end of the *estancia* continuum. The food is heavy on Argentine standards like *milanesa.* Estancia La Angostura (tel. 02902/49-1208, estancialaangostura@yahoo.com.ar) is open mid-October–April. If RN 40 is rerouted to Gobernador Gregores, this will be an off-the-paved-track place to experience the old highway.

North of La Angostura, the 200 or so kilometers of northbound RN 40 to Bajo Caracoles is almost service-free, especially since the owner's death forced closure of the landmark Hotel Las Horquetas, an out-of-the-wind dive near the junction with westbound RP 37. Some campers like the free sites beneath the bridge over the Río Chico near the junction of RN 40 and RP 25, but the best spots go early.

Gobernador Gregores

Though it's 60–70 kilometers east of RN 40 via either RP 29 or RP 25, Gobernador Gregores (pop. 2,513) can be an essential detour for bikers or motorists running short of gasoline. It's also the easiest place to obtain other supplies and to hire a car and driver to Parque Nacional Perito Moreno, some 200-plus kilometers northwest. RN 40's presumed paving and rerouting to Gregores figures to reinvigorate the town as a tourist service center, especially as a base for improved park access.

The **Camping Municipal Nuestra Señora del Valle** (Roca and Chile, tel. 02962/49-1228, free) has hot showers. The best accommodations are at **Hotel Cañadón León** (Roca 397, tel. 02962/49-1082, US$12 s, US$17 d), which also has the best restaurant. The next best dining is at **Pizzería Chicho** (Belgrano 319, tel. 02962/49-1391).

The **Dirección Municipal de Turismo** (Avenida San Martín 514, tel. 02962/49-1259, gregores@epatagonia.gov.ar) can help with general information; it also keeps a kiosk at the western approach to town. The **APN** (San Martín 882, tel./fax 02962/49-1477,

peritomoreno@apn.gov.ar) deals with Parque Nacional Perito Moreno.

Cerro San Lorenzo (San Martín and Alberdi) has buses to San Julián (US$15) at 6 P.M. Monday–Saturday.

El Pulgarcito (San Martín 704, tel. 02962/49-1102) goes to Río Gallegos (5.5 hours, US$24) daily at 7 A.M. and 5 P.M.

◖ Parque Nacional Perito Moreno

The Sierra Colorada's intensely colored sedimentary summits are the backdrop for the lake-laden, wind-whipped, and wildlife-rich high country of Parque Nacional Perito Francisco P. Moreno, named for the founder of Argentina's park system. Possibly Patagonia's wildest park, where Paleo-Indians covered cave walls with images of guanacos and human hands, it's a major reason travelers are braving the rigors of La Cuarenta.

Comprising 115,000 hectares of Patagonian steppe, subantarctic forest, glacial lakes and fjords, and high Andean pastures, the park is 220 kilometers northwest of Gobernador Gregores via RP 25, RN 40, and RP 37. It's 310 kilometers southwest of the town of Perito Moreno via RN 40 and RP 37.

At 900 meters above sea level, its base altitude is higher than Los Glaciares, and its climate is colder, wetter, and more unpredictable. Its highest summit is 2,254-meter Cerro Mié, but snowcapped 3,700-meter Cerro San Lorenzo, north of the park boundary, is even higher.

In the drier eastern steppes, the dominant vegetation consists of bunch grasses known collectively as *coirón;* to the west there's a transitional wind-flagged forest of *lenga* and *ñire,* the ubiquitous southern beeches. In more sheltered areas, there are dense and nearly pure *lenga* stands along the shores of Lago Azara and Lago Nansen.

Troops of guanacos patrol the steppes and even some of the high country where there's summer pasture; the *huemul* (Andean deer) grazes the uplands in summer but winters at lower altitudes. The puma is the alpha predator,

SOUTHERN PATAGONIA

but there are smaller killers in red and gray foxes. The *pilquín* or *chinchillón anaranjado* is a species of viscacha unique to Santa Cruz Province and southernmost Chile.

The largest birds are the Andean condor and the flightless rhea, but other impressive species include the *águila mora* (black-chested buzzard eagle), the large owl *ñacurutú*, Patagonian woodpeckers, and the *carancho* (crested caracara). The many lakes and streams support abundant wildfowl, including flamingos, black-necked swans, grebes, wild geese, and steamer ducks. Unlike other Patagonian lakes, those within the park have remained free of introduced fish species.

SIGHTS AND RECREATION

While **Lago Burmeister** is worth a visit, the cave paintings have been closed to public access. There are large troops of guanacos on **Península Belgrano,** reached by an isthmus immediately west of Estancia Belgrano (which is not a tourist *estancia*).

One of the best day hikes is 1,434-meter **Cerro León,** a 2.5-hour climb immediately north of Estancia La Oriental, which offers the area's best easily accessible panoramas (hikers must be prepared for the changeable weather). The volcanic overhang known as the **Cerro de los Cóndores** is the flight school for condor chicks.

ACCOMMODATIONS AND FOOD

There are free but barren campsites with pit toilets at the APN's Centro de Informes, at the park entrance; the more appealing Lago Burmeister campground consists of Tehuelche-style lean-tos in dense *lenga* forest. The water is potable, but no supplies are available; campers must bring everything.

Open November–April, on Lago Belgrano's north shore, **Estancia La Oriental** (Rivadavia 936, San Julián, tel./fax 011/4152-6901 in Buenos Aires, elada@videodata.com.ar, US$90 s, US$115 d) has both conventional accommodations (seven rooms sleeping up to 22 guests) and protected campsites (US$22 per tent for up to 3 people, with hot showers) near the lodge. The US$10 breakfasts of homemade

scones, bread, jam, ham, and cheese deserve a detour, but the dinners (US$28 pp) are nothing special.

Just outside the park boundary, **【 Estancia Menelik** occupies a windy, oddly exposed site—most *estancieros* chose protected valley-bottom locations—but the popular explanation is that its original German homesteader wanted to advertise his presence and spot the approach of any strangers. Despite the barren landscape, the welcome is warm at both the comfortably furnished farmhouse, which has ample bedrooms (US$100 pp with full board) plus a large sitting room (with library) and dining areas, and at its simpler **Refugio Río Belgrano** (a rehabbed bunkhouse, US$25 pp). Though well off the beaten path, it does get tour groups, so reservations are advisable; for details, contact Cielos Patagónicos (tel. 011/4836-3502 in Buenos Aires, www.cielospatagonicos.com). Given Menelik's isolation, the quality of the food (breakfast US$6, lunch or dinner US$18) is good. It's open November–April.

OTHER PRACTICALITIES

Rangers at the Centro de Informes, at the park entrance, provide maps and brochures and offer guided hikes and visits; they can also be reached through the APN (Avenida San Martín 882, tel./fax 02962/49-1477, peritomoreno@apn.gov.ar) in Gobernador Gregores. You can also write for information at their postal address: Casilla de Correo 103, (9311) Gobernador Gregores.

Rental cars offer the greatest flexibility, though it's possible to hire a car and driver in Gobernador Gregores or the town of Perito Moreno. Hitching from the highway junction is feasible but uncertain.

Bajo Caracoles

Midway between Las Horquetas and the town of Perito Moreno, barren Bajo Caracoles is an oasis for automobiles and motorcycles, with the only gas station in nearly 500 kilometers of RN 40. Southbound travelers should fill the tank here; others should buy enough to reach Perito Moreno, 128 kilometers north.

Bajo Caracoles is also the southern gateway to the rock-art site of Cueva de las Manos, 41 kilometers northeast via RP 57, but there are alternative access points farther north. RP 39 leads east to the hamlet of Hipólito Yrigoyen and **Lago Posadas,** near the Chilean border, while RP 41, a short distance north of Bajo Caracoles, goes directly to the border crossing at **Paso Roballos.**

Better than expected in this remote outpost, with recently modernized bathrooms, the legendary **Hotel Bajo Caracoles** (tel. 02963/49-0100, US$48 s or d) fills up early despite its cantankerous operator. It also has groceries and surprisingly good meals.

The hotel now has shoestring competition in the nearby **Hostel Ruta 40** (US$10 pp dorm), and there's also cheap camping across the highway.

Cueva de las Manos

Beyond Baja Caracoles, rugged RN 40 traverses the northern steppe until the point where, over millions of years, the Río Pinturas has cut a deep, scenic canyon. In the process, erosion has left countless *aleros,* stony overhangs often mistakenly called *cuevas* (caves). One of these is the Cueva de las Manos, a UNESCO World Heritage Site where stencils of hundreds of human hands, guanacos, and abstract forms cover the walls in orange, red, and yellow tones.

Dating from around 7370 B.C., the oldest paintings represent hunter-gatherers from immediate postglacial times, but the more abstract designs, which are fewer, are more recent. Oddly enough, nearly all the hands from which the site takes its name are left hands.

Along with Parque Nacional Perito Moreno, this is one of La Cuarenta's finest detours, with two main access points. From Bajo Caracoles in the south, gravel RP 41 goes directly to the site, where the municipality of Perito Moreno operates a small *confitería* and a rocky campground, and charges US$4 admission to the caves. Metal bars now block close access to the paintings, to discourage vandalism and prevent repeated touching that could damage the paintings, but they do not obscure the view.

Another access point is the Pinturas drainage itself, with two separate alternatives (both of which also offer accommodations). From **Estancia Casa de Piedra,** 45 kilometers north of Bajo Caracoles, there's a 12-kilometer access road, at the end of which it's a three-kilometer hike to the paintings; from **Estancia Cueva de las Manos,** another 23 kilometers north and seven kilometers east, another 15-kilometer access road permits a close approach. By either the northern or southern route, mountain bikers can avoid backtracking to RN 40 by hauling their bikes over the river (there's a footbridge) and out the other direction.

On the east side of RN 40, ideal for cyclists, the bucolic **Estancia Casa de Piedra** (tel. 02963/43-2199) allows camping for $6 pp, plus US$2 for showers; it also rents basic but passable rooms for US$131–139 s or d with shared baths. It's not always dependably staffed, however.

Estancia Cueva de las Manos (tel. 011/5237-4043 in Buenos Aires, www.cuevadelasmanos.net) has four modern carpeted rooms with private baths (US$90 s, US$100 d, with breakfast) as well as fine hostel accommodations (US$26 pp, without breakfast). Restaurant lunches and dinners cost about US$18, and afternoon tea is US$8. It's open November–March and sometimes for Semana Santa. Staff will also arrange other excursions in the area.

Estancia Telken

Only 30 kilometers south of Perito Moreno, just off the newly paved highway, Estancia Telken is a working ranch that doubles as a restful guesthouse and campground. Dating from 1915, the main house comprises two rooms with private baths and one with a shared bath; two separate new rooms can sleep up to five people, and an apartment can hold another four or five. The grassy campground has a covered *quincho* with a full kitchen and a full bath with hot showers.

The new absentee ownership at Telken (tel. 02963/43-2079, tel. 0297/447-1780 in Comodoro Rivadavia, telkenpatagonia@yahoo.

com.ar) has stated its intention to continue the previous owners' hospitality, but it's hard to imagine things won't change under hired help. Open October–end of April, Telken offers bed-and-breakfast for US$70 s, US$80 d, with shared bath; US$100 s, US$110 d, with private bath. Lunch costs US$20, and dinner is US$40 with drinks. Camping costs US$6 per tent or vehicle, plus US$6 pp.

Perito Moreno

Where RN 40 meets the smoothly paved international highway from Comodoro Rivadavia to Chile Chico, nondescript Perito Moreno marks the return to civilization for northbound travelers and the start of the adventure for the Calafate-bound. Often confused with its namesake national park, as well as the eponymous glacier in Parque Nacional Los Glaciares, it has pretty good services, but many visitors prefer the lakeside town of Los Antiguos to the west.

Perito Moreno (pop. 3,598) is 398 kilometers southwest of Comodoro Rivadavia via Caleta Olivia, and 58 kilometers east of Los Antiguos via paved RP 43. It is 124 kilometers south of Río Mayo, Chubut Province, via one of RN 40's rougher stretches, which continues toward Esquel and the Andean Lake District. Note that there is no scheduled public transportation between Perito Moreno and Río Mayo.

Early February's **Festival Folklórico Cueva de las Manos** is a musical event that capitalizes on the proximity of the world heritage site.

PRACTICALITIES

Opposite Laguna de los Cisnes, the city park at Perito's south end, the sheltered **Camping Municipal** (Roca and Moreno, tel. 02963/43-2130, US$1.50 pp plus US$3 per vehicle or tent) is small but has flawless bathrooms with hot showers.

Otherwise, the pickings are slim. **Hotel Santa Cruz** (Belgrano 1565, tel. 02963/43-2133, US$26 s or d with shared bath) is a no-frills shoestring option. The respectable **Hotel Belgrano** (Avenida San Martín 1001, tel. 02963/43-2019, US$32 s, US$42 d) also has

a restaurant, but the best option is the homey three-room B&B **Posada del Caminante** (Rivadavia 937, tel. 02963/43-2204, posadadelcaminante@yahoo.com.ar, US$37 s, US$47 d); phone first, as it's often booked far ahead. **Hotel Americano** (San Martín 1327, tel. 02963/43-2074, hotelamericano_consultas@yahoo.com.ar, US$39 s, US$55 d) is comparatively overpriced.

In new quarters, the **Oficina Municipal de Turismo** (Avenida San Martín and Gendarmería Nacional, tel. 02963/43-2732, peritomoreno@santacruzpatagonia.gob.ar) is open 7 A.M.–11 P.M. daily in summer, 8 A.M.–8 P.M. daily the rest of the year.

Banco de la Nación (Avenida San Martín 1385) has an ATM.

Correo Argentino is at Avenida Juan D. Perón 1331; the postal code is 9040. The **Call Center** (Rivadavia 1055) has long-distance phones, while **CTC** (Perito Moreno 1070) has Internet access.

Bilingual **Guanacondor Tours & Expeditions** (Perito Moreno 1087, tel. 02963/43-2303, jarinauta@yahoo.com.ar, jarinauta@santacruz.com.ar) arranges excursions that include Cueva de las Manos and Cañadón del Arroyo Feo.

For medical services, go to the **Hospital Distrital** (Colón 1237, tel. 02963/43-2045).

LADE (Avenida San Martín 1065, tel. 02963/43-2055) has occasional flights into and out of Perito Moreno but is hard to rely on.

The sharp new **Terminal de Ómnibus** is at the north end of town, where RN 40 (Avenida San Martín) meets RP 43. La Unión (tel. 02963/43-2638) and Sportman (tel. 02963/43-2177) have westbound service to Los Antiguos (1 hour, US$7) and eastbound service to Comodoro Rivadavia (5 hours, US$26). Sportman and Taqsa (tel. 02963/43-2675) both have daily service to Río Gallegos (14 hours, US$51).

Chaltén Travel (tel. 02902/49-2480 in El Calafate) buses from Los Antiguos to El Calafate will pick up passengers at the terminal here; the service runs on alternate days during December–April or so. Passengers from El

Chaltén can board the northbound bus from El Calafate at the junction of RN 40 and RP 23 without having to return to El Calafate. Buses depart Calafate on odd-numbered days and return from Los Antiguos on even-numbered days. For southbound travel to El Chaltén, Chaltén Travel links up with its own buses between El Calafate and El Chaltén.

Los Antiguos

Rows of upright poplars announce the approach to Los Antiguos, a garden spot where vivid flowerbeds fill the median strip of Avenida 11 de Julio, flats of soft fruits like raspberries, cherries, and strawberries go for a song, and baskets of apples, apricots, pears, peaches, plums, and prunes adorn the storefronts.

Its microclimate has made Los Antiguos a getaway since Tehuelche times, its Spanish name ("the ancient ones") derived from an indigenous term meaning "place of the elders." After August 1991, when the eruption of Chile's nearby Volcán Hudson buried the area in ash, both the fruit harvest and the tourist trade suffered, but it has recovered nicely. Fishing and hiking are the main attractions.

On Lago Buenos Aires's south shore, Los Antiguos (pop. 2,047) is 58 kilometers west of Perito Moreno via RP 43. Entering town, the highway becomes the Avenida 11 de Julio, which continues to the Chilean border; the Argentine border post is at the western end, while the Chilean Carabineros are across the Río Jeinemeni, about five kilometers farther.

Early January's three-day **Fiesta de la Cereza** (cherry festival) can put a strain on accommodations. February 5's **Día de los Antiguos** marks the town's anniversary, while **Día del Lago Buenos Aires** takes place October 29.

For fresh fruit as well as preserves, try any of several farms such as **Chacra El Porvenir** (walking distance from Avenida 11 de Julio) and the lakeshore **Chacra El Paraíso.**

PRACTICALITIES

Protected by poplars and cypresses, the lakeshore **Camping Municipal** (Avenida 11 de Julio s/n, tel. 02963/49-1265, US$1.25 pp plus US$4 per tent) provides picnic tables and fire pits at every site. Hot showers are available 5:30–10 P.M. only.

Chaltén Travel has opened **Albergue Padilla** (San Martín 44, tel. 02963/49-1140, US$12 pp dorm, US$30 d), with a dozen beds for shoestring travelers. **Hotel Argentino** (Avenida 11 de Julio 850, tel. 02963/49-1132, hotelargentino_sc@hotmail.com, US$32 s, US$42 d) is a utilitarian hotel with a decent restaurant. On the eastern outskirts of town, **Hostería Antigua Patagonia** (RP 43 s/n, tel. 02963/49-1038, www.antiguapatagonia.net, US$53 s, US$63 d) is a three-story lakeshore hotel with a restaurant.

The **Subsecretaría de Turismo** (Avenida 11 de Julio 432, tel. 02963/49-1261, www.losantiguos.gov.ar) is open 8 A.M.–midnight daily December–March, 8 A.M.–8 P.M. daily the rest of the year.

Banco de Santa Cruz (Avenida 11 de Julio 531) has an ATM.

Correo Argentino is at Gobernador Gregores 19; the postal code is 9041. **Locutorio Los Antiguos** (Alameda 436) has long-distance telephone services but has been slow to enter the digital age.

La Unión (Alameda 428, tel. 02963/49-1078) and **Sportman** (Patagonia Argentina 170, tel. 02963/49-1175) both provide bus service to Caleta Olivia (5 hours, US$18) and Comodoro Rivadavia (6 hours, US$22). Sportman also has daily service to Río Gallegos.

Both La Unión and Tacsa offer weekday and occasional Saturday services to Chile Chico (30 minutes, US$4), but never on Sunday.

For up-to-date information on Chaltén Travel buses to El Chaltén (13 hours, US$57) and El Calafate (14 hours, US$72) via southbound RN 40, contact Albergue Padilla (San Martín 44, tel. 02963/49-1140).

TIERRA DEL FUEGO AND CHILEAN PATAGONIA

If Patagonia is exciting, Tierra del Fuego—the "uttermost part of the earth"—is electrifying. In the days of sail, its subantarctic weather and ferocious westerlies obsessed sailors whether or not they had ever experienced the thrill—or terror—of "rounding the Horn." After Richard Henry Dana survived the southern seas en route to California in 1834, he vividly recounted conditions that could change from calm to chaos in an instant:

> "Here comes Cape Horn!" said the chief mate; and we had hardly time to haul down and clew up, before it was upon us. In a few moments, a heavier sea was raised than I had ever seen before, and the little brig plunged into it, and all the forward part of her was under water; the sea pouring in through the bow ports and hawse-hole, and over the knight-heads, threatening to wash everything overboard. At the same time sleet and hail were driving with all fury against us.

In Dana's time, that was the price of admission to the earth's most spectacular combination of sea, sky, land, and ice. In a landscape whose granite pinnacles rise nearly 2,000 meters straight out of the ocean, only a handful of hunter-gatherers foraging in the fjords and forests knew the area with any intimacy. Today, fortunately, reaching the Fuegian archipelago involves less hardship—not to mention motion sickness—than Dana and his shipmates suffered.

In his memoirs, pioneer settler Lucas Bridges

© DAVID WILBANKS/FLICKR.COM

HIGHLIGHTS

◖ Museo Marítimo de Ushuaia: Much more than its name suggests, Ushuaia's best museum needs more than one visit to absorb its maritime heritage and appreciate the way one of the world's most remote prisons affected the city's development (page 496).

◖ Estancia Harberton: East of Ushuaia, this historic *estancia* is, arguably, the nucleus of the "uttermost part of the earth" (page 505).

◖ Glaciar Martial: Whether entirely by foot or partly by chairlift, the climb to Ushuaia's nearby glacier, part of Parque Nacional Tierra del Fuego, rewards visitors with panoramic views of the city and the storied Beagle Channel (page 507).

◖ Puerto Williams: On Isla Navarino, across the Beagle Channel from Ushuaia in Chile, tiny Williams retains much of the "uttermost part of the earth" ambience that the Argentine city once offered. It also provides access to the rugged hiking trails of the Dientes de Navarino, a series of summits that rise like inverted vampire's fangs (page 512).

◖ Casa Braun-Menéndez (Museo Regional de Magallanes): In Punta Arenas, Chile, Magallanes's regional museum occupies what was the mansion of Patagonia's wool aristocracy (page 520).

◖ Monumento Natural Los Pingüinos: In the summer season, penguins occupy every square centimeter of Isla Magdalena, also home to a historic lighthouse (page 529).

◖ Parque Nacional Pali Aike: Hugging the Argentine border, the caves of the northern Magallanes's volcanic steppe feature some of the continent's prime early-human sites (page 533).

◖ The Fjords of Fuegia: It may be expensive to cruise the ice-clogged inlets of the archipelago of Tierra del Fuego, from Punta Arenas to Ushuaia, Cape Horn, and back, but it's still cheaper than chartering your own yacht. Even backpackers sometimes splurge for a leg of this unforgettable itinerary (page 534).

◖ Torres del Paine: The granite needles that rise above the Patagonian steppe are a beacon drawing travelers from around the world to Chile's premier national park, Parque Nacional Torres del Paine (page 552).

◖ Cuernos del Paine: This jagged interface between igneous and metamorphic rock, also in Parque Nacional Torres del Paine, is some of the world's most breathtaking alpine scenery (page 552).

LOOK FOR ◖ TO FIND RECOMMENDED SIGHTS, ACTIVITIES, DINING, AND LODGING.

TIERRA DEL FUEGO

labeled Tierra del Fuego the "uttermost part of the earth" for its splendid isolation at the continent's southern tip. The "Land of Fire" is still a place where fur seals, sea lions, and penguins cavort in the choppy seas of the strait named for the celebrated navigator Ferdinand Magellan, where Charles Darwin sailed on the *Beagle,* and the first '49ers found their route to California. From the seashore, behind the Argentine city of Ushuaia, glacial horns rise like sacred steeples. The beaches and southern beech forests of Parque Nacional Tierra del Fuego, west of the city, are the terminus of the world's southernmost highway.

Tierra del Fuego may be an archipelago, but the Isla Grande de Tierra del Fuego is South America's largest island. Chile shares the territory with Argentina; while parts of the Argentine side are urbanized, the Chilean side has just a few small towns and isolated *estancias.* Roads are few but improving, especially on the Argentine side; the unpaved roads, though, can be hell on windshields, which are most cheaply replaced in the Chilean mainland city of Punta Arenas.

Two ferry routes connect the Chilean mainland to Tierra del Fuego: a shuttle from Punta Delgada, only 45 kilometers south of Argentina's Santa Cruz Province, across the Primera Angostura narrows to Puerto Espora; and a daily service from Punta Arenas to Porvenir, one of the widest parts of the strait.

Chilean Patagonia's exact boundaries are imprecise because, in a sense, the region exists only in the imagination. In Chile, Patagonia has no juridical reality, though nearly everybody would agree that both Region XI (Aisén) and Region XII (Magallanes) are at least part of it. Other more northerly areas would like to be included to partake of the Patagonian mystique; this chapter, however, covers only Magallanes, a popular destination in an area where travelers cross borders frequently.

Chile's most southerly region has acquired international fame thanks to the Torres del Paine, the magnificent granite needles that loom above the Patagonian plains. Pacific storms drench the nearly uninhabited western cordillera, feeding alpine and continental glaciers and rushing rivers, but rolling grasslands and seemingly unstoppable winds typify the eastern areas in the Andean rain shadow. Along the Strait of Magellan, the city of Punta Arenas is the center for excursions to a variety of attractions, including easily accessible penguin colonies and Tierra del Fuego's remote fjords. The region has no direct road connections to the rest of Chile—travelers must arrive by air, sea, or through Argentine Patagonia.

Administratively, Region XII includes all Chilean territory beyond 49° south to the South Pole, as Chile claims a slice of Antarctica between 53° and 90° west longitude. It also takes in the Chilean half of the Isla Grande de Tierra del Fuego, west of about 68°35', and most of archipelagic Tierra del Fuego.

Over the past decade, improved cross-border communications have meant that many visitors to the Argentine side also visit Chile to see Puerto Natales, Torres del Paine, and other Chilean attractions. As in Argentina, January and February are the peak months. Prices drop in the off-season—though many places also close. Like El Calafate, the area enjoys a lengthening season.

PLANNING YOUR TIME

Like the rest of southern South America, Tierra del Fuego and Chilean Patagonia deserve all the time you can give them, but most visitors have to make choices. On Tierra del Fuego, Ushuaia is the best sightseeing base, given its access to the nearby national park, the Beagle Channel, and Estancia Harberton, with a minimum of three days. Hikers may wish to spend several days more, and fly-fishing aficionados—who prefer the vicinity of Río Grande—can easily stay a week or two.

Exploring Chile's thinly populated sector requires a vehicle, or even an airplane—connections to Puerto Williams, though it's not far from Ushuaia as the crow flies, can be haphazard except by commercial flights from Punta Arenas. Once you're there, it takes at least a week to hike the Dientes circuit.

On the Chilean mainland, Punta Arenas can

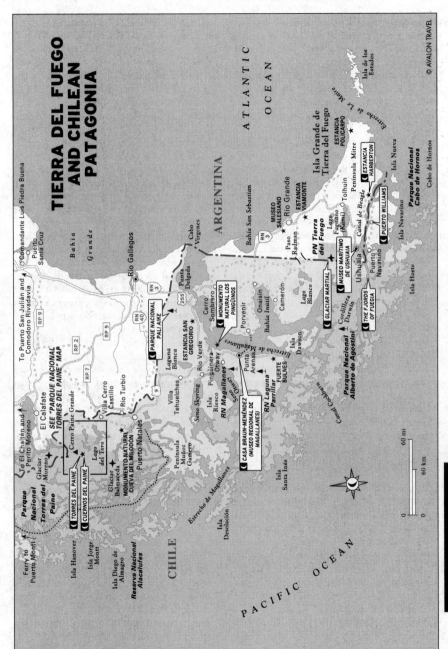

TIERRA DEL FUEGO
AND CHILEAN
PATAGONIA

© AVALON TRAVEL

ATLANTIC

OCEAN

Isla de los
Estados

Estrecho de Le Maire

Isla Grande de
Tierra del Fuego

ESTANCIA
POLICARPO ★

Península Mitre

ESTANCIA
HARBERTON ★

Isla Nueva

Parque Nacional
Cabo de Hornos

Cabo de Hornos

◀ PUERTO WILLIAMS

Isla Navarino

Isla Hoste

Canal de Beagle

Puerto
Navarino

◀ THE FJORDS
OF FUEGIA

Cordillera
Darwin ▲

Parque Nacional
Alberto de Agostini

Seno Almirantazgo

Brazo del Sudoeste

Isla
Santa Inés

Isla
Desolación

Estrecho de Magallanes

PACIFIC OCEAN

CHILE

Reserva Nacional
Alacalufes

Isla Diego de
Almagro

Isla Jorge
Montt

Isla Hanover

Ferry to
Puerto Montt

Parque
Nacional
Torres del
Paine

To El Chaltén and
Perito Moreno

◀ TORRES DEL PAINE
◀ CUERNOS DEL PAINE

SEE "PARQUE NACIONAL
TORRES DEL PAINE" MAP

Glaciar
Moreno

El Calafate

Cerro Paine Grande ★

Lago
del Toro

Glaciar
Balmaceda

MONUMENTO NATURAL
CUEVA DEL MILODÓN

Península
Muñoz
Gamero

Puerto Natales

Villa Cerro
Castillo

Río Turbio

ARGENTINA

To Puerto San Julián and
Comodoro Rivadavia

RP 9

RP 2

RP 7

RP 5

RN 40

Comandante Luis Piedra Buena

Puerto
Santa Cruz

Bahía
Grande

Río Gallegos

RN
3

Punta
Delgada

Cabo
Vírgenes

255

PARQUE NACIONAL
PALI AIKE ★

ESTANCIA SAN
GREGORIO ★

Laguna
Blanca

Villa
Tehuelches

Río Verde

9

Seno Skyring

Isla
Riesco

Seno Otway

Cerro
Sombrero

MONUMENTO
NATURAL LOS
PINGÜINOS

Porvenir

Bahía San Sebastián

RN
3

Paso
Radman

MUSEO
SALESIANO ★

Río Grande

ESTANCIA
VIAMONTE

Onaisin

Bahía Inútil

Camerón

Lago
Blanco

Lago
Fagnano
(Kami)

Tolhuin

PN Tierra
del Fuego

◀ MUSEO MARÍTIMO
DE USHUAIA

Ushuaia

◀ GLACIAR MARTIAL

Isla
Dawson

Fuerte
Bulnes

RN Laguna
Parrillar

CASA BRAUN-MENÉNDEZ
(MUSEO REGIONAL DE
MAGALLANES)

Punta
Arenas

RN Magallanes

Isla
Pingüinera

ATLANTIC
OCEAN

0   60 mi

0   60 km

N

be a sightseeing base, but usually only for a day or two; for those who haven't seen Magellanic penguins elsewhere, it's worth boating to Isla Magdalena. Punta Arenas is also the homeport for the spectacular shuttle cruise to Ushuaia and back via Tierra del Fuego's remotest fjords and Cape Horn, usually done in a three- or four-day segment. Based on an island in the western Strait of Magellan, summer whale-watching is attracting a small but growing public on three-day excursions.

Puerto Natales, the urban gateway to Torres del Paine, is primarily a place to prepare for trekking, but its seaside setting, youthful exuberance, and nearby hiking excursions often extend the stay. The park deserves no less than a week for day-hikers and overnight trekkers alike, but even a day trip is worth the trouble.

Another attraction is the five-night, four-day *Skorpios III* cruise through the fjords on the west side of the Campos de Hielo Sur, across the ice from Torres del Paine.

HISTORY

European familiarity with southernmost South America dates from 1520, when the Portuguese navigator Fernando Magalhaes, under the Spanish flag, sailed through the strait that now bears his name (Magallanes in Spanish, Magellan in English). Ranging from three to 25 kilometers in width, the strait became a maritime thoroughfare en route to the Pacific.

Prior to their "discovery" by Magellan, southern South America's insular extremes were inhabited by hunter-gatherer bands such as the Selk'nam (Ona), Kawésqar (Alacaluf), and Yámana (Yahgan). They lived off maritime and terrestrial resources that they considered abundant—only in the European view was this a land of deprivation. The archipelago acquired its name from the fires set by the region's so-called "Canoe Indians," the Kawésqar and Yámana, for heating and cooking; in this soggy region, though, it might have been more accurate to call it Tierra del Humo (Land of Smoke).

Early navigators dreaded Cape Horn's wild seas, and their reports gave their countrymen little reason to settle in or even explore the area.

In the early 1830s, Captain Robert Fitzroy of the *Beagle* abducted several Yámana, including the famous Jemmy Button, to England; he subjected them to missionary indoctrination before returning them to their home on a later voyage. On that voyage, a perplexed Charles Darwin commented on the simplicity of their society: "The perfect equality among the individuals composing the Fuegian tribes, must for a long time retard their civilization."

The first to try to bring civilization to the Yámana, rather than the opposite, were Anglican missionaries from the Falkland Islands, some of whose descendents still live here. After abortive attempts that included both Fuegian assaults and the starvation death of evangelist Allen Gardiner, the Anglican Thomas Bridges settled at present-day Ushuaia, on the Argentine side of the Isla Grande, where he compiled an English-Yámana dictionary. His son Lucas, who grew up with Yámana playmates, wrote the extraordinary memoir *The Uttermost Part of the Earth,* published a few years before his death in 1950.

In the meantime, both the Chilean and Argentine governments established their presence, and gigantic sheep *estancias* occupied the sprawling grasslands where native peoples once hunted guanaco and other game. As the guanaco slowly disappeared and the desperate Fuegians began to hunt domestic sheep, they often found themselves facing the wrong end of a rifle—though introduced European diseases such as typhoid and measles killed more native people than did bullets.

The archipelago's borders were never clearly defined, and the two countries nearly went to war over three small Beagle Channel islands in 1979. Positions were uncompromising—one adamant Argentine poster proclaimed that "We will never surrender what is ours!"—but papal mediation brought a settlement within a few years. There are lingering issues, though, such as transportation across the Channel from Ushuaia to Puerto Williams.

Since then, travel to the uttermost part of the earth has boomed, especially on the Argentine side in the summer months. Other important economic sectors are sheep farming and petroleum, on both the Chilean and Argentine sides.

Chilean Patagonia

Some of the oldest archaeological evidence for human habitation on the entire continent comes from Magallanes, from volcanic rock shelters in and near Parque Nacional Pali Aike along the Argentine border. Pleistocene hunter-gatherers once stalked now-extinct species such as giant ground sloths and native American horses, but later adopted more broad-spectrum forms of subsistence that included marine and coastal resources. These peoples were the predecessors of today's few surviving Tehuelche and Kawésqar (Alacaluf) peoples, and the nearly extinct Selk'nam (Ona) and Yámana (Yahgan) who gathered shellfish on the coast and hunted guanaco and rhea with bows and arrows and *boleadoras*.

Spain's 16th-century colonization attempts failed, as did the initial Chilean and Argentine efforts, but the city of Punta Arenas finally took hold after 1848—thanks partly to the fortuitous discovery of gold in California just a year later. Gold fever subsided, but the introduction of sheep brought a wool and mutton boom that benefited from the Franco-Prussian War of the 1870s and helped create sprawling *estancias* that dominated the region's political, social, and economic life for nearly a century.

While the livestock industry hangs on, commercial fisheries, the state-run oil industry, and the tourist trade have superseded it in the regional economy. Even these industries, though, have proved vulnerable to fluctuations, declining reserves, and international developments beyond their control, but Magallanes is presently one of Chile's most prosperous areas, thanks partly to the Zona Franca free-trade zone that has even drawn immigrants from the Chilean heartland.

Ushuaia

Beneath the Martial range's serrated spires, on the Beagle Channel's north shore, the city of Ushuaia is both an end (the virtual terminus of the world's southernmost highway) and a beginning (the gateway to Antarctica). The surrounding countryside attracts activities-oriented visitors for hiking, mountain biking, fishing, and skiing. In the summer season, the city gets hundreds of thousands of visitors, many of them merely day-trippers from the hundreds of cruise ships that anchor here.

After more than two decades of economic growth and physical sprawl, the provincial capital is both declining and improving. On the one hand, the duty-free manufacturing, fishing, and tourist boom that transformed a onetime penal colony and naval base into a bustling city has weakened. On the other, it has spruced up the waterfront and restored historic buildings, some of them becoming hotels or B&Bs. The streets are cleaner (though Avenida San Martín is tourist-trap ugly) and there are more parks, plazas, and green spaces. Still, Ushuaia has particulate pollution problems because high winds kick up dust in its unpaved newer neighborhoods.

HISTORY

Ushuaia dates from 1870, when the Anglican South American Missionary Society decided to place the archipelago's first permanent European settlement here. Pioneer missionary Thomas Bridges and his descendants have left an enduring legacy in Bridges's Yahgan (Yámana) dictionary, his son Lucas's memoir, and the family *estancia* at nearby Harberton (the Yahgans whom Thomas Bridges hoped to save, though, succumbed to introduced diseases and conflict with other settlers).

Not long after Ushuaia's settlement, Argentina, alarmed by the British presence, moved to establish its own authority at Ushuaia and did so with a penal settlement for its most infamous criminals and political

TIERRA DEL FUEGO

USHUAIA

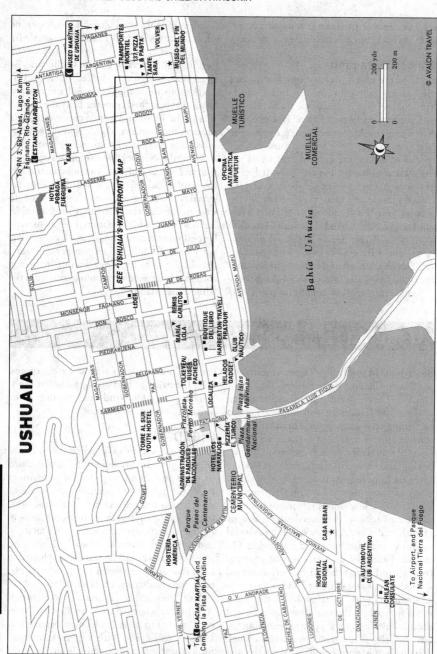

To RN 3; Srf. Areas, Lago Kami
Fagnano, Río Grande, and
ESTANCIA HARBERTON

MUSEO MARÍTIMO
DE USHUAIA

VAGANES

ANTÁRTIDA

ARGENTINA

TRANSPORTES
MONTIEL
137 PIZZA
TANTE & PASTA
SARA   VOLVER

MUSEO DEL FIN
DEL MUNDO

RIVADAVIA

MAGALLANES

KAUPÉ

GODOY

ROCA

AVENIDA SAN MARTÍN

MAIPÚ

HOTEL
POSADA
FUEGUINA

LASSERRE

GOBERNADOR DELOQUI

25 DE MAYO

AVENIDA

OFICINA
ANTÁRTICA
INFUETUR

MUELLE
TURÍSTICO

SEE "USHUAIA'S WATERFRONT" MAP

JUANA FADUL

9 DE JULIO

AVENIDA MAIPÚ

MUELLE
COMERCIAL

JM DE ROSAS

Bahía Ushuaia

SOLÍS

CAMPOS

MONSEÑOR FAGNANO

LÍDER

DON BOSCO

MARÍA
LOLA

REMIS
CARLITOS

BOUTIQUE
DEL LIBRO

HARBERTON TRAVEL /
PIRATOUR

PIEDRABUENA

BELGRANO

MAGALLANES

GOBERNADOR

PAZ

SARMIENTO

TORRE AL SUR
YOUTH HOSTEL

TOLKEYEN/
BUSES
PACHECO

HELADOS
GADGET

CLUB
NÁUTICO

Plaza Islas
Malvinas

LOCALIZA

Plazoleta
Perito Moreno

PATAGONIA

PASARELA LUIS FIQUE

ONAS

GOBERNADOR

ADMINISTRACIÓN
DE PARQUES
NACIONALES

PIZZERÍA
EL TURCO

HOTEL LOS
NARANJOS

Plaza
Gendarmería
Nacional

GOMEZ

Parque
Paseo del
Centenario

CEMENTERIO
MUNICIPAL

AVENIDA SAN MARTÍN

HOSTERÍA
AMÉRICA

DARWIN

To GLACIAR MARTIAL and
Camping la Pista del Andino

LUIS VERNET

PAZ

O V ANDRADE

FLORENCIA

SÁNCHEZ DE CABALLERO

LUGONES

12 DE OCTUBRE

HOSPITAL
REGIONAL

AVENIDA MALVINAS ARGENTINAS

3 DE AGOSTO

CASA BEBAN

AUTOMÓVIL
CLUB ARGENTINO

CHILEAN
CONSULATE

ONACHAGA

JAINEN

To Airport, and Parque
Nacional Tierra del Fuego

200 yds
200 m

© AVALON TRAVEL

undesirables. It remained a penal settlement until almost 1950, when Juan Domingo Perón's government created a major naval base to support Argentina's Antarctic claims. Since the 1976–1983 military dictatorship ended it has become a tourist destination, visited by cruise ships as well as overland travelers and air passengers who come to see the world's southernmost city.

ORIENTATION

Stretching east–west along the Beagle Channel's north shore, Ushuaia (pop. 64,107) is 3,220 kilometers south of Buenos Aires and 190 kilometers southwest of Río Grande, the island's only other city.

Bedecked with flowerbeds, the main thoroughfare is Avenida Maipú, part of RN 3, now expanded into a divided boulevard; it continues west to Bahía Lapataia in Parque Nacional Tierra del Fuego. The parallel Avenida San Martín, one block north, is the main commercial street; the focus of Ushuaia's nightlife, it gets gridlocked on summer nights as surely as any avenue in Buenos Aires. From the shoreline, the perpendicular northbound streets rise steeply—some so steeply that they become staircases.

SIGHTS

Even if it has leveled off, Ushuaia's economic boom provided the wherewithal to preserve and even restore some of the city's historic buildings. Two of them are now museums: Dating from 1903, the waterfront **Casa Fernández Valdés** (Avenida Maipú 175) houses the historical Museo del Fin del Mundo, while **Presidio de Ushuaia** (Yaganes and Gobernador Paz), dating from 1896, is now the misleadingly named Museo Marítimo (while not insignificant, its maritime exhibits are less interesting than those on the city's genesis as a penal colony).

Three blocks west of the Casa Fernández Valdés, dating from 1894, the classically Magellanic **Poder Legislativo** (Maipú 465) once housed the provincial legislature and is now part of the Museo del Fin del Mundo. Five blocks farther west, prisoners built the restored **Capilla Antigua** (Avenida Maipú and Rosas), a chapel dating from 1898. A branch of the municipal tourist office occupies the **Biblioteca Sarmiento** (1926) at San Martín 674, the city's first public library. At the west end of downtown, the waterfront **Casa Beban** (Avenida Malvinas Argentinas and 12 de Octubre) is a reassembled pioneer residence dating from

TIERRA DEL FUEGO

© WAYNE BERNHARDSON

A massive Carnival Lines ship dominates the passenger terminal at Ushuaia, Tierra del Fuego.

1913; it now houses the municipal Casa de la Cultura, a cultural center.

Museo del Fin del Mundo

Its block-style exterior handsomely restored, Ushuaia's evolving historical museum contains exhibits on the Yámana, Selk'nam, and other Fuegian Indians as well as on early European voyages. There remain permanent exhibits on the presidio, the Fique family's early general store, Banco de la Nación's original branch (which occupied the building for more than 60 years), and natural history, including run-of-the-mill taxidermy. Its celebrity artifact is a rare copy of Thomas Bridges's Yámana–English dictionary.

An open-air sector re-creates a Yámana encampment and dwellings alongside machinery used in early agriculture and forestry projects. The Museo del Fin del Mundo (Avenida Maipú 175, tel. 02901/42-1863, www.tierradelfuego.org.ar/museo, US$5 adults, US$2 students and retired people, free for children age 14 and under) also contains a bookstore–souvenir shop and a specialized library on southernmost Argentina, the surrounding oceans, and Antarctica. The exceptional website places much of this material online.

Hours are 9 A.M.–8 P.M. daily October–April, with guided tours at 11 A.M. and 2, 4, and 6 P.M.; the rest of the year, hours are noon–7 P.M. Monday–Saturday.

Admission to the museum includes access to the former Poder Legislativo (Provincial Legislature, Maipú 465). Both branches offer free guided tours several times daily.

C Museo Marítimo de Ushuaia

Misleadingly named, Ushuaia's maritime museum (Yaganes and Gobernador Paz, tel. 02901/43-7481, www.museomaritimo.com, US$12, US$8 for foreign students; Argentines and locals get a discount) most effectively tells the story of Ushuaia's inauspicious origins as a penal settlement for both civilian and military prisoners. Alarmed over the South American Missionary Society's incursions among the Beagle Channel's indigenous peoples, in 1884

BOUND FOR THE ICE

Since the Soviet Union's demise, Ushuaia has become the main jumping-off point for Antarctic excursions on Russian ice-breakers that, despite being chartered under U.S. officers, sometimes still show the hammer and sickle on their bows. For travelers with flexible schedules, it has been possible to make last-minute arrangements at huge discounts – no ship wants to sail with empty berths – but heavy demand has made it difficult to pay anything less than about US$4,000 for 9–14 days, including several days' transit across the stormy Drake Passage (seasickness medication advised).

On the waterfront Muelle Comercial, Ushuaia's **Oficina Antártida Infuetur** (tel. 02901/43-0015, antartida@tierradelfuego.org.ar) has the latest information on Antarctic cruises. At present, even last-minute arrangements go through Ushuaia travel agencies for the mid-November–mid-March season.

Argentina reinforced its territorial claims by building a military prison on Isla de los Estados (Staten Island), across the Strait of Lemaire at the southeastern tip of the Isla Grande.

Barely a decade later, in 1896, it established Ushuaia's civilian Cárcel de Reincidentes for repeat offenders; after finally deciding that Isla de los Estados was a hardship post even for prisoners, in 1902 the military moved its own facility to Ushuaia. Then, in 1911, the two institutions fused in this building, which held some of the country's most famous political prisoners, celebrated rogues, and notorious psychopaths of the first half of the 20th century, until it closed in 1947.

Divided into five two-story pavilions, with 380 cells intended to house one prisoner each, it held up to 600 prisoners at a time. Its most famous inmates were political detainees such as Russian anarchist bomber Simón Radowitzsky, who killed Buenos Aires police chief Ramón

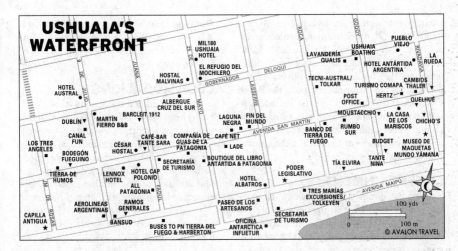

USHUAIA'S WATERFRONT

[Map labels: MIL180, USHUAIA HOTEL, EL REFUGIO DEL MOCHILERO, HOSTAL MALVINAS, GOBERNADOR, ALBERGUE CRUZ DEL SUR, BARCLEIT 1912, MARTÍN FIERRO B&B, DUBLÍN, HOTEL AUSTRAL, DE JULIO, JUANA, CANAL FUN, LOS TRES ANGELES, BODEGÓN FUEGUINO, CÉSAR HOSTAL, CAFÉ-BAR TANTE SARA, COMPAÑÍA DE GUAS DE LA PATAGONIA, TIERRA DE HUMOS, LENNOX HOTEL, HOTEL CAP POLONIO, SECRETARÍA DE TURISMO, ALL PATAGONIA, CAPILLA ANTIGUA, AEROLINEAS ARGENTINAS, RAMOS GENERALES, BANSUD, BUSES TO PN TIERRA DEL FUEGO & HARBERTON, LAGUNA NEGRA, FIN DEL MUNDO, AVENIDA SAN MARTÍN, CAFÉ NET, LADE, BOUTIQUE DEL LIBRO ANTÁRTIDA & PATAGONIA, HOTEL ALBATROS, PASEO DE LOS ARTESANOS, OFICINA ANTARCTICA INFUETUR, ROCA, GODOY, LAVANDERÍA QUALIS, USHUAIA BOATING, PUEBLO VIEJO, RIVADAVIA, LA RUEDA, HOTEL ANTÁRTIDA ARGENTINA, TECNI-AUSTRAL/TOLKAR, TURISMO COMAPA, CAMBIOS THALER, POST OFFICE, HERTZ, QUELHUÉ, MOUSTACCHIO, LA CASA DE LOS MARISCOS, CHICHO'S, BANCO DE TIERRA DEL FUEGO, RUMBO SUR, BUDGET, MUSEO DE MAQUETAS MUNDO YÁMANA, TÍA ELVIRA, TANTE NINA, PODER LEGISLATIVO, TRES MARÍAS EXCURSIONES/TOLKEYEN, AVENIDA MAIPÚ, SECRETARÍA DE TURISMO, LASSERRE, DELOQUI, MAYO, PADUL, M. DE ROSAS; scale bars: 100 yds, 100 m; © AVALON TRAVEL]

Falcón in 1909; Radical politicians Ricardo Rojas, Honorio Pueyrredón, and Mario Guido (the deceptively named Radicals are an ineffectual middle-class party); and Peronist politician Héctor Cámpora, who was briefly president in the 1970s.

Many, if not most, prisoners, however, were long-termers or lifers, such as the diminutive strangler Cayetano Santos Godino, a serial killer dubbed "El Orejudo" for his oversized ears (the nickname also describes a large-eared bat native to the archipelago). Julio Ordano has written a play, performed in Buenos Aires, about Santos Godino, titled *El Petiso Orejudo.*

Life-sized figures of the most infamous inmates, modified department-store dummies clad in prison stripes, occupy many cells. One intriguing exhibit is a wide-ranging comparison with other prisons that have become museums, such as San Francisco's Alcatraz and South Africa's Robben Island.

The museum does justify its name with a collection of scale models of ships that have played a role in local history, such as Magellan's galleon *Trinidad,* the legendary *Beagle,* the South American Missionary Society's three successive sailboats, each known as the *Allen Gardiner,* and Antarctic explorer and conqueror Roald Amundsen's *Fram.* In addition, there are materials on Argentina's Antarctic presence since the early 20th century, when the corvette *Uruguay* rescued Otto Nordenskjöld's Norwegian expedition, whose crew included the Argentine José María Sobral. On the grounds stands a full-size replica of the Faro San Juan de Salvamento, the Isla de los Estados (Staten Island) lighthouse that figures in Jules Verne's story "The Lighthouse at the End of the World."

In addition, the museum contains a philatelic room, natural history exhibits, and admirable accounts of the region's aboriginal peoples. It has only two drawbacks: There's too much to see in a single day, and the English translations could use some polishing—to say the least.

The Museo Marítimo is open 9 A.M.–8 P.M. daily October–April, and 10 A.M.–8 P.M. daily the rest of the year.

On request, staff will validate your admission ticket for another day; since there's so much here, splitting up sightseeing sessions is a good idea. It has an excellent book and souvenir shop as well as a *confitería* for snacks and coffee.

Museo de Maquetas Mundo Yámana

While both the Museo del Fin del Mundo and Museo Marítimo do a creditable job on Tierra del Fuego's indigenous heritage, this small private museum (Rivadavia 56, tel. 02901/42-2874, mundoyamana@infovia.com.ar, 10 A.M.–8 P.M. daily, US$4 adults, US$2 students and retired people, free for children under age 13) consists of skillfully assembled dioramas of pre-European life along the Beagle Channel, at a scale of 1:15. It also includes cartographic representations of the Yámana and their neighbors, interpretations of the European impact, and panels of historical photographs. The staff speak fluent English.

ENTERTAINMENT
Ushuaia has sprouted a plethora of pubs, some but not all with Irish aspirations or pretensions, such as **Dublin** (9 de Julio 168, tel. 02944/43-0744), with a standard menu of *minutas* (short orders).

SHOPPING
Boutique del Libro Antártida & Patagonia (25 de Mayo 62, tel. 2901/43-2117, www.antartidaypatagonia.com.ar) carries a wide choice of Argentine and imported books in Spanish, English, and other languages on the "uttermost part of the earth" and its surroundings, including current Moon handbooks at moderate markups; there are also novels for that long voyage across the Drake Passage to Antarctica. Relocated to more spacious quarters, its other **Boutique del Libro** (San Martín 1120, tel. 02901/42-4750) offers an excellent selection of Spanish-language books and a smaller choice of English-language titles.

Along with many similar venues along Ushuaia's main shopping street, **Fin del Mundo** (San Martín 505, tel. 02901/42-2971) has many kitschy souvenirs but also maps and books. Nearby **Laguna Negra** (San Martín 513, tel. 02901/43-1144) specializes in locally produced chocolates.

Tierra de Humos (San Martín 861, tel. 02901/43-3050, www.tierradehumos.com.ar) stocks locally produced leather, fleeces, handicrafts, and silverwork. For purchases directly from the artisans, there's the **Paseo de los Artesanos** (Maipú and Lasserre), at the entrance to the Muelle Comercial port.

Quelhué (San Martín 214, tel. 02901/43-5882, www.quelhue.com.ar) carries a fine selection of Argentine wines and imported duty-free liquors.

ACCOMMODATIONS
Ushuaia has abundant accommodations, but it has long been one of the most expensive destinations in the country. Demand is also high, especially in the summer months of January and February, when prices rise and reservations are advisable. One heartening development is the proliferation of good but moderately priced backpacker hostels and the arrival of several bed-and-breakfasts—known by the semi-English acronym ByB—some of them excellent alternatives.

US$10-25
Eight kilometers west of Ushuaia on the Lapataia road, the **Camping Municipal** has free but limited facilities (fire pits and pit toilets only). A stiff climb to the northwest of downtown, **La Pista del Andino** (Alem 2873, tel. 02901/43-5890 or 02901/15-56-8626, www.lapistadelandino.com.ar, US$6 pp) has slightly sloping sites at its ski area; the first transfer from downtown or the airport is free. Guests with sleeping bags can crash in the *refugio* above its bar-restaurant but shouldn't expect to get to sleep early.

US$25-50
Perched at downtown's western edge, with spectacular Beagle Channel views, HI affiliate **Torre al Sur Youth Hostel** (Gobernador Paz 1437, tel. 02901/43-0745, www.torrealsur.com.ar, US$14–15 pp dorm) has been one of Argentina's finest backpacker facilities, but overcrowding and noise have meant mixed reviews recently. Rooms have two or four beds as well as lockers; there's hot water, Internet access, and free luggage storage.

The HI affiliate 🄲 **Albergue Los Cormoranes** (Kamshen 788, tel. 02902/42-3459, www.loscormoranes.com, US$13–16 pp dorm, US$53–66 d with private bath, with breakfast) has attractive common areas, including a wind-sheltered garden, and better sleeping facilities than Torre al Sur. Most easily reached by climbing Don Bosco to its end and then taking a left, it's about eight steep blocks north of the waterfront (arrival transfers are free).

The more central **Albergue Cruz del Sur** (Deloqui 636, tel. 02901/43-4099, www.xdelsur.com.ar, US$16 pp dorm) is an independent hostel with four-, six-, or eight-bed rooms; there are also cable TV, Internet access, two kitchens, and a free initial pickup. Guests also get a series of discounts and specials at various services around town.

Half a block from the Lider bus terminal, the fast-expanding **Freestyle Backpackers Hostel** (Gobernador Paz 866, tel. 02901/43-2874, www.ushuaiafreestyle.com, US$16–19 pp dorm) is a gleaming purpose-built hostel with youthful energy, a spacious lounge and kitchen facilities, and secondary amenities including laundry service and parking.

US$50-100

On the hillside, the contemporary ◖ **Martín Fierro B&B** (9 de Julio 175, tel. 02901/43-0525, www.martinfierrobyb.com.ar, US$37 s, US$53 d) has two bunks in each of several small but well-designed rooms with shared baths. Host Javier Jury has created tasteful common areas that are simultaneously spacious and cozy, and the breakfast is varied and filling; the tiny shower stalls, though, make bathing with a friend impossible without being *really* intimate. Two downstairs "apart-hotel" rooms (US$53 s, US$74 d), with separate kitchens, sleep up to four people each.

Only a short walk from downtown, in an oasis neighborhood of sheltered gardens, ◖ **Galeazzi-Basily B&B** (Gobernador Valdés 323, tel. 2901/42-3213, www.avesdelsur.com.ar, US$37 s, US$52 d, with shared bath; US$69 s or d with private bath) is a comfortable family house that also has exterior *cabañas*. The hosts speak English fluently and are a great source of information on the rest of the island, including Estancia Harberton.

Pueblo Viejo (Deloqui 242, tel. 02901/43-

2098, www.puebloviejo.info, US$60 d with shared bath) is a B&B built on the foundations of an early Ushuaia house; replicating the traditional Magellanic style, it has added innovative contemporary touches. The street level rooms are more luminous than their semi-basement counterparts.

Responsive **Hostería América** (Gobernador Paz 1665, tel. 02901/42-3358, www.hosteriaamerica.com.ar, US$79 s, US$92 d) is a decent choice in a fine location above the Parque Paseo del Centenario.

Hostal Malvinas (Gobernador Deloqui 615, tel./fax 02901/42-2626, www.hostalmalvinas.net, US$70 s, US$80 d) provides simple but quiet and immaculate rooms with large baths and no frills—not even TV—but croissants and coffee are free all day.

Rehabbed **Hotel César** (Avenida San Martín 753, tel. 02901/42-1460, www.hotelcesarhostal.com.ar, US$58 s, US$87 d) has become one of the better values in a congested central area.

Just uphill from Martín Fierro, **Hotel Austral** (9 de Julio 250, tel. 02901/42-2223, www.hotel-austral.com.ar, US$84 s, US$95 d) is a 10-room hotel with soaring, light-filled common areas that offer panoramic views of the Beagle Channel (at least until new constructions block them some years from now). Painted in pastels, the rooms themselves are spacious and comfortable.

US$100-200

Hillside **Hotel Ushuaia** (Lasserre 933, tel. 02901/43-0671, www.ushuaiahotel.com.ar, US$90 s, US$120 d, with breakfast) is a good value in its price range.

Only its busy location detracts from the bright and cheerful **Hotel Cap Polonio** (San Martín 746, tel. 02901/42-2131, www.hotelcappolonio.com.ar, US$120 s or d, with breakfast). All rooms are carpeted and have cable TV; the private baths have tubs as well as showers, and there's a good restaurant *confitería*.

Though it's not really a view hotel, the 30-room **Mil 810 Ushuaia Hotel** (25 de Mayo 245, tel. 02901/43-7710, www.hotel1810.com,

US$101–149 s or d) is a central boutique hotel that occupies a prominent hillside site just a couple of blocks from the waterfront, close enough to walk everywhere but just beyond the congested center.

From its cul-de-sac perch, **〔** **Hotel Posada Fueguina** (Lasserre 438, tel. 02901/42-3467, www.posadafueguina.com.ar, US$116–182 s, US$182–234 d) offers awesome views along with cable TV and similar amenities. It has added *cabañas* to handle any overflow.

The spacious, rejuvenated **Hotel Albatros** (Avenida Maipú 505, tel. 02901/43-3446, www.albatroshotel.com.ar, US$195 s or d) is the pick of the waterfront accommodations.

In dense woods about 1.5 kilometers northeast of downtown, **〔** **Patagonia Villa Lodge** (Bahía Buen Suceso 563, tel. 02901/43-5937, www.patagoniavilla.com, US$200–240 s, US$260–300 d) has just five rooms in luminous semidetached cabins with a magnificently rustic architecture and comforts such as whirlpool tubs (in some, at least) and Wi-Fi. There is one double (US$110 s, US$130 d) that lacks significant natural light but suffers only by comparison with the others; elsewhere, it would count among the best in town. Owner Luciana Lupotti, a former Florida exchange student, speaks fluent English. Rates include airport pickup and drop-off.

Over US$200

Downtown's nearly new **Lennox Hotel** (San Martín 776, tel./fax 02901/43-6430, www.lennoxhotel.com.ar, US$228 s or d) has midsized rooms with either Beagle Channel or mountain views, but even with amenities such as whirlpool baths and Wi-Fi it's hard to think it's worth more than double the price of, say, Hotel César. It also follows the dubious practice of charging foreigners more than Argentines.

The interior is more impressive than the surprisingly plain exterior at the luxury **Hotel del Glaciar** (Luis Martial 2355, tel. 02901/43-0640, www.hoteldelglaciar.com, US$209–219 s or d). At Km 3.5 on the road to the Martial Glacier, each room has either a mountain view or an ocean view (which is slightly more

expensive), but it's questionable whether staffing is sufficient for a hotel of its category—and price.

About four kilometers west of downtown, in a still-developing neighborhood that's mostly residential, family-run **〔** **Hostería Tierra de Leyendas** (Tierra de Vientos 2448, tel. 02901/44-3565, www.tierradeleyendas.com.ar, US$189–229 s or d) is a new five-room boutique hotel with expansive views of the Beagle Channel. There are plans to add no more than two additional rooms. Owner Sebastián García Cosoleto, who cooked for eight years at the Buenos Aires Marriott Plaza Hotel, is also chef of its French-influenced restaurant (open for dinner only, reservations obligatory for nonguests).

At Km 3 on the glacier road, the **Hotel y Resort Las Hayas** (Luis Martial 1650, tel. 02901/43-0710, www.lashayas.com.ar, US$264–356 s or d) enjoys nearly all conceivable luxuries, including an elaborate buffet breakfast, a gym, a sauna, a hot tub, and a heated indoor pool; it picks up guests at the airport and offers a regular shuttle to and from downtown. Behind its surprisingly utilitarian exterior, some of its 93 rooms and suites suffer from hideous decor—the wallpaper is to cringe at—but all are comfortable, and its staff members are highly professional.

FOOD

Although the 2001–2002 peso collapse briefly reined in prices, they've since rebounded, and there are some truly expensive dining choices; the financially challenged should look for *tenedor libre* specials, or be cautious with extras like dessert and coffee.

Hotel Cap Polonio's **Marcopolo** (San Martín 730, tel. 02901/43-0001) is a café-restaurant that serves excellent coffee, chocolate, and croissants for breakfast—try the *submarino* for a cold morning's pickup. **Café de la Esquina** (Avenida San Martín 602, tel. 02901/42-3676) is a popular meeting place with similar offerings, as well as sandwiches for late-afternoon tea.

Open for lunch only on weekdays, but with Saturday evening hours, **Pizzería El Turco**

(San Martín 1440, tel. 02901/42-4711) is good and moderately priced but lacks variety. Well-established **Barcleit 1912** (Fadul 148, tel. 02901/43-3105, lunch and dinner daily) has fallen a step behind some of the other pizzerias but also offers a variety of moderately priced short orders.

In luminous quarters, **Tante Sara** (San Martín 175, tel. 02901/42-4118, lunch and dinner daily) made its name in sweets and snacks, which are still abundant, but it also produces a limited menu of well-crafted lunch and dinner dishes such as a rib eye with a malbec sauce (US$11). For breakfast, coffee, sandwiches, and desserts, try its **Café-Bar Tante Sara** (San Martín 701, tel. 02901/42-3912).

Formerly part of Tante Sara, now under new ownership, (◖ **137 Pizza & Pasta** (San Martín 137, tel./fax 02901/43-5005, lunch and dinner daily) still sets the pace in diverse pastas with a broad selection of imaginative sauces, as well as pizza. Most entrées, such as ravioli with king crab, fall into the US$7–10 range, with sauces extra.

Facing the waterfront, (◖ **Ramos Generales** (Maipú 749, tel. 02901/42-4317, www.ramos-generalesushuaia.com, noon–11 P.M. daily, US$8–15) is a bar and restaurant that recreates a pioneer general store with humor and museum-quality artifacts. It may romanticize the era, but its snacks (including sandwiches) and sweets reinforce the style to make it a must for any Ushuaia visitor. The menu is not elaborate, but the quality is outstanding.

Also in an artfully restored historic house, **Bodegón Fueguino** (San Martín 859, tel. 02901/43-1972, lunch and dinner daily) specializes in Fuegian lamb, prepared in a variety of styles for around US$10, but it also has seafood dishes, tangy beef empanadas, and good desserts.

La Rueda (San Martín 193, tel. 02901/43-6540, lunch and dinner daily) charges only slightly more for its own buffet *parrillada*. The well-established **Moustacchio** (Avenida San Martín 298, tel. 02901/42-3308, lunch and dinner daily) stresses seafood but also serves beef and other meats.

© WAYNE BERNHARDSON

Ushuaia's Ramos Generales is a wine bar/restaurant that mimics a pioneer general store.

Ushuaia has a wider choice of seafood restaurants than almost any other Argentine provincial city. **La Casa de los Mariscos** (San Martín 232, tel. 02901/42-1928, lunch and dinner daily) specializes in *centolla* (king crab) but has many other fish and shellfish options in the US$10–15 range. Looking like a Buenos Aires antique shop housed in a classic Magellanic residence, tango-themed **Volver** (Avenida Maipú 37, tel. 02901/42-3977, lunch and dinner daily) doesn't quite achieve its potential—the fish and seafood dishes can be disappointingly bland.

With a 30-year history and portside views, **Tante Nina** (Gobernador Godoy 15, tel. 02901/43-2444, www.tanteninarestaurant.com. ar, lunch and dinner daily) focuses on Fuegian fish and seafood; the food is fine and the service is efficient, but the ambience feels institutional. **Chicho's** (Rivadavia 72, tel. 02901/42-3469, lunch and dinner daily) also handles large crowds efficiently, serving dishes such as king crab (US$16), hake (US$16), and Fuegian trout stuffed with crab and shrimp (US$12).

Other possibilities include the **El Náutico** (Avenida Maipú and Belgrano, tel. 02901/43-0415, lunch and dinner daily), where entrées start around US$10–12; **Tía Elvira** (Avenida Maipú 349, tel. 02901/42-4725); and ☾ **Kaupé** (Roca 470, tel. 02901/42-2704, lunch and dinner daily), which serves an exclusively (and exclusive) à la carte menu. Kaupé has specialties such as king crab, exquisite lemon ice cream, carpaccio, and wine by the glass. Even post-devaluation, a full meal here can cost well upwards of US$35 pp, but some knowledgeable locals suggest the menu has stagnated.

Equally top-of-the-line—both literally and geographically—is the dining room with a panoramic view at ☾ **Chez Manu** (Luis Martial 2135, tel. 02901/42-3253, lunch and dinner daily), immediately below Hotel del Glaciar. Using local ingredients such as king crab and lamb, the French-run restaurant is *the* place for a truly elaborate meal at equally elaborate prices: US$30 and up. This is one Ushuaia restaurant with food to match its views, although portions are on the small side.

On a promontory, in a recycled building that once transmitted Argentina's first-ever color TV program—the 1978 World Cup—☾ **María Lola** (Deloqui 1048, tel. 02901/42-1185, www.marialolaresto.com.ar) may be Ushuaia's best restaurant, period. For items ranging from relatively simple but delicate pastas to more elaborate dishes such as stir-fried Patagonian lamb with vegetables, prices range US$10–25. The bar serves a diversity of mixed drinks at moderate prices. Open for lunch and dinner, it's closed Monday.

In bright new quarters, **Helados Gadget** (Avenida San Martín 1256, tel. 02901/43-4864) has all the conventional Argentine ice cream flavors—good enough in their own right—but also incorporates regional specialties such as *calafate* and, occasionally, rhubarb.

INFORMATION

Ushuaia's well-organized municipal **Secretaría de Turismo** (Maipú s/n, tel. 02901/43-7666, www.turismoushuaia.com) has moved its main office to a spacious new building opposite the tourist pier but will keep its other office (San Martín 674, tel. 02901/42-4550) in operation. Hours are 8 A.M.–10 P.M. weekdays and 9 A.M.–8 P.M. weekends and holidays. English-speaking staff are normally present. There's also an airport subsidiary (tel. 02901/42-3970) that's open for arriving flights only.

The provincial **Instituto Fueguino de Turismo (Infuetur)** has ground-floor offices at Hotel Albatros (Avenida Maipú 505, tel. 02901/42-3340, info@tierradelfuego.org.ar).

Motorists can consult the **Automóvil Club Argentino** (ACA, Malvinas Argentinas and Onachaga, tel. 02901/42-1121).

The **Administración de Parques Nacionales** (APN, Avenida San Martín 1395, tel. 02901/42-1315, tierradelfuego@apn.gov.ar) is open 9 A.M.–noon Monday–Friday.

At the waterfront Muelle Comercial, the **Oficina Antártica Infuetur** (tel. 02901/42-1423, antartida@tierradelfuego.org.ar, 8 A.M.–5 P.M. daily in summer, 9 A.M.–4 P.M. Mon.–Fri. the rest of the year) has the latest information on Antarctic sailings and tours.

TIERRA DEL FUEGO

SERVICES

Several banks have ATMs, including **BanSud** (Avenida Maipú 781) and **Banco de Tierra del Fuego** (San Martín 396); the latter accepts travelers checks at a 3 percent commission. **Cambio Thaler** (Avenida San Martín 209, tel. 02901/42-1911) also takes 3 percent but keeps longer hours (9:30 A.M.–1:30 P.M. and 4–8 P.M. Mon.–Fri., 10 A.M.–1:30 P.M. and 5:30–8 P.M. Sat., 5:30–8 P.M. Sun.).

Correo Argentino (San Martín 309) is the post office.

Café Net (San Martín 565, tel. 02901/42-2720) provides telephone, fax, and Internet access, including Wi-Fi.

The **Chilean consulate** (Jainén 50, tel. 02901/43-0970) is open 9 A.M.–1 P.M. weekdays only.

The **Dirección Nacional de Migraciones** (Beauvoir 1536, tel. 02901/42-2334) is open 9 A.M.–5 P.M. weekdays only.

Los Tres Angeles (Juan Manuel de Rosas 139, tel. 02901/42-2687) offers quick and reliable laundry service but can be overwhelmed in high season; try instead **Lavanderías Qualis** (Deloqui 368, tel. 02901/42-1996).

The **Hospital Regional** (Maipú and 12 de Octubre, tel. 02901/42-2950, tel. 107 for emergencies) handles medical issues.

GETTING THERE

Ushuaia has air links to Buenos Aires and intermediate points, and improving overland transportation from mainland Argentina and from Chile. Maritime transportation is either tenuous or expensive.

Air

Aerolíneas Argentinas (Maipú 823, tel. 02901/42-1218) normally flies two or three times daily to Buenos Aires's Aeroparque, sometimes via Río Gallegos, El Calafate, or Trelew. Occasional Buenos Aires–bound flights land at the international airport Ezeiza instead of Aeroparque.

The Chilean carrier LAN flies several times weekly to Punta Arenas, Chile (Ushuaia's only scheduled international service), while its affiliate LAN Argentina serves Aeroparque and other destinations. LAN tickets can be purchased at any local travel agency, including **All Patagonia** (Juana Fadul 60, tel. 02901/43-3622, www.allpatagonia.com), **Canal Fun** (9 de Julio 118, Local 1, tel. 02901/43-7395, www.canalfun.com), **Rumbo Sur** (San Martín 350, tel. 02901/42-1139, www.rumbosur.com.ar), **Tolkar** (Roca 157, Local 1, tel. 02901/43-1408, www.tolkarturismo.com.ar), and **Tolkeyén** (San Martín 1267, tel. 02901/43-7073, www.tolkeyenpatagonia.com).

In the Galería Albatros, **LADE** (Avenida San Martín 564, Local 5, tel. 02901/42-1123) flies irregularly to Río Gallegos, El Calafate, Comodoro Rivadavia, Bariloche, and Buenos Aires.

For Puerto Williams, across the Beagle Channel in Chile, it may be possible to arrange a private charter through the **Aeroclub Ushuaia** (tel. 02901/42-1717 or 02901/42-1892, www.aeroclubushuaia.org.ar).

Bus

At the foot of Juana Fadul, a new parking area now serves as a bus station, even though companies have their offices elsewhere. **Lider** (Gobernador Paz 921, tel. 02901/43-6421) goes to Tolhuin (1.5 hours, US$7) and Río Grande (3.5 hours, US$13) eight times daily Monday–Saturday and six times daily Sunday and holidays. **Transportes Montiel** (Deloqui 110, tel. 02901/42-1366) goes to Tolhuin and Río six or seven times daily except Sundays and holidays, when it goes five times only.

Represented by Tolkar Turismo (Roca 157, tel. 02901/43-1408), **Tecni-Austral** goes at 5 A.M. Monday–Saturday to Río Grande, sometimes continuing to Río Gallegos (13 hours, US$42) and others to Punta Arenas, Chile (12 hours, US$52). At the same office, **Buses Marga** goes at 6 A.M. daily to Río Gallegos. **Buses Pacheco** (San Martín 1267, tel. 02901/43-0727) goes to Punta Arenas Tuesday, Thursday, and Saturday, with connections to Puerto Natales.

Sea

The Chilean cruisers MV *Mare Australis* and MV *Via Australis* offer luxury sightseeing cruises to Puerto Williams, Cape Horn, and through the fjords of Chilean Tierra del Fuego to Punta Arenas; while not intended as simple transportation, they can serve that purpose for those who can afford them. It's possible to either disembark in Punta Arenas (four days) or return to Ushuaia (in a week). These cruises are usually booked far in advance, but on occasion—normally just before Christmas—it may be possible to make on-the-spot arrangements.

International political obstacles continue to complicate regular transportation across the Beagle Channel to Puerto Williams. Nevertheless, **Ushuaia Boating** (Godoy 190, tel. 02901/43-6193, www.ushuaiaboating.com.ar) occasionally shuttles passengers across the channel to Puerto Navarino and then overland to Puerto Williams (2 hours; US$130 pp, US$240 round-trip).

GETTING AROUND
To the Airport
A causeway links the city with **Aeropuerto Internacional Malvinas Argentinas,** which has the country's highest airport taxes: US$5 for flights elsewhere in Argentina, and US$20 for international flights. Taxis and *remises* cost about US$6 with **Remiscar** (San Martín 995, tel. 02901/42-2222, www.remiscar.com.ar).

Bus
From the new staging point at Avenida Maipú and Juana Fadul, several bus companies all charge around US$14 pp round-trip to Parque Nacional Tierra del Fuego; it's normally possible to camp in the park and return the following day. The most frequent services are with **Pasarela Tour** (tel. 02901/42-4582) and **Buses Eben-Ezer** (tel. 02901/43-1862), which between them have 18 buses daily to the park between 8 A.M. and 7 P.M., returning between 9 A.M. and 8 P.M. There are also services to the chairlift at the Glaciar Martial (US$7 pp), normally with a minimum of two passengers, and to Estancia Harberton (US$42 pp round-trip).

Car Rental
Car rentals start around US$38 per day and range up to US$143 per day for 4WD vehicles. Some agencies offer unlimited mileage within Tierra del Fuego Province, but others limit mileage to as few as 100 kilometers per day, so verify it before signing any contract.

Rental agencies include **Budget** (Gobernador Godoy 45, 1st floor, tel. 02901/43-7373, ushuaia@budgetargentina.com), **Hertz** (San Martín 245, tel. 02901/43-7529, hertzushuaia@infovia.com.ar), and **Localiza** (Sarmiento 81, tel. 02901/43-7780, localizaush@speedy.com.ar).

Vicinity of Ushuaia

Ushuaia has more than a dozen travel agencies offering excursions in and around Ushuaia, ranging from double-decker-bus city tours (1 hour, US$8) to Parque Nacional Tierra del Fuego (4–5 hours, US$30) and historic Estancia Harberton (8 hours, US$65). They also organize activities such as hiking, climbing, horseback riding, fishing, and mountain biking.

Local operators include **All Patagonia** (Juana Fadul 60, tel. 02901/43-3622, www.allpatagonia.com), which is the AmEx representative; **Canal Fun** (9 de Julio 118, Local 1, tel. 02901/43-7395, www.canalfun.com); **Rumbo Sur** (San Martín 350, tel. 02901/42-1139, www.rumbosur.com.ar);

Tolkar (Roca 157, Local 1, tel. 02901/43-1408, www.tolkarturismo.com.ar); and **Tolkeyén** (San Martín 1267, tel. 02901/43-7073, www.tolkeyen-patagonia.com).

The **Compañía de Guías de Patagonia** (San Martín 628, tel. 02901/43-7753, www.companiadeguias.com.ar) specializes in trekking.

BEAGLE CHANNEL BOAT EXCURSIONS
From the Muelle Turístico, at the foot of Lasserre, there are boat trips to Beagle Channel wildlife sites such as **Isla de los Lobos,** home to the southern sea lion (*Otaria flavescens*) and

the rarer southern fur seal (*Arctocephalus australis*), and **Isla de Pájaros,** a cormorant nesting site. These excursions cost around US$40 pp for a 2.5-hour trip on oversized catamarans such as the *Ana B, Ezequiel B,* and *Luciano Beta.* With extensions to the penguin colony at Estancia Harberton and a visit to the *estancia* itself, the cost is about US$68.

Rumbo Sur and Tolkeyén sell tickets for these excursions from offices at the foot of the Muelle Turístico, where Héctor Monsalve's **Tres Marías Excursiones** (tel./fax 02901/42-1897, www.tresmariasweb.com) operates four-hour trips (US$43–52 pp) on smaller vessels (four passengers minimum, 10 maximum) that can approach Isla de Lobos more closely than the large catamarans. They also land on Isla Bridges, a small but diverse island with cormorant colonies, shell mounds, and even the odd penguin.

FERROCARRIL AUSTRAL FUEGUINO

During Ushuaia's early days, prison labor built a short-line, narrow-gauge steam-driven railroad west into what is now Parque Nacional Tierra del Fuego to haul the timber that built the city. Only a few years ago, commercial interests rehabilitated part of the rail bed to create an antiseptic tourist version of the earlier line that pretty much ignores its unsavory history to focus on the Cañadon del Toro's admittedly appealing forest scenery.

The train leaves from the **Estación del Fin del Mundo** (tel. 02901/43-1600, www.trendelfindelmundo.com.ar), eight kilometers west of Ushuaia at the municipal campground. There are two to five departures daily October–mid-April; the rest of the year there's only one, or perhaps two if demand is sufficient. The two-hour-plus excursion costs US$24 pp in tourist class, US$48 pp in first class, and US$66 pp with food service. Fares do not include the US$14 park entry fee.

SKI AREAS

Most visitors see Ushuaia in summer, but it's also becoming a winter sports center given its proximity to the mountains. Downhill skiing, snowboarding, cross-country skiing, and even dogsledding are possibilities.

The major ski event is mid-August's **Marcha Blanca,** which symbolically repeats Argentine liberator José de San Martín's winter crossing of the Andes from Mendoza to assist his Chilean counterpart Bernardo O'Higgins against the Spaniards. Luring upwards of 400 skiers, it starts from the Las Cotorras cross-country area and climbs to Paso Garibaldi, the 430-meter pass between the Sierra Alvear and the Sierra Lucas Bridges. Ideally, it takes place August 17, the anniversary of San Martín's death. (Argentine novelist Tomás Eloy Martínez has called his countrymen "cadaver cultists" for their apparent obsession with celebrating the death dates rather than the birth dates of their national icons.)

There are two downhill ski areas. The aging **Centro de Deportes Invernales Luis Martial** (Luis Martial 3995, tel. 02901/15-61-3890 or 02901/15-56-8587, esquiush@tierradelfuego.org.ar), seven kilometers northwest of town at the end of the road, has a single 1,130-meter run on a 23-degree slope, with a double-seat chairlift capable of carrying 224 skiers per hour.

East of Ushuaia, **Cerro Castor** (RN 3 Km 27, www.cerrocastor.com) has up-to-the-minute facilities, including four lifts and 15 different runs. In high season (July), lift tickets cost US$28–41 per day, with discounts for multiday packages; in low and shoulder seasons, there are additional discounts.

Other areas east of town, along RN 3, are for cross-country skiers. These include **Tierra Mayor** (Km 21, tel. 02901/43-7454, www.tierramayor.com), **Las Cotorras** (Km 26, tel. 02901/49-9300), **Haruwen** (Km 35, tel./fax 02901/43-1099, www.haruwen.com.ar), and several newer options. All of them rent equipment and offer transfers from Ushuaia.

◀ ESTANCIA HARBERTON

Historic Harberton dates from 1886, when missionary Thomas Bridges resigned from Ushuaia's Anglican mission to settle at his new *estancia* at

Downeast, later renamed for the Devonshire hometown of his wife Mary Ann Varder. Thomas Bridges, of course, was the author of the famous English-Yámana dictionary, and their son Lucas continued their literary tradition with *The Uttermost Part of the Earth,* an extraordinary memoir of a boyhood and life among the indigenous Yámana and Ona (Selk'nam).

Harberton continues to be a family enterprise—its present manager and part-owner, Tommy Goodall, is Thomas Bridges's great-grandson. While the wool industry that spawned it has declined in recent years, the *estancia,* which still has about 1,000 cattle, has opened its doors to organized English- and Spanish-language tours of its grounds and outbuildings; these include the family cemetery, flower gardens, woolshed, woodshop, boathouse, and a native botanical garden whose Yámana-style lean-tos are more realistic than their Disneyfied counterparts along the Ferrocarril Austral Fueguino tourist train. Photographs in the woolshed illustrate the process of cutting firewood with axes and transporting it by raft and oxcart, and the tasks of gathering and shearing sheep.

In addition, American biologist Rae Natalie Prosser (Tommy Goodall's wife) has created the **Museo Acatushún de Aves y Mamíferos Marinos Australes** (www.acatushun.com, 10 A.M.–7 P.M. daily mid-Oct.–mid-Apr., US$4), a bone museum stressing the region's marine mammals but also seabirds and a few shorebirds. It's also possible to visit Magellanic penguin rookeries at Isla Martillo (Yecapasela) with Piratour for US$18 pp; a small colony of gentoo penguins has established itself on the island, making this a more intriguing trip for those who've seen Magellanic penguins elsewhere.

Estancia Harberton (contact Alejandro Galeazzi, tel. 02901/42-3123 in Ushuaia, alejandrogaleazzi@speedy.com.ar, www.estanciaharberton.com) is 85 kilometers east of Ushuaia via paved RN 3 and gravel RC-j, but work has stopped on a new coastal road from Ushuaia that would shorten the distance. The *estancia* is open for guided tours (US$8 pp) 10 A.M.–7 P.M. daily mid-October–mid-April except Christmas, New Year's Day, and Easter. Because of Harberton's isolation, there is no telephone, and email communications—which require a trip to Ushuaia—can be slow.

With written permission, free **camping** is permitted at unimproved sites; the *estancia* has also remodeled the former cookhouse (one double room and another with a bunk bed, with shared bath, US$70–90 pp) and the shepherds house (two triple rooms with private baths, US$90–120 pp). Dinner or lunch costs an additional US$25 pp.

Harberton's teahouse, **Mánacatush,** serves a three-course lunch without drinks for US$25. A separate afternoon tea is offered for nonguests, with a four-guest minimum. Its restaurant, **Parrilla Acawaia,** serves clients on the penguin tour.

In summer, several companies provide round-trip transportation from Ushuaia, but renting a car is more convenient. From Ushuaia's Muelle Turístico, **Piratour** (tel. 02901/15-60-4646, www.piratour.com.ar) offers a US$66 package with overland transportation and a visit to the penguin colony. It also operates out of **Harberton Travel** (San Martín 1162, tel. 02901/42-2367).

Catamaran tours from Ushuaia are more expensive and spend less time at Harberton but do include the farm-tour fee.

Parque Nacional Tierra del Fuego

For pilgrims to the uttermost part of the earth, mecca is Parque Nacional Tierra del Fuego's Bahía Lapataia, where RN 3 ends on the Beagle Channel's north shore. It's a worthy goal, but sadly most visitors see only the area on and around the highway because most of the park's mountainous interior, with its alpine lakes, limpid rivers, blue-tinged glaciers, and jagged summits, is closed to public access.

GEOGRAPHY AND CLIMATE

About 18 kilometers west of Ushuaia, Parque Nacional Tierra del Fuego hugs the Chilean border as its 63,000 hectares stretch from the Beagle Channel north across Lago Fagnano (Kami). Elevations range from sea level to 1,450 meters on the summit of Monte Vinciguerra.

The park has a maritime climate, with frequent high winds. Rainfall is moderate, about 750 millimeters per year, but humidity is high, as cool temperatures inhibit evapotranspiration—the summer average is only about 10°C. The record maximum temperature is 31°C, while the minimum is a fairly mild -12°C. At sea level, snow rarely sticks, but higher elevations have permanent snowfields and glaciers.

FLORA AND FAUNA

As in southernmost Chile, thick southern beech forests cover the Argentine sector of Tierra del Fuego. Along the coast, the deciduous *lenga* (*Nothofagus pumilio*) and the Magellanic evergreen *coigüe* (*Nothofagus betuloides*) are the main tree species; at higher elevations, the stunted, deciduous *ñirre* (*Nothofagus antarctica*) forms nearly pure stands. In some low-lying areas, where cool annual temperatures inhibit complete decomposition, dead plant material compresses into *sphagnum* peat bogs with a cover of ferns and other moisture-loving plants; the insectivorous *Drosera uniflora* swallows unsuspecting bugs.

Argentina's first coastal national park, Parque Nacional Tierra del Fuego has a seashore protected by thick kelp beds that help incubate fish fry. Especially around Bahía Ensenada and Bahía Lapataia, the shoreline and inshore waters swarm with cormorants, grebes, gulls, kelp geese, oystercatchers, flightless and flying steamer ducks, snowy sheathbills, and terns. The black-browed albatross skims the Beagle's waters, while the Andean condor sometimes soars overhead. Marine mammals, mostly sea lions but also fur seals and elephant seals, cavort in the ocean. The rare southern sea otter (*Lutra felina*) may exist here.

Inland areas are fauna-poor, though foxes and guanacos are present in small numbers. The most conspicuous mammals are the European rabbit and the Canadian beaver, both of which were introduced for their pelts but have proved to be pests.

◖ GLACIAR MARTIAL

Technically within park boundaries but also within walking distance of Ushuaia, the Glaciar Martial is the area's best single hike, offering expansive views of the Beagle Channel and even the jagged peaks of Chile's Isla Navarino. Reached by the zigzag Camino al Glaciar (also known as Luis Martial) that climbs northwest out of town, the trailhead begins at the Aerosilla del Glaciar, the ski area's chairlift, which operates 9 A.M.–7 P.M. daily. The 1.2-kilometer chairlift (US$6 pp) reduces the two-hour climb to the foot of the glacier by half. In summer there are occasional minibuses to the lift (9 A.M.–9 P.M., US$7 roundtrip) with Pasarela, Eben Ezer, and Bellavista, leaving from the corner of Avenida Maipú and Juana Fadul. Although it is easy to follow, the trail—especially the middle segment—is steep, and the descent requires particular caution because of loose rocks and soil. There is no admission charge to this sector.

OTHER SIGHTS AND ACTIVITIES

Where freshwater Lago Roca drains into the sea at Bahía Lapataia, the park's main sector has several short nature trails and a few longer ones; most of the backcountry is off-limits to casual hikers. Slightly less than one kilometer long, the **Senda Laguna Negra** uses a boardwalk to negotiate boggy terrain studded with ferns, wildflowers, and other water-tolerant species. The 400-meter **Senda de los Castores** (Beaver Trail) winds among southern beeches gnawed to death to form dams and ponds where the beavers themselves occasionally peek out of their lodges.

The five-kilometer **Senda Hito IV** follows Lago Roca's northeastern shore to a small obelisk that marks the Chilean border. If Argentine and Chilean authorities can someday get it together, this would be an ideal entry point to Estancia Yendegaia's wild backcountry, but at present it's illegal to continue beyond the marker. From a junction about one kilometer up the Hito IV trail, **Senda Cerro Guanaco** climbs four kilometers northeast up the Arroyo Guanaco to its namesake peak's 970-meter summit.

From Bahía Ensenada, near the park's southeastern edge, there are boat shuttles to **Isla Redonda** (10 A.M.–5:30 P.M., US$27 pp).

PRACTICALITIES
Accommodations and Food
Camping is the only option in the park itself, where there are free sites with little or no infrastructure at **Camping Ensenada, Camping Río Pipo, Camping Las Bandurrias, Camping Laguna Verde,** and **Camping Los Cauquenes.** While these are improving, they're less tidy than the commercial **Camping Lago Roca** (tel. 02901/43-3313, lagoroca@speedy.com.ar, US$4 pp), which has hot showers, a grocery, and the restaurant *confitería* **La Cabaña del Bosque.**

Information
At the park entrance on RN 3, the APN has a Centro de Información where it collects a US$14 pp entry fee. Argentine residents pay half.

Several books have useful information on the park, including William Leitch's *South America's National Parks* (Seattle: The Mountaineers, 1990), which is now out of print. Two good hiking guides are the fifth edition of Tim Burford's *Backpacking in Chile & Argentina* (Chalfont St Peter, UK: Bradt Publications, 2001) and the fourth edition of *Trekking in the Patagonian Andes* (Melbourne: Lonely Planet, 2009).

Birders may want to acquire Claudio Venegas Canelo's *Aves de Patagonia y Tierra del Fuego Chileno-Argentina* (Punta Arenas: Ediciones de la Universidad de Magallanes, 1986), Ricardo Clark's *Aves de Tierra del Fuego y Cabo de Hornos* (Buenos Aires: Literature of Latin America, 1986), or Enrique Couve and Claudio Vidal Ojeda's bilingual *Birds of the Beagle Channel* (Punta Arenas: Fantástico Sur Birding & Nature, 2000).

Getting There and Around
The transportation details provided for Ushuaia apply to the park as well.

Río Grande and Vicinity

Most visitors who stay in and around Río Grande, on the Isla Grande's blustery Atlantic shoreline, do so for the fishing. For the rest, this once-desolate city is more a place to change buses, but thanks to smoothly paved streets, the huge dust clouds that once blew through this wool and oil burg have subsided. There are limits to beautification, though—all the trees planted in Plaza Almirante Brown are stiffly wind-flagged.

Bus schedules used to dictate that travelers spend the night here, but recent improvements mean quicker overland connections to Ushuaia. Still, services have improved, and there's enough to do that an afternoon spent here need not be a wasted one.

On the north bank of its namesake river, Río Grande (pop. 52,786) is 79 kilometers southeast of the Chilean border post at San Sebastián and 190 kilometers northeast of Ushuaia via

THE FALKLAND ISLANDS (ISLAS MALVINAS)

In 1982, Britain and Argentina fought a 10-week war over the isolated Falkland Islands (which Argentines claim as the Malvinas), ending in a decisive British victory that derailed a brutal military dictatorship. The territorial dispute has not disappeared, but in the interim the islands have become an important destination for a select group of international travelers interested primarily in subantarctic wildlife.

What the Falklands can offer, 500 kilometers east of the continent in the open South Atlantic, is at least five species of penguins, including the uncommon king and gentoo; marine mammals including elephant seals, sea lions, and fur seals; enormous nesting colonies of black-browed albatrosses; and several species of cormorants. Most of these are not easily seen on the continent, and some would normally require a trip to Antarctica.

For several years after the war, the only way to reach the islands was an expensive Royal Air Force flight from England, but for the last several years LAN has offered Saturday flights to and from Punta Arenas; one flight per month picks up and drops off passengers in the Argentine city of Río Gallegos. Cruise ships pay frequent visits in the southern summer as well.

Despite their small population, only about 2,500, the islands have good infrastructure in the capital of Stanley and at wildlife sites in offshore island farms that resemble Argentine and Chilean *estancias*. The big drawback is that most, though not all, of these sites are only accessible by expensive air taxis.

Because of complicated logistics, Falklands-bound visitors should consider arranging an itinerary in advance to take maximum advantage of their time – accommodations are relatively few and internal flights have limited capacity. Contact **International Tours and Travel** (P.O. Box 408, Stanley, Falkland Islands, tel. 500/22041, www.falklandstravel.com).

For further information, consult *Moon Patagonia*, which has a detailed chapter on the Falklands, and the Falkland Islands Tourist Board's thorough, well-organized website (www.tourism.org.fk).

RN 3, which is now completely paved (though some deteriorating segments south toward Tolhuin will soon need repaving).

SIGHTS AND ENTERTAINMENT

Occupying the former storehouses of the Asociación Rural de Tierra del Fuego, the **Museo de La Ciudad Virginia Choquintel** (Alberdi 555, tel. 02964/42-1767, 9 A.M.–7 P.M. Mon.–Fri., 3–7 P.M. Sat., free) does a lot with a little, with good materials on natural history, sophisticated exhibits on ethnology and aboriginal subsistence, and historic displays on maps and mapmaking, island communications, and astronomy.

Río Grande has few architectural landmarks—or few buildings of any antiquity, for that matter—but the **Obras Sanitarias** waterworks tower (Lasserre 386), at the Plaza's northeast corner, dates from the Juan Perón era (circa 1954).

El Cine 1 & 2 (Perito Moreno 211, tel. 02962/43-3260) shows current films in modern facilities, but it sometimes cranks up the volume to excruciating levels—bring or improvise ear plugs, just in case.

ACCOMMODATIONS

Accommodations are few, particularly at the budget end, where quality varies dramatically. Nearly every mid-range-to-upscale place offers a 10 percent discount for cash payment.

Río Grande's first backpacker hostel, at the south end of town, the **Albergue Turístico Argentino** (San Martín 64, tel. 02964/42-2546, hostelargentino@gmail.com, US$13–16 pp dorm) gets high marks for hospitality, good beds, and good common areas including kitchen access. Prices with shared or private baths are acceptable, but make reservations for the latter; a couple of rooms are run-down and it sometimes suffers water shortages. Staff will fetch guests from the bus terminal for free.

TIERRA DEL FUEGO

The simple but spotless family-run **Hospedaje Noal** (Obligado 557, tel. 02964/42-7516, US$14 pp, US$34 d) has spacious rooms with shared baths but plenty of closet space and good beds, and some rooms with private baths. **B&B El Puesto** (Juan Bautista Thorne 345, tel. 02964/42-0923, bybelpuesto@yahoo.com. ar, US$32 s, US$40 d), the only one of its kind, is one of Río Grande's best values.

Around the corner from the former bus terminal, the seaside **Hotel Isla del Mar** (Güemes 936, tel. 02964/42-2883, isladelmar@hotmail. com, US$44 s, US$52 d) is frayed, not just worn around the edges, with loose doorknobs, scuffed walls, and eroding wooden built-ins. Still, it exudes a certain funky charm, even if "sea view" is a relative term here—with the enormous tidal range, the ocean sometimes seems to be on the distant horizon. Rates include breakfast, and there's a small discount for cash payments.

Possibly Río Grande's best value for money, rehabbed **Hotel Villa** (San Martín and Espora, tel. 02964/42-4998, hotelvillarg@hotmail. com, US$65 s or d) has cheerful contemporary rooms and assiduous service. It offers 10 percent cash discounts.

With its rooms and public areas upgraded, **Hotel Federico Ibarra** (Rosales 357, tel. 02964/43-0071, www.federicoibarrahotel.com. ar, US$72 s, US$87 d) is well worth consideration, with breakfast and cash discounts. A glass palace that's an architectural sore thumb, **Hotel Atlántida** (Avenida Belgrano 582, tel./ fax 02964/43-1914, www.atlantidahotel.com. ar, US$74 s, US$92 d) has improved its accommodations and offers similar discounts.

Río Grande's most professional operation, **(Posada de los Sauces** (Elcano 839, tel. 02964/43-2895, www.posadadelossauces.com. ar, US$74–90 s, US$85–111 d) is easily top of the line. One of the suite bathrooms could hold a hot-tub party, and the restaurant is the city's most elegant.

FOOD

Leymi (25 de Mayo 1335, tel. 02964/42-1683, lunch and dinner daily) serves inexpensive fixed-price lunches and has a broad *parrillada*

and pasta menu, plus other short orders. **El Rincón de Julio** (Elcano 805, tel. 02964/15-60-4261, lunch and dinner daily) is a hole-in-the-wall *parrilla,* highly regarded by locals, with lunch counter–style service.

Recent opened on the site of the classic La Nueva Piamontesa, **Tante Sara** (Belgrano 402, tel. 02964/42-4366, www.tantesara.com) is a branch of Ushuaia's fine café-restaurant.

Mamá Flora (Belgrano 1101, tel. 02964/42-4087, breakfast and lunch daily) is a good breakfast choice that also has coffee and exquisite chocolates. At the plaza's northwest corner, **Limoncello** (Rosal and Fagnano, tel. 02964/42-0134) is an exceptional ice creamery.

Several hotels have their own restaurants, most notably the **(Posada de los Sauces** (Elcano 839, tel. 02964/43-0868, lunch and dinner daily), which deserves special mention for superb service, the cooked-to-order *lomo a la pimienta* (pepper steak, US$10) and its complimentary glass of wine. There's also a 10 percent cash discount.

INFORMATION

On Plaza Almirante Brown, Río Grande's **Oficina de Información Turística** (Rosales 350, tel. 02964/43-1324, www.riogrande.gov. ar, 9 A.M.–5 P.M. daily in summer, 9 A.M.–5 P.M. Mon.–Fri. the rest of the year) is exceptionally helpful.

The provincial **Instituto Fueguino de Turismo** (Infuetur, Espora 533, tel. 02962/42-2887) is open 9 A.M.–6 P.M. weekdays only.

SERVICES

Cambio Thaler (Rosales 259, tel. 02964/42-1154) is the only currency exchange house. Banks with ATMs include **Banco de Tierra del Fuego** (San Martín 193) and **HSBC** (San Martín 194).

Correo Argentino (Rivadavia 968) is two blocks west of San Martín; the postal code is 9420. **Locutorio Cabo Domingo** (San Martín 458) has long-distance telephone and Internet services.

El Lavadero (Perito Moreno 221) handles the washing.

For medical services, contact the **Hospital Regional** (Ameghino s/n, tel. 02964/42-2088).

GETTING THERE

Aerolíneas Argentinas (San Martín 607, tel. 02964/42-2748) flies daily to Río Gallegos and Buenos Aires. **LADE** (Lasserre 429, tel. 02964/42-2968) flies with some frequency to Río Gallegos, less often to Comodoro Rivadavia.

The **Terminal Fueguina** (Obligado and Finocchio) is Río Grande's new bus terminal, but companies also retain their old offices, some of them more central. **Lider** (Perito Moreno 635, tel. 02964/42-0003, www.lidertdf.com.ar) and **Transportes Montiel** (25 de Mayo 712, tel. 02964/42-0997) have multiple departures to Tolhuin (US$10) and Ushuaia (US$17). At the new terminal, **Buses Pacheco** (tel. 02964/15-40-8717, www.busespacheco.com) goes to Punta Arenas, Chile (8 hours, US$33), at 10 A.M. Tuesday, Thursday, and Saturday and has summer connections to Puerto Natales, Chile.

Tecni-Austral (Moyano 516, tel. 02964/43-0610) goes to Punta Arenas at 8 A.M. Monday, Wednesday, and Friday, to Río Gallegos (8 hours, US$34) via Chile at 8:30 A.M. Monday–Saturday, and to Ushuaia (4 hours, US$17) at 4 P.M. daily.

Buses Marga (Mackinlay 545, tel. 02964/43-4316) goes daily to Río Gallegos (9 hours, US$34).

GETTING AROUND

City bus Línea C goes directly to **Aeropuerto Internacional Río Grande** (tel. 02964/42-0600), a short distance west of downtown on RN 3, for US$0.50. It's also a reasonable cab ride.

Europcar (Avenida Belgrano 423, tel. 02964/43-2022) rents cars and light trucks.

VICINITY OF RÍO GRANDE

As the surrounding area lacks a well-developed transport infrastructure, hiring a vehicle is worth consideration.

Reserva Provincial Costa Atlántica de Tierra del Fuego

From Cabo Nombre, at Bahía San Sebastián's north end, to the mouth of the Río Ewan,

FISHING IN FUEGIA

Fishing for Atlantic salmon, brown trout, and rainbow trout is a popular pastime throughout Argentine Tierra del Fuego, but fees differ according to the period of time, the lake or river in question, and residence status.

Daily rates range US$20-79 for foreigners; there's a weekly license for US$66-158, and seasonal rates are US$92-263. Fuegian and Argentine residents pay a fraction of these rates.

In Ushuaia, licenses are available at the **Asociación Caza y Pesca** (Maipú 822, tel. 02901/42-3168, cazpescush@infoviar.com.ar). In Río Grande, contact the **Asociación Riograndense de Pesca con Mosca** (Montilla 1040, tel. 02964/42-1268).

southeast of Río Grande, the Isla Grande's entire shoreline is a bird sanctuary because of the abundant plovers and sandpipers, some of which migrate yearly between the Arctic and South America. Near the San Sebastián border post is the privately owned **Refugio de Vida Silvestre Dicky,** a prime wetland of 1,900 hectares.

Misión Salesiana

One exception to Río Grande's lack of historic sites is the Salesian mission (RN 3 Km 2980, tel. 02964/43-0667, www.misionrg.com.ar), founded by the order to catechize the Selk'nam; after the aboriginals died out from unintentionally introduced diseases and intentional slaughter, the fathers turned their attention to educating rural youth in their boarding school. The well-preserved **Capilla** (chapel), a national historic monument, and similar Magellanic buildings make up part of the mission's **Museo de Historia, Antropología y de Ciencias Naturales** (9:30 A.M.–noon and 3–5 P.M. Tues.–Sun., US$1 adults, US$0.50 children), whose facilities display their natural history and ethnography exhibits far better than in the not-too-distant past.

From Río Grande, the Línea D bus goes hourly to the Misión Salesiana, about 11 kilometers north of Río Grande, 7:30 A.M.–8:30 P.M.

Historic *Estancias*

Several of the region's largest and most important *estancias* are in the vicinity of Río Grande. Founded by the Menéndez dynasty's Sociedad Explotadora de Tierra del Fuego, **Estancia María Behety,** 17 kilometers west via gravel RC-c, is home to the world's largest shearing shed.

Also Sociedad Explotadora property, **Estancia José Menéndez,** 25 kilometers southwest of town via RN 3 and RC-b, is one of the island's most historic ranches. RC-b continues west to an obscure border post (open Nov.–Mar. only) at **Radman,** where few visitors of any kind cross the line to Lago Blanco on the Chilean side.

For potential overnighters, though, the Sea View Guest House at the Simon and Carolina Goodall family's **Estancia Viamonte** (tel. 02964/43-0861, www.estanciaviamonte.com, US$145 pp with half board, US$175 pp with full board, including wine and soft drinks) is the only place on the island that can offer the opportunity to sleep in Lucas Bridges's bedroom. Directly on RN 3, about 42 kilometers southeast of Río Grande, it fronts on a bird-rich beach; the house itself can sleep up to six people with two shared baths, plus living and dining rooms. There are extensive gardens and chances for fishing, riding, and farm activities.

Lago Fagnano (Kami)

Named for the priest who spearheaded Salesian evangelism among the Selk'nam, this elongated lake fills a structural depression that stretches across the Chilean border to the west. Also known by its Selk'nam name Kami, its shoreline is nearly 200 kilometers long, and its surface covers nearly 600 square kilometers.

The lake's most westerly part, along the Chilean border, lies within Parque Nacional Tierra del Fuego but is virtually inaccessible except by boat. As might be expected, the lake is popular with fishing enthusiasts.

At the east end, about midway between Río Grande and Ushuaia, pilgrims pause at the town of **Tolhuin** to sample the goods at ◖ **Panadería la Unión** (www.panaderialaunion.com), a legendary bakery whose celebrity visitors have included former president Carlos Menem, folk-rocker León Gieco, hard-rockers Los Caballeros de la Quema, and actress China Zorrilla. It has the usual fine bread but also loads of *facturas* (pastries), *alfajores,* and sandwiches; what it lacks, astonishingly for Argentina, is any coffee other than machine-dispensed instant.

For a full meal, there's nearby **La Posada de los Ramírez** (Avenida de los Shelk'nam 411, tel. 02901/49-2382, lunch and dinner daily), which has excellent pastas at bargain prices, but also meats and, on occasion, local specialties such as trout.

Chilean Tierra del Fuego

◖ PUERTO WILLIAMS

On Isla Navarino's north shore, across the Beagle Channel from Argentine Tierra del Fuego, Puerto Williams is the so-called "Capital of Antarctica" and gateway to the rugged Los Dientes backcountry circuit, a five-day slog through soggy mountainous terrain. Local residents look forward to a permanent ferry link to nearby Argentina, but there is political opposition across the channel because myopic Ushuaia impresarios fear losing business to tiny Williams—however unlikely that possibility.

Founded in the 1950s, formerly known as Puerto Luisa, the town (pop. 1,952) has paved sidewalks but gravel streets. Most residents are Chilean naval personnel living in relatively stylish prefabs, but there are also some 60 remaining Yámana descendents, only a few of whom speak the language—now a hybrid including many Spanish and English words—among themselves.

Sights

Overlooking the harbor is the **Proa del Escampavía Yelcho,** the prow of the cutter that, under Luis Pardo Villalón, rescued British explorer Edward Shackleton's crew from Elephant Island on the Antarctic Peninsula in 1916. A national monument, the bow survived collisions with icebergs to reach its destination; returning to Punta Arenas, the entire ship makes a cameo appearance in original newsreel footage in British director George Butler's *Endurance,* an extraordinary documentary of Shackleton's adventure.

Very professional for a small-town museum, Williams's **Museo Martin Gusinde** (Aragay 1, tel. 061/62-1043, www.museoantropologicomartingusinde.cl, 9 A.M.–1 P.M. and 2:30–7:18 P.M. Mon.–Thurs., 2:30–6:30 P.M. Sat.–Sun., free) has exhibits on geology, economic plants and taxidermy, a marker for the former post office, and a sign for the coal mine at Caleta Banner, on nearby Isla Picton, which provisioned the *Yelcho* on its rescue mission. Nearby is the **Parque Botánico Omora,** an organized selection of native plants.

Built in Germany for operations on the Rhine, the **MV *Micalvi*** shipped supplies between remote *estancias* and other settlements before sinking in Puerto Williams's inner harbor in 1962; the upper deck and bridge remain as the yacht club's bar-restaurant.

Accommodations, Food, and Nightlife

At **Residencial Pusaki** (Piloto Pardo 242, tel. 061/62-1116, pattypusaki@yahoo.es, US$21 s, US$46 d), rates vary according to shared or private bath. **Refugio Coirón** (Ricardo Maragaño 168, tel. 061/62-1227, www.simexpeditions.com, US$50 s, US$60 d) has good accommodations with kitchen privileges and private baths, but it has had to close on occasion because of labor shortages.

The top choice is the utterly transformed 24-room **Hotel Lakutaia** (tel. 061/62-1733, www.lakutaia.cl, US$200 s, US$250 d), which is more a destination than just a hotel, with multiday activities programs; it also has a fine restaurant. Off-season (May–mid-Oct.) rates are about 25 percent lower.

South America's southernmost bar-restaurant, the **Club de Yates Micalvi,** occupies the main deck and bridge of the historic vessel that lies grounded in the inner harbor.

The **Pingüino Pub** is at the Centro Comercial.

Services

Nearly all services are concentrated around the Centro Comercial, a cluster of storefronts just uphill from the Muelle Guardián Brito, the main passenger pier. These include the post office, several telephone offices, Banco de Chile, the Cema-Chile crafts shop, and Manualidades, which rents mountain bikes.

Transportation

Aerovías DAP (tel. 061/62-1051), at the Centro Comercial, flies 20-seat Twin Otters to Punta Arenas (US$103) Monday and Wednesday–Saturday, April–October. Flights leave Monday–Saturday the rest of the year. DAP flights are often heavily booked, so make reservations well in advance.

Regular connections between Puerto Williams and Ushuaia, on Argentine Tierra del Fuego, continue to be problematic, but hitching a lift across the channel with a yacht is feasible—for a price. For up-to-date information, contact the **Gobernación Marítima** (tel. 061/62-1090), the **Club de Yates** (tel. 061/62-1041, ext. 4250), or **Sim Expeditions** (tel. 061/62-1150). There are occasional charter flights as well.

In summer, the **ferry** *Bahía Azul* sails to Punta Arenas (34 hours) at 10 P.M. Saturday. Fares are US$210 for a bunk, US$175 for a reclining seat.

VICINITY OF PUERTO WILLIAMS

The Williams-based German-Venezuelan **Sea & Ice & Mountains Adventures Unlimited** (Austral 74, tel. 061/62-1227, tel./fax 061/62-1150, www.simexpeditions.com) organizes

TRAVEL IN CHILE

Many visitors to Argentine Patagonia also cross the border into Chilean Patagonia and Tierra del Fuego. In fact, anyone traveling overland to Argentine Tierra del Fuego *must* pass through Chile, though air passengers can avoid Argentina's neighbor. Not that they would necessarily want to, as there's plenty to see and do there.

Because so many travelers to Patagonia visit bordering Magallanes and the Chilean side of Tierra del Fuego, key destinations like Punta Arenas, Parque Nacional Torres del Paine, and Puerto Williams are covered in detail in this book. For details on the rest of the country, see *Moon Chile*.

VISAS AND OFFICIALDOM
Very few nationalities need advance visas, but requirements can change – if in doubt, check Chilean consulates in Río Gallegos, Río Grande, or Ushuaia. Ordinarily, border officials grant foreign tourists an automatic 90-day entry permit, but if arriving by air some nationalities must pay a so-called reciprocity fee, equivalent to what their own countries charge Chileans for a visa application. In the case of U.S.

citizens, for instance, it's US$131, but the fee is normally collected only in Santiago.

The paramilitary Carabineros serve as both immigration and customs officials at some Patagonian crossings; at the larger ones, most notably San Sebastián (Tierra del Fuego) and Monte Aymond (south of Río Gallegos), the Policía Internacional (International Police), the Servicio Nacional de Aduanas (National Customs Service), and the Servicio Agrícola y Ganadero (SAG, Agriculture and Livestock Service) have separate presences. Fresh fruit is the biggest taboo.

HEALTH
Chile requires no vaccinations for visitors entering from any country, and public health standards are high. Generally, tap water is safe to drink, but short-term visitors should be cautious. As in Argentina, both Chagas' disease and hantavirus are present, but health risks in Patagonia and Tierra del Fuego are small indeed.

MONEY AND PRICES
Until the Argentine economic meltdown of early 2002, Chile had been relatively inex-

---

trekking, climbing, and riding expeditions on Isla Navarino and the Cordillera Darwin, week-long yacht excursions around the Beagle Channel and to Cape Horn, and even excursions to Antarctica. Advance booking is imperative.

The Coastal Road
From Puerto Williams, a coastal road runs 54 kilometers west to the village of Puerto Navarino, now a legal port of entry, and 28 kilometers east to Caleta Eugenia; only two kilometers east of Williams, **Villa Ukika** is the last Yámana refuge. From Caleta Eugenia, the road is advancing southeast to **Puerto Toro,** where some 60 boats employ about four workers each in search of *centolla* (king crab).

Cordón de los Dientes
Immediately south of Puerto Williams, Cordón

de los Dientes is a range of jagged peaks rising more than 1,000 meters above sea level that offers the world's southernmost trekking opportunities. There are, however, few trails through this rugged countryside—anyone undertaking the four- to five-day "circuit" should be experienced in route finding.

PORVENIR
Chilean Tierra del Fuego's main town, Porvenir sits on a sheltered harbor on the Strait of Magellan's eastern shore. It dates from the 1880s, when the area experienced a brief gold rush, but stabilized with the establishment of wool *estancias* around the turn of the 20th century. After the wool boom fizzled in the 1920s, it settled into an economic torpor that has left it a collection of corroding metal-clad Magellanic buildings. Construction of a

pensive compared with its larger neighbor, but Argentina's devaluation reversed this relationship. It was not that Chilean prices increased significantly, but rather that Argentine prices dropped so precipitously that Chile became relatively more expensive. Since 2003, a steady revaluation of the Chilean peso against the U.S. dollar has made Chile increasingly costly.

Nevertheless, Chile has maintained economic stability and a low-inflation economy for at least a decade and a half. Travelers should keep a close eye on exchange rates, however.

Travelers checks are relatively easy to cash, but ATM cards are more convenient. A small cash dollar reserve is also a good idea.

One economic advantage of travel in Chile is that mid-range to upscale hotels deduct IVA (value added tax) for foreign tourists who pay in U.S. dollars or by credit card. This means, for instance, that a US$100 hotel becomes a US$80 hotel, but it's not automatic – you must ask for it. The very cheapest accommodations, which are usually IVA-exempt, rarely follow this practice.

SCHEDULES AND HOURS

Chileans, in general, rise later than Argentines, many businesses do not open until 10 A.M., and it's often difficult to get breakfast in a Chilean hotel before 8 A.M. Lunch tends to be a bit later than in Argentina, around 2 P.M., but dinner is as early as 8 P.M.

COMMUNICATIONS

Telephone, Internet, and postal services are all moderately priced. Chile's country code is 56; the area code for Magallanes and Chilean Tierra del Fuego is 061. Prefixes for cell phones in the entire country are 098 and 099.

GETTING AROUND

Distances in Chilean Patagonia are shorter than in Argentina, and the main highways are excellent. On the Chilean side of Tierra del Fuego, some roads are paved, but most are gravel or dirt. Gasoline and diesel are significantly more expensive in Chile, so fill the tank on the Argentine side.

Chilean buses mostly resemble those in Argentina – modern, spacious, and fast. Prices resemble those in Argentina.

salmon-processing plant has jump-started the local economy, and it's more presentable than in the recent past.

Porvenir's inner harbor is a great place for spotting kelp geese, gulls, cormorants, steamer ducks, and other seabirds, but the lack of public transportation to the Argentine border has marginalized the tourist sector—all buses from the mainland to Argentine Tierra del Fuego take the longer Primera Angostura route, with a shorter and more frequent ferry crossing. Small local enterprises do offer access to parts of the archipelago that up to now have only been accessible through expensive cruises.

Only 30 nautical miles east of Punta Arenas, Porvenir (pop. 4,734) occupies a protected site at the east end of Bahía Porvenir, an inlet of the Strait of Magellan. Its port, though, is three kilometers west of the town proper.

From Porvenir, Ruta 215 (a smooth gravel road) leads south and then east along the Bahía Inútil shoreline to the Argentine border at San Sebastián, 150 kilometers away; an alternate route leads directly east through the Cordón Baquedano before rejoining Ruta 215 about 55 kilometers to the east. If it's too late to catch the ferry back to Punta Arenas, another gravel road follows the coast to Puerto Espora, 141 kilometers northeast.

Sights

Directly on the water, **Parque Yugoslavo** memorializes the earliest gold-seeking immigrants, mostly Croats; it's also one of Porvenir's best birding spots. The tourist office provides a small map/brochure, in English, of the city's architectural heritage; many of its houses and other buildings were also Croatian-built.

TIERRA DEL FUEGO

Most public buildings surround the neatly landscaped **Plaza de Armas,** two blocks north of Parque Yugoslavo. Among them is the **Museo de Tierra del Fuego Fernando Rusque Cordero** (Zavattaro 402, tel. 061/58-1800, www.museoporvenir.cl, 9 A.M.–4 P.M. Mon., 9 A.M.–5 P.M. Tues.–Fri., 10 A.M.–1:30 P.M. and 3–5 P.M. Sat.–Sun., US$1), a regional museum dealing with the island's natural history, indigenous heritage, the early gold rush, the later but longer-lasting wool rush, and even cinematography—German-born filmmaker José Bohr went to Hollywood in 1929 and enjoyed a long if inconsistent career. It has added a skillfully produced replica of an early rural store and a good photographic display on local architecture.

The museum takes its name from a Carabineros officer who helped found it—and was no doubt responsible for the permanent exhibit on police uniforms.

Accommodations and Food

There's no sign outside homey **Hospedaje Shinká** (Santos Mardones 333, tel. 061/58-0491, US$23 s, US$38 d), but it offers better facilities and amenities—immaculate midsize rooms with comfortable beds, private baths, and cable TV—for less money than any other place in town. The breakfast is forgettable, but that's a minor fault for a place this good.

All rooms at **Hotel Rosas** (Philippi 269, tel. 061/58-0088, hotelrosas@chile.com, US$34 s, US$45 d) have private baths and include breakfast; its restaurant is one of Porvenir's better values in a town with admittedly few other choices.

All rooms now have private baths at upgraded and expanded **Hotel España** (Croacia 698, tel. 061/58-0160, www.hotelespana.cl, US$28 s, US$46 d), whose utilitarian addition masks large new rooms; in the older section, some slightly smaller rooms are still adequate. It also has a restaurant.

Other than hotel restaurants, the main dining options include the basic **Puerto Montt** (Croacia 1169, tel. 061/58-0207, lunch daily, dinner Mon.–Sat.) and the **Club Social Catef** (Zavattaro 94, tel. 061/58-1399, lunch daily, dinner Mon.–Sat.). **El Chispa** (Señoret 202,

tel. 061/58-0054, lunch daily, dinner Mon.–Sat.) is a *picada* with good home cooking at moderate prices.

At Bahía Chilote, **La Picá de Pechuga** (tel. 099/888-6380, lunch daily, dinner Mon.–Sat.) is a moderately priced seafood *picada* that gets its fish fresh off the boat. The waterfront **Club Social Croata** (Señoret 542, tel. 061/58-0053, lunch daily, dinner Mon.–Sat.) is more formal and has good fish and wine by the glass, though service can be erratic.

Information and Services

In the same offices as the museum, Porvenir's helpful **Oficina Municipal de Turismo** (Padre Mario Zavattaro 434, tel. 061/58-1800, www.muniporvenir.cl) keeps the same hours as the museum (9 A.M.–4 P.M. Mon., 9 A.M.–5 P.M. Tues.–Fri., 10 A.M.–1:30 P.M. and 3–5 P.M. Sat.–Sun.).

Banco del Estado (Philippi 263) has an ATM.

Correos de Chile (Philippi 176) is at the southwest corner of the Plaza de Armas. Almost alongside the bank, the **Centro de Llamados** (Philippi 277) has long-distance telephones.

For medical services, try the **Hospital Porvenir** (Carlos Wood s/n, between Señoret and Guerrero, tel. 061/58-0034).

Getting There and Around

Porvenir has regular but infrequent connections to the mainland but none to the San Sebastián border crossing into Argentina; those with their own vehicles (including cyclists) will still find this a shorter route from Punta Arenas to Ushuaia.

Aerovías DAP (Manuel Señoret s/n and Muñoz Gamero, tel. 061/58-0089) operates air taxi service to Punta Arenas (15 minutes, US$37) at least daily, often more frequently.

At 3:45 P.M. Tuesday and Friday there's a municipal bus from the DAP offices on Señoret to Camerón and Timaukel (2 hours, US$3) in the southwestern corner of the island; another goes to **Cerro Sombrero** (1.5 hours, US$5) at 5 P.M. Monday, Wednesday, and Friday from Zavattaro 432.

In the same office as DAP, **Transbordadora Broom** (Manuel Señoret s/n, tel. 061/58-0089) sails the car-passenger ferry *Crux Australis* to Punta Arenas (2.5 hours) Tuesday–Sunday, seas permitting. The ferry leaves from Bahía Chilote, about three kilometers west of town. Adult passengers pay US$9 pp except for the drivers, whose own fare is included in the US$58 per-vehicle charge (motorcycles pay US$15). Children cost US$4.50 each.

VICINITY OF PORVENIR

"Vicinity" is a relative term on Tierra del Fuego, as some fascinating locales are difficult or expensive—or both—to reach. To reach the remote south-side fjords, the main option is the luxury cruises on the MV *Mare Australis* and MV *Via Australis*.

Monumento Natural Laguna de los Cisnes

International birding groups often detour to this 25-hectare saline lake reserve, which sometimes dries out, just north of Porvenir. While it takes its name from the elegant black-necked swan, it's home to many other species.

Cordón Baquedano

After Chilean naval officer Ramón Serrano Montaner found gold in the rolling hills east of Porvenir in 1879, panners from Chile and Croatia flocked to the Río del Oro Valley, between the Cordón Baquedano and the Sierra Boquerón. Living in sod huts that shielded them from the wind and cold, hoping to eke out a kilogram per year, more than 200 worked the placers until they gave out. By the turn of the century, California miners introduced dredges and steam shovels, but decreasing yields ended the rush by 1908–1909. A century later, a few hardy panners hang on.

From Porvenir, the eastbound road through the Cordón Baquedano passes several gold-rush sites, some marked with interpretive panels; the literal high point is the **Mirador de la Isla,** an overlook 500 meters above sea level. In many places guanacos, which seem to outnumber sheep, gracefully vault meter-high fences that stop the sheep cold.

Onaisín

About 100 kilometers east of Porvenir, a major north-south road crosses Ruta 215 at Onaisín, a former Sociedad Explotadora *estancia* whose **Cementerio Inglés** is a national historical monument. Northbound, the road goes to the petroleum company town of Cerro Sombrero, while southbound it goes to Camerón and Lago Blanco.

Lago Blanco

Some 50 kilometers southwest of Onaisín, the road passes through **Camerón,** an erstwhile picture-postcard *estancia* that is now a municipality. The road then angles southeast to Lago Blanco, an area known for its fishing, and continues toward Yendegaia, though it'll be a while before it's finished; in summer there's a bumpy border crossing to Río Grande, Argentina, via a dirt road with many livestock gates and a ford of the Río Rasmussen. The Argentine border post is called Radman.

Estancia Yendegaia

Visited primarily by Chilean cruise ships and private yachts, Yendegaia conserves 44,000 hectares of Fuegian forest in the Cordillera Darwin between the Argentine border and Parque Nacional Alberto de Agostini. While the owners hope to establish a private national park and create an unbroken preservation corridor along the Beagle Channel (Yendegaia borders Argentina's Parque Nacional Tierra del Fuego), there's government pressure to pave the airstrip at Caleta María, at the property's north end, and a road south from Lago Blanco has reached the Chilean side of Lago Fagnano. The owners, for their part, would rather see the border opened to foot traffic from Argentina, but they have consulted with public-works officials to minimize the road's environmental impact.

In the meantime, the *estancia* is open to visitors, although access is difficult without chartering a plane or boat, or taking an expensive tour like the MV *Mare Australis* cruise through the Fuegian fjords; even this cruise stops only occasionally. Naval boats between Punta Arenas and Puerto Williams may drop passengers here but are so infrequent that getting back could be problematic.

CERRO SOMBRERO

About 70 kilometers north of Onaisín and 43 kilometers south of the Puerto Espora ferry landing, Cerro Sombrero is a company town where employees of the Empresa Nacional de Petróleo (ENAP, National Petroleum Company) reside in orderly surroundings with remarkable amenities for a town with only about 150 houses. Dating from the early 1960s, it boasts an astronomical observatory, a bank, a botanical garden, a cinema, a hospital, recreational facilities that include a heated swimming pool, and restaurants. Buses between Río Grande and Punta Arenas take a meal break at **Restaurant El Conti** just outside town.

Overnighters will find accommodations at vastly improved **Hostería Tunkelén** (Arturo Prat 101, tel. 061/29-6696, www.hosteriatunkelen.cl, US$53 s, US$66 d), which also has a good (but expensive) restaurant.

Punta Arenas (Chile)

Patagonia's largest city, Punta Arenas is also the regional capital and the traditional port of entry, whether by air, land, or sea. Stretching north-south along the Strait of Magellan, the city boasts an architectural heritage that ranges from the Magellanic vernacular of metal-clad houses with steeply pitched roofs to elaborate Francophile mansions commissioned by 19th-century wool barons. Home to several museums, it's a good base for excursions to historical sites and nearby penguin colonies.

The diverse economy depends on fishing, shipping, petroleum, duty-free retail, and tourism. Historically, it's one of the gateways to Antarctica for both research and tourism, but the Argentine port of Ushuaia has absorbed much of this traffic. Ironically, in a region that grazes millions of sheep, it's hard to find woolens because of the influx of artificial fabrics through the duty-free Zona Franca.

HISTORY

After collapse of Chile's initial Patagonian settlement at Fuerte Bulnes, Governor José Santos Mardones relocated north to a site on the Strait of Magellan's western shore, long known to British sailors as "Sandy Point." Soon expanded to include a penal colony, the town adopted that name in Spanish translation.

The timing was propitious, as California's 1849 Gold Rush spurred a surge of shipping that helped keep the new city afloat—even if supplying sealskins, coal, firewood, and lumber did not exactly portend prosperity. A mutiny that resulted in Governor Benjamín Muñoz Gamero's death did not improve matters, and traffic soon fell off.

What finally brought prosperity was Governor Diego Dublé Almeyda's introduction of breeding sheep from the Falkland Islands. Their proliferation on the Patagonian plains, along with a vigorous immigration policy that brought entrepreneurs such as the Portuguese José Nogueira, the Spaniard José Menéndez, and the Irishman Thomas Fenton—not to mention the polyglot laborers who made their fortunes possible—helped transform the city from a dreary presidio to the booming port of a pastoral empire. Its mansions matched many in Buenos Aires, though the maldistribution of wealth and political power remained an intractable issue well into the 20th century.

As the wool economy declined after World War II, petroleum discoveries on Tierra del Fuego and commercial fishing sustained the economy. Creation of Zona Franca duty-free areas gave commercial advantages to Punta Arenas in the 1970s, and tourism has flourished since Pinochet's dictatorship ended in 1989.

ORIENTATION

Punta Arenas (pop. 116,105) is 210 kilometers southwest of Río Gallegos via the Argentine RN 3 and the Chilean Ruta 255 and Ruta 9; it is 241 kilometers southeast of Puerto Natales via Ruta 9. A daily vehicle ferry connects Punta with Porvenir, while a partly paved road, the continent's most southerly, leads to Fuerte Bulnes and Cabo San Isidro.

On the Strait of Magellan's western shore, Punta Arenas occupies a narrow wave-cut terrace, but the ground rises steeply farther west. Only in recent years has the city begun to spread eastward rather than north to south.

Most landmarks and services are within a few blocks of the central Plaza Muñoz Gamero; street names change on each side of the plaza, but the numbering system is continuous.

SIGHTS

For panoramas of the city's layout, the Strait of Magellan, and Tierra del Fuego in the distance, climb to **Mirador La Cruz,** four blocks west of Plaza Muñoz Gamero via a staircase at Fagnano and Señoret.

Plaza Muñoz Gamero and Vicinity

Unlike plazas founded in colonial Chilean cities, Punta Arenas's central plaza was not the initial focus of civic life, but European immigration and the wealth generated by mining, livestock, commerce, and fishing made it so by the 1880s. Landscaped with Monterey cypress and other exotic conifers, the plaza and surrounding buildings constitute a *zona típica* national monument; the plaza proper underwent a major renovation in 2004.

It takes its name from early provincial governor Benjamín Muñoz Gamero, who died in an 1851 mutiny. Among its features are the Victorian kiosk (1910), which houses the municipal tourist office, and sculptor Guillermo Córdova's elaborate monument sponsored by wool magnate José Menéndez on the 400th anniversary of Magellan's 1520 voyage. Magellan's figure, embellished with a globe and a copy of his log, stand above a Selk'nam Indian representing Tierra del Fuego,

Plaza Muñoz Gamero, Punta Arenas

© WAYNE BERNHARDSON

a Tehuelche symbolizing Patagonia, and a mermaid with Chilean and regional coats-of-arms. According to local legend, anyone touching the Tehuelche's now well-worn toe—enough have done so to change its color—will return to Punta Arenas.

After about 1880, the regional elite began to build monuments to their own good fortune, such as the ornate **Palacio Sara Braun** (1895), a national monument in its own right, at the plaza's northwest corner. Only six years after marrying José Nogueira, Punta's most prominent businessman, the newly widowed Sara Braun contracted French architect Numa Mayer, who designed a two-story Parisian-style mansard that helped upgrade the city's earlier utilitarian architecture. Now home to the Club de la Unión and Hotel José Nogueira, the building retains most original features, including the west-facing winter garden that now serves as the hotel's bar-restaurant.

Mid-block, immediately east, the **Casa José Menéndez** belonged to another of Punta's wool barons, while at the plaza's northeast

TIERRA DEL FUEGO

corner, the Comapa travel agency now occupies the former headquarters of the influential **Sociedad Menéndez Behety** (Magallanes 990). Half a block north, dating from 1904, the **Casa Braun-Menéndez** (Magallanes 949) houses the regional museum.

At the plaza's southwest corner, the **Iglesia Matriz** (1901) now enjoys cathedral status. Immediately north, both the **Residencia del Gobernador** (Governor's Residence) and the **Gobernación** date from the same period, filling the rest of the block with offices of the Intendencia Regional, the regional government. On the south side, directly opposite the Victorian tourist kiosk, the former **Palacio Montes** now holds municipal government offices; at the southeast corner, the **Sociedad Braun Blanchard** belonged to another powerful commercial group (their surnames suggest that Punta Arenas's first families were, commercially at least, an incestuous bunch).

◖ Casa Braun-Menéndez (Museo Regional de Magallanes)

Like European royalty, Punta's first families formed alliances sealed by matrimony, and the Casa Braun-Menéndez (1904) is a classic example: the product of a marriage between Mauricio Braun (Sara's brother) and Josefina Menéndez Behety (daughter of José Menéndez and María Behety, a major wool-growing family in Argentina—though international borders meant little to wool barons).

Still furnished with the family's belongings, preserving Mauricio Braun's office and other rooms virtually intact, the house boasts marble fireplaces and other elaborate architectural features. The basement servants' quarters expose the early-20th-century's upstairs-downstairs divisions.

Today, the Casa Braun-Menéndez (Magallanes 949, tel. 061/24-4216, www.museodemagallanes.cl, 10:30 A.M.–5 P.M. Mon.–Sat., 10:30 A.M.–2 P.M. Sun., US$2 adults, US$1 children) serves as the regional museum, replete with pioneer settlers' artifacts and historical photographs. There are imperfect but readable English descriptions of the exhibits.

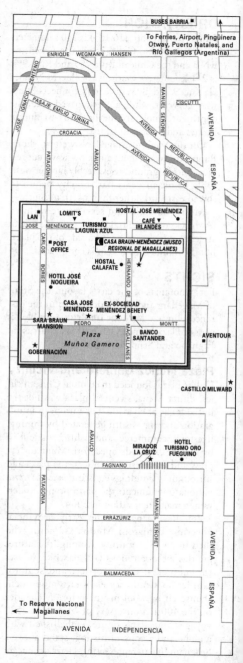

PUNTA ARENAS

To Cementerio Municipal, Museo del Recuerdo, Zona Franca, Ferries, Airport, Pingüinera Otway, Puerto Natales, and Río Gallegos (Argentina)

To Hospedaje Costanera

MUSEO REGIONAL SALESIANO MAYORINO BORGATELLO ★

LAVASECO VICARS

FANTASTICO SUR

AV BUNES
SARMIENTO DE GAMBOA
ARMANDO
SANHUEZA
CHILOE
CARLOS BORIES
DON BOSCO
CROACIA
HERNANDO DE MAGALLANES
LAUTARO
NAVARRO
O'HIGGINS
QUILLOTA

SABORES

MEJICANA

DONDE MARIANO

HOSPEDAJE MEJICANA
MEJICANA

SALA ESTRELLA

Plaza Sampaio

TURISMO AONIKENK

LA MARMITA BISTRO

EL ASADOR PATAGÓNICO

IGNACIO CARRERA PINTO

CHILE TÍPICO

HOSTAL ART NOUVEAU

HOSTAL AYELEN

HOSTAL TERRASUR

BUSES FERNÁNDEZ

Río de las Minas

VALESSE

SCOTT CAMBIOS/ CENTRAL DE PASAJEROS

BUSES PACHECO

JORGE MONTT

HOTEL DIEGO DE ALMAGRO

HOTEL CÓNDOR DE PLATA

HOTEL TIERRA DEL FUEGO

HOTEL FINIS TERRAE

AVENIDA COLÓN

HOTEL MONTECARLO

SANTINO

HOSTAL FITZROY

LUBAG

MURAL GABRIELA MISTRAL ★

PULLMAN BUS SUR

LA CARIOCA

TURISMO PEHOÉ

AEROVÍAS DAP

QUILLOTA

HOTEL CHALET CHAPITAL

PJE DUBLE ALMEYDA

JOSÉ MENÉNDEZ

SEE DETAIL

ENTEL

HERTZ

WALDO SEGUEL

BUSES GHISONI/ TECNI-AUSTRAL/ QUELLÉN

BUDGET RENT A CAR

O SOLE MIO

LAVANDERÍA RECORD

SERNATUR

ADEL RENT A CAR

PEDRO MONTT

Plaza

EL TEMPLO ★

MUSEO NAVAL Y MARÍTIMO

LA LUNA

RESIDENCIA DEL GOBERNADOR ★

Muñoz

HOTEL CABO DE HORNOS

HOSTAL AL FIN DEL MUNDO

JEKUS

PJE KÖRNER

Gamero

IGLESIA MATRIZ ★

PALACIO MONTES

BROCCOLINO

QUIJOTE

AVIS

ROCA

TURISMO VIENTO SUR

TELEFÓNICA CTC

HOTEL MERCURIO

HOTEL PLAZA

LA TASCA

EXPEDICION FITZ ROY

SKY AIRLINE

ARMANDO

SANHUEZA

CHILOE

NOGUEIRA

PJE J PEDRALS

SOCIEDAD BRAUN BLANCHARD

WHALESOUND

TURISMO PALI AIKE

SOTITO'S BAR

PUERTO VIEJO

OLIJOE PUB

ERRÁZURIZ

21 DE MAYO

HOTEL ISLA REY JORGE

LAUTARO

NAVARRO

TURISMO YAMANA

Estrecho de Magallanes

AVENIDA INDEPENDENCIA

LA LEYENDA DEL REMEZÓN

PUERTO DEL ESTRECHO

To Reserva Nacional Laguna Parrillar and Fuerte Bulnes

MUELLE FISCAL ARTURO PRAT

0   200 yds
0   200 m

© AVALON TRAVEL

TIERRA DEL FUEGO

Museo Regional Salesiano Mayorino Borgatello

From their base at Punta Arenas, the Salesian order evangelized among southern Patagonia's native peoples, on both sides of the border, in the 19th century. While their rosy view of Christianity's impact here may be debatable, figures such as the Italian mountaineer priest Alberto de Agostini (1883–1960) made key contributions to both physical geography and ethnographic research.

Agostini left a sizeable collection of photographs in the museum, which also has a library and a regionally oriented art gallery. Permanent exhibits deal with regional flora and fauna, a handful of early colonial artifacts, regional ethnography, the missionization of Isla Dawson and other nearby areas, cartography, and the petroleum industry. For Darwinians, there's a scale model of the *Beagle* and, for Chilean patriots, one of the *Ancud*, which sailed from Chiloé to claim the region in 1843.

The Museo Regional Salesiano (Avenida Bulnes 336, tel. 061/22-1001, US$3 adults, US$0.30 children) is open 10 A.M.–6 P.M. Tuesday–Sunday.

Museo Naval y Marítimo

Pleasantly surprising, Punta Arenas's naval and maritime museum provides perspectives on topics like ethnography—in the context of the Strait of Magellan's seagoing peoples—even while stressing its military mission. It features interactive exhibits, such as a credible warship's bridge, a selection of model ships, and information on the naval history of the southern oceans.

The most riveting material, though, concerns Chilean pilot Luis Pardo Villalón's 1916 rescue of British explorer Ernest Shackleton's crew at Elephant Island on the Antarctic peninsula. On the cutter *Yelcho*, with neither heat, electricity, nor radio in foggy and stormy winter weather, Pardo soon returned the entire crew to Punta Arenas; he later served as Chilean consul in Liverpool.

The Museo Naval (Pedro Montt 981, tel. 061/20-5479, terzona@armada.cl, US$2 adults, US$1 children) is open 9:30 A.M.–5 P.M. Tuesday–Saturday.

Museo del Recuerdo

Run by the Instituto de la Patagonia, part of the Universidad de Magallanes, the Museo del Recuerdo is a mostly open-air facility displaying pioneer agricultural implements and industrial machinery, reconstructions of a traditional house and shearing shed, and a restored shepherd's trailer house (hauled across the Patagonian plains on wooden wheels). In addition to a modest botanical garden, the institute has a library-bookshop with impressive cartographic exhibits.

The Museo del Recuerdo (Avenida Bulnes 01890, tel. 061/20-7056, 8:30 A.M.–11 A.M. and 2–5 P.M. weekdays, US$2 adults, children free) can be reached from downtown Punta Arenas by *taxi colectivos* (duty-free to the Zona Franca), which stop directly opposite the entrance.

Other Sights

Four blocks south of Plaza Muñoz Gamero, at the foot of Avenida Independencia, naval vessels, freighters, cruise ships, Antarctic ice-breakers, and private yachts dock at the **Muelle Fiscal Arturo Prat,** the city's major port facility until recently. It's still a departure point for cruises to the fjords of Tierra del Fuego and to Antarctica but, unfortunately, international security hysteria has closed it to spontaneous public access.

The late gifted travel writer Bruce Chatwin found the inspiration for his legendary vignettes of *In Patagonia* through tales of his eccentric distant relative Charley Milward, who built and resided at the **Castillo Milward** (Milward's Castle, Avenida España 959). Described by Chatwin as "a Victorian parsonage translated to the Strait of Magellan," with "high-pitched gables and gothic windows," the building features a square street-side tower and an octagonal one at the rear.

At the corner of Avenida Colón and O'Higgins, gracing the walls of the former **Liceo de Niñas Sara Braun** (Sara Braun Girls School), and honoring Chile's Nobel

Prize poetess, the seven-meter **Mural Gabriela Mistral** has undergone a recent restoration.

Ten blocks north of Plaza Muñoz Gamero, the **Cementerio Municipal** (Avenida Bulnes 029) is home to the extravagant crypts of José Menéndez, José Nogueira, and Sara Braun; the multinational immigrants who worked for them—English, Scots, Welsh, Croat, German, and Scandinavian—repose in more modest circumstances. A separate monument honors the vanished Selk'nam (Ona) Indians who once flourished in the strait, while another memorializes German fatalities of the Battle of the Falklands (1914).

ENTERTAINMENT

Except on Sunday, when the city seems deader than the cemetery, there's usually something to do. It has one surviving cinema, the **Sala Estrella** (Mejicana 777, tel. 061/24-1262).

El Templo (Pedro Montt 951, tel. 061/22-3667) is primarily a dance club. The stylish **Olijoe Pub** (Errázuriz 970) has the feel of an upscale English pub, with paneled walls, ceiling, and bar, and reasonably priced drinks; the music, though, can get a little loud for conversation. The Sara Braun mansion's basement **Taberna Club de la Unión** (Plaza Muñoz Gamero 716, tel. 061/61-7133) is popular on weekends.

Santino (Avenida Colón 657, tel. 061/71-0882, www.santino.cl) is a spacious and informal pub where everyone (except nonsmokers) feels welcome; there's also food, but it's not the star.

At the north end of town, **Makanudo** (El Ovejero 474, tel. 09/649-2031) has happy hours 7–10 P.M. Monday–Thursday, and live music from around 1:30 A.M. Friday and Saturday nights.

The **Club Hípico** (municipal racetrack) fronts on Avenida Bulnes between Coronel Mardones and Manantiales, north of downtown. Professional soccer matches take place at the **Estadio Fiscal** (stadium), a few blocks north at Avenida Bulnes and José González.

SHOPPING

Though it has faltered in recent years, Punta Arenas's major shopping destination is the duty-free **Zona Franca,** four kilometers north of downtown but easily reached by *taxi colectivo* from Calle Magallanes. Consumer electronics were once the big attraction—Santiaguinos even flew here for the bargains—but price differentials are smaller now.

Puerto del Estrecho (O'Higgins 1401, tel. 061/24-1022) is a good if pricey souvenir shop; in addition, it has an upstairs café, Internet access, and long-distance telephone service.

For crafts such as metal (copper and bronze), semiprecious stones (lapis lazuli), and woolens, visit **Chile Típico** (Ignacio Carrera Pinto 1015, tel. 061/22-5827). For books (including some local guidebooks and travel literature in English), maps, and keepsakes, try **Southern Patagonia Souvenirs & Books,** which has outlets at the airport (tel. 061/21-1591) and at the Zona Franca (tel. 061/21-6759).

ACCOMMODATIONS

Sernatur maintains a complete list of accommodations with current prices. What in many other parts of Chile would be called *residenciales* are *hostales* (B&Bs) here. Some relatively expensive places have cheaper rooms with shared baths that can be excellent values.

US$10-25

With the fluctuating Chilean peso, finding truly shoestring accommodations can be a matter of timing, but economical **Hospedaje Mejicana** (Mejicana 1174, tel. 061/22-7678, yoya_h@hotmail.com, US$7 pp, US$13 s, US$23 d) has made good impressions.

US$25-50

Often full despite mixed reviews, **Hostal Dinka's House** (Caupolicán 169, tel./fax 061/24-4292, www.dinkaspatagonia.com, US$19–28 d) has rooms with either private or shared baths. East of the racetrack at the foot of Quillota, the shoreline **Hospedaje Costanera** (Rómulo Correa 1221, tel. 061/24-0175, hospedajecostanera@hotmail.com, US$19 s, US$33 d) has drawn favorable commentary and has responsive management.

◖ **Hostal Fitz Roy** (Lautaro Navarro 850,

tel./fax 061/24-0430, www.hostalfitzroy.com, US$15 pp, US$32 s, US$43 d, with shared bath) is an old-fashioned B&B offering some modern comforts—notably cable TV and phones in each room—along with peace and quiet, thoughtful English-speaking ownership, and an excellent breakfast that includes fresh homemade bread and eggs. Returned to their original configuration, the rooms are spacious, but buildings of this vintage still have creaky floors and staircases. At the back of the property are separate private-bath *cabañas* (US$65 d), and there's ample parking.

In a large old house that's been subdivided, rooms at **Hostal al Fin del Mundo** (O'Higgins 1026, tel. 061/71-0185, www.alfindelmundo.cl, US$28 s, US$46 d, with shared bath) vary in size and quality, but it has its good points (including proximity to some of the city's best restaurants).

Thanks to the weakening peso, prices have slipped a notch at well-regarded, cul-de-sac **Hostal Sonia** (Pasaje Darwin 175, tel. 061/24-8543, www.hostalsk.cl, US$28 s, US$48 d, with breakfast), which has rooms with private baths and Wi-Fi throughout.

Though it's well kept, some rooms are small at **Hostal José Menéndez** (José Menéndez 882, tel. 061/22-1279, www.chileaustral.com/josemenendez, US$38 s, US$49 d). Still, it's friendly and central, arranges tours, has parking, and offers a decent breakfast; rates vary according to shared or private bath.

US$50-100

Rehabbed **Hotel Montecarlo** (Avenida Colón 605, tel. 061/22-2120, www.montecarlohotel.cl, US$19 pp with shared bath; US$44 s, US$52 d, with private bath) is once again worth consideration; the more expensive rooms are significantly better.

Low-key, tobacco-free **Hostal Terrasur** (O'Higgins 723, tel. 061/22-5618, www.hostalterrasur.cl, US$44 s, US$56 d) is one of the more appealing B&B-style places in its range. Rates include cable TV, telephone, and continental breakfast.

Hostal Ayelen (Lautaro Navarro 763, tel. 061/24-2413, www.ayelenresidencial.com, US$46 s, US$59 d) is a friendly family-run hostelry with small but efficient singles along with larger doubles and triples. Rates include satellite TV, Wi-Fi, and parking, but at midday the yippy poodles in the garden can be a nuisance (they're indoors, and quiet, at other hours).

Despite its misleadingly small street-side facade, **Hostal Calafate** (Magallanes 926, www.calafate.cl, tel./fax 061/24-1281, US$31–46 s, US$50–66 d) is a rambling building with spacious rooms that once held the former Hotel Oviedo; remodeled just a few years ago, it keeps a couple of so-called *celdas de castigo* ("prison cells") for as little US$16 per person—a pretty good deal in a well-kept, central facility—but tour guides usually have priority for these. It also has some of Punta's best Internet facilities, also open to nonguests.

Hotel Cóndor de Plata (Avenida Colón 556, tel. 061/24-7987, www.condordeplata.cl, US$60 s, US$70 d) has always been a good choice, and local competition is keeping prices reasonable.

Across from Hostal Ayelen, **Hostal Art Nouveau** (Lautaro Navarro 762, tel. 061/22-8112, www.hostalartnouveau.cl, US$54 s, US$74 d) is less pretentious than it sounds—a lovingly restored period house with attractive common spaces and breakfast. Some rooms, though, lack exterior windows, and others are small.

Prices have fallen at **Hotel Isla Rey Jorge** (21 de Mayo 1243, tel. 061/22-2681, www.islareyjorge.com, US$67 s, US$80 d), a favorite with foreign tour groups that is showing signs of deferred maintenance. Still, it's now a good value.

The stylishly modernized **Hotel Mercurio** (Fagnano 595, tel./fax 061/24-2300, www.chileaustral.com/mercurio, US$69 s, US$83 d) offers both convenience and charm, with gracious staff to boot.

New in late 2007, the 11-room **Hotel Chalet Chapital** (Sanhueza 974, tel. 061/73-0100, www.hotelchaletchapital.cl, US$72 s, US$89 d) occupies a handsomely restored historic building, with contemporary furnishings, Wi-Fi, and whirlpool tubs in every room.

Hostal Turismo Oro Fueguino (Fagnano 356, tel. 061/24-9401, www.orofueguino.cl, US$75 s, US$90 d) is still a good hotel, but cheap aluminum siding and faux brick have marred its deco-style exterior. Rates include cable TV, telephone, central heating, breakfast, and private baths; some rooms are windowless but have skylights.

US$100-200

Half a block south of Plaza Muñoz Gamero, **Hotel Plaza** (Nogueira 1116, tel. 061/24-1300, www.hotelplaza.cl, US$93–121 s, US$115–121 d) is a classic of its era; for a double, at least, the slightly more expensive "superior" room is worth the small price difference.

The contemporary **Hotel Tierra del Fuego** (Avenida Colón 716, tel./fax 061/22-6200, www.puntaarenas.com, US$125 s, US$140 d) is a business-oriented facility.

Corner rooms have the best views at **Hotel Diego de Almagro** (Avenida Colón 1290, tel. 061/20-8800, www.dahoteles.com, US$139 s, US$149 d), a welcome addition to Punta's accommodations roster that overlooks the rejuvenated waterfront. It's part of a small chain, but the rooms are large and the service gracious.

Part of the Best Western chain, the contemporary **Hotel Finis Terrae** (Avenida Colón 766, tel. 061/22-8200, www.hotelfinisterrae.com, US$154 s, US$185 d) is decent enough, but it's not in the class of the city's historic hotels or even the cheaper Diego del Almagro.

The most historic accommodations, though, can be found at the **(Hotel José Nogueira** (Bories 959, tel. 061/71-1000, www.hotel-nogueira.com, US$170 s, US$190 d), which occupies part of the Sara Braun mansion. Its greenhouse bar-restaurant, with its snaking grape arbor, merits a visit even if you can't afford to book a room.

Over US$200

Built by the Sociedad Ganadera Tierra del Fuego, the 1960s high-rise **Hotel Cabo de Hornos** (Plaza Muñoz Gamero 1025, tel. 061/71-5000, www.hotelesaustralis.com, US$190 s, US$210 d) has undergone not just a face-lift but a full-scale makeover under new ownership—the same as the Cruceros Australis cruise line. The public spaces are spectacular and the rooms attractive, but they have their shortcomings—Wi-Fi can't penetrate its thick walls, for instance, and the Ethernet cables are awkwardly remote from any potential workspace.

FOOD

Punta Arenas's gastronomic scene ranges from fast food to haute cuisine, with regional twists. Dining out here, though, is no bargain.

Quijote (Lautaro Navarro 1087, tel. 061/24-1225) serves inexpensive lunches. Upstairs in the Casa del Turista, at the entrance to Muelle Prat, **Café Puerto del Estrecho** (O'Higgins 1401, tel. 061/24-1022) has a variety of espresso-based specialty coffees, such as mocha and amaretto, plus snacks and desserts to accompany them.

The best fast-food option is **(Lomit's** (José Menéndez 722, tel. 061/24-3399), a dependable sandwich-and-beer chain that's almost always packed. Sandwiches cost around US$5. **La Carioca** (José Menéndez 600, tel. 061/22-4809), by contrast, is a one-of-a-kind sandwich outlet that also serves passable pizza, pasta, and draft beer. The **Café Irlandés** (José Menéndez 848, tel. 061/24-6082) is similar but more spacious and comfortable, though there's little Irish about it except a long bar.

Dónde Mariano (O'Higgins 504, tel. 061/24-5291, lunch and dinner daily) delivers on its modest pretensions, serving simply prepared fish entrées, including a side order, in the US$9–12 range. The decor has improved, and the service is adept.

Under the same management as the landmark restaurant La Luna, **O Sole Mio** (O'Higgins 974, tel. 061/24-2026, lunch and dinner daily) serves a diversity of pastas with seafood sauces, but the quality varies. Prices are moderate, around US$8 per entrée, and the atmosphere is informal.

Half a block south, **(La Luna** (O'Higgins 1017, tel. 061/22-8555, www.laluna.cl, lunch and dinner daily) still buzzes with activity—pins stuck on wall maps indicate the origins of

TIERRA DEL FUEGO

the clientele—but it has lost some of its informality. Even the *chupe de centolla* (king crab casserole, US$12) isn't quite what it was, and they may be trying a little too hard.

New in late 2007, alongside La Luna, **Jekus** (O'Higgins 1021, tel. 061/24-5851, jekus.patagonia@gmail.com, lunch and dinner daily) has a sunken bar and dining room of natural woods, with a separate upstairs for smokers. The food is demonstrably Patagonian in dishes such as the tender lamb chops (US$14) flavored with a spicy *merkén*. Some reports suggest uneven initial results, but at its best it's outstanding.

La Marmita Bistro (Plaza Sampaio 678, tel. 061/22-2056, lunch and dinner daily) has risen to near the top of Punta's restaurant scene for creative seafood (no Italian would recognize the scallop appetizer as "lasagna," but it's outstanding) and roast lamb (US$13) with a Mapuche *tomaticán* sauce of mushroom, onion, and tomato. With an atmosphere that is both historic and casual, it also serves unusual vegetarian plates and varied desserts.

For US$22, **Sabores** (Mejicana 702, 2nd floor, tel. 061/22-7369, www.restaurantsabores.com, lunch and dinner daily) serves a four-course "Magellanic menu" that includes both king crab and salmon as well as a *pisco* sour and half a bottle of wine; Wednesdays are all-you-can-eat pasta nights (US$7 pp).

Expanding from its Puerto Natales base, **El Asador Patagónico** (O'Higgins 694, tel. 061/22-2463, lunch and dinner daily) opened here in late 2008, and the early returns are mixed. The menu is virtually identical to that of the original, it's a little cheaper and a little smaller, but the service is erratic even when it's not crowded.

In expanded quarters, the nautically themed **Puerto Viejo** (O'Higgins 1166, tel. 061/22-5103, US$10–20) continues doing bang-up business with an almost exclusively seafood menu, but the service has deteriorated. Open for lunch and dinner, it serves specialties such as *centolla* (king crab) and *merluza* (hake).

Under the same management, a couple of kilometers north of the plaza, **Los Ganaderos** (Avenida Bulnes 0977, tel. 061/21-

4597, www.parrillalosganaderos.cl, lunch and dinner daily) is a classy *parrilla* specializing in succulent Patagonian lamb grilled on a vertical spit for US$15 pp *tenedor libre* (all-you-can-eat). There is also a more diverse *parrillada* for two (about US$25), and pasta dishes in the US$8–10 range. Try the regional Patagonian desserts, such as *mousse de calafate* and *mousse de ruibarbo* (rhubarb).

Four blocks south of the plaza, the creative **La Leyenda del Remezón** (21 de Mayo 1469, tel. 061/24-1029, lunch and dinner daily) serves game dishes (beaver and guanaco are now being farmed in the region) in the US$25 and up range—not cheap, but unique. Seafood specialties include krill, king crab, and spider crab, and most dishes are substantially cheaper than the game.

In the old Centro Español, the upstairs **La Tasca** (Plaza Muñoz Gamero 771, tel. 061/24-2807, lunch and dinner daily) has been reborn as a cheerful mid-range-to-upmarket Spanish restaurant with creative variants on traditional dishes, such as *merluza* (hake) stuffed with king crab and avocado (US$12). The *pisco* sours are excellent, and the wine list greatly improved, but it has also become a smokers' refuge.

Broccolino (O'Higgins 1049, tel. 061/71-0479, lunch and dinner daily) serves a fine risotto with *centolla* and scallops, along with beef, lamb, and pastas in the US$10–12 range. Traditionally, **Sotito's Bar** (O'Higgins 1138, tel. 061/24-5365, lunch and dinner daily) has set the seafood standard here, and it still deserves consideration.

INFORMATION

One block east of the plaza, **Sernatur** (Lautaro Navarro 999, tel. 061/22-5385, infomagallanes@sernatur.cl, 8:30 A.M.–7 P.M. Mon.–Fri., 9 A.M.–6 P.M. Sat.–Sun. in summer, 8:30 A.M.–7 P.M. Mon.–Fri. the rest of the year) is one of Chile's better regional offices, with English-speaking personnel and up-to-date accommodations and transportation information.

In summer, Plaza Muñoz Gamero's municipal **Kiosko de Informaciones** (tel. 061/20-0610, informacionturistica@puntaarenas.cl) is open

8 A.M.–4:30 P.M. Monday, 8 A.M.–5:30 P.M. Tuesday–Friday, and 9 A.M.–6 P.M. Saturday. **Conaf** (Avenida Bulnes 0309, 4th floor, tel. 061/23-8581) provides information on the region's national parks.

SERVICES

Punta Arenas is one of the easier Chilean cities in which to change both cash and travelers checks, especially at travel agencies along Lautaro Navarro. Most close by midday Saturday, but **Scott Cambios** (Avenida Colón and Magallanes, tel. 061/24-5811) will cash travelers checks then.

Several banks around Plaza Muñoz Gamero have ATMs, such as **Banco Santander** (Magallanes 997).

Just north of Plaza Muñoz Gamero, **Correos de Chile** (Bories 911) is the post office.

Long-distance call centers include **Telefónica CTC** (Nogueira 1116), at the southwest corner of Plaza Muñoz Gamero, and **Entel** (Lautaro Navarro 931). Try also **Hostal Calafate** (Magallanes 922), which has the best Internet café and call center in town.

The **Argentine consulate** (21 de Mayo 1878, tel. 061/26-1912) is open 10 A.M.–3:30 P.M. weekdays only.

For clean clothes, try **Lavandería Record** (O'Higgins 969, tel. 061/24-3607) or **Lavaseco Vicars** (Sarmiento de Gamboa 726, tel. 061/24-1516).

Punta Arenas's **Hospital Regional** (Arauco and Angamos, tel. 061/24-4040) is north of downtown.

GETTING THERE

Punta Arenas has good air links with mainland Chile, frequent air service to Chilean Tierra del Fuego, infrequent flights to Argentine Tierra del Fuego, and weekly service to the Falkland Islands. There are roundabout overland routes to mainland Chile via Argentina, regular bus service to Argentine Tierra del Fuego via a ferry link, direct ferry service to Chilean Tierra del Fuego, and expensive (but extraordinarily scenic) cruise-ship service to Ushuaia in Argentine Tierra del Fuego.

Air

LAN (Bories 884, tel. 061/24-1232) flies four times daily to Santiago, normally via Puerto Montt, but some flights stop at Balmaceda, near Coyhaique. It also flies three times weekly to Ushuaia, Argentina, and Saturday to the Falkland Islands; one Falklands flight per month stops in the Argentine city of Río Gallegos.

Sky Airline (Roca 935, tel. 061/71-0645) also flies north to Santiago and intermediate points. The Uruguayan airline **Pluna** (tel. 02/595-2879, www.pluna.aero) is due to begin service on this route.

Aerovías DAP (O'Higgins 891, tel. 061/61-6100, www.aeroviasdap.cl) flies seven-seat Cessnas to and from Porvenir (15 minutes, US$37) at least daily Monday–Saturday, more often in summer. DAP also flies 20-seater Twin Otters to and from Puerto Williams on Isla Navarino (US$103) Monday and Wednesday–Saturday. In addition, it has extensive charter services and occasionally goes to Antarctica.

Bus

Punta Arenas has no central bus terminal, though some companies share facilities, and the **Central de Pasajeros** (Avenida Colón and Magallanes, tel. 061/24-5811) sells tickets for all of them. Most terminals are within a few blocks of each other, north of Plaza Muñoz Gamero. Services vary seasonally but are most numerous in January–February.

Carriers serving Puerto Natales (3 hours, US$8–10) include **Pullman Bus Sur** (José Menéndez 552, tel. 061/61-4224, www.bussur.cl), with six buses daily; **Buses Fernández** (Armando Sanhueza 745, tel. 061/24-2313, www.busesfernandez.com), seven daily; **Buses Pacheco** (Avenida Colón 900, tel. 061/22-5527, www.busespacheco.com), five daily; and **Buses Barría** (Avenida España 264, tel. 061/24-0646).

Several carriers go to Río Gallegos (4 hours, US$12): **Buses Pingüino** (Armando Sanhueza 745, tel. 061/22-3898), **Buses Ghisoni** (Lautaro Navarro 975, tel. 061/61-3420, busesghisoni@123.cl), and Buses Pacheco.

Tecni-Austral (Lautaro Navarro 975, tel.

061/22-2078) goes to Río Grande (8 hours, US$40) and Ushuaia (11.5 hours, US$59) in Argentine Tierra del Fuego at 8:30 A.M. on Tuesday, Thursday, and Saturday. **Buses Pacheco** goes at 9 A.M. on Monday, Wednesday, and Friday to Río Grande, with connections to Ushuaia.

Sea
Transbordadora Austral Broom (Avenida Bulnes 05075, tel. 061/21-8100, www.tabsa.cl) sails from Punta Arenas to Porvenir (2.5 hours) at 9 A.M. Monday–Saturday and 9:30 A.M. Sunday. Adult passengers pay US$9 pp except for the drivers, whose fare is included in the US$58 charge per vehicle (motorcyclists pay US$15, but bicyclists pay nothing extra). The rate for children is half the adult fare. Given limited vehicle capacity, reservations are a good idea on the *Crux Australis,* which leaves from Terminal Tres Puentes at the north end of town, easily reached by *taxi colectivo* from the Casa Braun-Menéndez on Magallanes, half a block north of Plaza Muñoz Gamero.

Broom also operates the ferry *Bahía Azul* to Puerto Williams (32 hours) at 6 P.M. every Wednesday, returning at 10 P.M. Friday. The fare is US$210 for a bunk, US$175 for a reclining seat.

It's neither cheap nor a conventional way of getting to Argentina, but the luxury cruisers MV *Mare Australis* and MV *Via Australis* shuttle to Ushuaia as part of a weeklong circuit through the fjords of Chilean Tierra del Fuego, and passengers can disembark in Ushuaia (or board there, for that matter). Normally both ships require reservations well in advance.

GETTING AROUND
Aeropuerto Presidente Carlos Ibáñez del Campo is 20 kilometers north of town on Ruta 9, the Puerto Natales highway. **Transfer Austral** (Lautaro Navarro 975, tel. 061/61-7202) arranges door-to-door transfers (US$6 pp).

Buses returning from Puerto Natales will normally drop passengers at the airport to meet outgoing flights on request, but make arrangements before boarding. Natales-bound buses will also pick up arriving passengers, but again make arrangements in advance.

Punta Arenas has numerous car-rental options, including **Adel Rent a Car** (Pedro Montt 962, tel. 061/22-4819, www.adel.cl), **Budget** (O'Higgins 964, tel./fax 061/24-1696, www.budgetpatagonia.com), **Avis** (Roca 1044, tel./fax 061/61-4381, www.emsarentacar.cl), **Hertz** (O'Higgins 931, tel. 061/61-3087), and **Lubag** (Avenida Colón 975, tel./fax 061/71-0484, www.lubag.cl).

Vicinity of Punta Arenas (Chile)

Punta Arenas's myriad travel agencies operate various excursions to nearby destinations such as Reserva Nacional Magallanes, Fuerte Bulnes, the Seno Otway penguin colony, Río Verde, Estancia San Gregorio, and even Parque Nacional Torres del Paine. The most popular half-day excursions, such as Fuerte Bulnes and Otway, cost US$21–30 pp, while full-day trips such as Pali Aike can cost up to US$112 pp with a three-person minimum.

Among the established operators are **Aventour** (Patagonia 779-A, tel. 061/24-1197, www.aventourpatagonia.com), **Turismo Aónikenk** (Magallanes 619, tel. 061/22-1982, www.aonikenk.com), **Turismo Laguna Azul** (José Menéndez 786, tel. 061/22-5200, www.turismolagunaazul.cl), **Turismo Pali Aike** (Lautaro Navarro 1125, tel. 061/61-5750, www.turismopaliaike.com), **Turismo Viento Sur** (Fagnano 585, tel. 061/22-2590, www.vientosur.com), and **Turismo Yámana** (Errázuriz 932, tel. 061/71-0567, www.yamana.cl).

RESERVA NACIONAL MAGALLANES
Only eight kilometers west of downtown, 13,500-hectare Reserva Nacional Magallanes is a combination of Patagonian steppe and

southern beech forest that, in good winters, amasses enough snow for skiing. Despite its proximity to Punta Arenas, official statistics say it gets barely 11,000 visitors per year, and only 1,300 of those are foreigners.

Westbound Avenida Independencia, a good gravel road that may require chains in winter, climbs gradually to a fork whose southern branch leads to the **Sector Andino,** where the local Club Andino's **Centro de Esquí Cerro Mirador** includes a *refugio* that serves meals, as well as a ski school and a single well-maintained chairlift. In summer, try the **Sendero Mirador,** a two-hour loop hike that winds through the forest and crosses the ski area; there's also a mountain-bike circuit.

The northwesterly **Sector Las Minas,** which includes a gated picnic area, charges US$1.80 pp for adult admission but nothing for kids. A longer footpath links up with the trail to the El Mirador summit, which offers panoramas east toward Punta Arenas, the strait, and Tierra del Fuego, and west toward Seno Otway.

Though some travel agencies offer tours to the reserve, it would also be a good mountain-bike excursion from town.

PINGÜINERA SENO OTWAY

Burrowing Magellanic penguins abound along Argentine Patagonia's Atlantic shoreline, but they are fewer in Chile. Barely an hour from Punta Arenas, though, the Otway colony of *Spheniscus magellanicus* is the closest to any major city on the continent. Under the administration of the nonprofit Fundación Otway, it grew in a decade from no more than 400 penguins to about 11,000 at present. From October, when the first birds arrive, to April, when the last stragglers head to sea, it draws up to 40,000 visitors. The peak season is December–February.

While the site is fenced to keep human visitors out of critical habitat, the birds are relatively tame and easy to photograph; on the downside, this fence did not prevent stray dogs from killing more than a hundred birds in 2001. The landowning Kusanovic family has taken over management from the Fundación Otway.

During the season, any number of Punta Arenas operators shuttle visitors to and from Otway for about US$30 pp, not including the US$11 pp admission charge. Half-day tours take place either in the morning (which photographers may prefer) or afternoon. For visitors with private vehicles, there's also a US$2 toll.

Otway is only about 60 kilometers northwest of Punta Arenas via Ruta 9 and a gravel road that leads west from a signed junction at Parque Chabunco, about 19 kilometers north of the city.

While Otway is a worthwhile excursion, visitors with flexible schedules and a little more money should consider the larger Isla Magdalena colony in Monumento Natural Los Pingüinos, in the Strait of Magellan.

◖ MONUMENTO NATURAL LOS PINGÜINOS

From early October, more than 60,000 breeding pairs of Magellanic penguins paddle ashore and waddle to burrows that cover nearly all of 97-hectare Isla Magdalena, 20 nautical miles northeast of Punta Arenas, before returning to sea in April. Also the site of a landmark lighthouse, Isla Magdalena is the focal point of Monumento Natural Los Pingüinos, one of Conaf's smallest but most interesting reserves.

While the mainland Otway colony gets upwards of 40,000 visitors per year, Isla Magdalena gets fewer than 20,000—and 90 percent of them are foreigners—because of limited accessibility. In summer, though, the ferry *Melinka* visits the island daily from Punta Arenas. Though more expensive than Otway tours, these excursions also offer the chance to see penguins and dolphins in the water, as well as black-browed albatrosses, cormorants, kelp gulls, skuas, South American terns, and other seabirds in the surrounding skies.

From a floating dock on the east side of the island, a short trail leads along the beach and up the hill to Scottish engineer George Slight's **Faro Magdalena** (1901), a lighthouse whose iron tower rises 13.5 meters above the island's highest point; still functioning, the light has

PINGÜINOS AND *PINGÜINERAS*

Punta Arenas is close to two breeding colonies of the burrowing Magellanic penguin, *Spheniscus magellanicus*. The Otway Sound colony, about 45 minutes from the city, is interesting enough, but the larger colony on Isla Magdalena, in the Strait of Magellan, is two hours away by ferry or slightly less by bus and rigid inflatable.

Also known to English speakers as the jackass penguin because its call resembles that of a braying burro, the Magellanic is present from October to April. It is most numerous in January and February, when the chicks hatch in the sandy burrows that the birds have dug beneath the coastal turf. After the chicks have hatched, the parents alternate fishing trips for food that they later regurgitate to their young (combined with the scent of bird droppings, this makes any visit to a penguin colony an olfactory as well as a visual and auditory experience).

While the birds appear tame, they are wild animals, and their sharp beaks can draw blood – maintain a respectful distance for photography. Though both colonies have fenced walking routes to restrain tourists, the birds themselves frequently cross these routes.

Besides the countless seabirds and dolphins en route, the Magdalena trip has the added bonus of a historic lighthouse that now serves as a visitors center on an island that's one big warren of penguin burrows. While neither trip is strenuous, any walk in Patagonia's roaring winds can be a workout.

a range of 10 nautical miles. A narrow spiral staircase ascends the tower.

In the building's first five decades, a resident caretaker maintained the acetylene light, but after its automation in 1955 the abandoned building was vandalized. In 1981, though, the Chilean navy entrusted it to Conaf; declared a national monument, it has since become a visitors center. It boasts remarkably good exhibits on the island's history, including discovery, early navigation, cartography, and the lighthouse's construction, as well as natural history in both Spanish and English (though the English text is less complete). U.S. archaeologist Junius Bird, best known for his 1930s work at the mainland site of Pali Aike, also undertook excavations here.

For ferry excursions to Isla Magdalena, contact **Turismo Comapa** (Magallanes 990, tel. 061/20-0200, tcomapa@entelchile.net). December–March, the ferry *Melinka* makes a passengers-only trip to Isla Magdalena (US$46 adults, US$23 children) from Terminal Tres Puentes; sailing time is 3 P.M., and bring food—the *Melinka's* snack bar is pretty dire. Visitors spend about 1.5 hours on the island, returning to Punta Arenas around 8 P.M.

Passengers on the luxury MV *Mare Australis*

and MV *Via Australis* cruises through Tierra del Fuego's fjords stop here on the return leg of the trip, but there's also an intermediate alternative that's more frequent than either of the above options. Since 2005, **Solo Expediciones** (José Nogueira 1255, tel. 061/71-0219, www.soloexpediciones.com) offers half-day excursions (US$76 pp) that shuttle passengers from the mainland in Zodiacs and include an approach to nearby Isla Marta, where the overflow from penguin-saturated Magdalena has migrated.

FUERTE BULNES

In 1584, Spanish explorer Pedro Sarmiento de Gamboa organized an expedition of 15 ships and 4,000 men to control the Strait of Magellan, but after a series of disasters only three ships with 300 colonists arrived to found **Ciudad del Rey don Felipe,** at Punta Santa Ana south of present-day Punta Arenas. Even worse for the Spaniards, the inhospitable climate and unsuitable soils made agriculture impossible; when British privateer Thomas Cavendish landed three years later, in 1587, he found only a handful of survivors and gave it the name Port Famine, which has survived as the Spanish **Puerto del Hambre.**

For many years, the consensus was that

starvation alone determined the fate of Puerto Hambre, but regional historian Mateo Martinic has suggested that disease, mutual acts of violence, Tehuelche attacks, and a simple sense of anguish or abandonment contributed to its demise. Unfortunately, the Chilean military control much of the area, making archaeological excavations that might resolve the question difficult.

The area remained unsettled until 1843, when President Manuel Bulnes ordered the cutter *Ancud* south from Chiloé with tools, construction materials, food, and livestock to take possession for the expansionist Chilean state. The result was Fuerte Bulnes, a military outpost that survived only a little longer than the original Spanish settlement before being relocated to Punta Arenas in 1848.

Modern Fuerte Bulnes, on the site of the first Chilean settlement, is a national monument more for its site than for its reconstructions of 19th-century buildings and the defensive walls—with sharpened stakes—that surround them. Among the structures were residences, stables, a blockhouse, a chapel, a jail, and a warehouse.

Archaeologists located nearby remnants of Ciudad del Rey don Felipe in 1955, and later excavations turned up human remains, bullets, tombs, and ruins of Puerto Hambre's church. A more recent plaque (1965) celebrates the 125th anniversary of the Pacific Steam Navigation Company's ships *Chile* and *Perú* and their routes around the Horn.

Puerto Hambre and Fuerte Bulnes are 58 kilometers south of Punta Arenas via Ruta 9, which is paved about halfway; the rest is bumpy but passable. There is no regular public transportation, but most Punta Arenas tour operators offer half-day excursions. Admission is free.

PARQUE MARINO FRANCISCO COLOANE

Established in July 2003, named for a Chilean author who chronicled the southern seas, this 67,000-hectare maritime park is the result of five years' research that pinpointed the area around Isla Carlos III, in the southwestern Strait of Magellan, as summer feeding grounds for the southern humpback whale. In addition to the humpbacks, which migrate the length of the South American coast from Colombia, the park's seas and shores are home to breeding Magellanic penguins, cormorants, many other southern seabirds, fur seals, and sea lions. Orcas are also present.

From mid-December to late April, **Whalesound** (Lautaro Navarro 1175, 2nd floor, Punta Arenas, tel. 061/71-0511, ext. 201, cel. 09/9349-3862, www.whalesound. com) offers three-day expeditions (US$890 pp, minimum 2 persons) to the park, where guests sleep in geodesic dome tents with comfortable Japanese beds and solar-powered electricity, on Isla Carlos III. The cost includes daily excursions with specialized bilingual guides and gourmet meals. Sea kayaks are also available.

Aventura Sur (Avenida Roca 825, Oficina 3, tel. 061/61-3933, www.expedicionfitzroy. com) also offers three-day expedition tours to Isla Carlos III (US$1,022 pp), with accommodations aboard the refitted British-built MN *Forrest* rather than on land.

RÍO VERDE

Some 43 kilometers north of Punta Arenas on Ruta 9, a gravel road loops northwest along Seno Otway to Seno Skyring and Estancia Río Verde, which has seemingly made the transition from a shipshape sheep farm to a model municipality of exquisitely maintained public buildings in the Magellanic style. Note particularly the manicured gardens surrounding the **Escuela Básica,** the local boarding school.

Off to a good start, in one wing of the boarding school, the **Museo Comunal Río Verde** (10 A.M.–5 P.M. daily, US$1) has exhibits on local history, natural history (taxidermy), ethnology, and local and regional literature.

Unfortunately, only the foundations of the recently created *municipalidad* remain after it burned to the ground a few years ago and the museum exhibits were lost; municipal offices have since moved to the former Hostería Río Verde, 90 kilometers from Punta Arenas and six kilometers south of the *estancia*.

Across from the former *hostería,* a small ferry shuttles vehicles and passengers to **Isla Riesco** (warning: it's free to travel to the island, but costs US$30 to get your vehicle back to the mainland). Nearby, Paola Vizzani González's *Escultura Monumental,* a beached whale built of concrete and driftwood, honors the region's early colonists. Also nearby, the **Hito El Vapor** marks the final resting place of the steamer *Los Amigos,* which carried coal to outlying farms until it ran aground in a storm.

The loop road rejoins Ruta 9 at Villa Tehuelches, a wide spot in the road about 90 kilometers from Punta Arenas. This makes a good alternative route north or south for both motorists and mountain bikers.

While the *hostería* at the ferry crossing no longer provides accommodations, the Chilean-Uruguayan **Estancia Río Verde** (Km 98 Norte, tel. 061/31-1123 or 061/31-1131, www.estanciarioverde.cl, US$90 s, US$120 d) offers stylish accommodations (one suite has a sunny tower with sea and pampas views), day tours that can include horseback riding and fishing, and *asados,* lunches, and tea in its restaurant. Open November–March, with gracious English-speaking ownership, it's a bargain by *estancia* standards.

ESTANCIA RÍO PENITENTE

Founded by Falkland Islands immigrants in 1891, Río Penitente has turned one of the best-preserved historic houses on any Patagonian sheep ranch into a guesthouse that feels like a step back in time, but still has essential comforts such as private baths. Most guest rooms in this two-story Victorian have period furniture, in immaculate condition, and fireplaces for heat. Activities include horseback riding and fly-fishing in its namesake river, but it's an ideal place for just relaxing. The restaurant serves lamb-on-a-stake barbecues (US$35 pp) to tour groups on weekends.

Hostería Estancia Río Penitente Ruta 9 Km 137, tel. 061/33-1694, www.hosteriariopenitente.com, US$115 s, US$135 d with breakfast) is open October–Semana Santa.

ESTANCIA SAN GREGORIO

From a highway junction about 45 kilometers north of Punta Arenas, paved Ruta 225 leads east-northeast to the Argentine border at Monte Aymond, passing the former Estancia San Gregorio, once one of Chilean Patagonia's largest landholdings. Part of the Menéndez wool empire, San Gregorio dates from the 1890s, though it reached its peak between 1910 and 1930. Besides wool, it produced frozen mutton, hides, and tallow.

Now run as a cooperative, 120 kilometers from Punta Arenas, San Gregorio is a *zona típica* national historical monument. It exemplified the Anglo-Scottish model of the Patagonian sheep *estancia,* in which each unit was a self-sufficient hierarchy with a nearly omnipotent administrator at the top. Geographically, it consisted of discrete residential and production sectors: The former included the administrator's house, employee residences, shearers' dormitories, chapel, and the like, while the latter comprised the shearing shed, warehouses, a smithy, a company store, and similarly functional buildings. It had its own pier and railroad to move the wool clip directly to freighters.

Most of San Gregorio's constructions date from the 1890s, but a descendent of the Menéndez dynasty still occupies French architect Antoine Beaulier's **Casa Patronal** (1925). The farm featured an extensive system of windbreaks ranging upwards of five meters in height, later planted with Monterey cypress for beautification.

While technically not open to the public, many of San Gregorio's buildings line both sides of the highway to Monte Aymond. Beached on shore are the corroded hulks of the British clipper *Ambassador* (a national monument) and the company steamer *Amadeo,* which gave up the ghost in the 1940s.

PUNTA DELGADA

About 30 kilometers east of San Gregorio, paved Ruta 257 leads southeast to Punta Delgada, the port for the ferry crossing to Tierra del Fuego via the Primera Angostura narrows. Depending sometimes on tidal conditions, the ferries *Patagonia* and *Pionero* shuttle across the channel every 1.5 hours 8:30 A.M.–11:45 P.M. Fares are US$3 pp for adult passengers, US$1.50 for kids ages 10–14, US$26 for automobiles, and US$8 for motorcycles. Most buses to Argentine Tierra del Fuego use this route because the longer ferry to Porvenir goes only once daily and is subject to delay or cancellation for rough seas.

☾ PARQUE NACIONAL PALI AIKE

Hugging the Argentine border north of Kimiri Aike and west of the Monte Aymond border crossing, little-visited Pali Aike is an area of volcanic steppe and rugged lava beds that once supported megafauna such as the *Mylodon* ground sloth and the native American horse, both of which disappeared soon after humans first inhabited the area some 11,000 years ago.

Paleo-Indian hunters may have contributed to their extinction, but environmental changes after the last major glaciation probably also played a role. In the 1930s, self-taught archaeologist Junius Bird, of New York's American Museum of Natural History, conducted the earliest systematic excavations of Paleo-Indian sites such as Cueva Pali Aike, within the park boundaries, and Cueva Fell, a short distance west. These archaeologically rich volcanic shelters (not truly caves) are the prime reason Chilean authorities have nominated the area as a UNESCO World Heritage Site.

Findings at Pali Aike include human remains that have yielded insights on Paleo-Indian funerary customs, while materials from Cueva Fell have helped reveal the transition from relatively simple hunting to more complex forms of subsistence. These include sophisticated hunting tools such as the bow and arrow and *boleadoras,* and a greater reliance on coastal and marine resources. There are also indicators of ceremonial artifacts.

Geography and Climate

Part of arid eastern Magallanes, 5,030-hectare Pali Aike consists of rolling steppe grasslands whose porous volcanic soils and slag absorb water quickly. Almost constant high winds and cool temperatures make it a better summer or autumn excursion.

Flora and Fauna

While the *Mylodon* and native horse may have disappeared, the park's grasslands swarm with herds of wild guanaco and flocks of rheas, upland geese, ibis, and other birds. Pumas and foxes are the major predators.

Sights and Recreation

Accessible by road, **Cueva Pali Aike** is a volcanic tube seven meters wide and five meters high at its mouth; it is 17 meters deep but tapers as it advances. In the 1930s, Bird discovered both human and megafauna remains, at least 8,600 years old and probably much older, in the cave.

Tours from Punta Arenas visit Cueva Pali Aike and usually hike the 1.7-kilometer trail through the **Escorial del Diablo** (the appropriately named Devil's Slag Heap, which is hell on hiking boots). The trail ends at the volcanic **Crater Morada del Diablo.**

From Cueva Pali Aike, a nine-kilometer footpath leads to **Laguna Ana,** where waterfowl are abundant, and the main road, five kilometers from the park entrance. Mountain bikes should be ideal for this sort of rolling terrain, but it could be even tougher on tires than it is on boots.

Practicalities

As of 2010, a campground is supposedly in the works, but there are no tourist services as yet, so bring supplies.

At the main entrance, Conaf has a ranger station but collects no admission fee. A great destination for solitude seekers, Pali Aike officially gets only about 1,600 visitors per year, a third of them foreigners.

Pali Aike is 196 kilometers northeast of Punta Arenas via Ruta 9, Ruta 255, and a graveled secondary road from the hamlet of Cooperativa Villa O'Higgins, 11 kilometers beyond Kimiri Aike. Just south of the Chilean border post at Monte Aymond, a hard-to-follow dirt road also leads to the park.

There is no public transportation, but Punta Arenas travel agencies can arrange visits. Renting a car, though, is probably the best option, especially if shared among several people.

◖ THE FJORDS OF FUEGIA

Short of Antarctica itself, some of the Southern Hemisphere's most awesome scenery occurs in the Beagle Channel and southern Tierra del Fuego. And as usual, Charles Darwin left one of the most vivid descriptions of the channel named for the vessel on which he sailed:

The scenery here becomes even grander than before. The lofty mountains on the north side compose the granitic axis, or backbone of the country, and boldly rise to a height of between three and four thousand feet, with one peak above six thousand feet. They are covered by a wide mantle of perpetual snow, and numerous cascades pour their waters, through the woods, into the narrow channel below. In many parts, magnificent glaciers extend from the mountain side to the water's edge. It is scarcely possible to imagine anything more beautiful than the beryl-like blue of these glaciers, and especially as contrasted with the dead white of the upper expanse of the snow. The fragments which had fallen from the glacier into the water, were floating away, and the channel with the icebergs presented, for the space of a mile, a miniature likeness of the Polar Sea.

Even today, few visitors see Tierra del Fuego's splendid fjords, barely changed since Darwin described them in 1833; many do so onboard excursions from Punta Arenas to the Argentine port of Ushuaia or back on the twin Chilean vessels *Mare Australis* and *Via Australis*. Unlike the Navimag ferry from Puerto Natales to Puerto Montt, these are cruises in the traditional sense—the passengers are waited on hand and foot, and they're not cheap. Yet for the foreseeable future, this remains the only

way to see the area short of sailing your own yacht or chartering someone else's, and for that reason it's worth consideration even for those with limited finances.

Though it's possible to do the entire loop from either Punta Arenas or Ushuaia, most visitors do either four days and three nights from Punta Arenas to Ushuaia, or five days and four nights from Ushuaia to Punta Arenas. The boats sometimes undertake variants that involve four nights from Punta Arenas and three from Ushuaia, and there's usually some duplication; both legs, for instance, visit the western Beagle Channel's **Glaciar Pía,** and sometimes the boats are there simultaneously.

Routes can vary depending on weather conditions in this notoriously capricious climate. After an evening departure from Punta Arenas's Muelle Prat, the vessel crosses the Strait of Magellan to enter the **Seno del Almirantazgo** (Admiralty Sound), a westward maritime extension of the freshwater Lago Fagnano trough. Passengers usually go ashore at **Bahía Ainsworth,** near the **Glaciar Marinelli,** where there's a short hiking trail through what was once forest until feral beavers dammed the area into a series of ponds; the most interesting site is a small elephant seal colony. Farther west, at **Isla Tucker,** there's a Magellanic penguin colony (usually observed from an inflatable Zodiac) and it's also possible to see the rare striated caracara (*Phalcoboenus australis*).

After a night's sailing, the ship may enter the **Fiordo D'Agostini,** a glacial inlet named for the early-20th-century Italian priest and mountaineer who explored the Cordillera Darwin's farthest recesses. When high winds make it impossible to approach the **Glaciar Serrano** (named for Chilean naval Lieutenant Ramón Serrano Montaner, who charted the Strait in 1879), an option is the more sheltered **Glaciar D'Agostini.** Even here, though, seracs crack off the glacier's face, touching off a rapid surge of water and ice that runs parallel to a broad gravel beach and, when it subsides, leaves the beach littered with boulders of ice.

Darwin described the dangers of travel in

outlet of Glacier Pía, Avenida de los Glaciares, Chilean Tierra del Fuego

a land that sea kayakers are just beginning to explore:

> The boats being hauled on shore at our dinner hour, we were admiring from the distance of half a mile a perpendicular cliff of ice, and were wishing that some more fragments would fall. At last, down came a mass with a roaring noise, and immediately we saw the smooth outline of a wave traveling toward us. The men ran down as quickly as they could to the boats; for the chance of their being dashed to pieces was evident. One of the seamen just caught hold of the bows, as the curling breaker reached it: he was knocked over and over, but not hurt; and the boats, though thrice lifted on high and let fall again, received no damage. I had previously noted that some large fragments of rock on the beach had been lately displaced; but until seeing this wave, I did not understand the cause.

After navigating Canal Cockburn, where open ocean swells can rock the boat at least briefly, the vessel turns into the calmer **Canal Ocasión** and eventually enters the Beagle Channel's north arm, sailing past the so-called **Avenida de los Glaciares,** a series of glaciers named for various European countries; passengers normally disembark at **Glaciar Pía,** where dozens of waterfalls cascade down sheer metamorphic slopes from the glacier and passengers take a short hike.

Weather permitting, the ship sails south to **Cabo de Hornos** (Cape Horn) and, wind permitting (less than 45 knots), passengers disembark to visit the small Chilean naval detachment and hike to the stylized albatross sculpture that symbolizes sailors who lost their lives "rounding the Horn." On occasion, the captain can choose to round the Horn himself before proceeding north to **Bahía Wulaia,** on Isla Navarino's western shore. Here passengers visit the site of an early mission where, in a notorious incident, the Yámana massacred all but one of the Anglicans and their crew. There is then the option of a short but steep hike with panoramic views of the bay, or an easier shoreline walk to see birdlife that includes Magellanic oystercatchers.

© WAYNE BERNHARDSON

TIERRA DEL FUEGO

Northbound, emigration formalities now take place at **Puerto Navarino,** at the western end of **Isla Navarino.** Proceeding to **Ushuaia,** all passengers spend the night aboard; those returning to Punta Arenas have the day free in Ushuaia before returning to the ship, while new passengers check their bags downtown before boarding in late afternoon.

After reentering Chile at Puerto Navarino, the ship sails south to Wulaia and Cabo de Hornos and then, returning to the Beagle Channel, the ship veers westward through the Beagle Channel's north arm, again passing the Avenida de los Glaciares and entering Fiordo Pía. Proceeding through the afternoon and the night, the boat starts the last full day navigating the **Fiordo Chico** (Little Fjord), where passengers board Zodiacs to approach but not land at **Glaciar Plüschow,** named for a German pioneer aviator who took the first aerial photos of the Cordillera Darwin.

In the afternoon, the **Glaciar Águila** is the site of an easy shoreline walk or a more demanding slog through knee-deep mud in a southern beech forest (the video footage of this hike, shown the night before in an orientation session, is priceless). On the final morning, the boat sails north to **Isla Magdalena** (see *Monumento Natural Los Pingüinos*) before returning to Punta Arenas.

Practicalities

Well-organized without being regimented, the cruise is informal in both dress and behavior. As the start, passengers sign up for meal tables; places are fixed for the duration except at the buffet breakfast, when people tend to straggle in at different times. In general, passengers are grouped according to language, though they often place together people who speak English as a second language. The staff themselves can handle Spanish, English, German, French, and occasionally other languages.

After introduction of the captain and crew, and an obligatory safety drill, there's a welcome drink and a brief folklore show (in Punta Arenas) or tango demonstration (in Ushuaia). Smoking is prohibited everywhere except outdoors and at the rear of the fourth deck pub; bar consumption is now included in the package.

The cabins themselves are spacious, with either a double or twin beds, built-in reading lights, a closet with hangers and a small lock box for valuables, and a private bath with excellent hot showers. Some rooms also have a fold-down bunk for children or a third person. The food is abundant and occasionally excellent, though breakfasts are a little monotonous; the wine is superb, and the service exceptional. Vegetarian menus are available on request.

For those who tire of the landscape or when the weather is bad, onboard activities include karaoke, slide lectures on flora and fauna, engine-room tours, and culinary demonstrations of cucumbers, peppers, zucchinis, and other vegetables carved in the shapes of birds and flowers. The farewell dinner is a gala affair, followed by champagne on the topmost deck.

Punta Arenas is the homeport for fjordbound cruises; check-in takes place at Turismo Comapa (Magallanes 990, tel. 061/20-0200) 1–5 P.M., while boarding takes place 5–6 P.M. at the entrance to Muelle Prat. Some passengers begin or end the trip in Argentine Tierra del Fuego, where check-in takes place at Comapa's Ushuaia office (San Martín 245, tel. 02901/43-0727, 9 A.M.–4 P.M.); boarding takes place at the Muelle Turístico 5–6 P.M.

Usually this popular cruise runs full October–April, but the global recession has meant occasional last-minute bargains; in this case, it may be possible to negotiate a deal in Punta Arenas, getting a private cabin without paying a single supplement, for instance. The best time is around Christmas, when days are so long that it's possible to enjoy the landscape until after 11 P.M., and there's sufficient light to read by 4 A.M.

Make reservations through **Cruceros Australis** (Avenida Bosque Norte 0440, 11th floor, Las Condes, Santiago, tel. 02/442-3110, fax 02/203-5173, www.australis.com), which also has offices in Buenos Aires (Carlos Pellegrini 989, 6th floor, Retiro, tel. 011/43-25-8400) and in Miami (4014 Chase Ave.,

Suite 202, Miami Beach, FL 33140, tel. 305/695-9618 or 877/678-3772). Per-person rates for four days and three nights start at US$840–1,510 in low season and go up to US$1,330–2,390 in high season. For five days and four nights, the comparable rates are US$1,120–2,010 in low season to US$1,770–3,110 in high season.

Puerto Natales (Chile)

In the past 20 years, Puerto Natales has changed from a sleepy wool and fishing port on what seemed the aptly named Seno Última Esperanza—"Last Hope Sound"—to a bustling tourist town whose season has lengthened well beyond the traditional summer months. Its proximity to Torres del Paine, coupled with its status as the southern terminus for the scenic ferry route from Puerto Montt, has placed it on the international travel map, utterly transforming the local economy.

While Natales has no knockout attractions in its own right, the town enjoys a magnificent seaside setting, with the snow-capped Cordillera Sarmiento and Campo de Hielo Sur, the southern Patagonian ice cap, visible over the water to the west, and the waterfront is more presentable than in the past. For visitors to Paine and other regional sights, it has abundant services, including tour operators and rental equipment, plus connections to the Argentine town of El Calafate and Parque Nacional Los Glaciares. The strength of the Chilean peso had reduced its competitiveness with nearby Argentine attractions such as the Moreno Glacier, but a readjustment has made the city a good value again.

Another possible strong point is the possible construction of a 150-meter cruise-ship pier, which would simplify land transfers from both the ferry (which does have an improved dock) and visiting cruisers, but in 2010 this remained at the talking stage. Meanwhile, private initiative has built a smaller jetty for local cruises near Puerto Bories, north of town.

HISTORY
Última Esperanza acquired its name because expeditions led by 16th-century explorers Juan

© WAYNE BERNHARDSON

Ferry passengers disembark for Puerto Natales.

Ladrilleros and Pedro Sarmiento de Gamboa failed to find a westbound route to the Pacific here. Puerto Natales proper dates from the early 20th century, a few years after German explorer Hermann Eberhard founded the area's first sheep *estancia* at Puerto Prat. Within a few years, the Sociedad Explotadora de Tierra del Fuego had built a slaughterhouse at nearby Bories to process and pack mutton for the export market. While the livestock economy declined in the second half of the 20th century, the tourist boom has reactivated and diversified the economy.

TIERRA DEL FUEGO

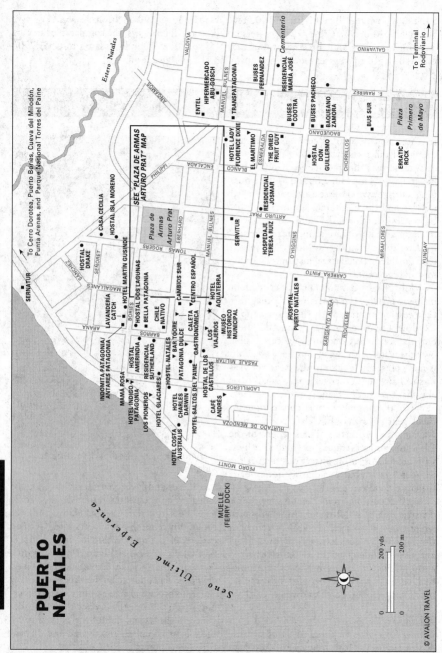

TIERRA DEL FUEGO

PUERTO NATALES

Seno Última Esperanza

Estero Natales

To Cerro Dorotea, Puerto Bories, Cueva del Milodón, Punta Arenas, and Parque Nacional Torres del Paine

MUELLE (FERRY DOCK)

SERNATUR

HOSTAL DRAKE

CASA CECILIA
HOSTAL ISLA MORENO

HOTEL MARTÍN GUSINDE

LAVANDERÍA CATCH

HOSTAL DOS LAGUNAS
BELLA PATAGONIA
CHILE NATIVO

CAMBIOS SUR

CENTRO ESPAÑOL

HOTEL AQUATERRA

CALETA GASTRONÓMICA

MUSEO HISTÓRICO MUNICIPAL

LOS VIAJEROS

BAR T'OORE
PATAGONIA DULCE

HOSTAL AMERINDIA
RESIDENCIAL SUTHERLAND
HOSTEL NATALES

INDÓMITA PATAGONIA/ ANTARES PATAGONIA

MAMA ROSA

HOTEL ÍNDIGO PATAGONIA
LOS PIONEROS
HOTEL GLACIARES

HOTEL COSTA AUSTRALIS

HOTEL CHARLES DARWIN
HOTEL SALTOS DEL PAINE

HOSTAL DE LOS CASTILLOS

CAFÉ ANDRÉS

Plaza de Armas Arturo Prat

SEE "PLAZA DE ARMAS ARTURO PRAT" MAP

SERVITUR

HOSPEDAJE TERESA RUIZ

HOTEL LADY FLORENCE DIXIE

EL MARÍTIMO
THE DRIED FRUIT GUY

RESIDENCIAL JOSMAR

HOSTAL DON GUILLERMO

HOSPITAL PUERTO NATALES

ERRATIC ROCK

ENTEL

HIPERMERCADO ABU-GOSCH

TRANSPATAGONIA

BUSES FERNÁNDEZ

RESIDENCIAL MARÍA JOSÉ

BUSES COOTRA

BUSES PACHECO
BAQUEANO ZAMORA

BUS SUR

Plaza Primero de Mayo

To Terminal Rodoviario

Cementerio

Streets: VALDIVIA, ANGAMOS, PHILIPPI, EBERHARD, TOMÁS ROGERS, BLANCO, ENCALADA, MANUEL BULNES, ARTURO PRAT, ESMERALDA, BAQUEDANO, CHORRILLOS, MIRAFLORES, YUNGAY, CARRERA PINTO, CHIGGINS, SARGENTO ALDEA, RIQUELME, E. RAMÍREZ, GALVARINO, SÁNCHEZ, SEÑORET, MAGALLANES, BORIES, BARROS, LADRILLEROS, PASAJE MILITAR, HURTADO DE MENDOZA, PEDRO MONT, ARANA

200 yds
200 m

© AVALON TRAVEL

PLAZA DE ARMAS ARTURO PRAT

DON JORGE
BORIES
Plaza de Armas
Arturo Prat
PHILLIPI
MAGALLANES
LA CASA DE PEPE
ROGERS
LA OVEJA NEGRA
CAFE CIELO DE PALO
RESIDENCIAL
PATAGONIA AVENTURA
EL EMPORIO
DE LA PAMPA
ÚLTIMA ESPERANZA
TOMÁS
EL LIVING
EL ASADOR
PATAGÓNICO
ÑANDÚ
ARTESANÍA
AFRIGONIA
FORTALEZA
PATAGONIA
MAGALLANIA
BACKPACKER
POST
OFFICE
MUNICIPALIDAD
★
IGLESIA PARROQUIAL
MARÍA AUXILIADORA
ARTURO PRAT
LA MESITA
GRANDE
TURISMO
CUTTER 21
DE MAYO
EBERHARD
BUSES
GOMEZ
TURISMO
COMAPA
TURISMO ZAAHJ
BUSES JB
HOSTAL
SOUTH WIND
CAFÉ
EVASIÓN
BLANCO ENCALADA
PUEBLO ARTESANAL
ETERH AIKE
WORLD'S
END
CAMBIO MILY
LA REPIZZA
LA BURBUJA
HOSTAL
DICKSON
EL BAR DE
RUPERTO
MASAY
LA MADDERA
PUMATOUR/
TRANS VIA PAINE
MANUEL BULNES
BANCO
SANTANDER
SANTIAGO
TELEFÓNICA CTC
SKY AIRLINE
COFFEE
PL@NET
LA TRANQUERA
HELADOS
BRUNA

0   100 yds
0   100 m

© AVALON TRAVEL

ORIENTATION

On the eastern shores of Seno Última Esperanza, Puerto Natales (pop. 16,978) is 250 kilometers northwest of Punta Arenas via paved Ruta 9. It is 150 kilometers south of Parque Nacional Torres del Paine, also by Ruta 9, which goes to Cerro Castillo, 52 kilometers north of the city.

Entering town from the north, Ruta 9 becomes the roughly north–south Costanera Pedro Montt; most services and points of interest are within easy walking distance to the east. The principal commercial streets are east–west Manuel Bulnes and north–south Avenida Baquedano. A new northwesterly route has cut the distance to the park border.

SIGHTS

The Sociedad Explotadora de Tierra del Fuego, owner of large pasture tracts in both Chile and Argentina, financed construction of the gingerbread-style **Municipalidad,** dating from 1929 (the powerful Sociedad Explotadora was, in some ways, the region's de facto government). Immediately east, the **Iglesia Parroquial María Auxiliadora** dates from the same era and shares its Magellanic style.

In the same exterior fashion but with a roomier interior that displays its holdings to advantage, the **Museo Histórico Municipal** (Bulnes 285, tel. 061/41-1263, muninata@ ctcinternet.cl, 8 A.M.–7 P.M. weekdays, 10 A.M.–1 P.M. and 3–6 P.M. weekends, US$1 for Chileans, US$2 for foreigners) offers displays on natural history, archaeology, and the region's aboriginal peoples, European settlement, and the rural economy (including the Sociedad Explotadora), Natales's own urban evolution, and the Carabineros police, who played a role in the museum's creation. Noteworthy individual artifacts include a Yámana (Yahgan) dugout canoe and Aónikenk (Tehuelche) *boleadoras,* plus historical photographs of Captain Eberhard and the town's development.

ENTERTAINMENT

Nightlife is limited mostly to dining out and to low-key bars such as **Bar Toore** (Eberhard 169), a new entrant in the nightlife sweepstakes. The well-established **El Bar de Ruperto** (Bulnes 371) takes its name from the *pisco*-swilling burro once popular on Chilean TV ads.

Upstairs at the restaurant **Mamá Rosa** (Ladrilleros 105), a separate **Pisco Sour Café &**

TIERRA DEL FUEGO

Bar has snacks, a diversity of *pisco* sour specials, including one made with the Mapuche spice *merkén,* Wi-Fi, occasional slide shows on the park and other travel-related topics, and even movies, projected onto a wall screen, to watch from comfortable sofas. In summer, these start late because sunset falls after 10 P.M.

SHOPPING

In new quarters, **Ñandú Artesanía** (Eberhard 301, tel. 061/41-4382) sells maps and books in addition to a selection of quality crafts. Across the street, with more style, **El Emporio de la Pampa** (Eberhard 302, tel. 061/41-3279) also sells crafts, but it's also a deli with gourmet cheeses, finer wines than usually found in Natales, and real coffee (as opposed to Nescafé).

World's End (Blanco Encalada 226, tel. 061/41-4725, www.patagoniax.com) is a map specialist that also carries a big selection of used books in English and other languages, available on a purchase-or-exchange basis.

The **Pueblo Artesanal Ehterh Aike** (Philippi 660) has a variety of crafts but is also the best place in town to buy fresh fruit and other produce.

ACCOMMODATIONS

Over the past two decades–plus, Natales has developed one of Chile's densest offerings of accommodations. This is especially true in the budget category, where competition keeps prices low, and in exceptional new upscale options—but there are plenty of mediocre and ordinary places in all ranges. Off-season rates can drop dramatically at upscale places.

US$10-25

In new quarters, **Residencial María José** (Esmeralda 869, tel. 061/41-2218, patagoniamj@hotmail.com, US$11 pp, US$15 pp with breakfast) is Natales's Israeli favorite. **Residencial Josmar** (Esmeralda 517, tel. 061/41-1685, www.josmar.cl, US$11 pp, US$34 s or d with private bath) has also built a spacious campground (US$6 pp) with clearly delineated sites, privacy from the street, electricity, hot showers, and a place to barbecue.

Hospedaje Teresa Ruiz (Esmeralda 463, tel. 061/41-0472, www.hieloenpatagonia.cl, US$9 pp) gets high marks for congeniality, cleanliness, and outstanding breakfasts with homemade rhubarb preserves.

Residencial Sutherland (Barros Arana 155, tel. 061/41-0359, US$11 pp, US$34 d) has recently added rooms with private baths.

US$25-50

Run by expatriate Oregonians, the informal hostel **Erratic Rock** (Baquedano 719, tel. 061/41-0355, www.erraticrock.com, US$15 pp) occupies a creaky house with character. It also serves a better-than-average breakfast, has a large book exchange, and rents quality gear for Paine-bound travelers.

Friendly **Residencial Patagonia Aventura** (Tomás Rogers 179, tel. 061/41-1028, www.apatagonia.com, US$17 pp, US$39 d) provides a bit more privacy than others in its range, with knowledgeable operators who also rent equipment.

Relocated in improved quarters, **Hostal Nancy** (Ramírez 540, tel. 061/41-0022, www.nateslodge.cl, US$14 pp with shared bath, US$19 pp with private bath, breakfast included) has long been a popular choice in its price range.

In an older house with substantial character, steadily improving ◖ **Hostal Dos Lagunas** (Barros Arana 104, tel. 061/41-5733, www.hostaldoslagunas.com, US$20 pp, US$33 s, US$46 d) is fast becoming a favorite; rates include an ample and varied breakfast. The five rooms share three baths, though private baths are under construction.

Stuck in an off-the-beaten-sidewalk location, the immaculate **Hostal Don Guillermo** (O'Higgins 657, tel./fax 061/41-4506, www.hostaldonguillermo.com, US$26–48 s, US$41–56 d) is underpriced compared to nearby competitors. Though the singles are small, some rooms now have private baths, and the breakfast is excellent.

At friendly **Hostal Dickson** (Bulnes 307, tel. 061/41-1871, www.hostaldickson.com, US$37 d with shared bath, US$45 d with private bath), look at the rooms closely—some have windows so small that they're more like jail cells. On the other hand, there's central heating, the beds are good, the shared baths are numerous, it now has Wi-Fi, and rates include breakfast.

US$50-100

With what may be Natales's most colorful garden—the summer roses are a sight—**Hostal de los Castillos** (Bulnes 241, tel. 061/41-3641, www.hostalcastillos.com, US$39 s, US$56 d, with breakfast) is also a popular teahouse. The rooms themselves are comfortable and spacious, though one picture-window double faces the street (heavy curtains give it sufficient privacy).

Rehabbed **Hostal Drake** (Philippi 383, tel./fax 061/41-1553, www.hostalfrancisdrake.com, US$41 s, US$56 d) is a comfortable hostelry in a quiet location that tour operators often choose for their clients. Rates include breakfast and Wi-Fi, but you may need persistence to get IVA discounts.

Hostería Isla Moreno (Tomás Rogers 68, tel. 061/41-4773, www.islamorena.cl, US$46 s, US$56 d) enjoys fine natural light in modern rooms with private baths; a couple of rooms lack exterior windows but have skylights. It also has a restaurant with a limited nightly menu.

Now a Natales institution, **《 Casa Cecilia** (Tomás Rogers 60, tel. 061/41-1797, www.casaceciliahostal.com, US$24-47 s, US$40-60 d) deserves credit for improving accommodations standards here—it's such a legend that, on occasion, nonguests even ask for tours of the hospitable Swiss-Chilean bed-and-breakfast. The rooms are simple, and some are small, but all enjoy central heating, some have private baths and cable TV, and the cheerful atrium is a popular gathering place. Rates include the usual sumptuous breakfast.

A few years ago, **Hostel Natales** (Ladrilleros 209, tel. 061/41-0081, www.hostelnatales.cl, US$29 pp, US$61 s, US$81 d) transformed the aging Hotel Palace into warm, luminous accommodations with private baths; some rooms have two or four bunk beds, while others have standard doubles for couples. While prices have risen, especially in high season, the lobby and atrium (which includes a fountain) are spacious and inviting, with comfortable chairs and sofas; the rooms are sparsely furnished, and sounds carry from the lobby (which is also an Internet café with Wi-Fi) to the nearest ones. An ample breakfast costs US$5 extra.

Expanded **Hostal Amerindia** (Barros Arana 135, tel. 061/41-1945, www.hostelamerindia. com, US$56-84 s or d, with a 6 percent surcharge for credit cards) is an artfully decorated 13-room bed-and-breakfast. Seven of the rooms have private baths, but the other six share three baths. It also has Wi-Fi and serves a buffet breakfast.

US$100-200

The striking **《 Hotel Lady Florence Dixie** (Manuel Bulnes 659, tel. 061/41-1158, www.chileanpatagonia.com/florence, US$92-110 s, US$112-130 d) has expanded and upgraded what was already a good hotel, but prices have recently risen accordingly.

Hotel Glaciares (Eberhard 104, tel./fax 061/41-1452, www.hotelglaciares.com, US$109 s, US$119 d) is also a respectable option, with a full buffet breakfast. The handsome **Hotel Saltos del Paine** (Bulnes 156, tel. 061/41-3607, fax 061/41-0261, www.saltosdelpaine.cl, US$100 s, US$120 d) is comparable.

Just a couple of years ago **《 Hotel Aquaterra** (Bulnes 299, tel. 061/41-2239, www.aquaterra-patagonia.com, US$125 s, US$140 d), a purpose-built hotel that combines style (native woods) and substance (comfortable furnishings), was almost unique. Though the competition is catching up, it's still worth consideration, as is its unconventional restaurant menu.

If only for honoring history's greatest scientist, **Hotel Charles Darwin** (Bulnes 90, tel. 061/41-2478, www.hotelcharlesdarwin.com, US$127 s, US$153 d) deserves some attention; painted in pastels, the 22 rooms range from smallish to midsize, but they're flooded with natural light and have state-of-the-art baths. Management is accommodating, and the restaurant has an interesting menu as well.

One of the best values in its category, the modern, well-located ❰❰ **Hotel Martín Gusinde** (Bories 278, tel. 061/41-2770, www. hotelmartingusinde.com, US$139 s, US$168 d) prides itself on good service.

Over US$200

Natales's most distinctive new accommodations are at the subtly landscaped **Hotel Altiplánico del Sur** (Ruta 9 Norte, Huerto 258, tel. 061/41-2525, www.altiplanico.cl, US$180 s, US$220 d), which has built all its rooms into the hillside along the Paine highway about two kilometers north of town. Only the windows and roof rise above ground level, while blocks of peat insulate the concrete structure and help integrate it into its site. The common areas, the rooms, and the furnishings all display an elegant design simplicity.

Rates at the waterfront classic **Hotel Costa Australis** (Costanera Pedro Montt 262, tel. 061/41-2000, www.hotelesaustralis.com, US$220–275 s, US$248–300 d), rebuilt after nearly being destroyed by fire a couple of years ago, depend on whether the room has a city or sea view. It's hard-pressed, though, to match stylish newer choices such as the Altiplánico and Indigo.

Opened in late 2006, on the site of what was once a modest bed-and-breakfast, **Hotel Indigo Patagonia** (Ladrilleros 105, tel. 061/41-3609, www.indigopatagonia.com, US$260–350 s or d) is an audacious new hotel and spa with 29 rooms, including half a dozen suites. Facing the waterfront, it bids to help transform the shoreline.

FOOD

Known for seafood, Natales has several moderately priced eateries and improving mid-range-to-upscale choices.

To stock up on supplies for that Paine trek, visit **Hipermercado Abu-Gosch** (Bulnes 742). More specialized, for your trail mix, is **The Dried Fruit Guy** (Baquedano 443).

Decor-free **Masay** (Bulnes 427, tel. 061/41-5008) has decent inexpensive sandwiches and pizzas. **Café Evasión** (Eberhard 595-B,

tel. 061/41-4605) is a moderately priced café with daily lunch specials. Basic Chilean dishes outshine the Italian at **La Repizza** (Blanco Encalada 294, tel. 061/41-0361).

Patagonia Dulce (Barros Arana 233, tel. 061/41-5285, www.patagoniadulce.cl) serves several varieties of hot chocolate (expensive at around US$4–5 each, but welcome on a cold morning) and desserts, including kuchen and mousses, along with rich homemade chocolate candies sold by weight. Unfortunately it doesn't open until 11 A.M.

On the east side of the Plaza de Armas, the British-run vegetarian ❰❰ **El Living** (Arturo Prat 156, tel. 061/41-1140, 11 A.M.–11 P.M. daily mid-Oct.–Apr., US$5–6 for sandwiches) also serves breakfast, economical sandwiches, and desserts (try especially the Sachertorte). Its owner arrived here by way of Torres del Paine's extravagant Hotel Salto Chico, but his food is more upmarket than his prices.

In the same style, the cozy **Café Cielo de Palo** (Tomás Rogers 179, tel. 061/41-1028, lunch and dinner daily) serves tasty vegetarian dishes such as falafel and a variety of fine desserts, not to mention freshly brewed coffee, tea, juices, and sandwiches.

El Marítimo (Baquedano 379-A, tel. 061/41-3166, www.restaurantelmaritimo.com, lunch and dinner daily) and **Los Pioneros** (Pedro Montt 166, tel. 061/41-0783, lunch and dinner daily) set the standard in quality fish and seafood at moderate prices, but lack flair. For better atmosphere, try the casual **La Tranquera** (Bulnes 579, tel. 061/41-1039, lunch and dinner daily).

La Caleta Gastronómica (Eberhard 261, tel. 061/41-3969, lunch and dinner daily) is a moderately priced (US$6–10) locale that offers excellent value—try the salmon with king crab sauce. Another well-established option is **Café Andrés** (Ladrilleros 381, tel. 061/41-2380, lunch and dinner daily) for cooked-to-order seafood.

Don Jorge (Bories 430, tel. 061/41-0999, lunch and dinner daily) and **El Asador Patagónico** (Prat 158, tel. 061/41-3553, lunch and dinner daily) are both *parrillas* facing the

Plaza de Armas. The latter prepares meat to order, including lamb on a stake; provides a selection of by-the-glass wines that is uncommonly flexible for the provinces; and features assiduous service.

La Burbuja (Bulnes 300, tel. 061/41-4204, lunch and dinner daily) specializes in seafood and meats, but also has vegetarian offerings; try the *ostiones al pil pil* (US$8), a mildly spicy scallops appetizer, and the *congrio* (conger eel) for an entrée.

In a relaxed setting, ((**La Casa de Pepe** (Tomás Rogers 131, tel. 061/41-0950, lunch and dinner daily) prepares refined versions of Chilean standards such as *pastel de choclo* (US$10) and *cazuela de ave* (US$7.50) with the freshest ingredients. On the Plaza de Armas, it's also tobacco-free (though the owner himself is an occasional smoker).

Rarely does Chilean pizza merit special mention, but the thin-crusted pies at ((**Mesita Grande** (Arturo Prat 196, tel. 061/41-1571, www.mesitagrande.cl, lunch and dinner daily) do. Individual pizzas (US$5–9), of four ample slices, range from simple mozzarella to spinach and garlic to ground lamb and just about everything in between; diners sit at either of two long but solid tables that promote conversation with neighboring parties.

Greatly improved, opposite the plaza, ((**La Oveja Negra** (Tomás Rogers 169, tel. 061/41-5711, lunch and dinner daily, US$8–12) is the choice for a quiet meal in relaxed, if not quite intimate, surroundings. For either seafood or beef, its upscale aspirations make for more elaborate dining than at most of its competitors, but it's also a free-fire zone for tobacco junkies.

Part of its eponymous hotel, **Aquaterra** (Bulnes 299, tel. 061/41-2239, lunch and dinner daily, entrées US$9–12) is an upscale restaurant with menu items such as Mexican fajitas and Japanese *gyoza* (pot stickers) rarely seen in this part of the world. For more conservative palates, it offers traditional beef dishes.

Underrated ((**Última Esperanza** (Eberhard 354, tel. 061/41-3626, lunch and dinner daily) deserves more attention than it gets for exceptional seafood at reasonable prices with outstanding service. **Los Viajeros** (Bulnes 291, tel. 061/41-1156, lunch and dinner daily) is a recent entry in the seafood category but also serves grilled Patagonian lamb. The **Centro Español** (Magallanes 247, tel. 061/41-1181, lunch and dinner daily) promises Spanish cuisine, but it remains a work in progress.

The surprising **Afrigonia** (Eberhard 343, tel. 061/41-2232, lunch and dinner daily) attempts to fuse Patagonian standards with East African touches in dishes such as lamb with a mint sauce (US$12) along with curry and tandoori. Early signs are positive, but whether it can survive the low season, when the critical mass of foreign tourists that form its clientele shrinks, is open to question. The service is uneven and the kitchen can be slow, but reservations are advisable because it's small.

Reopened and relocated after an unfortunate absence, ((**Angélica's** (Bulnes 501, tel. 061/41-0007, lunch and dinner daily) has great fish and seafood such as king crab cannelloni (US$13), but the service is an anomaly—often great when it's crowded, but distracted when it's barely a third full. Still, this would be a good restaurant just about anywhere.

Hotel Indigo's adjacent restaurant ((**Mamá Rosa** (Ladrilleros 105, tel. 061/41-3609, ext. 218, lunch and dinner daily) offers bay-view dining on sophisticated versions of Chilean seafood standards, such as hake and salmon, in the US$8–12 range. The flavors are delicate and the side orders thoughtfully assembled, and service has improved.

At Natales's best ice creamery, **Helados Bruna** (Bulnes 585), calafate and rhubarb are the regional specialties.

INFORMATION

In a freestanding waterfront chalet, the local delegation of **Sernatur** (Pedro Montt 19, tel./fax 061/41-2125) is open 8:15 A.M.–7 P.M. weekdays, 10:30 A.M.–1:30 P.M. and 3–6 P.M. weekends December–March; the rest of the year, it's open 8:15 A.M.–7 P.M. weekdays only. It has helpful personnel, occasionally English-speaking, and fairly thorough information on accommodations, restaurants, and transportation.

Two relocated Oregonians publish the

monthly freebie tabloid *Black Sheep* (www. patagoniablacksheep.com), with engaging articles and frequently updated information on Natales, Torres del Paine, and services throughout the region. It's widely available around town.

SERVICES

Puerto Natales has several currency exchange houses, including **Cambio Mily** (Blanco Encalada 266) and **Cambios Sur** (Eberhard 285). **Banco Santander Santiago** (Bulnes 598) has an ATM.

Correos de Chile (Eberhard 429), at the southwest corner of Plaza Prat, is the post office.

Long-distance operators include **Telefónica CTC** (Blanco Encalada and Bulnes) and **Entel** (Baquedano 270).

Internet connections are improving and getting cheaper, with new outlets appearing all the time and Wi-Fi ubiquitous at places like **Coffee Pl@net** (Bulnes 555).

Lavandería Catch (Bories 218) can do the washing.

Hospital Puerto Natales (Ignacio Carrera Pinto 537, tel. 061/41-1582) handles medical emergencies.

GETTING THERE
Air

LAN no longer keeps a separate office here, but **Turismo Comapa** (Eberhard 555, tel. 061/41-4300, www.comapa.com) handles reservations and tickets. Punta Arenas–bound buses will drop passengers at that city's Aeropuerto Presidente Carlos Ibáñez del Campo.

In summer, up to three times weekly, **Sky Airline** (Bulnes 692, Local 4, tel. 061/41-0646, www.skyairline.cl) offers service from Santiago, stopping here before continuing to Punta Arenas and then back to Santiago.

Bus

As of 2010, Puerto Natales was building a new Terminal Rodoviario at Santiago Bueras (the eastward extension of Yungay) and Bolívar, destined to be more efficient but less convenient than individual companies' scattered, but

In Puerto Natales, the spreading ozone hole over Antarctica is a concern every summer.

mostly central, bus terminals. There's frequent service to and from Punta Arenas and Torres del Paine, and regular but less frequent service to the Argentine destinations of Río Turbio, Río Gallegos, and El Calafate.

Carriers serving Punta Arenas (3 hours, US$7–10) include **Bus Sur** (Baquedano 668, tel. 061/61-4220, www.bus-sur.cl), **Buses Fernández** (Ramírez 399, tel. 061/41-1111, www.busesfernandez.com), and **Buses Pacheco** (Ramírez 224, tel. 061/41-4800, www.busespacheco.com). Round-trip tickets offer small discounts but less flexibility. In summer, Pacheco goes to Ushuaia, Argentina (US$60, 14 hours), at 7:30 A.M. Sunday–Friday, which involves changing buses just outside Punta Arenas.

Services to Torres del Paine (2.5 hours, US$14) vary seasonally, and there is frequent turnover among agencies; again, there are small discounts for round-trip fares. Carriers include **Buses J.B.** (Prat 258, tel. 061/41-0242), **Buses Gómez** (Arturo Prat 234, tel. 061/41-1971), **Buses María José** (Bulnes 386, tel. 061/41-2218), and **Trans Vía Paine** (Bulnes 518, tel.

061/41-3672). **Vía Terra** (061/61-3840, puerto-natales@vientosur.com) operates a door-to-door service (US$35 pp) as far as Hostería Lago Grey as part of its full-day tours.

For the Argentine border town of Río Turbio (1 hour, US$6), where there are connections to El Calafate and Río Gallegos, try **Buses Cootra** (Baquedano 454, tel. 061/41-2785), which has 5–7 buses Monday–Friday, and two or three Saturday–Sunday. Bus Sur has fewer departures.

To the Argentine town of El Calafate (5 hours, US$19), the carriers are Buses Cootra, Bus Sur, and **Turismo Zaahj** (Prat 236, tel. 061/41-2260, www.turismozaahj.co.cl). Services are frequent in high season, but in winter they may be weekly only.

Ferry

Turismo Comapa/Navimag (Eberhard 555, tel. 061/41-4300, www.navimag.cl) operates the weekly car/passenger ferry MV *Magallanes* to the mainland Chilean city of Puerto Montt. In early season, it's fairly easy to get a north-bound berth, but later in the season reservations are advisable.

Northbound departures are normally at 6 A.M. Friday, but weather and tides can change schedules. Passengers usually spend the night on board before these early-morning departures, but Navimag also has a Sala de Espera (waiting room) immediately across from the new pier.

GETTING AROUND

The selection of rental cars is growing, though it's better in Punta Arenas. Agencies include **Transpatagonia** (Blanco Encalada 330, tel. 061/41-4930, www.transpatagonia.cl) and **Punta Alta** (Blanco Encalada 244, tel. 061/41-0115, www.puntaalta.cl).

World's End (Blanco Encalada 226, tel. 061/41-4725) rents bicycles and motorcycles.

Vicinity of Puerto Natales (Chile)

A growing number of operators arrange excursions to nearby sites of interest and, of course, to Parque Nacional Torres del Paine and even Argentina's Parque Nacional Los Glaciares. Day tours of Paine, more feasible since completion of a new road permits loops rather than time-consuming backtracking to return to Natales, cost around US$33 pp (plus the park entrance fee, of course). The most reliable are **Tour Express** (Manuel Bulnes 769, tel. 061/41-0734, www.tourexpress.cl) and **Kipaventour Patagonie** (Bulnes 90-B, tel. 061/41-3615, www.kipaventourpatagonie.com).

Several operators supply services, including accommodations and meals at park *refugios,* and activities within the park. These include **Fantástico Sur** (Sanhueza 579, Punta Arenas, tel./fax 061/61-3410, www.fantasticosur.com), with its own accommodations; **Turismo Stipe** (Baquedano 571, tel./fax 061/41-1125, turismostipe@entelchile.net); **Chile Nativo** (Eberhard 230, tel. 061/41-1385, www.chilenativo.com), for riding, trekking, and birding; **Fortaleza Patagonia** (Tomás Rogers 235, tel. 061/61-3395, www.fortalezapatagonia.cl); and **Servitur** (Prat 353, tel./fax 061/41-1858, www.servitur.cl). **Baqueano Zamora** (Baquedano 534, tel. 061/61-3531, www.baqueanozamora.com) specializes in horseback trips in the park and is also the concessionaire for Posada Río Serrano and Hostería El Pionero.

Three companies have united to form the **Centro de Turismo Aventura de Patagonia** (Bories 206), all with different contacts: **Antares Patagonia** (tel. 061/41-4611, www.antarespatagonia.com) for trekking; **Indómita Patagonia** (tel. 061/41-4525, www.indomita-patagonia.com) for kayaking and sea kayaking; and **Big Foot Patagonia** (tel. 061/41-4525, www.bigfootpatagonia.com) for expeditions.

Several other companies work together on sea kayaking in particular, including Fortaleza Patagonia; **Bella Patagonia** (Barros Arana

160, tel. 061/41-2489, www.bellapatagonia. com); **Sendero Aventura** (Tomás Rogers 179, tel. 061/41-5636, www.senderoaventura.com), in the same building as Residencial Patagonia Aventura; and **La Maddera** (Arturo Prat 297, tel. 061/41-3318), though the latter is more a gear rental place.

FRIGORÍFICO BORIES

Four kilometers north of Puerto Natales, the Sociedad Explotadora de Tierra del Fuego built this state-of-the-art (for its time) meat freezer to process livestock, primarily sheep, for shipment to Europe. Built of brick between 1912 and 1914, in the Magellanic style, it's the only plant of its kind in a reasonable state of preservation. After its 1971 expropriation by the Allende government, the plant was partially dismantled and finally shut down a few years back.

Among the remaining structures are the rendering plant, which converted animal fat into tallow; the tannery, which prepared hides for shipment; and the main offices, smithy, locomotive repair shop (Bories had its own short line), freight jetty, power plant, and boilers. The power plant still works.

Accommodations and food are available at **Hotel Cisne Cuello Negro** (tel. 061/41-1498, US$93 s, US$130 d, with half board); make reservations through **Turismo Pehoé** (José Menéndez 918, Punta Arenas, tel. 061/24-4506, www.pehoe.com).

PUERTO PRAT AND VICINITY

About 15 kilometers northwest of Puerto Natales via a gravel road, sheltered Puerto Prat is the nearest thing to a beach getaway for Natalinos—on rare hot days, its shallow waters warm up enough to let the truly intrepid dip their toes into the sea. It's also the paddling point for half-day sea kayak trips to **Fiordo Eberhard** (about US$75 pp); for details, contact any of several kayaking companies in Puerto Natales.

A short distance north, settled by Captain Hermann Eberhard, **Estancia Puerto Consuelo** was the area's first sheep farm. It's

open to the public, but usually only for those on horseback excursions.

DIFUNTA CORREA SHRINE

About six kilometers east of Puerto Natales, on the south side of Ruta 9, the spreading mountain of water-filled plastic bottles at this spontaneous roadside shrine suggests one of two things: Either many Argentines are traveling here, or Chileans are becoming devoted to Argentina's favorite folk saint. Or it may be a changing combination of the two, as the Argentine economic crisis of 2001–2002 reversed the traditional flow of Argentine tourists into Chile.

CERRO DOROTEA

About seven kilometers east of town on Ruta 9, nudging the Argentine border, the hike to the Sierra Dorotea ridge makes an ideal half-day excursion, offering some of the area's finest panoramas. Well-marked with red blazes and signs, the route to Cerro Dorotea's 549-meter summit is, after the initial approach, unrelentingly uphill but never exhaustingly steep. This is not pristine nature—much of the lower slopes are cutover *lenga* forest, some of which has regenerated itself into an even-aged woodland. The ridge itself is barren, with a telephone relay antenna on the top.

Trailhead access is over private property, where farmer Juan de Dios Saavedra Ortiz collects US$8 pp. The fee, though, includes a simple but welcome Chilean *onces* (afternoon tea with homemade bread, butter, ham, and cheese) on your return from the hike.

MONUMENTO NATURAL CUEVA DEL MILODÓN

Northwest of present-day Puerto Natales, on the shores of a small inlet known as Fiordo Eberhard, the giant Pleistocene ground sloth known as the *Mylodon* (*Mylodon darwini*) took shelter in this wave-cut grotto some 30 meters high, 80 meters wide at its mouth, and 200 meters deep. While the *Mylodon* has been extinct nearly as long as humans have inhabited the area—some 11,000 years—the discovery of its remains caused a sensation, as their state of preservation induced some European scientists to speculate the animal might still be alive.

German pioneer Hermann Eberhard gets credit for discovering the cave in 1895, but Erland Nordenskjöld was the first scientist to study it, in 1900, taking sample bones and skin back to Sweden. Its manure has been carbon-dated at roughly 10,400 years before the present, meaning the large herbivore coexisted with humans, but it was definitely *not* domesticated. In all probability, hunting pressure contributed to its demise (and to that of other Pleistocene megafauna). Oddly enough, no complete skeleton has been found.

The *Mylodon* has gained a spot in the Western imagination, both among scientists and the lay public. U.S. archaeologist Junius Bird described the animal in his journals, published as *Travel and Archaeology in South Chile* (Iowa City: University of Iowa Press, 1988), edited by John Hyslop of the American Museum of Natural History. Family tales inspired Bruce Chatwin to write his masterpiece *In Patagonia*, which relates far-fetched legends that Paleo-Indians penned the *Mylodon* in the cave and that some animals survived into the 19th century.

Conaf's **Museo de Sitio** (8 A.M.–8 P.M. daily) has excellent information on the 192-hectare park, which attracted 68,702 visitors in 2008, about half of them foreigners. A tacky life-sized statue of the *Mylodon* stands in the cave itself.

Summer admission costs US$5 for adult foreigners, US$2.50 for Chilean residents, with nominal rates for children. Many Natales-based tours take in the site, but there is no regular public transport except for Paine-bound buses that pass on Ruta 9, five kilometers east. Mountain-bike rental could be a good option. In addition to the park's picnic area, **Café Restaurant Caverna** is a view restaurant directly opposite the visitors center.

GLACIAR BALMACEDA (PARQUE NACIONAL BERNARDO O'HIGGINS)

Chile's largest national park, covering 3,525,901 hectares of islands and icecaps from near Tortel in Region XI (Aisén) to Última Esperanza in Region XII (Magallanes), has few easy access points, but the Balmaceda Glacier at the Río Serrano's outlet is one of them. From Puerto Natales, the closest approach is a four-hour sail northwest—where Juan Ladrilleros and Pedro de Sarmiento de Gamboa ended their futile quests for a sheltered route to the Pacific—past Puerto Bories, several wool *estancias* reachable only by sea, and nesting colonies of seabirds and breeding colonies of southern sea lions, among U-shaped valleys with glaciers and waterfalls. Andean condors have been sighted in the area.

At the end of the excursion, passengers disembark for an hour or so at **Puerto Toro,** where a half-hour walk through southern beech forest leads to the fast-receding Glaciar Balmaceda. Visitors remain for about an hour before returning to Natales, unless they take advantage of the option to travel upriver to Torres del Paine, which may be visible in the distance.

A new option for visiting remote parts of the park, in comfort, is the five-day, four-night *Skorpios* cruise of the so-called "Ruta Kawéskar."

Accommodations and Food

The park lacks formal accommodations. Across the sound from Puerto Toro, though, in virtually the most peaceful location imaginable—except for the wind—the nearly new **Hostería Monte Balmaceda** (c/o Turismo 21 de Mayo, Eberhard 560, Puerto Natales, tel. 061/61-4420, www.turismo21demayo.cl) charges US$150 s, US$180 d, with breakfast; lunch and dinner cost another US$25 each.

As it's mostly accessible by sea, a stay here is usually part of a package including a visit to the park and/or Torres del Paine. There is, however, a footpath suitable for a two-day trek to or from Torres del Paine.

Getting There

Natales operators sail up the sound to the Balmaceda Glacier, usually daily in summer, less frequently the rest of the year. Bad weather and high winds may cause cancellations at any time of year.

TIERRA DEL FUEGO

The traditional operator is **Turismo 21 de Mayo** (Eberhard 560, tel. 061/41-1978, www.turismo21demayo.cl), which sails its eponymous cutter or the yacht *Alberto de Agostini* to the park. Fares are US$110 pp; on the return the boat stops for lunch at Hostería Monte Balmaceda, sometimes an *asado,* at Estancia Los Perales.

Recently, though, **Punta Alta** (Blanco Encalada 244, tel. 061/41-0115, www.puntaalta.cl) has provided competition with newer catamarans that cover the route faster and in greater comfort ($125 pp), and good food is provided on board.

Instead of returning to Puerto Natales, it's possible to continue upriver to Torres del Paine with either Turismo 21 de Mayo or Punta Alta. In open Zodiac rafts, supplying all passengers with warm raingear, the route traverses scenic areas not normally seen by Paine visitors, makes a lunch stop, and requires a brief portage around the Serrano rapids before arriving at the Río Serrano campground. The total cost is about US$165 with lunch; the excursion can also be done in the opposite direction, or as a round-trip from either Puerto Natales or the park.

CERRO CASTILLO AND VICINITY

One of Chile's most thinly populated municipalities, the *comuna* of Torres del Paine has only 739 inhabitants, according to the last census; more than half reside in the hamlet of Cerro Castillo, 60 kilometers north of Puerto Natales on Ruta 9, alongside the Río Don Guillermo border crossing. Called Cancha Carrera on the Argentine side, this is the most direct route from Parque Nacional Torres del Paine to El Calafate (Argentina) and Parque Nacional Los Glaciares. Previously seasonal, it is now open all year.

Formerly an *estancia* of the powerful Sociedad Explotadora de Tierra del Fuego,

Cerro Castillo has an assortment of services, including a dismal museum at the municipal **Departamento de Turismo** (Avenida Bernardo O'Higgins s/n, tel. 061/69-1932) and the only gas station north of Puerto Natales (if continuing to Argentina, gasoline—but not diesel—is cheaper on the Argentine side).

En route to and at Cerro Castillo, there are several accommodations options. The most southerly, on the site of an older namesake that burned to the ground, **Hotel Tres Pasos** (Km 38 Norte, tel. 02/196-9630 or 02/196-9631, www.hotel3pasos.cl, US$120 s, US$148 d) is a contemporary roadside inn that's above average for the area. Lunch or dinner costs US$20 at its restaurant.

At Cerro Castillo itself, there are good lodgings at **Hostería El Pionero** (Baquedano 534, Puerto Natales, tel. 061/61-3531, www.baqueanozamora.com, US$35 pp, US$107 s, US$130 d); the cheaper rates correspond to an annex *refugio.* Open September–April only, it also serves meals to nonguests and rents horses.

On what is still a working sheep ranch on Estancia Cerro Guido, about midway between Cerro Castillo and Torres del Paine, **Lodge Cerro Guido** (tel. 02/196-4807, tel. 061/22-7716 in Punta Arenas, www.lodgecerroguido.cl, US$236–305 s or d) has rehabbed and modernized its historic *casco* and another structure into attractive guesthouses with 10 rooms in total. About 12 kilometers north of the road that leads to the park's Laguna Amarga entrance, Cerro Guido gets less traffic than Paine's accommodations, but its facilities equal or better most of them; there's also a restaurant-bar whose wines come from the ownership's own Matetic family vineyards near Valparaíso. Rates include breakfast, while lunch or dinner costs about US$30 extra. Activities include horseback riding (multiday excursions are possible), hiking, and observing farm activities such as summer shearing.

Parque Nacional Torres del Paine (Chile)

Several years ago, when a major Pacific Coast shipping company bought a two-page spread in Alaska Airlines' in-flight magazine, the landscape chosen to represent Alaska's grandeur was Parque Nacional Torres del Paine! An ignorant photo editor may have been the culprit—fittingly enough for a Southern Hemisphere destination, the image was reversed—but the soaring granite spires of Chile's premiere national park have truly become an international emblem of alpine majesty.

But there's more—unlike many South American parks, Torres del Paine has an integrated network of hiking trails suitable for day trips and backpack treks, endangered species such as the wild guanaco in a UNESCO-recognized World Biosphere Reserve, and accommodations from rustic campgrounds to cozy trail huts and five-star luxury hotels. It is so popular that some visitors prefer the shoulder seasons of spring (November–December) or fall (March–April); the park receives more than 140,000 visitors annually, about 70 percent of them foreigners. While Torres del Paine has become a major international destination, it's still wild country.

Almost everybody visits the park to behold extraordinary natural features such as the **Torres del Paine,** the granite needles that defy erosion even as the weaker sedimentary strata around them have weathered, and the jagged **Cuernos del Paine,** with their striking interface between igneous and metamorphic rocks. Most hike its trails uneventfully, but for all its popularity, this can still be treacherous terrain. Hikers have disappeared, the rivers run fast and cold, the weather is unpredictable, and there is one documented case of a tourist killed by a puma.

ORIENTATION

Parque Nacional Torres del Paine is 112 kilometers northwest of Puerto Natales via Ruta 9 through Cerro Castillo; 38 kilometers beyond

© WAYNE BERNHARDSON

Cuernos del Paine, Parque Nacional Torres del Paine

TIERRA DEL FUEGO

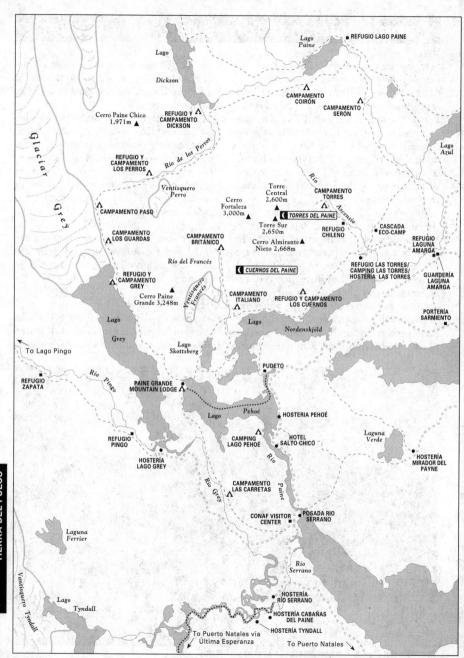

Castillo, a westbound lateral traces the south shore of Lago Sarmiento de Gamboa to the isolated Laguna Verde sector. Three kilometers beyond the Laguna Verde junction, another westbound lateral leaves Ruta 9 to follow Lago Sarmiento's north shore to Portería Sarmiento, the main gate; it continues southwest for 37 kilometers to the Administración, the park headquarters at the west end of Lago del Toro.

Twelve kilometers east of Portería Sarmiento, another lateral branches northwest and, three kilometers farther on, splits again; the former leads to Guardería Laguna Azul, in the little-visited northern sector, while the latter enters the park at Guardería Laguna Amarga, the most common starting point for the popular Paine Circuit, and follows the south shore of Lago Nordenskjöld and Lago Pehoé en route to the visitors center. Most public transportation takes this route.

A new bridge over the Río Serrano now permits access to park headquarters via Cueva del Milodón and Lago del Toro's western shore, but this has not affected regular public transportation.

GEOGRAPHY AND CLIMATE

Parque Nacional Torres del Paine comprises 181,414 hectares of Patagonian steppe, lowland and alpine glacial lakes, glacier-fed torrents and waterfalls, forested uplands, and nearly vertical granite needles. Altitudes range from only about 50 meters above sea level on the lower Río Serrano to 3,050 meters atop Paine Grande, the central massif's tallest peak.

Paine has a cool temperate climate characterized by high winds, especially in spring and summer. The average summer temperature is about 10.8°C, with highs reaching around 23°C, while the average winter minimum is around freezing. Average figures are misleading, though, as the weather is changeable. The park lies in the rain shadow of the Campo de Hielo Sur, where westerly storms drop most of their load as snow, so it receives only about 600 millimeters of rainfall per year. Still, snow and hail can fall even in midsummer.

TIERRA DEL FUEGO

Spring is the windiest season; in autumn, March–April, winds tend to moderate, but days are shorter.

It should go without saying that at higher elevations temperatures are cooler and snow is likelier to fall. In some areas it's possible to hut-hop between *refugios,* eliminating the need for a tent and sleeping bag—but not for warm clothing and impermeable raingear.

FLORA AND FAUNA

Less diverse than in areas farther north, Paine's vegetation still varies with altitude and distance from the Andes. Bunch grasses of the genera *Festuca* and *Stipa,* known collectively as *coirón,* cover the arid southeastern steppes, often interspersed with thorny shrubs such as the calafate (*Berberis buxifolia*), which produces edible fruit, and *neneo.* There are also miniature ground-hugging *Calceolaria* orchids such as the *zapatito* and *capachito.*

Approaching the Andes, deciduous forests of southern beech (*Nothofagus*) species such as *lenga* blanket the hillsides, along with the related evergreen *coigüe de Magallanes* and the deciduous *ñirre.* At the highest elevations, little vegetation of any kind grows among alpine fell fields.

Among Paine's mammals, the most conspicuous is the llama-like guanaco, whose numbers—and tameness—have increased dramatically over two decades. Many of its young, known as *chulengos,* fall prey to the puma. A more common predator, or at least a more visible one, is the gray fox, which feeds off the introduced European hare and, beyond park boundaries, off sheep. The endangered *huemul* (Andean deer) is a rare sight.

The monarch of South American birds, of course, is the Andean condor, not a rare sight here. Filtering the lake shallows for plankton, the Chilean flamingo summers here after breeding in the northern altiplano. The *caiquén* (upland goose) grazes the moist grasslands around the lakes, while the black-necked swan paddles peacefully on the surface. The fleet, flightless rhea or *ñandú* scampers over the steppes.

◖ TORRES DEL PAINE

Some of the Andes' youngest peaks, the Torres del Paine are among the most emblematic in the entire range. Some 10 million years ago, a magma intrusion failed to reach the earth's surface, cooling underground into resistant granite; in the interim, water, ice, and snow have eroded softer terrain to liberate the spires as one of the world's most dramatic landscapes.

So strong a draw are the Torres that some visitors pressed for time settle for day tours that allow only a few hours in the park. Others walk to their base from Hostería Las Torres, a relatively easy day hike where it's hard to avoid crowds. A longer and more tiring alternative, up the steep canyon of the Río Bader, provides a different perspective and the Andean solitude that many hikers seek.

◖ CUERNOS DEL PAINE

Many park visitors misidentify the Cuernos del Paine (Horns of Paine) as the Torres. Located almost immediately south of the Torres proper, the saw-toothed Cuernos retain a cap of darker but softer metamorphic rock atop a broader granitic batholith that, like the Torres, never reached the surface before cooling. It's the contrast between the two that gives the Cuernos their striking aspect.

As with the Torres, day-trippers can admire the Cuernos from the highway through the park. The best views, though, come from the "W" trail along the north shore of Lago Nordenskjöld, between Hostería Las Torres and Lago Pehoé.

HIKING THE PAINE CIRCUIT

Nearly three decades ago, under a military dictatorship, Chile attracted few foreign visitors, and hiking Torres del Paine was a solitary experience—on a 10-day trek over the now-famous circuit, the author met only three other hikers, two Americans and a Chilean. Parts of the route were easy-to-follow stock trails (the park once belonged to an *estancia*); others, on the east shore of Lago Grey and into the Río de los Perros Valley in particular, were barely boot-width tracks on steep slopes, or involved scrambling over granite boulders and fording waist-deep glacial meltwater.

In the interim, as raging rivers have destroyed bridges at the outlets of Lago Nordenskjöld and Lago Paine, the original trailhead on Lago Pehoé's north shore no longer exists. Completion of a trail along Lago Nordenskjöld's north shore several years back, though, created a new loop and simultaneously provided access to the Torres's south side, offering easier access up the Río Ascencio and Valle del Francés on the shorter "W" route to Lago Pehoé. Where the former circuit crossed the Río Paine and continued along its north bank to the Laguna Azul campground, the new circuit now follows the river's west bank south to Laguna Amarga (a Laguna Azul exit or entrance is still feasible, though, by crossing the Río Paine by a cable raft at the river's Lago Dickson outlet, with help from the staff at Refugio Dickson).

In the interim, trail maintenance and development have improved, rudimentary and not-so-rudimentary bridges have replaced fallen logs and traversed stream fords, and comfortable concessionaire *refugios* and organized campgrounds have supplanted the lean-tos and *puestos* (outside houses) that once sheltered shepherds. It's theoretically possible to complete most of the circuit without a tent or even a sleeping bag, showering and eating at the *refugios,* but hikers must remember that this is still rugged country with unpredictable weather.

Most hikers now tackle the circuit counterclockwise from Guardería Laguna Amarga, where buses from Puerto Natales stop for passengers to pay the park admission fee. An alternative is to continue to Pudeto and take a passenger launch to Refugio Pehoé, or else to the park's Administración (involving a longer and less interesting approach); both of these mean doing the trek clockwise.

At least a week is desirable for the circuit; before beginning, registration with park rangers is obligatory. Camping is permitted only at designated sites, a few of which are free. Purchase supplies in Puerto Natales, as only limited goods are available with the park, at premium prices.

Accommodations and Food

For counterclockwise hikers beginning at Laguna Amarga, there is no *refugio* until Lago Dickson (roughly 11 hours), though there is a fee campground at **Campamento Serón** (4–5 hours).

All the *refugios* are presently under concession to Puerto Natales's **Vértice Patagonia** (Esmeralda 671, tel. 061/41-2742, Puerto Natales, www.verticepatagonia.cl) including **Refugio Lago Grey** and **Refugio Lago Dickson,** where there are also campgrounds and backpackers still crash at the old *puesto,* plus the **Campamento Río de los Perros.**

Both *refugios* resemble each other, with 32 bunks charging US$28 pp, with kitchen privileges and hot showers, but without sheets or sleeping bags, which are technically available for rental but sometimes scarce. Breakfast costs US$9, lunch US$13, dinner US$19; a bunk with full board costs US$63 pp. Campers pay US$6.50 each (*refugio* guests, though, have shower priority). Rental tents, sleeping bags, mats, and camp stoves are also available.

Replacing the cramped and overcrowded Refugio Lago Pehoé, the **Paine Grande Mountain Lodge** (tel. 02/196-0051) is the newest option along the Paine Circuit. Rates are US$39–56 pp without breakfast (US$9 extra); lunch (US$13) and dinner (US$16) are available separately, but full-board packages (US$71–87 pp) mean a small savings. Camping costs US$8.50 pp (US$48 with full board), with rental tents, pads, and sleeping bags available. There's also phone and even (expensive) Internet access.

HIKING THE "W" VARIANT

From Guardería Laguna Amarga, a narrow undulating road crosses the Río Paine on a narrow suspension bridge to the grounds of **Estancia Cerro Paine,** at the base of 2,640-meter Monte Almirante Nieto. The *estancia* operates a hotel, *refugios,* and campgrounds, and staff also shuttle hikers back and forth from Laguna Amarga for US$5 pp.

From Estancia Cerro Paine, a northbound trail parallels the route from Guardería Laguna

Amarga, eventually meeting it just south of Campamento Serón. The *estancia* is more notable, though, as the starting point for the "W" route to Lago Pehoé, a scenic and popular option for hikers lacking time for the full circuit. On the western edge of the grounds, the trail crosses the Río Ascencio on a footbridge to a junction where a northbound lateral climbs the river canyon to Campamento Torres, where a short but steep trail ascends to a nameless glacial tarn at the foot of the Torres proper. This is a reasonable day hike from the *estancia,* though many people prefer to camp or spend the night at the *refugio.*

From the junction, the main trail follows Lago Nordenskjöld's north shore, past another *refugio* and campground, to the free Campamento Italiano at the base of the **Río del Francés** Valley. While the main trail continues west toward Lago Pehoé, another northbound lateral climbs steeply up the valley, between the Cuernos del Paine to the east and the 3,050-meter summit of Paine Grande to the west, to the free Campamento Británico.

Hikers in search of peace and quiet can make a strenuous detour up the **Valle Bader,** a steep rugged river valley that's home to a climber's camp at the base of the Cuernos. The route is mostly unmarked, but experienced cross-country walkers can handle it.

Accommodations and Food

Most of the "W" route crosses private property belonging to **Fantástico Sur** (Sarmiento 846, Punta Arenas, tel./fax 061/36-0360, www.fs-lodges.com), which runs the 96-bunk **Refugio Las Torres Norte** and the new, nearby **Refugio Las Torres Central** on the *estancia's* main grounds; the 36-bunk **Refugio Chileno** in the upper Río Ascencio Valley; and the 28-bunk **Refugio Los Cuernos,** all of which also have campgrounds. Fantástico Sur's *refugios* are more spacious, diverse, and attractive in design than the park *refugios,* and the food is better as well.

Bunks at Fantástico Sur *refugios* cost US$32 pp (US$68 with full board), except for the slightly more expensive Las Torres Central

(US$35 pp, US$71 with full board). Camping costs US$7.50 pp with hot showers. Refugio Los Cuernos also has two-person *cabañas* (US$116 d with breakfast and hot tub; US$148 s, US$185 d, with full board).

Separately, breakfast costs US$9, lunch US$13, or dinner US$17. Rental tents, sleeping bags, mats, and stoves are also available.

OTHER TRAILS

After heavy runoff destroyed the once-sturdy bridge at Lago Paine's outlet in the early 1980s, the Río Paine's north shore became, and has remained, isolated from the rest of the park. A good road, though, still leads from Guardería Laguna Amarga to Laguna Azul's east end, where there are a campground and *cabañas,* and the **Sendero Lago Paine,** a four-hour walk to the lake and a simple *refugio.* A trekkers' alternative is the **Sendero Desembocadura,** which leads north from Guardería Laguna Amarga through open country to Laguna Azul's west end and continues to Lago Paine, but this takes about eight hours. From Lago Paine's north shore, the **Sendero Lago Dickson** (5.5 hours) leads to the Dickson Glacier.

Several easy day hikes are possible near Guardería Lago Pehoé, directly on the road from Laguna Amarga to the Administración visitors center. The **Sendero Salto Grande** trail leads quickly to the thunderous waterfall, at Lago Sarmiento's outlet, that was the Circuit's starting point until unprecedented runoff swept away the iron bridge to Península Pehoé in 1986. From Salto Grande, the **Sendero Mirador Nordenskjöld** is a longer but still easy walk to a lakeshore vista point, directly opposite the stunning Cuernos.

From Guardería Lago Grey, 18 kilometers northwest of the Administración by road, a short footpath leads to a sandy beach on Lago Grey's south shore, where steady westerlies often beach icebergs from Glaciar Grey. The longer and less visited **Sendero Lago Pingo** ascends the Río Pingo Valley to its namesake lake (5.5–6 hours); there are a basic *refugio* and two free campgrounds along the route.

FURTHER RECREATION

Though popular, hiking is not Paine's only recreational option.

Despite similar terrain, Paine attracts fewer climbers than Argentina's neighboring Parque Nacional Los Glaciares, perhaps because fees for climbing permits have been high here. At present, permits are free of charge; before being granted permission, though, climbers must present Conaf with climbing résumés, emergency contacts, and authorization from their consulate.

When climbing in sensitive border areas (meaning most of Andean Chile), climbers must also have permission from the Dirección de Fronteras y Límites (Difrol, www.difrol.cl) in Santiago. It's possible to do this through a Chilean consulate overseas or at Difrol's Santiago offices or, preferably, online; if you arrive in Puerto Natales without permission, it's possible to request it through the **Gobernación Provincial** (tel. 061/41-1423, fax 061/41-1992), the regional government offices on the south side of Plaza Arturo Prat. The turnaround time is 48 hours.

While climbing and mountaineering activities may be undertaken independently, local concessionaires can provide training and lead groups or individuals with less experience on snow and ice. **Rutas Patagonia** (tel. 061/61-3874, www.rutaspatagonia.com) has a Refugio Grey base camp, where it leads half-day traverses of Glaciar Grey's west side (US$130 pp). Except for warm, weatherproof clothing, the company provides all equipment.

Kayaking specialist **Indómita** (Bories 206, tel./fax 061/41-4525, www.indomitapatagonia.com) arranges guided three-day, two-night descents of the Río Serrano (US$600–742 pp, depending on group size).

The only concessionaire offering horseback trips is Río Serrano–based **Baqueano Zamora** (Baquedano 534, Puerto Natales, tel. 061/61-3531, www.baqueanozamora.com). Just outside the park boundaries, though, Hostería Las Torres has its own stables.

ACCOMMODATIONS

Park accommodations range from free trailside campgrounds to first-rate luxury hotels with just about everything in between; in summer, reservations are almost obligatory at hotels and advisable at campgrounds and *refugios*.

Camping

At Estancia Cerro Paine, **Camping Las Torres** (US$7.50 pp, US$50 pp with full board) draws hikers heading up the Río Ascencio Valley to the Paine overlook and/or west on the "W" route to Lago Pehoé, or finishing up the circuit here. Formerly insufficient shower and toilet facilities have improved.

On a bluff above Refugio Las Torres, the **Cascada EcoCamp** (www.ecocamp.travel) is a geodesic dome-tent facility designed for minimum-impact accommodations; on raised platforms, each tent is five meters wide, with wooden floors and two single beds, with towels and bedding including down comforters. Two larger domes contain a common living area, dining rooms, and a kitchen; the separate bathrooms have hot showers and composting toilets (from some domes, it's a long walk for middle-of-the-night toilet visits).

Electricity comes from solar collectors, windmills, and a small hydroelectric turbine. Cascada's organized tour clients have priority, but its half-dozen luxury "Dome Suites" with woodstoves, king-size beds, private baths and showers, and exterior decks with views of the Torres are available to private parties on a space-available basis. Contact them through the website or, alternatively, through their Puerto Natales office (Barros Arana 166, tel. 061/41-4442).

On the small peninsula on its namesake lake's eastern shore, just west of the road to the Administración, sites at concessionaire-run **Camping Lago Pehoé** (tel. 02/196-0377, www.campingpehoe.com, US$9 pp) hold up to six people; fees include firewood and hot showers. It has also added dome tents (US$120 d with breakfast).

About six kilometers south of park headquarters, **Vista Paine Camping** (www.campingchile.com, US$7.50 pp) has reopened with notable improvements, including cooking shelters at each site, and also offers horseback riding.

In Paine's remote northeastern sector, which

some visitors prefer, is **Camping Laguna Azul** (tel. 061/61-3531 in Puerto Natales, www.baqueanozamora.cl, US$7.50 pp).

Hosterías and Hotels

Posada Río Serrano (tel. 061/61-3531 in Puerto Natales, www.baqueanozamora.com, US$96–130 d) is a former *estancia* house retrofitted as a B&B. Rates, which include breakfast, depend on whether the room has shared or private bath; there is a restaurant/bar for so-so meals and drinks. While it has improved under new management, and quadruples (US$42 pp) and sextuples (US$34 pp) can be cheaper, it's overpriced for what it offers.

Reachable by road along Lago Sarmiento's south shore or by foot or horseback from the Río Paine, well-regarded **Hostería Mirador del Payne** (tel. 061/41-0498, www.miradordelpayne.com, US$200 s, US$245 d) lies in the isolated southeastern Laguna Verde sector.

Where Lago Grey becomes the Río Grey, the 30-room **Hostería Lago Grey** (US$301 s, US$348 d, with breakfast) hosts visitors to the park's lesser-visited western sector; it also has a restaurant open to the public. For reservations, contact the hotel through **Turismo Lago Grey** (tel. 061/71-2100, www.lagogrey.cl).

The park's oldest hotel, on a five-hectare island linked to the mainland by a footbridge, the 25-room **Hostería Pehoé** (US$195–213 s, US$213–269 d) has improved since the operator began to reinvest in what had been a run-down facility with substandard service in an undeniably spectacular setting. For reservations, contact **Turismo Pehoé** (José Menéndez 918, Punta Arenas, tel. 061/24-1373, www.pehoe.com).

At Estancia Cerro Paine, seven kilometers west of Guardería Laguna Amarga, the sprawling but well-run (**Hostería Las Torres** (Sarmiento 846, Punta Arenas, tel. 061/36-0360, www.lastorres.com, US$267 s, US$305 d) is a gem for its setting beneath Monte Almirante Nieto, its professionalism, the recent addition of a spa offering saunas and massages, and even Wi-Fi access (expensive because of a costly satellite link). While it's

an elite option, it's conscientiously ecofriendly in terms of waste disposal, and management is constantly seeking feedback from guests. It now offers all-inclusive packages as well as just lodging. Off-season hotel rates are about half. Open to both guests and nonguests, the tobacco-free restaurant prepares quality food in cruise-ship quantities.

Open for packages only, (**Hotel Salto Chico** is a mega-luxury resort that somehow manages to blend inconspicuously into the landscape while providing some of the grandest views on the globe. Rates start at US$3,748 s, US$5,320 d, for four nights in the least expensive room, ranging up to US$11,360 s, US$14,032 d, for eight nights in the costliest suite, including transfers to and from Punta Arenas and unlimited excursions. Off-season rates are about 20 percent cheaper. For reservations, contact **Explora Hotels** (Américo Vespucio Sur 80, 5th floor, Las Condes, Santiago, tel. 02/206-6060, www.explora.com).

Just beyond park boundaries, reached by launch over the Río Serrano, the stylish **Hotel Lago Tyndall** (tel. 061/61-4682, www.hoteltyndall.cl, US$195–213 s, US$213–250 d) enjoys peace, quiet, and magnificent views from its balconies. Nearby is the less stylish **Hotel Cabañas del Paine** (tel. 061/21-0179 in Punta Arenas, www.cabanasdelpaine.cl, US$240 s, US$250 d).

INFORMATION

Conaf's principal facility is its **Centro de Informaciones Ecológicas** (tel. 061/69-1931, www.parquetorresdelpaine.cl, 8:30 A.M.–8 P.M. daily in summer), at the Administración building on the shores of Lago del Toro near the Río Paine outlet, with good natural-history exhibits.

Ranger stations at Guardería Laguna Amarga, Portería Lago Sarmiento, Guardería Laguna Azul, Guardería Lago Verde, and Guardería Lago Grey can also provide information.

The private Hostería Las Torres has an excellent audiovisual salon with sophisticated environmental exhibits.

Entry Fee

For foreigners, Torres del Paine is Chile's most expensive national park—the entry fee is US$28 pp, except May 1–September 30, when it's US$14; families get a break as children cost only US$1. The fee is valid for three days, though that's a little misleading—anyone staying longer without leaving the park and returning is unlikely to be asked for additional payment.

Rangers at Portería Lago Sarmiento, Guardería Laguna Amarga (where most inbound buses now stop), Guardería Lago Verde, or Guardería Laguna Azul collect the fee, issue receipts, and provide a 1:100,000 park map suitable for trekking.

Books and Maps

Still serviceable, Tim Burford's *Chile & Argentina: The Bradt Trekking Guide* (Chalfont St Peter, UK: Bradt Publications, 2001) is overdue for a new edition; the maps are only so-so. The new 4th edition of *Trekking in the Patagonian Andes* (Melbourne: Lonely Planet, 2009) has significantly better maps than the Bradt guide's and expanded coverage compared to its own previous editions. Only a few of those maps, though, are as large as the 1:100,000 scale that's desirable for hiking, though the rest are suitable for planning hikes.

Climbers should look for Alan Kearney's *Mountaineering in Patagonia* (Seattle: The Mountaineers, 1998), which includes both historical and practical information on climbing in Torres del Paine and Argentina's Parque Nacional Los Glaciares. Gladys Garay N. and Oscar Guineo N. have collaborated in *The Fauna of Torres del Paine* (1993), a locally produced guide to the park's animal life.

GETTING THERE

Most people find the bus the cheapest and quickest way to and from the park, but the more expensive trip up Seno Última Esperanza and the Río Serrano by cutter and Zodiac is a viable, more interesting alternative.

The new road from Puerto Natales has opened, so tour companies usually enter the park at Laguna Amarga and loop back on the new road, but bus companies continue to use the old highway.

Bus

Bus companies enter the park at Guardería Laguna Amarga, where many hikers begin the Paine circuit, before continuing to the Administración at Río Serrano and then returning by the same route. Round-trips from Natales are slightly cheaper, but companies do not accept each others' tickets.

In summer only, there may be direct bus service to El Calafate, Argentina, the closest town to that country's Parque Nacional Los Glaciares. Inquire in Puerto Natales at Calafate Travel (Baquedano 459, tel. 061/41-4456).

River

Transportation up and down the Río Serrano, between the park and Puerto Natales, has become a popular if more expensive alternative to the bus. **Turismo 21 de Mayo** (Eberhard 560, Puerto Natales, tel. 061/41-1978, www.turismo-21demayo.cl) and **Punta Alta** (Blanco Encalada 244, Puerto Natales, tel. 061/41-0115, www.puntaalta.cl) ply the route in open Zodiac rafts, supplying all passengers with warm raingear; the route traverses scenic areas not normally seen by Paine visitors, makes a lunch stop, and requires a brief portage around the Serrano rapids before arriving at the Río Serrano campground. The total cost is about US$165 with lunch; the excursion can also be done in the opposite direction, or as a round-trip from either Puerto Natales or the park. Visitors who only want to see this sector of the river, without continuing to Puerto Natales, can do so as a day trip to Puerto Toro and back.

GETTING AROUND

Buses to and from Puerto Natales will also carry passengers along the main park road, but as their schedules are similar, there are substantial periods with no public transportation. Hitching is common, but competition is heavy and most vehicles are full with families. There is a regular shuttle between Guardería Laguna

TIERRA DEL FUEGO

Amarga and Estancia Cerro Paine (Hostería Las Torres, US$5 pp) that meets arriving and departing buses.

October–April, reliable transportation is available from Pudeto to Refugio Pehoé (30 minutes; US$21 one-way, US$34 round-trip) with the catamaran **Hielos Patagónicos** (tel. 061/41-1380 in Puerto Natales). The first two weeks of October and in April, there is one departure daily, at noon, from Pudeto, returning at 12:30 P.M. From mid-October to mid-November and the last two weeks of March, there's an additional service at 6 P.M.,

returning at 6:30 P.M. From mid-November to mid-March, there are departures at 9:30 A.M., noon, and 6 P.M., returning at 10 A.M., 12:30 P.M., and 6:30 P.M. Schedules may be postponed or canceled due to bad weather, and there are no services on Christmas and New Year's Day.

Also in season, the catamaran *Grey II* goes daily from Hostería Lago Grey to Glaciar Grey (US$80 round-trip) at 9 A.M. and 3 P.M. daily. There is a US$16 shuttle between the Administración and Hotel Lago Grey that connects with the excursion.

BACKGROUND

The Land

Stretching from the northern desert tropics through the temperate pampas grasslands to the subantarctic and rising from sea level to puna zones well above 4,000 meters, alpine fell fields, and continental glaciers, Argentina's diverse geography contains almost every possible South American environment.

GEOGRAPHY

With an area of about 2.8 million square kilometers (apart from its South Atlantic and Antarctic claims), Argentina is the world's eighth-largest country, only slightly smaller than India. From the tropical latitudes of the Bolivian border, around 22° south, it stretches more than 3,700 kilometers as the crow flies to almost exactly 55° south at the city of Ushuaia, on the Argentine side of Tierra del Fuego. It's more than 1,300 kilometers across at its widest, in the north, but narrows to barely 400 kilometers at the tip.

Most of Argentina is temperate lowlands, but its natural landscapes range from northeastern subtropical wetlands to the endless pampas grasslands, Andean uplands, and sprawling Patagonian steppes.

Pampas

On the right bank of the Río de la Plata, the capital city of Buenos Aires sits atop the coastal

margin of the flat, fertile, sedimentary pampas, whose beef and grain exports made Argentina a wealthy country throughout much of the 19th and 20th centuries. Receiving up to 1,200 millimeters of rainfall per annum, Buenos Aires Province's easterly pampas are lush, green, and vulnerable to flooding; rainfall diminishes as the landscape stretches westward into Córdoba and La Pampa Provinces, where it is nearly desert.

Mountains

Argentina's most imposing physiographic feature is the longitudinal Andean range that runs from its northern borders with Chile and Bolivia to southernmost Patagonia, where it gradually disappears beneath the oceans. The highest point in the Americas is Cerro Aconcagua's 6,962-meter summit, west of the city of Mendoza, but much of the northern Andes and altiplano (high steppe) or puna exceeds 4,000 meters. The southern Patagonian Andes are not so high but have glaciated peaks because of their higher latitude.

In addition to the Andes, there are several lesser ranges. The interior of northern Misiones Province is undulating hill country that rarely exceeds 600 meters. Near the country's geographical center, most of the rolling Sierras de Córdoba top out around 1,500 meters, though the highest peaks fall just short of 3,000 meters; the range extends into neighboring San Luis Province. In southern Buenos Aires Province, the Tandil and Ventania ranges lie mostly below 1,000 meters but still offer relief from the otherwise numbingly flat pampas.

Steppes

In Jujuy, Salta, and other northwestern provinces, sparse pasture grasses and prostrate shrubs cover the broad level areas of the high-altitude puna, between the soaring volcanoes along the Chilean and Bolivian borders. In Patagonia's high latitudes, similar grasses and shrubs punctuate the *meseta* between the Atlantic coast and the Andean foothills to the west.

Rivers

The Río de la Plata, misleadingly glossed into English as the River Plate, is one of the world's great river systems, approaching the Amazon, the Nile, and the Mississippi in terms of length, width, and flow. Originating in the Bolivian altiplano, draining an area of more than 3.1 million square kilometers, it is in reality an estuary at the confluence of the Río Paraná (3,945 kilometers long) and the Río Uruguay (1,650 kilometers long).

Its delta, northwest of Buenos Aires proper, is a series of islands in a maze of muddy channels whose sedimentary surface is largely covered by dense gallery forest. United, the waters of the Paraná and Uruguay carry sediments far out into the South Atlantic.

In the west, descending from the Andes, rushing rivers create recreational rafting runs and water to irrigate the vineyards of Mendoza Province and other wine-growing areas. Some of these reverse direction to flow through gaps into the Pacific on the Chilean side, while others traverse the Patagonian steppe to reach the Atlantic.

Wetlands

Between the Río Paraná and the Río Uruguay, the Mesopotamian lowland provinces of Entre Ríos, Corrientes, and Misiones are home to lush gallery forests along the rivers and shallow, biologically rich wetlands between them. The most notable, one of the country's most spectacular attractions, is Corrientes's Esteros del Iberá.

Lakes

Argentina is famous for its southern lakes district, where the melting ice of Pleistocene glaciers has left a legacy of indigo-filled troughs. Even in the desert north, though, there are surprises like Laguna Pozuelos, which is home to a wealth of birdlife that includes flamingos and giant coots.

CLIMATE

Located in the southern hemisphere, Argentina's seasons are reversed from the northern hemisphere: The summer solstice falls on December 21, the autumn equinox on March 21, the winter solstice on June 21, and the spring equinox on September 21. For most Argentines, the summer months are January and February, when schools are out of session and families take their holidays.

Because Argentina stretches from the desert tropics, where the amount of sunshine and daylight hours vary little over the year, to far southern latitudes where blustery maritime conditions are the rule and seasonal variations can be dramatic, it's difficult to generalize about climate. Moreover, altitude plays a major role everywhere.

Thanks to their midlatitude setting and proximity to the ocean, Buenos Aires and the surrounding pampas have a humid temperate climate, with annual precipitation of about 1,200 millimeters distributed evenly throughout the year. Summer can be hot, wet, and sticky, as temperatures frequently exceed 30°C and thunderstorms are common. Pamperos (southwesterly cold fronts) and *sudestadas* (cool high winds from the southeast) are the most problematic climatic phenomena; winter temperatures are mild, frosts rare, and snow almost unheard of.

Between the Río Paraná and the Río Uruguay, the Mesopotamian provinces of Entre Ríos, Corrientes, and Misiones can be hot, humid, and flood-prone, but nighttime winter temperatures occasionally approach freezing even in the subtropical areas near the Brazilian and Paraguayan borders. West of the Paraná, the arid Chaco encompasses parts of northern Santa Fe and Córdoba Provinces, plus Santiago del Estero, Chaco, and Formosa; rainfall diminishes toward the west in this summertime furnace, whose dry winter is the best time to visit. Santiago del Estero gets less than half of Corrientes's 1,200-millimeter annual rainfall.

In the desert canyons and high puna of the northernmost Andes, warm or even hot daytime temperatures often fall to or near freezing at night. Summer thunderstorms can bring heavy rains and even floods or, at higher elevations, snow; nearly rain-free, the winter

months of July and August are an ideal time to travel here. In some favored microclimates, such as Tucumán, rainfall is sufficient for unirrigated agriculture. South of Tucumán, summer can be brutally hot (especially in La Rioja and Catamarca) and rainfall is inadequate for agriculture, but irrigation has turned the Cuyo region (primarily Mendoza and San Juan Provinces) into the country's vineyard. The dry katabatic wind known as El Zonda brings stifling heat and even physical distress.

Its receding glaciers sensitive to warming, Patagonia is a living laboratory for climate-change studies. While it's the country's coolest region, its inclemency is often overstated—despite its geographical position at the continent's tip, it is not Antarctica. Eastern portions of the Patagonian provinces are even arid steppe, with low rainfall but frequent high winds, especially in summer. Climatically, Tierra del Fuego is an extension of mainland Patagonia.

ENVIRONMENTAL ISSUES

Like other countries, Argentina suffers from environmental degradation, though not all indicators are negative.

Air, Water, and Noise Pollution

Aging diesel buses may be the primary culprit in deteriorating urban air quality, but private vehicles (some still using leaded gasoline) and taxis contribute more than their share (some taxis and private vehicles, though, burn natural gas). Superannuated factories, with their subsidized smokestacks, are another source.

A different sort of air pollution is the deterioration of the antarctic ozone layer, which has exposed both humans and livestock in far southern Argentina to ultraviolet radiation in summer. Though ozone depletion is a global problem over which Argentines have little control, they suffer the consequences of the growing ozone hole.

Just as motor vehicles cause urban air pollution, they also produce most of its noise pollution, due partly to inadequate mufflers. According to one study, vehicular noise accounts for 80 percent of noise levels that, at corners like Rivadavia and Callao in Buenos Aires, exceed 80 decibels. Buses and motorcycles are the worst offenders.

Drinking water is normally potable, but a historical legacy of polluted waterways derives from, first, the proliferation of European livestock on the pampas, followed by the processing of hides and livestock, and then by heavy industry. The textbook case is Buenos Aires's Riachuelo, in the working-class barrio of La Boca, which more closely resembles sludge than water; its bottom sediments, thanks to chemical runoff from factories here and in nearby Avellaneda, are an even greater toxic hazard. The construction of riverside pulp plants in Uruguay continues to be a hot-button issue in Entre Ríos Province, but this is a complex issue characterized by much cynical posturing on the Argentine side.

In the provinces, mining is also a factor; near the town of Esquel, Chubut Province, vociferous opposition caused abandonment of a Canadian project that would have used cyanide, which could have found its way into streams and aquifers, to extract gold from local ores. In San Juan Province, Canada's Barrick Gold is promoting a binational project that could mean the destruction of several glaciers on the Chilean side of the border and pollution of downstream irrigation water.

Solid Waste

Buenos Aires and other cities produce prodigious amounts of garbage—Buenos Aires alone, for instance, generates 5,000 tons of solid waste per day. The capital ships its garbage as far away as the city of Olavarría, 400 kilometers to the southwest, but a new law stipulates that it will reduce the waste sent to landfills by half by 2012, and by 75 percent by 2017.

Sidewalk pickups take place daily, but in the aftermath of the 2002 economic crisis, garbage-strewn streets became more common because of spontaneous recycling by *cartoneros* who ripped open plastic bags in search of reusable materials like cardboard. There's another dark side to this recycling, as

some *cartoneros*—apparently in league with criminal elements—have also absconded with valuable metals covering utility boxes and other similar objects accessible from the street. Sold and melted into ingots of bronze and other metals, these are almost untraceable.

Another sort of solid waste is even more problematic. Greenpeace Argentina has protested an agreement with Australia to import that country's nuclear waste for reprocessing near the Buenos Aires suburb of Ezeiza. Argentina's constitution prohibits storage of nuclear waste, though Argentina has its own 357-megawatt Atucha I reactor near the town of Lima, northwest of the capital.

Energy

Mismanagement and disinvestment are threatening Argentina's self-sufficiency in fossil fuels, so that the country is now having to import natural gas, at above-market prices, from Bolivia. The country does have hydroelectric resources in the subtropical north and along the Andean foothills, but Argentine governments have promoted nuclear power since the 1950s. While the country has renounced any intention to build nuclear weapons, the 357-megawatt Atucha I reactor has powered the capital's electrical grid since 1974. For much of the time since then it has operated at reduced capacity thanks partly to cheaper hydroelectricity, but also due to inadequate maintenance; the controlling Comisión Nacional de Energía Atómica (CNEA, National Atomic Energy Commission) is not known for its transparency. Atucha I is due to close in 2014.

Even hydroelectricity is no panacea, as the creation of the massive Yacyretá dam along the Paraguayan border in Corrientes Province may be raising water levels in the Iberá marshlands; this could sever the "floating islands," on which their wildlife depends, from their anchoring soils. Similarly, upstream water diversions on the Río Iguazú could affect the flow over the spectacular falls that are one of the continent's greatest natural features.

Soil Conservation and Deforestation

Centuries of livestock impacts, both grazing and trampling, have caused serious erosion even in areas where there were never native forests, such as the pampas and the Patagonian steppes. Even today, some forested national parks—most notably Lanín and Los Glaciares—have been unable to eliminate grazing within their boundaries. There has been pressure to create presumably sustainable forest-exploitation projects in the Magellanic woodlands of Tierra del Fuego.

The hot-button forest issues, though, are in the northern subtropical forests. In Misiones Province, agricultural colonists and commercial tea and *yerba mate* plantations have cut over much of the *selva misionera,* a diverse, wildlife-rich rain forest that cannot easily reestablish itself when its natural recycling mechanisms are disturbed. In Jujuy and Salta Provinces, the *yungas* cloud forest on the edge of the Andes has already suffered deforestation from construction of a nearly pointless natural gas pipeline over the Andes to Chile, and from widespread clear-cutting to extract just a few prize timber species.

Conservation and Outdoors Organizations

For information on protected areas, contact the **Administración de Parques Nacionales** (APN, Avenida Santa Fe 680, Retiro, Buenos Aires, tel. 011/4312-0820, www.parquesnacionales.gov.ar). While its selection of brochures on national parks and other protected areas is improving, the staff themselves are best informed on the country's most high-profile destinations, such as Parque Nacional Iguazú and Parque Nacional Los Glaciares. Hours are 10 A.M.–5 P.M. weekdays. The APN maintains branch offices in many provincial cities and towns, while rangers staff information offices at parks and reserves.

Argentina has three main categories of protected areas: *parques nacionales* (national parks), *reservas nacionales* (national reserves), and *monumentos naturales* (natural monuments), though the practical distinctions among them are not always clear. According to law, national parks are "areas to be preserved in their natural state, which are representative of a biogeographical region and have natural beauty or scientific interest." Often contiguous with national parks, national reserves may be buffers that permit "conservation of ecological systems…or the creation of independent conservation zones."

Natural monuments are "places, things, and live animal or plant species, of aesthetic, historic, or scientific interest, to which is granted absolute protection." They usually have one outstanding geographical feature, but may also consist of a rare or endangered species such as the southern right whale and the *huemul* (Andean deer).

Argentina's main wildlife advocacy organization is the **Fundación Vida Silvestre Argentina** (Defensa 251, Monserrat, Buenos Aires, tel. 011/4331-3631, www.vidasilvestre.org.ar). Annual membership rates start around US$37; it publishes the bimonthly magazine *Revista Vida Silvestre,* which is excellent reading for those proficient in Spanish.

For bird-watchers, it's the **Asociación Ornitológica del Plata** (Matheu 1246/1248, Buenos Aires, tel. 011/4943-7216, www.avesargentinas.org.ar); hours are 3–9 P.M. weekdays.

The international conservation organization **Greenpeace** also has a Buenos Aires branch (Zabala 3873, Chacarita, tel. 011/4551-8811, www.greenpeace.org.ar).

For general information on mountaineering, contact the **Centro Andino Buenos Aires** (Rivadavia 1255, Oficina 2, tel. 011/4381-1566, www.caba.org.ar). There are also numerous local and provincial mountaineering clubs, described in the destination chapters of this book.

Flora

With latitudinal limits comparable to those between Havana and Hudson Bay, and elevations ranging from oceanic to alpine, Argentina possesses a diversity of flora. Much of it will be novel to foreign visitors, especially those from the northern hemisphere.

VEGETATION ZONES

Floral associations are strongly, but not perfectly, correlated with latitude and altitude. The environments below are described in more detail in the listings for individual national parks and other locations in the destination chapters.

Temperate Grasslands

As European sheep, cattle, and horses consumed the succulent native grasses of the pampas, they so impoverished the native vegetation that opportunistic colonizers like thistles turned much of the region into a botanical desert. As the land grew too valuable for grazing, grain farms supplanted the livestock industry in many areas.

Gallery Forests

Dense, nearly impenetrable forests still cover large areas along the banks and on the islands of the Paraná, the Uruguay, and other northern rivers. Twisted trunks of the *ceibo* (whose blossom is Argentina's national flower) mix with *sauces* (willows), *canelones,* and lesser species.

Subtropical Forests and Savannas

Argentina has no truly tropical rain forests, but Misiones Province is a panhandle of verdant subtropical forest jutting northeast between Paraguay and Brazil; araucaria pines punctuate its interior uplands. On the most easterly Andean slopes, in Salta, Jujuy, and Tucumán Provinces, the *yungas* are a narrow longitudinal fringe of cloud forest with a unique microclimate.

Between these two geographical extremes, the Gran Chaco of Formosa, Chaco, and Santiago del Estero Provinces is a mix of broad savannas and dense thorn forests. Away from the rivers, *yatay* palm savannas survive on the higher ground of Entre Ríos.

Puna

In the canyons of the northwest, the dry hillsides sprout stands of the *cardón* cactus; at higher altitudes, these yield to broad level areas of the perennial bunch grasses *ichu,* interspersed with shrubs known collectively as *tola.* Their sparse vegetation provides year-round pasture for wild guanacos and vicuñas, and domestic llamas and sheep.

Broadleaf and Coniferous Forest

In the Patagonian lakes district, various species of broad-leafed southern beech (*Nothofagus* spp.), both evergreen and deciduous, are the most abundant trees. There are, however, several notable conifers, particularly the *pewen* or *paraguas* (umbrella, *Araucaria araucaria*), so named because its crown resembles an umbrella. It's also known as the monkey-puzzle tree because its limbs seem to take the shape of a monkey's curled tail. The long-lived *alerce* or *lawen* (*Fitzroya cupressoides*) is an endangered species because of its high timber value, though most stands of the tree are now protected.

Note that Argentines other than specialists refer indiscriminately to conifers as *pinos* (pines), even though the Southern Hemisphere has no true pines (of the genus *Pinus*) other than garden ornamentals or timber species in plantations.

Patagonian Steppe

In the rain shadow of the Andes, on the eastern Patagonian plains, Chilean Magallanes, and even parts of Tierra del Fuego, decreased rainfall supports extensive grasslands where the wind blows almost ceaselessly. In some areas, thorn scrub such as the fruit-bearing *calafate* (a barberry) is abundant. From the late 19th century, sheep-grazing for wool had a tremendous detrimental impact on these natural pastures.

Magellanic Forest

From southern Patagonia to the tip of Tierra del Fuego, Argentine woodlands consist primarily of dense southern beech (*Nothofagus*) forests that, because of winds and climatic extremes, are nearly prostrate except where high mountains shelter them.

Fauna

As with the flora, Argentina's fauna is largely correlated with latitude and altitude. In the warm northeastern lowlands, for instance, the range of many species overlaps into the South American tropics, while the high altitudes of the Andean northwest have much in common with the high latitudes of the Patagonian steppe.

MARINE, COASTAL, AND AQUATIC FAUNA

Argentina's lengthy Atlantic coastline and many estuaries are a storehouse of biological wealth, though that wealth is more abundant in terms of individuals than diverse in terms of species.

Saltwater Fish and Shellfish

In the murky sediment-saturated waters of the La Plata estuary, it can be difficult to spot any aquatic fauna, but it's there in oceangoing **fish** species such as the **yellow corvina** and **black corvina**, as well as crustaceans such as **crabs** and shellfish such as **mussels**. *Congrio* (conger eel) and the overexploited *merluza* (hake) are among the top pelagic fish.

Shellfish and crustaceans include the relatively commonplace *ostión* (scallop) and *calamares* (squid).

Freshwater Fish

In the upper reaches of the Plata estuary, as far as the confluence of the Paraná and the

elephant seals

Uruguay, freshwater game fish such as the **boga,** the **dorado** (a 30-kilogram fighter), **sábalo,** the 80-kilogram **surubí** (a giant catfish), and **tararira** mix with some of the oceanic species. These freshwater species, though, are abundant throughout the Mesopotamian provinces.

In the Andean region, introduced species include **brook trout, European brown trout, rainbow trout,** and landlocked **Atlantic salmon.** Native species (catch-and-release only) include **perca bocona** (big-mouthed perch), **perca boca chica** (small-mouthed perch), **puyén,** Patagonian **pejerrey,** and **peladilla.**

Marine Mammals

The most important aquatic mammal in the estuaries is the endangered La Plata **river dolphin.** The **southern sea lion** inhabits the coastline from the River Plate all the way south to Tierra del Fuego. From Chubut south, the **southern elephant seal** and **southern fur seal** are both on Appendix II of the Endangered Species List (CITES), classified as threatened or regionally endangered.

The most famous of Argentine whales is the **southern right whale,** which breeds in growing numbers in the sheltered waters around Península Valdés. Other cetaceans found in South Atlantic waters include the **blue whale,** the **humpback whale,** the **fin whale,** and the **sei whale.** The **orca** or killer whale is also present, along with smaller marine mammals such as **Commerson's dolphin.**

TERRESTRIAL FAUNA

Argentina's land fauna, especially large mammals, are often nocturnal or otherwise inconspicuous, but they are a diverse lot.

Mammals

The largest, most widely distributed carnivore is the secretive **puma** or mountain lion. The most spectacular feline, though, is the **yaguareté** (jaguar), limited to Misiones Province, the *yungas* of Jujuy and Salta, and possibly parts of the Gran Chaco. Other wild cats include the smaller **Andean cat** and the **jaguarundi,** both endangered species.

Two otters are also endangered: the **long-tailed otter** and the **southern river otter.** The only **wolf** is the nocturnal **aguará guazú** (maned wolf) of the northern wetlands; there are several foxes, including the threatened **Argentine gray fox.**

The northern subtropical forests are also home to the rarely sighted **tapir,** related to the horse, along with the **tufted capuchin monkey** and **howler monkey.** A much more common sight is the **coatimundi,** a raccoon relative. The world's largest rodent, the **carpincho** (capybara) has a wide distribution from the Paraná Delta north into Corrientes and the Gran Chaco.

Wild grazing mammals include the **vicuña,** an endangered relative of the domestic **llama** and **alpaca** that occurs only in the northern puna. Their more widely distributed cousin, the wild **guanaco,** is most abundant on the Patagonian steppe but also inhabits parts of the high Andes. **Domestic livestock** like cattle, horses, burros, and goats are of course very common.

The **South Andean huemul,** a cervid that appears on Chile's coat of arms, is the subject of a joint conservation effort between the two countries. In the mid-19th century, there were some 22,000 in both countries, but at present only about 1,000 survive in each country south of Chile's Río Biobío because of habitat destruction, contagious livestock diseases, and unregulated hunting.

The closely related **North Andean huemul** inhabits the Andean northwest. The **pudú** is a miniature deer found in densely wooded areas on both sides of the Patagonian Andes. Farther north, the main cervids are the subtropical **marsh deer** and the declining **pampas deer.**

The northern puna is home to two noteworthy rodent species, the Andean **viscacha** and its smaller nocturnal cousin the short-tailed **chinchilla.** Inhabiting large rookeries, the former is fairly easy to spot.

Reptiles and Amphibians

The northeastern wetlands have two small species of **yacaré** (caimans), which ignore humans unless provoked. Ranging from the northern-most lowlands well into the pampas and be-yond, several species of the deadly pit vipers known collectively as **yarará** (*Bothrops* spp.) can be aggressive. The mostly widely distrib-uted is the **yarará ñata,** which reaches alti-tudes upward of 2,000 meters in the Sierras de Córdoba, and latitudes south of Península Valdés. They are less common in the south than in the subtropical north, however.

The amphibian **rana criolla** (Creole frog) is large (up to 130 millimeters in length) and meaty enough that it's occasionally eaten.

BIRDS

Argentina can be a wonderland for bird-watch-ers, especially in the northeastern marshes and gallery forests along the great river systems, the humid pampas, and southern Patagonia's steppes and seas. For visitors and especially dedicated bird-watchers from the Northern Hemisphere, the great majority are new addi-tions to their life lists.

In the gallery forests along the Plata estuary, common birds include the **boyero negro** (black cacique), an oriole-like species that breeds in hanging nests; the **rufous-capped antshrike,** and the **pava de monte** (black guan). Common aquatic species include **coots, ducks,** and **swans.**

Marshland species include the **junquero** (marsh wren), the polychrome **sietecolo-res** (literally, "seven colors"), and the strik-ing **federal,** with black plumage crowned by a scarlet hood. There are also several species of **rails** and **crakes.**

Many of these same species extend across the pampas, especially in inundated low-lying areas, which also attract large numbers of mi-gratory birds. The pampas' signature species is the **tero** (southern lapwing), whose local name derives from its call, but it and other simi-lar species have a wide distribution. With its curved beak, the widely distributed **bandurria** (buff-necked ibis) is a striking presence.

In the Mesopotamian marshlands, the di-versity is astounding—Iberá has more than 250 species, including large conspicuous ones

a rare crested caracara on Cabo de Hornos (Chilean Tierra del Fuego)

like the **chajá** (horned screamer), **cormorants,** several species of **storks, herons,** and **egrets,** and many waterfowl. Subtropical Misiones is habitat for overlapping tropical species like the **red-breasted toucan.**

The Andean condor soars above the deserts and puna of the north, while migratory birds like **flamingos,** along with **coots, ducks,** and **geese,** frequent its shallow lakes. Common throughout the Andes, the **condor** reaches its most easterly point in the Sierras de Córdoba.

In northern Patagonia's dense forests, some birds are heard as often as they're seen, especially the reticent songbird **chucao.** Others, like the flocks of squawking **Patagonian parakeets** that flit through the woods, are more conspicuous.

Some 240 bird species inhabit the South Atlantic coastline and Tierra del Fuego, including the **wandering albatross,** with its awesome four-meter wingspan, the **black-necked swan, Coscoroba swan, flightless steamer duck, kelp gull,** and several species of **penguins,** most commonly the Magellanic or jackass penguin.

Its numbers reduced on the pampas, where it roamed before cattle, horses, and humans turned native grasslands into ranches and granaries, the ostrich-like **choike** or **ñandú** (greater rhea) still strides across some less densely settled parts of the country. The smaller **ñandú petiso** (lesser rhea) is fairly common in the Patagonian provinces of Neuquén, Río Negro, Chubut, and Santa Cruz; a rare subspecies survives on the heights of the northwestern puna.

INVERTEBRATES

For purely practical purposes, visitors should pay attention to pests and dangers like mosquitoes, flies, and ticks, which can be serious disease vectors, even though maladies like malaria and dengue are almost unheard of (the mosquito vector for dengue has been spreading southward from the tropics, but the disease itself has not yet been detected). In well-watered rural areas like the Paraná Delta, mosquitoes can be a real plague, so a good repellent is imperative.

The *vinchuca* (reduviid or assassin bug), which carries the protozoa that cause Chagas' disease, is present in Argentina, though it is hardly cause for hysteria.

Cultural Landscape

While Argentina's natural landscapes, flora, and fauna are fascinating and enchanting, the country also has a cultural landscape, one transformed by human agency over the millennia. Few parts of the country are truly pristine, but their landscapes are no less interesting for all that.

As an outlier of the great Andean civilizations, northwestern Argentina shows tangible testimony of those times. While their monuments are not as grand as those of Perú and Bolivia, many *pukarás* (fortresses), *pircas* (walls), agricultural terraces, and pre-Columbian roads survive in sites like the Quebrada de Humahuaca and Quilmes.

Except for the shifting cultivators of the upper Mesopotamian provinces, most of the rest of pre-Columbian Argentina was a thinly populated place of hunter-gatherers who left few conspicuous landmarks—notwithstanding aboriginal rock-art sites like Santa Cruz Province's Cueva de las Manos. Some of the continent's most important early human archaeological sites are just over the border from Santa Cruz, in the Chilean region of Magallanes.

In immediate pre-Columbian times, bands of nomadic Querandí hunter-gatherers peopled what is now Buenos Aires and its surrounding pampas. Living in smallish bands with no permanent settlements, they relied on wild game like the guanaco (a relative of the domestic llama) and the flightless ostrich-like *ñandú* (rhea) as well as fish for subsistence.

What remains of their material culture is primarily lithic (arrowheads, spear points, and the rounded stone balls known as *boleadoras*) and ceramic.

AGRICULTURE AND THE LANDSCAPE

In some areas, such as the more remote parts of Quebrada de Humahuaca, local communities have retained control of their better lands and constructed durable terrace systems that have conserved soil and maintained productivity. Native crops such as quinoa are still grown here, while indigenous llama herders persist in the northwestern puna well upward of 3,000 meters. Cultivation along the eastern Andean slopes extended south into what is now Mendoza Province.

The pre-Columbian peoples of northern Mesopotamia were shifting cultivators, and as such their impact on the landscape is less obvious. Because they cut the forest and used fire to clear the fields before planting, their impact was significant, but long fallow periods allowed the woodlands to recover. Much of what seems to be virgin forest may in fact be secondary growth.

The arrival of the Spaniards, of course, brought major transformations. At first content to collect tribute from the indigenous population, they became landholders as that population declined from various causes, primarily introduced diseases. Their large rural estates, known as haciendas, consisted of relatively small areas of intensively cultivated land surrounded by large areas that grazed cattle, horses, and other European livestock.

From the pampas south, the European invasion utterly transformed the landscape into first an open-range cattle zone and then, successively, sprawling sheep and cattle ranches known as *estancias* that dominated the rural economy for more than a century. Parts of the pampas, in turn, became large-scale grain ranches. In Patagonia, the sprawling sheep *estancia,* producing wool for export to Europe and North America, was the dominant agricultural institution.

SETTLEMENT LANDSCAPES

After the Spaniards took control of Argentina, as in the rest of their American dominions, they tried to institute a policy of *congregación* or *reducción.* This meant concentrating native populations in villages or towns for the purpose of political control, tribute (taxation), and religious evangelization.

The only area where this really worked was the Andean northwest, which had much in common with the highland civilizations of Perú and Bolivia; still, descendents of the same natives who had resisted the 15th-century Inka invasions made things difficult for the Spaniards. For indigenous peoples, who lived in dispersed settlements near their fields or their animals, this was an inconvenience at best, and contributed to land disputes both within indigenous communities and between indigenous communities and Spaniards.

Still, in many areas, the need to be close to one's fields or animals has reinforced a dispersed rural settlement pattern—in the puna, for instance, some villages have become primarily ceremonial sites where people gather for the festival of their patron saint. The standard house is often an adobe, usually with a thatched or tiled roof, and small windows to conserve heat; frequent earthquakes, though, have encouraged reinforced-concrete-block construction, and galvanized roofing has become more common.

A different model prevailed in the northeast, where Jesuits organized Guaraní-speaking peoples into self-sufficient missions against the raids of Brazilian slavers. While the Jesuits may have been paternalistic, they also taught useful skills, such as carpentry and masonry, which helped create the monumental mission architecture that survives in ruins along the upper Paraná drainage in Argentina, Paraguay, and Brazil.

In the Mapuche country of the northern Patagonian lakes district, traditional *rucas,* plank houses with thatched roofs traditionally erected with community labor rather than by individual families, have nearly disappeared; they are more common on the Chilean side, where the indigenous population is larger and more cohesive. In southern Patagonia, 19th century "Magellanic" houses often affect a Victorian style, with wooden framing covered by metal cladding and topped by corrugated zinc roofs.

Cities, of course, differ greatly from the countryside. By royal decree, Spanish cities in the Americas were organized according to a rectangular grid surrounding a central plaza where all the major public institutions—*cabildo* (town council), cathedral, and market—were located. Buenos Aires and other Argentine cities were no exception to the rule; though the transformation from colonial city to modern metropolis obliterated some landmarks, the essential grid pattern remains.

Traditionally, as in Buenos Aires, colonial houses fronted directly on the street or sidewalk, with an interior patio or garden for family use; any setback was almost unheard of. This general pattern has persisted, though building materials have mostly changed from adobe to concrete, and high-rise apartment blocks have replaced single-family houses in many city neighborhoods.

At the same time, many wealthier Argentines have built houses with large gardens, on the North American suburban model, in a frenzy of conspicuous consumption—but still surrounded by high fences and state-of-the-art security in so-called *countrys* (gated communities) that surround Buenos Aires.

History

From inauspicious beginnings, Argentina has fashioned an epic but contentious and often divisive history. Both Argentine and foreign historians find it hard to separate scholarship from politics—even when they have no overt political agenda, almost everyone interprets their work in an ideological context.

PREHISTORY

Human occupation of the Americas, unlike that of Africa, Europe, and Asia, is relatively recent. The earliest immigrants reached North America from East Asia more than 12,500 years ago, when sea levels fell during the last major period of continental glaciation and united the two continents via a land bridge across the Bering Strait. Some researchers believe this migration, interrupted by various interglacials during which rising sea levels submerged the crossing, began tens of thousands of years earlier. Nevertheless, by the time the bridge last closed about 10,000 years ago, the entire Western Hemisphere was populated, at least thinly, with hunter-gatherer bands in environments ranging from barren torrid deserts to sopping rain forests to frigid uplands.

Evidence of Paleo-Indian hunter-gatherers is relatively scarce in Argentina, but one of the continent's oldest confirmed archaeological sites is at Monte Verde, Chile, just across the Andes from present-day Bariloche. Radiocarbon dating here has given a figure of 13,000 years at a site that, according to University of Kentucky archaeologist Tom Dillehay, has some of the continent's earliest evidence of architecture, as well as use of wild potatoes and other native tubers. The most geographically proximate early human sites—later than Monte Verde—are 900 kilometers or more to the north.

As important as hunting was, gathering wild foods probably contributed more to the diet. As population gradually reached the saturation point under hunter-gatherer technology, they began to rely on so-called incipient agriculture, one of whose hearths was the Peruvian highlands. In the process of gathering, incipient agriculturalists had acquired knowledge of the annual cycles of seed plants, and they selected, scattered, and harvested them in a lengthy domestication process. In fact, the earliest domesticated plants could have been root crops like manioc in the Amazon lowlands, but as these are perishable tubers rather than durable seeds, there is little archaeological evidence to support this supposition.

In any event, starting about 6000 B.C., beans (*Phaseolus* spp.), squash (*Cucurbita* spp.), and potatoes (*Solanum* spp.) became the staples of an agricultural complex that, as population grew, supported a settled village life and, eventually, the great Andean civilizations. Maize was a later addition, acquired from Mexico. In Argentina, outliers of these civilizations appeared on the eastern Andean slopes as far south as present-day San Juan Province and in the highlands of Córdoba; across the Gran Chaco, in Mesopotamia, semisedentary shifting cultivators raised maize, manioc (cassava), and sweet potatoes.

When the Spaniards finally arrived, according to one scholar, they found "the richest assemblage of food plants in the Western Hemisphere." Domestic animals were few, however—only the dog (sometimes raised for food), the guinea pig (definitely raised for food), and the llama and alpaca (both raised for food and fiber, with the llama also serving as a pack animal).

Slower to develop than the Andean region, due partly to late demographic saturation, most indigenous societies in what is now Argentina remained nomadic or semisedentary until shortly before the Spanish invasion. In Patagonia, some indigenous peoples sustained a hunter-gatherer lifestyle even into the 20th century.

PRE-COLUMBIAN CIVILIZATION AND CULTURES

In pre-Columbian times, what is now Argentina comprised a diversity of native peoples who ranged from small isolated bands of hunter-gatherers to semiurbanized outliers of Inka Cusco (in present-day Perú). The Inka were never quite able to impose their will on the agricultural Diaguita peoples, who exercised autonomy in what are now Salta, Tucumán, La Rioja Catamarca, and San Juan Provinces.

Likewise, the Inka had little control over the southerly Araucanians—the semisedentary Mapuche and the closely related Pehuenche and Puelche—who withstood both the Inka expansion and, for more than three centuries, the Spanish invasion. More numerous on the Chilean side of the Andes, they survived because of distance from Cusco, their mobility as shifting cultivators, and their decentralized political structure—not easily conquered or co-opted by the bureaucratic Inka. Likewise, the decentralized Guaraní of Mesopotamia were a more or less independent people.

In Patagonia, groups like the Chonos, Tehuelche (Aónikenk), Kawésqar (Alacaluf), Yámana (Yahgan), and Selk'nam (Ona) subsisted by hunting, fishing, and gathering, but introduced European diseases and outright extermination devastated their already small numbers, and sheep displaced the guanaco and rhea on which many of them relied.

The Inka Empire and Its Collapse

At the time of the Spanish invasion, the Inka ruled a centralized but unwieldy empire; their hold was especially tenuous on the southern Araucanian (Mapuche) frontier, just as it would be for the Spaniards in just a few years. Though Inka political achievements were impressive, their realm having stretched into present-day Colombia in the north, they were relative late-comers in the pre-Columbian Andes, only consolidating their power around A.D. 1438. Building on earlier Andean advances in mathematics, astronomy, and other sciences, they were a literate and administratively sophisticated society, but their hierarchical organization, like that of the modern Soviet Union, was ultimately unsustainable.

Toward the end of the 15th century, just prior to the Spanish invasion of the New World, the Inka empire was no monolith, but rather a diverse realm with a mosaic of peoples who resisted domination, especially on its most remote frontiers. Because of internal divisions after the premature deaths of the Inka ruler Huayna Capac and his immediate heir, there developed a struggle between potential successors Atahualpa and Huáscar. That the Inka state was a house divided against itself helps explain why a relatively small contingent of Spanish invaders could overcome vastly superior numbers, but it's only part of the story.

EARLY HISTORY

Early Argentine history is complex because of multiple currents of European exploration and settlement. The Florentine Amerigo Vespucci's 1501 expedition, in the service of Portugal, brought what were probably the first Europeans to enter the Río de la Plata estuary, followed by Cristóbal de Haro (1514); Juan Díaz de Solís (1516), who died at the hands of the Charrúa on the Uruguayan side of the river; and Sebastian Cabot (1527), who went some distance up the river and returned to Spain with small amounts of Peruvian silver—giving the river the name that has survived to the present.

Solís's crew, who landed on Isla Martín García, was probably the first European group to actually set foot in what is now Argentina. Ferdinand Magellan's legendary 1519 expedition, though, spent the winter of 1520 in San Julián, Santa Cruz Province; Magellan himself died before returning to Spain on the first circumnavigation of the globe, but his Italian chronicler Antonio Pigafetta aroused European imaginations with exaggerated tales of Patagonian "giants."

Cabot's expedition, combined with the first news from wealthy Cajamarca and Cusco, spurred Pedro de Mendoza's massive expedition (1535), which founded Buenos Aires on the right bank of the river. Mendoza's effort failed within five years due to poor planning, supply shortages, and stiff resistance from the native Querandí, whom the Spaniards treated with disdain. A contingent of Mendoza's forces had headed north to Asunción, Paraguay, where the Guaraní proved more receptive to the Spaniards; in 1580, moving south from Asunción, Juan de Garay reestablished Buenos Aires. In the meantime, more momentous events in the central Peruvian Andes were to have a greater impact on Argentina.

From the North

Christopher Columbus's so-called "discovery" of the "New World" was, of course, one of global history's signal events. While Columbus may have bungled his way into fame—according to geographer Carl Sauer, "the geography in the mind of Columbus was a mixture of fact, fancy, and credulity"—the incompetently audacious Genovese sailor excited the interest and imagination of Spaniards and others who, within barely half a century, brought virtually all of what is now known as Latin America under at least nominal control.

Europeans had roamed the Caribbean for more than three decades after Columbus's initial voyage, but the impulse toward conquest in South America came from Mexico and especially Panama, which Francisco Pizarro and his brothers used as a base to take Perú. From there, in 1535, Pizarro's partner/rival Diego de Almagro made the first attempt to take Chile by traveling south through Jujuy, Salta, and Catamarca. Crossing the 4,748-meter Paso de San Francisco from the east, Almagro's expedition ended in grisly failure as most of his personnel, retainers, and even livestock died, but this marked the start of Spain's presence in Argentina.

The Spanish Imposition

Spain had contradictory goals in the Americas. Most Spaniards came to get rich, but there were also Christian idealists who sought to save the souls of the millions of people they found in highland Mexico, Perú, and elsewhere (ignoring, for the moment, that these millions already had their own elaborate religious beliefs).

Consequently, the Spanish Crown obliged its forces to offer their opposition the option to accept papal and Spanish authority in lieu of military subjugation. Whether or not they accepted, the result was the same—they became subject to a Spanish colonial system that was overwhelmingly stacked against them.

Many prisoners of war became Spanish slaves and were shipped elsewhere in the Americas. Others who remained were obliged to work for individual Spaniards through forced-labor systems like *repartimiento* and geographically based tribute systems like the *encomienda*. In principle, the Spanish *encomendero* (holder of an *encomienda*) was to provide Spanish-language and Catholic religious instruction, but this was almost unenforceable. The *encomienda*, it should be emphasized, was *not* a land grant, though many *encomenderos* became large landholders.

Spanish institutions were most easily imposed in areas that had been under Inka influence, as a long history of hierarchical government made it possible for the Spaniards to place themselves atop the pyramid. Subjects accustomed to paying tribute to the Inka's delegate now paid it to the *encomendero*, the Spanish Crown's representative. This was different, though, with the unsubjugated Araucanians of the south.

The Demographic Collapse and Its Consequences

One of the invasion's perpetual mysteries, at least on its face, was how so few Spaniards could overwhelm such large indigenous populations in so little time. Spanish weapons were not markedly superior to their indigenous equivalents—it took longer to reload a harquebus than a bow, for instance, and the bow and arrow were probably more accurate. Mounted cavalry gave the Spaniards a tactical edge in open terrain, but this was only occasionally decisive. Certainly the Spaniards took advantage of indigenous factionalism, but that was not the entire story either. The Spaniards' greatest allies may have been microbes.

From the time the Bering Strait land bridge closed, the Americas had been geographically isolated from Europe and Asia. Diseases that had evolved and spread in the Old World, such as smallpox, measles, plague, and typhus, no longer took a catastrophic toll there, but in the New World they encountered immunologically defenseless populations and spread as the plague did in 14th-century Europe. In some lowland tropical areas, fatal infections reduced the population by nearly 95 percent in less than a century.

In the cooler, drier highlands, disease spread more slowly and less thoroughly but was still devastating. In some places disease even preceded direct contact with the Spaniards—the

Inka Huayna Capac's death may have been the result of European smallpox spread indirectly. For this reason, historian Murdo Macleod has called introduced diseases "the shock troops of the conquest."

While the population was numerous, *encomiendas* were a valuable source of wealth for those who held them (including the Catholic church). As the population plummeted, though, *encomiendas* lost their value—dead Indians paid no tributes. Without large indigenous populations to exploit, Spaniards took economic refuge in large rural estates, or haciendas, though they struggled to find labor to work them.

European settlement, then, proceeded south from Lima (capital of the Viceroyalty of Perú) and the silver-rich highland town of Potosí (in present-day Bolivia). Before Juan de Garay reestablished Buenos Aires in 1580, southbound Spaniards had founded Santiago del Estero (1553); San Miguel de Tucumán (1571), which supplied cloth, food, and mules to high, cold, barren Potosí; and Córdoba (1573). Salta (1582), La Rioja (1591), and Jujuy (1593) soon followed. Spaniards from Chile settled the Cuyo cities of Mendoza (1561), San Juan (1562), and San Luis (1596), which produced wine and grain. Remote Buenos Aires, legally barred from trade with the mother country except overland through Lima, suffered in isolation from the viceregal capital.

In the southern lakes region, on both sides of the Andes, mobile Araucanians staved off the Spaniards and then the Argentines and Chileans for more than three centuries. In far-off Patagonia, the situation was even more tenuous, as tentative Spanish colonization efforts failed disastrously because of poor planning and extreme environmental conditions.

COLONIALISM

Barred from direct contact with Europe by Spain's mercantile bureaucracy, early Buenos Aires had to survive on the resources of the sprawling pampas grasslands. The Querandí and other indigenous groups had subsisted on guanacos, rheas, and other game in addition to edible fruits and plants they gathered, but these resources were inadequate and culturally alien to the Spaniards.

The Mendoza expedition, though, had left behind horses that proliferated on the lush pastures, and the multiplication of escaped cattle from the Garay expedition soon transformed Buenos Aires's backcountry into a fenceless feral-cattle ranch. The presence of horses and cattle, nearly free for the taking, resulted in the gaucho culture for which Argentina became famous. Durables were the primary product; perishable beef had little value.

Buenos Aires had no easily accessible markets, though, because hides were too low-value a product to ship to Spain via Lima and Panama; thus there developed a vigorous contraband with British and Portuguese vessels in the secluded channels of the Paraná Delta. As this trade grew, Spain acknowledged Buenos Aires's growing significance by making it capital, in 1776, of the newly created Virreinato del Río de la Plata (Viceroyalty of the River Plate). Reflecting its significance and the need to curb growing Portuguese influence, the viceroyalty even included the silver district of Potosí.

Buenos Aires's population grew slowly at first, but by the time of the new viceroyalty it exceeded 24,000, and nearly doubled by the early 19th century. Open to European commerce, as Madrid loosened its control, the livestock economy expanded with the development of *saladeros* (meat-salting plants), giving value to a product that was almost worthless before.

Unlike the densely populated central-Andean area, Buenos Aires lacked an abundant labor force. The improving economy and growing population, which previously consisted of peninsular Spaniards, criollos (creoles, or American-born Spaniards), *indígenas* (Indians), and mestizos (the offspring of Spaniards and *indígenas*), soon included African slaves. Increasing political autonomy and economic success paved the way for the end of Spanish rule.

The Dissolution of Colonial Argentina

Appointed by the Spanish Crown, all major viceregal officials governed from Buenos Aires,

and economic power was also concentrated there. Outside the capital, provincial bosses created their own power bases. When Napoleon invaded Spain in the early 19th century, the glue that held Spain's colonies together began to dissolve, leading to Argentine independence in several steps.

Contributing to this tendency was a changing sense of identity. In the early generations, of course, people identified themselves as Spaniards, but over time criollos began to differentiate themselves from *peninsulares* (European-born Spaniards). It bears mention that while the mestizos and even the remaining indigenous population may have identified more closely with Argentina than with Spain, it was the criollo intelligentsia to whom independence had the greatest appeal.

South America's independence movements commenced on the periphery, led by figures like Argentina's José de San Martín, Venezuela's Simón Bolívar, and Chile's Bernardo O'Higgins, but their heroism rested on a broader base. In Buenos Aires, this base crystallized as opportunistic and unauthorized British forces, exploiting Spain's perceived weakness, occupied the city in 1806 and 1807.

As the shocked Viceroy Rafael de Sobremonte fled to Córdoba, city residents organized a covert resistance that, led by Frenchman Santiago de Liniers, dislodged the invaders. On the rationale that Spain's legitimate government had fallen, the *porteños* of the capital chose Liniers as viceroy in an open *cabildo* (town meeting). The royalist Liniers, ironically, died at the hands of independence fighters during the Revolution of 1810.

Returning from Spain, San Martín led independence forces against the royalists, deployed from Perú, in what is now northwestern Argentina, and over the Andes into Chile. In 1816, in the city of Tucumán, delegates of the Provincias Unidas del Río de la Plata (United Provinces of the River Plate) issued a formal declaration of independence, but this was only a loose confederation that papered over differences between "Federalist" caudillos—provincial warlords intent on preserving their fiefdoms—and the cosmopolitan "Unitarists" of Buenos Aires.

The struggle between Federalists and Unitarists was slow to resolve itself; in the words of historian James Scobie, "It took seventy years for Argentina to coalesce as a political unit." Even today, tensions between the provinces and the central government have not disappeared, but it took a Federalist to ensure Buenos Aires's supremacy.

REPUBLICAN ARGENTINA

Having achieved independence but united in name only, the Provincias Unidas became an assortment of quarrelsome mini-states. In 1829, after they failed to agree upon a constitution, the Federalist Juan Manuel de Rosas took command of Buenos Aires, the largest and most populous province, and ruled it ruthlessly until his overthrow in 1852. Ironically enough, the opportunistic Rosas did more than anyone else to ensure the city's primacy, though it did not become the country's capital until 1880.

In the early independence years, Unitarist visionaries like Mariano Moreno and Bernardino Rivadavia had advocated an aggressive immigration policy to Europeanize the new republic, but Rosas's dictatorial rule, obstinate isolationism, and military adventures discouraged immigration. His defeat at the battle of Caseros, followed by his departure for England, opened the country to immigration. It also helped diversify the economy from extensive *estancias* and *saladeros* to the more intensive production of wool and grains for export.

War, Expansion, and Consolidation

Rosas's exile did not mean the end of conflict, as it took nearly a decade of civil war for General Bartolomé Mitre's Buenos Aires army to defeat the other provinces, led by Justo José Urquiza of Entre Ríos, and unite the country. Even then, Federalist resistance lingered in provinces such as La Rioja, and only a few years later Argentina became embroiled in the bloody War of the Triple Alliance (1864–1870)

against Paraguay. Allied with Brazil and Uruguay, Argentina gained the provinces of Misiones and Formosa, but the real challenge was the Patagonian frontier south and west of Buenos Aires Province.

With encouragement from foreign minister Guillermo Rawson, Welsh colonists had given Argentina a beachhead in the southern territory of Chubut in 1865. General Julio Argentino Roca, though, wanted to complete the job begun by Rosas, who had driven the Araucanians westward toward the Andean lakes in the 1830s. The Araucanians, for their part, continued to raid the frontier for cattle and horses.

In 1879 the politically ambitious Roca initiated the Conquista del Desierto (Conquest of the Desert), a euphemistically titled military campaign that rode ruthlessly across La Pampa, Neuquén, and Río Negro to dispossess the Mapuche and Tehuelche east of the Andes; at the same time it was a preemptive strike against Chilean ambitions. On the strength of his military victory, Roca became president in 1880 and made prosperous Buenos Aires a separate federal district (the Capital Federal). Economically and politically, the provinces beyond the pampas lagged far behind.

Around the same time, the government began to encourage settlers, primarily British sheep farmers from the Falkland Islands, into the southern territories of Chubut, Santa Cruz, and Tierra del Fuego. With the definitive settlement of southern Patagonia, Argentina reached its maximum territorial expansion, though precise boundaries with Chile remained to be settled.

The Argentine Transformation

Rosas's expulsion reversed Argentina's inward-looking isolationism, opening the country to "liberalism" through foreign immigration, investment, and export opportunities. The first beneficiary was the wool industry, as sheep *estancias* in Buenos Aires Province provided countless bales of wool for England's mills, while traditional cattle *estancias* floundered except on the frontier. Close to the capital, intensively farmed *chacras* produced food for the burgeoning urban market.

After 1880, the humid pampa of Buenos Aires, along with Santa Fe and parts of Córdoba and Mesopotamia, became one of the world's great granaries, as it still is today. This also resulted, however, in the rise of latifundios, large landholdings that precluded the rise of any independent class of freehold farmers.

Meanwhile, the influx of British capital modernized the transportation system. Supplanting cart roads, rail lines fanned out from Buenos Aires like the spokes of a wheel. The export economy, though, was susceptible to negative developments like the 1879 depression that followed the Franco-Prussian War, and to land speculation by *latifundistas* (large landholders) that resulted in financial collapse as the century drew to a close.

In the new century, the economy recovered thanks to grain and meat exports, but the latifundios failed to achieve a broader prosperity. Urban Argentina grew dramatically, but at a cost; as immigrants streamed into Argentina from Spain, Italy, Britain, Russia, and other European countries, a growing gap between rich and poor intensified social tensions. In 1913, Buenos Aires became the first South American city to open a subway system, but in poorer neighborhoods large families squeezed into *conventillos* (tenements) and struggled on subsistence wages. Conflicts exploded into the open—in 1909, following police repression of a May Day demonstration, anarchist immigrant Simón Radowitzky killed police chief Ramón Falcón with a bomb, and in 1919, President Hipólito Yrigoyen ordered the army to crush a metalworkers' strike during "La Semana Trágica" (The Tragic Week).

Yrigoyen, ironically enough, pardoned Radowitzky a decade later. His second administration, though, was the first to suffer one of repeated military coups that plagued the country for most of the 20th century. This opened the way for the ascendancy of Juan and Eva Perón, the most loved—and loathed—figures in modern Argentine politics.

THE PERÓNS AND THEIR LEGACY

Unlike most of the military caste, Juan Domingo Perón (1895–1974) came from relatively humble origins in the Buenos Aires Province town of Lobos, about 100 kilometers southwest of the capital. During his youth, Argentina was prosperous, but certain sectors—most notably the *oligarquía terrateniente* (landed elite)—were far more prosperous than others. Many Argentines attributed the maldistribution of wealth to foreign "liberal" sectors, especially the British, who used Argentina as a source of raw commodities but discouraged the industrialization that would bring a broader-based prosperity.

Opportunistically or not, Perón shared this outlook. In the course of his military travels, he got to know most of Argentina (as well as Fascist Italy) first-hand, but his career was undistinguished until 1944, when he turned a moribund labor department into a power base as the Secretaría de Trabajo y Bienestar Social (Secretariat for Labor and Social Welfare). Ideologically, he appealed to labor bosses and their clientele (whom he co-opted with extravagant benefits), leftist intellectuals (who distrusted foreign capital), and conservative nationalists (who distrusted foreigners, period).

Thanks partly to his wife Eva, whose charismatic populism exceeded even his own, the demagogic Perón managed to convince both left- and right-wing extremists that he was their champion—even as they trained their rifle sights on each other. After the loss of his post and a brief imprisonment, he won the presidency in 1946 and 1952, and used his power to raise wages and pensions, improve working conditions, and guarantee job security. While Perón and his allies threatened their critics, "Evita" Perón capriciously dispensed favors to their supporters through her own private foundation until her death from cancer in 1952.

Meanwhile, Perón's administration expanded the bureaucracy and splurged on pharaonic works projects, heavy and heavily subsidized industry, and unsustainable social spending that squandered post–World War

II surpluses. By 1955, amidst growing social disorder and economy disarray, General Pedro Aramburu's so-called Revolución Libertadora (really a coup) commenced three disastrous decades of dictatorships, punctuated by brief periods of civilian rule.

With Perón in Spanish exile and his "Justicialist" party banned, the downward spiral continued. By the early 1970s, several guerrilla groups (inspired by Fidel Castro's Argentine ally Ernesto "Che" Guevara) had begun operations in the northwestern sierras, the pro-Peronist left-wing Montoneros had become an urban guerrilla movement, and bank robberies, political kidnappings, and assassinations were almost everyday events. From Madrid the aging Perón, with help from right-wing spiritualist José López Rega (known as El Brujo, "The Witch"), cynically manipulated leftist sympathizers (whom he later called "callow and stupid") in Argentina.

After winning the presidency in 1973, Perón's stand-in Hector Cámpora permitted the caudillo's return on the chaotic night of June 20, when hundreds may have died in clashes between right-wing Peronists and leftist Montoneros on the Ezeiza airport road. Perón won the presidency again in September of that year, but he lived less than a year. His successor was his hapless "running mate" María Estela "Isabelita" Martínez de Perón, an exotic dancer whom he had met and married (after Evita's death) while in exile. Meanwhile, López Rega's sinister Alianza Anticomunista Argentina (AAA, Argentine Anticommunist Alliance) battled the Montoneros and other "subversive" organizations and individuals.

THE DIRTY WAR AND ITS AFTERMATH

Continued political instability emerged into almost-open warfare until 1976, when the military ousted Isabelita in a bloodless coup that became the bloodiest reign of terror in Argentine history. General Jorge Rafael Videla headed a three-man junta that imposed a ferocious military discipline on the country.

Under its euphemistically titled Proceso de Reorganización Nacional (Process of National Reorganization), the military's *Guerra Sucia* (Dirty War) killed up to 30,000 Argentines, ranging from leftist urban and rural guerrillas to suspected sympathizers and large numbers of innocent bystanders whose links to armed opposition groups were tenuous at most. Many more were imprisoned and tortured, or sent (or escaped) into exile. Only a few courageous individuals and groups, such as Nobel Peace Prize winner Adolfo Pérez Esquivel and the famous Madres de Plaza de Mayo, who marched around Buenos Aires's central plaza in quiet defiance, dared to risk public opposition.

One rationale for taking power was civilian corruption, but the military and their civilian collaborators were just as adept in diverting international loans to demolish vibrant but neglected neighborhoods and create worthless public works like dead-end freeways. Much of the money found its way into offshore bank accounts. The horror ended only after the military underestimated the response to their 1982 invasion of the British-ruled Falkland (Malvinas) Islands; after a decisive defeat, the military meekly ceded control to civilians. The main coup plotters and human-rights violators even went to prison—an unprecedented occurrence in Latin America (though they later received pardons).

Following a 1983 return to constitutional government, Argentina underwent several years of hyperinflation in which President Raúl Alfonsín's Radical-party government squandered an enormous amount of good will. President Carlos Menem's succeeding Peronist administration overcame hyperinflation by pegging the peso at par with the U.S. dollar through a "currency basket" that ensured it would print no more pesos than it had hard currency reserves to back.

Menem's strategy—really the brainchild of Economy Minister Domingo Cavallo—brought a decade of stability during which foreign investment flowed into Argentina. Privatization of inefficient state-run monopolies, which had had thousands of so-called *ñoquis* ("ghost employees"—who may or may not

On Avenida del Libertador is the Navy Mechanics school where some of the worst torture and executions from "The Dirty War" took place.

actually work for their paychecks) on the payroll, brought major improvements in telecommunications, transportation, and other sectors. The financial and service sectors flourished, giving many Argentines a sense of optimism through most of the 1990s.

The boom had a dark side, though, in the form of "crony capitalism" in which the president's associates enriched themselves through favorable privatization contracts. At the same time, reform barely brushed the patronage-ridden provinces, which maintained large public payrolls and even printed their own *bonos* (bonds), "funny money" that further reduced investor confidence. The Menem years also saw still-unsolved terrorist incidents in the bombings of Buenos Aires's Israeli Embassy in 1992 and AMIA Jewish cultural center in 1994. (In August 2003, Britain arrested the former Iranian ambassador to Argentina, Hade Soleimanpour, in connection with the AMIA bombing but refused to extradite him to Buenos Aires. He was later released for lack of evidence, but the British agreed to keep the case open.)

COLLAPSE AND RECOVERY

Even before the partial debt default of late 2001, the economy contracted and Argentines began to suffer. After the resignation of Menem's feckless and luckless successor Fernando de la Rúa in December, the country had a series of caretaker presidents before the congress chose Peronist Eduardo Duhalde (whom De la Rúa had defeated two years earlier) to serve until elections in late 2003. In a controversial move, Duhalde ended Cavallo's convertibility policy and devalued the peso, which lost nearly 75 percent of its value within a few months. At the same time, he continued De la Rúa's *corralito* policy, which restricted bank withdrawals to maintain hard currency reserves, but also strangled the country's economy.

As the economy stagnated and unemployment rose, homelessness also rose and scavengers became a common sight even in prosperous neighborhoods. Strikes, strident pickets blocking bridges and highways, and frustration with politicians and institutions like the International Monetary Fund (IMF) contributed to the *bronca* (aggravation). Under pressure, the ambitious Duhalde advanced presidential elections to early 2003, but also manipulated Peronist primary rules to favor his chosen successor, left-of-center Santa Cruz governor Néstor Kirchner, over his political nemesis Carlos Menem. (*Buenos Aires Herald* columnist Martín Gambarotta described the political maneuvers of Duhalde and Menem as "two men playing a chess match with boxing gloves.")

Facing near-certain defeat after finishing a weak second in the primary, Menem declined to participate in the runoff, leaving Kirchner the winner by default. Without a mandate, though, Kirchner soon acted as if he had one by consolidating his own power base and simultaneously marginalizing pro-Duhalde Peronists.

At the same time, Kirchner took full credit for Argentina's economic rebound in a country that had nowhere to go but up after the 2001–2002 collapse. To keep domestic peace, he co-opted labor and picket forces by controlling prices for utilities and primary goods—even prohibiting the export of beef to make it more affordable for the domestic market.

As an economic nationalist from a thinly populated province, the confrontational Kirchner blew off concerned European businesspeople and diplomats as well as presumptive Mercosur allies such as Brazil's President Luiz Inácio Lula da Silva and Uruguay's Tabaré Vásquez, in favor of populists such as Bolivia's Evo Morales and especially Venezuela's erratic Hugo Chávez. He also upset neighboring Chile by failing to honor existing natural gas contracts and then passing on higher prices for gas exports after negotiating high prices for Bolivian natural gas with Morales.

In 2007, Kirchner declined to seek a second term, instead supporting his wife Cristina Fernández, then a senator—making the husband-wife team suitable successors to the Peróns in governing on personal charisma and loyalties rather than through institutions. In 2009, however, the effects of the international economic crisis, Fernández's own confrontational approach, and concern over issues such as manipulation of the federal statistics agency INDEC, brought a midterm electoral catastrophe for the ruling party. It has even brought speculation that Fernández—who has denounced a "conspiracy" among Vice President Julio Cobos, the middle-of-the-road *Clarín* newspaper, and even the federal courts—might not finish her term.

Government and Politics

Argentine politics are often contentious, with little consensus, but since the end of the 1976–1983 military dictatorship it has been fairly stable and peaceful. The major exception was the storm of political and economic protest that led to the deaths of five demonstrators in Buenos Aires's Plaza de Mayo on December 20, 2001, and brought the resignation of President Fernando de la Rúa. The country then had three provisional presidents in two weeks before Buenos Aires Province Senator Eduardo Duhalde, who had lost the 1999 presidential election to De la Rúa, assumed the office in an extra-constitutional congressional vote.

Argentines' lack of faith in institutions, though, has led to barrio activism through spontaneous *asambleas populares* (popular assemblies) and less-constructive practices such as *escrache,* in which groups of citizens loudly and publicly demonstrate against politicians, judges, bankers, or representatives of other institutions at their homes or work places. *Escraches,* which began after a series of pardons and other measures limited prosecutions of alleged torturers and murderers of the military dictatorship, often deteriorate into shouting matches.

Another questionable form of protest has been the emergence of *piqueteros* (pickets), who block roads and highways to pressure politicians for assistance or handouts to the unemployed. When unemployment was around 20 percent, the issue was legitimate, but picket leaders managed to dispense this assistance as patronage for their followers. Surveys show that Argentines are, overwhelmingly, fed up with picket abuses, but politicians—including the otherwise confrontational Kirchners—are loath to challenge them.

Unlike 1970s Argentina, though, early-21st-century Argentina appears to be imploding rather than exploding, and the villains are less obvious than they once were. *Buenos Aires Herald* analyst James Neilson has suggested that, despite vocal protests, inertia rather than genuine activism characterizes the country's politics.

ORGANIZATION

Formally in force but often ignored in practice, the Constitution of 1853 created a checks-and-balances system of executive, legislative, and judicial branches resembling that of the United States. The bicameral Congreso Nacional (National Congress—the legislative branch) consists of a 257-member Cámara de Diputados (Chamber of Deputies) and a 72-member Senado (Senate), whose members represent 23 provinces and the Ciudad Autónoma de Buenos Aires (Autonomous City of Buenos Aires). The Cámara is subject to redistricting following each decennial census.

In reality, however, the president wields great discretionary powers, often governs by decree, and frequently intervenes in provincial affairs. A 1994 constitutional amendment reduced the executive's term from six years to four, but also allowed him or her to run for immediate re-election to a second term. The same amendment abolished a provision that required the president to be Roman Catholic.

Argentina's constitution is federal; each province and the city of Buenos Aires has its own autonomous government. Its federalism is one-sided, though, as the central government funds provincial governments through revenue-sharing; in practice, this is a burden, as fiscally irresponsible provinces can blame

revenue shortages on Buenos Aires. La Rioja, for instance, collects only 10 percent of its budget in local tax revenue.

In addition to the city of Buenos Aires and 23 provinces, Argentina claims the Islas del Atlántico Sur (including the British-ruled Falkland/Malvinas Islands and South Georgia) and Antártida Argentina (a wedge of Antarctica below 60° south latitude between 25° and 74° west longitude). While Argentina is persistent and vocal in its claims to the Falklands and South Georgia, it acknowledges that Antarctic claims are on hold by international treaty.

POLITICAL PARTIES

For all its factionalism, the Partido Justicialista (PJ, the Peronist or Justicialist party) is the country's largest and most cohesive political entity. For most of the past century, the next most important has been the misnamed Unión Cívica Radical (UCR), a middle-class party that seems to function better in opposition than in power. After the collapse of the Radical president Fernando de la Rúa's administration in 2001, though, the party nearly dropped off the map; the two top vote-getters in the 2007 presidential election were Peronist Cristina Fernández de Kirchner and ex-Radical Elisa Carrió, and Fernández co-opted dissident Mendoza Radical Julio Cobos as her vice-presidential candidate.

The Peronists, Radicals, and similar entities, however, are barely parties in the European or North American sense—in some ways, it might be more accurate to call them movements. When Carrió ran in the 2003 primary, she did so at the head of her own hastily created Alternativa por una República de Iguales (ARI, Alternative for a Republic of Equals) to finish a weak fourth; in 2007, she made a better showing as the candidate of the Coalición Cívica (Civic Coalition), which included additional factions, but she still garnered barely a quarter of the vote (about half what Fernández won).

As of early 2010, Fernández de Kirchner's Peronist Frente para la Victoria held a majority in the Senado, with 44 seats, while there were 10 Radicals; several other parties shared the remaining 18. In the Cámara de Diputados, the Frente para la Victoria holds 153 seats, the Radicals 30, and the Coalición Cívica 27, with several other parties holding the remaining 47; with intra-party defections, though, the Kirchnerites no longer have a working majority. The Peronists hold a substantial majority of provincial governorships.

Historically, many officeholders have used their supporters for political intimidation instead of dialogue. Voters, for that matter, cannot vote directly for candidates, but only for lists chosen by party bosses at the provincial level. More often than not, the parties serve as patronage machines that, after mobilizing their most militant members for elections, reward them with well-paid public posts that may or may not actually involve working for their paychecks. Such "ghost employees" are called *ñoquis* (gnocchi) after the inexpensive potato pasta traditionally served on the 29th of each month in restaurants and cash-strapped households. The insinuation is that they start showing up at the office just in time to collect their salary on the first of the following month.

Many Argentines express a "plague on all your houses" attitude toward politicians in general, but the Peronists have still managed to dominate the even more divided opposition parties in most of the country.

ELECTIONS
Dating from 1853, amended in 1994, Argentina's constitution now stipulates a four-year presidential term; no president may serve more than two consecutive terms. There are no term limits on senators, elected for six years, or deputies, who serve four.

Elections and dates are ostensibly fixed, but military coups, other political crises, and simple expediency have often disrupted orderly transitions. In 1989, for instance, economic chaos forced the resignation of Radical president Raúl Alfonsín, and newly elected Carlos Menem took office early. Radical president Fernando de la Rúa's late 2001 collapse led to five caretakers within two weeks.

Likewise, in early 2003, caretaker president Eduardo Duhalde stage-managed the elections so that his chosen successor, Néstor Kirchner, would not have to face former president Menem (whose constitutional eligibility was questionable, in any event) in a Peronist primary; he also advanced the general-election date by more than six months. Menem and Kirchner were the first-round leaders, but when Menem withdrew because unfavorable polls made his defeat look inevitable (though he claimed otherwise), the runoff never took place. The next presidential elections are to take place in October 2011.

JUDICIAL AND PENAL SYSTEMS
According to the constitution, the courts act independently, but in practice they are subject to political influence and even whim. When former president Carlos Menem encountered judicial opposition to administrative reforms, for instance, he managed to expand the Supreme Court from five to nine members, with one of the new appointees being his former tennis coach. This gave Menem a so-called "automatic majority" for his projects, and insurance against political scandals such as an illegal arms sale to Croatia.

When the political winds shifted, though, congressional allies of president Néstor Kirchner managed to force the resignation of Chief Justice Julio Nazareno and Justice Guillermo López. They also successfully impeached Justice Eduardo Moliné O'Connor, who now has more free time for the tennis courts. Kirchner has been slow to appoint replacements, and some observers have questioned whether the new appointees will be the best legal scholars or simply more political cronies.

Meanwhile, important cases in the lower courts drag on for years and even decades due to corruption, inefficiency, or political influence. The most high-profile example is the investigation of the 1994 bombing of the AMIA Jewish cultural center in Buenos Aires's Once neighborhood, which killed 87 people. Former president Kirchner pledged to pursue the matter—in which both former Iranian diplomats and Buenos Aires provincial police have been implicated—with greater diligence, but neither his administration nor his wife's brought any significant new developments.

Justice may also vary according to social class. The military caste, for instance, escaped judgment for their Dirty War crimes with almost complete impunity except for a handful of top officers (all of whom were later pardoned by Menem, though he himself had been imprisoned during the dictatorship). Rich and powerful civilians have avoided detention even when the charges have been murder, but petty thieves can count on jail time. The Kirchner administration voided an amnesty that had limited prosecutions of Dirty War suspects, though, and some of them are currently on trial.

BUREAUCRACY

The government institutions most travelers are likely to come into contact with are immigration, customs, and police. Immigration and customs generally treat foreigners fairly, but Argentine police are notoriously corrupt. The capital's Policía Federal is generally better than provincial forces, particularly the Buenos Aires provincial police—a "mafia with badges" that is often involved with illegal activities. Its members are infamous for shaking down motorists for bribes for minor equipment violations.

The politicized bureaucracy remains one of Argentina's most intractable problems, thanks to the continuing presence of *ñoquis* (ghost employees) at the federal, provincial, and municipal levels. While abuses are less extreme than in the past, when individuals often drew multiple paychecks without performing any work whatsoever, bloated state payrolls are still cause for concern.

While the privatizations of the 1990s reduced federal-sector employment by nearly two-thirds, they had little impact on the provinces. Provincial payrolls still include well over 1 million Argentines in what, for the most part, might be more honestly called positions rather than jobs. For the tourist, it may be gratifying to find an obscure museum open 60 hours per

week, staffed by three people, but the cumulative economic impact of such practices has been catastrophic.

In practical terms, the absence of a professional civil service means a lack of continuity, as officials lose their jobs with every new administration; continuing political influence means an abundance of uninterested and often ill-qualified officials who take their time dealing with any but the most routine matter. It also means, of course, nepotism and corruption—Argentina consistently performs poorly in Transparency International's (www.transparency.org) annual survey of perceived corruption. In 2006, Argentina ranked 106th of 180 countries surveyed (the highest rating indicates the least perceived corruption), tied with several African countries and just ahead of Algeria.

THE MILITARY

Thanks to repeated 20th-century coups and the vicious dictatorship of the 1976–1983 "Dirty War," the Argentine military earned a reputation as one of Latin America's worst even in a region infamous for armed repression. Its ignominious collapse in the 1982 Falkland Islands War, followed by public revelations of state terrorism and the conviction of the top generals and admirals responsible for kidnapping, torture, and murder, helped overcome the worst aspects of its traditional impunity.

Since the 1983 return to constitutional rule, civilian governments have eliminated conscription, the military budget has declined to barely 1 percent of GDP (about half that of neighboring Chile, which has less than half Argentina's population and a smaller territory), and Argentine forces have undertaken more strictly military operations such as peacekeeping in the Balkans and humanitarian missions such as earthquake relief in Haiti. While periods of political disorder such as 2001–2002 always bring coup rumors, the military appears to have little or no interest in taking the reins of government.

The size of the military services has also been reduced, and the army, navy, and air force all have lower troop strengths than Chile.

Argentine forces are strongly weighted toward noncommissioned officers, though, and their hardware—ships and planes, especially—is more abundant than Chile's.

Despite the country's reputation for dictatorial bellicosity, two Argentines have won Nobel Peace Prizes: foreign minister Carlos Saavedra Lamas (1936) for mediating a Chaco War settlement between Paraguay and Bolivia, and Adolfo Pérez Esquivel (1984) for publicizing the 1976–1983 military dictatorship's human-rights atrocities.

Economy

To most foreign observers, Argentina's economy is an enigma. Rich in natural resources, with a well-educated populace and modern infrastructure, for most of seven decades it has lurched from crisis to crisis, with the notable exception of the stable, prosperous 1990s. In late 2001 it stunned the world and even many Argentines by defaulting on part of its US$141 billion foreign debt, triggering a political and economic meltdown comparable to the Great Depression of the 1930s. In the first quarter of 2002, the economy shrank 16.3 percent, marking 14 consecutive quarters of contraction.

Argentina actually emerged from World War II in an enviable position, but the government of the charismatic General Juan Domingo Perón and its successors squandered enormous budget surpluses from agricultural exports on bloated state enterprises that, in collusion with corrupt labor leaders, became industrial dinosaurs impossible to reform. Then, during the 1970s and 1980s, large loans destined for massive public works projects filled the pockets—or Swiss bank accounts—of the nefarious generals and their civilian collaborators who ruled the country.

Corruption and deficit spending resulted in hyperinflation that reached levels of 30 percent or more *per month*. Shortly after taking power in 1989, President Carlos Menem's administration became the first Argentine government in recent memory to tackle the inflation problem through Economy Minister Domingo Cavallo's "convertibility" policy; this "currency basket" fixed the peso's value at par with the U.S. dollar, and required the government to back every peso printed with a dollar or other hard currency.

Selling off unprofitable state enterprises such as Aerolíneas Argentinas, the state telecommunications enterprise Entel, and most of the extensive railroad networks made convertibility possible. Inflation dropped to zero, and after an initial glitch, there was steady economic growth, but the 1995 Mexican crisis and a subsequent Brazilian devaluation that reduced Argentine competitiveness led to increasing unemployment and recession. After a brief recovery, convertibility proved to be an economic straitjacket that, by the De la Rúa administration's second year, was unsustainable.

In a desperation move, De la Rúa reappointed Cavallo to the Economy Ministry, but a run on bank deposits brought severe restrictions on withdrawals, known collectively as the *corralito* (literally, "little fence"), whose unpopularity triggered Cavallo's resignation and De la Rúa's downfall. De la Rúa's successor, Eduardo Duhalde, made things even worse by eliminating convertibility, pesifying dollar savings accounts at a 1:1.4 rate, and floating the peso so that those accounts soon lost most of their value. At the same time, in a classic case of Argentine "crony capitalism," the caretaker president pesified dollar debts at a rate of 1:1, benefiting the large industrialists who were his political base.

With devaluation, according to the Economist Intelligence Unit, in less than a year Buenos Aires went from the world's 22nd most expensive city (of 131 surveyed) to the 120th. As the dollar-to-peso ratio plummeted from 1:1 to 1:3.5 in only a few months, citizens with the discipline to save saw their frozen wealth evaporate; those who had accumulated large debts saw their burdens reduced. Devaluation also meant the return of inflation—about 25 percent for 2002—though it failed to reach the nightmarish 1980s levels because banking restrictions limited cash in circulation. It dropped to about 4 percent in 2003, but exceeded 12 percent in 2005 and probably reached at least 15 percent in 2009 (though the government, which has intervened in the state statistics agency INDEC, claims it is only around eight percent).

In theory, a devalued peso should make Argentine exports more competitive, but it's never quite that simple. The Duhalde administration, for instance, slapped an export tax on all profits over US$5 million. His populist successor Kirchner went so far as to prohibit beef exports to maintain low domestic prices, and his successor (and wife) Cristina Fernández de Kirchner slapped such high taxes on soybean exports as to discourage production in a time of record prices—thus, counterproductively, reducing government revenues.

In 2002 the Argentine GDP contracted by more than 11 percent, but after 2003 it has averaged 9 percent growth (from an admittedly low base) for several years. Despite the recovery, Kirchner tackled the country's monstrous US$185 billion debt by unilaterally declaring a "haircut" of some 35 percent; he then used a third of Argentina's foreign currency reserves to pay off its obligations to the International Monetary Fund and thus avoid the IMF's stringent budgetary constraints. In 2008, meanwhile, Fernández de Kirchner confiscated private pension funds to compensate for revenue shortages, and in early 2010 she precipitated a political crisis by trying to fire independent Central Bank president Martín Redrado and use part of the bank's reserves to pay foreign debt.

It's not that Argentina doesn't have money, but much of it is not in Argentina—by some estimates Argentines hold more than US$100 billion overseas, with another US$20 billion in the country but "beneath the mattress." According to Uruguay's Central Bank, Argentine citizens' deposits in that country increased by more than 20 percent in 2009, and growth rates within Argentina slowed considerably.

In the long run, economists such as Arturo Porcezanski believe the only way to stabilize prices is to adopt the dollar as Argentina's currency, as "any effort to convince Argentines that the peso is worth anything are in vain. They only have faith in the dollar." In a similar vein, Cavallo remarked that "forcing Argentines to save in pesos would be as difficult as forcing them to learn to speak Chinese instead of Spanish."

This, of course, has long been the case—for many decades, Argentines have speculated on the dollar in times of crisis. In the 1970s, when Montoneros guerrillas headed by Rodolfo Galimberti kidnapped impresario Jorge Born, they demanded and got a ransom of US$60 million—at a time when that was *real* money. In an only-in-Argentina scenario, the pardoned Galimberti later became the business partner of the man he abducted.

EMPLOYMENT, UNEMPLOYMENT, AND UNDEREMPLOYMENT

The 2002 peso collapse triggered an economic decline that, on a single-country level, could only be compared to the 1930s Great Depression. As the official unemployment figure approached 25 percent, street, bus, and subway vendors became far more numerous than in the past, and the numbers of people rummaging through garbage for recyclables shocked almost everyone. Unemployed individuals even spent the night in line at Banco de la Nación and private exchange houses in hopes of selling their spot to those who had sufficient pesos to purchase dollars. Similarly, individuals waited outside the Italian consulate and other European missions to sell their place in line for passports and visas.

At the end of 2009, President Fernández de Kirchner claimed that unemployment had fallen to 8.4 percent and the worst of the crisis had passed. Most independent observers, though, feel the figure is at least 10 percent, and that it also disguises underemployment; numbers are also worse in the provinces than in Buenos Aires and are especially bad in the capital's desperate southern suburbs.

The 2002 crisis also created an increasingly militant sector of publicly protesting *piqueteros* (pickets), who have blocked highways and put enormous pressure on the government for remedial action and, many would argue, handouts for graft.

AGRICULTURE

Since the 19th century, the Argentine pampas have developed from the meat locker and woolshed of the world to one of its main granaries, growing corn, wheat, oats, sorghum, and soybeans, among other crops. The country's agriculture has diversified, though, to include vegetables such as potatoes, onions, carrots, squash, beans, and tomatoes, and to fruit crops like apples, pears, and grapes—the latter of which help make Argentina the world's fifth-largest wine producer.

Other commercial crops include subtropical cultigens such as sugar cane, olives, tea, *yerba mate,* and tobacco, mostly in provinces to the north and west of the capital. Agriculture accounts for roughly 10 percent of GDP but nearly 60 percent of exports by value, nearly US$41 billion per year, because of high commodity prices.

INDUSTRY

Argentina's industrial heyday was the immediate post–World War II period, when Juan Domingo Perón invested vast sums in manufacturing products such as steel, chemicals, and petrochemicals; the military controlled large parts of the economy, including its own weapons-manufacture and support industries.

Despite the privatizations of the 1990s, much of Argentine industry is still inefficient and unable to compete without state assistance—or cronyism. In the aftermath of the 2002 economic meltdown, frustrated unemployed workers occupied some factories that had closed and began to run them as cooperatives. Some were successful, at least in the short term, and others

were not. In the absence of capital investment, the long-term prognosis for low-productivity installations was not good.

Accounting for about a third of GDP, industry includes food processing, motor vehicles, consumer durables, textiles, printing, metallurgy, and steel. Much of this activity is concentrated in the southern Buenos Aires suburbs of Avellaneda and Quilmes, across the Riachuelo, and in large cities like Rosario, Córdoba, and Mendoza.

DISTRIBUTION OF WEALTH

The gap between rich and poor, once an issue of the landed and the landless, is more complex today. When giant *estancias* and wheat farms ruled the rural landscape, land meant power, but this is less true in contemporary Argentina's urbanized society.

More important is the difference between hereditary wealth and a nouveau-riche plutocracy on the one hand, and a declining middle class and struggling working class on the other. Over the past three decades, the gap between rich and poor has increased.

Historically, the disparity between rich and poor has been less extreme than in other Latin American countries, but the 2001–2002 meltdown, with its devastating impact on the middle class, has resurrected the issue. As of late 2008, a study of 31 major metropolitan areas (covering about two-thirds of all Argentines) showed a poverty rate of 15.3 percent, about half what it had been three years earlier, but government interference in the previously nonpartisan official statistics agency makes these figures open to question.

According to World Bank figures from the 2000 calendar year, with the Argentine peso at par with the U.S. dollar, the country's per capita GDP was US$7,460; in 2002 it fell to US$4,080, but by 2005 it had recovered to almost US$4,700 and by 2008 to US$7,200. In practice, purchasing power was even higher than that would suggest, but 2009 statistics are likely to show at least a slight reversal with the global recession. In any event, there is no doubt the scenario is less encouraging for the lower and middle classes than for the well-to-do. White-collar crimes (fraud and tax evasion) by the rich are also common.

Despite Peronist platitudes about sharing the wealth, more than half a century of dominating the country's politics has had little success in anything other than minor patronage handouts. According to one survey, Argentina ranks 27th of 134 countries in the maldistribution of wealth—in the same league with Perú, Sri Lanka, and Zimbabwe (for the most part, the Scandinavian social democracies are the world's most egalitarian states).

The gap between rich and poor has geographical as well as social dimensions. Poverty affects nearly 20 percent of *porteños,* primarily in the capital's run-down southern neighborhoods and adjacent suburbs, while the northern barrios and areas beyond them in Buenos Aires Province remain relatively wealthy.

EDUCATION

Argentina's formal literacy rate of nearly 97 percent is one of the highest in the Americas, but that statistic disguises some serious problems. Education is free through high school and compulsory to age 12, and the curriculum is rigid; more importantly, though, many schools are disorderly and continual teachers' strikes have meant that students often only get half a year, or less, of instruction.

Geographically, there are vast differences. The level of instruction at rural public schools can be appallingly low, but other public secondary schools, most notably the Colegio Nacional Buenos Aires, are even more prestigious than some of their private bilingual counterparts in the capital.

Public universities like the capital's Universidad de Buenos Aires and the Universidad Nacional de La Plata, in the provincial capital, are generally superior to private universities. Public university education is free of charge but has generated a surplus of high-status degrees in fields like law and intellectually stimulating but less obviously practical subjects like psychology and sociology—and not enough in hands-on disciplines like engineering and computer science. It is also highly politicized, with activists insisting on open admissions to careers such as medicine, and claiming that any rejection is discriminatory.

Schoolteachers generally do not receive university degrees but attend special teachers colleges. There is vocational and technical training as well, but these skills enjoy little respect even when those jobs pay more than white-collar positions or office work.

Several Argentine scientists have won Nobel Prizes, including Bernardo Houssay (Medicine, 1946), Luis Federico Leloir (Chemistry, 1972), and César Milstein (Medicine, 1984). One continual concern is the "brain drain" of educated Argentines overseas; Milstein, for instance, spent his most productive years in England because political pressures at Argentine universities made research impossible. Many talented individuals, though, have left simply because the economy has failed them.

TOURISM

Both international tourism (which accounts for about 10 percent of Argentine exports) and domestic travel are significant factors in the economy. In the aftermath of the 2001 terrorist attacks on the United States and Argentina's own domestic instability, long-distance tourist traffic diminished, but visitors from neighboring countries soon appreciated the bargains that devaluation had wrought. Budget travelers soon streamed into a country that had been intolerably expensive for more than a decade, and more affluent long-distance travelers began to return in greater numbers than before.

In 2006, the most recent year for which full statistics are available, the number of foreign visitors exceeded 4.1 million, and tourism revenues for the year were about US$3.5 billion. Tourism employed 1 million Argentines directly and another half million indirectly, and tourism was the country's biggest export earner after agriculture and petroleum.

In that year, most visitors came from other South American countries, mainly Chile (993,000), Paraguay (313,000), Uruguay (514,000), Brazil (559,000), and Bolivia

(155,000). These figures can also be misleading, though, as many such visits involve weekend excursions or even short shopping trips across the border.

Visitors from the United States and Canada numbered 400,000, while those from Europe totaled 658,000. Long-distance visitors spent substantially more money on travel-related expenses such as accommodations, food, and transportation—while accounting for only 26 percent of visitors, the 1,058,000 North American and European travelers spent more than US$1.4 billion—nearly 45 percent of total tourism income. Their stays tended to be longer—about two weeks for U.S. citizens and nearly three weeks for Europeans—than those of visitors from neighboring countries, who averaged about a week.

As Argentina's main gateway, Buenos Aires benefits more than any other locality from the tourist trade, with more than two million foreign visitors per annum. Many other visitors to the capital, of course, come from elsewhere in the country.

People and Culture

POPULATION GEOGRAPHY

According to the 2001 census, Argentina has 36,223,947 inhabitants, an increase of about 3.6 million over 1991 figures; the projected figure for 2010, when a new census was due to take place, is about 40.5 million.

Roughly one-third of all Argentines live in the Capital Federal (a little more than 3 million) and the 24 counties of Gran Buenos Aires (about 9.5 million), a total of some 12.5 million.

Most of the rest of Argentines are also city dwellers, in population centers such as Rosario, Córdoba, Mar del Plata, Mendoza, Salta, and other provincial capitals and cities. The southern Patagonian provinces of Chubut, Santa Cruz, and Tierra del Fuego are very thinly populated, as are the hot northern provinces of Chaco and Formosa, but Tierra del Fuego is the country's fast-growing province, with an increase of more than 45 percent between censuses.

Indigenous Peoples

Argentina has the smallest indigenous population of any South American country except Uruguay, but certain provinces and regions have substantial concentrations. The most numerous are the Mapuches of Patagonia, who reside mostly in La Pampa, Neuquén, and Río Negro, and Kollas (Quechuas) of northwestern Argentina. There are also significant numbers of Guaraní in the northeast, and Mataco, Mocoví, and Toba in Santa Fe and the Gran Chaco.

Until the 2001 census, when the government statistics agency INDEC questionnaire asked whether "there is in this household any person who considers himself or herself a member or descendent of an indigenous group," there were only estimates of the country's indigenous population. While INDEC's methodology itself is questionable, an update in 2004–2005 gave a figure of about 600,000 indigenous people, including 114,000 Mapuches, 70,000 Kollas, 70,000 Tobas, 40,000 Wichís, 32,000 Diaguitas, and smaller numbers of other groups.

Ethnic Minorities

Argentina is a country of immigrants, both recent and not-so-recent, and the capital reflects that history. Spaniards, of course, first colonized what is now Argentina, but a 19th-century tidal wave of Italians, Basques, English, Irish, Welsh, Ukrainians, and other nationalities made Buenos Aires a mosaic of immigrants; Italo-Argentines even came to outnumber Argentines of Spanish origin.

Some immigrant groups retain a high visibility, most notably a Jewish community that numbers at least 200,000 and is historically concentrated in the Once district of Buenos Aires. During and after the 2001–2002

THE AFRO-ARGENTINES AND THEIR "DEMISE"

In a country of immigrants, the heritage of many Argentines is often conspicuous. According to some accounts, even more Argentines have Italian surnames than Spanish ones. Anglo-Argentines are prominent enough to have their own daily newspaper, and German-Argentines still support a weekly. Buenos Aires has numerous Jewish landmarks, and so-called *turcos* of Middle Eastern descent, such as former President Carlos Menem, have made their mark in politics.

Yet an Afro-Argentine population that by official statistics once comprised nearly a third of Buenos Aires's population has been nearly invisible. When the revolutionary government of 1810 tentatively banned the slave trade three years later, almost a third of 32,000 *porteños* were of African origin. As late as 1838, the figure was nearly 15,000 of almost 63,000. Yet by 1887, there were only 8,000 among more than 430,000 city residents.

After the turn of the century, Afro-Argentines virtually fell off the city map. In the 1970s, newspaper and magazine articles even puzzled over the disappearance of a community that fought honorably in the 19th-century civil and regional conflicts, supported social and charitable organizations, sponsored a lively local press, and contributed to the arts. How and why this could have happened was seemingly an enigma.

Two plausible hypotheses were widely accepted. One was that Afro-Argentines were frontline cannon fodder, particularly in the Paraguayan war, where they suffered disproportionate casualties. Another was that the 19th-century yellow-fever epidemics in San Telmo, where many Afro-Argentines lived, decimated their numbers as wealthier criollos moved to higher, healthier ground in the northern suburbs.

Historian George Reid Andrews argued that there was slim evidence for either hypothesis and, moreover, little for the disappearance of the community itself. What he learned by examining archival materials and the capital's Afro-Argentine press was that the community itself was unconcerned with demographic decline but clearly worried about its socioeconomic status.

As the slave trade ended by the mid-19th century and European immigration transformed the city a couple of decades later, Afro-Argentines were clearly a declining *percentage* of the population, but that does not explain their plunging absolute numbers. Andrews, though, found that Argentine authorities and opinion-makers consciously excised the Afro-Argentine presence to help promote the country as a European outpost in the Americas.

Some of this certainly owed its origins to racism that was present from early independence times. Political opponents of Bernardino Rivadavia, presumably of mixed European and African ancestry and who served as president in 1826–1827 before his forced resignation, stigmatized him with the epithet "Dr. Chocolate." Argentine schoolchildren hear that their country abolished slavery in 1813, but these measures were so half-hearted that the institution lingered nearly another half-century.

More insidiously, though, census-takers systematically undercounted Afro-Argentines in equally half-hearted efforts that sometimes even avoided their neighborhoods. When summarizing the data, they minimized the black presence by creating vague racial categories such as *trigueño* (wheat-colored) to describe individuals with African ancestry. Eventually, in Andrews's words, Buenos Aires's Afro-Argentines were "forgotten, but not gone."

Even as more and more European immigrants streamed into Argentina, Afro-Argentines kept alive institutions such as the Shimmy Club, a social organization that sponsored dances only half a block off Avenida Corrientes in the 1970s. Here rhythmic drum-based *malambo, milonga,* and *zamba* filled the hall and, on occasion, spilled out into the street.

Andrews thought that Argentine society was absorbing blacks and, indeed, defining them as whites in accordance with an unspoken ideology, even as their contributions to society survived. In recent years, though, there has been a small but complex revival of black culture in Buenos Aires that involves Afro-Argentines (estimated at about 3,000) as well as Afro-Uruguayans, Afro-Brazilians, Cape Verde Portuguese (perhaps 8,000), Cubans, and Africans. This has not always been convivial, as the remaining Afro-Argentines distinguish themselves from the latecomers even as they share some cultural traits.

Still, Argentine society's continued refusal to acknowledge their presence and its own African heritage may be their greatest adversary. Created in 1996, the Fundación Africa Vive (Africa Lives Foundation) claims there are more than 2 million Argentines of African descent; according to director María Magdalena Lamadrid, "A single drop of blood is enough" to define an Afro-Argentine.

Yet in 2002, when Lamadrid herself attempted to fly to Panama to participate in a conference on Dr. Martin Luther King Jr.'s life, immigration officials detained her on suspicion of carrying a false passport. One allegedly said, "she can't be black and Argentine."

economic crisis, though, many needed assistance from Jewish community organizations, and some Argentine Jews emigrated or considered emigrating to Israel despite the insecurity there. It's worth mentioning that still-unsolved terrorist incidents in Buenos Aires killed 29 people in Retiro's Israeli Embassy, and 87 people in Once's Asociación Mutua Israelita Argentina (AMIA), a Jewish cultural center, in 1994; most Jewish community landmarks are well fortified.

Numbering roughly half a million, Middle Eastern immigrants and their descendants have occupied high-profile positions—the most notable being former president Carlos Menem, of Syrian descent. Palermo's Saudi-funded Islamic Center is disproportionately large compared to the capital's observant Muslim population. Argentines misleadingly refer to anyone of Middle Eastern descent as *turcos* (Turks), a legacy of the initial immigration from the region.

In recent years, Asian faces have become more common. There has long been a community of about 30,000 Japanese-Argentines, concentrated in the capital and the Greater Buenos Aires suburb of Escobar, but Belgrano also has a modest Chinatown near the Barrancas. Many Koreans work in Once and live in the southern barrio of Nueva Pompeya.

Other South Americans, mostly Bolivians, Paraguayans, and Peruvians, flocked to Argentina during the early-1990s boom. They generally work at menial jobs, and many returned home after the economic meltdown of 2001–2002. They are mostly concentrated in certain Buenos Aires neighborhoods—Peruvians in Congreso, Paraguayans in Constitución, and Bolivians in Nueva Pompeya.

RELIGION

Roman Catholicism remains Argentina's official and dominant religion, though church membership is no longer a requirement for the presidency. Evangelical Protestantism, with its street preachers and storefront churches, is growing even in sophisticated Buenos Aires, mostly but not exclusively among working-class people. Other religions have fewer adherents.

Catholicism in particular has left the country with many of its greatest landmarks, ranging from the colonial chapels, churches, and cathedrals of Córdoba and the northwest to the neoclassical dignity of Buenos Aires's Catedral Metropolitana. Immigrant Protestant communities are responsible for Buenos Aires landmarks like San Telmo's Danish and Swedish churches, and the impressive Russian Orthodox dome opposite Parque Lezama.

Roman Catholicism

Starting with the famous Dominican Bartolomé de las Casas in Mexico, factions

THE PROMISED LAND OF THE SOUTH

Argentina's Jewish community of about 200,000 is Latin America's greatest and the world's sixth-largest. Still, it draws little international attention except when it literally explodes onto the news – as in 1992 when a car bomb destroyed Buenos Aires's Israeli embassy and in 1994 when a similar event leveled the city's main Jewish cultural center. Ever since the first Jews arrived in the mid-19th century, though, the community has endured a cycle of ups and downs in both the capital and the countryside.

In the mid-19th century, Buenos Aires's first Jews were professionals who arrived as representatives of British, French, and German exporters; about 50 of them formed the first Congregación Israelita de la República Argentina in 1862. The first Moroccan Jews arrived in the early 1880s, but the main impetus for organized immigration began in 1881, when President Julio Argentino Roca appointed an honorary agent in Paris, with special attention to Jewish refugees from Tsarist pogroms.

Still, nearly eight years passed before the first 120 farming families arrived, but their welcome was less than even lukewarm – an immigration inspector separated them for two days and nearly shipped them back on the steamer that brought them. Finally admitted as *colonos* who had purchased property from Rafael Hernández (brother of the author of the *gauchesco* poem *Martín Fierro*), they never received their property. Hernández reneged on the deal due to increased land prices.

Many Jews settled in Buenos Aires, of course, but the French baron Maurice de Hirsch responded to Hernández's duplicity by sponsoring a program to settle the *colonos* in Santa Fe Province, where they created the Colonia Agrícola Moisesville. Riding like gauchos and introducing new crops such as rice and sunflowers, the new settlers prospered in a community (pop. about 2,000) that still today has four synagogues (only one of which remains open, however).

In all, between 1888 and 1938, perhaps 250,000 Jewish immigrants entered Argen-

tina; another 10,000 or so were Holocaust survivors. As birthrates fell after 1960, the young preferred the cities, upwards of 30,000 emigrated to Israel through 1983, and the community's profile began to change.

Traditionally middle-class, the Jewish population suffered along with the rest of Argentina in the 2001-2002 crisis, and nearly 20 percent fell below the poverty line. Despite assistance from overseas organizations, the situation was dire enough that some have chosen to emigrate to Israel – preferring the political uncertainties of a war zone to jobless futility in the country of their birth. Some speculated that up to 10 percent of the population might leave for Israel, where new immigrants receive jobs and government subsidies to get started.

Moisesville, for its part, retains much of its identity – even though only about 15 percent of the remaining population is Jewish and the majority is now Roman Catholic, the town shuts down for Jewish holidays. With the movement to the cities, many Jewish landowners now lease their properties to gentile farmers.

Coincidentally, Jewish themes appear in Argentine literature and, more recently, the cinema (though not so prominently as in Hollywood). Russian immigrant Alberto Gerchunoff (1884–1950) left a series of vignettes republished in English as *The Jewish Gauchos of the Pampas* (Albuquerque: University of New Mexico Press, 1998), while Nina Barragan reconstructed the Moisesville experience in *Losers and Keepers in Argentina* (Albuquerque, NM: University of New Mexico Press, 2001).

A version of Gerchunoff's *Los Gauchos Judíos* made it to the screen in the early 1970s. More recently, director Antonio Ottone made the early colony the setting for *Un Amor en Moisesville* (2000), known in English as *Divided Hearts*. The well-known actors Federico Luppi and Norma Aleandro appeared in director Eduardo Mignogna's *Sol de Otoño* (1996), a Buenos Aires-based comedy-drama about a love affair between an older couple, a Jew and a non-Jew.

within the Catholic Church have wrestled with the contradictions between its official mission of recruiting and saving souls and its duty to alleviate the misery of those who have experienced secular injustice and persecution. Argentina is no exception—figures such as the late cardinal Antonio Quarracino were outright apologists for the vicious military dictatorship of 1976–1983, but others lobbied against its excesses and in favor of a return to democracy. Some more-militant clergy worked the slums under the influence of "liberation theology," and some lost their lives in the aftermath of the 1976 coup.

Folk Catholicism, including spiritualist practices, often diverges from Church orthodoxy in the veneration of unofficial saints such as San Juan's Difunta Correa and Corrientes's Gaucho Antonio Gil, and even historical figures like Juan and Evita Perón, tango legend Carlos Gardel, and healer Madre María, all of whose tombs are in Buenos Aires's landmark cemeteries Recoleta and Chacarita. Novelist Tomás Eloy Martínez has sardonically labeled his countrymen as "cadaver cultists" for their devotion to the dead.

Protestantism

Anglicans were the original bearers of Protestantism in Argentina, but Scandinavian communities were numerous enough to justify construction of Lutheran churches. More-recent Protestant denominations are often shrill evangelicals; nearby Uruguay's capital city of Montevideo is one of the centers of Reverend Sun Myung Moon's cultish Unification Church (no relation to Moon Handbooks!).

Other Religions

The Argentine constitution guarantees freedom of religion, and adherents of non-Christian faiths are not rare, if not exactly numerous. The largest and most conspicuous of these is Judaism, as the capital's Jewish community is at least 200,000 strong (a planned community census may well reveal a larger number). Saudi Arabia sponsored the construction of Palermo's Centro Islámico Rey Fahd, whose vastness overshadows the capital's relatively small community of observant Muslims.

HOLIDAYS, FESTIVALS, AND EVENTS

Argentina observes the typical national holidays and quite a few special events on top of that. The summer months of January and February, when most Argentines leave on vacation, are generally a quiet time; things pick up after school starts in early March.

January

January 1 is **Año Nuevo** (New Year's Day), an official holiday.

February or March

Dates for the pre-Lenten **Carnaval** (Carnival) vary year to year but most celebrations take place on weekends rather than during the week. While unlikely ever to match the spectacle of Brazilian festivities, Carnaval is enjoying a revival in Buenos Aires neighborhoods and Mesopotamian cities like Gualeguaychú and Corrientes.

March/April

Semana Santa (Holy Week) is widely observed in Catholic Argentina, though only the days from **Viernes Santo** (Good Friday) through **Pascua** (Easter) are official holidays. Many Argentines use the long weekend for a mini-vacation.

May

May 1 is **Día del Trabajador** (International Labor Day), an official holiday. On May 25, Argentines observe the **Revolución de Mayo** (May Revolution of 1810), when *porteños* made their first move toward independence by declaring the viceroy illegitimate.

June

June 10 is **Día de las Malvinas** (Malvinas Day), an official holiday celebrating Argentina's claim to the British-governed Falkland Islands. June 20, also an official holiday, is **Día de la Bandera** (Flag Day).

July

July 9's **Día de la Independencia** celebrates the formal declaration of Argentine independence at the northwestern city of Tucumán in 1816. Later in the month, when school lets out, many Argentines take **Vacaciones de Invierno** (Winter Holidays), when flights and even buses fill up fast.

August

August 17 is **Día de San Martín**, the official observance of the death (not birth) of Argentina's independence hero.

October

October 12 is **Día de la Raza** (equivalent to Columbus Day), an official holiday.

November

November 2's **Día de los Muertos** (Day of the Dead) is when Argentines visit the graves of their loved ones, though this is not the colorful event it is in, say, Mexico or Guatemala.

December

December 25 is **Navidad** (Christmas Day), an official holiday.

LANGUAGE

Spanish is the official language, but English is widely spoken at tourist offices, airlines, travel agencies, upscale hotels, and in business settings. In the provinces it's less common, though its use is spreading, especially in the travel and tourism sector.

Foreign-language use is also vigorous among ethnic communities such as Italo-Argentines, Anglo-Argentines, and German-Argentines. The Anglo-Argentine and business communities even support a daily tabloid, the *Buenos Aires Herald*, while the German-Argentine community has the weekly *Argentinisches Tageblatt*. Welsh is making a comeback in Chubut Province.

Buenos Aires also has its own street slang, *lunfardo*, which owes its origins to working-class immigrant communities. Many *lunfardo* words have worked their way into everyday Argentine speech even though they may be unintelligible to those who have learned Spanish

---

VOSEO

Along with Uruguayans, Paraguayans, and some Central Americans, Argentines commonly use the distinctive second-person-familiar form of address known as *voseo* (use of the pronoun *vos*). Spaniards and most other Latin Americans, by contrast, employ the *tuteo* (use of the pronoun *tú*).

Use of the *voseo*, a somewhat archaic form dating from the 16th and 17th centuries, involves different verb endings for all regular and most irregular verbs. This means adding a last-syllable accent for stress – instead of *tú hablas*, for instance, Argentines will say *vos hablás*. Likewise, with an irregular verb such as *decir* (to say), Argentines will also say *vos decís* rather than *tú dices*.

In the imperative form, there are also differences – instead of *ven* (come), Argentines say *vení*. Negative imperatives, however, are the same in both the *tuteo* and *voseo*, as in *no vengas* (don't come). Some common verbs, such as *ir* (to go) and *estar* (to be) are similarly irregular in both *voseo* and *tuteo*, but others are not. In *voseo*, for instance, *tú eres*... becomes *vos sos*...

Despite the differing verb forms, Argentines still use the possessive article *tu* and the reflexive or conjunctive object pronoun *te* (¿*te vas?*). Alert travelers will quickly recognize the differences, but they may wish to refrain from using the form, considered substandard in some contexts, unless absolutely certain that it is appropriate. The *tuteo* is never incorrect, though it may sound quaint in some contexts.

---

elsewhere. Some are fairly obvious in context, such as *laburar* instead of *trabajar* for work or labor, but others are obscure.

While many of its idioms are crude by standards of formal Spanish, *lunfardo* has acquired a certain legitimacy among Argentine scholars. There is even an academy for the study of *porteño* slang, the **Academia Porteña del Lunfardo** (Estados Unidos 1379, Monserrat, Buenos Aires, tel. 011/4383-2393, www.aplunfardo.org.ar).

The Arts

Even during Argentina's 2002 economic crisis, one sector of Argentine society that showed real resilience was the arts. After Tucumán native Tomás Eloy Martínez, a professor of Spanish at Rutgers, won the Spanish Alfaguara literary prize for *El Vuelo de la Reina,* a novel about crime and corruption, he remarked that "One of Argentina's riches is forgotten, but it is the quality, the leadership of our culture. [In that field] we can speak as equals to the U.S. or France."

LITERATURE

In the 19th century, even as the free-roaming gaucho was becoming a wage laborer, Argentine literature created a romanticized *gauchesco* (gauchesque) stereotype in José Hernández's epic poem *Martín Fierro* (1872); Ricardo Güiraldes's *Don Segundo Sombra* (1926) novelized the genre. Both are widely available in translation.

Distinctly unromanticized despite his own provincial origins, educator and politician Domingo F. Sarmiento's *Life in the Argentine Republic in the Days of the Tyrants* (1845) is an eloquent tirade against rural caudillos.

Born in Buenos Aires Province of Anglo-American parents, William Henry Hudson (1841–1922) left for London at age 33, but his memoir *Long Ago and Far Away* (1922) is a staple of public education (Argentines know him as Guillermo Enrique Hudson). *Idle Days in Patagonia* (1893) describes his bird-watching explorations.

No Argentine author has ever won a Nobel Prize, but three have won the Premio Cervantes, the Spanish-speaking world's most important literary honor: essayist, poet, and short-story writer Jorge Luis Borges (1979), novelist Ernesto Sábato (1984), and novelist Adolfo Bioy Casares (1990).

Globally, the most prominent is Borges (1899–1986). Ironically enough for an urbane figure with a classical education and who loathed Perón and Peronism, his short stories, poetry, and essays often focus on urban lowlifes and rural themes, including gaucho violence. Borges never wrote a novel; his most frequently read works are obscure and even surrealistic stories such as those in *Labyrinths* (1970, in English). Eliot Weinberger has edited a wide-ranging collection of the author's short pieces, many previously untranslated, in *Jorge Luis Borges: Selected Non-Fictions* (New York: Viking, 1999).

Borges's friend Bioy Casares (1914–1999) collaborated with the older man on detective stories under the pseudonym Honorio Bustos Domecq, but his own fantastical novella *The Invention of Morel* (Austin: University of Texas Press, 1985) is a purposefully disorienting work that director Eliseo Subiela transformed into the award-winning film *Man Facing Southeast.*

Sábato (born 1911) acquired renown in the English-speaking world as the coordinator of *Nunca Más,* an official account of the brutalities of the 1976–1983 military dictatorship. The ultimate Buenos Aires novel may be his psychologically engrossing *On Heroes and Tombs* (1961; New York: Ballantine, 1991).

Son of a diplomatic family, Brussels-born Julio Cortázar (1914–1984) was a short-story writer, experimental novelist, and committed leftist who chose Parisian exile after a Peronist purge in the university. Michelangelo Antonioni turned one of Cortázar's stories into the film *Blowup,* but the author is also known for the novels *Hopscotch* (1963; New York: Random House, 1966), about a failed Francophile poet in Buenos Aires, and *62: A Model Kit* (1968; New York: Random House, 1972).

Enthralled with popular culture, especially movies, Manuel Puig (1932–1990) authored a series of readable novels including *Betrayed by Rita Hayworth* (1968); *The Buenos Aires Affair* (New York: Dutton, 1968); and *Kiss of the Spider Woman* (New York: Vintage, 1991), which Brazilian director Héctor Babenco made into an award-winning English-language film.

Journalist and novelist Osvaldo Soriano (1943–1997) wrote satirical fiction such as *A Funny*

Dirty Little War (Columbia, LA, and London: Readers International, 1989), depicting the consequences of national upheaval in a small community. His *Shadows* (New York: Knopf, 1993), whose Spanish title, *Una Sombra Ya Pronto Serás*, comes from a classic tango, became a disorienting road movie under Héctor Olivera's direction.

Essayist Victoria Ocampo (1891–1979), whose poetess sister Silvina (1909–1994) was Bioy Casares's wife, founded the literary magazine *Sur;* some of her essays appear in Doris Meyer's biography *Victoria Ocampo: Against the Wind and the Tide* (Austin: University of Texas Press, 1990). Borges was one of her collaborators at *Sur,* which became a prestigious publishing house that brought works by Aldous Huxley, D. H. Lawrence, and even Jack Kerouac to Spanish-speaking readers.

Tomás Eloy Martínez, quoted above on Argentina's cultural resilience and vitality, is author of several novels dealing with the Argentine condition through fictionalized biography, most notably *The Perón Novel* (New York: Pantheon, 1988). *Santa Evita* (New York: Knopf, 1996), by contrast, can only be called postbiographical, as it traces the odyssey of Evita's embalmed body to Italy, Spain, and back to Buenos Aires.

Novelist Federico Andahazi, also a psychiatrist, outraged heiress Amalia Fortabat when an independent jury awarded him her self-anointed literary prize for *The Anatomist* (New York: Doubleday, 1998), a sexually explicit (but unerotic) tale of medieval Italy.

VISUAL ARTS

With its small, dispersed settlements, colonial Argentina lacked the great religious art tradition of the populous Perú and Bolivia, which developed their own "schools" of painting and sculpture. *Porteño* art critic Jorge Glusberg has even argued that the colonial period, "characterized by subordination to the European models currently in vogue," lasted until the 1940s. Glusberg may underrate some earlier painters and sculptors, but many innovative artists have flourished (if not always financially) since then—in both figurative and abstract modes.

Painting

European-trained Prilidiano Pueyrredón (1823–1870) painted landscapes and people of rural Buenos Aires. Eduardo Sívori (1847–1918) and Ernesto de la Cárcova (1866–1927) both displayed concern with social causes such as poverty and hunger.

After losing his right forearm to a grenade in battle against Paraguay, army officer Cándido López (1840–1902) painted more than 50 oils of war scenes with his left hand; more remarkably, his works were not romanticized scenes of combat heroism but vivid landscapes depicting routine activities—ordinary encampments and river crossings, for instance—plus the occasional battle.

Benito Quinquela Martín (1890–1977) portrayed immigrant factory workers and stevedores in his vivid oils of La Boca. The watercolors of Borges's friend Xul Solar (1887–1963; real name Alejandro Schulz Solari) dealt with esoteric and mystical themes.

The versatile Antonio Berni (1905–1981) worked in painting, drawing, engraving, collage, and sculpture. His socially conscious canvases, such as *Juanito Laguna Bañándose entre Latas* (Juanito Laguna Bathing in the Trash), have fetched astronomical prices at auction.

Berni, along with Lino Spilimbergo (1896–1964), Juan Carlos Castagnino (1908–1972), Galician-born Manuel Colmeiro (1901–1999), and Demetrio Urruchúa (1902–1978), were part of the Nuevo Realismo (New Realism) movement that created the ceiling murals in Buenos Aires's Galerías Pacífico shopping center.

When not collaborating on such projects, Spilimbergo specialized in geometric forms, still life, and lighted landscapes. Castagnino specialized in rural, even gauchesque, landscapes, while Colmeiro and Urruchúa were both socially oriented painters and muralists.

Modern Argentine painting's current star, Guillermo Kuitca (born 1960) contrasts small figures with large environments, transforms everyday abstractions such as floor plans and road maps, and creates abstract visual expressions of popular music themes like the antilynching classic "Strange Fruit" and the Rolling Stones' "Gimme Shelter."

ARGENTINE SPECTATOR SPORTS

As in most of the rest of Latin America, *fútbol* (soccer) is by far the most popular spectator sport. For a country born on horseback, equestrian sports like horse racing, polo, and the gaucho-derived *pato* all enjoy popularity.

Argentina has had an international boxing presence ever since Luis Angel Firpo (1894–1960), the "Wild Bull of the Pampas," nearly won the world heavyweight championship from Jack Dempsey in New York in 1923. Although the sport has declined since then, it may be making a comeback.

Argentine tennis has long enjoyed an international reputation through stars such as Guillermo Vilas and Gabriela Sabatini. In 2002, David Nalbandian, of Córdoba Province, became the first Argentine to reach the men's finals at Wimbledon before losing to Lleyton Hewitt of Australia. In 2009, Juan Martín del Potro of Tandil made headlines by defeating the nearly invincible Roger Federer at the U.S. Open.

Argentina has had a nationwide professional basketball league since 1984. By winning gold medals at the 2004 Olympics, the national team has gained international respect, especially for their strong fundamentals and team play. The NBA success of San Antonio's 6-foot-6 (1.98-meter) Emanuel Ginóbili has spurred interest in the sport; fellow Argentines Fabricio Oberto (Ginóbili's former teammate, now with the Washington Wizards), Andrés Nocioni (Sacramento Kings), Carlos Delfino (Milwaukee Bucks), and Luis Scola (Houston Rockets) have earned more playing time, but haven't yet matched Ginóbili's achievements. Walter Herrmann, formerly with Charlotte and Detroit, now plays in Spain.

Rugby is an amateur endeavor here, but Los Pumas, the national team, has earned a global reputation.

SOCCER

Argentina is a perpetual soccer power – having won the World Cup in 1978 and 1986 – and the birthplace of Diego Armando Maradona, one of the sport's all-time legends. The national team disappointed its fans by losing to Germany in the quarter-finals of the 2006 World Cup and, under Maradona's erratic coaching, barely made the 2010 World Cup in South Africa.

What its English creators like to call "the beautiful game" often falls short of its billing; the *Buenos Aires Herald* once said it best with the headline "Another Boring 0-0 Tie." Still, Argentina is a soccer-mad country, with six first-division teams in Buenos Aires, another seven in its suburbs, and the rest of the country not far behind. The season runs March-December; for current information, check the Asociación de Fútbol Argentina's website (www.afa.org.ar), which appears in both English and Spanish.

Sculpture

Buenos Aires is a city of monuments but many, if not most, are pretentious busts of ostensible statesmen and colossal equestrian statues of military men. The Rodin-influenced Rogelio Yrurtia (1879–1950) found better outlets for his talents in statues like his working-class tribute *Canto al Trabajo* (Ode to Labor), on San Telmo's Plazoleta Olazábal.

Those who followed Yrurtia have been more daring. León Ferrari (born 1920) created the prescient *La Civilización Occidental y Cristiana* (Western and Christian Civilization, 1965), a sardonic Vietnam-era work that portrays Christ crucified on a diving F-105. Similarly, Juan Carlos Distéfano (born 1933) blends sculpture and painting in works like *El Rey y La Reina* (1977), a thinly disguised portrayal of extrajudicial executions carried out by death squads after the 1976 military coup.

Alberto Heredia (1924–2000) mocked the pomposity of monumental public art in *El Caballero de la Máscara* (The Masked Horseman). The misleading title describes a collage that's a headless parody of an equestrian statue that ridicules 19th-century strongmen and their contemporary counterparts.

ARCHITECTURE

Because Buenos Aires languished as a backwater of Spain's empire until the creation of the Viceroyalty of the River Plate in the late 18th century, little remains of its precarious early architecture. The northwestern provinces, though, retain significant colonial monuments in their capital cities and in the countryside. Many are ecclesiastical constructions, ranging from modest chapels in the Quebrada de Humahuaca to full-fledged cathedrals in Córdoba.

For most of the 19th century, *porteño* architecture evolved from Spanish colonial origins to an Italianate style but, from the early 20th century, the reigning architectural fashion was a beaux arts academicism, both for public buildings and landowning oligarchy's ornate *palacetes* (mansions). Many French professionals, including landscape architect Charles Thays, worked on projects in Buenos Aires and provincial cities.

From the 1930s, the capital developed greater residential and commercial density with buildings such as Retiro's Edificio Kavanagh, a 30-story art deco high-rise that was the country's first air-conditioned structure. The late 20th century saw some hideous developments, such as Clorindo Testa's brutalist Biblioteca Nacional (National Library) in Palermo. One positive development is the recycling of historical structures, such as the Galerías Pacífico, into contemporary shopping centers, and the brick warehouses at Puerto Madero into fashionable restaurants and residential lofts.

Architect Alejandro Bustillo created a magnificent northern Patagonian style with Bariloche's landmark Centro Cívico. His imitators, though, have failed to achieve the same harmony of nature and culture.

It would be misleading to ignore vernacular architecture styles, ranging from Andean adobes to the distinctive *casa chorizo,* a long narrow construction on a deep lot. La Boca's wood-frame metal-clad houses owe their bright primary colors to the fact that early residents scavenged their paint from ships on the Riachuelo. Houses in the Río Paraná Delta sit atop stilts to avoid flooding.

MUSIC

Argentines are musical people, their interests ranging from folk, pop, rock, and blues to classical. Popular music takes many forms, from Andean folk tradition to the accordion-based immigrant *chamamé* of the northeastern lowlands and the hard-nosed *rock nacional* of Buenos Aires. Both instrumentally and with lyrics, the signature sound and dance is the plaintive, melancholy tango, the Argentine blues. Performers are versatile and quick to cross boundaries—the late folksinger Mercedes Sosa, for instance, collaborated with erratic rocker Charly García, and classical composers and performers have adapted tango into their repertoire.

Classical Music and Dance

Since its completion in 1908, Buenos Aires's Teatro Colón has been the continent's preeminent high-culture venue. Thanks to the Colón, the Teatro Avenida, and other classical venues, early-20th-century Argentina produced an abundance of classical composers, particularly in opera and ballet.

Contemporary Argentine classical music can boast figures like Daniel Barenboim (born 1942), a pianist and conductor who has held posts at the Orchestre de Paris, the Chicago Symphony Orchestra, and the Deutsche Staatsoper Berlin. Barenboim is a versatile figure who has, among other achievements, recorded tango and other popular music (also an Israeli citizen, he has played the West Bank in defiance of that government's objections).

Though she lives in Brussels, pianist Martha Argerich (born 1941) has sponsored competitions in Buenos Aires. She has drawn rave reviews from the *New York Times* for her Carnegie Hall concerts, and has won a Grammy for best instrumental soloist.

Rosario-born but Europe-based tenor José Cura (born 1962) has drawn attention as a credible successor to Luciano Pavarotti on the international opera scene. The most significant ballet performer is Julio Bocca (born 1967), a prodigy who performed in New York, Paris, and elsewhere. He has formed his own company, the Ballet Argentino, but retired from performing himself.

Tango

Tango overlaps the categories of music and dance, and even within those categories there are distinctions. As music, the tango can be instrumental, but it earned its popularity and international reputation through the *tango canción* (tango song) of the legendary Carlos Gardel and others. One *porteño* songwriter has described the tango as "a sad feeling that is danced," and it clearly appeals to nostalgia for things lost—whether an old flame or the old neighborhood.

The charismatic Gardel (died 1935), whose birth date and birthplace are topics of controversy, attained immortality after perishing in a Colombian plane crash. According to diehard admirers, "Gardel sings better every day." Uruguayan-born Julio Sosa (1926–1964), who also died young in an auto accident, was nearly as important; at a time when Peronism was outlawed, his subtle smile and on-stage gestures evoked the exiled caudillo.

As opposed to the *tango canción,* orchestral tango is the legacy of bandleaders and composers like Osvaldo Pugliese (1905–1995), Aníbal "Pichuco" Troilo (1914–1975), and especially Astor Piazzola (1921–1992), whose jazz influences were palpable. Key lyricists included Enrique Santos Discépolo (1908–1992) and Homero Manzi (1907–1951).

Practiced by skilled and sexy dancers, the tourist-oriented floor show tells only part of the story. The tango is not just for the young and lithe—one could argue that its nostalgia lends it to older individuals with longer memories—and a recent revival has raised its popularity with mixed-age audiences at *milongas* (informal dance clubs).

Tango remains a daily presence in Buenos Aires, with both a 24-hour FM radio station (FM 92.7, www.la2x4.gov.ar) and a cable TV channel, Sólo Tango. Contemporary performers of note include Eladia Blásquez (1931–2005), Susana Rinaldi (born 1935), and Adriana Varela (born 1958). Pop singers such as Sandro (1945–2010) and Cacho Castaña

© BERNARDO ERTL/123RF.COM

a couple dancing tango in Buenos Aires

(born 1942) have also sung tango, while the much younger Omar Giammarco produces tango-flavored music using accordion instead of *bandoneón*.

Folk

Tango may be an urban folk music, but the true folk tradition stems from *payadores*, gauchos who sang verses to guitar accompaniment; in dance, it can take the form of *malambo*, a competitive male-only affair with echoes of flamenco. An older current derives from the northwestern Andean highlands, featuring the *zampoña* (panpipes) and *charango*, a stringed instrument whose sound box is an armadillo shell.

Born in Buenos Aires Province, the late Atahualpa Yupanqui (1908–1992) belongs to these purist traditions, as does the Salta-based group Los Chalchaleros, an institution for over half a century. Tucumán native Mercedes Sosa (1935–2009) was less a purist, having performed with rock musician Charly García. Their contemporary León Gieco (born 1951) crosses the line into folk-rock and even rap.

Tomás Lipán, an Aymará Indian from Jujuy, embodies the Andean tradition, but adds urban touches like the *bandoneón* to create a hybrid. Soledad Pastorutti (born 1980), who performs under her first name only, is a self-conscious folkie who sings and dresses in *gauchesco* style.

Immigrant communities have left their mark in accordion-based *chamamé*, typical of the northern Mesopotamian provinces. Notable performers include Antonio Tarragó Ros and Chango Spasiuk (born 1968), from a Ukrainian community in Misiones Province.

Rock and Pop

Despite the handicap of trying to fit a multisyllabic language into a monosyllabic musical idiom, the practitioners of *rock nacional* have had remarkable success. In terms of live music, there's something almost every night; the downside is that some top bands have a small but pugnacious hard core of fans who often crowd the stage; visitors unaccustomed to the scene may prefer to stand back.

Argentine rock's pioneer is Roberto Sánchez (1945–2010). Better known by his stage name, Sandro, also a movie idol with a domineering manager, he draws obvious comparisons with Elvis Presley, but "El Maestro" was also a credible tango singer and the first Argentine to appear at Madison Square Garden.

Charly García (born 1951) transcends generations—many of his fans are in their twenties and often younger. García, who sings and plays mostly keyboards, incorporates women into his backing bands even as lead guitarists and saxophonists; he displays a sense of history in adapting Spanish-language lyrics to classics like Eddie Cochran's "Summertime Blues."

Nearly as revered is Dylanesque León Gieco (born 1951); his album *Bandidos Rurales* (2002) bears thematic resemblance to Dylan's *John Wesley Harding*. Fito Páez (born 1963) and García protégé Andrés Calamaro (born 1961) also have major solo careers.

Many acts have a stronger group than individual identity. Among them are Attaque 77, Babasónicos, Los Divididos (famous for versions of the Mexican folk song "Cielito Lindo" and the Doors' "Light My Fire"), Las Pelotas, Los Piojos, and the Stones-influenced Los Ratones Paranóicos. Almafuerte and the power trio A.N.I.M.A.L. are the leading heavy-metal bands.

Grammy winners Los Fabulosos Cadillacs (best alternative Latin rock group in 1998) have toured North America, playing salsa- and reggae-influenced rock at venues like San Francisco's Fillmore Auditorium. Others in this idiom include Los Auténticos Decadentes, Los Cafres, and especially Bersuit Vergarabat.

Buenos Aires has a robust blues scene thanks to performers like guitarist Norberto Napolitano (better known as Pappo, 1950–2005) and groups like La Mississippi and Memphis La Blusera. The female vocal trio Las Blacanblus, who broke up in 2006, treated blues standards in a distinctive style with minimal accompaniment (only guitar and piano).

In a category of their own are Les Luthiers, an eclectic bunch that makes its own instruments (which defy description) and caricatures society's most authoritarian and bourgeois sectors. While musically sophisticated, the band's shows are as much theater as concert.

Jazz

Both traditional and free-form jazz play a part in Argentina's musical history. A fixture in the former idiom is Buenos Aires's Fénix Jazz Band, whose vocalist Ernesto "Cachi" Carrizo says he can't sing blues in Spanish because "the blues in Spanish seems as absurd to me as tango in English."

Better known beyond strictly Argentine circles is saxophonist Gato Barbieri (born 1932), also composer of the soundtrack for *The Last Tango in Paris*. Famous for TV and movie soundtracks like *Bullitt, Cool Hand Luke,* and *Mission Impossible,* Hollywood regular Lalo Schifrin (born 1932) originally moved to the United States to play piano with Dizzy Gillespie. His father, Luis, was concertmaster of the Teatro Colón's orchestra.

CINEMA

Given the country's political and economic instability, it's surprising that Argentine cinema has been as productive and successful as it has. In 2000, for instance, Argentine directors managed to make 30 full-length features and four documentaries.

Special effects are generally limited, and Argentine films, like those in Europe, tend to be more character-driven than plot-driven. There are plenty of outstanding directors and actors, though, and quite a few films from the last 20 years–plus are available on video or DVD in Argentina and abroad.

Not only have Argentines made good films, but foreign directors have found Argentina an appealing location—all the more so now that the peso's collapse has made it inexpensive to shoot here.

Argentine Directors, Movies, and Actors

In its earliest years, Argentine cinema dealt almost exclusively with *porteño* themes such as Carnaval. Later, tango legend Carlos Gardel worked in Hollywood as well as Buenos Aires,

leaving films such as *El Día Que Me Quieras* (The Day You Love Me, 1935).

Over the decades, Argentine films have made respectable Oscar showings. Based on a story by Uruguayan writer Mario Benedetti, Sergio Renán's *La Tregua* (The Truce, 1975) was the first nominated for best foreign-language film. María Luisa Bemberg (1922–1995), astonishingly enough, made her first feature at the age of 58, but made up for lost time with films like the 1984 nominee *Camila,* based on the true story of 19th-century heiress Camila O'Gorman, her Jesuit lover, and their persecution by the Rosas dictatorship. Among its virtues, the film does an excellent job of representing the era's Afro-Argentine population.

In 1985, Luis Puenzo's *The Official Story* won the Oscar for his treatment of the controversial issue of military adoptions of "disappeared" parents' babies during the 1976–1983 Dirty War; it stars Norma Aleandro, a highly respected theater actress and director as well.

Based partly on Adolfo Bioy Casares's novella *The Invention of Morel,* Eliseo Subiela's *Man Facing Southeast* was considered for an Oscar nomination in 1986. Juan José Campanella's maudlin *Hijo de la Novia* (Son of the Bride) was a 2002 Oscar nominee, but his noirish *The Secret of Her Eyes* was a more deserving contender in 2010.

The Oscars, though, showcase only a small percentage of Argentine films and are not necessarily representative. Often subtly and sometimes overtly political, independent films may be eloquent and passionate but also introspective—partly due, perhaps, to the popularity of psychoanalysis.

Subiela's *The Dark Side of the Heart* (1992), an erotic love story with both humor and pathos, takes place in Buenos Aires and Montevideo; based loosely on *porteño* poet Oliverio Girondo's life, it features a cameo by Uruguayan poet Mario Benedetti. Puenzo (born 1946) used San Telmo, La Boca, and Palermo as settings for his adaptation of Albert Camus's *The Plague* (1992), with the (notoriously difficult) William Hurt, as well as Raúl Juliá and Robert Duvall.

Bemberg cast Julie Christie in the title role of her English-language *Miss Mary* (1986), the tale of an English governess on an Argentine *estancia*. Starring the late Marcelo Mastroianni, Bemberg's *I Don't Want to Talk About It* (1992) is a peculiar romance set in a conservative provincial town (filming took place in the Uruguayan city of Colonia, across the river from Buenos Aires).

Adolfo Aristarain (born 1943) directed the versatile Federico Luppi in *A Place in the World* (1992), a socially conscious drama disqualified for an Oscar because it was unclear whether it was an Uruguayan, Argentine, or Spanish production (most of the filming took place in Argentina's scenic San Luis Province).

In what may be the ultimate *porteño* film, Ricardo Darín and Gastón Pauls share the lead in Fabián Bielinsky's *Nine Queens* (2001), the twist-filled tale of con men who strike up a partnership in crisis-racked Buenos Aires. Uruguayan-born Adrián Caetano (born 1969) portrays the Argentine underclass in *Bolivia* (2001), which highlights hostility toward undocumented immigrants in a fictional but realistic milieu.

Fernando "Pino" Solanas (born 1936), a left-wing Peronist recently elected to Congress, dealt with the theme of expatriation in *The Exile of Gardel* (1985), with a soundtrack by tango legend Astor Piazzola. The prolific Leopoldo Torre Nilsson (1924–1978), who shot nearly 30 features in his relatively short lifetime, adapted Manuel Puig's novel *Boquitas Pintadas* (Painted Lips), a story of hypocrisy and petty jealousies in a small provincial town, to the screen in 1974.

Director Héctor Olivera (born 1931) turned Osvaldo Soriano's satirical novel *A Funny Dirty Little War* (1983), depicting the comic consequences of a military coup in a provincial town, into a movie. Starting with a bungled robbery in Buenos Aires, Marcelo Piñeyro's *Wild Horses* (1995) becomes a road romance that ends with a chase in the Patagonian province of Chubut.

THEATER

Argentines, especially *porteños*, are avid theatergoers. The tradition dates from late colonial times, when creation of the Viceroyalty of the River Plate gave the capital a certain legitimacy and pretensions, at least, to high culture. Over the 19th century, it developed through institutions like the *sainete*, a humorous performance dealing with immigrant issues.

Formal theater dates from the late 19th century, thanks to the patronage of the Montevideo-born Podestá family, who built theaters in Buenos Aires and La Plata. Influential early playwrights included Montevideo-born Florencio Sánchez (1875–1910), who wrote *sainetes* but drew much of his inspiration from Ibsen; Gregorio de Laferrere (1867–1913), who wrote comic plays; and Roberto Payró (1867–1928).

In the days before jet travel, twentieth-century European dramatists such as Federico García Lorca and Jean Cocteau found the Buenos Aires theater scene justified the long voyage across the Atlantic and beyond the Equator. Among Argentina's best-loved 20th-century performers are comedian Luis Sandrini (1905–1980) and Lola Membrives (1888–1969); the best-known contemporary playwright is Juan Carlos Gené (born 1929). Primarily known for her films, Norma Aleandro (born 1936) is also active as a theater director.

Ranging from vulgar burlesque with elaborate stage shows to Shakespearean and avant-garde drama, the Buenos Aires theater scene is busiest June–August. Avenida Corrientes is the traditional locus of live theater, but it's worth seeking out "off-Corrientes" alternatives such as La Boca's imaginative, politically committed Teatro Catalinas Sur.

CRAFTS

Argentina's artisanal heritage is less obvious than, say, the indigenous textile traditions of the Peruvian or Guatemalan highlands, but both the city and the countryside have characteristic crafts. The finest urban expression of folk art is *filete*, the rainbow signage that, in the hands of skilled painters, approaches fine calligraphy.

Befitting their origins on the Río de la Plata (literally, "River of Silver"), Argentine silversmiths create truly intricate jewelry, plus adornments such as the *facón* (knife) and *espuelas* (spurs) that accompany traditional gaucho clothing. The major silverwork center is the Buenos Aires provincial town of San Antonio de Areco.

Expert leatherworkers, in turn, produce gaucho-style clothing and horse gear such as *rastras* (belts), reins, and saddles. Both traditions come together in paraphernalia for *mate,* the herbal "Paraguayan tea" whose consumption is a cultural bellwether. Traditionally, *mate* (the herb) is sipped with a silver *bombilla* (straw) from a *mate* (gourd, in a different context), which may be mounted in a leather holder.

In the northwestern Andean provinces, indigenous weaving traditions are apparent in blankets, ponchos, sweaters, and similar garments. The Huarpe styles of Cuyo and the Mapuche of northern Patagonia differ in their approaches to such goods.

ESSENTIALS

Getting There

Most overseas visitors arrive in Argentina by air, mostly at Buenos Aires, but smaller regional airports get some of this traffic. Many also arrive overland from Chile, Bolivia, Uruguay, Paraguay, and Brazil. Almost all of the latter arrive by bus or private vehicle; there is no international rail service. There are ferry connections to Uruguay.

BY AIR

Buenos Aires has regular air links with North America, Europe, and Australia/New Zealand, plus less frequent routes from southern Africa across the Atlantic (some via Brazil). It is, however, a relatively expensive destination during peak periods such as the Christmas–New Year's and Holy Week (Easter) holidays; an Advance Purchase Excursion (Apex) fare can reduce the bite considerably, but may have minimum- and maximum-stay requirements, allow no stopovers, and impose financial penalties for any changes. Economy-class (Y) tickets, valid for 12 months, are more expensive but allow maximum flexibility. Travelers staying more than a year, though, have to cough up the difference for any interim price increases.

Discount ticket agents known as consolidators in the United States and "bucket shops" in Britain may offer the best deals through so-called "bulk fares," but they often have other

© EDUARDO RIVERA/123RF.COM

drawbacks—they may not, for instance, allow mileage credit for frequent-flyer programs. Courier flights, on which passengers surrender some or all of their baggage allowance to a company sending equipment or documents to overseas affiliates or customers, may be even cheaper, but are less common to Latin America than to other parts of the world. They are available for short periods only, and often leave on short notice.

Other options include Round the World (RTW) and Circle Pacific routes that permit numerous stopovers over the course of much longer multicontinental trips, but putting these itineraries together requires some effort. Two useful resources for researching airfares and many other aspects of international travel are the fourth edition of Edward Hasbrouck's *The Practical Nomad: How to Travel Around the World* (Berkeley, CA: Avalon Travel Publishing, 2007).

Many airlines reduced their services to Argentina after the economic collapse of 2001–2002, as debt default and devaluation meant far fewer Argentines could splurge on overseas travel. Schedules are expanding now, though, as the recovering economy has augmented business travel and the cheap peso has made the country a travel bargain for foreigners.

From North America

The main gateways to Buenos Aires are Miami, Atlanta, Washington, D.C. (Dulles), New York (JFK), Dallas, Houston, and Los Angeles. Canadian passengers may also use Toronto.

Aerolíneas Argentinas is the traditional carrier, but other options include Aerosur de Bolivia, American Airlines, Avianca, Continental, Copa, Delta, Gol/Varig, LAN, LAN Argentina, LAN Peru, Mexicana, Transportes Aéreos Mercosur (TAM), TACA, United Airlines, and US Airways. Aerolíneas Argentinas, American, Continental, LAN Argentina, United and US Airways have the only nonstop or direct services; others require changing planes elsewhere in Central or South America.

Air Canada flies from Toronto to Buenos Aires via Santiago, three or four times per week. By taking this route, non-Canadians can avoid the hassle of getting a U.S. visa just for transit purposes.

From Mexico, Central America, and the Caribbean

Aeroméxico and Mexicana fly regularly from Mexico City. Cubana has two or three flights weekly from Havana, while Avianca has connections to the Caribbean, Central America, and Mexico via Bogotá.

Copa flies daily from Panama, with connections throughout the region.

From Europe

There are direct services to Buenos Aires with Aerolíneas Argentinas (from Paris and Madrid, Barcelona, and Rome); Air Europa (from Madrid); Air France (from Paris); Alitalia (from Milan and Rome); British Airways (from London Heathrow); Iberia (from Madrid); and Lufthansa (from Frankfurt via São Paulo). TAM has connections from Paris via São Paulo.

From Asia, Africa, and the Pacific

The most direct service from the Pacific is Aerolíneas Argentinas's twice-weekly service from Sydney. From Australia, Qantas links up with LAN via Tahiti, Easter Island, and Santiago, or with LAN via Los Angeles; from Auckland, it also connects with LAN. From Japan, it's easiest to make connections via Los Angeles.

South African Airways now has nonstops from Johannesburg to Buenos Aires's Ezeiza Airport.

Within South America

Buenos Aires has connections to the neighboring republics of Uruguay, Brazil, Paraguay, Bolivia, and Chile, and elsewhere on the continent except the Guyanas.

Some major international airlines fly to and from Ezeiza Airport to Montevideo, Uruguay, but most flights to the Uruguayan capital leave from close-in Aeroparque. There

INTERNATIONAL AIRLINES IN BUENOS AIRES

Unless otherwise indicated, the addresses below are in the Microcentro and vicinity.

- **Aerolíneas Argentinas:** Perú 2, Monserrat, tel. 011/4320-2000

- **AeroMéxico:** Paraguay 555, tel. 011/5648-2205

- **AeroSur:** Avenida Santa Fe 849, 1st floor, tel. 011/4516-0999

- **Air Canada:** Avenida Córdoba 656, tel. 011/4327-3640

- **Air Europa:** Avenida Santa Fe 850, tel. 011/5219-4545

- **Air France:** San Martín 344, 23rd floor, tel. 011/4317-4700

- **Alitalia:** Suipacha 1111, 28th floor, Retiro, tel. 011/4310-9999

- **American Airlines:** Avenida Santa Fe 881, Retiro, tel. 011/4318-1111

- **Avianca:** Carlos Pellegrini 1163, 4th floor, Retiro, tel. 011/4394-5990

- **British Airways:** Avenida del Libertador 498, 13th floor, tel. 0800/222-0075

- **Continental Airlines:** Carlos Pellegrini 527, tel. 0800/333-0425

- **Copa:** Emma de la Barra 353, 7th floor, Puerto Madero, tel. 011/4132-3535

- **Cubana de Aviación:** Sarmiento 552, 11th floor, tel. 011/4326-5291

- **Delta:** Avenida Santa Fe 899, Retiro, tel. 011/4898-8170

- **Gol:** tel. 0810/266-3131, www.voegol.com

- **Iberia:** Carlos Pellegrini 1163, 1st floor, Retiro, tel. 011/4131-1000

- **LAN:** Cerrito 866, Retiro, tel. 0800/999-9526

- **Lufthansa:** Marcelo T. de Alvear 590, 6th floor, Retiro, tel. 011/4319-0600

- **Mexicana:** Avenida Córdoba 1131, 1st floor, Retiro, tel. 011/4136-4136

- **Pluna:** Libertad 1133, 4th floor, Retiro, tel. 011/4132-4444

- **Qantas:** Avenida Madero 900, 27th floor, Puerto Madero, tel. 011/4114-5800

- **South African Airways:** Avenida Santa Fe 846, Retiro, tel. 011/4319-0099

- **Swiss International:** Avenida Santa Fe 846, Retiro, tel. 011/4319-0000

- **Taca:** Carlos Pellegrini 1075, Retiro, tel. 0810/333-8222

- **Transportes Aéreos de Mercosur (TAM):** Cerrito 1030, Retiro, tel. 011/4819-4800

- **United Airlines:** Avenida Eduardo Madero 900, 9th floor, Retiro, tel. 0810/777-8648

- **US Airways:** tel. 011/4314-1600

are also flights from Aeroparque to Punta del Este, Uruguay's popular summer resort and weekend getaway. Aerolíneas Argentinas and Pluna are the main carriers.

To Brazil, the main destinations are São Paulo and Rio de Janeiro, but there are also flights to Florianópolis, Porto Alegre, and Bahía (Salvador), with connections to other cities. The main carriers are Aerolíneas Argentinas, TAM, and Gol/Varig.

Paraguay-bound flights go mostly to the capital city of Asunción, with Aerolíneas Argentinas, TAM, and Gol/Varig; some TAM flights go to Ciudad del Este, however, and on to Brazil.

AeroSur flies three times weekly to the Bolivian cities of Santa Cruz, Cochabamba, and La Paz. Aerolíneas also flies to Santa Cruz, while TAM has connections to Santa Cruz and Cochabamba via Asunción.

Discounted fares are less common in Latin America than in North America; the main exception is the highly competitive Buenos Aires–Santiago (Chile) route, where LAN has some excellent advance purchase fares.

LAN also has flights from Santiago to Mendoza and Córdoba, and occasionally to the northern Patagonian city of Bariloche.

Flights to Perú, Ecuador, Colombia, and Venezuela are all via capital cities, though some carriers stop elsewhere en route. Aerolíneas Argentinas goes to Lima and Caracas, LAN Perú to Lima, Grupo Taca to Lima en route to Mexico City, and Avianca to Bogotá.

OVERLAND
From North America, Mexico, and Central America

Overland travel from North America or elsewhere is problematic because Panama's Darien Gap to Colombia is impassable for motor vehicles. It is time-consuming, difficult, and potentially dangerous even for those on foot, as it passes through areas controlled by drug smugglers, guerrillas, and/or brutal Colombian paramilitaries.

Those visiting other parts of the continent and remaining for an extended period may want to consider shipping a vehicle. To locate a shipper, check the Yellow Pages of your local phone directory under Automobile Transporters, who are normally freight consolidators rather than the company that owns the ship, which will charge higher container rates. Since many more people ship vehicles to Europe than to South America, finding the right shipper may take patience; one reliable U.S. consolidator is **McClary, Swift & Co.** (360 Swift Ave., South San Francisco, CA 94080, tel. 650/872-2121, www.mcclaryswift.com), which has affiliates at many U.S. ports.

Argentine bureaucracy has improved in recent years, and clearing customs with a vehicle is simpler than it used to be. Vehicles arrive at the **Estación Marítima Buenos Aires** (Dársena B, Avenida Ramón Castillo y Avenida Maipú, Retiro, tel. 011/4311-0692 or 011/4317-0675 or 011/4312-8677); here it is necessary to present your passport, vehicle title, and the original *conocimiento de embarque* (bill of lading), and to fill out a customs application. You will then obtain an appointment with a customs inspector to retrieve the vehicle, which will cost about US$300 for port costs and another US$200 for the shipper; if the vehicle has been in port longer than five days, there will be additional charges. The vehicle can remain in Argentina legally for eight months, with an eight-month extension possible; any visit to a neighboring country restarts the clock. In event of any difficulty, consult a private *despachante de aduana* (customs broker), such as **José Angel Vidal Labra** (tel. 011/4345-7887, vidla@sinectis.com.ar).

Another possibility is Chile, whose ports are less bureaucratic and safer for the vehicle than Argentine ports. The most probable ports of entry are San Antonio, southwest of Santiago, and Valparaíso, northwest of the capital. It does pay to be there within a couple of days of the vehicle's arrival, or storage charges can mount up. Leave the gas tank as nearly empty as possible (for safety's sake) and leave no valuables, including tools, inside.

To arrange a shipment from San Antonio or Valparaíso, contact the Santiago consolidator **Ultramar** (Avenida Bosque Norte 500, 18th floor, Las Condes, tel. 2/630-1000, www.ultramar.cl). For a trustworthy customs agent to handle the paperwork, contact the office of **Juan Alarcón Rojas** (Fidel Oteíza 1921, 12th floor, Providencia, Santiago, tel. 02/328-5100, fax 02/328-5140, www.alarcon.cl); Chile's country code is 56.

Bicycles, of course, can be partially dismantled, packaged, and shipped aboard airplanes, sometimes for no additional charge. Except that there is rarely any additional paperwork for bringing a bike into the country, many of the same cautions apply as to any other overland travel.

From Neighboring South American Countries

Argentina has numerous border crossings with Chile, a few with Bolivia and Paraguay, many with Brazil, and a few with Uruguay. Relatively few Chilean crossings have scheduled public transportation, nor do those with Bolivia, but the Paraguayan, Brazilian, and Uruguayan borders are heavily transited.

International bus service is available from the neighboring republics, and also from more-distant destinations such as Perú, Ecuador, and Colombia.

Both international and domestic bus services normally have comfortable reclining seats (with every passenger guaranteed a seat), clean toilets, air-conditioning, and meals and refreshments served on board, at least on the longest trips. If not, they make regular meal stops. Between Santiago and Mendoza, there are minibuses and *taxi colectivos,* shared taxis that are slightly more expensive but faster than full-size buses.

From the settlements of San Pedro de Atacama and Calama in Northern Chile, there are buses to Salta and Jujuy via the smoothly paved highway over the Paso de Jama. The busiest crossing, though, is the Los Libertadores tunnel between Mendoza and Santiago.

In northern Patagonia, there are buses from Temuco to Neuquén over the 1,884-meter Paso de Pino Hachado via Curacautín and Lonquimay; the alternative 1,298-meter Paso de Icalma is slightly to the south. There is also bus service from Temuco to San Martín de los Andes via the Paso de Mamuil Malal (Paso Tromen to Argentines); a bus-ferry combination from Panguipulli to San Martín de los Andes via the 659-meter Paso Huahum and Lago Pirehueico; a paved highway from Osorno to Bariloche via the Paso de Cardenal Samoré that is the second-busiest crossing between the two countries; and the scenic bus-boat shuttle from Puerto Montt and Puerto Varas to Bariloche.

There are many southern Patagonian crossings, but the roads are often bad and only a few have public transportation. Those served by scheduled transport include the mostly gravel road from Futaleufú, Chile, to Esquel (local buses only); Coyhaique to Comodoro Rivadavia on a mostly paved road via Río Mayo on comfortable coaches; Chile Chico to Los Antiguos

(shuttles with onward connections); Puerto Natales to El Calafate via Río Turbio on a route that should soon be entirely paved; Punta Arenas to Río Gallegos via a paved highway; and Punta Arenas to Ushuaia and Río Grande.

In addition, many crossings are suitable for private motor vehicles and mountain bikes, and a few by foot.

There are three major crossings to Bolivia in northernmost Argentina, most importantly the walk-across from Villazón to La Quiaca, on RN 9 in Jujuy Province. The other two are in Salta Province, at Aguas Blancas (on RN 50 from Tarija, Bolivia) and Pocitos (from Yacuiba and Santa Cruz de la Sierra), on RN 34.

At the confluence of the Pilcomayo and the Paraguay Rivers, the Formosa Province border town of Clorinda sits directly across from Paraguay's capital of Asunción. There are several minor border crossings along the Paraguay and the Paraná Rivers, but the only other major one is the Misiones provincial capital of Posadas, opposite the smaller Paraguayan city of Encarnación. At both major crossings, bridges connect the two countries.

One of the continent's most important border zones is the controversial *Triple Frontera* at the confluence of the Paraná and Iguazú Rivers, where Argentina, Brazil, and Paraguay converge in northernmost Misiones Province. A bridge connects Argentina's Puerto Iguazú with Brazil's Foz do Iguaçu.

In addition to several minor river crossings, there are two major bridges over the Río Uruguay in Corrientes Province: between Santo Tomé and the Brazilian town of São Borja, and between Paso de los Libres and the larger Brazilian city of Uruguaiana.

From Uruguay, there are three highway bridges over the Río Uruguay into Entre Ríos Province: between Gualeguaychú and the Uruguayan town of Fray Bentos, between Colón and the Uruguayan city of Paysandú, and between Concordia and the Uruguayan city of Salto.

BY BOAT

From Buenos Aires, there are ferry connections across the river to the Uruguayan capital of Montevideo, but also to the resort town of Piriápolis (summer only) and to the 18th-century town of Colonia. From the suburban river port of Tigre, there are launches to the Uruguayan river ports of Carmelo and Nueva Palmira.

In addition, there is the popular and scenic but increasingly expensive bus-boat shuttle between Bariloche and the Chilean city of Puerto Montt, and a relatively short cruise (three days–plus) that carries passengers between Punta Arenas (Chile) and Ushuaia.

Getting Around

BY AIR

In addition to international air service, Argentina has a wide network of domestic airports and a handful of airlines centered on Buenos Aires; to fly between Argentine cities, more often than not it's unavoidable to change planes in BA. Most of these use Aeroparque Jorge Newbery, the city airport, but some use the international airport at Ezeiza.

Aerolíneas Argentinas has domestic as well as international flights, while its affiliate Austral (the distinction between the two is vague) serves exclusively Argentine destinations from Jujuy and Puerto Iguazú in the north to Ushuaia in Tierra del Fuego.

LAN Argentina, an affiliate of Chile's LAN, has an expanding route system that includes Salta, Tucumán, San Juan, Córdoba, Mendoza, Puerto Iguazú, Neuquén, Comodoro Rivadavia, El Calafate, Río Gallegos, Ushuaia, and Bariloche.

Other domestic airlines come and go, with the exception of Líneas Aéreas del Estado (LADE, www.lade.com.ar), the air force's heavily subsidized commercial-aviation branch. Miraculously surviving budget crises and privatizations, it flies to southern Buenos Aires Province and out-of-the-way Patagonian destinations on a wing and a subsidy.

Fares

Airfares fell with the 2002 devaluation and have remained reasonable, though foreigners are not eligible for discount fares available to Argentine citizens and residents. This means, in effect, that foreigners are paying full Y-class fares, but this also means greater flexibility in

purchasing one-way *cabotaje* tickets and "open jaws" routes that land at one city and return from another, and to mix and match airlines.

Typical Aerolíneas Argentinas destinations, with one-way fares from Aeroparque, include Bariloche (US$215), Córdoba (US$122), El Calafate (US$248), Puerto Iguazú (US$156), Mar del Plata (US$133), Mendoza (US$156), Salta (US$190), Trelew (US$146), and Ushuaia (US$262). Fares can be either higher or lower, though, depending on date, time, and advance purchase.

Available only in conjunction with international travel to Buenos Aires, Aerolíneas Argentinas's "Visit Argentina" pass gives discounts to foreigners and nonresident Argentines who arrange their itinerary in advance. Passengers arriving on Aerolíneas get bigger discounts, but the pass requires considerable planning to eke out maximum advantage.

LAN Argentina, an affiliate of Chile's flagship airline, serves fewer destinations but does not discriminate against foreign passengers. Andes Líneas Aéreas is a new carrier that flies from Aeroparque to Córdoba, Salta and Jujuy, Puerto Iguazú, and Puerto Madryn.

LADE, which flies smaller, older planes and makes many stops, is known for bargain-basement fares; from Buenos Aires, for instance, Bariloche costs just US$162. It is infamous, though, for unreliability in making and honoring reservations, and in keeping to its schedules.

BY BUS

Buses along the principal highways, and those connecting other main cities and resorts, are

A suspension bridge crosses the Río Paine on the edge of Chile's Parque Nacional Torres del Paine.

frequent and almost invariably spacious and comfortable, sometimes even luxurious. On a few back-road routes, they're only a little better than Central American "chicken buses," and may be infrequent, but distances are relatively short.

So-called Pullman buses have reclining seats, four across, and for short to medium runs, say up to seven hours, they're more than adequate. Seats are guaranteed. For truly long distances, some travelers prefer the more spacious *servicio diferencial* or *coche cama,* with greater leg room in seats that recline almost horizontally. Fares are reasonable by international standards—the 16-hour trip from Buenos Aires to Puerto Iguazú costs about US$80 in *coche cama,* including onboard and/or roadside meal service. For the 20-hour trip to Bariloche, in northern Patagonia, fares are around US$100.

Most cities have a central *terminal de buses* (bus terminal), but in a few places there are multiple terminals for long-distance, regional, and rural services, or for individual companies.

Some companies also have separate ticket offices in more central locations than the terminals themselves.

Bus services are so frequent that reservations are rarely necessary except for a few infrequently traveled routes and some international services, or during holiday periods like Semana Santa (Holy Week), Christmas–New Year's, and occasionally during the January–February summer vacation season. Note also that fares rise and fall with demand, depending on the season.

BY TRAIN

Once the primary mode of interurban transportation, domestic rail service is now limited to a handful of long-distance domestic services, mostly to the Atlantic beach resorts of southern Buenos Aires Province but also to Rosario, Tucumán, and Posadas. There is also service between the Río Negro provincial capital of Viedma and the resort city of Bariloche.

Schedules, though, are infrequent, the trains are mostly slow, and high demand from impoverished Argentines makes reservations essential, often far in advance. Fares are low—only US$15–24 pp for the 404 kilometers from Constitución to Mar del Plata, for instance, and just US$12–34 pp for the 1,200 kilometers from Retiro (Buenos Aires) to Tucumán.

The best long-distance line is the one between Constitución (Buenos Aires) and Mar del Plata. This route, perhaps the only line in the country that could be justified on economic grounds, may see a high-speed upgrade, though there has been talk of building one to Córdoba.

In addition to regular passenger trains, there are also tourist excursions, including Salta's popular Tren a las Nubes (Train to the Clouds) and the narrow-gauge La Trochita, in Río Negro and Chubut Provinces; the latter was immortalized in Paul Theroux's overrated opus *The Old Patagonian Express*.

BY CAR OR MOTORCYCLE

Driving in Argentina, especially in Buenos Aires, is not for the timid. In the words of *Buenos Aires Herald* columnist Martín Gambarotta, this is a country "where pedestrians and not cars have to stop at a zebra crossing." According to United Nations statistics, the traffic death rate of 25 per 100,000 is South America's highest, nearly twice that of Chile and the United States, and almost three times that of Germany.

According to another *Herald* article,

Argentines' penchant for speed – evident in many urban drivers who weave in and out of fast-moving city traffic for no evident reasons, and in the yearly death toll that makes their roads among the most dangerous in the world – is reflected by their veneration of Formula One race car drivers like the legendary Juan Manuel Fangio and Carlos Reutemann, the former governor of Santa Fe.

In 2002, Buenos Aires provincial governor Felipe Solá named RN 2, the Buenos Aires–Mar del Plata freeway, in honor of Fangio, and the YPF oil company has named its highest-octane fuel for the famous racer.

Argentine highways are divided into *rutas nacionales* (abbreviated here as RN, for which the federal government is responsible), and *rutas provinciales* (RP, which each province maintains). Generally, but not necessarily, the federal highways are better maintained; the exception is prosperous provinces like Santa Cruz, which has large oil royalty revenues.

Speed limits on most highways are generally around 100 kilometers per hour, but 120 kilometers per hour on four-lane divided roads. Officially, helmets are obligatory for motorcyclists, but enforcement is lax. The most thickheaded riders appear to believe their skulls are strong enough—some even hook their helmets over their elbows—but emergency-room results have proved them wrong.

Vehicle Documents, Driver's License, and Equipment

Most South American countries, including Argentina, Chile, Uruguay, and Brazil, have dispensed with the cumbersome *Carnet de Passage en Douanes* that required depositing a large bond in order to import a motor vehicle. Officials at the port of arrival or border post will usually issue a 90- or 180-day permit on presentation of the vehicle title, registration, bill of lading (if the vehicle is being shipped), and your passport. For shipped vehicles, there are some fairly substantial port charges (which rise rapidly if the vehicle has been stored more than a few days).

Argentine police generally recognize foreign drivers' licenses, but theoretically visitors should have an International or Interamerican Driving Permit (visitors to Uruguay should note that that country officially recognizes only the latter, though in practice they're more flexible). These permits are available through the American Automobile Association (AAA) or its counterpart in your home country, and are normally valid for one calendar year from date of issue. Strictly speaking, they are not valid without a state or national driver's license. Legally, another form of identification, such as national ID card or passport, is also necessary.

The police, though, pay close attention to vehicle documents—*tarjeta verde* (green card) registration for Argentine vehicles, customs permission for foreign ones. Vehicles without registration may be impounded on the spot. Argentine vehicles should have proof of a *verificación técnica* (safety inspection).

Though many Argentines drive without liability insurance, foreign vehicles cannot clear customs without coverage. Policies from neighboring countries except Chile may be valid in Argentina; it is now possible, though, to purchase short-term Argentine policies in Chile, often near the border.

At roadside checkpoints, Argentine police are also rigid about obligatory equipment such as headrests for the driver and each passenger, *valizas* (triangular emergency reflectors), and *matafuegos* (one-kilogram fire extinguishers). Provincial police may threaten excessive fines for document irregularities or minor equipment violations, but they're usually soliciting *coimas* (bribes). A firm but calm suggestion that you intend to call your consulate may help overcome any difficulty.

Road Hazards

Argentine traffic is fast and ruthless, many roads are narrow with little or no shoulder, and others are poorly surfaced or potholed. Heavy truck traffic can make all these routes dangerous, and not just because of excess speed—impatient Argentine drivers will often try to pass in dangerous situations, and head-on crashes—even between passenger buses—are disturbingly common.

Porteño drivers in Buenos Aires and stray cattle in the countryside might seem to be enough to deal with, but the 2001–2002 economic crisis led to a major increase of *piquetes* (roadblock demonstrators) protesting unemployment and other issues, which has not abated. *Piqueteros* (pickets), though they tend to focus on stopping commercial traffic, manage to slow down everything else as well; never try to run one of these roadblocks, which can raise their wrath.

Rather, try to show solidarity and, in all likelihood, you'll pass without incident. The poor northern provinces of Jujuy and Salta have been hotbeds of picket activity.

Note that members of the American Automobile Association (AAA), Britain's Automobile Association (AA), and similar foreign automobile clubs are often eligible for limited roadside assistance and towing through the **Automóvil Club Argentina** (www.aca.org.ar), which has offices throughout the country.

Unleaded fuel is available everywhere, though some older vehicles still use leaded. In remote areas where gas stations are few, carry additional fuel.

Expenses

Prior to devaluation, Argentina had some of the most expensive gasoline in the Americas except for Uruguay, but prices have fallen in dollar terms—at least temporarily, even as they rose in peso terms. Prices are about US$0.85 per liter for regular, US$0.96 for super, and US$1.05 for Fangio. *Gasoil* (diesel) is typically cheaper than most gasolines, about US$0.87 per liter, but the differential is shrinking. Because gasoline prices are unregulated, they may rise quickly.

Note, however, that so-called "Patagonian prices" south of Sierra Grande on RN 3 and El Bolsón on RN 40 are more than one-third cheaper for gasoline; there is no price differential for diesel. Fortunately, the government has eliminated the decree that made vehicles with foreign license plates pay across-the-border prices—much higher in Chile, Brazil, Uruguay, and Paraguay—while Argentine vehicles continued to pay local prices.

Repairs are cheap in terms of labor but can be expensive in terms of parts, many of which must be imported and, in provincial cities, often brought by special order from Buenos Aires. Fortunately, Argentine mechanics are skilled at rehabilitating virtually any salvageable part.

Car Rental

Aggressive drivers, traffic congestion, and limited parking make driving in Buenos Aires inadvisable, but beyond the capital a vehicle can be useful, especially in the wide-open spaces of northwestern Argentina or Patagonia. To rent a car, you must show a valid driver's license and credit card, and be at least 21 years old.

Both local and international agencies maintain offices in Buenos Aires, where rental costs are typically lower than elsewhere in the country but higher than in North America. Since the 2002 devaluation, prices are more volatile, but they usually involve a fixed daily amount plus a per-kilometer charge; unlimited-mileage deals are normally for weekly or longer periods. Insurance is additional.

It is also possible to rent campers and motor homes through **Gaibu Motorhome Time** (Avenida Maipú 2517, Oficina 11, Olivos, Vicente López, tel. 011/5368-1544, www.gaibu.com), in the northern suburbs of Buenos Aires.

BY BICYCLE

For the physically fit or those intending to become physically fit, cycling can be an ideal way to see the country. Because so many roads are unpaved in the most scenic areas, a *todo terreno* (mountain bike) is a better choice than a touring bike. Cyclists should know basic mechanics, though the increasing availability of mountain bikes means that parts and mechanics are easier to find than they once were. In an emergency, it's easy to put a bicycle onboard a bus.

Some cyclists dislike the main highways because their narrowness, coupled with fast drivers and the lack of shoulders, can make them unsafe. There are many alternative routes with less traffic, though, and some really interesting ones, such as RN 9 between Salta and Jujuy, and RP 52 from Uspallata to Mendoza. High winds can make Patagonian roads, such as coastal RN 3 and the interior RN 40, difficult for cyclists.

BY ORGANIZED TOUR

Because of Argentina's complex logistics, organized tours can be a useful option for visitors with limited time, and many reputable U.S. and Argentine operators offer and even coordinate tours. Sometimes these take in sights in neighboring countries, usually Chile but sometimes Uruguay or Brazil. Within each category, the companies listed here appear in alphabetical order.

United States-Based Operators

Primarily but not exclusively for cyclists, **Backroads** (801 Cedar St., Berkeley, CA 94710, tel. 510/527-1555 or 800/462-2848, fax 510/527-1444, www.backroads.com) offers a nine-day "Chile & Argentina Biking" tour that takes in Bariloche, Villa la Angostura, and vicinity, along with Chile's Lago Llanquihue area, for US$4,498 pp. Their nine- or 10-day "Patagonia Walking & Hiking" trip stays at luxury lodgings in Chile's Parque Nacional Torres del Paine and Argentina's Parque Nacional Los Glaciares; rates range US$4,498–8,398 pp, depending on accommodations (the higher price includes top-of-the-line choices such as Hostería Los Notros and Hostería Helsingfors). A new eight-day "Argentina Biking" tour (US$3,998 pp) explores Salta Province and its Andean wine country.

For travelers at least 55 years of age, **Exploritas** (formerly Elderhostel, 11 Ave. de Lafayette, Boston, MA 02111, tel. 800/454-5768, www.exploritas.org) has a variety of southern South American trips, including an eight-day "Argentina 101" tour (US$1,866 pp) and a 15-day "Patagonia and the Andean Lake Region" tour (US$4,194) that takes in Chile and Argentina, including the Punta Tombo and Península Valdés wildlife reserves.

Nature Expeditions International (7860 Peters Rd., Suite F-103, Plantation, FL 33324, tel. 954/693-8852 or 800/869-0639, fax 954/693-8854, www.naturexp.com) operates upscale "soft adventure" and culture-oriented tours to the Southern Cone countries, among other destinations. A 15-day "Journey to Patagonia," taking in Buenos Aires, Punta Tombo, Península Valdés, Bariloche, El Calafate, and Iguazú, starts at US$4,955 pp; other trips include parts of Brazil and Chile.

Orvis (1711 Blue Hills Dr., Roanoke, VA 24012-8613, tel. 800/547-4322, www.orvis.com) arranges fishing holidays in the vicinity of northern Patagonia's Junín de los Andes, southern Patagonia's Río Gallegos, and the Argentine side of Tierra del Fuego.

Powderquest Tours (7108 Pinetree Rd., Richmond, VA 23229, tel. 888/565-7158, www.powderquest.com) runs five or six 9–13-day Southern Cone ski tours annually. Las Leñas, Chapelco, Cerro Bayo, Cerro Catedral, and Ushuaia are the Argentine resorts included.

REI Adventures (P.O. Box 1938, Sumner, WA 98390-1938, tel. 800/622-2236, www.rei.com) offers an increasing variety of hiking, cycling, and multisport trips in the Mendoza wine region (including parts of Chile), the Chilean-Argentine lakes district, and southern Patagonia, in the US$3,699–4,399 range.

Wilderness Travel (1102 Ninth St., Berkeley, CA 94710, tel. 510/558-2488 or 800/368-2794, www.wildernesstravel.com) offers several 10–16-day trips focused primarily on Patagonia, with extensions to Iguazú, but it has also recently begun to visit the northwestern canyon country of Salta and Jujuy Provinces. Rates fall into the US$4,295–6,695 range, including some private trips with as few as two clients.

Wildland Adventures (3516 NE 155th St., Seattle, WA 98155, tel. 800/345-4453, www.wildland.com) operates small group tours (2–8 people) through locally based guides. The 10-day Best of Argentina (US$3,250) takes in the wildlife rich coast and the southernmost Andes, including the Moreno Glacier. Starting in Chile and ending in Buenos Aires, the 16-day "In the Wake of Magellan" trip (from US$7,395) includes Torres del Paine and a segment of the scenic luxury cruise between Punta Arenas and Ushuaia as well as Argentina's Moreno Glacier.

United Kingdom-Based Operators
Explore Worldwide (55 Victoria Rd., Farnborough, Hampshire GU14 7PA, tel. 0870/333-4001, www.exploreworldwide.com) organizes 16–22-day tours primarily to Patagonia and the Chilean and Argentine lakes districts.

Journey Latin America (12/13 Heathfield Terrace, Chiswick, London W4 2JU, tel. 020/8747-8315, www.journeylatinamerica.co.uk) specializes in small-group tours throughout Latin America, including Argentina.

Australia-Based Operators
Peregrine Adventures (380 Lonsdale St., Melbourne, Victoria 3000, tel. 03/8601-4444, www.peregrineadventures.com) offers tours throughout the country, some of which overlap with Brazil, Uruguay, and Chile.

World Expeditions (71 York St., Level 5, Sydney, NSW 2000, tel. 02/8270-8400, www.worldexpeditions.com.au), one of Australia's biggest operators, has a variety of tours to Patagonia and elsewhere in Argentina. It also has branches in other Australian cities, New Zealand, and Canada.

Argentina-Based Operators
The operators below invariably have English-speaking personnel and have services in many parts of Argentina. Many locally focused operators, though, have very good services as well.

The Buenos Aires–based **Asatej Group** (Florida 835, Oficina 320, tel. 011/4114-7600, www.asatej.com) is Argentina's youth- and budget-oriented operator, which has refocused on incoming tourism since the peso collapse of early 2002.

Salta-based **Clark Expediciones** (Mariano Moreno 1950, Salta, tel. 0387/497-1094, www.clarkexpediciones.com) is a bird-watching specialist but also does general natural history and hiking tours.

Bariloche-based **Meridies** (Calle 4 (Meli) 12040, tel. 0294/51-2073, www.meridies.com.ar) is primarily an adventure-oriented climbing company with strenuous trips like Volcán Lanín and Cerro Aconcagua, but it also does a weeklong driving and hiking safari along the southern portion of Patagonia's RN 40 (La Cuarenta). Guides speak English and French.

Buenos Aires–based **Sendero Sur** (Perú 359, Oficina 608, Monserrat, tel./fax 011/4343-1571, www.senderosur.com.ar) organizes activity-oriented trips that include cycling in the Argentine and Chilean lake districts, stays at Patagonian *estancias,* and hiking in and around Parque Nacional Los Glaciares and Ushuaia.

Chile-Based Operators

Several Chilean operators figure in Chilean Patagonia and Tierra del Fuego, and some of them also work the Argentine side of the border. Chile's country code is 56.

From October to April, **Cruceros Australis** (Avenida Bosque Norte 0440, 11th floor, Las Condes, Santiago, tel. 02/442-3110, www.australis.com), offers three-day, four-day, and seven-day cruises through the fjords of southern Tierra del Fuego and Cape Horn on its small luxury liners. Rates vary during the season. Cruceros Australis also has offices in Buenos Aires (Carlos Pellegrini 989, Retiro, tel. 011/4325-8400) and Miami (4014 Chase Ave., Suite 202, Miami Beach, FL 33140, tel. 305/695-9618 or 877/678-3772).

Explora Hotels (Américo Vespucio Sur 80, 5th floor, Las Condes, Santiago, tel. 02/206-6060, www.explora.com) offers expensive, all-inclusive packages, ranging from three days to a week, at its magnificently sited hotel in Parque Nacional Torres del Paine, and it's building a companion on the Argentine side of the border.

Cruceros Australis's sister company **Navimag Ferries** (Avenida El Bosque Norte 0440, 11th floor, Las Condes, Santiago, tel. 02/442-3120, www.navimag.com) sails between the Patagonian town of Puerto Natales and the mainland city of Puerto Montt. While these are not cruises in the traditional sense, they are more than just transportation as they pass through archipelagic Chile's spectacular fjord lands.

In the summer months, Puerto Williams–based, German-run **Sea & Ice & Mountains Adventures Unlimited** (tel./fax 061/62-1150 or 061/62-1227, www.simexpeditions.com) operates yacht tours through Tierra del Fuego and Cape Horn.

LOCAL TRANSPORTATION

Even as cars clog the streets of Buenos Aires and other cities, most Argentines still rely on public transport to get around. Services in the capital, Gran Buenos Aires, and even relatively small provincial cities are frequent and reasonably well integrated.

Underground

Buenos Aires has the country's only subway system, popularly known as the Subte (www.metrovias.com.ar). Though it dates from 1913, it moves city residents efficiently and is expanding to underserved neighborhoods.

Colectivos (Buses)

Even small cities and towns are well-served by local buses, which often run 24-7. Fares are mostly in the US$0.35 range, but vary according to distance. In Buenos Aires *colectivos* are due to change to a magnetic card system in lieu of fare boxes; in some cities, they accept coins (though they may not make change), *fichas* (tokens), or magnetic cards.

Trains

With a few exceptions, suburban trains are less useful to short-term visitors than they are to commuters from Buenos Aires Province. They are cheap, and while they may be improving, most are not improving nearly so fast as the Subte.

Taxis and *Remises*

Buenos Aires and other cities have abundant taxis, painted black with yellow roofs. Since a spate of robberies that began some years ago, nearly all of them are now *radio taxis,* and some people prefer the security of phoning for a cab, but many if not most *porteños* still flag them down in the street. If in doubt, lock the back doors so that no one can enter the cab by surprise.

All regular cabs have digital meters. In Buenos Aires, it costs about US$1.20 to *bajar la bandera* ("drop the flag," meaning switch on the meter) and another US$0.12 per 200 meters; provincial cities tend to be cheaper. Verify that the meter is set at zero.

Drivers do not expect tips; sometimes, to avoid making change, they will even round the fare *down*. Carry small bills instead of relying on the driver making change, especially if he has just come on shift; to deter a potentially dishonest driver when paying with a large note, ask whether he has the proper change for that amount.

Remises are radio taxis that charge an agreed-upon rate based on distance; the dispatcher will let you know the fare when you call, based on the pickup and drop-off points.

Hotels, restaurants, and other businesses will gladly ring radio taxis and *remises* for customers and clients, especially when the hour is late.

Bicycles

Cycling may not be the safest way to navigate Argentina's chaotic traffic, but the number of cyclists is growing. If riding around Buenos Aires or other Argentine cities, side streets may be safer than fast-moving avenues, but they are also narrower, with less room to maneuver. Weekend traffic is not as wild as on weekdays, and parts of downtown are virtually deserted on Sunday. There are a few dedicated bike paths, most of which go through city parklands, and some bike lanes (that motor vehicles tend to ignore).

Walking

Most Argentine cities are compact enough that walking suffices for sightseeing and other activities, but the first rule of pedestrian safety is that you are invisible—for many Argentine drivers, crosswalks appear merely decorative. While making turns, drivers weave among pedestrians rather than slowing or stopping to let them pass. Jaywalking is endemic, perhaps because it's not much more hazardous than crossing at the corner with the light.

Despite the hazards, pedestrians in congested areas can often move faster than automobiles. Much of the country has hot, humid summers, so carry and consume plenty of fluids. Frequent thunderstorms in the humid pampas and Mesopotamia make an umbrella advisable.

Visas and Officialdom

Citizens of neighboring countries—Bolivians, Brazilians, Uruguayans, and Paraguayans—need only national identity cards, but most other nationalities needs passports to enter Argentina. U.S. and Canadian citizens, along with those of the European Community and Scandinavian countries, Switzerland, Israel, Australia, New Zealand, and other Latin American countries, need passports but not advance visas. Citizens of nearly every African and Asian country, with the exceptions of South Africa and Japan, need advance visas.

Regulations change, however, and it may be helpful to check the visa page of Argentina's **Ministerio de Relaciones Exteriores** (Foreign Relations Ministry, www.mrecic.gov.ar). See the accompanying sidebar for contact information for the most important Argentine embassies and consulates overseas.

Argentina routinely grants 90-day entry permits to foreign visitors in the form of a tourist card. For some nationalities, however, it has also instituted a "reciprocity fee" that corresponds to the value of the visa application fee that their countries impose on Argentine visa applicants. Collected only at Buenos Aires's international airport at Ezeiza, at least for the moment, the fee is US$131 for United States citizens (valid for 10 years), US$100 for Australians (single entry), and US$70 for Canadians (single entry).

Theoretically, the tourist card must be surrendered on departure; in practice, it's the passport stamp that counts. For US$80, the entry is renewable for 90 days at the **Dirección**

CONSULATES

Embassies and consulates are often, though not always, at the same address. Consulates, rather than embassies, are primarily responsible for dealing with individuals traveling for either business or pleasure, however. Intending visitors should visit consulates for visas or other inquiries.

ARGENTINE CONSULATES IN OTHER COUNTRIES

- **Australia:** 7 National Circuit, 2nd floor, Barton ACT, tel. 02/6273-9111

  44 Market Street, 20th floor, Sydney NSW, tel. 02/9262-2933
- **Bolivia:** Aspiazu 497, La Paz, tel. 02/241-7737
- **Brazil:** Praia de Botafogo 228, Sobreloja, Rio de Janeiro, tel. 021/2553-1646

  Avenida Paulista 1106, Entreloja, São Paulo, tel. 011/3897-9522
- **Canada:** 81 Metcalfe, 7th floor, Ottawa, Ontario K1P 6K7, tel. 613/236-2351

  5001 Yonge St., Suite 201, Toronto, Ontario M2N 6P6, tel. 416/955-9075

  2000 Peel St., Suite 600, Montréal, Québec H3A 2W5, tel. 514/842-6582
- **Chile:** Vicuña Mackenna 41, Santiago, tel. 02/582-2606

  Pedro Montt 160, 6th floor, Puerto Montt, tel. 065/25-3996

  21 de Mayo 1878, Punta Arenas, tel. 061/26-1912
- **New Zealand:** 142 Lambton Quay, Level 14, Wellington, tel. 04/472-8330
- **Paraguay:** Palma 319, 1st Floor, Asunción, tel. 021/44-2151

  Artigas 960, Encarnación, tel. 071/20-1066
- **United Kingdom:** 27 Three Kings Yard, London W1Y 1FL, tel. 020/7318-1340
- **United States:** 1811 Q St. NW, Washington, DC 20009, tel. 202/238-6460

  5550 Wilshire Blvd., Suite 210, Los Angeles, CA 90036, tel. 323/954-9155

  1101 Brickell Ave., Suite 600, North Tower, Miami, FL 33131, tel. 305/373-1889

  245 Peachtree Center Ave., Suite 2101, Atlanta, GA 30303, tel. 404/880-0805

  205 N. Michigan Ave., Suite 4209, Chicago, IL 60601, tel. 312/909-0308

  12 W. 56th St., New York, NY 10019, tel. 212/603-0400

  2200 West Loop South, Suite 1025, Houston TX 77027, tel. 713/871-8935
- **Uruguay:** Wilson Ferreira Aldunate 1281, Montevideo, tel. 02/902-8623

  Avenida General Flores 209, Colonia, tel. 052/22-086

  Edificio Espigón Gorlero, Avenida Gorlero and Calle 19 (Comodoro Gorlero), Sala H, Punta del Este, tel. 042/44-6162 (mid-Dec.-mid-Mar. only)

FOREIGN CONSULATES IN BUENOS AIRES

Unless otherwise indicated, addresses below are in the Microcentro and vicinity.

- **Australia:** Villanueva 1400, Palermo, tel. 011/4779-3550
- **Bolivia:** Bartolomé Mitre 2815, 1st floor, Balvanera, tel. 011/4381-0539
- **Brazil:** Carlos Pellegrini 1363, 5th floor, Retiro, tel. 011/4515-6500
- **Canada:** Tagle 2828, Palermo, tel. 011/4805-3032
- **Chile:** Roque Sáenz Peña 547, 2nd floor, tel. 011/4331-6228
- **New Zealand:** Carlos Pellegrini 1427, 5th floor, Retiro, tel. 011/4328-0747
- **Paraguay:** Viamonte 1851, Balvanera, tel. 011/4812-0075
- **United Kingdom:** Dr. Luis Agote 2412, Recoleta, tel. 011/4803-7070
- **United States:** Colombia 4300, Palermo, tel. 011/5777-4533
- **Uruguay:** Avenida Las Heras 1915, Recoleta, tel. 011/4807-3045

Nacional de Migraciones (Avenida Argentina 1355, Retiro, Buenos Aires, tel. 011/4317-0237, 8 A.M.–2 P.M. weekdays).

In the provinces, renewal can be done at any office of the Policía Federal (Federal Police), but in smaller towns they may not be accustomed to doing so. Buenos Aires visitors may find it cheaper and simpler to take a ferry trip to Colonia, Uruguay.

Formally, arriving visitors must have a return or onward ticket, but enforcement is inconsistent—if you have a Latin American, North American, or Western European passport, for instance, it's unlikely you'll be asked to show the return ticket (in the western hemisphere, only Cubans need a visa to enter Argentina). The author has entered Argentina dozens of times over many years, at Buenos Aires's international airport and some of the most remote border posts, without ever having been asked for either.

Airlines, though, may not permit a passenger without a round-trip ticket to board a flight to Argentina. Likewise, if the arriving passenger presents an Eastern European, Asian, or African passport, he or she may well be asked for proof of return transport. Immigration officials have considerable discretion in these matters.

Always carry identification, since either the federal or provincial police can request it at any moment, though they rarely do so arbitrarily. Passports are also necessary for routine transactions like checking into hotels, cashing travelers checks, or even payment by credit card.

Dependent children under age 14 traveling without both parents presumably need notarized parental consent, but the author's daughter visited Argentina many times with only one parent and was never asked for such a document.

Argentine-born individuals, even if their parents were not Argentines or if they have been naturalized elsewhere, sometimes attract unwanted attention. Generally, they may enter the country for no more than 60 days on a non-Argentine document. Argentine passports renewed outside the country expire on reentry, making it necessary to renew them with the Policía Federal, which can be a bothersome and time-consuming process on a short trip.

LOST OR STOLEN PASSPORTS

Visitors who suffer a lost or stolen passport must obtain a replacement at their own embassy or consulate. After obtaining a replacement passport, it's necessary to visit the Dirección Nacional de Migraciones to replace the tourist card.

CUSTOMS

Traditionally notorious for truly flagrant corruption, Argentine customs has improved from the days of the so-called *aduana paralela* (parallel customs) and normally presents no obstacle to tourists. Short-term visitors may import personal effects including clothing, jewelry, medicine, sporting gear, camping equipment and accessories, photographic and video equipment, personal computers, and the like, as well as 400 cigarettes, two liters of wine or alcoholic beverages (adults over age 18 only), and up to US$300 of new merchandise.

Customs inspections are usually routine, but at Buenos Aires's international airports, river ports, and some land borders, incoming checked baggage may have to pass through X-ray; do not put photographic film in checked baggage. Fresh food will be confiscated at any port of entry.

At some remote border posts, the Gendarmería Nacional (Border Guards) handles all formalities, including immigration, customs, and agricultural inspections. Visitors arriving from drug-producing countries like Colombia, Perú, and Bolivia may get special attention, as may those from Paraguay, with its notorious contraband economy.

POLICE AND MILITARY

Argentina is notorious for police corruption. For this reason, Argentines scornfully call both federal and provincial police *la cana*—an insult that should never be used to their faces.

The Policía Federal (Federal Police) are more professional than provincial forces like that of Buenos Aires Province; the latter is almost universally detested for harassing motorists for minor equipment violations and, even worse, for their *gatillo fácil* (hair-trigger) response to minor criminal offenses. In fairness, many police officers have died at the hands of well-armed criminals (who are sometimes police officers themselves).

Nevertheless, officers often solicit *coimas* (bribes) at routine traffic stops. To avoid paying a bribe, either state your intention to contact your consulate, or use broken Spanish even if you understand the language well. Either one may frustrate a corrupt official sufficiently to give up the effort.

Since the end of the 1976–1983 military dictatorship, the military has lost prestige and appears to have acknowledged its inability to run the country, despite occasional clamor for a coup by fringe figures. Still, security is heavy around military bases and photography is taboo—though mostly a thing of the past, signs proclaiming that "the sentry will shoot" are sometimes posted.

Accommodations

Argentina has an abundance of accommodations in all categories, from campgrounds and youth-hostel dormitories to extravagant luxury suites and everything in between. National and municipal tourist officials offer accommodations lists and brochures, but these frequently exclude budget options and may even omit some mid-range and high-end places.

Prices are often negotiable; do not assume the *tarifa mostrador* (rack rate) is etched in stone. Visitors also should not take hotel ratings too seriously, as they often represent an ideal rather than a reality, and some one- or two-star places are better than others that theoretically rank higher.

Prices in Buenos Aires proper often fall during the summer season of January and February, as business travel slows to a crawl; for excursion destinations, though, prices usually rise as *porteños* flee the capital for sand, sun, and sex on the beach. The same is true for popular provincial destinations like San Antonio de Areco. Other peak seasons, when prices may rise, are Semana Santa (Holy Week) and July's winter school vacations, which coincide with patriotic holidays.

Note also that Argentine hotels levy 21 percent in *impuesto de valor agregado* or IVA (Value Added Tax or VAT). Unless otherwise indicated, rates in this book include IVA, but if there's any question at the front desk, ask for clarification to avoid unpleasant surprises when paying the bill.

CAMPING

Organized camping is common throughout Argentina; campgrounds are generally spacious, with shade, clean toilets, and bathrooms with hot showers, and even groceries and restaurants. They are often surprisingly central, and they are almost always cheap, rarely more than a few dollars per person.

In the peak summer season and on weekends, the best sites can be crowded and noisy, as families on a budget take advantage of bargain prices. It's usually possible to find a quiet—but less desirable—site on the periphery. But remember that Argentines stay up late—very late—for their barbecues.

HOSTELS

For youthful and budget travel, Argentina has growing hostel networks and many independent hostels as well, where bunks start at around US$8–10 pp. Since the 2002 devaluation, these are no longer the only budget options, but they do offer an opportunity to get together with like-minded travelers. In addition to the customary dorms, many offer more expensive private rooms for individuals and couples.

For up-to-the-minute information on official Argentine hostels, contact **Hostelling International Argentina** (Florida 835, Buenos Aires, tel. 011/4511-8723, www.hostels.org.

A DAY (OR MORE) IN THE COUNTRY

Over the past decade-plus, facing economic reality, many of Argentina's great rural estates have opened themselves to the tourist trade. From the subtropical north to the subantarctic south, diversification has become the word for *estancia* owners, some of which earn more income from hosting visitors than they do growing grain or raising livestock. For many visitors, staying at an *estancia* is their entire vacation.

According to the Buenos Aires-based Red Argentina de Turismo Rural (Ratur), more than 1,000 *estancias* are open to the public, and hundreds of thousands of people spend some time in the countryside every month. For nearly all of these farms, tourism comprises a significant portion of their income, and for some of them, most notably in Patagonia, it exceeds 90 percent.

Throughout the country, some *estancias* are reasonably priced places with limited services, but others are magnificent properties with castle-like *cascos* (big houses), elaborate service that includes gourmet meals, and recreational activities such as horseback riding, tennis, and swimming. Some *estancias* aim at day-trippers – weekending in the countryside of Buenos Aires Province has become an increasingly popular option for escaping the capital – but most of them prefer overnight guests.

Many *estancias* get detailed individual coverage in this book, but various others are open to the public. Several groups of them have formed networks to promote themselves as tourist destinations.

Affiliated with the Sociedad Rural Argentina, the traditionally powerful landowners' organization, the **Red Argentina de Turismo Rural** (Ratur, Florida 460, 4th floor, Buenos Aires, tel. 011/4328-0499, www.raturestancias.com.ar) represents a number of *estancias* in northern and southern Buenos Aires Province, and a few more in Mesopotamia, the Cuyo region, and Patagonia.

Estancias Argentinas (Diagonal Roque Sáenz Peña 616, Oficina 910, Buenos Aires, tel. 011/4343-2366, www.estanciasargentinas.com) has expanded in recent years, with a broader geographical representation than it once had, but not all of its members are *estancias* – some are even urban hotels.

The best-organized provincial group is **Estancias de Santa Cruz** (Suipacha 1120, Retiro, Buenos Aires, tel./fax 011/4325-3098 or 011/4325-3102, www.estanciasdesantacruz.com). Most of its affiliates are in the southwestern corner of its home province, but there are also a few members on the Argentine side of Tierra del Fuego.

La Pampa Province has its own network, **Red de Estancias Turísticas de La Pampa** (Suipacha 346, Buenos Aires, tel. 011/4326-5111, www.lapampaestancias.com.ar).

ar). There are also, however, many independent hostels whose quality can vary, but some of them are excellent.

Note that most Argentine hostels now avoid the term *albergue;* in Argentine Spanish, an *albergue transitorio* is a by-the-hour hotel. Many have adopted the English word *hostel* or Hispanicized it into *hostal* (a term more common in Chile, where it's a step above an *hospedaje*).

OTHER BUDGET ACCOMMODATIONS

Budget accommodations in Argentina can cost as little as US$10 pp, but they're usually a bit dearer. They go by a variety of names that may camouflage their quality—they can range from dingy fleabags with mattresses that sag like hammocks to simple but cheerful and tidy places with firm new beds.

An *hospedaje* is generally a family-run lodging with a few spare rooms; *pensiones* and *casas de huéspedes* are comparable, nearly interchangeable terms. All may often have long-term residents as well as overnight guests. *Residenciales* (singular *residencial*) are generally buildings constructed with short-stay accommodations in mind, but they may also have semipermanent residents. All of these places may even go by the term *hotel,* though usually that belongs to a more-formal category.

That said, there are some exceptionally good values in all these categories. Many will have a shared bath and toilet (*baño general* or *baño compartido*) or offer a choice between shared and private bath (*baño privado*); tubs are unusual. In some cases, they will have ceiling fans and even cable TV, but there is often an extra charge for cable and almost always a surcharge for air-conditioning.

Travelers intending to stay at budget accommodations should bring their own towels, though some provide them. Many, but by no means all, include breakfast in their rates; ask to be certain.

MID-RANGE ACCOMMODATIONS

Mid-range hotels generally offer larger, more comfortable, and better-furnished rooms, almost always with private baths, than even the best budget places. Ceiling fans, cable TV, and even air-conditioning are common, but they may not have on-site parking. Some have restaurants. Rates can range from US$50 up to US$100 d; some are better values than their high-end counterparts.

HIGH-END ACCOMMODATIONS

Luxury hotels with top-flight service, which can range well upwards of US$100 per night, are few outside the capital and major resort areas. In the capital they will usually offer amenities such as restaurants, swimming pools, gym facilities, business centers, Wi-Fi, and conference rooms; outside the capital these are mostly resort hotels and may lack the business facilities. Invariably they will offer secure parking.

Some of the best options in this category are country-inn resorts on *estancias,* offering traditional hospitality and ambience with style unmatchable at other high-end places. Again, prices may be upward of US$100, often substantially upward.

Food and Drink

Food and drink range from the economical and ordinary to the truly elegant and everything in between. For most of the 1990s, eating well at restaurants was financially challenging except for cheap cafeteria lunches and *tenedor libre* (literally, "free fork") buffets, but the 2002 peso collapse has made it possible to eat diverse and imaginative food for a fraction of its former price—at least for visitors with dollars or euros in their wallets.

Stereotypically, the Argentine diet consists of beef and more beef. This common perception is not entirely mistaken, but the local diet has always had a Spanish touch and, for more than a century, a marked Italian influence with pizza and pasta. Over the past decade, though, the restaurant scene has become far more cosmopolitan, adventurous, and nuanced, with Brazilian, Japanese, Thai, Vietnamese, and many other once-exotic cuisines—not to mention high-quality variations on Argentine regional dishes. Certain Buenos Aires neighborhoods, such as Palermo Viejo and Las Cañitas, seem to have sprouted stylish and sophisticated new eateries on every corner and in between.

For a succinct but detailed guide to Argentine cuisine, look for Dereck Foster and Richard Tripp's *Food and Drink in Argentina* (El Paso, TX: Aromas y Sabores, 2006). Dan Perlman's English-language blog Salt Shaker (www.saltshaker.net) is another savvy resource on Argentine food in general, though it focuses on the Buenos Aires food scene in particular.

RESTAURANT TERMINOLOGY

The term *restaurante* (occasionally *restorán* or, more fashionably, *restó*) usually refers to places with sit-down service, but within this definition there can be great diversity. Most often the term refers to a locale with a printed menu and table service, but it can range from any place

DINING VOCABULARY AND ETIQUETTE

Restaurant vocabulary is mostly straightforward. The usual term for menu is *la carta; el menú* is almost equally common, but can also mean a fixed-price lunch or dinner. The bill is *la cuenta. Cubiertos* are silverware, while a *plato* is a plate and a *vaso* a glass. A *plato principal* is a main dish or entrée.

Note that one might ask for a *vaso de agua* (glass of water), but never for a *vaso de vino* (literally but incorrectly, a glass of wine); rather, ask for a *copa de vino* (when speaking English, native Spanish-speakers often err similarly in requesting "a cup of wine").

Many but not all Argentine restaurants assess a small *cubierto* (cover charge) for dishes, silverware, and bread. This is not a *propina* (tip); generally, a 10 percent tip is the norm, but Argentines themselves often ignore this,

especially in times of economic crisis. Women in a group will often tip little or nothing, but a good rule of thumb is that anyone able to afford a restaurant meal can afford a tip.

It's worth emphasizing that the occupation of waiter is traditionally male and professional, rather than a short-term expedient for university students or aspiring actors. This is changing in the new, stylish restaurants, where servers are just as likely to be young and female. Note that *mozo*, a common and innocuous term for an Argentine waiter, suggests an insulting servility in Chile (parts of which are covered in this book). When in doubt, use *mesero* or *jóven*, even if the individual in question is not particularly young; for a female, use *señorita* unless the individual is of at least late middle-age.

---

with a basic beef and pasta menu to truly elegant settings with complex cuisine, elaborate wine lists, and professional waiters.

The usual international fast-food villains have franchises here, but the best cheap food comes from *rotiserías* (delis), which serve excellent takeaway fare and may have basic seating. Likewise, supermarkets such as Coto and Disco have budget *cafeterías* that are excellent options for budget visitors.

Bares and *comedores* are no-frills eateries, with indifferent service, offering *minutas* (short orders); the term *comedor* can also mean a hotel breakfast nook or dining room. A *café*, by contrast, is a place whose patrons may dawdle over coffee and croissants, but its de facto purpose is to promote social interaction in personal affairs, business deals, and other transactions—even though it also serves snacks, *minutas*, and alcoholic drinks (beer, wine, and hard liquor).

Confiterías, by contrast, serve breakfast, light meals that include sandwiches, cakes and other desserts, and coffee-based drinks. Generally more formal than cafés, some of them prestigious, they are suitable for afternoon tea; some have full-scale restaurant menus, often in a separate sector.

WHAT TO EAT

Argentina is famous for beef—in abundance—and grains, but fresh fruit, vegetables, and an underrated wealth of seafood add diversity to the country's cuisine. While the stereotypical diet of beef and more beef may have serious shortcomings, visitors will easily find alternatives, especially in Buenos Aires.

According to historian John C. Super, whatever the Spanish invasion's negative consequences, it actually improved a diet that was, by some accounts, nutritionally deficient (often protein-poor) in late pre-Columbian times. In Super's opinion,

The combination of European and American foods created diversified, nutritionally rich diets. Crop yields were higher than those in Europe, and longer or staggered growing seasons made fresh food available during much of the year. The potential for one of the best diets in the history of the world was evident soon after discovery of the New World. For Europeans, the introduction of livestock and wheat was an essential step in creating that diet.

© DAVID WILBANKS/FLICKR.COM

choripán

When Europeans first set foot in South America, in the densely populated Andean region, the staples were beans, squash, and a variety of potatoes and other tubers, but the diet was low in animal protein—only the llama, alpaca, guinea pig, and wild game were readily available, and even those were unevenly distributed. Spanish introductions such as wheat and barley, which yielded only a four-to-one harvest ratio in Europe, reached at least two to three times that in the Americas.

The Spanish introductions blended with the indigenous base to create many of the edibles found on Argentine tables today. The abundance of seafood, combined with European animal protein and high-productivity European fruits such as apples, apricots, grapes, pears, and many others, resulted in a diverse food production and consumption system which, however, is changing today.

Consumption of red meat, the hallmark of the diet, may be decreasing among more affluent Argentines, but it remains the entrée of choice among the lower classes. Thanks to the Italian-immigrant influence, an assortment of pastas is available almost everywhere.

Legumes, Vegetables, and Tubers

Salads are almost invariably safe, and all but the most sensitive stomachs probably need not be concerned with bugs from greens washed in tap water. Restaurant salads are often large enough for two diners.

Porotos (beans of all sorts except green beans) are traditional in families of Spanish descent. Other common legumes include *chauchas* (green beans), *arvejas* (peas), *lentejas* (lentils), and *habas* (fava beans).

In many varieties, *zapallo* (squash) is part of the traditional diet, as is the *tomate* (tomato). Other Old World vegetables include *acelga* (chard), *berenjena* (eggplant), *coliflor* (cauliflower), *lechuga* (lettuce), and *repollo* (cabbage). *Chiles* (peppers) are relatively uncommon; Argentine cuisine is rarely *picante* (spicy) except in the Andean Northwest, and even those dishes rarely challenge palates accustomed to Mexican or Thai cuisine.

Native to the central Andes, *papas* (potatoes) grow in well-drained soils at higher elevations in northwestern Argentina; *papas fritas* (French fries) are almost universal, but spuds also appear as *purée* (mashed potatoes) and in Italian dishes such as *ñoquis* (gnocchi). Other common tubers include *zanahorias* (carrots) and *rábanos* (radishes).

Vegetarianism

While vegetarian restaurants are few except in Buenos Aires proper, the ingredients for quality vegetarian meals are easy to obtain, and many eateries prepare dishes such as pasta and salads that are easily adapted into a vegetarian format. Before ordering any pasta dish, verify whether it comes with a meat sauce—*carne* means "beef" here, and waiters or waitresses may consider chicken, pork, and similar items as part of another category—sometimes called *carne blanca* (literally, "white meat"). Faced with a reticent cook, you can always claim *alergia* (allergy).

Fruits

As its seasons are reversed from those in the Northern Hemisphere, temperate Argentina produces many of the same fruits as the north, often available as fresh juices. Items like *manzana* (apple), *pera* (pear), *naranja* (orange), *ciruela* (plum), *sandía* (watermelon), *membrillo* (quince), *durazno* (peach), *frambuesa* (raspberry), and *frutilla* (strawberry) will be familiar to almost everyone. When requesting *jugo de naranja* (orange juice), be sure it comes *exprimido* (fresh-squeezed) rather than out of a can or box.

Also widely available, mostly through import, are tropical and subtropical fruits like banana and *ananá* (pineapple). Mango, *maracuyá* (passion fruit), and similar tropical fruits are less common but not unknown.

The *palta* (avocado), a Central American domesticate known as *aguacate* in its region of origin, often appears in Argentine salads.

Meats and Poultry

Prior to the Spaniards, South America's only domesticated animals were the *cuy* (guinea pig, rare in what is now Argentina), the llama and alpaca, and the dog, sometimes used for food. The Spaniards enriched the American diet with their domestic animals, including cattle, sheep, pigs, and poultry (chickens and ducks).

Carne, often modified as *carne de vacuno,* or *bife* (beef) is the most common menu item, and comes in a variety of cuts. Among them are *bife de chorizo* (sirloin or rump steak), *bife de lomo* (tenderloin), *asado de tira* (rib roast), *matambre* (rolled flank steak), and *entraña* (skirt steak). *Milanesa* is a breaded cutlet or chicken-fried steak that, at cheaper restaurants, can be intolerably greasy.

The widest selection is usually available in the *parrillada* or *asado,* a mixed grill that includes prime cuts but also *achuras,* a broad term that encompasses offal such as *chinchulines* (small intestines), *mollejas* (sweetbreads), *criadillas* (testicles), *morcilla* (blood sausage), and *riñones* (kidneys). *Asado* can also mean a simple roast. *Chimichurri* is a garlic-based sauce that often accompanies the *parrillada.*

Sausages such as the slightly spicy *chorizo* may also form part of the *asado;* in a hot-dog bun, it becomes *choripán. Panchos* are basic hot dogs, while *fiambres* are processed meats.

Cordero (lamb), often roasted on a spit over an open fire, is more common in Patagonia. *Cerdo* (pork) appears in many forms, ranging from simple *jamón* (ham) to *chuletas* (chops) to *lomito* (loin) and *matambre de cerdo. Chivo* (goat) or *chivito* (the diminutive) is a western-Argentine specialty that sometimes appears on menus in the capital; note that the Uruguayan *chivito* is very different, a steak sandwich or plate slathered with eggs, fries, and other high-calorie extras.

Stews and casseroles include *carbonada* (beef, rice, potatoes, sweet potatoes, corn, squash, and fruit like apples and peaches) and *puchero:* beef, chicken, bacon, sausage, *morcilla* (blood sausage), cabbage, corn, garbanzos, peppers, tomatoes, onions, squash, and sweet potatoes. Broth-cooked rice serves as a garnish.

Ave (poultry) most often means *pollo* (chicken), which sometimes appears on menus as *gallina* (literally, hen) in a casserole or stew;

CATTLE CULTURE AND THE ARGENTINE DIET

From his hotel room on Buenos Aires's Avenida de Mayo, American poet Robert Lowell once wrote, he could hear "the bulky, beefy breathing of the herds." Ever since feral livestock changed the face of the pampas in the 16th century, displacing the native guanaco and rhea, cattle have been a symbol of wealth and the foundation of the Argentine diet. Riding across the pampas, Charles Darwin found the reliance on beef remarkable:

I had now been several days without tasting any thing besides meat: I did not at all dislike this new regimen; but I felt as if it would only have agreed with me with hard exercise. I have heard that patients in England, when desired to confine themselves exclusively to an animal diet, even with the hope of life before their eyes, have scarce been able to endure it. Yet the Gaucho in the Pampas, for months together, touches nothing but beef.... It is, perhaps, from their meat regimen that the Gauchos, like other carnivorous animals, can abstain long from food. I was told that at Tandeel, some troops voluntarily pursued a party of Indians for three days, without eating or drinking.

Recent research has suggested that this diet has not been quite so universal – urban archaeologist Daniel Schávelzon has unearthed evidence that fish consumption, for instance, was much greater in colonial Buenos Aires than once thought – but there is no doubt that the *parrilla* is a culinary institution. Beef may not be healthy in the quantities that some Argentines enjoy, and many will even admit that. But few can bypass restaurants where flamboyantly clad urban gauchos stir the glowing coals beneath grilled meat on a vertical spit without craving that savory beef.

For most Argentines, *bien cocido* (well done) is the standard for steak, but *jugoso* (rare) and *a punto* (medium) are not uncommon.

eggs are *huevos. Pavo* (turkey) is becoming more common.

Fish and Seafood

Argentine fish and seafood may not have the international reputation of its beef, but the long coastline, large territorial seas, and huge freshwater rivers and lakes provide abundant options. Buenos Aires, Mar del Plata, and other coastal cities have fine seafood restaurants, but these are less common in the interior.

Seafood, among the most abundant animal-protein sources in pre-Columbian times, includes both *pescado* (fish) and *mariscos* (shellfish and crustaceans). The most common fish are *congrio* (conger eel, covering a variety of species), sometimes called *abadejo; lenguado* (sole or flounder); *merluza* (hake); and *trucha* (trout). *Salmón* (salmon) normally comes from fish farms in Patagonia and in Chile.

Note that the cheapest restaurants may ruin perfectly good fish by preparing it *frito* (deep-fried), but on request almost all will prepare it *a la plancha* (grilled, usually with a dab of butter) or *al vapor* (steamed). Higher-priced restaurants will add elaborate sauces, often including shellfish.

Among the shellfish, visitors will recognize the relatively commonplace *almejas* (clams), *calamares* (squid), *camarones* (shrimp), *cangrejo* (crab), *centolla* (king crab), *mejillones* (mussels), *ostiones* or *callos* (scallops, but beware—the latter word can also mean tripe), *ostras* (oysters), and *pulpo* (octopus). Spanish restaurants normally serve the greatest variety of fish and shellfish.

"Fast Food" Snacks

Ignoring the invasion of international franchises, Argentina has some of the continent's best snack food. Best of the best is the empanada, a flaky dough turnover most frequently filled with ground beef, hard-boiled egg, and olive, but it may also come with ham and cheese, chicken, onion, and (rarely) tuna or fish. The spicier ground-beef *salteña* comes from northwestern Argentina but is available in Buenos Aires; the tangy *empanada árabe* (lamb with a touch of lemon juice) is more difficult to find. Empanadas *al horno* (oven-baked) are lighter than *fritas* (fried, sometimes in heavy oil).

Argentine pizza can be exceptional, though it's often cheese-heavy and generally less diverse in its toppings than in North America. For slices, try the cheeseless *fugazza* with Vidalia-sweet onions or its cousin *fugazzetta,* enhanced with ham and mozzarella. Argentines often embellish their slices with *fainá,* a baked chickpea dough that fits neatly atop.

Desserts

Many Argentines have a sweet tooth. At home, the favorite *postre* is fresh fruit, including grapes (most single-family homes have their own arbors) along with apples, pears, and oranges. In restaurants, this becomes *ensalada de frutas* (fruit salad) or, somewhat more elaborately, *macedonia. Postre vigilante,* consisting of cheese and *membrillo* (quince) or *batata* (sweet potato) preserves, is another fruit-based dessert; it also goes by the name *queso y dulce.*

Arroz con leche (rice pudding) and *flan* (egg custard, often topped with whipped cream) are also good choices, as is the Spanish custard known as *natillas.* An acquired taste is *dulce de leche,* which one international travel magazine referred to as "its own major food group." Argentines devour this sickly sweet caramelized milk, spread on just about anything and often spooned out of the jar in private homes, in prodigious quantities.

Though it stems from the Italian tradition, Argentine ice cream lacks the high international profile of gelato—when a pair of *porteños* opened an ice creamery in Oakland, California, they chose the compromise name of Tango Gelato, stressing its Italian origins without suppressing its Buenos Aires way station. Argentina has a remarkable number of high-quality ice creameries and a remarkable

diversity of flavors, ranging from the standard vanilla and chocolate (with multiple variations on those standards, including white chocolate and bittersweet chocolate) to lemon mousse, *sambayón* (resembling eggnog), the staple *dulce de leche* (caramelized milk), and countless others.

MEALS AND MEALTIMES

Despite some regional differences, Argentine food is relatively uniform throughout the country, except in Buenos Aires, where diverse ethnic and international cuisine is abundant; the Andean northwest, where some dishes resemble those of highland Bolivia and Perú; and Patagonia, where game dishes are not unusual (most of this, such as boar and venison, is farmed).

By North American and European standards, Argentines are late eaters except for *desayuno* (breakfast). *Almuerzo* (lunch) usually starts around 1 P.M., *cena* (dinner) around 9 P.M. or later—sometimes much later. *Porteños* often bide their time between lunch and dinner with a late-afternoon *té* (afternoon tea) that consists of a sandwich or some sort of pastry or dessert; it can be very substantial.

Since Argentines often eat *after* the theater or a movie, around 11 P.M. or even later on weekends, anyone entering a restaurant before 9 P.M. may well dine alone.

Breakfast and Brunch

Most Argentines eat a light breakfast of coffee or tea and *pan tostado* (toast, occasionally with ham and/or cheese), *medialunas* (croissants), or *facturas* (pastries, also eaten for afternoon tea); *medialunas* may be either *de manteca* (buttery and sweet) or *salada* (saltier, baked with oil). *Mermelada* (jam) usually accompanies plain *tostados.*

As a side dish, eggs may be either *fritos* (fried) or *revueltos* (scrambled), or sometimes *duros* (hardboiled). In some fashionable restaurant zones, a more elaborate Sunday brunch has become an option.

Lunch

Lunch is often the day's main meal, usually including an *entrada* (appetizer), followed by a *plato principal* (entrée), accompanied by a *guarnición* (side dish) and a *bebida* (soft drink) or *agua mineral* (mineral water), and followed by *postre* (dessert).

Many upscale restaurants offer a *menú ejecutivo* (fixed-priced "executive" lunch) that makes it possible to eat well and stylishly without busting the budget. It's also possible to find local fast-food items like *hamburguesas* (hamburgers), sandwiches, pizza, and pasta without resorting to international franchises.

Té

Té, the fourth meal of the typical Argentine day, can range from a late-afternoon sandwich to the equivalent of afternoon tea, with elaborate cakes and cookies, and is often a social occasion as well. Presumably intended to tide people over until their relatively late dinnertime, it often becomes larger and more elaborate than its name would imply.

Dinner

Dinner resembles lunch, but in formal restaurants it may be substantially more elaborate (and more expensive), and it can be a major social occasion. Argentines dine late—9 P.M. is early, and anything before that will likely earn incredulous "What are you doing here?" stares from waiters. The exception to this rule is at tourist-oriented areas like BA's Puerto Madero complex, where restaurateurs have become accustomed to North Americans and Europeans who, lodged at nearby chain and luxury hotels, often can't wait any later than 7 P.M.

BEVERAGES
Coffee, Tea, and Chocolate

Unreconstructed caffeine addicts will feel at home in Argentina, where espresso is the norm even in small provincial towns. *Café chico* is a dark viscous brew in a miniature cup, supplemented with enough sugar packets to make it overflow onto the saucer. A *cortado* comes diluted with milk—for a larger portion request a *cortado doble*—and follows lunch or dinner. *Café con leche,* equivalent to a latte, is a breakfast drink; ordering it after lunch or dinner is a serious faux pas.

Té negro (black tea) usually comes in bags and is insipid by most standards. Visitors wanting British-style tea with milk should ask for tea first and milk later; otherwise, they may get a tea bag immersed in lukewarm milk. Herbal teas range from the nearly universal *manzanilla* (chamomile) and *rosa mosqueta* (rose hips) to *mate de coca* (coca leaf), but *yerba mate,* the so-called "Paraguayan tea," is one of the country's most deeply embedded customs.

Chocolate-lovers will enjoy the *submarino,* a bar of bittersweet chocolate that dissolves in steamed milk from the espresso machine. Powdered chocolate is also available but is less flavorful.

Water, Juices, and Soft Drinks

Argentine tap water is potable almost everywhere except in some of the northerly tropical deserts; ask for *agua de la canilla.* For ice, request it *con hielo.* Visitors with truly sensitive stomachs might consider bottled water, which is widely available. Ask for *agua pura* or *agua mineral;* some brands, such as Eco de los Andes and Villavicencio, are springwater, while others are purified. For carbonated water, add *con gas* or ask for the even cheaper *soda,* which comes in large siphon bottles.

Gaseosas (singular *gaseosa*) are sweetened bottled soft drinks (including most of the major transnational brands, but also local versions such as the tonic water Paso de los Toros).

Fresh-squeezed *jugos* (fruit juices) are good though limited in their diversity. *Naranja* (orange) is the standard; to ensure freshness, ask for *jugo de naranja exprimido.*

Alcoholic Drinks

Argentina may be less famous for its wines than Chile is, perhaps because domestic consumption overshadows exports, but it's the world's fifth-largest wine producer and its profile is higher every year. Most production takes place in the western and northwestern provinces of Mendoza, San Juan, and Salta, but it's increasing in the Patagonian provinces of Neuquén and Río Negro.

Tinto is red wine, while *blanco* is white. Good

THE RITUAL OF *MATE*

It's rarely on the menu, but the single most important social drink in Argentina and most of the River Plate region – including Uruguay, Paraguay, and southern Brazil – is *mate*, made from the dried, shredded leaf of *Ilex paraguayensis*.

Espresso, in its many forms, may dominate café society, but the *mate* infusion transcends commercialism. Its production is a major industry, but its consumption belongs to home and hearth. Native to the forests of the upper Río Paraná Delta, a relative of the everyday holly, *yerba mate* became a commercial crop in plantations on colonial Jesuit missions.

Transplanted Europeans took to it – Austrian Jesuit Martin Dobrizhoffer asserted that *mate* "speedily counteracts the languor arising from the burning climate, and assuages both hunger and thirst" – but unlike coffee and tea it never really established markets across the Atlantic or even elsewhere in the Americas, except for parts of Chile.

Production diminished with the Jesuits' expulsion from the Americas in 1767, but the so-called "Paraguayan tea" kept its place in humble households and privileged palaces alike. According to English sailor Emeric Essex Vidal, who visited Buenos Aires in the 1820s,

> *Mate is in every house all day long, and the compliment of the country is to hand the mate cup to every visitor, the same cup and tube serving for all, and an attendant being kept in waiting to replenish for each person. Throughout the provinces, the weary traveler, let him stop at what hovel soever he may, is sure to be presented with the hospitable mate-cup, which, unless his prejudices are very strong indeed, will be found a great refreshment.*

In fact, the purpose of *mate* is hospitality; preparing and serving it is a ritual. It is also an equalizer, as everyone sips in turn from the same *bombilla* (metallic tube or straw), placed in the same *yerba*-stuffed *mate* (a term which also means "gourd"), filled with slightly below-boiling water by the *cebador* (brewer).

It is customary to drink the gourd dry, and then return it to the *cebador,* who passes it clockwise around the group. Note that, in this context, to say *gracias* (thank you) means that you want no more.

Not all rituals are equal, though, and *mate*'s material culture can differ dramatically among classes. The servant whose sole job was to prepare and serve it is a thing of the past, but upper-class households own far more elaborate paraphernalia than working-class families – just as British peers have more ornate tea sets than the untitled. While simple gourds might be plain calabashes or even plastic, others might be elaborately carved wood set in silver or even gold; the *bombilla*, likewise, can range from utilitarian aluminum to ceremonial silver.

Most Argentines prefer *mate amargo* (bitter, i.e. without sugar), but northerners often take it *dulce*, with sugar and fragrant herbs known as *yuyos* (literally, "weeds"). While it's a mostly homebound custom in Argentina, Uruguayans (who consume even more than Argentines) make it a public affair as they walk the streets with leather-encased gourds and enormous thermoses. In the ferocious Paraguayan summer, street vendors sell ice-cold *yerba* in the form of *tereré*.

Supermarkets sell *yerba* in bulk packages with engaging designs that look half a century old. It's also available in tea bags as *mate cocido*, which is weaker, and may be more palatable to neophytes, than the first bitter swallows from the freshly prepared gourd. Do not confuse it with *mate de coca*, an equally innocuous infusion that's made from the leaf of the notorious coca plant.

Fortunately for its aficionados, *mate* is inexpensive. No one really has to worry anymore, as did Dobrizhoffer, that,

> *If many topers in Europe waste their substance by an immoderate use of wine and other intoxicating liquors, there are no fewer in America who drink away their fortunes in potations of the herb of Paraguay.*

wine is almost always reasonably priced, even during times of high inflation. The best restaurants have a wide selection, usually in full bottles, though sometimes it's possible to get a *media botella* (half bottle) or, increasingly frequently, wine by the glass. Argentines often mix their table wines—even reds—with soda water or ice.

An increasing number of wine bars also offer Spanish tapas, sushi, and other light meals. Keep an eye out for torrontés, a unique white varietal from the vineyards around Cafayate, in Salta Province, and the signature red malbec. Wine tourism is popular here and in the Cuyo provinces of Mendoza and San Juan.

For more information on Southern Cone wines and wineries, look for Christopher Fielden's *The Wines of Argentina, Chile, and Latin America* (New York: Faber and Faber, 2001), though it doesn't account for some recent developments. Harm de Blij's *Wine Regions of the Southern Hemisphere* (Lanham, MD: Rowman and Littlefield, 1985) is a more intellectually sophisticated overview but is now rather outdated.

While Argentine wines are more than worthwhile, Argentines now lean more toward beer, which tastes best as *cerveza tirada,* direct from the tap, rather than from bottles or cans. The most widely available beer is Quilmes, produced in its namesake suburb across the Riachuelo from La Boca.

Hard liquor is not so popular, but whiskey, gin, and the like are readily available. *Ginebra bols* (differing from gin) and *caña* (cane alcohol) are local specialties.

Argentina's legal drinking age is 18.

Conduct and Customs

Argentines and especially *porteños* (like New Yorkers) have a stereotyped reputation for brusqueness. Still, politeness goes a long way with officials, shopkeepers, and others with whom you may have contact. Always offer the appropriate polite greeting: *buenos días* (good morning), *buenas tardes* (good afternoon), or *buenas noches* (good evening or good night).

In terms of general conduct, both women and men should dress inconspicuously when visiting churches, chapels, and sacred sites. This again is an issue of respect for local customs, even if Argentines themselves don't always observe it.

GENDER ROLES
Like other Latin American societies, Argentina has a strong *machista* (chauvinist) element. Argentine women are traditionally mothers, homemakers, and children's caregivers, while men are providers and decision-makers, although there are increasing numbers of female professionals and other working women.

Many Argentine men view foreign women as sexually available, but this is not necessarily discriminatory—they view Argentine women the same way. Harassment often takes the form of *piropos,* sexist comments which are often innocuous and can even be poetic, but are just as likely vulgar. It is best to ignore verbal comments, which are obvious by tone of voice even if you don't understand them; if they're persistent, seek refuge in a café or *confitería.*

Despite challenges, women have acquired political prominence. The most prominent and notorious, of course, was Evita Perón, but her rise to the top was an unconventional one. The highest-profile females in current politics are President Cristina Fernández—wife of former President Néstor Kirchner—and legislator and former presidential candidate Elisa Carrió, a vociferous anticorruption campaigner who, unfortunately, is better at identifying problems than offering solutions.

GAYS AND LESBIANS
Despite its conspicuous Catholicism, Argentina is surprisingly tolerant to both gays and lesbians, and public displays of affection—men kissing on the cheek, women holding hands—are relatively common even among heterosexuals.

PHOTOGRAPHIC ETIQUETTE – AND A WARNING

Few Argentines, especially *porteños*, are camera-shy. Generally, if a person's presence in a photograph is incidental, as in a townscape, it's unnecessary to ask permission, but avoid the in-your-face approach. If in doubt, ask; if rejected, don't insist. If a person is the photograph's primary subject, try to establish a rapport before asking permission to photograph, if you can manage Spanish or have another language in common. If you're purchasing something from a market vendor, he or she will almost certainly agree to be photographed. Photographers should be particularly respectful of the indigenous peoples of northwestern Argentina and Patagonia, however.

Visitors should be circumspect about photographing political protests – the police are notorious for cataloguing dissidents, so protestors may be suspicious of people with cameras. Likewise, avoid photography near military installations, although "The Sentry Will Shoot" signs are a thing of past.

There is one absolute no-no – without explicit permission, don't even think about photographing Israeli or Jewish community sites anywhere. Since car-bomb attacks on Retiro's Israeli Embassy in 1992 and Once's Jewish cultural center in 1994, federal police are stationed outside all these sites. They will politely or, if necessary, not so politely discourage would-be photographers.

In 2002 the capital's legislature established domestic-partner regulations applicable to gay couples (and to other unmarried couples as well), with regard to health insurance and pension rights. There was opposition from the Catholic Church and from the Buenos Aires Bar Association (the latter on a legal technicality, that only the federal government could establish such legislation).

In late 2009, meanwhile, Buenos Aires mayor Mauricio Macri decided not to appeal a court judgment that permitted Alejandro Freyre and José María Di Bello to marry, but a federal judge blocked the ceremony until it could be considered by Argentina's supreme court. In the interim, governor Fabiana Ríos of Tierra del Fuego Province issued a decree that allowed the couple to marry there despite legal ambiguity. And in July 2010, Argentina became the first country in Latin America to legalize same-sex marriage.

The Buenos Aires–based **Comunidad Homosexual Argentina** (CHA, Tomás Liberti 1080, La Boca, tel. 011/4361-6352, www.cha.org.ar), the country's foremost gay-rights organization, was instrumental in lobbying for the domestic partner legislation.

SMOKING

About a third of Argentines smoke, including nearly 40 percent of the male population; tobacco directly causes about 40,000 deaths per annum. According to one survey, 3 of every 10 Argentine *cardiologists* smoke, as do 3 of every 10 students between the ages of 13 and 15.

Still, there is widespread recognition that the habit is unhealthy; the city of Buenos Aires and an increasing number of provinces have enacted stringent antismoking ordinances that have purified the air in restaurants and other enclosed areas (though one ironic effect has been to concentrate smokers at patio and sidewalk tables where tobacco is still permitted). If faced with secondhand smoke in inappropriate places, such as buses or taxis, it's easiest to appeal to courtesy with a white lie such as *"soy asmático"* (I'm asthmatic).

Sin Pucho (Gallo 812, Buenos Aires, tel. 011/4862-6913, www.sinpucho.org.ar) is an ex-smokers' support group.

Tips for Travelers

OPPORTUNITIES FOR STUDY AND EMPLOYMENT

After the 2002 peso collapse, with upwards of 20 percent unemployment, remunerative work was hard to come by even for legal residents, let alone visitors on tourist or student visas. Even then, foreigners found work teaching English or another foreign language, working in the tourist industry, or performing casual labor in bars or restaurants. The problem with such jobs is that they either require time to build up a clientele (in the case of teaching), may be seasonal (tourism), and can be poorly paid (restaurants, except in a handful of places where tips are high). Language teachers, in any event, may find that few Argentines can afford the luxury of one-on-one lessons.

Ideally, obtaining a work permit from an Argentine consulate is better than attempting to obtain one in-country, as employment may not begin until the permit is actually granted. No matter what, the process requires submitting documents and takes some time.

BUSINESS TRAVEL

There are few legal restrictions on foreign businesses in Argentina, but the recent business climate, due largely to the government's debt default and banking restrictions, has not been conducive to investment. In country risk assessments, featured like sports scores on the front page of many newspapers, Argentina has ranked among the world's highest—in August 2002, this key statistic soared to 7,222 compared to 1,200 for its beleaguered neighbor Uruguay and only 150 for Chile.

In September 2003, after more than a year of relative stability, the country risk was still 5,100; by late 2006 it had fallen to about 289, nearly the lowest in Argentine history, but this still contrasted with Chile's 57 and Brazil's 211. Following the 2009 global recession and the Fernández de Kirchner administration's clumsy attempt to fire Central Bank president Martín Redrado in early 2010, the figure rebounded to 1,426, as opposed to Chile's 96, Uruguay's 231, and Brazil's 326.

Corruption remains an issue, as a Transparency International survey for 2009 ranked Argentina 106th of 180 countries evaluated, on par with several African countries. Political officeholders have an unfortunate reputation for shaking down foreign companies for bribes, and customs procedures can be trying despite efforts to professionalize the service. Intellectual-property rights for computer software, CD and cassette recordings, and DVDs and videotapes are problematic.

Good background sources on business, at least for those who read Spanish, are the businesses dailies mentioned under *Media* later in this chapter, and the magazine *Mercado* (www.mercado.com.ar). The most accessible English-language source is the U.S. State Department's Country Commercial Guide service (www.export.gov), though it often lags behind events. Its best bets for investment include travel and tourism services, hotel and restaurant equipment, computer equipment and software, alternative energy technology, medical equipment and supplies, residential building materials and supplies, sporting goods, and biotechnology.

Some investors believe that Argentine businesses may offer high yields on investments because devaluation has depressed prices in dollar terms. Residential real estate, for instance, has experienced a boom, though that has also meant rebounding prices. In any event, before signing any business deal, consult a local lawyer recommended by your embassy, consulate, or a trusted friend.

Business Etiquette

Conducting business is as much a personal and social activity as an economic one; initial contacts may be formal, with appointments arranged well in advance, but topics such as family and sports are often part of the conversation. Formality in dress and appearance is

PROVINCIAL AND MUNICIPAL TOURIST OFFICES

Every Argentine province and several municipalities maintain tourist representatives in Buenos Aires.

- **Buenos Aires:** Avenida Callao 237, San Nicolás, tel. 011/4371-7045, www.turismo.gba.gov.ar

- **Catamarca:** Avenida Córdoba 2080, Balvanera, tel. 011/4374-6891, www.turismocatamarca.gov.ar

- **Chaco:** Avenida Callao 328, Balvanera, tel. 011/4372-5209

- **Chubut:** Sarmiento 1172, San Nicolás, tel. 011/4382-2009, www.chubutur.gov.ar

- **Córdoba:** Avenida Callao 332, Balvanera, tel. 011/4373-4277, www.cordobaturismo.gov.ar

- **Corrientes:** San Martín 333, 4th floor, Microcentro (San Nicolás), tel. 011/4394-9490, www.corrientes.gov.ar

- **Entre Ríos:** Suipacha 844, Retiro, tel. 011/4326-2573, www.turismo.entrerios.gov.ar

- **Formosa:** Hipólito Yrigoyen 1429, Monserrat, tel. 011/4384-7048, www.casadeformosa.gov.ar

- **Jujuy:** Avenida Santa Fe 967, Retiro, tel. 011/4393-6096, www.turismo.jujuy.gov.ar

- **La Pampa:** Suipacha 346, Microcentro (San Nicolás), tel. 011/4326-0511, www.turismolapampa.gov.ar

- **La Rioja:** Avenida Callao 745, San Nicolás, tel. 011/4815-1929, www.larioja.gov.ar/turismo

- **Mar del Plata (municipal):** Avenida Corrientes 1660, Local 16, San Nicolás, tel. 011/4384-5722, www.mardelplata.gov.ar

- **Mendoza:** Avenida Callao 445, San Nicolás, tel. 011/4371-0835, www.turismo.mendoza.gov.ar

- **Misiones:** Avenida Santa Fe 989, Retiro, tel. 011/4317-3700, www.turismo.misiones.gov.ar

- **Neuquén:** Maipú 48, Microcentro (San Nicolás), tel. 011/4343-2324, www.neuquentur.org

- **Pinamar (municipal):** Florida 930, 5th floor, Retiro, tel. 011/4315-2679, www.pinamar.gov.ar

- **Río Negro:** Tucumán 1916, Balvanera, tel. 011/4371-7078

- **Salta:** Diagonal Norte (Roque Sáenz Peña) 933, Microcentro (San Nicolás), tel. 011/4326-1314, www.turismosalta.gov.ar

- **San Juan:** Sarmiento 1251, Microcentro (San Nicolás), tel. 011/4382-5580, www.turismo.sanjuan.gov.ar

- **San Luis:** Azcuénaga 1087, Recoleta, tel. 011/5778-1621, www.sanluis.gov.ar

- **Santa Cruz:** Suipacha 927, Retiro, tel. 011/4314-4880, www.epatagonia.gov.ar

- **Santa Fe:** Montevideo 373, 2nd floor, San Nicolás, tel. 011/5811-4327, delegacionsantafe@ciudad.com.ar

- **Santiago del Estero:** Florida 274, Microcentro (San Nicolás), tel. 011/4326-9418, www.turismosantiago.gov.ar

- **Tierra del Fuego (Instituto Fueguino de Turismo):** Marcelo T. de Alvear 790, Retiro, tel. 011/4311-0233, infuebue@arnet.com.ar

- **Tucumán:** Suipacha 140, Microcentro (San Nicolás), tel. 011/4322-0564, www.tucumanturismo.gov.ar

- **Villa Carlos Paz (municipal):** Lavalle 623, Oficinas 38/39, Microcentro (San Nicolás), tel. 011/4322-0348, www.villacarlospaz.gov.ar

- **Villa Gesell (municipal):** Carlos Pellegrini 1275, Retiro, tel. 011/4393-0429, www.gesell.gov.ar

less rigid than it once was, but in sectors like banking it's still the rule.

An ability to speak Spanish well is a plus, though many Argentine business figures speak English well (and more than a few have been educated in English-speaking countries). The best business travel months are April–November; in January and February, when school lets out and Argentines take their summer vacations, Buenos Aires can seem almost deserted. Many people also leave for winter holidays, the last two weeks of July.

Useful Organizations

Nearly all important business-oriented organizations are in Buenos Aires. One critically important and unavoidable contact is the national customs headquarters, the **Administración Nacional de Aduanas** (Azopardo 350, Monserrat, tel. 0810/999-2347, www.afip.gov.ar). If importing equipment for permanent use, it's essential to deal with them through a *despachante de aduanas* (private customs broker).

U.S. citizens can get advice at the **Cámara de Comercio de los Estados Unidos en Argentina** (U.S. Chamber of Commerce, Viamonte 1133, 8th floor, Microcentro, tel. 011/4371-4500, www.amchamar.com.ar).

Their local counterpart is the **Cámara Argentina de Comercio** (Argentine Chamber of Commerce, Avenida Leandro N. Alem 36, Planta Baja, Microcentro, tel. 11/5300-9000, www.cac.com.ar).

Importers may want to consult with the **Cámara de Importadores de la República Argentina** (Argentine Chamber of Importers, Avenida Belgrano 427, 7th floor, Monserrat, tel./fax 011/4342-1101 or 011/4342-0523, www.cira.org.ar).

Argentina's main stock exchange is the **Bolsa de Comercio de Buenos Aires** (Sarmiento 299, 1st floor, Microcentro, tel. 011/4316-7000, www.bcba.sba.com.ar).

For agricultural contacts, visit the **Sociedad Rural Argentina** (Argentine Agricultural Association, Florida 460, Microcentro, tel. 011/4324-4700, www.ruralarg.org.ar).

TRAVELERS WITH DISABILITIES

For people with disabilities, Argentina can be a problematic country. The narrow, uneven sidewalks in many cities, not to mention the fast-moving traffic, are unkind to people with disabilities, especially to the wheelchair-bound.

Public transportation can rarely accommodate passengers with disabilities, though the capital's newer Subte stations have elevators, and others are being retrofitted. Avis has introduced rental vehicles with hand controls.

Few older buildings are specifically equipped for disabled people, but many of these are low and can often accommodate people with disabilities. Newer hotels are usually high-rises, and disabled access is obligatory.

TRAVELING WITH CHILDREN

Argentina is a child-friendly country, and Buenos Aires is a child-friendly city. In fact, since many Argentines enjoy large extended families, they may feel little in common with people in their late twenties and older who do *not* have children, and traveling with kids can open doors.

Many parks and plazas have playground equipment, so it's easy to mix with Argentine families there. What foreign parents may find unusual is that toddlers and their families may be out on the swings and slides at 11 P.M. or even later. Likewise, kids are off across the street, around the neighborhood, and even on the buses and Subte at ages when anxious North American parents are driving their kids three blocks to school and waiting until the doors close behind them.

On public transportation, strangers may spontaneously but gently touch small children and even set them on their laps. While this may be disconcerting to non-Argentines, it's not necessarily inappropriate in cultural context.

Many cultural activities are child-oriented, particularly during late July's winter school holidays.

WOMEN TRAVELERS

Like other Latin American societies, Argentina has strong *machista* (male chauvinist) elements.

Though nearly everybody visits and leaves without experiencing any unpleasantness, women are certainly not exempt from harassment and, rarely, violence. The most common form of harassment is the *piropo*, a sexist remark that can range from clever and humorous to crude and insulting.

If you do receive unwanted attention, the best strategy is to ignore it, and the odds are that the problem will just go away. If not, the next best option is to return to your hotel, enter a restaurant, or find some other public place where harassment will be more conspicuous and you're likely to find support. Some women have suggested wearing a bogus wedding ring, but truly persistent suitors might see this simply as a challenge.

GAY AND LESBIAN TRAVELERS

Argentine public opinion in general, and that of Buenos Aires in particular, has turned remarkably tolerant of gays and lesbians, if not necessarily of public homosexual behavior. Buenos Aires has an active gay scene that revolves around Barrio Norte's Avenida Santa Fe, Recoleta, Palermo, and San Telmo. Early November's Marcha de Orgullo Gay (Gay Pride Parade) leads from BA's Plaza de Mayo to Congreso.

Other popular areas include outlying areas like the Paraná Delta; other large cities have their own enclaves. Within Mar del Plata's city limits, for instance, there's a gay-oriented resort area known as Calú Beach.

Demonstrative contact such as kissing between males (on the cheek, at least) and holding hands for females does not have the same connotations as it might in North America or some European countries, and it is common among heterosexuals. This does not mean that gays and lesbians can always behave as they wish in public, however—police have beaten and jailed individuals who have offended their unenlightened sensibilities. If in doubt, be circumspect.

Health and Safety

Midlatitude Buenos Aires and vicinity offer few major health risks beyond those associated with any large city; public health standards are good, and tap water is potable. In some parts of northernmost subtropical Argentina, though, there's a small risk of malaria or similar tropical diseases, and the dengue mosquito vector has moved southward to the capital.

A good general source on foreign health matters is the fourth edition of Dr. Richard Dawood's *Travelers' Health* (Oxford: Oxford University Press, 2006), a small encyclopedia on the topic. The 13th edition of Dr. Stuart R. Rose's *International Travel Health Guide* (Amsterdam: Elsevier, 2006) is updated annually and regionally focused. Try also the fifth edition of Dirk G. Schroeder's *Staying Healthy in Asia, Africa, and Latin America* (Berkeley, CA: Avalon Travel Publishing, 2000).

For up-to-date information on health issues in Argentina and elsewhere in the Southern Cone, visit the U.S. Centers for Disease Control (CDC) travel page (wwwnc.cdc.gov/travel). Another good source is the United Kingdom's Department of Health (www.dh.gov.uk), which provides a chart of recommended prophylaxis by country.

Thanks to devaluation of the peso, quality medical care has been so cheap as to justify a trip to Buenos Aires, at least in some cases. As the peso has recovered and inflation risen, the price differential is no longer so great, but it may be worth at least a consultation.

Visitors considering medical care, however, should choose private hospitals and clinics, especially since the economic crisis has strained the resources of public hospitals. One outstanding choice is **Clínica Fleni** (Montañeses 2325, Belgrano, tel. 011/5777-

3200, www.fleni.org.ar), whose focus is pediatrics and neurology but which also has outstanding orthopedists. Another possibility is the **Fundación Favaloro** (Avenida Belgrano 1746, Monserrat, tel. 011/4378-1200, www.fundacionfavaloro.org), whose specialty is cardiology. Nearly all the doctors at both are English-speaking.

BEFORE YOU GO

Theoretically, Argentina demands no proof of vaccinations, but if you are coming from a tropical country where yellow fever is endemic, authorities could ask for a vaccination certificate.

Traveling to Argentina or elsewhere without adequate medical insurance is risky. Before leaving your home country, obtain medical insurance that includes evacuation in case of serious emergency. Foreign health insurance may not be accepted in Argentina, so you may be required to pay out of your own pocket for later reimbursement. Often, however, private medical providers accept international credit cards in return for services.

Numerous carriers provide medical and evacuation coverage; an extensive list, including Internet links, is available at the U.S. State Department's website (www.travel.state.gov).

GENERAL HEALTH MAINTENANCE

Common-sense precautions can reduce the possibility of illness. Washing the hands frequently with soap and water and drinking only bottled, boiled, or carbonated water diminish the likelihood of contagion for short-term visitors—though Argentine tap water is potable almost everywhere.

Where purified water is impossible to obtain, such as backcountry streams where there may be livestock or problems with human waste, pass drinking water through a one-micron filter and purify it further with iodine drops or tablets (avoid prolonged consumption of iodine-purified water). Nonpasteurized dairy products, such as goat cheese, can be problematic and are best avoided.

FOOD- OR WATERBORNE DISEASES

While relatively few visitors to Argentina run into problems of this sort, contaminated food and drink are not unheard of. In many cases, it's simply exposure to different sorts of bugs to which your body soon becomes accustomed, but if symptoms persist, the problem may be more serious.

Traveler's Diarrhea

Colloquially known as *turista,* the classic traveler's diarrhea (TD) usually lasts just a few days and almost always less than a week. Besides "the runs," symptoms include nausea, vomiting, bloating, and general weakness. The usual cause is the *Escherichia coli* bacterium from contaminated food or water; in rare cases *E. coli* infections can be fatal.

Fluids, including fruit juices, and small amounts of bland foods such as freshly cooked rice or soda crackers may relieve symptoms and help regain strength. Dehydration can be a serious problem, especially for children, who may need to be treated with an oral rehydration solution (ORS) of carbohydrates and salt.

Over-the-counter remedies like Pepto-Bismol, Lomotil, and Immodium may relieve symptoms but can also cause problems. Prescription drugs such as doxycyline and trimethoprim/sulfamethoxazole can also shorten the cycle. These may not be suitable for children, and it's better for everyone to avoid them if at all possible.

Continuing and worsening symptoms, including bloody stools, may mean dysentery, a much more serious ailment requiring a physician's attention.

Dysentery

Bacterial dysentery, resembling a more intense form of TD, responds to antibiotics, but amoebic dysentery is far more serious, sometimes leading to intestinal perforation, peritonitis, and liver abscesses. Like diarrhea, its symptoms include soft and even bloody stools, but some people may be asymptomatic even as they pass on *Entamoeba hystolica* through unsanitary toilet and food-preparation practices. Metronidazole, known by the brand names Flagyl or Protostat, is an effective treatment, but a physician's diagnosis is advisable.

Cholera

Resulting from poor hygiene, inadequate sewage disposal, and contaminated food, modern cholera is less devastating than its historic antecedents, which produced rapid dehydration, watery diarrhea, and imminent death without almost equally rapid rehydration. While today's cholera strains are highly infectious, most carriers do not even come down with symptoms. Existing vaccinations are ineffective, so health authorities now recommend against them.

Treatment can only relieve symptoms. On average, about five percent of victims die, but those who recover are immune. It's not a common problem in Argentina, but it's not unheard of either, especially in northern subtropical areas.

Hepatitis A

Usually passed by fecal-oral contact under poor hygiene and overcrowding, hepatitis A is a virus. The traditional gamma globulin prophylaxis has limited efficacy and wears off in just a few months. New hepatitis A vaccines, though, are more effective and last longer.

Typhoid

Typhoid is a serious disease common under unsanitary conditions, but the recommended vaccination is an effective prophylaxis.

INSECT-BORNE DISEASES

Argentina is not quite malaria-free, but there is none in or around Buenos Aires; a few other insect-borne diseases are present if not exactly prevalent.

Dengue Fever

Like malaria, mosquito-borne dengue is a disease of the lowland tropics, but it's less common than malaria and only rarely fatal. Often debilitating in the short term, its symptoms include fever, headache, severe joint pain, and skin rashes, but most people recover fairly quickly even though there is no treatment. Uncommon but often fatal, the more severe dengue hemorrhagic fever sometimes occurs in children, particularly those who have suffered from the disease previously.

Eradicated in Argentina in 1963, the mosquito vector *Aedes egypti* is once again present as far south as Buenos Aires. There were several hundred confirmed cases in lowland subtropical areas of Salta Province in 1997, and health authorities believe outbreaks are possible in Buenos Aires. The best prophylaxis is to avoid mosquito bites by covering exposed parts of the body with insect repellent or appropriate clothing.

Chagas' Disease

Also known as South American trypanosomiasis, Chagas' is most common in Brazil but affects about 18 million people between Mexico and Argentina; 50,000 people die from it every year. Not a tropical disease per se, it has a discontinuous distribution—Panamá and Costa Rica, for instance, are Chagas'-free.

Since it is spread by the bite of the night-feeding cone-nose or assassin bug, which lives in adobe structures, avoid such structures (these still exist in the countryside); if it's impossible to do so, sleep away from the walls. DEET-based insect repellents offer some protection. Chickens, dogs, and opossums may carry the disease.

Chagas' appears first as a swollen bite accompanied by fever, which soon subsides. In the long run, though, it may cause heart damage leading to sudden death, intestinal constipation, and difficulty in swallowing; there is no cure. Charles Darwin may have been a chronic sufferer.

HANTAVIRUS

Hantavirus is an uncommon but deadly disease contracted by breathing, touching, or ingesting feces or urine of the long-tailed rat. Primarily a rural phenomenon and most prevalent in southerly Patagonia, the virus thrives in enclosed areas; when exposed to sunlight or fresh air, it normally loses its potency. Avoid places frequented by rodents, particularly abandoned buildings, but note that there have been apparent cases in which hikers and farm workers have contracted the disease in open spaces.

RABIES

Rabies, a virus transmitted through bites or scratches by domestic animals (like dogs and cats) and wild mammals (like bats), is a concern; many domestic animals go unvaccinated, especially in rural areas. Human prophylactic vaccination is possible, but may be incompatible with malaria medication.

Untreated rabies can cause an agonizingly painful death. In case of an animal bite or scratch, clean the affected area immediately with soap and running water, and then with antiseptic substances like iodine or 40 percent-plus alcohol. If possible, try to capture the animal for diagnosis, but not at the risk of further bites; in areas where rabies is endemic, painful postexposure vaccination may be unavoidable.

SNAKEBITE

The federal capital does not have poisonous snakes, but the aggressive and highly venomous pit viper *yarará* is found in parts of Buenos Aires Province and elsewhere in the country. The timid but even more venomous coral snake is found in humid areas such as the Paraná Delta.

The *yarará,* whose venom paralyzes the nervous system, is responsible for most snakebite incidents, but strikes are not common. Death is not instantaneous and antivenins are available, but the wisest tactic is to be alert and avoid confrontation. If bitten, get to medical facilities as quickly as possible, but avoid excessive movement that helps the venom circulate.

ALTITUDE SICKNESS

At the highest elevations, above about 3,000 meters in the northern and the central Andes, *apunamiento* or *soroche* can be an annoyance and even a danger, especially to older people or those with respiratory problems. Even among young, robust individuals, a quick rise from sea level to *puna* within a couple of hours can cause intense headaches, vertigo, either drowsiness or insomnia, shortness of breath, and other symptoms. Combined with hypothermia, it can be life-threatening.

For most people, rest and relaxation help relieve these symptoms as the body gradually adapts to the reduced oxygen; aspirin or a comparable painkiller will combat headache. Should symptoms persist or worsen, moving to a lower elevation will usually have the desired effect. Some individuals have died at elevations above 4,000 meters; it is better to stay at an intermediate altitude than to travel to very high elevations in a single same day. Do not overeat, avoid or limit alcohol consumption, and drink extra fluids.

The second edition of Stephen Bezruchka's *Altitude Illness, Prevention & Treatment* (Seattle: The Mountaineers, 2005) deals with the topic in great detail; the fifth edition of James A. Wilkerson's edited collection *Medicine for Mountaineering & Other Wilderness Activities* (Seattle: The Mountaineers, 2001) discusses other potential problems as well.

HYPOTHERMIA

Hypothermia is a dangerously quick loss of body heat, most common in cold and damp weather at high altitudes or high latitudes—be particularly careful in areas with major temperature changes between day and night, or sun and shade. Symptoms include shivering, disorientation, loss of motor functions, skin numbness, and physical exhaustion. The best remedy is warmth, shelter, and food; unlike cottons, woolen clothing retains warmth even when wet. Avoid falling asleep; in truly hazardous conditions, it's possible you will not regain consciousness. Carry drinking water and high-energy snacks.

SUNBURN

Since Buenos Aires and vicinity lie within temperate latitudes comparable to those in the northern hemisphere, sunburn is not quite the problem it is in subtropical northern Argentina, where nearly vertical solar rays are far more intense. In southernmost Patagonia and Tierra del Fuego, ozone-destroying aerosols have increased the entry of ultraviolet radiation and caused skin problems for people and even for livestock like cattle and sheep.

Still, Argentine sun worshippers put themselves at risk whenever the sun breaks through the clouds. If you dress for the beach, use a heavy sunblock; on city streets, walk in the shade whenever possible.

SEXUALLY TRANSMITTED DISEASES

While AIDS (SIDA in Spanish) is the most lethal of sexually transmitted diseases (STDs) and gets the most press, other STDs are far more prevalent and also serious if left untreated. All are spread by unprotected sexual conduct; use of latex condoms reduces the possibility of contracting sexually transmitted diseases, but does not eliminate it.

Most STDs, including gonorrhea, chlamydia, and syphilis, are treatable with antibiotics, but some strains have developed immunity to penicillin and alternative treatments. If taking antibiotics, complete the prescribed course, since an interrupted treatment may not kill the infection and could even help it develop immunity.

The most common STD is **gonorrhea**, characterized by a burning sensation during urination, and penile or vaginal discharge; it may cause infertility. **Chlamydia** has milder symptoms but similar complications. **Syphilis,** the only major New World disease to spread to Europe after the Spanish invasion, begins with ulcer and rash symptoms that soon disappear; long-term complications, however, can include cardiovascular problems and even mental derangement.

Herpes, a virus causing small but irritating genital ulcers, has no effective treatment. It is likely to recur, spreads easily when active, and can contribute to cervical cancer. **Hepatitis B,** though not exclusively an STD, can spread through the mixing of bodily fluids such as saliva, semen, and menstrual and vaginal secretions. It can also spread through unsanitary medical procedures, inadequately sterilized or shared syringes, during body piercing, and under similar circumstances. Like hepatitis A it can lead to liver damage but is more serious; vaccination is advisable for high-risk individuals, but it's expensive.

HIV/AIDS

As in most countries, HIV/AIDS is an issue of increasing concern. According to official statistics, there are about 120,000 AIDS and HIV-infected individuals, but fears are that the figure may be higher—many carriers are probably unaware they are infected. There are about 7,000 AIDS-related fatalities in Argentina yearly.

HIV/AIDS is not exclusively a sexually transmitted disease (IV drug users can get it by sharing needles), but unprotected sexual activity is a common means of transmission; the use of latex condoms can reduce the possibility of infection.

The health ministry's **Línea SIDA** (tel. 0800/333-3444) provides toll-free over the phone AIDS and HIV information. The **Fundación Cooperación, Información y Ayuda al Enfermo de SIDA** (Coinsida, Finocchieto 1263, Constitución, tel. 011/4304-6664) is a support organization.

LOCAL DOCTORS

Top-quality medical services, with the latest technology, are readily available in Buenos Aires. Foreign embassies sometimes maintain lists of English-speaking doctors, who may have overseas training and are numerous in the capital and other large cities. On the downside, devaluation has nearly tripled the cost of imported equipment in dollar terms.

PHARMACIES

Pharmacies serve an important public-health role, but also carry certain risks. Pharmacists may provide drugs on the basis of symptoms that they don't completely comprehend, especially if there's a language barrier; while the cumulative societal impact may be positive, individual recommendations may be erroneous.

Many medications available by prescription only in North America or Europe may be sold over the counter in Argentine pharmacies. Travelers should be cautious about self-medication even when such drugs are available; check expiration dates, as out-of-date drugs sometimes remain on the shelf.

In large cities and even some smaller towns, pharmacies remain open all night for emergency prescription service on a rotating basis. The *farmacia de turno* and its address will usually be posted in the windows of other pharmacies, or advertised in the newspaper.

CRIME

Though many Argentines believe assaults, rapes, homicide, and property crimes are increasing, Argentina is a safe country by most standards. Because *porteños* and other Argentines keep late hours, there are plenty of people on the street at most times, and rarely will you find yourself walking alone down a dark alleyway.

Still, certain precautions almost go without saying—most crimes are crimes of opportunity. Never leave luggage unattended, store valuables in a hotel safe, keep close watch on your belongings at sidewalk cafés, and carry a photocopy of your passport with the date of entry into the country. Leave valuable jewelry at home, keep conspicuous items such as photo and video cameras out of sight as much as possible, and do not carry large amounts of cash (money belts or leg pouches are good alternatives for hiding cash). Do not presume that any area is totally secure.

If you should be accosted by anyone with a firearm or other potentially lethal weapon, do not resist. While guns are uncommon—knives are the weapon of choice—and truly violent crime against tourists is unusual, misjudgments can be lethal. Certain barrios are more crime-prone than others.

Most common is the crime of distraction, in which an individual bumps into the victim and spills a substance like ice cream or mustard; while the perpetrator apologizes profusely, his or her accomplice surreptitiously lifts items of value. Pickpocketing is also common on crowded public transportation; carry wallets and other valuable items in a front trouser pocket or, even better, an interior jacket pocket.

Information and Services

MONEY

While traveling in Argentina, it makes sense to have a variety of money alternatives. International credit cards are widely accepted, and foreign ATM cards work almost everywhere. Because ATMs are open 24 hours, many visitors prefer this alternative, but economic instability and occasional regulations that limit cash withdrawals for Argentines have made Argentine ATMs iffy at times; carry a cash reserve in U.S. dollars (rather than euros; though the European currency is gaining credibility, it's not an everyday item, especially outside Buenos Aires). Argentine ATMs have recently imposed fees (about US$4) on each withdrawal, so it pays to make fewer withdrawals of larger amounts.

Travelers checks may be the safest way to carry money, since they're refundable in case of loss or theft, but changing them outside Buenos Aires can be a frustrating experience even when stability reigns.

If carrying an emergency cash reserve, use an inconspicuous leg pouch or money belt—not the bulky kind that fits around the waist, which thieves or robbers easily recognize, but a zippered leather belt that looks like any other.

Currency

Throughout the 1990s, money was a simple matter. The Argentine peso (Ar$) was at par with the U.S. dollar, which circulated almost interchangeably alongside it, but the economic collapse of late 2001 has complicated matters.

Many merchants still accept cash dollars, but exchange rates vary and any change will come in pesos.

Banknotes exist in denominations of 2, 5, 10, 20, 50, and 100 pesos. Coins exist in denominations of 1, 5, 10, 25, and 50 centavos, and one peso; one-centavo coins have nearly disappeared and most businesses generally round off prices to the nearest 5 or 10 centavos.

Counterfeiting of both U.S. and foreign currency appears to be increasing. Merchants will often refuse a U.S. banknote with the smallest tear or writing on it; at the same that they will accept any peso note that is not flagrantly *trucho* (bogus). On any Argentine banknote, look for the conspicuous watermark with the initials of the historical figure depicted on it— JSM for José de San Martín on the five-peso note, for instance.

Exchange Rates

Following the early-2002 debt default, caretaker president Eduardo Duhalde devalued the peso from 1 to 1.4 per dollar, but when that proved unsustainable, he soon floated the currency. By midyear it had fallen to 3.5 to the dollar before stabilizing; by early 2004 it had recovered to the 2.8–2.9 range, but it's now about 3.8 per dollar.

For the most up-to-date exchange rates, consult the business section of your daily newspaper or an online currency converter such as www.oanda.com. The exchange rate is front-page news on virtually every Argentine daily. The best sources on exchange-rate trends are the financial dailies *Ambito Financiero* and *Buenos Aires Económico*.

During the 1990s, when the peso was at par with the dollar and the two circulated side-by-side, changing money was a nonissue. The peso float of 2002, however, made banks and *casas de cambio* (exchange houses) relevant again.

ATMs, abundant and becoming universal except in a few remote areas, match the best bank rates and are accessible 24-7. Most ATMs, unfortunately, dispense large banknotes, often of Ar$100 and rarely smaller than Ar$50. One way around this problem is to punch in an odd amount, such as Ar$790, in order to ensure getting some smaller notes.

Travelers Checks and Refunds

Despite their safeguards, travelers checks have drawbacks here. In addition to the time-consuming bureaucracy of changing them at banks and exchange houses, they often carry a penalty in terms of commission— up to 3 percent or even more in some cases. Businesses other than exchange houses rarely accept them under any circumstances and, in out-of-the-way places, nobody will. Travelers checks, unfortunately, should be a last-resort means of carrying and changing money here; cash (despite the risks) and ATM cards are better options.

Bank Transfers

Many Argentine exchange houses, post offices, and other businesses are affiliated with Western Union, making it relatively straightforward to send or receive money from overseas. For a list of Western Union affiliates in Argentina, visit the company's website (www. westernunion.com). The American Express Money Gram is another alternative; Amex has a large headquarters in Retiro, Buenos Aires, and affiliates throughout the country.

In an emergency, it's possible to forward money to U.S. citizens via the U.S. embassy in Buenos Aires by establishing a Department of State trust account through its **Overseas Citizens Services** (Washington, D.C., tel. 202/647-5225); there is a US$20 service charge for setting up the account. It is possible to arrange this as a wire or overnight mail transfer through Western Union (tel. 800/325-6000 in the U.S.); for details, visit the State Department's website (www.travel.state.gov).

Credit and Debit Cards

Credit cards have been common currency for many years, and in the aftermath of the 2002 peso crisis, when Argentines could not withdraw their savings, their use became even more widespread. Visa and MasterCard are most widely accepted, but there are inconsistencies—a significant number of businesses prefer American Express, sometimes to the exclusion of the others, or even Diner's Club. Debit cards are also widely accepted, at least those with Visa or MasterCard affiliation, but some automatic readers consider them credit cards (making them impossible to use at places that do not accept credit cards).

There are possible drawbacks to using credit cards. During the 1990s boom years, Argentine merchants generally refrained from the *recargo,* a surcharge on credit card purchases, because of slow bank payments; many have reinstituted the *recargo,* which can be up to 10 percent. Note that hotels in particular may offer discounts for payments in cash.

Fluctuating exchange rates may affect the charge that eventually appears on your overseas account. If the rate has changed in the interim between your payment in Buenos Aires and its posting to the home account, it may be either greater or smaller in terms of dollars (or other foreign currency), depending on the peso's performance.

Note that, in general, *propinas* (gratuities) may *not* be added to charged restaurant meals. Keep some cash, either dollars or pesos, for tips.

To deal with lost or stolen cards, the major international credit card companies have Buenos Aires representatives: **American Express** (Arenales 707, Retiro, tel. 011/4310-3000), **Diner's Club** (tel. 0800/444-6464), **MasterCard** (0800/555-0507), and **Visa** (Avenida Corrientes 1437, 3rd floor, tel. 011/4379-3333).

Costs

For most of the 1990s, Argentina was South America's most expensive country, so much so that even North Americans and Europeans cringed at the cost. Wealthy Argentines, meanwhile, partied in Miami, Madrid, Rome, and other "inexpensive" destinations.

This anomaly was a function of then economy minister Domingo Cavallo's "convertibility" exchange-rate policy, which reduced previous hyperinflation to near zero. It also froze prices at a relatively high but unsustainable level, however, that eventually made Argentine exports noncompetitive and contributed to the late-2001 default.

After the 2002 peso float, Argentina became a bargain for visitors from hard-currency countries. Though the peso has solidified since then—some even argue that it's undervalued—travel remains inexpensive by global standards. Much depends on the traveler's expectations, though; there are suitable services for everyone from bare-bones budget backpackers to pampered international business travelers. Budget travelers will still find hostel or hotel rooms for US$10 pp or so, and some excellent values for only a little more money. Prices have rebounded at hotels and resorts of international stature, such as the Hyatt and Sheraton chains and their local equivalents, which had to lower rates during the crisis.

Likewise, meals range from a few dollars or less at the simplest *comedores,* but restaurants with sophisticated international cuisine can charge a lot more; even the latter, though, often serve moderately priced lunchtime specials.

As of press time, true shoestringers could still get along on US$25 per day or conceivably less for accommodations and food. For US$50 or so per day it's possible to live comfortably and eat a bit better, but a budget over US$100 per day is far from extravagant. It's worth adding that economic volatility—hyperinflation was a recurrent phenomenon in the late 20th century—makes it impossible to guarantee that prices will not rise.

Taxes

Argentina imposes a 21 percent *impuesto de valor agregado* (IVA, value-added tax or VAT) on all goods and services, though this is normally included in the advertised price; if in doubt, ask *¿Incluye los impuestos?* Tax evasion is a national sport, though, and hotel owners often ignore the tax for cash payments.

Tourists, however, may request IVA refunds for purchases of Argentine products valued more than about US$25 from shops that display a "Global Refund" decal on their windows. Always double-check, however, that the decal is not out of date.

When making any such purchase, request an invoice and other appropriate forms. Then, on leaving the country, present these forms to Argentine customs; customs will then authorize payment to be cashed at Banco de la Nación branches at the main international airport at Ezeiza, Aeroparque Jorge Newbery (for flights to neighboring countries), or at Dársena Norte (for ferries to Uruguay). Refunds can also be assigned to your credit card..

At smaller border crossings, however, do not expect officials to be prepared to deal with tax refunds. Some crossings do not even have separate customs officials, but rather are staffed by the Gendarmería (Border Guards), a branch of the armed forces.

Tipping

In restaurants with table service, a 10 percent gratuity is customary, but in smaller family-run eateries the practice is rare. Taxi drivers are customarily not tipped, but rounding off the fare to the next-highest convenient number is appropriate. Where there is no meter, this is not an issue.

Bargaining

Bargaining is not the way of life in Argentina that it is in some Latin American countries, but in flea or crafts markets the vendor may start at a higher price than he or she expects to receive—avoid insultingly low offers or such a high offer that the vendor will think you a fool. Depending on your language and bargaining skills, you should be able to achieve a compromise that satisfies everybody.

Even in some upscale Buenos Aires shops, prices for items like leather jackets may be open to negotiation.

Student Discounts

Student discounts are relatively few, and prices are so low for most services that it's rarely worth arguing the point. Students, though, may arrange discount international airfares.

COMMUNICATIONS
Postal Services

Correo Argentino, the Argentine post office, is more reliable than in the past, but it has once again reverted to state control. Domestic services remain generally cheap, international services more expensive. Major international couriers provide fast, reliable services at premium prices.

General delivery at Argentine post offices is *lista de correos*, literally a list arranged in alphabetical order. There is a small charge for each item addressed to you.

By custom, the number follows rather than precedes the street name; instead of "1343 Washington Avenue," for example, a comparable Argentine address would read "Avenida Callao 272." Argentines and other Spanish speakers normally omit the word *calle* (street) from addresses; where an English speaker might write "499 Jones Street," an Argentine would simply use "Tucumán 272," for example. It is not unusual for addresses to lack a number, as indicated by *s/n* (*sin número*), especially in small provincial towns.

Telephone and Fax

Argentina has two major telephone companies, **Telecom** (north of Avenida Córdoba in Buenos Aires) and **Telefónica** (south of Avenida Córdoba). The country code is 54; the *característica* (area code) for the Capital Federal and Gran Buenos Aires is 011, but there is a bewildering number of area codes for individual cities, smaller cities and towns, and rural areas. All telephone numbers in the Capital Federal and Gran Buenos Aires have eight digits, while those in other provincial cities and rural areas vary. When calling out of the area code, it's necessary to dial zero first. In addition, certain toll-free and other specialty numbers have six or seven digits with a three-digit prefix.

Cellular phone numbers in Argentina are all prefixed by 15. Some landlines are blocked from calling cell phones directly, but phone cards may be used for such calls.

Public telephones are abundant; some operate with coins only, but most also accept rechargeable-account cards. The basic local phone rate is Ar$0.25 (about US$0.10) for five minutes or so; domestic long-distance is considerably more expensive. Phone cards are convenient for in-country calls but less useful for more-expensive overseas calls.

For long distance and overseas calls, as well as for fax services, it's simplest to use *locutorios* (call centers), which are abundant in both Buenos Aires and the provinces. Prices are increasingly competitive, and usually much cheaper than placing *cobro revertido* (collect) or *tarjeta de crédito* (credit card) calls to the United States or any other country. Calls are more expensive during peak hours, 8 A.M.–8 P.M. weekdays and 8 A.M.–1 P.M. Saturday.

It's also possible to make home-country credit card calls through overseas operators.

Travelers interested in having a **cell phone** while in Argentina will find that opening an account without a permanent Argentine address is something of a nuisance, but it's easy to purchase a rechargeable prepaid phone (though calls are more expensive than on a plan). Some upscale hotels include cell phones in their rates, but rentals are available through **Nolitel** (Ricardo Rojas 401, 11th floor, Retiro, Buenos Aires, tel. 011/4311-3500, www.nolitelgroup. com.ar).

Internet Access

In the last few years, public Internet access has become both abundant and so cheap that, if price trends continue, providers will soon be paying customers to use their services. Rarely does access cost more than US$1 per hour, and it's often even cheaper. Many *locutorios* offer access, but there are also numerous Internet cafés, and Wi-Fi is also becoming widespread.

MEDIA
Newspapers

Historically, freedom of the press has been tenuous, as Argentine governments have controlled the supply of newsprint and withheld official advertising from newspapers and magazines that have published items not to their liking. Nevertheless, since the 1976–1983 dictatorship ended, the trend has been largely positive for liberty of expression. Many newspapers and periodicals mentioned below have websites.

Buenos Aires papers, some to a greater degree than others, are also national papers sold widely throughout the provinces. The middle-of-the-road tabloid *Clarín,* the Spanish-speaking world's largest-circulation daily, sells about 340,000 copies weekdays and nearly twice that on Sundays, but its circulation is more sensitive to hard economic times than papers with a steadier niche clientele. Part of a consortium that includes TV and radio outlets, it also publishes *¡Ole!,* a sports daily.

According to Anglo-Argentine journalist Andrew Graham-Yooll, until your obituary appears in *La Nación,* you're not really dead— a comment that reflects the social standing of the capital's most venerable (1870) daily. With a circulation of about 150,000—a quarter million on Sundays when it has an exceptional cultural section—the center-right paper was the creation of Bartolomé Mitre, who later became president.

Página 12 is the tabloid voice of Argentina's intellectual left, and while its outspokenness is admirable, it would benefit from more rigorous editing—many articles are far too long and err on the side of hyperanalysis. Since the election of President Néstor Kirchner and his wife and successor Cristina Kirchner, it has abdicated much of its critical approach.

As *Página 12* has become more establishmentarian, the new weekly *Perfil* (www.perfil. com, circulation about 55,000) has assumed the mantle of Argentina's most aggressively investigative national newspaper.

The capital has three financial newspapers, which publish weekdays only: the morning *Ambito Financiero,* which also publishes an outstanding arts and entertainment section; the afternoon *El Cronista;* and *Buenos Aires Económico.*

With a circulation of only about 12,000, the *Buenos Aires Herald* is an English-language daily whose niche market correlates highly with hotel occupancy. It stresses commerce and finance, but also produces intelligent analyses of political and economic developments; its thicker Sunday edition relies on material from the *Washington Post, Bloomberg News,* and other international sources, and includes a locally published version of *Newsweek.*

The German-language *Argentinisches Tageblatt* (www.tageblatt.com.ar) began as a daily in 1889 but is now a Saturday weekly.

Magazines and Newsletters

Noticias (www.noticias.uol.com.ar) is the Argentine counterpart to English-language weeklies such as *Time* and *Newsweek. Veintitres* (www.veintitres.com) is more critical and innovative.

Radio and Television

What was once a state broadcast monopoly is now far more diverse, thanks to privatization and the advent of cable, but conglomerates like the Clarín and El Cronista groups control much of the content. Both radio and TV tend to stress entertainment at the expense of journalism.

Radio Rivadavia, Argentina's most popular station (AM 630, www.rivadavia.com.ar), plays popular music and also hosts talk programs. Radio Mitre (AM 790, www.radiomitre.com.ar) is the voice of the Clarín group. Buenos Aires's FM Tango 92.7 (www.la2x4.gov.ar) plays all tango, all the time, while Radio Folclorísimo (AM 1410, www.radiofolclorisimo.com.ar) plays folk music 24-7.

Clarín and El Cronista also control TV stations and some cable service (where overseas media like CNN, ESPN, BBC, Deutsche Welle, and others are available). TV news coverage, though, can be surprisingly deep.

MAPS AND TOURIST INFORMATION
Maps

The **Automóvil Club Argentino** (ACA, Argentine Automobile Club, Avenida del Libertador 1850, Palermo, tel. 011/4808-4000, www.aca.org.ar) publishes the most comprehensive series of highway maps (including major city plans) of all Argentine provinces. Members of overseas affiliate automobile clubs like the AAA in the United States and the AA in Britain can buy these maps at discount prices. ACA has offices in all provincial capitals and many smaller cities as well.

For official topographic maps, visit the **Instituto Geográfico Militar** (Avenida Cabildo 301, Palermo, tel. 011/4576-5576, www.igm.gov.ar). The growing series of topographical maps by Bariloche-based **Pixmap** (tel. 02944/15-642152, www.macarenaperezcorrea.com) are pretty much the best available for recreation-oriented visitors.

Tourist Offices

The **Secretaría Nacional de Turismo** (www.turismo.gov.ar), the national tourism service, has its main office in Buenos Aires, but every province also maintains a tourist information representative in the capital.

Each province also operates an information office in its own capital, and often in specific tourist destinations as well. Almost every other locality has its own tourist office—even in very small towns; these usually keep long summer hours but may be limited the rest of the year.

FILM AND PHOTOGRAPHY

For those who still use color print film, it is still available; color slide film much less so. As film tends to be cheaper in North America and Europe, it's best to bring as much as possible. If purchasing film in Argentina, check the expiration date, especially in out-of-the-way places. In the capital and larger tourist centers, competent print-film processing is readily available and moderately priced, but it's better to hold slide film until returning to your home country if possible (but store it under cool, dark, and dry conditions).

Environmental conditions can affect the quality of your shots and the type of film you should use. Bright sun can wash out photographs; in these circumstances, it's best to use a relatively slow film, around ASA 64 or 100, and a polarizing filter to reduce glare. A polarizing filter also improves contrast, dramatizing the sky and clouds, but can result in a dark foreground.

WEIGHTS AND MEASURES
Time

Argentina is three hours behind GMT for most of the year, and does not observe daylight savings (summer time). When the U.S. Eastern Time Zone is on daylight savings (during the Northern Hemisphere summer) and Argentina is on standard time, Buenos Aires is one hour ahead of New York; the rest of the year, there is a two-hour difference.

Electricity

Throughout the country, nearly all outlets are 220 volts, 50 cycles, so converters are necessary for North American appliances like computers and electric razors (except for dual-voltage appliances). Traditional plugs have two rounded prongs, but more recent ones have three flat blades that form, roughly, an isosceles triangle; cheap adapters are widely available.

Adequately powered converters, though, are hard to find, so it's better to bring one from overseas.

Measurements

The metric system is official, but this doesn't completely eliminate the variety of vernacular measures in everyday life. Rural folk often use the Spanish *legua* (league) of about five kilometers as a measure of distance, and the *quintal* of 46 kilos is also widely used, especially in wholesale markets and agricultural statistics.

RESOURCES

Glossary

acequia irrigation canal, especially in the Cuyo provinces

aduana customs

aduana paralela "parallel customs"; corrupt customs officials

agua de la canilla tap water; in adjacent Chile, this is *agua de la llave*

albergue juvenil youth hostel

albergue transitorio a by-the-hour-hotel, frequently used by young and not-so-young couples in search of privacy

algarrobos desert tree, related to mesquite

altiplano high steppe of northern Argentine Andes; synonymous with puna

andén platform at a train station or bus terminal

anexo telephone extension

argentinidad nebulous notion of Argentine nationalism, often associated with the gaucho

arrabales geographically and socially peripheral parts of Buenos Aires, identified with immigrants and the rise of the tango

autopista freeway

avenida avenue

balneario bathing or beach resort

bandoneón accordion-like instrument in tango music

baño compartido shared bath (at hotel or other accommodations)

baño general shared or general bath (at hotel or other accommodations)

baño privado private bath

barrancas natural levee on the original banks of the Río de Plata, now far inland in San Telmo, Belgrano, and other parts of Buenos Aires because of continual landfill

barras bravas "soccer hooligans," violent gangs affiliated with soccer teams

barrio borough or neighborhood

bis used to modify addresses, bus routes, and the like that have the same number; Paseo 110 and Paseo 110 bis, for example

boleadoras rounded stones, tied together with leather thong, used for hunting by Pampas and Patagonian Indians; also known as *bolas*

boliche dance club

bronca a singularly *porteño* combination of aggravation and frustration; there is no precise English equivalent, the closest being "wrath" or, in Britain, "aggro"

cabildo colonial governing council

cabotaje full-fare domestic airline ticket

cacique indigenous chief or headman

cajero automático automated teller machine (ATM)

calle street

camarote sleeper berth on a train

camioneta pickup truck

campo countryside

candombe music and dance of Afro-Argentine *porteños*, of whom few remain

Carabinero Chilean policeman

característica telephone area code

carne beef; other meats are *carne blanca* ("white meat")

carretera highway

cartelera discount ticket agency

cartonero a scavenger who picks recyclables from the garbage on Buenos Aires streets; synonymous with *ciruja* (literally, "surgeon")

casa chorizo "sausage house," a narrow residence on a deep lot

casa de cambio official money-exchange facility, often just "cambio"

casco "big house" of an *estancia*

casilla post office box

caudillo in early independence times, a provincial warlord, though the term is often used for populist leaders such as Juan Domingo Perón

centolla king crab

cerro hill

chacra intensely cultivated agricultural plot

chamamé accordion-based folk music of northeastern Argentine littoral

charqui jerked meat, normally llama, in Andean northwest

chopp draft beer

cobro revertido collect or reverse-charge telephone call

coche cama spacious, fully reclining, long-distance bus seat

cocoliche pidgin blend of Italian and Spanish spoken by southern European immigrants

coima bribe

colectivo a city bus

comedor simple eatery or dining room

confitería a restaurant/café with a menu of *minutas* (short orders)

conventillo tenement, often an abandoned mansion occupied by squatters

cospel bus token, still used in some provincial cities (pl. *cospeles*)

costanera any road along a seashore, lakeshore, or riverside

criollo in colonial times, an Argentine-born Spaniard; in the present, normally a descriptive term meaning "traditionally" Argentine

desaparecido "disappeared one," victim of the 1976-1983 dictatorship

descamisados "shirtless ones," working-class adherents of Juan and Evita Perón

día de campo "day in the countryside" on a tourist *estancia*

dique deep water basin dredged in Buenos Aires harbor

doble tracción four-wheel drive, also known as *cuatro por cuatro* (the latter written as "4X4")

edificio building

embalsado "floating island" in the Iberá marshes

encomienda in colonial times, a grant of Indian labor within a given geographical area; the *encomendero* (the *encomienda*'s holder) incurred the reciprocal obligation to provide instruction in the Spanish language and Catholic religion, though such obligations were rarely honored

entrerriano resident of Entre Ríos province

escrache public demonstration, originally identifying human-rights violators at their residences, but since extended to perceived corrupt officials and institutions

estancia cattle or sheep ranch controlling large extents of land, often with an absentee owner, dominant manager, and resident employees

estanciero owner of an *estancia*

estatuas vivas "living statues," mimes in touristed areas of Buenos Aires

estero estuary

facón gaucho knife

farmacia de turno pharmacy open all night for emergencies, on a rotating basis

feria artisans market

ficha token, formerly used on Buenos Aires subway and still used on city buses in some parts of the country

filete traditional calligraphic art of *porteño* sign painters

fileteador *filete* artist

gasoil diesel fuel

gauchesco adjective describing romantic art or literature about, as opposed to by, gauchos

golfo gulf

golpe de estado coup d'état

Gran Aldea "great village," Buenos Aires prior to 20th-century immigration

heladería ice creamery

hipódromo horserace track

hospedaje family-run lodging

indígena indigenous person

indigenista adjective describing romantically pro-Indian literature, music, and art

infracción traffic violation

ingenio industrial sugar mill of northwestern Argentina

intendencia park headquarters

isla island

islote islet
istmo isthmus
IVA *impuesto de valor agregado*, or value added tax (VAT)
lago lake
laguna lagoon
latifundio large landholding, usually an *estancia*
local numbered office or locale, at a given street address
locutorio telephone call center
lunfardo *porteño* street slang, often inappropriate in formal situations
machista male chauvinist
malevo street bully
media pensión half board, at hotel or guesthouse
menú menu; also, a fixed-price meal
meseta Patagonian steppe
mestizo individual of mixed indigenous and Spanish ancestry
microcentro downtown of Buenos Aires or other large cities
Migraciones Immigration department
milonga informal neighborhood dance club, which often includes tango as a participant rather than spectator activity
minuta a short-order meal like pasta
mirador overlook or viewpoint
mozo term of address for a restaurant waiter; note that in neighboring Chile, this would be extremely rude
museo museum
ñoqui "ghost employee," collecting a state salary despite performing little or no work
oligarquía terrateniente traditional land-owning "aristocracy" of the pampas
onces Chilean afternoon tea
palacete mansion
pampa broad, flat expanse in and around Buenos Aires Province
pampero southwesterly cold front on the pampas
parada bus stop
parque nacional national park
partido administrative subdivision of an Argentine province, equivalent to a county
pasarela catwalk in wet or marshy area (or at fashion show)

paseaperros professional dog walker
payador spontaneous gaucho singer
peaje toll booth
peatonal pedestrian mall
pensión family-run accommodation
pensión completa full board, at a hotel or guesthouse
picante spicy-hot; Argentines' tolerance for spicy food is low, however, and visitors may find foods labeled spicy relatively bland
pingüinera penguin colony
piquete protestors' roadblock
piquetero picketer, manning a roadblock
pirca pre-Columbian Andean fortress
piropo sexist remark, ranging from humorous and innocuous to truly vulgar; also, on *filete*, an aphorism
pisco grape brandy
playa beach
polideportivo sports club
porteño native or resident of Buenos Aires
propina tip, as at a restaurant
puente bridge
puerto port
Pullman first-class bus or train, with reclining seats and luggage storage underneath
pulpería general store, often the only retail outlet in a rural area
puna high steppe of northern Andes; synonymous with altiplano
Puntano native of San Luis Province
quebrada canyon
quincho roofed outdoor dining area
quinta country estate
ramal branch of a bus or rail line
rastra studded gaucho belt
recargo surcharge on credit card purchases
recova colonnade
reducción colonial settlement where missionaries concentrated indigenous population for catechization
refugio shelter, in a national park or other protected area
remise meterless radio taxi charging a fixed rate within a given zone
reserva nacional national reserve
residencial permanent budget accommodations, often also called hotel

restó fashionable, even pretentious, term for a restaurant

río river

rotisería delicatessen

ruca Mapuche plank house, with thatched roof

ruta route or highway

ruta nacional federal highway

ruta provincial provincial highway

saladero meat-salting plant of late-colonial and early-republican times

Semana Santa Holy Week, the last week of Lent and the week before Easter

s/n *sin número,* a street address without a number

sudestada cold wind out of the southeast

tango canción "tango song," with music and lyrics expressing nostalgia

tanguero tango dancer

tarifa mostrador hotel "rack rate," from which there are often discounts

tenedor libre literally "free fork"; an all-you-can-eat restaurant

toldo tent of animal skins, inhabited by mobile Pampas Indians in pre-Columbian times

trasnoche late-night cinema, often starting at 1 A.M. or later

trucho bogus

turco Argentine of Middle Eastern descent

ventanilla ticket window at bus terminal or train station

villa miseria urban shantytown

viveza criolla "artful deception," ranging from small-scale cheating to audacious chutzpah

voseo use of the second-person-singular pronoun *vos* and its distinct verb forms in Argentina, Uruguay, Paraguay, and some other countries

Yanqui Yankee, any North American (US citizen)

yungas subtropical cloud forest of northwestern Argentina

zafra sugar harvest of northwestern Argentina

ABBREVIATIONS

4WD four-wheel drive

ACA Automóvil Club Argentino

APN Administration de Parques Nacionales (National Parks Administration)

BA Buenos Aires

int. *interno,* like ext. (extension) in English

IVA *impuesto de valor agregado* (value-added tax)

HI Hostelling International

RN Ruta Nacional (National Highway)

RP Ruta Provincial (Provincial Highway)

Spanish Phrasebook

Spanish is Argentina's official language, but the stereotypical *porteño* intonation – equivalent to a Bronx accent in New York – is unmistakably different from any other variant. Argentine Spanish in general is distinctive, often Italian-inflected, most notable for pronouncing the "ll" diphthong and "y" as "zh." "Llegar" (to arrive), for example, is pronounced "zhe-gar," while "yo" (I) is pronounced "zho."

Another distinguishing feature is use of the familiar pronoun "vos" instead of "tú." Verb forms of the *voseo* differ from those of the *tuteo,* although Argentines will always understand speakers who use "tú." In the western Cuyo provinces, it's not unusual to hear the *tuteo.*

Visitors spending any length of time in Buenos Aires, especially students and businesspeople, should look for Tino Rodríguez's *Primer Diccionario de Sinónimos del Lunfardo* (Buenos Aires: Editorial Atlántida, 1987), which defines *porteño* street slang – some of whose usage requires *great* caution for those unaware of their every meaning.

PRONUNCIATION GUIDE

Spanish is a more phonetic language than English, but there are still occasional variations in pronunciation, especially in Argentina.

Consonants

c as c in "cat," before a, o, or u; like s before e or i

d as d in "dog," except between vowels, then like th in "that"

g before e or i, like the ch in Scottish "loch"; elsewhere like g in "get"

h always silent

j like the English h in "hotel," but stronger

ll like the z in "azure"

ñ like the ni in "onion"

r always pronounced as strong r

rr trilled r

v similar to the b in "boy" (not as English v)

y like ll, it sounds like the z in "azure." When standing alone, it's pronounced like the e in "me."

z like s in "same"

b, f, k, l, m, n, p, q, s, t, w, x as in English

Vowels

a as in "father," but shorter

e as in "hen"

i as in "machine"

o as in "phone"

u usually as in "rule"; when it follows a q the u is silent; when it follows an h or g, it's pronounced like w, except when it comes between g and e or i, when it's also silent (unless it has an umlaut, ü, when it is again pronounced as English w)

Stress

Native English speakers frequently make pronunciation errors by ignoring stress; all Spanish vowels – a, e, i, o, and u – may carry accents that determine which syllable gets emphasis. Often, stress seems unnatural to nonnative speakers – the surname Chávez, for instance, is stressed on the first syllable – but your failure to observe this rule may confuse native speakers.

NUMBERS

zero cero
one uno (masculine)
one una (feminine)
two dos
three tres
four cuatro
five cinco
six seis
seven siete
eight ocho
nine nueve
10 diez
11 once
12 doce
13 trece
14 catorce
15 quince
16 diez y seis
17 diez y siete
18 diez y ocho
19 diez y nueve
20 veinte
21 veinte y uno
30 treinta
40 cuarenta
50 cincuenta
60 sesenta
70 setenta
80 ochenta
90 noventa
100 cien
101 ciento y uno
200 doscientos
1,000 mil
10,000 diez mil
1,000,000 un millón

DAYS OF THE WEEK

Sunday domingo
Monday lunes
Tuesday martes
Wednesday miércoles
Thursday jueves
Friday viernes
Saturday sábado

TIME

While Argentines normally use the 12-hour clock (A.M. and P.M.), they sometimes use the 24-hour clock, usually associated with plane or bus schedules. Under the 24-hour clock, for example, las diez de la noche (10 P.M.) would be las 22 horas (2200 hours).

What time is it? *¿Qué hora es?*
It's one o'clock. *Es la una.*
It's two o'clock. *Son las dos.*
at two o'clock *A las dos*
It's 10 to three. *Son las tres menos diez.*
It's 10 past three. *Son las tres y diez.*
It's three fifteen. *Son las tres y cuarto.*
It's two forty five. *Son las tres menos cuarto.*
It's two thirty. *Son las dos y media.*
It's six A.M. *Son las seis de la mañana.*
It's six P.M. *Son las seis de la tarde.*
It's 10 P.M. *Son las diez de la noche.*
today *hoy*
tomorrow *mañana*
morning *la mañana*
tomorrow morning *mañana por la mañana*
yesterday *ayer*
week *la semana*
month *mes*
year *año*
last night *anoche*
the next day *el día siguiente*

BASIC AND COURTEOUS EXPRESSIONS

Argentines and other Spanish-speaking people consider formalities important. Whenever approaching anyone for information or some other reason, use the appropriate salutation good morning, good evening, etc. Standing alone, the greeting *hola* (hello) can sound brusque.

Most of the words below are fairly standard, common to all Spanish-speaking countries. Many, however, have more idiomatic Argentine equivalents; refer to the Glossary for these.

Hello. *Hola.*
Good morning. *Buenos días.*
Good afternoon. *Buenas tardes.*
Good evening. *Buenas noches.*
How are you? *¿Cómo está?*
Fine. *Muy bien.*
And you? *¿Y usted?*
So-so. *Más o menos.*
Thank you. *Gracias.*
Thank you very much. *Muchas gracias.*
You're very kind. *Muy amable.*
You're welcome. *De nada* (literally, "It's nothing.")

yes *sí*
no *no*
I don't know. *No sé.*
It's fine; OK. *Está bien.*
good; OK *Bueno*
please *por favor*
Pleased to meet you. *Mucho gusto.*
Excuse me (physical). *Perdóneme.*
Excuse me (speech). *Discúlpeme.*
I'm sorry. *Lo siento.*
goodbye *adiós, chau*
See you later. *Hasta luego* (literally, "until later").
more *más*
less *menos*
better *mejor*
much, a lot *mucho*
a little *un poco*
large *grande*
small *pequeño, chico*
quick, fast *rápido*
slowly *despacio*
bad *malo*
difficult *difícil*
easy *fácil*
He/She/It is gone; as in "She left," "He's gone." *Ya se fue.*
I don't speak Spanish well. *No hablo bien el español.*
I don't understand. *No entiendo.*
How do you say...in Spanish? *¿Cómo se dice...en español?*
Do you understand English? *¿Entiende el inglés?*
Is English spoken here? (Does anyone here speak English?) *¿Se habla inglés aquí?*

TERMS OF ADDRESS

When in doubt, use the formal *usted* (you) as a form of address. If you wish to dispense with formality and feel that the desire is mutual, you can say *Me podés tutear* (you can call me "tu") even though Argentines use the slightly different verb forms that correlate with the familiar pronoun "vos."

I *yo*
you (formal) *usted*
you (familiar) *vos*

he/him *él*
she/her *ella*
we/us *nosotros*
you (plural) *ustedes*
they/them (all males or mixed gender) *ellos*
they/them (all females) *ellas*
Mr., sir *señor*
Mrs., madam *señora*
Miss, young lady *señorita*
wife *esposa*
husband *marido* or *esposo*
friend *amigo* (male), *amiga* (female)
sweetheart *novio* (male), *novia* (female)
son, daughter *hijo, hija*
brother, sister *hermano, hermana*
father, mother *padre, madre*
grandfather, grandmother *abuelo, abuela*

GETTING AROUND
Where is . . . ? *¿Dónde está . . . ?*
How far is it to . . . ? *¿A cuanto está . . . ?*
from...to . . . *de...a . . .*
highway *la carretera*
road *el camino*
street *la calle*
block *la cuadra*
kilometer *kilómetro*
north *norte*
south *sur*
west *oeste; poniente*
east *este; oriente*
straight ahead *derecho; adelante*
to the right *a la derecha*
to the left *a la izquierda*
bus stop *la parada*
bus terminal *terminal de buses*
airport *el aeropuerto*
launch *lancha*
dock *muelle*
I want a ticket to . . . *Quiero un pasaje a . . .*
I want to get off at . . . *Quiero bajar en . . .*
Here, please. *Aquí, por favor.*
Where is this bus going? *¿Adónde va este autobús?*
round-trip *ida y vuelta*
What do I owe? *¿Cuánto le debo?*

ACCOMMODATIONS
Is there a room? *¿Hay habitación?*
May I (we) see it? *¿Puedo (podemos) verla?*
What is the rate? *¿Cuál es el precio?*
Is that your best rate? *¿Es su mejor precio?*
Is there something cheaper? *¿Hay algo más económico?*
single room *un sencillo*
double room *un doble*
room for a couple *matrimonial*
key *llave*
with private bath *con baño privado*
with shared bath *con baño general; con baño compartido*
hot water *agua caliente*
cold water *agua fría*
shower *ducha*
towel *toalla*
soap *jabón*
toilet paper *papel higiénico*
air conditioning *aire acondicionado*
fan *ventilador*
blanket *frazada; manta*
sheets *sábanas*

FOOD
menu *la carta; el menú*
glass *vaso*
fork *tenedor*
knife *cuchillo*
spoon *cuchara*
napkin *servilleta*
soft drink *gaseosa*
coffee *café*
cream *crema*
tea *té*
sugar *azúcar*
drinking water *agua pura; agua potable*
bottled carbonated water *agua con gas*
bottled uncarbonated water *agua sin gas*
beer *cerveza*
wine *vino*
milk *leche*
juice *jugo*
eggs *huevos*
bread *pan*
watermelon *sandía*
banana *banana*

apple *manzana*
orange *naranja*
peach *durazno*
pineapple *ananá*
meat (without) *carne (sin)*
beef *carne de res*
chicken *pollo; gallina*
fish *pescado*
shellfish *mariscos*
shrimp *camarones*
fried *frito*
roasted *asado*
barbecued *a la parrilla*
breakfast *desayuno*
lunch *almuerzo*
dinner, or a late night snack *cena*
the check or bill *la cuenta*

MAKING PURCHASES

I need ... *Necesito...*
I want ... *Deseo... or Quiero...*
I would like...(more polite) *Quisiera...*
How much does it cost? *¿Cuánto cuesta?*

What's the exchange rate? *¿Cuál es el tipo de cambio?*
May I see ...? *¿Puedo ver...?*
this one *ésta/ésto*
expensive *caro*
cheap *barato*
cheaper *más barato*
too much *demasiado*

HEALTH

Help me please. *Ayúdeme por favor.*
I am ill. *Estoy enfermo.*
It hurts. *Me duele.*
pain *dolor*
fever *fiebre*
stomachache *dolor de estómago*
headache *dolor de cabeza*
vomiting *vomitar*
diarrhea *diarrhea*
drugstore *farmacia*
medicine *medicina*
pill, tablet *pastilla*
birth control pills *pastillas anticonceptivas*
condom *condón; preservativo*

Suggested Reading

ARCHAEOLOGY, ETHNOGRAPHY, AND ETHNOHISTORY

McEwan, Colin, Luis A. Borrero, and Alfredo Prieto, eds. *Patagonia: Natural History, Prehistory and Ethnography at the Uttermost End of the Earth.* Princeton, NJ: Princeton University Press, 1997. First published under the auspices of the British Museum, this is a collection of learned but accessible essays on topics ranging from Patagonia's natural environment to early human occupation, first encounters between Europeans and indigenes, the origins of the Patagonian "giants," and even Patagonian travel literature.

ENVIRONMENT AND NATURAL HISTORY

Hudson, William Henry. *The Bird Biographies of W. H. Hudson.* Santa Barbara, CA: Capra Press, 1988. A partial reprint of the romantic naturalist's detailed description of the birds he knew growing up in Buenos Aires Province, with illustrations.

GUIDEBOOKS AND TRAVELOGUES

Darwin, Charles. *Voyage of the Beagle* (many editions). Perhaps the greatest travel book ever written, Darwin's 19th-century narrative bursts with insights on the people, places, and even politics he saw while collecting the plants and animals that led to his revolutionary theories. The great scientist observed the city of Buenos Aires, the surrounding pampas and Patagonia, and met key figures in the country's history, including the dictator Rosas.

France, Miranda. *Bad Times in Buenos Aires.* Hopewell, NJ: Ecco Press, 1998. A timeless title, perhaps, but it refers to the author's sardonic analysis of her early 1990s residence in the Argentine capital.

Green, Toby. *Saddled with Darwin.* London: Phoenix, 1999. An audacious if uneven account by a young, talented writer of his attempt to retrace the hoof prints—not the footsteps—of Darwin's travels through Uruguay, Argentina, and Chile. Self-effacing but still serious, the author manages to compare Darwin's experience with his own, reflect on contemporary distortions of the great scientist's theories, and stay almost completely off the gringo trail.

Guevara, Ernesto. *The Motorcycle Diaries: A Journey around South America.* New York and London: Verso, 1995. Translated by Ann Wright, this is an account of an Argentine drifter's progress from Buenos Aires across the Andes and up the Chilean coast by motorcycle and, when it broke down, by any means necessary. The author is better known by his nickname, "Che," a common Argentine interjection.

Moreno, Francisco Pascasio. *Perito Moreno's Travel Journal: A Personal Reminiscence.* Buenos Aires: Elefante Blanco, 2002. Absorbing translation of the great Patagonian explorer's northern Patagonian letters and journals, including his thrilling escape down the Río Limay from his indigenous captors.

Naipaul, V. S. *The Return of Eva Perón.* New York: Knopf, 1980. The great but controversial British Nobel Prize–winning author's acerbic observations on Argentine society, in the context of his visit during the vicious 1976–1983 dictatorship.

Roosevelt, Theodore. *A Book Lover's Holiday in the Open.* New York: Scribner's, 1916. After retiring from politics, the still vigorous U.S. president undertook numerous overseas adventures; among other stories, this collection retells his crossing of the Andes from Chile into the lakes district of northern Argentine Patagonia, and his meeting with legends like Perito Moreno.

Symmes, Patrick. *Chasing Che: A Motorcycle Journey in Search of the Guevara Legend.* New York: Vintage, 2000. Symmes follows the tire marks of Che's legendary trip from Buenos Aires through Argentina and Chile in the early 1950s.

Willis, Bailey. *A Yanqui in Patagonia.* Palo Alto, CA: Stanford University Press, 1947. Out of print but well worth seeking, this U.S. geologist's memoir is a vivid account of the northern Patagonian frontier in the early 20th century. It's also fascinating for his assessment of the region's potential, and for his account of intrigues within the Argentine governments of the day.

Wilson, Jason. *Buenos Aires: A Cultural and Literary Companion.* New York: Interlink, 2000. Part of the "Cities of the Imagination" series, this is a breathlessly thorough summary of what *porteño,* other Argentine, and foreign authors have written about the capital. It's particularly good at providing a sense of what untranslated Argentine authors have written about the city.

GOVERNMENT AND POLITICS

Castañeda, Jorge G. *Utopia Unarmed: The Latin American Left After the Cold War.* New York: Knopf, 1993. A former academic and Mexican foreign minister makes Argentina the starting point in his analysis of the democratization of Latin America's revolutionary left, with a particularly good analysis of the Montoneros urban guerrilla movement.

HISTORY

Andrews, George Reid. *The Afro-Argentines of Buenos Aires, 1800–1900.* Madison, WI: University of Wisconsin Press, 1980. Path-breaking research on the so-called "disappearance" of the capital's Afro-Argentine community, which once made up nearly a third of its total population.

Dujovne Ortiz, Alicia. *Eva Perón.* New York: St. Martin's Press, 1996. Filled with controversial assertions, this nevertheless absorbing biography is most eloquent in describing the transformation of a poor provincial girl into a powerful international figure through relentless and bitterly ruthless ambition, blended with a genuine concern for the truly destitute. Shawn Fields's translation to English, unfortunately, is awkward.

Goñi, Uki. *The Real Odessa.* New York and London: Granta, 2002. A remarkable account of the controversial links between the Juan Perón government and the shadowy organization that spirited Nazi war criminals from Europe to Argentina. Employing a variety of archival sources on a topic that most often relies on rumor, Goñi implicates the Vatican and its Argentine branch as go-betweens in negotiations with the Nazi regime's remnants.

Nouzeilles, Gabriela, and Gabriela Montaldo, eds. *The Argentina Reader: History, Culture, Politics.* Durham, NC: Duke University Press, 2002. It's too big and heavy to carry along on the road, but this diverse collection of essays and extracts is an excellent introduction to the country through the eyes of Argentines, and visitors to Argentina, since colonial times.

Rock, David. *Argentina 1516–1987: From Spanish Colonization to the Falklands War and Alfonsín.* London: I. B. Taurus, 1987. A comprehensive narrative and analysis of Argentine history prior to Carlos Menem's presidency.

Scobie, James R. *Buenos Aires: From Plaza to Suburb, 1870–1910.* New York: Oxford University Press, 1974. A classic account of the city's explosive growth of the late 19th century, and the transition from "Gran Aldea" to "Paris of the South."

Shumway, Norman. *The Invention of Argentina.* Berkeley, CA: University of California Press, 1991. An intellectual history of Argentina's founding myths, and the degree to which elitist debate excluded entire sectors of society from participation and resulted in frequent ungovernability.

Slatta, Richard. *Cowboys of the Americas.* New Haven and London: Yale University Press, 1990. A spectacularly illustrated comparative analysis of New World horsemen, including both Argentine gauchos and Chilean *huasos.*

LITERATURE AND LITERARY CRITICISM

Fuentes, Carlos. *The Campaign.* New York: Farrar, Straus and Giroux, 1991. He's not an Argentine himself, but Mexico's great contemporary novelist has managed to express the epic contradictions of the independence era through the character of a criollo from Buenos Aires.

Gerchunoff, Alberto. *Jewish Gauchos of the Pampas.* Albuquerque, NM: University of New Mexico Press, 1998. Evocative vignettes of life in the Jewish agricultural colonies of Entre Ríos, some of them romanticized but others portraying violence and deceit on the frontier.

Martínez, Tomás Eloy. *The Perón Novel.* New York: Pantheon Books, 1988. Based on the author's own lengthy interviews with the exiled caudillo, for which fiction seemed the appropriate outlet. According to Jorge Castañeda, "Whether Perón ever actually uttered these words is in the last analysis irrelevant: he could have, he would have, and he probably did."

Martínez, Tomás Eloy. *Santa Evita.* New York: Knopf, 1996. One of Argentina's leading contemporary writers tackles the Evita myth in a fictionalized version of her postmortem odyssey from Argentina to Italy, Spain, and back to Buenos Aires.

Vásquez Montalbán, Manuel. *The Buenos Aires Quintet*. London: Serpent's Tail, 2003. In this seemingly disjointed but ultimately coherent and insightful novel, first published in 1997, the late Spanish journalist sent his fictional gourmet detective Pepe Carvalho to Buenos Aires to track down a returned Dirty War exile.

Wilson, Jason. *Traveler's Literary Companion: South & Central America, Including Mexico*. Lincolnwood, IL: Passport Books, 1995. An edited collection of excerpts from literature, including fiction, poetry, and essays, that illuminates aspects of the countries from the Río Grande to the tip of Tierra del Fuego, including Argentina and Chile.

Woodall, James. *Borges: A Life*. New York: Basic Books, 1997. An analytical—in the Freudian sense—biography of Argentina's most prominent literary figure. Originally appeared in Britain under the title *The Man in the Mirror of the Book* (London: Hodder & Stoughton, 1996).

Internet Resources

Aconcagua
www.aconcagua.com.ar
Clearinghouse for climbers and hikers on the highest peak in the Americas.

Administración de Parques Nacionales
www.parquesnacionales.gov.ar
Primary government agency in charge of national parks and other conservation areas.

Aerolíneas Argentinas
www.aerolineas.com.ar
Home page for Argentina's struggling flagship airline.

Aeropuertos Argentinos 2000
www.aa2000.com.ar
Private concessionaire operating most of Argentina's international and domestic airports, including Buenos Aires's Ezeiza and Aeroparque; in English and Spanish.

Ambitoweb
www.ambitoweb.com
Online version of *porteño* financial daily *Ambito Financiero*.

AmeriSpan
www.amerispan.com
Information on language instruction throughout the Americas, including Argentina.

Argentina Travel Net
www.argentinatravelnet.com
Portal for Argentine travel sites, though not nearly all the links are closely related to travel; in Spanish and English.

Argentine Wines
www.argentinewines.com
Close-to-comprehensive introduction to Argentine wines and wine regions; in Spanish with some English links.

Asociación Argentina de Albergues de la Juventud (AAAJ)
www.aaaj.org.ar
Argentine hostelling organization, with limited facilities throughout the country. Site in Spanish and French only.

Asociación de Fútbol Argentina
www.afa.org.ar
Argentina's professional soccer league; in English and Spanish.

Asociación Ornitológica del Plata
www.avesargentinas.org.ar
Buenos Aires–based bird-watching and conservation organization.

Automóvil Club Argentino (ACA)
www.aca.org.ar
Argentine automobile association, useful for both information and up-to-date road maps. Offers discounts for members of affiliated clubs, such as AAA in the United States and the AA in Britain.

Buenos Aires Herald
www.buenosairesherald.com
Improved online version of the capital's venerable English-language daily, though its full content is only available by subscription or, alternatively, after 2 P.M. Argentine time.

B y T Argentina
www.bytargentina.com
Short-term apartment rentals and other information on Buenos Aires; in English and Spanish.

Centers for Disease Control
www.cdc.gov
U.S. government page with travel health advisories.

CIA Factbook
www.cia.gov/library/publications/the-world-factbook/geos/ar.html
The notorious spooks perform at least one admirable public service in their annual encyclopedia of the world's countries, which appears complete online.

Clarín
www.clarin.com
Outstanding online version of the capital's tabloid daily, the Spanish-speaking world's largest-circulation newspaper.

Currency Converter
www.oanda.com
Present and historic exchange rate information.

Department of Health
www.doh.gov.uk
British government agency with country-by-country health advice.

Department of State
www.travel.state.gov
Travel information and advisories from the U.S. government; while it has useful material, its warnings are often exaggerated.

Feria del Libro
www.el-libro.com
Buenos Aires's heavily attended annual book fair.

Fondo Nacional de las Artes
www.fnartes.gov.ar
Official federal government site with information on performing arts, architecture, cinema, and related fields.

Fundación Vida Silvestre Argentina
www.vidasilvestre.org.ar
Nongovernmental wildlife and habitat advocates.

Greenpeace
www.greenpeace.org.ar
Argentine affiliate of the international conservation organization.

Hostelling International Argentina
www.hostels.org.ar
Argentine Hostelling International affiliate, with information on travel and activities throughout the country.

Instituto Geográfico Militar
www.igm.gov.ar
Military geographical institute, preparing and selling maps of the country.

Instituto Nacional de Estadísticas y Censos (INDEC)
www.indec.mecon.ar
Home page for the federal government statistical agency, but not always reliable because of political interference.

Interpatagonia
www.interpatagonia.com
Probably the most complete site for content and services on both the Argentine and Chilean sides of the Southern Cone's southernmost region.

La Nación
www.lanacion.com.ar
Major *porteño* daily, with an excellent Sunday cultural section.

La Plata
www.laplata.gov.ar
Portal of Buenos Aires Province's capital city.

Latin American Network Information Center (LANIC)
www.lanic.utexas.edu
Organized by the University of Texas, this site has a huge collection of quality links to Argentina and other Latin American countries.

Líneas Aéreas del Estado (LADE)
www.lade.com.ar
Commercial passenger arm of the Argentine air force.

Mercopress News Agency
www.falkland-malvinas.com
Montevideo-based Internet news agency covering politics and business in the Mercosur common market countries of Argentina, Brazil, Uruguay, and Paraguay, as well as Chile and the Falkland/Malvinas Islands; in English and Spanish.

Metrovías
www.metrovias.com.ar
Details on Buenos Aires's subway system.

Ministerio de Relaciones Exteriores
www.mrecic.gov.ar
Argentine foreign ministry, with information on visas and consulates; in English and Spanish.

Páginas Amarillas
www.paginasamarillas.com.ar
Yellow Pages for the entire country.

Página 12
www.pagina12.com
Outspoken left-of-center Buenos Aires daily, which has shifted from reporting toward opinion but features some of the country's best writers.

Secretaría Nacional de Turismo
www.turismo.gov.ar
National tourism authority, with information in Spanish and English.

Turismo Buenos Aires
www.bue.gov.ar/home
Official city tourist information in English and Portuguese as well as Spanish.

UkiNet
www.ukinet.com
A freelancer's human rights–oriented website, with an archive of his best work from Britain's *Guardian* and other sources.

U.S. Commercial Service
www.buyusainfo.net
U.S. Department of Commerce's summary of business climate and possibilities in Argentina and other foreign countries.

What's Up Buenos Aires
www.whatsupbuenosaires.com
Definitive online guide to the city's nightlife.

Index

List of Maps

www.moon.com

DESTINATIONS | ACTIVITIES | BLOGS | MAPS | BOOKS

MOON.COM is ready to help plan your next trip! Filled with fresh trip ideas and strategies, author interviews, informative travel blogs, a detailed map library, and descriptions of all the Moon guidebooks, Moon.com is all you need to get out and explore the world—or even places in your own backyard. While at Moon.com, sign up for our monthly e-newsletter for updates on new releases, travel tips, and expert advice from our on-the-go Moon authors. As always, when you travel with Moon, expect an experience that is uncommon and truly unique.

MOON IS ON FACEBOOK—BECOME A FAN!
JOIN THE MOON PHOTO GROUP ON FLICKR

MAP SYMBOLS

═════	Expressway	◖	Highlight	✕	Airfield	⌁	Golf Course
┄┄┄	Primary Road	○	City/Town	✈	Airport	P	Parking Area
┅┅┅	Secondary Road	◉	State Capital	▲	Mountain	⏚	Archaeological Site
┈┈┈	Unpaved Road	⊛	National Capital	✦	Unique Natural Feature	♦	Church
------	Trail	★	Point of Interest			⛽	Gas Station
··········	Ferry	•	Accommodation	⌇	Waterfall		Glacier
━·━·━	Railroad	▼	Restaurant/Bar	♠	Park		Mangrove
▓▓▓	Pedestrian Walkway	▪	Other Location	◻	Trailhead		Reef
▥▥▥	Stairs	Λ	Campground	⛷	Skiing Area		Swamp

CONVERSION TABLES

$°C = (°F - 32) / 1.8$
$°F = (°C \times 1.8) + 32$
1 inch = 2.54 centimeters (cm)
1 foot = 0.304 meters (m)
1 yard = 0.914 meters
1 mile = 1.6093 kilometers (km)
1 km = 0.6214 miles
1 fathom = 1.8288 m
1 chain = 20.1168 m
1 furlong = 201.168 m
1 acre = 0.4047 hectares
1 sq km = 100 hectares
1 sq mile = 2.59 square km
1 ounce = 28.35 grams
1 pound = 0.4536 kilograms
1 short ton = 0.90718 metric ton
1 short ton = 2,000 pounds
1 long ton = 1.016 metric tons
1 long ton = 2,240 pounds
1 metric ton = 1,000 kilograms
1 quart = 0.94635 liters
1 US gallon = 3.7854 liters
1 Imperial gallon = 4.5459 liters
1 nautical mile = 1.852 km

MOON ARGENTINA
Avalon Travel
a member of the Perseus Books Group
1700 Fourth Street
Berkeley, CA 94710, USA
www.moon.com

Editor: Tiffany Watson
Series Manager: Kathryn Ettinger
Copy Editor: Christopher Church
Graphics Coordinator: Kathryn Osgood
Production Coordinator: Domini Dragoone
Cover Designer: Domini Dragoone
Map Editor: Albert Angulo
Cartographers: Kat Bennett, Allison Rawley, and
    Chris L. Henrick
Proofreader: Jamie Andrade
Indexer: Judy Hunt

ISBN-13: 978-1-59880-675-5
ISSN: 1550-2627

Printing History
1st Edition – 2004
3rd Edition – October 2010
5 4 3 2 1

Text © 2010 by Wayne Bernhardson.
Maps © 2010 by Avalon Travel.
All rights reserved.

Title page photo: cocoi heron in Esteros del Iberá ©
Wayne Bernhardson
Front color photos: pgs. 4, 5 (left), 6 (bottom),
7 (top left), 10, 16 (bottom), 19, and 20 © David
Wilbanks/flickr.com; pgs. 5 (center and right),
6 (top), 7 (top right), 9, 11, 15, 16 (top), and 21 ©
Wayne Bernhardson; pgs. 7 (bottom left) and 23
© Gagea/commons.wikimedia.org; pgs. 7 (bottom
right), and 12 © Pablo Caridad/123rf.com; pg. 13 ©
123rf.com; pg. 14 © Galina Barskaya/123rf.com; pg.
18 © Adam Jones/adamjones.freeservers.com; pg.
24 © bigstockphoto.com.

Printed in Canada by Friesens

KEEPING CURRENT

If you have a favorite gem you'd like to see included in the next edition, or see anything
that needs updating, clarification, or correction, please drop us a line. Send your
comments via email to feedback@moon.com, or use the address above.